CLASSICS IN PSYCHOLOGY

CLASSICS
IN PSYCHOLOGY

Edited by

THORNE SHIPLEY

PHILOSOPHICAL LIBRARY

NEW YORK

To Linda

TABLE OF CONTENTS

Page

INTRODUCTION 1
PREFACE 19

PSYCHOLOGY AS A SCIENCE, NEWLY FOUNDED UPON EXPERIENCE, METAPHYSICS AND MATHEMATICS

JOHANN FRIEDRICH HERBART

"Foundations of the statics of the soul"
"Sum and ratio of inhibition in complete contrast"

The complete contrast of two ideas. Inhibition to a degree. A function of the strength of ideas. The summation of inhibitions. For total contrast, one or the other idea must be the sum of the inhibitions. The sum of the inhibitions must be conceived of as small as possible. The natural condition of ideas is uninhibited. Extension to more than two ideas. Tensions in our ideas. The ratio of inhibitions. Conflict of ideas

"Calculation of the inhibition in complete contrast and the first demonstration of the thresholds of consciousness"

The calculation of what is to be inhibited takes place through proportions. Degree of the remaining vitality of the idea. Negative ideas. Suppression from consciousness. Threshold of consciousness. Computation of the threshold. The narrowness of the human mind. Threshold tables. Thresholds of three ideas 22

CONTRIBUTIONS TO THE THEORY OF SENSORY PERCEPTION

WILHELM WUNDT

"Introduction. On the methods in psychology"

Progress in science and progress in methods. Psychology has retrogressed. Psychology vs. metaphysics. Philosophy must start from experience. The importance of grasping psychic phenomena at their origin. The history of the evolution of the psyche and comparative psychology supplement general psychology. Confusion between perception, and imagination or sensation. Only two methods in psychology: self-observation and deduction from metaphysical hypotheses. All psychology begins with self-observation. But self-observation can never go to causes, beyond the facts of consciousness. Criticism of the metaphysical method. Sociology as a deductive science. Mathematical psychology; its limitations. The application of mathematics to the moral sciences is not impossible. To improve the methods: broadened self-observation and experimentation. Statistical investigations. An experimental study of the personal equation. Primarily the sensory side of the psychic life is open to experiment. Sensory stimuli as experimental tools. The psychophysical law. The physical law. Experiment has already taught us two laws: of the mutual interdependence of the psychic functions, and of their evolution from each other 51

VII

TREATISE ON PHYSIOLOGICAL OPTICS

HERMANN VON HELMHOLTZ

"Concerning the perceptions in general"
Visual perceptions. Psychic energy. Psychology, physiology, and physics. Avoidance of metaphysical questions. Illusions of the senses vs. illusions of the judgment. Unconscious conclusions by analogy. Their irresistibility. Widespread influence of experience. Difficulty of the discovery of subjective sensations. Illustrations. True of both qualitative differences and of space relations. Apperceptions from sensations or experience. Empirical theory vs. intuitive theory. The perceptual-image can be traced to the memory-image. Influence of the comprehension of the sensation. Sensations cannot be converted into their opposite by experience. Training in the interpretation of immediate perceptions. Theory of identity vs. theory of projection. Arguments against the intuitive theory. The assumption of a pre-established harmony. The *practical* truth of our ideas. Properties of objects as sensory effects. Representation of space-relations. Inductive conclusions. Those which are unconsciously formed. Experimental determination vs. simple repetition. We recognize an external cause of sensations. The law of causation cannot be deduced from experience. Law of sufficient reason 79

THE ANALYSIS OF SENSATIONS AND THE RELATION OF THE PHYSICAL TO THE PSYCHICAL

ERNST MACH

"The chief points of view for the investigation of the senses"
Retention of habits of thought. The principle of continuity vs. the principle of sufficient determination. To analyze sensations by following up the connexion between psychologically observable data and the corresponding physical (physiological) processes. Principle of complete parallelism. Concrete examples. Concerning the theory of color-sensation. The sense-organ as a fragment of soul. The problem of memory. Raising a sparrow. The fear of ghosts is the true mother of religion. Memory reaching beyond the individual into evolution. The danger of teleology 128

PRINCIPLES OF PSYCHOLOGY

WILLIAM JAMES

"The stream of thought"
The simplicity of sensations cannot be postulated, only the fact of thinking. Five characters in thought. Thought tends to personal form. Thought is in constant change. Within each personal consciousness, thought is sensibly continuous. Human thought appears to deal with objects independent of itself; that is, it is cognitive, or possesses the function of knowing. It is always interested more in one part of its object than in another, and welcomes and rejects, or chooses, all the while it thinks 151

THE POSTULATES OF A STRUCTURAL PSYCHOLOGY

Edward B. Titchener

Modern psychology as the exact counterpart of biology. Morphology and experimental psychology. To analyze the structure of the mind. Dissection of the higher mental processes. Functional psychology over and above the psychology of structure. Ontogenetic psychology. Taxonomic psychology. Functional psychology of the collective mind. Phylogenetic psychology. The structural elements of mind, their number and nature: sensations; simple affective processes. Our justification for looking upon them as last things of the mind. Indispensable determinants: quality and intensity. The hope of psychology lies in a continuance of structural analysis   224

GENERAL PSYCHOLOGY FROM THE PERSONALISTIC STANDPOINT

William Stern

"Personalistic foundations of psychology"
The substratum and empirical facts of mind. The original unity of the individual. Definition of the person. The modalities of life: vitality; experience; introception. Consonance of multiplicity. Experience is life under cleavage and tension. The inner picture that one has of himself *must* necessarily contain illusory items. The person's budget of energy. The progressive correction of internal and external illusions as one of the principle aspects of consciousness. Definition of mind. Phenomena as the original material of psychology. Dispositions as the dependent radiations of a single personal entelechy. Factors from the external world *converge* at all times with dispositions. Experience lies intermediate between vitality and introception. Distinction between animals and man. The relation of the mental and the physical. The radial significance of the body. The person-world. The inward-outward dimension. The dimensionality proper to the person is extended homogeneously to the world   243

II. Psychopathology

TREATISE ON INSANITY

Philippe Pinel

Importance of accurate observation and analytical investigation. The method of descriptive history. The author's inducements to study the principles of moral treatment. The conduct of the Governor of Bicetre, upon the revolutionary orders he received to destroy the symbolic representations of religion. The most violent and dangerous maniacs described, with expedients for their repression. An instance illustrative of the advantage of obtaining an intimate acquaintance with the character of the patient. A case of convalescent insanity aggravated by neglect of encouraging the patient's taste for the fine arts. An attempt to cure a case of melancholia produced by a moral cause. The effects of the cold and warm bath, and especially of the bath of surprise, in the cure of maniacal disorders. Circumstances to be adverted to in forming an opinion of the author's success in the treatment of mental derangement   291

MENTAL MALADIES: A TREATISE ON INSANITY

(Jean) Etienne Dominique Esquirol

"Symptoms of insanity"

"Definition of term. . . . Illustrations. Primitive type in some of the passions. Vital forces often greatly exalted. Physical and moral sensibility modified or changed. Divisions of Insanity in lypemania, etc."— Author's summary . . . .

"Treatment of insanity"

"Isolation, and treatment at home, compared and considered at length. Effects of isolation upon the brain. Moral therapeutics highly esteemed. Principles of physical treatment. Site suited to the insane. Clothing, bedding, diet, drinks, corporal exercises. Medical treatment. Use of water. Evacuants, purgatives, emetics, blood-letting. Tonics, and sedatives. General regimen. Counter-irritants. Electricity, galvanism. magnetism, Prophylactics. . . ."—Author's summary 313

CLINICAL LECTURES ON CERTAIN DISEASES OF THE
NERVOUS SYSTEM

Jean Martin Charcot

"On six cases of hysteria in the male subject"

"Hysteria in the male is not so rare as one might suppose. Role of traumatism in the development of this affection; railway spine. Tenacity of hysterical stigmata in typical cases in both sexes. Account of three typical and complete cases of hystero-epilepsy in the male. Striking resemblance which these cases bear to each other, and to corresponding cases observed in the female sex."—Author's summary

"On six cases of hysteria" (*continued*)

"Abdominal forms of the hysterical attack in man. Detail of a case in which the seizures took the aspect of a partial epilepsy. Diagnosis of this case; importance of the hysterical stigmata. The convulsive seizure may be wanting in hysteria of the male. Description of a case of brachial monoplegia in a man aged nineteen years, hysterical. Difficulties of diagnosis in these cases."—Author's summary 370

DEMENTIA PRAECOX OR THE GROUP OF SCHIZOPHRENIAS

(Paul) Eugen Bleuler

"The fundamental symptoms—the compound functions"

Association and affectivity. *Autism* and detachment from reality. Case discussions. Indifference of patients, and apathy toward the outer world. Case discussion. The reality of the autistic world. Hallucinations. Entanglement of real and autistic worlds. Wishes and fears are autistic thought. Autism vs. unconsciousness. *Attention.* Variable span of attention. *Will.* Abulia. Hyperbulia. Blocking of will. Autopsychic orientation. *Schizophrenic "Dementia."* Conflicting evidence. Pseudodementia. Organic dementia is different. Inadequacy of usual intelligence tests. Specific dementia instead of general. Disintegration. Condensations. Emotionally toned complexes. Fragmentary concepts. Suggestibility. Hypnosis with schizophrenics. Reduced influence of experiences. Association disturbances vs. logical thought. Abrupt emergence of ideas. Pseudo-motivations. Indifference to contradictions. Impeded comprehension. Inability to learn. Aesthetic capacities damaged. Poetic talent suffers. Activity and behavior. High irritability. Unpredictability   417

LECTURES ON CLINICAL PSYCHIATRY

EMIL KRAEPELIN

"Depressed stages of maniacal-depressive insanity (circular stupor)"

Presentation of a patient. Emotional depression. Difficulty of all action of will, an impediment. We give this the name *maniacal-depressive insanity.* Series of isolated attacks. Impediment of cognition. Another patient . . . .

"Maniacal excitement"

The same malady in spite of the extraordinary rapid transition of the alternating pictures. Presentation of a patient. A stage of maniacal-depressive insanity. Another patient. The extraordinary mutability of the individual psychical process. Divertibility. The flight of ideas. Another patient. The tendency to repetition of episodes . . . . .

"Mixed conditions of maniacal-depressive insanity"

Presentation of a patient. Mixing of symptoms. Melancholia and loquacity. Impediment of thought. Another patient. Further course of the malady. Delusions. Differences from dementia praecox **464**

MEDICAL INQUIRIES AND OBSERVATIONS, UPON THE
DISEASES OF THE MIND

BENJAMIN RUSH

"Of the faculties and operations of the mind, and on the proximate cause and seat of intellectual derangement"

To lessen a portion of some of the greatest ills of human life. The faculties of the mind. The principle operations of the mind. Internal senses. Derangement in the understanding. Rejected proximate causes of intellectual derangement: liver; spleen; peritoneal coat of the intestines; disease of the nerves; disease of the mind. The cause of madness is seated primarily in the blood-vessels of the brain . . .   499

THE DISSOCIATION OF A PERSONALITY

MORTON PRINCE

"Miss Beauchamp"

Description of the first personality of Miss Beauchamp. Her childhood, and history . . . .

XI

"The birth of Sally"

The use of hypnosis and the emergence of the second personality. Origin of double consciousness. Difficult to describe the hypnotic personality. Problem of whether personalities developed under hypnosis are artificial or not. Notes from the patient-interviews. A personality vs. an hypnotic state. Continuous vs. discontinuous memories .   514

III. Organic Therapy

THE EFFECT OF MALARIA ON PROGRESSIVE PARALYSIS

JULIUS WAGNER VON JAUREGG

Specific and general treatments. Need for a balance between them. Inoculation of blood from a malaria patient. Reactions of the paralytic patients. Slow psychic improvement. Case reports. Of nine patients, four returned to an active life, two improved sufficiently to live outside the clinic, three had relapses. Recommendations for further experiments   543

THE PHARMACOLOGICAL SHOCK TREATMENT OF
SCHIZOPHRENIA

MANFRED SAKEL

"Therapeutic mechanism of pharmacological shock: working hypothesis"

Hormonal influence on the nerve cell. Picture of the therapeutic effect: neutralization of the hormone and blockage of the nerve cell; shock; neutralization of toxins. Hypothetical considerations in the development of the treatment. Analogy to the fuel engine. Phylogeny of the nerve cell. Syntonic manic-depressives do not fit into the scheme. The seat of the action of the treatment lies in the vegetative centers. Importance of the amount of adrenalin . . . .

"Clinical observations and conclusions"

Aphasia. Progressive reactivation of the entire series of successive functions of the central nervous system in the order of their development. Entire ontogenetic development partially and briefly recapitulated. Most recent phylogenetic and ontogenetic functions most sensitive to hypoglycemia. Psychotic reactions during hypoglycemia. Hunger-excitement. Hypoglycemia as a test for psychotic predisposition. Hysterical reactions. Amnesia. Results   559

IV. Neurology

ON AFFECTIONS OF SPEECH FROM DISEASE OF THE BRAIN

(JOHN) HUGHLINGS JACKSON

Loss of speech: psychological, anatomical, physiological, and pathological sides. Physiology vs. pathology. Anatomy of the speech centers. Cooperation of speech and perception. Imperceptions vs. loss of speech. Difficult symptom called ataxy of articulation. Organized actions.

Principle of dissolution. Other classes of nervous disease. Popular division: speech, articulation, voice. Loss of intellectual not of emotional language. Aphasia. To speak is to propositionize. Speech and words are psychical. Psychic states arise during, not from, neural functionings. Defect of speech. Loss of speech. Loss of language. The patient's negative condition. The patient's positive condition. Speech is not necessary for the perception, recognition, or thinking of simple relations. Internal and external speech. Deaf-mute vs. one who has lost speech 582

THE INTEGRATIVE ACTION OF THE NERVOUS SYSTEM

Sir Charles Scott Sherrington

"The physiolog al position and dominance of the brain"
"The primitive reflex-arc. The diffuse nervous system and the grey-centered nervous system; the central nervous system a part of the latter. Nervous integration of the segment. The three receptor fields. Richness of the extero-ceptive field. Special refinements of the receptor-organs of the 'leading' segments. The refined receptors of the leading segments are 'distance-receptors.' 'Distance-receptors'; the projicience of sensations. Extensive internuncial paths belonging to 'distance-receptors.' 'Distance-receptors' initiate precurrent reactions. Consummatory reactions; strong affective tone of the sensations adjunct to them. Receptive range and locomotion. The 'head' as physiologically conceived. Proprio-ceptive arcs excited secondarily to other arcs. Close functional connexion between the centripetal impulses from muscles and from the labyrinth. Tonic reflexes (of posture, etc.) and compensatory reflexes are characteristic reactions of this combined system. Nervous integration of the segmental series. Restriction of segmental distribution a factor in integration. The cerebellum is the main ganglion of the proprio-ceptive system. The cerebrum is the ganglion of the 'distance-receptors.' "—Author's summary 613

V. Psychoanalysis

STUDIES ON HYSTERIA

Josef Breuer and Sigmund Freud

"On the psychical mechanism of hysterical phenomena: preliminary communication"
Symptoms. Point of origin. Necessity of hypnotism. Role of external events. Hallucination of precipitating event. Childhood event. Case discussion. Resemblance to dreams in a healthy person. Analogy between the etiology of common and traumatic-hysteria. Partial traumas from a group of provoking causes. Symptom disappears permanently only when patient describes both the event and the affect in detail. Hysterics suffer mainly from reminiscences. Cathartic effect. Abreaction. Cases. Repressed. Denial of normal forgetting. Double conscience. Hypnoid states. Dispositional vs. psychically acquired-hysteria. Motor aspects of hysteria. *Condition seconde.* Typical course of hysteria. Theory of psychotherapeutic procedure 667

THE PRACTICE AND THEORY OF INDIVIDUAL
PSYCHOLOGY

ALFRED ADLER

"New leading principles for the practice of individual psychology"
Understanding neurosis. Path of neurosis. Estrangement from reality.
Counter-compulsion. Needs of communal life. Community-feeling.
Method of comparison. Community demands. Desire for power. In-
tolerance of neurotics. Ideal of superiority. Compulsions. A case report
"Individual psychology, its assumptions and its results"
Limitations of psychologists. Comparative individual-psychology. Unity
of the individual. To know the goal is to know what will happen.
Necessary perception of some goal. Objectives for the psychic life.
Psychic phenomena as preparations for a goal. Procedure in indi-
vidual-psychology. Cause of poor memory. Anxiety is a weapon of
aggression. Milieu as a subjective evaluation. General goal of man.
Goal of superiority as principle factor of our life. Case reports.
Neurotic distance. Goal of god-likeness. Child's feeling of inferiority   687

TWO ESSAYS IN ANALYTICAL PSYCHOLOGY

C. G. JUNG

"The personal unconscious and the super-personal or collective unconscious"
Physician as parental authority. Physician with uncanny powers. Primordial image belonging to the common mental history of humanity.
Recognition of two levels in the unconscious: personal and super-
personal (collective). The idea of the conservation of energy as a
primordial image. Energy as God. Men must always have gods. Consciousness and the rational; collective unconsciousness and the irrational. Enantiodromia—everything tends to its opposite. Difference
between the handling of young and of old people. The old cling
to the illusions of youth . . . .
"The dominants of the collective unconscious"
Case discussion. Physician as uncanny, blockage of treatment. Transference. Personal memories cannot account for demons. Problem of the
distinction between the personal and the collective unconscious. Dominants as representations of average regularities in the sequence of
secular processes. Dominants appear projected upon the persons of
the immediate environment. Fear in dreams as dread of the dominants of the collective unconscious. Animal-symbol points especially
to the super-personal. Hero-myths from the unconscious. Dream analyses. The dream function of compensation   715

VI. Behavior Theory

CONDITIONED REFLEXES: AN INVESTIGATION OF THE
PHYSIOLOGICAL ACTIVITY OF THE CEREBRAL CORTEX

IVAN PETROVICH PAVLOV

*"The development of the objective method in investigating the physio-
logical activities of the cerebral hemispheres"*

XIV

Cerebral hemispheres as the height of neural development. Hemispheres and some special psychical activity. It is open to doubt whether psychology is a science. The idea of a reflex. Time is ripe for an objective analysis. Rejection of anthropomorphism. Psychic secretion of the digestive glands. Genuine scientific concepts imply necessity, e.g. reflex. Reflexes are units of perpetual equilibration. Two kinds of reflexes: excitatory and inhibitory. Reflexes vs. instincts. Nervous activity founded on aggregates of reflexes. Freedom reflex. Investigatory reflex. Internal vs. external reflexes. Reflex of self-defence. Signal reflex as the most fundamental physiological characteristic of the hemispheres . . . .

"Technical methods employed in the objective investigation of the functions of the cerebral hemispheres"
Extension of purely objective method from lower parts to the hemispheres. Inborn reflexes inadequate to maintain the organism. Appropriateness of alimentary and mild defence reflex for study. Two components: motor and secretory. The latter can be measured very accurately, i.e. number of drops per unit time. Salivary fistula. Experimental procedure. Necessary laboratory conditions. Demonstrations. The importance of signals. Conditioned vs. unconditioned reflexes. Necessary conditions for the development of conditioned reflexes 756

PSYCHOLOGY AS THE BEHAVIORIST VIEWS IT

JOHN B. WATSON

Psychology as a purely objective natural science. No division between man and brute. The independent value of behavioral material. Fallacy of the analogical interpretation of all behavior from the point of view of consciousness. Psychology must discard all reference to consciousness. Behaviorism avoids the dangers of parallelism and of interactionism. Animals and men are to be studied in the same way. Dissatisfaction with the fact that psychology has no realm of application. Avoidance of introspection. Denial that the realm of psychics is open to experimentation 798

MIND, MECHANISM, AND ADAPTIVE BEHAVIOR

CLARK L. HULL

Man's preeminence in adaptive behavior. Mind as an hypothetical entity. Typical phenomena of adaptive behavior. Two main theories of the nature of adaptive behavior: non-physical vs. physical. Does the problem lie within the range of scientific methodology? Essential characteristics of a sound scientific theoretical system. Illustration of such a system. Philosophical speculation vs. comparison with direct observation. The importance of observational checks. Theoretical methodology applied to adaptive behavior. Consideration of the thirteen theorems of the system. Adaptive behavior—a scientific theoretical system in miniature. The nature of adaptive behavior. Consciousness . . . 822

VII. Individual Differences

MENTAL TESTS AND MEASUREMENTS

JAMES McK. CATTELL

Psychology based on experiment. Application of mental tests. General test procedure. Dynamometer pressure; rate of movement; sensation areas; pressure causing pain; least noticeable difference in weight; reaction time for sound; time for naming colours;bi-section of a 50 cm. line; judgment of ten seconds time; number of letters remembered on one hearing. Experimental psychology in the schools. Tests of sight, hearing, taste and smell, touch and temperature, sense of effort and movement, mental time, mental intensity, mental extensity   860

THE DEVELOPMENT OF INTELLIGENCE IN CHILDREN

ALFRED BINET AND THEODORE SIMON

"Upon the necessity of establishing a scientific diagnosis of inferior states of intelligence"

Education of subnormal. Problem of tests to be used. Introduction of the exactness of science. Definitions of feeble-mindedness lack precision. Constant disagreement as to diagnosis. No means for reliable differential diagnosis . . . .

"New methods for the diagnosis of the intellectual level of subnormals"

To measure the intellectual capacity of the child. Exclude from consideration the unstable child and all forms of insanity and decay. Differences between idiots and children. Three methods: medical, pedagogical and psychological. The psychological method and the graded series of tests. General remark on the tests. Intelligence is good judgment. The scale: general recommendations; the thirty tests themselves   872

PSYCHODIAGNOSTICS: A DIAGNOSTIC TEST BASED ON PERCEPTION

HERMANN RORSCHACH

Apparatus. The interpretation of accidental forms. Method of construction. Symmetry and the interpretation of whole scenes. *Procedure.* "What might this be?" At least one answer per plate. *Interpretation of the figures as perception.* Perception as integration of available engrams. This experiment as test of perception. *Statement of problems.* Form responses: Normal vs. abnormal. Movement responses: Normal vs. abnormal. *Mode of apperception of the figures.* To interpret the plate as a whole. The fictitious normal. *Scoring the mode of apperception.* Primary and secondary whole responses. Confabulation. Successive-combinatory answers. Simultaneous-combinatory wholes. Confabulatory-combined wholes. Contaminated wholes. Detail vs. small detail   920

XVI

VIII. Child Psychology

WAYWARD YOUTH

AUGUST AICHHORN

"The meaning of the reality principle in social behavior"
Education expands experience. Education presents antisocial potentialities. Freud and the pleasure principle. Instincts and wishes from the
unconscious. Infant instinctual demands. Constant childhood disappointments. Ego conforms to demands of life. Suppression. Reality
principle acts to safe-guard the ego. Pain endured for pleasure later.
Educators must recognize the nature of the reality principle. Social
adaptability through education. Strength of ego. Danger of totally
permissive education. Approval in order to bring the child to renunciation. Education with rewards vs. education with punishment. The
delinquent and immediate pleasure. Cases: excess of love and excess
of severity. Nature of remedial training. The role of the modern
training school 943

ADOLESCENCE: ITS PSYCHOLOGY AND ITS RELATIONS TO PHYSIOLOGY, ANTHROPOLOGY, SOCIOLOGY, SEX, CRIME, RELIGION, AND EDUCATION

G. STANLEY HALL

*"Evolution and the feelings and instincts characteristic of normal ado-
lescence"*
Psychic changes of adolescence. All-sided mobilization. Threatening
dangers. Beckoning of vocations. The love of struggle. Longings for
immortality. Youth is passionately fond of excitement. The 'teens'
are emotionally unstable. Emotions develop by reaction into the opposite. Overenergetic action vs. languor. Pleasure vs. pain. The curve
of despondency. Egoism vs. sinking of heart. Selfishness vs. altruism.
Good vs. bad conduct. Love for solitude vs. love for companionship.
Exquisite sensitiveness vs. imperturbability. Curiosity vs. cultivated
indifference. Knowing vs. doing. Radical vs. conservative. Reciprocity
between sense and intellect. Wisdom vs. folly. Asymmetry of growth.
Need for suddenly widened liberty. Mental unity comes later. Man's
enmity against the lower races. The past and future contend for mastery 963

THE LANGUAGE AND THOUGHT OF THE CHILD

JEAN PIAGET

"The questions of a child of six"
What are the logical functions to which questions testify? All questions
asked by a child to a given person. 1125 spontaneous questions.
Whys of place and name precede *whys* of cause and time. Questions
not calling for an answer. Three big groups of children's whys:
causal explanation; motivation; justification. Intermediate types.
Statistical review. Anthropomorphism as artificialism. Causal order
vs. order of ends. Whys of motivation outnumber all the others.
Genetic table of *whys*, a working hypothesis 994

XVII

IX. GESTALT PSYCHOLOGY

EXPERIMENTAL STUDIES ON THE SEEING OF MOTION

MAX WERTHEIMER

One actually sees motion. Psychic supplementation. A review of the theories of seen motion. Central vs. peripheral explanations. Stroboscopic demonstrations. What is psychically given when one sees motion? Possible experimental approaches. Visibility of object vs. impression of motion. Indistinguishability of actual and apparent motion. Experimental variables and controls. Tachistoscopic methods. The plan of the experiment. Independence from the effect of eyemovements. Two possible theories of ϕ. The ϕ-phenomenon with only one object. The ϕ-phenomenon with haplioscopic presentation. Motion is unthinkable without a thing which moves. Pure ϕ can be experienced without any conception of the objects themselves. ϕ-phenomena in everyday situations. Summary of the findings. Discussion of the theories in the light of the present findings. We must refer to processes which lie behind the retina. A physiological explanation. An overflowing of stimulation. The range effects in the neighborhood of the stimulation 1032

THE MENTALITY OF APES

WOLFGANG KÖHLER

"The making of implements—Building"

To pile two or more boxes on top of one another in order to reach the food. Descriptions of the chimpanzee's attempts and solutions. To pile up boxes is something quite different than simply to use one box alone. Conclusions: chimpanzees possess an almost absolute lack of insight with respect to statics. Absolute visual orientation in space. Distinction between impression of humanness and the degree of insight and the level of achievement. Problem of the function of the tool as used and realized by the chimpanzee. Building in common vs. building altogether. To see the task from the point of view of the other animal 1090

PERCEPTION: AN INTRODUCTION TO THE GESTALT-THEORIE

KURT KOFFKA

General critical review. Introduction for American readers. More than a theory of perception. Sensations. The constancy hypothesis. Association. Attention. Physiological side. Divisions of the cortex. Gestaltqualität vs. Gestalt. The clash of the old and the new methods of thinking. Differential threshold and Weber's law. Neglect of the step-concept. Structures not separate, sensations underlie all psychophysical experiments. Learning of relations vs. learning of absolutes. "Member-character." "Level-experiences." Attitude as a readiness to carry out a structural process. Report of experiments. Pure *ground* experience. A *good* figure is always a *closed* figure. "Figure attitude." "Figural after-effect." "Thing"-character vs. "substance"-character. Can a ground exist without a figure? Theory of the perception of illumination. The "spatial level." Points of anchorage in the visual field. The stability of objects depends on the quality of the object. Phenomenally there is no relativity of movement. 1128

X. Social Psychology

A TREATISE ON THE MEDICAL JURISPRUDENCE OF
INSANITY

Issac Ray

"Legal consequences of mania"

Man possesses the liberty of regulating his conduct. Hence, he is morally responsible. Moral vs. legal responsibility. Legal Consequences of Intellectual Mania. Common law is open to censure. Incarceration would probably aggravate their disorder. The delicacy of the question when mania annuls criminal responsibility. The special problem of monomania. The validity of a marriage contracted in a state of partial mania. The civil rights of the insane. Partial mania vs. total insanity. Validity of wills. The sense of the *fitness of things*. Partial mania excludes the idea of culpability. Wrong notion that the insane reason correctly from wrong premises. Legal Consequences of Moral Mania. The power of the intellect must also suffer. Perverted notions of right and wrong. The blind irresistible impulse. Such a patient is not restrained by the fear of punishment, therefore should not be punished. Homicidal monomania. The homicidal monomaniac often seeks his own death, i.e., punishment. Epidemic murders of children (venial sin) rather than to commit suicide (mortal sin). Punishment is not a deterrent to the insane. Insanity may be completely veiled from observation. Problem of the discovery of the motive. The defence of the maniac is secure for him by the law of nature 1197

INTENTION, WILL AND NEED

Kurt Lewin

"A Few Facts"

1. The influence of Time on the Effect of the Intention: the Immediate Cessation of the Effect after Consummation Action.

2. The Effect of Intentions when occasion and consummation action are not predetermined, or when the occasion fails to appear.

3. The resumption of interrupted activities.

4. The forgetting of intentions.

"The theory of intentional action"

    1. The effect of the act of intending is a quasi-need. 2. The effects of quasi-needs and genuine-needs. 3. Fixation in genuine-needs and quasi-needs. 4. Substitute consummation.

"Summary"   1234

AN INTRODUCTION TO SOCIAL PSYCHOLOGY

WILLIAM McDOUGALL

"The mental characters of man of primary importance for his life in society. The nature of instincts and their place in the constitution of the human mind"

    Innate tendencies as motive of all thought and action. Their different relative strengths. Mind as the sum of these innate tendencies. Two main classes: specific (instincts) and general. Loose use of the word 'instinct.' Pre-human instincts. Instincts are more than dispositions to certain kinds of movements. Mental process as striving towards the natural end of the process. Instinctive process as of the nature of perception. Four kinds of complications of instinctive processes in man: initiation by ideas of objects, the bodily movements are modifiable, several instincts may come into play simultaneously, systematic organization about objects of ideas. Modes of instinct modification: experience; operation of resemblances. Instincts vs. acquired habits of thought. Habits are formed only in the service of instincts . .

"The principal instincts and the primary emotions of man"

    Each instinct conditions some emotion. Simple and complex emotions. The instinct of flight and the emotion of fear. The instinct of repulsion and the emotion of disgust. The instinct of curiosity and the emotion of wonder. The instinct of pugnacity and the emotion of fear. The instinct of self-abasement and of self-assertion, and the emotions of subjection and elation. The parental instinct and the tender emotion   1290

INDEX   1337

XX

CLASSICS IN PSYCHOLOGY

INTRODUCTION

The historian in his description of the past depends on his own judgment as to what constitutes the importance of human life . . .

There is no history but our idea of history. Ideas, not things are the true reality. They alone are victors over whatsoever has been. Proper history is the complex growth of ideas down through the ages. Ideas created by one generation become a part only of the next. Benedetto Croce has said that all history is current history. Each generation, he said, must rewrite its own. Even this is not sufficient.

Each individual man must weave the pivotal ideas of the past into the pattern of his own personality. The courageous man becomes estranged from his time. He welcomes ideas more quickly than his generation. He seeks estrangement deliberately by his courtship of the future. The history of modern psychology begins with a Prince among such men.

Philippe Pinel discovered the special rationality of the insane. Enigmatic as it had so long appeared, Pinel nevertheless finally made public proclamation of the immense idea that reason could appear in unreasonable guise. Mental disorder is a *disease entity*. The mad, the deluded, the possessed, the debauched all could be reached, therefore, by the deepest reason of all, the reason of love, "the moral treatment of insanity." The precise rationality of Aquinas was not the way of all men. The Platonic syllogism itself, this quintessential height of thought, was fairly jettisoned at Pinel's disclosure of the vast chain of reasons between the premise of a man and his conclusion.

Already incensed with the hot blood of the Revolution coursing through France in 1794 the people of Paris reacted violently to this idea. A mob attacked Pinel in

1

the fear that he was unleashing devils into the streets. That Pinel himself was not drawn into the violence of the Revolution is one of the small but special miracles in the history of ideas.[1] Pinel struggled against the problems brought by the new calendar, against the diverted concern which cut his hospital budget manifold, and reduced his food rations to starvation levels. The madman is sick, he proclaimed with ever increasing vigor. The chains had to fall.

There is a touching delicacy in Pinel's writings, as we read them today. And Esquirol, his successor at the Salpetriere[2] (the Parisian home for outcast and insane women built from the old arsenal of Louis XIII), displayed a particularly beautiful, even reverent sensibility.

Moreover, there was hardly a single French doctor of the early and middle nineteenth century, working with the insane, who was not taught by one of these two men.

Continuing the great French tradition in psychiatry, Charcot also at the Salpetriere, approached the profound issue of the rationality of man from a different side. Charcot lectured on hysteria in the male. Originally hysteria in the Greek, simply meant *womb*. Having become the name of a behavior disorder, it nevertheless still could not apply to men. This recognition of hysteria as a legitimate disorder in men can be considered, in the historical sense, as perhaps the first major insight into the psychogenesis of mental disorder.

As none before them, Charcot, and then Freud, understood the meaning of the psychic voyage to conclusion. The premise becomes the conclusion. An intellectual idea becomes a physiological event, an hysteria a symptom. The mind, in some wondrous sense, becomes the body. One of Freud's most important papers, written in

---

[1] He did, however, once shelter Condorcet among the male patients at the Bicetre.

[2] By 1795 Pinel had left the Bicetre, and took over the direction of the Salpetrière.

French under Charcot's inspiration, showed that hysterical paraesthesias can be distinguished from organic forms from the fact that the hysterical patient becomes numbed as he thinks he ought, not as we infer he should, from his neurology (*e.g.* the well-known "glove-anaesthesia").

This was the first inroad. And, in a sense, it is actually as far as we can go. More recently "psychosomatics" has entered the common jargon of us all. Yet, the concept often strikes us strangely. In our inner minds we still really do not believe it. We are, for instance, so easily swayed by the negative evidence. In spite of ourselves, the physical world constantly flaunts its arbitrary authority.

The clinician in his daily rounds, cannot help but be stirred constantly by the deepest philosophical problems. The psychosomatic solution of the mind-body problem, however, is not the only one which he may find in the wards. There are many others. And an examination of them here, in historical perspective, may help to set the stage for the critical reading of the essays which follow in the book.

Descartes, for example, at first denied psychophysical interaction altogether. The impossible, said he, could not happen—that the soul and the body ever meet. However, if we are compelled to admit that they do meet then it can only be at one point—the intersection of the mental and the physical pathways. It would be a horror beyond imagination should the soul of man be confronted with his body along its whole extent. Such an intercourse could take place only in a very small and restricted region, the pineal gland. This is as close as Descartes could come, in physiological terms, to the mathematical ideal of a point, to a locus without dimension. Even while admitting the intercourse, he thus maintained his denial.

In spite of the ubiquity of similar sentiments in modern

3

times, physiologists tell us that we learn 'all-over'. The mind does not lie exclusively in the brain, but seeps out through our whole body. The severely brain-injured patient, for example, with no verbal memory, with hardly a name and little identity, can often drive his car, or ride his bike, or engage in complex athletics or social recreations. The memory lies in his hands, his feet, in the neuro-musculature itself. The phantom-limb phenomenon, quite common in recent amputees, is a further example. Modern physiology has much to say of such peripheral intelli-, gence. Lotze introduced the theory of local signs (peripheral self-localization); Sherrington described peripheral neural induction; Lapique measured the chronaxy (peripheral neural reaction time); Dewey elaborated the concept of the peripheral reflex arc; and Pavlov spoke of the "conditioned" reflex. Actually, the oldest notion in physiology, that of the "common" sensibility, implies a peripheral intelligence.

The mind-body problem is one of the most tenacious of the perennial philosophical issues. All possible formulations seem fraught with ambivalence. Of the basic questions, it is the one which most deeply pervades the everyday life of men. It is, to be sure, the basic enigma of the religious life. In this sense, it is the essential problem of a human existence. Perhaps this is why no philosophical resolution can ever be entirely satisfactory.

The lay solution, however, is very attractive. Because he is unwilling consciously to admit that his mental life is totally isolated, man strives without consciousness to meld into the obviously real physical universe. From this he borrows the conviction of his own reality. The world of mankind is thoroughly alive. The evocation of anthropomorphic interaction is man's primary motivation. And it compounds man's punishment that even in this he is afraid.

At times he may grow bold, and claim a mastery over

4

the rocky world, but by an inevitable reversal, we are forced to retrench behind our lines. The necessity of our retreat before nature was never heralded with more devastating frankness than by Charles Darwin. The theory of evolution is as much a theory of the mind as of the body; and today, within its compass, we believe ourselves to belong to nature more completely than previous generations could have ever granted. This terribly close psychic association, with its intimation of absolute inanimation, is the ultimate source of our repugnance against the theory of evolution.

Lytton Strachey has said that the two most obvious characteristics of nature are loveliness and power. Modern man plunges back into nature, enticed and entrapped by the loveliness. Forced to remain aloof from himself, his mind from his body, he seeks death as the only possible unity: ugliness is beauty, life is death, mind and body are eternally chained.

Such a broad philosophical entanglement subsumes lesser ones of special interest in the history of psychology. In particular, the unity between stimulus and sensation, between occasion and experience. Exploration of this unity is the major task of psychology. The starting point in modern psychology was John Locke's conviction that the senses alone were the doorways to the mind. Nothing he said, is in the mind which is not first in the senses.[3] The problem, then, is the nature of these stimuli which are first in the senses. What is the essence of that precious moment between the terse physical and the shimmering psychic?

A recent school of psychology, the Gestalt psychology, provides a key. Our basic knowledge, it is said, is pure phenomenal experience. This only do we know. From it we can infer the stimulus. And such inference is the only

---

[3] The existential problem of the nature of the mind itself was later formulated by Leibnitz, when he postulated an *intelligence* propadeutic to experience.

possible activity of the mind. Happily, however, these inferences need not be made in a random fashion. There is an inherent isomorphism between experience and occasion, and this is the proper path for our inferences. Moreover, this inferential knowledge is as valid, and as concrete as our knowledge of pure experience.

Previously, Kant taught us that we can never know true reality, the thing in itself. The inferential path was a maze for him, with no exit; a *cul de sac*. The true nature of Strachey's powerful and beautiful world lay always beyond our grasp. Entities were bashful; they hid behind "appearances". Thus, the Gestalt psychology, giving us a logical link to reality, is an explicit denial of the Kantian epistemology.

But, the Gestalt psychologists recognized that, in a sense, Kant was probably correct. The quality of the experience of *inference-to-reality*, however valid and concrete it may seem, is different from the quality of a pure sensory experience. The isomorphism of the Gestalt psychology is a psycho-physiological one, not a psycho-physical one, for the mind is trapped inside. There is a boundary to the outward penetration of· isomorphic inferences.

For example, if at one instant we have an experience, then immediately preceding it in time an event must have occurred of the same form (isomorphic) as the experience itself. The existence of this heraldic event is probably assured. A theory of psycho-physiological isomorphism seems to be unavoidable. Spinoza once wrote that " ... the orders of the actions and passions of our body are simultaneous in nature with the orders of the actions and passions of our mind." But this isomorphism stops inside the body. Even the most casual observation reveals that the form of experience often differs from the form of external events. Will or no, the isomorphic linkage does not provide an escape outside the self. The real

6

world remains just as far away as ever.

Many years before Gestalt psychology, the two physiologists, Johannes Müller (German) and Charles Bell (English), simultaneously and independently of each other, formulated a second limitation on isomorphic inferences, this time on its inner penetration. This also originated as a criticism of Kant. They maintained that in many instances we do not even know the Kantian "appearances." We often know only the special (specific) qualities of our nerves. We experience 'red' as 'red-nerves-responding', 'b-sharp' as 'b-sharp-nerves-responding'. While the mind may need training, or practice, or encouragement of its emergent properties, the nerves themselves cannot be instructed. Their specific quality emerges from them at the proper stimulation. From the moment of birth, hot is not cold, sweet is not sour, pain is not comfort, red is not blue.

Such, then, is our inner knowledge. To the extent of the truth of this concept, this knowledge (of specific nerve energies) is essentially an internal generic limitation on isomorphic inference. An experience of pure quality (neural energy) need not be the same as an experience of pure form (isomorphism). Thus there exist both inner and outer boundaries, beyond which our inferences cannot go.

These barriers to the complete resolution of the mind-body problem forced the second great issue in the history of psychology to the fore—i.e. the problem of individuality. If man is not one with the universe, does he still at least possess an inner unity, an inner proof of the existence of God? The covert recognition of these limitations on isomorphism by earlier thinkers gave rise to the popular concept of the blunt individuality (divisibility, separability) of men. The British Associationists denied isomorphism entirely, and they carefully shunned all isomorphic inferences. Man is what he has learned to be. Each

7

man stands aloof from his fellows. Each man, alone, is held accountable for himself and for his progeny. Each lineage is marked with a singular cast. All things must be studied on their own. Unfortunately, the study of the individual will always be hampered by a particularly great difficulty in identifying the individual essence. Understanding, suffering, or the sudden surprise of success, are unmeasurable in the individual. It is not too hard to show progress in knowledge, or in goods, but who dares to point out the "happy" man? Who dares claim that we have learned, at last to improve ourselves by raising better children?

John B. Watson did indeed make this claim. And he was cheered for his boldness. However pretentious his words may sound today, they seemed to assuage important tensions in the American public of the post World War I era. As the fear of Pinel was fear of the indeterminate within ourselves, so the accolade for Watson was joy at regaining control over our children. If man was not in unity with his environment, if nature incessantly squirmed away beyond the limited grasp of psychophysiological isomorphism, at least man's destiny, his progeny, was clearly in his own hands.

With perhaps more restraint, the rationalists had claimed that the only thing of which they could be certain was the existence of their own minds. All else could be doubted, even denied. Thinking alone was proof of being. Watson maintained, rather, that consciousness was an hypothesis of which he felt no need. The influence of John Dewey, with whom Watson studied in Chicago, is seen here in its literal sense. Being was doing; existence was action. A stern judgment!

Even today, many people are slightly embarrassed whenever some one mentions consciousness, or spirit, or any of these mere "thinkables". It is one of the strangest phenomena in the history of science, though certainly not

8

without parallel in other fields, that the definitive basis of psychology (the psyche itself) was explicitly denied existence by many of those who sought eagerly after it.

Another, perhaps more fruitful approach to the investigation of individual differences, had begun in England many years previously. The story is now legend, how the astronomer, Maskelyne, at the Greenwich Observatory in the year 1796, fired his assistant, Kinnebrook, because he was late. Had Kinnebrook really been tardy, say by a minute or two, this would not have been important. That he was consistently just about one-half second late, this was too much! The point is that the measuring procedure for timing the transit of stars past the telescope reticule was felt to be accurate to about one-tenth of a second. That Kinnebrook could be so habitually out of line with Maskelyne's own readings reflected only his own unwillingness to dedicate himself wholeheartedly to his work. Legitimate expectancies for such refined individual differences simply did not exist. That the process of ideation, or imagination, should possess a duration, much less a measurable one, was an idea which did not occur in the older philosophies. Yet it is interesting to note that the 'speed' of the understanding, the rate of the flight of ideas, was measured, by the astronomers, only 150 years after they measured the speed of light.

The idea that men differ grossly from one another is most certainly a primitive one, emerging in the infant simultaneously with the idea of self. All peoples have their way of referring to a *strong* man, to a *proud* man, and to a *selfish* man. All peoples have notions and linguistic categories for *bravery-cowardice,* for *wisdom-stupidity,* for *honesty-deception.* Nevertheless, a hierarchy can be established among the attributes of man and of situations. Some are simpler, more superficial, and more easily comprehended than others. Among the more subtle ones are irony, for example, and tragedy, or self-reproach, imagi-

9

nation, restraint, intelligence. Aspects of spiritual function are always more elusive than those of bodily function. Our introduction to mental attributes is always through physical ones.

Historically, the first such psychophysical attribute of which science became aware was the *reaction time,* the time-span of intellectual activity. It was not until some fifty or sixty years after Kinnebrook, that the meaning of the regularity of his disagreement with Maskelyne was fully understood. The astronomers eventually realized that such fixed differences were general phenomena. They were incorporated into transformation equations, "personal equations" as they were called, from one astronomer to another, so that transit readings by different men could be accurately compared.[4]

The struggle to abstract the purity of events from its contamination by human observers is a great one. We seem dedicated to it, though certain to fail. We constantly buck against the outer boundary of the isomorphic inference. We avoid it. We measure. And so postpone the inevitable and compelling inference. Why, for example, was there this delay of fifty years? What is it that is so fundamentally different between the scale of temperaments and humors of Galen, for example, and the personal equation of the astronomer?

The idea of the overt measurability of pure mental processes, of the quantitative equation between the mind of one man and that of another, of the human spirit as a null instrument, of the instantaneous and deliberate transmigration of souls—such an idea is justifiably slow in developing.

Wundt, in a criticism of Herbart's rationalism,[5] first formulated this concept in the early nineteenth century.

_____

[4] See Boring (b-Chap. 8) for an excellent introduction to this concept, also a bibliography of further studies on it.

[5] Herbart's influence, however was extremely wide. It is quite interesting, for example, though little known, that Herbart had an important influence on the

The pragmatic application of this idea reached its height at about the turn of the twentieth century, in the work of Alfred Binet in France, of Francis Galton in England, and of James Cattell in the United States.[6] Within some small span of years, these men established on a sound basis the theory and practice of mental testing. They drew heavily on the philosophically parallel developments in the field of mathematical statistics. Some few years later, Hermann Rorschach, influenced particularly by certain of Jung's contributions to psychoanalysis, expanded the concept of the reckoning of individual differences and of the measurement of personality into the hitherto impregnable realm of psychopathology.

Perhaps the highest forms of such analysis are the case history, the biography, and the autobiography: Freud on *Leonardo Da Vinci;* Albert Schweitzer on the *Psychiatric Study of Jesus;* and James Joyce on his own youth (*Portrait of an Artist as a Young Man*). There seems to be nothing we cannot measure,—no private Elan Vital into which the probe of test, of analysis, of polls and of quotients cannot penetrate. Whether this adventure into the secret gardens of the human spirit is a healthy one, whether we have pursued it sufficiently without malice, are moot points. Psychological measurement, in any case, does seem destined to become one of the basic themes of our civilized life.

What then, was the essence of the Personal Equation that made it so difficult to conceive, so long to accept? To build up an endurance against the destruction of intimacy (or perhaps a tolerance for it), which is inherent

---

great mathematician, Georg Friedrich Bernard Riemann (1826-1866), whose work released us from the Euclidean restrictions on our inferences about space and geometry.

[6] Wundt's greatest pupil, however, was the psychiatrist Kraepelin, and not a psychologist as one might think. The cooperation between Wundt and Kraepelin, —experimental psychology and psychiatry,—was one of the most fruitful examples of reciprocity in the history of the two sciences.

11

in mental and personality testing, necessarily required a shift in the intellectual, emotional and spiritual concepts of man;—a shift which embodied the insights of Enlightenment, both religious and secular, and not a little of the brutality of the manipulative societies. This concept could not have emerged from the Catholic or the Jewish view of man. The cosmic harmony of the universe is disturbed by the deliberate weighing of men by men in a man-made balance. Directly we seize power to judge ourselves, to know ourselves, a knowledge which the Hebrew God has forbidden us. In its attainment, the great chain of being is sundered at its highest link.

To measure something is to cast it apart from its fellows. This above all else, is the meaning of measurement. One soon becomes disappointed by a lack of distinction. At best, one becomes bored. Hence, differences become virtues, and all things become relative. Events must titillate. Man must be true only to himself. He need reach only as high as the modern psychiatric goal of self-consistency, a complacent and emasculating motivation at best.[7] The grand theme of associationism was the harbinger of this image of man; and psychometrics, in its fundamentals, rests upon the very same recognition of the limits of isomorphism. It seeks to know perfectly, almost as the pure experience of the psychometrist, the nature and being of another man—but by measurement, not by inference. Since the psychometrist's man is *nothing but* the sum total of his experiences, then men can resemble each other only in the exceedingly rare contingency of a multitude of overlapping episodes. These can be known only through measurement, through partial resurrection and recitation. The only generic commonality between men is the Tabula Rasa itself, the men-

---

[7] The aim of psychotherapy is so meager, because the therapists themselves have been unable to reach any agreement (largely for sociological reasons) on the definition of mental health.

tal anlage of evolution. And this is not within the domain of psychometrics.

To explore behind the Tabula is a special task of present day psychology. It is our preordained failure to discover measuring scales which reach behind the Tabula which makes psychometrics a limited approach to human understanding. Psychometrics must necessarily describe a lesser man. It is inference, not measurement which can take us behind, which can span the full compass of the human soul.

Through the insights of the Gestalt psychologists, for example, logic, perception, ethics, aesthetics are all seen to be founded upon origins lying well back of the Tabula, outside of experience, beyond relativity. This is exactly the meaning of Leibnitz' modification of the associationist's dictum: the mind itself, he said, is in the mind before sensory experience. This is exactly the meaning of Jung's search for archetypes, for inherited predispositions which lie behind the Tabula.[8]

The first important paper of the German psychologist, Max Wertheimer, in 1912, reported an experiment which successfully challenged the reigning postulate of a one-to-one association between physical stimuli and phenomenal experience. There is no such thing as an empty mind. The mind itself, Wertheimer showed, had something to say as to what was to be a "stimulus" in the first place. The mind imposed its own order upon experience, or, rather, that order which was its own because the mind partakes in (is ruled by) the laws of physical causality. Causes, as Wertheimer phrased it, proceed from above.

As far back as the eighteenth century, Kant, arguing from experience, had insisted, in an analogous manner,

---

[8] This concept can be traced from Jung, through Mach, to the physiologist Ewald Hering—and beyond.

13

on the Euclidean nature of these laws.[9] He was wrong, we now know, but the essence of his idea is still with us. Phenomenological analysis, the primary method of the Gestalt approach, takes us directly into the geometry of experience. This geometry, in fact, is the Gestalt definition of mind.[10] We seek, therefore, to know this geometry, entirely independently of experience. We seek after the pure core, equally a property of the event as of the experience. In fact, such study holds our only chance for success. Once we discover this geometry, we shall know it with certainty. Actually, we recognize it. It is this claim to noetic truth, to perfect recognition, which is the challenge of Gestalt psychology, though perhaps also its point of greatest vulnerability.

The philosophical implications are clear. Men have far more in common than hitherto thought. We can even infer the pure experiences of others via isomorphic inferences from the pure experiences of ourselves. The transmigration of souls is a spiritual event, not a measurable one. The laws of logic are the same for all men simply because logical behavior is pulled out from behind the ubiquitous Tabula by man's environment. The form of events requires that a man be logical. One could as easily cease to be logical, by will or by lack of it, as he could cease to breathe . . . with the same disastrous consequences. Indeed, it is the self-conscious logic of insanity wherein lies its greatest tragedy.

So we find Pinel's early thoughts resurrected. The old theory that only the intellectual premises of the insane were wrong, is not entirely without basis. And, certainly, a vast quantity of psychotherapy today consists in highly biased argumentation with the patient over questions of right and wrong. The unsolved questions of social ethics

---

[9] Kant recognized that he could infer action pathways but not things.
[10] It is, after Kurt Lewin, the crux of the definition of the personality and of the group as well.

(i.e. sociologically determined ethics) constitute the basic dilemma of psychiatry.

Similarly, only environments are relative, never experience or meaning or behavior. An environment is a perceptual event. *Esse est percipi* is the basic tenet. We perceive in accordance with the laws governing physical causality. The principles of equilibrium, of least effort, of rest and symmetry, of field and boundary . . . these rule in the realm of our perceptions,—not experience, nor the laundry-basket of unconscious or inherited habits. If all behavior has significance, as Freud has shown, then it cannot be illogical. Our thoughts may sometimes ride tornado within us, kick about and rattle till we collapse, but in any single cross section they do have shape and meaning. To be logical means to be lawful; it is not a synonym for health. Something entirely unlawful cannot be experienced. In the event, experience emerges with its own legality.

Likewise, the significance of ethics and aesthetics is inherent in the requiredness of events. The ethical consequences of a human situation are inevitably the demands of structure. Whatever may be that universal aspect of an event between men which demands good from them, and love, and however gossamer it may be, the optimism of the philosophy of Gestalt sets us out after it with high hopes.

Yet in one important area of the mind-body problem all these recent movements in psychology have remained silent. Modern man is somehow ashamed of his own compelling religiosity. Political involvement is essentially our blush at religion. The two greatest lacunae in Freud, for example, were religion and ethics. In both, we owe far more to anthropology than to psychology. Freud understood neither, and claimed to find no place for religious experiences in his own life. Nevertheless, the most serious intellectual upheaval which Freud experi-

15

enced, his break with Jung, was basically over this issue. While the enigma of Jung is his ambivalence. At the very invocation of his acknowledgement of the high religious spirit of man, he implies its degradation. Jung has touched aspects of our unconscious towards which Freud did not deign to point. But religion seems old to Jung, wrinkled, atavistic, demiurgical.

These two areas, religion and ethics, are the cosmic meeting grounds. All great philosophies must come to stand or fall upon them. A rapprochement, on these issues, between the two great movements in modern psychology,—Gestalt and Psychoanalysis,—is probably the most important challenge in the field today. There are elements in each, which, on both sides of the Tabula, should eventually blend into a more healthy and a more generous description of the human personality than we have yet been able to comprehend.

Those references cited by author only in the Introduction and editor's Notes are given here in full title.

Baldwin, J. M. (ed.)—*Dictionary of Philosophy and Psychology.* N.Y.: Macmillan, 1905, 3 vol.

Bennett, S. & Boring, E. G.—*Psychological Necrology* (1928-1952). *Psychol. Bull.* 1954, 51:75-81.

Boring, E. G.—
  a) *Sensation and Perception in the History of Experimental Psychology.* N. Y.: D. Appleton-Century, 1929.
  b) *A History of Experimental Psychology.* N. Y. D. Appleton-Century, 1929.
  c) *Psychological Necrology.* (1903-1927). *Psychol. Bull.* 1928, 25:302-305, 621-625.

Castiglioni, A.—*A History of Medicine.* N. Y.: Knopf, 1941. Trans. & ed. by E. B. Krumbhaar.

Grinstein, A.—*The Index of Psychoanalytical Writings.* N. Y.: International Universities Press, 1956-1958, 3 vol. (to *Rowley*).

Hall, G. S.—*Founders of Modern Psychology.* N. Y.: Appleton, 1912.

Hall, J. K. (ed.)—*One Hundred Years of American Psychiatry.* N. Y.: Columbia University Press, 1944. esp. Moore, T. V. "A century of psychology in its relation to psychiatry."

Louttit, C. M.—*Bibliography of Bibliographies on Psychology,* 1900-1927. *Bull. Nat. Res. Council.* 1928, 65 (November).

Murchison, C. (ed.)—

a) *History of Psychology in Autobiography.* Worcester, Mass.: Clark Univ. Press, 1930, 4 vol. (vol. 4 edited by E. G. Boring et al.).

b) *The Psychological Register.* Worcester, Mass.: Clark Univ. Press, 1929 (vol. 2), 1932 (vol. 3). Volume 1 was never completed. An excellent compilation of bibliographies.

Rand, B.—*The Classical Psychologists.* Boston: Houghton Mifflin, 1912.

Zilboorg, G. *A History of Medical Psychology.* in collab. with G. Henry, N. Y.: Norton, 1941.

PREFACE

A book such as this has value in direct proportion to the deference which it shows to the original sources. Whenever possible I have tried to include the full text of each selection. Certain of the essays have not been previously translated into English: the selections from Herbart, Wertheimer, and Wundt. The editor wishes to acknowledge the assistance of Frank Gaynor in making the first, and very fine drafts of the Herbart and the Wundt, and of Dagobert Runes in preparing the working draft of the Wertheimer. The final form of the translations is the full responsibility of the editor. Because of the difficulty of Herbart's writing, the translation of his work is quite free. The selection from Wertheimer has been substantially shortened, because of limitations of space. In all these translations an attempt has been made to catch the spirit of the original text as well as its literal meaning. Hence archaic and even Germanic construction has at times been intentionally retained. Several of the selections were taken from fairly rare sources: Charcot, Esquirol, Herbart, Pinel, Ray, Rush, Stern, Wagner-Jauregg, and Wundt.

I have learned a great deal in the process of organizing this book. It has helped me to place many of the important issues of psychology in new historical perspectives, and, I confess, given me a much deeper respect for the difficulties which the historian of science must overcome. It has pinpointed major weaknesses in our knowledge both of people and of events. For example, several of the birthdates are still unceitain: equally reliable French sources (i.e. reliable as far as I can tell), give Binet's date of birth variously as July 3, July 8, and July 11, 1857. Even the very important date of Pinel's Grand Geste is not known exactly. Hence, often only approximate or conflicting dates can be given in the text. And then, there are the many people who are simply lost from the records of history. For example, to cite a surprisingly recent instance, *Th.* Simon seems only to be known because of his connection with Binet, at least in America, though he certainly is important in his own right as a greatly loved and respected child psychiatrist. And his correct name seems to have almost entirely disappeared from American (and most secondary French) records. Many academic libraries (e.g. Clark, Harvard, Columbia) list it as *Theodore,* as do the Medical Dictionaries; but the great New York Public Library lists it as *Thomas;* and, finally, certain American texts in psychology, and the Library of Congress, list him as *Théophile.* Nor is the library of the Vineland Training School, in New Jersey, out of which came the major English translations of Simon's work with Binet, able to supply me with the correct name.*

Recognizing these limitations, and trusting the reader to have compassion for the difficulties of historical reportage, I do hope that those who are more learned than I in specialized fields will forgive and understand my having overlooked so many references, facts, and contributions. The definition of "classic" must necessarily have been my own.

I am deeply aware of the drawbacks of anthologies, and am admittedly disturbed by the ever present trend towards capsule scholarship. This book is not intended to contribute in this manner. My purpose has not been to survey a whole field, but rather to give a very small introduction to the mileposts. If many readers stop with this book and do not go on, then I have failed.

Moreover, it is surprising how much of the knowledge, even of the scholars, comes from secondary sources. Most of us, surely, know this, and are willing to accept it because we believe ourselves to be surrounded, somewhere,

---

* It happens that his name is Théodore (see biographical note, p. 919).

20

by colleagues who have studied the originals. Upon closer questioning, however, more often than not, we find that our colleagues are at best relying on a different secondary source, or, mirrorlike, are relying on us! This book has been prepared in the hope that this fruitless reciprocity may be partially alleviated.

A sourcebook of this kind is, for me, a long awaited opportunity to give a lecture in the history of psychology, entirely without concern for the traditions in the academic courses (History and Systematic Psychology, Proseminars, etc.), which usually represent the lowest point in the course curriculum. It is clear, of course, that this book can serve only as a short introduction, but perhaps this must be true of historical investigations, no matter how involved. Someone, some generations later, will inevitably feel compelled to repeat it. I am grateful to Dagobert Runes for the concrete conception of this book in approximately its present form. My special thanks go also to the authors and publishers who have graciously consented to the reprinting in the present manner.

For intellectual guidance, I am ever in debt to Professor Eric Gutkind, of the Department of Philosophy of City College, New York. My introduction to the history of psychology comes from an early reading of Professor E. G. Boring's great books. No work can be done today in America in this field, without a very special acknowledgement to these two works. As far as my own approach is concerned, the reader will sense a favorable bias towards the Gestalt Psychology. This stems in part, from my years as Graduate Student at the New School for Social Research, under Professor Mary Henle.

My wife has, with her special grace, volunteered as private librarian and secretary, and has struggled valiantly to correct my literary errors. I am afraid, however, that her criticisms have set standards of expression far higher than I have been able to attain.

PSYCHOLOGY AS A SCIENCE, NEWLY FOUNDED ON EXPERIENCE, METAPHYSICS AND MATHEMATICS

Johann Friedrich Herbart

Foundations of the statics of the soul
Sum and ratio of inhibition in complete contrast

41

The contrast between two ideas is complete, or as great as possible when one of the two must be totally inhibited in order that the other remain inhibited. However, this will never be the case, for an idea is inhibited only if it resists, and its resistance must always produce a certain inhibition in the contrasting idea as well. We may, nevertheless, adopt the fiction that the entire strength of the contrast, and consequently the entire compulsion to decline, affects only one of the two; the most that can happen then is a total decline of this one, or a total extinction of the product of its ideation by a transformation of its entire activity into a mere striving against the contrasting idea. It can do no more than decline, however, and it would be senseless to wish to conceive of the quantum of actual ideation as decreasing still further beyond zero, and thus as being negative.

A diminished contrast, however, may easily be conceived. Consequently, a given idea could remain totally uninhibited if only a certain fraction of the other idea were inhibited; that is, rather, if the other one were inhibited only to a certain degree.

The difference between complete and diminished contrast is independent of the strength of the ideas. Let one idea equal *a*, and the other one equal *b*, where *a* and

22

b represent numbers by means of which the strength of the two [ideas] may be compared. Moreover, let the [strength of the] contrast [between them] equal *m*, where *m* stands for some fraction, or at most for unity. So, in the case of complete contrast (where $m=1$), *a* must decline completely if *b* is to remain uninhibited, likewise *b* must decline completely in order that *a* remain uninhibited. For the inhibited idea must yield fully and completely if all inhibition is to be removed from the contrasting idea, and if complete freedom [of the latter] is to return; and this is fully and equally necessary regardless of which may be the stronger and which the weaker one. In the case of diminished contrast, *mb* must decrease if *a* is to remain uninhibited, or *ma* must decrease if *b* is to remain uninhibited; the more of the inhibiting element present, the more must yielding occur, in the same ratio, if the contrasting idea is to remain untouched. If *b* consisted of an infinite number of small parts, each of these would have to be ascribed with the propensity for forming a contrast to *a*, and specifically to the degree *m*. Moreover, this tendency towards contrast would multiply in proportion to the total number of the parts in *b*, and would therefore be equivalent to the product *mb*.

This assumption of complete contrast will facilitate the investigations which follow immediately; this is the reason why we begin with it.

42

The sum of the inhibitions is that quantum of ideation which must be inhibited by the mutually opposing ideas taken simultaneously.

This sum of the inhibitions must necessarily be determined beforehand if the inhibition of each individual idea is to be found, because . . . the dynamic mutual opposition of all the ideas is only incidental. Ideas express themselves accordingly as forces only insofar as it is called for by the quantum of contrast which forms between them. The stronger the degree of contrast (the above mentioned *m*), and the more [forceful] the contrasting ideas (owing to the strength of the individual ideas), the greater will be the quantum of that which must retreat from the consciousness. This quantum also forms, then, so to speak, the burden which distributes itself among the different ideas which have to bear it; this includes all those which mutually oppose each other. But we cannot speak properly of the distribution before we know [the magnitude of] the burden that is to be distributed.

Now, for complete contrast, involving two ideas *a* and *b*, at least so much is immediately evident that either *a* or *b* must constitute the sum of the inhibitions, since certainly, both will exert some inhibition. The idea that either of the two should yield fully is a mere fiction that can by no means be made to agree with reality, for necessarily both ideas must suffer a little from the forces acting in opposition to them: in whatever manner the burden may be distributed, it [the burden] still always remains one and the same. However, we have already mentioned, in the preceding section, that this burden, or the idea to be inhibited [the total strength of the inhibition] would be *a* if *b* were to remain uninhibited, whereas it would be *b* if *a* were to be conceived as free from the inhibition. Assuming, then, that the sum of the inhibitions equals *a* in magnitude, nevertheless this would not result in an inhibition of the entire idea *a*. The sole reason for this would be that a part of this sum of inhibitions would fall on *b*. The magnitude of that which would devolve upon *b*, should be precisely equal to that which would now cease to inhibit *a*. Assuming the contrary case, that the sum of the inhibitions equals *b* in magnitude, only that much of *b* would be able to remain uninhibited as would of *a*, on the other hand, be [in its turn also] suppressed from the consciousness.

24

We waver, therefore, between these two possible definitions of the sum of the inhibitions [i.e. a or b]. The decision as to which of these two is the right one may appear at first glance, to be difficult.

However, the decisive basis presents itself easily enough. Namely, one must consider the sum of the inhibitions to be as small as possible. This is because the natural condition of ideas is the uninhibited one, and ideas surely approach, as nearly they can, this condition to which they all strive to return. It follows from this that if a is the stronger idea, and b is the weaker one, the sum of the inhibitions will equal b in magnitude, and not a.

Even a preliminary glance at the distribution of the sum of the inhibitions will make it clear that, while the stronger idea must predominate, it may not possibly do so more than is necessary for the weaker one to be wholely inhibited; and that this limit [of predominance] remains absolutely the same, no matter how much the stronger one may grow. Let us assume, for example, that $a = 10$, and $b = 1$; if so, b will certainly be inhibited almost entirely; but it will not be possible to inhibit more than the whole of b even if a should no longer equal 10, but 100. There is simply nothing more available than b in opposition to a! *Consequently an increase in the* [strength of the] *strongest one of the ideas does not produce an increase in the sum of the inhibitions.* On the other hand, let us assume that $a = 10$, and $b = 2$; in this case, the contrast has certainly become greater. [Maximum contrast occurs when $a = b$.] For inasmuch as b has increased from 1 to 2. a must resist a stronger force than before, and this makes it exert more power; and the same applies to b, though it now suffers relatively less than before.

Now then, since the sum of the inhibitions cannot be greater than b, and neither can it be smaller (because in the case of complete contrast, b is totally and fully in contrast to a), then it certainly equals b. This same conclusion is

25

also evident from the following consideration. Let a be uninhibited; b is then totally inhibited. Now, improve the distribution so that a part of the burden also falls on a; while b, on the contrary, increases. Nevertheless, as a result of this changed distribution, the quantum of the [striving of] one in opposition to the other still cannot possibly increase or decrease, because the effective idea [a], and its singular character, by virtue of which it manifests a definite contrast to the other one [in the first place], remain exactly as before; the sum of the inhibitions must, therefore, be and remain equal to b.

But exactly this latter method of reasoning might also be used to formulate an objection. Let us assume the reverse (so one might say), that b is uninhibited, and consequently that a is totally inhibited. In the case of an improved distribution, then, the quantum of the inhibition nevertheless, still cannot become depleted precisely for the reason that this quantum is independent of the distribution; it follows that the sum of the inhibitions equals a, and not b. Moreover, if it should be demonstrated in the same manner that the sum of the inhibitions is a, and that also it is b, this would then be a revelation of the weakness of the method of proof, which is self-contradictory.

If, however, one recalls what was demonstrated previously, it becomes obvious that in the assumption that a is totally inhibited, the quantum of the inhibition is taken to be greater than it need be in accordance with the nature of a and b. These two can, undeniably, assume a position in contrast to each other in which less [than a] of them is inhibited, and just for that very reason they will never fail to do so as soon as the distribution changes, although this is not [strictly speaking], a result of the new distribution. Rather, the same ascending tendency in both ideas, which brings a better proportion into the distribution, is the very thing that also opposes the excess

26

quantity of inhibition and reduces the inhibition to the necessary amount.—Hence, it does seem that our determination of the sum of the inhibitions is [can be] sufficiently definite.

Moreover, under the assumption of complete contrast, this same determination can be extended very readily from two ideas to several, in any desired number. Let us say that besides a, the strongest one, there are present also $b, c, d, \ldots n$; the sum of the inhibitions is then $= b + c + d + \ldots + n$. Since b, and the others, are fully in opposition to a, the quantum of the inhibition cannot be less than their sum,—but neither can it be greater, for if they were all fully repressed, the strongest one would remain completely uninhibited.—If on the other hand, we wish to try to conceive of b as uninhibited. the sum of the inhibitions is $= a + c + d + \ldots + n$; in other words, it is greater than previously; and so it is in the case of every other similar assumption. Consequently, only the above mentioned statement [that the sum of the inhibitions equals the sum of the strength of the weaker ideas] is admissible.

But before we close our consideration of the sum of the inhibitions, we must still eliminate a possible misunderstanding that might arise out of the comparison of that sum with the burden intended for distribution. Namely, quite in conformity with the spirit of our established principles, it will be found that the ideas, all also transformed into dynamic forces in the same degree as they suffer, are put under tension [i.e. exert a resistance] by the repression, and that the equilibrium sets in as soon as resistance and repression mutually cancel each other. From this it seems to follow that the sum of what is actually inhibited must amount to far less than is required by the original compulsion to decline [i.e. the sum of the inhibitions]. Then, this compulsion and the resistance of the ideas will act against each other; and thus the

27

former [compulsion] cannot reach the point towards which it is striving. This is apparent, but nevertheless wrong. Namely it is taken for granted in this, that the ideas can actively oppose the sum of the inhibitions. But it is more likely, rather, that the ideas actively oppose one another. The sum of the inhibitions is nothing different from [the ideas] themselves; it is not a burden imposed upon them more or less from the outside, that they have to bear collectively, but is merely the expression of the quantum of the opposition that arises among them and remains among them, insofar as they meet in the consciousness. Therefore, what an idea gains through its resistance cannot cause a decrement in the original opposition [the inhibition sum] that is based on the nature of the ideas (or else they would have to change their character); but each idea wins out, as much as it can, over the other ideas, which it inhibits by exactly as much as the magnitude by which it prevents the eclipsing of its own object in the consciousness. And far from assuming that the sum of the inhibitions should encounter a counterforce in the resistance, it is rather precisely the manifestation of this very resistance which is identical with the opposition, insofar as the latter is regarded as the sum of the active strivings of the individual ideas. Later on, we shall find the opportunity to express this, as well as the opposing incorrect view, in mathematical equations, for it will be shown that quite different laws of the gradual decline of the sum of the inhibitions follow from them [i.e. from the equations].

Finally, should it not be asked whether we are also conscious of such resistance of our ideas? According to our entire argument presented above, the ideas fail to be actual ideations to the extent to which they have changed into mere strivings—in other words, to the extent to which they are placed under tension [and so exert resistance]. It is impossible to encounter this tension directly in the

28

consciousness, else there would have to exist a consciousness of that which is not ideation, but which is precisely
the absence thereof. Therefore, our ambitions, desires,
etc., of which we [ourselves] are really conscious, must
not rashly be explained by means of that tension, even
though they are essentially connected to it.

43

The inhibition ratio is that ratio in which the sum of
the inhibitions distributes itself over [each of] the separate, active mutually contrasting ideas.

Each idea maintains itself, as best it can, amongst all
the others; it must, however, not be regarded as an
originally aggressive force, but merely as a resisting one.
Now, it is right here at the beginning that we must eliminate a possible error that would lead to erroneous calculations. It could be believed, namely, that each force might
act on the others in proportion to its strength. Therefore,
if, for example, the idea a were $= 2$, and the idea $b = 1$,
and that [amount] of b which were inhibited were $= x$;
then, for $a = 4$ that [amount] of b which were inhibited
would have to be $2x$, since the inhibiting force has been
doubled. This is incorrect, however, because $a = 4$ is
affected by $b = 1$ less than is $a = 2$ by this same b. But a
can have an effect only insofar as it is driven to it by its
opposite. If b has also become double, simultaneously
with a, then and only then, would the stimulation [of b
on a] and consequently the effect, also become double.

But the better each idea resists the opposition, which
has arisen among the multiplicity of ideas, the stronger
that idea is. It suffers, therefore, in inverse proportion
to its strength.

And, finally, we can easily clarify these concepts in
full. Three considerations must first be distinguished, and
then linked together again.

First: Every idea acts in proportion to its strength = i.

Second: It acts in the proportion in which it suffers, $= 1/i$.

Third: It suffers in inverse proportion to its intensity, *i.e.* in the proportion $1/i$.

The proportion of activity [First and Second statements] is composed of i and $1/i$, and thus it is $= 1$ at all times [$i \times 1/i = 1$]; consequently, it may be omitted from the calculation. The proportion of suffering [repression], $1/i$, alone remains, and it alone determines the distribution of the sum of inhibitions.

This is the situation in the case of complete contrast. which we are discussing now. In the case of diminished contrast, another factor exerts its effect in the proportion of activity which will be discussed later on.

In complete contrast, each individual idea is acted upon in an equal degree by all the others, no matter hou unequal they may be in strength.

In order to make this principle entirely clear, we shall start with the easiest assumption. Let there be, at first only two ideas in conflict with one another, the stronger one $= a$, and the weaker one $= b$. The sum of the inhibitions which indicates the intensity of the conflict, is then that from which both ideas suffer. Now, to be sure, a suffers in the proportion $1/a$ and b suffers in the proportion $1/b$. Both exert a counteraction on this suffering (only not just in reaction, but exactly insofar as they suffer the [initial] action) in the integrated proportion of their suffering and their own strength, which is $= a \times 1/a$ and $b \times 1/b$, or $= 1$. This counteraction of b affects a, and the counter-action of a affects b, but the two reactions are equal and cancel each other out; therefore. only the first proportion, that of the suffering of the [i.e. caused by the] sum of the inhibitions is decisive

Now let there be three ideas in conflict, namely a, l

and c, where $a > b$ and $a > c$. The idea a suffers from the sum of the inhibitions in the proportion $1/a$, b suffers from it in the proportion $1/b$, and c in the proportion $1/c$. All counter-actions are $= 1$. Each of these counter-actions distributes its force in equal parts onto each of the opposing ones (for it cannot have a special direction, more than against another), and each part is then cancelled out by one that is equal and opposite to it.

In order to proceed still more carefully, we shall shift our attention: we set the sum of the inhibitions aside, and view the ideas in pairs, in order not only to observe each one acting against all the rest [as a totality], but each one acting against every single other one in the conflict.

First: in the conflict between a and b, they both suffer, as found previously, in the proportions $1/a$ and $1/b$. We do not know as yet how much they suffer, but let the suffering of a [due to b] equal x/a, in which case that of b [due to a] equals x/b.—Secondly: let c also be in conflict with a. Now, in so far as c suffers from a, greater or less than does b, this can only be the result of the ratio $b:c$, which determines the proportion of the resistance, which the two [respectively] can present to the same force, a, in response to their being equally put under pressure. According to the proportion

$$c : b = x/b : x/c$$

x/c is what c suffers from a. Consequently, a suffers x/a from c.—Thirdly: in conflict between b and c, we may determine the suffering of each in two ways. Namely, we already know how much a suffers from b [i.e. x/a]; it can be ascertained from this just how much c must suffer from the very same force [b], under the very same tension. We also know how much a suffers from c [i.e. also x/a]; it can be ascertained from this just how much b must suffer from the very same force [c]. Finally, the two results must agree with each other. We have, thus,

31

$$c : a = x/a : x/c,$$
and
$$b : a = x/a : x/b,$$

where the fourth terms are in the inverse ratio of c and b, as they should be. Now, to summarize, the suffering of a is $= 2x/a$ [x/a, from c, plus x/a, from b], that of b is $= 2x/b$, and that of c is $= 2x/c$. These values [added] together must equal the sum of the inhibitions, so that x can be ascertained from it. At the same time, the principle noted above is proven, because a suffers equally from b and from c, b suffers equally from c and from a, and c suffers equally from b and from a.

It is unnecessary to demonstrate this for four or more ideas as well, for the easy method of extrapolation may be clearly indicated.

Now, let the ideas $a, b, c, \ldots n$ be given, the inhibition ratios are then $1/a$, $1/b$, $1/c$, $\ldots 1/n$. Concerning the calculation, the only thing to note [further] is that some combining occurs here, because these magnitudes will have to be reduced to whole numbers. This yields for a, b, c the binary combinations bc, ac, ab; for a, b, c, d, the ternaries bcd, acd, abd, abc, etc.

Calculation of the inhibition in complete contrast, and the first demonstration of the thresholds of consciousness

44

The calculation of the amount which is to be inhibited by each idea [i.e. the magnitude of ideation which is to be suppressed] must be based upon proportionalities, the first two terms of which derive from the inhibition ratios, and the third term of which is furnished by the sum of the inhibitions.

Let us assume that the ideas a and b are given as acting against one another in the consciousness, and as being in complete contrast; in this case, in conformity with our previous discussions, the sum of the inhibitions equals the [strength of the] weaker idea, or $= b$; the inhibition ratio, thus, is as $b : a$. Consequently, we shall conclude that: the magnitude [of inhibition] to be distributed [throughout the consciousness] (i.e. the sum of the inhibitions [here $= b$]) is to each separate part [of the inhibition] as the sum of the ratio numbers is to each individual ratio number; or*

$$(a + b) \left\{ \begin{array}{l} : b \\[2em] : a \end{array} \right. = b \left\{ \begin{array}{l} : \dfrac{b^2}{a + b} \\[2em] : \dfrac{ab}{a + b} \end{array} \right. .$$

The ratio number b belongs [is the total amount of inhibition acting] (because of the inversion of the ratio [number a]) to a [$ab = 1, b = 1/a.$]; consequently

the residual of a: $a = a - \dfrac{b^2}{a + b}$.

and the residual of b: $b = b - \dfrac{ab}{a + b} = \dfrac{b^2}{a + b}$.

These residuals are naturally not actually severed parts of the ideas a and b, but are rather the amounts of

---

*EDITORS NOTE: In the ratio x/y, both x and y are "ratio numbers", i.e. numbers which partake in the aspect of being ratioed, each to each other. Hence, a and b are the ratio numbers referred to in the text. The case of two ideas is unique in that only here are the ratio numbers and the strength of the original ideas one and the same. Moreover, $b = \dfrac{ab}{a + b} + \dfrac{b^2}{a + b}$ i.e. the sum of the inhibitions active in the momentary consciousness is equal to that operating to suppress $\left(a \text{ i.e.} \dfrac{b^2}{a + b} \right)$, plus that operating to suppress b $\left(\text{i.e.} \dfrac{a + b}{ab} \right)$. That Herbart's equation is valid can be seen easily in a numerical example:
Given: 7/5 then we have $(7 + 5 =)$ 12 : 7 and 12 : 5.
Given: 14/10 then we have $(14 + 10 =)$ 24 : 14 and 24 : 10.

the still remaining vitality of the ideas, after the previously computed component of the actual ideation has been cancelled by the inhibition and transformed into a mere striving at ideation.

Let three ideas be given in this same fashion, designated as a, b and c, of which a is the strongest and c is the weakest. In this case, the sum of the inhibitions $= b + c$, and the inhibition ratios $1/a$, $1/b$, $1/c$, or bc, ac, ab;** and the proportionalities are:

$$(bc + ac + ab) : \begin{cases} bc \\ ac \\ ab \end{cases} = (b + c) : \begin{cases} \dfrac{bc(b + c)}{bc + ac + ab} \\ \dfrac{ac(b + c)}{bc + ac + ab}, \\ \dfrac{ab(b + c)}{bc + ac + ab} \end{cases}$$

from which the residuals are:

$$\text{of } a, = a - \frac{bc(b + c)}{bc + ac + ab},$$

$$\text{of } b, = b - \frac{ac(b + c)}{bc + ac + ab},$$

$$\text{of } c, = c - \frac{ab(b + c)}{bc + ac + ab}.$$

It is easy to see how this extends to four and more ideas. Here are a few numerical computations. First, for two ideas:

If $a = 1$, and $b = 1$, the residual of a is $1/2$, that of b is $1/2$.

If $a = 2$, and $b = 1$, the residual of a is $5/3$, that of b is $1/3$.

**EDITORS NOTE: For example: if $abc = 1 =$ the totality of consciousness, and the amount of inhibition exerted on a given idea is in inverse proportion to its strength; then the amount of inhibition operating on a is $1/a = bc$. And so forth.

If $a = 10$, and $b = 1$, the residual of a is 100/11, that of b is 1/11.

If $a = 11$, and $b = 10$, the residual of a is 131/21, that of b is 100/21.

It is obvious that the residuals differ by a far bigger proportion than do the ideas themselves. Yet the residual of b can never become $= o$, for only when $a = \infty$ does the value of the formula $\dfrac{b^2}{a + b}$ become infinitely small.***

Now for three ideas:

If $a = 1$, $b = 1$, $c = 1$, the residuals are:
of a, $= 1/3$; of b, $= 1/3$; of c, $= 1/3$.

If $a = 2$, $b = 1$, $c = 1$, the residuals are:
of a, $= 8/5$; of b, $= 1/5$; of c, $= 1/5$.

If instead of b and c one single idea having the strength $b + c$ had been present here, then the residual of this would have been the same as that of a, namely, the residual of each would have been $= 1$. In the present case eight times as much remains from a as from b and from c, this difference is of so great an importance, i.e. whether the same identical quantum of ideation acts as one collective force or whether it is divided into two, also mutually opposing ideas.—Finally, let us take the case where
$a = 6$, $b = 5$, $c = 4$; then,
the residual of a, $= 132/27$,
the residual of b, $= 77/37$,
the residual of c, $= 13/37$.

A total force equal to $b + c$, instead of the two separate forces b and c, would have produced here, a much smaller sum of inhibitions; it would have become $= 6$, instead of $+ 9$. Also, only a small residual would have been left over from a and, consequently the larger would be the residual

---

***EDITORS NOTE: This formula equals zero also, when $b = o$. Herbart denies both these possibilities: $a \neq \infty$, for no idea can be infinitely strong; and $b < o$, for should $b = o$ then be cannot be in consciousness (*i.e.* it is totally suppressed) and should $b < o$ then we would have an absurdity (See also Boring, a, p. 248 et passim).

which would have been left over from the collective force.

The residual from b cannot become $= o$ for three ideas, as well as for two; otherwise ($bbc + abb - acc$) could $= o$. This is not possible, for b is not smaller than c, and consequently either $abb < acc$, or at worst $abb = acc$; so that the equation is always positive.

On the other hand, the residual of c can in fact become $= o$; this is a very important circumstance, about which more will be said soon.

45

The purpose of the general equations in the present investigation is essentially to attain a survey of an entire field of possibilities, or, to be more precise, of the consequences of all possible presuppositions. This purpose is very greatly advanced by small tables which show the values of the equations, when computed numerically for assumed basic magnitudes. In order, however, to shorten the work necessitated by such tables, it is advisable to select a few simple cases for the actual calculation, so that, whenever possible, the other [complex] cases can be thought of as being interpolated between them.

Let us begin here with the following: for three ideas, let the residual of a, be $= p$, that of b, $= q$, and that of c, $= r$. Let us first of all equate b and c, from which it must follow that $q = r$. Secondly, let us equate b and a, from which it must follow that $p = q$. After proper derivation, on the basis of equation of the preceding section, we shall find:

for $b = c$,

$$p = a - \frac{2b^2}{b + 2a},$$

$$q = r = \frac{b^2}{b + 2a}.$$

for $b = a$,

$$p = q = a - \frac{c(a + c)}{2c + a},$$

$$r = \frac{2c^2 - a^2}{2c + a}.$$

36

In the first case, let us make $b = 10$; in the second case, $c = 10$; then:

$$(1) \quad q = a = \frac{200}{10 + 2a}, \qquad (2) \quad p = q = a - \frac{10(10 + a)}{20 + a},$$

$$p = r = \frac{100}{10 + 2a}, \qquad\qquad r = \frac{200 - a^2}{20 + a},$$

$$b = c = 10. \qquad\qquad\qquad a = b, \text{ and } c = 10.$$

TABLE 1

	p	$q = r$		$p = q$	r
$a = 10$	3,33..	3,33..	$a = b = 10$	3,33..	3,33..
$a = 11$	4,75..	3,12..	$a = b = 11$	4,22..	2,54..
:	:	:	$a = b = 12$	5,17..	1,75
$a = 15$	10	2,5	$a = b = 13$	6,03..	0,93..
:	:	:	$a = b = 14$	6,94..	0,11..
$a = 20$	16	2	$a = b = 15$	7,5	0
:	:	:	:	:	:
$a = 40$	37,77	1,11..	$a = b = 20$	10	0

46

It may not be without value to mention, now, the additional problem of finding the (strength of the) ideas themselves, by working backwards from the given values of the residuals. Thus, in the equations

$$p = a - \frac{bc(b + c)}{bc + ac + ab},$$

$$q = b - \frac{ac(b + c)}{bc + ac + ab},$$

$$r = c - \frac{ab(b + c)}{bc + ac + ab},$$

let a, b and c be unknown; if so, the equation $a = p + q + r$ becomes immediately obvious, from the nature of the

37

matter, as well as from the formulas themselves.

Furthermore, let

$$\frac{b + c}{bc + ac + ab} = F,$$

then one has

$$a - p = bcF; \; b - q = acF; \; c - r = abF;$$

consequently:

$$\frac{a - p}{b - q} = \frac{b}{a}; \qquad \frac{a - p}{c - r} = \frac{c}{a},$$

or: $\qquad a^2 - ap = b^2 - bq = c^2 - cr.$

Let us equate already known magnitude $a^2 - ap$ to h; so that

$$b = \tfrac{1}{2}q + \sqrt{\tfrac{1}{4}q^2 + h} \; ; \; c = \tfrac{1}{2}r + \sqrt{\tfrac{1}{4}r^2 + h} \, .$$

It is obvious that only the + sign can be used before the radical sign, since b and c must be greater than half their residuals.

47

The previous remark that the residual of c can become negative is a primary concept which may lead us into very far-reaching investigations.

It is easy to answer the question as to what a negative idea could mean: namely, it can mean absolutely nothing. For, according to the previous discussions, the most that can happen to an idea is that it is transformed fully and outright into a mere striving at ideation, or that the residual of the actual ideation becomes $= o$. Therefore, the equation $r = o$ sets a limit to the applicability of the preceding method of calculation, for in our case a negative r is as good as an impossible magnitude.

From $r = o$, it follows $c = b \sqrt{\dfrac{a}{b + a}}$. Insofar as c

is smaller in relation to b and a, then, according to this formula, any more exact determination of its magnitude for the above calculation of the inhibition is quite unnecessary, because it is totally inhibited in any case. Consequently its share [that which bears on it] in the sum of the inhibitions is exactly equal to its contribution to that sum, and the stronger ideas divide their contributions precisely as if c had not been present at all. Therefore, the state of consciousness, insofar as it can be determined statically, is not at all dependent on c; even less is it dependent on any *still weaker* ideas, *an infinite number of which might be present without their being in the least perceptible in the consciousness as long as the consciousness is and remains in the state of equilibrium of all ideas.*

This proposition, which is derived here with the highest mathematical rigor, gives us now an explanation of the most widespread of all psychological wonders. We all observe within ourselves, that, of all our knowledge, our thoughts, and our desires, an incomparably smaller quantity actually occupies our consciousness in any single instant, than that quantity which could emerge within us upon appropriate stimulation. In what state in us, is this knowledge which is absent, yet not lost, but remaining and abiding in our possession? How does it happen that although it is present, it still does not make any contribution to the determination of our affective state until it once again occurs to us? What [is it that] can prevent our most vivid convictions, our best intentions, our concrete feelings, from becoming effective, often for long periods of time? What can instill into them that unfortunate inertia through which they so often make us the victims of vain regret? *Other thoughts* have occupied us [our consciousness] too vividly! We know this directly through experience. And yet some people have preferred to lose themselves in the false teachings of the transcendental freedom, and of the radical evil, which destroy all sound metaphysics, rather than to investigate more thoroughly the psychological mechanism which obviously must be at fault.

The proposition just now formulated, is the first, though as yet very limited, beginning of our insight into this mechanism. Two ideas are sufficient to repress a third one completely from the consciousness, and to bring about an effective state entirely independent of it. One idea alone is not capable of accomplishing this against a second one, as we have already seen when we noted that the residual of b can never become $= o$. But, whatever is possible for two ideas to do against a third, they can also do against any number of weaker ideas no matter how many. Further investigations will show that exactly similar psychological events can also take place, under certain circumstances, without the ideas which are repressed from the consciousness having necessarily to be weaker than the ideas which drive them out.

But, meanwhile, let us, right now indicate the generality of these events by a technical term, the use of which often become necessary again in the following discussions. As it is customary to speak of an entry of the ideas into the consciousness, so I call *threshold of consciousness* that boundary which an idea appears to cross as it passes from the totally inhibited state into some [any] degree of actual ideation. *Computation of the threshold* is an abbreviated expression for the computation of all those conditions under which an idea is still just able to maintain even an infinitely small degree of actual ideation,—under which it thus stands precisely at the threshold. As we may speak of the intensification and weakening of ideas, so I refer to an idea as *below the threshold* if it lacks the strength to satisfy those conditions. Although the state in which the idea is then, is always equivalent to total inhibition, nevertheless, it may be *more* or *less far below the threshold,* according as it lacks more or less of the

40

strength which would still have to be added to it in order for it to reach the threshold. Likewise, an idea is *above the threshold* insofar as it has reached a certain degree of actual ideation.

When the conditions under consideration are such that in the state of equilibrium, an idea is just at the threshold, the latter is referred to as the *static* threshold. Further below this, *mechanical* thresholds will also appear, which depend on the laws of motion of the ideas. Among the static thresholds, there are some which depend upon the complications and fusions of several ideas. In contradistinction to these, those thresholds which are determined solely by the intensity and contrast of simple ideas are designated as *common* thresholds. The first type of common threshold is the one which occurs in complete contrast, such as we have considered up to the present, and which we have defined by the formula $c = b \sqrt{\dfrac{a}{a+b}}$.

48

This is the place for reexamining a few earlier remarks. It was indicated [previously] . . . what the expression, "facts of consciousness", was to be understood to mean. We also spoke [earlier] . . . of the difference between that which comes into the consciousness and that of which one is conscious. This differentiation is necessitated by the linguistic deficiency, which is produced by a defect in our psychological insight. Namely, many people consider ideation and the self-observation of this ideation to be inseparable; or they mistake one outright for the other. This is how the term. "consciousness," becomes ambiguous, in that it is used at times to designate the entire actual ideation—in other words, the prominence of certain ideas above the threshold, their elevation above the totally inhibited state—and at other times to desig-

41

nate the observation of this ideation *as ours,* [that is] its connection with the Ego. Here we take the word, "consciousness," always in the first sense, whereas for the second sense we employ the phrase: "one is conscious of a thing."

This is not meant, though, to be decisive on the question of the so-called unconscious ideas, or, as we would express it, the ideas which are in the consciousness without one's being conscious of them. In the first place, moreover, in the light of all the previous discussion, it is clearly evident that the laws, according to which ideas enter the consciousness, begin to reveal themselves to us much earlier than do those laws, according to which the Ego may be viewed as the actor in the ideation. Self-observation is doubtless something incomparably more complicated than the mere crossing of the threshold, and it must, therefore, be completely separated in our investigation from this latter concept. *Secondly, we need a name for the totality of the moment by moment simultaneously concurrent ideation,* and a more suitable expression than the word "consciousness," could hardly be found for this. This [concurrent ideation] is of such great importance because it constitutes the sphere of action for every idea which is contained in it at a given moment, in that all simultaneously active ideas interact with each other and produce, jointly, the existing affective state. Should it appear contrary to proper linguistic usage to speak of ideas in the consciousness, of which we are supposed to be effectively unconscious, let it be recalled that even the most colloquial language uses the phrase, "he is without consciousness," to designate a state of mind that is very different from the one, for example, which a thinker or a poet approaches to the extent that he, *forgetting himself,* becomes scientifically or artistically absorbed in his subject.

[Previously, we] ... had the occasion to recall Locke's

42

justified amazement at the "narrowness of the human mind." It can be seen already at this moment, that this apparent peculiarity of the psyche—the ability to activate only a small number of ideas, simultaneously, and, in the exchange of ideas, to always let the old ideas pass over the new ones, yet without losing them—is no peculiarity of the psyche at all, but is merely a necessary result of the contrasts between our ideas. What thoughts would we have to entertain, indeed, if we wished to conceive of the mind as more or less equipped with a narrow pupil, perhaps with some sort of an iris, which dilated and contracted according to its own laws? The previous discussion makes it clear that the quantum of that which can be present together in the consciousness in the state of equilibrium has no *general* law at all, but depends *in each individual instance* on the strength and the contrasts of the *concurrent* ideas. However, we can not speak here, as yet, of the physiological influences which modify this to some extent and which might bring us a little closer to the analogy with that pupil.

49

The importance of this subject requires that we present a few computed values of the very simple threshold formula, $c = b \sqrt{\dfrac{a}{a+b}}$. We combine this with a study of the respective residuals of a and of b.

As we know, the equation derived in # 46,

$$r = c - \frac{ab(b+c)}{bc + ac + ab} = o,$$

has yielded the formula, $c = b \sqrt{\dfrac{a}{a+b}}$. Instead of substituting this value of c in the equations shown there for p

and for q, let us take the equation which was further along in the same section.

$$c = \tfrac{1}{2}r + \sqrt{\tfrac{1}{4}r^2 + h} \quad,$$

where

$$h = a^2 + ap.$$

For $r = o$ there follows from this that $c = \sqrt{h} = \sqrt{a^2 - ap}$, or $c^2 = a^2 - ap$, or $ap = a^2 - c^2 = (a + c)\,(\dot{a} - c)$.

Furthermore, now, $a = p + q$ and $p = a - q = a - \dfrac{c^2}{a}$ whence $q = \dfrac{c^2}{a}$, or $aq = c^2$.

This gives an easily comprehensible relation between q (the residual of b), and a (the strongest of the three ideas) and c, whenever it has its threshold value. We can imagine q as a constant magnitude, as the parameter of a parabola; in that case, there is a correlated constant sequence of values for c and a, namely as ordinates and abscissae taken from the vertex on the axis. Since a is not $< b$, this [axis] starts from $a = b$, for which a obtains a value that depends on q (namely $a = 2q$, from an equation that follows immediately), and then it continues as far as $a = \infty$ (for which b and c become infinites of the order of $\tfrac{1}{2}$. [If $a = \infty$, $\sqrt{a} =$ an infinity of the order of $\tfrac{1}{2}$], as $b = \tfrac{1}{2}q + \sqrt{\tfrac{1}{4}q^2 + qa}$.

From $a = p + q$ and $\dfrac{a - p}{b - q} = \dfrac{b}{a}$, furthermore, we

obtain $\dfrac{q}{b - a} = \dfrac{b}{a}$ or $q = \dfrac{bb}{a + b}$, identical to the equation

given in # 44. This is as it should be because only a and b have the sum of the inhibitions i.e. b, to divide, so long as c is at the threshold.

Therefore, if we wish to compute all the correlated

magnitudes at once, it is convenient, for arbitrarily assumed a and b, to calculate first

$$\frac{a+b}{bb} = q \text{ then } p = a - q, \text{ and then } c = \sqrt{aq}.$$

We can relate the present examples to the residuals previously calculated in # 44 for two ideas, in that we need add here only the threshold values for the third idea.

TABLE 2

a	b	p	q	c
1	1	$\frac{1}{2} = 0.5$	$\frac{1}{2} = 0,5$	0,707..
2	1	$\frac{5}{3} = 1,666..$	$\frac{1}{3} = 0,333..$	0,816..
10	1	$\frac{109}{11} = 9,909..$	$\frac{1}{11} = 0,090..$	0,953..
11	10	$\frac{131}{21} = 4,761..$	$\frac{100}{21} = 4,761..$	7,237..

A slightly more coherent series of threshold values for c follows in the next Table, which has been computed under the constant assumption that $b = 1$:

TABLE 3

a	c	a	c
1	0,7071	2	0,8164
1,1	0,7237	3	0,8660
1,2	0,7385	4	0,894
1,3	0,7518	5	0,912
1,4	0,7637	6	0,925
1,5	0,7745	7	0,935
1,6	0,7844	8	0,942
1,7	0,7934	9	0,948
1,8	0,8017	10	0,953
1,9	0,8094	∞	1

45

It is understood that if instead of the value 1, another value is adopted for b, the other figures must increase in the same proportion. Thus, if $b = 10$, $a = 11$, and $c = 7.237$ instead of 0.7237, as it is indicated by the preceding Table.

50

If we wish to apply the calculation of inhibition given in # 44 to assumed magnitudes of three ideas, we must first ascertain whether or not the applicability of the calculation is altered by the fact that the weakest of the three ideas must decline below the threshold in comparison to the others, in which case, the calculation, from the very start, is to be referred only to the two stronger ideas.

For instance, let the intensities of the ideas be to each other in the ratio of 1, 2 and 3. In order to apply the preceding Table here, [it is only necessary to] divide the given figures by 2, to make $b = 1$. Then $a = 3/2 = 1.5$, and $c = 0.5$. The Table shows now that $c = 0.77\ldots$ would already decline to its threshold, in comparison to a and b; in other words, a great deal [of strength] is lacking [from c]in order that $c = 0.5$ be taken into account here. Hence, the calculation of inhibition proceeds according to the equation for two ideas; this gives the residual of a, $= 11/5$, and of b, 4/5.

This example shows the usefulness, in fact almost the indispensability, of threshold tables. Unfortunately, the thresholds depend in reality on so many highly involved definitions (as it will become more and more evident soon), and even the general equations which can still be found, are so numerous and, partly, so difficult to employ, that no little patience will be required if speculative psychology is ever to be provided with tools of this nature.

But it is already a great gain in itself if simply correct

46

concepts are acquired concerning these subjects, and a general view is obtained of the possibility and the laws according to which something happens and can happen in the psyche.

Moreover, in the present basic outline we cannot yet conceive of complete elucidations. We want, therefore, only to mention the thresholds for *more than three* ideas [not to try to discuss them fully].

#51

Let us assume that the ideas a, b, c and d are given, and arranged, as we always assume, in the order of their strength, from the strongest to the weakest one. The sum of the inhibitions is then $= b + c + d$; the inhibition ratios are $bcd : acd : abd : abc$, and the residual of d:

$$s = d - \frac{abc\,(b + c + d)}{bcd + acd + abd + abc}.$$

It follows from $s = o$ that $d =$

$$d = \sqrt{\frac{abc\,(b + c)}{bc + ac + ab}}.$$

In precisely the same fashion the residual of e or t would be found, in the case of five [simultaneously opposing] ideas:

$$t = e - \frac{abcd\,(b + c + d + e)}{bcde + acde + abde + abce + abcd},$$

and, from $t = 0$,

$$e = \sqrt{\frac{abcd\,(b + c + d)}{bcd + acd + abd + abc}}.$$

For the sake of comparison, let us write the already known equation,

47

$$ c = b \ \sqrt{\dfrac{a}{a+b}} $$

as

$$ c = \sqrt{\dfrac{ab \cdot b}{a+b}} \ ; $$

the method of extrapolation will then be so clearly evident that it would be superfluous to add anything more.

Now let all ideas be $= 1$, except for whichever is the weakest one in each particular instance. The threshold equations then yield:

$$ c = \sqrt{\tfrac{1}{2}} \ = 0.707, $$

$$ d = \sqrt{2/3} \ = 0.816, $$

$$ e = \sqrt{\tfrac{3}{4}} \ = 0.866. $$

which series infinitely converges toward the value of unity. That is, the more ideas there are [simultaneously in the consciousness], the less may the weakest one be removed [in magnitude] from the stronger ones, (in order not to decline to the threshold). This holds true all the more definitely when the other ideas are different [in magnitude from each other]. For, if a increases, the sum of the inhibitions remains the same, but a bears less of it [the inhibition] and so shifts all the more [of it] onto the weaker ideas. If b increases also however, the sum of the inhibitions itself actually increases, and the weaker ones must succumb all the sooner.

The possibility of the co-existence of more than three ideas in the conscious seems, thus, to be confined within very narrow limits. But this applies only to cases of complete contrast, and it is modified, moreover, by many circumstances as well.

JOHANN FRIEDRICH HERBART (b.-Oldenburg, Germany, May 4, 1776; d.-Gottingen, Aug. 11, 1841).

Herbart studied philosophy under Fichte, at Jena, for three years, from 1794 to 1797. He visited Pestalozzi in Switzerland, in 1799. Herbart received his PhD. from Gottingen, in 1802, and continued on as Dozent. In 1805 he became Ausserordentlicher Professor in Philosophy. In 1809 he went to Konigsberg, to occupy the chair in Philosophy left vacant by Kant (d.-1804). He remained here, where he published his most important works, until 1833. He then returned to Gottingen, where he held the chair of Philosophy until his death, some eight years later.

Herbart is perhaps better known as the founder of scientific pedagogy than he is as the founder of scientific psychology—yet in a very real sense, this is his just due. He can be credited with having written the first formal textbook in psychology in 1813 (v.i.), which gives a simplified version of his psychological theories for the beginning student. Moreover, his magnum opus (1824) is the first attempt to formally abstract the science of psychology from its philosophical nexus.

For us today, Herbart's threefold base of psychology is still perhaps its most accurate description. Experience has become reemphasized by Hoffding and the Gestalt school. Metaphysics, in the form of the mind-body problem and of Philosophical Anthropology, is perhaps the most important aspect of modern psychological thought. Neurologists for example, constantly struggle with problems of the location of consciousness, semanticists with problems of the nature of man implied in a particular linguistic description of the universe, and so on. While the mathematical foundations of psychology are manifest in the domain of experimental psychology and psychophysics. Herbart had denied that psychological experiments could be done, but it was, in fact, the application of his very own mathematics by Fechner (1860) which eventually proved him wrong (*Elemente der Psychophysik*). Moreover, the recent topological psychology of Kurt Lewin resembles in its very essence the primitive mathematizations of Herbart.

The frankly literal rationalism of Herbart is his greatest appeal for us today. We envy his freedom in this intellectual game, which we can no longer play because the weight of 'tough-minded' facts presses in upon us, and hampers our thoughts. Herbart could say, simply: "Let there be an idea, *a*, in the consciousness. Let the strength of this idea be 10!" And already we are lost: by what right 10? Exactly 10? Not 10.5 or 10.05, or even 7.345? What is the 'strength' of an idea in the first place? Indeed, what is an 'idea'? Herbart soon leaves us far behind

49

in the wonderful flow of his ideas. The first time that mathematics is applied to a new field, it always has that same fresh blush of excitement and enthusiasm which we see here in Herbart. It is only with time and its distant perspective that we can see our efforts in the proper light. The present selection is Herbart's most important attempt at mathematization, and illustrates his method at its best.

HERBART, J. F. *Psychology as science, newly based upon experience, metaphysics, and mathematics*. Vol. I, Synthetic part, section 2: "Foundations of the statics of the soul." Chap. I: "Sum and ratio of inhibition in total contrast." Chap. II: "Calculation of the inhibition in total contrast and the first demonstration of the threshold of consciousness." Translated from Herbart's important work: *Psychologie als Wissenschaft, neu gegründet auf Erfahrung, Metaphysik und Mathematik**. Konigsberg: A. W. Unzer, 1824. Vol. I, Synthetische Theil, Zweyter Abschnitt: "Grundlinien der Statik des Geistes." Erstes Capitel: "Summe und Verhältnis der Hemmung bey vollem Gegnsatz." Zweytes Capitel: "Berechnung der Hemmung bey vollem Gegensatz, und erste Nachweisung der Schwellen des Bewuseyns."

See also:

HERBART, J. F. *Sämmtliche Werke*. Leipzig: G. Hartenstein, 1850-1852, 12 vol.
In particular:
Psychologische Untersuchungen über die Stärke einer Vorstellung —1912, vol. 7.
Lehrbuch zur Psychologie—1813, vol. 5. This is available in English translation: *A textbook in psychology*. N. Y.: D. Appleton Century, 1897 (1894, 1891). Trans. M. K. Smith.
Uber die Moglichkeit und Nothwendigkeit Mathematik auf Psychologie anzuwenden—1822, vol. 7.

BALDWIN (Vol. III, pp. 253-257) gives a readily available bibliography.

BORING (Chap. 12) gives a survey of Herbart's importance to psychology.

---

* Editor's note—As a reflection of Herbart's time, this book was published at Herbart's own expense.

CONTRIBUTIONS TO THE THEORY OF SENSORY PERCEPTION

WILHELM WUNDT

Introduction: *On the methods in psychology*

It is a maxim, impressed upon us from all sides, by the history of the natural sciences, that advances in science are intimately linked with advances in the methods of investigation. The entire natural science of recent years owes its origin to a revolution in methodology, and where great results are achieved, we may be sure that they were preceded by an improvement in previous methods or by discovery of new ones.

When psychology is considered as a natural science, one cannot help but find it extremely remarkable that those great changes, which have completely reshaped the physical sciences since the days of Baco* and Galileo, have had no effect on it whatsoever. There is even more justification for applying to psychology the comment that Kant once made about logic, namely that it had not advanced one single step since Aristotle. Logic has, at least, become stationary, but psychology has retrogressed in many respects.

However, if we take a look at the problems with which psychologists especially like to deal, we cannot [really] find the slow progress in this science surprising. The questions concerning the nature, seat, origin and future destiny of the psyche have been the objects of psychological research from time immemorial. Some even believed, at times, that as long as these questions were undecided, the phenomena of psychic life [Seelenlebens] could not be understood in their causal relationship. Investigations of this kind still play the main role in contemporary psychology, nevertheless some [slight] advance

---

* Editor's note: The latinized name of Francis Bacon.

towards the methods of natural science has certainly taken place.

These questions, however, belong for the most part, not to natural scientific psychology, but to metaphysics which, since it is not a natural science, has also been unable to derive any benefit from the improvements in the methods of natural science. Even though one may concede a certain justification to the discussion of the metaphysical problems which stand behind psychology, one must still insist that up to now they have deserved no more of a place in scientific psychology than views on the first cause of things have deserved in physics.

An unbiased criticism must admit that all these investigations into the nature of the psyche and its relationship to corporeality have produced extraordinarily little result to this moment. We move perpetually in a circle. That which is brought to light as something new has always been present in some similar form, while the last word always remains, only, a negative criticism which reaches out in all directions and has at least the one consequence that it questions all supposedly positive results.

A stubborn pursuit of these metaphysical investigations is, however, so much the less advisable since an infinity of problems stand open in psychology, which are totally unrelated to basic metaphysical questions and which are amenable to independent solutions; so that it truly appears to be a useless waste of energy to keep returning to such aimless discussions about the nature of the psyche, which were in vogue for a while, and practically still are, instead, rather, of applying one's energies where they will produce real results.

It would be a sad state of affairs for physics if the physicists, instead of taking direct action in the midst of the wide variety of phenomena, had chosen—say—to speculate on the nature of matter, and had put all problems aside until the basic solution of this speculative question [was found]. Why does psychology not follow the example of the natural sciences? Why does it insist stubbornly on beginning where it will, at best, be able to finish? The great multitude of psychic phenomena is so distinct in itself that it is very well capable of being subjected to independent scientific investigation. And if we do decide to undertake this investigation, uninfluenced by preconceived views, we shall finally return, unexpectedly, to the basic metaphysical questions of psychology, but we shall then stand much closer to them than we can today.

It is an unmistakable fact that in the psychology of today lies the possibility of great progress . . . This progress is linked with an essential reform in our views about the nature and tasks of philosophy in general. The view is continually gaining ground that philosophy, like every science, must start out from the basis of *experience*. Even metaphysics, which for a while appeared not only to dominate all science, but in fact to create it, is being relegated again to [a position] within the limits which were already marked out for it by Aristotle, who regarded it as the science that takes the results of all the other sciences as the objects of its special study.

However, the more philosophy itself begins to take deliberate cognizance of the realm of real events, the greater significance and consideration which psychology acquires; indeed, psychology was even in the past, that philosophical discipline which, to a certain point at least, represented itself as an experimental science. Thus, this previous step-child of the idealistic systems, has advanced more and more into the forefront in our time, and has gained ground to the same extent that metaphysics has retreated. One can almost say, at the present time, that our entire philosophy is psychology.

Nevertheless, it can hardly be claimed that any fundamental progress has already taken place in psychology.

53

Psychology still furnishes us with hardly anything more than a multitude of facts, without order and without correlation. And, still, the path taken by most philosophical thinkers today, in order to find this order and this correlation, seems to be little suited for reaching a better goal. New viewpoints and new ideas are sought, and, it is [somehow] hoped, that the idea, as a glowing spark, will all of a sudden be able to bring light into the dark chaos of unorganized knowledge. But the idea needs a content, which it can obtain only from the facts: and as regards the facts, we still adhere essentially to what is supplied by the most superficial observation of consciousness. Our psychology today is, therefore, still what it was for Aristotle, and even more a science of the facts of consciousness than it was for him. But it is beyond all doubt that the consciousness itself, and everything that happens within it, are already involved phenomena. Here, as everywhere in nature, the fact is that only the complicated phenomenon is immediately accessible to our observation, while that which is simple at first remains hidden from us. This simple element, which we can reach only through the dissection of the composite phenomena, but which in turn furnishes us with the principles for the exploration of these composite phenomena, constitutes, in psychology, the beginnings of psychic life—the beginnings in the individual animated being as well as in the entire scale of animal life. Just as anatomy entered its scientific stage only since microscopic dissection and embryological research began to teach us of the beginning of forms, through which the laws of the structure of tissue and of the organism can be explored, so perhaps psychology also will not free itself from the investitures of metaphysical hypotheses which still surround it, and stand on the ground of its own laws, until we succeed in grasping psychic phenomena at their very beginning and in making them accessible to dissection. There are two sciences which, in this sense, must come to the aid of general psychology: the *history of the evolution of the psyche* and *comparative psychology*. The task of the former is to elaborate the gradual development of psychic life in man, that of the latter is to describe its differences in the animal kingdom and in the races of mankind.

If one should work diligently on these undeveloped sciences, in which a vast treasure of observations lies unused and in which an even greater treasure is still to be discovered, this would lead to an immeasurable advance. The difficulties which arise here are, of course, not minor ones, but at least they are not insuperable, as the metaphysical problems have been up to now, and perhaps will be for a long time to come.

In fact, various beginnings have already been made in these . . . ancillary sciences of psychology. But these initial steps, it seems to me, in most cases still do not approach this matter in the proper fashion. Thus, in comparative psychology we are still unable to free ourselves from the traditional prejudice which ascribes all psychic phenomenon in the animal kingdom to an instinct, by which the entire psychic life is predestined, in some inexplicable manner. Furthermore, the psychology of nations [Völkerpsychologie] still offers a rich, open field, in which great preliminary works are already in existence, on linguistics, cultural history and the history of morals, but which as yet have hardly been utilized in the service of psychology.

In the history of the evolution of the psyche we have also failed to proceed in a manner likely to promise an insight into the nature of this evolution. In most cases, we have limited ourselves to direct observation. I believe, that this [direct observation] can be applied generally only as a control on results gained through other channels; because man, in the first stages of his evolution,

55

is just as strange to himself as is a creature of another species. We are able to attain positive results here only because we are entitled to presuppose a continuity of the evolution, and to use observations on the evolved human being as the basis for far-reaching conclusions concerning the laws of his evolution.

The genesis of sensation and perception is, certainly, one of the most important events of this evolution. In sensation, the domains of physical and psychic events are in direct contact, and perception is the first and perhaps simplest event of a purely psychic character. To find out how the physical sensory impression becomes sensation—this problem has hardly been studied as yet. We still seem to be far from the answer to this fundamental question in psychology, which is, at the same time, a basic question in all philosophical speculation. The problem of perception is indubitably much nearer to its solution. Here we possess a great number of valuable physiological observations, which would perhaps have led long ago to a completed theory of the perceptive processes, if [only] we had defined the concept of perception with sufficient clarity and had not constantly confused it with sensation and imagination. Since, however, we always considered only complex phenomena and did not penetrate into their correlations, it happened here, as everywhere, that, on the one hand, we severed what was inherently connected and, on the other hand we grouped together what was inherently distinct. But why was our penetration into the correlations of the psychical phenomena so very imperfect? Obviously because we were almost universally satisfied with the crudest observations, and made no effort to sharpen and to expand our observations by better methods. Thus, no matter from which side we may undertake a psychological investigation, we are always led back to the point from which we started—the improvement of the methods. If

56

the methods previously employed do not lead to a satisfactory solution of the questions that clamor for our
attention—well, then, we must try to seek other ways,
to discover new methods which will reveal new facts to
us, and, along with them, perhaps, an access to the laws
of psychic life.

We intend to consider, first, those methods heretofore
employed in psychology: if we apply the yardstick of
natural-scientific criticism to them, their shortcomings
will be easy to discover. Once we know these shortcomings,
it will, perhaps, not be difficult to find ways and means for
their correction.

In psychology, until now, only two methods of investigation have been applied: self-observation, and deduction
of the phenomena of psychic life from metaphysical
hypotheses. The former is deficient because it encompasses only a small part of the phenomena, while the
latter is to be rejected as a matter of principle.

All psychology begins with self-observation, and this
always remains an indispensable aid for interpreting
those psychic phenomena that are external to us. Self-
observation, however, is totally insufficient, when one's
intention is to go back to the beginnings and to the causes
of the phenomena. Self observation can never go beyond
the facts of consciousness; moreover, a science, based
[only] upon self-observation begins with these [facts],
whereas it [a science] ought, rather, to end with them.
For the phenomena of consciousness are composite
products of the unconscious psyche. Their nature is such,
that,—once they have already entered the consciousness,
—they will seldom still allow direct conclusions concerning their formation. The psychology based on self-
observation, which preferred to designate itself *empirical*
psychology, must therefore limit itself to an unsystematic
juxtaposition of the facts of the consciousness; and, since
it is unable to discover an inner connection between these

57

facts, it splits up those components which belong together into a large number of dissociated details. This is how empirical psychology came to represent every expression of the activity of the psyche as the expression of a special psychic capacity. This differentiation among the psychic capacities [Seelenvermogen] is the true expression of a state of science in which the whole is completely divisible into its individual phenomena, and in which the system itself is replaced by the external separation of disconnected facts.

Opposition to this confusion within empirical psychology was put forth very successfully by [those] philosophical schools which set themselves the task of deducing psychic phenomena from certain metaphysical hypotheses. The advantage of this psychology lay in the fact that the very weaknesses of the empirical school constituted the strengths of [this] the metaphysical method. While in the former, everything fell apart into a disordered mass of experiences, the latter presented a self-contained system in which every detail possessed its [own] definite place. On the other hand, the great disadvantage of this method consisted in the fact that, as soon as the metaphysical foundation, on which the structure had been erected, was no longer sustained, then the entire building also collapsed. Empirical psychology produced only a little, but that little was secure, metaphysical psychology gave everything, but if just one [component] was doubted, everything within it became questionable. Empiricism, however, was never without [some] influence on the metaphysician, whose conclusions fell mostly into either of two categories: there were the conclusions which did not lend themselves to confirmation by experience, and there were those which had to be recognized as definite facts of observation. Usually, however, only the conclusions of the first category were really deduced from the metaphysical hypothesis; the conclusions of the second category were very often merely smuggled into the system.

Empirical psychology proceeded according to the *inductive* method, as is indicated in most instances for an incomplete state of science, but it certainly did not exhaust all the instruments of induction. Metaphysical psychology proceeded *deductively*, but one must take objection, in principle, to the manner in which it reached its deductions. For the fundamental laws which served as starting point had not been attained inductively from the mass of all individual phenomena, nor were they taken at all from the psychic domain; rather, they were purely metaphysical hypotheses placed at the apex of the system. Metaphysics, however, is a science that is at first alien to psychology. Nevertheless, in the vast realm of knowledge, it is not unusual, that one region receive its light from another. Every advance in theoretical mechanics has also [served to] advance the physical sciences, and progress in mechanics itself has been intrinsically bound to geometry, the general knowledge of space. A further example that is directly connected with our topic is given by national economics. Sociology has existed as a science only since Adam Smith conceived of the fortunate idea of extending the psychology of the individual human being to the human race. And this [sociology] was deductive to begin with; it took the simplest facts of practical psychology as a starting point, and with these it opened up an entire special field for itself. There is far more justification for designating national economics the "psychology of society" then there [ever] was for referring to it as the "physics of society."

Things are different, however, with respect to metaphysics. Anyone who is familar with the schisms in the views about all metaphysical questions must admit, insofar as he has not entirely learned to doubt the possibility of a metaphysics, that our contemporary metaphysics is not only far removed from any firm foundation, but that there is, as yet, nothing sufficiently established here to have led, even, to any accord among the thinkers. It must appear, therefore, as a dangerous undertaking, to say the least, to wish to make such a questionable science the basis of another one, which has at least already reached a clear conclusion about many facts. There is, however, a still greater criticism that can be made against such a foundation for psychology. We may ask, namely, whether there is any relation at all between psychology and metaphysics similar to that between mechanics and geometry, or to that between sociology and psychology.

In the case of the latter sciences, the relationship is such that the science [psychology] upon which the other one was founded was itself completely independent from that other one, at least in its fundamental development. We can conceive of a geometry without any knowledge of the laws of motion, but motion cannot be conceived of without [a conception of] the space in which it takes place. Psychology has reached its fundamental facts solely through observation without any consideration of human society as a whole, but the laws which control the life of human society become understandable only when one began to study them through self-observation. The situation is totally different with respect to metaphysics. If we really possessed a metaphysics, it would perhaps be possible to derive psychology from it, but everything supports the view that psychology does not need metaphysics; but, on the contrary, at least in the entire domain of inner experience, metaphysics is in need of psychology for its firm foundation. In addition, the metaphysics of today always starts out from psychological experiences; but, to be sure because it wants in principle to disavow experience [altogether], though unable to do without it, it steals, only surreptitiously, some of the riches of the psychological facts which would be wholly and freely at its disposal.

The attempt to build psychological facts on a metaphysical basis is most essentially linked with the mathematical method of treatment in psychology. This [treatment] is an almost necessary result of the fact that metaphysical psychology encompasses the deductive method. In a science when a major portion of the facts can be deduced from a few axioms through a series of more or less complicated conclusions, and when the simple procedural methods of formal logic are insufficient for this deduction, then the science is compelled to resort to the aid of the mathematical language of symbols.

[However], this [language of symbols] is merely an efficient instrument of thought [it is] only a repetitive application of the logical laws which, by means of certain symbols, fixes the results of thinking at each individual step in logical sequence.* The mathematical method of treatment occurs, therefore, to an increased extent, as soon as a science has become completely deductive, in other words as soon as it has arrived at the ultimate phenomena, from which its entire domain of experience can be deduced. Therefore, as soon as people thought that the totality of psychic phenomena could be deduced from metaphysical axioms the idea of resorting to the aid of mathematics lay very near.

Considering that the metaphysician has always proceeded deductively in psychology, the expanded application of mathematics in this science is actually a rather late occurrence. It made its first appearance only at that moment when the endeavor was not merely to deduce the intrinsically metaphysical problems of psychology, but

---

*The mathematician might easily find this definition to be too loose, because mathematics has up to now, in fact not yet found such a general application. It seems unmistakable to me, however, that the entire modern mathematics is headed toward this generalization of the calculus, which would make it essentially into an expanded logic.

when an attempt was made to extend this deduction from metaphysical propositions to the entire domain of experience. Aristotle divides psychology in two parts: a deductive part, in which the nature of the psyche is developed from concepts [preconceptions] and an inductive part, in which those properties of the psyche, which are revealed by experience, are made the object of investigation. The same distinction appears again later, in a much sharper form, in the views of Christian Wolff who seeks, in [his] rational psychology, to determine the supra-sensory nature of the psyche according to Leibnitzian metaphysics, and who treats, in [his] *empirical* psychology, the different psychic capacities as he believes them to be given by observation. This differentiation, into a rational and an empirical psychology, was lost once again in the idealistic systems of this century. But psychology in general, was given a very subordinate consideration in them [i.e. the idealistic systems]. These systems, which were, above all, intended to proceed in the most rigorous deductive fashion, in that they constructed the sciences from a definite set of concepts, were applied in psychology with the greatest lassitude; they extracted primarily only the general pattern from the system, but then they filled out this pattern with a content that remained entirely within the boundaries of the traditional empiricism, and in which only the experientially given genetic connection between phenomena was disrupted, to be replaced by the semblance of a conceptual connection that dissolved into an arbitrary disorder at the hand of [serious] criticism. This was done, lately, in the most conspicuous fashion, by Hegel and his school. Recently, however, a more realistic trend of metaphysics, which found its expression in Herbart, has devoted greater attention to psychology; and it is in this manner that Herbart became the creator of mathematical psychology.

Herbart was of the opinion that, by mathematical treatment, psychology would at least attain the same security which has been reached by those natural sciences which are [already] capable of a complete mathematical method of treatment. If we examine the actual results of mathematical psychology, it must appear strange, in contrast to these high expectations, to see that in the explanation of individual phenomena (which must, after all, always be the yardstick of progress in the whole), this mathematical psychology essentially does not go beyond that which was known long ago to certain perspicacious observers of the psychic life: in fact it does not go beyond what Aristotle, in large part, had already stated about the psyche in his writings, so rich in observations and ideas, as long as two thousand years ago. Mathematical psychology has only in part reduced such well known facts to formulae; in part it has arrived by means of calculation at results that must be called doubtful or obviously incorrect.* An impartial scrutiny of the individual results, therefore, proves irrefutably that no way has yet been found here, to achieve [by means of them] a better explanation of psychic phenomena.

On the other hand, let it not be denied that mathematical psychology has one great merit—a merit, to be sure, which is linked most immediately to its weakest side. Namely, as long as they [the mathematical psychologists] endeavored to deduce mathematically all the details of science from one single axiom, through this procedure they recognized a unity of psychological science, a unity of psychic phenomena (although—as it was frequently believed—even a problematic unity of the psyche had not yet been shown). This step, actually carried out by the mathematical school for the first time, was, indeed, an especially important one. The previous psychology had

---

* The very metaphysical axiom on which the entire psychology of Herbart is built can be refuted directly by experiment.

done nothing but list, somewhat aimlessly, whatever the crudest observations had revealed. Each of the principal manifestations of the activity of the psyche was represented as the expression of a special psychic capacity, hence, the entire psychic life was merely a composite of its details.·Mathematical psychology was the first to consider psychic life as a whole, and to regard [all] the individual psychic expressions as specific modes of manifestation of a unified fundamental entity. Thus, essentially, it has paved the way for a systematic science, and this merit remains even if its own structure should completely collapse.

The basic fault of every metaphysical method in psychology, however, was also shared by mathematical psychology. The principle which it used as the starting point of its deductions had not grown out of the science itself, but had been borrowed from an extraneous science which was itself still wholly undeveloped, and which was dependent on psychology; ultimately, the facts did not flow forth necessarily from the principle, rather the principle was adjusted to the facts.

But, in addition, in the carrying out of the deductive method, mathematical psychology went in a direction which would not be the right one, even if it should ever be possible to treat psychology successfully by the deductive method. The entire structure of this mathematical psychology consists, namely, of a statics and a mechanics of ideas. It regards the ideas as masses which act upon each other with definite forces and which thereby produce certain motions among each other; that is, it makes its material accessible to a mathematical method of treatment by representing it spatially. This is a limitation, however, that is not demanded either by the subject matter, which has absolutely nothing whatever to do with spatial masses and motions, or by the tool, i.e. the mathematical calculus. Geometry and mechanics, these purest sciences of space, are, nevertheless, the fields to which mathematics is most usually applied, and in which in fact, lay its origin. The physical natural sciences move in the region of spatial events; they are linked, therefore, directly to geometrical and mechanical considerations; when they are developed entirely through deduction, they can be regarded as immediate applications of those two basic sciences. If mathematics should consist wholly and exclusively of the sciences of space from which it had originally evolved (as was the case at a certain stage of its development), we could hardly speak at all of an extended application of mathematics to the moral sciences. But mathematics achieved a far more general meaning some time ago. The step by which it attained this meaning lay above all in the discovery of the differential calculus; by this [discovery] mathematics embarked on a calculus which, while it did become extremely productive in geometry and mechanics, is nevertheless totally independent of these sciences. Even though the differential calculus begins with mathematical functions which can be represented spatially and which were also found at first by geometrical means, [it is independent of them] inasmuch as it passes from these continually over into functions which are no longer capable of a spatial representation. Moreover, in this case, we are not dealing with a primary distinction, as, for instance, between number theory and a geometry which makes each of these branches capable only of a limited application. Rather, the whole broad meaning of this calculus exists also in the mathematical method. In a sense, this demonstrates to us that the limitation of space to three dimensions is merely a special property of our sensory nature. There is no such limitation in pure thought.

The application of mathematics to the moral sciences, even though it has been a narrowly limited one, and will surely remain so for a long time to come, is by no means to be regarded as an impossibility *per se*. First of all, mathematics has advanced, through the discovery of the differential calculus, from [the status of] a limited tool of the physical sciences to the position of a general tool of thought. This advance has made it possible, in fact necessary, that application of the mathematical methods be made wherever the facts are such as to imply far-reaching conclusions. It is significant in this respect that a discoverer of the differential calculus devoted a large part of his endeavors to the idea of the mathematical treatment of the moral sciences. This was a trait that accompanied Leibnitz throughout his entire life. Twice he started to carry out this idea: first, in the elaboration of the theory of combination, and then in the invention of the differential calculus. Perhaps he did find in the latter the tool he was seeking, but first of all, the new method was not yet sufficiently developed, and the time was not yet ripe for the extended application that he had in mind. So it happened that Leibnitz himself fell short of recognizing the significance of his discovery to its full extent; he still kept searching constantly for that universal tool of thought which he perhaps had already in his hands.*

If it has turned out as a result of our criticism that the former methods of psychology were insufficient, the question now arises as to how these methods are to be improved. I believe that this question is, in general, not difficult to answer. In this connection, since, as we have shown, the deductive method is to be rejected as a matter of principle, the only starting point available is the inductive process, which empirical psychology has fol-

---

* In the first presentations of his new method of calculation, Leibnitz came much closer to a clear philosophical view of the concept of the differential than later on, when he adopted increasingly the habit of designating the differentials as infinitely small magnitudes of various orders—a mode of designation which will do well enough for practical purposes, but which is not really sufficient, either mathematically or philosophically.

66

lowed for a long time. But it will still have to be investigated whether induction cannot be given a far wider application in psychological investigations than has been the case until now. In my opinion, there are two ways by which this can be done: the first one consists in a broadening of the method of observation heretofore in use, the second one in the utilization of the experiment as a tool of the investigation.

I mentioned above that sociology in its present form was created by an extension of the results of the psychological observation of the individual, to the lives of the nations. Now, however, this science has gradually begun to free itself from the basis on which it rests, and to establish its own foundation. This foundation consists in the determination of a great number of facts through *statistics*. It is with the aid of statistical investigations that national economics, as such, is first beginning to raise itself to [the status of] a true *natural history of human society,* resting far more safely on its own laws than on foreign territory. It is an unmistakable fact that in our times sociology is in the process of experiencing this great revolution; but the revolution has not been completed as yet, it has hardly gone through its initial stages. The material offered by statistics is by far still insufficient for erecting the science on it anew. To the extent, however, to which sociology becomes an independent science, its relationship to psychology also begins to invert itself. It is now no longer dependent on psychology, as it used to be; but, on the contrary, the statistical disclosures of the national economists contain a multitude of facts which are directly relevant to important psychological conclusions. In this respect, the new statistics, little as its achievement appears in terms of its total task, has nevertheless produced extremely rich material for the psychologist, which has remained effectively unexploited. But, in this way, not only may something new be gained for psychology, but this method also has the infinite advantage that it replaces vague suppositions by an unshakable conviction, that instead of uncertain inferences it permits the drawing of conclusions with a mathematical certainty.

Let us demonstrate this by just a few examples. The external causes of suicide were, in general, known also to psychologists in the past, but only in a very indefinite fashion, for the conclusions were based on individual cases, and unaccountable random factors are always at play in the individual case. Statistics, above everything, has brought a greater certainty here. Based as it is on a great number of cases, it has determined numerically the relative frequency of the causal factors, and has even discovered definite relationships between the form of the suicide and its cause. But statistics has gone still further here; it has permitted us, for the first time, to inspect the more remote causes of suicide, by furnishing information concerning its occurrence according to the age, sex, the national character and the occupation of the individual, according to the climate, the weather, the season of the year, and to many other external factors. Similarly: it had always been observed, concerning the proclivity of the sexes, that a young man will occasionally idolize an older sweetheart, and, the other way around, that a more aged man will not infrequently take to his fancy a girl [still] half-child. But statistics have proven that love follows psychological laws, and that these facts are not striking chance occurrences, but that they contain the law of the proclivity of the sexes according to their age.

Other examples could be cited as well. It can be stated without exaggeration that we can learn more psychology from statistical data than from all the philosophers, with the exception of Aristotle. Of course, statistical facts are immediately of importance only for practical *psychology* not for the *theory* of psychic phenomena. But practical psychology forms the foundation from which we must start out. Even if we only learn from statistics what factors determine the most important life-destinies [Lebensschicksale] of man, this is already of great importance because our knowledge here [then] has a scientific certainty for the first time. Statistics was the first [of the branches of applied mathematics] to create material out of long observed facts, that is useful and important to psychology. We are unable to appraise the significance of this material as yet, precisely because the earlier observations of practical psychology, which always dealt with the single individual, remained so vague and so indefinite that there was not much that could be done with them. Moreover, the little thing that could be concluded from them, passed into the general consciousness such a long time ago that its influence on the formation of our fundamental views can no longer be judged at all.

The only tool heretofore utilized for the observation of single individuals was the study of *history*. But neither did this tool endow the investigations with any greater certainty. For also in history, the role of a determinant factor is played by the indeterminant freedom of the individual, and history has heretofore preponderantly considered just exactly this influence of the single outstanding individual on the course of events. The situation would be quite different if, as it always happens when statistics is brought in, we took the *natural history* of mankind as the tool for psychological observation. Mankind or individual national units as wholes lead a natural-historical existence which is entirely dependent on the state of the total society. Wherever the material for the observations is sufficiently large, the law of the greater number applies, i.e., individual deviations occur which we attribute to chance or to individual volition, and the natural-historical law manifests itself with perfect clarity. The statistician, in so far as he seeks to gather the greatest possible number of cases, acts exactly like the observer in natural science who, by accumulating his observations or experiments, thereby endows his results with sufficient certainty; and in this, the statistical method is closely akin to the second tool which we regard as necessary in psychological investigations.

This second tool consists of the extensive application of the *experiment*. The importance which experimentation will eventually have in psychology can hardly be visualized to its full extent as yet. We do have, surely, many noteworthy beginnings in the field of psychological investigations, but as a coherent science, experimental psychology still awaits its foundations. These beginnings relate predominantly to the borderline areas where physiology and psychology touch each other, in the area of sensation and perception. It has often been held that the area of sensation and perception is the only one wherein the application of the experimental method remains a possibility, because this is the very area where physiological factors always play a role; whereas—so holds this view—it is a futile attempt to try to penetrate into the realm of the higher psychic activities by experimental methods. Surely, this is a prejudice. As soon as the psyche is viewed as a natural phenomenon, and psychology as a natural science, the experimental methods must also be capable of full application to this science. In point of fact, we already possess experimental investigations which are removed from the psycho-physical area and which concern themselves with purely psychic events, insofar as there is such a thing at all.

In the last chapter of these Contributions, reference is made repeatedly to the fact observed by astronomers and called the *personal equation*, which can be explained only on the ground that the course of ideation and of thinking is bound to a definite temporal extent. I have

70

lately attempted to determine this temporal extent more accurately through experiment. The astronomical observations are not suited to this purpose, since only relative determinations are obtained through them, and, furthermore, since a greater complexity of psychological factors is present in them. I have tried, therefore, to first of all determine the speed of the course of the process of ideation in the simplest case, the succession of only two different ideas. I let a pendulum swing in front of a circular scale. At a given point of its path [the pendulum] struck against a lever. It was then possible to compare exactly the true position of the pendulum, in the instant when it produced the sound, with the position which made it appear to occupy, in the instant when the sound was heard. In this way, a constant scale difference was found, from which together with the duration of the pendular motion, the time interval between the auditory and the visual image formation could be computed. The average length of this time interval was found to be one-eighth of one second, and this difference was positive in one instance and negative in another; that is, the observer was either able to see first and then to hear, or to hear first and to see later.

I believe that I may designate this investigation of the speed of image formation as a *purely* psychological one, even though sensory excitations are utilized in it, because the sensory excitations are by no means the essential element here, but are used merely as experimental aids; it is not to be doubted, that the ideation and thinking which is completely independent of external excitations, takes place according to these same laws and during the same temporal extent. The opposite assumption would, in fact, embody such an improbability that it need not be discussed more specifically: it would presuppose a double consciousness, inasmuch as it would claim that the consciousness for the [self] reproduced images was

71

something totally different from the consciousness for those images resulting from direct excitation by external impressions.

Through the measurements cited here, it was not only possible to determine a specific psychic constant, which had been completely unknown until now, but certain general conclusions concerning the nature of consciousness, which seem to me quite noteworthy, also follow from it. It was here that good evidence was first obtained for the psychological law of the unity of the imagination. This [concept] was already probable, in accordance with the observations of the astronomers, but owing to their having complicated vision and hearing with a third activity (i.e. the counting of the blows of the pendulum), it perhaps had not yet really been established with sufficient certainty. Many facts discussed in Chapter 5 of these Contributions already point to this law, but the criticism of the Herbartian psychology presented in Chapter 6, and the theory (presented there) of the common sensibility, specifically receive their essential support from this law.

Thus if we feel justified in making the statement that experiments can find application in the purely psychological domain (although, admittedly, the sensory excitations can never be disposed with as *aids* in the investigation), it must nevertheless be admitted that it is primarily the *sensory* side of psychic life which accords the widest prospect for experimental investigation. This is, therefore, where the first begining is to be made; further advances [could] then follow by themselves, in the course of investigation, for the psychic domains are not so sharply delimited as to make it impossible to find a continual transition from one to the other.

It would be a fundamental error to insist, in reference to the experimental exploration of the sensory and the perceptive processes, that all that one can find in this manner are laws which possess a validity only for the psyche in its attitude toward external sensory stimuli, and that in the life which is independent from these [stimuli], in pure thought, quite deviant laws might be valid, about which the results of our experiments could disclose nothing. Although attention was already called to the absurdity of this assumption, because it introduced an inexplicable schism in psychic phenomena, I must refer to it here once again because it includes at the same time a total misunderstanding of experimental methodology, and of the role which sensory stimuli play in it.

When a chemist wishes to determine the nature of a substance that he has found, he investigates how it behaves in relation to other substances, but what he wants to find and actually does find through his experiments is not merely its behavior in relation to other substances, but the chemical nature itself of the object in question. In precisely the same way in psychology, it will hardly be possible to do away with external influences in the experiment, and yet it would be totally wrong to say that only the behavior of those influences with respect to the psyche is determined through the experiment. The behavior of the psyche with respect to the external influences is determined as well, and by varying those external influences we arrive at the laws to which the psychic life as such is subject. The sensory stimuli are, for us, nothing else than *experimental tools,* to express it succinctly. By effecting manifold changes in the sensory stimuli, while continually studying the psychic phenomena, we are merely applying the principle that constitutes the essence of the experimental method; "we change," to say it with Baco, "the circumstances in which the phenomena occur."

In the borderline areas between psychic and physical events, the ground was prepared for experimental manipulation by physiological investigations a long time ago.

Above all, however, in most recent times a great impetus was given by the important works of G. Th. Fechner.* Fechner succeeded, by making use of previous observations as well as new ones of his own, in demonstrating the law for all the senses, according to which the intensity of the sensation changes when the intensity of the stimulus is changed by a given magniude. This law, which states that the sensation does not increase in direct proportion to the stimulus, but in proportion to the relative increase in the stimulus, was designated by Fechner as a *psychophysical* law. This designation was meant to indicate that it was a law which determined the interrelations between the external impressions and the psyche. It is easily demonstrable that this law is actually not a physical law, that it does not express the way in which the excitation of the sensory nerves is determined by external impressions. But the term "psychophysical law" still says too much if the law is meant to be restricted to the interrelations of the psyche with the ouside world. Fechner already demonstrated that not only the *intensive* sensations, but also the *extensive* ones are to be subsumed under the law. But that which Fechner calls extensive sensation is nothing other than spatial perception, and we shall show that this develops from the sensation only through psychic processes. Therefore, if the same thing applies to the so-called extensive sensation as to the intensive one, this means merely that the dependent relationship between perception and sensation follows the same law as the dependency between sensation and stimulus. It is easy to prove in general, even if it is difficult to confirm by exact measurement, that this same law also retains its validity in the domain of the higher psychic activities. Everyone has observed for himself that the smallest annoyance, which a person who is

---

* G. T. Fechner, *Elemente der Psychophysik* Volumes I and II. Leipzig, 1860.

already in a bad mood does not even notice, is completely able to destroy a gay frame of mind; this is simply a special case of the law. We do not have here a psycho-physical, but a psychic law before us, which states that *where two psychic functions are in immediate dependence on one another, the dependent function always increases proportionally to the logarithm of the independently variable one.*

The following investigations deal with another problem. It is attempted in them to penetrate the *evolution* of the psychic processes, primarily with respect to the genesis of the perceptions from the sensations. The beginnings of a theory of the perceptive processes are, surely, already in existence here and there, yet an adequate examination on an experimental basis has not been attempted anywhere. These first attempts suffer specifically from the weakness that either the experimental material is not sufficiently utilized in the theory, or that the theoretical speculations are set forth without any experimental support at all. It was my intention to fill in the gaps in both directions as much as possible; I tried to decide the question about the nature of the perceptive processes solely on the basis of observation and experimentation, and after this question was decided, I endeavored, through the application of the discovered law to the specific case at hand, to gain an understanding of each individual form of perception and of each individual perceptive act. I am, now, by no means of the opinion that I have constructed the theory in this fashion with sufficient thoroughness, on the basis of empirical validation. Such [thoroughness] was unattainable for the very reason that these investigations do not embrace the entire domain of perception. But I do believe that the validation which did become possible extends at least far enough to warrant our regarding the given theory as secured in its essential points. In contradistinction to the currently

75

prevailing confusion of opinions, this does seem to me to be some gain after all.

The law, to which the analysis of individual perceptive processes leads back again and again, is the law of the *logical evolution* of the psyche. This law has therefore been selected as the foundation of the theory, and I hope to have shown that a successive application of this law (given by experience) is all that is needed to deduce the phenomena of the unconscious and the conscious psychic life, from sensation to image formation, in an orderly sequence. It is in this sense that I can preface the following investigations with the principle of Locke, the sensualist, together with the supplement added to it by Leibnitz, the idealist: *Nihil est in intellectu quod non fuerit in sensu —nisi intellectus ipse.* But I am far from placing in the psyche with this *intellectus,* an entire world of congenital ideas as Leibnitz did; I understand by *intellectus* only that empirical fact of logical evolution in which lies not the cognition itself, but the possibility of its attainment.

We have cited here two laws as valid for the totality of psychic phenomena. Both laws are already known, but not yet sufficiently respected as to their general significance. The first one was believed to be valid only for the dependence between sensation and stimulus, the second one was accepted only within the facts of consciousness (and here, too, mostly just for the moments of the deductive cognitive process). We owe the knowledge of the extended validity of these laws essentially to the experimental method. Experimentation in psychology, new as its application is, has already borne its fruits; it has opened up points of view to us about which it can be said with certainty that they could never have been reached through the road of immediate observation. Experimentation made it possible to subject the course of psychic phenomena to a temporal measure, and it has taught us two general laws which are of the greatest importance for our outlook on psychic life: a law of the *mutual inter-dependence of the psychic functions*, and a law of the *evolution of the psychic functions from each other.*

WILHELM MAX WUNDT (b.-Neckarau, Baden, Aug. 16, 1832; d.-Leipzig, Aug. 31, 1920)

Wundt went, for the year 1851, to Tübingen, then to Heidelberg till 1855. In 1856 he went to Berlin, for one term of study under Müller. In the same year he returned to Heidelberg and received his M.D., and then remained as Dozent and Instructor in Physiology until 1864. In this same year he was appointed Professor. Ten years later, in 1874, he was appointed to the Chair of Inductive Philosophy at Zürich. Then, shifting after one year to the Chair of Philosophy at Leipzig (1875), Wundt settled permanently, for 45 years. This was perhaps the longest span in a single position for anyone in the history of psychology. Here, in 1879, Wundt founded the first laboratory in psychology in the world, the Psychologisches Institut. In 1881 Wundt founded the journal *Philosophische Studien,* which carried the reports of the laboratory, and was second to *Mind* (founded by Bain in 1879) as the earliest journal in psychology. In 1889, Wundt was made rector of Leipzig.

It was in the years 1873-1874 Wundt published his monumental *Grundzüge der Physiologischen Psychologie.* It covered six editions, to 1911, and is partly available in English translation (v.i.). Boring calls this ". . . the most important book in the history of modern psychology". This book set the spirit and tone of Wundt's great laboratory. It grew out of the many years of lecturing at Heidelberg in physiology and medicine, and fulfilled certain of the major goals stated many years before in the Introduction to his *Beiträge.* The Leipzig laboratory was the forerunner of similar laboratories all over the world. Most of these were founded by students who had worked directly with Wundt, and who were inspired by him. The revealing list of Wundt's students (given in Boring), indicates that the breadth of Wundt's influence on academic psychology was probably greater than that of any other man. He is certainly to be credited with establishing the legitimacy of the experimental approach (e.g. as opposed to Herbart), and with spreading its influence into the farthest reaches of modern society. His most important European students were: E. Kraepelin, H. Münsterberg, H. Lehmann, O. Külpe, A. Kirschmann, E. Meuman, K. Marble, F. Kiesow, A. F. Lipps, G. W. Storring, F. Kruegar, W. Wirth. His American students were: G. S. Hall, J. McK. Cattell, H. M. Wolfe, E. A.

Pace, E. W. Scripture, F. Angell, E. B. Titchener, L. Witmer, H. Z. Warren, H. Gale, G. T. W. Patrick, G. M. Stratton, C. H. Judd, G. A. Tawney. The present selection is the Einleitung to Wundt's *Beiträge*, of 1862. Of this, Titchener (who probably knew Wundt better than any other American) comments that it constitutes a statement of Wundt's life goal, a goal which he actually carried out. A true picture of Wundt can only be formed by a direct acquaintance with his works. Their sheer number and diversity is of importance, not only the ideas in them. It is only by keeping in mind that Wundt, unlike most men, did in fact create the great science which he had conceived of in his Introduction, that one may begin to picture the enormity of his contribution. This essay appears here for the first time in English.

WUNDT, W. *Contributions to the theory of sensory perception.* Introduction: "On the methods of psychology." Trans. from: *Beiträge zur Theorie der Sinneswahrnehmung.* Leipzig: C. F. Winter, 1862. "Einleitung Ueber die Methoden in der Psychologie".

See also:

WUNDT, W.

a) *Vorlesungen über die Menschen-und Tierseele.* Leipzig: Voss, 1863. Available in translation—London: Sonnenschein, 1901 (2nd German edition.) Trans.: J. E. Crieghton & E. B. Titchener.

b) *Grundzüge der Physiologische Psychologie.* Leipzig: Engelmann, 1874. A partial translation of the 5th edition is available. London: Sonnenschein, 1904 (Germany, 1902). Trans.: E. B. Titchener.

c) *Einführung in die Psychologie.* Leipzig: Voigtländer, 1911. Also in translation.

d) *Volkerpsychologie: eine Untersuchung der Entwicklungsgesetz von Sprache, Mythus und Sitte.* Leipzig: Engelmann, 1911-1920, 10 vol.

TITCHENER, E. B. et al. "A bibliography of the scientific writings of Wilhelm Wundt" *Amer. J. Psychol.* 1908, 19: 541-556, and *Ibid.* 20-25 inc., 33.

"Wilhelm Wundt". *Amer. J. Psychol.* 1921, 32: 161-178 ". . . I am prepared to say that Wundt is the founder not of experimental psychology alone, but of psychology."—So said Titchener.

BORING (Chap. 15, pp. 310-344). This is a superb summary. It includes excellent related bibliographic material.

TREATISE ON PHYSIOLOGICAL OPTICS

HERMANN VON HELMHOLTZ

Concerning the Perceptions in General

The sensations aroused by light in the nervous mechanism of vision enable us to form conceptions as to the existence, form and position of external objects. These ideas are called *visual perceptions*. In this third subdivision of Physiological Optics we must try to analyze the scientific results which we have obtained concerning the conditions which give rise to visual perceptions.

Perceptions of external objects being therefore of the nature of ideas, and ideas themselves being invariably activities of our psychic energy, perceptions also can only be the result of psychic energy. Accordingly, strictly speaking, the theory of perceptions belongs properly in the domain of psychology. This is particularly true with respect to the mode of the mental activities in the case of the perceptions and with respect to the determination of their laws. Yet even here there is a wide field of investigation both in physics and physiology, inasmuch as we have to determine, scientifically as far as possible, what special properties of the physical stimulus and of the physiological stimulation are responsible for the formation of this or that particular idea as to the nature of the external objects perceived. In this part of the subject, therefore, we shall have to investigate the special properties of the retinal images, muscular sensations, etc., that are concerned in the perception of a definite position of the observed object, not only as to its direction but as to its distance; how the perception of the form of a body of three dimensions depends on certain peculiarities of the images; and under what circumstances it will appear single or double as seen by both eyes, etc. Thus, our main purpose will be simply to investigate the material of sensation whereby we are enabled to form ideas, in those relations that are important for the perceptions obtained from them. This problem can be solved entirely by scientific methods. At the same time, we cannot avoid referring to psychic activities and the laws that govern them, as far as they are concerned with the perception of the senses. But the discovery and description of these psychic activities will not be regarded as an essential part of our present task, because then we might run the risk of losing our hold of established facts and of not adhering steadily to a method founded on clear, well-recognized principles. Thus, for the present at least, I think the psychological domain of the physiology of the senses should be kept separate from pure psychology, whose province really is to establish as far as possible the laws and nature of the processes of the mind.

Still we cannot altogether avoid speaking of the mental processes that are active in the sense-perceptions, if we wish to see clearly the connection between the phenomena and to arrange the facts in their proper relation to one another. And hence, to prevent any misconception of the plan I have in mind, I intend to devote the latter part of this chapter to a discussion of the conclusions which I think can be inferred with respect to these mental processes. And yet we know by experience that people very seldom come to any agreement as to abstract questions of this nature. The keenest thinkers, philosophers like KANT for instance, have long ago analyzed these relations correctly and demonstrated them, and yet there is no permanent and general agreement about them among educated people. And, therefore, in the subsequent chapters devoted specially to the theory of the visual perceptions, I shall endeavour to avoid all reference to opinions as to mental activity, as involving questions that always have been, and perhaps always will be, subjects of debate

80

between the various metaphysical schools; so as not to distract the reader's attention from those facts about which an agreement may possibly be reached, by wrangling over abstract propositions that are not necessarily involved in the problem before us.

Here I shall merely indicate at the outset certain general characteristics of the mental processes that are active in the sense-perceptions, because they will be constantly encountered in connection with the various sub jects to be considered. Without some previous explanation of their general significance and wide range of activity, the reader might be apt in some special case to regard them as paradoxical and incredible.

The general rule determining the ideas of vision that are formed whenever an impression is made on the eye, with or without the aid of optical instruments, is that *such objects are always imagined as being present in the field of vision as would have to be there in order to produce the same impression on the nervous mechanism, the eyes being used under ordinary normal conditions.* To employ an illustration which has been mentioned before, suppose that the eyeball is mechanically stimulated at the outer corner of the eye. Then we imagine that we see an appearance of light in front of us somewhere in the direction of the bridge of the nose. Under ordinary conditions of vision, when our eyes are stimulated by light coming from outside, if the region of the retina in the outer corner of the eye is to be stimulated, the light actually has to enter the eye from the direction of the bridge of the nose. Thus, in accordance with the above rule, in a case of this kind we substitute a luminous object at the place mentioned in the field of view, although as a matter of fact the mechanical stimulus does not act on the eye from in front of the field of view nor from the nasal side of the eye, but on the contrary, is exerted on the outer surface of the eyeball and more from behind. The general

81

validity of the above will be shown by many other instances that will appear in the following pages.

In the statement of this rule mention is made of the ordinary conditions of vision, when the visual organ is stimulated by light from outside; this outside light, coming from the opaque objects in its path that were the last to be encountered, and having reached the eye along rectilinear paths through an uninterrupted layer of air. This is what is meant here by the normal use of the organ of vision, and the justification for using this term is that this mode of stimulation occurs in such an enormous majority of cases that all other instances where the paths of the rays of light are altered by reflections or refractions, or in which the stimulations are not produced by external light may be regarded as rare exceptions. This is because the retina in the fundus of the firm eyeball is almost completely protected from the actions of all other stimuli and is not easily accessible to anything but external light. When a person is in the habit of using an optical instrument and has become accustomed to it, for example, if he is used to wearing spectacles, to a certain extent he learns to interpret the visual images under these changed conditions.

Incidentally, the rule given above corresponds to a general characteristic of all sense-perceptions, and not simply to the sense of sight alone. For example, the stimulation of the tactile nerves in the enormous majority of cases is the result of influences that affect the terminal extensions of these nerves in the surface of the skin. It is only under exceptional circumstances that the nerve-stems can be stimulated by more powerful agencies. In accordance with the above rule, therefore all stimulations of cutaneous nerves, even when they affect the stem or the nerve-centre itself, are perceived as occurring in the corresponding peripheral surface of the skin. The most remarkable and astonishing cases of illusions of this sort are those in which the peripheral area of this particular portion of the skin is actually no longer in existence, as, for example, in case of a person whose leg has been amputated. For a long time after the operation the patient frequently imagines he has vivid sensations in the foot that has been severed. He feels exactly the places that ache on the one toe or the other. Of course, in a case of this sort the stimulation can affect only what is left of the stem of the nerve whose fibres formerly terminated in the amputated toes. Usually, it is the end of the nerve in the scar that is stimulated by external pressure or by contraction of the scar tissue. Sometimes at night the sensations in the missing extremity get to be so vivid that the patient has to feel the place to be sure that his limb is actually gone.

Thus it happens, that when the modes of stimulation of the organs of sense are unusual, incorrect ideas of objects are apt to be formed; which used to be described, therefore, as *illusions of the senses*. Obviously, in these cases there is nothing wrong with the activity of the organ of sense and its corresponding nervous mechanism which produces the illusion. Both of them have to act according to the laws that govern their activity once for all. It is rather simply an illusion in the judgment of the material presented to the senses, resulting in a false idea of it.

The psychic activities that lead us to infer that there in front of us at a certain place there is a certain object of a certain character, are generally not conscious activities, but unconscious ones. In their result they are equivalent to a *conclusion,* to the extent that the observed action on our senses enables us to form an idea as to the possible cause of this action; although, as a matter of fact, it is invariably simply the nervous stimulations that are perceived directly, that is, the actions, but never the external objects themselves. But what seems to differentiate them from a conclusion is an act of conscious thought. An astronomer, for example, comes to real conscious conclusions of this sort, when he computes the positions of the stars in space, their distances, etc., from the perspective images he has had of them at various times and as they are seen from different parts of the orbit of the earth. His conclusions are based on a conscious knowledge of the laws of optics. In the ordinary acts of vision this knowledge of optics is lacking. Still it may be permissible to speak of the psychic acts of ordinary perception as *unconscious conclusions,* thereby making a distinction of some sort between them and the common so-called conscious conclusions. And while it is true that there has been, and probably always will be, a measure of doubt as to the similarity of the psychic activity in the two cases, there can be no doubt as to the similarity between the results of such unconscious conclusions and those of conscious conclusions.

These unconscious conclusions derived from sensation are equivalent in their consequences to the so-called *conclusions from analogy.* Inasmuch as in an overwhelming majority of cases, whenever the parts of the retina in the outer corner of the eye are stimulated, it has been found to be due to external light coming into the eye from the direction of the bridge of the nose, the inference we make is that it is so in every new case whenever this part of the retina is stimulated; just as we assert that every single individual now living will die, because all previous experience has shown that all men who were formerly alive have died.

But, moreover, just because they are not free acts of conscious thought, these unconscious conclusions from analogy are irresistible, and the effect of them cannot be overcome by a better understanding of the real relations. It may be ever so clear how we get an idea of a luminous phenomenon in the field of vision when pressure is exerted on the eye; and yet we cannot get rid of the conviction that this appearance of light is actually there at the given place in the visual field; and we cannot seem to comprehend that there is a luminous phenomenon at the place where the retina is stimulated. It is the same way in case of all the images that we see in optical instruments.

On the other hand, there are numerous illustrations of fixed and inevitable associations of ideas due to frequent repetition, even when they have no natural connection, but are dependent merely on some conventional arrangement, as for example, the connection between the written letters of a word and its sound and meaning. Still to many physiologists and psychologists the connection between the sensation and the conception of the object usually appears to be so rigid and obligatory that they are not much disposed to admit that, to a considerable extent at least, it depends on acquired experience, that is, on psychic activity. On the contrary, they have endeavoured to find some mechanical mode of origin for this connection through the agency of imaginary organic structures. With regard to this question, all those experiences are of much significance which show how the judgment of the senses may be modified by experience and by training derived under various circumstances, and may be adapted to the new conditions. Thus, persons may learn in some measure to utilize details of the sensation which otherwise would escape notice and not contribute to obtaining any idea of the object. On the other hand, too, this new habit may acquire such a hold that when the individual in question is back again in the old original normal state, he may be liable to illusions of the senses.

Facts like these show the widespread influence that experience, training and habit have on our perceptions. But how far their influence really does extend, it would perhaps be impossible to say precisely at present. Little enough is definitely known about infants and very young animals, and the interpretation of such observations as have been made on them is extremely doubtful. Besides, no one can say that infants are entirely without experience and practice in tactile sensations and bodily movements. Accordingly, the rule given above has been stated in a form which does not anticipate the decision of this question. It merely expresses what the result is. And so it can be accepted even by those who have entirely different opinions as to the way ideas originate concerning objects in the external world.

Another general characteristic property of our sense-perceptions is, that *we are not in the habit of observing our sensations accurately, except as they are useful in enabling us to recognize external objects. On the contrary, we are wont to disregard all those parts of the sensations that are of no importance so far as external objects are concerned.* Thus in most cases some special assistance and training are needed in order to observe these latter subjective sensations. It might seem that nothing could be easier than to be conscious of one's own sensations; and yet experience shows that for the discovery of subjective sensations some special talent is needed, such as PURKINJE manifested in the highest degree; or else it is the result of accident or of theoretical speculation. For instance, the phenomena of the blind spot were discovered by MARIOTTE from theoretical considerations. Similarly, in the domain of hearing, I discovered the existence of those combination tones which I have called summation tones. In the great majority of cases, doubtless it was accident that revealed this or that subjective phenomenon to observers who happened to be particularly interested in such matters. It is only when subjective phenomena are so prominent as to interfere with the perception of things, that they attract everybody's attention. Once the phenomena have been discovered, it is generally easier for others to perceive them also, provided the proper precautions are taken for observing them, and the attention is concentrated on them. In many cases, however—for example, in the phenomena of the blind spot, or in the separation of the overtones and combination tones from the fundamental tones of musical sounds, etc.—such an intense concentration of attention is required that, even with the help of convenient external appliances, many persons are unable to perform the experiments. Even the after-images of bright objects are not perceived by most persons at first except under particularly favourable external conditions. It takes much more practice to see the fainter kinds of after-images. A common experience, illustrative of this sort of thing, is for a person who has some ocular trouble that impairs his vision to become suddenly aware of the so-called *mouches volantes* in his visual field, although the causes of this phenomenon have been there in the vitreous humor all his life. Yet now he will be firmly persuaded that these corpuscles have developed as the result of his ocular ailment, although the truth simply is that, owing to his ailment, the patient has been paying more attention to visual phenomena. No doubt, also there are cases where one eye has gradually become blind, and yet the patient has continued to go about for an indefinite time without noticing it, until he happened one day to close the good eye without closing the other, and so noticed the blindness of that eye.

When a person's attention is directed for the first time to the double images in binocular vision, he is usually greatly astonished to think that he had never noticed them before, especially when he reflects that the only objects he has ever seen single were those few that happened at the moment to be about as far from his eyes as the point of fixation. The great majority of objects, comprising all those that were farther or nearer than this point, were all seen double.

Accordingly, the first thing we have to learn is to pay heed to our individual sensations. Ordinarily we do so merely in case of those sensations that enable us to find out about the world around us. In the ordinary affairs of life the sensations have no other importance for us. Subjective sensations are of interest chiefly for scientific investigations only. If they happened to be noticed in the ordinary activity of the senses, they merely distract the attention. Thus while we may attain an extraordinary degree of delicacy and precision in objective observation, we not only fail to do so in subjective observations, but indeed we acquire the faculty in large measure of overlooking them and of forming our opinions of objects independently of them, even when they are so pronounced that they might easily be noticed.

The most universal sign by which subjective visual phenomena can be identified appears to be by the way they accompany the movement of the eye over the field of view. Thus, the after-images, the *mouches volantes,* the blind spot, and the "luminous dust" of the dark field all participate in the motions of the eye, and coincide successively with the various stationary objects in the visual field. On the other hand, if the same phenomena recur again invariably at the same places in the visual field, they may be regarded as being objective and as being connected wih external bodies. This is the case with contrast phenomena produced by after-images.

The same difficulty that we have in observing subjective sensations, that is, sensations aroused by internal causes, occurs also in trying to analyze the compound sensations, invariably excited in the same connection by any simple object, and to resolve them into their separate components. In such cases experience shows us how to recognize a compound aggregate of sensations as being the sign of a simple object. Accustomed to consider the sensation-complex as a connected whole, generally we are not able

88

to perceive the separate parts of it without external help and support. Many illustrations of this kind will be seen in the following pages. For instance the perception of the apparent direction of an object from the eye depends on the combination of those sensations by which we estimate the adjustment of the eye, and on being able to distinguish those parts of the retina where light falls from those parts where it does not fall. The perception of the solid form of an object of three dimensions is the result of the combination of two different perspective views in the two eyes. The gloss of a surface, which is apparently a simple effect, is due to differences of colouring or brightness in the images of it in the two eyes. These facts were ascertained by theory and may be verified by suitable experiments. But usually it is very difficult, if not impossible, to discover them by direct observation and analysis of the sensations alone. Even with sensations that are much more involved and always associated with frequently recurring complex objects, the oftener the same combination recurs, and the more used we have become to regarding the sensation as the normal sign of the real nature of the object, the more difficult it will be to analyze the sensation by observation alone. By way of illustration, it is a familiar experience that the colours of a landscape come out much more brilliantly and definitely by looking at them with the head on one side or upside down than they do when the head is in the ordinary upright position. In the usual mode of observation all we try to do is to judge correctly the objects as such. We know that at a certain distance green surfaces appear a little different in hue. We get in the habit of overlooking this difference, and learn to identify the altered green of distant meadows and trees with the corresponding colour of nearer objects. In the case of very distant objects like distant ranges of mountains, little of the colour of the body is left to be seen, because it is mainly shrouded in the colour of the illuminated air. This vague blue-grey colour, bordered above by the clear blue of the sky or the red-yellow of the sunset glow, and below by the vivid green of meadows and forests, is very subject to variations by contrast. To us it is the vague and variable colour of distance. The difference in it may, perhaps, be more noticeable sometimes and with some illuminations than at other times. But we do not determine its true nature, because it is not ascribed to any definite object. We are simply aware of its variable nature. But the instant we take an unusual position, and look at the landscape with the head under one arm, let us say, or between the legs, it all appears like a flat picture; partly on account of the strange position of the image in the eye, and partly because, as we shall see presently, the binocular judgment of distance becomes less accurate. It may even happen that with the head upside down the clouds have the correct perspective, whereas the objects on the earth appear like a painting on a vertical surface, as the clouds in the sky usually do. At the same time the colours lose their associations also with near or far objects, and confront us now purely in their own peculiar differences.[1] Then we have no difficulty in recognizing that the vague blue-grey of the far distance may indeed be a fairly saturated violet, and that the green of the vegetation blends imperceptibly through blue-green and blue into this violet, etc. This whole difference seems to me to be due to the fact that the colours have ceased to be distinctive signs of objects for us, and are considered merely as being different sensations. Consequently, we take in better their peculiar distinctions without being distracted by other considerations.

The connection between the sensations and external objects may interfere very much with the perception of

---

[1] This explanation is given also by O. N. ROOD, SILLIMAN'S *Journ.*, (2) xxxii. 1861. pp. 184, 185.

their simplest relation. A good illustration of this is the difficulty about perceiving the double images of binocular vision when they can be regarded as being images of one and the same external object.

In the same way we may have similar experiences with other kinds of sensations. The sensation of the *timbre* of a sound, as I have shown elsewhere,[2] consists of a series of sensations of its partial tones (fundamental and harmonics); but it is exceedingly difficult to analyze the compound sensation of the sound into these elementary components. The tactile sensation of wetness is composed of that of coldness and that of smoothness of surface. Consequently, on inadvertently touching a cold piece of smooth metal, we often get the impression of having touched something wet. Many other illustrations of this sort might be adduced. They all indicate that we are exceedingly well trained in finding out by our sensations the objective nature of the objects around us, but that we are completely unskilled in observing the sensations *per se*; and that the practice of associating them with things outside of us actually prevents us from being distinctly conscious of the pure sensations.

This is true also not merely with respect to qualitative differences of sensation, but it is likewise true with respect to the perception of space relations. For example, the spectacle of a person in the act of walking is a familiar sight. We think of this motion as a connected whole, possibly taking note of some of its most conspicuous singularities. But it requires minute attention and a special choice of the point of view to distinguish the upward and lateral movements of the body in a person's gait. We have to pick out points or lines of reference in the background with which we can compare the position of his head. But look through an astronomical telescope

---

[2] HELMHOLTZ, *Die Lehre von den Tonempfindungen.* Braunschweig 1862.

at a crowd of people in motion far away. Their images are upside down, but what a curious jerking and swaying of the body is produced by those who are walking about! Then there is no trouble whatever in noticing the peculiar motions of the body and many other singularities of gait; and especially differences between individuals and the reasons for them, simply because this is not the everyday sight to which we are accustomed. On the other hand, when the image is inverted in this way, it is not so easy to tell whether the gait is light or awkward, dignified or graceful, as it was when the image was erect.

Consequently, it may often be rather hard to say how much of our apperceptions (*Anschauungen*) as derived by the sense of sight is due directly to sensation, and how much of them, on the other hand, is due to experience and training. The main point of controversy between various investigators in this territory is connected also with this difficulty. Some are disposed to concede to the influence of experience as much scope as possible, and to derive from it especially all notion of space. This view may be called the *empirical theory* (*empiristische Theorie*). Others, of course, are obliged to admit the influence of experience in the case of certain classes of perceptions; still with respect to certain elementary apperceptions that occur uniformly in the case of all observers, they believe it is necessary to assume a system of innate apperceptions that are not based on experience, especially with respect to space-relations. In contradistinction to the former view, this may perhaps be called the *intuition theory* (*nativistische Theorie*) of the sense-perceptions.

In my opinion the following fundamental principles should be kept in mind in this discussion.

Let us restrict the word *idea* (*Vorstellung*) to mean the image of visual objects as retained in the memory, without being accompanied by any present sense-impressions; and use the term *apperception* (*Anschauung*) to mean a perception (*Wahrnehmung*) when it is accompanied by the sense-impressions in question. The term *immediate perception* (*Perzeption*) may then be employed to denote an apperception of this nature in which there is no element whatever that is not the result of direct sensations, that is, an apperception such as might be derived without any recollection of previous experience. Obviously, therefore, one and the same apperception may be accompanied by the corresponding sensations in very different measure. Thus idea and immediate perception may be combined in the apperception in the most different proportions.

A person in a familiar room which is brightly lighted by the sun gets an apperception that is abundantly accompanied by very vivid sensations. In the same room in the evening twilight he will not be able to recognize any objects except the brighter ones, especially the windows. But whatever he does actually recognize will be so intermingled with his recollections of the furniture that he can still move about in the room with safety and locate articles he is trying to find, even when they are only dimly visible. These images would be utterly insufficient to enable him to recognize the objects without some previous acquaintance with them. Finally, he may be in the same room in complete darkness, and still be able to find his way about in it without making mistakes, by virtue of the visual impressions formerly obtained. Thus, by continually reducing the material that appeals to the senses, the perceptual-image (*Anschauungsbild*) can ultimately be traced back to the pure memory-image (*Vorstellungsbild*) and may gradually pass into it. In proportion as there is less and less material appeal to the senses, a person's movements will, of course, become more and more uncertain, and his apperception less and less accurate. Still there will be no peculiar abrupt transi-

93

tion, but sensation and memory will continually supplement each other, only in varying degrees.

But even when we look around a room of this sort flooded with sunshine, a little reflection shows us that under these conditions too a large part of our perceptual-image may be due to factors of memory and experience. The fact that we are accustomed to the perspective distortions of pictures of parallelopipeds and to the form of the shadows they cast has much to do with the estimation of the shape and dimensions of the room, as will be seen hereafter. Looking at the room with one eye shut, we think we see it just as distinctly and definitely as with both eyes. And yet we should get exactly the same view in case every point in the room were shifted arbitrarily to a different distance from the eye, provided they all remained on the same lines of sight.

Thus in a case like this we are really considering an extremely multiplex phenomenon of sense; but still we ascribe a perfectly definite explanation to it, and it is by no means easy to realize that the monocular image of such a familiar object necessarily means a much more meagre perception than would be obtained with both eyes. Thus too it is often hard to tell whether or not untrained observers inspecting stereoscopic views really notice the peculiar illusion produced by the instrument.

We can see, therefore, how in a case of this kind reminiscences of previous experiences act in conjunction with present sensations to produce a perceptual image (*Anschauungsbild*) which imposes itself on our faculty of perception with overwhelming power, without our being conscious of how much of it is due to memory and how much to present perception.

Still more remarkable is the influence of the comprehension of the sensations in certain cases, especially with dim illumination, in which a visual impression may be misunderstood at first, by not knowing how to attribute

94

the correct depth-dimensions; as when a distant light, for example, is taken for a near one, or *vice versa.* Suddenly it dawns on us what it is, and immediately, under the influence of the correct comprehension, the correct perceptual image also is developed in its full intensity. Then we are unable to revert to the previous imperfect apperception.

This is very common especially with complicated stereoscopic drawings of forms of crystals and other objects which come out in perfect clearness of perception the moment we once succeed in getting the correct impression.

Similar experiences have happened to everybody, proving that the elements in the sense-perceptions that are derived from experience are just as powerful as those that are derived from present sensations. All observers who have thoroughly investigated the theory of the sense-perceptions, even those who were disposed to allow experience as little scope as possible, have always admitted this.

Hence, at all events it must be conceded that, even in what appears to the adult as being direct apperception of the senses, possibly a number of single factors may be involved which are really the product of experience; although at the time it is difficult to draw the line between them.

Now in my opinion we are justified by our previous experiences in stating that no indubitable present sensation can be abolished and overcome by an act of the intellect; and no matter how clearly we recognize that it has been produced in some anomalous way, still the illusion does not disappear by comprehending the process. The attention may be diverted from sensations, particularly if they are feeble and habitual; but in noting those relations in the external world, that are associated with these sensations, we are obliged to observe the sensations themselves. Thus we may be unmindful of the temperature-sensation of our skin when it is not very keen, or of the contact-sensations produced by our clothing, as long as we are occupied with entirely different matters. But just as soon as we stop to think whether it is warm or cold, we are not in the position to convert the feeling of warmth into that of coldness; maybe because we know that it is due to strenuous exertion and not to the temperature of the surrounding air. In the same way the apparition of light when pressure is exerted on the eyeball cannot be made to vanish simply by comprehending better the nature of the process, supposing the attention is directed to the field of vision and not, say, to the ear or the skin.

On the other hand, it may also be that we are not in the position to isolate an impression of sensation, because it involves the composite sense-symbol of an external object. However, in this case the correct comprehension of the object shows that the sensation in question has been perceived and used by the consciousness.

My conclusion is, that *nothing in our sense-perceptions can be recognized as sensation which can be overcome in the perceptual image and converted into its opposite by factors that are demonstrably due to experience.*

Whatever, therefore can be overcome by factors of experience, we must consider as being itself the product of experience and training. By observing this rule, we shall find that it is merely the qualities of the sensation that are to be considered as real, pure sensation; the great majority of space-apperceptions, however, being the product of experience and training.

Still it does not follow that apperceptions, which persist in spite of our better conscious insight and continue as illusions, might not be due to experience and training. Our knowledge of the changes of colour produced in distant objects by the haziness of the atmosphere, of perspective distortions, and of shadow is undoubtedly a matter of experience. And yet in a good landscape picture we shall get the perfect visual impression of the distance and the solid form of the buildings in it, in spite of knowing that it is all depicted on canvas.

Similarly our knowledge of the composite sound of vowels is certainly obtained from experience; and yet we get the auditory impression of the vowel sound by combining the individual tones of tuning forks (as I have demonstrated) and grasp the sound in its entirety, although in this instance we know that it is really compound.

Here we still have to explain how experience counteracts experience, and how illusion can be produced by factors derived from experience, when it might seem as if experience could not teach anything except what was true. In this matter we must remember, as was intimated above, that the sensations are interpreted just as they arise when they are stimulated in the normal way, and when the organ of sense is used normally.

We are not simply passive to the impressions that are urged on us, but we *observe,* that is, we adjust our organs in those conditions that enable them to distinguish the impressions most accurately. Thus, in considering an involved subject, we accommodate both eyes as well as we can, and turn them so as to focus steadily on the precise point on which our attention is fixed, that is, so as to get an image of it in the fovea of each eye; and then we let our eyes traverse all the noteworthy points of the object one after another. If we are interested in the general shape of the object and are trying to get as good an idea as we can of its relative dimensions, we assume a position such that, without having to turn the head, we can survey the whole surface, enabling us at the same time to view as symmetrically as possible those dimensions we wish to compare. Thus, in looking at an object, as, for example, a building with prominent horizontal and

97

vertical lines, we like to stand opposite to it with the centres of rotation of the two eyes in a horizontal line. This position of the eyes can be controlled at any moment by separating the double images; which in the case mentioned here are in the same horizontal plane.

Unquestionably, our reason for choosing this definite mode of seeing is because in this way we can observe and compare most accurately; and, consequently, in this so-called *normal* use of the eyes we learn best how to compare our sensations with the reality. And so we obtain also the most correct and most accurate perceptions by this method.

But if, from necessity or on purpose, we employ a different mode of looking at objects, that is, if we view them merely indirectly or without focusing both eyes on them, or without surveying them all over, or if we hold the head in some unusual position, then we shall not be able to have as accurate apperceptions as when the eyes are used in the normal fashion. Nor are we so well trained in interpreting what we see under such circumstances as in the other case. Hence there is more scope for interpretation, although, as a rule, we are not clearly aware of this uncertainty in the explanation of our sense-perceptions. When we see an object in front of us, we are obliged to assign it to some definite place in space. We cannot think of it as having some dubious intermediate position between two different places in space. Without any recollections coming to our aid, we are wont to interpret the phenomenon as it would have to be interpreted if we had received the same impression in the normal and most accurate mode of observation. Thus certain illusions enter into the perception, unless we concentrate our eyes on the objects under observation, or when the objects are in the peripheral part of the visual field, or if the head is held to one side, or if we do not focus the object with both eyes at once. Moreover, the agreement between the images on the two retinas is most constant and regular in looking at distant objects. The fact that the horizontal floor usually happens to be in the lower part of the visual field, apparently influences the comparison of the fields of the two eyes in a peculiar manner. Thus, our judgment as to the position of near objects is not entirely correct when we observe them with the look tilted decidedly up or down. The retinal images presented in this way are interpreted just as if they had been obtained by looking straight ahead. We run across many illustrations of this sort. Our training in interpreting immediate perceptions is not equally good in all directions of the eyes, but simply for those directions which enable us to have the most accurate and most consistent perceptions. We transfer the latter to all cases, as in the instances just cited.

Now it is quite possible that the similarity between a visual impression of this kind and one of the possible impressions obtained by normal observation may not be so overwhelming and striking as to preclude many other comparisons and corresponding interpretations of that impression. In such cases the explanation of the impression varies. Without any change of the retinal images, the same observer may see in front of him various perceptual images in succession, in which case the variation is easy to recognize. Or else one observer may incline more toward one comparison and interpretation, and another toward another. This has been a source of much controversy in physiological optics, because each observer has been disposed to consider the apperception which he obtained by the most careful observation he could make as being the only valid one. But supposing that we have such confidence in the observers to assume that their observations were careful and unprejudiced, and that they knew how to make them, it would not be proper in such cases to adopt one of the conflicting interpretations of the visual phenomenon as being the only correct one. And yet that is what they are disposed to do who try to derive the origin of perceptual images mainly from innate factors. The truth rather is, that in a case of this sort various perceptual images may be developed; and we should seek rather to discover what circumstances are responsible for the decision one way or the other.

It is true we meet with a difficulty here that does not exist in the other parts of the natural sciences. In many instances we have simply the assertions of individual observers, without being in the position to verify them by our own observation. Many idiosyncrasies are manifested in this region, some of which are doubtless due to the structure of the eyes, others to the habitual way of using the eyes, and others still perhaps to previous impressions and apperceptions. Of course, nobody save the person who has peculiarities of this nature can observe their effects, and nobody else can give an opinion about them. On the other hand, observation in this region is by no means so easy as might be supposed at first. Steady fixation of a point for a long time while observations are being made in indirect vision; controlling the attention; taking the mind away from the ordinary objective interpretation of sense-impression; estimation of difference of colour and of difference of space in the visual field— all these things take much practice. And hence a number of facts in this region cannot be observed at all without having had previous long training in making observations in physiological optics. It cannot be done even by persons who are skilled in making other kinds of observations. Thus, with respect to many matters we have to depend on the observations of a very limited number of individuals, and hence when the results found by somebody else are different, it is much harder in this subject than anywhere else to judge rightly whether secondary influences have not contributed in an observation of this sort. Accordingly, I must apprise the reader in advance that much of the material that is perhaps new in the following chapters may possibly be due to individual peculiarities of my own eyes. Under such circumstances, there was no alternative for me except to observe as carefully as possible the facts as they appeared to my own eyes, and to try to ascertain their connection. Discrepancies that have been found by other observers have been noted. But how widespread this or the other mode of vision may be, is something that has to be left to the future to determine.

Incidentally, the more the visual impressions are unlike the normal ones, the greater will be the variety of interpretations as a rule. This is a natural consequence of the view which I hold, and is an essential characteristic of the activity of psychic influences.

Heretofore practically nothing has been ascertained as to the nature of psychic processes. We have simply an array of facts. Therefore, it is not strange that no real explanation can be given of the origin of sense-perceptions. The *empirical theory* attempts to prove that at least no other forces are necessary for their origin beyond the known faculties of the mind, although these forces themselves may remain entirely unexplained. Now generally it is a useful rule in scientific investigation not to make any new hypothesis so long as known facts seem adequate for the explanation, and the necessity of new assumptions has not been demonstrated. That is why I have thought it incumbent to prefer the empirical view essentially. Still less does the *intuition theory* attempt to give any explanation of the origin of our perceptual images; for it simply plunges right into the midst of the matter by assuming that certain perceptual images of space would be produced directly by an innate mechanism, provided certain nerve fibres were stimulated. The earlier forms of this theory implied some sort of self-observation of the retina; inasmuch as we were supposed to know by intuition about the form of this membrane and the positions of

101

the separate nerve terminals in it. In its more recent development, especially as formulated by E. HERING, there is an hypothetical subjective visual space, wherein the sensations of the separate nerve fibres are supposed to be registered according to certain intuitive laws. Thus in this theory not only is KANT's assertion adopted, that the general apperception of space is an original form of our imagination, but certain special apperceptions of space are assumed to be intuitive.

The naturalistic view has been called also a special *theory of identity,* because in it the perfect fusion of the impressions on the corresponding places of the two retinas has to be postulated. On the other hand, the *empirical* theory is spoken of as a *theory of projection,* because according to it the perceptual images of objects are projected in space by means of psychic processes. I should like to avoid this term, because both supporters and opponents of this view have often attached undue importance to the idea that this projection must take place parallel to the lines of direction; which was certainly not the correct description of the psychic process. And, even if this construction were admitted as being valid simply with respect to the physiological description of the process, the idea would be incorrect in very many instances.

I am aware that in the present state of knowledge it is impossible to refute the intuition theory. The reasons why I prefer the opposite view are because in my opinion:

1. The intuition theory is an unnecessary hypothesis.
2. Its consequences thus far invariably apply to perceptual images of space which only in the fewest cases are in accordance with reality and with the correct visual images that are undoubtedly present; as will be shown in detail later. The adherents of this theory are, therefore, obliged to make the very questionable assumption, that the *space sensations,* which according to them are present

originally, are continually being improved and overruled by knowledge which we have accumulated by experience. By analogy with all other experiences, however, we should have to expect that the sensations which have been overruled continued to be present in the apperception as a conscious illusion, if nothing else. But this is not the case.

3. It is not clear how the assumption of these original *"space sensations"* can help the explanation of our visual perceptions, when the adherents of this theory ultimately have to assume in by far the great majority of cases that these sensations must be overruled by the better understanding which we get by experience. In that case it would seem to me much easier and simpler to grasp, that all apperceptions of space were obtained simply by experience, instead of supposing that the latter have to contend against intuitive perceptual images that are generally false.

This is by way of justifying my point of view. A choice had to be made simply for the sake of getting at least some sort of superficial order amid the chaos of phenomena; and so I believed I had to adopt the view I have chosen. However, I trust it has not affected the correct observation and description of the facts.

To prevent misunderstandings as to my meaning, and to make it clearer to the natural intelligence of those readers who have never thought much about their sense-perceptions, the following explanations will be added.

Thus far the sensations have been described as being simply *symbols* for the relations in the external world. They have been denied every kind of similarity or equivalence to the things they denote. Here we touch on the much disputed point as to how far our ideas agree in the main with their objects; that is, whether they are true or false, as one might say. Some have asserted that there is such an agreement, and others have denied it. In favour of it, a *pre-established harmony* between nature and mind was assumed. Or it was maintained that there was an *identity* of nature and mind, by regarding nature as the product of the activity of a general mind; the human mind being supposed to be an emanation from it. The *intuition theory* of space-apperceptions is connected with these views to the extent that, by some innate mechanism and a certain pre-established harmony, it admits of the origin of perceptual images that are supposed to correspond with reality, although in a rather imperfect fashion.

Or else the agreement between ideas and their objects was denied, the ideas being explained therefore as illusions. Consequently, it was necessary to deny also the possibility of all knowledge of any objects whatsoever. This was the attitude of certain so-called "sensational" philosophers in England in the eighteenth century. However, it is not my purpose here to undertake an analysis of the opinions of the various philosophical schools on this question. That would be much too extensive a task in this place. I shall confine myself therefore merely to inquiring what I think should be the attitude of an investigator toward these controversies.

Our apperceptions and ideas are *effects* wrought on our nervous system and our consciousness by the objects that are thus apprehended and conceived. Each effect as to its nature, quite necessarily depends both on the nature of what causes the effect and on that of the person on whom the effect is produced. To expect to obtain an idea which would reproduce the nature of the thing conceived, that is, which would be true in an absolute sense, would mean to expect an effect which would be perfectly independent of the nature of the thing on which the effect was produced; which would be an obvious absurdity. Our human ideas, therefore, and all ideas of any conceivable intelligent creature, must be images of objects whose mode is essentially co-dependent on the nature of the

104

consciousness which has the idea, and is conditioned also by its idiosyncrasies.

In my opinion, therefore, there can be no possible sense in speaking of any other truth of our ideas except of a *practical* truth. Our ideas of things *cannot* be anything but symbols, natural signs for things which we learn how to use in order to regulate our movements and actions. Having learned correctly how to read those symbols, we are enabled by their help to adjust their actions so as to bring about the desired result; that is, so that the expected new sensations will arise. Not only is there *in reality* no other comparison at all between ideas and things—all the schools are agreed about this—but any other mode of comparison is entirely *unthinkable* and has no sense whatever. This latter consideration is the conclusive thing, and must be grasped in order to escape from the labyrinth of conflicting opinions. To ask whether the idea I have of a table, its form, strength, colour, weight, etc., is true *per se,* apart from any practical use I can make of this idea, and whether it corresponds with the real thing, or is false and due to an illusion, has just as much sense as to ask whether a certain musical note is red, yellow, or blue. Idea and the thing conceived evidently belong to two entirely different worlds, which no more admit of being compared with each other than colours and musical tones or than the letters of a book and the sound of the word they denote.

Were there any sort of similarity or correspondence between the idea in the head of a person *A* and the thing to which the idea belongs, another intelligent person *B,* conceiving both the thing itself and *A*'s idea of it, according to the same laws, might be able to find some similarity between them or at least to suppose so; because the same sort of thing represented (conceived) in the same way would have to give the same kinds of images (ideas). Now I ask, what similarity can be imagined between the pro-

105

cess in the brain that is concomitant with the idea of a table and the table itself? Is the form of the table to be supposed to be outlined by electric currents? And when the person with the idea has the idea that he is walking around the table, must the person then be outlined by electric currents? Perspective projections of the external world in the hemispheres of the brain (as they are supposed to be) are evidently not sufficient for representing the idea of a bodily object. And granted that a keen imagination is not frightened away by these and similar hypotheses, such an electrical reproduction of the table in the brain would be simply another bodily object to be perceived, but no idea of the table. However, it is not simply persons with materialistic opinions who try to refute the proposed statement, but also persons with idealistic views. And for the latter I should think the argument would be still more forcible. What possible similarity can there be between the idea, some modification of the incorporeal mind that has no extension in space, and the body of the table that occupies space? As far as I am aware, the idealistic philosophers have never once investigated even a single hypothesis or imagination in order to show this connection. And by the very nature of this view it is something that cannot be investigated at all.

In the next place as to the *properties* of objects in the external world, a little reflection reveals that all properties attributable to them may be said to be simply *effects* exerted by them either on our senses or on other natural objects. Colour, sound, taste, smell, temperature, smoothness, and firmness are properties of the first sort, and denote effects on our organs of sense. Smoothness and firmness denote the degree of resistance either to the gliding contact or pressure of the hand. But other natural bodies may be employed instead of the hand. And the same thing is true in testing other mechanical properties such as elasticity and weight. Chemical properties are described by certain reactions, that is, by effects exerted by one natural body on others. It is the same way with any other physical property of a body, optical, electrical, or magnetic. In every case we have to do with the mutual relations between various bodies and with the effects depending on the forces that different bodies exert on each other. For all natural forces are such as are exerted by one body on others. When we try to think of mere matter without force, it is void of properties likewise, except as to its different distribution in space and as to its motion. All properties of bodies in nature are manifested therefore simply by being so situated as to interact with other bodies of nature or with our organs of sense. But as such interaction may occur at any time, particularly too as it may be produced by us voluntarily at any moment, and as then we see invariably the peculiar sort of interaction occurring, we attribute to the objects a permanent capacity for such effects which is always ready to become effective. This permanent capacity is a so-called characteristic *property*.

The result is that in point of fact the characteristic *properties* of natural objects, in spite of this name, do not denote something that is peculiar to the individual object by itself, but invariably imply some relation to a second object (including our organs of sense). The kind of effect must, of course, depend always on the peculiarities both of the body producing it and of the body on which it is produced. As to this there is never any doubt even for an instant, provided we have in mind those properties of bodies that are manifested when two bodies belonging to the external world react on each other, as in the case of chemical reactions. But in the case of properties depending on the mutual relations between things and our organs of sense, people have always been disposed to forget that here too we are concerned with the

107

reaction toward a special reagent, namely, our own nervous system; and that colour, smell, and taste, and feeling of warmth or cold are also effects quite essentially depending on the nature of the organ that is affected. Doubtless, the reactions of natural objects to our senses are those that are most frequently and most generally perceived. For both our welfare and convenience they are of the most powerful importance. The reagent by which we have to test them is something we are endowed with by nature, but that does not make any difference in the connection.

Hence there is no sense in asking whether vermilion as we see it, is really red, or whether this is simply an illusion of the senses. The sensation of red is the normal reaction of normally formed eyes to light reflected from vermilion. A person who is red-blind will see vermilion as black or as a dark gray-yellow. This too is the correct reaction for an eye formed in the special way his is. All he has to know is that his eye is simply formed differently from that of other persons. In itself the one sensation is not more correct and not more false than the other, although those who call this substance red are in the large majority. In general, the red colour of vermilion exists merely in so far as there are eyes which are constructed like those of most people. Persons who are red-blind have just as much right to consider that a characteristic property of vermilion is that of being black. As a matter of fact, we should not speak of the light reflected from vermilion as being red, because it is not red except for certain types of eyes. When we speak of the properties of bodies with reference to other bodies in the external world, we do not neglect to name also the body with respect to which the property exists. Thus we say that lead is soluble in nitric acid, but not in sulphuric acid. Were we to say simply that lead is soluble, we should notice at once that the statement is incomplete, and the question would have to be asked immediately, Soluble in what? But when we say that vermilion is red, it is implicitly understood that it is red for our eyes and for other people's eyes supposed to be made like ours. We think this does not need to be mentioned, and so we neglect to do so, and can be misled into thinking that red is a property belonging to vermilion or to the light reflected from it, entirely independently of our organs of sense. The statement that the waves of light reflected from vermilion have a certain length is something different. That is true entirely without reference to the special nature of our eye. Then we are thinking simply of relations that exist between the substance and the various systems of waves in the aether.

The only respect in which there can be a real agreement between our perceptions and the reality is the time sequence of the events with their various peculiarities. Simultaneity, sequence, the regular recurrence of simultaneity or sequence, may occur likewise in the sensations as well as in the events. The external events, like their perceptions, proceed in time; and so the temporal relations of the latter may be the faithful reproduction of the temporal relations of the former. The sensation of thunder in the ear succeeds the sensation of lightning in the eye, just in the same way as the sound vibrations in the air due to the electrical discharge reach the place where the observer is later than the vibrations of the luminiferous aether. Yet here it certainly should be noted that the time-sequence of the sensations is not quite a faithful reproduction of the time-sequence of the external events, inasmuch as the transmission from the organs of sense to the brain takes time, and in fact a different time for different organs. Moreover, in case of the eye and the ear, the time has to be added that it takes light and sound to reach the organ. Thus at present we see the fixed stars as they were various long periods of years ago.

As to the representation of space-relations, there certainly is something of this sort in the peripheral nerve terminals in the eye and to a certain extent in the tactile skin, but still only in a limited way; for the eye gives only perspective surface-images, and the hand reproduces the objective area on the surface of a body by shaping itself to it as congruently as possible. A direct image of a portion of space of three dimensions is not afforded either by the eye or by the hand. It is only by comparing the images in the two eyes, or by moving the body with respect to the hand, that the idea of solid bodies is obtained. Now since the brain itself has three dimensions, of course, there is still another conceivable possibility, and that is to fancy by what mechanism in the brain itself images of three dimensions can arise from external objects in space. But I cannot see any necessity for such an assumption nor even any probability for it. The idea of a body in space, of a table, for instance, involves a quantity of separate observations. It comprises the whole series of images which this table would present to me in looking at it from different sides and at different distances; besides the whole series of tactile impressions that would be obtained by touching the surface at various places in succession. Such an idea of a single individual body is, therefore, in fact a *conception* (*Begriff*) which grasps and includes an infinite number of single, successive apperceptions, that can be deduced from it; just as the species "table" includes all individual tables and expresses their common peculiarities. The idea of a single individual table which I carry in my mind is correct and exact, provided I can deduce from it correctly the precise sensations I shall have when my eye and my hand are brought into this or that definite relation with respect to the table. Any other sort of similarity between such an idea and the body about which the idea exists, I do not know how to conceive. One is the mental symbol of the other. The kind of symbol was not chosen by me arbitrarily, but was forced on me by the nature of my organ

110

of sense and of my mind. This is what distinguishes this sign-language of our ideas from the arbitrary phonetic signs and alphabetical characters that we use in speaking and writing. A writing is correct when he who knows how to read it forms correct ideas by it. And so the idea of a thing is correct for him who knows how to determine correctly from it in advance what sense-impressions he will get from the thing when he places himself in definite external relations to it. Incidentally, it does not matter at all what sort of mental symbols we employ, provided they constitute a sufficiently varied and ordered system. Nor does it matter either how the words of a language sound, provided there are enough of them, with sufficient means of denoting their grammatical relations to one another.

On this view of the matter, we must be on our guard against saying that all our ideas of things are consequently *false*, because they are not *equal* to the things themselves, and that hence we are not able to know anything as to the *true nature* of things. That they cannot be equal to things is in the nature of knowledge. Ideas are merely pictures of things. Every image is the image of a thing merely for him who knows how to read it, and who is enabled by the aid of the image to form an idea of the thing. Every image is similar to its object in one respect, and dissimilar in all others, whether it be a painting, a statue, the musical or dramatic representation of a mental mood, etc. Thus the ideas of the external world are images of the regular sequence of natural events, and if they are formed correctly according to the laws of our thinking, and we are able by our actions to translate them back into reality again, the ideas we have are also the *only true* ones for our mental capacity. All others would be false.

In my opinion, it is a mistake, therefore, to try to find preestablished harmony between the laws of thought and those of nature, an identity between nature and mind, or whatever we may call it. A system of signs may be more or less perfect and convenient. Accordingly, it will be more or less easy to employ, more exact in denoting or more inexact, just as is the case with different languages. But otherwise each system can be adapted to the case more or less well. If there were not a number of similar natural objects in the world, our faculty of forming shades of conception would indeed not be of any use to us. Were there no solid bodies, our geometrical faculties would necessarily remain undeveloped and unused, just as the physical eye would not be of any service to us in a world where there was no light. If in this sense anybody wishes to speak of an adaptation of our laws of mind to the laws of nature, there is no objection to it. Evidently, however, such adaptation does not have to be either perfect or exact. The eye is an extremely useful organ practically, although it cannot see distinctly at all distances, or perceive all sorts of aether vibrations, or concentrate exactly in one point all the rays that issue from a point. Our intellectual faculties are connected with the activities of a material organ, namely the brain, just as the faculty of vision is connected with the eye. Human intelligence is wonderfully effective in the world, and brings it under a strict law of causation. Whether it necessarily must be able to control whatever is in the world or can happen—I can see no guarantee for that.

We must speak now of the manner in which our ideas and perceptions are formed by inductive conclusions. The best analysis of the nature of our conclusions I find in J. S. MILL's Logic. As long as the premise of the conclusion is not an injunction imposed by outside authority for our conduct and belief, but a statement related to reality, which can therefore be only the result of experience, the conclusion, as a matter of fact, does not tell us anything new or something that we did not know already before we made the statement.

Thus, for example:

112

Major: All men are mortal.
Minor: Caius is a man.
Conclusion: Caius is mortal.

The major premise, that all men are mortal, which is a statement of experience, we should scarcely venture to assert without knowing beforehand whether the conclusion is correct, namely, that Caius, who is a man, either is dead or will die. Thus we must be sure of the conclusion before we can state the major premise by which we intend to prove it. That seems to be proceeding in a circle. The real relation evidently is, that, in common with other folks, we have observed heretofore without exception that no person has ever survived beyond a certain age. Observers have learned by experience that Lucius, Flavius and other individuals of their acquaintance, no matter what their names are, have all died; and they have embraced this experience in the general statement, that *all* men die. Inasmuch as this final result occurred regularly in all the instances they observed, they have felt justified in explaining this general law as being valid also for all those cases which might come up for observation hereafter. Thus we preserve in our memory the store of experiences heretofore accumulated on this subject by ourselves and others in the form of the general statement which constitutes the major premise of the above conclusion.

However, the conviction that Caius would die might obviously have been reached directly also without formulating the general statement in our consciousness, by having compared his case with all those which we knew previously. Indeed, this is the more usual and original method of reasoning by induction. Conclusions of this sort are reached without conscious reflection, because in our memory the same sort of thing in cases previously observed unites and reinforces them; as is shown especially in those cases of inductive reasoning where we cannot

113

succeed in deducing from previous experiences a rule with precisely defined limits to its validity and without any exceptions. This is the case in all complicated processes. For instance, from analogy with previous similar cases, we can sometimes predict with tolerable certainty what one of our acquaintances will do, if under certain circumstances he decides to go into business; because we know his character and that he is, let us say, ambitious or timid. We may not be able to say exactly how we have estimated the extent of his ambition or timidity, or why this ambition or timidity of his will be enough to decide that his business will turn out as we expect.

In the case of conclusions properly so-called, which are reached consciously, supposing they are not based on injunctions but on facts of experience, what we do therefore, is really nothing more than deliberately and carefully to retrace those steps in the inductive generalizations of our experiences which were previously traversed more rapidly and without conscious reflection, either by ourselves or by other observers in whom we have confidence. But although nothing essentially new is added to our previous knowledge by formulating a general principle from our previous experiences, still it is useful in many respects. A definitely stated general principle is much easier to preserve in the memory and to be imparted to others than to have to do this same thing with every individual case as it arises. In formulating it we are led to test accurately every new case that occurs, with reference to the correctness of the generalization. In this way every exception will be impressed on us twice as forcibly. The limits of its validity will be recalled much sooner when we have the principle before us in its general form, instead of having to go over each separate case. By this sort of conscious formulation of inductive reasoning, there is much gain in the convenience and certainty of the process; but nothing essentially new is added that did not

114

exist already in the conclusions which were reached by analogy without reflection. It is by means of these latter that we judge the character of a person from his countenance and movements, or predict what he will do in a given situation from a knowledge of his character.

Now we have exactly the same case in our sense-perceptions. When those nervous mechanisms whose terminals lie on the right-hand portions of the retinas of the two eyes have been stimulated, our usual experience, repeated a million times all through life, has been that a luminous object was over there in front of us on our left. We had to lift the hand toward the left to hide the light or to grasp the luminous object; or we had to move toward the left to get closer to it. Thus while in these cases no particular conscious conclusion may be present, yet the essential and original office of such a conclusion has been performed, and the result of it has been attained; simply, of course, by the unconscious processes of association of ideas going on in the dark background of our memory. Thus too its results are urged on our consciousness, so to speak, as if an external power had constrained us, over which our will has no control.

These inductive conclusions leading to the formation of our sense-perceptions certainly do lack the purifying and scrutinizing work of conscious thinking. Nevertheless, in my opinion, by their peculiar nature they may be classified as *conclusions,* inductive conclusions unconsciously formed.

There is one circumstance quite characteristic of these conclusions which operates against their being admitted in the realm of conscious thinking and against their being formulated in the normal form of logical conclusions. This is that we are not able to specify more closely what has taken place in us when we have experienced a sensation in a definite nerve fibre, and how it differs from corresponding sensations in other nerve fibres. Thus,

115

suppose we have had a sensation of light in certain fibres of the nervous mechanism of vision. All we know is that we have had a sensation of a peculiar sort which is different from all other sensations, and also from all other visual sensations, and that whenever it occurred, we invariably noticed a luminous object on the left. Naturally, without ever having studied physiology, this is all we can say about the sensation, and even for our own imagination we cannot localize or grasp the sensation except by specifying it in terms of the condition of its occurrence. I have to say, "I see something bright there on my left." That is the only way I can describe the sensation. After we have pursued scientific studies, we begin to learn that we have nerves, that these nerves have been stimulated, and that their terminals in fact lie on the right-hand side of the retina. Then for the first time we are in a position to define this mode of sensation independently of the mode in which it is ordinarily produced.

It is the same way with most sensations. The sensations of taste and smell usually cannot be described even as to their quality except in terms of the bodies responsible for them; although we do have a few rather vague and more general expressions like "sweet," "sour," "bitter" and "sharp."

These judgments, in which our sensations in our ordinary state of consciousness are connected with the existence of an external cause, can never once be elevated to the plane of conscious judgments. The inference that there is a luminous object on my left, because the nerve terminals on the right-hand side of my retina are in a state of stimulation, can only be expressed by one who knows nothing about the inner structure of the eye by saying, "There is something bright over there on my left, because I see it there." And accordingly from the standpoint of everyday experience, the only way of expressing the experience I have when the nerve terminals on the right-hand side of my eyeball are stimulated by exerting pressure there, is by saying, "When I press my eye on the right-hand side, I see a bright glow on the left." There is no other way of describing the sensation and of identifying it with other previous sensations except by designating the place where the corresponding external object appears to be. Hence, therefore, these cases of experience have the peculiarity that the connection between the sensation and an external object can never be expressed without anticipating it already in the designation of the sensation, and without presupposing the very thing we are trying to describe.

Even when we have learned to understand the physiological origin and connection of the illusions of the senses, it is impossible to get rid of the illusion in spite of our better knowledge. This is because inductive reasoning is the result of an unconscious and involuntary activity of the memory; and for this very reason it strikes our consciousness as a foreign and overpowering force of nature. Incidentally, manifold analogies for it are to be found in all other possible modes of *apparition*. We might say that all apparition originates in premature, unmeditated inductions, where from previous cases conclusions are deduced as to new ones, and where the tendency to abide by the false conclusions persists in spite of the better insight into the matter based on conscious deliberation. Every evening apparently before our eyes the sun goes down behind the stationary horizon, although we are well aware that the sun is fixed and the horizon moves. An actor who cleverly portrays an old man is for us an old man there on the stage, so long as we let the immediate impression sway us, and do not forcibly recall that the programme states that the person moving about there is the young actor with whom we are acquainted. We consider him as being angry or in pain according as he shows us one or the other mode of countenance and demeanour. He arouses fright or sympathy in us, we tremble for the moment, which we see approaching, when he will perform or suffer something dreadful; and the deep-seated conviction that all this is only show and play does not hinder our emotions at all, provided the actor does not cease to play his part. On the contrary, a fictitious tale of this sort, which we seem to enter into ourselves, grips and tortures more than a similar true story would do when we read it in a dry documentary report.

The experiences we have that certain aspects, demeanours and modes of speech are indicative of fierce anger, are generally experiences concerning the external signs of certain emotions and peculiarities of character which the actor can portray for us. But they are not nearly so numerous and regular in recurrence as those experiences by which we have ascertained that certain sensations correspond with certain external objects. And so we need not be surprised if the idea of an object which is ordinarily associated with a sensation does not vanish, even when we know that in this particular instance there is no such object.

Finally, the tests we employ by voluntary movements of the body are of the greatest importance in strengthening our conviction of the correctness of the perceptions of our senses. And thus, as contrasted with purely passive observations, the same sort of firmer conviction arises as is derived by the process of experiment in scientific investigations. The peculiar ultimate basis, which gives convincing power to all our conscious inductions, is the law of causation. If two natural phenomena have frequently been observed to occur together, such as thunder and lightning, they seem to be regularly connected together, and we infer that there must be a common basis for both of them. And if this causal connection has invariably acted heretofore, so that thunder and lightning

118

accompany each other, then in the future too like causes must produce like effects, and the result must be the same in the future. However, so long as we are limited to mere observations of such phenomena as occur by themselves without our help, and without our being able to make experiments so as to vary the complexity of causes, it is difficult to be sure that we have really ascertained all the factors that may have some influence on the result. There must be an enormous variety of cases where the law is obeyed, and the law must define the result with great precision, if we are to be satisfied with a case of mere observation. This is the case with the motions of the planetary system. Of course, we cannot experiment with the planets, but the theory of universal gravitation as propounded by NEWTON gives such a complete and exact explanation of the comparatively complicated apparent motions of the heavenly bodies, that we no longer hesitate about considering it as being sufficiently proved. And yet there are REICH's experiments on the gravitational attraction of lead balls, FOUCAULT's experiment on the deviation of the plane of vibration of a pendulum in consequence of the earth's rotation, and the experimental determinations of the velocity of light in traversing terrestrial distances as made by FOUCAULT and FIZEAU, that are of the utmost value in strengthening our conviction experimentally also.

Probably there is no event of pure observation that has been found to be so unexceptionally correct as the general statement previously used by way of illustration, namely, that all human beings die before they have passed a certain age. In many millions of human beings not a single exception has been found. If one had occurred, we might assume that we should have heard of it. Among those who have died there are individuals who have lived in the most varied climates on the most various kinds of nourishment, besides having been engaged in the most diverse

119

occupations. Nevertheless, the statement that all men are bound to die, cannot be said to have the same degree of certainty as any law of physics whose consequences have been precisely compared experimentally with experience in manifold modifications. I do not know the causal connection for the death of human beings. I cannot state the causes that inevitably entail old age, in case life has not been terminated sooner by some rougher external injury. I have not been able to verify by experiments that when I allow these causes to operate, old age inevitably occurs, and that it does not occur when I remove those causes of its occurrence. Anyone who tells me that the life of a man can be indefinitely prolonged by employing certain means may be treated, of course, with the utmost incredulity, but he cannot be positively contradicted without knowing certainly that individuals have actually lived in the circumstances he describes, and yet have ultimately perished. On the other hand, when I assert that all liquid mercury will expand when it is heated, if it is free to do so, I know that whenever I have observed the two together, not only higher temperature and expansion of mercury were due to the action of an unknown common third cause, as I might have supposed from pure observation alone, but I know by experiment that the heat by itself was enough to cause the expansion of the mercury. At various times I have often heated mercury. I have deliberately selected the moment when I wished the experiment to begin. If therefore the mercury expanded under these circumstances, the expansion must have been dependent on those conditions that I produced in the experiment. Consequently, I know that the heating by itself was a sufficient cause for the expansion, and that no other latent influences were needed to bring about this result. By comparatively few carefully executed experiments we are enabled to establish the causal conditions of an event with more certainty than can be done by a million observations where we have not been able to vary the conditions as we please. For instance, if I had merely seen mercury expand in a thermometer which was inaccessible to me, and in a place where the air was saturated with moisture at all temperatures, I should have to inquire whether mercury expands on account of heat or on account of the moisture. The only way to determine this would be by experiment, and by finding out whether the volume of mercury changes with change of humidity, when the temperature is kept constant, or with change of temperature, when the humidity is kept constant.

The same great importance which experiment has for the certainty of our scientific convictions, it has also for the unconscious inductions of the perceptions of our senses. It is only by voluntarily bringing our organs of sense in various relations to the objects that we learn to be sure as to our judgments of the causes of our sensations. This kind of experimentation begins in earliest youth and continues all through life without interruption.

If the objects had simply been passed in review before our eyes by some foreign force without our being able to do anything about them, probably we should never have found our way about amid such an optical phantasmagoria; any more than mankind could interpret the apparent motions of the planets in the firmament before the laws of perspective vision could be applied to them. But when we notice that we can get various images of a table in front of us simply by changing our position; and that we can sometimes have one view and sometimes another, just as we like at any time, by a suitable change of position; and that the table may vanish from sight, and then be there again at any moment we like, simply by turning the eyes toward it; we get the conviction based on experiment, that our movements are responsible for the different views of the table, and that whether we see it just at this moment or do not see it, still we can see

121

it whenever we like. Thus by our movements we find out that it is the stationary form of the table in space which is the cause of the changing image in our eyes. We explain the table as having existence independent of our observation, because at *any moment we like,* simply by assuming the proper position with respect to it, we can observe it.

The essential thing in this process is just this principle of experimentation. Spontaneously and by our own power, we vary some of the conditions under which the object has been perceived. We know that the changes thus produced in the way that objects look depend solely on the movements we have executed. Thus we obtain a different series of apperceptions of the same object, by which we can be convinced with experimental certainty that they are simply apperceptions, and that it is the common cause of them all. In fact we see children also experimenting with objects in this way. They turn them constantly round and round, and touch them with the hands and the mouth, doing the same things over and over again day after day with the same objects, until their forms are impressed on them; in other words, until they get the various visual and tactile impressions made by observing and feeling the same object on various sides.

In this sort of experimentation with objects some of the changes in the sense-impressions are found to be due to our own will; whereas others, that is, all that depend on the nature of the object directly before us, are urged upon us by a necessity which we cannot alter as we like, and which we feel most when it arouses disagreeable sensations or pain. Thus we come to recognize something independent of our will and imagination, that is, an external cause of our sensations. This is shown by its persisting independently of our instantaneous perception; because at any moment we like, by suitable manipulations and movements, we can cause to recur each one of the series of sensations that can be produced in us by this external

122

cause. Thus this latter is recognized as an object existing independently of our perception.

The idea and the cause here combine, and it is a question whether we have a right to assume this cause in the original perception of the senses. Here again the difficulty is that we are not able to describe the processes except in the language of metaphysics, whereas the reflection of the consciousness in itself is not yet distinctly contained in the original form of the conscious perception.

Natural consciousness, which is entirely absorbed in the interest of observing the external world, and has little inducement to direct its attention to the Ego that appears always the same amid the multi-coloured variations of outside objects, is not in the habit of noticing that the *properties* of the objects that are seen and touched are their effects, partly on other natural bodies, but mainly on our senses. Now as our nervous system and our sensation-faculty, as being the constant reagent on which the effect is exerted, is thus left out of account entirely, and as the difference of the effect is regarded as being simply a difference in the object from which it proceeds, the effect can no longer be recognized as an effect (for every effect must be the effect on something else), and so comes to be considered objectively as being a property of the body and merely as belonging to it. And then as soon as we recall that we perceive these properties, our impression, consequently, seems to us to be a pure image of the external state of affairs reflecting only that external condition and depending solely on it.

But if we ponder over the basis of this process, it is obvious that we can never emerge from the world of our sensations to the apperception of an external world, except by inferring from the changing sensation that external objects are the causes of this change. Once the idea of external objects has been formed, we may not be concerned any more as to how we got this idea, especially

123

because the inference appears to be so self-evident that we are not conscious of its being a new result.

Accordingly, the law of causation, by virtue of which we infer the cause from the effect, has to be considered also as being a law of our thinking which is prior to all experience. Generally, we can get no experience from natural objects unless the law of causation is already active in us. Therefore, it cannot be deduced first from experiences which we have had with natural objects.

This statement has been made in many ways. The law of causation was supposed to be a law of nature arrived at by induction. Recently it has been again interpreted in that way by J. S. Mill. He has even suggested the possibility of its not being valid in other parts of the universe. As opposed to that view, I shall merely say, for what it is worth, that there is good reason to think that the empirical proof of the law is extremely doubtful. For the number of cases in which we think we can trace perfectly the causal connection between natural processes is small as compared with the number of those in which we are absolutely unable to do so at present. The former cases belong almost exclusively to inorganic nature. The cases that are not understood include the larger part of the phenomena of organic nature. In fact, by the evidence of our own consciousness, we positively assume both in beasts and in man a principle of free will, for which we claim most decidedly complete independence of the force of the law of causation. And in spite of all theoretical speculations as to possible mistakes about this conviction, I am of the opinion that our natural consciousness will hardly ever be free from it. Thus the case of conduct itself, which we know best and most accurately, we consider as being an exception to that law. Were therefore the law of causation a law of experience, its inductive proof would seem to be in a very bad shape. The best we could say is that it was not any more valid than rules of meteorology like the law of rotation of the wind, etc. Perhaps, we could not positively controvert the vitalistic physiologists who maintain that the law of causation is valid in inorganic nature; although in the organic world they relegate it to a lower sphere of action.

Finally, the law of causation bears on its face the character of a purely logical law, chiefly because the conclusions derived from it do not concern actual experience, but its interpretation. Hence it cannot be refuted by any possible experience.[1] For if we founder anywhere in applying the law of causation, we do not conclude that it is false, but simply that we do not yet completely understand the complex of causes mutually interacting in the given phenomenon. And when at length we have succeeded in explaining certain natural processes by the law of causation, the conclusions we derive from it are that certain masses of matter exist and move in space and act on each other with certain motive forces. But the conceptions of both matter and force are entirely abstract in nature, as is shown by their attributes. Matter without force is assumed to exist only in space, but not to act or to have any properties. Thus it would be of no importance whatever for all other affairs in the world or for our perceptions. It would be practically non-existent. Force without matter is indeed said to act; but it cannot exist independently, for whatever exists is matter. Thus the two conceptions are inseparable; they are merely abstract modes of regarding the same objects of nature in various aspects. For that very reason neither matter nor force can be direct objects of observation, but are always merely the revealed causes of the facts of experience. Hence, if we conclude by proposing certain abstractions, which can never be objects of experience, as the final and

---

[1] HELMHOLTZ, *Uber das Sehen des Menschen, ein popular wissenschaftlicher Vortrag.* Leipzig 1855.

sufficient bases of natural phenomena, how can we say that experience proves that the phenomena have sufficient bases?

The law of sufficient basis amounts simply to the requirement of wishing to understand everything. The process of our comprehension with respect to natural phenomena is that we try to find *generic notions* and *laws of nature*. Laws of nature are merely generic notions for the changes in nature. But since we have to assume the laws of nature as being valid and as acting independently of our observation and thinking whereas, as generic notions they would concern at first only the method of our thinking, we call them *causes* and *forces*. Hence, when we cannot trace natural phenomena to a law, and therefore cannot make the law objectively responsible as being the cause of the phenomena, the very possibility of comprehending such phenomena ceases.

However, we must try to comprehend them. There is no other method of bringing them under the control of the intellect. And so in investigating them we must proceed on the supposition that they are comprehensible. Accordingly, the law of sufficient reason is really nothing more than the *urge* of our intellect to bring all our perceptions under its own control. It is not a law of nature. Our intellect is the faculty of forming general conceptions It has nothing to do with our sense-perceptions and experiences, unless it is able to form general conceptions or laws. These laws are then objectified and designated as causes. But if it is found that the natural phenomena are to be subsumed under a definite causal connection, this is certainly an objectively valid fact, and corresponds to special objective relations between natural phenomena, which we express in our thinking as being their causal connection, simply because we do not know how else to express it.

Just as it is the characteristic function of the eye to

have light-sensations, so that we can *see* the world only as a *luminous* phenomenon, so likewise it is the characteristic function of the intellect to form general conceptions, that is, to search for causes; and hence it can *conceive* (*begreifen*) of the world only as being *causal* connection. We have other organs besides the eye for comprehending the external world, and thus we can feel or smell many things that we cannot see. Besides our intellect there is no other equally systematized faculty, at any rate for comprehending the external world. Thus if we are unable to *conceive* a thing, we cannot imagine it as existing.

HERMANN LUDWIG FERDINAND, BARON VON HELMHOLTZ
(b.-Potsdam, Prussia, Aug. 31, 1821; d.-Sept. 8, 1894).

Helmholtz received an M.D. from the Royal Medical and Surgical Friedrich-Wilhelms Institute in Berlin in 1842. He was Professor of Physiology at Konigsberg (1849); at Bonn (1855); at Heidelberg (1859). He finally became Professor of Physics at Berlin (1871).

The breadth of Helmholtz' contribution to science is enormous, extending from the short epoch-making paper *Uber die Erhaltung der Kraft,* delivered before the Berlin Society of Physics on July 23, 1847, to the still unsurpassed *Handbook of Physiological Optics,* written over the years 1856-1866 in three volumes. His invention of the ophthalmoscope, in 1851, can, without exaggeration, be said to have solved the major problem in the development of a science of opthalmology in one instant.

The present selection is his most important statement of basic principles in the field of sensory psychology.

HELMHOLTZ, H. *v. Treatise on Physiological Optics.* Optical Society of America, 1925. Editor: J.P.C. Southall (from the 3rd German edition, 1909-1911). Chap. 26: "Concerning the perceptions in general". This essay is reproduced in its entirety, with the kind permission of the Optical Society of America.

See aiso:
HELMHOLTZ, H. v. *On the sensation of tone as a physiological basis for the theory of music.* N. Y.: Dover Pub. Co., 1954 (1863). Trans, A. J. Ellis. (This book contains a readily available bibliography of Helmholtz' writings, in English translation.)

KONIGSBERGER, L. *Hermann von Helmholtz.* F. Vieweg & Sons, 1902-1903, 3 vol. This is the best biography.

THE ANALYSIS OF SENSATIONS
AND THE RELATION OF THE PHYSICAL
TO THE PSYCHICAL

ERNST MACH

The Chief Points of View for the
Investigation of the Senses

1.

In order to get our bearings, we will now try to obtain from the standpoint we have reached, a broad view of the special problems that will engage our attention.

When once the inquiring intellect has formed, through adaptation, the habit of connecting two things, A and B, in thought, it tries to retain this habit as far as possible, even where the circumstances are slightly altered. Wherever A appears, B is added in thought. The principle thus expressed, which has its root in an effort for economy, and is particularly noticeable in the work of the great investigations, may be termed the *principle of continuity.*

Every actually observed variation in the connexion of A and B which is sufficiently large to be noticed makes itself felt as a disturbance of the above-mentioned habit, and continues to do so until the habit is sufficiently modified to prevent the disturbance being felt. Suppose, for instance, that we have become accustomed to seeing light deflected when it impinges on the boundary between air and glass. But these deflections vary noticeably in different cases, and the habit formed by observing some cases cannot be transformed undisturbed to new cases, until we are able to associate with every particular angle of incidence (A) a particular angle of refraction (B), which we are able to do by discovering the so-called law of refraction, and by making ourselves familiar with the rules contained in that law. Thus another and modifying principle confronts that of continuity; we will call it the *principle of sufficient determination, or sufficient differentiation.*

The joint action of the two principles may be very well illustrated by a further analysis of the examples cited. In order to deal with the phenomena exhibited in the change of color of light, the idea of the law of refraction must be retained, but with every particular color a particular index of refraction must be associated. We soon perceive that with every particular temperature also, a particular index of refraction must be associated; and so on.

In the end, this process leads to temporary contentment and satisfaction, the two things A and B being conceived as so connected that to every change of the one that can be observed at any moment there corresponds an appropriate change of the other. It may happen that both A and B are conceived as complexes of components, and that to every particular component of A a particular component of B corresponds. This occurs, for example, when B is a spectrum, and A the corresponding sample of a compound to be tested, in which case to every component part of the spectrum one of the components of the matter volatilized before the spectroscope is correlated, independently of the others. Only through complete familiarity with this relation can the principle of sufficient determination be satisfied.

2.

Suppose, now, that we are considering a color-sensation B, not in its dependence on A, the heated matter tested, but in its dependence on the elements of the retinal process, N. By doing this we change, not the kind, but only the direction of our point of view. None of the preceding observations lose their force, and the principles to be followed remain the same. And this holds good, of course, of all sensations.

129

Now, sensation may be analysed in itself, immediately, that is, psychologically (which was the course adopted by Johannes Müller), or the physical (physiological) processes correlated with it may be investigated according to the methods of physics (the course usually preferred by the modern school of physiologists), or, finally, the connexion of psychologically observable data with the corresponding physical (physiological) processes may be followed up—a mode of procedure which will carry us farthest, since in this method observation is directed to all sides, and one investigation serves to support the other. We shall endeavor to attain this last-named end whereever it appears practicable.

This being our object, then, it is evident that the principle of continuity and that of sufficient determination can be satisfied only on the condition that with the same B (this or that sensation) we always associate the same N (the same nerve-process) and discover for every observable change of B a corresponding change of N. If B is psychologically analysible into a number of independent components, then we shall rest satisfied only on the discovery, in N, of equivalent components corresponding to these. If, on the other hand, properties or aspects have to be noticed in B which cannot appear in isolation, as, for instance, pitch and intensity in tones, we shall have to expect the same state of things in N. In a word, for all psychically observable details of B we have to seek the correlated physical details of N.

I do not of course maintain that a (psychologically) simple sensation cannot also be conditioned by very complicated circumstances. For the circumstances would hang together like the links of a chain and would not issue in a sensation, unless the chain extended to the nerve. But since the sensation may also appear in the form of a hallucination, namely when no physically conditioned circumstances are present outside the body, we see that a certain nervous process, as the final link in the chain, is the essential and immediate condition of the sensation. Now we cannot think of this immediate condition as being varied without conceiving of the sensation as being varied, and *vice versa*. For the connexion between this final link and the sensation we will regard the principle which we have laid down as valid.

3.

We may thus establish a guiding principle for the investigation of the sensations. This may be termed the *principle of the complete parallelism of the psychical and physical*. According to our fundamental conception, which recognizes no gulf between the two provinces (the psychical and the physical), this principle is almost a matter of course; but we may also enunciate it, as I did years ago, without the help of this fundamental conception, as a heuristic principle of research.[1]

The principle of which I am here making use goes further than the widespread general belief that a physical entity corresponds to every psychical entity and *vice versa;* it is much more specialized. The general belief in question has been proved to be correct in many cases, and may be held to be probably correct in all cases; it constitutes moreover the necessary presupposition of all exact research. At the same time the view here advocated is different from Fechner's conception of the physical and psychical as two different aspects of one and the same reality. In the first place, our view has no metaphysical background, but corresponds only to the generalized expression

---

[1] Compare my paper, *Ueber die Wirkung der räumlichen Vertheilung des Lichtreizes auf die Netzhaut (Sitzungsberichte der Wiener Akadamie,* Vol. LII., 1865); further *Reichert's und Dubois' Archiv,* 1865, p. 634, and *Grundlinien der Lehre von den Bewegungsempfindungen* (Leipzig, Engelmann, 1875, p. 63). The principle is also implicitly contained in an article of mine in Fichte's *Zeitschrift fur Philosophie* (Vol. XLVI., 1865, p. 5), which is printed also in my *Popular Scientific Lectures,* Chicago, Open Court Publishing Co.

of experiences. Again, we refuse to distinguish two different aspects of an unknown *tertium quid;* the elements given in experience, whose connexion we are investigating, are always the same, and are of only one nature, though they appear, according to the nature of the connexion, at one moment as physical and at another as psychical elements.[1] I have been asked whether the parallelism between psychical and physical is not meaningless and a mere tautology, if the psychical and physical are not regarded as essentially different. The question arises from a misunderstanding of the analysis which I have given above. When I see a green leaf (an event which is conditioned by certain brain processes) the leaf is of course different in its form and color from the forms, colors, etc., which I discover in investigating a brain, although all forms, colors, etc., are of like nature in themselves, being in themselves neither psychical nor physical. The leaf which I see, considered as dependent on the brain-process, is something psychical, while this brain-process itself represents, in the connexion of *its* elements, something physical. And the principle of parallelism holds good for the dependence of the former immediately given group of elements on the latter group, which is only ascertained by means of a physical investigation which may be extremely complicated.

4.

I have perhaps stated the principle in rather too abstract a form. A few concrete examples may now help to explain it. Wherever I have a sensation of space, whether through the sensation of sight or through that of touch, or in any other way, I am obliged to assume the presence

---

[1] For the various aspects of the problem of parallelism, see C. Stumpf's address to the Psychological Congress at Munich (Munich, 1897); G. Heymans, "Zur Parallelismusfrage," *Zeitschrift fur Psychologie der Sinnesorgane,* Vol. XVII.; O. Kulpe, *Ueber die Beziehung zwischen korperlichen und seelischen Vorgängen, Zeitschrift fur Hypnotismus,* Vol. VII,. J. von Kries, *Uber die materiellen Grundlagen der Bewusstseinserscheinungen,* Freiburg im Breisgau, 1898; C. Hauptmann, *Die Metaphysik in der Psychologie,* Dresden, 1893.

of a nerve-process of the same kind in all cases. For all time-sensations, also, I must suppose like nerve-processes.

If I see figures which are the same in size and shape but differently colored, I seek, in connexion with the different color-sensations, certain identical space-sensations and corresponding identical nerve-processes. If two figures are similar (that is, if they yield partly identical space-sensations) then the corresponding nerve-processes also contain partly identical components. If two different melodies have the same rhythm, then, side by side with the different tone-sensations there exists in both cases an identical time-sensation with identical corresponding nerve-processes. If two melodies of different pitch are identical, then the tone-sensations as well as their physiological conditions, have, in spite of the different pitch, identical constituents. If the seemingly limitless multiplicity of color-sensations is susceptible of being reduced, by psychological analysis (self-observation), to six elements (fundamental sensations), a like simplification may be expected for the system of nerve-processes. If our system of space-sensations appears in the character of a threefold manifold, the system of the correlated nerve-processes will likewise present itself as such.

5.

This principle has, moreover, always been more or less consciously, more or less consistently, followed.

For example, when Helmholtz[1] assumes for every tone-sensation a special nerve-fibre (with its appurtenant nerve-process), when he resolves clangs, or compound sounds, into tone-sensations, when he reduces the affinity of compound tones to the presence of like tone-sensations (and nerve-processes), we have in this method of pro-

---

[1] Helmholtz, *Die Lehre von den Tonempfindungen,* Brunswick, Vieweg, 1863. English translation by Alex. J. Ellis, London, Longmans, Green, & Co. 2nd edition, 1885.

133

cedure a practical illustration of our principle. It is only the application that is not complete, as will be later shown. Brewster,[1] guided by a psychological but defective analysis of color-sensations, and by imperfect physical experiments,[2] was led to the view that, corresponding to the three sensations, red, yellow, and blue, there existed likewise physically only three kinds of light, and that, therefore, Newton's assumption of an unlimited number of kinds of light, with a continuous series of refractive indices, was erroneous. Brewster might easily fall into the error of regarding green as a compound sensation. But had he reflected that color-sensations may occur entirely without physical light, he would have confined his conclusions to the nerve-process and left untouched Newton's assumptions in the province of physics, which are as well founded as his own. Thomas Young corrected this error, at least in principle. He perceived that an unlimited number of kinds of physical light with a continuous series of refractive indices (and wave-lengths) was compatible with a small number of color-sensations and nerve processes,—that a discrete number of color sensations did answer to the continuum of deflexions in the prism (to the continuum of space-sensations). But even Young did not apply the principle with full consciousness or strict consistency, wholly apart from the fact that he allowed himself to be misled, in his psychological analysis, by physical prejudices. Even he first assumed, as fundamental sensations, red, yellow, and blue, for which he later substituted red, green, and violet

---

[1] Brewster, *A Treatise on Optics*, London, 1831. Brewster regarded the red, yellow, and blue light as extending over the whole solar spectrum, though distributed there with varying intensity, so that, to the eye, red appears at both ends (the red and the violet), yellow in the middle, and blue at the end of greater refrangibility.

[2] Brewster believed that he was able to alter by absorption the nuances of the specrum—colors regarded by Newton as simple—a result, which, if correct, would really destroy the Newtonian conception. He experimented, however, as Helmholtz (*Physiological Optics*) has shown, with an impure spectrum.

—misled, as Alfred Mayer, of Hoboken, has admirably shown,[1] by a physical error of Wollaston's. The direction in which the theory of color-sensation, which has reached a high degree of perfection through Hering, has still to be modified, was pointed out by me many years ago in another place.

6.

Here I will merely state shortly what I have to say concerning the treatment of the theory of color-sensation. We frequently meet with the assertion, in recent works, that the six fundamental color-sensations, white, black, red, green, yellow, blue, which Hering adopted, were first proposed by Leonardo da Vinci, and later by Mach and Aubert. From the very first it seemed to me highly probable, in view of the conceptions prevalent at this time, that the assertion was founded upon an error, as far as Leonardo da Vinci was concerned. Let us hear what he himself says in his *Book of Painting* (Nos. 254 and 255 in the translation of Heinrich Ludwig, *Quellenschriften zur Kunstgeschichte*, Vienna, Braumuller, 1882, Vol. XVIII).

[1] *Philosophical Magazine,* February 1876, p. III. Wollaston was the first to notice (1802) the dark lines of the spectrum, later named after Fraunhofer, and believed that he saw his narrow spectrum divided by the strongest of these lines into a red, a green, and a violet part. He regarded these lines as the dividing lines of the physical colors. Young took up this conception, and substituted for his fundamental sensations red, yellow, and blue, the colors red, green, and violet. Thus, in his first conception, Young regarded green as a composite sensation, in his second, both green and violet as simple. The questionable results which psychological analysis may thus yield, are well calculated to destroy belief in its usefulness in general. But we must not forget that there is no principle in the application of which error is excluded. Here, too, practice must determine. The circumstance that the physical conditions of sensation almost always give rise to composite sensations, and that the components of sensation seldom make their appearance separately, renders psychological analysis very difficult. Thus, green is a simple sensation; a given pigment or spectrum-green, however, will as a rule excite also a concomitant yellow or blue sensation, and thus favor the erroneous idea (based upon the results of pigment-mixing) that the sensation of green is compounded of yellow and blue. Careful physical study, therefore, is also an indispensable requisite of psychological analysis. On the other hand, physical observation must not be overestimated. The mere observation that a yellow and blue pigment mixed, yield a green pigment, cannot by itself determine us to see yellow and blue in green, unless one or the other color is actually contained in it. Certanly no one sees yellow and blue in white, although, as a fact, spectrum-yellow and spectrum-blue mixed give white.

135

"254. Of simple colors there are six. The first of these is white, although philosophers admit neither white nor black into the number of colors, since the one is the cause of color, the other of its absence. But, *inasmuch as the painter cannot do without them*, we shall include these two also among the other colors and say that white in this classification is the first among the simple colors, yellow the second, green the third, blue the fourth, red the fifth, black the sixth. And the white we will let represent the light, without which one can see no color, the yellow the earth, the green the water, blue the air, red fire, and black the darkness which is above the element of fire, because in that place there is no matter or solid substance upon which the sunbeams can exert their force, and which as a result they might illumine." "255. Blue and green are not simple colors by themselves. For blue is composed of light and darkness, as, the blue of the air, which is made up of the most perfect black and perfectly pure white." "Green is composed of a simple and a composite color, namely, of yellow and blue." This will suffice to show that Leonardo da Vinci is concerned partly with observations concerning pigments, partly with conceptions of natural philosophy, but not with the subject of fundamental color-sensations. The many remarkable and subtle scientific observations of all sorts which are contained in Leonardo da Vinci's book lead to the conviction that the artists, and among them especially he himself, were the true fore-runners of the great scientists who came soon afterwards. These men were obliged to understand nature in order to reproduce it agreeably; they observed themselves and others in the interest of pure pleasure. Yet Leonardo was far from being the author of all the discoveries and inventions which Groth, for example (*Leonardo da Vinci als Ingenieur und Philosoph*, Berlin, 1874), ascribes to him.[1]

---

[1] Marie Herzfeld, *Leonardo da Vinci, Auswahl aus den veroffenlichten Handschriften*, Leipzig, 1904.

My own scattered remarks concerning the theory of color-sensations were perfectly clear. I assumed the fundamental sensations white, black, red, yellow, green, blue, and six different corresponding (chemical) processes (not nerve-fibres) in the retina. (Compare *Reichert's und Dubois' Archiv*, 1865, p. 633, et seq.) As a physicist, I was of course familiar with the relation of the complementary colors. My conception, however, was that the two complementary processes together excited a new— the white—process. (*Loc. cit.*, p. 634.) I gladly acknowledge the great advantages of Hering's theory. They consist for me in the following. First, the black process is regarded as a *reaction* against the white process; I can appreciate all the better the facilitation involved in this, as it was just the relation of black and white that for me presented the greatest difficulty. Further, red and green, as also yellow and blue, are regarded as antagonistic processes which do not produce a new process, but mutually annihilate each other. According to this conception white is not subsequently produced but is already present beforehand, and still survives on the annihilation of a color by the complementary color. The only point that still dissatisfies me in Hering's theory is that it is difficult to perceive why the two opposed processes of black and white may be simultaneously produced and simultaneously felt, while such is not the case with red-green and blue-yellow. This objection has been partly removed by a further development of Hering's theory.[1] The full explanation of this relation lies undoubtedly in the proof, which W. Pauli has provided, that certain processes in colloidal and in living substances can be reversed by opposite processes along the same path, or "homodromously," while other processes can only be reversed by opposite processes along a different path, or "hetero-

---

[1] *Zur Lehre vom Lichtsinne,* Vienna, 1878, p. 122. Cp. also my paper, previously cited, in the *Sitzungsberichte der Wiener Akademie,* Vol. LII., 1865, October.

dromously,'"[1] I myself shewed long ago that certain sensations are related to one another as positive and negative magnitudes (*e.g.*, red and green), while others do not stand in this relation (*e.g.*, white and black).[2] Now all difficulties are reconciled if we suppose with Pauli that the opposed processes as assumed by Hering, which correspond to the first pair, are homodromous, and that the processes underlying the second pair are heterodromous.[3]

7.

The examples adduced will suffice to explain the significance of the above-enunciated principle of inquiry, and at the same time to show that this principle is not entirely new. In formulating the principle, years ago, I had no other object than that of making quite clear to my own mind a truth which I had long instinctively felt.

It seemed to me a simple and natural, nay, an almost self-evident supposition, that similarity must be founded on a partial likeness or identity, and that consequently, where sensations were similar, we had to look for their common identical constituents and for the corresponding common physiological processes. I wish, however, to make it quite clear to the reader that this view by no means meets with universal agreement. We constantly find it maintained in philosophical books that similarity may be observed without there being any question at all of such identical constituents. Thus a physiologist[4] can speak as follows of the principle under discussion: "The application of this principle to the above problems leads him (Mach) to ask, what is the physiological factor that corresponds to the qualities thus postulated? Now it seems

---

[1] W. Pauli, *Der Kolliodale Zustand und die Vorgänge in der lebendigen Substanz, Brunswick,* Vieweg, 1902, pp. 22, 30.

[2] *Grundlinien der Lehre von den Bewegungsempfindungen,* 1895, pp. 57, seq.

[3] A recent exposition of Hering's views will be found in Graefe-Saemisch's *Handbuch der ges. Augenheilkunde,* Leipzig, 1905, Vol. III.

[4] J. Von Kries, *Ueber die materiellen Grundlagen der Bewusstseinserscheinungen,* Freiburg im Breisgau, 1898.

to me that, of all axioms and principles, none is more doubtful, none is exposed to greater misunderstandings than is this principle. If it is nothing more than a periphrasis for the so-called principle of parallelism, then it cannot be considered either new or particularly fruitful, and it does not deserve the importance that is attached to it. If, on the other hand, it is intended to mean that a definite element or constituent of a physiological event must correspond to everything which we can distinguish as having some sort of psychological unity,—to every relation, to every form, in a word to everything that we can denote by a general conception,—then this formulation can only be characterized as dubious and misleading." And I am taken as holding that the principle in question must be understood in this last "dubious and misleading" sense. I must leave it entirely to the reader to choose whether he will accompany me any further and enter with me on that preliminary stage of inquiry which is clearly defined by means of our principle, or whether, bowing to the authority of my opponents, he will turn back and satisfy himself merely with considering the difficulties which confront him. If he chooses the former alternative, he will, I hope, discover, that when simpler cases have been disposed of, the difficulties in cases of deeper-lying abstract similarity no longer appear in such a formidable light as before. All I will add at present is, that in these more complicated cases of similarity the similarity arises not from the presence of *one* common element, but from a common *system* of elements, as I shall explain at length in connexion with conceptual thinking.

8.

As we recognize no real gulf between the physical and the psychical, it is a matter of course that, in the study of the sense-organs, general physical as well as special biological observations may be employed. Much that appears to us difficult of comprehension when we draw a parallel between a sense-organ and a physical apparatus, is rendered quite obvious in the light of the theory of evolution, simply by assuming that we are concerned with a living organism with particular memories, particular habits and manners, which owe their origin to a long and eventful race-history. The sense-organs themselves are a fragment of soul; they themselves do part of the psychical work, and hand over the completed result to consciousness. I will here briefly put together what I have to say on this subject.

9.

The idea of applying the theory of evolution to physiology in general, and to the physiology of the senses in particular, was advanced, prior to Darwin, by Spencer (1855). It received an immense impetus through Darwin's book *The Expression of the Emotions*. Later, P. R. Schuster (1879) discussed the question whether there were "inherited ideas" in the Darwinian sense. I, too, expressed myself in favor of the application of the idea of evolution to the theory of the sense-organs (*Sitzungsberichte der Wiener Akademie,* October 1866). One of the finest and most instructive discussions, in the way of a psychologico-physiological application of the theory of evolution, is to be found in the Academic Anniversary Address of Hering, *On Memory as a General Function of Organized Matter,* 1870 (English translation, Open Court Publishing Company, Chicago, 1913). As a fact, memory and heredity almost coincide in one concept if we reflect that organisms, which were part of the parent-body, emigrate and become the basis of new individuals. Heredity is rendered almost as intelligible to us by this thought as, for example, is the fact that Americans speak English, or that their state-institutions resemble the English in many respects, etc. The problem involved in the fact that organisms possess memory, a property which is apparently lacking to inorganic matter, is, of course, not affected by these considerations, but still exists. If we want to avoid criticizing Hering's theory unfairly, we must observe that he uses the conception of memory in a rather broad sense. He perceived the affinity between the lasting traces imprinted on organisms by their racial history and the more evanescent impressions which the individual life leaves behind it in consciousness. He recognizes that the spontaneous reappearance, in response to a slight stimulus, of a process which has once been set up, is essentially the same event, whether it can be observed within the narrow framework of consciousness or not. The perception of this common feature in a long series of phenomena is an essential step in advance, even though this fundamental feature itself still remains unexplained. Recently Weissmann (*Ueber die Dauer des Lebens*, 1882) has conceived death as a phenomenon of heredity. This admirable book, also, has a very stimulating effect. The difficulty which might be found in the fact that a characteristic should be inherited which can make its appearance in the parent-organism only after the process of inheritance is ended, lies probably only in the manner of statement. It disappears when we consider that the power of the somatic cells to multiply can increase, as Weismann shows, at the cost of the increase of the germ-cells. Accordingly, we may say that greater length of life on the part of the cell-society and lessened propagation are two phenomena of adaptation which mutually condition each other.—While a Gymnasium student, I heard it stated that plants from the Southern Hemisphere bloom in our latitudes, when it is spring in their native place. I recall clearly the mental shock which this communication caused me. If it is true, we may actually say that plants have a sort of memory, even though it be admitted that the chief point involved is the periodicity of the

141

phenomena of life. The so-called reflex movements of animals may be explained in a natural manner as phenomena of memory outside the organ of consciousness. I was a witness of a very remarkable phenomenon of this kind—in 1865, I think—with Rollett, who was experimenting with pigeons whose brains had been removed. These birds drink whenever their feet are placed in a cold liquid, whether the liquid is water, mercury, or sulphuric acid. Now since a bird must ordinarily wet its feet when it seeks to quench its thirst, the view arises quite naturally that we have here a habit adapted to an end, which is conditioned by the mode of life and fixed by inheritance, and which, even when consciousness is eliminated, takes place with the precision of clockwork on the application of the stimulus appropriate to its excitation. Goltz in his wonderful book *Die Nervencentren des Frosches,* 1869, and in later writings, has described many phenomena of the sort.—I will take this opportunity of mentioning some further observations which I recall with a great deal of pleasure. In the autumn vacation of 1873, my little boy brought me a sparrow a few days old, which had fallen from its nest, and wanted to bring it up. But the matter was not so easy. The little creature could not be induced to swallow, and would certainly have succumbed to the indignities that would have been unavoidable in feeding it by force. I then fell into the following train of thought: "Whether or not the Darwinian theory is correct, the new-born child would certainly perish if it had not the specially formed organs and inherited impulse to suck, which are brought into activity quite automatically and mechanically by the appropriate stimulus. Something similar (in another form) must exist likewise in the case of the bird." I exerted myself to discover the appropriate stimulus. A small insect was stuck upon a sharp stick and swung rapidly about the head of the bird. Immediately the bird opened its bill, beat its wings, and eagerly devoured the proffered food. I had thus discovered the right stimulus for setting the impulse and the automatic movement free. The creature grew perceptibly stronger and greedier, it began to snatch at the food, and once seized an insect that had accidentally fallen from the stick to the table; from that time on it ate, without ceremony, of itself. In proportion as its intellect and memory developed, a smaller portion of the stimulus was required. On reaching independence, the creature took on, little by little, all the characteristic ways of sparrows, which it certainly had not learnt by itself. By day, with its intellect awake, it was very trustful and friendly. In the evening, other phenomena were regularly exhibited. It grew timid. It always sought out the highest places in the room, and would become quiet only when it was prevented by the ceiling from going higher. Here again we have an inherited habit adapted to an end. On the coming of darkness, its demeanour changed totally. When approached, it ruffled its feathers, began to hiss, and showed every appearance of terror and real physical fear of ghosts. Nor is this fear without its reasons and its purpose in a creature which, under normal circumstances, may at any moment be devoured by some monster.

This last observation strengthened me in an opinion already formed, that my children's terror of ghosts did not have its source in nursery tales, which were carefully excluded from them, but was innate. One of my children would regard with anxiety an arm-chair, which stood in the shadow; another carefully avoided, in the evening, a coal-scuttle by the stove, especially when this stood with the lid open, looking like gaping jaws. The fear of ghosts is the true mother of religions. Neither scientific analysis nor the careful historical criticism of a David Strauss, as applied to myths, which, for the strong intellect, are refuted even before they are invented, will all at once do away with and banish these things. A motive which has so long answered, and in a measure still answers, to actual economic needs (fear of something worse, hope of something better), will long continue to exist in mysterious and uncontrollable instinctive trains of thought. Just as the birds on uninhabited islands (according to Darwin) learn the fear of man only after the lapse of generations, so we shall unlearn, only after many generations that useless habit known as the creeping of flesh. Every presentation of Faust may teach us the extent to which we are still in secret sympathy with the conceptions of the age of witchcraft. The exact knowledge of nature and of the conditions of this life gradually becomes more useful to man than fear of the unknown. And in time the most important thing of all for him is to be on his guard against his fellow-men who want to oppress him violently or abuse him treacherously by misleading his understanding and emotions. I will here relate one other curious observation, for the knowledge of which I am indebted to my father (an enthusiastic Darwinian and in the latter part of his life a landed proprietor in Carniola). My father occupied himself with silk-culture, raised the yammai in the open oak-woods, etc. The ordinary mulberry silkworm has, for many generations, been raised indoors, and has consequently become exceedingly helpless and dependent. When the time for passing into the chrysalitic state arrives, it is the custom to give the creatures bundles of straw, upon which they spin their cocoons. Now it one day occurred to my father not to prepare the usual bundles of straw for a colony of silk-worms. The result was that the majority of the worms perished, and only a small portion, the geniuses (those with the greatest power of adaptation) spun their cocoons. Whether, as my sister believes she has observed, the experiences of one generation are utilized, in noticeable degree, in the very next generation, is a question which probably requires to be left to further investigation. The experiments made by

144

C. Lloyd Morgan (*Comparative Psychology*, London, 1894) with young chickens, ducks, etc., shew that, at any rate in the case of the higher animals scarcely anything is innate but the reflexes. The newly hatched chick at once begins to peck with great assurance at everything that it sees; but it has to learn what is suitable to pick up by its individual experience. The simpler the organism the smaller the part played by individual memory. From all these remarkable phenomena we need derive no mysticism of the Unconscious. A memory reaching beyond the individual (in the broader sense defined above) renders them intelligible.—A psychology in the Spencer-Darwinian sense, founded upon the theory of evolution, but supported by detailed positive investigation, would yield richer results than all previous speculation has done.—These observations and reflections had long been made and written down when Schneider's valuable work, *Der thierische Wille*, Leipzig, 1880, which contains many that are similar, made its appearance. I agree with the details of Schneider's discussions (in so far as they have not been made problematical by Lloyd Morgan's experiments) almost throughout, although his fundamental conceptions in the realms of natural science with regard to the relation of sensation and physical process, the significance of the survival of species, etc., are essentially different from mine, and although I hold, for instance, the distinction between sensation-impulses and perception-impulses to be quite superfluous.—An important rvvolution in our views on heredity may perhaps be produced by Weissmann's work. *Ueber die Vererbung, Jena,* 1883 (English translation, *Essays on Heredity and Kindred Biological Problems,* Oxford, The Clarendon Press, 1889). Weissmann regards the inheritance of traits acquired by use as highly improbable, and finds in chance variation of the germ-elements and in the selection of the germ-elements the most important factors. Whatever attitude

145

we adopt towards Weissmann's theories, the discussion initiated by him must contribute to the elucidation of these questions. No one will refuse to recognize the almost mathematical acuteness and depth of the way in which he states the problem, and it cannot be denied that his arguments have much force. He makes, for instance, the extremely suggestive remark that it is impossible that the peculiar and unusual forms of sexless ants, which must apparently be referred to use and adaptation, and which moreover deviate so remarkably from the forms of ants that are capable of propagation, should be produced by inheritance of characteristics acquired by use.[1] That the germ-elements themselves may be altered by external influences appears to be clearly shewn by the formation of new races, which maintain themselves as such, transmit their racial traits by inheritance, and are themselves, again, capable of transformation, under other circumstances. Accordingly, some influence must certainly be exerted on the germ-plasm by the body which envelops it (as Weissmann himself admits). Thus an influence of the individual life upon its descendants can certainly not be entirely excluded, even although a direct transmission to the descendants of the results of use in the individual can (according to Weissmann) no longer be expected. In entertaining the notion that the germ-elements vary accidentally, we must bear in mind that chance is not a principle of action. When periodic circumstances of different kinds and different periodicities coincide in accordance with definite causal laws, the circumstances overlap in such a way that in any particular case it is impossible to see that any law is involved. But the law reveals itself with the lapse of a long enough time, and

---

[1] But perhaps the powerful mandibles of the sexless ants are the *original* acquisition of the species, and merely appear in an atrophied form in the individuals to whom propagation of the race is confined.

permits us to calculate on certain average values or probabilities of effects.[1] Without some such principle of action, chance or probability is meaningless. And what principle of action can be conceived as exercising more influence on the variation of the germ-elements than the body of the parent? Personally I cannot understand how it is possible that the species should succumb to the influence of varying circumstances, and yet that these circumstances should not affect the individual. Moreover, I am certain that I myself vary with every thought, every memory, every experience; all these factors undoubtedly change my whole physical behaviour.[2]

Although it is scarcely necessary, I should like to add explicitly that I regard the theory of evolution, in whatever form, as a working scientific hypothesis, capable of being modified and of being made more precise, which is valuable in so far as it facilitates the provisional understanding of what is given in experience. I have been a witness of the powerful impetus which Darwin's work gave in my time not merely to biology, but to all scientific enquiry, and it is not likely that I should underestimate the value of the theory of evolution. But I would not quarrel with anyone who should rate its value very low. As long ago as 1883 and 1886 I dwelt on the necessity of advancing by means of more precise conceptions obtained by the study of biological facts for their own sakes.[3] Thus I am by no means committed to a refusal to understand investigations such as those of Driesch. But whether Driesch's criticism of my attitude towards the theory of evolution is justified,[4] I leave to anyone to

---

[1] *Vorlesungen uber Psychophysik, Zeitschrift fur prakt. Heilkunde*, pp. 148, 168, 169, Vienna, 1863.

[2] *Popular Scientific Lectures*, Chicago, Open Court Publishing Co.

[3] Cp. *Popular Scientific Lectures, and Analyse der Empfindungen*, 1886, pp. 34, seq.

[4] Driesch, *Die organisatorischen Regulationen*, pp. 165, seq., 1901.

decide who, even after this criticism, still cares to be at the pains of reading my works.

10.

Teleological conceptions, as aids to investigation, are not to be shunned. It is true, our comprehension of the facts of reality is not enhanced by referring them to an unknown World-Purpose, itself problematical, or to the equally problematical purpose of a living being. Nevertheless, the question as to the value that a given function has for the existence of an organism, or as to what are its actual contributions to the preservation of the organism, may be of great assistance in the comprehension of this function itself.[1] Of course we must not suppose, on this account, as many Darwinians have done, that we have

---

[1] Such teleological conceptions have often been useful and instructive to me. The remark, for example, that a visible object under varying intensity of illumination can be recognized as the same only when the sensation excited depends on the ratio of the illumination-intensities of object and surroundings, makes intelligible a whole train of organic properties of the eye. (Cp. Hering in Graefe-Saemisch's *Handbuch der Augen heilkunde*, Vol. III., Ch. 12, pp. 13, seq.). In this way we understand also, how the organism, in the interest of its survival, was obliged to adjust itself to the requirement mentioned and to adapt itself to feel the ratios of light-intensity. The so-called law of Weber, or the fundamental psycho-physical formula of Fechner, thus appears not as something fundamental, but as the explicable result of organic adjustments. The belief in the universal validity of this law is, naturally, herewith relinquished. I have given the arguments on this point in various papers. (*Sitzungsberichte der Wiener Akademie*, Vol. LII., 1865; *Vierteljahrsschrift fur Psychiatrie*, Neuwied and Leipzig, 1868; *Sitzungsberichte der Wiener Akademie*, Vol. LVII., 1868). In the last-named paper, proceeding from the postulate of the parallelism between the psychical and the physical, or, as I then expressed myself, from the proportionality between stimulus and sensation, I abandoned the metrical formula of Fechner (the logarithmic law), and brought forward another conception of the fundamental formula, the validity of which for light-sensation I never disputed. This is apparent beyond all doubt from the way in which that paper is worked out. Thus one cannot say, as Hering has done, that I everywhere take the psycho-physical law as my foundation, if by this is understood the *metrical formula*. How could I have maintained the *proportionality* between stimulus and sensation at the same time with the *logarithmic dependence?* It was sufficient for me to render *my* meaning clear;—to criticize and contest Fechner's law in detail, I had, for many obvious reasons, no need. Strictly speaking I consider the expression "proportionality" also to be inappropriate, since there can be no question of an actual measurement of the sensations; all that can be done is to characterize them exactly and make an inventory of them by numerical means. Cp. what I have said about the characterization of states of heat (*Prinzipien der Warmelehre*, p. 56).

148

"mechanically explained" a function, when we discover that it is necessary for the survival of the species. Darwin himself is doubtless quite free from this short-sighted conception. By what physical means a function is developed, still remains a physical problem; while the how and why of an organism's voluntary adaptation continues to be a psychological problem. The preservation of the species is only one, though an actual and very valuable, point of departure for inquiry, but it is by no means the last and the highest. Species have certainly been destroyed, and new ones have as certainly arisen. The pleasure-seeking and pain-avoiding will,[1] therefore, is directed perforce beyond the preservation of the species. It preserves the species when it is advantageous to do so, and destroys it when its survival is no longer advantageous. Were it directed merely to the preservation of the species, it would move aimlessly about in a vicious circle, deceiving both itself and all individuals. This would be the biological counterpart of the notorious "perpetual motion" of physics. The same absurdity is committed by the statesman who regards the state as an end in itself.

---

[1] Schopenhauer's conception of the relation between Will and Force can quite well be adopted without seeing anything metaphysical in either.

ERNST MACH (b.-Turas, in Moravia, Austria, Feb. 18, 1838; d.-Haar, near München, Feb. 9, 1916.)

Mach received his Ph.D. from Vienna in 1860. He was appointed Professor of Physics at the University of Vienna in 1895, and remained for six years, till 1901.

As physicist and philosopher, Mach made a deep and lasting impression on psychology by his astute discussion of sense perception. He gave rise to, or rather expressed most succinctly, two themes, which, though united in him, grew over the years into majestic opposing camps. As the inspiration for Ehrenfels' work on the *Gestaltqualitat,* Mach directly influenced the development of Gestalt Psychology. As background and direct reference for such work as Karl Pearson's *Grammar of Science,* Mach's work constitutes one of the earliest bulwarks for the positivistic approach to psychology, and to science in general.

MACH, E. *The analysis of sensations and the relation of the physical to the psychical.* Chicago: Open Court Pub. Co., 1914 (1886). Trans. C. M. Williams from the 1st German edition; rev. and suppl. by S. Waterflow from the 5th German edition. Chap. IV: "The chief points of view for the investigation of the senses."

See also:

MACH, E. a) *Popular scientific lectures.* Chicago: Open Court, 1895. Trans. T. J. McCormack.

b) *Erkenntnis und Irrtum. Skizzen zur Psychologie zur Forschung.* Leipzig: Barth, 1905.

FRANK, P. "Ernst Mach—the centenary of his birth." *Erkenntnis.* 1938, 7:247-256.

PRINCIPLES OF PSYCHOLOGY
William James

THE STREAM OF THOUGHT

We now begin our study of the mind from within. Most books start with sensations, as the simplest mental facts, and proceed synthetically, constructing each higher stage from those below it. But this is abandoning the empirical method of investigation. No one ever had a simple sensation by itself. Consciousness, from our natal day, is of a teeming multiplicity of objects and relations, and what we call simple sensations are results of discriminative attention, pushed often to a very high degree. It is astonishing what havoc is wrought in psychology by admitting at the outset apparently innocent suppositions, that nevertheless contain a flaw. The bad consequences develop themselves later on, and are irremediable, being woven through the whole texture of the work. The notion that sensations, being the simplest things, are the first things to take up in psychology is one of these suppositions. The only thing which psychology has a right to postulate at the outset is the fact of thinking itself, and that must first be taken up and analyzed. If sensations then prove to be amongst the elements of the thinking, we shall be no worse off as respects them than if we had taken them for granted at the start.

The first fact for us, then, as psychologists, is that thinking of some sort goes on. I use the word thinking for every form of consciousness indiscriminately. If we could say in English 'it thinks,' as we say 'it rains' or 'it blows,' we should be stating the fact most simply and with the minimum of assumption. As we cannot, we must simply say that *thought goes on.*

How does it go on? We notice immediately five important characters in the process, of which it shall be the duty of the present chapter to treat in a general way:

1) Every thought tends to be part of a personal consciousness.

2) Within each personal consciousness thought is always changing.

3) Within each personal consciousness thought is sensibly continuous.

4) It always appears to deal with objects independent of itself.

5) It is interested in some parts of these objects to the exclusion of others, and welcomes or rejects—*chooses* from among them in a word—all the while.

1) *Thought tends to Personal Form.*

When I say *every thought is part of a personal consciousness*, 'personal consciousness' is one of the terms in question. Its meaning we know so long as no one asks us to define it, but to give an accurate account of it is the most difficult of philosophic tasks. This task we must confront in the next chapter; here a preliminary word will suffice.

In this room—this lecture-room, say—there are a multitude of thoughts, yours and mine, some of which cohere mutually, and some not. They are as little each-for-itself and reciprocally independent as they are all-belonging-together. They are neither: no one of them is separate, but each belongs with certain others and with none beside. My thought belongs with my other thoughts, and your thought with your other thoughts. Whether anywhere in the room there be a mere thought, which is nobody's thought, we have no means of ascertaining, for we have no experience of its like. The only states of consciousness

152

that we naturally deal with are found in personal consciousnesses, minds, selves, concrete particular I's and you's.

Each of these minds keeps its own thoughts to itself. There is no giving or bartering between them. No thought even comes into direct *sight* of a thought in another personal consciousness than its own. Absolute insulation, irreducible pluralism, is the law. It seems as if the elementary psychic fact were not *thought* or *this thought* or *that thought*, but *my thought*, every thought being *owned*. Neither contemporaneity, nor proximity in space, nor similarity of quality and content are able to fuse thoughts together which are sundered by this barrier of belonging to different personal minds. The breaches between such thoughts are the most absolute breaches in nature. Everyone will recognize this to be true, so long as the existence of *something* corresponding to the term 'personal mind' is all that is insisted on, without any particular view of its nature being implied. On these terms the personal self rather than the thought might be treated as the immediate datum in psychology. The universal conscious fact is not 'feelings and thoughts exist,' but 'I think' and 'I feel.' No psychology, at any rate, can question the *existence* of personal selves. The worst a psychology can do is so to interpret the nature of these selves as to rob them of their worth. A French writer, speaking of our ideas, says somewhere in a fit of anti-spiritualistic excitement that, misled by certain peculiarities which they display, we 'end by personifying' the procession which they make,—such personification being regarded by him as a great philosophic blunder on our part. It could only be a blunder if the notion of personality meant something essentially different from anything to be found in the mental procession. But if that procession be itself the very 'original' of the notion of personality, to personify it cannot possibly be wrong. It

153

is already personified. There are no marks of personality to be gathered *aliunde,* and then found lacking in the train of thought. It has them all already; so that to whatever farther analysis we may subject that form of personal selfhood under which thoughts appear, it is, and must remain true that the thoughts which psychology studies do continually tend to appear as parts of personal selves.

I say 'tend to appear' rather than 'appear,' on account of those facts of sub-conscious personality, automatic writing, etc., of which we studied a few in the last chapter. The buried feelings and thoughts proved now to exist in hysterical anaesthetics, in recipients of post-hypnotic suggestion, etc., themselves are parts of *secondary personal selves.* These selves are for the most part very stupid and contracted, and are cut off at ordinary times from communication with the regular and normal self of the individual; but still they form conscious unities, have continuous memories, speak, write, invent distinct names for themselves, or adopt names that are suggested; and, in short, are entirely worthy of that title of secondary personalities which is now commonly given them. According to M. Janet these secondary personalities are always abnormal, and result from the splitting of what ought to be a single complete self into two parts, of which one lurks in the background whilst the other appears on the surface as the only self the man or woman has. For our present purpose it is unimportant whether this account of the origin of secondary selves is applicable to all possible cases of them or not, for it certainly is true of a large number of them. Now although the *size* of a secondary self thus formed will depend on the number of thoughts that are thus split-off from the main consciousness, the *form* of it tends to personality, and the later thoughts pertaining to it remember the earlier ones and adopt them as their own. M. Janet caught the actual moment of inspissation (so to speak) of one of these secondary personalities in his anaesthetic somnambulist Lucie. He found that when this young woman's attention was absorbed in conversation with a third party, her anaesthetic hand would write simple answers to questions whispered to her by himself. "Do you hear?" he asked. *"No,"* was the unconsciously written reply. "But to answer you must hear." *"Yes, quite so."* "Then how do you manage?" *"I don't know."* "There must be some one who hears me." *"Yes."* "Who?" *"Someone other than Lucie."* "Ah! another person. Shall we give her a name?" *"No."* "Yes, it will be more convenient." *"Well, Adrienne, then."* "Once baptized, the subconscious personage," M. Janet continues, "grows more definitely outlined and displays better her psychological characters. In particular she shows us that she is conscious of the feelings excluded from the consciousness of the primary or normal personage. She it is who tells us that I am pinching the arm or touching the little finger in which Lucie for so long has had no tactile sensations."*

In other cases the adoption of the name by the secondary self is more spontaneous. I have seen a number of incipient automatic writers and mediums as yet imperfectly 'developed,' who immediately and of their own accord write and speak in the name of departed spirits. These may be public characters, as Mozart, Faraday, or real persons formerly known to the subject, or altogether imaginary beings. Without prejudicing the question of real 'spirit-control' in the more developed sorts of trance-utterance, I incline to think that these (often deplorably unintelligent) rudimentary utterances are the work of an inferior fraction of the subject's own natural mind, set free from control by the rest, and working after a set pattern fixed by the prejudices of the social environment. In a spiritualistic community we get optimistic messages,

---

* L'Automatisme Psychologique, p. 318.

whilst in an ignorant Catholic village, the secondary personage calls itself by the name of a demon, and proffers blasphemies and obscenities, instead of telling us how happy it is in the summer-land.[*]

Beneath these tracts of thought, which, however, rudimentary, are still organized selves with a memory, habits, and sense of their own identity, M. Janet thinks that the facts of catalepsy in hysteric patients drive us to suppose that there are thoughts quite unorganized and impersonal. A patient in cataleptic trance (which can be produced artificially in certain hypnotized subjects) is without memory on waking and seems insensible and unconscious as long as the cataleptic condition lasts. If, however, one raises the arm of such a subject it stays in that position, and the whole body can thus be moulded like wax under the hands of the operator, retaining for a considerable time whatever attitudes he communicates to it. In hysterics whose arm for example, is anaesthetic, the same thing may happen. The anaesthetic arm may remain passively in positions which it is made to assume; or if the hand be taken and made to hold a pencil and trace a certain letter, it will continue tracing that letter indefinitely on the paper. These acts, until recently, were supposed to be accompanied by no consciousness at all: they were physiological reflexes. M. Janet considers with much more plausibility that feeling escorts them. The feeling is probably merely that of the position or movement of the limb, and it produces no more than its natural effects when it discharges into the motor centers which keep the position maintained, or the movement incessantly renewed. Such thoughts as these, says M. Janet, "are known by *no one*, for disaggregated sensations

---

[*] Cf. A. Constans: Relation sur une Epidémie d'hystero-demonopathie en 1861. 2me ed. Paris, 1863.—Chiap e Franzolini: L'Epidemia d'isterodemonopatie in Verzegnis. Reggio, 1879.—See also J. Kerner's little work: Nachricht von dem Vorkommen des Besessenseins. 1836.

reduced to a state of mental dust are not synthetized in any personality."* He admits, however, that these very same unutterably stupid thoughts tend to develop memory,—the cataleptic ere long moves her arm at a bare hint; so that they form no important exception to the law that all thought tends to assume the form of personal consciousness.

2) *Thought is in Constant Change.*

I do not mean necessarily that no one state of mind has any duration—even if true, that would be hard to establish. The change which I have more particularly in view is that which takes place in sensible intervals of time; and the result on which I wish to lay stress is this, that *no state once gone can recur and be identical with what it was before.* Let us begin with Mr. Shadworth Hodgson's description:

"I go straight to the facts, without saying I go to perception, or sensation, or thought, or any special mode at all. What I find when I look at my consciousness at all is that what I cannot divest myself of, or not have in consciousness, if I have any consciousness at all, is a sequence of different feelings. I may shut my eyes and keep perfectly still, and try not to contribute anything of my own will; but whether I think or do not think, whether I perceive external things or not, I always have a succession of different feelings. Anything else that I may have also, of a more special character, comes in as parts of this succession. Not to have the succession of different feelings is not to be conscious at all.... The chain of consciousness is a sequence of *differents*."†

Such a description as this can awaken no possible protest from any one. We all recognize as different great classes of our conscious states. Now we are seeing, now hearing; now reasoning, now willing; now recollecting, now expecting; now loving, now hating; and in a hundred other ways we know our minds to be alternately engaged. But all these are complex states. The aim of science is

* Loc. cit. p. 316.
† The Philosophy of Reflection, I. 248, 290.

always to reduce complexity to simplicity; and in psychological science we have the celebrated 'theory of *ideas*' which, admitting the great difference among each other of what may be called concrete conditions of mind, seeks to show how this is all the resultant effect of variations in the *combination* of certain simple elements of consciousness that always remain the same. These mental atoms or molecules are what Locke called 'simple ideas.' Some of Locke's successors made out that the only simple ideas were the sensations strictly so called. Which ideas the simple ones may be does not, however, now concern us. It is enough that certain philosophers have thought they could see under the dissolving-view-appearance of the mind elementary facts of *any* sort that remained unchanged amid the flow.

And the view of these philosophers has been called little into question, for our common experience seems at first sight to corroborate it entirely. Are not the sensations we get from the same object, for example, always the same? Does not the same piano-key, struck with the same force, make us hear in the same way? Does not the same grass give us the same feeling of green, the same sky the same feeling of blue, and do we not get the same olfactory sensation no matter how many times we put our nose to the same flask of cologne? It seems a piece of metaphysical sophistry to suggest that we do not; and yet a close attention to the matter shows that *there is no proof that the same bodily sensation is ever got by us twice.*

What is got twice is the same OBJECT. We hear the same *note* over and over again; we see the same *quality* of green, or smell the same objective perfume, or experience the same *species* of pain. The realities, concrete and abstract, physical and ideal, whose permanent existence we believe in, seem to be constantly coming up again before our thought, and lead us, in our carelessness, to suppose that our 'ideas' of them are the same ideas.

When we come, some time later, to the chapter on **Perception**, we shall see how inveterate is our habit of not attending to sensations as subjective facts, but of simply using them as stepping-stones to pass over to the recognition of the realities whose presence they reveal. The grass out of the window now looks to me of the same green in the sun as in the shade, and yet a painter would have to paint one part of it dark brown, another part bright yellow, to give its real sensational effect. We take no heed, as a rule, of the different way in which the same things look and sound and smell at different distances and under different circumstances. The sameness of the *things* is what we are concerned to ascertain; and any sensations that assure us of that will probably be considered in a rough way to be the same with each other. This is what makes off-hand testimony about the subjective identity of different sensations well-nigh worthless as a proof of the fact. The entire history of Sensation is a commentary on our inability to tell whether two sensations received apart are exactly alike. What appeals to our attention far more than the absolute quality or quantity of a given sensation is its *ratio* to whatever other sensations we may have at the same time. When everything is dark a somewhat less dark sensation makes us see an object white. Helmholtz calculates that the white marble painted in a picture representing an architectural view by moonlight is, when seen by daylight, from ten to twenty thousand times brighter than the real moonlit marble would be.*

Such a difference as this could never have been *sensibly* learned; it had to be inferred from a series of indirect considerations. There are facts which make us believe that our sensibility is altering all the time, so that the same object cannot easily give us the same sensation over

---

* Populäre Wissenschaftliche Vorträge, Drittes Heft (1876), p. 72.

again. The eye's sensibility to light is at its maximum when the eye is first exposed, and blunts itself with surprising rapidity. A long night's sleep will make it see things twice as brightly on wakening, as simple rest by closure will make it see them later in the day.* We feel things differently according as we are sleepy or awake, hungry or full, fresh or tired; differently at night and in the morning, differently in summer and in winter, and above all things differently in childhood, manhood and, old age. Yet we never doubt that our feelings reveal the same world, with the same sensible qualities and the same sensible things occupying it. The difference of the sensibility is shown best by the difference of our emotions about the things from one age to another, or when we are in different organic moods. What was bright and exciting becomes weary, flat, and unprofitable. The bird's song is tedious, the breeze is mournful, the sky is sad.

To these indirect presumptions that our sensations, following the mutations of our capacity for feeling, are always undergoing an essential change, must be added another presumption, based on what must happen in the brain. Every sensation corresponds to some cerebral action. For an identical sensation to recur it would have to occur the second time *in an unmodified brain.* But as this, strictly speaking, is a physiological impossibility, so is an unmodified feeling an impossibility; for to every brain-modification, however small, must correspond a change of equal amount in the feeling which the brain subserves.

All this would be true if even sensations came to us pure and single and not combined into 'things.' Even then we should have to confess that, however we might in ordinary conversation speak of getting the same sensation again, we never in strict theoretic accuracy could do

---

* Fick, in L. Hermann's Handb. d. Physiol., Bd. III. Th. I. p. 225

so; and that whatever was true of the river of life, of the river of elementary feeling, it would certainly be true to say, like Heraclitus, that we never descend twice into the same stream.

But if the assumption of 'simple ideas of sensation' recurring in immutable shape is so easily shown to be baseless, how much more baseless is the assumption of immutability in the larger masses of our thought!

For there it is obvious and palpable that our state of mind is never precisely the same. Every thought we have of a given fact is, strictly speaking, unique, and only bears a resemblance of kind with our other thoughts of the same fact. When the identical fact recurs, we *must* think of it in a fresh manner, see it under a somewhat different angle, apprehend it in different relations from those in which it last appeared. And the thought by which we cognize it is the thought of it-in-those-relations, a thought suffused with the consciousness of all that dim context. Often we are ourselves struck at the strange differences in our successive views of the same thing. We wonder how we ever could have opined as we did last month about a certain matter. We have outgrown the possibility of that state of mind, we know not how. From one year to another we see things in new lights. What was unreal has grown real, and what was exciting is insipid. The friends we used to care the world for are shrunken to shadows; the women, once so divine, the stars, the woods, and the waters, how no so dull and common; the young girls that brought an aura of infinity, at present hardly distinguishable existences; the pictures so empty; and as for the books, what *was* there to find so mysteriously significant in Goethe, or in John Mill so full of weight? Instead of all this, more zestful than ever is the work, the work; and fuller and deeper the import of common duties and of common goods.

But what here strikes us so forcibly on the flagrant

161

scale exists on every scale, down to the imperceptible transition from one hour's outlook to that of the next. Experience is remoulding us every moment, and our mental reaction on every given thing is really a resultant of our experience of the whole world up to that date. The analogies of brain-physiology must again be appealed to to corroborate our view.

Our earlier chapters have taught us to believe that, whilst we think, our brain changes, and that, like the aurora borealis, its whole internal equilibrium shifts with every pulse of change. The precise nature of the shifting at a given moment is a product of many factors. The accidental state of local nutrition or blood-supply may be among them. But just as one of them certainly is the influence of outward objects on the sense-organs during the moment, so is another certainly the very special susceptibility in which the organ has been left at that moment by all it has gone through in the past. Every brain-state is partly determined by the nature of this entire past succession. Alter the latter in any part, and the brain-state must be somewhat different. Each present brain-state is a record in which the eye of Omniscience might read all the foregone history of its owner. It is out of the question, then, that any total brain-state should identically recur. Something like it may recur; but to suppose *it* to recur would be equivalent to the absurd admission that all the states that had intervened between its two appearances had been pure nonentities, and that the organ after their passage was exactly as it was before. And (to consider shorter periods) just as, in the senses, an impression feels very differently according to what has preceded it; as one color succeeding another is modified by the contrast, silence sounds delicious after noise, and a note, when the scale is sung up, sounds unlike itself when the scale is sung down; as the presence of certain lines in a figure changes the apparent form of the other

162

lines, and as in music the whole aesthetic effect comes from the manner in which one set of sounds alters our feeling of another; so, in thought, we must admit that those portions of the brain that have just been maximally excited retain a kind of soreness which is a condition of our present consciousness, a codeterminant of how and what we now shall feel.*

Ever some tracts are waning in tension, some waxing, whilst others actively discharge. The states of tension have as positive an influence as any in determining the total condition, and in deciding what the *psychosis* shall be. All we know of submaximal nerve-irritations, and of the summation of apparently ineffective stimuli, tends to show that *no* changes in the brain are physiologically ineffective, and that presumably none are bare of psychological result. But as the brain-tension shifts from one relative state of equilibrium to another, like the gyrations of a kaleidoscope, now rapid and now slow, is it likely that its faithful psychic concomitant is heavier-footed than itself, and that it cannot match each one of the organ's irradiations by a shifting inward iridescence of its own? But if it can do this, its inward iridescences must be infinite, for the brain-redistributions are in infinite variety. If so coarse a thing as a telephone-plate can be made to thrill for years and never reduplicate its inward condition, how much more must this be the case with the infinitely delicate brain?

I am sure that this concrete and total manner of regarding the mind's changes is the only true manner, difficult

---

* It need of course not follow, because a total brain-state does not recur, that no *point* of the brain can ever be twice in the same condition. That would be as improbable a consequence as that in the sea a wave-crest should never come twice at the same point of space. What can hardly come twice is an identical *combination* of wave-forms all with their crests and hollows reoccupying identical places. For such a total combination as this is the analogue of the brain-state to which our actual consciousness at any moment is due.

as it may be to carry it out in detail. If anything seems obscure about it, it will grow clearer as we advance. Meanwhile, if it be true, it is certainly also true that no two 'ideas' are ever exactly the same, which is the proposition we started to prove. The proposition is more important theoretically than it at first sight seems. For it makes it already impossible for us to follow obediently in the footprints of either the Lockian or the Herbartian school, schools which have had almost unlimited influence in Germany and among ourselves. No doubt it is often *convenient* to formulate the mental facts in an atomistic sort of way, and to treat the higher states of consciousness as if they were all built out of unchanging simple ideas. It is convenient often to treat curves as if they were composed of small straight lines, and electricity and nerve-force as if they were fluids. But in the one case as in the other we must never forget that we are talking symbolically, and that there is nothing in nature to answer to our words. *A permanently existing 'idea' or 'Vorstellung' which makes its appearance before the footlights of consciousness at periodical intervals, is as mythological an entity as the Jack of Spades.*

What makes it convenient to use the mythological formulas is the whole organization of speech, which, as was remarked a while ago, was not made by psychologists, but by men who were as a rule only interested in the facts their mental states revealed. They only spoke of their states as *ideas of this or of that thing*. What wonder then, that the thought is most easily conceived under the law of the thing whose name it bears! If the thing is composed of parts, then we suppose that the thought of the thing must be composed of the thoughts of the parts. If one part of the thing have appeared in the same thing or in other things on former occasions, why then we must be having even now the very same 'idea' of that part which was there on those occasions. If the thing is simple, its thought

164

is simple. If it is multitudinous, it must require a multitude of thoughts to think it. If a succession, only a succession of thoughts can know it. If permanent its thought is permanent. And so on *ad libitum*. What after all is so natural as to assume that one object, called by one name, should be known by one affection of the mind? But, if language must thus influence us, the agglutinative languages, and even Greek and Latin with their declensions, would be the better guides. Names did not appear in them inalterable, but changed their shape to suit the context in which they lay. It must have been easier then than now to conceive of the same object as being thought of at different times in non-identical conscious states.

This, too, will grow clearer as we proceed. Meanwhile a necessary consequence of the belief in permanent self-identical psychic facts that absent themselves and recur periodically is the Humian doctrine that our thought is composed of separate independent parts and is not a sensibly continuous stream. That this doctrine entirely misrepresents the natural appearances is what I next shall try to show.

3) *Within each personal consciousness, thought is sensibly continuous.*

I can only define 'continuous' as that which is without breach, crack, or division. I have already said that the breach from one mind to another is perhaps the greatest breach in nature. The only breaches that can well be conceived to occur within the limits of a single mind would either be *interruptions, time-gaps* during which the consciousness went out altogether to come into existence again at a later moment; or they would be breaks in the *quality,* or content, of the thought, so abrupt that the segment that followed had no connection whatever with the one that went before. The proposition that within each personal consciousness thought feels continuous, means two things:

165

1. That even where there is a time-gap the consciousness after it feels as if it belonged together with the consciousness before it, as another part of the same self;

2. That the changes from one moment to another in the quality of the consciousness are never absolutely abrupt.

The case of the time-gaps, as the simplest, shall be taken first. And first of all, a word about time-gaps of which the consciousness may not be itself aware.

[Earlier] we saw that such time-gaps existed, and that they might be more numerous than is usually supposed. If the consciousness is not aware of them, it cannot feel them as interruptions. In the unconsciousness produced by nitrous oxide and other anaesthetics, in that of epilepsy and fainting, the broken edges of the sentient life may meet and merge over the gap, much as the feelings of space of the opposite margins of the 'blind spot' meet and merge over that objective interruption to the sensitiveness of the eye. Such consciousness as this, whatever it be for the onlooking psychologist, is for itself unbroken. It *feels* unbroken; a waking day of it is sensibly a unit as long as that day lasts, in the sense in which the hours themselves are units, as having all their parts next each other, with no intrusive alien substance between. To expect the consciousness to feel the interruptions of its objective continuity as gaps would be like expecting the eye to feel a gap of silence because it does not hear, or the ear to feel a gap of darkness because it does not see. So much for the gaps that are unfelt.

With the felt gaps the case is different. On waking from sleep, we usually know that we have been unconscious, and we often have an accurate judgment of how long. The judgment here is certainly an inference from sensible signs, and its ease is due to long practice in the particular field.* The result of it, however, is that the consciousness is, *for itself,* not what it was in the former case, but inter-

---

* The accurate registration of the 'how long' is still a little mysterious.

rupted and continuous, in the mere time-sense of the words. But in the other sense of continuity, the sense of the parts being inwardly connected and belonging together because they are parts of a common whole, the consciousness remains sensibly continuous and one. What now is the common whole? The natural name for it is *myself, I* or *me*.

When Paul and Peter wake up in the same bed, and recognize that they have been asleep, each one of them mentally reaches back and makes connection with but *one* of the two streams of thought which were broken by the sleeping hours. As the current of an electrode buried in the ground unerringly finds its way to its own similarly buried mate, across no matter how much intervening earth; so Peter's present instantly finds out Peter's past, and never by mistake knits itself on to that of Paul. Paul's thought in turn is as little liable to go astray. The past thought of Peter is appropriated by the present Peter alone. He may have a *knowledge,* and a correct one too, of what Paul's last drowsy states of mind were as he sank into sleep, but it is an entirely different sort of knowledge from that which he has of his own last states. He *remembers* his own states, whilst he only *conceives* Paul's. Remembrance is like direct feeling; its object is suffused with a warmth and intimacy to which no object of mere conception ever attains. This quality of warmth and intimacy and immediacy is what Peter's *present* thought also possesses for itself. So sure as this present is me, is mine, it says, so sure is anything else that comes with the same warmth and intimacy and immediacy, me and mine. What the qualities called warmth and intimacy may in themselves be will have to be matter for future consideration. But whatever past feelings appear with those qualities must be admitted to receive the greeting of the present mental state, to be owned by it, and accepted as belonging together with it in a common self.

This community of self is what the time-gap cannot break in twain, and is why a present thought, although not ignorant of the time-gap, can still regard itself as continuous with certain chosen portions of the past.

Consciousness, then, does not appear to itself chopped up in bits. Such words as 'chain' or 'train' do not describe it fitly as it presents itself in the first instance. It is nothing jointed; it flows. A 'river' or a 'stream' are the metaphors by which it is most naturally described. *In talking of it hereafter, let us call it the stream of thought, of consciousness, or of subjective life.*

But now there appears, even within the limits of the same self, and between thoughts all of which alike have this same sense of belonging together, a kind of jointing and separateness among the parts, of which this statement seems to take no account. I refer to the breaks that are produced by sudden *contrasts in the quality* of the successive segments of the stream of thought. If the words 'chain' and 'train' had no natural fitness in them, how came such words to be used at all? Does not a loud explosion rend the consciousness upon which it abruptly breaks, in twain? Does not every sudden shock, appearance of a new object, or change in a sensation, create a real interruption, sensibly felt as such, which cuts the conscious stream across at the moment at which it appears? Do not such interruptions smite us every hour of our lives, and have we the right, in their presence, still to call our consciousness a continuous stream?

This objection is based partly on a confusion and partly on a superficial introspective view.

The confusion is between the thoughts themselves, taken as subjective facts, and the things of which they are aware. It is natural to make this confusion, but easy to avoid it when once put on one's guard. The things are discrete and discontinuous; they do pass before us in a train or chain, making often explosive appearances and

168

rending each other in twain. But their comings and goings and contrasts no more break the flow of the thought that thinks them than they break the time and the space in which they lie. A silence may be broken by a thunder-clap, and we may be so stunned and confused for a moment by the shock as to give no instant account to ourselves of what has happened. But that very confusion is a mental state, and a state that passes us straight over from the silence to the sound. The transition between the thought of one object and the thought of another is no more a break in the *thought* than a joint in a bamboo is a break in the wood. It is a part of the *consciousness* as much as the joint is a part of the *bamboo*.

The superficial introspective view is the overlooking, even when the things are contrasted with each other most violently, of the large amount of affinity that may still remain between the thoughts by whose means they are cognized. Into the awareness of the thunder itself the awareness of the previous silence creeps and continues; for what we hear when the thunder crashes is not thunder *pure,* but thunder-breaking-upon-silence-and-contrasting-with-it.* Our feeling of the same objective thunder, coming in this way, is quite different from what it would be were the thunder a continuation of previous thunder. The thunder itself we believe to abolish and exclude the silence; but the *feeling* of the thunder is also a feeling of the silence as just gone; and it would be difficult to find in the actual concrete consciousness of a man a feeling so limited to the present as not to have an inkling of anything that went before. Here, again, language works against our perception of the truth. We name our thoughts simply, each after its thing, as if each knew its own thing and nothing else. What each really knows is

* Cf. Brentano; Psychologie, vol. *I*. pp. 219-20. Altogether this chapter of Brentano's on the Unity of Consciousness is as good as anything with which I am acquainted.

clearly the thing it is named for, with dimly perhaps a thousand other things. It ought to be named after all of them, but it never is. Some of them are always things known a moment ago more clearly; others are things to be known more clearly a moment hence.* Our own bodily position, attitude, condition, is one of the things of which *some* awareness, however inattentive, invariably accompanies the knowledge of whatever else we know. We think; and as we think we feel our bodily selves as the seat of the thinking. If the thinking be *our* thinking, it must be suffused through all its parts with that peculiar warth and intimacy that make it come as ours. Whether the warmth and intimacy be anything more than the feeling of the same old body always there, is a matter for the next chapter to decide. Whatever the content of the ego may be, it is habitually felt *with* everything else by us humans, and must form a *liaison* between all the things of

---

* Honor to whom honor is due! The most explicit acknowledgment I have ever found of all this is in a buried and forgotten paper by the Rev. Jas. Wills, on 'Accidental Association,' in the Transactions of the Royal Irish Academy, vol. xxi. part I (1846). Mr. Wills writes:

"At every instant of conscious thought there is a certain sum of perceptions, or reflections, or both together, present, and together constituting one whole state of apprehension. Of this some definite portion may be far more distinct than all the rest; and the rest be in consequence proportionally vague, even to the limit of obliteration. But still, within this limit, the most dim shade of perception enters into, and in some infinitesimal degree modifies, the whole existing state. This state will thus be in some way modified by any sensation or emotion, or act of distinct attention, that may give prominence to any part of it; so that the actual result is capable of the utmost variation, according to the person or the occasion. . . . To any portion of the entire scope here described there may be a special direction of the attention, and this special direction is recognized as strictly what is *recognized* as the idea present to the mind. This idea is evidently not commensurate wth the entire state of apprehension, and much perplexity has arisen from not observing this fact. However deeply we may suppose the attention to be engaged by any thought, any considerable alteration of the surrounding phenomena would still be perceived; the most abstruse demonstration in this room would not prevent a listener, however absorbed, from noticing the sudden extinction of the lights. Our mental states have always an *essential unity,* such that each state of apprehension, however variously compounded, is a single whole, of which every component is, therefore, strictly apprehended (so far as it is apprehended) as a part. Such is the elementary basis from which all our intellectual operations commence."

which we become successfully aware.*

On this gradualness in the changes of our mental content the principles of nerve-action can throw some more light. When studying, in Chapter III, the summation of nervous activities, we saw that no state of the brain can be supposed instantly to die away. If a new state comes, the inertia of the old state will still be there and modify the result accordingly. Of course we cannot tell, in our ignorance, what in each instance the modifications ought to be. The commonest modifications in sense-perception are known as the phenomena of contrast. In aesthetics they are the feelings of delight or displeasure which certain particular orders in a series of impressions give. In thought, strictly and narrowly so called, they are unquestionably that consciousness of the *whence* and the *whither* that always accompanies its flows. If recently the brain-tract a was vividly excited, and then b, and now vividly c, the total present consciousness is not produced simply by c's excitement, but also by the dying vibrations of a and b as well. If we want to represent the brain-process we must write it thus: a^b_c—three different processes coexisting,

and correlated with them a thought which is no one of the three thoughts which they would have produced had each of them occurred alone. But whatever this fourth thought may exactly be, it seems impossible that it should not be something *like* each of the three other thoughts whose tracts are concerned in its production, though in a fast-waning phase.

It all goes back to what we said in another connection only a few pages ago. . . . As the total neurosis changes, so does the total psychosis change. But as the changes of neurosis are never absolutely discontinuous, so must the successive psychoses shade gradually into each other, although their *rate* of change may be much faster at one moment than at the next.

* Compare the charming passage in Taine on Intelligence (N. Y. ed.), I. 83-4.

This difference in the rate of change lies at the basis of a difference of subjective states of which we ought immediately to speak. When the rate is slow we are aware of the object of our thought in a comparatively restful and stable way. When rapid, we are aware of a passage, a relation, a transition *from* it, or *between* it and something else. As we take, in fact, a general view of the wonderful stream of our consciousness, what strikes us first is this different pace of its parts. Like a bird's life, it seems to be made of an alternation of flights and perchings. The rhythm of language expresses this, where every thought is expressed in a sentence, and every sentence closed by a period. The resting-places are usually occupied by sensorial imaginations of some sort, whose peculiarity is that they can be held before the mind for an indefinite time, and contemplated without changing; the places of flight are filled with thoughts of relations, static or dynamic, that for the most part obtain between the matters contemplated in the periods of comparative rest.

Let us call the resting-places the 'substantive parts,' and the places of flight the 'transitive parts,' of the stream of thought. It then appears that the main end of our thinking is at all times the attainment of some other substantive part than the one from which we have just been dislodged. And we may say that the main use of the transitive parts is to lead us from one substantive conclusion to another.

Now it is very difficult, introspectively, to see the transitive parts for what they really are. If they are but flights to a conclusion, stopping them to look at them before the conclusion is reached is really annihilating them. Whilst if we wait till the conclusion *be* reached, it so exceeds them in vigor and stability that it quite eclipses and swallows them up in its glare. Let anyone try to cut a thought across in the middle and get a good look at its section, and he will see how difficult the introspective

172

observation of the transitive tracts is. The rush of the thought is so headlong that it almost always brings us up at the conclusion before we can arrest it. Or if our purpose is nimble enough and we do arrest it, it ceases forthwith to be itself. As a snowflake crystal caught in the warm hand is no longer a crystal but a drop, so, instead of catching the feeling of relation moving to its term, we find we have caught some substantive thing, usually the last word we were pronouncing, statically taken, and with its function, tendency, and particular meaning in the sentence quite evaporated. The attempt at introspective analysis in these cases is in fact like seizing a spinning top to catch its motion, or trying to turn up the gas quickly enough to see how the darkness looks. And the challenge to *produce* these psychoses, which is sure to be thrown by doubting psychologists at anyone who contends for their existence, is as unfair as Zeno's treatment of the advocates of motion, when, asking them to point out in what place an arrow *is* when it moves, he argues the falsity of their thesis from their inability to make to so preposterous a question an immediate reply.

The results of this introspective difficulty are baleful. If to hold fast and observe the transitive parts of thought's stream be so hard, then the great blunder to which all schools are liable must be the failure to register them, and the undue emphasizing of the more substantive parts of the stream. Were we not ourselves a moment since in danger of ignoring any feeling transitive between the silence and the thunder, and of treating their boundary as a sort of break in the mind? Now such ignoring as this has historically worked in two ways. One set of thinkers have been led by it to *Sensationalism*. Unable to lay their hands on any coarse feelings corresponding to the innumerable relations and forms of connection between the facts of the world, finding no *named* subjective modifications mirroring such relations, they have

173

for the most part denied that feelings of relation exist, and many of them, like Hume, have gone so far as to deny the reality of most relations *out* of the mind as well as in it. Substantive psychoses, sensations and their copies and derivatives, juxtaposed like dominoes in a game, but really separate, everything else verbal illusion, —such is the upshot of this view.* The *Intellectualists,* on the other hand, unable to give up the reality of relations *extra mentem,* but equally unable to point to any distinct substantive feelings in which they were known, have made the same admission that the feelings do not exist. But they have drawn an opposite conclusion. The relations must be known, they say, in something that is no feeling, no mental modification continuous and consubstantial with the subjective tissue out of which sensations and other substantive states are made. They are known, these relations, by something that lies on an entirely different plane, by an *actus purus* of Thought, Intellect, or Reason, all written with capitals and considered to mean something unutterably superior to any fact of sensibility whatever.

But from our point of view both Intellectualists and Sensationalists are wrong. If there be such things as feelings at all, *then so surely as relations between objects exist in rerum natura, so surely, and more surely, do feelings exist to which these relations are known.* There is not a conjunction or a preposition, and hardly an ad-verbial phrase, syntactic form, or inflection of voice, in human speech, that does not express some shading or other of relation which we at some moment actually feel to exist between the larger objects of our thought. If we speak objectively, it is the real relations that appear revealed; if we speak subjectively, it is the stream of

---

* E.g.: "The stream of thought is not a continuous current, but a series of distinct ideas, more or less rapid in their succession; the rapidity being measurable by the number that pass through the mind in a given time." (Bain: E. and W., p. 29.)

consciousness that matches each of them by an inward coloring of its own. In either case the relations are numberless, and no existing language is capable of doing justice to all their shades.

We ought to say a feeling of *and*, a feeling of *if,* a feeling of *but*, and a feeling of *by*, quite as readily as we say a feeling of *blue* or a feeling of *cold.* Yet we do not: so inveterate has our habit become of recognizing the existence of the substantive parts alone, that language almost refuses to lend itself to any other use. The Empiricists have always dwelt on its influence in making us suppose that where we have a separate name, a separate thing must needs be there to correspond with it; and they have rightly denied the existence of the mob of abstract entities, principles, and forces, in whose favor no other evidence than this could be brought up. But they have said nothing of that obverse error, of which we said a word in Chapter VII, . . . of supposing that where there is *no* name no entity can exist. All *dumb* or anonymous psychic states have, owing to this error, been coolly suppressed; or, if recognized at all, have been named after the substantive perception they led to, as thoughts 'about' this object or 'about' that, the stolid word *about* engulfing all their delicate idiosyncrasies in its monotonous sound. Thus the greater and greater accentuation and isolation of the substantive parts have continually gone on.

Once more take a look at the brain. We believe the brain to be an organ whose internal equilibrium is always in a state of change,—the change affecting every part. The pulses of change are doubtless more violent in one place than in another, their rhythm more rapid at this time than at that. As in a kaleidoscope revolving at a uniform rate, although the figures are always rearranging themselves, there are instants during which the transformation seems minute and interstitial and almost absent, followed by others when it shoots with magical rapidity, relatively stable forms thus alternating with forms we should not distinguish if seen again; so in the brain the perpetual rearrangement must result in some forms of tension lingering relatively long, whilst others simply come and pass. But if consciousness corresponds to the fact of rearrangement itself, why, if the rearrangement stop not, should the consciousness ever cease? And if a lingering rearrangement brings with it one kind of consciousness, why should not a swift rearrangement bring another kind of consciousness as peculiar as the rearrangement itself? The lingering consciousnesses, if of simple objects, we call 'sensations' or 'images,' according as they are vivid or faint; if of complex objects, we call them 'percepts' when vivid, 'concepts' or 'thoughts' when faint. For the swift consciousnesses we have only those names of 'transitive states,' or 'feelings of relation,' which we have used.* As the brain-changes

---

* Few writers have admitted that we cognize relations through feeling. The intellectualists have explicitly denied the possibility of such a thing—e.g., Prof. T. H. Green ('Mind,' vol. VII. p. 28): "No feeling, as such or as felt, is [of?] a relation. . . . Even a relation between feelings is not itself a feeling or felt." On the other hand, the sensationists have either smuggled in the cognition without giving any account of it, or have denied the relations to be cognized, or even to exist at all. A few honorable exceptions, however, deserve to be named among the sensationists. Destutt de Tracy, Laromiguière, Cardaillac, Brown, and finally Spencer, have explicitly contended for feelings of relation, consubstantial with our feelings or thoughts of the terms 'between' which they obtain. Thus Destutt de Tracy says (Eléments d'Idéologie, T. Ier. chap. IV): "The faculty of judgment is itself a sort of sensibility, for it is the faculty of feeling the relations among our ideas; and to feel relations is to feel." Laromiguière writes (Lecons de Philosophie, IIme Partie, 3me Lecon):
"There is no one whose intelligence does not embrace simultaneously many ideas, more or less distinct, more or less confused. Now, when we have many ideas at once, a peculiar feeling arises in us: we feel, among these ideas, resemblances, differences, relations. Let us call this mode of feeling, common to us all, the feeling of relation, or relation feeling (*sentiment-rapport*). One sees immediately that these relation-feelings, resulting from the propinquity of ideas, must be infinitely more numerous than the sensation-feelings (*sentiments-sensations*) or the feelings we have of the action of our faculties. The slightest knowledge of the mathematical theory of combinations will prove this . . . *Ideas* of relation originate in feelings of relation. They are the effect of our comparing them and reasoning about them."
Similarly, de Cardaillac (Etudes Elémentaires de Philosophie, Section I.

176

are continuous, so do all these consciousnesses melt into

chap. VII):

"By a natural consequence, we are led to suppose that at the same time that we have several sensations or several ideas in the mind, we feel the relations which exist between these sensations, and the relations which exist between these ideas. . . . If the feeling of relations exists in us, . . . it is necessarily the most varied and the most fertile of all human feelings: 1° the most varied, because, relations being more numerous than beings, the feelings of relation must be in the same proportion more numerous than the sensations whose presence gives rise to their formation; 2°, the most fertile, for the relative ideas of which the feeling-of-relation is the source . . . are more important than absolute ideas, if such exist. . . .If we interrogate common speech, we find the feeling of relation expressed there in a thousand different ways. If it is easy to seize a relation, we say that it is *sensible,* to distinguish it from one which, because its terms are too remote, cannot be as quckly perceived. A sensible difference, or resemblance. . . . What is taste in the arts, in intellectual productions? What but the feeling of those relations among the parts which constitutes their merit? . . . Did we not feel relations we should never attain to true knowledge , . . . for almost all our knowledge is of relations. . . . We never have an isolated sensation; . . . we are therefore never without the feeling of relation. . . . An *object* strikes our senses; we see in it only a sensation. . . . The relative is so near the absolute, the relation-feeling so near the sensation-feeling, the two are so intimately fused in the composition of the object, that the relation appears to us as part of the sensation itself. It is doubtless to this sort of fusion between sensations and feelings of relation that the silence of metaphysicians as to the latter is due; and it is for the same reason that they have obstinately persisted in asking from sensation alone those ideas of relation which it was powerless to give."

Dr. Thomas Brown writes (Lectures, XLV. *init.*): "There is an extensive order of our feelings which involve this notion of relation, and which consist indeed in the mere perception of a relation of some sort. . . . Whether the relation be of two or of many external objects, or of two or many affections of the mind, the feeling of this relation . . . is what I term a relative suggestion; that phrase being the simplest which it is possible to employ, for expressing, without any theory, the mere fact of the rise of certain feelings of relation, after certain other feelings which precede them; and therefore, as involving no particular theory, and simply expressive of an undoubted fact. . . . That the feelings of relation are states of the mind essentially different from our simple perceptions, or conceptions of the objects, . . . that they are not what Condillac terms *transformed sensations,* I proved in a former lecture, when I combatted the excessive simplification of that ingenious but not very accurate philosopher. There is an original tendency or susceptibility of the mind, by which, on perceiving together different objects, we are instantly, without the intervention of any other mental process, sensible of their relations in certain respects, as truly as there is an original tendency or susceptibility by which, when external objects are present and have produced a certain affection of our sensorial organ, we are instantly affected with the primary elementary feelings of perception; and, I may add, that as our sensations or perceptions are of various species, so are there various species of relations;—the number of relations, indeed, even of external things, being almost infinite, while the number of perceptions is, necessarily, limited by that of the objects which have the power of producing each other like dissolving views. Properly they are but one protracted consciousness, one unbroken stream.

Feelings of Tendency

So much for the transitive states. But there are other

some affection of our organs of sensation. . . . Without that susceptibility of the mind by which it has the feeling of relation, our consciousness would be as truly limited to a single point, as our body would become, were it possible to fetter it to a single atom."

Mr. Spencer is even more explicit. His philosophy is crude in that he seems to suppose that it is only in transitive states that outward relations are known; whereas in truth space-relations, relations of contrast, etc., are felt along with their terms, in substantive states as well as in transitive states, as we shall abundantly see. Nevertheless Mr. Spencer's passage is so clear that it also deserves to be quoted in full (Principles of Psychology, §65):

"The proximate components of Mind are of two broadly-contrasted kinds—Feelings and the relations between feelings. Among the members of each group there exist multitudinous unlikenesses, many of which are extremely strong; but such unlikenesses are small compared with those which distinguish members of the one group from members of the other. Let us, in the first place, consider what are the characters which all Feelings have in common, and what are the characters which all Relations between feelings have in common.

"Each feeling, as we here define it, is any portion of consciousness which occupies a place sufficiently large to give it a perceivable individuality; which has its individuality marked off from adjacent portions of consciousness by qualitative contrasts; and which, when introspectively contemplated, appears to be homogeneous. These are the essentials. Obviously if, under introspection, a state of consciousness is decomposable into unlike parts that exist either simultaneously or successively, it is not one feeling but two or more. Obviously if it is indistinguishable from an adjacent portion of consciousness, it forms one with that portion—is not an individual feeling, but part of one. And obviously if it does not occupy in consciousness an appreciable area, or an appreciable duration, it cannot be known as a feeling.

"A Relation between feelings is, on the contrary, characterized by occupying no appreciable part of consciousness. Take away the terms it unites, and it disappears along with them; having no independent place, no individuality of its own. It is true that, under an ultimate analysis, what we call a relation proves to be itself a kind of feeling—the momentary feeling accompanying the transition from one conspicuous feeling to an adjacent conspicuous feeling. And it is true that, notwithstanding its extreme brevity, its qualitative character is appreciable; for relations are (as we shall hereafter see) distinguishable from one another only by the unlikenesses of the feelings which accompany the momentary transitions. Each relational feeling may, in fact, be regarded as one of those nervous shocks which we suspect to be the units of composition of feelings; and, though instantaneous, it is known as of greater or less strength, and as taking place with greater or less facility. But the contrast between these relational feelings and what we ordinarily call feelings is so strong that we must class them apart. Their extreme brevity, their small variety, and their dependence on the terms they unite, differentiate them in an unmistakable way.

178

unnamed states or qualities of states that are just as important and just as cognitive as they, and just as much unrecognized by the traditional sensationalist and intellectualist philosophies of mind. The first fails to find them at all, the second finds their *cognitive function,* but denies that anything in the way of *feeling* has a share in bringing it about. Examples will make clear what these inarticulate psychoses, due to waxing and waning excitements of the brain, are like.*

Suppose three successive persons say to us: 'Wait!' 'Hark!' 'Look!' Our consciousness is thrown into three quite different attitudes of expectancy, although no defi-

---

"Perhaps it will be well to recognize more fully the truth that this distinction cannot be absolute. Besides admitting that, as an element of consciousness, a relation is a momentary feeling, we must also admit that just as a relation can have no existence apart from the feelings which form its terms, so a feeling can exist only by relations to other feelings which limit it in space or time or both. Strictly speaking, neither a feeling nor a relation is an independent element of consciousness; there is throughout a dependence such that the appreciable areas of consciousness occupied by feelings can no more possess individualities apart from the relations which link them, than these relations can possess individualities apart from the feelings they link. The essential distinction between the two, then, appears to be that whereas a relational feeling is a portion of consciousness inseparable into parts, a feeling, ordinarily so called, is a portion of consciousness that admits imaginary division into like parts which are related to one another in sequence or coexistence. A feeling proper is either made up of like parts that occupy time, or it is made up of like parts that occupy space, or both. In any case, a feeling proper is an aggregate of related like parts, while a relational feeling is undecomposable. And this is exactly the contrast between the two which must result if, as we have inferred, feelings are composed of units of feelings, or shocks."

* M. Paulhan (Revue Philosophique, xx. 455-6), after speaking of the faint mental images of objects and emotions, says: "We find other vaguer states still, upon which attention seldom rests, except in persons who by nature or profession are addicted to internal observation. It is even difficult to name them precisely, for they are little known and not classed; but we may cite as an example of them that peculiar impression which we feel when, strongly preoccupied by a certain subject, we nevertheless are engaged with, and have our attention almost completely absorbed by, matters quite disconnected therewithal. We do not then exactly think of the object of our preoccupation; we do not represent it in a clear manner; and yet our mind is not as it would be without this preoccupation. Its object, absent from consciousness, is nevertheless represented there by a peculiar unmistakable impression, which often persists long and is a strong feeling, although so obscure for our intelligence." "A mental sign of the kind is the unfavorable disposition left in our mind towards an individual by painful incidents erewhile experienced and now perhaps forgotten. The sign remains, but is not understood; its definite meaning is lost." (P. 458.)

nite object is before it in any one of the three cases. Leaving out different actual bodily attitudes, and leaving out the reverberating images of the three words, which are of course diverse, probably no one will deny the existence of a residual conscious affection, a sense of the direction from which an impression is about to come, although no positive impression is yet there. Meanwhile we have no names for the psychoses in question but the names hark, look, and wait.

Suppose we try to recall a forgotten name. The state of our consciousness is peculiar. There is a gap therein; but no mere gap. It is a gap that is intensely active. A sort of wraith of the name is in it, beckoning us in a given direction, making us at moments tingle with the sense of our closeness, and then letting us sink back without the longed-for term. If wrong names are proposed to us, this singularly definite gap acts immediately so as to negate them. They do not fit into its mould. And the gap of one word does not feel like the gap of another, all empty of content as both might seem necessarily to be when described as gaps. When I vainly try to recall the name of Spalding, my consciousness is far removed from what it is when I vainly try to recall the name of Bowles. Here some ingenious persons will say: "How *can* the two consciousnesses be different when the terms which might make them different are not there? All that is there, so long as the effort to recall is vain, is the bare effort itself. How should that differ in the two cases? You are making it seem to differ by prematurely filling it out with the different names, although these, by the hypothesis, have not yet come. Stick to the two efforts as they are, without naming them after facts not yet existent, and you'll be quite unable to designate any point in which they differ." Designate, truly enough. We can only designate the difference by borrowing the names of objects not yet in the mind. Which is to say that our psychological vocabulary is wholly inadequate to name the differences that exist, even such strong differences as these. But namelessness is compatible with existence. There are innumerable consciousnesses of emptiness, no one of which taken in itself has a name, but all different from each other. The ordinary way is to assume that they are all emptiness of consciousness, and so the same state. But the feeling of an absence is *toto coelo* other than the absence of a feeling. It is an intense feeling. The rhythm of a lost word may be there without a sound to clothe it; or the evanescent sense of something which is the initial vowel or consonant may mock us fitfully, without growing more distinct. Every one must know the tantalizing effect of the blank rhythm of some forgotten verse, restlessly dancing in one's mind, striving to be filled out with words.

Again, what is the strange difference between an experience tasted for the first time and the same experience recognized as familiar, as having been enjoyed before, though we cannot name it or say where or when? A tune, an odor, a flavor sometimes carry this inarticulate feeling of their familiarity so deep into our consciousness that we are fairly shaken by its mysterious emotional power. But strong and characteristic as this psychosis is —it probably is due to the submaximal excitement of wide-spreading associational brain-tracts—the only name we have for all its shadings is 'sense of familiarity.'

When we read such phrases as 'naught but,' 'either one or the other,' '*a* is *b*, but,' 'although it is, nevertheless,' 'it is an excluded middle, there is no *tertium quid*,' and a host of other verbal skeletons of logical relation, is it true that there is nothing more in our minds than the words themselves as they pass? What then is the meaning of the words which we think we understand as we read? What makes that meaning different in one phrase from what it is in the other? 'Who?' 'When?' 'Where?' Is the difference of felt meaning in these interrogatives nothing more than their difference of sound? And is it not (just like the difference of sound itself) known and understood in an affection of consciousness correlative to it, though so impalpable to direct examination? Is not the same true of such negatives as 'no,' 'never,' 'not yet'?

The truth is that large tracts of human speech are nothing but *signs of direction* in thought, of which direction we nevertheless have an acutely discriminative sense, though no definite sensorial image plays any part in it whatsoever. Sensorial images are stable psychic facts; we can hold them still and look at them as long as we like. These bare images of logical movement, on the contrary, are psychic transitions, always on the wing, so to speak, and not to be glimpsed except in flight. Their function is to lead from one set of images to another. As they pass, we feel both the waxing and the waning images in a way altogether peculiar and a way quite different from the way of their full presence. If we try to hold fast the feeling of direction, the full presence comes and the feeling of direction is lost. The blank verbal scheme of the logical movement gives us the fleeting sense of the movement as we read it, quite as well as does a rational sentence awakening definite imaginations by its words.

What is that first instantaneous glimpse of some one's meaning which we have, when in vulgar phrase we say we 'twig' it? Surely an altogether specific affection of our mind. And has the reader never asked himself what kind of a mental fact is his *intention of saying a thing* before he has said it? It is an entirely definite intention, distinct from all other intentions, an absolutely distinct state of consciousness, therefore; and yet how much of it consists of definite sensorial images; either of words or of things? Hardly anything! Linger, and the words and things come into the mind; the anticipatory intention, the divination is there no more. But as the words that replace it arrive, it welcomes them successively and calls them

182

right if they agree with it, it rejects them and calls them wrong if they do not. It has therefore a nature of its own of the most positive sort, and yet what can we say about it without using words that belong to the later mental facts that replace it? The intention *to-say-so-and-so* is the only name it can receive. One may admit that a good third of our psychic life consists in these rapid premonitory perspective views of schemes of thought not yet articulate. How comes it about that a man reading something aloud for the first time is able immediately to emphasize all his words aright, unless from the very first he have a sense of at least the form of the sentence yet to come, which sense is fused with his consciousness of the present word, and modifies its emphasis in his mind so as to make him give it the proper accent as he utters it? Emphasis of this kind is almost altogether a matter of grammatical construction. If we read 'no more' we expect presently to come upon a 'than'; if we read 'however' at the outset of a sentence it is a 'yet,' a 'still,' or a 'nevertheless,' that we expect. A noun in a certain position demands a verb in a certain mood and number, in another position it expects a relative pronoun. Adjectives call for nouns, verbs for adverbs, etc., etc. And this foreboding of the coming grammatical scheme combined with each successive uttered word is so practically accurate that a reader incapable of understanding four ideas of the book he is reading aloud, can nevertheless read it with the most delicately modulated expression of intelligence.

Some will interpret these facts by calling them all cases in which certain images, by laws of association, awaken others so very rapidly that we think afterwards we felt the very *tendencies* of the nascent images to arise, before they were actually there. For this school the only possible materials of consciousness are images of a perfectly definite nature. Tendencies exist, but they are facts for the outside psychologist rather than for the subject of the observation. The tendency is thus a *psychical* zero; only its *results* are felt.

Now what I contend for, and accumulate examples to show, is that 'tendencies' are not only descriptions from without, but that they are among the *objects* of the stream, which is thus aware of them from within, and must be described as in very large measure constituted of *feelings* of *tendency,* often so vague that we are unable to name them at all. It is, in short, the re-instatement of the vague to its proper place in our mental life which I am so anxious to press on the attention. Mr. Galton and Prof. Huxley have, as we shall see in Chapter XVIII, made one step in advance in exploding the ridiculous theory of Hume and Berkeley that we can have no images but of perfectly definite things. Another is made in the overthrow of the equally ridiculous notion that, whilst simple objective qualities are revealed to our knowledge in subjective feelings, relations are not. But these reforms are not half sweeping and radical enough. What must be admitted is that the definite images of traditional psychology form but the very smallest part of our minds as they actually live. The traditional psychology talks like one who should say a river consists of nothing but pailsful, spoonsful, quartpotsful, barrelsful, and other moulded forms of water. Even were the pails and the pots all actually standing in the stream, still between them the free water would continue to flow. It is just this free water of consciousness that psychologists resolutely overlook. Every definite image in the mind is steeped and dyed in the free water that flows round it. With it goes the sense of its relations, near and remote, the dying echo of whence it came to us, the dawning sense of whither it is to lead. The significance, the value, of the image is all in this halo or penumbra that surrounds and escorts it, —or rather that is fused into one with it and has become bone of its bone and flesh of its flesh; leaving it, it is

184

true, an image of the same *thing* it was before, but making it an image of that thing newly taken and freshly understood.

What is that shadowy scheme of the 'form' of an opera, play, or book, which remains in our mind and on which we pass judgment when the actual thing is done? What is our notion of a scientific or philosophical system? Great thinkers have vast premonitory glimpses of schemes of relation between terms, which hardly even as verbal images enter the mind, so rapid is the whole process.* We all of us have this permanent consciousness of whither our thought is going. It is a feeling like any other, a feeling of what thoughts are next to arise, before they have arisen. This field of view of consciousness varies very much in extent, depending largely on the degree of mental freshness or fatigue. When very fresh, our minds carry an immense horizon with them. The present image shoots its perspective far before it, irradiating in advance the regions in which lie the thoughts as yet unborn. Under ordinary conditions the halo of felt relations is much more circumscribed. And in states of extreme brain-fag the horizon is narrowed almost to the passing word,—the associative machinery, however, providing for the next word turning up in orderly sequence, until at last the tired thinker is led to some kind of a conclusion. At certain moments he may find himself doubting whether his thoughts have not come to a full stop; but the vague sense of a *plus ultra* makes him ever struggle on towards a more definite expression of

---

* Mozart describes thus his manner of composing: First bits and crumbs of the piece come and gradually join together in his mind; then the soul getting warmed to the work, the thing grows more and more, "and I spread it out broader and clearer, and at last it gets almost finished in my head, even when it is a long piece, so that I can see the whole of it at a single glance in my mind, as if it were a beautiful painting or a handsome human being; in which way I do not hear it in my imagination at all as a succession—the way it must come later—but all at once, as it were. It is a rare feast! All the inventing and making goes on in me as in a beautiful strong dream. But the best of all is the *hearing of it all at once*."

185

what it may be; whilst the slowness of his utterance shows how difficult, under such conditions, the labor of thinking must be.

The awareness that our *definite* thought has come to a stop is an entirely different thing from the awareness that our thought is definitively completed. The expression of the latter state of mind is the falling inflection which betokens that the sentence is ended, and silence. The expression of the former state is 'hemming and hawing,' or else such phrases as '*et cetera,*' or 'and so forth.' But notice that every part of the sentence to be left incomplete feels differently as it passes, by reason of the premonition we have that we shall be unable to end it. The 'and so forth' casts its shadow back, and is as integral a part of the object of the thought as the distinctest of images would be.

Again, when we use a common noun, such as *man,* in a universal sense, as signifying all possible men, we are fully aware of this intention on our part, and distinguish it carefully from our intention when we mean a certain group of men, or a solitary individual before us. In the chapter on Conception we shall see how important this difference of intention is. It casts its influence over the whole of the sentence, both before and after the spot in which the word *man* is used.

Nothing is easier than to symbolize all these facts in terms of brain-action. Just as the echo of the *whence,* the sense of the starting point of our thought, is probably due to the dying excitement of processes but a moment since vividly aroused; so the sense of the whither, the foretaste of the terminus, must be due to the waxing excitement of tracts or processes which, a moment hence, will be the cerebral correlatives of some thing which a moment hence will be vividly present to the thought. Represented by a curve, the neurosis underlying consciousness must at any moment be like this:

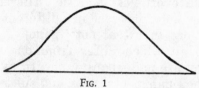

Fig. 1

Each point of the horizontal line stands for some brain-tract or process. The height of the curve above the line stands for the intensity of the process. All the processes are *present,* in the intensities shown by the curve. But those before the latter's apex *were* more intense a moment ago; those after it *will be* more intense a moment hence. If I recite *a, b, c, d, e, f, g,* at the moment of uttering *d,* neither *a, b, c,* nor *e, f, g,* are out of my consciousness altogether, but both, after their respective fashions, 'mix their dim lights' with the stronger one of the *d,* because their neuroses are both awake in some degree.

There is a common class of mistakes which shows how brain-processes begin to be excited before the thoughts attached to them are *due*—due, that is, in substantive and vivid form. I mean those mistakes of speech or writing by which, in Dr. Carpenter's words, "we mispronounce or misspell a word, by introducing into it a letter or syllable of some other, whose turn is shortly to come; or, it may be, the whole of the anticipated word is substituted for the one which ought to have been expressed."* In these cases one of two things must have happened: either some local accident of nutrition *blocks* the process that is *due,* so that other processes discharge that ought as yet to be but nascently aroused; or some opposite local accident furthers the *latter processes* and makes them explode before their time. In the chapter on Association of Ideas, numerous instances will come before us of the actual effect on consciousness of neuroses not yet maximally aroused.

---

* Mental Physiology, §236. Dr. Carpenter's explanation differs materially from that given in the text.

It is like the 'overtones' in music. Different instruments give the 'same note,' but each in a different voice, because each gives more than that note, namely, various upper harmonics of it which differ from one instrument to another. They are not separately heard by the ear; they blend with the fundamental note, and suffuse it, and alter it; and even so do the waxing and waning brain-processes at every moment blend with and suffuse and alter the psychic effect of the processes which are at their culminating point.

Let us use the words *psychic overtone, suffusion,* or *fringe,* to designate the influence of a faint brain-process upon our thought, as it makes it aware of relations and objects but dimly perceived.*

If we then consider the *cognitive function* of different states of mind, we may feel assured that the difference between those that are mere 'acquaintance,' and those that are 'knowledges-*about'* . . . is reducible almost entirely to the absence or presence of psychic fringes or overtones. Knowledge *about* a thing is knowledge of its relations. Acquaintance with it is limitation to the bare impression which it makes. Of most of its relations we are only aware in the penumbral nascent way of a 'fringe' of unarticulated affinities about it. And, before passing to the next topic in order, I must say a little of this sense

---

* Cf. also S. Stricker: Vorlesungen uber allg. u. exp. Pathologie (1879), pp. 462-3, 501, 547; Romanes: Origin of Human Faculty, p. 82. It is so hard to make one's self clear that I may advert to a misunderstanding of my views by the late Prof. Thos. Maguire of Dublin (Lectures on Philosophy, 1885). This author considers that by the 'fringe' I mean some sort of psychic material by which sensations in themselves separate are made to cohere together, and wittily says that I ought to "see that uniting sensations by their 'fringes' is more vague than to construct the universe out of oysters by platting their beards" (p. 211). But the fringe, as I use the word, means nothing like this; it is part of the *object cognized,*—substantive *qualities* and *things* appearing to the mind in a *fringe of relations.* Some parts—the transitive parts—of our stream of thought cognize the relations rather than the things; but both the transitive and the substantive parts form one continuous stream, with no discrete 'sensations' in it such as Prof. Maguire supposes, and supposes me to suppose, to be there.

of affinity, as itself one of the most interesting features of the subjective stream.

In all our voluntary thinking there is some topic or subject about which all the members of the thought revolve. Half the time this topic is a problem, a gap we cannot yet fill with a definite picture, word, or phrase, but which, in the manner described some time back, influences us in an intensely active and determinate psychic way. Whatever may be the images and phrases that pass before us, we feel their relation to this aching gap. To fill it up is our thought's destiny. Some bring us nearer to that consummation. Some the gap negates as quite irrelevant. Each swims in a felt fringe of relations of which the aforesaid gap is the term. Or instead of a definite gap we may merely carry a mood of interest about with us. Then, however vague the mood, it will still act in the same way, throwing a mantle of felt affinity over such representations, entering the mind, as suit it, and tingeing with the feeling of tediousness or discord all those with which it has no concern.

Relation, then, to our topic or interest is constantly felt in the fringe, and particularly the relation of harmony and discord of furtherance is there, we are 'all right;' with the sense of hindrance we are dissatisfied and perplexed, and cast about us for other thoughts. Now *any* thought the quality of whose fringe lets us feel ourselves 'all right,' is an acceptable member of our thinking, whatever kind of thought it may otherwise be. Provided we only feel it to have a place in the scheme of relations in which the interesting topic also lies, that is quite sufficient to make of it a relevant and appropriate portion of our train of ideas.

For the important thing about a train of thought is its conclusion. That is the *meaning,* or, as we say, the topic of the thought. That is what abides when all its other members have faded from memory. Usually this conclusion is a word or phrase or particular image, or practical attitude or resolve, whether rising to answer a problem or fill a pre-existing gap that worried us, or whether accidentally stumbled on in revery. In either case it stands out from the other segments of the stream by reason of the peculiar interest attaching to it. This interest *arrests* it, makes a sort of crisis of it when it comes, induces attention upon it and makes us treat it in a substantive way.

The parts of the stream that precede these substantive conclusions are but the means of the latter's attainment. And, provided the same conclusion be reached, the means may be as mutable as we like, for the 'meaning' of the stream of thought will be the same. What difference does it make what the means are? *"Qu'importe le flacon, pourvu qu'on ait l'ivresse?"* The relative unimportance of the means appears from the fact that when the conclusion is there, we have always forgotten most of the steps preceding its attainment. When we have uttered a proposition, we are rarely able a moment afterwards to recall our exact words, though we can express it in different words easily enough. The practical upshot of a book we read remains with us, though we may not recall one of its sentences.

The only paradox would seem to lie in supposing that the fringe of felt affinity and discord can be the same in two heterogeneous sets of images. Take a train of words passing through the mind and leading to a certain conclusion on the one hand, and on the other hand an almost wordless set of tactile, visual and other fancies leading to the same conclusion. Can the halo, fringe, or scheme in which we feel the words to lie be the same as that in which we feel the images to lie? Does not the discrepancy of terms involve a discrepancy of felt relations among them?

If the terms be taken *qua* mere sensations, it assuredly does. For instance, the words may rhyme with each

190

other,—the visual images can have no such affinity as *that*. But *qua* thoughts, *qua* sensations *understood,* the words have contracted by long association fringes of mutual repugnance or affinity with each other and with the conclusion, which run exactly parallel with like fringes in the visual, tactile and other ideas. The most important element of these fringes is, I repeat, the mere feeling of harmony or discord, of a right or wrong direction in the thought. Dr. Campbell has, so far as I know, made the best analysis of this fact, and his words, often quoted, deserve to be quoted again. The chapter is entitled "What is the cause that nonsense so often escapes being detected, both by the writer and by the reader?" The author, in answering this question, makes (*inter alia*) the following remarks:[*]

"That connection [he says] or relation which comes gradually to subsist among the different words of a language, in the minds of those who speak it, . . . is merely consequent on this, that those words are employed as signs of connected or related things. It is an axiom in geometry that things equal to the same thing are equal to one another. It may, in like manner, be admitted as an axiom in psychology that ideas associated by the same idea will associate with one another. Hence it will happen that if, from experiencing the connection of two things, there results, as infallibly there will result, an association between the ideas or notions annexed to them, as each idea will moreover be associated by its sign, there will likewise be an association between the ideas of the signs. Hence the sounds considered as signs will be conceived to have a connection analogous to that which subsisteth among the things signified; I say, the sounds considered as signs; for this way of considering them constantly attends us in speaking, writing, hearing, and reading. When we purposely abstract from it, and regard them merely as sounds, we are instantly sensible that they are quite unconnected, and have no other relation than what ariseth from similitude of tone or accent. But to consider them in this manner commonly results from previous design, and requires a kind of effort which is not exerted in the ordinary use of speech. In ordinary use they are regarded solely as signs, or, rather, they are confounded

---

[*] George Campbell: Philosophy of Rhetoric, book II. chap. VII.

with the things they signify; the consequence of which is that, in the manner just now explained, we come insensibly to conceive a connection among them of a very different sort from that of which sounds are naturally susceptible.

"Now this conception, habit, or tendency of the mind, call it which you please, is considerably strengthened by the frequent use of language and by the structure of it. Language is the sole channel through which we communicate our knowledge and discoveries to others, and through which the knowledge and discoveries of others are communicated to us. By reiterated recourse to this medium, it necessarily happens that when things are related to each other, the words signifying those things are more commonly brought together in discourse. Hence the words and names by themselves, by customary vicinity, contract in the fancy a relation additional to that which they derive purely from being the symbols of related things. Farther, this tendency is strengthened by the structure of language. All languages whatever, even the most barbarous, as far as hath yet appeared, are of a regular and analogical make. The consequence is that similar relations in things will be expressed similarly; that is, by similar inflections, derivations, compositions, arrangement of words, or juxtaposition of particles, according to the genius or grammatical form of the particular tongue. Now as, by the habitual use of an language (even though it were quite irregular), the signs would insensibly become connected in the imagination wherever the things signified are connected in nature, so by the regular structure of a language, this connection among the signs is conceived as analogous to that which subsisteth among their archetypes."

If we know English and French and begin a sentence in French, all the later words that come are French; we hardly ever drop into English. And this affinity of the French words for each other is not something merely operating mechanically as a brain-law, it is something we feel at the time. Our understanding of a French sentence heard never falls to so low an ebb that we are not aware that the words linguistically belong together. Our attention can hardly so wander that if an English word be suddenly introduced we shall not start at the change. Such a vague sense as this of the words belonging together is the very minimum of fringe that can accompany them,

192

if 'thought' at all. Usually the vague perception that all the words we hear belong to the same language and to the same special vocabulary in that language, and that the grammatical sequence is familiar, is practically equivalent to an admission that what we hear is sense. But if an unusual foreign word be introduced, if the grammar trip, or if a term from an incongruous vocabulary suddenly appear, such as 'rat-trap' or 'plumber's bill' in a philosophical discourse, the sentence detonates, as it were, we receive a shock from the incongruity, and the drowsy assent is gone. The feeling of rationality in these cases seems rather a negative than a positive thing, being the mere absence of shock, or sense of discord, between the terms of thought.

So delicate and incessant is this recognition by the mind of the mere fitness of words to be mentioned together that the slightest misreading, such as 'casualty' for 'causality,' or 'perpetual' for 'perceptual,' will be corrected by a listener whose attention is so relaxed that he gets no idea of the *meaning* of the sentence at all.

Conversely, if words do belong to the same vocabulary, and if the grammatical structure is correct, sentences with absolutely no meaning may be uttered in good faith and pass unchallenged. Discourses at prayer-meetings, re-shuffling the same collection of cant phrases, and the whole genus of penny-a-line-isms and newspaper-reporter's flourishes give illustrations of this. ''The birds filled the tree-tops with their morning song, making the air moist, cool, and pleasant,'' is a sentence I remember reading once in a report of some athletic exercises in Jerome Park. It was probably written unconsciously by the hurried reporter, and read uncritically by many readers. An entire volume of 784 pages lately published in Boston* is composed of stuff like this passage picked out at random.

---

* Substantialism or Philosophy of Knowledge, by 'Jean Story' (1879).

"The flow of the efferent fluids of all these vessels from their outlets at the terminal loop of each culminate link on the surface of the nuclear organism is continuous as their respective atmospheric fruitage up to the altitudinal limit of their expansibility, whence, when atmosphered by like but coalescing essences from higher altitudes,—those sensibly expressed as the essential qualities of external forms,—they descend, and become assimilated by the afferents of the nuclear organism."*

There are every year works published whose contents show them to be by real lunatics. To the reader, the book quoted from seems pure nonsense from beginning to end. It is impossible to divine, in such a case, just what sort of feeling of rational relation between the words may have appeared to the author's mind. The border line between objective sense and nonsense is hard to draw; that between subjective sense and nonsense, impossible. Subjectively, any collocation of words may make sense—even the wildest words in a dream—if one only does not doubt their belonging together. Take the obscurer passages in Hegel: it is a fair question whether the rationality included in them be anything more than the fact that the words all belong to a common vocabulary, and are strung together on a scheme of predication and relation,—immediacy, self-relation, and what not,—which has habitually recurred. Yet there seems no reason to doubt that the subjective feeling of the rationality of these sentences was strong in the writer as he penned them, or even that some readers by straining may have reproduced it in themselves.

---

* M. G. Tarde, quoting (in Delbœuf, Le Sommeil et les Reves (1885), p. 226) some nonsense-verses from a dream, says they show how prosodic forms may subsist in a mind from which logical rules are effaced. . . . "I was able, in dreaming, to preserve the faculty of finding two words which rhymed, to appreciate the rhyme, to fill up the verse as it first presented itself with other words which, added, gave the right number of syllables, and yet I was ignorant of the sense of the words. . . . Thus we have the extraordinary fact that the words called each other up, without calling up their sense. . . . Even when awake, it is more difficult to ascend to the meaning of a word than to pass from one word to another; or to put it otherwise, *it is harder to be a thinker than to be a rhetorician,* and on the whole nothing is commoner than trains of words not understood."

To sum up, certain kinds of verbal associate, certain grammatical expectations fulfilled, stand for a good part of our impression that a sentence has a meaning and is dominated by the Unity of one Thought. Nonsense in grammatical form sounds half rational; sense with grammatical sequence upset sounds nonsensical; e.g., "Elba the Napoleon English faith had banished broken to he Saint because Helena at." Finally, there is about each word the psychic 'overtone' of feeling that it brings us nearer to a forefelt conclusion. Suffuse all the words of a sentence, as they pass, with these three fringes or haloes of relation, let the conclusion seem worth arriving at, and all will admit the sentence to be an expression of thoroughly continuous, unified, and rational thought.*

Each word, in such a sentence, is felt, not only as a word, but as having a *meaning*. The 'meaning' of a word taken thus dynamically in a sentence may be quite different from its meaning when taken statically or without context. The dynamic meaning is usually reduced to the bare fringe we have described, of felt suitability or unfitness to the context and conclusion. The static meaning, when the word is concrete, as 'table,' 'Boston,' consists of sensory images awakened; when it is abstract, as 'criminal legislation,' 'fallacy,' the meaning consists of other words aroused, forming the so-called 'definition.'

Hegel's celebrated dictum that pure being is identical with pure nothing results from his taking the words statically, or without the fringe they wear in a context. Taken

---

* We think it odd that young children should listen with such rapt attention to the reading of stories expressed in words half of which they do not understand, and of none of which they ask the meaning. But their thinking is in form just what ours is when it is rapid. Both of us make flying leaps over large portions of the sentences uttered and we give attention only to substantive starting points, turning points, and conclusions here and there. All the rest, 'substantive' and separately intelligible as it may *potentially* be, actually serves only as so much transitive material. It is *internodal* consciousness, giving us the sense of continuity, but having no significance apart from its mere gap-filling function. The children probably feel no gap when through a lot of unintelligible words they are swiftly carried to a familiar and intelligible terminus.

195

in isolation, they agree in the single point of awakening no sensorial images. But taken dynamically, or as significant, — as *thought*, — their fringes of relation, their affinities and repugnances, their function and meaning, are felt and understood to be absolutely opposed.

Such considerations as these remove all appearance of paradox from those cases of extremely deficient visual imagery of whose existence Mr. Galton has made us aware (see below). An exceptionally intelligent friend informs me that he can frame no image whatever of the appearance of his breakfast-table. When asked how he then remembers it at all, he says he simply '*knows*' that it seated four people, and was covered with a white cloth on which were a butter-dish, a coffee-pot, radishes, and so forth. The mind-stuff of which this 'knowing' is made seems to be verbal images exclusively. But if the words 'coffee,' 'bacon,' 'muffins,' and 'eggs' lead a man to speak to his cook, to pay his bills, and to take measures for the morrow's meal exactly as visual and gustatory memories would, why are they not, for all practical intents and purposes, as good a kind of material in which to think? In fact, we may suspect them to be for most purposes better than terms with a richer imaginative coloring. The scheme of relationship and the conclusion being the essential things in thinking, that kind of mind-stuff which is handiest will be the best for the purpose. Now words, uttered, or unexpressed, are the handiest mental elements we have. Not only are they very *rapidly* revivable, but they are revivable as actual sensations more easily than any other items of our experience. Did they not possess some such advantage as this, it would hardly be the case that the older men are the more effective as thinkers, the more, as a rule, they have lost their visualizing power and depend on words. This was ascertained by Mr. Galton to be the case with members of the Royal Society. The present writer observes it in his own person most distinctly.

On the other hand, a deaf and dumb man can weave his tactile and visual images into a system of thought quite as effective and rational as that of a word-user. *The question whether thought is possible without language* has been a favorite topic of discussion among philosophers. Some interesting reminiscences of his childhood by Mr. Ballard, a deaf-mute instructor in the National College at Washington, show it to be perfectly possible. A few paragraphs may be quoted here.

"In consequence of the loss of my hearing in infancy, I was debarred from enjoying the advantages which children in the full possession of their senses derive from the exercises of the common primary school, from the every-day talk of their school-fellows and playmates, and from the conversation of their parents and other grown-up persons.

"I could convey my thoughts and feelings to my parents and brothers by natural signs or pantomime, and I could understand what they said to me by the same medium; our intercourse being, however, confined to the daily routine of home affairs and hardly going beyond the circle of my own observation. . . .

"My father adopted a course which he thought would, in some measure compensate me for the loss of my hearing. It was that of taking me with him when business required him to ride abroad; and he took me more frequently than he did my brothers; giving, as the reason for his apparent partiality, that they could acquire information through the ear, while I depended solely upon my eye for acquaintance with affairs of the outside world. . . .

"I have a vivid recollection of the delight I felt in watching the different scenes we passed through, observing the various phases of nature, both animate and inanimate; though we did not, owing to my infirmity, engage in conversation. It was during those delightful rides, some two or three years before my initiation into the rudiments of written language, that I began to ask myself the question: *How came the world into being?* When this question occurred to my mind, I set myself to thinking it over a long time. My curiosity was awakened as to what was the origin of human life in its first appearance upon the earth, and of vegetable life as well, and also the cause of the existence of the earth, sun, moon, and stars.

"I remember at one time when my eye fell upon a very large old stump which we happened to pass in one of our rides, I asked myself, 'Is it possible that the first man that ever came into the world rose out of that stump? But that stump is only a remnant of a once noble magnificent tree, and how came that tree? Why, it came only by beginning to grow out of the ground just like those little trees now coming up.' And I dismissed from my mind, as an absurd idea, the connection between the origin of man and a decaying old stump. . . .

"I have no recollection of what it was that first suggested to me the question as to the origin of things. I had before this time gained ideas of the descent from parent to child, of the propagation of animals, and of the production of plants from seeds. The question that occurred to my mind was: whence came the first man, the first animal, and the first plant, at the remotest distance of time, before which there was no man, no animal, no plant; since I knew they all had a beginning and an end.

"It is impossible to state the exact order in which these different questions arose, i.e., about men, animals, plants, the earth, sun, moon, etc. The lower animals did not receive so much thought as was bestowed upon man and the earth; perhaps because I put man and beast in the same class, since I believed that man would be annihilated and there was no resurrection beyond the grave,— though I am told by my mother that, in answer to my question, in the case of a deceased uncle who looked to me like a person in sleep, she had tried to make me understand that he would awake in the far future. It was my belief that man and beast derived their being from the same source, and were to be laid down in the dust in a state of annihilation. Considering the brute animal as of secondary importance, and allied to man on a lower level, man and the earth were the two things on which my mind dwelled most.

"I think I was five years old, when I began to understand the descent from parent to child and the propagation of animals. I was nearly eleven years old, when I entered the Institution where I was educated; and I remember distinctly that it was at least two years before this time that I began to ask myself the question as to the origin of the universe. My age was then about eight, not over nine years.

"Of the form of the earth, I had no idea in my childhood, except that, from a look at a map of the hemispheres, I inferred there were two immense disks of matter lying near each other. I also believed the sun and moon to be round, flat plates of illuminating matter; and for those luminaries I entertained a sort of reverence on account of their power of lighting and heating the earth. I

198

thought from their coming up and going down, travelling across the sky in so regular a manner that there must be a certain something having power to govern their course. I believed the sun went into a hole at the west and came out of another at the east, travelling through a great tube in the earth, describing the same curve as it seemed to describe in the sky. The stars seemed to me to be tiny lights studded in the sky.

"The source from which the universe came was the question about which my mind revolved in a vain struggle to grasp it, or rather to fight the way up to attain a satisfactory answer. When I had occupied myself with this subject a considerable time, I perceived that it was a matter much greater than my mind could comprehend; and I remember well that I became so appalled at its mystery and so bewildered at my inability to grapple with it that I laid the subject aside and out of my mind, glad to escape being, as it were, drawn into a vortex of inextricable confusion. Though I felt relieved at this escape, yet I could not resist the desire to know the truth; and I returned to the subject; but as before, I left it, after thinking it over for some time. In this state of perplexity, I hoped all the time to get at the truth, still believing that the more I gave thought to the subject, the more my mind would penetrate the mystery. Thus I was tossed like a shuttlecock, returning to the subject and recoiling from it, till I came to school.

"I remember that my mother once told me about a being up above, pointing her finger toward the sky and with a solemn look on her countenance. I do not recall the circumstance which led to this communication. When she mentioned the mysterious being up in the sky, I was eager to take hold of the subject, and plied her with questions concerning the form and appearance of this unknown being, asking if it was the sun, moon, or one of the stars. I knew she meant that there was a living one somewhere up in the sky; but when I realized that she could not answer my questions, I gave up in despair, feeling sorrowful that I could not obtain a definite idea of the mysterious one living up in the sky.

"One day, while we were haying in a field, there was a series of heavy thunder-claps. I asked one of my brothers where they came from. He pointed to the sky and made a zig-zag motion with his finger, signifying lightning. I imagined there was a great man somewhere in the blue vault, who made a loud noise with his voice out of it; and each time I heard* a thunder-clap I was frightened,

---

* Not literally *heard*, of course. Deaf mutes are quick to perceive shocks and jars that can be felt, even when so slight as to be unnoticed by those who can hear.

199

and looked up at the sky, fearing he was speaking a threatening word."*

Here we may pause. The reader sees by this time that it makes little or no difference in what sort of mind-stuff, in what quality of imagery, his thinking goes on. The only images *intrinsically* important are the halting places, the substantive conclusions, provisional or final, of the thought. Throughout all the rest of the stream, the feelings of relation are everything, and the terms related almost naught. These feelings of relation, these psychic overtones, halos, suffusions, or fringes about the terms, may be the same in very different systems of imagery. A diagram may help to accentuate this indifference of the mental means where the end is the same. Let *A* be some experience from which a number of thinkers start. Let Z be the practical conclusion rationally inferrible from it. One gets to the conclusion by one line, another by another; one follows a course of English, another of German, verbal imagery. With one, visual images predominate; with another, tactile. Some trains are tinged with emotions, other not; some are very abridged, synthetic and rapid, others, hesitating and broken into many steps. But when the penultimate terms of all the trains, however differing *inter se*, finally shoot into the same conclusion, we say and rightly say, that all the thinkers have had sub-

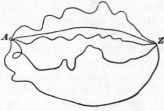

Fig. 2

---

* Quoted by Samuel Porter: 'Is Thought possible without Language?' in Princeton Review, 57th year, pp. 108-12 (Jan. 1881 ?). Cf. also W. W. Ireland: The Blot upon the Brain (1886), Paper X, part II; G. J. Romanes: Mental Evolution in Man, pp. 81-83, and references therein made. Prof. Max Muller gives a very complete history of this controversy in pp. 30-64 of his 'Science of Thought' (1887). His own view is that Thought and Speech are inseparable; but under speech he includes any conceivable sort of symbolism or even mental imagery, and he makes no allowance for the wordless summary glimpses which we have of systems of relation and direction.

stantially the same thought. It would probably astound each of them beyond measure to be let into his neighbor's mind and to find how different the scenery there was from that in his own.

Thought is in fact a kind of Algebra, as Berkeley long ago said, "in which, though a particular quantity be marked by each letter, yet to proceed right, it is not requisite that in every step each letter suggest to your thoughts that particular quantity it was appointed to stand for." Mr. Lewes has developed this algebra-analogy so well that I must quote his words:

"The leading characteristic of algebra is that of operation on relations. This also is the leading characteristic of Thought. Algebra cannot exist without values, nor Thought without Feelings. The operations are so many blank forms till the values are assigned. Words are vacant sounds, ideas are blank forms, unless they symbolize images and sensations which are their values. Nevertheless it is rigorously true, and of the greatest importance, that analysts carry on very extensive operations with blank forms, never pausing to supply the symbols with values until the calculation is completed; and ordinary men, no less than philosophers, carry on long trains of thought without pausing to translate their ideas (words) into images. . . . Suppose some one from a distance shouts 'a lion!' At once the man starts in alarm. . . . To the man the word is not only an . . . expression of all that he has seen and heard of lions, capable of recalling various experiences, but is also capable of taking its place in a connected series of thoughts without recalling any of those experiences, without reviving an image, however faint, of the lion—simply as a sign of a certain relation included in the complex so named. Like an algebraic symbol it may be operated on without conveying other significance than an abstract relation: it is a sign of Danger, related to fear with all its motor sequences. Its logical position suffices. . . . Ideas are *substitutions* which require a secondary process when what is symbolized by them is translated into the images and experiences it replaces; and this secondary process is frequently not performed at all, generally only performed to a very small extent. Let anyone closely examine what has passed in his mind when he has constructed a chain of reasoning, and he will be surprised at the fewness and faintness of the images which have accompanied the ideas. Suppose you inform me that 'the blood rushed violently from the man's heart, quickening his pulse at the sight of his enemy.' Of the many latent images in this phrase, how many were salient in your mind and in mine? Probably two—the man and his enemy—and these images were faint. Images of blood, heart, violent rushing, pulse, quickening, and sight, were either not revived at all, or were passing shadows. Had any such images arisen, they would have hampered thought, retarding the logical process of judgment by irrelevant connections. The symbols had substituted *relations* for these *values*. . . . There are no images of two things and three things, when I say 'two and three equal five,' there are simply familiar symbols having precise relations. . . . The verbal symbol 'horse,' which stands for all our experiences of horses, serves all the purposes of Thought, without recalling one of the images clustered in the perception of horses, just as the sight of a horse's form serves all the purposes of *recognition* without recalling the sound of its neighing or its tramp, its qualities as an animal of draught, and so forth."*

It need only be added that as the Algebrist, though the sequence of his terms is fixed by their relations rather than by their several values, must give a real value to the *final* one he reaches; so the thinker in words must let his concluding word or phrase be translated into its full sensible-image-value, under penalty of the thought being left unrealized and pale.

This is all I have to say about the sensible continuity and unity of our thought as contrasted with the apparent discreteness of the words, images, and other means by which it seems to be carried on. Between all their substantive elements there is 'transitive' consciousness, and the words and images are 'fringed,' and not as discrete as to a careless view they seem. Let us advance now to the next head in our description of Thought's stream.

4. *Human thought appears to deal with objects independent of itself; that is, it is cognitive, or possesses the function of knowing.*

For Absolute Idealism, the infinite Thought and its

---

* Problems of Life and Mind, 3d Series, Problem IV, chapter 5. Compare also Victor Egger: La Parole Intérieure (Paris, 1881), chap. VI.

objects are one. The Objects are, through being thought; the eternal Mind is, through thinking them. Were a human thought alone in the world there would be no reason for any other assumption regarding it. Whatever it might have before it would be its vision, would be there, in *its* 'there,' or then, in *its* 'then'; and the question would never arise whether an extra-mental duplicate of it existed or not. The reason why we all believe that the objects of our thoughts have a duplicate existence outside, is that there are *many* human thoughts, each with the *same* objects, as we *cannot* help supposing. The judgment that *my* thought has the same object as *his* thought is what makes the psychologist call my thought cognitive of an outer reality. The judgment that my own past thought and my own present thought are of the same object is what makes *me* take the object out of either and project it by a sort of triangulation into an independent position, from which it may *appear* to both. *Sameness* in a multiplicity of objective appearances is thus the basis of our belief in realities outside of thought.*

To show that the question of reality being extra-mental or not is likely to arise in the absence of repeated experiences of the *same*, take the example of an altogther unprecedented experience, such as a new taste in the throat. Is it a subjective quality of feeling, or an objective quality felt? You do not even ask the question at this point. It is simply *that taste*. But if a doctor hears you describe it, and says: "Ha! Now you know what *heartburn* is," then it becomes a quality already existent *extra mentem tuam*; which you in turn have come upon and learned. The first spaces, times, things, qualities, experienced by the child probably appear, like the first heartburn, in this absolute way, as simple *beings*, neither in

---

* If but one person sees an apparition we consider it his private hallucination. If more than one, we begin to think it may be a real external presence.

nor out of thought. But later by having other thoughts than this present one, and making repeated judgments of sameness among their objects, he corroborates in himself the notion of realities, past and distant as well as present, which realities no one single thought either possesses or engenders, but which all may contemplate and know. This, as was stated in the last chapter, is the *psychological* point of view, the relatively uncritical non-idealistic point of view of all natural science, beyond which this book cannot go. A mind which has become conscious of its own cognitive function, plays what we have called 'the psychologist' upon itself. It not only knows the things that appear before it; it knows that it knows them. This stage of reflective condition is, more or less explicitly, our habitual adult state of mind.

It cannot, however, be regarded as primitive. The consciousness of objects must come first. We seem to lapse into this primordial condition when consciousness is reduced to a minimum by the inhalation of anaesthetics or during a faint. Many persons testify that at a certain stage of the anaesthetic process objects are still cognized whilst the thought of self is lost. Professor Herzen says:*

"During the syncope there is absolute psychic annihilation, the absence of all consciousness; then at the beginning of coming to, one has at a certain moment a vague, limitless, infinite feeling—a sense of *existence in general* without the least trace of distinction between the me and the not-me."

Dr. Shoemaker of Philadelphia describes during the deepest conscious stage of ether-intoxication a vision of "two endless parallel lines in swift longitudinal motion . . . on a uniform misty background . . . together with a constant sound or whirr, not loud but distinct . . . which seemed to be connected with the parallel lines. . . . These phenomena occupied the whole field. There were present no dreams or visions in any way connected with human affairs, no ideas or impressions akin to anything in past experience, no emotions, of course no idea of personality. There was no conception as to what being it was that was regarding the

---

* Revue Philosophique, vol. XXI. p. 671.

two lines, or that there existed any such thing as such a being; the lines and waves were all."*

Similarly a friend of Mr. Herbert Spencer, quoted by him in 'Mind' (vol. III. p. 556), speaks of "an undisturbed empty quiet everywhere except that a stupid presence lay like a heavy intrusion *somewhere*—a blotch on the calm." This sense of objectivity and lapse of subjectivity, even when the object is almost indefinable, is, it seems to me, a somewhat familiar phase in chloroformization, though in my own case it is too deep a phase for any articulate after-memory to remain. I only know that as it vanishes I seem to wake to a sense of my own existence as something additional to what had previously been there.†

Many philosophers, however, hold that the reflective consciousness of the self is essential to the cognitive function of thought. They hold that a thought, in order to know a thing at all, must expressly distinguish between the thing and its own self.‡ This is a perfectly wanton assumption, and not the faintest shadow of reason exists for supposing it true. As well might I contend that I

---

* Quoted from the Therapeutic Gazette, by the N. Y. Semi-weekly Evening Post for Nov. 2, 1886.

† In half-stunned states self-consciousness may lapse. A friend writes me: "We were driving back from —— in a wagonette. The door flew open and X., alias 'Baldy,' fell out on the road. We pulled up at once, and then he said, 'Did anybody fall out?' or 'Who fell out?'—I don't exactly remember the words. When told that Baldy fell out, he said, 'Did Baldy fall out? Poor Baldy!'"

‡ Kant originated this view. I subjoin a few English statements of it. J. Ferrier, Institutes of Metaphysic, Proposition I: "Along with whatever any intelligence knows it must, as the ground or condition of its knowledge, have some knowledge of itself." Sir Wm. Hamilton, Discussions, p. 47: "We know, and we know that we know,— these propositions, logically distinct, are really identical; each implies the other. . . . So true is the scholastic brocard: *non sentimus nisi sentiamus nos sentire*." H. L. Mansel, Metaphysics, p. 58: "Whatever variety of materials may exist within reach of my mind, I can become conscious of them only by recognizing them as mine. . . . Relation to the conscious self is thus the permanent and universal feature which every state of consciousness as such must exhibit." T. H. Green, Introduction to Hume, p. 12: "A consciousness by the man . . . of himself, in negative relation to the thing that is his object, and this consciousness must be taken to go along with the perceptive act itself. Not less than this indeed can be involved in any act that is to be the beginning of knowledge at all. It is the minimum of possible thought or intelligence."

cannot dream without dreaming that I dream, swear without swearing that I swear, deny without denying that I deny, as maintain that I cannot know without knowing that I know. I may have either acquaintance-with, or knowledge-about, an object O without thinking about myself at all. It suffices for this that I think O, and that it exist. If, in addition to thinking O, I also think that I exist and that I know O, well and good; I then know one more thing, a fact about O, of which I previously was unmindful. That, however, does not prevent me from having already known it a good deal. O *per se,* or O *plus* P, are as good objects of knowledge as O *plus me* is. The philosophers in question simply substitute one particular object for all others, and call it *the* object *par excellence.* It is a case of the 'psychologist's fallacy' . . . *They* know the object to be one thing and the thought another; and they forthwith foist their own knowledge into that of the thought of which they pretend to give a true account. To conclude, then, *thought may, but need not, in knowing, discriminate between its object and itself.*

We have been using the word Object. *Something must now be said about the proper use of the term Object in Psychology.*

In popular parlance the word object is commonly taken without reference to the act of knowledge, and treated as synonymous with individual subject of existence. Thus if anyone ask what is the mind's object when you say 'Columbus discovered America in 1492,' most people will reply 'Columbus,' or 'America,' or, at most, 'the discovery of America.' They will name a substantive kernel or nucleus of the consciousness, and say the thought is 'about' that,—as indeed it is,—and they will call that your thought's 'object.' Really that is usually only the grammatical object, or more likely the grammatical subject, of your sentence. It is at most your 'fractional object;' or you may call it the 'topic' of your thought, or the 'subject of your discourse.' But the *Object* of your thought is really its entire content or deliverance, neither more nor less. It is a vicious use of speech to take out a substantive kernel from its content and call that its object; and it is an equally vicious use of speech to add a substantive kernel not articulately included in its content, and to call that its object. Yet either one of these two sins we commit, whenever we content ourselves with saying that a given thought is simply 'about' a certain topic, or that topic is its 'object.' The object of my thought in the previous sentence, for example, is strictly speaking neither Columbus, nor America, nor its discovery. It is nothing short of the entire sentence, 'Columbus-discovered-America-in-1492.' And if we wish to speak of it substantively, we must make a substantive of it by writing it out thus with hyphens between all its words. Nothing but this can possibly name its delicate idiosyncrasy. And if we wish to *feel* that idiosyncrasy we must reproduce the thought as it was uttered, with every word fringed and the whole sentence bathed in that original halo of obscure relations, which, like an horizon, then spread about its meaning.

Our psychological duty is to cling as closely as possible to the actual constitution of the thought we are studying. We may err as much by excess as by defect. If the kernel or 'topic,' Columbus, is in one way less than the thought's object, so in another way it may be more. That is, when named by the psychologist, it may mean much more than actually is present to the thought of which he is reporter. Thus, for example, suppose you should go on to think: 'He was a daring genius!' An ordinary psychologist would not hesitate to say that the object of your thought was still 'Columbus.' True, your thought is *about* Columbus. It 'terminates' in Columbus, leads from and to the direct idea of Columbus. But for the moment it is not fully and immediately Columbus, it is only 'he,' or rather 'he-was-a-daring-genius;' which though it may be an unimportant difference for conversational purposes, is, for introspective psychology, as great a difference as there can be.

The object of every thought, then, is neither more nor less than all that the thought thinks, exactly as the thought thinks it, however complicated the matter, and however symbolic the manner of the thinking may be. It is needless to say that memory can seldom accurately reproduce such an object, when once it has passed from before the mind. It either makes too little or too much of it. Its best plan is to repeat the verbal sentence, if there was one, in which the object was expressed. But for inarticulate thoughts there is not even this resource, and introspection must confess that the task exceeds her powers. The mass of our thinking vanishes for ever, beyond hope of recovery, and psychology only gathers up a few of the crumbs that fall from the feast.

The next point to make clear is that, *however complex the object may be, the thought of it is one undivided state of consciousness.* As Thomas Brown says:[*]

"I have already spoken too often to require again to caution you against the mistake into which, I confess, that the terms which the poverty of our language obliges us to use might of themselves very naturally lead you; the mistake of supposing that the most complex states of mind are not truly, in their very essence, as much one and indivisible as those which we term simple—the complexity and seeming coexistence which they involve being relative to our feeling[†] only, not to their own absolute nature. I trust I need not repeat to you that, in itself, every notion, however seemingly complex is, and must be, truly simple—being one state or affection, of one simple substance, mind. Our conception of a whole army, for example, is as truly this one mind existing in this one state, as our conception of any of the individuals that compose an army. Our notion of the abstract numbers, eight, four, two, is as truly one feeling of the mind as our notion of simple unity."

---

[*] Lectures on the Philosophy of the Human Mind, Lecture 45.
[†] Instead of saying to *our feeling only*, he should have said, to the *object* only.

The ordinary associationist-psychology supposes, in contrast with this, that whenever an object of thought contains many elements, the thought itself must be made up of just as many ideas, one idea for each element, and all fused together in appearance, but really separate.* The enemies of this psychology find (as we have already seen) little trouble in showing that such a bundle of separate ideas would never form one thought at all, and they contend that an Ego must be added to the bundle to give it unity, and bring the various ideas into relation with each other. We will not discuss the ego just yet, but it is obvious that if things are to be thought in relation, they must be thought together, and in one *something*, be that something ego, psychosis, state of consciousness, or whatever you please. If not thought with each other, things are not thought in relation at all. Now most believers in the ego make the same mistake as the associationists and sensationists whom they oppose. Both agree that the elements of the subjective stream are discrete and separate and constitute what Kant calls a 'manifold.' But while the associationists think that a 'manifold' can form a single knowledge, the egoists deny this, and say that the knowledge comes only when the manifold is subjected to the synthetizing activity of an ego. Both make an identical initial hypothesis; but the egoist, finding it won't express the facts, adds another hypothesis to correct it. Now I do not wish just yet to 'commit myself' about the existence or non-existence of the ego, but I do contend that we need not invoke it for this particular reason—namely, because the manifold of ideas has to be

---

* "There can be no difficulty in admitting that association does form the ideas of an indefinite number of individuals into one complex idea; because it is an acknowledged fact. Have we not the idea of an army? And is not that precisely the ideas of an indefinite number of men formed into one idea?" (Jas. Mill's Analysis of the Human Mind (J. S. Mill's Edition), vol. I. p. 264.)

reduced to unity. *There is no manifold of coexisting ideas;* the notion of such a thing is a chimera. *Whatever things are thought in relation are thought from the outset in a unity, in a single pulse of subjectivity, a single psychosis, feeling, or state of mind.*

The reason why this fact is so strangely garbled in the books seems to be what on an earlier page ... I called the psychologist's fallacy. We have the inveterate habit, whenever we try introspectively to describe one of our thoughts, of dropping the thought as it is in itself and talking of something else. We describe the things that appear to the thought, and we describe other thoughts *about* those things—as if these and the original thought were the same. If, for example, the thought be 'the pack of cards is on the table,' we say, "Well, isn't it a thought of the pack of cards? Isn't it of the cards as included in the pack? Isn't it of the table? And of the legs of the table as well? The table has legs—how can you think the table without virtually thinking its legs? Hasn't our thought then, all these parts—one part for the pack and another for the table? And within the pack-part a part for each card, as within the table-part a part for each leg? And isn't each of these parts an idea? And can our thought, then, be anything but an assemblage or pack of ideas, each answering to some element of what it knows?"

Now not one of these assumptions is true. The thought taken as an example is, in the first place, not of 'a pack of cards.' It is of 'the-pack-of-cards-is-on-the-table,' an entirely different subjective phenomenon, whose Object implies the pack, and every one of the cards in it, but whose conscious constitution bears very little resemblance to that of the thought of the pack *per se.* What a thought *is,* and what it may be developed into, or explained to stand for, and be equivalent to, are two things, not one.*

An analysis of what passes through the mind as we utter the phrase *the pack of cards is on the table* will, I hope, make this clear, and may at the same time condense into a concrete example a good deal of what has gone before.

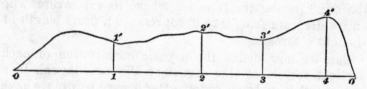

The pack of cards is on the table
FIG. 3.—The Stream of Consciousness.

It takes time to utter the phrase. Let the horizontal line in Fig. 3 represent time. Every part of it will then stand for a fraction, every point for an instant, of the time. Of course the thought has *time-parts*. The part 2-3 of it, though continuous with 1-2, is yet a different part from 1-2. Now I say of these time-parts that we cannot take any one of them so short that it will not after some fashion or other be a thought of the whole object 'the pack of cards is on the table.' They melt into each other like dissolving views, and no two of them feel the object just alike, but each feels the total object in a unitary undivided way. This is what I mean by denying that in the thought any parts can be found corresponding to the object's

---

* I know there are readers whom nothing can convince that the thought of a complex object has not as many parts as are discriminated in the object itself. Well, then, let the word parts pass. Only observe that these parts are not the separate 'ideas' of traditional psychology. No one of them can live out of that particular thought, any more than my head can live off my particular shoulders. In a sense a soap-bubble has parts; it is a sum of juxtaposed spherical triangles. But these triangles are not separate realities; neither are the 'parts' of the thought separate realities. Touch the bubble and the triangles are no more. Dismiss the thought and out go its parts. You can no more make a new thought out of 'ideas' that have once served than you can make a new bubble out of old triangles. Each bubble, each thought, is a fresh organic unity, *sui generis.*

211

parts. Time-parts are not such parts.

Now let the vertical dimensions of the figure stand for the objects or contents of the thoughts. A line vertical to any point of the horizontal, as 1-1′, will then symbolize the object in the mind at the instant 1; a space above the horizontal, as 1-1′-2′-2, will symbolize all that passes through the mind during the time 1-2 whose line it covers. The entire diagram from 0 to 0′ represents a finite length of thought's stream.

Can we now define the psychic constitution of each vertical section of this segment? We can, though in a very rough way. Immediately after 0, even before we have opened our mouths to speak, the entire thought is present to our mind in the form of an intention to utter that sentence. This intention, though it has no simple name, and though it is a transitive state immediately displaced by the first word, is yet a perfectly determinate phase of thought, unlike anything else. . . . Again, immediately before 0′, after the last word of the sentence is spoken, all will admit that we again think its entire content as we inwardly realize its completed deliverance. All vertical sections made through any other parts of the diagram will be respectively filled with other ways of feeling the sentence's meaning. Through 2, for example, the cards will be the part of the object most emphatically present to the mind; through 4, the table. The stream is made higher in the drawing at its end than at its begining, because the final way of feeling the content is fuller and richer than the initial way. As Joubert says, "we only know just what we meant to say, after we have said it." And as M. V. Egger remarks, "before speaking, one barely knows what one intends to say, but afterwards one is filled with admiration and surprise at having said and thought it so well."

This latter author seems to me to have kept at much closer quarters with the facts than any other analyst of

212

consciousness.* But even he does not quite hit the mark, for, as I understand him, he thinks that each word as it occupies the mind *displaces* the rest of the thought's content. He distinguishes the 'idea' (what I have called the total *object* or meaning) from the consciousness of the words, calling the former a very feeble state, and contrasting it with the liveliness of the words, even when these are only silently rehearsed. "The feeling," he says, "of the words makes ten or twenty times more noise in our consciousness than the sense of the phrase, which for consciousness is a very slight matter." And having distinguished these two things, he goes on to separate them in time, saying that the idea may either precede or follow the words, but that it is a 'pure illusion' to suppose them simultaneous.† Now I believe that in all cases where the words are *understood,* the total idea may be and usually is present not only before and after the phrase has been spoken, but also whilst each separate word is uttered.‡ It is the overtone, halo, or fringe of the word, *as spoken in that sentence.* It is never absent; no word in an understood sentence comes to consciousness as a mere noise. We feel its meaning as it passes; and although our object differs from one moment to another as to its verbal kernel

---

* In his work, La Parole Intérieure (Paris, 1881), especially chapters VI and VII.

† To prove this point, M. Egger appeals to the fact that we often hear some one whilst our mind is preoccupied, but do not understand him until some moments afterwards, when we suddenly 'realize' what he meant. Also to our digging out the meaning of a sentence in an unfamiliar tongue, where the words are present to us long before the idea is taken in. In these special cases the word does indeed precede the idea. The idea, on the contrary, precedes the word whenever we try to express ourselves with effort, as in a foreign tongue, or in an unusual field of intellectual invention. Both sets of cases, however, are exceptional, and M. Egger would probably himself admit, on reflection, that in the former class there is some sort of a verbal suffusion, however evanescent, of the idea, when it is grasped—we hear the echo of the words as we catch their meaning. And he would probably admit that in the second class of cases the idea persists after the words that came with so much effort are found. In normal cases the simultaneity, as he admits, is obviously there.

‡ A good way to get the words and the sense separately is to inwardly articulate word for word the discourse of another. One then finds that the meaning will often come to the mind in pulses, after clauses or sentences are finished.

or nucleus, yet it is *similar* throughout the entire segment of the stream. The same object is known everywhere, now from the point of view, if we may so call it, of this word, now from the point of view of that. And in our feeling of each word there chimes an echo or foretaste of every other. The consciousness of the 'Idea' and that of the words are thus consubstantial. They are made of the same 'mind-stuff,' and form an unbroken stream. Annihilate a mind at any instant, cut its thought through whilst yet uncompleted, and examine the object present to the cross section thus suddenly made; you will find not the bald word in process of utterance, but that word suffused with the whole idea. The word may be so loud, as M. Egger would say, that we cannot *tell* just how its suffusion, as such, feels, or how it differs from the suffusion of the next word. But it does differ; and we may be sure that, could we see into the brain, we should find the same processes active through the entire sentence in different degrees, each one in turn becoming maximally excited and then yielding the momentary verbal 'kernel,' to the thought's content, at other times being only sub-excited, and then combining with the other sub-excited processes to give the overtone or fringe.*

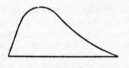

Fig. 4

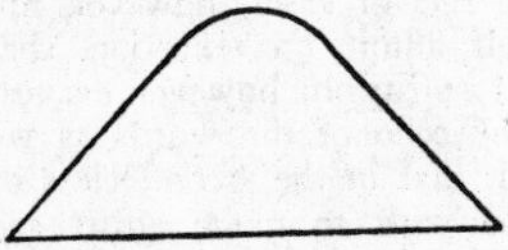

Fig. 5

We may illustrate this by a farther development of the diagram. Let the objective content of any vertical section through the stream be represented no longer by a line, but by a plane figure, highest opposite whatever part of the object is most prominent in consciousness at the moment when the section is made. This part, in verbal thought will usually be some word. A series of sections 1-1',

---

* The nearest approach (with which I am acquainted) to the doctrine set forth here is in O. Liebmann's *Zur Analysis der Wirklichkeit*, pp. 427-438.

214

taken at the moments 1, 2, 3, would then look like this :

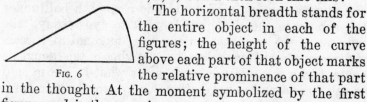

FIG. 6

The horizontal breadth stands for the entire object in each of the figures; the height of the curve above each part of that object marks the relative prominence of that part in the thought. At the moment symbolized by the first figure *pack* is the prominent part; in the third figure it is *table*, etc.

We can easily add all these plane sections together to make a solid, one of whose solid dimensions will represent time, whilst a cut across this at right angles will give the thought's content at the moment when the cut is made.

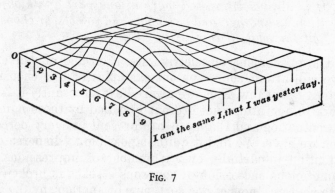

FIG. 7

Let it be the thought, 'I am the same I that I was yesterday.' If at the fourth moment of time we annihilate the thinker and examine how the last pulsation of his consciousness was made, we find that it was an awareness of the whole content with *same* most prominent, and other parts of the thing known relatively less distinct. With each prolongation of the scheme in the time-direction, the summit of the curve of section would come further towards the end of the sentence. If we make a solid wooden frame with the sentence written on its front, and the time-scale on one of its sides, if we spread flatly a

215

sheet of India rubber over its top, on which rectangular co-ordinates are painted, and slide a smooth ball under the rubber in the direction from 0 to 'yesterday,' the bulging of the membrane along this diagonal at successive moments will symbolize the changing of the thought's content in a way plain enough, after what has been said to call for no more explanation. Or to express it in cerebral terms, it will show the relative intensities, at successive moments, of the several nerve-processes to which the various parts of the thought-object correspond.

The last peculiarity of consciousness to which attention is to be drawn in this first rough description of its stream is that

5) *It is always interested more in one part of its object than in another, and welcomes and rejects, or chooses, all the while it thinks.*

The phenomena of selective attention and of deliberative will are of course patent examples of this choosing activity. But few of us are aware how incessantly it is at work in operations not ordinarily called by these names. Accentuation and Emphasis are present in every perception we have. We find it quite impossible to disperse our attention impartially over a number of impressions. A monotonous succession of sonorous strokes is broken up into rhythms, now of one sort, now of another, by the different accents which we place on different strokes. The simplest of these rhythms is the double one, tick-tóck, tick-tóck, tick-tóck. Dots dispersed on a surface are perceived in rows and groups. Lines separate into diverse figures. The ubiquity of the distinctions, *this* and *that, here* and *there, now* and *then,* in our minds is the result of our laying the same selective emphasis on parts of place and time.

But we do far more than emphasize things, and unite some, and keep others apart. We actually *ignore* most of

216

the things before us. Let me briefly show how this goes on.

To begin at the bottom, what are our very senses themselves but organs of selection? Out of the infinite chaos of movements, of which physics teaches us that the outer world consists, each sense-organ picks out those which fall within certain limits of velocity. To these it responds, but ignores the rest as completely as if they did not exist. It thus accentuates particular movements in a manner for which objectively there seems no valid ground; for as Lange says, there is no reason whatever to think that the gap in Nature between the highest sound-waves and the lowest heat-waves is an abrupt break like that of our sensations; or that the difference between violet and ultra-violet rays has anything like the objective importance subjectively represented by that between light and darkness. Out of what is in itself an undistinguishable, swarming *continuum,* devoid of distinction or emphasis, our senses make for us, by attending to this motion and ignoring that, a world full of contrasts, of sharp accents, of abrupt changes, of picturesque light and shade.

If the sensations we receive from a given organ have their causes thus picked out for us by the conformation of the organ's termination, Attention, on the other hand, out of all the sensations yielded, picks out certain ones as worthy of its notice and suppresses all the rest. Helmholtz's work on Optics is little more than a study of those visual sensations of which common men never become aware — blind spots, *muscæ volitantes,* after-images, irradiation, chromatic fringes, marginal changes of color, double images, astigmatism, movements of accommodation and convergence, retinal rivalry, and more besides. We do not even know without special training on which of our eyes an image falls. So habitually ignorant are most men of this that one may be blind for years of a single eye and never know the fact.

Helmholtz says that we notice only those sensations

217

which are signs to us of *things*. But what are things? Nothing, as we shall abundantly see, but special groups of sensible qualities, which happen practically or æsthetically to interest us, to which we therefore give substantive names, and which we exalt to this exclusive status of independence and dignity. But in itself, apart from my interest, a particular dust-wreath on a windy day is just as much of an individual thing, and just as much or as little deserves an individual name, as my own body does.

And then, among the sensations we get from each separate thing, what happens? The mind selects again. It chooses certain of the sensations to represent the thing most *truly,* and considers the rest as its appearances, modified by the conditions of the moment. Thus my table-top is named *square,* after but one of an infinite number of retinal sensations which it yields, the rest of them being sensations of two acute and two obtuse angles; but I call the latter *perspective* views, and the four right angles the *true* form of the table, and erect the attribute squareness into the table's essence, for æsthetic reasons of my own. In like manner, the real form of the circle is deemed to be the sensation it gives when the line of vision is perpendicular to its centre—all its other sensations are signs of this sensation. The real sound of the cannon is the sensation it makes when the ear is close by. The real color of the brick is the sensation it gives when the eye looks squarely at it from a near point, out of the sunshine and yet not in the gloom; under other circumstances it gives us other color-sensations which are but signs of this—we then see it looks pinker or blacker than it really is. The reader knows no object which he does not represent to himself by preference as in some typical attitude, of some normal size, at some characteristic distance, of some standard tint, etc., etc. But all these essential characteristics, which together form for us the genuine objectivity of the thing and are contrasted with what we call

218

the subjective sensations it may yield us at a given moment, are mere sensations like the latter. The mind chooses to suit itself, and decides what particular sensation shall be held more real and valid than all the rest.

Thus perception involves a twofold choice. Out of all present sensations, we notice mainly such as are significant of absent ones; and out of all the absent associates which these suggest, we again pick out a very few to stand for the objective reality *par excellence*. We could have no more exquisite example of selective industry.

That industry goes on to deal with the things thus given in perception. A man's empirical thought depends on the things he has experienced, but what these shall be is to a large extent determined by his habits of attention. A thing may be present to him a thousand times, but if he persistently fails to notice it, it cannot be said to enter into his experience. We are all seeing flies, moths, and beetles by the thousand, but to whom, save an entomologist, do they say anything distinct? On the other hand, a thing met only once in a lifetime may leave an indelible experience in the memory. Let four men make a tour in Europe. One will bring home only picturesque impressions—costumes and colors, parks and views and works of architecture, pictures and statues. To another all this will be non-existent; and distances and prices, populations and drainage-arrangements, door- and window-fastenings, and other useful statistics will take their place. A third will give a rich account of the theatres, restaurants, and public balls, and naught beside; whilst the fourth will perhaps have been so wrapped in his own subjective broodings as to tell little more than a few names of places through which he passed. Each has selected, out of the same mass of presented objects, those which suited his private interest and has made his experience thereby.

If, now, leaving the empirical combination of objects,

we ask how the mind proceeds *rationally* to connect them, we find selection again to be omnipotent. In a future chapter we shall see that all Reasoning depends on the ability of the mind to break up the totality of the phenomenon reasoned about, into parts, and to pick out from among these the particular one which, in our given emergency, may lead to the proper conclusion. Another predicament will need another conclusion, and require another element to be picked out. The man of genius is he who will always stick in his bill at the right point, and bring it out with the right element—'reason' if the emergency be theoretical, 'means' if it be practical—transfixed upon it. I here confine myself to this brief statement, but it may suffice to show that Reasoning is but another form of the selective activity of the mind.

If now we pass to its æsthetic department, our law is still more obvious. The artist notoriously selects his items, rejecting all tones, colors, shapes, which do not harmonize with each other and with the main purpose of his work. That unity, harmony, 'convergence of characters,' as M. Taine calls it, which gives to works of art their superiority over works of nature, is wholly due to *elimination*. Any natural subject will do, if the artist has wit enough to pounce upon some one feature of it as characteristic, and suppress all merely accidental items which do not harmonize with this.

Ascending still higher, we reach the plane of Ethics, where choice reigns notoriously supreme. An act has no ethical quality whatever unless it be chosen out of several all equally possible. To sustain the arguments for the good course and keep them ever before us, to stifle our longing for more flowery ways, to keep the foot unflinchingly on the arduous path, these are characteristic ethical energies. But more than these; for these but deal with the means of compassing interests already felt by the man to be supreme. The ethical energy *par excellence* has to go

220

farther and choose which *interest* out of *several*, equally coercive, shall become supreme. The issue here is of the utmost pregnancy, for it decides a man's entire career. When he debates, Shall I commit this crime? choose that profession? accept that office, or marry this fortune?—his choice really lies between one of several equally possible future Characters. What he shall *become* is fixed by the conduct of this moment. Schopenhauer, who enforces his determinism by the argument that with a given fixed character only one reaction is possible under given circumstances, forgets that, in these critical ethical moments, what consciously *seems* to be in question is the complexion of the character itself. The problem with the man is less what act he shall now choose to do, than what being he shall now resolve to become.

Looking back, then, over this review, we see that the mind is at every stage a theatre of simultaneous possibilities. Consciousness consists in the comparison of these with each other, the selection of some, and the suppression of the rest by the reinforcing and inhibiting agency of attention. The highest and most elaborated mental products are filtered from the data chosen by the faculty next beneath, out of the mass offered by the faculty below that, which mass in turn was sifted from a still larger amount of yet simpler material, and so on. The mind, in short, works on the data it receives very much as a sculptor works on his block of stone. In a sense the statue stood there from eternity. But there were a thousand different ones beside it, and the sculptor alone is to thank for having extricated this one from the rest. Just so the world of each of us, howsoever different our several views of it may be, all lay embedded in the primordial chaos of sensations, which gave the mere *matter* to the thought of all of us indifferently. We may if we like, by our reasonings unwind things back to that black and jointless continuity of space and moving clouds of

221

swarming atoms which science calls the only real world. But all the while the world *we* feel and live in will be that which our ancestors and we, by slowly cumulative strokes of choice, have extricated out of this, like sculptors, by simply rejecting certain portions of the given stuff. Other sculptors, other statues from the same stone! Other minds, other worlds from the same monotonous and inexpressive chaos! My world is but one in a million alike embedded, alike real to those who may abstract them. How different must be the worlds in the consciousness of ant, cuttle-fish, or crab!

But in my mind and your mind the rejected portions and the selected portions of the original world-stuff are to a great extent the same. The human race as a whole largely agrees as to what it shall notice and name, and what not. And among the noticed parts we select in much the same way for accentuation and preference or subordination and dislike. There is, however, one entirely extraordinary case in which no two men ever are known to choose alike. One great splitting of the whole universe into two halves is made by each of us; and for each of us almost all of the interest attaches to one of the halves; but we all draw the line of division between them in a different place. When I say that we all call the two halves by the same names, and that those names are '*me*' and '*not-me*' respectively, it will at once be seen what I mean. The altogether unique kind of interest which each human mind feels in those parts of creation which it can call *me* or *mine* may be a moral riddle, but it is a fundamental psychological fact. No mind can take the same interest in his neighbor's *me* as in his own. The neighbor's me falls together with all the rest of things in one foreign mass, against which his own *me* stands out in startlng relief. Even the trodden worm, as Lotze somewhere says, contrasts his own suffering self with the whole remaining

222

universe, though he have no clear conception either of himself or of what the universe may be. He is for me a mere part of the world; for him it is I who am the mere part. Each of us dichotomizes the Kosmos in a different place. . . .

WILLIAM JAMES (b.-Jan. 11, 1842; Aug. 26, 1910).

James' early years were spent in travel. He entered Harvard in 1861. Upon graduation he entered the medical college, but interrupted his studies in order to accompany Louis Agassiz on one of his expeditions to Brazil, in 1865. He returned to medical college in 1866-67. In 1867-68, he studied in Germany with Helmholtz. He then returned to Harvard and took his M.D. in 1869. In 1872 he was appointed Instructor at Harvard. In 1884 he founded the American Society for Psychical Research. (It was during the dark mood of a nervous breakdown, extending roughly from 1868 to 1872 that James' interest in this field was aroused.) In 1897, he was appointed Professor of Philosophy at Harvard, which position he held until his resignation in 1907.

James wrote, on academic psychological issues, with a freedom and power that few have attained. His influence is not so much in what he wrote, as in the dignity and compelling nature of his convictions. It was as a teacher, rather than as an innovator, that James has had his greatness. In particular, the concept of the onrushing continuity of consciousness has received its most brilliant explication in James. The refreshing intellectual strength and health of this great idea stands in sharp contrast to James' own life, fraught as it was with emotional and psychological upheavals. The "stream of consciousness" is James' most famous and, probably his most important single contribution. Perhaps, it was the ultimate source of his own peace of mind.

JAMES, W. *Principles of psychology*. New York: Henry Holt & Co., Inc. 1890, Vol. I, chap. IX: "The stream of thought."

See also:

JAMES, W. a) *Psychology: briefer course*. N.Y.: Henry Holt, 1892.
   b) *Talks to teachers on psychology: and to students on some of life's ideals*. N.Y. Henry Holt, 1899.

PERRY, R. B. *The thought and character of William James*. Boston: Little, Brown, 1935, 2 vol.

FAY, J. W. *American psychology before William James*. New Brunswick, N. J.: Rutgers University Press, 1939.

THE POSTULATES OF A STRUCTURAL PSYCHOLOGY.[1]

Edward B. Titchener

Biology, defined in its widest sense as the science of life and of living things, falls into three parts, or may be approached from any one of three points of view. We may enquire into the structure of an organism, without regard to function,—by analysis determining its component parts, and by synthesis exhibiting the mode of its formation from the parts. Or we may enquire into the function of the various structures which our analysis has revealed, and into the manner of their interrelation as functional organs. Or, again, we may enquire into the changes of form and function that accompany the persistence of the

---

[1] At the Ithaca meeting of the American Psychological Association, December, 1897, Professor Caldwell read a paper (printed in the *Psychological Review* of July, 1898) upon the view of the psychological self sketched in my *Outline of Psychology.* The present article contains a part of my reply to the criticism of Professor Caldwell; a full answer would require a definition of science and a discussion of the relation of science to philosophy. I hope to publish, later on, a second article, dealing with these topics. Since Professor Caldwell is really attacking, not an individual psychologist, but a general psychological position, the discussion of the questions raised by him can take an objective form. A polemic is always more telling if it be directed against an individual, and Professor Caldwell doubtless recognized this fact when he selected my book as whipping-boy. But a rejoinder in kind would, I think, be dreary reading, while the issues involved are serious enough to justify a broader treatment.

As I shall not return to the point, I may note here that a few of Professor Caldwell's objections rest upon technical errors. This is true at least of nos. 1, 8, and 9 of his twelve arguments. Such lapses are hardly to be avoided by any one who travels out of his own special field into that of another discipline; they do not at all impair the value of Professor Caldwell's contentions regarded as a whole.

organism in time, the phenomena of growth and decay. Biology, the science of living things, comprises the three mutually interdependent sciences of morphology, physiology, and ontogeny.

This account is, however, incomplete. The life which forms the subject matter of science is not merely the life of an individual; it is species life, collective life, as well. Corresponding to morphology, we have taxonomy or systematic zoology, the science of classification. The whole world of living things is here the organism, and species and sub-species and races are its parts. Corresponding to physiology, we have that department of biology—it has been termed 'œcology'—which deals with questions of geographical distribution, of the function of species in the general economy of nature. Corresponding to ontogeny we have the science of phylogeny (in Cope's sense): the biology of evolution, with its problems of descent and of transmission.

We may accept this scheme as a 'working' classification of the biological sciences. It is indifferent, for my present purpose, whether or not the classification is exhaustive, as it is indifferent whether the reader regards psychology as a subdivision of biology or as a separate province of knowledge. The point which I wish now to make is this: that, employing the same principle of division, we can represent modern psychology as the exact counterpart of modern biology. There are three ways of approaching the one, as there are the three ways of approaching the other; and the subject matter in every case may be individual or general. A little consideration will make this clear.[1]

1. We find a parallel to morphology in a very large portion of 'experimental' psychology. The primary aim of the experimental psychologist has been to analyze the structure of mind; to ravel out the elemental processes

---

[1] The comparison has been drawn, in part, by Professor Ebbinghaus. See his *Grundzüg der Psychologie*, I, pp. 161 ff.

from the tangle of consciousness, or (if we may change the metaphor) to isolate the constituents in the given conscious formation. His task is a vivisection, but a vivisection which shall yield structural, not functional results. He tries to discover, first of all, what is there and in what quantity, not what it is there for. Indeed, this work of analysis bulks so largely in the literature of experimental psychology that a recent writer has questioned the right of the science to its adjective, declaring that an experiment is something more than a measurement made by the help of delicate instruments.[1] And there can be no doubt that much of the criticism passed upon the new psychology depends on the critics' failure to recognize its morphological character. We are often told that our treatment of feeling and emotion, of reasoning, of the self is inadequate; that the experimental method is valuable for the investigation of sensation and idea, but can carry us no farther. The answer is that the results gained by dissection of the 'higher' processes will always be disappointing to those who have not themselves adopted the dissector's standpoint. Protoplasm consists, we are told, of carbon, oxygen, nitrogen, and hydrogen; but this statement would prove exceedingly disappointing to one who had thought to be informed of the phenomena of contractility and metabolism, respiration and reproduction. Taken in its appropriate context, the jejuneness of certain chapters in mental anatomy, implying, as it does, the fewness of the mental elements, is a fact of extreme importance.

2. There is, however, a functional psychology, over and above this psychology of structure. We may regard mind, on the one hand, as a complex of processes, shaped and moulded under the conditions of the physical organism. We may regard it, on the other hand, as the

---

[1] G. Wolff, in *Zeits. f. Psych. u. Physiol. d. Sinnesorgane,* XV, p. 1 (August 1897).

collective name for a system of functions of the psycho-physical organism. The two points of view are not seldom confused. The phrase 'association of ideas,' *e. g.,* may denote either the structural complex, the associated sensation group, or the functional process of recognition and recall, the associating of formation to formation. In the former sense it is morphological material, in the latter it belongs to what I must name (the phrase will not be misunderstood) a physiological psychology.[1]

Just as experimental psychology is to a large extent concerned with problems of structure, so is 'descriptive' psychology, ancient and modern, chiefly occupied with problems of function. Memory, recognition, imagination, conception, judgment, attention, apperception, volition, and a host of verbal nouns, wider or narrower in denotation, connote, in the discussions of descriptive psychology, functions of the total organism. That their underlying processes are psychical in character is, so to speak, an accident; for all practical purposes they stand upon the same level as digestion and locomotion, secretion and excretion. The organism remembers, wills, judges, recognizes, etc., and is assisted in its life-struggle by remembering and willing. Such functions are, however, rightly included in mental science, inasmuch as they constitute,

---

[1] An article by Professor Dewey, entitled "The Reflex Arc Concept in Psychology," *Psychological Review,* July, 1896, seems to contain this idea of a functional psychology: *cf.* pp. 358, 364 f., 370. The article is especially valuable in that it has direct reference to the experimental work of Angell and Moore (*Psychological Review,* May 1896). Professor Caldwell, too, insists on the importance of the study of psychological function, but forgets that function presupposes structure (*International Journal of Ethics,* July, 1898, p. 466).

It may be mentioned, further, that a good deal of the introductory writing in works upon modern logic and theory of knowledge—Bosanquet, Bradley, Hobhouse, Wundt—falls within the scope of functional psychology as here defined. Professor Creighton, indeed, suggests that logic may be distinguished from the psychology of thought as physiology, the science of function, from morphology, the science of structure (*An Introductory Logic,* p. 6). I think that, in spite of present overlapping, logic has a field of its own, which is not the field of functional psychology—though the question cannot be gone into in this place.

in sum, the actual, working mind of the individual man. They are not functions of the body, but functions of the organism, and they may—nay, they must—be examined by the methods and under the regulative principles of a mental 'physiology.' The adoption of these methods does not at all prejudice the ultimate and extra-psychological problem of the function of mentality at large in the universe of things. Whether consciousness really has a survival-value, as James supposes, or whether it is a mere epiphenomenon, as Ribot teaches, is here an entirely irrelevant question.

It cannot be said that this functional psychology, despite what we may call its greater obviousness to investigation, has been worked out either with as much patient enthusiasm or with as much scientific accuracy as has the psychology of mind structure. It is true, and it is a truth which the experimentalist should be quick to recognize and emphasize, that there is very much of value in 'descriptive' psychology. But it is also true that the methods of descriptive psychology cannot, in the nature of the case, lead to results of scientific finality. The same criticism holds, as things stand, of individual psychology, which is doing excellent pioneer work in the sphere of function. Experimental psychology has added much to our knowledge, functional as well as structural, of memory, attention, imagination, etc., and will, in the future absorb and quantify the results of these other, new coordinate branches. Still, I do not think that anyone who has followed the course of the experimental method, in its application to the higher processes and states of mind, can doubt that the main interest throughout has lain in morphological analysis, rather than in ascertainment of function. Nor are the reasons far to seek. We must remember that experimental psychology arose by way of reaction against the faculty psychology of the last century. This was a metaphysical, not a scientific, psychology. There is, in reality, a great difference between, say, memory regarded as a function of the psychophysical organism, and memory regarded as a faculty of the substantial mind. At the same time, these two memories are nearer together than are the faculty memory and the memories or memory complexes of psychological anatomy. There is, further, the danger that, if function is studied before structure has been fully elucidated, the student may fall into that acceptance of teleological explanation which is fatal to scientific advance: witness, if witness be necessary, the recrudescence of vitalism in physiology.[1] Psychology might thus put herself for the second time, and no less surely though by different means, under the dominion of philosophy. In a word, the historical conditions of psychology rendered it inevitable that, when the time came for the transformation from philosophy to science, problems should be formulated, explicitly or implicitly, as static rather than dynamic, structural rather than functional. We may notice also the fact that elementary morphology is intrinsically an easier study than elementary physiology, and that scientific men are so far subject to the law of inertia, whose effects we see in the conservatism of mankind at large, that they prefer the continued application of a fruitful method to the adoption of a new standpoint for the standpoint's sake.

I may, perhaps, digress here for a moment, to raise and attempt to answer two questions which naturally suggest themselves: the questions whether this conservatism is wise, and whether it is likely to persist. I believe that both should be answered in the affirmative. As has been indicated above, the morphological study of mind serves, as no other method of study can, to enforce and sustain the thesis that psychology is a science, and not a province of metaphysics; and recent writing shows clearly enough

[1] *Cf.* Burdon Sanderson, in *Science Progress,* March, 1896.

229

that this truth has need of constant reiteration. Moreover, there is still so much to be done in the field of analysis (not simply analysis of the higher processes, though these will of course benefit in the long run, but also analysis of perception and feeling and idea) that a general swing of the laboratories towards functional work would be most regrettable. It seems probable, if one may presume to read the signs of the times, that experimental psychology has before it a long period of analytical research, whose results, direct and indirect, shall ultimately serve as basis for the psychology of function; unless, indeed,— and this is beyond predicting,—the demands laid upon psychology by the educationalist become so insistent as partially to divert the natural channels of investigation.[1]

The remaining four psychologies may be dismissed with a briefer mention. 3. Ontogenetic psychology, the psychology of individual childhood and adolescence, is now a subject of wide interest, and has a large literature of its own. 4. Taxonomic psychology is not yet, and in all likelihood will not be, for some time to come, anything more than an ingredient in 'descriptive,' and a portion of individual, psychology. It deals with such topics as the classification of emotions, instincts and impulses, temperaments, etc. , the hierarchy of psychological 'selves,' the typical mind of social classes (artists, soldiers, literary men), and so forth. 5. The functional psychology of the collective mind is, as might be expected, in a very rudimentary condition. We can delimit its sphere and indicate its problems; minor contributions to it may be found here and there in the pages of works upon psychology, logic, ethics, æsthetics, sociology, and anthropology; and a few salient points—the question, *e.g.*, of the part played by the æsthetic sentiment in the make-up

---

[1] I have elsewhere given reasons for the opinion that it is functional psychology which may be expected to bring direct assistance to the teacher: *e.g.*, in the *Amer. Jour. of Psych.*, April, 1898, pp. 420 f.

of a national mind—have been touched upon in essays. But we must have an experimental physiology of the individual mind, before there can be any great progress. 6. Lastly, the labors of the evolutionary school have set phylogenetic psychology upon a fairly secure foundation, and the number of workers is a guarantee of rapid advance in our understanding of mental development.

The object of the present paper is to set forth the state of current opinion upon the question of the structural elements of mind, their number and nature. It may be doubted, at first sight, whether anything like a consensus of opinion can be made out. "Every psychologist of standing," wrote Kulpe in 1893, "has his own laws of association."[1] Every psychologist of standing in the year of grace 1898, so the reader may think, has his own favorite 'unique' process. Does not Brentano advocate an ultimate 'judgment,' and James a 'fiat of the will,' and Stout an ultimate 'thought'? Is there not the perennial controversy about the 'third conscious element,' the process of conation, the 'activity experience'? Are not even the clear waters of the psychology of sensation troubled by the possibility of an 'efferent' conscious process, a sensation of innervation? The questions are importunate, and cannot be lightly brushed aside. We will begin, therefore, by examining a test case: Brentano's irreducible 'judgment.' I select this, because Professor Ebbinghaus, in his recent Psychology, seems to put a structural interpretation upon it. He himself classifies the elements of mind (we shall return to this classification later) as sensations, ideas, and feelings; Brentano, he says, ranks alongside of ideas the element of judgment.[2] If this account is correct, we must admit that the morph-

---

[1] *Outlines of Psychology,* p. 190.

[2] *Grundzüge,* p. 168. It is only fair to say that Professor Ebbinghaus' remarks here are very brief, and that he promises to return to the subject in his second volume.

ology of mind is still a battlefield for individual opinions; we shall hardly escape the difficulty by the mere statement that Ebbinghaus is an experimentalist, and Brentano not.

When, however, we turn to Brentano himself, the matter assumes a different complexion. Brentano's principal criterion of psychical, as contradistinguished from physical phenomena, is that of 'intentional inexistence' or 'immanent objectivity,' which we may paraphrase as reference to contents, direction upon something as object.[1] "Every psychical phenomenon contains in it something as object, though not every one in the same way. In ideation something is ideated, in judgment something admitted or rejected, in love and hate something loved and hated, in desire something desired, etc."[2] This is evidently the language of function, not of structure. Indeed, Brentano uses the phrases *psychisches Phanomen* and *Seelenthatigkeit* interchangeably; his 'fundamental' or 'principal classes of psychical phenomena' are the 'mental activities' of ideation (not 'idea!'), judgment and interest (love and hate, the emotive processes).[3] The spirit of his whole psychology is physiological; and when, on occasion, he discusses a point in anatomy,[4] he leaves his reader in no doubt as to the shift of *venue*. Now the mental elements of the experimentalists, the bare sensation and the bare feeling, are abstractions, innocent of any sort of objective reference.[5] We cannot fairly compare Brentano's 'judgment' with them. Nay, more, we cannot fairly say that he would have posited an ultimate judgment process *if* he had adopted the anatomical point of view; since he has not adopted it, the speculation is absurd. The 'psychology from the empirical standpoint' is a systematization of mental 'activities,' *i.e.*, of the

[1] *Psychologie vom empirischen Standpunkte,* I, pp. 101 ff.; esp. p. 127.
[2] *Ibid.,* p. 115.
[3] *Ibid.,* pp. 44, 50, etc.; pp. 256 ff.
[4] As in Book ii, ch. I, §3.
Reference to contents, meaning, comes with the mental formation. I have attempted to show its relation to structure in my *Primer of Psychology,* pp. 95, 297, etc.

232

mental functions of the human organism.

This wave, then, has not overwhelmed us. Escaping it, we may turn now to the positive side of our enquiry. Our appeal will lie, in the first instance, to the experimentalists; but the omission of references to works on descriptive psychology is largely due to considerations of space, and does not by any means necessarily imply that the authors of these works differ from the writers quoted. Some of the 'unique' processes still left outstanding will be taken up at the end of this discussion.

We set out from a point of universal agreement. Everyone admits that *sensations* are elementary mental processes. There is, it is true, diversity of opinion as to the range of contents that the term shall cover. Wundt identifies the peripherally excited and the centrally excited processes. ''For the psychological attributes of a sensation the circumstance [of external or internal initiation] is entirely irrelevant. . . . It is only the central stimulus that always accompanies sensation.'' Külpe retains the name 'sensation' for both classes, but declares that they ''must be treated separately, as they normally present characteristic differences.'' Ziehen and Ebbinghaus, on the other hand, draw a sharp line of distinction between the 'sensation,' which is externally aroused, and the 'idea' (in Lotze's sense), which is its centrally aroused substitute, and so recognize two elements where Wundt and Külpe see only one.[1] The divergence, however, is not serious. It seems to depend, primarily, upon the admission or exclusion of genetic considerations. If we rule that these are foreign to a strictly morphological exami-

[1] Wundt, *Grundriss d. Psych.*, 2te Aufl., pp. 43, 46 (Eng. trans. of 1st ed., pp. 36, 39); Külpe, *Outlines*, p. 35; Ebbinghaus, *Grundzüge*, I, pp. 167 ff.; Ziehen, *Leitfaden d. phys. Psych.*, 4te Aufl., pp. 17, 19, 128 ff. (Eng. trs., 2d ed., pp. 22, 25, 153 ff.); Münsterberg, *Beitr. z. exp. Psych.*, I, Einleitung, §§ iv, v; *Die Willenshandlung*, ch. ii, and elsewhere. In his recently published book, *The New Psychology*, Dr. Scripture puts aside the question of mental classification altogether (pp. 39, 305), and groups the chief psychological experiments under physical headings. I cannot but regard this as a retrograde step. There is, surely, no reason for giving up, without a struggle, what our predecessors have so hardly won.

nation of mind, the question of one sense element or two becomes a problem set by analysis to analysis, capable of resolution by analytic methods; it is a subject for dispute 'inside the ring,' and is thus upon a quite different level from the question, *e.g.*, of an elementary will process.— We may note, in passing, that the innervation sensation, while it remains a theoretical possibility,[1] has been generally given up by the experimental school.[2]

Simple *affective* processes, again, are regarded by a large majority as elemental. Both Wundt and Kulpe are at some pains to make clear the essential difference between sensation and affection. Lehmann and Ebbinghaus are equally explicit. Ziehen does not give a place to feeling beside sensation and idea; his chapters are entitled 'The Affective Tone of Sensation' and 'The Affective Tone of Ideas,' and his treatment makes affective tone an attribute, coordinate with the intensity and quality of sensation and the clearness and contents (meaning) of idea. Nevertheless, he speaks in one passage of the cortical substrate of this tone as "an entirely new psychophysiological process." Munsterberg, on the other hand, denies the ultimateness of feeling altogether, and seeks to reduce it to the sensations accompanying movements of flexion and extension, reflexively released.[3] There is further, an 'inside' controversy as to the number of affective qualities. But analysis will some day settle the question whether there are two of these (Kulpe), or two

---

[1] See, *e. g.*, A. D. Waller, *The Sense of Effort, an Objective Study. Brain*, xiv, p. 179.

[2] Wundt, *Phys. Psych.*, 4te Aufl., I, p. 431; Külpe, *Outlines*, p. 267; Ziehen, *Leitf.*, p. 57 (trs., p. 71); Münsterberg, *Beitr.*, I, pp. 23, 26; *Willenshandlung*, pp. 75 f.; Müller, *Grdl. d. Psych.*, pp. 311 f. (cf. Müller und Schumann, in *Pfl. Arch.*, xlv, pp. 80f.); Stumpf, *Tonpsych.*, I, pp. 166 f.

[3] Wundt, *Grundriss*, pp. 34, 39 ff. (trs., pp. 29, 33 ff.); Külpe, *Outlines*, pp. 20, 225 ff.; Lehmann, *Hauptgesetze d. menschl. Gefühlslebens*, pp. 12 f., 17, 22; Ebbinghaus, *Grundzüge*, p. 168; Ziehen, *Leitf.*, pp. 35, 127, 143 (trs., pp. 44, 151, 171). Cf. Fechner, *Vorschule d. Aesthetik*, I, pp. 8 ff. Münsterberg, *Beitr.*, I, p. 23; IV, pp. 216 ff. Exner holds a position somewhat simliar to that of Münsterberg.

in the sphere of sensation and many more in that of idea (Ziehen), or an inexhaustible variety under the six heads of pleasantness and unpleasantness, tension and relaxation, excitement and tranquilization (Wundt).[1]

It is natural, in view of the intrinsic difficulty of the subject, that the psychology of feeling should be in a less settled state than the psychology of sensation.[2] All the more striking, when we consider the close relation that obtains between 'feeling' and 'will,' is the unanimity with which experimentalists reject the doctrine of a specific will process. "There is no reason," writes Ebbinghaus, "for looking upon acts of will or appetitions as elementary forms of the mental life." And Wundt, Kulpe, Ziehen, and Munsterberg are of the same manner of thinking.[3]

No fourth candidate for elemental rank has appeared. No trace has been found, in all the minute analysis of the last twenty years, of a mental krypton or argon. It seems safe, then, to conclude that the ultimate processes are two, and two only, sensations and affections, though we must not forget that the first class, that of sensations, includes the two well-defined sub-species, 'sensation' and 'idea.'

How, now, are these different processes to be distinguished? What is our justification for looking upon them as last things of mind? Disregarding function, and trying to answer the question upon the anatomical plane, we can

---

[1] Külpe, *Outlines*, p. 232; Ziehen, *Leitf.*, pp. 127, 149 (trs., pp. 152, 178); Wundt, *Grundriss*, pp. 91 ff. (trs., pp. 77ff.); *Vorlesungen*, 3te Aufl., p. 239.

[2] It is, I think, a noteworthy phenomenon that the drift of thought in experimental psychology should be towards a structural dualism, and not towards Münsterberg's monism. On the modern revival of dualistic theories at large, see Külpe, *Introduction to Philosophy*, pp. 133 ff., 144, and a paper by G. Heymans, entitled *Zur Parallelismusfrage* (*Zeits f. Psych.*, XVII, pp. 62 ff.), with the literature there cited.

[3] Ebbinghaus, *Grundzüge*, I, p. 168; Wundt, *Grundriss*, pp. 35, 187, 214 ff. (trs., p. 29, 159, 183 ff.); Külpe, *Outlines*, p. 267; Ziehen, *Leitf.*, pp. 19 f. (trs., p. 26); Münsterberg, *Beitr.*, I, p. 23; *Die Willenshandlung*, ch. II (cf. p. 55). Wundt's remarks are especially worthy of attention, in view of the voluntaristic attitude of the *Logik* and the *Grundriss*. The voluntarism here is, of course, methodological only.

point at least to three valid criteria. We may refer to experience itself, and note that sensation and affection are irreducible for introspection. The one cannot be derived from, identified with, the other; they 'look' different or 'feel' different, however far analysis be pushed. Or we may have recourse to physiology. Since the structure of mind is conditioned upon the physical organization, we may differentiate sensation and affection by reference to their physical substrates. Or, again, we may seek a descriptive formula, which shall sum up the essential characteristics of the two processes. It is in this sense that Wundt is speaking, when he says that sensation qualities range between maxima of *difference,* and affective qualities between maxima of *opposition* or antithesis. Any one of these statements is adequate to the psychological requirements. The last of them, however, as Wundt's exposition shows, implies that we are already familiar with the *attributes* of which sensation and affection are constituted. We must devote a brief space to their consideration.

Once more, we set out from a point of universal agreement. "There are two indispensable determinants of every psychical element, quality and intensity." But discussion is not slow to begin. For these two attributes or determinants are, evidently of different kinds. Quality is specific and individual; it is quality that makes the elemental process a blue or a sweet, a pleasant or a *c* of the third octave. Intensity, on the contrary, is a general attribute, common to all modalities of sensation and qualities of affection. Hence, while some psychologists rank the two determinations together, as coordinate, others set aside quality for itself, and count intensity along with extent and duration as equipollent characteristics, whether of all the mental elements or of certain great groups of qualities. There is also much difference of opinion as to the precise place to be ascribed to the attributes of extent and duration. For Wundt, who holds a genetic theory, psychological space is the resultant of a two-dimensional system of qualitative local signs multiplied into, or fused with, a one-dimensional intensive system of sensations aroused by movement. It is, primarily, tactual or visual. Psychological time, in the same way, is the resultant of qualitatively varied feelings multiplied into, or fused with, the same intensive system of sensations. The affective processes, in abstraction, are timeless; the primary sources of temporal ideas are audition and 'internal touch.' It follows that space and time, extent and duration, can be predicated only of formations, not of elements. Spatial arrangement (Wundt makes no distinction between 'spatial arrangement' and 'space' as 'absolute contents') cannot "be an original attribute of the elements, analogous to the intensity or quality of sensations;" it "results from the bringing together of these elements," which means the "arising of new psychical conditions;" and the same thing is true of time. Opposed to this genetic theory is the nativistic view, represented for space, *e. g.*, by Stumpf, according to which every sensation has about it something of tridimensionality, a certain bigness or voluminousness, and every elemental process a certain duration.[1]

It is, indeed, hardly possible to keep the psychological problem of space and time clear of epistemology, on the one hand, and of psychogenesis, on the other. It would, perhaps, be unwise to make any attempts to do so, in a work meant to serve the purpose of instruction; for the

---

[1] Wundt, *Grundriss*, pp. 36, 121, f., 168, 185 (trs., pp. 30, 103, 143, 157). Ebbinghaus, *Grundzüge*, I, p. 169. Henry, *Raumwahrn. d. Tastsinnes*, pp. I, 159 f. Ziehen speaks of space and time as *Merkmale* of sensations. He gives a local-sign theory of space, but offers no theory of time. *Leitf.*, pp. 35, 62 ff., 99 ff., 109, 252 (trs., pp. 45, 76 ff., 121 ff., 130, 305). Külpe seems to have been led by the results of his structural analysis into a nativistic theory (*Outlines*, pp. 30, 328, 373, etc.), though there is no necessary connection between the two. For Münsterberg's position, see *Beitr.*, II, III. *Cf.*, further, Stumpf, *Raumvorstellung*, p .301; James, *Principles*, II, p. 135.

attempt would invoke a total disregard of historical conditions. Nevertheless, there can be little doubt as to the anatomical facts. I am wholly unable to conceive of a sensation or affective process as timeless, as lacking duration; analysis of mind as it is leaves me, always, with a process-lasting-some-time. I am equally unable to conceive of a visual sensation or sensation of pressure as spaceless, punctual; analysis leaves me, always, with a process-spread-out. On the other hand, I feel no constraint to regard the spreading-out as tridimensional. Neither does the surface itself necessarily imply the depth perception, nor need the relation of the surface to the ideating subject be present in consciousness. And the other sensations, tones, tastes, etc., as well as the affections seem to be entirely devoid of space attributes. In mental morphology, the perfect element (say, a sensation of color) shows us quality, intensity, duration, and superficial extension.

A similar difficulty confronts us with regard to the attribute of clearness. Variation in degree of clearness of the constituent processes in ideas is the anatomical equivalent of what is functionally termed the 'distribution of attention.' Wundt places degree of clearness on the same level with spatial and temporal arrangement. "As these attributes [clearness and obscurity, distinctness and indistinctness] arise always and only from the interconnection of the various psychical formations, they cannot be considered as determinants of the psychical elements." Yet, on Wundt's own principle of relativity, the same thing would be true of sensation intensity; we cannot say anything of the intensity of a sensation unless a formation—at least two sensations, side by side—be there for 'comparison.' Moreover, we must exclude genetic arguments here as before. If we make analytic introspection the test, we cannot but admit that the ultimate sensation may be conceived of as clear or obscure.[1]

I conclude, then, that the affective element is constituted of quality, intensity, and duration; the sense element (sensation or idea) of quality, intensity, duration, clearness, and (in some cases) extent.[2] Quality is intrinsic and individual; intensity and clearness are 'relative' characteristics; duration and extent are, very probably, extrinsic translations into structure of the lowest terms of a functional series. And the corollary is that the 'elements' of the experimentalists, as they themselves have been the first to urge, are artifacts, abstractions, usefully isolated for scientific ends, but not found in experience save as connected with their like.

It is unnecessary to pursue further our examination of structural psychology. Just as morphology proper, passing beyond the cell, becomes a morphology of organs, so does structural psychology, passing beyond the elementary processes, become an anatomy of functional complexes. The experimental psychologies deal, as do the descriptive works, with the perceptions and emotions and actions handed down in popular and psychological tradition. Külpe, working out a distinction which was quite clearly drawn in the physiological psychology of the younger Mill, has reduced all the 'higher' processes to two structural patterns: mixtures of intensities and qualities (fusions), and connections of spatial and tem-

---

[1] Wundt, *Grundriss*, pp. 36, 244 f. (trs., pp. 31, 208 f.). Külpe, *Outlines*, pp. 424 f. Ziehen's view is somewhat different: *Leitf.*, pp. 143 f. (trs., 171 ff.). I have used the phrase 'distribution of attention,' in the text, advisedly, since I have been brought by introspection to put little faith in the graded 'fringes' and tailings-off of obscure and obscurer processes which figure largely in some psychological systems.

[2] 'Locality,' Stumpf's *Tonfarbe*, Passy's *pouvoir odorant*, Müller's *Eindringlichkeit*, etc., are all attributes which admit of resolution into constituents. Miss Washburn has recently maintained the thesis that *familiarity* is a "peculiar property of centrally excited sensations." I do not think that this view of recognition will find general acceptance. In any event, however, familiarity would be a *fundierte* attribute, predicable not of the sensation but of the sensation complex. See this REVIEW, May, 1897.

poral attributes (colligations).[1] This reduction marks a decided step in advance; but its chief value lies in the suggestion of a plan of arrangement for the results gained by analysis of the basal functions. A discussion of these results themselves would far transgress the limits of the present paper.

What remains, now, is to assure ourselves that the various 'unique' processes of current psychology, not recognized in the preceding analysis, are conceived of in terms of function, and not in terms of structure. There is no room for doubt of this, in the case of Stout's *Analytic Psychology*. The author's use of the phrase 'mental functions,' his constant reference to Brentano, his insistence upon mental 'activity,' are indications enough.[2] In view of the similarity of standpoint, it may be interesting to compare his final classification with that of Brentano. The latter, as we have seen, ranks ideation, judgment, and interest as the fundamental functions of mind. Stout distinguishes two primary attitudes of consciousness: the cognitive and the volitional. Cognition includes thought and sentience as 'fundamentally distinct mental functions,' and thought, again, subdivides into simple apprehension and judgment. Volition, in its turn, includes "two fundamentally distinct modes of reference to an object," feeling and conation. We have, then, five 'fundamental modes of consciousness,' grouped under the two primary conscious attitudes.[3] The difference between

[1] *Outlines,* pp. 21, 276 ff. *Cf.* J. S. Mill, *System of Logic,* Bk. VI, ch. 4, § 3 (People's ed., p. 558).

[2] I take this opportunity, in view of Mr. Stout's criticism of my *Outline of Psychology* (*Mind,* July, 1897), of saying that there is no reason, as the universe is constituted, why he should not accept my analysis of structure, and I his analysis of function. If we disagree, it is not because our points of departure are logically incompatible.

[3] *Analytic Psychology,* I, pp. 50, 113 ff. It is, perhaps, worth while to remind the reader of the ambiguity of the term 'process,' according as it occurs in a morphological or a physiological context. Stout's use of the word is, naturally, very different from that of this article. The word 'function,' too, is not seldom employed by experimental psychologists—I am myself among the guilty—with a meaning different from that which it bears here. *Tantae molis erit* to found a terminology!

Brentano and Stout is at least as apparent as their agreement.

James' 'fiat of the will,' or "express consent to the reality of what is attended to," is also a functional process:

"This consent . . . seems a subjective experience *sui generis,* which we can designate but not define. We stand here exactly where we did in the case of belief. When an idea *stings* us in a certain way, makes as it were a certain electric connection with our self, we believe that it *is* a reality. When it stings us in another way, makes another connection with our self, we say *let it be* a reality. To the words 'is' and 'let it be' correspond peculiar attitudes of consciousness which it is vain to seek to explain."[1]

Lastly, I may refer in this connection to Dr. Irons' contention that emotion is an 'irreducible' process, an "ultimate and primary aspect of mind."[2] Dr. Irons has stated that the method of his enquiry is not genetic;[3] and his definition of emotion as 'feeling attitude' implies, that it is not anatomical.[4] But while his words are the words of function ('cognition,' etc.), his criticism is very largely criticism of the morphologists. It would seem that he has not fully recognized the difference between the two standpoints.[5] No one among the experimentalists has hitherto expressed a doubt—I venture to assert that no one ever will—as to the composite nature of the emotive process.

The burden of the argument has been that there is reasonable agreement, within the experimental camp, as to the postulates of a purely structural psychology, whereas there is pretty radical disagreement among the psychologists of function. Let it not be supposed, now,

[1] *Principles,* II, pp. 568, 569.
[2] This REVIEW, May, 1897.
[3] This REVIEW, May, 1898; *cf.* the no. of Nov., 1897.
[4] *Mind,* Jan., 1894.
[5] Although it has been clearly brought out by Professor H. N. Gardiner, in a criticism published in the *Psych. Rev.,* Jan., 1898, p. 100.

that this latter state of affairs is anything else than a disadvantage for psychology at large; above all, let it not be thought that the experimentalist rejoices at the lack of unanimity among his colleagues. It is a commonplace of the biological sciences that structure and function are correlative terms, and that advance in knowledge of the one conditions and is conditioned by advance in the understanding of the other. Only, in psychology, functional analysis—required by the living of our daily life—had been carried out to a degree sufficient for the successful prosecution of anatomical work, before the experimental method appeared. Structural psychology might proceed far on its way, even if the psychology of function had halted at Kant or, for that matter, at Aristotle. I believe that physiological psychology (in the sense of this paper) has a great future; and I subscribe fully to all that has been said of the critical subtlety of Brentano's discussions, of the delicacy of discrimination shown in Stout's recent book, of the genius of James' work. Nevertheless, I believe as firmly that the best hope for psychology lies today in a continuance of structural analysis, and that the study of function will not yield final fruit until it can be controlled by the genetic and, still more, by the experimental method—in the form both of laboratory experimenting and of interpretation of that natural experiment which meets us in certain pathological cases.

EDWARD BRADFORD TITCHENER (b.-Chichester, England, Jan. 11, 1867; d.-Ithaca, New York, Aug. 3, 1927).

Titchener studied primarily at Brasenose College, Oxford. However, he finished his training with Wundt, receiving Ph.D. from the University of Leipzig in 1892. In this same year, Titchener accepted an assistant Professorship at Cornell University. In 1910 he was appointed Sage Professor of Psychology at Cornell where he remained until his death.

It is not so much Titchener himself who concerns us, but his role as the spokesman of a major psychological outlook: the structural psychology. The primary datum of psychology is experience, the

242

trained introspective report of sophisticated observers (a descendent of Wundt's concept of *Selbstbeobachtung*). In such an approach, the accurate description of experience, not yet the cause, becomes the essential objective: modes of experience, elements, attributes, and their manner of interaction. It is not the individual who matters, but the general underlying laws of thought and experience which he helps to reveal. This is a modern Cartesian position in its most dynamic form.

Titchener's influence spread to almost every psychology department in the United States; in 1928 his students and associates formally organized themselves as the Society of Experimental Psychologists (having met informally since 1904), which exists today as a specialty and as a subdivision of the American Psychological Association. The present selection is Titchener's classic statement of his approach.

TITCHENER, E. B. "The postulates of a structural psychology." *Philos. Rev.* 1898, VII: 449-465. This is reprinted in its entirety by permission of the Managing Editor of the *Philosophical Review*.

See also:

TITCHENER, E. B.

a) *Experimental psychology: a manual of laboratory practice.* N.Y.: Macmillan, 1901-1904. This is the formal introduction of Wundt's methods and ideas to the United States.
b) *Lectures on the experimental psychology of the thought-process.* N.Y.: Macmillan, 1909.
c) *Systematic psychology. Prolegomena.* N.Y.: Macmillan, 1929.

BORING, E. G. "Edward Bradford Titchener" Amer. J. Psychol. 1927, 38: 489-506.

GENERAL PSYCHOLOGY
FROM THE PERSONALISTIC STANDPOINT
WILLIAM STERN

PERSONALISTIC FOUNDATIONS OF PSYCHOLOGY

I. THE SUBSTRATUM OF MIND

In the opening pages of this book the subject-matter of *all* psychology was designated in a twofold way as embracing the essential nature and activity of mind. Or in more general terms, the *substratum* and the *empirical facts* of mind. It was also stated ... that these two aspects cannot be studied independently of each other; they are mutually conditioned. The manner of conceiving the substratum of mind necessarily gives direction to the psychological study of mental data and makes possible explanation and interpretation of the empirical phenomena.

1. *Introductory Questions*

Do mental data have any "substratum"? Is there an entity *by which* they are substantiated and *from which* they issue? The question must be answered in the affirmative. In itself mentality is only a state of being or attribute, and not an entity. (That is why we purposely prefer the *adjectival* terms "psychical" and "mental" in order to express this contingent, "inherent" character.)

The attempt has often been made to deny a substratum to mind or at least to exclude it from all scientific investigation. In consequence the contents of mind as such were substantialized; ideas, conations, character traits, instincts, etc. were treated as entities that somewhere and somehow had existence, and supposedly dangled in space. This view disregarded the fact that within psychological experience itself—quite independently, thus far, of philosophical hypotheses—mental phenomena, processes, and states are simply *properties* of the concomitant individual self that "has" them. Not the existence of a substratum but only its *nature* is open to question.

Is the substratum to be thought of as an independent "soul"? This second question signifies: Does the substratum itself belong to the mental category? Does its sole essence consist in generating, in owning, in governing the mental realm? And is the substratum accordingly to be contrasted with the individual's non-mental being, with his body, as with something different and alien? This question is answered in the negative.

The assumption of a substantial mind would require (*a*) that the *mentality* of the individual, as the product of his mind, comprise a closed system of interrelations, (*b*) that the *individual* represent a substantial duality of mind and body, (*c*) that the relationships *between* mind and body be secondary as compared with the primary relationships that hold *within* each category, (*d*) that everything subsisting and taking place in the individual come *wholly* under the heading of mind on the one hand or of body on the other. ... As one existing counter-proposal we find the extreme view of materialism, which holds that material substance is the only reality; the substratum of what is called mind is simply the body; mind is constituted by physiological, bodily processes. It is not necessary to restate here the frequently reiterated philosophical arguments against materialism. *Psychology* disposes of it with indirect but telling contrary evidence: its own existence. There *is* a science of mind, and this science deals with something quite different from physiological processes that have been, as it were, merely translated into other terms; it deals with internal experience and events and the ability to have experience; and these categories are different from those of the purely physical world.

There remains but one possibility: The substratum of mind must be something *that has existence going beyond or prior to the differentiation into the mental and the physical,* thereby certifying the original unity of the individual. This formula sounds "monistic," for all monism attacks the substantial duality of *physics* and *psyche,* viewing both simply as characteristics of a single substrate (thus Spinoza: "Thought and extension are attributes of the sole substance."). But current monism neglects the question as to the *nature* of the substratum, for this is defined merely as being "at once physical and psychical"; other specifications are not admitted or pass for unknowable. Consequently monism remains on the same plane that was supposedly transcended by its denial of the duality, and it must rest content with affirming the persisting coexistence of the two disparate attributes ("parallelism") without being able to grasp the *meaning* of this correlation.

There remains the crucial question as to whether the substratum may be defined by *positive* criteria that in themselves belong neither to the purely psychical nor to the purely physical sphere; in other words, whether the categories "physical" and "psychical" can themselves be subordinated as secondary to another category that appropriately defines its essential nature. The affirmation of this view is the fundamental task of the personalistic theory. Not only from the philosophical point of view is the person a "psychophysically neutral" being, but he may also be characterized and *empirically* apprehended through qualities that exist apart from the differentiation into body and mind.

2. *Definitions*

We define the person as follows:

The "person" is a living whole, individual, unique, striving toward goals, self-contained and yet open to the world around him; he is capable of having experience.

Except for the criterion of "experiencing," which was purposely placed at the end, the specifications throughout are *psychophysically neutral*. Into the totality of the person are interwoven both his physical and psychical aspects. Goal-directed activity is manifested in breathing and limb movements as well as in thinking and striving. Independence of and exposure to the environment apply both to bodily functions and to conscious phenomena. The attribute "capable of having experience" is dis-

246

tinct from all the others in that it is *non-compulsory*.
Every person *must* be at all times and in all respects a
totality possessing life, individual uniqueness, goal-
directed activity, independence of and openness to the
world, *but not always consciousness*. Even at times when
nothing is being "experienced" the person exists, while
the loss of any one of the other attributes would suspend
existence.

There is a *science* of the human "person," that studies
him in his totality and psychophysical neutrality; it is
personalistics. It furnishes common hypotheses for all
specialized scientific studies of the person: for the
biology, the physiology, the pathology, the psychology,
of the person. *Psychology is the science of the person as
having experience or as capable of having experience*.
It studies this personal attribute, experience, in regard to
the conditions of its appearance, its nature, mode of
functioning and regularity, and its significance for
personal existence and life considered as a whole.

II. LIFE AND EXPERIENCE

1. *The Modalities of Life*

Only that which lives can have experience. "Life" is
the unity of being and acting in a totality open to the
environment. A living being is of such character that its
total *nature* is constantly being actualized through its
activity while likewise remaining a whole in its incessant
intercourse with the environment. This "having life"
is the basic principle from which any consideration of the
person takes its departure. Life comprises the fundament
from which all experience develops, that supports all
experience, into which all experience discharges. Life is
complete, while in comparison experience is fragmentary
and intelligible only in terms of life.

247

The question must here be brought up as to why the term "experience" (*Erleben*) and not the long-established term consciousness (*Bewusstsein*) is preferred in characterizing mind. The term "consciousness" originally had a completely intellectualistic meaning; it designated the condition in which the individual is a *knower* (of facts or of himself). Later the word was used more and more loosely (permitting references also to a foggy kind of feeling-consciousness, etc.), but its original purpose was always suggested whenever it was employed. It has become a matter of grave concern for the entire modern conception of mind, that mind came thus to be explained in terms of its latest and most refined characteristic, "knowledge." In the role of knower the individual is furthest removed from the estate of continuous and autonomous vital functioning.

Two quite different consequences may be derived from the orientation about "consciousness," both of which however, lead into *culs-de-sac*. As one possible consequence consciousness is separated abruptly from everything that is not consciousness, and psychology is limited strictly to the investigation of "conscious phenomena." Here the connection between experience and the background of life is sacrificed. The other possibility acknowledges this connection but defines the prerequisite of consciousness only by negating it. The indefinite negative term "the Unconscious" proceeds to signify a mysterious basic force that is regarded partly as a contradiction, partly as the origin of consciousness.

In the philosophy and psychology of the "Unconscious" from Leibniz through Schelling and Edward von Hartmann to modern depth psychology, was developed the basic principle that conscious phenomena cannot be understood or explained in terms of themselves alone. But this view was one that looked backward from the conscious mind, and its descriptions were necessarily affected by the prevailing conception of the conscious mind.

The thesis of personalistics, that "experience develops out of and into life," reverses the approach. The primary thing is really conceived as primary, that is, as bearing the stamp of life.[1] But here a fundamental question arises. What do we mean by "life" in reference to the *human* "person"? Not simply that life which is the subject-matter of current biology. In human beings life appears in *three modalities,* and in going from one to the other the personal world also, to which life is open, takes on diverse aspects.

The first modality was just mentioned as the *biological* in a narrow sense. Human life holds in common with vegetable and animal life those functions which bring the individual naturally and unquestionably into conformity with his environment. Self-maintenance and "self-steering," growth and maturing, reproduction, adaptation, mneme, are such *vital functions.* The "world" is present with respect to these functions as but an extended domain of life, as stimulus or raw material, as shelter or menace; it constitutes the vital world or *biosphere* of the person.

We may skip the second modality for the moment and proceed to describe the third, which contrasts with the first since it deals with the purely *human* sphere in the life of the person. Every trace of this third modality of life is absent in animals and plants. In this sphere every human being constitutes a substrate of value and at the same time the unique, meaningful center of a world that also consists of independent substrata of value, be they

---

[1] The use of the *terms* "conscious" and "unconscious" in psychological discussion can no longer be dodged. They have become currency that cannot be withdrawn from the every day commerce of science. We ourselves are not able wholly to dispense with the terms on the grounds of verbal simplification. But if the fundamental conceptions of this chapter be heeded, misinterpretations are no longer to be feared.

other individuals, societies, cultural, historical, or religious facts and ideals.

MODALITIES OF LIFE

Person	World
I. Vitality	Biosphere
II. Experience	World of Objects
III. Introception	World of Values

The aim of human life involves the affirmation by the individual, in his being and acting, both of his own intrinsic significance *and* of the objective significance of the world, so that he acquires reality as a person through the coalescence of the world of objective values with his own substance. This coalescence or incorporation the personalistic theory designates as *introception;* it denotes the activity that gives direction and form to all genuinely human life. The unitary and meaningful pattern of life that introception endeavors to establish is called *personality*. Although the concept of "person" in the sense given above may be applied to any individual animal, *personality* is an uniquely human category.

The concept introception is psychophysically neutral, covering as it does the purposes of life functions and not merely a mode of experience. This is also true of all specific forms of introception: loving, understanding, creating, consecrating, etc. While these are wholly inconceivable in the absence of consciousness, their true nature consists in personal modes of conduct and formative tendencies, in enacting intentions, which in view of their ultimate aim, project far beyond the limits of any "awareness." It is on this account that the theory of introception belongs not to psychology but to personalistics.

Between the first modality of life, vitality, and the third, introception, there is another, with which *psy-*

chology is directly concerned: the modality of *experience*. The "world" that belongs to this modality likewise occupies a position between the simple biosphere and the world of values. It is the *world of objects.*

2. *Experience*

a. Cleavage. The person is a totality, that is, a *unitas multiplex.* This must be taken literally. All the multiplicity included in the person, the hegemony of elements, events, phases, strata, is *integral* to the totality and not just superficially cemented to it or supported and conditioned by it; it is the *consonance* of multiplicity with the personal whole and of the person with the world, that makes human life possible.[2]

But this consonance is not merely a perpetuated harmony. The more amply a living totality is articulated and the more various the multiplicity integral to it, *the less self-evident* is its life. Whenever the simple modality of vitality is surpassed but the modality of complete introception is not attained, there is tension and dissonance in life, which resist immediate coalescence with the totality; a *dis-living* sets in. But since these cleavages affect the totality, which cannot be abandoned, they become life functions, assuming the special form "experience."

Experience, then, is life under cleavage and tension. Cleavage and tension can never exist as quiescent conditions; they are dynamic processes. Therefore dissonance is constantly being augmented or diminished. All experience consequently tends to become either *salient* against or *embedded* within the totality. Or more accurately, in any experience both tendencies are always simultaneously

---

[2] It is therefore absurd to project the essence of life back into a single tendency, some *particular* life-principle, some vital force, or whatever else may be suggested. The biological "soul" of "vitalism," as a special factor in a living creature, is quite as untenable as is the psychological soul-substance of spiritualism.

present, for complete cleavage would destroy the unity of the person while complete embedding would break off the tension and disrupt experience. *The different proportions of salience and embedding* give the process and content of every experience its special character.

The following examples may serve as an introductory illustration of these paired concepts. . . . When the initially vague feeling of danger leads to definite thoughts and to organized acts of will we have an instance of increasing salience. And when recollections of a loved one who has recently died gradually lapse into generalized and vague melancholy, embedding is on the increase.

Modern Gestalt psychology operates with the concepts Gestalt and "surrounding field." As conscious content the Gestalt occupies the outermost position at the pole of salience; while in contrast with it, the surrounding field recedes into the total state of the person and is thus embedded.

The proof that experience has cleavage is expressed first of all in the fact that it has *objects*. Living, with the individual, is absolute and unconditional, but his experience is always *of something*. Experience is transitive; it transfers to and aims at something that is not itself experience.

What *is* this "something" that is experienced? Here we have a new cleavage between the outside world and the person himself. That is, while these two components are one in the immediate vital modality and in the higher totality of introception, in experience they belong to life apart from each other. The individual experiences the outside world; external objects, values, laws, that are potential or actual, past, present, future, timeless; or else he experiences *himself;* his own strivings, values,

252

dispositions, inarticulate tendencies, former states of being, future possibilities. The scale of *objectified experiences* runs from the first tingle of a touch impression through perceptions, ideas, thoughts, to a complete world-view. The scale of *subjectified experiences* runs from the infant's vague feeling of being alive to the adult's completely formed consciousness of self and sense of his own importance.

Neither the one nor the other end of experience is ever fully reached because the complete sundering of person and world would destroy personal life and experience with it. Even so highly objectified a mode of experience as scientific knowledge never finds the "pure object" and is never able to extricate the world wholly from personal entanglements. And the highest level of development of subjectified experience, "self-knowledge," does not exactly reflect back the self in its undisguised essence; for the one experiencing and the thing experienced would then be one and the same, and the necessary condition of experience—cleavage and tension—would be destroyed.

Experiences that objectify and subjectify are thus like endless *voyages of discovery* into the objective world and the subjective self; the ultimate ports of "thing in itself" and "self in essence" are never arrived at in experience. The passage of objectification and subjectification through many stages constitutes another of the leading *motifs* of this book.

b. Appearance. Now although a gap always remains between the experience and its object, on the other hand a *positive* connection obtains between the two; for every experience *points to* some existence (in the external world or in one's own person). This positive relation is suggested by the terms mirroring, *appearing.* (For example, past events appear in a remembrance; the personal weakness of the subject is mirrored in a feeling of inferiority.)

253

In experience the object is given a second time, not, to be sure, actually duplicated, but as a reflection that is both similar and dissimilar to, close to and distant from, that which it reflects. It is *appearance,* but not disembodied appearance; on the contrary it is *authenticated appearance.*

Under this double aspect conscious phenomena must consequently be regarded now as approximations of reality, now as aberrations of it, i.e., as "illusions." It is a fact of importance that not only are there illusions of objectifying experience, that is, sensory illusions, memorial illusions, illusions of judgment; but that illusions of subjectifying experience also arise in a corresponding manner; the inner picture that anyone has of himself *must* necessarily contain illusory items. (Here kinship may be found between insights of modern depth psychology and the basic principles of personalistics.)

As measured by its objects, then, experience is imperfect and non-congruent; still it deals with appearance and reflection. This raises the question: *What is the significance for the person of this double nature of all experience?*

Experience is fragmentary. The sum total of life processes and contents is not convertible into experience, nor does it need to be. Only such particular occurrences within life as involve *tensions* are at the same time experienced internally. The individual is mirrored in his own experience in so far as he is in a *struggling* state, i.e., in so far as internal resistance and inhibition interrupt the plain current of life. And the world is reflected in his experience in so far as it deviates from the individual and his course of life as something salient, alien, questionable and even hostile.

The more acute the tensions, the more multiform the frictions, the more impermanent—and hence uncertain—

the objective situations under which the individual lives, the stronger is the conscious representation of his life. It is on this account that: (1) the life of the adult has so much more of awareness than that of the child; (2) civilized man has so many more possibilities and so much more need of experience than primitive man; and (3) changes and catastrophes in life, new impressions, and new developmental phases, are endowed with consciousness in a wholly different manner than are the more quiescent states and conservative phases of existence.

Yet the life-modality of tension and indeterminateness is not a domain of life set apart by itself, but is always in close connection with both the other modalities, vitality on the one hand, introception on the other. Hence experience itself merges under a thousand imperceptible shadings into those life modalities that have no need of consciousness, just as it continually arises from them in the reverse order. The marginal states comprise an especially interesting object for psychology, for in them experience no longer possesses the easily identifiable character of clearly salient patterns of consciousness, but becomes more and more deeply embedded in life until it entirely disappears within it.

In other instances, to be sure, the *point* can be assigned at which an inner tension or an external disturbance gives rise to a conscious phenomenon. This point constitutes the *threshold* of experience. Thus the concept of threshold extends much further in personalistic psychology than in psychophysics, where it is restricted solely to the coming to consciousness of sensory impressions.

While experience is fragmentary, this incompleteness is not *capricious* and meaningless, but fits perfectly into significant and purposeful connections of personal life. For life is dammed up in experience; energy used up is accordingly drained from some other immediate process.

(For example, as long as the individual has full awareness of voluntary motives and conflicts of motives, his
capability of acting is crippled.) On this account the
economy of experience is an essential factor in the person's budget of energy. This is regulated effectively by
appropriate *selectivity,* which shunts life processes into
experience in accordance with the *personal relevance* of
the tensions and disturbances. This is alike true of subjectified and objectified experience. The individual himself becomes his own object of awareness only with
respect to those items which maintain some distance from
him, and similarly for external things; only that small
sector of his world may become his objective world which
is still too remote to be merged with his biosphere or his
sphere of introception, while yet close enough to attract
notice as something split off and alien. *Exclusion* by
selection also has personal significance; forgetting, suppression, "being taken for granted," automatization, in
short, any process generally ascribed to the "Unconscious," is organized within the total purposes of the
personal life-process.

A similar situation obtains for the *incongruence* of the
content of experience with its object. In designating such
dissonances as "illusions" we did not do justice to their
positive role in the life of the person. As we have seen,
experience is always on the offensive. It must therefore
serve in the struggle as weapon and instrument, as prevention and cure. For this reason, experience cannot be
a smooth and unyielding plane mirror, uniform in clarity,
reproducing self and world with equal exactitude and
unerring accuracy; rather is it an elastic envelope of
many folds about the person, reflecting, with its wrinkles
and hollows, tangles and variations of form, in accordance with the demands of the personal state of tension,
so that the proportions are altered, the reflected light is
strengthened, weakened, or extinguished. The individual

experiences *himself* so as to live on the best possible terms with himself. And he experiences the *world* in such a way that the foreground appears large, the background small, important items clear, incidental items blurred, the thing loved worthy of love, and life worthy of being lived.

This reduction of internal and external reality to patterns of experience is, to be sure, never final; for the incongruence of image with reality produces new cleavages of life that in turn engender new experience; thus the supplanting of naive experience by more critical experience, the progressive correction of internal and external illusions. is in itself one of the principal activities of consciousness.

III. MIND

Our theory must now be brought into alliance with the central concept of the science of psychology. What is "mind"? What things may be called "mental?" And in what sense do they become objects of psychological study? We begin with this definition: *"Mind" is everything about the person that is experience or that is essentially related to experience.* In explaining this definition we shall follow a course contrary to that of the foregoing section; we shall work up from *below,* i.e., from actual, singular items of experience, through the capacity for experience, to the person.

1. *Experiencing*

a. Patterns of experience. Contemporary experience may run its course in continuous, flowing activity; it is then *unpatterned,* vague, deeply embedded in the personal totality. But it may also appear as a unitary pattern, clearly marked off from other patterns of experience. Such a total configuration of experience has its com-

257

mencement, rise, climax, decline, and termination, and is structured and formed in terms of itself. Thus there are patterns of thought-experience, of volitional experience, of aesthetic experience.

The general relation mentioned above between experiencing and living is naturally repeated for each individual item of awareness; every such pattern of experience is the partitive appearance of a "life pattern." The concept "life pattern" proves to be necessary since life as such may also become actualized in relatively delimited part-wholes. A circumscribed act of will is a life pattern; only a few portions and aspects of it are represented in the experiential pattern of volitional consciousness belonging with it.

b. Phenomena. The *content* of what is presently conscious to the experiencing person, is called a mental *phenomenon.* It is mind in its purest but also in its narrowest sense, without admixture of the non-mental; and hence in its delimited state it is unrelated to that to which it is attached and which gives it significance.

A pure psychology of phenomena would necessarily be smothered by pure description. Nevertheless phenomena play a fundamental part in psychology since they constitute, as it were, the *original material* that psychology must describe, analyze, and classify in order to be able to interpret and explain it.

The differentiation of phenomena (into sensations, ideas, feelings, thoughts, conations, etc.) as well as their articulation (as Gestalten or grounds, complexes, chains of ideas and the like) is an object of psychological investigation. *But all further activities of psychological research are removed from the phenomenal plane.* For the subsequent concern is with data that are no longer themselves contents of experience, but are related to experience and may therefore be called "mental" in a *broader* sense.

"Phenomena that are not experienced" is a self-contradiction. The designations "unconscious idea," "unconscious feeling" are handy—but absurd. The contents of experience are not things that may be taken out of experience and placed somewhere else, and that may perhaps be later repossessed by experience with their identity preserved. If the term "unconscious" is not to be renounced, it must at all events be restricted to mind in the *broader* sense, that is, to personal states, acts, and dispositions.

c. States and acts. The relationship of the person to his contemporary experiences is both of having and acting. The individual *has* experience and he *acts* through experience. This is simultaneous, for there is no experience in which both are not united. But the relative importance of each may be so variable that we have a right to designate many experiences as *passive,* and other experiences in which the person is involved as a directive, formative, selective agent, as *active.* Striking examples of passive experience are the mood of coziness, daydreaming; of active experience, a vigorous and concentrated train of thought, an inner conflict between inclination and duty.

The *act* that governs an experience is itself no longer a content of experience, and is thus not "mental" in the narrow sense. It may indeed be *represented* in consciousness by phenomena, as a feeling of activity, sensations of strain, etc., but such phenomena are only precipitates or reflections (that may be imperfect or even deceptive), and not the act itself. The designation "mental act" is nevertheless applicable in the *broader* sense to an act that is directed upon mental phenomena, or *in so far* as it is directed upon such phenomena. An act of thought is thus "mental" because the contents and process of thought that it produces and directs are mental phenomena. An act of will is "mental" in so far as it includes volitional experiences (phenomena of need, motivation, choice, decision). But this second example shows that the usefulness of the term "mental" is limited. For the act of will as a whole takes its meaning from the purposive unity of mental experiences and bodily actions; it is a psychophysically neutral, a *personal* act. The psychologist has the right and the duty to separate and analyze the mental aspects which it contains, and to consider them for themselves; but if he consequently calls the whole a "mental" act, he must constantly keep in mind that he is designating only dependent partial aspects, and that he is missing the meaningful *totality* of the act. It may be seen once more from this how immediately personal categories are superordinate to both the purely mental and the purely somatic.

2. *Dispositions*

A particular pattern of experience is restricted to a definite present. It begins and ceases; some other kind of experience or activity without experience both precedes and succeeds it. Are we to limit the concept "mind" or "mental" solely to the fragmentary and chaotic occurrence of phenomena, states, and acts? In the general usage of language it was long ago decided otherwise, and this usage we shall follow; for under the personalistic theory we are justified in broadening the concept "mind" to cover *potential experience* as well. The person is a meaningful unity in his total conduct of life; his goal-directedness impels us to insert every single item into the *personal-historical* relationship and to see in this relationship, as it were, the potential background; i.e., the tendency and readiness, in short, the "disposition," for the production of present items.

After the 18th century doctrine of "mental faculties" (*Vermogenslehre*) had been shipwrecked in the 19th century, psychology was for a long time determined to succeed without any "dispositional" categories whatever. We now know that this is impossible. Concepts like memory, imagination, intelligence, temperament, character-trait, suggestibility, etc., are more than a mere classification of ideas, feelings, and actions. These signify at the same time the *lasting* attitude and capacity of the person to actualize such items, given the opportunity, in definite ways. Dispositional concepts are, however, scientifically useful in modern psychology only if they are distinguished from mental "faculties."

a. Dispositions are not rigid and compartmentalized mental powers that might exist independently side by side, but are the *dependent radiations* of a single personal entelechy. There is not in reality an isolated memory or an isolated intelligence, etc. On the contrary all these are only moments, aspects, perspectives, of the person's total life. But science must assimilate these perspectives which were laid down in the structure of the person, and is therefore obliged to emphasize one or another disposition from time to time, without ever forgetting that various dispositional trends are shared by every single *concrete* experience.

b. Dispositions are possibilities for action having a range of free play, not powers discharging a sole function, and are consequently not the only basis for what actually occurs within the person. Other factors deriving from the external world *converge* at all times with dispositions. There is no pattern of life or of experience, no condition or mode of behavior of the person that could be derived exclusively from dispositions, just as there is no such item that could be uniquely determined by the milieu. The milieu has an effect only because *susceptivity* to its influences is preestablished in dispositions. For their part, dispositions must be supplemented; they eventuate into explicit action only because the environmental situation affords them the stimulus or material for doing so.

This *convergence* theory makes it possible to transcend the equally one-sided points of view of nativism and empiricism. We must neither seek to explain man solely in terms of the "inborn" and specific qualities that he possesses at the outset, nor may we regard him merely as a passive mechanism for receiving fortuitous external influences.

c. Dispositions, viewed teleologically, are possibilities in a twofold sense; as implements and as directional determinants of personal functioning.

Example: A mnemic disposition includes the *ability* to make use of the effect of previous patterns as well as the *readiness* to utilize them in a specific manner (e.g., to enrich ideational activity with visual imagery).

Thus in every disposition there lodges at once *potency* and *tendency*. But according to the one perspective or the other either the potency or the tendency may be considered the primary characteristic of a disposition; accordingly *instrumental and directional* dispositions may be distinguished. As between the two, *intelligence* is an instrumental disposition, because of the *instrumental* significance that it has for the most varied purposes. In contrast, *interest* is a directional disposition, for it includes the lasting attitude of the person toward definite *aims.*

d. Dispositions may *vary* according to time, potency, and tendency. While dispositions are indeed *lasting possibilities,* it does not signify that they must necessarily accompany the *entire life* of the person from birth to death. There are dispositions of quite diverse temporal structure.

The mental instability and lack of balance of many people at the time of puberty is doubtless dispositional in character. Yet when the period of puberty is over no trace of this "epochal" disposition need any longer be present.

Dispositions may also be connected with very definite life-situations; during an illness or before an examination the individual is quite differently "disposed," bodily and mentally, than at other times.

But even *lasting* dispositions, which cannot be conceived apart from the life of the person, are not always present in exactly the same aspect. Instinctive tendencies, the capacity for mneme, the capacity for thought, etc. are part of the nature of every individual, but undergo many alterations in the course of life. From a completely latent state they develop sooner or later into a state of readiness; in this process their potency acquires force and their tendency becomes definitive. What was originally only a vague, highly ambiguous "potentiality" gradually solidifies into a characteristic trait. Even the *direction* of their tendency may be changed in the course of time; character traits and bents of interest may vary within certain limits. And the *degree* of readiness may undergo periodic or aperiodic fluctuations; a disposition may be so charged with energy that the slightest impetus suffices to actualize it; at other times it is difficult to set off or is wholly latent.

This variability of particular dispositions prompts us to raise again the question of causation. They are clearly not, as the doctrine of "faculties" insisted, permanent original powers that, being irreducible in themselves, furnish the causation through life and experience. Rather are they influenced in part by the natural and cultural conditions of the milieu (climate, education, influence of society, etc.), and in part by the totality and the singularity of the person, whose radiations they are. Again the convergence theory proves true.

e. The term "mental" is applicable to dispositions in its *broad* sense only. These do not, of course, *appear* as such in consciousness; in its dispositional guise intelligence, for example, is not a thought phenomenon but the basis for possible thought phenomena. In this case, however, the designation "mental" as applied to the disposition is not likely to be misunderstood because its activity is directed upon mental phenomena (content and process of thought).

It is otherwise when the manifestations of a disposition are themselves no longer exclusively mental or physical, but are psychophysically neutral. Then the disposition may be called "personal" rather than "mental."

Here are three examples. *Temperament* is the provision sort of personal dynamic; this dynamic (e.g., of a "sanguine" individual) is manifested in the tempo, abundance, change, openness, lack of restraint of personal activity generally, be it a matter of goal-directed and expressive *movements* of the body only, or solely of *experiences* in the domain of temper and conation. *Character traits* signify permanent attitudinal sets for certain kinds of acts of will; but acts of will are personal acts, i.e., psychophysically neutral processes which include motor activities as well as aspects of experience, but are not purely mental phenomena and acts. *Mnemic* dispositions too, such as exercise, are not purely mental in nature; verbal memory, for example, covers the readiness for speech movements as well as for images of words.

3. The "Person" and "Personality"

The path from below upward took us from concrete, particular phenomena to states and acts that include them but are still concrete in every case, and from these to both temporary and lasting dispositions. But since the multiplicity and coexistence of the latter cannot be final, these too must be brought into an inclusive unity; and this unity is the person. In what sense is the designation "mental" to be applied to the person as such?

We may preface the answer with a few words in regard

264

to *animals,* for the problems relating to man will thereby gain in clarity.

According to our definition, to be sure, the animal individual is likewise a "person," but almost wholly a "vital person" (organism). Its activities are virtually confined to the lowest of the three life-modalities, i.e., "vitality." Accordingly the modality of experience has but a rudimentary significance for animals as compared with man. Consciousness is merely appended as an incidental epiphenomenon which accompanies inhibited and strained vital functions.

Since the modality of introception is entirely lacking, all functions of consciousness which direct and prepare introception are also lacking. (Similarly the animal's *world* is almost solely biosphere; an objective world is present in scanty traces at best.)

This structure of the animal individual implies that the science of animal life is and must remain essentially biology. There can never be an animal *psychology* possessing the independence and systematic organization of human psychology; and it is no accident that behaviorism, which is restricted to the study of vital modes of behavior and their relation to the biosphere, developed directly from animal investigations. In *man* the modality of experience plays a totally different part, and therefore the human person is "mental" in quite another sense and to another degree than the individual animal.

It is characteristic of man that *experience has an intermediate position between vitality and introception.* The human mind is both a superstructure built upon the foundation of "unconscious" vital activity and a substructure for the introceptive acme of life. The individual must become alienated from the self-evidentness of his merely biological nature and thereby try to raise himself and the world to the plane of objectivity; and he is constantly dominated by the striving to transcend this alienation on the still higher level of life charged with value in a world of values. And this dual import of his life can be achieved only by *experience*. Consciousness is sublimated—refined, subjugated, shaded—vitality; on the other hand it is an adjustment to one's values of existence and to those without.

Here are two preliminary examples of this mediating function of consciousness: From purely vital sensitivity develops conscious perception that leads to the comprehension of an objective world, and ultimately to its introception into a systematic scheme of the world and of life. The purely vital sexual function becomes sublimated to feeling-experiences of longing and desire, which, as love-experiences, proceed to make ready for the introception of another self into one's own personality.

The capacity for experience thus changes the *human* being from a purely animalistic, vital person into a human, introceptive personality; it transforms his *world* from a mere sector of life into a system of objects that invite introception. On this account the human mind has great instrumental and radial (symbolic) significance. On the one hand, the *service* of mind is a broadly outlined mediating function of the activities of personal life; on the other, mind *represents*—illustrates, symbolizes—the location of the individual between vitality and value.

But the instrumental and the radial significance of mind, however inclusive they may be, are never anything but derived meanings. "Mind" does *not* have any intrinsic meaning, in the sense of final irreducible import. Human personality simply cannot be characterized as mental because mind must in turn be characterized by its significance within and for human personality.

4. *The Relation of the Mental and the Physical*
a. *General aspect.* Under the personalistic conception

the ancient "mind-body" problem receives a new direction, and at the same time loses much of its former significance. The individual is not partly body and partly mind, but a person with the capacity for experience. He is a portion of a world that, although bounded on the outside, nevertheless continually exchanges substance and function with all other portions of the world; this is his corporeality. And he also has the capacity to reflect himself and the world inwardly; this is his mentality. The life of the person includes *both; accordingly there is no experience and no capacity for experience that is not bound up with the physical aspect of life and with bodily functions.*

How, specifically, is this connection to be regarded? Certainly not as an "interaction" in the Cartesian sense. For that theory assumes the existence of *two* substances in the individual that are to act upon each other, and the hypothesis falls with the rejection of a substantial mind. Nor is it to be regarded as a "psychophysical parallelism," which in theory asserts a thoroughgoing, unambiguous, and constant correlation of mental and physical items. According to this view a definite physiological excitation corresponds to each elementary mental phenomenon, a succession of excitations to each succession of mental phenomena, a physical pattern or Gestalt to a mental Gestalt ("isomorphism") and a region of the body to every mental disposition, as its seat (doctrine of localization).

This conception is inadmissible simply because of its elementaristic assumptions. For there are no special mental or physical items in the personal totality that are at once so isolable and so stable that they could form *among themselves* a direct relationship, independent, as it were, of the person. Every relationship of the physical and the mental *passes through the person,* and is first set

267

up and afterward directed by his total activity and total aims. Moreover, whether the correlation is constant or variable depends upon its significance within the personal entelechy.

Example: A particular brain cell does not "experience" a definite idea when it is excited; rather does the *person* respond to a definite stimulus *situation* with a *total* reaction that is physically concentrated chiefly in certain cerebral tracts and that mentally results in an ideational experience.

It must not be considered a piece of sophistry to introduce the "total person" between the physiological and mental processes, and no mere obvious truism should be seen in the fact that physiological and mental processes occur in the same identical person. For the person is not here regarded as a mere go-between or passive theatre of psychophysical events, but as their true generator and carrier, governor and regulator.

The reference to the person of both the physical and the mental alike permits the psychophysical relationship to be conceived as a *meaningful* connection, whereas ordinary parallelism or isomorphism must rest its case with establishing the conjunction of two series that are wholly disparate from each other. When we called attention above to the fact that everything pertaining to the person has *instrumental* and *radial* significance for him, we intended it also to hold by inclusion for the meaningful relationships of *physical* items to the *experiencing* person.

b. Instrumental significance of the body. The person makes use of his body as an implement in the service of his experience. There is considerable *teleological* correlation which is nevertheless quite different from psychophysical parallelism. The total end of the person implies that a system of bodily organs is available for the highly *salient,* graduated, and structured modes of experience; this organization is itself highly differentiated and adapted to graduated special functions. This is the central nervous system. On the other hand, the *embedded,* more diffuse modes of experience and the dispositional states of mind are connected with the functions of circulation of the blood, assimilation, internal secretion, etc., that is, with such functions as are interwoven with the organism in its totality.

Moreover stability or variability of bodily functions is adapted to the special activities that they must perform in the service of experience. Those experiences that scarcely go beyond the vital sphere are relatively constant in nature, both phylogenetically and ontogenetically; thus the corresponding bodily processes may be established in a fixed manner for the most part in race and individual alike. That is why psycho-physical correspondence in the domain of instinct and habit has for the most part a stereotyped character. Contrariwise, it is a peculiarity of higher types of experience that they are continually being readjusted to the changing activities of life through a process of give-and-take, and become connected with perpetually new patterns. They thus require organic implements that are mobile, capable of changing position, and capable of forming new combinations.

This is true of the peripheral as well as the central regions of the body. Why is the human hand adapted to playing the piano? Because each finger movement is *not* associated with a definite touch, a definite tone, a definite impulse to movement, but is predisposed for endless coordinations. The same proves true within the central nervous system. In contrast to the spinal cord, with its stereotyped and inherited sensori-motor coordinations, the cerebrum is the properly qualified instrument for the admission of changing experiences, for the production of different syntheses in thought and imagination, for creative activity that is not closely tied to the past but is in line with the future. It is *able* to serve as such an instrument because its parts and their functions are *not* associated irrevocably with definite contents of experience, acts, and abilities.

This contrast between the stereotyped and the flexible in bodily functioning must not be understood as a dualism. Both modify every organ and every organic activity; but the manner in which stability and liability are *connected* with the person's activities through special bodily organs or functions differs radically according to the nature of the service to be performed.

It is therefore a justifiable and fruitful psycho-physiological inquiry to seek relatively generic and constant correlations between mental and physical items. But this is only *one* perspective; the rigid coordination must be tempered by recognition of the capacity of such correlations to be transformed and made novel and individual, and to have more than one meaning.

It is very instructive to follow the periodic alternation of these two views in the study of nerve and brain physiology during the past century and a half. At one time detailed hypotheses were set up along the line of "specific energies"; i.e., with every particular place and process in the nervous system was correlated a quite definite, unique mode of experience (sensation, idea, volition). And in the same way even the mental dispositions were conceived to be connected with fixed regions of the cerebrum (phrenology in the eighteenth century, the doctrine of sensory, association, speech, and motor centers in the nineteenth century). But such a parallelism of parts was repeatedly dissipated by a totality view that rejected the specific assigning of mental activities to isolated regions and elements of the brain and emphasized the many-sidedness and

270

plasticity of the cerebral apparatus in its relations to the person's total end.

At the present time this latter view is again decidedly in the ascendant (Lashley, Goldstein, and others). This time, however, onesidedness is avoided, and the attempt is being made so to conceive the *twofold function of the nervous system,* in a manner analogous to the personalistic interpretation indicated above, as to ascribe both specificity and elasticity to it. The existence of "centers" in the cerebrum is consequently not disputed (how indeed would that be possible in view of the countless proofs from anatomy, physiology, pathology, and clinical examinations?), but these centers are no longer regarded as fixed local organs that are solely and immutably the determinants for storing up, associating, and promoting the activity of definite mental functions. They are simply regions that have peculiar *readiness* for the performance of special functions for which they are predisposed (but not predestined) by heredity.

How greatly the elasticity of psychophysical correlations is influenced by the person's total goal-structure is shown by the phenomena of *substitution.* These may likewise be peripheral or central. A person whose right hand is injured writes (although imperfectly) with the left. The blind man cannot of course "see" with his groping hand, but he can exercise the mental functions of recognition and discrimination with it that would otherwise require an optical receiver. And even the incapacitation of a brain center need not result in the utter disruption of the mental phenomena connected with it; restoration of function, though of course to a restricted degree, can take place through the medium of other portions of the brain. Deaf, dumb, and blind people are able to learn to speak (by means of a language of touch). Their "speech center" must accordingly have a wholly different structure and arrangement from that of people with normal senses, for it possesses its functional capacity not by virtue of appropriate nervous connections with the ear and the vocal organs, as in their case, but by virtue of connections with the hand, which transmits signals and receives impressions of touch.

c. Radial significance of the body. The meaning of the body for the person is not however simply its instrumentality; it also has radial or symbolical meaning, i.e., bodily states and movements portray the nature of the person. Since the inner experiences likewise have radial or symbolizing significance of this sort ... the one and the other class of phenomena are *united* in producing the psychophysically neutral *expression* of the person.

Once again elementaristic psychophysical parallelism is conquered. It is not a question of the nature of some unknowable arrangement by which certain feelings are linked up with certain postural movements, accelerations of the pulse, etc. *The arrangement by which the person expresses his life inwardly and outwardly includes both components in one.* Rise of the tide of personal life, for example, is expressed as a unity in acceleration of tempo of both ideas and movements; in expansiveness of feeling as well as in extension of the body and spread of the arms. *Feeling could not be experienced at all if it did not at the same time achieve bodily expression.* In the same way, lasting mental dispositions have their bodily expression in permanent features and states of the physiognomy, of gesticulation, bodily build, demeanor, etc.

IV. The Person-World Relation

a. The "personal world." As a totality that is "open to the world" the person, in living and experiencing, is occupied with incessant intercourse with the world. But every person has his own personally relevant world, briefly, his *personal world.* There are a number of general

272

specifications of the nature and structure of this world of every person, which differentiate it in principle from the other "worlds" (mathematical, physical-cosmological, sociological, and historical).

In contrast to the cosmic world, the personal world is *centered;* each person is the center of his own world. But this center is not, like the origin in a mathematical system of coordinates, a point lacking extensity and quality. Being the person, it is possessed of structure and content. All other characteristics of the personal world are generated from the structural and meaningful correspondence of the personal center with the world.

In accordance with the three modalities of personal life, the personal world also takes on three modalities (mentioned above in passing): *biosphere,* the domain of vital functions; *objective world,* the goal of objectifying experience; *introceptible world,* the cosmos of individualized carriers of significance and value, and of claims that become related to the person's center.

b. Valence and materiality. Not only the person but also *his* world is *developed* in perpetual commerce of events between person and world. The "milieu" of a person is not that portion of the objective world that happens to be nearby and consequently influential; the environment is rather the portion of the world that the person *brings* near to himself because he possesses receptivity or sensitivity for it, and to which he also *seeks to give* that form which is appropriate to his essential nature. Two persons who live long amid the same scenery, in the same society, or even in the same room, nevertheless do not have the same milieu; for each person exerts diverse selection and shaping upon things, events, and circumstances; on this account the total pattern and the atmosphere of the two personal milieus also vary.

This commerce between person and world is so intimate that there is no separating cause from effect in any given case. With regard to ends, however, it is possible to distinguish two directions of activity in the person-world relation; the one is centripetal (world-person), the other centrifugal (person-world). In the first case the person is receptive and responsive in encountering the world, in the second he is seeking and giving. The person's activity is thus consummated in *reactions* in the former instance, in *spontaneous actions* in the latter; in the former the personal world has *valence,* in the latter, *materiality.*

These principles put into the shade the impoverished "reaction" theories which view all that transpires in the person, even mental activity, solely as processes of response to environmental stimuli. While such a conception may be efficacious to a considerable extent in zoology (although even here it is insufficient by itself), it is at all events wholly inadequate for human beings. Those specifically human modes of living that are accompanied in large measure by experience are certainly never consummated through mere responses; under them, on the contrary, the person has in his own right a determinative effect upon the world; his relations with the world are extended and multiplied by reason of his *spontaneous* activities. The world is the point of attack, the raw material, for these spontaneous actions, though it also proceeds to offer resistance and to set limits, so that spontaneous action is integrated with reaction and is thereby made specific. The sovereignty of pure creativity is quite as impracticable a principle as passive acquiescence to the world; in reality there is simply endless oscillation between spontaneity and reactivity. *The personal world is at all times both the destiny and the product of the person.*

c. Homogeneity and heterogeneity. As to quality, the person-world relationship is sometimes "homogeneous," sometimes "heterogeneous," in each of the two directions described above.

Centripetal homogeneity; "assimilation." By virtue of his membership in and his devotion to the world the person participates in that entire transpersonal nexus which constitutes his world. In him are actualized the characteristics of breed and clan, of nation and race; from his environment he takes over customs and usages, values and convictions, modes of action and conduct.

This process of assimilation is in itself psychophysically neutral; to it are subject bodily form and style of movement as well as ideational content and mental set. It operates, moreover, both in phylogeny and ontogeny; inherited tendencies make the individual an homogeneous member of the racial order; imitation, cultural acceptance, suggestion, bring about his assimilation into the rest of the world.

Centrifugal homogeneity; "impress." From his spontaneous inner activity every individual leaves by impress upon his personal world the stamp of his essential nature. He translates his intimately personal ideas into transpersonal performances; he serves, consciously and unconsciously, as a model and suggestive influence; he extends, as it were, the sphere of his personality into the surrounding atmosphere and thereby forms the community, the home; he determines the spirit, the form, even the substance of his sector of influence *in accordance with his own nature.* He also determines the *future.* Indeed, the most significant effects of impress are those that outlast the individual originator and constitute his immortality, through the survival of his personal cast in descendants, and of his personal ideas and accomplishments in human culture.

To be sure, homogeneity, whether centripetal or centrifugal, never results in out-and-out duplication; its actual effect can be but one of *similarity.* This limitation is due to the fact that no community of person and world can ever entirely silence the rhythm and specific melody of either factor. However great the power exerted by the world to make the individual fall in with its trend, he nevertheless continues to be a ''person'' and can react to its influence only as a person, thereby modifying and deflecting its very tendency. And vice versa, however strikingly novel and penetrating the effect of the impress by which the genius of an artist, the founder of a religion, a statesman, puts a new face upon the world; since this modified world has no creative genius, it can absorb novelty only in a diluted, simplified form; and since it meanwhile follows its own laws and is subject to still other influences, it perforce modifies all acquisitions. In other words, there is some *heterogeneity within* every homogeneous relationship between person and world, and its importance is not confined to this point.

The *meaningful relationship* between person and world is a *resultant,* and its total meaning can be achieved only because each factor contributes a *different* part-meaning, according to the diverse nature of each. When the one component is dominant, the other is subordinate; the reaction to danger is defence or flight. A similar *heterogeneity* affects a future relation; the farmer plants now to harvest in the future; the merchant's present negotiations bring future profits. Everywhere the two terms have complementary significance. Since they occupy different positions in the relationship, they *differ* from each other; as stimulus and response, means and end, cause and effect, need and gratification, motive and act. In every case a single term is incomplete by itself, it takes the other to *complete* it.

Paired terms give the most clear-cut appearance of heterogeneity when they form an antithesis. But an antithesis is itself a particularly strong relationship. The person-world relation is dialectical in that *what is denied by its antithesis contrives to be completed by its antithesis*. The person seeks in the world that which he *lacks*, and reacts against the world with the force of a *counteraction* whenever his own being must be asserted in opposition to the process of assimilation.

V. The Personal Dimensions

"Space" and "time" are categories that are treated by widely divergent scientific disciplines, but in a special way by each. To these various doctrines of dimension we must subjoin a *personalistic* view. The "personalistics of dimensions" occupies a position between objective science, which treats space and time as items of epistemology, mathematics, physics, history, etc., and psychology, which deals with the consciousness of space and the consciousness of time. Its subject matter is the *personal dimensions, i.e., those extensions in definite directions through which every person actualizes himself and his personal world*. In contrast to the "dimensions" of mathematics the personal dimensions are not pure formal principles but qualitative attributes sustained by a constant inner development. Along certain dimensions personal life is *partially* converted into experience, and it is this experience with which the psychology of space and time is concerned.

1. *The Inward-Outward Dimension*

The mathematical and physical world is without a center, for any desired point may be taken as an origin and this may be replaced by any other point. *The personal world has a natural center* from which and toward which everything pertaining to it extends; this is the person himself, about whom it is oriented . . . This center is essential and indispensable as long as the person and his world exist.

277

The origins in mathematical dimensional systems are "points," that is, simply bare loci of coordination having no consistence or form of their own. *The center of the personal world,* the person, is a finite, structured totality which as such *includes extension within itself.* On this account we shall have later to distinguish between personal dimensions proper to the person and those proper to the world. The person-world relationship is thus the relationship of *two* systems of dimensions, and this relationship may in turn be expressed dimensionally as *inward-outward.* This comprises the basal polarity within the personal world; in the non-personal world there is nothing analogous to the inward-outward dimension. (A mathematical point has no "inwardness"; everything related to it is "outer.")

The *polarity* of the inward-outward dimension involves the assumption that person and world confront each other in basic opposition. Wherever they are one, as in the first and third modalities of the person-world relationship, this *dimensional polarity is lacking.* In the primitive state of the infant, who as yet exists wholly in the biosphere, nothing is inward or outward. This is also true in the exalted state of introception; for the lover the loved one, for the devout man divinity, is no longer something "outer" that is opposed to his "inner" being. Thus the *poles* inward-outward exist only for the middle modality, where the world becomes *objectified.* The things and processes of my world, other people who are alien to me, together with their life-patterns and experiences, are "outside," whereas my heart and my lungs, my thoughts and feelings, are "inside." It may be perceived from this criterion that the inward-outward dimension is psychophysically neutral. "Inside" and "outside" may alike be both physical and mental.

The present. Since inward-outward polarity is not in

278

existence at all times, we need a term for that primordial principle of dimensionality which obtains *before* a state of opposition is reached and *after* it has been left behind. ... In what dimensional sphere does the infant live who does not yet distinguish himself from the external things? And the lover to whom the loved person has ceased to be as an external object? This fundamental sphere may be called the present, or more precisely *the personal present*. Its nature harbors the germ of the entire personal dimension-system.

In the personal present, the incident life pattern (of the person) and the coincident *situation* (of the personal world) are completely *fused into one*. For example, at this very instant there belong to *my* present the thought that is forming and the impulse to guide the pen, as well as the object "pen" and the objective writing that is appearing on the paper.

The personal present is "spatio-temporally" neutral; it is the unseparated "here-now." In this respect our concept of present differs from the purely temporal present of objective science.

The personal present is not inextensive, but has *extension and structure*. A melody to which I am listening, or the action of writing that I am pursuing, is given to me in a "now" without any contingent loss of the temporal pattern of the melody (or of the action). At the same time the action of writing is taking place *here;* no point may be assigned for this "here"; not only my body but also objects extending out from it in space, the paper, the desk, belong to the "here." The structure of the present at any given time depends upon the personal relevance of the factors contained in the life pattern and the situation.

There is *superposition of personal* presents. "Here" is the desk, but "here" also is my room, and even the city in which I reside; *always according to the personal perspective.* Thus I have "here" a book that I need at the present instant; i.e., I need not go elsewhere to buy or borrow it. But it is not "here" (within reach of where I am at the instant), but "there" in the bookcase, over to which I have to go. It is the same in the case of time. "Now" I am occupied with writing this line, but I am also "now" writing out the chapter on "dimensions"; indeed, I am "now" writing a *General Psychology* (in comparison with my past and future concern with other subjects).

The two branches. The *two branches* of inward-outward dimensionality extend from the personal present, "inward" into the person and away from the world, "outward" through the world and away from the person. The branches differ in characteristics; *along* each there are both gradations and qualitative shadings (Fig. I).

The inward direction leads first to the regions of the person that are nearest his present; in so far as these are separate from the world while still confronting it, they constitute the personal *surface.* Further inward the personal *depths* are reached, i.e., those moments of the person that have no *immediate* reference to the direct external situation, but which represent in a specific way the self-contained being of the person. Further progress in the same direction signifies passage from the explicit and concrete to the implicit, the underlying, the potential. At the fictitious limit of this incursion into the personal depths is the complete indeterminateness and inner infinity of the person.

The outward direction covers the world-zones of the near and the far. Here too progress is from the definite to the indefinite, from the actual to the possible, until it finally lapses fictively into the wholly contentless, into outer infinity.

Those external features are *"personally near"* that maintain meaningful relations with the personal present;

they surround it like an aura. The near region still possesses immediate personal relevance, and is the echo of contact or readiness for contact. Protection or danger is "near"; it is in this domain that the person expressively manifests his essential nature. "Near" is the goal of present striving; "near" is the just completed action whose consequences are still at hand.

That is *"personally distant"* which either lies *below the threshold* of personal relevance or is *split off* from the present and the near region in opposition. Thus the unknown seat-mate of a street-car passenger is "distant"; while yesterday, when he was still happy, is "distant" to the person visited by sudden misfortune.

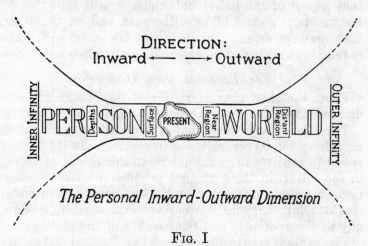

The Personal Inward-Outward Dimension

FIG. I

All the features of the inward-outward dimension that were discussed above are *"spatio-temporally"* neutral. Just as "present" has more than a merely temporal meaning, so have "surface," "depths," "near region," "distant region" more than purely spatial significance.

Both examples show that the *graduations* along these

dimensions need not be commensurable with objective measures of space or time. My seat-mate in the street car is distant from me while the friend toward whom I am riding is already near to me—in contradiction of the linear distance from both;—all that counts is personal relevance to my present life.

The attributes of the inward-outward dimension are also in themselves neutral in regard to *value*. "Superficiality" is to be considered inferior only in connection with certain definite personal trends; from other points of view immediate contact with the world may be a requirement for the person and therefore have positive value. Similarly, "depths" may signify on the one hand that aspect of the individual which is still activated by rudimentary phases of primitiveness, and on the other, such features as are constitutive of his truest self, when it remains unfalsified by externals or by alien influences.

2. *The Person's Own Dimensions*

From the chief characteristics of the person are also derived the chief characteristics of his dimensionality.

The life of any individual is directed; this direction may, however, be *reversible* or *irreversible*. In the former case life consists in continual re-establishment of being, in the latter, in the continual production of new being. Conservative maintenance on the one hand and progressive development on the other are expressed dimensionally as the *spatiality* and *temporality* of the person.

The explicit separation of these two dimensional modes is possible, to be sure, only in abstraction; the living reality of the person always consists in a greater or lesser amount of stability *and* lability, of self-conservation *and* self-development. Consequently the person has spatiality that is temporarily charged, temporality of a spatial order, common features and similarities of spatial *and* temporal attributes.

282

The person extends *spatially* in all directions, but not uniformly so. External limitation and internal structuring make extension especially prominent in three directions. But because of the very fact that this *tridimensionality of the person* is bound up with his essential constitution, it has a quite different character from the tridimensional space of Euclidean geometry, which is deprived of quality. The three chief personal dimensions, *above-below, before-behind, left-right,* are saturated with quality and are not interchangeable; and for *each* dimension the two poles are not distinguished solely by positive and negative signs, but in terms of quality and rank.

The *above-below* dimension is the principal axis of the person (the "vertical" axis). "Above" is a specifically human localization; in thought and speech "to be above" is the symbol of power and conquest. The *before-behind* dimension is highly charged with temporal dynamics; "forward" indicates personal aims; the individual's actions proceed from his forward surface; by his forward surface he presents himself expressively to the world. The *right-left* dimension produces the basic semblance of symmetry; the poles of this dimension are interchangeable to a certain degree.

The time proper to the person is first of all the span of single life-patterns. The present for each particular life-pattern includes both duration and succession; think of the immediately lived rhythm of dance movements, or of a cohesive yet articulated act of will.

Personal time is *not simply undimensional* like mathematical time. It would be so if it consisted solely of duration. Within it there would then be only differences in length. But in reality there are, for periods of equal duration, the most varied temporal *patterns;* for example, an endless number of rhythms, melodies, etc. This is possible only in multidimensionality. As a matter of fact, personal time also has its dimension of breadth; *simultaneity*. The salient features of a temporal pattern; for example, the tones in a melody do not supersede the continuum of duration, but are superposed upon this continuum which simultaneously marches in the background of the event. Now if the melody is not composed of single tones at all, but of full chords (each of which signifies ample "simultaneity"), the temporal current of this life pattern accordingly increases in volume.

The irreversibility in the progression of a life-pattern stamps the sequent items dimensionally as "earlier and later," and with respect to their connectedness, gives them the signs of position "before" and "after." Only the fact that all these essential time references appear in a single, concrete life-pattern makes it possible for them to be applied to more inclusive personal periods of time and ultimately to the life-span. Duration progressively covers each single pattern of life and takes into itself new patterns and leaves earlier ones behind.

In this manner a peculiar double motion arises which divides off personal time fundamentally from mathematical time. The latter has uniquely and solely a forward direction. Essential to personal time, however, is its (unstable) *center*, the temporal present, which moves *forward* constantly under the steady conductance of duration, while its concrete contents assume the reverse motion, that is, *backward*, and continue to recede further and further. Consequently *future* and *past* are regarded in personalistics as "progressive" present (development) and "recessive" present (history). Combined with the actual present at a given time, they constitute the unity of the course of personal life.

All this is beyond the province of pure psychology. Even though he does not know it, the person has a future in the form of the fulfillment of the tendency of life, and

284

though remembrance is lacking, he has a past in the sense of the continued effect of what has already been experienced ("mneme").

Since the direction of time is irreversible, all that is *purely* temporal in the life of the person is *unique and irrevocable*. The end-points of personal time, birth and death, are likewise unique and irrevocable. In this uniqueness lies that which is specifically *historical* about each personal life, the incomparable dignity of each instant of life. But life itself resists the absolute character of the uniqueness because it constantly strives for reestablishment and stability. Thus personal time contains features that offer resistance to its own incessant progression and it thus seems to contradict the abstract concept of temporality while tinging it with some spatial flavor. Such an indication is the tendency to return into oneself by rhythmatizing the activities of life, by constant repetition of customs and habits. Finally, the irrevocability of the very bounds may be denied, both through action (by influencing the future after one's death, by stabilizing power in making wills, etc.) and through belief (in metempsychosis and immortality).

3. *Dimensional Intercourse between Person and World*
   a. The dimensionality proper to the person is extended homogeneously into the world. The example just suggested of disposal by will is pertinent, for it assumes that "my" time will continue its passage after my death. It is the same in regard to space; the three personal dimensions of space become extended beyond the limits of the body. "Above" does not stop with my head but includes the hat upon it and the ceiling above it; "behind" is not only my back but also the wall nearest to my back.
   b. But the objects of the world are not present solely in relation to "me" as the center, but have their own

significance and their own proper dimensionality. From this fact results a personified *recentralizing* of all dimensions. The object (whether living or lifeless) has *its* before and behind *its* past and future, etc. *about its own center*. Examples: The cupboard which, according to my orientation, stands "behind" me, nevertheless has its own "before" and "behind" that are independent of my position in relation to it. I may say of my great-great-grandchildren, "They will long since have overcome the turmoil of the twentieth century," meaning that what is the present for me is the remote past for the *new* centre of reference of my descendants, which is set in *my* future.

c. None the less it is not sufficient for the person to *attribute* dimensions to objects and persons outside himself; he must also come to terms with the dimensions of the world, and adapt himself to them. This is the occasion for a development in two directions; certain extensions proper to the person must be made manifest as proper *only* to the person, and are therewith *subjectified;* others become recognized as having community with others and are therewith *objectified.* Let four persons be seated at a square table; then the cupboard against the wall is to the right for one of them, in front for the second, to the left for the third, in back for the fourth; these dimensional specifications are thus entirely bound up with the subjects and their position at the instant. On the other hand, the ceiling is "above" for all of them; this specification is consequently far more objective. It may be supposed that "above" even has *cosmic* objectivity for a naive person; the sky is not above for him alone but for everybody; it is "really" above—while *his* objective world has no "right" and "left." In the cosmological system of science even the objectivity of "above" has disappeared. In this case qualitative differences in general, which we found to pertain to the personal dimensions, are sacrificed to objectification. All qualities of personal dimensions are likewise expunged from the space of Euclidean geometry as "merely subjective"; but in such space tridimensionality and perpendicularity are still objectified, and the symmetry arising from the personal right-left dimension is transferred to all three dimensions. Non-Euclidean geometry has at last banished even tridimensionality to the domain of subjectivity; its space is completely de-personalized.

A corresponding de-personalizing is exhibited in the quantitative features of dimensions. "Near" and "far," "large" and "small," etc., are determined altogether by personal relevance in the system of the person's own dimensions. But life in an objective world demands identification, comparison, and measurement,—and incidentally the de-subjectification of quantities.

It is a matter of moment for personalistics that these objectified dimensional modes and measures be again *introcepted* into the system of dimensions proper to the person. The *life-space* of the mature adult is no longer so lacking in objectivity as the "vital space" of the infant, but it is also not as impersonal as the fictitious, decentralized, and non-qualitative space of mathematics. As a special structure "my home" is wholly centered about me; it is an expressive extension of my personality, it is attuned to my aims, and serves as my mete, bounds and shelter. At the same time, it is also articulated with sociological space (through limitation of property and through communality), with terrestrial and cosmic space ("my" dwelling-place in this street, this city, this country, etc., projection of my personal locality on objective maps, etc.), with mathematical space (through the application of measures that make "my" space "comparable" with all other space). But even while the relatively circumscribed space and locality of the person become coordinated with these transpersonal spatial arrangements, the latter are introcepted on their part into the now enlarged and refined space of the person; despite all its connections with objectivity it continues to be *the space of this person's living.*

The objective *time-periods* of the seasons of the calendar, of holidays, as well as the incisive determinations of time by political world events (which affect all contemporary people in common), accordingly belong also to the personal structure *of my personal life-time.* Thus, for example, the temporalization ''before and after the world war'' has constituted for all people of a certain generation the most trenchant landmark in their individual courses of life.

4. *The Psychology of the Dimensions*

Transition from the personalistic theory of the dimensions to the *psychology of the dimensions* is effected through the question: how does the individual *experience* space and time?

That which we have portrayed thus far as dimensional aspects of the person and the personal patterning of the world, extends far beyond the reaches of human consciousness; yet in principle each of these relations *can* become the content of experience at any given time.

One answer to the above question must be negative: there is no *specific* mental function by means of which the individual experiences his dimensions, that is, there is no special ''space sense'' or ''time sense.'' Or to state it in positive terms, the individual can experience his dimensions and those of his world through all his mental functions. There exist the feeling of space, the perception of space, the idea of space, the thought of space, imagined space, spatial conations; and similar functions for time. *Space and time are psychologically interfunctional.* This of course does not silence the question as to how each of

288

these special modes of experience is constituted. It must not be thought that independent departments of mind are involved at those times when space perception alone, imaginal space alone, etc., are considered; for it is always a question of the same personal space, the same personal time, being projected differently in experience on each occasion; and there are intermediate forms and transitions by the thousand between the various modes of experience.

This warning against pigeonholing must be made especially emphatic in the case of one particular problem with which the psychologist is deeply concerned: that of the *perception* of the dimensions. The fact that sense perception happens to be constituted under different "modalities" has led to the practice of cutting up the investigation of dimensions and treating visual space, tactual space, auditory space, etc., as independent. These special forms of psychological space are artificial fictions; indeed they are misrepresentations of the true nature of mind. In so far as the individual experiences space in general, this is the *one* space of his personal existence and world; specific sensory constituents of vision, touch, etc., contribute materially to this experiential structure of space, but they remain submerged and interdependent aspects. This is similarly true of time. *Space and time are psychologically intersensorial.*

A second mode of attack for all psychological investigation of dimensions is furnished by the fact that there are two dimensional systems, one of the person and one of the world. I can experience my own spatiality and temporality in a subjectifying manner and the world in an objectifying manner. In either case I can experience the totality of the spatio-temporal structure, or an isolated dimension, a pattern, a direction, an extent. Moreover, I can apprehend the relations of both systems to each other as conscious content, as for example when I perceive, imagine, or think of the position of any external object in relation to my own position at the time.

LOUIS WILLIAM STERN (b.-Berlin, April 29, 1871; d.- Durham, North Carolina, U.S.A., Mar. 27, 1938).

Stern received his Ph.D. from the University of Berlin in 1892. He became Instructor of Psychology at the University of Breslau in 1897; Associate Professor in 1907. He remained at Breslau until 1916, when he became Director of the Hamburg Psychological Institute and Professor at the new University. In 1934 he left Germany and came to Duke University as Professor of Psychology. He remained here until his death, four years later.

Stern introduced the concept of the Intelligence Quotient (I.Q.) in 1911 as a means of giving quantitative expression to the concept of intelligence. His early work in founding the modern approach (Stern influenced such people as Piaget, for example) is of great importance in its own right. Stern's meaning for us today, however, lies not so much in child psychology, as in his statement of basic principles. The task of Psychology is pre-eminently the conscious life of man. The inherent unity of the human personality, the salient (conscious) human motives, the healthy dynamism of the vital adult ego,—these are concepts which the recent and more brilliant achievements in the theories of psychopathology have overshadowed. In the manner in which Stern has described the structural levels of the human personality, and de-emphasized the embedded (unconscious) levels, he has expressed some cf the growing dissatisfaction with extrapolations from the psychopathological approach to the human person. In this, his ideas resemble those of Kurt Lewin. The present selection is his most concise statement of this philosophical anthropology.

STERN, W. *General psychology from the personalistic standpoint.* N.Y.: Macmillan, 1938 (1935). Trans. H. D. Spoerl. Chap. IV: "Personalistic foundations of psychology."

See also:
STERN, W. a) *Die differentielle Psychologie in ihren methodischen Grundlagen.* Leipzig; Barth, 1911. Introduction of the I. Q.
b) *Person und Sache: System des Kritischen Personalimus.* Leipzig: Barth, 1906-1924, 3 vol. This is Stern's major philosophical statement.

c) *Psychology of early childhood.* N. Y. Holt, 1926.

STERN, W. & STERN, C. *Monographien über die seelische Entwicklung des Kindes. I. Die Kindersprache. Eine psychologische und sprachtheoretische Untersuchung.* Leipzig: Barth. 1907.

ALLPORT, G. "The personalistic psychology of William Stern." *Character & Personal.* 1937, 5:231-246.

CALKINS, M. "Psychology as the science of selves." *Philos. Rev.* 1900, 9:490-501.

MACLEOD, R. B. "William Stern (1871-1938)." *Psycho. Rev.* 1938, 45:347-353.

MURCHISON (a—Vol. I, p. 335-388; b—Vol. II, p. 470-473; c—Vol. III, p. 876-880).

TREATISE ON INSANITY

PHILIPPE PINEL

GENERAL PLAN OF THE WORK

Nothing has more contributed to the rapid improvement of modern natural history, than the spirit of minute and accurate observation which has distinguished its votaries. The habit of analytical investigation, thus adopted, has induced an accuracy of expression and a propriety of classification, which have themselves, in no small degree, contributed to the advancement of natural knowledge. Convinced of the essential importance of the same means in the illustration of a subject so new and difficult as that of the present work, it will be seen that I have availed myself of their application, in all or most of the instances of this most calamitous disease, which occurred in my practice at the Asylum de Bicetre. On my entrance upon the duties of that hospital, every thing presented to me the appearance of chaos and confusion. Some of my unfortunate patients laboured under the horrors of a most gloomy and desponding melancholy. Others were furious, and subject to the influence of a

291

perpetual delirium. Some appeared to possess a correct judgement upon most subjects, but were occasionally agitated by violent sallies of maniacal fury; while those of another class were sunk into a state of stupid idiotism and imbecility. Symptoms so different, and all comprehended under the general title of insanity, required, on my part, much study and discrimination; and to secure order in the establishment and success to the practice, I determined upon adopting such a variety of measures, both as to discipline and treatment, as my patients required, and my limited opportunity permitted. From systems of nosology, I had little assistance to expect; since the arbitrary distribution of Sauvages and Cullen were better calculated to impress the conviction of their insufficiency than to simplify my labour. I, therefore, resolved to adopt that method of investigation which has invariably succeeded in all the departments of natural history, viz. to notice successively every fact, without any other object than that of collecting materials for future use; and to endeavour, as far as possible, to divest myself of the influence, both of my own prepossessions and the authority of others. With this view, I first of all took a general statement of the symptoms of my patients. To ascertain their characteristic peculiarities, the above survey was followed by cautious and repeated examinations into the condition of individuals. All our new cases were entered at great length upon the journals of the house. Due attention was paid to the changes of the seasons and the weather, and their respective influences upon the patients were minutely noticed. Having a peculiar attachment for the more general method of descriptive history, I did not confine myself to any exclusive mode of arrangeing my observations, nor to any one system of nosography. The facts which I have thus collected are now submitted to the consideration of the public, in the form of a regular treatise.

The Author's Inducements to Study the Principles of Moral Treatment.

All civilised nations, however different in their customs, and manner of living, will never fail to have some causes of insanity in common; and, it is natural to believe, that all will do their utmost to remedy the evil. Why may not France, as well as England, adopt the means, from the use of which, no nation is by nature proscribed, and which are alone discovered by observation and experience? But success, in this department of medical enquiry, must depend upon the concurrence of many favourable circumstances. The loss of a friend, who became insane through excessive love of glory, in 1783, and the inaptitude of pharmaceutic preparations to a mind elated, as his was, with a high sense of its independence, enhanced my admiration of the judicious precepts of the ancients, and made me regret that I had it not then in my power to put them in practice.

About that time I was engaged to attend, in a professional capacity, at an asylum, where I made observations upon this disease for five successive years. My opportunities for the application of moral remedies, were, however, not numerous. Having no part of the management of the interior police of that institution, I had little or no influence over its servants. The person who was at the head of the establishment, had no interest in the cure of his wealthy patients, and he often, unequivocally, betrayed a desire, that every remedy should fail. At other times, he placed exclusive confidence in the utility of bathing, or in the efficacy of petty and frivolous recipes. The administration of the civil hospitals, in Paris, opened to me in the second year of the republic a wide field of research, by my nomination to the office of chief physician to the national Asylum de Bicetre, which I continued to fill for two years. In order, in some degree, to make up for the local disadvantages of the hospital, and the numerous inconveniences which arose from the instability and successive changes of the administration, I determined to turn my attention, almost exclusively, to the subject of moral treatment. The halls and the passages of the hospital were much confined, and so arranged as to render the cold of winter and the heat of summer equally intolerable and injurious. The chambers were exceedingly small and inconvenient. Baths we had none, though I made repeated applications for them; nor had we extensive liberties for walking, gardening or other exercises. So destitute of accommodations, we found it impossible to class our patients according to the varieties and degrees of their respective maladies. On the other hand, the gentleman, to whom was committed the chief management of the hospital, exercised towards all that were placed under his protection, the vigilance of a kind and affectionate parent. Accustomed to reflect, and possessed of great experience, he was not deficient either in the knowledge or execution of the duties of his office. He never lost sight of the principles of a most genuine philanthropy. He paid great attention to the diet of the house, and left no opportunity for murmur or discontent on the part of the most fastidious. He exercised a strict discipline over the conduct of the domestics, and punished, with severity, every instance of ill treatment, and every act of violence, of which they were guilty towards those whom it was merely their duty to serve. He was both esteemed and feared by every maniac; for he was mild, and at the same time inflexibly firm. In a word, he was master of every branch of his art, from its simplest to its most complicated principles. Thus was I introduced to a man, whose friendship was an invaluable acquisition to me. Our acquaintance matured into the closest intimacy. Our duties and inclinations concurred in the same

294

object. Our conversation, which was almost exclusively professional, contributed to our mutual improvement. With those advantages, I devoted a great part of my time in examining for myself the various and numerous affections of the human mind in a state of disease. I regularly took notes of whatever appeared deserving of my attention; and compared what I thus collected, with facts analogous to them that I met with in books, or amongst my own memoranda of former dates. Such are the materials upon which my principles of moral treatment are founded.

Insanity From Religious Enthusiasm Extremely Difficult to Cure.

To say that the attempts, which have been made in England and France, to cure the insanity of devotees, have been generally ineffectual, is not precisely to assert its incurability. It certainly is not impossible, that by a judicious combination of moral and physical means, a cure might, in many instances, be effected. My plan would have been, could the liberties of the Bicetre have admitted of it, to separate this class of maniacs from the others; to apportion for their use a large piece of ground to till or work upon, in the way that mine or their own inclination might dispose them; to encourage employments of this description, by the prospect of a moderate recompense, want or more exalted motives; to remove from their sight every object appertaining to religion, every painting or book calculated to rouse its recollections; to order certain hours of the day to be devoted to philosophical reading, and to seize every opportunity of drawing apt comparisons between the distinguished acts of humanity and patriotism of the ancients, and the pious nullity and delirious extravagances of saints and anchorites; to divert their minds from the peculiar object of their hallucination, and to fix their interest upon pursuits of contrary influence and tendency.

*The Conduct of the Governor of Bicetre, Upon the
Revolutionary Orders He Received to Destroy the
Symbolic Representations of Religion.*

In the third year of the republic, the directors of the
civil hospitals, in the excess of their revolutionary zeal,
determined to remove from those places the external
objects of worship, the only remaining consolation of
the indigent and the unhappy. A visit for this purpose
was paid to the hospital de Bicetre. The plunder, impious
as it was and detestable, was begun in the dormitories of
the old and the infirm, who were naturally struck at an
instance of a robbery so new and unexpected, some with
astonishment, some with indignation, and others with
terror. The first day of visitation being already far spent,
it was determined to reserve the lunatic department of
the establishment for another opportunity. I was present
at the time, and seized the occasion to observe, that the
unhappy residents of that part of the hospital required
to be treated with peculiar management and address; and,
that it would be much better to confide so delicate a business to the governor himself, whose character for prudence and firmness was well known. That gentleman, in
order to prevent disturbance, and perhaps an insurrec-
tion in the asylum, wished to appear rather to submit to a
measure so obnoxious than to direct it. Having purchased
a great number of national cockades, he called a meeting
of all the lunatics who could conveniently attend. When
they were all arrived he took up the colours and said,
"Let those who love liberty draw near and enrol themselves under the national colours." This invitation was
accompanied by a most gracious smile. Some hesitated;
but the greatest number complied. This moment of enthusiasm was not allowed to pass unimproved. The con-

verts were instantly informed, that their new engagement required of them to remove from the chapel the image of the Virgin, with all the other appurtenances of the catholic worship. No sooner was this requisition announced than a great number of our new republicans set off for the chapel, and committed the desired depredation upon its sacred furniture. The images and paintings, which had been objects of reverence for so many years, were brought out to the court in a state of complete disorder and ruination. Consternation and terror seized the few devout but impotent witnesses of this scene of impiety. Murmurs, imprecations and threats expressed their honest feelings. The most exasperated amongst them prayed that fire from heaven might be poured upon the heads of the guilty, or believed that they saw the bottomless abyss opening to receive them. To convince them, however, that heaven was deaf equally to their imprecations and prayers, the governor ordered the holy things to be broken into a thousand pieces and to be taken away. The good-will and attachment, which he knew so well how to conciliate, ensured the execution of this revolutionary measure. A great majority immediately seconded his wishes. The most rigid devotees, who were comparatively few in number, retired from the scene, muttering imprecation, or agitated by fruitless fury. I shall not enquire into the propriety of so harsh a measure, nor how far its universal enactment might consist with the principles of a wise and enlightened administration. It is very certain, that melancholia or mania, originating in religious enthusiasm, will not admit of a cure, so long as the original impressions are allowed to be continued, or renewed by their appropriate causes.

The Most Violent and Dangerous Maniacs Described,
With Expedients for Their Repression.

The madmen most remarkable for their activity and

turbulence, most subject to sudden explosions of maniacal fury, and most difficult of management at lunatic hospitals, exhibit almost all the external characters, which Cabanis, in his general considerations upon the study of man, has described with so much truth and eloquence as peculiarly characteristic of the sanguine temperament. "A bold and well marked physiognomy; brilliant expressive eyes; a yellow or dark complexion; face remarkably thin; jet black hair and frequently curled; a strong athletic person, with the bones projecting, but seldom fat; strong, quick and hard pulse. These men are perpetually hurried away, sometimes on the buoyant streams of imagination, and at others on the torrents of passion. Their purposes are formed rashly, and executed with violence and impetuosity. Their diseases even participate in the violence of their temperament." We may easily imagine how dangerous madmen of this temperament are, when we consider that their strength and audacity are frequently increased by the influence of their unfortunate maladies. The great secret of mastering maniacs of this character, without doing them injury or receiving violence from them, consists in going up to them boldly and in a great body. Convinced of the inutility of resistance, and impressed with a degree of timidity, the maniac thus surrounded will often surrender without further opposition or reluctance. An instrument of offence will, however, sometimes arm him with extraordinary resolution. A madman shall be suddenly seized with a paroxysm of phrenitic delirium, with perhaps a knife, or a stone, or a cudgel in his hand at the time. The governor, ever faithful to his maxim of maintaining order without committing acts of violence, will, in defiance of his threats, march up to him with an intrepid air, but slowly and by degrees. In order not to exasperate him, he takes with him no offensive weapon. As he advances he speaks to him in a firm and menacing tone, and gives his calm advice or issues his threatening summons, in such a manner as to fix the attention of the hero exclusively upon himself. This ceremony is continued with more or less variation until the assistants have had time, by imperceptible advances,[1] to surround the maniac, when, upon a certain signal being given, he finds himself in instant and unexpected confinement. Thus a scene which threatened so much tragedy, generally ends in an ordinary event. Disturbances will occasionally interfere with the tranquility of all institutions, where the passions are licentiously gratified. Lunatic establishments are peculiarly liable to such commotions. The prevention of conspiracies and tumults by anticipation, is always preferable to their suppression by violence or active contest: either will frequently require such a variety and combination of measures as the greatest sagacity and longest experience can supply. Lunatics, even during their lucid intervals and convalescence, are disposed to be passionate upon very slight causes. Quarrels amongst the patients— specious complaints of injustice—the sight of a sudden

---

[1] The situation of the madman at the time must determine the choice of different means of arrest. A piece of iron of a semicircular form, with a long handle attached to it and adapted by its convexity in the middle for its intended purpose, is sometimes found of great service in the mastering of maniacs, by forcing them up to a wall, and incapacitating them in that position for using their hands. In other cases, when with impunity they can be more nearly approached, a piece of cloth thrown over their faces so as to blind them will enable their keepers to secure them without much difficulty. By harmless methods of this description, a maniac may be sufficiently repressed, without subjecting him to the danger of a wound or the indignity of a blow. Of this mode of coercion, the predecessor of the present governor of Bicetre adopted entirely the reverse. During his superintendence the refractory were abandoned to the unrestrained cruelty of the domestics. Consistent with their policy, the great object was to bring the unruly maniac to the ground by a brutal blow: when one of the other keepers or servants instantly jumped upon him, and detained him in that position, until he was secured, by pressing his knees against his chest and stomach—a process by which that important part was frequently crushed and injured. I cannot speak without horror of the barbarous methods for the repression of maniacs, which are still employed at some hospitals, and which I know to be in too many instances the cause of a premature death.

seizure by a maniacal paroxysm—any object, real or imaginary, of murmur or discontent, may become a source of great disorder, and be communicated, like a shock of electricity, from one end of the hospital to the other. Meetings are called, parties are formed, and commotions stirred up as in popular insurrections, which, if not suppressed in their very commencement, may be succeeded by very unpleasant and possibly by disastrous or fatal consequences. Upon the appearance of tumults of this kind, I have more than once seen the governor of Bicetre brave with wonderful courage the violence that threatened him, move about and mingle in the effervescence with the rapidity of thought, seize the most mutinous, and provide for their instant security, and thus, in a very short time, restore tranquility to the institution.

An Instance Illustrative of the Advantage of Obtaining an Intimate Acquaintance with the Character of the Patient.

A man, in the vigour of life, confined at Bicetre, fancied himself to be a king, and always spoke with the voice of command and authority. He had been for sometime at the Hotel Dieu, where blows and other indignities, received from the keepers, had greatly exasperated his fury. Thus rendered suspicious and unmanageable, it was extremely difficult to fix upon a proper method of treating him. To have recourse to coercive means might still further aggravate his disorder, whilst condescension and acquiescence appeared likely to confirm him in his chimerical pretensions. I determined to wait the further developement of his character, and taking advantage of any favourable circumstance that might happen. I was not long kept in suspence. He one day wrote a letter to his wife full of passionate expressions, accusing her with great bitterness of prolonging his detention, in order to

300

enjoy her own entire liberty. He moreover threatened her with all the weight of his vengeance. Before this letter was sent off, he gave it to read to another patient, who reproved his passionate conduct, and remonstrated with him in a friendly manner, for endeavoring, as he did, to make his wife miserable. This remonstrance was kindly received. The letter was not sent, and another, replete with expressions of esteem, was substituted in its place. Mr. Poussin, the governor, saw in the effects of this friendly advice, the evident symptoms of a favourable change which was about to take place. He immediately availed himself of the occasion, and went to the maniac's apartment, where, in the course of conversation, he led him by degrees to the principal subject of his delirium. "If you are a sovereign," observed the governor, "why do you not put an end to your detention; and wherefore do you remain here, confounded with maniacs of every description?" He repeated his visits daily, when he assumed the tone of friendship and kindness. He endeavoured from time to time to convince him of the absurdity of his pretensions, and pointed out to him another maniac, who had for a long time indulged in the conviction that he was invested with sovereign power, and on that account, was now become an object of derision. The maniac was soon shaken in his convictions. In a short time he began to doubt his claim to sovereignty; and, at last, he was entirely convinced of his pretensions being chimerical. This unexpected revolution was accomplished in the course of a fortnight, and after a few months' longer residence in the house, this respectable husband and father was restored to his family.

A Case of Convalescent Insanity Aggravated by Neglect of Encouraging the Patient's Taste for the Fine Arts.

The gloomy and irritable character of maniacs, even

301

when convalescent, is well known. Endowed, in most instances, with exquisite sensibility, they resent with great indignation the slightest appearances of neglect, contempt or indifference, and they forsake for ever what they had before adopted with the greatest ardour and zeal. A sculptor, a pupil of the celebrated Lemoin, was defeated in his endeavours to be admitted a member of the academy. From that moment he sunk into a profound melancholy, of which the only intermissions consisted in invectives against his brother, whose parsimony he supposed had arrested his career. His extravagance and violence rendered it necessary to confine him for lunacy. When conveyed to his apartment, he gave himself up to all the extravagances of maniacal fury. He continued in that state for several months. At length a calm succeeded, and he was permitted to go to the interior of the hospital. His understanding was yet feeble, and a life of inactivity was not a little irksome to him. The art of painting, which he had likewise cultivated, presented its renascent attractions to him, and he expressed a desire of attempting portrait painting. His inclination was encouraged and gratified and he made a sketch of the governor and his wife. The likeness was striking; but incapable of much application, he fancied that he perceived a cloud before his eyes. He allowed himself to be discouraged by a conviction of his insufficiency to emulate the models of fine taste, of which the traces were not yet effaced from his memory. The talent which he had discovered, his disposition to exercise it, and the probability of rescueing for his country the abilities of so promising a youth, induced the board of Bicetre to request of him a pledge of his genius; leaving to him the choice of his subject, that his imagination might not be cramped. The convalescent, as yet but imperfectly restored, shrunk from the task which was thus imposed upon him; requested that the

302

subject might be fixed upon, and that a correct and proper sketch might be given him for a model. His application was evaded, and the only opportunity of restoring him to himself and to his country was thus allowed to escape. He felt exceedingly indignant; considered this omission, as an unequivocal mark of contempt; destroyed all the implements of his art; and with angry haughtiness declared, that he renounced for ever the cultivation of the fine arts. This impression upon his feelings so unintentionally communicated, was so profound, that it was succeeded by a paroxysm of fury of several months' continuance. To this violence again succeeded a second calm. But now the brilliant intellect was for ever obscured, and he sunk irrecoverably into a sort of imbecility and reverieism, bordering upon dementia. I ordered him to be transfered to the hospital infirmary, with a view of trying the effects of a few simple remedies, combined with the tonic system of regimen. Familiar and consolatory attentions to him, and such other assistance as his case appeared to suggest, were recurred to, more as they were dictates of humanity than as probable means of recovery. His taste for the fine arts, with his propensity to exertion of any kind, had for ever disappeared. Ennui, disgust with life, his gloomy melancholy and apathy made rapid progress. His appetite and sleep forsook him, and a colliquative diarrhea put an end to his degraded existence.

An Attempt to Cure a Case of Melancholia Produced by a Moral Cause.

The fanciful ideas of melancholics are much more easily and effectually diverted by moral remedies, and especially by active employment, than by the best prepared and applied medicaments. But relapses are exceedingly difficult to prevent upon the best founded system of treatment. A working man, during an effervescent period of the revolution, suffered some unguarded expressions to escape him, respecting the trial and condemnation of Louis XVI. His patriotism began to be suspected in the neighborhood. Upon hearing some vague and exaggerated reports of intentions on the part of government agents to prosecute him for disloyalty, he one day betook himself in great tremour and consternation to his own house. His appetite and sleep forsook him. He surrendered himself to the influence of terror, left off working, was wholly absorbed by the subject of his fear; and at length he became fully impressed with the conviction that death was his unavoidable fate. Having undergone the usual treatment at the Hotel Dieu, he was transferred to Bicetre. The idea of his death haunted him night and day, and he unceasingly repeated, that he was ready to submit to his impending fate. Constant employment at his trade, which was that of a tailor, appeared to me the most probable means of diverting the current of his morbid thoughts. I applied to the board for a small salary for him, in consideration of his repairing the clothes of the other patients of the asylum. This measure appeared to engage his interest in a very high degree. He undertook the employment with great eagerness, and worked without interruption for two months. A favourable change appeared to be taking place. He made no complaints nor any allusions to his supposed condemnation. He even spoke with the tenderest interest of a child of about six years of age, whom it seemed he had forgotten, and expressed a very great desire of having it brought to him. This awakened sensibility struck me as a favourable omen. The child was sent for, and all his other desires were gratified. He continued to work at his trade with renewed alacrity, frequently observing, that his child, who was now with him altogether, constituted the happiness of his life. Six months passed in this way without any disturbance or accident. But in the very hot weather of Messidore, (June and July) year 5, some precursory symptoms of returning melancholy began to show themselves. A sense of heaviness in the head, pains of the legs and arms, a silent and pensive air, indisposition to work, indifference for his child, whom he pushed from him with marked coolness and even aversion, distinguished the progress of his relapse. He now retired into his cell, where he remained, stretched on the floor, obstinately persisting in his conviction, that there was nothing left for him but submission to his fate. About that time, I resigned my situation at Bicetre, without, however, renouncing the hope of being useful to this unfortunate man. In the course of that year, I had recourse to the following expedient with him. The governor, being previously informed of my project, was prepared to receive a visit from a party of my friends, who were to assume the character of delegates from the legislative body, dispatched to Bicetre to obtain information in regard to Citizen......, or upon his innocence, to pronounce upon him a sentence of acquittal. I then concerted with three other physicians whom I engaged to personate this deputation. The principal part was assigned to the eldest and gravest of them, whose appearance and manners were most calculated to command attention and respect. These commissaries, who were dressed in black robes suitable to their pretended office, ranged themselves round a table and caused the melancholic to be brought before them. One of them interrogated him as to his profession, former conduct, the journals which he had been in the habits of reading, and other particulars respecting his patriotism. The defendant related all that he had said and done; and insisted on a definitive judgement, as he did not conceive that he was guilty of any crime. In order to make a deep impression on his imagination, the president of the delegates pronounced in a loud voice the following sentence. "In virtue of the power which has been delegated to us by the national assembly, we have entered proceedings in due form of law, against Citizen......: and having duly examined him, touching the matter whereof he stands accused, we make our declaration accordingly. It is therefore, by us declared, that we have found the said Citizen......a truly loyal patriot; and, pronouncing his acquittal, we forbid all further proceedings against him. We furthermore order his entire enlargement and restoration to his friends. But inasmuch as he has obstinately refused to work for the last twelve months, we order his detention at Bicetre to be prolonged six months from this present time, which said six months he is to employ, with proper sentiments of gratitude, in the capacity of tailor to the house. This our sentence is entrusted to Citizen Poussin, which he is to see executed at the peril of his life." Our commissaries then retired in silence. On the day following the patient again began to work, and, with every expression of sensibility and affection, solicited the return of his child. Having received the impulse of the above stratagem, he worked for some time unremittingly at his trade. But he had completely lost the use of his limbs from having remained so long extended upon the cold flags. His activity, however, was not of long continuance; and its remission concurring with an imprudent disclosure of the above well intended plot, his delirium returned. I now consider his case as absolutely incurable.

The Effects of the Cold and Warm Bath, and Especially of the Bath of Surprise, in the Cure of Maniacal Disorders.

A young gentleman, twenty-two years of age, of a

306

robust constitution, was deprived of part of his property by the revolution. He gave way to melancholy, began to look forward to futurity with extreme despondency, and lost his sleep. He was, at length, seized by violent maniacal fury. He was put upon the treatment for acute mania, in the town of his department. With his hands and feet tied he was suddenly immersed in the cold bath. Notwithstanding the violence with which he resisted this treatment, it was practiced upon him for some time. His delirium chiefly consisted in supposing himself to be an Austrian general, and he commonly assumed the tone and manner of a commander. During the process of bathing his fury was greatly exasperated by the mortifying consideration that his rank was neglected and despised. His disorder becoming more and more aggravated by this method, his relations came to the determination to convey him to Paris to be under my care. Upon my first interview with him he appeared exceedingly enraged. To conciliate his favour and obtain his good opinion, I felt the necessity of assenting to his illusive ideas. The bath was never mentioned to him. He was treated with mildness and put upon a diluent regimen, with the liberty of walking at all hours in a pleasant garden. The amusement which he derived from this liberty, exercise and familiar conversation, in which from time to time I engaged him, gradually induced a state of calmness, and towards the end of a month he was not remarkable either for haughtiness or diffidence. In about three months his delirium had completely left him. But towards the autumn of that year, and the spring of the succeeding, some threatening symptoms of a return of his disorder betrayed themselves in his manner and conduct. His looks became more animated, and he was unusually petulant and loquacious. In those circumstances I ordered him a gentle purge to be repeated at intervals, with frequent

307

draughts of whey. He was continued upon this plan for a fortnight. I then advised him to take the warm bath. Not to rouse his former repugnance to bathing, this indication was suggested to him as a practice merely agreeable and conducive to cleanliness. By those means his paroxysms were prevented. To ascertain, however, the permanence of his cure he was detained at my house for a twelve month. Upon his departure he returned into the country, where, for the last two years, he has been occupied partly by literary pursuits, and partly by those of agriculture. No symptom of his delirium has since appeared.

"Cold bathing," says Mr. Haslam, "having for the most part been employed in conjunction with other remedies, it becomes difficult to ascertain how far it may be exclusively beneficial in this disease. The instances in which it has been separately used for the cure of insanity, are too few to enable me to draw any satisfactory conclusions. I may, however, safely affirm, that in many instances, paralytic affections have in a few hours supervened on cold bathing, especially when the patient has been in a furious state, and of a plethoric habit." Dr. Ferriar appears more decidedly favourable to the practice of bathing. In cases of melancholia he advises the cold, and in mania the warm bath. The only case, however, which he adduces in support of the practice must be acknowledged to be equivocal, inasmuch as it was treated, especially in its advanced stages, successively by opium, camphor, purgatives and electricity. General experiments of this nature are, perhaps, more calculated to perpetuate than to dissipate uncertainty. The real utility of bathing in maniacal disorders, remains yet to be ascertained. To establish the practice upon a solid foundation, it must be tried with constant and judicious reference to the different species of insanity. A raving female manic was put upon the use of the warm bath. She bathed twenty-five times, great debility was the immediate consequence, and her mania was shortly after succeeded by dementia. I am led to suppose, that the warm bath may be resorted to with more probability of success, as a preventative of approaching maniacal paroxysms.

It has been said, that the bath of surprise has been found a valuable remedy in some cases of insanity which had resisted the effects of the warm bath, the cold shower bath, and other remedies. This superiority of the unexpected application of cold water, has been ascribed to an interruption of the chain of delirious ideas, induced by the suddenness of the shock, and the general agitation of the system experienced from this process. It is well known that the enthusiast Van Helmont, has made some valuable remarks upon the durable effects of sudden immersion in cold water in some cases of mental derangement. His practice was to detain the patient in the bath for some minutes. It may be proper to observe, that this method, however successful in some instances, might in others be extremely dangerous, and that it can only be resorted to with propriety in cases almost hopeless, and where other remedies are ineffectual; such as in violent paroxysms of regular periodical mania, inveterate continued insanity, or insanity complicated with epilepsy.

Circumstances to be Adverted to in Forming an Opinion of the Author's Success in the Treatment of Mental Derangement.

Before we conclude, it may not be improper to advert to certain circumstances which ought not to be overlooked, in judging of the success of our labours and researches on the subject of the present treatise. It is necessary to mark the point from which we set out, that at which we have arrived, and the circumstances by which we were guided in our hospital duties. The maniacs of either sex, who were admitted at Bicetre and Saltpêtriere, whether as convalescents or incurables, had at other places previously to their admission into those hospitals, undergone the usual system of treatment, by bleeding, bathing and pumping. Among the facts which were most constantly observed, are to be enumerated the permanent recovery of some, the death soon after their arrival of others, and the recurrence of paroxysms which in some instances terminate in complete re-establishment, but most frequently in a state of incurable dementia. Establishments of this kind seldom afford an opportunity of drawing up correct tables of their mortality, of determining accurately the proportion of the cases that are cured, and of fixing with precision the conversions which occur among the different species of insanity. I have, therefore, devoted my principal attention to such objects as were within my power; to the study of the different species of insanity, to the examination of the effects of certain remedies, and to the determination of principles of moral and physical regimen at lunatic asylums. To have surmounted many of the prejudices and other obstacles which present themselves in the organization and discipline of hospitals, is a merit which we hope it will be deemed no arrogance to lay some claim to. The fundamental principles advanced in this treatise will enable us, at a future period, to erect a superstructure for the reception and treatment of lunatics, superior to any of the boasted establishments of neighbouring nations. For the accomplishment of these our earnest wishes, we look up to the councils of a firm government, which overlooks not any of the great objects of public utility.

PHILIPPE PINEL (b.-St. André d'Alayrac, France, April 20, 1745*; d.-Oct. ca. 25, 1826).

In the year 1773, Pinel received his M.D. from Toulouse. On April 25, 1793 he was nominated as Director of the Bicetre, the hospital in Paris for insane men. (The exact date on which he took office is not known. In any case, the date of 1792 usually cited in American literature is wrong by one year.) In 1795 Pinel became Professor of Internal Pathology and Director of the Salpetrière, the corresponding hospital in Paris for insane women.

The best estimate of the date of Pinel's removal of the chains from the male patients at the Bicetre is Sept. 2, 1793 (probably Fructidor 15, in the first year of the Republic) on which day he released about 50 patients. On Sept. 3, 1793, he released some 30 more. The formal order to remove the chains had to be approved by governmental authority, since the chaining of such patients was required by law. Hence, Pinel made direct appeal to the Comité du Salut Public, and Couthon himself (Member of the Comité as of July, 1793, and soon to preside) came to visit the Bicetre. The exact date of these events is not known, however, as few records seemed to have survived the years of the Revolution.

Pinel's Grand Geste has become a symbol in men's minds of the humane and moral treatment of the insane. It may stand, also, as a mark in history commemorating the birth of man's introspective study of himself,—the origin of the social ego.

Though Pinel was certainly not alone in his struggles,** and perhaps not the very first, nevertheless the cleanness of his break and the proud perseverance with which he held to his principles earns for him a very special recognition, the title of Father of Psychiatry, and the love of all future generations.

PINEL, P. *A treatise on insanity, in which are contained the principles of a new and more practical nosology of maniacal disorders than has yet been offered to the public, exemplified by numerous and accurate historical relations of cases from the author's public and private practice: with plates illustrative of the craniology of maniacs and idiots.* London: Cadell & Davis, 1806 (1800). Trans. D. D. Davis.

---

*The date of Pinel's birth is given in H. Sigerist (*The great doctors.* N.Y.: Norton, 1933) as 1755. This must be a misprint. 1745 is the accepted date.
**William Tuke founded the humane asylum, the York Retreat, for example, in 1796.

See also:

PINEL, P. *Nosographie philosophique, ou la méthode de l'analysis appliquée a la médecine.* 1798, 3 vol.

DE SAUSSURE, R. "Phillippe Pinel and the reform of the insane asylums" *Ciba Symp.* 1950, 11: 1222-1252.

TIFFANY, F. "Philippe Pinel (1745-1826)" A Privately printed pamphlet.

TRIBOUILLIER, J.E.L. "Le Geste de Pinel." *M.D. Thesis:* Faculté de Médicine de Paris, 1955.

CASTIGLIONO (esp. p. 633).

MENTAL MALADIES:
A TREATISE ON INSANITY
(JEAN) ÉTIENNE DOMINIQUE ESQUIROL

General Description of the Mental Characteristics of
the Inmates of an Institution for the Insane.

What reflections engage the mind of the philosopher,
who, turning aside from the tumult of the world, makes
the circuit of a House for the insane! He finds there the
same ideas, the same errors, the same passions, the same
misfortunes, that elsewhere prevail. It is the same world;
but its distinctive characters are more noticeable, its
features more marked, its colors more vivid, its effects
more striking, because man there displays himself in all
his nakedness; dissimulating not his thoughts, nor con-
cealing his defects; lending not to his passions seductive
charms, nor to his vices deceitful appearances.

Every House for the insane has its gods, its priests,
its faithful, its fanatics. It has its emperors, its kings,
its ministers, its courtiers, its opulent, its generals,
its soldiers, and a people who obey. One believes himself
inspired of God, and in communication with the Holy
Spirit. He is charged with the conversion of the world;
whilst another, possessed of a demon, given over to all
the torments of hell, groans, and is frantic with despair;
cursing heaven, earth, and his own existence. Another,
bold and audacious, commands the universe, and makes
war with the four quarters of the globe; which he has subjected to his laws, or delivered over to the chains of

313

despotism. A third, proud of the name he has given himself, looks with disdain upon his companions in affliction; lives alone, retired, and preserves a seriousness, as affecting as it is vain. *This one,* in the pride of his heart, thinks himself to possess the science of Newton, and the eloquence of Bossuet; and requires the applauses of those about him to the productions of his genius, with a comic pretension and assurance. *That,* stirs not; nor makes the least movement; always in the same place, and in the same position, he utters not a word. We might take him for a statue. He lives within himself; his inaction is destroying him. Withered by remorse, his neighbor drags out the feeble remnant of a life, which he with difficulty sustains. Uttering reproaches, he curses himself, and invokes death, as terminating the evils that are preying upon him. Near him, is a man who, appearing happy and in the perfect enjoyment of his reason, calculates the moment of his dissolution with frightful indifference. He prepares with calmness, and even joy, the means of terminating his existence. This wretched man, both day and night, with eye and ear, watches for secret enemies. Darkness and light, sound and silence, motion and repose, all frighten and terrify him; he fears himself. How many imaginary terrors consume the days and nights of this lypemaniac! Proceeding onward, we see one, who believing himself betrayed, persecuted and dishonored, has become agitated, exasperated, furious. Suspicion and hatred raise up enemies on every hand. In his unbridled vengeance, he spares no one. Another, the sport of a morbid sensibility, and an excited imagination, suffers from habitual anger. He breaks, rends, and destroys, whatever comes within his reach. He cries aloud, threatens, and strikes, alledging always a motive to justify the frightful disorder of his actions. He whom you see confined, is a fanatic, who vociferates, blasphemes, and con-

314

demns to the fires of hell. He pretends to convert men; and as it is by the baptism of blood that he would purify them, he has already sacrificed two of his children. This senseless being, amid the noisy ravings of his delirium, is of an incoercible petulance. He would injure no one, though ready, apparently, to commit the greatest disorders. To witness his eager activity, you would believe that some great subject engaged his attention, and that his destiny depended upon his movements. In his devious course, he shocks and offends every one that surrounds him, and overthrows whatever opposes his progress. He follows and assails you with his unintelligible babble; but notwithstanding this torrent of words, he says nothing, thinks nothing.

Another, quite at his ease, passes a happy life, laughing incessantly: yet who can excite his joy, and for what can he hope? He has no recollection of the day just past, nor any desire for the morrow.

Thus, in a House for the insane, one can hear at the same time, the shouts of gladness mingled with the sentiments of sorrow; expressions of joy, in connection with the groans of despair. He may see contentment in some, and tears flowing from the eyes of others.

In these establishments, the social bonds are broken; habits are changed; friendships cease; confidence is destroyed. Their inmates do good without benevolence; injure without dislike, and obey through fear. Each has his own ideas, affections and language. With no community of thoughts, each lives alone, and for himself. Egotism isolates all. Their language is extravagant, and disordered, like the thoughts and passions which it expresses. An asylum of this character is not exempt from crime. They denounce, calumniate, conspire. They give themselves up to brutish libertinism; ravish, rob, assassinate. The son curses his father, the mother strangles her children.

If we proceed farther, we see man, fallen from the high rank which places him at the head of creation, despoiled of his privileges, deprived of his most noble character, and reduced to the condition of the most stupid and vilest creature. He thinks not. Not only is he destitute of ideas and passions, but has not even the determinations of instinct.

Unable to provide for his subsistence, he is also incapable of conveying to his lips the aliment that tenderness or benevolence provides. He rolls about amid his own ordure, and remains exposed to all external and destructive influences; rarely recognizing his fellow beings, and having no proper sentiment of his own existence. In this assemblage of enemies, who know only how to shun, or injure each other; what application, what devotion to duty, what zeal are necessary, to unfold the cause, and seat of so many disorders; to restore to reason its perverted powers; to control so many diverse passions, to conciliate so many opposing interests; in fine, to restore man to himself! We must correct and restrain one; animate and sustain another; attract the attention of a third, touch the feelings of a fourth. One may be controlled by fear, another by mildness; all by hope. For this untiring devotion, an approving conscience must be our chief reward. For what can a physician hope, who is always considered wrong when he does not succeed, who rarely secures confidence when successful; and who is followed by prejudices, even in the good which has been obtained.

For our guidance, in this chaos of human miseries, we will reduce to four principal divisions, what we have to say concerning insanity: 1st, we will analyze the symptoms which characterize this malady; 2d, seek for its causes; 3d, trace its progress and mark out its different terminations; 4th, and finally, we will lay down the general principles of its treatment.

I. SYMPTOMS OF INSANITY

Insanity, or mental alienation, is a cerebral affection, ordinarily chronic, and without fever; characterized by disorders of sensibility, understanding, intelligence, and will.

I say ordinarily, because insanity is sometimes of brief duration; and because at its commencement, and sometimes during its course, febrile symptoms are manifested.

Among the insane, sensibility is exalted, or perverted; and their sensations are no longer in relation with external or internal impressions. They seem to be the sport of the errors of their senses, and of their illusions. Many insane persons do not read, because the letters appear to be mingled in a confused mass, so that they are unable to arrange them, in such a manner as to form syllables and words. A thousand illusions of sight, produce, and continue their delirium. They recognize neither their parents nor friends, and regard them either as strangers or enemies. They are no longer correct in the appreciation of the qualities and properties of surrounding objects; many believing themselves at their usual places of abode, when, indeed, they are very far removed from them, and reciprocally.

An officer of talent, of strong constitution, and about forty-six years of age, experiences some disappointments in the service. He becomes irritable, is remanded to Paris, and is not received as he had anticipated. His imagination becomes excited. After some days, he leaves his own residence at eleven o'clock in the evening, traverses the Place Louis XV, and finds not the Column, elevated in the Place Vendome. He at once persuades himself that the insurgents have overturned it, and threaten the

317

government. He stations himself upon the bridge Louis XVI to defend the passage against the pretended insurgents. He arrests all who would pass. The guard appear. He contends desperately against these enemies of the State, is wounded, and yields only to numbers.

A lady aged twenty-seven years in the last stage of phthisis, becomes exceedingly annoyed by the odor of burning charcoal. She believes that they wish to suffocate her; accuses the proprietor of the house, and hastens to denounce him to her friends. This odor follows her everywhere. Every where she is assailed by the fumes of charcoal. She quits her lodgings, changing them many times in a month. The principal disease continues to make progress, and the patient dies, tormented to the last by her hallucination.

Very often the insane repulse with horror, and obstinately refuse aliments after having smelled them for a considerable time. Frequently, at the commencement of insanity, the taste is perverted, and the alienated reject all kinds of nourishment. This symptom, alarming to those who have no experience among the insane, is dissipated with the inconvenience which causes it, viz., gastric irritation.

A student breakfasts with a friend, gets tipsy, becomes furious, and remains convinced that they have mingled drugs with his wine.

How frequently do the insane deceive themselves with respect to the volume, form, and thickness of those bodies which they touch! The greater part become unskillful in labors of the hands, in the mechanic arts, music and writing. They are very awkward, and the touch has lost its singular property of rectifying the errors of the other senses.

These errors of sensation appear to affect, sometimes but one sense, often two, more rarely three, sometimes four, and even all. When mental alienation manifests itself, and sometimes long before, both the senses of smell and taste are altered, but errors of hearing and sight, characterize, and continue more generally, the delirium of the greater part of the insane.

There are insane persons who hear voices speaking very distinctly, and with which they hold successive conversations. *These voices* proceed from the clouds, and from trees; they penetrate walls and pavements; they pursue and fatigue, those who hear them, day and night; while walking, in society, amidst assemblies, as well as in retirement. They take the accent and tone of a relative, a friend, a neighbor, or an enemy. They make proposals, gay, erotic, threatening or injurious in their nature. They advise to actions, contrary to honor, to interest, or to the preservation of the patient. A gentleman, after a dreadful catastrophe, thinks himself accused; attempts suicide, and passes more than two years, in listening to the threatening voices of his accusers.

Mrs. A. entertains the belief that men enter her chamber during the night. On being shown that this is impossible, she replies, they pass through the lock. A lypemaniac speaks aloud, when by himself, and as if in conversation with another person. I remarked upon its impropriety, assuring him that no person could hear, or reply to him. In the midst of our discussion, he says to me: *Do you not sometimes think? Doubtless, I replied. You think silently, he continued, but I aloud.* If insanity is characterized and maintained by errors of sensation, by illusions and hallucinations; it is also, by the multiplicity of sensations, by the abundance of ideas, the versatility of the affections, which are produced in melancholy confusion, without order, end, or coherence. This exuberance of thought, permits not the patient to arrest his attention sufficiently long upon each sensation or idea,

319

to separate those which have no relation among themselves, or to remove those, which exist in excess. He can no longer seize upon the qualities or relations of things; neither compare, nor abstract. There results from this disposition a volatile delirium, whose object is unceasingly renewed, and takes every variety of form. Both the language and actions participate in this mobility, and give at times, a very elevated, and even sublime character, to the thoughts. Under other circumstances, the attention exercises itself with so much energy as to become fixed upon a single subject. Constantly confined to this, nothing can turn it aside. All reasonings and determinations, are derived from this all-absorbing idea. Monomania offers a thousand examples of this form of delirium.

The faculty which the mind possesses, of associating our sensations and ideas, of arranging them among themselves, of combining them with our determinations, presents very remarkable alterations among the insane. The slightest impression, or the most remote coincidence, provokes the strangest associations.

The city of *Die* is overlooked by a neighboring rock, which is called the *U*. A young man suggested to himself the propriety of adding the letter U to the word Die, making it the word *Dieu,* (God). Hence all the inhabitants of Die, became gods in his opinion. He immediately perceives the absurdity of this Polytheism, and concentrates the divinity in the person of his father, as the most reputable man of that country. His father, although at two hundred leagues distance acts in him, and he acts only by his father. A general becomes agitated, cries aloud, and takes the tone of a commander, the moment that he hears the drum or the cannon. Often the delirium allies itself so closely to the cause which has excited it, to the intellectual and moral condition of the patient at the period of the attack, that this vicious association, persists during the whole disease, characterizes it, and becomes the only obstacle to its cure. An emigrant soldier, thirty-five years of age, having returned to France, is arrested, put in prison, and loses his reason. Restored to liberty, he sees himself everywhere surrounded by spies, and agents of the police.

A young artist, a passionate admirer of Rousseau, not obtaining the first prize for sculpture, of which he thought himself deserving, gives himself up to despair. He vows eternal hatred to men, and wishes no longer to live except after the manner of brutes. He walks upon all fours, and if placed upon a bed rolls himself off upon the ground. If confined, he has convulsions. He will eat nothing but herbs, or crude fruits which he picks up from the ground. If helped to them, he refuses to use them. This condition persists for more than two months, after which he falls into a state of dementia, to which he has a strong predisposition, having several brothers and sisters affected with this form of disease.

With another class of the insane, the enfeebled organs perceive but feebly, sensations; impressions are not sufficiently felt; memory retains them not, and is unfaithful. These persons remember only events long since passed. Imperfectly served by their sensations and memory, they cannot seize upon affinities. They can no longer arrest their attention, as it is not excited by the impression of external objects. Their determinations are uncertain. They seem to act only from recollections.

Memory presents also striking anomalies among the insane, the ideas either requiring an actual sensation to awaken them, or a continual effort to recall them. Memory is not wanting with these patients, but the faculty of directing and fixing their attention being impaired, memory serves them imperfectly.

In some cases of mental alienation, man, deprived, in

some sort, of the control of the will, seems no longer to be master of his determinations. The insane, controlled by their predominant ideas and impressions, are drawn away to the performance of acts which they themselves disapprove. Some, condemning themselves to repose, to silence and inaction, cannot control the power which represses their activity. Others walk about, sing, dance, and write, without the power to refrain. We have seen some escape from their relatives with no other motive than the desire of moving about, hasten from point to point for many days, scarcely stopping to take nourishment; while others give themselves up to acts of madness, which cause them intense agony. These impulses, these irresistible propensities, these automatic determinations as authors call them, seem to be independent of the will. However, they result generally, from motives, of which the insane, and those conversant with them, can, to a certain extent, give an account.

The insane are, as Locke remarks, like those who lay down false principles, from which they reason very justly, although their consequences are erroneous.

A public receiver, after long and difficult labor upon the finances, is stricken with mania. The attack terminates in melancholy complicated with dementia and paralysis. He refuses for some days to drink at his repasts. They insist—he becomes enraged; exclaiming, *rascal, would you have me swallow my brother!* Reflecting upon this strange notion, I perceive that the patient sees his own image in the bottle placed upon the table. I remove it, and from thenceforth he drinks without difficulty. A vine-dresser slays his children, says Pinel, but he does it that they may not be damned. A woman forty years of age, having fallen into the most abject misery, throws herself into the river. She assured me that during twenty-four hours, while walking upon its banks, she had suffered

322

indescribably, and had resolved upon suicide, only to prevent the anguish of the most profound misery.

The moral affections provoke insanity. The symptoms which characterize it, impress often, every feature of the passions. The determinations which the passions produce, are not in harmony with those by which the patient was formerly affected, nor with what are observed among other individuals.

A madman is passionate, jealous; he commits murder. He is impatient of restraint; and if he cannot otherwise escape, will precipitate himself from the house in which he is confined, or set fire to it. Among the insane, some are stricken with terror, believe themselves ruined, tremble lest they shall become the victims of a conspiracy, fear death. Others are happy and gay; think only of the good which they enjoy, or of the benefits which they can dispense. They feel persuaded that they are elevated to the greatest dignity,—that the homage of the world is their due,—that they inhabit a superior region, where they are eternally to dwell, intoxicated with delight. Witness for example, the madman of Athens, who believed that all the vessels entering the Pyræus were his own.

A young chemist, aged twenty-seven years, and of a strong constitution, labors night and day in researches appropriate to his department. He becomes greatly excited, and is at the same time amorous. He precipitates himself from the fourth story of the house, and fractures the fibula. Replaced in bed, the delirium continues intense. The patient distributes millions, and promises that all the world shall be happy. At the expiration of three months he is restored.

The first sentence which he wrote his parents is thus expressed: *'I feel that I must renounce my illusions. Never shall I be so happy as during the three months which have just passed.'* This happy state of some deranged persons, has been the cause of many errors respecting this class of people. Some who see them thus, conclude that the insane are all happy, that they do not suffer; whilst, generally, they suffer as much physically as morally.

The passions of the insane are impetuous, especially in mania and monomania. They are of a depressing character in lypemania. In dementia and imbecility, those only exist, which spring from the first wants of man,—love, anger, jealousy.

He who should say that rage is but an attack of anger prolonged, might also say, that erotomania is love carried to excess,—that religious lypemania is zeal or religious fear carried beyond due limits,—that suicide is an attack of despair. Thus, from a condition the most calm, one becomes excited, by insensible gradations, to the most violent passion, and even to the most furious mania, or sinks into the profoundest melancholy,—almost all forms of insanity, having their primitive type in some of the passions.

The insane sometimes surrender themselves to the most disgraceful acts.

Here is one of strict integrity, of irreproachable morals, connected even with the highest class in society; but who, becoming insane, makes infamous proposals, indulges in indecent gestures, and is the opposite, in every respect, to what his past conduct would lead us to expect.

There are, in fine, those who rob.

M. ***, forty years of age, after the storms of the revolution had passed away, returns to France and obtains an honorable subsistence. Two years subsequently, he suffers from loss of memory, and his friends perceive a change in his character. At length, while dining with one of them, he carries off certain pieces of silver plate.

On arriving at Paris, he betakes himself to the cafe de Foy, orders a cup of chocolate, breakfasts, and leaves without paying, carrying off in his waistcoat, a spoon and saucer. It is unnecessary to relate here, the excesses which the hysterical and nymphomaniacs commit.

The insane become pusillanimous in the extreme. They permit themselves to be easily intimidated. They are fearful, diffident, jealous. It is this which occasions their restlessness, which makes them anxious to be anywhere, rather than where they happen to be,—to distrust themselves, and to withdraw from their parents and friends. This feeling of distrust, is found among people of little intelligence. Men the least suspicious, and the most confident, are, beyond contradiction, those who cultivate their minds; so true is it, that moral force is in proportion to mental development. But notwithstanding this distrust, the insane are improvident, to a degree which can be compared only with that of savages. They have no care for the moment which has just past, but are extremely anxious for the present. This improvidence exposes them to privations of every kind, if a careful watch is not exercised over them, and their wants carefully supplied.

The insane often entertain an aversion towards persons who were previously dear to them. They insult, misuse, and fly from them. It is a result, however, of their distrust, jealousy and fear. Opposed to all, they fear all. Some, appear to constitute an exception to this general law, and seem to preserve a sort of affection for their relatives and friends. But this tenderness, which is sometimes excessive, exists without confidence, and without intimacy with those persons, who, before their illness, directed the ideas, and actions of the patient. This melancholic person adores his wife, but is deaf to her advice and prayers. This son would sacrifice his life for his father; but would do nothing through deference to his counsels, from the moment they have his delirium for their object.

This moral alienation is so constant, that it would appear to me to be an essential characteristic of mental alienation.

There are insane persons whose *delirium* is scarcely noticeable; none whose passions and moral affections, are not disordered, perverted, or annihilated. The return of the moral affections within their just bounds, the wish to see his children and friends once more, the tears of sensibility, the desire of unfolding the affections, of finding himself again in the midst of his family, and of returning to his accustomed habits, are certain signs of a cure; while the contrary had been a sign of approaching insanity, or the index of a threatening relapse.

The diminution of delirium is a certain sign of returning health, only when the insane return to their first affections.

Closing this long summary of the intellectual and moral symptoms of insanity, let us pass to the principal physical alterations, which the insane present.

The vital forces acquire, among this class of persons, an exaltation which permits them to resist influences, most calculated to affect the health; but this exaltation is not so general as is commonly believed.

Examples are rare, though repeated on all sides. Some insane persons experience an internal heat, so intense, that they throw themselves into water, and even amid ice, or refuse all clothing at the coldest season of the year.

With others the muscular system acquires an energy, the more formidable, as force is joined to audacity, and their delirium renders them indifferent to danger.

We have seen madmen pass many days without food or drink, and preserve all their muscular energy. I repeat it, these examples are rare. Almost all the insane crowd around the fire when there is occasion for its use, and almost all eat much, and very frequently.

Scrofula affects so many of the insane in every hospital, because their habitations are damp, cold, and imperfectly ventilated; and because this class of patients live in idleness and inactivity. Epidemics and contagions spare them not, which proves that they are not so insusceptible to external influences as is pretended.

The features of the insane are convulsed, and their physiognomy wears the impress of pain. How different the changeful features of the maniac; the fixed and lengthened visage of the melancholic; the relaxed features, and extinct expression of one in dementia, from those of the same individuals after restoration to health!

Among the insane, some are plethoric, others lymphatic; some are strong, others feeble; the pulse is full, voluminous and hard among the former; with the latter, slow, soft, and concentrated. Tormented with hunger and thirst, they are more agitated or melancholic after, than before their repasts. Some have acid nidorous eructations; some debility of the stomach, which induces them to drink wine and liquors; while others suffer from abdominal pains, and heat of the intestines.

Maniacs, monomaniacs and lypemaniacs, do not sleep; insomnia continuing for several months. If they sleep, they have the nightmare, frightful dreams, and are awoke by surprise, while imbeciles and those in dementia would like to sleep constantly.

There are those, who are troubled with a constipation, which persists for eight, thirteen and twenty-one days, —those whose urine is retained for twenty-four, sixty, and one hundred and twenty hours. With others, the alvine dejections and urine, pass off involuntary.

All the secretions acquire a penetrating odor, impreg-

327

nating both the clothing and furniture, and which nothing can remove.

Many insane persons suffer from violent pains in the head, which cause them to beat it; also from pains in the chest, abdomen and limbs, which they attribute often, to their enemies, to the devil, or to harsh treatment. In fine, they are subject to cutaneous affections, sores, hemorrhoids, convulsions, organic diseases, etc.

From all that precedes we conclude, that among the insane the vital properties are changed; that physical and moral sensibility; the faculty of perceiving, comparing and associating ideas; the memory and will; the moral affections, and the functions of organic life; are all more or less impaired. As I have interdicted myself from all explanation, I must content myself with saying, behold the facts. However, I will add a few brief observations, which will aid, perhaps, in shedding some light on the subject of delirium.

A young man sees around him all the persons composing the court. He prostrates himself before the feet of him, whom he believes to be the sovereign, and refuses the attentions they are about to render him; unwilling to be served by such august personages. He becomes furious, when the servants treat with familiarity the sovereign of his creation. I cause his eyes to be bandaged for two days, and his delirium ceases; but on removing the covering, it again returns.

Reil states that a lady, seeing spectres and monsters about her, fell into a convulsive delirium; and that her chambermaid, in order to protect her, placed her hand over the eyes of the patient, who immediately exclaimed: *I am cured.* This experiment was renewed with the same success, before the physician.

The insane, when restored, preserve the most perfect recollection of their sensations, whether true or false.

328

They recall without difficulty their reasonings, and the determinations resulting from them, and the recollection even of the smallest details, acquire distinctness, as they advance towards the enjoyment of perfect health. Hence during delirium, they possess the knowledge and capacity requisite for reasoning.

As to lesions of the understanding, they can be reduced to that of the attention; Jean Jacques has said, "*The state of reflection, is a state, contrary to nature. Man who meditates is a depraved animal.*" Instead of this misanthropic freak of thought, Rousseau should have said, that all reasoning supposes an effort, and that we are not naturally reasoning beings; that is to say, our ideas are not conformed to objects, our comparisons exact, our reasonings just, but by a succession of efforts of the attention; which supposes in its turn, an active state of the organ of thought; just as a muscular effort is necessary to produce motion, although the movement may no more exist in the muscle, than thought in the brain.

If we reflect upon what passes through the mind of even the most sensible man for a single day, what incoherences shall we notice in his ideas and determinations, from the time that he awakes in the morning, until he retires to rest at night! His sensations, ideas and determinations, have some connection among themselves, only when he arrests his attention; and then only does he reason. The insane, no longer enjoy the faculty of fixing, and directing their attention, and this privation is the primitive cause of all their errors.

We observe this among children, who, although very impressible, have nevertheless few sensations, for want of attention. The same thing happens to the aged, because their attention is no longer solicited by external objects, in consequence of the feebleness of organs.

The impressions are so fugitive and numerous, the

ideas so abundant, that the maniac cannot fix his attention sufficiently upon each object and idea. With the monomaniac, the attention is so concentrated, that it cannot turn itself aside upon surrounding objects, and accessory ideas. Hence these madmen feel, but do not think. Among those in a state of dementia or the contrary, the organs are too much enfeebled to sustain the attention, and there are no longer sensations or understanding.

The attention of all the insane is essentially disturbed by one of these three causes, that if sensation, strong, agreeable, painful or unexpected, fixes the attention of the maniac, or turns aside that of the monomaniac; if a violent commotion arouses the attention of him who is in a state of dementia; he immediately becomes rational, and this return of reason, lasts as long as the effect of the sensation; that is, whilst the patient retains the power of directing and sustaining his attention.

Imbeciles and idiots are deprived of this faculty, and hence are incapable of education. I have very often repeated this experiment among them. Having taken casts of a great many insane people, I have succeeded in placing in a suitable attitude, maniacs, the furious even, and the melancholic; but could never cause the imbeciles to close their eyes sufficiently long for the plaster to flow, whatever degree of good will they might bring to the undertaking. I have even seen them weep, because the casting of their heads had not succeeded, and undertake many times, but unsuccessfully, to preserve the posture that had been given them. They were unable, also, to close their eyes longer than one or two minutes.

Will the pathological study of the faculties of the soul, conduct to the same results with those to which M. Laromiguiere has arrived, in his eloquent discourses on philosophy?

Numerous facts will justify this psychological view,

upon which reposes a principle, fruitful, with respect to the cure of mental diseases.

After having reduced insanity in some sort to its elements; after having isolated them; to obtain the general forms of insanity, we have only to reunite these elements. Now these general forms are embraced in the terms following, and constitute five varieties.

1. Lypemania (melancholy of the ancients), delirium with respect to one or a small number of objects, with predominance of a sorrowful and depressing passion.

2. Monomania, in which the delirium is limited to one or a small number of objects, with excitement, and predominance of a gay, and expansive passion.

3. Mania, in which the delirium extends to all kinds of objects, and is accompanied by excitement.

4. Dementia, in which the insenate utter folly, because the organs of thought have lost their energy, and the strength requisite to fulfill their functions.

5. Imbecility, or idiocy, in which the conformation of the organs has never been such, that those who are thus afflicted, could reason justly.

These forms, sufficiently well distinguished in the engravings appended to these memoirs, in which are described the varieties of insanity, have served as the basis of classification with Pinel; and express the generic characters of mental alienation. Being common to many mental affections, whose origin, nature, treatment and termination, are widely different, they cannot characterize the species and varieties which are reproduced with infinite shades of difference.

Insanity may assume successively, all these forms; monomania, and dementia, may alternate and replace each other, and become complicated in the course of the same disorder, and in the person of the same individual. It is this circumstance that has caused some physicians to reject all distinctions, and to admit, in insanity, but one and the same malady, which masks itself under various forms. I do not concur with them in this opinion, and regard the varieties of which I have just spoken, as too distinct ever to be confounded.

We could wish to establish the numerical relation which subsists between the different forms of insanity. Some authors believe that melancholy is the most frequent. Pinel would seem to be of this opinion. However, in the second edition of his *"Treatise on Insanity,"* he makes six hundred and four maniacs, and only two hundred and ten melancholics or monomaniacs.

To compare the returns which have been made in different places, and by different authors, it would be necessary that each should give the same signification to the terms, *dementia, idiocy, mania* and *melancholy;* a fact which does not exist.

According to the foregoing definition of these varieties, I think that monomania is more frequent than mania. Dementia and idiocy are more rare, particularly the latter, which is endemic in certain mountainous districts.

V. Treatment of Insanity

It is doubtless, less difficult to establish systems, and to imagine brilliant hypotheses respecting mental alienation, than to observe the insane, and put up with the disgusting circumstances of whatever kind, to which those are exposed, who would, by observation, study the history of this most serious infirmity.

The difficulty of catching the varied and fugitive forms of insanity, the savage rudeness of certain monomaniacs, the obstinate silence of some, the scorn and abuse of others, the threats and blows of maniacs, the disgusting filthiness of imbeciles, together with the prejudices which aggravate the lot of these unfortunates, have discouraged those who wished to cultivate this branch of the healing art.

They shun the maniacs. They fear them, and leave them in their chains.

Monomaniacs are a little less neglected. They submit more readily to observation. Their delirium is more amenable to theories and explanations.

But we must live with the insane, in order to obtain exact notions respecting the causes, symptoms, course, crises, and terminations of their malady. We must live with them, in order to appreciate the infinite cares and numberless details, which their treatment requires. How great the good which the patient derives from friendly and frequent intercourse with his physician! How valuable the lesson, which the latter acquires, relative to the influence of the physical over the moral man, and reciprocally!

In the gestures, movements, looks, and general aspect; in his proposals, actions, and shades of conduct which are imperceptible to others, the physician often derives his first thought, respecting the treatment which is suited to each patient committed to his care.

Mental alienation offers three orders of phenomena, whether we study the causes which produce it, or the symptoms which characterize it.

We have seen physical as well as intellectual and moral causes, acting upon the brain, sometimes individually, sometimes collectively, produce insanity. These causes have, now a general, now a local action; now primitive and immediate; now secondary and sympathetic. Their action varies with the individual cases, and their effects are diverse, and even opposite.

We have seen physical disorders as well as moral and intellectual, marking all the periods of the malady, in degrees, more or less intense. We have sometimes seen nature herself, bear the whole burthen of a cure, and restore the patient to health, by means that had escaped the most practiced observers. Generally, mental alienation is terminated by sensible crises. It is not rare to witness surprising cures, which are produced by moral influences, either accidental, or otherwise.

Thus, in a general view of the treatment of the insane, we should propose to ourselves, the removal of physical disorder, the aberrations of the understanding and the disturbance of the passions.

We must, therefore, skillfully control the mind and passions, and make a suitable use of the physical means, which ought to be employed in the treatment of the insane. We must never lose sight of the causes which have predisposed to, and provoked insanity; nor by any means forget the habits of the patient, and the sickness which existed, previous to the appearance of mental alienation, and which ceased a little before, or at the moment of the attack.

Among the ancients, the treatment of insanity was made to consist in the use of hellebore.

An accident was the means of proposing the bath of surprise. The discovery of the circulation of the blood, caused physicians to bleed largely. The humorists returned to the use of purgatives. The English vigorously employed the precepts which Areteus and Cœlius had suggested, and of which Erasistratus and Gallienus had made a most happy application. They made a secret of them; but Pinel made himself a master of it, and changed the lot of the insane. The chains were broken,* the insane were treated with humanity, hope gained hearts, and a more rational system of therapeutics, directed the treatment.

*Bicetre in 1792 or the abolishment of chains (Memoirs of the Royal Academy of Medicine, Paris, 1836, t. v. pag. 31.)

It will often be necessary to vary, combine and modify the means employed; for there is no specific treatment of insanity.

As this malady is not identical in every case; as in every instance it depends upon different causes, and presents varied characteristics, and requires new combinations; a new problem is to be solved, for every patient whom we are called to treat.

I will limit myself to general considerations, which are adapted to all; and will set a due value upon certain medicaments, denominated heroic.

In the study of symptoms, we have seen that the lesions of sensations, together with that of the association of ideas, and of the will, caused by defective attention, produced, and kept up the delirium, as well as the perversion of the passions.

Whatever can act upon the brain, either directly or indirectly, and modify the principle of thought; whatever can control and direct the passions, should be the object of moral treatment.

The first question that presents itself, is relative to isolation. Ought every insane person to be removed from all familiar scenes, his mode of life changed—separated from those with whom he has always lived,—placed in a situation altogether new, and committed to the care of strangers?

The English, French, and German physicians, agree with respect to the necessity and utility of isolation.

Willis, who was so long known, and sought for, in consequence of his success in the treatment of insanity, was accustomed to remark, that foreigners were with more certainty cured, than the English. The same is true in France.

The cures are more frequent among those patients who visit Paris from abroad, than those who reside at the capital. The latter are not sufficiently isolated.

The first effect of isolation is, to produce new sensations, to change and break up the chain of ideas, from which the patient could not free himself.

New and unexpected impressions strike, arrest, and excite his attention, and render him more accessible to those councils, that ought to bring him back to reason.

Besides, from the moment that an insane man is shut out from the world, surprised, astonished, and disconcerted, he always experiences a remission, of great value to the physician, who then, finding the patient without prepossessions, can more readily acquire his confidence.

Isolation is not less useful, in combating the disorder of the moral affections of the insane. The disturbance unexpectedly occurring in the nervous system, changes the nature of the sensations, and often renders them painful. The natural relations with the external world are no longer the same. Externally, every thing seems to be thrown into confusion. The patient who believes not that the cause of these phenomena is within himself, is at variance with all that he either sees or hears; a circumstance which excites his mind, and places him in opposition to others and himself. He persuades himself that his friends wish to oppose him, since they disapprove of his errors and excesses. Not comprehending fully what is said to him, he most frequently misinterprets the language which is addressed to him:—proofs of the tenderest affection are regarded as injuries, or as enigmas which he cannot solve:—the most devoted attentions are vexations:—his heart, ere long, nourishes only distrust.

The insane man becomes timid and suspicious. He fears every one that he approaches; and his suspicions extend to those who were most dear to him. The conviction that every one is endeavoring to torment and slander him, to render him miserable, and to ruin him, in body and estate, put the finishing stroke to this moral perversion.

Hence that *symptomatic suspicion,* which often grows up without motive; sometimes, in consequence of necessary opposition, which increases by reason of the alteration of the intellectual faculties, and which is depicted so strikingly upon the physiognomy of the insane.

With such moral dispositions, leave an insane person in the bosom of his family, and immediately this tender son, whose happiness once consisted in residing at home, will desert the paternal mansion. The despairing lover hopes, by his counsels, to bring back the wandering reason of her whom he adores. Her unfortunate condition renders the blow only the more severe.

She who once loved him so tenderly, will now see in him only a wretch, who offers his attentions, only the better to betray.

This friend, whose heart is weighed down with grief, hopes, by his affectionate attentions, to restore that sensibility and reason, which had been the source of his attachment and happiness.

But soon, unhappy one, thou wilt be embraced in the general prescription; and thy cares for thy suffering friend, will be but proofs, that thou also hast yielded to the corrupting influence of his enemies.

What are we to hope for, if we change not the moral condition of that unfortunate class, whose prejudices are so strongly excited?

Who of us has not experienced the difference which exists, between being deceived, thwarted and betrayed, by his neighbors and friends, and by those who are strangers to him?

This unfortunate man, suddenly becomes master of the world, gives out his sovereign orders, to all who surround him. He pretends to be blindly obeyed, by those who had ever yielded to his wishes, through respect or affection. His wife, children, friends and domestics, are his subjects. They have always obeyed; will they now dare to be disobedient? He is in his dominions, and commands a despot; and he is ready to punish with the greatest severity whoever shall dare to make the least remonstrance. What he wills is impossible; suppose it is, he wills it; and shall the will of the great be met by insurmountable obstacles? The affliction of his family, the regrets of his friends, the agitation of all, their deference for his wishes and caprices; the repugnance of every one to oppose him through fear of exasperating his madness; do not all these serve to confirm this wretched man in his notions of power and domination? Remove him from the seat of his pretensions:—take him from his home. Stripped of his empire and subjects, he will collect his thoughts, direct his attention to the study of himself in this new world, and to the establishment of relations with those around him.

The cause of mental alienation often exists within the family circle. The malady originates from chagrins, domestic dissensions, reverses of fortune, privations; and the presence of the parents and friends of the patient, exasperates the evil. Sometimes, an excess of tenderness keeps up the disease.

A husband persuades himself that he cannot secure the happiness of his wife; and resolves to fly from her, or to terminate his existence, as the only means by which he can render her happy. The tears of his wife, and her sad countenance, are only new motives for inducing him to commit the act.

Has the first commotion amid the intellectual and moral faculties, originated in the house of the insane man, and in the midst of his neighbors? The sight of this house and his acquaintances, will constantly revive in the mind of the insane person, his peculiar ideas and sensations. The only means by which we can break up this fatal association, must consist in preventing a renewal of the impression; and, in order to effect this, the patient must be removed from the causes that produce it.

We would remark generally, that the insane conceive a dislike and aversion to certain individuals, without any motive, and nothing induces them to change their views. The object of their hatred is usually the person who, before their illness, enjoyed their love. It is this circumstance, which renders this class of person so indifferent, and sometimes so dangerous to their friends; whilst strangers are agreeable to them, and suspend their delirium; either because novelty with respect to persons and things is always useful, or because they have no recollection, no painful back thought, to attach to the person of a stranger; or because, through a secret sentiment of self-love, they wish to conceal their condition.

I have seen patients appear very calm before their physician and strangers, at the same time that they would abuse in a low voice, their relatives or friends; and conceal themselves, in order to pinch, prick, or scratch them. Such are the obstacles and inconveniences, which present themselves in view of the sojourn of the insane in their families, when we desire to subject them to medical treatment. Let us now look at the advantages which patients will derive, from treatment in an establishment especially devoted to their use; where, placed in circumstances quite unusual, and committed to the care of strangers, they will receive new impressions.

Where shall we isolate the patient? We have already said that the insane man should be placed in an institution devoted to the treatment of mental diseases. We prefer a house of this kind to a private one, where our object is effected at great expense. Partial isolation rarely succeeds. It presents many inconveniences, which we would wish to shun, by withdrawing the insane from their accustomed places of abode; and offers very few of the advantages of a house in which many patients are assembled.

The strongest objection that can be urged against establishments devoted to this kind of treatment, is founded upon the frightful effects that may result from mingling with companions in misfortune. I reply, that, generally, it does not injure them,—that it is not an obstacle to a cure—that it is a valuable means of treatment, because it obliges the insane to reflect upon their condition, because that, common objects no longer making an impression upon their minds, they are diverted from themselves, by the extravagances of their companions. They are obliged to live, *out of themselves,* and to occupy their thoughts with what is going on around them,—to forget themselves, as it were, which is, in itself, a means of cure. The desire of being free, and the need of seeing parents and friends, grow out of the privation of these privileges, and replace imaginary and unreasonable wants and desires.

Ennui exercises, in its way, a favorable influence upon the ideas and affections of the insane. The presence and conduct of their companions, serves as a text to the physician, who wishes to address himself to the imagination. However, there are cases in which isolation, like all other remedies, even the most useful, may prove injurious; when it is not modified by the susceptibility of the insane, and the character of the delirium; and with a reference also, to their passions, habits, and mode of life. We should never be absolute in practice. Art consists, in happily distinguishing the indications which ought to lead to a modification of principles, however great the efficacy that experience may attribute to them.

In an Establishment devoted to the treatment of the insane, the arrangements are better adapted to their wants than in a private house. With less suffering to the patient, he is more faithfully attended to. What can be done with a furious patient in an apartment of a private house, however large? A suitable regard for his security, will render it necessary that he should be bound, and confined to his bed; a painful condition, which augments the delirium and fury; while, in a suitable house, he could be indulged in his propensities, with less danger to himself and his attendants. In a house of this kind, his wants are better understood, and the domestics better instructed. The distribution of buildings permit the patient to be removed, from one habitation to another, as his condition, his disposition to injure himself, or his progress towards recovery may render expedient. These truths, useful in the management of the rich who are insane, are of rigorous application in the treatment of the poor.

An Establishment for the insane must be governed by regulations, to which all must submit. This will serve as a response to all objections, and aid in surmounting all repugnance, at the same time that it furnishes motives to obedience, less unpleasant, than the will or caprice of a principal.

There is, in a house of this kind, a movement, an activity, a vortex, into which by degrees, all enter. The most infatuated and jealous lypemaniac finds himself, almost without knowing it, forced to live out of himself; carried along by the general movement, by the example, and by the impressions often strange, which are perpetually striking his senses. The maniac himself, attracted by the harmony, order and regularity of the house, defends himself better against his impulses, and abandons himself less to his eccentric actions.

In an Establishment for the insane, there must be a Head, and a single Head, from whom all authority should emanate. Reil, and those who, after him, have desired that a hospital for the insane should be directed by a physician, a psychologist and moralist, had no practical experience, and did not appreciate the inconveniences attending a division of powers. When there are several coordinate powers, and the mind of the insane knows not upon whom to repose, it wanders in doubt; confidence is not established. Now, without confidence, there is no cure. A spirit of independence evades obedience, when authority is divided. It is to prevent this double inconvenience, that we admit with caution, of interviews between the insane and their friends. The insane are but grown up children, children too, who have received false notions, and a wrong direction. So many points of resemblance do they bear to children and young persons, that it will not be surprising, if both one and the other should be governed on similar principles.

The physician who, in an establishment of this kind, gives an impulse to every thing; to whom is referred whatever interests each individual;—sees his patients more frequently than he would otherwise do, is more frequently informed of whatever affects them,—interferes in their dissensions and quarrels,—governs them by principles more clear and positive,—controls their actions and causes them to be attended by people who are accustomed to the care of the insane. Attendants should set an example of deference and obedience to the regulations, and head of the house. By their numbers, they present an array of force, which renders its employment unnecessary; they persuade those most excited, that all resistance would be vain; in fine, living among the sick, the latter are not alone, nor always surrounded by irrational persons. Example, which exerts such power over

342

the determinations of man, has also great influence with the insane. We must not forget what has been said respecting the sagacity of the insane, in comprehending what is passing around them. The restoration and discharge of a patient inspires confidence in the hearts of others. It establishes in their minds the hope of a cure, and the certainty of being set at liberty. The convalescent, by their contentment, their advice and counsels, console and encourage the sick, and are, in this way, of great service to them. Thus, the inmates of a house of this kind, produce a happy influence, one upon another, and every thing concurs to favor the success of treatment. The arrangements also, are such that the sick can neither injure themselves nor their companions in misfortune, nor those who serve them.

The quietude which the insane enjoy, far from tumult and noise; the moral repose which their withdrawal from their former habits, their business, and domestic cares procure, are very favorable to their restoration. Subjected to a regular life, to discipline, and a well ordered regimen, they are constrained to reflect upon the change in their situation. The necessity of restraining and composing themselves with strangers, and the dwelling together with companions in misfortune, are powerful auxiliaries in restoring their lost reason.

The attentions, which an insane person receives in his family, pass for nothing, though all around him be eager in offering them. But away from home, the care that is bestowed upon him is appreciated, because it is new, and is not strictly due. Civilities, attentions and mildness, will produce an effect, because he has little right to expect them at the hands of those with whom he is not acquainted. Let a man, practiced and skillful, profit by this disposition; let him command confidence and esteem, and the insane will shortly find in the unknown, a person

343

whom they must control, or to whose kindness submit. The necessity of a dependence from which they cannot escape, hope, fear, ennui even, will begin to make them suspicious that they are sick. Having acquired this conviction, the cure is not far distant.

Sometimes the insane, when placed in a new situation, think themselves abandoned by their relatives and friends. But let those to whom they are brought, be prodigal of consolations and regards, let them promise to assist in renewing the connection which binds these unhappy people to moral existence, and they pass from a state of despair to that of hope. This contrast of sentiments, springing from their presumed abandonment, and the tender cares and sympathy bestowed upon them by strangers, provoke an internal struggle, from which reason sometimes comes off victorious. Others imagine that they have been brought to this new abode, only to be given up to their enemies or to punishment. If these fears are overcome by civil and affable conduct, on the part of those by whom they are surrounded, a cure will soon be effected.

Thus reason comes to the support of experience, to strengthen the doctrine of isolation, as a preliminary condition to all rational treatment of mental alienation.

But, says an objector, it may happen, that by dwelling together, the insane may injure each other. The soundest mind would be disturbed, were its habits abruptly changed, and brought into contact only with the insane. Besides, after a cure has been effected, how can we conceal from the patient the condition in which he has been? Why tear away from the seat of all his affections, a miserable man, whom misfortunes have overcome? Why shut up a man who, above all things, dreads a prison.— But, how many objections have already been made? How many may not still be offered? These objections however, do not do away with the inconveniences and advantages that we have pointed out above, and to which experience returns a favoring response.

But, it may be said, that there are insane persons who are cured at home. This is true. These cures however, are rare, and cannot impair the general rule. They prove only, that isolation, like all other curative means, ought always to be prescribed by a physician. I will say more,—that isolation has been fatal to some insane persons. And what shall we conclude from this? That we should recommend it with caution; especially when it is to be prolonged; and also, that it is the nature of the best and most useful things, not to be always exempt from inconveniences. To the wise, judicious and experienced physician does it belong, to foresee and prevent them.

It is not easy to determine the period at which isolation should cease. To prevent abuse, extreme caution and tact are requisite. Here, experience is slow to decide. I recommend nothing positive with respect to it, except that when isolation has had no effect, the visits of relatives and friends should be encouraged, exercising much discretion in the choice of the first persons who may be admitted. Visits, in these cases, should be sudden and unexpected, in order to produce a strong impression upon the patient. With respect to convalescents, visits are to be allowed with great caution. Experience shows, that isolation unduly prolonged, is attended with consequences less injurious than its premature cessation.

We should ever bear in mind, that at the commencement of insanity, this affection strongly resembles febrile delirium—that a mistake is easily made, and that unseasonable isolation may compromise the cure of the patient, and the moral responsibility of the physician. In doubtful and difficult cases, we should delay a few days, in order that the characteristics of mental alienation may become evident.

In dementia and idiocy, isolation is only indicated, to prevent accidents which may be grave, and to maintain order and security. Some lypemaniacs are injured by confinement, in consequence of their excessive sensibility. Monomaniacs and maniacs must of necessity be isolated. Confinement is indispensable for the insane poor, because they are deprived of necessary attentions at home, and can, in a thousand ways, compromise their own, and the existence of their friends.

Isolation is not always effected in the same manner. It is partial, when the patient remains at home, and is only separated from the members of his family, and persons with whom he has habitually lived. We isolate an insane man, by causing him to travel with his near connections, friends or strangers. We isolate him, by placing him alone in a habitation unknown to him, as well as those who serve him. In fine, he is isolated in a public or private establishment, devoted to the reception of many people, affected with mental alienation.

Isolation acts directly upon the brain, and forces this organ to repose, by withdrawing the insane man from irritating impressions,—by repressing the vivacity and mobility of impressions,—by moderating the exaltation of the ideas and affections. By reducing the maniac to the smallest possible number of sensations, we are enabled to fix his attention, by unexpected and oft-repeated impressions. We must, on the contrary, use strong measures with the monomaniac and lypemaniac, to draw them away from their concentrated ideas, and force them to direct their attention upon objects, foreign to their meditations, disquietudes, and delirious pretensions. We must excite the enfeebled attention of him who is in a state of dementia; but the happy effects which we may propose to ourselves are obtained only by means of strong mental impressions, unexpected events, lively, animated, and brief conversations; for it is not by long arguments that we are to expect to benefit the insane. We should ever speak with truth and sincerity to the insane, and only employ the language of reason and kindness. To expect however, to cure the insane by syllogisms and reasoning, indicates little knowledge of the clinical history of mental alienation. *"I understand you perfectly,"* said a young lypemaniac, *"and if I were convinced, I should be cured."* Said another, *"I know what I ought to do, I would do it; but give me the power, the ability which is wanting, and you will have cured me."*

It is here that we must employ a perturbing mode of treatment;—breaking up one spasm by another, by provoking moral shocks, which may dissipate the clouds which obscure the reason,—rend the veil which interposes between man and the external world,—break the vicious chain of ideas,—bring to an end injurious associations,— destroy their despairing concentration of thought, and break the chain which paralyzes all the active powers of the insane. We effect this object by arousing the attention of the insane, now by presenting to them new objects, now by causing them to witness new and surprising phenomena; now, by putting them in opposition to themselves; and sometimes, by taking up their ideas, caressing and flattering them. By complying with their desires, we secure their confidence,—a sure test of an approaching cure. We must bring into subjection the whole character of some patients, conquer their pretensions, control their freaks of passion, break down their pride; while we must arouse and encourage others.

We repress the passionate transports of the maniac, and sustain the broken spirit of the lypemaniac. We oppose the passions of the one to those of the other, and from this struggle, reason sometimes comes off victorious. Fear is a depressing passion, which exercises such an

347

influence over the economy, as to suspend, and even extinguish vital actions.

Can we hope to cure those whom fear pursues and devours, if we do not inspire them with confidence? Many insane persons sleep not; aroused by panic terrors. Encourage them, by causing someone to sleep in their chamber, or by allowing them a light during the night. It is above all, important to substitute a real for an imaginary passion. This monomaniac becomes dissatisfied, although using every thing with an unsparing hand. Cut him off from this habit, and impose upon him real privations; then will satiety, founded on reason, prove a powerful means of cure. A lypemaniac believes that he is abandoned by his friends. Deprive him of those proofs of affection which he forgets; then will he regret their loss, and desire them; and this natural uneasiness, these reasonable desires, will prove a means of cure.

To combat the self-love and vanity of some insane persons, certain allusions may be made to the superiority of others, and to the embarrassments of their own position. Sometimes displeasure opportunely manifested, has been useful. Great experience however, is necessary, to control these passions. The exciting passions of love and ambition, have been called in, to aid in the treatment of the insane. A melancholic is in despair. A law suit is supposed to be instituted against him. The desire to defend his interests restores his intellectual energy. A soldier becomes a maniac. After some months, he is told that a campaign is about to commence. He demands permission to rejoin his general, returns to the army, and arrives there in good health.

Pinel offers some remarkable observations, on the art of directing the intelligence and passions of the insane.

I have published several in my dissertation on the

passions, and proved by facts, how valuable is moral treatment, whether we desire to prevent the outbreak of an attack of insanity, or are called to treat the malady, or propose to confirm a convalescence. This treatment besides, is not confined exclusively to mental maladies: it is applicable to all others. It is not enough to say to the sick, *courage, you will be better*. A feeling heart must dictate these consoling words, that they may reach the mind and heart of him who suffers. How happens it, that in an age in which we have so triumphantly established the influence of the moral over the physical man, that these researches upon man in a state of disease, have not been extended? Gaubius complains of the negligence of physicians in this respect.

The ancients attached great importance to moral therapeutics, which are so much neglected by the moderns. From the highest antiquity, the art of healing was committed to the ministers of the altar. There were temples celebrated for the cures they had wrought. A long voyage, a new climate, the salubrity of holy places, the change of habits and modes of life, purifications, processional marches, the use of thermal waters, and diet, prepared the way for the moral influence which their ceremonies and mysterious practices were to produce upon the sick. The Egyptians, Greeks and Romans, had their Aesculapii, whose priests preserved a medical liturgy, and to whom they were accustomed to come, seeking health. The moderns made their pilgrimages to the revered remains of some saint. In some cities, festivals were celebrated, to which were conducted with pomp, both epileptics and the insane, who were sometimes cured. In our day we have found a great physician. His name, his consolations, his councils, are often more useful than his remedies, because his reputation commands confidence, and permits us not to doubt respecting a cure.

349

The ancients have boasted of the wonderful effects of music. Herodotus and Pausanias assure us, that most legislators were musicians,—that music was used to civilize men. The phrygian measure excited to fury,—the lydian, soothed to melancholy—the eolian was devoted to the amorous passions. Each passion had a rhythm which was proper to it; while the moderns have sacrificed every thing to harmony. The Jews, Greeks, and Romans were all equally aware of the power of music.

Every body knows the effect which the "*ranz des vaches*" produced upon the Swiss. Music acts upon the physical system, by producing gentle shocks upon the nerves, by quickening the circulation, as Gretry observed in his own person. It acts upon our moral nature, or the mind, in fixing the attention by mild impressions, and in exciting the imagination and even the passions, by agreeable recollections. Did they wish success in the treatment of the insane, they would make choice of a small number of instruments,—place the musicians out of sight of the patient, and execute airs familiar to his infancy, or which were agreeable to him after his illness. I have often employed music, but have rarely been successful with it. It brings peace and composure of mind, but does not cure. I have seen those whom music rendered furious; one, because all the tones appeared false; another, because he thought it dreadful that people should amuse themselves near a wretch like him. Finally, I believe that the ancients have exaggerated the effects of music, as well as many other things. The facts, reported by the moderns, are not sufficiently numerous to enable us to determine the circumstances in which music may be useful. However, it is a valuable remedial agent, particularly in convalescence. It ought not to be neglected, however indeterminate may be the principles of its application, or uncertain its efficacy.

350

The means of diverting the mind are, nevertheless, after labor, the most efficacious agents in the cure of the insane, but we cannot rely upon the success of those which exalt the imagination and passions.

The lypemaniac, always suspicious, appropriates to himself whatever strikes his senses, and makes it serve as aliment to his delirium. The maniac becomes still more excited by the representation of the passions, by the vivacity of the dialogue, and the playing of the actors, if he is present at a theatrical representation. Our opinion respecting amusements of this kind is supported by the example of the Egyptians and Greeks. But with them these exhibitions partook of a religious character, adapted to calm the passions, and to impose upon the imagination, at the same time that the mind was diverted by the pomp of the ceremonies. A mind at all accustomed to reflection, is astonished that theatrical representations should formerly have been permitted at Charenton; and a German author regards the multiplication of theatres as one of the causes of the great number of insane people in Germany. The maniacs could never be present at the theatrical representations of Charenton, the monomaniacs rarely,—and imbeciles could not be benefited by them. Those to whom the spectacle could be useful, were already cured, and it would have been more profitable to restore them to liberty than to shut them up for three hours in a place, confined, heated and noisy, where every things tended to produce cephalalgia. Thus there were few representations that were not signalized by some violent explosion of delirium, or by some relapse. This mode of amusement, by which the public were imposed upon by being informed that the insane themselves played comedies, never obtained the approbation of the Physician in chief of the Establishment. Royer-Collard exerted himself vigorously against it, and was ultimately successful in bringing it to an end. I once accompanied a young convalescent to a Comic Opera. He everywhere saw his wife conversing with men. Another, after the space of a quarter of an hour, felt the heat in his head increasing—and says, let us go out, or I shall relapse. A young lady, being at the Opera, and seeing the actors armed with sabres, believed that they were going to assail her. All this happened, notwithstanding I had selected both the individuals I was to accompany, and the pieces that were to be acted. A theatrical spectacle can never be suited to the condition of the insane, and I much fear, not even to that of convalescents.

Seneca says, that traveling is of little benefit in moral affections. He cites on this subject, the reply of Socrates to a melancholic, who was complaining that he had derived little advantage from his travels. *"I am not surprised; do you not travel with yourself?"* However, the ancients prescribed traveling, and sent their patients to take the hellebore of Antycira, or to make the leap at Leucates. The English now send their melancholics into the southern provinces of France, into Italy, and even into the colonies. I have always observed that the insane are relieved by a long voyage, especially if they have visited distant countries, whose situation and aspect took strong hold of their imagination; and if they experienced diffi-culties, opposition, disappointments, and the fatigues incident to travel. Traveling acts moreover, by exciting all the assimilative functions. It promotes sleep, the appetite and secretions. Convalescents, who fear to re-enter the world, where they will be called upon to speak of their complaint, are less uneasy, after a journey which may be made the subject of conversation with their friends. Such are the agents which exercise a direct in-fluence over the brain, and consequently over the intel-lectual and moral disorders of the insane; and such are the general views of their application, which I would suggest. They have for their object, to restrain the mental operations of the maniac, and to draw out and fix upon external objects the mind and thoughts of the monomaniac. The principles of physical treatment cannot be reduced to propositions so general. No one doubts the necessity of acting upon the brain, in combating the causes which have produced and keep up insanity; but the nature of these causes often escapes us. The brain is not always the primitive seat of their action, and this, moreover, does not produce the same effect in every case. The physical means, therefore, adapted to avoid the fatal effects of these causes, must be varied. They are hygienic, or pharmaceutic.

The constitution of the insane becomes rapidly enfeebled. They contract affections of the skin, lymphatic engorgements and scurvy; a circumstance which shows the importance of a suitable site, as well as a mode of construction of their habitations. In building a house for the insane, we should select a site, in our country, with a southeastern exposure; with an exposure to the west in warm countries; and to the south, at the north. The soil should be dry, and light. The lodging rooms should be protected against humidity and cold; and favorably disposed for ventilation. It is a grave error to support that the insane are insensible to atmospheric influences. The greater part of them avoid cold, and desire warmth.

The ancients recommended that maniacs should be placed in a situation cool and obscure. This precept is excellent during the acute period of the malady; but when it has passed into the chronic state, Pinel advises that they be left to all the activity of their movements, and in the open air. Situations well lighted, cheerful and picturesque, are suited to lypemaniacs. Those who have become insane in warm climates, will be more likely to

353

recover their reason by returning to a cold one; and reciprocally. Those afflicted with nostalgia will be restored only by returning to their country, the places where they were born, and where their infancy was passed.

The clothing, especially that of the lypemaniac, should be warm. The use of woolen garments next to the skin, and of dry frictions, will be found of service. The bedding may consist of a mattress and hair-quilt, together with a bolster and pillow of horse-hair. The patient should repose upon a bed of horse-hair. The covering should be light, and the head usually uncovered. Alimentation should be varied according to the nature and period of the malady,—the individual circumstances and complications. At its commencement we prescribe the diet to which most patients are subjected during the early stages of acute disorders; at a later period the quantity and quality of aliments are modified. They should always be simple, prepared without spices, and easy of digestion. During convalescence, the aliment should be more substantial than previously, without ever being excitant, and in some very rare cases should be more abundant. The food should be distributed with discretion. We should avoid furnishing at once a day's supply, as is done in some hospitals. It results, from a neglect of this precaution, that the patients devour or destroy a day's provision at once; and, tormented by hunger during the remainder of it, they become more furious or sorrowful, supposing that they are maliciously refused a supply of their wants, or that the design of starving them to death, is entertained by those who have the charge of them. The greater part of maniacs and monomaniacs are distressed by thirst. We must satisfy this desire by placing appropriate drinks at their doors, or by distributing them at certain hours during the day.

Those aliments and drinks which excite the patient,

should be proscribed during every period of the malady. Nevertheless, they may be adapted to some cases of dementia, or monomania, and to the period of convalescence, as I have just remarked. Both the secretions and excretions should be favored in every possible manner. We should watch with care, the condition of the bowels; for constipation is a frequent symptom, and one which exasperates the delirium.

Corporeal exercises, riding on horseback, the game of tennis, fencing, swimming and traveling, especially in melancholy, should be employed, in aid of other means of treatment. The culture of the earth, with a certain class of the insane, may be advantageously substituted for all other exercises. We know the result to which a Scotch farmer arrived, by the use of labor. He rendered himself celebrated by the cure of certain insane persons, whom he obliged to labor in his fields.

Bourgoin, in his *Travels in Spain*, remarks, that the rich at the Hospital for the insane at Saragossa, are not restored, because they are not obliged to labor; whilst the poor work and are cured. Pinel recommends that an Establishment for the insane should have a farm connected with it, on which the patients can labor. The cultivation of the garden, has succeeded happily in the cure of some insane persons. At the Salpetriere, the best results follow the manual labor of the women in that Hospital. They are assembled in a large working room, where some engage in sewing or knitting; while others perform the service of the house, and cultivate the garden. This precious resource is wanting in the treatment of the rich of either sex. An imperfect substitute is furnished, in walks, music, reading, assemblages, etc. The habit of idleness among the wealthy, counterbalances all the other advantages which this class enjoy for obtaining a cure.

To establish the basis of a certain therapeutic treatment of mental alienation, it would be necessary to understand all the general and individual causes of this malady; to distinguish by certain signs, the source from whence all disorders spring; to determine whether the physical reacts upon the moral, or the moral upon the physical; to establish the varieties of insanity that are cured spontaneously; those which call for moral aids; those which require medication; and finally, those which yield only to a mixed treatment. What accidents have befallen, what obstacles opposed those physicians, who have been unwilling to see but one disorder, in all the forms of insanity that they have been called to treat! They inferred that delirium being symptomatic of almost all maladies at the approach of their fatal terminations, insanity might also be symptomatic. They were not ignorant that there were forms of insanity evidently sympathetic; they knew that a thousand predisposing and exciting causes lead to insanity; but having regard only to the most apparent symptoms, they have permitted themselves to be diverted by the impetuosity, violence, and changefulness of the symptoms, and neglected the study of the causes of insanity, and the relations which they bear to the symptoms. Drawn away by theories, some have seen nothing but inflammation; have charged upon the blood the production of insanity, and employed bleeding to excess. Others believed that the bile was the source of irritation, and that it restrained and interfered with the due performance of organic functions. They were prodigal of emetics and drastic purgatives. Others still have taken account only of the nervous influence, and employed antispasmodics in excess. All have forgotten, that if the practitioner ought always to have before his mind great general truths,—systematic views, which are to predominate, and which constitute medical science; art should

356

confine itself to the most careful study of the circumstances and symptoms, which will best acquaint us with the causes and seat; in a word, with the nature of the malady which we are to combat.

When called to visit an insane person, after having acquired a knowledge of his history, together with the predisposing and exciting causes of his attack, we should inquire if there are no urgent indications to fulfill. To ascertain the cause of the malady, will, in general, furnish a clue to the best mode of treatment. To recall the menses when suppressed, to reestablish old ulcers, to provoke cutaneous affections, and to insert issues, if the patient had formerly been accustomed to them, will be peculiarly proper. If there is active excitement attended with plethora, these symptoms must be controlled by sanguine evacuations, tepid baths and emollients long continued; together with cooling and laxative drinks. Sometimes it will be necessary to apply to the skin rubefacient derivatives. At the same time, the strictest attention should be paid to the diet and regimen of the patient. Treated as an acute disorder, almost always at the expiration of 8, 15, 21, or 30 days, there is a remission, and sometimes a very marked intermission. Then, in connection with those moral means appropriate to the character of the delirium, we must set ourselves to combating these material causes, whether hygienic or pathological, which had preceded and induced the malady; in every case, following the individual indications. Let it suffice, to point out a few of these indications. A man becomes insane, who has been subject to hemorrhages which no longer exist. The physician succeeds in establishing this evacuation, and at the same time in restoring reason to his patient. A cutaneous affection disappears; an ulcer dries up, and mania or monomania bursts forth. On recalling the disorder of the skin, and reopening the ulcer, it is almost certain that

357

the insanity will cease.

When we have attacked and overcome the general derangements, the painful effects of particular causes, if the insanity is not cured, we may have recourse to an empirical treatment. We may here vary without ceasing, those measures which experience suggests. We shall point them out, when speaking of the different forms of insanity. We shall content ourselves for the present, by stating our opinion respecting the mode of action of certain remedies denominated heroic, in the treatment of this disease.

Water by all methods, and at every temperature, has been administered to the insane. Tepid baths, from 20° to 25° Reaumur, are the most useful. We may even prolong their use for several hours in succession, among lean, nervous and very irritable subjects. When there is a strong determination of blood to the head, we find it advantageous to apply bladders filled with very cold water, or cloths saturated with the same to the head, during the continuance of the bath. The cold bath is adapted to young, strong, and robust subjects, who are devoured by heat. The cold acts by removing to some extent, the excess of heat, or by exciting the tonic action of the skin. Some authors have advised hot baths. Prosper Alpin advises them; perhaps we neglect them too much. The baths are rendered more active by mingling with the water divers kinds of substances, more or less medicinal.

The bath of immersion consists in plunging the patient into cold water, and withdrawing him immediately. This may be repeated three, four, five and six times. The bath of effusion, following the method of Currie, is administered by placing the patient in an empty bathing tub, and pouring upon his head cold water, whose temperature is reduced at each bath. The baths of immersion and effusion are particularly useful to subjects enfeebled by masturbation, or by long grief, and in whose cases we wish to produce a reaction, by withdrawing from the centre, nervous power, and calling it to the circumference. These baths differ from the bath of surprise. The latter consists in plunging the patient into the water when he least expects it. We administer it, by precipitating him into a reservoir, a river, or the sea. It is the fright which renders this means efficacious in overcoming sensibility. We can conceive the vivid impression that a patient experiences, who falls unexpectedly into the water, with the fear of being drowned.

Van Helmont recommends that the patient be kept under water, till loss of consciousness takes place. Van Swieten, commenting upon Boerhaave, insists upon this means, which was almost the only one, in connection with blood-letting, employed during the last century. However, we have no fact illustrating the effects of this practice. Pinel proscribed the bath of surprise. I have never made use of it, but am certain that it has been fatal. When I hear of its being prescribed, I should prefer rather, that they advised to precipitate the patient from the third story, because we have known some insane persons cured by falling upon the head. The douche consists in pouring water upon the head from a greater or less height. It was known to the ancients; and is administered in different ways. At Avignon, the tube of the douche, with a flute-like termination, is placed about a foot above the head of the patient. At Bordeaux, it terminates in a head like that of a watering pot. At the Salpetriere, the douches terminate in tubes of four, six and twelve lines in diameter, and the water falls from different heights. The water is usually at the atmospheric temperature. It has been proposed to employ hot water in some cases of dementia. The patient receives the douche, seated in an arm chair; or better, plunged into a bath of tepid or cold water.

The douche produces its effects, both by the action of the cold, and the percussion. It exercises a sympathetic influence upon the region of the epigastrium. It causes cardialgia, and desires to vomit. After its action ceases, the patients are pale, and sometimes sallow. It acts also morally, as a means of repression; a douche often sufficing to calm a raging excitement, to break up the dangerous resolutions, or force a patient to obedience. It is that class of the insane who are young, strong and active, who require the douche. They experience after having received it, a sensation of coolness about the head, which is very agreeable to them, and often very useful. It is especially proper in cases attended with cephalalgia. The douche ought to be employed with discretion, and never immediately after a repast. It is necessary to obviate constipation before employing it. Its employment ought to be continued but a few minutes at a time, and its administration never to be left to servants. They may abuse it, and we ought not to be ignorant that the douche is not exempt from grave accidents. Ice has been applied to the head. Its long continued application calms the cephalalgia and fury which resists blood-letting, general baths, and the douche, especially at the commencement of mania; when there is redness and heat of face, threatening cerebral congestion. This application succeeds much better when the feet of the patient are plunged into very warm water, or enveloped in an irritating cataplasm.

Revulsive pediluvia, produce a remote irritation, which is often salutary. We render them irritant, by the elevated temperature of the water, by the addition of the muriates of soda, ammonia, and powdered mustard. We ought to remember, that if the water is too warm at first, it causes pain, which reacts upon the brain. By plunging the legs into an emollient decoction, slightly warmed, and allowing them to remain there for a considerable period, we relieve the patient of cramps. We moreover make use

360

of water by jets, frequently repeated; throwing it upon the faces of some, who are laboring under a stupor. These slight excitements, frequent and unexpected, have sometimes aroused patients from their lethargy. Water has been prescribed by injections; sometimes pure, sometimes combined with purgative, and soothing or antispasmodic remedies, as the indications required. The douche by the rectum has also been advised, to overcome obstinate constipation,—to unload the large intestines, and to relieve the spasm of the alimentary canal; sometimes to give tone to this tract, or to provoke a derivative irritation.

Avenbrugger recommended the internal use of cold water, drank in large quantities, at the rate of a tumbler every hour. Hufeland regards this means as of service in mania. Leroi d'Anvers has published an account of the advantages of cold water, as a preventive of suicide. Many facts seem to justify this practice. The most interesting is that of Theden, a very distinguished Prussian surgeon, who having been hypochondriacal in his youth, at length became melancholic, with a disposition to commit suicide. The copious use of cold water restored him to health. He drank of it from twenty-four to thirty pints a day. From a favorable opinion of its utility, as well as from the force of habit, Theden has reported, that at the age of eighty years, he drank every day, several pints of cold water. Hufeland confirms this fact by two cases which he has collected. This means has been particularly advised, as a preventive of suicide.

Evacuants have been celebrated from the highest antiquity, and for a long time formed the basis of treatment in insanity, particularly, lypemania. Far from being adapted to all cases, they may augment the evil. The moderns have advised emetics, which ought to hold a high place in the treatment of some forms of monomania, and lypemania with stupor. Emetics are suited to those cases in which the sensibility is blunted, where the patient seems stricken with atony, whilst they would be injurious, did irritation exist. Mason Cox places emetics in the front rank of remedies, in every stage of insanity. Rush believes emetics most useful in hypochondriacal melancholy. They repeat them many days in succession. Besides the sensible evacuations which they provoke, they excite the transpiration, and cause succussions useful in relieving spasms of the abdominal viscera. Purgatives are also praised. The choice of purgatives is not a matter of indifference. In some cases, we prefer those which have a special action upon the hepatic system, the hemorrhoidal vessels, upon intestinal worms, etc. Purgatives often cause irritation, thereby suspending the activity of the skin. To prevent these accidents, or consecutive effects, we alternate them with the tepid bath. Many insane persons think themselves very well, and refuse all medication. We may triumph over this repugnance by causing them to take without their knowledge, some substance which, by irritating the stomach or intestines, provokes pains, and even evacuations. These accidents, by causing uneasiness in the mind of the patient respecting his health, render him docile. Hellebore, gamboge, bryony, aloes, submuriate of mercury, and especially the tartrate of antimony and potassa, together with purgative mineral waters, are the therapeutic agents, which we may at such times employ with advantage.

M. Chrestien, a celebrated practitioner of Montpellier, proposes colocynth, administered by friction upon the abdomen, as a sure purgative. He goes so far as to recommend this substance as a specific in insanity. I have repeated the experiments of M. Chrestien, upon twenty insane persons, but have not been equally successful with himself. The colocynth not only failed to effect a cure, but did not purge, except in two instances after confinement.

On the discovery of the circulation of the blood, it was believed that we had discovered the cause of every disorder, and a remedy for all ills. Blood was shed abundantly. The blood of the insane was the more freely shed, as by bleeding them to faintness, it was believed that they were cured. This treatment was extended to all the insane. In every hospital, there was established what was called, the treatment of the insane on this principle; that the blood being too abundant and too much heated, ought to be evacuated and cooled. Besides, in the hospitals of France, where some attention was paid to the insane, in spring and autumn, they bled them once or twice, and bathed them in cold water; or cast them, bound hand and foot, into a river or reservoir. If a few victims of such gross mismanagement escaped, they cried out, a miracle! Such was the prejudice not long since even at Paris, in favor of bleeding, that we were accustomed to receive pregnant women, who were bled by way of precaution, before being sent to a house where bleeding was proscribed. Excess in this respect has sometimes been so great, that I have had in charge an insane man, who had been bled thirteen times in forty-eight hours. Pinel set himself against this abuse, and cites examples which ought to be presented to the observation of all physicians. I can add, that I have many times seen insanity increase after abundant menstrual flows, after hemorrhages, and after one, two and even three bleedings. I have seen a state of sadness pass into mania and fury, immediately after bleeding; and dementia to replace, reciprocally, the condition of mania. I do not believe it necessary to proscribe blood-letting in the treatment of insanity. It is indispensable in plethoric subjects, when the head is strongly congested, and hemorrhages, or habitual sanguine evacuations have been suppressed. At the commencement of insanity, if there is plethora, if the blood

363

rushes violently to the head, if some habitual hemorrhage is suppressed, we bleed largely, once, twice, or thrice; apply leeches to the jugular veins and temporal arteries, and cups to the base of the brain. At a later period, sanguine evacuations are local, and employed as revulsives, or as supplementary to suppressed evacuations, etc. The use of energetic tonics and antispasmodics, ought also to be appreciated. Camphor, musk, iron, quinine and antimony, have been employed in very large doses, as specifics in insanity. These medicines are useful, but of individual utility. They succeed surprisingly well, when one is sufficiently happy to seize the proper indication for their use, which the disease presents; but are hurtful and dangerous if employed indiscriminately.

Some insane persons sleep little; passing weeks and months without repose. Narcotics are employed to produce sleep. These medicines are rather hurtful than salutary, especially when there is plethora, or congestion of the head. For a long time, Valsalva and Morgagni proscribed opiates, and daily practice confirms the judgment of these great masters. Regimen, labor and exercise, are the true remedies for insomnia. Tepid or cool baths provoke sleep, are truly efficacious, and are in no way dangerous. Setons, moxas, the actual cautery, cups, vesicatories, irritating and mercurial frictions have been employed. These means are excellent auxiliaries to provoke a revulsion, to bring back a cutaneous eruption which has been suppressed, to arouse the sensibility of the skin, which is often in a state of atony, to excite a general reaction, etc., etc. It has been proposed to envelope the head with epispastics, or some other irritating compositions; and to employ a saturated solution of tartrate of antimony and potassa, in water. I must confess, that I have never seen those means succeed, which augment irritation,—torment and disturb the sick, and

364

persuade them that we wish to punish them. It is almost always among monomaniacs, or persons in a state of dementia, that we prescribe a course of medication, so active and perturbating. I do not deny, that in some cases, success may have followed this treatment; but I believe that those cases are very rare, and the indications very difficult to appreciate.

I cannot omit making some remarks respecting the use of fire and moxa, applied to the top of the head, and over the occiput or neck in mania. Doctor L. Valentin has published some valuable observations concerning the cure of mania by the application of fire.* I have many times applied the iron at a red heat to the neck, in mania complicated with fury, and sometimes with success. I made very many attempts, which always proved fruitless, when I addressed myself to subjects which presented symptoms of paralysis. The seton in the neck, has succeeded better in my hands, except when I have applied it to individuals who did not experience the same complications, and who were in that stage of dementia which is confounded with idiocy.

Gmelin and Perfect affirm, that they have effected cures by electricity. At the Salpetriere, during two summers, those of 1823 and 1824, I submitted to the influence of electricity a large number of our insane women. One only was cured, in the course of my experiments. This was a young and very strong girl, who had become a maniac in consequence of a fright, which suppressed her menses. She had been insane for a month, and was electrized for fifteen days. At the menstrual period, the discharge appeared, and she was immediately restored. Wennolt tried galvanism. I also employed it, in connection with Professor Aldini, in 1812. Twice the menses were restored,

---

* An Essay and Observations concerning the good effects of the actual cautery, applied to the head in various disorders. Nancy, 1815, in 8vo.

but the delirium persisted. Experiments have been made with magnetism, particularly in Germany. The facts reported in France, in relation to it, are neither exact, nor well observed. In 1813 and 1816, I made experiments with the late M. Faria, upon eleven insane women, maniacs or monomaniacs. One only, who was remarkably hysterical, yielded to the magnetic influence; but her delirium underwent no change. Magnetism produced no effect upon ten other insane persons. These experiments were made in presence of M. Desportes, governor of the hospitals, and others, besides several physicians. I repeated the same trials, several times, with divers magnetizers, with no better success.*

I ought to say a word respecting the machine of Darwin. This instrument which, nearly enough, resembles a circular swing, has passed from the arts, to be employed in medicine. Mason Cox made much use of it. Hufeland and Horn employed it at Berlin. One of them remains at Geneva, which furnished Odier an opportunity to observe its effects. Doctor Martin, physician of the hospital at Antiquaille, where to this day the insane of Lyons are treated, has informed me that he had been frightened at the accidents which the insane had met with, who had been submitted to the influence of this machine. They fell into a state of syncope, and had also copious evacuations both by vomiting and purging, which prostrated them extremely. This mode of treatment, employed with prudence, may be useful to such insane persons as refuse all kinds of medicine, and who present symptoms of gastric derangement.†

---

* Georget has given an account of the experiments in magnetism, which he made at the Salpetriere, in a work entitled: *"Physiology of the Nervous System."* Paris, 1821, tome I, Page 267, and tome II. p. 404. M. Dechambre, who repeated the experiments which he performed, is convinced that Georget was the dupe of his pretended somnambulist. See *Medical Gazette,* year 1835, for a very witty account of the experiments made by M. Dechambre.

† Since the first edition of this article was published, the rotary machine has been everywhere abandoned.

We should not complete all that relates to the treatment of insanity, did we neglect to speak of the modes of preventing it. Prophylactic measures have for their object the preventing of the disorder, or the return of an attack. These measures are either general or particular. They have been already indicated, by an exposition of the causes of insanity. We should avoid marriages with persons descended from insane parents. The education of man begins in infancy, and we should guard against the recital of such stories and fables to children, as disturb the brain, or painfully excite the imagination. While cultivating the mind, we should at the same time form the heart, and never lose sight of the fact that education consists less in what we learn, than in correct habits of mind, feeling and action. If education is neither religious nor moral; if the child meets with no opposition to his wishes or caprices; if every one yields to his desire; how will he familiarize himself to the difficulties with which life abounds? We should not force the principles of feeling and intelligence, by early fatiguing the brain with lessons of inordinate length. We should avoid errors of regimen, which often, at the tenderest age, predispose to insanity. We should control, and direct the passions of the young.

The education of those who are born of parents already insane, should be less devoted to the cultivation of the mind, than the strengthening of the physical powers. The preceptor, informed beforehand of the mental state of their parents, and the wanderings of their passions, will educate his pupils with reference to this knowledge,—will moderate their undue ardor of mind,—check their wayward propensities, and fortify them against the seductive influence of the passions; whilst the physician, aware of the physical causes which have provoked the disease in the persons of their parents, will prevent the development

367

of these causes, or diminish their deplorable effects, by regimen and medicines adapted to the wants of their children.

How can we assure ourselves of his convalescence, and prevent relapses, if the patient is not submitted during a period, more or less protracted, to a mode of life appropriate to his constitution, and to the causes and character of the malady from which he has just been restored? if he avoid not the predisposing, physical and moral causes,—if he is not watchful against errors of regimen, excess of study, and transports of passion? Experience has taught us that relapses often take place, in consequence of the simultaneous development of physical and moral causes. We must attack with energy, these causes, from the moment that they manifest themselves, without awaiting the explosion of the delirium. An emetic, and purgatives given in season, may arrest an attack of insanity. The application of leeches, and blood-letting, in cases of slight menstrual disorder, prevent attacks, which might otherwise have taken place. The disappearance of a cutaneous eruption, of the gout, or rheumatism, or an habitual evacuation, has preceded a first attack of insanity. We must be ever watchful of these metastases and suppressions. What has been said respecting the precautions which the physical state of those who have been insane, demands, is equally true with respect to the moral. One man is choleric; he will relapse unless he exercise all his strength to overcome this passion. Another has lost his reason in consequence of domestic trials. He ought from henceforth to be spared from these afflictions. A third remains in imminent danger of a relapse, if he does not reform his conduct, and abandon the excesses that have preceded his first attack. It is for want of foresight that insanity is so often hereditary; and in consequence of imprudences, that persons who have had one attack of insanity are subject to a recurrence of the same malady.

(JEAN) ÉTIENNE DOMINIQUE ESQUIROL (b.—Toulouse, France, Feb. 3, 1772; d.—Paris, Dec. 12, 1840).

Esquirol studied under Pinel at the Salpetrière. In 1817 he instituted the first formal instruction in psychiatry, at the Salpetrière,—which he directed after Pinel's death. These were the famous "cours cliniques." Later he became physician-in-chief of the Maison Royale des Aliénés de Charenton. Together with the great Quaker, William Tuke (founder of the York Retreat in 1796 in England), Vincenzo Chiarugi of Florence (who even antedates Pinel), and Benjamin Rush of Philadelphia, Esquirol stands foremost in the development of mental hospitals. In his lifetime, he established hospitals and clinics throughout France, all thoroughly founded on Pinel's teachings of the moral treatment of insanity.

Letting Esquirol's voice represent both his own, and the equally courageous sentiments of William Tuke, we find in the preface of Esquirol's major work (v.i.), a statement of dedication reflecting the highest aims of humanity:

Happy shall I be, if this new publication, notwithstanding its imperfections, may contribute to overcome prejudices, to dissipate errors, to throw light upon obscure points connected with mental diseases, and to make known truths of useful application in the treatment and regimen, of that unfortunate class, to whom I have dedicated my life.

The substantive import of Esquirol's writings today is largely historical. But comparisons with similar writings today are both instructive, and not a little unfavorable to our modern methods. The humility and the gentle philosophy of Esquirol stand as models for us all.

ESQUIROL, E. *Mental maladies: a treatise on insanity.* Lea & Blanshard, 1845. Trans. E. K. Hunt, with additions. "Insanity: General description of the mental characteristics of the inmates of an institution for the insane." Chap. I, No. 1: "Symptoms of insanity." Chap. I, No. V: "Treatment of insanity."

See also: (These are all rare books.)

ESQUIROL, E.

a) *Des établissements consacrés aux aliénés en France, et des moyens de les améliorer.* Paris: Renouard, c. 1818.

b) *Mémoire historique et statistique sur la Maison royale de Charenton.* Paris: Renouard, 1835.

c) *Des maladies mentales considerées sous les rapports médical, hygiénique et médico-légal.* Paris: Baillière, 1838.

CLINICAL LECTURES
ON
CERTAIN DISEASES
OF THE
NERVOUS SYSTEM
Jean Martin Charcot

LECTURE VII
ON SIX CASES OF HYSTERIA IN THE MALE SUBJECT

SUMMARY.- Hysteria in the male is not so rare as one might suppost. Role of traumatism in the development of this affection; railway spine. Tenacity of hysterical stigmata in typical cases in both sexes.

Account of three typical and complete cases of hystero-epilepsy in the male. Striking resemblance which these cases bear to each other, and to corresponding cases observed in the female sex.

GENTLEMEN: We shall study to-day hysteria in the male sex, and in order the better to compass the subject, we shall consider male hysteria more particularly in adolescent subjects, or such as are in the vigor of age and in full maturity, that is to say, in men of from twenty to forty years, and we shall give attention more especially to that intense, very pronounced form which corresponds to what is called in the female great hysteria, or hystero-epilepsy with mixed crises. If I have decided to take up this subject which I have touched upon many times already, it is because we have actually in our clinical service at the present time a truly remarkable collection of patients whom I shall cause to appear before you, and whom I shall study with you. I have for my object especially to make you recognize and prove by your senses the identity of the great neurosis in both sexes, for in the comparison which we shall make as we go on of the symptoms of hysteria major in the female and in the male, everywhere we shall have occasion to remark the most striking similarities, and here and there only, certain differences which as you will see, are of but secondary importance.

Moreover, this question of hysteria in the male subject is one of the questions regarded as of special interest at the present day. In France, during the last few years it has much occupied the attention of physicians. From 1875 to 1880 five inaugural dissertations on hysteria in the male were defended before the Faculty of Paris, and Klein, author of one of these theses written under the direction of Dr. Olivier, succeeded in compiling eighty cases of this affection. Since then the important publications of Bourneville and his pupils have appeared; of Debove, Raymond, Dreyfus and some others; and all these works tend to prove, among other things, that cases of male hysteria may be met with quite frequently in ordinary practice. Quite recently, male hysteria has been studied in America by Putnam and Walton, principally in connection with and as a sequel of traumatisms, and more especially of railroad accidents. They have recognized, along with Page, who has also interested himself in this question in England, that many of those nervous accidents designated under the name of *railway spine,* and which, in his opinion, might better be called *railway brain,* are in reality, whether appearing in man or in woman, simply hysterical manifestations. It is easy, then, to understand the interest which such a question has to the practical mind of our confreres of the United States. The victims of railroad accidents quite naturally claim damages of the companies. The case goes into court; thousands of dollars are at stake. Now, I repeat, often it is hysteria which is at the bottom of all these nervous lesions. Those neuropathic states, so grave and so tenacious, which present themselves as the sequel of "collisions" of that kind, and which render their victims unable to work or pursue any regular occupation for months and for even years, are often only hysteria, nothing but hysteria. Male hysteria is then worthy of being studied and known by the medico-legalist, for he is often called upon to give his opinion, in matters concerning which great pecuniary interests are at stake, before a tribunal which would be likely to be influenced (and this circumstance renders his task the more difficult) by the disfavor which is still attached to the word hysteria on account of prejudices profoundly rooted. A thorough acquaintance not only with the disease, but also with the conditions under which it is produced, will be on such occasions the more useful from the fact that the nervous disorders often ensue without any traumatic lesion, and simply as a consequence of the psychical nervous shock resulting from the accident; frequently, moreover, they do not come on immediately after the accident, but some time afterwards, when, for instance, one of the victims of the collision, who may have been disabled by fracture of the leg, will have got well after being incapacitated for work for three or four months; another, perhaps, may have been suffering from nervous troubles which are destined to prevent him from working for six months or a year, but which have not reached their full intensity. You see how delicate in such cases is the mission of the medical jurist, and it is this medico-legal side of the question which seems among our American confreres to have awakened a new interest in the study of hysterical neuroses heretofore a little neglected.

In proportion as the disease has been better studied and better known (as habitually happens in similar circumstances), cases become apparently more and more frequent, and at the same time, more easy of analysis. I just told you that four or five years ago, Klein, in his thesis, had collected eighty cases of hysteria in men; to-day, Batault who is preparing in our hospital service a special work on the subject, has been able to gather together 218 cases of the same kind, none of which belong to our clinic.

Male hysteria is, then, far from being rare. Indeed, gentlemen, if I were to judge from what I see every day among us, these cases are very often misunderstood, even by very distinguished physicians. It is granted that an effeminate young man may, after certain excesses, disappointments, deep emotions, present various phenomena of an hysterical nature, but that a vigorous mechanic, well developed, not enervated by an indolent or too studious mode of life, a fireman of a locomotive, for instance, never before emotional, at least in appearance, may, as the result of a railroad accident, a collision, a car running off from the track, become hysterical just like a woman— all this has never entered into the imagination of some people. Nothing, however, is better proved, and pathology must adjust itself to this new conception, which will hereafter take its place along with other propositions which are to-day received as demonstrated truths, after having long fought their way through scepticism, and often through ridicule.

There is a prejudice which doubtless contributes much to oppose the diffusion of right knowledge relative to hysteria in the male sex; I refer to the relatively false notion generally entertained of the clinical tableau of this neurosis in the female. In the male, in fact, the disease often presents itself as an affection remarkable by the permanence and tenacity of the symptoms which characterize it. In the female, on the contrary—and this is without doubt that which seems to constitute the capital difference between the two sexes in the estimation of anyone who does not thoroughly and radically know the disease

373

in the female—what is generally believed to be the characteristic feature of hysteria is the instability, the mobility of the symptoms. In hysteria, it is said, observations of the disease in the female being naturally taken as the basis of this opinion, the phenomena are mobile, fugacious, and the capricious march of the affection is often interrupted by scenes of the most unexpected nature. Very well, but, gentlemen, this mobility, this fugaciousness is far from being a universal characteristic of hysteria, even in the female, as I have shown you by numerous examples.

Yes, even in females there are cases of hysteria with durable, permanent phenomena, extremely difficult to modify, and which sometimes resist all medical interference. Cases of this kind are numerous, very numerous, if, indeed, they do not constitute the majority. This is a point to which I shall return shortly. But for the moment I content myself by remarking, only, that the permanence of the hysterical symptoms in the male, and their tenacity often prevent the medical attendants from recognizing their true character. Some, in presence of phenomena which resist all therapeutic modifiers, will believe, I imagine, if there exist sensorial troubles with nervous crises simulating more or less the epileptic fit, that they have to do with an organic localized lesion (lesion en foyer), an intra-cranial neoplasm, or if it is a case of paraplegia, with an organic spinal lesion. Others will willingly admit, or will even affirm, that there can be no question in these cases of an organic alteration, but simply of a dynamic lesion; but in view of symptoms whose tenacity does not comport with the scheme which they have in mind of hysteria, they will think that they have before them a special disease, not yet described, and which merits a place by itself.

A mistake of this kind seems to me to have been committed by M. M. Oppenheim and Thomsen, of Berlin, in a memoir which contains, however, a great number of interesting facts, carefully observed, if not always well interpreted, at least according to my way of thinking. These gentlemen have observed hemi-anæsthesia, sensitive and sensorial, like in all points to that of hysterical patients, in seven observations similar to those of Putnam and Walton. These cases had to do with firemen, conductors, workingmen, victims of rail-road or other accidents, all of whom had sustained a blow on the head, a concussion, or a general shock. Alcoholism, lead-poisoning, etc., were not factors in these cases, and the fact was recognized that, according to every probability, there existed no organic lesion in these subjects.

We have here, then, a set of cases quite like those of Putnam and Walton, but differing from the latter in this respect that the German authorities are not willing to concede that these are cases of hysteria, which to their minds constitute something peculiar, some undefined, undescribed pathological state, demanding a new place in the nosological category. The principal arguments which Oppenheim and Thomsen adduce to the support of their thesis are the following: 1. The anæsthesia is obstinate; we do not see there those capricious changes which are characteristic(?) of hysteria. It lasts just as it is for months and for years. 2. Another reason is that the psychical state of the patient is not that of the hysterical. The troubles of this order in these patients have not the changing, mobile traits of hysterical manifestations. The patients are conspicuously depressed, melancholic after a permanent sort, and without great fluctuations in the degree of their melancholy.

It is impossible for me to agree with the conclusions of M. M. Oppenheim and Thomsen, and I hope to show you, gentlemen, 1, that the sensorial hysterical troubles may in the female, even, present a remarkable tenacity, and that in the male it is often so; 2, that in the male in particular, the depression and the melancholic tendency are most commonly observed in the most marked, the least contestable cases of hysteria. We do not indeed ordinarily observe in the male subject, although this is assuredly not a distinctive characteristic of the first order, those caprices, those changes of character and humor, which belong more commonly, but not necessarily, to the hysteria of the female.

But it is time, gentlemen, to bring to end these preliminary remarks, in order to come to the principal object of our lesson today. We shall proceed by clinical demonstration to study together in detail a certain number of perfectly characteristic cases of male hysteria. While thus engaged we shall bring to view the likenesses and the differences that exist between the symptoms of hysteria observed in men and those with which we are familiar every day in the corresponding form of the disease in women. Lastly, I intend to present after the manner of a summary, certain general considerations on the great hysteria (hysteria major) as seen in the male sex.

But before coming to my subject proper, I desire briefly to remind you by two examples to what extent in the female the permanent symptoms of hysteria, the hysterical stigmata, as we are wont to call them for convenience, may show themselves fixed, tenacious, and consequently exempt from that proverbial mobility which has been attributed to them, and which some writers regard as characteristic of the disease. I shall not refer now to the six or eight subjects of great hysteria actually assembled in our wards. Certain of them have presented for months and even for years a simple or double anæsthesia which our best and most appropriate therapeutic modifiers can influence only for a few hours. I will limit myself to presenting to you two women who are veritable veterans of hystero-epilepsy, and who now, being rid for several years of their great attacks, and discharged from the medical service, exercise in the hospital the functions of domestics. The first, L. by name, well known in the history of hystero-epilepsy, and noted for the "demoniacal" character which her convulsive crises presented, is to-day 63 years of age. She entered the Salpetriere in 1846, and I have not ceased to have her under observation since 1871. At this time she was affected, as she is still to-day, with a right hemi-anæsthesia, complete, absolute, sensorial and sensitive, with ovaria on the same side, which, during this long period of fifteen years, has never been modified, *even temporarily,* whether by the action many times tried of æsthesiogenous agents, whether by the progress of age and the menopause. Six years ago, at the time when our attention was more particularly directed to the modifications which the visual field undergoes in the hysterical, we detected in this patient the existence in a marked degree of the classic contraction of the visual field, which was pronounced on both sides, but much more so on the right. The repeated examination once or twice every year since then has never failed to reveal the permanence of this contraction.

The other patient, Aurel by name, aged 62 years, and in whom the great seizures, replaced sometimes by certain symptoms of angina pectoris, have only ceased within a dozen of years, presented as far back as 1851, according to a precious note dated that very year, a left hemianæsthesia, complete and absolute, sensorial and sensitive, which, as you can observe for yourselves, exists this very day, after a lapse of 34 years. This patient has been under our observation for fifteen years, and never has the hemianæsthesia in question ceased to present itself

377

during our often-repeated examinations. The double contraction of the visual field, very plain on both sides, but more pronounced on the left, which the campimetric examination has enabled us at the present time to find, already existed with her five years ago.

This is enough, I think, to show you how stable and permanent in these women are the stigmata of which no one would think of disputing the hysterical nature, and how little this corresponds to the notion, erroneous by reason of being carried too far, which is generally entertained of the evolution of the symptoms of the disease.

I come now to the study of our male hysterics.

Case I.—Rig * * *, aged 44 years, clerk in an oil factory, entered the Salpetriere May 12, 1884, or about a year ago. He is a large strong man, of firm muscles; was formerly a cooper, and endured without fatigue arduous toil. The hereditary antecedents in this patient are very remarkable. His father is still living, aged 76 years. From the age of 38 to 44 the latter, by reason of disappointments and pecuniary losses, suffered *nervous attacks,* as to the nature of which the patient can give us but little information. His mother died at the age of 63, of asthma. His mother's *great uncle* was *epileptic,* and died in consequence of a fall into the fire during one of his fits. The *two daughters of this uncle* were also *epileptic.* Rig * * * has had seven brothers and sisters who have never had any nervous diseases. Four are dead; among the three living, one sister is asthmatic. He himself has had nine children, four of whom died young. Of the five who are still living, *one daughter fifteen years old has nervous crises; another, aged ten years, has attacks of hystero-epilepsy* which Dr. Marie has witnessed in this very place; *another daughter is feeble in intelligence;* lastly, two boys present nothing in particular to note.

In the personal antecedents we find the following facts:

At the age of 19 or 20 years, the patient was attacked with acute articular rheumatism, without lesions of the heart. The last attack lasted six months, and it is, perhaps, to the rheumatism that we are to attribute the deformation of the hands, which we note in this patient. While a child, he was very timid, his sleep was troubled by dreams and nightmares, and besides he was addicted to somnambulism. He would often rise in the night-time and go to work, and the next morning he would be much surprised to find his job done. This state continued from 12 to 15 years. He married at 28 years of age. We do not find in his antecedents either syphilis or alcoholism, vices from which coopers are not always exempt. He came to Paris when 32 years old, working at first with his father, then employed as shop clerk in an oil refinery.

In 1876, when 32 years of age, he met with his first accident. He cut himself quite deeply with a razor which he was sharpening, as some people are in the habit of doing, by straping it back and forth on the front aspect of the fore arm. A vein was cut, and the blood spurted; under the influence of the hemorrhage and the fright, the patient lost consciousness and fell to the ground. He was a long time in recovering, remaining two months profoundly anæmiated, pale and without power to work.

In 1882, consequently about three years ago, he was lowering a barrel of wine into the cellar, when the cord which held it gave way; the barrel rolled down the stairway and would certainly have crushed him if he had not jumped to one side, he did not, however, save himself sufficiently to avoid a slight wound of the left hand. Despite the fright which he experienced, he was able to get up and help raise the cask. But five minutes afterward, he had an attack of loss of consciousness which lasted twenty minutes. Coming to himself, he was unable to walk, so weak had his limbs become, and he was taken home in a carriage. For two days, it was absolutely impossible for him to work; during the night his sleep was disturbed by frightful visions and interrupted by cries of : help! I am killed! He went over again in dreams the scene in the cellar. He had nevertheless resumed his work, when ten days after the accident, in the middle of the night, he had his first attack of hystero-epilepsy. Since this time, the attacks returned almost regularly every two months; and often in the interval, during the night, whether at the moment of the first sleep or about the time of waking, he would be profoundly disturbed by visions of ferocious animals.

Formerly as he came out of these fits, he remembered that he had been dreaming during the attack, a phenomenon which no longer exists. He imagined that he was in a dark forest pursued by robbers or frightful animals, or the scene of the cellar was acted over again, and he saw wine casks rolling upon him and threatening to crush him. He affirms that never, during these seizures, or in the interval, has he had dreams or hallucinations of a gay or agreeable character.

About this time, he went to St. Anne's Hospital for advice and treatment. The physicians there prescribed for him bromide of potassium, and this medicine (a fact to be noticed) has never had the least influence on the attacks, although administered for a long time till the organism was saturated with it. It was under these conditions that Rig...., was admitted to the Salpetriere, and at his entrance we made note of the following state.

The patient is pale, anæmic, has but little appetite, especially for meat, to which he prefers acid foods; in short, the general condition is far from satisfactory. The *hysterical stigmata* in this patient are very well marked. They consist in *a double anaesthesia in patches* of great extent, for pain (pinching, pricking) and for cold. Sen-

380

sorial anæsthesia in general does not exist, except to a very mild degree; taste and smell are normal; hearing is nevertheless quite perceptibly blunted, especially in the left ear; the patient hears no better when the sonorous object is applied to the cranium. As far as vision is concerned, the symptoms are much plainer, and alone suffice, in a measure, to enable us to affirm the hysterical nature of the affection. He presents, in fact, on both sides *a notable contraction of the visual field,* more marked, however, on the right. He distinguishes all the colors, but the visual field of the blue is more contracted than that of the red, and passes within the latter, a phenomenon when it is met with, which is quite characteristic, as far as I know, of the visual field of hysterical patients; of this I have many times shown you examples. Lastly, to finish what I say of the permanent stigmata, there exist in Rig** *two hysterogenous* points, the one cutaneous, seated below the last right false ribs, the other deeper, in the popliteal space of the right side, at a point where the patient has a cyst, which is the seat of extreme pain of spontaneous origin. There does not exist in this patient any testicular point. Pressure exercised over the spasmogenous points, whether accidentally or voluntarily, produces all the phenomena of the hysterical aura; precordial pain, constriction of the neck, with the sensation of a ball, hissings in the ears, and beatings in the temples, these two last phenomena constituting, as you know, the cephalic aura. Those points whose excitation may provoke the attack with singular facility are, on the other hand, but feebly *spasm-checkers (spasmo-frenateurs),* that is to say, their excitation, even when intense and prolonged, arrests but imperfectly the attack in the process of evolution.

In the mental state of Rig...., today as in the past, it is always anxiety, fear, distress, that predominate. He cannot sleep in the dark; in full day he does not like to be alone; he is of excessive sensitiveness, and he experiences great fright at the sight or remembrance of certain animals, such as rats, mice, toads, which he often sees, moreover, in terrifying nightmares, or in hallucinations occurring when half asleep. He is always sad; "I am weary of myself," he says. He manifests a certain mobility of mind characterized by the fact that he can apply himself to nothing, and that he undertakes and abandons with the same facility five or six tasks at a time. He is intelligent and has a fair amount of education. He is, moreover, of a mild disposition, and totally devoid of vicious propensities.

The attacks are spontaneous or provoked. Whatever may be the manner of their origin, they always begin by a keen sensation of smarting or burning in the region of the spasmogenous points, to which succeed first a pain in the epigastrium, then the sensation of constriction of the neck and of a ball, finally the cephalic aura consisting of sibilant noises in the ears, and beatings in the temples. At this moment the patient loses consciousness and the *paroxysm* proper begins. It is divided into *four periods* which are quite clear and distinct. In the first, the patient executes certain epileptiform convulsive movements. Then comes the period of great gesticulations of salutation, which are of extreme violence, interrupted from time to time by an arching of the body which is absolutely characteristic, the trunk being bent bow fashion, sometimes in front (emprosthotonos), sometimes backward (opisthotonos), the feet and head alone touching the bed, the body constituting the arch. During this time the patient utters wild cries. Then comes the third period, called period of passional attitudes, during which he utters words and cries in relation with the sad delirium and terrifying visions which pursue him. Sometimes it is the woods, the wolves, or other frightful animals, sometimes it is the cellar, the stairway, the rolling cask. Finally he regains consciousness, recognizes the persons around him and calls them by name, but the delirium and hallucinations still continue for some time. He looks all around and under the bed for the black beasts which threaten him; he examines his arms, thinking to find there the bites of the animals which he thinks he has felt. Then he comes to himself, and the attack is over, although it is generally sure to be repeated a few minutes later, and so on, till after three or four successive paroxysms, the patient at last completely regains the normal state. Never during the course of these crises has he bitten his tongue or wet his bed.

For more than a year, R. has been subjected to treatment by static electrization, which, in cases of this kind, as you know, often gives us good results; we have prescribed at the same time all the tonics and reconstituents imaginable. Nevertheless, the phenomena which we have just described, the permanent stigmata and fits, persist just as they were, without appreciable changes; they seem, in short, having already existed almost three years, to be of the kind that undergo very slow modification. We have, however, certainly here, as you will all agree, a case of hystero-epilepsy with mixed crises (epileptiform hysteria) as clearly characterized as possible, and it is plain that the stability of the stigmata, on which we have sufficiently insisted, should not an instant stay our diagnosis.

To conclude this case, so perfectly typical, I will still further call your attention to certain particulars which the clinical analysis has disclosed. In the first place. I will mention particularly the nervous heredity, so strongly pronounced in his family: hysteria in the father (very probable at least) ; great uncle and cousins-german of the mother epileptic; two daughters, one of whom is hysterical, the other hystero-epileptic. You will frequently, gentlemen, meet with these conditions of heredity in the hysterical male patient, and find them, perhaps, more marked even than in the female.

I must remind you, moreover, how in our patient the hysterical manifestations were developed on the occasion and as the result of an accident which threatened his life. Could the traumatism which was the consequence of the accident (and it was nothing but a trifling wound of the finger) have sufficed of itself to cause the development of the nervous symptoms? This is possible, but I would not affirm it. It is always necessary, alongside of the traumatism, to take account of a factor which very probably has played a more important part in the genesis of these accidents than the wound itself. I refer to the terror experienced by the patient at the moment of the accident, and which found expression shortly afterwards in loss of consciousness followed by temporary paresis of the inferior extremities. This same psychical element is found, apart from the traumatism, in some of the cases described by Putnam, Walton, Page, Oppenheim and Thomsen, where its influence, often predominant, cannot be misunderstood.

This fact of the development of the hysterical phenomena on the occasion and as the result of a shock with or without traumatism, where emotion has played a great part, you will also find, gentlemen, in most of the other patients who will presently be shown to you.

The cases which are now to be presented for your study are in many respects patterned after the preceding, and this will be my excuse for not entering into lengthy details respecting them.

Case 2.—Gil * * *, aged 32 years, a gilder of metals, entered the Salpetriere in Jan. 1885. There is nothing

384

peculiar to note in his *hereditary antecedents*. His father, who was a very passionate man, died at the age of 60 years from paralysis, which did not, however, follow a fit of any kind. His mother, who died of tuberculosis, was a nervous woman, but never had any fits.

The *personal antecedents* are much more interesting to study. When 10 years old, he was addicted to somnambulism. Since his childhood, he has been afraid of the dark, and during the night has been subject to hypnagogic-hallucinations and to nightmares. In early life, he made an abuse of coitus; he feels from time to time a sort of irresistible impulsion towards women. He would often leave his work to run after some woman of the town, and after obtaining his desire, would return immediately to resume his occupation. He is, moreover, an insatiable masturbator. He is, nevertheless, intelligent, is a clever workman, and learns easily. On occasions he is given to music; he plays the violin and accordion. He is very fond of going to the theatre; nevertheless is of a rather gloomy and taciturn disposition, and habitually seeks solitude.

His occupation, in which large use is made of mercury, has never produced in him any accidents which may be referred to mercurial poisoning. There are no signs of alcoholism; none of syphilis.

His first fit took place at the age of twenty, without known cause. He was seated on the imperial of an omnibus, when he felt the first warnings of the coming seizure. He had just time to get down, when the convulsive attack took him in the street. The fits thereafter returned quite frequently. He reckoned at one time as many as four or five a month. It seems that at this time in some of the paroxysms he would make urine. The convulsive crises were for several years becoming less and less frequent, and he was having considerable exemption from his malady, when in 1880 he was the victim of an assault in

385

the night-time. He received a blow from a hammer *on the head,* in the right parietal region, fell without consciousness, was robbed, and left for dead on the spot. He was picked up and carried to the Charity, to M. Gosselin's ward, where he remained for three or four days without consciousness. An erysipelas developed several days later around the wound on the head produced by the blow, and at the moment of recovery there began an intense headache of a peculiar character which still continues today.

For a long time after this accident he remained plunged in a sort of hebetude from which he came out by degrees, although incompletely, for since this time, even in his best days, it is impossible for him to apply himself to work or to any occupation whatever, even to reading for any length of time. So he fell into a state of utter wretchedness. Moreover, the convulsive seizures, from which for a while he had obtained respite, returned and became more intense and more frequent than ever, and for this reason, in February, 1883, he presented himself at the Hotel Dieu, where he was admitted. He remained there till March, 1884.

It was there that the left hemianæsthesia, complete and absolute, just as we find it to-day, was for the first time noted. The fits which were then frequent, and were regarded, it would seem, by the hospital staff, as due to epilepsy, were for almost thirteen months treated by bromide of potassium in large doses, but without the least result.

When the patient was admitted to the Salpetriere in January, 1885, this is what we found: The general state, as far as the functions of nutrition are concerned, appears to be quite satisfactory. He eats well, and is not anæmic. On the other hand, one would not fail to note in him a psychical depression which is very marked. He is gloomy, taciturn, distrustful, avoids the gaze of people, and has very little intercourse with the other patients in the wards. He does not interest himself during the day in any occupation, in any diversion. The left hemianæsthesia, already noticed at the Hotel Dieu, is complete and absolute as far as common sensibility is concerned. The sensorial troubles on this same left side are also very pronounced. There is notable dullness of hearing; complete loss of smell and of taste; in the left eye, complete achromatopsia regularly noted by M. Parinaud, and contraction of the visual field extremely pronounced for white light. Contrarily to what usually happens in cases of this kind, the extent of the visual field, and the notion of colors, are absolutely normal on the right side. There does not, moreover, exist any trace of lesion of the fundus of the eye on either side.

He constantly complains of an intense headache, which is gravitative, or rather constrictive, general, occupying the occiput, the top of the head, the forehead, the temples especially, and more pronounced on the left side than on the right. He seems to himself to be wearing a heavy and tight helmet, which compresses and constricts his head. This cephalalgia, which, as I have said, is permanent, is somewhat exaggerated just before and after the fits. It is especially violent when the patient undertakes any occupation, when he attempts, for instance, to read, or to write a letter.

The attacks of which we have been many times witness in our wards, present the following characters: They may be spontaneous or provoked, in both cases differing by no essential character. Three hysterogenous zones have been discovered: two of these occupy on the right and on the left the infra-mammary regions; the third is in the right iliac region; on this side, however, pressure of the cord and testicle do not produce any abnormal sensation.

When you press lightly on the hysterogenous patches whose seat has just been indicated, the patient immediately experiences all the symptoms of the cephalic aura, to wit, beatings in the temples, sibilant noises in the ears, vertigo, etc. But, if you persist ever so little in your compression, the attack inevitably comes on rapidly. A few epileptoid spasms, of but short duration, open the scene. They are soon followed by divers contortions and great movements of salutation, interrupted from time to time by the *arching* attitude (*arc de cercle*); during this time the patient does not cease to utter wild cries. A convulsive laugh, tears, and sobs terminate the attack. On waking, G—— retains no recollection of what has happened. The hysterogenous points are in this patient but incompletely spasm-restraining; when they are compressed during the attack, the fit is suspended for an instant, but speedily resumes its customary course. Whether provoked or spontaneous, the attacks generally repeat themselves successively a certain number of times so as to constitute a series; never, in such cases, is the rectal temperature higher than 37.8° C.

According to the brief description above given, you will notice that the case of G. resembles in many particulars that of Rig. (Case 1), from which it differs in only a few particulars. In both cases, there are the same hysterical stigmata, the same melancholic tendencies; the same kind of attacks, with this peculiarity relative to G., that in him the aura is evolved with great rapidity, and that in the crisis the passional attitudes are wanting. Let us note the few differences to which it is worth the while to call the attention relatively to the second case.

We have said that in some of the attacks, G. bites his tongue and urinates in his clothes. This fact has been sufficiently noticed by us. We were for a short time led to believe from this that we had here a case of hystero-epilepsy with distinct crises, to wit: true epilepsy on one side, hysteria major on the other, manifesting themselves under this form of separate attacks. A more attentive examination has convinced us that it is not so. All the attacks in G. have the character of hysteria major, and it is during the course of these attacks that sometimes he bites his tongue, and that sometimes he urinates in his clothes. But biting the tongue and the involuntary emission of urine are far from being univocal characters of the falling sickness. These accidents may be observed in hystero-epilepsy apart from all complication of true epilepsy. This fact is of rare occurrence, it is true; I have, nevertheless, observed and published a certain number of cases which were perfectly demonstrative thereof.*

In finishing what concerns this case, I will call your attention to the headache from which G. suffers continually, and which is exasperated by application to the least occupation. With all the particularities which I have mentioned above, cephalægia of this kind does not belong to the tableau of hysteria; it is met with, on the contrary, almost as a necessary element in neurasthenia, of which it constitutes one of the predominant characters, and in which we equally observe the physical and mental depression which exist at so high a degree in our patient. I have endeavored to impress upon you the fact that in him these divers symptoms came on as the result of a blow which he received on his head. Now, gentlemen, the neurasthenic state with the entire congeries of phenomena which Beard assigns to it in his remarkable monograph, is one of the nervous affections which are developed most frequently in consequence of shocks, particularly in railroad accidents. To this fact testify many of the observations reported by Page in his monograph on "Injuries of

* Some months later this patient died suddenly after taking surreptitiously an enormous dose of chloral. The autopsy, absolutely negative as far as the nervous centres were concerned, completely confirmed the diagnosis.

389

the Spinal Cord and Nervous Shock.'' I have myself met with two instances absolutely like those published by this writer, one of which concerns one of our confreres in Paris. From this there is reason to believe that two quite distinct elements coexist in our patient G. In the first place, the neurasthenic state, the immediate and direct consequence of the shock of which he was a victim three years ago; in the second place, the hystero-epilepsy with all the train of symptoms which characterize it. The latter existed before the accident; it has been, however, considerably aggravated since then, as you can judge by referring to the details of the case.

I come now to the examination of the third patient, who belongs absolutely to the same group as the two preceding.

Case 3.—The patient whom you see before you, Gui. by name, is twenty-seven years of age, by occupation a lock-smith. He entered February 20, 1884, in the service of my colleague, Luys. Of his parentage he knows only that his father died at the age of forty-eight years, a confirmed drunkard; his mother is still living, and never seems to have suffered from nervous affections. He has had seven brothers and sisters; only one of his brothers is living; this one has never been sick and is not nervous.

At about the age of twelve or thirteen years, Gui. became very cowardly, and could not remain alone in a room without a feeling of fear and anxiety. He was not, however, irritable or petulant. At school, he learned easily, and later, at about the age of seventeen or eighteen, he showed himself adroit and intelligent in his occupation. Several times, even, in the competition for prizes offered for excellence in his special branch of work, he obtained medals. Unhappily, about this time an immoderate passion for women and for strong drink was developed in him. He worked all day long, like his comrades, but when the day was done, he was often in the habit of going to balls, or passing the night in some groggery, or house of ill-fame. These excesses were repeated on occasions several times a week, and naturally deprived him of the necessary sleep. They did not, however, seem to fatigue him, for the next day he would go back to his work as ordinarily and acquit himself of his tasks satisfactorily.

In 1879, when he was twenty-one years of age, during one of his nocturnal expeditions, he received a blow from a knife which penetrated the left eye. He was immediately carried to the Hotel Dieu, to the service of M. Panas, who shortly afterward practiced enucleation of this eye. On leaving the hospital G. speedily renewed his disorderly life.

About the beginning of 1882, it frequently happened that at the moment when he closed his eyes to sleep, he seemed to see a monster in human form advancing towards him. In alarm he would utter a cry, open his eyes, and the vision would disappear, to return, however, as soon as he would again attempt to go to sleep. He then fell into an extremely painful state of anxiety, and often remained thus a part of the night without being able to obtain any sleep.

These hypnagogic hallucinations had already lasted about six months, when, in July, 1882, he was the victim of a new accident, more terrible than the first. He was occupied in propping a balcony at the third story of a house, at a time when he was, perhaps, under liquor, and fell down upon the street, alighting upon his feet, as he affirms. For more than an hour he remained unconscious. On waking, he was again carried to the Hotel Dieu, to the ward of Prof. Panas. It seems that the surgeons at that time feared the existence of a fracture of the cranium. Recovery, nevertheless, was not long delayed, and at the end of two months, the patient was able to return home. Shortly afterwards, the terrifying nocturnal hallu-

391

cinations reappeared, and the spasmodic seizures began to manifest themselves for the first time. These were not at first as characteristic as they subsequently became. They consisted, chiefly, in attacks of vertigo coming on all at once, and followed by rigidity, then by trembling of the limbs. There was no loss of consciousness. These attacks were, however, not very frequent.

Things remained in the same condition for almost eighteen months. At the end of this time, the remedial measures adopted by the various physicians to whom the responsibility of the case had been committed having remained without effect, Gui. made up his mind to enter the Salpetriere (service of Luys).

Shortly after his admission, Gui. became subject to frequent attacks of abdominal and gastric colic, followed by a feeling of constriction of the pharynx, and subsequently by spells of vomiting which supervened without effort. These symptoms, which would yield to no treatment, ceased suddenly at the end of about six weeks. About this time, there was first noticed the existence of the right hemianæsthesia, and also of the peculiar trembling of the right hand, to be presently considered.

In January, 1885, by reason of a change in the hospital staff, the patients of Dr. Luys passed over to our wards, and it was then that I saw Gui, for the first time. He is, as you know, a man of good muscular development, and vigorous; his general health seems good. The mental condition has not presented any great deviation from the normal. The hypnagogic hallucinations have for more than a year completely disappeared. Gui. is not melancholy. He converses freely with the other patients and makes himself useful in the hospital.

The hemianæsthesia is complete and absolute on the right side; neither touching nor pricking is perceived on this side of the body. The organs of sense are also profoundly affected on this same side, hearing, smell and taste in particular. As far as the organ of vision is concerned, a methodical examination discloses very characteristic modifications. On the right side—you have not forgotten that the left eye is gone—the visual field is extremely contracted. The red only is perceived by this eye, and the circle of this color is reduced almost to a point.

The trembling, of which mention was made above, and which occupies the right hand, is remarkable by the perfect regularity of its rhythm as noted by the aid of the enregistering apparatus. It consists in oscillations, of which the number is five per second on an average. In this respect, it holds consequently the medium between the trembling with slow oscillations, such as characterizes paralysis agitans, for instance, and the vibratory tremblings—with rapid oscillations—of general paralysis, and of Basedow's disease. It is not exaggerated under the influence of voluntary movements. The patient can use his hand in eating and drinking, and can even write passably well, provided that he supports with his left hand his right wrist, a maneuvre which causes the trembling to cease for an instant. The muscular sense is wholly intact in the entire extent of the right superior member.

The only hysterogenous zone noted in Gui. occupies the testicle and the tract of the spermatic cord almost as far as the groin of the right side. The skin of the scrotum on this side is very sensitive, and when you pinch it rather strongly you produce exactly the same effects as if you compress the testicle itself, or the cord, i. e., the development or the arrest of the attack, as the case may be.

These attacks, whether they are spontaneous or provoked by the artificial excitation of this hysterogenous zone, are always preceded by a sensation of painful aura perfectly characteristic, which takes its origin in the right testicle, mounts up toward the epigastric and cardiac regions, then to the throat, where it determines a strong constriction, and finally attains the head where sibilant noises are produced, especially in the right ear, and beatings, principally in the temple of the same side. The patient then loses consciousness completely; the epileptoid period is begun; at first the trembling of the right hand is augmented and precipitated, the eyes are convulsed upwards, the limbs are extended, the fists clenched, then writhed in exaggerated pronation. Presently the arms approach each other in front of the abdomen by reason of convulsive contraction of the pectoral muscles. After this supervenes the period of contortions, characterized chiefly by extremely violent movements of salutation which are intermingled with disorderly gesticulations. The patient breaks or tears everything which is in reach of his hands. He takes postures and attitudes the oddest imaginable, so as fully to legitimize the denomination of *clownism* which I have proposed, to designate this part of the second period of the fit. From time to time the contortions above described stop for an instant to give place to the attitude so characteristic called *"arc de cercle"* (a bowing or arching of the body). Sometimes it is a veritable opisthotonos in which the loins are separated from the plane of the bed by a distance of more than fifty centimetres, the body resting on the head and heels. At other times, the arching is made in front, the arms being crossed upon the chest, the legs in the air, the head and trunk bent upwards, the hips and loins alone resting on the bed. Lastly, at other times, in the attitude of *arc de cercle* the patient rests upon one side or the other. All this part of the seizure is very fine, if I may so express myself, and every one of these details deserves to be fixed by the process of instantaneous photography. I pass before you the figures which have thus been obtained by M. Londe. You see that from the point of view of art they leave nothing to be desired, and moreover they are very instructive. They show, in fact, that in what concerns the regularity of the periods and the typical character of the divers attitudes, the attacks in Gui. yield in nothing to those which we observe every day in our hystero-epileptics of the female sex, and this perfect resemblance is the more worthy of note from the fact that Gui. has never entered the dormitories where the females are placed during their seizures, so that we cannot assume in his case the influence of contagious imitation.

Only the period of hallucinations and of passional attitudes is wanting in this patient. Sometimes, however, we have seen towards the end of the crisis his physiognomy express alternately fright or joy, while with his hands extended in vacancy he would clutch at some imaginary object.

The end of the attack in our patient is often marked by a sort of motor aphasia which in general does not last more than eight or ten minutes, but which on one occasion continued almost six days. Then, when the patient wishes to speak, certain hoarse, inarticulate sounds are all that he can utter; he becomes impatient and excited, but nevertheless succeeds in making himself understood by very expressive gestures. It sometimes has happened to him on such occasions to take his pen and write very legibly a few quite correct sentences.

I have said enough respecting these cases, which from every point of view are quite typical. But I have not yet finished with hysteria in the male subject. We shall find it, in the next lecture, quite as characteristic in three other patients belonging to our clinical service as in the cases which I have just presented.

LECTURE VIII.
CONCERNING SIX CASES OF HYSTERIA IN THE MALE SEX.

(*Continued.*)

SUMMARY.—Abdominal forms of the hysterical attack in man.— Detail of a case in which the seizures took the aspect of partial epilepsy.—Diagnosis of this case; importance of the hysterical stigmata.

The convulsive seizure may be wanting in hysteria of the male.—Description of a case of brachial monoplegia in a man aged nineteen years, hysterical.—Difficulties of diagnosis in these cases.

GENTLEMEN :—I am intending to finish to-day the study which we began in the last lecture. I shall proceed as I did on the previous occasion, mainly by the method of clinical demonstration. Our material of male hysterics is far from being exhausted. Three new patients are going to be presented to you; in connection with them the principal details of the observations which concern them will be communicated to you; I shall let the facts speak for themselves, and I shall only set forth by a few short commentaries the more important lessons which these cases furnish.

Case 4.—The subject who is about to be presented to you does not quite belong to the class of cases with which we have thus far been occupied, in this respect that he is still quite a boy, and yet nearly a full grown man. But the disease, as you will see, seems in him endowed with that character of permanence and tenacity which we have already met in the previous cases.

The patient Mar. aged sixteen years, entered our clinical service April 29th, 1884, *i. e.* a year ago. He was born and lived till the age of fourteen years in the country. His mother is said to have had in 1872 several attacks of hysteria. His paternal grandfather was intemperate and of a very violent character. This is all we can elicit relative to his hereditary antecedents. As for the patient himself, he is a large boy, well developed, although he had in his childhood certain strumous manifestations, to wit: runnings from the ears, glandular swellings in the mastoid region. He is intelligent, of a rather gay character, and has never been timid; but he has been subject to very violent fits of anger, going so far in these paroxysms as to break everything in his reach. Two years ago he became apprentice in Paris to a baker. Shortly after he had an attack of congestion of the lungs and the enfeeblement which this sickness produced was certainly not without influence in the development of the nervous symptoms which shortly followed. Some time afterward, while still convalescent, he had a severe fright. He was, he says, attacked by two young men one night in the street; he fell almost immediately without consciousness, and was carried in this state to his employer's house. He did not show any mark of injury. From this moment he remained for several days plunged in a sort of hebetude. He began to be subject nights to very painful nightmares, which still torment him to-day. He believed that he was a party in a fight, and he awoke often with loud outcries. Lastly, at the end of a fortnight the attacks of hysteria commenced. They took place at first every day, presenting themselves in series of eight or ten; sometimes the attendants counted two series in the same day; then the fits diminished little by little in number and intensity.

At the moment when the patient entered the Salpetriere we noted the following state: "The hysterical stigmata are very plain; they consist in an *anæsthesia in patches*, scattered irregularly over the whole body, and in which the insensibility is complete to touch, to cold, and to pain. Hearing, smell, and taste are obnubilated on the left side, and, as concerns vision, we notice the existence of a *double contraction of the visual field,* more pronounced on the right side. On this side the patient does not distinguish violet, while on the left side he recognizes all the colors; but on both sides (a remarkable phenomena to which I have many times called your attention, and which we have already met with in the first of our subjects) the visual field of the red is more extended than that of the blue— the opposite of what takes place, you know, in the normal conditions. There exists but one *hysterogenous point,* which occupies the left iliac region. To-day, moreover, although the disease began two years ago, the attacks come on spontaneously, at quite short intervals, about every ten or twelve days. They may be very easily provoked by a certain amount of even moderate pressure over the hysterogenous point. A more energetic pressure exercised over the same point arrests the attack.

The fit, whether spontaneous or provoked, is always preceded by an aura; an iliac pain on the level of the hysterogenous point, a sensation of a ball which rises from the epigastrium to the throat, buzzings in the ears and beatings in the temples. Then the fit begins; the eyeballs roll upward in their sockets, the arms stiffen in extension, and the patient, if he is standing, loses consciousness and falls. The epileptoid phase is in general little pronounced and very short, but the period of great movements and of contortions which follows is excessively violent and of long duration. The patient utters cries, bites everything in his reach, tears his clothes, makes the great classic movements of salutation, which he interrupts from time to time by taking the attitude so characteristic of arching of the body (*arc de cercle*). The scene terminates by the phase of passional attitudes, which is very well pronounced in him, and differs a little according to the occasion. Thus, when the fit has been spontaneous,

398

it may happen that the hallucinations accompanying the attack may have a gay character, while, if the crisis has been provoked by excitation of the hysterogenous zone, the delirium is always sad, furious, accompanied with abusive words: "wretches, villains, devils!"

Generally several attacks follow in succession, so as to constitute a series.

In regard to this patient, I will limit myself to signalizing the permanence and fixedness of the constituent elements of the hysteria, and in this respect this case is an instance of what is often observed in the male subject. Thus, as you have already remarked in our young patient, although two years have elapsed since the onset of the disease, the convulsive crises are still frequent to-day, despite all we have been able to do, and the hysterical stigmata, the sensorial and sensitive anæsthesia, have not sensibly varied since the day when we studied these signs for the first time. There is nothing to indicate that there is likely now to be any change.

It is not ordinarily so with young boys, particularly when the disease is developed in them before the age of puberty. At this age (at least this appears to be the result of the numerous observations which I have been able to make) the hysterical symptoms are generally much more fugacious, much more mobile, however well marked they may have been, and generally yield readily to an appropriate treatment.

The case which I am now about to bring before you, and which concerns a young man of 22 years, belongs, like the preceding, despite an anomaly in the form of the attacks to which I shall presently return, to the type of hystero-epilepsy.

Case 5.—The patient, Ly., mason, aged 22 years, entered the clinical service of the Salpetriere March 24, 1885. He was born in the country in the suburbs of Paris;

is a young man of medium height, poorly developed, and of rather debilitated appearance. His father, who is a carter, is a drunkard. His mother, who died of tuberculosis, formerly had attacks of hysteria. Lastly, we find in the family a maternal grandmother still hysterical, although she has attained the age of 82 years, and two maternal aunts, both affected with hysteria. Here are antecedents of capital importance; four hysterical persons and one drunkard in the same family! The personal antecedents are not less interesting to recount. Our patient has always been of little intelligence, feeble minded; he never could learn anything at school, but apart from this mental weakness, he does not present any very characteristic psychical troubles. He confesses to having been in the habit for a long time of drinking five or six glasses of brandy a day, and a considerable quantity of wine, but he assures us that he has given up this habit since he has been sick. Three years ago, he had an attack of erysipelas of the face, followed shortly by an attack of acute rheumatism, which was, however, quite light, as it did not keep him in bed but a fortnight. The same year he was under treatment for a tape-worm, and took pomegranate bark. The remedy produced the desired effect; the patient first voided fragments of the worm, then the entire worm. But the sight of the tænia which he found in his stools affected him very unpleasantly, and the emotion which he experienced was so vehement that for several days he suffered from slight nervous disorders, such as cramps, pains, and convulsive shocks of his limbs.

A year ago, while working at his trade in Sceaux, the son of one of his comrades was rudely struck by his father; L., who was a witness of the scene, attempted to interpose, but evil happened to him in consequence, for his infuriated comrade turned his blows upon him; and when he took to flight, threw a large stone at him, which fortunately did not hit him. The fright, however, which L. experienced was very severe; immediately he was taken with trembling in his limbs, and on the night which followed it was impossible for him to sleep. The insomnia persisted on the following day; moreover, night and day he was troubled with distressing notions. He fancied himself suffering again from the assaults of his tænia, and going through the treatment which he had endured in its removal; moreover, he had pricking sensations in his tongue, could not eat, felt weak, and worked in pain. This state had lasted a fortnight, when one evening about six o'clock his first convulsive seizure came on. Since the morning of that day, he had been suffering from pain in the epigastrium with the sensation of a ball rising, of choking, and of buzzings in the ears. At the moment when the attack began, he felt (so he says) his tongue drawn to the left side by a sort of involuntary, irresistible traction. Then he lost consciousness, and when he came to himself, we were told that his frame was contorted toward the left, his limbs agitated with trembling; and when once the convulsions had stopped, he began talking in a loud tone of voice without waking. During the months which followed, he continued to have fits just like this every eight or ten days, and he was obliged during this long period to refrain from all work by reason of the state of weakness in which he found himself. These crises were considered as epileptiform attacks of alcoholic origin, and for almost a year he was subjected to treatment by bromide of potassium in large doses, but without any benefit whatever being derived therefrom. On the day which followed his admission to the Salpetriere, there was a succession of five fits which came on without provocation, and at which I was not present.

The next day, a methodical examination of the patient revealed the following condition; generalized anæsthesia in disseminated patches; considerable contraction of the visual field on both sides; the field of red is more extended than that of blue; monocular diplopia. There exist two spasmogenous points, the one over the right clavicle, the other below the last false ribs of the same side. Rather hard pressure made over this latter spot caused immediately, on our first examination, a fit which we were able to study in all its details. It is preceded by the classic aura; epigastric constriction, a feeling of a ball in the neck, etc. At that very moment, and before the patient has lost consciousness, the tongue becomes stiff, and is drawn in the mouth towards the left side; we can tell by means of the finger that its point is carried behind the molars of that side. The mouth, half open, is also drawn to one side, the left labial commissure is deviated to the left, and all the left side of the face takes part in this deformation; even the head is strongly twisted toward the left. The patient at that period, and for some time previous, has lost consciousness. Then the upper limbs become rigid in extension, the right first, then the left. The inferior members, however, remain flaccid, or, at least, are but slightly rigid. The movement of torsion toward the left, at first so well marked in the face, rapidly becomes generalized, and the patient rolls upon his left side; then clonic convulsions replace the tetanic. The limbs are agitated with frequent, short, vibratory movements. The face is the seat of sudden starts, then supervenes a complete relaxation without stertor. But at this moment the patient seems tormented with fearful dreams. He doubtless goes over again mentally, the scene of the struggle with his comrade. "Wretch! Prussian! he would kill me, the villain!" Such are the words which he utters with perfect distinctness. Then, all at once, he changes his attitude; you see him, seated on his bed, by turns passing his hand down his leg as if he were endeavoring to rid

402

himself of some reptile which, winding itself about the leg, was trying to creep up his thigh; he speaks of the "tape worm" which was so long a terror to him. The scene of Sceaux again comes back: "I will kill him, I will shoot him!" After this period, marked by delirium and the corresponding passional attitudes, the epileptic period reproduces itself, thus ushering in a new fit, which is distinguished in nothing from the first, and which may be followed by several others. Pressure over the hysterogenous points may however interrupt the paroxysm in the divers phases of its evolution. On awakening L. seems astounded, stupefied, and he assures us that he remembers nothing that has taken place.

All the attacks which we have witnessed (and these have been quite numerous), whether spontaneous or provoked, have presented exactly the same character. Always we have seen reproduced in the same order, systematically, and even in respect to the least details, the divers incidents of the epileptoid phase, beginning by the tongue and face, just as I have described them, then the various scenes of the delirious phase.

You have here, gentlemen, an attack of hystero-epilepsy, which, by one side, differs notably from the classic type. In the first period, in fact, we see the convulsive accidents reproduce, even to an almost perfect imitation, the symptoms of partial epilepsy, while the contortions, the great movements, the arching of the body are absolutely wanting. But we are acquainted with this variety of the hystero-epileptic fit in the female; although it is quite rare, I have nevertheless had occasion to show you latterly several typical examples of it. It was, moreover, last year the subject of an attentive study by my former clinical chief, Dr. Ballet, physician to the hospitals. In comparing the case which has just been before us with the cases which are the subject of this memoir, you will be led to recognize once more the truly striking features of resemblance which affiliate the hystero-epilepsy of the male with that of the female, even when, ceasing to consider exclusively the fundamental type, you open the chapter of anomalies.

Another anomaly, less rare indeed and less unexpected, in the hysteria of the female is the absence of convulsive crises. You know, in fact, that according to the teachings of Briquet, about one-quarter part of hysterical women do not have fits. The disease in such a case, without losing any of its autonomy, is only represented symptomatically by the permanent stigmata, to which are sometimes added several morbid accidents, spasmodic or otherwise, such as a nervous cough, permanent contractures, certain arthralgias, certain paralyses, hemorrhages taking place by divers passages, etc.; now the convulsive attacks may equally be wanting in the hysteria of the male. The case which I am going to bring before you now, when it was first presented to us, was a good example of this kind. The disease has in a certain sense undergone completion since then, for the patient now has fits. But for a long period of eleven months this was one of those masked cases which are not very easy of interpretation, at least in certain respects, as you will be able to judge.

It was, then, the 10th of last March that the boy whom you now see, first appeared at our clinic, suffering from a left brachial monoplegia, without any trace of rigidity, the limb being flaccid and flexible to a perfectly normal degree. This paralysis had now lasted ten months, and came on several days after a traumatism affecting the anterior part of the left shoulder. There was no trace of paralysis or even of paresis in the corresponding inferior extremity or in the face; there were, moreover, despite the already remote date of the onset, no traces of atrophy of the paralyzed muscles, a circumstance which, joined to the absence of any modification in the electric reaction of the muscles, led us immediately to eliminate the influence (at least the local, direct influence) of traumatism. We were struck, moreover, at seeing the skin of the carotid regions lifted by violent arterial throbbings. The Corrigan pulse was well marked. Auscultation of the heart revealed the existence of a murmur with the second sound and at the base, and, moreover, we found in the antecedents of the patient the history of an attack of acute articular rheumatism, which had kept him in bed five or six weeks. The idea came to us, in consequence, quite naturally, that this monoplegia depended on a localized cerebral lesion in the cortex, strictly limited to the motor zone, in the brachial centre, and itself consecutive to the valvular affection of the heart. But a more attentive study of the case soon undeceived us. Without doubt, the monoplegia in question takes its origin in a cerebral cortical lesion for the most part localized in the motor zone of the arm; but we have not to do here with a gross material alteration—the lesion is purely "dynamic," "*sine materia*," of the kind of those, in fact, whose existence we are obliged to assume in order to explain the development and persistence of divers permanent symptoms of hysteria. This is, at least, what results very clearly from the detailed examination which we are about to make of our patient.

Case 6.—The patient, named Pin., aged 18 years, mason by occupation, entered the Salpetriere March 11, 1885. His mother died at the age of 46 years from the effect of "rheumatism"; his father is a drunkard. One of his sisters, aged 16 years, is subject to frequent nervous attacks. The patient is a young man of robust appearance and vigorous muscles, but the functionment of the nervous system has always left much to be desired. From the age of five to seven years he suffered incontinence of urine.

He has always been deficient in intelligence; his memory is weak; and he never learned much at school. Moreover he was timid, and suffered from nightly terrors. From a moral point of view he is ill balanced. From the time that he was nine years old he often left his home and slept under bridges, or in the waiting rooms of railway stations. His father apprenticed him to a fruit dealer, then to a confectioner, and to other tradespeople, but he was always getting into scrapes. One night he was arrested, in company with a band of young vagabonds, and sentenced to the Reformatory of Roquette, where his father left him for a year.

Two years ago, when he was 16 years old, he was taken with an attack of acute articular rheumatism, preceded by an attack of erysipelas of the face, and it is quite probable that from this period we must date the organic alteration of the heart which we note in him to-day.

May 24, 1884, or eighteen months afterward, P., then a mason's apprentice, fell from a height of about two metres, and remained for several minutes without consciousness upon the place where he fell. He was carried to his home, and there several contusions were found on the anterior aspect of the left shoulder, knee, and ankle; these contusions were slight, and did not seriously interfere with the use of the affected parts.

For several days, it was thought that things would remain where they were; but on the 27th of May, *i.e.*, three days after the accident, P. perceived that his left upper limb was becoming feeble. He then went to see a physician, who detected, it would seem, a paresis of all the movements of the left arm, with anæsthesia of this member. On the 8th of June, that is, 15 days after his fall, and 11 days after the commencement of the paresis, he entered the Hotel Dieu. There he was examined with care, and the physicians recognized the well characterized signs of aortic insufficiency. The parts which were bruised were not the seat of any pain, whether spontaneous or provoked by active or passive movements. Incomplete paralysis of the left superior member. The patient could still, though incompletely, flex the hand on the forearm, and the latter on the arm, but all movements of the shoulder were impossible. The paralyzed limb was quite flexible in all its joints; there were no traces of rigidity. The face and the left inferior extremity were absolutely normal; as far as motility was concerned, it was a clear case of monoplegia in the true sense of the word. The study of the sensibility gave the following results: There existed already at this period a generalized left-sided hemi-analgesia; the anæsthesia was complete and confined to the paralyzed limb. At this time there was noted the binocular contraction of the visual field, much more marked, however, on the left side, and which we shall find so existing to-day. In fine, the 25th of June, *i. e.*, 22 days after the onset of the paralysis, the latter had become absolutely complete. The diagnosis remained uncertain, the treatment inefficacious. Faradization, several times applied to the left side, had for its effect only to render the sensibility less obtuse on the trunk, face, and inferior extremity. The anæsthesia and paralysis remained as they were in the left upper limb. The contraction of the visual field had undergone no modification at the time that P. quit the Hotel Dieu.

It was on the eleventh of March of this year, ten months after the fall, and nine months after the complete establishment of the monoplegia, that P. entered the service of the clinic of the Salpetriere. We then verified the antecedents as I have just stated them, and, moreover, a minute clinical examination disclosed a pronounced aortic insufficiency. There exists a murmur with the second sound and at the base; the arteries of the neck are lifted by beatings which are apparent to the sight; Corrigan pulse; capillary pulse perceptible on forehead.

The motor paralysis of the left upper limb, which is seen to be inert, hangs along the side of the body, and falls heavily when, on being raised, it is abandoned to itself, is complete, absolute. There is no trace of voluntary movement, or of contracture. The muscular masses have preserved their volume; their normal relief and electric reactions, faradic as well as galvanic, are in no respect modified. Very slight relative augmentation of the tendinous reflexes of the elbow and forearm. Cutaneous anæsthesia absolute to contact, to cold, to pricking, to the most intense faradization, along the whole extent of the limb, hand, forearm, arm and shoulder. In its relation to the trunk, this anæsthesia is limited by a circular line producing an almost vertical plane, which, passing by the hollow of the arm-pit, trenches a little on the sub-clavicular hollow in front, the external two-thirds of the shoulder blade behind. The insensibility extends in the same degree to the deep parts; you may, in fact, faradize powerfully the muscles, the nerve trunks themselves, make energetic traction on the articular ligaments, subject the different joints to movements of violent torsion, without the patient having the least consciousness of it. The loss of the different notions attached to the muscular sense is equally complete; the patient is unable to determine, even approximately, the attitude which has been impressed on divers segments of his limb, the place which they occupy in space, the direction and nature of the movements to which they are subjected, etc.

Aside from the left upper member, there does not exist on that half the body any modification of motility, whether of the face, trunk or inferior extremity, but all over this side we find the analgesia already noticed during the sojourn of the patient at the Hotel Dieu. The examination

408

of the visual field gives us on the right side the normal state, while on the left there is an enormous contraction; moreover, the circle of red is transferred outside of that of blue. There has then been produced in the visual field since the sojourn in the Hotel Dieu a modification which it is interesting to note. Moreover, we find that hearing, smell, taste, tested by the ordinary methods, present a very marked diminution of their acuteness on the left side.

It now became our task to determine as far as possible the nature of this singular monoplegia, supervening after a traumatism. The absence of atrophy and of all modification of the electric reactions of the muscles in a case where the paralysis goes back ten months, ought to cause us to reject at once the hypothesis of a lesion of the brachial plexus; while the absence of amyotrophy of itself, as well as the intensity of the troubles of sensibility, compel us to set aside the notion that this may be one of those paralyses so well studied by Lefort and Valtat, which come on in consequence of traumatisms affecting a joint.

A brachial monoplegia may supervene, though very exceptionally, it is true, as the result of certain lesions of the internal capsule, as is shown by a fact recently published by Drs. Bennett and Campbell in Brain; but in such cases we do not certainly meet with the sensorial and sensitive hemianæsthesia which is sometimes superadded to total hemiplegia of the ordinary kind following lesion of the capsule.

The production in the right hemisphere of a small *foyer* (local lesion), whether from hemorrhage or from softening determined by embolism in consequence of the organic affection of the heart, a disease-focus which we might suppose limited strictly to the motor zone of the arm—such a lesion, I say, might account for the existence of a left brachial monoplegia. But on this supposition, the paralysis would have come on all at once, after a shock, however slight, and not progressively; it would almost certainly, several months after the onset, have been characterized by a certain degree of contracture, and by a well marked exaggeration of the tendon-reflexes; lastly, it would not surely have been accompanied with trouble of the cutaneous and deep sensibility so pronounced as those which we observe in our patient.

We are compelled then to eliminate in our diagnosis this last hypothesis, and that of a spinal lesion will not bear discussion for an instant. On the other hand, our attention has been drawn from the very first to the very significant hereditary antecedents of the subject, to his psychical state and to his habits, to the troubles of sensibility, diffused, though unequally, over all of one side of the body, to the contraction of the visual field so pronounced on the left side, and marked by the transposition of the circle of the red; in fine, to the modifications of activity of the other sensorial apparatuses on the same side; all this has led us almost irresistibly, in the absence of any other hypothesis equally probable, to interpret this case as an example of hysteria. Moreover, the clinical characters of the monoplegia, its traumatic origin even— and in reference to this latter point I must refer you to what I have said before—were not at all at variance with this view. In fact, the limitation of the motor paralysis to one member, without participation at any time of the corresponding side of the face; the absence of marked exaltation of the tendinous reflexes, of muscular atrophy, and of all modification of the electric reactions, the absolute resolution of the limb remaining several months after the onset of the paralysis; the anæsthesia cutaneous and profound, so complete in the paralyzed member, and the utter loss of all notions relative to the muscular sense; all these phenomena, when we find them united and clearly marked as they are in our patient, suffice

410

largely to reveal the hysterical nature of a paralysis.

In consequence, the diagnosis "hysteria" was frankly, resolutely adopted. It was true that the convulsive seizure was wanting; but you well know that this is not at all necessary to the constitution of the disease, and this circumstance ought not, we felt, to stand in the way of a diagnosis. As a result of this view of the case, the prognosis changed completely its character; we were no longer in the presence of an affection of organic cause, perhaps incurable; we could then hope, despite the long duration of the malady, to see supervene spontaneously, or under the influence of certain practices, some one of those sudden modifications which are not rare in the history of hysterical paralyses, and of those in particular which are attended with resolution. At all events we could foresee that sooner or later the patient would get well. A subsequent event was destined soon to justify our previsions and at the same time fully confirm our diagnosis.

The fifteenth of March, four days after the entrance of the patient, we made careful search—a thing which had not been done before—to see if we could find any hysterogenous zones. We found one situated under the left mamma, another over each of the iliac regions; still another over the right testicle. We remarked that even a slight excitation of the infra-mammary zone readily determined the phenomena of the aura: sensation of constriction of the thorax, then of the neck; beatings in the temples, sibilant sounds in the ears, especially in the left ear. On pressing a little harder we saw P. all at once lose consciousness and fall over backwards with stiffening of his members; and we witnessed the first attack of hystero-epilepsy which the patient had ever had. This attack was, moreover, quite typical; to the epileptoid phase soon succeeded that of the great movements. These were of extreme violence, the patient in his movements of salutation went so far as to smite his face against his knees. A little after, he tore his clothes, his bed curtains, and turning his fury upon himself, he bit his left arm. The phase of passional attitudes then set in; P. seemed a prey to a furious delirium; he reproaches, provokes and excites to violence some imaginary personages. "Hold! take your knife; come, strike!" Lastly he recovers consciousness and affirms that he has no remembrance of anything that has happened.

It is to be remarked that during the entire continuance of the first attack, *the left superior member took no part in the convulsions;* it remained flaccid and completely inert. From this time onward, the fits were repeated every day, spontaneously, several times during the day with precisely the same characters as the provoked attack. During one of these, which took place on the night of the 17th of March, the patient wet his bed. There were two fits on the 19th. On the 21st there was a new crisis *during which the left arm trembled.* On waking, the patient, to his great astonishment found that he could move the divers segments of this member, of the use of which he had been totally deprived during the long period of almost 10 months. The motor paralysis was not completely cured, however, for there remained a certain degree of paresis, but there was a considerable improvement. Only, the troubles of sensibility persisted to the same degree as in the past.

This cure, gentlemen, or more properly speaking, this attempt at a cure, after the diagnosis which we were led to make, did not surprise us. But in our judgment, it supervened prematurely, unseasonably. In fact, it was no longer possible to enable you to witness *de visu,* in all their plenitude (as we had hoped to do), the character of this monoplegia, so excellent a subject for

412

study. The idea then occurred to me that perhaps by acting on the mind of the patient *by way of suggestion in the waking state* (I had previously found that the subject was not hypnotizable) we might reproduce the paralysis, at least for a while. Therefore the next morning, finding P. just coming out of a fit which had in no way modified the state of things, I endeavored to persuade him that he was again paralyzed. ''You believe yourself cured,'' I said to him with assurance, ''it is a mistake; you can not raise your arm or bend it; see, you can not move your fingers, you are unable to grasp my hand.'' The experiment succeeded wonderfully, for after a few minutes, while I was talking, the monoplegia returned just as it was the day before. I was not at all disturbed, I may here say, as to the result of this paralysis artificially reproduced, for I knew by experience that in a matter of hypnotic suggestion, *what one has made one can unmake.* The paralysis, however, did not last longer than 24 hours. The next day a new attack came on, following which, the voluntary movements were definitely reestablished. This time, all the new attempts of suggestion which we made were absolutely powerless. It now remains for me to inform you of the modifications which, as far as voluntary movement is concerned, have been effected in the limb formerly completely paralyzed.

The patient as you see, can move at will all the parts of this member. But these movements have but little energy, they yield to the least resistance opposed to them, and while on the right, the dynamometric force expresses itself in the hand by the figure 70, on the left it gives only the figure 10. If then, the motor impotence is not as absolute as formerly, it still persists to a sufficiently high degree. Moreover, the troubles of sensibility are just as they were, not only in the limb which is the subject of paresis, but also on all the left side of the body including the organs of sense; the fits, besides, remain frequent. Truly, as you see, we have here only an improvement in the condition of the arm, and we are far from having attained a cure.

I propose in connection with this study of hysterical paralysis by traumatism, which I intend soon to bring before you at length, to take up again certain of the facts contained in this interesting case, in order to give them their full value. For the present, leaving to one side the monoplegia, which really constitutes but an episode in the history of the disease, I shall dismiss the subject by expressing the hope that I have made it plain to you that in this man, as in the other five cases, before presented, the great hysteria (hysteria major) exists, endowed with its characteristic attributes.

Gentlemen, in studying with you, in these two lectures, these six cases, so significant and instructive, which chance has placed in our way, I have desired especially to convince you that hysteria, even grave hysteria, is not a rare disease in the male, and that it is likely to appear now and then in private and hospital practice, where only the prejudices of another age could cause a failure to recognize it. I have dared here to hope that after so many proofs which have been accumulating these last five years, this notion is destined hereafter to keep in your minds the place which it deserves to hold.

JEAN MARTIN CHARCOT (b.-Paris, Nov. 29, 1825; d.-Paris, Aug. 16, 1893).

Charcot received his M.D. from Paris, in 1853, after which he remained to intern at the Salpetrière. He spent his whole subsequent professional life primarily at this one institution. From 1853 to 1855 he was head of the clinic at the Medical College. In 1856 he was nominated Doctor of the Hospitals of Paris. In 1862 Charcot established his eventually renowned clinic in neurology at the Salpetrière. In 1872 he became Professor of Pathological Anatomy, in which position he remained for the next ten years. On Jan. 2, 1882 Charcot was appointed, by public decree, to the newly created chair of Nervous Diseases, the first formal recognition of neurology as a separate medical discipline.

Having given up his youthful dreams to become a painter, Charcot turned his artistry to clinical instruction. He succeeded, during his many years at the Salpetrière, in establishing without doubt the most important teaching center in the history of neuro-psychiatry. His famous *Lecons du Mardi* (later *Lecons du Vendredi*) were given in a great amphitheatre before audiences often numbering more than 600. Many of his published works consist of edited notes taken by his students at these lectures, and during his ward tours. His influence on the present thought cannot be overestimated, if only for the inspiration which he gave to his most famous students: Babinsky, Binet, Bleuler, Freud, Janet, Marie, and many more. (See Guillain, below, Chap. VI). This alone would be sufficient to mark him with a singularity even amidst greatness.

Charcot's major contributions to the understanding of psychopathology lie in the field of conversion hysteria. In particular, he gave to hysteria the dignity of a true disease (Charcot always preferred the term 'neurosis' to the term 'hysteria', however), and clearly established it as a disorder in the male. The present selection is perhaps his most forthright statement of this finding.

CHARCOT, J. M. *Clinical lectures on certain diseases of the nervous system.* Detroit, Mich.: G. S. Davis, 1888. Trans. E. P. Hurd. Lect. VII & VIII: "On six cases of hysteria in the male subject." Reprinted here substantially in their entirety.

See also:

CHARCOT, J. M.

a) *Lectures on the diseases of the nervous system.* London: New Sydenham Society, 1877-1889, 3 vol. Trans. G. Sigerson from the first three volumes of the complete works.

b) *Lecons du Mardi a la Salpetrière.* Paris: 1892. L. Battaille, Vol. I (1887-1888); E. Lecrosnier et Babé, Vol. 2 (1888-1889). Notes by his students.

c) *La médecine empirique et la médecine scientifique. Parallèle entre les anciens et les modernes.* Paris: A. Delahaye, 1867.

415

d) *Lecons sur les localizations dans les maladies du cerveau et de la Moelle épinière.* Paris: A. Delahaye, 1875- Recueilliées et publiées par Bourneville, Chef de Bureaux du Progrès Médical. In translation: E. P. Fowler, W. Wood & Co., N.Y., 1876.

e) *Les difformes et les malades dans l'art,* with P. Richer. Paris: Lecrosnier et Babé, 1889.

f) *Les démoniaques dans l'art,* with P. Richer. Paris: Delahaye et Lecrosnier, 1887. These latter two books testify to Charcot's life-long interest in painting, and, in their beauty and delicacy of execution, constitute two of the very finest essays in the history of ideas. Cf. Prinzhorn, H. *Bildnerei der Geisteskranken.* Berlin: J. Springer, 1922.

MACKAY, F. H. & LEGRAND, E. "Jean Martin Charcot, 1825-1893." *Arch. Neurol. Psychiat.* 1935, 34: 390-400.

TOMLINSON, J. C. & HAYMAKER, W. "Jean-Martin Charcot" *Arch. Neurol. Psychiat.* 1957, 77: 44-48.

GUILLAIN, G. *J.-M. Charcot* (1825-1893). *Sa Vie—Son Oeuvre.* Paris: Masson, 1955. This is the best available source on Charcot and contains Charcot's bibliography, and a list of references on him.

JANET, P. "J.-M. Charcot. Son oeuvre psychologique." *Rev. Philos., France et Étranger.* 1895, 39: 567-604.

DEMENTIA PRAECOX
OR
THE GROUP OF SCHIZOPHRENIAS

(Paul) Eugen Bleuler

The Compound Functions

The complex functions which result from the coordinated operations of the functions previously discussed, such as attention, intelligence, will, and action, are, of course, disturbed to the extent that the elementary (simple) functions on which they depend are altered. Only association and affectivity may have to be considered here. However, schizophrenia is characterized by a very peculiar alteration of the relation between the patient's inner life and the external world. The inner life assumes pathological predominance (autism).

(a) *Relation to Reality: Autism*

The most severe schizophrenics, who have no more contact with the outside world, live in a world of their own. They have encased themselves with their desires and wishes (which they consider fulfilled) or occupy themselves with the trials and tribulations of their persecutory ideas; they have cut themselves off as much as possible from any contact with the external world.

This detachment from reality, together with the relative and absolute predominance of the inner life, we term autism.

In less severe cases, the affective and logical significance of reality is only somewhat damaged. The patients are still able to move about in the external world but neither evidence nor logic have any influence on their hopes and delusions. Everything which is in contradiction to their complexes simply does not exist for their thinking or feeling.

An intelligent lady who for many years was mistaken for a neurasthenic "had built a wall around herself so closely confining that she often felt as if she actually were in a chimney." An otherwise socially acceptable woman patient sings at a concert, but unfortunately once started she cannot stop. The audience begins to whistle and hoot and create a disturbance; she does not bother a bit, but continues singing and feels quite satisfied when she finally ends. A well-educated young woman, whose illness is hardly noticeable suddenly moves her bowels before a whole social gathering and cannot comprehend the embarrassment which she causes among her friends. During the course of about ten years, a patient gave me from time to time a note on which the same four words were always written and which signified that he had been unjustly incarcerated. It did not make any difference to him if he handed me a half-dozen of these notes at the same time. He did not understand the senselessness of his action when one discussed it with him. Withal, this patient showed good judgment about other patients and worked independently in his ward. Very frequently schizophrenics will give us numerous letters without expecting any answer; or they will ask us a dozen questions one after the other without even giving us time to answer. They predict an event for a certain day, but are so little bothered when the prophecy does not come to pass that they do not even seek to find explanations. Even where reality has apparently become identical with the patient's pathological creations, it will often be ignored.

The wishes and desires of many patients revolve around their release from the hospital. Yet they remain indifferent to the actual discharge. One of our patients

418

who has a marked complex about children made an attempt to murder his wife because she only bore him four children in ten years. Yet he is quite indifferent to the children themselves. Other patients are in love with someone. If this person is actually present, he makes no impression on them at all; if he dies, they do not care. One patient constantly begs to be given the key to the door of his ward. When it is finally given to him, he does not know what to do with it and returns it almost at once. He tries a thousand times each day to open the door. If it is left unlocked, he becomes embarrassed and does not know what to do. He continuously pursues the doctor at each of his visits with the words: "Please, Doctor." Asked what he desires, he appears surprised and has nothing further to say. A woman patient asked to see her doctor. When she was summoned to the interview, she at least was able after a few minutes of perplexity to make her wishes known by pointing to his wedding ring. For weeks on end, a mother exerts every means at her command to see her child. When permission is granted her, she prefers to have a glass of wine. For years a woman longs for a divorce from her husband. When at long last she gets her divorce, she refuses to believe in it at all, and becomes furious if she is not addressed by her husband's name. Many a patient consumes himself with anxiety over his imminent death but will not take the least precaution for his self preservation and remains totally unmoved in the face of real danger to his life.

Autism is not always to be detected at the very first glance. Initially the behavior of many patients betrays nothing remarkable. It is only on prolonged observation that one sees how much they always seek their own way, and how very little they permit their environment to influence them. Even severe chronic patients show quite good contacts with their environment with regard to indifferent, everyday affairs. They chatter, participate in games, seek out stimulation—but they are always selective. They keep their complexes to themselves, never saying a word about them and not wishing to have them touched upon in any way from the outside.

Thus the indifference of patients toward what would be considered their nearest and dearest interest becomes understandable. Other things are of far greater importance to them. They do not react any more to influences from the outside. They appear "stuporous" even where no other disturbance inhibits their will or actions. The external world must often appear to them as rather hostile since it tends to disturb them in their fantasies. However, there are also cases where the shutting off from the outside world is caused by contrary reasons. Particularly in the beginning of their illness, these patients quite consciously shun any contact with reality because their affects are so powerful that they must avoid everything which might arouse their emotions. The apathy toward the outer world is then a secondary one springing from a hypertrophied sensitivity.

Autism is also manifested by many patients externally. (Naturally, this is, as a rule, unintentional.) Not only do they not concern themselves with anything around them, but they sit around with faces constantly averted, looking at a blank wall; or they shut off their sensory portals by drawing a skirt or bed clothes over their heads. Indeed, formerly, when the patients were mostly abandoned to their own devices, they could often be found in bent-over, squatting positions, an indication that they were trying to restrict as much as possible of the sensory surface area of their skin.

Misunderstandings stemming from the autistic thought processes can hardly ever, or only with great difficulty, be corrected by the patients.

420

A hebephrenic lies on a bench in a thoroughly vile mood. As she catches sight of me, she attempts to sit up. I beg her not to disturb herself. She answers in an irritated tone that if she could sit up she would not be lying down, apparently imagining that I was reproaching her for lying on the bench. Several times, using different words, I repeat the suggestion that she remain lying quietly as she was. She merely becomes more and more irritated. Everything I say is interpreted falsely by her in the sense and direction of her autistic train of thought.

The autistic world has as much reality for the patient as the true one, but his is a different kind of reality. Frequently, they cannot keep the two kinds of reality separated from each other even though they can make the distinction in principle. A patient heard us speaking of a certain Dr. N. Immediately afterwards he asks whether it was a hallucination or whether we had spoken of a Dr. N.

The reality of the autistic world may also seem more valid than that of reality itself; the patients then hold their fantasy world for the real, reality for an illusion. They no longer believe in the evidence of their own senses. Schreber described his attendants as "miracled up, changeable individuals." The patient may be very aware that other people judge the environment differently. He also knows that he himself sees it in that form but it is not *real* to him. "They say, that you are the doctor, but I don't know it," or even, "But you are really Minister N." To a considerable extent, reality is transformed through illusions and largely replaced by hallucinations (twilight states, *Dammerzustande*).

In the usual hallucinatory conditions, more validity is, as a rule, ascribed to the illusions; yet the patients continue to act and orient themselves in accordance with reality. Many of them, however, no longer act at all, not

421

even in accordance with their autistic thinking. This may occur in stuporous conditions, or the autism itself may reach such a high degree of intensity, that the patients' actions lose all relation to the blocked-off reality. The sick person deals with the real world as little as the normal person deals with his dreams. Frequently both disturbances, the stuporous immobility and the exclusion of reality, occur simultaneously.

Patients who show no clouding of consciousness often appear much less autistic than they really are because they are able to suppress their autistic thoughts or, like certain hysterics, seem to be occupied with them only in a theoretical way, and ordinarily allow them only very little influence upon their actions. These patients rarely remain under our observation for very long because we are inclined to discharge them as improved or cured.[*]

A complete and constant exclusion of the external world appears, if at all, only in the most severe degree of stupor. In milder cases the real and the autistic world exist not only side by side, but often become entangled with one another in the most illogical manner. The doctor is at one moment not only the hospital-physician and at another the shoemaker S., but he is both in the same thought-content of the patient. A patient who was still fairly well-mannered and capable of work, made herself a rag-doll which she considered to be the child of her imaginary lover. When this "lover" of hers made a trip to Berlin, she wanted to send "the child" after him, as a precautionary measure. But she first went to the police, to ask whether it would be considered as illegal to send "the child" as luggage instead of on a passenger ticket.

---

[*] The very common preoccupation of young hebephrenics with the "deepest questions" is nothing but an autistic manifestation. The "questions" about which they are so concerned are those that cannot be decided because reality has no part in them. Freud considers doubt and uncertainty as a preliminary stage of what he calls auto-erotism. (cf. *Jahrbuch fur Psychoanalyse*, Vol. 1, p. 410.)

Wishes and fears constitute the contents of autistic thinking. In those rare cases where the contradictions to reality are not felt at all, it is the wishes alone which are involved; fears appear when the patient senses the obstacles to the fulfillment of his wishes. Even where no true delusions arise autism is demonstrable in the patients' inability to cope with reality, in their inappropriate reactions to outside influences (irritability), and in their lack of resistance to every and any idea and urge.

In the same way as autistic feeling is detached from reality, autistic thinking obeys its own special laws. To be sure, autistic thinking makes use of the customary logical connections insofar as they are suitable but it is in no way bound to such logical laws. Autistic thinking is directed by affective needs; the patient thinks in symbols, in analogies in fragmentary concepts, in accidental connections. Should the same patient turn back to reality he may be able to think sharply and logically.

Thus we have to distinguish between realistic and autistic thinking which exist side by side in the same patient. In realistic thinking the patient orients himself quite well in time and space. He adjusts his actions to reality insofar as they appear normal. The autistic thinking is the source of the delusions, of the crude offenses against logic and propriety, and all the other pathological symptoms. The two forms of thought are often fairly well separated so that the patient is able at times to think completely autistically and at other times completely normally. In other cases the two forms mix, going on to complete fusion, as we saw in the cases cited above.

The patient need not become conscious of the peculiarity, of the deviation of his autistic thinking from his previous realistic type of thinking. However, the more intelligent patients may for years gauge the difference.

They experience the autistic state as painful; only rarely as pleasurable. They complain that reality seems different from what it was before. Things and people are no longer what they are supposed to be. They are changed, strange, no longer have any relationship to the patient. A released patient described it, "as if she were running around in an open grave, so strange did the world appear." Another "had started to think herself into an entirely different life. By comparison, everything was quite different; even her sweetheart was not the way she had imagined him." A still very intelligent woman patient considered it a change for the better that at will, she could transpose herself into a state of the greatest (sexual and religious) bliss. She even wanted to give us instructions to enable us to do likewise.

Autism must not be confused with "the unconscious." Both autistic, and realistic thinking can be conscious as well as unconscious.

(b) Attention

As a partial phenomenon of affectivity . . . attention is affected with it by deterioration. Insofar as interests are extant—in milder cases this means for the majority of events, in severe cases at least for the emotionally charged activity (such as the working out of plans for escape)— attention appears to be normal at least according to our present methods of observation. However, where affect is lacking, there will also be lacking the drive to pursue the external and internal processes, to direct the path of the senses and the thoughts; i.e. active attention will be lacking.

Passive attention is altered in an entirely different manner. On the one hand it is evident that the uninterested or autistically encapsulated patients pay very little attention to the outer world. On the other hand, however, it is remarkable how many of the events which the patients seem to ignore are registered nevertheless. The selectivity which normal attention ordinarily exercises among the sensory impressions can be reduced to zero so that almost everything is recorded that reaches the senses. Thus, the facilitating as well as the inhibiting properties of attention are equally disturbed.

Events on the ward which did in no way refer to the patients, newspaper reports which they heard only in passing, can be reproduced after years in every detail by patients who appeared completely absorbed in themselves, who always sat gazing into some corner, so that one can hardly understand how these people managed to learn of these matters. One of our catatonics, who for months on end had been constantly occupied with pantomiming toward the wall, showed after some improvement that she was fully familiar with what had happened in the Boer War during the period of her illness. She must have snatched single remarks from her demented environment and preserved them in an orderly fashion. Another patient, who for many years had not uttered one reasonable word, had never carried out a sensible action (not even fed herself), knew the name of the new Pope a number of years after his investiture, although she herself had always lived in a Protestant environment where no reference was ever made to Rome.

The tenacity and vigility of attention can be altered independently of each other in both a positive as well as a negative sense, but there is nothing characteristically schizophrenic about the disturbances. (A part of the concept of vigility coincides with that of distractability.) Indeed, there are specific inner disturbances which give rise to a condition of hypovigility, as for example when "thoughts are withdrawn." On the other hand, if the train of thought loses itself in deviations tenacity is no longer extant.

The extent of the span of attention is variable; it may be quite normal. On the other hand, the intensity of attention can be so disturbed that the patient can hardly concentrate, even though he makes a very special effort to do so. In that event, the extensity of attention suffers as well. The patient is then incapable of drawing on all the associations necessary for proper reflection. Such disturbances may be conditioned by primary obstacles in the psychic processes which are as yet unknown to us. However, apart from the affects the success of attention is mostly dependent on association disturbances. If the train of thought has disintegrated entirely, correct thinking becomes impossible without abnormally intensive efforts.

The general tendency to fatigue in some cases also causes the rapid dwindling of attention. Most chronic patients, however, show a normal or even hypernormal capacity to maintain the span of attention whenever it is possible to engage their active attention.

Preoccupation due to complexes, blockings, inhibitions, often prevents the patients continuously or momentarily from following a definite chain of thought or from thinking in a desired direction. Thus, many can only follow in a very fragmented way the story they are reading or the dramatic performance they are watching. Others can relate to perfection what was heard or seen, even though throughout the entire time of their listening, they were constantly in conversation with their "voices." *Even attention can be "split."* Very often the attention, like the other functions, is blocked: the patients, in the midst of a conversation or while working, appear to be following another train of thought or not to be thinking at all. Peculiarly, in either case, they can continue to think with full knowledge of what went on during the period of inattention; and for example, later answer a question which seemed not to have been comprehended at the time.

Many catatonics demonstrate a compulsion to direct their attention to specific external or preferably internal activities. The hallucinations, in particular, often seem to compel continuous attention against the patient's will. . . .

(c) *Will*

The will, a resultant of all the various affective and associative processes, is of course disturbed in a number of ways, but above all by the breakdown of the emotions. Even mild cases frequently come into conflict with their environment because of their abulia. The patients appear lazy and negligent because they no longer have the urge to do anything either of their own initiative or at the bidding of another. They can spend years in bed. In mild cases, where wishes and desires still exist, they will nevertheless do nothing toward the realization of these wishes. However, we also see the opposite form of weakness of will which consists in the patient's inability to withstand impulses coming from within or from without. Whatever desire, whatever notion strikes their fancy, many of them proceed to carry out at once. Some do this because they do not consider the possible consequences; others have full insight into these same consequences but totally lack resistance, or are indifferent to the consequences. In a state of affect they are thus capable of anything, even of committing serious crimes.

However, under certain conditions, one may even see what can well be termed hyperbulia. There are patients who carry out with the greatest energy whatever they may have taken into their heads to do, whether it be something reasonable or something senseless. They can be utterly ruthless even towards themselves, exert themselves to the utmost, bear pain and hardships of every kind, and will allow nothing to distract them from their

427

purpose. In such instances they can show a perseverance which can be maintained for years under certain conditions.

On the other hand, we often see the combination, found frequently in normal people, of weakness of will with stubbornness in which one or the other prevails, depending on the circumstances.* In general, most of the patients evidence peevishness, capriciousness and vacillation. They will make all sorts of promises without keeping any. Hospital patients, for example, may ask for work but on being assigned a task prove unable to cope with it. Likewise their threats usually remain unfulfilled.

In the sphere of will, blocking is particularly striking. Frequently a patient really wants to do something but is unable to carry it out because his psychomotor apparatus fails him. Persistent blockings of will then constitute a form of catatonic stupor. Under different circumstances, compulsive or automatic acts and the various forms of command-automatism may occur.

(d) The Person

The auto-psychic orientation is usually quite normal. The patients know who they are in so far as delusions do not falsify the person. But the ego is never entirely intact. Certain modifications reveal themselves regularly, especially the tendency to "splitting." However, these disturbances are not sufficiently explicit in the simpler cases to lend themselves well to description.

(e) Schizophrenic "Dementia"

The schizophrenic disorder of intelligence is really most clearly characterized by the state of the associations and of the affectivity. No description of the resultants of

---

* We use "weakness of will" here in the sense of a lack of strength of drive (= apathy) as well as of a lack of tenacity and unity of will (= flightiness, capriciousness), and of a defect of inhibition.

these functions could ever do adequate justice to their endless variety. Therefore, we can only hope to illustrate the most important trends that this disturbance takes by means of random examples. Here we propose to discuss only the true schizophrenic dementia, not the special coloring it takes on through the accessory symptoms.

In no other disease is the disturbance of intelligence more inadequately designated by the terms "dementia" and "imbecility" than in schizophrenia. We see absolutely nothing in this disease of "definitive loss of memory images" or other memory disturbances which properly belong to the concept of dementia. Thus some psychiatrists are able to maintain that even the severest schizophrenics are not demented; others, mostly French authorities, feel the need to separate this disorder of intellect under the term of "pseudo-dementia" from the other types.

Dementia, in the sense of the organic psychoses, is something fundamentally different. Equally different are the manifold forms of congenital idiocy even though the defective intellectual attainments in these various kinds of disorder may ultimately give an externally similar result, leading to inadequate reactions to the external world. In other words, the concept "dementia" is nearly as broad as that of mental disease in general, and contains nearly as many subdivisions as does the latter.†

It is of prime importance to establish that even in a very severe degree of schizophrenia all the fundamental functions that are accessible to present tests are preserved. In mental deficiency complicated connections of ideas and associations are never formed; in organic cases

---

† How obscure the concept of dementia really is, is best illustrated by the discussion and controversy concerning the presence of dementia in paranoia. Some consider the paranoiacs to be demented because they think and act in such an illogical fashion; others insist they are not demented because they can still very ably exercise such professions as judges, architects, and teachers.

much has been lost, if not by actual brain-damage at least by the very poor utilization of the psyches. In contrast, even the most demented schizophrenic can under proper conditions suddenly demonstrate productions of a rather highly integrated type (cunning attempts at escape, etc.). Aside from the pronounced lack of interest and activity, the severe schizophrenic dementia is characterized by the fact that in all thinking and acting there occurs a large number of mistakes ("Fehlleistungen"); the relative difficulty of the task is of secondary importance. Conversely, in the mildest cases the dementia is characterized by the fact that, though these people are usually quite sensible, they are also capable of every possible stupidity and foolishness. The mild paretic or mental defective demonstrates his ineptitude when reflections are necessitated which, for him, are too complicated. In simpler situations he behaves normally. In such patients, the degree of dementia can be gauged by the extent of the possible accomplishments, and even then only by careful testing which takes into consideration the total constellation, mood, fatigue, individual peculiarities, etc. Patients who are incapable of doing multiplication are even less apt to do division; those who cannot get the point of a fable will not understand a novel; on the other hand, whoever can understand the whole context of a novel should find no difficulties in grasping a simple story. It is quite different in schizophrenia. A patient who at a certain moment cannot add 17 and 14, even when he earnestly tries, will suddenly be able to solve a difficult arithmetical problem or to give a well-composed and successful speech. A schizophrenic can estimate with excellent judgment the behavior, the pathology and the expediency of the therapeutic measures applied to his ward-mates. But at the same time he is unable to understand that he cannot possibly maintain himself outside the hospital since he

430

causes a row each night and beats up his neighbors.

A patient may have sat around for years in a demented euphoria, uttering nothing but the most banal phrases; then all of a sudden he may take part in every kind of work and appear recovered in every respect. Therefore, the external picture of schizophrenic dementia is characterized much more by the state of affectivity and, in particular, by interest and spontaneity, than by the intellectual disturbance in the narrower sense. The latter is essentially a numerical concept and cannot be graded in accordance with the degree of possible attainments but only according to the ratio of correct to incorrect performances.

Thus, it is wrong in every respect to compare the dementia of schizophrenics with the intelligence of a child of a certain age.... It shows a complete misunderstanding of the peculiarities of schizophrenia if one believes that schizophrenic dementia can be proved or excluded by means of an "intelligence test," whether it be one which takes but a few minutes or several days to perform. The actual amount of knowledge remains preserved on the whole but it is not always available or it is employed in the wrong way. What may be inaccessible in one constellation of the psyche, may be freely utilized in another. That is why the Ebbinghaus completion experiments, as well as the Heilbronner . . . picture-tests frequently fail and are not at all applicable in this disease precisely when we desire to estimate the degree of intelligence.‡ The habits of life, the lack of adaptation to the environment only can show in the milder cases how far the dementia has progressed. In the hospital the quickest way is to use a brief test consisting of questioning the patient about

‡ Indeed, many of these patients need abnormally long periods of time for correct solutions, while many of the more severe cases are not capable of solving such problems at all. They fill the gaps with inappropriate or even completely false words disregarding meanings, as well as grammatical structure.

his present situation, the reasons for his confinement, his relations to his superiors and those in charge, and about his future plans. Even then there may be complete understanding and comprehension present, although very severe defects are to be noted in other spheres.

Therefore, if one wishes to speak of intellectual dementia in our patients, one must express oneself approximately as follows: the schizophrenic is *not* generally demented but he is demented with regard to certain periods, to certain constellations, and to certain complexes. In mild cases, the defective functions are the exception. In most severe cases, those who sit around in our mental institutions taking no part in anything, the defective functions are the rule. And in between we find every transitional form. The difference between moderate and severe dementia is an extensive, not an intensive one. The mildest case of schizophrenia can commit as great a piece of folly as the most severe, but he commits it far more rarely.

Nonetheless, the intellectual defect does occur not entirely haphazardly. The particularly poor intellectual performances are, for example, tied up with emotionally toned complexes. Furthermore, it is self-evident that in each stage of the disease alterations of intellectual functions will increase with the complexity of the specific function. When on an average one out of one hundred associations is pathological, then the function which involves merely a few associations will only rarely be disturbed, while the one which involves several hundreds of individual functions is almost always disturbed. In addition, in schizophrenics the capacity for condensation of many ideas under one unified logical viewpoint is evidently rendered more difficult, which in turn impairs the complex functions more than the simple functions. Thus, on the whole, the higher mental functions are more severely disturbed.

The anomaly called schizophrenic dementia consists of the effects of association disturbance, indifference and irritability in the affective sphere and the autistic seclusion from the influences of the outside world. The disintegration of the associations effects the concept formation. To be sure, the majority of concepts does not seem to be much less clear cut in the permanent clinical conditions of this disease than in the healthy. For example, one sees very little of the vagueness which is so striking in the concepts of the demented epileptics, even though now and then there is a tendency to apply general ideas where specific ones would be indicated. Thus our patients call an instrument made of iron, "iron," or call a dustpan, "a domestic utensil." Although the use of such terminology is rare except in response to explicit questions yet it reveals an anomaly of concepts and not simply of expression. I have not met with an actual schizophrenic reduction in concepts in the sense of some having been lost entirely. On the other hand, the concepts frequently lack some of their component parts. All these disturbances may fluctuate from one moment to the next. More or less consistent and constant defects are displayed only in concepts which are woven into delusions or else are composed of emotionally accentuated complexes.

Wernicke's method of asking the patient to differentiate between related ideas is therefore entirely inadequate for investigation of this disturbance, even though it is evident that, under certain circumstances, comparison and differentiation of incompletely conceived ideas must be impaired. It is highly probable that the hebephrenic ... knew quite well the difference between city and village in spite of her very bizarre answers which incidentally did not at all indicate her ignorance but were primarily a "para-functioning" of her actual associations. Just as little can I believe that Wernicke's patient, who mistook the attendant for his sister, Laura, had forgotten the memory picture of male and female clothing. As a rule, lucid schizophrenics have a fairly good grasp of such ideas and memory pictures. Exceptions are noted only in definite psychic constellations, e.g., when complexes are activated, in states of distraction, and in all probability in states of organic disturbance. Thus a hebephrenic associates "wheel" to "barrel" and indicates that the ideas, "wheel" and "hoop," were really almost identical for him at the time. The same patient can later differentiate these two ideas quite well without the disease having shown any change whatsoever. Often objects are mistaken because only a part of their properties is noted (the other properties are not entirely "forgotten"), and then freely associated to form another object. A picture on a wall with a deep frame is therefore a spittoon. The fire-ladder in front of the ward becomes "our barn-ladder." The director of the psychiatric service is Reverend F., because he administers here as does Reverend F. in the hospital. The cotton mill where the patient worked is called a "clothing-factory."

By means of condensation several concepts are compressed into one. Particularly often, several persons are conceived of as one. A patient is his father and mother, and his children. During an acute, although mildly cloudy episode of his illness, another patient does not distinguish between his children as they are now and as they were as infants. When the conversation turns to sexual matters and the education of children, his wife and his own ego seem to run together into an indivisible concept; likewise he confuses the institution with his home. On questioning or other stimulation it does not make any difference of which part of this conceptual pair he or the observer are talking since he says the same things about either part and it is quite impossible to force a separation. A female

434

patient identifies the story of Moses' childhood with that of Herod's slaughter of the Bethlehem infants.

Often enough the emotionally toned complexes determine the transformation of concepts. Thus a patient, who expects something extraordinary to happen to her in the future, speaks of her "future parents" as if it were something entirely self-evident. An ambitious paranoid patient has seen himself portrayed as a "general in a French and Swiss uniform." The confusion of both armies does not seem to disturb him in the least. To the objection that Switzerland has no general, he replies that a colonel is also a general. In such cases it is easy to demonstrate that not only the terms but the concepts themselves are altered. A hebephrenic signs a letter to his mother with "your hopeful nephew." How he arrived at this conclusion could not be discovered. The patient defends this nonsense with the argument that his mother did have a sister and that he was her (the sister's) nephew. However, it is certain that at least for a few moments his ideas about family relations had become obscured. A female catatonic had received a watch as a present, which gave her much pleasure. But she also found pleasure in all of her other possessions as well as in her sweetheart. All this had merged into one single concept which she designated mainly with the term "gift." The inappropriate expressions of hallucinating patients frequently conceal grossly extended concepts. A hebephrenic "had pain twice, and that is murder by poisoning."

The identification of two concepts on the basis of one common component, in many instances, leads to symbolism which plays such an outstanding role in delusions. A patient signs himself as "The Beginning and End of the World." His delusion is expressed in this phrase. For our patients the symbol is readily transposed into reality. They may come to believe in real people burning them with real fire when their secret love "burns" within them. The following ideas are somewhat similar: a catatonic makes a certain movement of his eyebrows in exact imitation of a Miss N.; then he insists that he had sexual relations with her. Miss N.'s gesture executed by his own body is equated with Miss N. herself.

The alteration of concepts in schizophrenia has the peculiarity that simple ideas can just, or almost as easily be disturbed and distorted as complex ones. The decisive element is, above all, the relation to an emotionally toned complex which, at times, facilitates and, at others, impedes conceptualizations. But aside from this, the disturbance varies with the oscillations of the disease, which at times may involve the major part of the thought processes and at other times again recede to involve only a few isolated functions.

Of course, no clear and accurate thinking operations can be carried out with fragmentary concepts.

A rather lazy patient had finally been induced to do some work for a half-hour. He then believed that he had a right to obtain all sorts of rewards. When these were not forthcoming he again stopped working. He was still correct in his thinking that he should be compensated for his work but he did not distinguish between half-an-hour of work and persistent work; and just as little did he distinguish between small and large compensation. A short bit of work was to him *work* in general. By the idea of compensation he understood anything which his heart desired. His concepts of accomplishment and recompense were unclear, therefore a correct quantitative correlation between the two ideas was impossible.

The inaccurate delimitation of concepts favors quite senseless generalizations of some ideas. A paranoid patient suddenly no longer hears the hallucinated noise of a machine; therefore the whole hospital ceases to exist

436

for him. Another paranoid had solemnly made peace with an enemy of his; he then wanted to act as peacemaker everywhere. A hebephrenic had given his father a rude answer. He then believed that he had to purify himself for that sin. Finally, he extended this purification to everything around him. He not only washed himself and the furniture but also laid his clothes out on the roof so that the rain could clean them. Delusions proper frequently extend into such generalizations.*

The disturbances of affect influence the intelligence in a multiplicity of ways. When interest is lacking there is little thinking or the thinking is not carried through to its proper end. Whenever the patient has an earnest aspiration, he shows himself capable of making exceptionally sharp-witted and complex deductions to achieve his desired ends. Conversely, many paranoids think incorrectly only when their complexes are involved. Schreber could criticize the expert opinions on his tutelage most pertinently at the very time when he was defending his most preposterous delusions.

In general, the intellectual accomplishments vary with the emotionally charged complexes, which at times suppress reflection and at others make use of and favor reflection. (These functional variations are not to be mistaken for oscillations of the disease itself. A patient often appears to be much more demented at certain periods because the disease process has become more intense.)

The disturbances of affect are the most important cause of "the loss of the psychic value system" (Schuele). Mental defectives and organic cases also may lack the feeling for the difference between the essential and the unessential; the defectives because they are unable to grasp complex ideas in their totality; the organics for

---

* Here the extension of the concept is at the same time a displacement; the feeling of moral uncleanliness leads, as it so frequently does in neurotics, to exaggerated physical cleanliness.

the same reasons and also because their chains of ideas are limited to those which correspond to the dominant affect.

The process is far more complicated in schizophrenia. Ideas are thought of in entirely haphazard fragments which frequently retain far-fetched connections and miss the closer related ones. The affects inhibit and facilitate the associations to a far larger degree than in organics, and moreover are themselves changed both qualitatively and quantitatively. If it does not make any difference to the patient whether he and his family go to rack and ruin, whether or not he remains institutionalized forever, or whether he lies in filth or not, then these ideas, so vitally important for most other people, can have no influence on the patient's reflections. If such a patient is given the choice of renouncing a whim or losing his job, he will decide for the latter course without thinking twice because only the whim is affectively charged. This is one of the most important aspects of schizophrenic dementia.

Suggestibility is also altered in conjunction with the affectivity. It is generally lowered. This impedes psychological influence from the outside but facilitates the utilization of judgment where such is still possible. In this respect, the more intelligent schizophrenics have an advantage in the carrying through of new ideas. Due to flexibility of their associations, they can more easily than the normal person conceive and comprehend ideas which deviate from the normal. But they are also more independent of the opinions of others and therefore have the mettle to carry through ideas and plans which would appear unthinkable to a healthy person. I was once consulted about a schizophrenic who at the present time is executing some highly important economic plans with governmental aid in many different foreign countries— plans (of his own invention) which a normal person might have thought up but which he would not have considered feasible. Every new movement, good or bad, usually draws its quota of schizophrenics into its orbit.

In other cases there is a combination of superficiality of affect with the associative disturbance of thinking resulting in an exaggerated gullibility. An externally entirely lucid hebephrenic, who worked as a compositor in between attacks of illness, permitted himself to be taken to the hospital on four different occasions under the same pretense of having to go to see a doctor about some physical ailment. In complicated business transactions, the patients easily become the dupes of those who know how to take advantage of them. Hypochondriacally disposed patients can have an illness easily suggested to them merely by an injudicious question. Naturally, the tenor of the complexes determines the direction of this partial suggestibility. The condition of an intellectually well preserved patient with hypochondriacal ideas was considerably improved by us in the course of a two months treatment by means of various suggestions. But close association with a melancholic patient for only a few days was sufficient to reduce her to her former state. Paranoids can be talked by any dumbbell into believing that this or that one is their friend or enemy, yet will remain inaccessible to logical influence.

It is also amazing how easily schizophrenics react to neutral influences. I once answered a paranoid with "noi" instead of "no", using a word from the Swabian dialect which had absolutely no connection with our conversation. The patient began to imitate me immediately, using the Swabian idiom, although she herself had no closer connection with this dialect than would any other native of Zurich. She kept this up till the end of our conversation, though I gave her no further reason for it.

Both recent or old cases of schizophrenia can be hypnotized. However, the power of hypnotic suggestion does not go very far in combating this disease. Many schizophrenics can resist mass-suggestibility far better than the healthy. Still, here, too, the influence of a suggestion increases when given to a number of people simultaneously. Peculiarly, schizophrenics are also the most delicate re-agents to the *spiritus loci*. It cannot be mere accident that the external forms of this disease should vary so markedly from institution to institution, from physician to physician, from attendant to attendant. Catalepsy, negativism, hyperkinesis, violence, suicidal tendencies, necessity for tube-feeding, and restraint, all these are quantitatively very variable, according to time and place, even when the members of the administrative staff do their utmost to make the handling of the patients as uniform as possible. Also suggestion does not only come from the hospital personnel and the hospital set-up but equally as much from the other patients. A single patient can disrupt an entire ward. If someone cleverly sets the tone on the ward, then he will quickly have any number of imitators among the active schizophrenics. In one ward, for example, a certain dish of food is disliked; in another ward, it is another type of food which is detested. This will go on till the instigator of this fad is removed.

The power of suggestion also manifests itself in the induced psychoses whereby an active schizophrenic frequently will impose his delusional system on a family member who is a latent schizophrenic. A very special increase in suggestibility appears in "command-automatism" which will be discussed later under the catatonic symptoms.

Naturally the state of schizophrenic intelligence is also in a reciprocal relationship to the autism. The latter cannot arise without concomitant weakness of intelligence and thus brings about the really demented logical errors

440

by the exclusion of reality from the material of thought.

Thus, an erotomanic, hebephrenic, young girl believes that a certain highly placed gentleman is going to marry her, whereas in reality he does not want to have anything to do with her. A hebephrenic promotes his uncle to the rank of general so that the uncle will be in a better position to help him than he is in his present rank of colonel. The association that this promotion can have absolutely no effect is simply not made. Another patient answers to the question, "Have you been in a mental hospital before?", with "No, but unjustly."

Autism is also connected with the reduced influence of experience. A burnt schizophrenic does not always fear the fire! No matter how painful the consequences, they permit themselves again and again to be misled by their distorted ideas or by their negligence. However, this does not hold good for all experiences. Often disciplinary punishments or rewards still have some influence, even on the quite severely sick patients.

Of course, the association disturbances are responsible for most of the confusion in logical thinking. Logical thinking is a reproduction of associations which are equivalent or analogous to those which experience has taught us. Through the loosening of the customary connections between concepts, thinking becomes detached from experience and takes a turn into deviant pathways. Blocking occurs precisely at the important points so that the patient is incapable of completing his thinking on certain subjects. What is worse, instead of the blocked associations, others crop up which do not belong at all to this train of thoughts or belong to another juncture of it. Thus, the story about the donkey crossing the brook first with a load of salt and then with a load of sponges may be repeated as follows: "They overloaded the donkey so much that it was crushed . . . now it is the custom in the

Catholic religion . . ., it has been said that was the last rites given to the dying.''

If the inappropriate idea-connections become very numerous, the train of thought cannot reach any conclusion since the direction of thinking is constantly changing.

Therefore, many logical operations fail because any one thought is immediately linked to the dominant complex (delusions of reference), or, conversely, because the patients are unable to find any connection with their complex. Therefore most direct questions about affective occurrences determining symptomatology are answered at first or persistently in the negative, or the patients evade the question. The patient has come to the institution, ''because he sprained his ankle;'' or (to the question, why?) ''I came in a cab.'' These are really cases of ''misdirected thinking'' and not merely of ''misdirected talking.''

(What do the voices say?) ''I also have two children.'' (Repeating the question), ''People say so many things here.'' (Repeating the question again), ''Not much.'' (Repeating.) ''I do not talk much anyway.'' (Repeating.) ''Yes, not much.'' (Repeating.) ''Yes, I can't say it.'' (Why not?) ''I don't know.'' (What do the voices say?) ''Yes, we talk with each other, but I don't talk much.''

This kind of thinking can be carried over to neutral topics; indeed, it can become quite generalized. The question as to what date it is can then be answered with, ''The same.'' (The same what?) ''The same date that we have today.'' Such types of responses can be given by perfectly lucid patients even when they make an effort to think correctly. They never get beyond such generalized phrases.

The impression of a high degree of dementia can easily be evoked by the very frequent responses of a type which may be termed ''at random replies'' (*In-den-Tag-hinein-*

442

antworten): (When were you born?) "1876." (Is that correct? When?) "1871." (Which is right?) "1872." (In reality none of these answers was correct.) It is particularly in questions that can be answered by a Yes or No that one must be wary of taking the response at its face value. Often we get something like this: (Do you want to get up?), "Yes." (Do you wish to stay in bed?) "Yes."

The inadequate application of necessary associations also causes a premature termination of reflections. Often, the patient will give an answer before one has completed the question, therefore, the many incomplete, "demented" judgments.

The abrupt emergence of new ideas leads to pathological notions. Suddenly a catatonic demands in all earnestness that he wants to see Niagara Falls. On his admission to the hospital, another patient found nothing more important to ask than whether the Sahara was still in Africa.

The results are particularly senseless where there is a split between the logical directives of the thought-train and the substance and content of the associations and where each of these functions goes its own independent way.

I asked a patient what a gentleman acquaintance could do for him. The answer was, "Nothing, except if I could receive a poem from him." Thus, formally, he did give me an answer to my question. The poem is named as the desired object in a perfectly correct and logical form. In truth, however, the patient picked up this idea only because shortly before I had conversed with another patient about poetry; he had no real desire for any poem. I argue with a patient as to the fact that she claims to own a house. "Yes," she answers, "the music proves it." Actually, music could be heard in the distance, and thus she obtained the idea which is immediately used as a proof against my objections.

443

The thought-content is often determined by some passing notion or sudden fancy; (Why do you shake hands?, "Because I can't eat any students"), or by a wish or fear which happens to preoccupy the patient. (The patient smears "in order to get transferred to a better ward.") Then again he gets his content from the outside world (see the examples cited above); or the notion belongs to the circle of thoughts involved in the question. Thus it is not a question of motivation by the content when Stransky's patient declares that he flies into a rage because the doctor is wearing a grey suit. According to my experience the patient really becomes furious for quite different reasons which have some relationship to his complexes. He then, purely at random, mentions the grey suit, as the reason for his fury.

Such ex post-facto pseudo-motivations in which the patient himself believes are quite common in schizophrenia. One of our patients was quite aware that he always made up the motivations subsequently, "after he himself had been startled by the stupidities which he had committed." After an attempted suicide, a woman patient was brought back to bed and then insisted that she had attempted the suicide because she had to lie in bed. We have the same sort of after-the-fact justification of behavior when a very good-for-nothing hebephrenic tells us that he got into debt only in order to show his wife that he could obtain money without her assistance; or when a dangerously aggressive patient allegedly bought his revolver only to prove to his wife that he would not hurt her even though he had a revolver. In such cases, the hindsight type of justification can appear as the real reason to a superficial observer, so that often even intelligent people allow themselves to be fooled into attributing sound judgment to the patient.

It is amazing to see the indifference of the patient to

444

his grossest contradictions. A hebephrenic can complain in the main clause that he never gets a night's sleep, while in the subordinate clause he indicates how wonderfully well he slept. Patients complain bitterly and emphatically to their relatives that they are not allowed to do something or other. As soon as they receive permission to do what they desire, they do not wish to exercise the privilege. A patient requests in a letter to his wife that firstly, she should send him his razor so that he may commit suicide; secondly, that she should come and get him out of the institution; and finally, she should bring him a pair of shoes.

Except on rare occasions, it does not help much to draw the patient's attention to the contradictions. Generally the necessity to shape things into some logical order, to reflect on them and to bring them under a common heading, is markedly reduced. At the other extreme, we have the alcoholics who liberally invent elaborations of their stories in order to round them out, and seek a causal motivation for their actions. In contrast, the schizophrenics' thinking is composed of logical fragments. Causality frequently does not seem to exist for them. Few of them are concerned with where their "voices" come from. They may remain confined to the hospital for long periods without asking the reason. This appears to be not only an affective but also a logical defect.

In certain respects, the patients lack the capacity for discussion. They think about something, and then take it for granted. As supporting evidence, they will offer sham-proofs, and the most logical counter-evidence remains utterly ineffectual.

If confronted with complicated tasks, the patients often appear so confused, their psyche so split, that it is not easy to discover the genesis of their thinking errors. Nevertheless, with some patience, it is possible even in

445

such cases to find cues here and there.

The thinking disturbance in its various forms reveals itself in the recognition of pictures. Certainly, many patients can recognize simple and complex pictures as well as the healthy. The paranoid B. St. (described by Jung) was superior in the comprehension of pictures to the attendant personnel subjected to the same test. On the other hand, many patients are not at all, or only partially, capable of comprehending complicated pictures; or they give wrong interpretations, particularly when the pictures are in some way associated with their complexes. However, even illustrations of simple objects are mistaken.

A mildly agitated hebephrenic calls a student a "tobacco-pipe;" she pays attention only to that one detail. She calls a hammer, "Nature sperm, the hammer;" the hammer's handle is still the hammer's handle but in connection with her sexual complexes, it is also the penis. A clock becomes for her the "electrolyzer-clock" because she connects it in some way with her sexual hallucinations. Shown the picture of a pine-cone in its natural size and colors, she calls it an "ear of corn." She takes note only of its form, and even that very inadequately. Another patient calls the ears of a zebra "a hair-bow on the head," in accordance with her tendencies toward grandeur and adornment. A part-concept is indicated in the following answers: "hung" (instead of wash hanging on the line), "a heap" (instead of potatoes). Often the blocking becomes as systematized as the abnormal linkings (of ideas): (Bride?) "I don't know what;" (What are they [musicians] doing?), "Making noise." (The bride is shown again), "a woman, wearing a hat" (the nose-gay is designated as a hat). Objects such as asparagus and snakes are readily falsely designated usually in conjunction with other indications of an aroused sexuality.

446

Sometimes no associations at all are given to pictures shown to otherwise attentive patients. (Just as we do with thousands of things which we see as we pass along the street without paying any attention to them.)

Sometimes the narration of things experienced or read is also very characteristic. Frequently there is a difference between experiences undergone before and after onset of the illness. In the latter case, the various disturbances of comprehension may of course affect the result. Occasionally, even cooperative patients with good comprehension evidently do not assimilate something new any more. They then relate stories read in former times, in fragments, but still in proper context; whereas recently read stories are repeated inadequately. At times they also insert new ideas into the old stories. Thus, an educated hebephrenic calls William Tell a "ship's captain." Or it is too much for them to recall memories and we then get as answer to the question: "What do you know about William Tell?", such remarks as, "There has been already a good deal of discussion about the matter."

Stories which have been read* can be repeated perfectly and also summarized and applied in other connections by many patients who otherwise commit the grossest stupidities or are occupied with the most senseless delusions. But for the most part, hospital patients fail completely in such tasks; or the moral is deduced in the sense of their complexes, or from purely accidental associations.

---

* For various reasons, the following story was found an appropriate test for simple achievements: "The Donkey Carrying A Load of Salt." A donkey loaded with bags of salt had to wade across a river. He slipped and fell and remained lying comfortably in the cool water for a few moments. Standing up, he noticed how much lighter his load had become because the salt had dissolved in the water. Long-ears registered this advantage and decided to use it the following day when he was carrying a load of sponges across the same river. This time, he fell deliberately but was badly disappointed. The sponges had soaked up a great deal of water and were far heavier than before. Indeed, the load was so heavy that it drowned him.

"One means does not hold good in every case."

447

Thus a patient drew the moral from the test-story that one must not get frightened if faced with a difficult task.

The comprehension of a story may be impeded by blocking even for patients whose thinking is otherwise unimpeded. A usually attentive and naturally intelligent patient was unable to get a simple little tale into his head, although he strained his attention so intensely that he got red in the face, perspired and breathed heavily. "The voices interfered too much." Sometimes repeated readings help, but not always is the result improved by this means.

Some patients will relate a story entirely different from the one read, about a donkey, salt, etc. Others bring fragments of the given ideas into a new context. Thus we will hear "that a donkey wanted to drown himself." Then again disconnected fragments are reproduced, often with schizophrenic additions. "A donkey was loaded up heavily with salt and bolted—through the desert." Occasionally the patients notice the disjointedness or obscurity of their own story. (After the second reading): "A donkey was carrying a load of salt and had to go through a river; then along came a sponge—I don't know, is it a sponge, or a swan—or a goose?" (Here the patient noted that a sponge cannot very well move along, and then changed the sponge into a swan.)

In more severe cases, the various ideas of the stories are mixed up and then simply linked up grammatically: "A donkey waded through a stream in which there were sponges, and then the load became too heavy." Conversely, if the causal connections are especially stressed or further elaborated by means of unnecessary additions, then we are as a rule dealing with a complicating alcoholic condition. "A donkey had a load of sponges. He was thirsty and went down to the river in order to drink water. . . ."

448

Actual transformations of the story usually reveal themselves as results of the influence of the complexes. A woman patient who was conscience-stricken because she had not defended herself vigorously enough against an attack, was supposed to say that the axe fell into the river. But instead of "river," she said a "hole." When it was pointed out to her that it was a river, she said, "Yes, it was a hole full of water." Aside from such cases, we see remarkably little of this kind of personal reference in the reading of the fables in schizophrenia, whereas organic depressives, as a rule, refer the story of being drowned or overloaded to themselves. Also, most alcoholics find a reference to their weakness in the mention of water.

In this disease, the majority of changes appear as accidental; nevertheless they can be maintained very persistently. A hebephrenic insisted that she had just read about a "deep river;" and as the book was shown to her she insisted that the printed words had been changed in the meantime. Real fantasies hardly seem to prevail. But if they are present, they are given free play due to the lack of a sense of reality. A hebephrenic painter described the technique of painting quite accurately. Yet his own experiences, as well as stories from the Bible and William Tell were reproduced incorrectly—"as they might have occurred."

The general impediments of thinking may become obvious in sudden interruptions of the narration, and in the slow progress of the thought process. "It was a donkey." (What was he doing?) "He went through a river." (And then?) "He fell down." (And then?) "Remained lying there." (And then?) ". . . got up." Another patient answered to the repeated, "and then?", only with single words. "Long-ears—swims—heavily loaded—raised head —wade—He stop one's ear—shake off—street to—must be beaten. . . ."

Insight into one's illness has served as a time-honored measure of intelligence, and this insight is quite characteristic in schizophrenia. As in other mental diseases, at the height of the disease insight is lacking either completely or at least partially. However, at the onset many of the patients consider themselves not only to be "nervous" but they also recognize the anomalies of thought, the abulia and many other symptoms. If they do not think themselves insane, they fear that they will "become insane," whereas in later phases of their illness they insist that "they were made insane." Even in those cases, partial insight is not rare although the patients only exceptionally draw practical consequences from this insight. The paranoids are most remarkable in this respect. They will come to consult the physician with complaints that they suffer from delusions of persecution or from hallucinations, and describe the anomalies as objectively as possible. A normal part of their ego judges the abnormal correctly in all details without, however, being able to influence it. Of course, there are also periods when these patients are completely dominated by delusions, and even during examinations one can regularly find associations in which insight is lacking or is at least very inadequate.

Many patients notice that they see things differently from before but they believe that they formerly were in error and that now they have recognized reality. They even claim to have "a re-inforced intellect." At the height of the disease they misjudge their own actions and motivations. Thus, even so intelligent a patient as Forel's Miss L. S. believed that she had borne everything with great patience, whereas actually she had been an exceedingly difficult patient for quite some time.

In each recurring episode of illness, the patients may repeat actions which they had acknowledged as wrong during their intervals of improvement, but which they now once more defend as entirely justifiable.

During good remissions, the delusions are recognized as such; but almost without exception one can demonstrate that under certain conditions they are still operative. Also, the "cured" patient may regard his behavior during the illness as abnormal and senseless, yet even then for the most part there is a lack of complete insight. I have seen a catatonic who, while she was in the hospital, was very violent toward herself and others,—smearing, refusing food, etc.—and who, during a period of the greatest agitation, was taken home by her father. From the very first day at home she was able to take charge of the household and eventually she even edited her father's memoirs. She remembered her stay in the hospital in all its details. She could indicate this or the other symptom as abnormal but she still maintained that she had been most unjustly committed. My cautious objections that her violence and refusal of food were hardly to be considered as signs of health she believed she could refute by stating that she had acted in that way "because she had wanted to disturb the administration of the institution in which she had been so badly abused."

The severely affected patients are hardly able to learn anything new. Often they are still able to adjust themselves to simple agricultural tasks. They can also be trained for some industrial activity, although they always have to have supervision. In the hospital for chronic mental disease at Rheinau, I made great effort to introduce basket-weaving. However, it was impossible to get even a single one of this group of severely ill patients to work independently.

This, of course, does not exclude the possibility that in another case a patient, who had been very severely catatonic for some years and who now suffered from paranoia hallucinatoria, could suddenly begin to study English and continue his auto-didactic activity in the hospital to the point where he was able to sell his translations.

According to Specht . . . the capacity for practice, as measured by the facility in adding, is normal. According to Reis, the progress made in practicing is somewhat reduced, as demonstrated by various psychological tests. In one case it was completely lacking. Further research on advanced cases is certainly still needed since attention and cooperation on the part of the patients naturally affect the results.

In the severe cases, the ability to calculate is easily altered, yet it can be re-established at any moment when the patient is sufficiently composed to be able to concentrate on the problem. Naturally, in hospital patients, mistakes of all sorts appear frequently, due to perplexity and poor attention. In addition they often do not have the desire to answer correctly. Even intelligent schizophrenics will be in no way embarrassed during a clinical presentation to say 3 x 4 is equal to 100. However, milder cases in the chronic stage sometimes adapt themselves very well to office work requiring calculations. They are not easily distracted, think very little except about what they are doing. They work like robots year-in and year-out with the greatest conscientiousness, or perhaps we should say with the greatest "exactitude."

In every kind of game the patients behave as they do in other mental performances; that is, extraordinarily variable. Many do not seem to have any need or desire for entertainment. Others who do have the drive to play often apply to this activity as complete attention as do the healthy. Indeed, not only can chronic cases take part in the usual games, especially card-playing, with cleverness and full understanding of the intricacies of the game, but even a seemingly confused catatonic in an acute state can surprise us with his virtuosity as a chess-player. Naturally the patients for the most part are not able to carry out those social games which require "esprit."

As a rule, the schizophrenics' imagination is markedly

452

affected. Most of them do not have the drive to think something new, and still less the ability to do anything new. Novel thoughts often result from peculiar combinations of their old stock of concepts; however, they are reshuffled without any intellectual goal. The ideas are therefore merely bizarre and not actually creative productions. A paretic patient, in a manic state, can produce more novel ideas in one day than can an entire ward-full of schizophrenics in years.

The aesthetic capacities are almost completely destroyed, or at least markedly damaged. This is due to the lack of consistent thinking, judgment, the emotional matrix, and above all, the initiative and capacity for productiveness. The sense of appreciation for a work of art is lacking for the most part.

Now and again we are astonished that a patient, who seemed to have deteriorated completely and who for many years never expressed an appropriate emotion or a sensible word, has been able to create in musical fantasy an artistic expression for the most varied moods. But moods and means of expression change very abruptly in most of the musically inclined patients. The schizophrenic way of thinking, with its sudden transitions, oddities, blockings and perseveration, reveals itself as clearly in musical productions as it does in speech. Sometimes one can make the diagnosis almost with certainty from listening to a short piano recital.

For the most part, the plastic artist is severely handicapped by this disease. Here the bizarre idea, technique and execution strikes the eyes almost at once. Obviously, productivity suffers. Yet there are painters who always, over a long period of time, repeat the same idea an endless number of times. Often art serves as a medium of expression for the delusional system, and it can then be recognized as morbid, almost at first glance.*

Naturally, poetic talent suffers greatly from the schizophrenic thinking process, from looseness, from lack of feeling and taste, and from the lack of productivity and initiative. While considerable amounts of schizophrenic poetry have been printed, little of it has been of any great significance or value. At best the productions are rather unimportant; most of them are quite revolting.

The later poems of Holderlin are good examples, among which "Patmos" is the best known. The schizophrenic train of thought has rarely been more beautifully illustrated. Christian . . . gives us the following pertinent example of emptiness and obscurity of ideas with preservation of a certain formal technical skill:

> "Sous le chaud soleil qui rayonne
> Cachee a l'ombre du Sumac,
> La dormeuse mele au tabac
> Sa criniere epaisse de lionne."

The banality of thought and form is shown in the verses published by Stawitz.

> "Der Chorgesang.
> Starker als die Sprache der Natur
> von bekannten Sangern schallte nur,
> eines Tags ein Lied mir zu.
> Manch Trane, die mein Herz verbarg,
> trat hervor, im Uberwinden karg,
> schaffte so der Seele Ruh!
> Mehr noch schatzte ich das Singen
> als vorher; es gab ja Schwingen
> Meinem Ruckblick in die Zeit.
> Meinem Ohr ward es zur Weid."

---

* In mild cases, the peculiarity of subject, conception and technique can make the schizophrenic painter quite famous.

The bizarre and strange is expressed in the following verses whose author I cannot recall any more:

> "Wie hat die Liebe mich entzuckt,
> Als ich noch schwer und kugelrund!
> Hier sitz ich jetzt und bin verruckt,
> und wiege kaum noch hundert Pfund."

In severe cases, the result is usually a word-salad, or merely a more or less versified string of unknown words.

Even where such blunders are not made, the mental productions of the schizophrenics suffer a great deal from the lack of integration, the vacuity of thought and the banality of content, or the lack of integration renders otherwise good ideas quite insipid.

All this is valid for the more severe cases which come to the attention of the physician. However, we also know that several very well-known artists and poets (e.g. Schumann, Scheffel, Lenz, van Gogh) were schizophrenics. It cannot be ruled out that very mild forms of schizophrenia may be rather favorable to artistic production. The subordination of all thought-associations to one complex, the inclination to novel, unusual range of ideas, the indifference to tradition, the lack of restraint, must all be favorable influences if these characteristics are not over-compensated by the association disturbances proper. In fact, almost all truly artistic natures are individuals with markedly split-off, emotionally charged complexes; perhaps for this reason they have hysteriform symptoms so frequently. Schizophrenics too are *"Komplexmenschen"* (people dominated by complexes). The question deserves a good deal more study.

In acute stages we even find a kind of pathological productivity. Forel's patient had been unable to write poems; in the preliminary stage of her illness she was all but "persecuted" by verses in formation.

(f) Activity and Behavior

Outspoken schizophrenic behavior is marked by lack of interest, lack of initiative, lack of a definite goal, by inadequate adaptation to the environment, i.e., by disregard of many factors of reality, by confusion, and by sudden fancies and peculiarities.

The mild latent cases live essentially like other people and are considered as healthy. What is striking is mainly their sensitivity and now and then some peculiarity. They are able to work both inside and outside the hospital, some very diligently, others in a more capricious, irregular fashion. They are active in all the simpler vocations, occasionally even in artistic or academic activities. Often they do well, sometimes even very well. However, in the latter case it is only in clearly defined jobs, e.g., as farm-helpers, or maid servants. Much more often they "are different." They are prone to change jobs and occupations frequently. One will even leave his work without waiting to draw his pay. A young sculptor, who did quite well in his profession, wandered around for a whole year with a phonograph. Most of these people limit their contacts with the external world to a more or less significant degree; some do so in general, and some only in certain respects.

What is most striking in these mild cases is usually their irritability and sensitivity. Because of some small matter which at a given moment displeases them, they will sulk, curse, run away. If the fiance does not show up, that is not right; should he come promptly then the girl will find plenty to scold him for. They develop an unpleasant stubbornness, in small matters as well as in large ones, besides which, they are moody, and occasionally they may run away in the middle of the night.

The tendency to seclusion from other people can be combined with excesses in dissolute company. The indifference to important things and their laziness often lands these people in the street or in some other unfavorable milieu. They become vagrants, thieves, more rarely swindlers and other types of criminals. I have also seen two schizophrenic pyromaniacs. Yet their apathy and lack of will power generally makes them relatively harmless. Though every prison has its share of schizophrenics, their number is in no way proportional to the number of those living in freedom, many of whom more or less lack social feelings or are prone actually to think and feel antisocially, either because of delusional ideas or because of rage about previous commitments. Nevertheless the absolute number of schizophrenic murderers is not quite inconsiderable.

Their striving is mostly ineffectual if it has not ceased entirely. Indeed, in isolated cases, it can even be overstrong, though one-sided (world-reformers, pseudo-poets, etc.). In work to which the patients are not accustomed it is the energy rather than the intelligence which seems to fail first. Many of the more severe cases will avoid any kind of work with some silly excuse, or even without one. Occasionally they work like machines. If one gives the patient a saw he will pull it back and forth till the wood is sawn through and remain standing apathetically till the attendant fixes a new piece of wood under the saw. Others make themselves very useful if one can give them some type of work which does not require much thinking or personal initiative. They can haul coal, weed, knit, keep certain rooms in order; they will fetch the mail. Now and then we find schizophrenics who seem to feel no fatigue and will work all day long, partly without thinking very much, partly even with an occasional reflection. They actually have to be protected from their own "addiction" to work.

Kraepelin's . . . observation of a case in which there was an utter inability to finish or stop what he was doing

457

is interesting and worthy of further study. This lack was to be expected where neither fatigue nor interest was present.

The defective intelligence in the narrower sense of the term makes these people, who are more severely ill, totally or partially unfitted for complicated work. Thus one of Kraepelin's patients could still copy fairly well but he could no longer draw a curve. Another could copy with exactitude but could not correctly apply the insertion marks. Altogether, these patients show little capacity for variation in their work. Many of them must do the work the way they figure it, no matter how inappropriate the method. Their inability to reflect is very noticeable. A retired teacher demands that he be re-instated, but in his letter he insults the authorities. A physician, who had been committed to the hospital because of his violent and dangerous threats believed in all earnestness that he could obtain every kind of concession by starting a lawsuit against me. Then I would be the defendant in the lawsuit and could not employ my power as expert and hospital director to restrain him. Every day we observe ill-considered attempts at escape of apparently lucid patients which they will execute before the very eyes of the attendants, or by dashing out of their room into the corridor, from where they would still have to pass several locked doors.

The patients' goals are often in obvious contradiction, not only with their actual abilities, but also with their mental predispositions in general. World-reform, poetry and philosophy are the cherished activities of many schizophrenics. Nevertheless, in large matters and small, they point out the truth which the healthy would not notice.

Also, in smaller matters they can appear quite impertinent and precocious. Thus an uneducated patient, in a long letter gives some excellent advice to his physician as to just how the doctor should treat his own relative. In another instance, one has a demented patient giving instructions in an impressive tone of voice, regarding good manners in polite society. This is, however, no worse than a newspaper article written by a patient, discussing the educational value of the circus for the Zurich public. At times, even in externals there is revealed an exaggerated vanity which may go on to the point of the wildest caricature. Yet it is far more usual to find the patients ultimately becoming dirty and slovenly in every respect.

However, sometimes even severely sick individuals can impress their fellowmen precisely because they leave all difficulties out of consideration. A schizophrenic woman succeeded in marrying almost against his consent a man of good standing who otherwise displayed quite a strong will of his own, and who had made a reputation for himself in a very prominent position. In public speeches such individuals can convince an entire auditorium of their health and many another equally fictitious matter. The poet-author of the song "Freut euch das Lebens" chose a schizophrenic bride precisely because of her "naive etourderie" which distinguished her from their stiff social circle.

In the moderate and severe cases it is the desultoriness in the intellectual sphere which often is most noticeable.

An educated lady writes a number of letters, marks them "registered mail," and then does not mail them. A teacher suddenly applies for a position paying 2,000 Swiss francs salary, and quits his present teaching position. An uneducated person wishes to study the theory of music. A sales clerk rides back and forth on the train between Romanshorn and Geneva because he had heard that some people had become engaged to nice young women while riding on the night trains. A man takes off all his clothes outdoors in winter, walks naked through the village in order to take a dip in a river which lies a half-hour's distance away. A young girl sews stockings upon a rug.

The pathological fancies make it impossible for some patients to earn their own living. Otherwise quite diligent individuals will one day not come to work without any obvious reason; and they consider it quite self-evident that they should later return to their job without even offering an excuse.

A hebephrenic who for years had spread the fertilizer over the spacious horticultural area of the hospital with never-failing industry was one fine day found cutting the roots of the dwarf trees in order "to raise" them, as he thought. In his vague idea of doing something useful he had ruined several hundred trees. There is no absurdity so great that our patients will not commit it regardless of consequences. One patient will merely hit the table a few times, or crow like a cock. Another, however, will set fire to a house or throw his mother down the well.

Often the patients depart more and more from the norm in their behavior and become progressively more "whimsical." This can go so far that three of our patients from good families while they were considered normal took to wrapping up their feces in pieces of paper and hiding them away in closets. One of our patients who did good work in the hospital would go home each Sunday for a visit and sit there from 1:45 p.m. to 5:30 p.m. on a certain chair always staring in the same corner, without having a single word to say to anyone in the house. More advanced cases show the habit of collecting all sorts of objects, useful as well as useless, with which they would fill their apartments so that there was hardly room to move around. Ultimately this collecting mania becomes so utterly senseless that their pockets are always crammed full of pebbles, pieces of wood, rags and all kinds of other

460

trash. The tendency to buffoonery can also become so overwhelming as to lead to the external picture of monotonous, chronic "clowning."

At times patients exhibiting the most incomprehensible behavior will again appear more or less normal. They can once again take up their jobs or often go through their periods of military training very satisfactorily.* Conversely, a sudden outbreak of excitement with or without provocation may disrupt a hitherto composed clinical picture. An "improved" patient wanted to kill a cat but was scolded by his father. Thereupon, the patient got very excited, exclaimed, "Now everything is over," jumped into the river, swam back to the bank and resumed working as he had before.

Intercourse with other people is not disturbed merely by the schizophrenics' irritability and their peculiarities. In their autism they can comport themselves in a crowded work-room as if they were alone; everything which concerns the others does not exist for them. On the ward, many patients will not change their position in any way whatsoever during the coming and going of the doctor, except to make their rejection more marked by mimic or attitude. They have turned their backs on the world, and seek to protect themselves from all influences coming from the outside. This may develop into a sort of stereotypy in which the patients feel comfortable only in some corner where they can hug the walls. Where they are left to themselves, one can even find them lying in the angle between wall and floor, their face to the wall, and often even covering it with a cloth or with their hands. In milder degrees of the illness, it can happen that a hebephrenic will return from America without any warning, make his nightly quarters in his parents' barn, where he is discovered only after some time since he gets up early to go to his distant

* It is indeed much more frequent that the latent schizophrenic does not succeed in adjusting to military life.

461

place of work. A desire for entertainment is usually absent even in those schizophrenics perfectly capable of work. The patient's life is then a monotonous cycle of working, eating, and sleeping.

Should schizophrenics have to have relations with others, they assume quite a peculiar form. Sometimes patients are obtrusive, continue endlessly to repeat the same thing over and over again, and are completely deaf to all objections. At other times, they comport themselves very disdainfully, curtly, rudely. A hebephrenic pharmacist reproached his customers when they brought prescriptions which involved much work.

* * *

Such are cases that are still capable of acting and having relations with people. However, when autism gets the upper hand, it creates a complete isolation around the sick psyche. The most severe schizophrenics live in their own rooms as if in a dream, at times moving about like automatons, without any external goal; at other times, they remain silent and motionless, their contact with the external world is reduced to an intangible minimum. Should accessory symptoms come to the fore at any stage of the illness, it is they which determine actions and behavior.

(PAUL) EUGEN BLEULER. (b.—Zollikon, near Zürich, ca. April 4, 1857; d.—Zollikon, July 15, 1939).

Bleuler received his degree of Medical Practice from Zürich University in 1881. He became Assistant Physician at Waldau asylum for about two years. He studied further with Charcot at the Salpetrière in 1884; also in London and Munich. Returning to Zürich in 1885, he became Assistant at the Cantonial Hospital at Burgholzli, the psychiatric clinic of Zürich. In this same year he received his M.D. from Bern. He then became clinic director at Rheinau, and later at Ellikon (1892). In 1898 he became director at Burgholzli, and Professor of Psychiatry at Zürich. He remained here 29 years, until his retirement in 1927.

462

Bleuler was a teacher and later colleague of Jung. It was he who introduced the term "ambivalence" into the modern psychiatric jargon. Bleuler's most important contributions deal with schizophrenia. If there is understanding in this area today, it is largely due to Bleuler. His description of this disease entity stands today practically unmodified. The present selection is taken from Bleuler's great monograph on this subject.

BLEULER, E. *Dementia praecox or the group of schizophrenias.* N. Y.: International Universities Press, 1950 (1911). Trans. J. Zinkin. Chap. 1, #B: "The fundamental symptoms—the compound functions." The present selection is reproduced substantially complete, with the permission of the publisher.

See also:

BLEULER, E. "The theory of schizophrenic negativism." *Nerv. Ment. Dis. Monogr.* 1912, 11: Trans. W. A. White.
Textbook of psychiatry. N. Y.: Macmillan, 1924. Trans. A. A. Brill. Contains a selective bibliography.
Affectivity, suggestibility, paranoia. Halle a.S.: Marhold, 1926 (1906). Trans. Ricksher.

KLAESIA, J. "Zum hundersten Geburtstag Eugen Bleulers." *Psychiatria, Basel.* 1957, 134: 353-361.

MURCHISON (b—Vol. III, p. 1165-1166).

LECTURES
ON
CLINICAL PSYCHIATRY
Emil Kraepelin

LECTURE II
DEPRESSED STAGES OF MANIACAL-DEPRESSIVE INSANITY (CIRCULAR STUPOR)

Gentlemen,—The patient you see before you to-day is a merchant, forty-three years old, who has been in our hospital almost uninterruptedly for about five years. He is strongly built, but badly nourished, and has a pale complexion, and an invalid expression of face. He comes in with short, wearied steps, sits down slowly, and remains sitting in a rather bent position, staring in front of him almost without moving. When questioned, he turns his head a little, and, after a certain pause, answers softly, and in monosyllables, but to the point. We get the impression that speaking gives him a great deal of trouble, his lips moving for a little while before the sound comes out. The patient is clear about time and place, knows the doctors, and says that he has been ill for more than five years, but cannot give any further explanation of this than that his spirits are affected. He says he has no apprehension. He gives short and perfectly relevant answers to questions about his circumstances and past life. He does exercises in arithmetic slowly but correctly, even when they are fairly hard. He writes his name on the blackboard, when asked to do so, with firm though hesitating strokes, after having got up awkwardly. No delusions, particularly ideas of sin, can be made out, the patient only declaring that he is in low spirits, without knowing of any cause for it, except that his illness has lasted so long, and worries him. He hopes, however, to get well again.

As you may see, it is evident that in reality we have to deal with *emotional depression* in this case, as well as in those already discussed. It is true that there are no delusions associated with it here, as there were in the other cases; but let us not be inclined to lay too much stress on this, after having learned by experience how widely delusions may vary in the same illness. On the other hand, it must strike us that this patient is not apprehensive, but only "low spirited," and still more that, unlike the patients already considered, he is apparently unable to move and express himself freely. In those cases there were lively gesticulations, lamentations, and complaints, and a certain necessity of giving vent to the oppression within, while here it is hard to draw any remark from the patient on his mental condition, or on questions of fact. This very circumstance, that the answers come so slowly, even on matters of indifference, shows that in this patient we have not to deal with a fear of expressing himself, but with some general obstacle to utterance in speech. Indeed, not only speech, but *all action of the will is extremely difficult to him.* For three years he has been incapable of getting up from bed, dressing, and occupying himself, and since that time has lain in bed almost without moving. But as he has the most perfect comprehension of his surroundings, and is able to follow difficult trains of thought, the disturbance must be essentially confined to the accomplishment of voluntary movements, or at any rate must find by far its strongest manifestations in this direction. We clearly recognise the pain he takes to act and to comply with our demands, and at the same time the delay and difficulty attending every effort of the will. Under these circumstances, it will be permissible here to speak of an *impediment* of *volition,* in the sense that the transformation of the impulses of the will into action meets with obstacles which cannot be overcome without difficulty, and often not at all by the patient's own strength.

This constraint is by far the most obvious clinical feature of the disease, and compared with this, the sad, oppressed mood has but little prominence. No other psychical disturbances can be made out at present.

Having established this, we have got an insight, on several points, into the nature of the disease before us. In the first place, we see that this condition differs from that of our melancholic patients, in a very definite way, through the strong impediment of volition, and the absence of the apprehensive restlessness so clearly marked in them. Experience shows that this condition is very characteristic of an entirely different disease, to which we will give the name of *maniacal-depressive insanity*, for reasons to be discussed immediately. This disease generally runs its course in *a series* of *isolated attacks*, which are not uniform, but present either states of depression of the kind described or characteristic states of excitement, which we will learn to know better later on. The isolated attacks are generally separated by longer or shorter intervals of freedom.

The conclusion we have drawn from our patient's present condition is correct. He first became ill when he was twenty-three years old, and was then depressed, as is generally the case in first attacks; but the depression was followed next year by a state of excitement, which led to his being brought to the asylum. Two years later he married a person very much beneath him, very probably when under slight excitement, but separated from her during the depression which ensued. At the age of thirty-one, probably when again in an excited state, he fell into the hands of an adventuress, who abandoned him when he became depressed again. Indeed, his relations held his depression to be the result of the melancholy experience he had been through. In his thirty-sixth and thirty-seventh years a further and stronger excitement followed, which again made treatment in the asylum necessary.

466

The patient's father, as well as his two brothers, was a drunkard, while his sister was ill in the same way as himself. He suffered for several years from diabetes insipidus. A doctor advised him, presumably on this account, to take a little wine, as too much water was not good for him. The patient followed this advice, and about five and a half years ago he suddenly fell ill of delirium tremens, immediately followed by a state of excitement, gradually and continually growing worse, which only disappeared slowly after two years. Only a few weeks after his discharge from our hospital, where he was then treated, the extraordinarily severe impediment of volition which you may still observe in a milder form set in rather suddenly. The patient remained motionless in bed, would not eat, was wet and dirty in his habits, could hardly speak, and expressed apprehensive ideas. Thought also seems to have been affected at first, and the patient made no answer, or replied only very slowly, alike to emphatic and to gentle questionings. But there were no actual delusions even then. The patient soon returned to the hospital, but in spite of the most careful nursing, his condition has improved only very slowly and immaterially in the course of the last three years. Yet we may expect that this attack also will end in recovery, like those which have preceded it, if only the patient can live through so severe a disturbance.* But it is no less probable that he will again fall ill of attacks of depression or excitement such as he has so often had before.

Fluctuations of *weight* are of special interest in the disease we are now discussing. In the last attack of excitement he had in the hospital our patient lost nearly 13 kilogrammes, and then gained 25 kilogrammes when he became calm. In the first eighteen months of the depres-

---

* Unfortunately, this expectation was not realized. The psychical disturbances still continued, and the patient succumbed to acute phthisis when the depression had lasted three and a half years.

sion, his weight fell from 91.5 kilogrammes to 56.5 kilogrammes, and has only risen 14 kilogrammes since. These figures show the violent revolutions in the province of general nutrition which take place in diseases of this kind. Little as we are yet able to account for the details of these occurrences, regular and continuous weighings afford us an excellent means of judging of the general state of the disease in this as in most other forms of insanity. A decided increase in the previously reduced weight in maniacal-depressive insanity is the most reliable sign that the attack has passed its worst.

In the light of the case we have just considered the meaning of what follows will, I think, be clearer to you than it formerly was to me. Here is a case of a woman, twenty-three years old, who was admitted only a fortnight ago. The patient, whose mother is mentally rather limited, bore her second child six weeks ago. Seventeen days later she got a great fright from a fire in her room, and she then became apprehensive and restless, saw flames, black birds and dogs, heard whistling and singing, began to pray, screamed out of the window, lamented her sins, promised to be good, and could not sleep. The patient is ill-nourished and anæmic. She sits almost motionless, with her eyes cast down, staring in front of her, and moving her lips slightly now and then. Her expression is strained, and rather apprehensive. When questioned about dates, the place where she is, and ·the people about her, she either makes no answer at all, or shakes her head, or says in a low, hesitating voice: "I do not know." She nods when I ask her if she is unhappy, and mutters to herself: "There are always so many carriages coming; a great number drive about outside." Now and then she uses isolated, broken expressions, in a tone of lamentation, often repeating them one after the other: "I want to go home, to get out. Alas! alas! only let me go away. I will not let myself be done to death. I cannot

stay here. Good heavens! there is poison in the food!"
She obeys orders with hesitation, and sometimes resists,
but can plainly be influenced by persuasion. When threatened with a needle, she screams and turns away hastily.
She generally has to be fed.

On consideration of the want of freedom in our
patient's bearing, and the slowness and constraint of her
movements, which will only become more active in apprehensive gestures of self-defence, you will clearly see that,
in this case, too, we have to deal with an impediment of
volition, particularly apparent in the almost entire falling
off of utterance in speech and of expressive movement.
But it presents a contrast with the previous case in the
more definite apprehension, which is far less amenable
to persuasion and influence, and also by the severe disturbance of comprehension. The patient has absolutely no
clear idea of her position, does not understand what goes
on around her, and cannot solve any mental problems.
A similar difficulty in thought is associated with the difficulty in the action of the will. You will remember that
a disturbance of this kind occurred at the beginning of
the last patient's attack, and that it was only later on
that it became less and less obvious. This *impediment of
cognition,* as we will call it, is in fact a symptom regularly
accompanying the state of depression in maniacal-depressive insanity. It is sometimes more, sometimes less clearly
defined, and is generally perceived very plainly by the
patients themselves.

As the intensity and colouring of the emotional depression may vary very widely in maniacal-depressive
insanity, we will conclude, in consideration of the well-
defined impediment of volition and cognition, that the
case which is before us now belongs to the same group
of diseases as the last case. Hence, it would seem probable that similar attacks, and also attacks of excitement,
will clearly be noticed sooner or later in our patient. This

conclusion is confirmed by the remarkable fact that, although she is so apprehensive, she begins, after a good deal of persuasion, to twist her face into an extraordinary smile. You will understand the meaning of this symptom at once if we glance back into the past. The patient was here four years ago. At that time she had aborted, after having been pregnant by a married man. A few weeks later she became dumb and rigid, expressed ideas of death, saw spirits, grew quite confused, mixed, perplexed, and apprehensive, and refused to eat—in short, a state of impediment of volition and cognition was developed very like the present condition, but even more severe, lasting about seven months. Then, quite suddenly, there was a *complete* change, and the patient became clear and collected, and was in high spirits. Finally, she passed through a very violent state of excitement, which gradually disappeared after nearly six months. During her convalescence, there was slight and transitory emotional depression, but after this the patient became well, and remained so till the beginning of the present attack.

Thus we see that the conclusion drawn from the patient's present condition was correct. The similarity of the two periods of depression of which we know leaves no room for reasonable doubt that they both belong to the same clinical picture of disease. We must indeed notice that both attacks followed a confinement, so that the same cause might have produced the same illness each time. But we saw the same characteristic symptoms of impediment of thought and will in the preceding case, where there had been no confinement, and the subsequent change from depression to excitement, occurring in the same way in both patients, is a fresh proof that our case is one of maniacal-depressive insanity. We will see later on that those representations of disease in which we really have grounds for regarding a confinement as the actual cause present entirely different clinical features. Finally, ex-

470

perience shows that single attacks of maniacal-depressive insanity are very often set free by injurious external influences. We must, therefore, expect our patient's next attack to break out once again without any very tangible cause.

On the strength of these considerations, we may venture to suppose that the patient will often fall ill again in the future course of her life, either of depression, as on this occasion, or of excitement, but that each attack may be expected to end in recovery. In the present attack, this may certainly be expected, yet it is very possible that a slighter state of excitement may first intervene, as has happened before.* The smile already mentioned might be the first sign of such a change.

The condition of severe impediment of volition is generally included with some other and outwardly similar states under the name of *stupor*. We may call the form now before us "circular stupor." as maniacal-depressive insanity is often called circular insanity (*folie circulaire*), on account of the cycle of recurrent conditions. The common characteristic of all forms of stupor is the absence of expression in speech or otherwise in response to external influences. Stupor is, however, no uniform condition, much less a separate disease, but a symptom which may arise from very different causes, and therefore may have very different clinical meanings. Even circular stupor meets us in such various forms that it is often difficult to recognise their real agreement. Here you see an innkeeper's wife, aged forty-four, who has been ill for about ten weeks. There has been no insanity in her family, and she has three healthy children. When her husband was obliged to change his inn a little while ago, she began to complain of heaviness in her head, and

---

* The patient recovered without any distinct maniacal excitement, after having spent five months in the asylum, and gained 13 kilogrammes in weight. She has been well for two years since then.

471

worried herself groundlessly—*e.g.*, with the idea that the children had no clothes, that everything was torn up, and that the house-moving would be the death of her. She thought she had made her husband unhappy, that the bailiffs were coming, that life was no longer possible at her home, and that everything was going to ruin. At the same time she spoke and ate but little, stared into space, and hardly slept at all. She also took a knife to bed with her at night, and expressed ideas of suicide, so she was brought to the hospital. Here she seemed quite collected and clear about her position, and, in answer to questions, gave a monosyllabic but consecutive account of her circumstances and her illness. For the last three months, she said, she had no rest, and had been absent-minded and forgetful; she had such a bad memory. She could not be happy now; everything was spoiled for her, and her work had grown so hard for her that she could not get through with it. The patient spoke little of her own accord, and generally lay still in bed with a downcast expression. She was obliged to think for a disproportionately long time over the answers to simple questions, was not quite clear about the chronological order of her experiences, and hardly knew at all where she was. All her expressions and movements were slow and hesitating, as if she did not quite know what she ought to say and do. She was low-spirited, and in particular cried a great deal when she had visitors. She described her complaint as "dejection," and burst into tears whenever it was discussed, without being able to give a more precise account of her condition. The picture the patient now presents still shows substantially the same features: a quiet, oppressed mood, a sad expression, low hesitating speech, and slow, tired movements, while at the same time she is quite collected. But the ideas of sin have grown much stronger. With tears, the patient calls herself the greatest of sinners, because she has brought her

472

husband and children into misfortune; she will certainly be executed. These are the same ideas of sin as we have learned to recognise in melancholia. We might, therefore, be tempted, especially in view of the patient's age, to take the illness for simple climacteric melancholia. But I think that this idea is contradicted by the obvious presence of the impediment of thought and will, which we have observed before, in just the same form, in maniacal-depressive insanity, but not in melancholia. I think that this symptom will justify our regarding the present case as one of the former disease. If this opinion of mine be correct, we need not expect a lingering, uniform course of disease, ending in recovery or in the characteristic state of weakness following melancholia, which has already been briefly described. We may hope for a much shorter duration of the disease, and for complete recovery, as the first attack of maniacal-depressive insanity generally runs a fairly rapid and favourable course. On the other hand, we must certainly be prepared to see it return, either as the same affection or in the form of excitement.

The course of the case until now would certainly tend to show that our conception is correct. The patient's downcast mood disappeared almost entirely after three or four weeks in the asylum. In its place she showed a rather impatient, discontented temper, with frequent smiling, of which we will learn the clinical meaning on a future occasion. The patient was so anxious to go home that her husband thought he ought to humour her homesickness, even against our advice. But her condition grew worse so quickly that she had to be brought back in four days. But probably we will soon effect an improvement even now.*

---

* The patient is still under treatment here, and has substantially improved. Unfortunately, her husband has again jeopardized her recovery by taking her home in the face of medical advice, and a serious attempt at suicide has been the result.

The milder form of impediment of volition seen in this case is noticed by patients themselves as "inability to come to a decision," and meets us as such in the numberless mild cases of maniacal-depressive insanity which never come into an asylum, and indeed, are never recognised as morbid states at all. Then we have the "psychological riddle" that, without any adequate cause, but in the opinion of the sufferers and those around them, as the result of some external influence or other, there arise times of complete inability to come to a decision, when every determination of the will costs the greatest effort, which alternate more or less regularly with periods of the most reckless enterprise. It is just these mildest forms of the illness, leading by an infinity of gradations to the severe forms, and the most severe, which show how deeply maniacal-depressive insanity is rooted in the natural disposition of certain individuals. Hence we frequently find it in several members of the same family. Often enough we see nearly a whole lifetime filled with slight attacks, succeeding one another almost uninterruptedly. But just as often the illness only appears a few times, as in the case described, either at a particular period of life, or as the result of some external influence. The attacks usually set in during the years of evolution, or later on at the time of reversion.

Many of the quite slight attacks—which, by the way, may always alternate with the severe—pass off without any treatment. Other cases are sent as "neurasthenia" to different asylums and watering places, or ordered to travel, and the patients then extol, with full conviction, the particular cure they were taking when the improvement or the change to excitement occurred. In all the more serious attacks, however, treatment in an asylum is urgently required, on account of the danger of suicide, which is greatest at the beginning or near the end of an attack, because at those times their indecision does

474

not make the patients incapable of pulling themselves together to act. In the asylum they must be carefully watched, and an intelligent and moderately strict treatment in bed should be carried out. Of drugs, bromides may be used, either alone or in combination with opium or other suitable hypnotics, but too much must not be expected of them. Prolonged warm baths sometimes do good service. Visits from near relations and premature discharge from the asylum are frequent causes of relapses.

LECTURE VII
Maniacal Excitement

GENTLEMEN,—In the course of our lectures hitherto we have considered widely different states of depression. It has been my aim to show you that sad or apprehensive depression permits in itself of no conclusions as to the disease through which it is engendered. It is far more our task to become clear as to the special clinical meaning of this symptom in each separate case. Under some circumstances we can draw important conclusions as to the nature of the underlying disease merely from the kind of depression, from its duration, from its repeated return, from its trifling depth, and so on; but often enough it is the consideration of the other symptoms of disease that will first lead us on the right track. Very similar conditions can, at the first glance, be apparent in the course of very different diseases. But inversely we frequently find that the most differentiated and apparently quite opposite conditions can make their appearance in succession as indications of the same malady. Here there is no question of the connection of different independent diseases, as was formerly often believed to be the case. Apart from the frequency of the phenomenon, this is proved to a certainty by the often extraordinarily rapid transition of the alternating pictures, by the occasional mixing of the separate features, and, lastly, by the similarity of the course and its termination.

The powerfully-built and well-nourished merchant, aged fifty, who is brought before you to-day, enters the room with a rapid step, and greets us in a loud voice; he takes a seat with a courteous bow, and looks about him expectantly and with curiosity. He answers quickly and with assurance as soon as we address him, and gives fluent and pertinent information as to his personal circumstances, as well as concerning his present position. Very soon he not only answers, but also leads the conversation; says jokingly that he is not going to relate everything so glibly, but will make the examination a little more difficult, in order that he may see whether we understand anything ourselves. He explains that he suffers from paralysis, makes quite senseless statements, and adds up incorrectly, but is as happy as a king if you go further into things. If you give him free scope, he talks a great deal and with animation, hardly allowing himself to be interrupted; but he easily loses the thread, forever bringing into his history some new irrelevant details. A short, concise answer cannot be obtained from him; he has always something to add and to exaggerate. During my lecture he, at intervals, frequently asks for "a hearing," but always draws back with a polite bow. He often addresses his discourse to you students, adverts to student life, interpolates verses from student songs, even making up some topical doggerel rhymes himself.

His frame of mind is joyous and exalted; he amuses himself with all sorts of jokes, even tolerably risky ones, makes fun of himself and of others, imitates well-known characters, laughs at his own tricks, which he knows how to put in a quite harmless light. For instance, the last few nights before his admission to the hospital he had gadded about to all sorts of taverns and disreputable houses, had drunk hard everywhere, behaved in the highest degree extravagantly, sprinkled himself from head to foot with water in the market-place, and had driven in a cab from one public-house to another in the neighbouring villages. Finally he smashed the mirror, crockery, and furniture in his own house, so that he had to be brought to the hospital under a strong escort of police. For all that, he observes cutely his wife alone is to blame, for she did not treat him properly, nor had she cooked anything decently for him. As a consequence, he had to go to the public-house, and, besides, he must give people something by which to earn a living. He does not consider himself to be ill, but, he adds with a significant smile, if it will give us pleasure, he will remain with us for awhile. The patient does not present any physical disturbance, except some wounds that he sustained in being conveyed by force to the hospital.

This case appears to us in every respect to be the exact opposite to certain states of depression that we have already learnt to recognise. Comprehension occurs quickly, ideas spring up unhindered, though soon driven out by something new. The spirits are cheerful, actions run untrammelled and without obstacles, without even those which act as a restraint in a normal life. This combination of symptoms of disease, which we frequently meet with in the same form, we designate by the name of *Mania,* or, if the individual disturbances are only slightly developed, as in the present case, by that of *Hypomania.* Our patient is, however, by no means always so considerate and jovially amiable as he is at present. For a time, especially at the beginning, he was quite confused and incoherent in his headlong talk, very irritated by his surroundings, smashed tables, chairs, and windowpanes, poured his soup over his head, and behaved in very disgusting ways. At other times, by teasing and ill-treating the other patients, slandering the attendants, and grumbling and making mischief at every opportunity, he was almost unbearable.

Mania, to a certain degree, is not only a true subversion of states of circular depression, but in itself is nothing but a stage of *maniacal-depressive insanity*. Where we really meet with maniacal excitements we are then able to draw the probable inference, not only that the excitements will recur often during life, but that states of depression of the kind already described will alternate with them. To return to our patient, we can state that he has already been in the asylum seven times. He is illegitimate; his mother died of an apoplectic fit; a sister of hers was insane. The patient had always been considered eccentric, but was sober and industrious. The first attack of the malady occurred in his thirty-seventh year, and exactly resembled the present one. At that time the patient, through the press, suddenly invited the whole "nobility of the place" to a "haute-volee soiree" at a belvedere, drove up to the police-station with the pretext that he had discovered a long-wanted anarchist criminal in the person of a gendarme, and indulged in all manner of practical jokes with the officials. He was at that time supposed to be suffering from general paralysis. The later attacks began with an inclination, for the time being, to extravagant expenditure, alcoholic and sexual excess, as well as every imaginable open misdemeanour; once on admission to the hospital he had all his pockets full of worthless rings, foreign coins, and cheap jewellery, which he had bought up everywhere, as well as numerous pawn-tickets.

At the beginning the attacks lasted from two to three months, and later on about six months. The patient generally soon became composed in the hospital, and scarcely presented even slight disturbances, yet a number of experiments of dismissal turned out badly because he at once began to drink again, and then quickly became re-

478

excited. After recovery, he was, in the intervals, a very sober man, leading an extremely retired life, and on good terms with his wife, whom he tormented and insulted in his excitement. For three months after the last dismissal but one, and for nine months after the last, he was deeply depressed, misanthropic, lay in bed a great deal, and expressed thoughts of suicide, until his mental equilibrium gradually became restored.

The expectation already expressed by us has been verified. Not only have a series of maniacal attacks occurred, but in the course of the year attacks of depression with distinctive features have also made their appearance. Most probably the future will bring a more or less regular return of one or the other of these states.* That in the course of time the duration and severity of the attacks have increased, while the intervals have become shorter and shorter, corresponds with the general experience of the disease. The future course will probably involve a gradual aggravation of the behaviour of the attacks, with fluctuations possibly.

As you may have already guessed from the noise outside, the second patient, who now storms into the room, is violently excited. She does not sit down, but walks about quickly, examines briefly what she sees, interferes unceremoniously with the students, and tries to be familiar with them. No sooner is she induced to sit down than she quickly springs up again, flings away her shoes, unties her apron, and begins to sing and dance. The next minute she stops, claps her hands, goes to the blackboard, seizes the chalk, and begins to write her name, but ends with a gigantic flourish which in an instant covers the whole board. She wipes it off perfunctorily with the sponge, again hastily writes some letters of the alphabet, suddenly flings away the chalk over the heads of the

---

* After the setting in of tranquility the patient was at first low-spirited for a long time, and a year later he again became maniacal.

audience, seizes the chair, swings it in a circle, and sits down on it with vigour, only to spring up again immediately and repeat the old game in other forms. During the whole time the patient chatters almost incessantly, though the purport of her rapid headlong talk is scarcely intelligible and quite disconnected. On addressing her impressively, one generally obtains a short, sensible answer, to which all kinds of disconnected sentences are, however, immediately joined. Still, one can sometimes follow up her erratic thoughts; they seem to be recollections springing up, fragments of phrases and verses, words and turns that she has heard formerly from her companions, and which she now interlaces into her stream of talk. The patient gives her age and her name, and knows that she is in a "mad-house," but gives quite arbitrary names to other people. She refuses to be led into a connected conversation, but at once digresses, jumps up, addresses one of the students, runs to the window, sings part of a song, and dances about. Her mood is extremely merry; she laughs and titters continuously between her talk, but easily becomes angry on slight provocation, and then breaks out into a torrent of the nastiest abuse, only to become tranquil a minute after with a happy laugh. In spite of her great restlessness, she is tolerably easy to manage, and obeys orders given in a friendly tone, although it must be admitted that she immediately does something else quite different. There is nothing to notice in the physical condition of the delicately-built patient, except a certain amount of anæmia, and an inflammation of the margin of the left eyelid, which she will not allow to be touched.

The extraordinary *mutability of the individual psychical processes* constitutes the characteristic feature of the condition under consideration. These processes are quickly and easily induced, but just as easily supplanted by others. Some accidental attraction at once arrests the attention, but only for the moment; every arising idea or mood, every impulse of the will, is already replaced by another before it is properly carried out. Evidently the patient is wanting in ability to prevent herself from being ruled in thought, mood, and action by the changing influences of the moment, or to work these out to their proper endings. It is in this way that the important symptom of *divertibility* arises—that is to say, increased liability to influence through outward and inward attractions. In the province of comprehension it makes itself perceptible in that it is not impressions of real importance that arrest the attention, but those which, presenting themselves directly, are chosen at haphazard, to be at once replaced, just as accidentally, by others. Thus, in the province of the course of ideas, there arises that phenomenon which we are accustomed to call the "flight of ideas." As the idea of a goal is wanting which gives its fixed direction to healthy thought and at once arrests all side issues, the train of thought is perpetually driven out of its course, while incidental and non-essential ideas, often only awakened through habit of speech or similarity of sound, intrude everywhere. That the succession of thought is not hastened by this, as is generally taken for granted, but that the generation of new ideas often goes on very inadequately and slowly, can easily be proved by suitable experiments. But the designation "flight of ideas" is so far quite appropriate, as, in point of fact, the *duration of the individual idea* appears to be very much shortened; the ideas are "fleeting," and soon fade again before they have actually attained clearness. Hence, as a rule, there exists at the height of such disturbance a more or less pronounced incomplete consciousness.

The divertibility can be recognised in the abrupt *change of colouring* of the frame of mind, which can *change* in a moment from exuberant merriment to angry irritation as well as to tearful despair. Lastly, in the form taken by expressions of the will, the disturbance shows as motor unrest, as *press of occupation*. There constantly spring up in the patient the most manifold impulses of the will, whose transposition into action is impeded by no checks, but is very soon crossed by new impulses.

Compare this description with the picture of the first patient, and you will easily see that there we were met by the same features that meet us here, only they were in a less aggravated form. There, too, we noticed the divertibility of the train of thought, the change of mood, and the unsteadiness of the will, and the tendency to give way unresistingly to every rising impulse. In both cases we have in reality the same picture of disease, that of *maniacal excitement*. That the differences, so striking at the first glance, are only a question of degree, becomes clear to us when we see the same state develop with growing excitement in the first patient as in the case we are now considering. But, again, our patient has from time to time presented the picture of "hypomania." Certainly that is not true of the present attack, which began pretty suddenly about two months ago, or at least is only true of the first few days. On the other hand, as we had to consider probable after our previous lecture, the patient has already gone through a whole series of maniacal attacks, some of which have passed off wonderfully mildly.

The woman is now thirty-two years of age; her father was very excitable; so also was his brother, who committed suicide; and a cousin of the father was insane. Her sister is feebleminded. The patient's illness began in her fourteenth year with an attack of depression, which was followed two years after by a state of excitement. Two years later another attack of depression came on, with self-accusations and severe impediment of the will. This was followed by an excitement, then again by a depression, and then another excitement. From that

482

time frequent fluctuations between slight depression and hypomaniacal states were observed, but were only recognised as morbid by the mother. The patient led, at that time, an unsettled life, published a notification of marriage, engaged in love affairs without discretion, which were not without results, but had only been considered by her friends as "full of spirits." Once she actually married while in such a state, only to separate again. Thrice the excitement was so strong that the patient had to be temporarily lodged in an asylum. In her states of depression she felt deep repentance for her behaviour during the excitement. Between the attacks long periods intervened, however, in which neither sad nor cheerful moods existed.

The whole development and course of this case is wonderfully diagnostic of maniacal-depressive insanity. The beginning at a youthful age with depressed states of mind, the later vacillation between mania and depression, the occurrence of a single severe attack after numerous slighter ones, which to the uninitiated scarcely appear as morbid, we find repeated in the same way innumerable times. We know from experience that patients of that kind are generally descended from families in which attacks of mental derangement have occurred. We may expect that our patient will have a series of different-coloured mild or severe attacks to go through in the future.*

The patient who next follows, a sea-captain, aged forty-nine, also begins to speak immediately on his entrance, and introduces himself as "The accused under chief command of Herr Professor General K." He answers the questions put to him promptly, and shows that he is quite clear as to time, residence, and surroundings. Very

---

* After five months' duration of the attack the patient recovered, with great increase of weight, but in the eight years elapsing since then she has again been through numerous slight depressions and excitements.

soon, however, he goes into long-winded, nineteen-to-the-dozen statements, which he suddenly brings to an end with the somewhat surprising remarks, "Either I am well or ill or off my head." To the name Katherine he adds "Kathereinen-Kneipps-Malzkaffee"—"Frohlich Pfalz, Gott erhalts" (Happy Palace, God uphold it!")—"all will be roasted." His comprehension and memory are very good; he makes his statement with a kind of joking minuteness; he came to the hospital on Friday, July 1, at ten minutes to six o'clock. He considers himself well; there was no need to bring him here. He makes derisive remarks about the doctors and the hospital, as well as about himself; he may talk nonsense, but he is clever—more clever than the doctors, who learnt nothing in Heidelberg. When he begins to "thee and thou" us, and we express our astonishment, he breaks out into a torrent of abuse, trying always to surpass himself, and ending in shouts of laughter. His mood is exalted and insolent, his behaviour jolly and vigorous; in answering, he holds his hand to his temple as in military salute, speaks loudly and abruptly as if making a military report, but soon relapses into the easy tone of a narrator.

The patient's real condition, as you will have already seen, is likewise one of maniacal excitement. The unstable nature of his train of thought, the exalted, changing mood, the motor unrest, and especially the passion for talk, are significant enough. You would also be astonished at his press of occupation in other ways if you saw him in the ward arranging his clothes in ever new and intricate ways, manufacturing a horse, on which he rides, out of his bedding, or an anchor, the emblem of his calling; how he bawls, dances, or sings, and also occasionally destroys what he gets hold of. Our previous conjecture, based on common experience, that the present attack was certainly not the first, proves to be true. The patient came here for the first time eight years ago; since then he has been here eight times. The attack set in each time quite suddenly—the two first after a fall into the water, the second at the burial of his daughter, the later ones without known cause. Each time he at once became very excited, and developed the most senseless delusions—that he was God, Joseph in Egypt, called his companions by the names of princes and emperors, and had to be put into a strait-waistcoat on account of his very violent resistance. The excitement disappeared regularly, however, after from one to two weeks, so that he could soon be let out again.

The last five admissions took place this year. For this reason we kept the patient in the hospital this time after the disappearance of the excitement, and during that time we were able to observe the beginning of two new attacks. We have tried to cut short the last attack by at once giving the patient 12 and then 15 grammes of bromide of sodium daily on the first symptoms of excitement. In point of fact, the attack passed off much more quickly and mildly than the previous ones; perhaps we might venture to hope that the next attack will be longer in coming.*

In addition to this, we have employed those remedies which are generally found to be of use in maniacal states —first, rest in bed; but when that was found impracticable, then prolonged warm baths, which we are accustomed, under certain circumstances, to employ, with the best results, for a month at a time, for the half or even for the whole of the day. Doses of hyoscin or sulphonal are often necessary at the commencement to accustom the patients to the baths; but afterwards they stay in the comfortable warm bath, in which they also take their meals and can sometimes amuse and occupy themselves without much resistance. As in this case, it

---

* After a very brief excitement four weeks later, also treated with bromide of sodium, the patient remained well for over five months, then had another slight relapse, and has now again been at home for more than four months.

is found that with many patients simple separation from others is an efficient calmative, the employment of which has, however, to be immediately abandoned if and so long as the patients show any inclination to uncleanliness or destruction. Under kindly, quiet, non-exciting treatment, these "delirious" patients are far less troublesome than one usually imagines.

So far we have only considered the states of excitement in our patients. As they generally come under observation, morbid phenomena of that kind are commonly designated simply as "periodic mania." Very marked *low spirits* have, however, been also observed here. Especially after the disappearance of the excitement the patient was often downcast and quiet for days, thought that he had no longer any friends left—it was misery to be in his position. There are also hours intervening in the maniacal excitement when he weeps bitterly and deplores his sad fate, soon to fall back into the old boisterous mood. It appears to me that not only the deep inward relationship of such apparently contradictory states, but also the clinical unity of all those cases, which one generally tries to distinguish as the different forms of simple and periodic mania and of circular insanity, are distinctly marked in these fluctuations, which are hardly ever absent, even in the most hilarious mania. The tendency to repeated relapses, as well as the usually favourable termination of a single attack, is common to all of them, even if the indications are very severe and of very long duration.

LECTURE VIII

Mixed Conditions of Maniacal-Depressive Insanity

GENTLEMEN,—If the different colouring, severity, and duration of even a single attack of maniacal-depressive insanity can give an extraordinarily varied form to the pictures of disease, this wealth of form will receive yet a substantial increase through the consideration of some further cases. You see before you a man, aged fifty, of uncommonly strong build, but badly nourished, who has been in the hospital for a few weeks. On my addressing him, the patient turns to me and answers questions as to his personal circumstances slowly and with difficulty, but correctly. Sometimes one has to repeat the questions several times, as the patient does not pay attention, but looks around the room, drums on the table with his fingers, suddenly gets up or stretches out his hand to the doctor. He gives the date of his admission quite incorrectly, says he is here, "in the Castle"; it is so beautiful here. He is not ill; he is very well; he is here "to make peace with us all." At this he breaks into a hearty laugh, so that one is not clear as to whether his remark is not intended for a joke. He knows the doctors, but not by name—"You must know that better than I." He does sums sometimes correctly and sometimes incorrectly, usually adding: "That squares wonderfully." As far as one can judge, his general knowledge is good, though the patient very often says: "I must first think"; and he has to be asked the same question several times, until at last, after some wrong answers, he gives the right one. His mood is cheerful and exalted; he sits there with beaming countenance, and often laughs away happily to himself, makes facetious remarks, and begins in a booming voice to sing a song. At the same time his behaviour is almost quiet; the movements are remarkably slow and awkward, but strong; he presses the hand offered to him very hard, and holds it firmly. He says little, breaks off abruptly, and soon comes to a standstill, ending with a laugh. When told to write his name on the blackboard, he draws the separate letters exceedingly slowly, pressing very hard on the board, and then adds a row of other names. On going away, he says good-bye in a loud voice, placing his hand in military fashion to his head. Except for a slight oscillation on shutting the eye, and a rupture in the left groin, the physical examination shows no disturbance worth remarking.

The condition under consideration cannot at first be classified with any of the conditions already considered. On the one hand we are met by symptoms of stupor, dimness of comprehension, forgetfulness, poverty of thought, and clumsiness of expression of the will; on the other hand, a certain divertibility shows itself, with exalted mood and slight motor unrest. Under these circumstances, the question must in the first place be raised whether we may not possibly have to deal with general paralysis, in which similar phenomena can occur. Only, the physical examination has furnished us with no good grounds for such a supposition; neither the pupils, nor the speech, nor the reflexes, nor the sensibility to pain, present the symptoms of general paralysis of the insane. Add to this that the memory also is less disturbed than at first appears, the patient is only stupefied and somewhat confused, so that, as he says himself, he must first consider even with simple answers. But in the end he usually finds the right answer, in contradistinction to the general paralytic, who does not at all notice the uncertainty and contradictions of his statements. That the condition is not to be considered as katatonic stupor is obvious. The attention of the patient is easily aroused, but he comprehends with difficulty; his mood is not indifferent or childish, but really cheerful and happy; no negativism, no stereotypism, or automatic obedience appears in his actions, but a singular mixture of constraint and excitement. Finally, the supposition of epileptic stupor, quite apart from the long duration of the condition, will also present difficulties in diagnosis, because the emotional tension and irritability which usually distinguish that state are here completely wanting.

488

The fact that the patient has already suffered three times from mental derangement shows us the way to the right interpretation of this particular clinical picture. The father and a brother drowned themselves; a sister became insane in her youth. He himself, as a child, suffered from St. Vitus' dance; later on he was always a very quiet, reserved, temperate man, who, since his twenty-fifth year, has lived in happy wedlock, but has no children. He became ill for the first time in his thirty-first year. He was sad, thoughtful, overanxious on account of a tapeworm from which he suffered, and of which one heard now for the first time, and left off working. After a short time he became well again. The second attack set in seven years later with ideas of grandeur. The patient wanted to bring out a new machine, thought he need no longer work, was sexually very excited, and was raving mad and violent towards his wife, so that he had to be put into a strait-waistcoat. He hardly ate or slept at all. Here, in the hospital, where he was brought at once, he was very confused and apprehensive, expressed ideas of persecution, and had to be fed artificially; then he became ill with septic pneumonia, and after four weeks was taken home again by his wife.

The third attack began four years later with melancholia, which was very soon succeeded by wild excitement. It appears that at that time the patient presented in the hospital a similar picture to what he does now—slight restlessness, with cheerful, occasionally irritable mood, and an inclination to funny pranks. Recovery followed after eight months. This time the attack began with sleeplessness, restlessness, and quickly increasing bewilderment. In the beginning the patient also appears to have had singular hallucinations; he heard singing, shouts, saw a red cushion signifying England, a shirt that represented a heart, declared that he was the Son of God, that he would redeem the world, that he could

489

heal all diseases, that he had transformed everything. He mistook people, called the doctor the King of Bavaria, and wanted to embrace and to kiss him, made stupid jokes, and shook hands violently, shook his sheet in other people's faces, but was easily managed, only now and then angrily excited, and always easily quieted with a cigar. Quite transitory and violent weeping and lamenting was observed.

As you will see, the two first attacks were both depressive, the two last expansive. But while in the second attack ideas of grandeur stepped in along with the apprehensive bewilderment, in the present and in the preceding attacks we have a combination of cheerful mood with impediment of thought and action. Thus, in a series of favourably resulting attacks, the clinical course of the malady quite corresponds with that of *maniacal-depressive insanity*. In point of fact, we have to do here with conditions in which the otherwise different attacks of related or successively recurring symptoms of disease *mix with each other* in wonderful ways. While a cheerful frame of mind with facility of expression of the will usually accompanies maniacal-depressive insanity, and impediments of the same go along with a depressive mood, here impediments of thought and action are connected with exaltation. In this way the picture of maniacal stupor is formed, in which the patients are forgetful, intellectually dull, clumsy, taciturn, sometimes almost dumb, but occasionally showing their wanton moods in all manner of tricks, adornments, facetious remarks, and play on words.

Quite another form of these mixed conditions is shown by a farmer of fifty-three years, whom I will now show you. The patient gives coherent information as to his personal circumstances, knows where he is, knows the doctors, but is not quite clear as to time. At first he behaves quietly, but in the course of the conversation

490

becomes more and more excited, begs urgently to be allowed to go home to his wife and children, entreats once more to be pardoned. Can they answer for keeping him always and for ever in the penitentiary? The attendants had said so; he had seen in the crossed spoons that they would shackle him; the five plates on the top of one another had meant that he would go no more to his family—four at home, and one here. He sees very well that they think him incurable, and will not eat another bite. He steals money from his children through his residence here. To-morrow he will certainly be put to death; but why has he not taken heed thereof of what was meant when the cup was broken and the vessel stood in that way on the table? He should have said, "I know not why," and demanded his clothes. In this confused way he talks on, only allowing himself to be interrupted for a short time, to immediately begin his lamentations anew. At the same time he shows active emotional excitement, wrings his hands, wishes to kneel down, groans and weeps aloud. All the same, his expression is not really sad. He looks round him with lively and sparkling eyes, answers questions between whiles quite to the purpose, is ready to make a compact that he will not speak and will eat regularly for eight whole days if he may go home, urging half jokingly that one must give him one's hand on it, but then falls again into his former loquacity. The physical examination shows no deviation from health worth noticing.

The patient's condition, therefore, is one of *depression*. If we ask what this signifies clinically, we shall first think of *melancholia,* as general paralysis is little probable on account of the want of physical disturbances; so also is a state of circular depression, there being full freedom of expression of the will. The only symptoms, perhaps, that do not so entirely fit into the picture of melancholia are the great *loquacity* of the patient, and the ease with which one succeeds in *diverting* him, if only for a time.

If we now look back at the development of the condition, we learn that the patient comes of a healthy family, but has a son who is insane; two other children are healthy. He was in the campaign of 1870, and was a quiet, sober workman, healthy till his forty-third year, when he was treated in this hospital for "melancholia," recovering after a short time. Now for about a year he has again been ill. The illness came on gradually. The patient had groundless anxieties, worked badly, and expressed thoughts of suicide. According to his own account, he did not know in the morning whether he was to go out or whether he was to go in, whether he was to take the manure here or there. At last his wife said: "Now, do go away once and for all." Some days things went well with him, then again he thought he could never any more be happy. Why should he go on living? Often he became excited and angry; subsequently he regretted this.

On admission to the hospital six weeks ago, the patient was in a cheerful mood, showed strong desire for talking, and had no feelings of illness. He said that now he could decide everything easily that had been so very difficult to him before. But next day the picture changed quite suddenly. The patient became forgetful, was only able with difficulty to give the names of his children, showed great apprehension, thought he was condemned to death, slid about the ground on his knees, and refused to eat. But this condition changed quickly also, and now there developed a quite erratic alternation between exalted and apprehensive moods, which sometimes occurred within a few hours.

The apprehensive mood, however, gradually gained the upper hand. Contradictory ideas of sin and persecution sprang up, and disappeared; at the same time the patient, in the way indicated, had the inclination to refer every occurrence in his surroundings to himself. He was es-

492

pecially tormented by the compulsion to add, "I know not why," to all his observations, so as to come to no harm from them. In his "delusions of reference" the great divertibility of the patient showed very distinctly, always allowing him to find out new connections, while the old would be quickly forgotten. Great motor unrest showed during the whole illness, manifesting itself in lively gesticulations, continual wandering about, and particularly in the exceedingly strong desire for talking. In that respect the enhancement of the excitement by speech itself was worthy of notice. As soon as one addressed the patient, his torrent of talk unfailingly quickly rose up, however much he had firmly resolved to remain quiet. Latterly, a more cheerful, hopeful mood has for the time stepped in again.

It is clear from the course of the attack that we have not here to do with a melancholic illness. The *distinct maniacal colouring* of the condition in the first weeks of the present attack, as well as the early appearance of the first attack of the illness, are contradictory to that throughout. At the same time, we see from the statements of the patient that *want of resolution,* which we have learnt to recognise as a symptom of circular depression, was very marked during the first time of the illness. We were also often able without difficulty to show an *impediment of thought.* The condition of the patient, therefore, in the beginning of the present attack showed symptoms already known to us as those of *circular depression*—that is to say, impediment of thought and will; later, from time to time those of *maniacal excitement*—namely, cheerful mood, with desire for talking, though without marked "flight of ideas." Then, after a time of fluctuations backwards and forwards, the sad apprehensive depression again became stronger, while the motor excitement continued. In our opinion, this picture also belongs to the embodiments of maniacal-depressive insanity, and is to be described as a *mixed condition of psycho-motor excitement with psychic depression.* The patient shows us, therefore, as we believe, the very opposite of the picture in the preceding case, in which we could establish cheerful moods side by side with psycho-motor impediment. The grounds for these opinions are drawn chiefly from the marked, if at the same time transitory prominence of the ordinary maniacal and depressive conditions in the same patient in the same or in different attacks, alongside of the mixed states already described.

The value of this interpretation consists in the fact that we gain through it a clear opinion as to the further course of the malady. If we know that conditions of this particular kind only represent maniacal-depressive insanity, we may expect recovery from the present attack, but in all probability a relapse will occur later on in this or in another form of the periodically recurring disease. This tendency to fall each time into mixed conditions of the same nature apparently often exists in the same patient; sometimes, as in our first case, this tendency comes out only later on, yet an ordinary attack may appear, in addition, between several mixed attacks. As a rule, mixed conditions seem to represent rather more severe forms of the disease than simple attacks.*

In maniacal-depressive insanity we have already been repeatedly met by *delusions,* usually ideas of sin and persecution, more rarely ideas of grandeur. These delusions do not necessarily belong to the indications of the disease. They can be entirely wanting, but can also be so strongly developed that they give a deceptive character to the whole condition. You see here before you a student of music, aged nineteen, who has been ill for about a year. His old father is disabled in consequence of several apoplectic fits; a brother of his became insane. The highly-

---

* After twenty months' duration of the attack, the patient has quite recovered, with great increase of weight.

494

gifted patient, without any tangible cause, while studying music, became depressed, felt ill at ease, and lonely, made all manner of plans, which he always gave up, for changing his place of residence and his profession, for he could come to no fixed resolutions. During a visit to Munich, he felt as if people in the street had something to say to him, and as if he were talked about everywhere. He heard an offensive remark at an inn at the next table, which he answered rudely. Next day he was seized with the apprehension that his remark might be taken as *lese majeste*. He heard that students asked for him at the door, and he left Munich post-haste with every precautionary measure, because he thought himself accompanied and followed on the way. Since then he overheard people in the street who threatened to shoot him, and to set fire to his house, and on that account he burned no light in his room. In the streets voices pointed out the way he ought to go so as to avoid being shot. Behind doors, windows, hedges, pursuers seemed everywhere to lurk. He also heard long conversations of not very flattering purport as to his person. In consequence of this, he withdrew altogether from society, but yet behaved in such an ordinary way that his relatives, whom he visited, did not notice his delusions. At last the many mocking calls which he heard at every turn provoked the thought of shooting himself.

After about six months he felt more free, "comfortable, enterprising, and cheerful," began to talk a lot, to compose, criticised everything, concocted great schemes, and was insubordinate to his teacher. The voices still continued, and he recognised in them the whisperings of master spirits. Hallucinations of sight now became very marked. The patient saw Beethoven's image radiant with joy at his genius; saw Goethe, whom he had abused, in a threatening attitude; masked old men and ideal female forms floated through his room. He saw lightning and glorious brilliancy of colours, which he interpreted partly as the flowing out of his great genius, partly as attestations of applause from the dead.

He regarded himself as the Messiah, preached openly against prostitution, wished to enter into an ideal connection with a female student of music, whom he sought for in strange houses, composed the "Great Song of Love," and on account of this priceless work was brought to the hospital by those who envied him, as he said.

The patient is quite collected, and gives connected information as to his personal circumstances. He is clear as to time and place, but betrays himself by judging his position falsely, inasmuch as he takes us for hypnotizers, who wish to try experiments with him. He does not look upon himself as ill; at the most as somewhat nervously overexcited. Through diplomatic questions we learn that all people know his thoughts; if he writes, the words are repeated before the door. In the creaking of boards, in the whistle of the train, he hears calls, exhortations, orders, threats. Christ appears to him in the night, or a golden figure as the spirit of his father; coloured signs of special meaning are given through the window. In prolonged conversation the patient very quickly loses the thread, and produces finally a succession of fine phrases, which wind up unexpectedly with some facetious question. His mood is arrogant, conceited, generally condescending, occasionally transitorily irritated or apprehensive. The patient speaks much and willingly, talks aloud to himself, and marches boisterously up and down the ward, interests himself more than is desirable in his fellow-patients, seeking to cheer them and to manage them. He is very busy, too, with letter-writing and composing, but only produces fugitive, carelessly jotted down written work, with numerous marginal notes. Physically, he is well.

The interpretation of this condition is not easy at the first glance. Of the diseases hitherto considered, dementia

496

præcox would perhaps come first and foremost under consideration, especially certain forms of it with which we shall have to deal later on. But the exceedingly fresh, active mood of the patient, his interest in his surroundings, his sociability, and his press of occupation, are decidedly opposed to this supposition. Also, the manifold peculiarities of action and behaviour which we saw stand out so prominently in that disease are entirely wanting. On the other hand, the *divertibility* which is seen in his ever flying off at a tangent and so easily losing the thread of his narratives, in his *cheerful, arrogant frame of mind, and in his urgent need to be talking and doing,* points to the relationship of the condition with maniacal-depressive insanity. And this opinion would be justified by the joyless, irresolute manifestations, so characteristic of the first stage, passing into the comfortable but active states, so noticeable in the second stage. Hallucinations and delusions are not such essential clinical indications that they would suffice to found another diagnosis, because they could be absent in one attack of the malady and present in another. If our supposition with regard to our patient be right, we are able to predict complete recovery in the near future, though the possibility of a subsequent relapse has to be admitted.*

EMIL KRAEPELIN (b.—Neustrelitz, Germany, Feb. 15, 1856; d.— München, Germany, Oct. 7, 1926).

Kraepelin began his studies in medicine at Leipzig in the winter 1874-1875. He went to Würzburg the following year (1876-1877). He also studied at München, after which he returned to Leipzig to complete his studies.

In Easter of the year 1882, Kraepelin became Assistant to Wundt. For ten years, there ensued an important collaboration, with Wundt as mentor and Kraepelin as investigator, on the problem of the interrelationships between pharmacological drugs and mental disorders (v.i.). In 1892 Kraepelin became Professor at Heidelberg, where, at the psychiatric clinic, he applied the Wundtian methods of experimental psychology for the first time to the field of psychopathology.

* The patient quite recovered, and has now been well for eight years.

It is certainly true that the influence and lifelong association of Wundt constantly reassured Kraepelin of the validity of the experimental approach, and was responsible for the great many experimental studies in psychopathology which came from Kraepelin's laboratory.

It was here at Heidelberg that Kraepelin developed his definitive psychiatric nosology. This is still today the basis of psychiatric diagnosis, with only nonessential modifications. Kraepelin was able to penetrate the complex array of unrelated psychiatric symptoms, to see how one symptom was so often linked with another, and to group them into significant recurrent disease patterns. There was, to be sure, much work of this nature before Kraepelin—psychiatric nosology had begun, actually, with Pinel, over one hundred years earlier—but Kraepelin was, by time and place, the first one able to survey the whole field from a sufficiently aloof vantage point. For the first time, a clear distinction was made between "symptom and disease."

The present selection from the nosology is Kraepelin's most important class of psychoses, the manic-depressive.

KRAEPELIN, E. *Lectures on clinical psychiatry.* New York: William Wood & Co., 1904. Authorized trans., rev. and ed.—T. Johnstone. Lect. II: "Depressed stages of maniacal-depressive insanity (circular stupor)." Lect. VII: "Maniacal excitement." Lect. VIII: "Mixed conditions of maniacal-depressive insanity."

See also:

KRAEPELIN, E. *Uber die Beeinflussung einfacher psychischer Vorgäng durch einige Arzneimittel.* Jena: G. Fischer, 1892. This bears a dedication to Wundt.

BRACELAND, F. J. "Kraepelin, his system and his influence." *Amer. J. Psychiat.* 1957, 113: 871-876.

KAHN, E. "Emil Kraepelin." *Amer. J. Psychiat.* 1956, 113: 289-294.

WIRTH, W. "Emil Kraepelin zum Gedächtnis!" *Arch. f. ges. Psychol.* 1927, 58: i-xxxiii. An important discussion of the relationship between Wundt and Kraepelin and of the application of experimental methods to psychopathology.

GAUPP, R. "Die Lehren Kraepelins in ihrer Bedeutung für die heutige Psychiatrie." *Z. f. g. Neurol. Psychiat.* 1939, 165: 47-75.

MEDICAL INQUIRIES
AND
OBSERVATIONS,
UPON
THE DISEASES OF THE MIND.

BENJAMIN RUSH

CHAPTER I.

Of the Faculties and Operations of the Mind, and on the Proximate Cause and Seat of Intellectual Derangement.

IN entering upon the subject of the following Inquiries and Observations, I feel as if I were about to tread upon consecrated ground. I am aware of its difficulty and importance, and I thus humbly implore that BEING, whose government extends to the thoughts of all his creatures, so to direct mine, in this arduous undertaking, that nothing hurtful to my fellow citizens may fall from my pen, and that this work may be the means of lessening a portion of some of the greatest evils of human life.

Before I proceed to consider the diseases of the mind, I shall briefly mention its different faculties and operations.

Its faculties are, understanding, memory, imagination, passions, the principle of faith, will, the moral faculty, conscience, and the sense of Deity.

Its principal operations, after sensation, are perception, association, judgment, reasoning and volition. All its subordinate operations, which are known by the names of attention, reflection, contemplation, wit, consciousness, and the like, are nothing but modifications of the five principal operations that have been mentioned.

The faculties of the mind have been called, very happily, *internal* senses. They resemble the external senses in being innate, and depending wholly upon bodily impressions to produce their specific operations. These impressions are made through the medium of the external senses. As well might we attempt to excite thought in a piece of marble by striking it with our hand, as expect to produce a single operation of the mind in a person deprived of the external senses of touch, seeing, hearing, taste, and smell.

All the operations in the mind are the effects of motions previously excited in the brain, and every idea and thought appears to depend upon a motion peculiar to itself. In a sound state of the mind these motions are regular, and succeed impressions upon the brain with the same certainty and uniformity that perceptions succeed impressions upon the senses in their sound state.

In inquiring into the causes of the diseases of the mind, and the remedies that are proper to relieve them, I shall employ the term derangement to signify the diseases of all the faculties of the mind.

As the understanding occupies the highest rank of those faculties, and as it is most frequently the seat of derangement, I shall begin by considering the causes, and all the states and forms of its diseases.

By derangement in the understanding I mean every departure of the mind in its perceptions, judgments, and reasonings, from its natural and habitual order, accompanied with corresponding actions. It differs from delirium, whether acute, or chronic, in being accompanied with a departure from habitual order, in incoherent conduct, as well as conversation. The latter however is not necessary to constitute intellectual madness, for we sometimes meet with the most incongruous actions without incoherent speech, and we now and then met with incoherent speech in mad people, in whom the disease does not destroy their habits of regular conduct. This is evinced by the correctness with which they sometimes perform certain mechanical and menial pieces of business. Madness is to delirium what walking in sleep is to dreaming. It is delirium, heightened and protracted by a more active and permanent stimulus upon the brain.

Let it not be supposed that intellectual derangement always affects the understanding exclusively in the manner that has been mentioned. Far from it. Two or more of the faculties are generally brought into sympathy with it, and there are cases in which all the faculties are sometimes deranged in succession, and rotation, and now and then they are all affected at the same time. This occurs most frequently in the beginning of a paroxysm of intellectual madness, but it rarely continues to affect the other faculties of the mind after two or three weeks, or after the liberal use of depleting remedies. Thus fever in its first attack, affects the bowels and nervous system, and in a few days settles down into a disease chiefly of the blood-vessels.

Derangement in the understanding has been divided into partial and general. The causes of both are the same. I should proceed immediately to enumerate them, but as the seat, or proximate cause, of a disease is generally the first object of a physician's inquiry on entering a sick room, it shall be the first subject of our consideration in the present inquiry.

1. The most ancient opinion of the proximate cause of intellectual derangement, or what has been called madness is, that it is derived from a morbid state of the liver, and that it discovers itself in a vitiated state of the bile. Hippocrates laid the foundation of this error by his encomium upon Democritus whom he found employed in examining the liver of a dumb animal in order to discover the cause of madness.

2. Madness has been said to be the effect of a disease in the spleen. This viscus is supposed to be affected in a peculiar manner in that grade of madness which has been

501

called hypochondriasis. For many years it was known in England by no other name than the spleen, and even to this day, persons who are affected with it are said to be spleeny, in some parts of the New England states.

3. A late French writer, Dr. Prost, in an ingenious work entitled "Medicine Eclairee par Observation et l'Overture des Corps," has taken pains to prove that madness is the effect of a disease in the intestines, and particularly of their peritoneal coat. The marks of inflammation which appear in the bowels, in persons who have died of madness, have no doubt favoured this opinion; but these morbid appearances as well as all those which are often met with in the liver, spleen, and occasionally in the stomach in persons who have died of madness, are the effects, and not the causes of the disease. They are induced either, 1, by the violent or protracted exercises of the mind attracting or absorbing the excitement of those viscera, and thereby leaving them in that debilitated state which naturally disposes them to inflammation and obstruction. Thus disease in the stomach induces torpor and costiveness in the alimentary canal. Thus too local inflammation often induces coldness and insensibility in contiguous parts of the body. Or, 2, they are induced by the reaction of the mind from the impressions which produce madness, being of such a nature as to throw its morbid excitement upon those viscera with so much force as to produce inflammation and obstructions in them. That they are induced by one, or by both these causes, I infer from the increased secretion and even discharge of bile which succeed a paroxysm of anger; from the pain in the left side, or spleen, which succeeds a paroxysm of malice or revenge; and from the pain, and other signs of disease in the bowels and stomach which follow the chronic operations of fear and grief. That the disease and disorders of all the viscera that have

502

been mentioned, are the effects, and not the causes of madness, I infer further from their existing for weeks, months and years in countries subject to intermitting fevers, without producing madness, or even the least alienation of mind.

4. Madness it has been said is the effect of a disease in the nerves. Of this, dissections afford us no proofs; on the contrary, they generally exhibit the nerves after death from madness in a sound state. I object further, to this opinion, that hysteria, which is universally admitted to be seated chiefly in the nerves and muscles, often continues for years, and sometimes during a long life, without inducing madness, or if the mind be alienated for a few minutes in one of its paroxysms, it is only from its bringing the vascular system into sympathy, in which I shall say presently the cause of madness is primarily seated. The reaction of the mind from the impressions which produce hysteria, discovers itself in the bowels, in the kidneys, and in most of the muscular parts of the body.

5, and lastly. Madness has been placed exclusively in the mind. I object to this opinion, 1, because the mind is incapable of any operations independently of impressions communicated to it through the medium of the body. 2, Because there are but two instances upon record of the brain being found free from morbid appearances in persons who have died of madness. One of these instances is related by Dr. Stark, the other by Dr. De Haen. They probably arose from the brain being diseased beyond that grade in which inflammation and its usual consequences take place. Did the cause of madness reside exclusively in the mind, a sound state of the brain ought to occur after nearly every death from that disease.

I object to it, 3, because there are no instances of primary affections of the mind, such as grief, love, anger, or despair, producing madness until they had induced some obvious changes in the body, such as wakefulness, a full or frequent pulse, costiveness, a dry skin, and other symptoms of bodily indisposition.

I know it has been said in favour of madness being an ideal disease, or being seated primarily in the mind, that sudden impressions from fear, terror, and even ridicule have sometimes cured it. This is true, but they produce their effects only by the healthy actions they induce in the brain. We see several other diseases, particularly hiccup, head-ache, and even fits of epilepsy, which are evidently affections of the body, cured in the same way by impressions of fear and terror upon the mind.

Having rejected the abdominal viscera, the nerves, and the mind, as the primary seats of madness, I shall now deliver an opinion, which I have long believed and taught in my lectures, and that is, that the cause of madness is seated primarily in the blood-vessels of the brain, and that it depends upon the same kind of morbid and irregular actions that constitute other arterial diseases. There is nothing specific in these actions. They are a part of the unity of disease, particularly of fever; of which madness is a chronic form, affecting that part of the brain which is the seat of the mind.

My reasons for believing the cause of madness to be seated in the blood-vessels of the brain are drawn,

I. From its remote and exciting causes, many of which are the same with those which induce fever and certain diseases of the brain, particularly phrenitis, apoplexy, palsy, and epilepsy, all of which are admitted to have their seats in a greater or less degree in the blood-vessels. Of thirty-six dissections of the brains of persons who had died of madness, Mr. Pinel says he could perceive no difference between the morbid appearances in them, and in the brains of persons who had died of apoplexy and epilepsy. The sameness of these appearances however do not prove that all those diseases occupy the same parts of the brain: I believe they do not, especially in their first stage: they become diffused over the whole brain, probably in their last stages, or in the paroxysm of death. Dr. Johnson, of Exeter, in speaking of the diseases of the abdominal viscera, mentions their sympathy with each other, by what he very happily calls "an intercommunion of sensation." It would seem as if a similar intercommunion took place between all the diseases of the brain. It is remarkable they all discover, in every part of the brain, marks of a morbid state of the blood-vessels.

II. From the ages and constitutions of persons who are most subject to madness. The former are in those years in which acute and inflammatory arterial diseases usually affect the body, and the latter, in persons who labour under the arterial predisposition.

III. I infer that madness is seated in the blood-vessels, 1. From its symptoms. These are a sense of fulness, and sometimes pain in the head; wakefulness, and a redness of the eyes, such as precede fever, a whitish tongue, a dry or moist skin, high coloured urine, a frequent, full, or tense pulse, or a pulse morbidly slow or natural as to frequency. These states of the pulse occur uniformly in recent madness, and one of them, that is frequency, is seldom absent in its chronic state.

I have taken notice of the presence of this symptom in my Introductory Lecture upon the Study of Medical Jurisprudence, in which I have mentioned, that seven-eighths of all the deranged patients in the Pennsylvania Hospital in the year 1811 had frequent pulses,* and that a pardon was granted to a criminal by the president of

* This fact was ascertained, at my request, with great accuracy, by Dr. Frederick Vandyke. It is probable the pulsations of the arteries in the brain were preternaturally frequent in the brain in the few cases in which they were natural at the wrists. Dr. Coxe, of Bristol, informs us that he had found the carotid artery to be full and tense, when the radial artery was weak and soft.

the United States, in the year 1794, who was suspected of counterfeiting madness, in consequence of its having been declared by three physicians that that symptom constituted an unequivocal mark of intellectual derangement.

The connection of this disease with the state of the pulse has been further demonstrated by a most satisfactory experiment, made by Dr. Coxe, and related by him in his Practical Observations upon Insanity. He gave digitalis to a patient who was in a furious state of madness, with a pulse that beat 90 strokes in a minute. As soon as the medicine reduced his pulse to 70, he became rational. Upon continuing it, his pulse fell to 50, at which time he became melancholy. An additional quantity of the medicine reduced it to 40 strokes in a minute, which nearly suspended his life. He was finally cured by lessening the doses of the medicine so as to elevate his pulse to 70 strokes in a minute, which was probably its natural state. In short there is not a single symptom that takes place in an ordinary fever, except a hot skin, that does not occur in the acute state of madness.

IV. From its alternating with several diseases which are evidently seated in the blood-vessels. These are consumption, rheumatism, intermitting and puerperile fever, and dropsy, many instances of which are to be met with in the records of medicine.

V. From its blending its symptoms with several of the forms of fever. It is sometimes attended with regular intermissions, and remissions. I have once seen it appear with profuse sweats, such as occur in certain fevers, in a madman in the Pennsylvania Hospital. These sweats, when discharged from his skin, formed a vapour resembling a thick fog, that filled the cell in which he was confined to such a degree as to render his body scarcely visible.

Again, this disease sometimes appears in a typhus

506

form, in which it is attended with coldness, a feeble pulse, muttering delirium, and involuntary discharge of fæces and urine. But it now and then pervades a whole country in the form of an epidemic. It prevailed in this way in England in the years 1355 and 1373, and in France and Italy in the year 1374, and Dr. Wintringham mentions its frequent occurrence in England in the year 1719.

A striking instance of the union of madness with common fever is mentioned by Lucian. He tells us that a violent fever once broke out at Abdera, which terminated by hæmorrhages, or sweats, on the seventh day. During the continuance of this fever the patients affected with it, repeated passages from the tragedy of Andromeda with great vehemence, both in their sick rooms and in the public streets. This mixture of fever and madness continued until the coming on of cold weather. Lucian ingeniously and very properly ascribes it to the persons affected, having heard the famous player Archilaus act a part in the above tragedy in the middle of summer, in so impressive a manner that it excited in them the seeds of a dormant fever which blended itself with derangement, and thus produced, very naturally, a repetition of the ideas and sounds that excited their disease.

VI. From the appearances of the blood which is drawn in this disease being the same as that which is drawn in certain fevers. They are, inflammatory buff, yellow, serum, and lotura carnium.

VII. From the appearances of the brain after death from madness. These are nearly the same as after death from phrenitis, apoplexy, and other diseases which are admitted to be primary affections of the blood-vessels of the brain. I shall briefly enumerate them; they are, 1, the absence of every sign of disease. I have ascribed this to that grade of suffocated excitement which prevents the effusion of red blood into the serous vessels. We observe

507

the same absence of the marks of inflammation after several other violent diseases. Dr. Stevens in his ingenious inaugural dissertation published in 1811, has called this apparently healthy appearance, the "anæmatous" state of inflammation. Perhaps it would be more proper to call it the "aimatous" state of disease. It is possible it may arise in *recent* cases of madness which terminate fatally, from the same retrocession of the blood from the brain which takes place from the face and external surface of the body, just before death. But,

2. We much oftener discover in the brain, after death from madness, inflammation, effusions of water in its ventricles, extravasation and intravasion of blood, and even pus. After chronic madness, we discover some peculiar appearances which have never been met with in any other disease of the brain, and these are a preternatural hardness, and dryness in all its parts. Lieutaud mentions it often with the epithets of "durum," "prædurum," "siccum," and "exsuccum." Morgagni takes notice of this hardness likewise, and says he had observed it in the cerebrum in persons in whom the cerebellum retained its natural softness. Dr. Bailie and Mr. John Hunter have remarked, that the brain in this state discovered marks of elasticity when pressed by the fingers. Mr. Mickell says a cube of six lines of the brain of a maniac, thus indurated, weighed seven drams, whereas a cube of the same dimension of a sound brain weighed but one dram, and between four and six grains. I have ascribed this hardness, dryness, elasticity and relative weight of the brain to a tendency to schirrus, such as succeeds morbid action or inflammation in glandular parts of the body, and particularly that early grade of it which occurs in the liver, and which is known by the name of hepitalgia. The brain in this case loses its mobility so as to become incapable of emitting those motions from im-

pressions which produce the operations of the mind.

3. We sometimes discover preternatural softness in the brain, in persons who die of madness, similar to that which we find in other viscera from common and febrile diseases. This has been observed to occur most frequently in the kidneys and spleen. The brain in this case partakes of its texture and imbecility in infancy, and hence its inability to receive, and modify the impressions which excite thought in the mind.

4, and lastly. We sometimes discover a preternatural enlargement of the bones of the head from madness, and sometimes a preternatural reduction of their thickness. Of 216 maniacs, whose heads were examined after death, Dr. Crichton says in 160 the skull was enlarged, and in 38 it was reduced in its thickness. Now the same thing succeeds rheumatism, and many other febrile diseases which exert their action in the neighbourhood of bones.

I might add further, under this head, that the morbid appearances in the spleen, liver, and stomach, which are seen after death from madness, place it still more upon a footing with fevers from all its causes, and particularly from koino-miasmatic exhalations, and in a more especial manner when they affect the brain, and thereby induce primary, or idiopathic phrenitis. In short madness is to phrenitis, what pulmonary consumption is to pneumony, that is a chronic state of an acute disease. It resembles pulmonary consumption further, in the excitement of the muscles, and in the appetite continuing in a natural, or in a preternatural state.

VIII. I infer madness to be primarily seated in the blood-vessels, from the remedies which most speedily and certainly cure it, being exactly the same as those which cure fever or disease in the blood-vessels from other causes, and in other parts of the body. They will be noticed in their proper place.

I have thus mentioned the facts and arguments which prove what is commonly called madness to be a disease of the blood-vessels of the brain. All the other and inferior forms of derangement, whether of the memory, the will, the principle of faith, the passions, and the moral faculties, I believe to be connected more or less with morbid action in the blood-vessels of the brain, or heart, according to the seats of those faculties of the mind.

In placing the primary seat of madness in the blood-vessels, I would by no means confine the predisposition to it exclusively to them. It extends to the nerves, and to that part of the brain which is the seat of the mind, both of which when preternaturally irritable, communicate more promptly, deranged action to the blood-vessels of the brain. I have called the union of this diffused morbid irritability, the phrenitic predisposition. It is from the constant presence of this predisposition, that some people are seldom affected with the slightest fever, without becoming delirious; and it is from its absence, that many people are affected with fevers and other diseases of the brain, without being affected with derangement. I am aware that it may be objected to the proximate cause or seat of madness, which has been delivered, that dissections have sometimes discovered marks of arterial diseases in the brain similar to those that have been mentioned, which were not preceded by the least alienation of mind. In these cases, I would suppose the diseases may have existed in parts of the brain which are not occupied by the mind, or that the mind may have been translated to another, and a healthy part of the brain. The senses of taste and hearing, we know, when impaired by disease, are often translated to contiguous, and sometimes to remote parts of the body. But did we admit the objection that I have met, to militate against madness being an arterial disease, it would prove too much, for we sometimes discover the same morbid appearances, which produce apoplexy and palsy, to be present in the brain after death, without any of the common symptoms of those diseases having been preceded by them.

Many other organic diseases are occasionally devoid of their usual characteristic symptoms. Neither vomiting, nor want of appetite, have taken place in stomachs in which mortification has been discovered after death; and abscesses have been found in the livers of persons, who have died without any one of the common symptoms of hepatitis. By allowing the same latitude to the "confused and irregular operations of nature," in the brain, in the production of madness, that we observe in the production of all the other diseases that have been mentioned, we can reconcile its occasional absence, with the existence of all the organic affections in the brain which usually produce it.

In reviewing the numerous proofs of madness, being seated primarily in the blood-vessels, and its being accompanied so generally with most of the symptoms of fever, we cannot help being struck with the histories of the disease that have been given by many ancient and modern physicians. Galen defines it to be "delirium sine febre." Aritæus says it is "semper sine febre." Dr. Arnold quotes a group of authors, who have adopted and propagated the same error. Even Dr. Heberden admits and reasons upon it. The antiquity and extent of this error should lead us never to lose sight of the blood-vessels in investigating the causes of diseases. They are, to a physician, what the meridian sun is to a mariner. There are but few diseases in which it will be possible for him to preserve the system in a healthy course, without daily, and often more frequent observations of the state of the blood-vessels, as manifested by the different and varying states of the pulse.

BENJAMIN RUSH (b.—Byberry, Penn., Dec. 24 o.s., 1745; d.—Philadelphia, April 19 o.s., 1813).

Rush received his A.B. from the College of New Jersey (now
Princeton) in 1760. He studied, as apprentice, under a Dr. John Redman during the years 1761-1766. He went to the University of Edinburgh in 1776, and received his degree two years later. He then went
to London, for some additional clinical experience, to St. Thomas'
Hospital. In 1779 he returned to Philadelphia, and was appointed
Professor of Chemistry at the Medical School. In 1791, he was appointed Professor of the Institutes and Practices of Medicine, and of
Clinical Practice. In 1799 he was appointed by President John Adams
as Treasurer of the Mint, in which position he remained until his death.

A guiding spirit in the American Revolution, Rush was a most
prolific writer on all subjects. They ranged lightly from the present
essay on the cause of insanity, to a defense of the Bible as a school
book, to an account of the manners of the German inhabitants of Pennsylvania. Rush, in his more restrictive role, may be considered as the
Father of Psychiatry in America.

Rush believed strongly in the physiological basis of mental derangements, in the blood vessels of the brain as the seat of the illness, yet at
the same time he introduced the psychiatric interview technique with
his patients, taking notes and discussing with them their experiences.
Pinel observed and recorded; Rush made an approach directly to the
patient. The moral treatment of the insane did find a place in Rush's
method of treatment, but it was secondary to the use of surgery, drugs,
and physical methods. Though it is perhaps true that Rush was somewhat
outside the mainstream of psychiatry, as epitomized by Pinel in France
at about this same time, nevertheless his influence on American psychiatry is unequalled.* Rush's textbook (v.i.) was almost the sole basis
of education in American Psychiatry until Ray's book on forensics, in
1838, some 26 years later (q.v.). Rush's vigorous writings and his
uncompromising statesmanship gave a momentum to the mental hospital
movement and to the dignity of the medical profession from which
several succeeding generations have taken comfort and strength. The
abolition of slavery; the abolition of the death penalty for criminals;
the separation of criminals from the insane; the institution of free
public education; the treatment, not punishment, of the criminal—these
were the basic themes of Rush's life. There are none greater.

---

* It was probably Dorothea Dix (1841) and not Rush who brought the strict
adherence to the moral treatment of insanity into the American hospitals.

RUSH, B. *Medical inquiries and observations, upon the diseases of the mind*. Philadelphia: Kimber and Richardson, 1812 (1818, 1827, 1830, 1835; in German translation 1825). Chap. I: "Of the faculties and operations of the mind, and on the proximate cause and seat of intellectual derangement."

See also:

GOODMAN, N. G. *Benjamin Rush, physician and citizen*. Philadelphia: Univ. of Pennsylvania Press, 1934.

RUNES, D. D. *The selected writings of Benjamin Rush*. N. Y.: Philosophical Library, 1947.

SHRYOCK, R. H. "The psychiatry of Benjamin Rush." *Amer. J. Psychiat.* 1944-1945, 101: 429-432.

MEYER, A. "A reevaluation of Benjamin Rush." *Amer. J. Psychiat.* 1944-45, 101: 433-442.

WITTELS, F. "The Contribution of Benjamin Rush to Psychiatry." *Bull. Hist. Med.* 1946, 20: 157166.

THE DISSOCIATION OF
A PERSONALITY
MORTON PRINCE

MISS BEAUCHAMP

MISS BEAUCHAMP—I mean the one who first presented herself for professional care in the spring of 1898 (B I)—is extremely reticent and dislikes intensely any discussion of herself or her circumstances. She is even reticent in reference to her physical ailments, so much so that it is never easy to discover any temporary indisposition from which she may be suffering. She dislikes the publicity which her psychical trouble tends to draw upon her, and has sought jealously to guard her secret. Indeed, all three personalities have endeavored by every artifice to conceal the knowledge of their trouble from friends, and have done so with a success that is astonishing. It has been at the expense of being considered a strange, incomprehensible person, "unlike other people," as may well be the case when three persons have to act one role in life's comedy. The publication of this study has been consented to by Miss Beauchamp, as a personal favor, at the sacrifice of all her instinctive tastes and inclinations. The constant answer to my frequent remonstrance about her reticence is, "I have never been in the habit of talking about my private affairs." All this is carried to the verge of morbidness, or to what more exactly might be termed *"fixed ideas."* I mention this merely as evidence of the absence of any desire for notoriety, or exaggeration. Nevertheless, I am acquainted with all the important details of her past and present life.

Besides the reticence in matters pertaining to herself, already mentioned, she is possessed of a conscientiousness which at times has proved embarrassing to her friends. It, too, is carried sometimes to a degree that may be characterized as morbid. For instance, while in college she was the recipient of a scholarship; consequently she considered it her duty, in return for this benefit, so diligently to apply herself to her studies that it was impossible for teacher or physician to enforce sufficient recreation, or even the rest and hygienic measures which were absolutely necessary to keep what little health she had.

Equally embarrassing from a therapeutic point of view is a morbid pride which makes her unwilling to be the recipient of favors or attention which she may not be able to repay. The other selves are not always so sensitive in this respect, and bitterly has Miss Beauchamp sometimes suffered when she has come to herself to find that she has, as one of her other selves, accepted obligations distasteful to her own pride.

A love of truth which is equally marked in her makeup, and which has been in constant conflict with the endeavor to conceal her mental troubles, has led to much mental perturbation. To be frank and open, and yet not to "give away" the fact that she has not the remotest idea, at moments when she comes to herself, of how she happens to be in a given situation, or what her interrogator is talking about, or even who he is, taxes her innate sense of truth, though it has developed a capacity for intellectual gymnastics and quick inference which is instructive. Her power in any one of the three characters of taking in a new situation, of jumping at correct inferences of what has gone before, of following leads without betraying her own ignorance, of formulating a reply which allows of an interpretation compatible with almost any set of conditions,—her ingenuity in these directions is surprising; and by showing what can be done by shrewd leads, guesses and deftly worded responses, gives one an inkling as to the possible origin of much of the supposed supernormal knowledge of mediums. In the case of Miss Beauchamp this is, of course, compulsory from the necessity of adapting her divided personality to the demands of social life.

If Miss Beauchamp's eye should peruse this paper, perhaps she will overlook the personality of the statement that her refinement of character is out of the ordinary. I do not mean by this only the kind of refinement which comes from social education, but rather, that natural refinement of thought and feeling which is inborn, and which is largely made up of delicacy of sentiment and appreciation of everything that is fine in thought and perceptions. This refinement is not easy to analyze, though readily recognized, and would not be mentioned here, were it not the basis of other peculiarities of her character which are of practical moment. It is largely the sponsor for her conscientiousness and honesty, her power of attracting friends, and, unfortunately, probably in part for her neurasthenic condition. It has also been the cause of no end of trouble in the prosecution of this study, for it has led to her unwillingness to ''inflict,'' as she calls it, her personal affairs on others, and to her reticence about her mental life. One could often wish she were less sensitive, and had a little of that mental and moral callousness which does not shrink from opening the mind to psychological analysis.

In ending this brief account of Miss Beauchamp's character, I would add, she is well educated and has marked literary tastes and faculties. She is essentially a bibliophile, and is never so happy as when allowed to delve amongst books, to live with them and know them.

The little that is known of her heredity from a neuro-pathic point of view is suggestive of nervous instability. Her grandfather on her father's side is said to have been a man of violent temper, and it would seem without balanced self-control. Her father apparently inherited the violent temper of her grandfather. He and her mother were unhappily married.

The subject of this study was a nervous, impressionable child, given to day-dreaming and living in her imagination. Her mother exhibited a great dislike to her, and for no reason, apparently, excepting that the child resembled her father in looks. The general impression left on Miss Beauchamp's mind to-day is that of her presence having been ignored by her mother excepting on occasions of a reprimand. On the other hand, she herself idealized her mother, bestowing upon her almost morbid affection; and believing that the fault was her own, and that her mother's lack of affection was due to her own imperfections, she gave herself up to introspection, and concluded that if she could only purify herself and make herself worthy, her mother's affection would be given her. The effect of all this upon the child was to suppress all disclosures of her own mental life, and to make her morbidly reticent. She never gave expression to the ordinary feelings of everyday child life; never spoke to say that she was tired, hungry, or sleepy. She lived within herself and dreamed.

When she was thirteen her mother died. This was a great shock to her mental system, and for a number of weeks she was probably half delirious, or, as we would now interpret it, disintegrated. The three years following her mother's death, when she lived with her father, were a period of successive mental shocks, nervous strains and frights. The details of this unhappy period, although of great importance from a psychopathic point of view, unfortunately cannot be given, as, being well known to neighbors and friends, they would lead to the identification of the subject. It is unlikely that even a strong constitution would withstand the continuous nervous strain and depressing emotional influences to which her whole childhood was subjected. At sixteen she ran away from home, and thus ended this hystero-genetic period. At a later period anxieties of another kind succeeded those of her youth.

517

In Miss Beauchamp's heredity and childhood, then, we find ample to account for the psychopathic soil which has permitted her present condition. She was never strong, as a child, became easily tired, and suffered from headaches and nightmares. Attacks of somnambulism also occurred. On one occasion when about fourteen years of age she walked out into the street at night in her nightgown and was brought home by a policeman. For years she was in the habit, from time to time, of going into spontaneous trance-like states, lasting a few minutes, and at the time when she first came under observation she was subject to these spells (as was subsequently learned), although they were not nearly so frequent or prolonged as formerly. For instance, one day, an attack came on while she was crossing the Public Garden. At the moment she was headed for Park Square. When she came to herself she was walking in an opposite direction, in a different part of the Garden.

As a child, then, the subject of our study was morbidly impressionable, given to day-dreaming and unduly under the influence of her emotions. She took everything intensely, lived in a land of idealism, and saw the people and the world about her not as they were but as they were colored by her imagination. That is to say, she saw people through her own ideas, which dominated her judgment, and which tended to be insistent. Even as a child she appeared to have hallucinations, or at any rate so mixed up her daydreams and imaginings with reality that she did not have a true conception of her environment.

Such a person, under the unhappy circumstances of her girlhood, surely never had half a chance. Her very differences from the conventional person stamped her an "original," and attracted other people to her. Intellectually she was keen, fond of books and study. The knowledge that she thus acquired being colored by the wealth of her imagination gave an attraction to her personality.

About 1893 she had a nervous shock which, unfortunately, only came to my knowledge long after I became acquainted with the fact of there being a division of personalities; unfortunately, for it played the principal role in the development of these phenomena. It will be described in its proper place.

When Miss Beauchamp first came under my professional care, in 1898, she was, as has been said, a student in one of our New England colleges; she was twenty-three years of age and a "neurasthenic" of an extreme type. The most salient features of her physical condition were headaches, insomnia, bodily pains, persistent fatigue, and poor nutrition. All this unfitted her for any work, mental or physical, and even for the amount of exercise that ordinary rules of hygiene required; but in spite of her disability nothing could dissuade her from diligent and, in fact, excessive study which she thought it her duty to persist in. My notes taken at this time, before it was known that there was any division of personalities, thus describe her general condition:

"Is a pronounced neurasthenic of extreme type; has never been able to pursue steadily any occupation in consequence. Tried three times to do professional nursing and broke down. Is now studying at - — College; ambitious; good student; does good work, but always ill; always suffering. Over-conscientious and mentally and morally stubborn. Is very nervous, and different parts of body in constant motion. General appearance of an hysteric; cannot sit still, cannot fix her eyes to properly test field of vision; probably slight visual limitation, but this is difficult to determine. *No objective anaesthesia,* or other physical stigmata."

At this time Miss Beauchamp was very suggestible and plainly manifested aboulia, although this was mistaken by her friends and at first by myself, to speak plainly, for stubbornness (which was one of her traits), or at least an unwillingness to be guided by the advice of friends when this conflicted with her prejudices. By *aboulia* is meant an inhibition of will by which a person is unable to do what he actually wishes to do.[1] There was also a decided limitation of the field of consciousness, in the sense that her mind at certain moments was strongly absorbed in and dominated by certain particular ideas. She was unable to correct her judgments by constant reference to and comparison with collateral facts, which is always necessary for wise conduct. In other words, she tended to be lost in abstraction. These are recognized psychical stigmata of hysteria. . . .[2]

THE BIRTH OF SALLY

IN April, 1898, inasmuch as Miss Beauchamp had failed to be improved by the conventional methods of treatment, and as it was impossible for her to pursue any vocation in the condition of health in which she was at the time, it was decided to try hypnotic suggestion. I have no intention of going into this aspect of the case, but I transcribe a few of the notes made at the time, as they show the extreme suggestibility of the subject, and make clear the beneficial effects which were obtained by this mode of treatment. By suggestion it was found possible to convert a condition of constant physical distress into one of at least temporary comfort. If this means proved ineffectual to remove the existing instability of the nervous system, which constantly allowed painful reactions to the environment, it was partly because of a primary faulty organization, but more particularly because of the condition of psychological disintegration which had al-

---

[1] In typical and extreme cases, for instance, a person with aboulia may find it impossible to pick up something from the table, or to rise from the chair, though strongly desiring to do so. In Miss Beauchamp's case I have often known her to come to my office for the express purpose of telling something important, but after struggling a few minutes with attempts to speak, to utter the words necessary, and finding herself unable, she would give it up and leave without accomplishing or even explaining her errand.

[2] Deleted is a long section discussing the multiple personalities which later developed.—*Editor*.

ready taken place, but which was unsuspected. There was no reason to suppose that the first Miss Beauchamp was psychologically other than she appeared to be, a whole person, so to speak. It was only after a prolonged study, which justified itself scientifically, that the secret leaked out. It then became clear that a permanent cure could come about only as a result of a synthesis of the disintegrated elements of personality. Yet it was something to banish pain whenever it arose.

Miss Beauchamp was hypnotized for the first time April 5th. She went at once into deep hypnosis, followed by amnesia (total loss of memory) for the period when she was in hypnosis. This was repeated on the 6th, 7th, and 8th, appropriate suggestions being given each time, and was always followed by immediate relief. From notebook:

April 8th. "Reports slept soundly all night without waking; ravenously hungry at meals; has felt well; little or no fatigue; pain returned in the side, *while in church,* and lasted for an hour; it was very severe, but suddenly ceased; no pain in the morning on awaking, but has now some headache and backache. Her friends comment on her great improvement in health, and she herself is astonished. In hypnosis patient said that pain in side was caused by sermon, which made her think how wicked she was (etc.). No pain from walking."

April 9th. "Reports herself remarkably well; has walked about all day—out and about since 9 A. M.; no pain in side, no headache or backache; slept well; quiet; thinks she is not nervous; feels like a different person; remarks that she 'can't understand it,' etc., etc.; eats well. Patient appears like a different person: that is, is much better."

April 25th. "General improvement since April 9th. Is becoming stronger; occasional pain in side, but not nearly so severe, occasionally brought on by walking, sometimes by being bothered; feels stronger and better than for years; has been walking about two miles a day, formerly not more than two or three blocks; can walk a mile at a stretch without feeling more than reasonably tired; no headache to speak of up to yesterday."

It has always been easy to remove from time to time the varying bodily discomforts as they appeared, although this improvement was not lasting. These somatic symptoms have a psychological interest in this case, for it has been easy to demonstrate that they are not based on underlying structural changes, but are by-products, so to speak, of emotional states, or fatigue, and in part "association phenomena," which are dragged into the field of consciousness by the psychical states to which they are attached.

Particular emotional states, like fear or anxiety, or general mental distress, have the tendency to disintegrate the mental organization in such a way that the normal associations become severed or loosened. Thus it happens that a mental shock like that of an accident, or an alarming piece of news, produces a dissociation of the mind, known as a state of hysteria, or "traumatic neurosis." Such states are characterized by persisting loss of sensation, paralysis, amnesia, and other so-called stigmata, which are now recognized to be manifestations of the dissociation of sensory, motor, and other images from the main stream of consciousness. A doubling of consciousness is thus brought about. The dissociated images may still be capable of functioning, more or less independently of the waking consciousness; and when they do, so-called automatic phenomena (hallucinations, tics, spasms, contractures, etc.) result. Sometimes the mental dissociation produces a complete loss of memory (amnesia) for long periods of the subject's life; when this is the case we have the fundamental basis for alternating personalities, of which this study will offer many examples. In other instances, the distintegration induced by the emotion results less in sharply defined somatic disturbances than in a general loosening of the mental and nervous organization. A general neurasthenic condition then results, revealed by all sorts of perverted reactions to the environment in the form of pains, fatigue, vasomotor disturbances, etc. Finally, when the neurasthenic

522

systems have been repeatedly awakened by an emotion, they form a habit, or what I have termed an "association neurosis."[1] It then comes about that (in subjects of nervous instability) when, through the vicissitudes of life, distressing emotions are awakened, the somatic symptoms, as a kind of tail to a mental kite, are brought into the field of consciousness. Fatigue and mental strain have the same genetic influence as emotion.

The whole history of the Beauchamp "family" has been like that of a person who has been exposed to an almost daily series of railroad accidents or nervous shocks. Owing primarily to a natural, and secondarily to a still greater acquired, instability of nervous organization, the contretemps of ordinary life have acted like a series of mild shocks, resulting in little traumatic neuroses.[2] The immediate effects have been removed from time to time by suggestion; but the original fundamental instability, magnified a hundred-fold by the psychological disintegration which was brought about by a mental accident of recent date, has made possible a frequent repetition of such shocks. Most instructive is the fact that with the complete synthesis of all the personalities into one, with the reintegration of the shattered mental organization, stability becomes reestablished and the physical health becomes normal.

Miss Beauchamp has already been described as a very reserved person. She never drops into familiarity of speech, nor does she invite it. Her personality is one that cannot be provoked into rudeness; rather her tendency is to bear in silence what others might resent. If any one has done ill to her she bears it in resignation, without idea of retaliation by word or deed. Personal dignity, a predominant characteristic, never lets her descend into the vulgarisms which ordinary, though refined, people

---

[1] Association Neuroses; Journ. of Nervous and Mental Disease, May, 1891
[2] Disturbances of the nervous system caused by accidents.

may be pardoned for falling into under the stress of petty annoyances. This I mention here, that the differing characteristics of the separate personalities, as the latter are developed, may be appreciated. With me and with those who know her trouble, she has a depressed, rather weary, expression and manner. Her voice, too, is strongly indicative of this frame of mind; but I am told that with strangers who know nothing of her infirmity she is more buoyant and light-hearted.

It is not easy to describe satisfactorily this Miss Beauchamp in hypnosis; at least in such a way as to give one who is not familiar with hypnosis an intelligible understanding of her in this state. In essential characteristics she is not very different from herself awake, except as any one in hypnosis differs from the waking self. If I said that she is herself intensified, but without the artificial reserve with which she ordinarily surrounds herself as a protection to her life, it would give the best idea of her. In manner, her air of sadness and weariness is accentuated, and her tastes and desires are the same; but she does not hesitate to give freely information which it is essential for her well-being should be known, and to ask for aid that will protect her even from herself. In the waking state, as Miss Beauchamp, she desires to give the same information and she often longs to make the same request, but is as often held back by that intense shrinking from talking about herself which has already been mentioned. So prohibitive has been this reserve that it has been difficult to obtain from her while awake, as B I, a reasonable amount of information regarding her infirmity. This amounts at times to an actual aboulia. I doubt if the hypnotic self could be made to do what she in her waking state would morally object to. Perhaps it is not too far-fetched to say, metaphorically, that the hypnotic self is the soul of Miss Beauchamp freed from the artificial restraints of conventionality.

The hypnotic self, then, let it be borne in mind, is distinctly the same personality as Miss Beauchamp awake. She speaks of herself as the same person, making no distinction whatsoever, except that she is now "asleep," or what "you call asleep." On the other hand, when awake, as already stated in the introduction, she has no knowledge or remembrance of herself in the hypnotic state. On awaking there is complete oblivion of everything said and done in hypnosis. There is also a large degree of passiveness in the hypnotic self. She sits with her eyes closed (never having been allowed to open them), and though she converses, and even sometimes argues and defends her own views, she tends to passiveness, like most subjects in hypnosis.

Up to this time the only personality with which I was acquainted, and the only one known to her friends, was the Miss Beauchamp whom I have just described as B I. But there now appeared upon the scene a new character, who was destined to play the leading role in the family drama that was enacted during a period of six years. This character at first appeared to be a second hypnotic state, but later proved a veritable personality, with an individuality that was fascinatingly interesting to watch; she largely determined the dramatic situations, and consequently the health, happiness, and fortunes of Miss Beauchamp. She became known successively as B III, Chris, and finally as Sally, according as acquaintance with her grew. The way this character first made herself known I shall let a resume of my notes, which were made at the time, tell.

One day in April, 1898, while in hypnosis, Miss Beauchamp surprised me by denying having made certain statements which she made during the previous state of hypnosis, and then again later when hypnotized, admitting freely, without reserve, what she had previously denied. She thus alternately denied and admitted the

525

same facts. The statements themselves were not matters of importance, but the denials of her own plain statements were puzzling. Being on my guard, my first suspicion of course was of an attempt at deception, but on a repetition of this experience her honesty became plainly beyond question. The solution was not long in coming. On one of the following occasions I was startled to hear her, when hypnotized, speak of herself in her waking state as "She." Previously, as already stated, she had always used the first person, "I," indifferently for herself, whether awake or asleep in hypnosis. She had never made any distinction whatever as to personalities, or suggested any difference between herself while awake and while in hypnosis; nor had I made any such suggestions, or even thought of the matter. I had regarded the hypnotic self simply as Miss Beauchamp asleep. But now the hypnotic self, for the first time, used the pronoun "She," in speaking of her waking self, as if of a third person; but used "I," of herself in hypnosis. The tone, address, and manner were also very different from what they had been. As bearing on the question of the possible unconscious education of the subject on the part of the experimenter, I may say here that my experience of this case entirely contradicted the view that I had held up to this time. My conviction had been growing that so-called personalities, *when developed through hypnotism,* as distinct from the spontaneous variety, were purely artificial creations,— sort of unspoken and unconscious mutual understandings between the experimenter and the subject, by which the subject accepted certain ideas unwittingly suggested by the experimenter. But in opposition to this view the personality known as B III, or Chris, which first made its appearance during hypnosis, came as a surprise to me; and so far from being the product of suggestion, originated and persisted against my protests and in spite of my scepticism. In view, therefore, of my own lack of preparedness, this complete change of attitude of the hypnotic self is noteworthy. I hastened to follow up the lead offered and asked, as if in ignorance of her meaning, who "She" was. The hypnotic self was unable to give a satisfactory reply.

"You are 'She,' " I said.

"No, I am not."

"I say you are."

Again a denial.

Feeling at the time that this distinction was artificial, and that the hypnotic self was making it for a purpose, I made up my mind that such an artifact should not be allowed to develop. I pursued her relentlessly in my numerous examinations, treated the idea as nonsense, and refused to accept it, but with what success will be noted.

Finally:

"Why are you not 'She'?"

"Because 'She' does not know the same things that I do."

"But you both have the same arms and legs, haven't you?"

"Yes, but arms and legs do not make us the same."

"Well, if you are different persons, what are your names?"

Here she was puzzled, for she evidently saw that, according to her notion, if the hypnotic self that was talking with me was Miss Beauchamp, the waking self was not Miss Beauchamp, and *vice versa.* She appeared to be between the horns of a dilemma, was evasive, unable to answer, and made every effort not to commit herself. On another occasion, in answer to the question why she (the *apparently* hypnotic state) insisted that Miss Beauchamp in her waking state was a different person from herself at that moment, the contemptuous reply was: "Because she is stupid; she goes round mooning, half asleep, with her head buried in a book; she does not know half the time what she is about. She does not know how to take care of herself." The contemptuous tone in which she spoke of Miss Beauchamp (awake) was striking, and her whole manner was very different from what it formerly had been when hypnotized. The weary, resigned, attitude was gone; she was bold, self-assertive, unwilling to accept suggestions, and anything but passive. A few days after this, when hypnotized, all became changed again; the former hypnotic manner returned.

"Who are you?" I asked.

"I am Miss Beauchamp."

Then, after a number of questions on another point:

"Listen: now you say you are Miss Beauchamp."

"Yes."

"Then why did you say you were not Miss Beauchamp?"

[Surprised.] "Why, I never said so."

"The last time we talked you said you were not Miss Beauchamp."

"You are mistaken. I did not. I said nothing of the sort."

"Yes, you did."

"No."

. . . .

"Well, you know who you are?"

"Yes, Miss Beauchamp."

"Exactly. You have got over that idea of being different from other persons,—that there is a 'She'?"

[Surprised and puzzled.] "What 'she'? I do not know what you mean."

"Yes, you do."

"No, unless you mean Rider Haggard's 'She'."

"You used to tell me that you were not Miss Beauchamp."

"I did not."

"That, when you were awake you were a different person."

528

[Remonstrating and astounded.] "Dr. Prince, I did not say so."

"What did you say?"

"I did not say anything. I told you about my back and shoulders." [Referring to an experiment tried to produce a blister by a suggestion given to the hypnotic self.]

Repeated experiences of this kind made it plain that Miss Beauchamp when hypnotized fell into one or the other of two distinct mental states, or selves, whose relations to the primary waking consciousness, as well as their memories, were strikingly different. From the very first they claimed different relations with the waking Miss Beauchamp. The first hypnotic self either definitely stated she was Miss Beauchamp asleep, or accepted that idea, as a technical expression, without objection; though she apparently recognized the paradox conveyed in the idea of a sleeping person talking. Still she regarded herself most distinctly as Miss Beauchamp, though not awake. For the sake of convenience at this early stage, to distinguish the different selves, this hypnotic self was noted as B II, in distinction from the waking Miss Beauchamp, who was now labelled for the first time B I. In contrast with this attitude of B II, the second hypnotic self, who was correspondingly named B III, refused from the very first to accept the idea of being asleep or being Miss Beauchamp asleep. She insisted she was wide awake, and resented in a way foreign to either B I or B II every attempt on my part to make her appear illogical in claiming to be a different person.

It may be well to repeat that B I's name was Christine. Desiring to have some distinctive term of address for B III, I gave her the name of *Chris*. Later, of her own volition, she adopted the name *Sally Beauchamp*, taking it, I think, from a character in some book.

The following notes of the interview of April 30 make evident the distinction between the hypnotic states.

529

April 30. "Patient has not been here since April 25th, when Miss Beauchamp had apparently lost her second personality; that is to say, she did not know in hypnosis who 'She' was, and denied all knowledge as claimed by B III of any other person than herself, and had no recollection of her previous statement as B III. It appeared as if the second phase of hypnosis had disappeared. To-day patient returned, stating that she has been unable to come before because of illness; has had a return of old symptoms, etc. *Remarks that she has been unable to read or fix her mind on a book.* To-day is much better. Thinks the cause of her relapse was catching cold, and possibly the effect of the sermon the previous Sunday. [This sermon had been the subject of considerable discussion between B II and myself at the previous visit.] Miss Beauchamp is now hypnotized and becomes, as at the last sitting, B II, the first hypnotic self. She makes the same statement as to the cause of her relapse as did B I. In response to inquiries she goes on to state that her name is 'Miss Beauchamp.' [Her manner at this early stage used to indicate great surprise that I should ask her name, as if both of us did not know.] She does not know anything about any other person, and expresses some annoyance at being told that she[1] has stated that there is another. (This talk about a 'she' evidently troubles her, as it did at the last interview, and is something she cannot understand. I take pains not to explain anything, only asking her such questions as will test her memory, leaving her in the dark as to the meaning of the questions and the existence of the other hypnotic self.) [Both B I and B II were kept in ignorance of B III for a long time.]

"Patient now, without being first waked up, is more deeply hypnotized by command. She goes into an apparently deeper trance. At once her whole manner changes. She begins to stutter, and again speaks of herself as being a different person from Miss Beauchamp, whom as before she refers to as 'She' and 'Her.' Explains that the cause of her illness was partly the effect of the sermon (referred to by B I), and partly due to the fact that 'the person in black' (my secretary, who was taking stenographic notes) was in the room, and partly to the fact that I had bothered 'Her' (i. e., B II) at the previous sitting by troubling 'Her' with all sorts of questions which 'She' did not understand.[2] B II, she asserts, does not know anything of the present person talking, and when I kept asking 'Her' questions concerning things 'She' did not

---

[1] That is, in testing her memory for what has been said by B III.

[2] That is, as if B II and B III were one and the same person.

know anything about, it upset 'Her' very much. It also troubled 'Her' (i. e., B I) having in the room some one to whom 'She' was afraid 'She' would expose 'Her' thoughts, having been told by me that 'She' talked in hypnosis. All these things conspired to upset 'Her;' hence 'Her' illness of the past week."

It should be noticed that in this explanation the third self *also* did not make any distinction between Miss Beauchamp and B II; but spoke of Miss Beauchamp as being upset by my questions, although the disturbing questions had been put to Miss Beauchamp in hypnosis. Yet, again, it was when awake that she dreaded being hypnotized with a stranger in the room. More important is the fact that B III showed a complete knowledge of all that was said to B II,—in fact, knew all about B II. She showed an intimate knowledge of the conversation in which B II was accused by me of having made the claim that she was a distinct person from ''She,'' and she professed at least a knowledge of her inmost thoughts and feelings. And so it was at every interview.

As a test of the memories of B II and B III, I was in the habit at each interview of asking each to repeat certain parts of a previous conversation, and to describe what had occurred during the earlier part of the interview, or during the previous interview, including insignificant details of my actions, etc. Miss Beauchamp never had any memory of what happened while she was Chris, any more than while she was B II. That was plain enough. Miss Beauchamp knew nothing of the other two. The hypnotic self, B II, on the other hand, remembered everything that she, B II, said during the preceding times when she had been in existence, and also everything about Miss Beauchamp's life. She would give at each visit an accurate account of everything that happened when Miss Beauchamp was awake, whether in my presence or at her own home. She would repeat my conversation with Miss Beauchamp, what I did when Miss Beauchamp was in

531

the room, and so on, *ad infinitum*. She was plainly the "hypnotic self." But she was in entire ignorance of the new self, Chris (B III). She always denied any knowledge of what she had said in this new state, nor could I ever trip her up, though I set many traps. For instance, at the close of the last interview, just referred to, the new hypnotic self, Chris, volunteered to give some information on a matter connected with Miss Beauchamp's affairs, but did not complete it. This was the last thing that she said before Miss Beauchamp was awakened. At the next interview I questioned B II as to what it was she was going to tell me, as if it were she and not the new self, Chris, with whom I had been talking.

"Do you remember the last thing you said yesterday? You were going to tell me something."

"Going to tell you something? No, I was not."

"Yes, you were."

"No, I am sure. I do not remember anything."

Later in the course of this same interview Chris was obtained. The same questions were put to her.

"Yesterday you were going to tell me something. What was it?"

Chris at once showed complete knowledge of the conversation and continued what she had begun at the interview in question. Thus it was shown that B II could give verbatim my conversation with herself and with B I, but nothing of that with B III. But B III could repeat that with all three selves; and so it was correspondingly with what was done at those times. So B III knew both B I and B II, although B I and B II knew nothing of B III.

This relationship may be expressed by the following diagram, the arrow indicating the direction of knowledge:

Chris, B III — B I (a personality)

(a personality) — B II (later known as B Ia, a hypnotic state)

Of course Chris's memory was continuous for the times of her own previous existence; that is, for the times when, Miss Beauchamp having been put to sleep, Chris was present as an alternating personality. As to her knowledge of Miss Beauchamp, besides her familiarity with outward circumstances, she could describe the latter's inmost thoughts and feelings, her moods and her emotions, as afterwards was verified over and over again. The marked individuality of Chris's character, her insistence upon herself being a separate personality, the wideness of her knowledge, and various other even more important peculiarities which later became known made her an interesting study. Although she first disclosed her existence through the hypnotizing process, she proved to be no ordinary hypnotic self, but a veritable personality which also exhibited itself at times as an organized *subconsciousness*.

One of the most interesting features when the change to Chris took place was the sudden alteration of character, which was almost dramatic. It was amazing to see the sad, anxious, passive B II suddenly become transformed into a new personality, stuttering abominably, and exhibiting a lively vivacity, boldness, and saucy deviltry, difficult to describe.

No longer sad, but gay and reckless, she resented any attempt to control her. For example: therapeutic suggestions given to B II were accepted with docility, but when they were tried on this new hypnotic self they were met at once by opposition. "You th-th-think you c-c-c-can c-c-control me," she stuttered, "b-b-because you c-c-control 'her.' You c-c-can't d-d-do it. I shall d-d-do as I p-p-please," etc., etc.[1]

---

[1] Chris, when she first appeared on the scene, stuttered badly. Later this difficulty disappeared, but in the early days of her career it was obtrusive. Sometimes she would remain silent on account of it, especially at the first moment of her appearance. She also used to keep her arms and hands in motion in a nervous way. It was as if she had not yet learned to co-ordinate her newly acquired muscles, and had general ataxia in consequence. This too disappeared later.

Finding that this tack would not work, another was tried.

"I want your co-operation to help me get Miss Beauchamp well. Will you help me?"

"Now that is a different kind of talk," she replied, mollified, though still stuttering.

Rebelliousness and above all sauciness like this was something entirely foreign to Miss Beauchamp's character. It was clear that there were three different selves, or at least three different mental states.

Some idea of the memories and characteristics of the different selves may be had from the following extract from the notes of the next interview, May 1. It was not easy to exactly transcribe the language, and above all to represent the tone and mannerism of each. It was found that the presence of a stranger in the room was so disturbing to Miss Beauchamp, who naturally feared lest she should betray her private affairs, that it was necessary to give up the plan of taking stenographic notes. The difficulty of taking down verbatim, in longhand, a rapidly held conversation necessarily obliged a condensation of sentences, so that the style is not fairly represented in these notes, but the accuracy of the facts as brought out may be insisted upon. On May 1, the ground of April 30th was gone over again as follows:

After hearing the report from Miss Beauchamp and questioning her on various matters, she was hypnotized, becoming plainly B II.

Q. "How has Miss Beauchamp been doing?"

A. [Changing the question to the first person.] "How have I been doing? I have been doing very well?"

Q. "How has 'she' been doing?"

A. " 'She'? Who?"

Q. "Don't you know who 'she' is?"

A. "You did not say."

Q. "Don't you know?"

A. "Do you mean Miss K.? No, I do not know whom you mean."

B II kept rubbing her eyes. She would not recognize the existence of any other personality than herself, nor could I get her to betray any knowledge of having, as Chris, referred to a "she."

Q. "Have you been going to sleep this past week during the daytime?" [Referring to spontaneous trances that had occurred.]

A. "No."

Q. "Are you sure?"

A. "Yes."

Q. "Have you been reading?"

A. "No."

Q. "Why?"

A. "I can't."

Q. "Why can't you? Have you been trying?"

A. "Yes."

Q. "What prevents you?"

A. "Nothing."

Q. "Do you mean you can't fix your mind?" [As already stated by her when awake as Miss Beauchamp at the interview of the previous day: . . .]

A. "Yes, that is what I mean. I can't read—can't fix my mind at all."

Q. "What happens?"

A. "I begin thinking of all sorts of things the minute I try to read. Sometimes I throw the book down on a chair or table. I throw it down hard and closed after trying to read." [Illustrates at my request.]

Q. "Have you ever been so before this past week?"

A. "No, never."

When pressed for an explanation of her unusual action her answer was characteristic of subjects exhibiting phenomena which they cannot explain: "People do not always have a reason for everything they do." This apparently simple action had more significance than would appear on the surface. Though not open to absolute proof, it is morally certain that it was an example of a suggested post-hypnotic phenomenon and the prelude to many similar exhibitions which I actually observed. For the benefit of the uninitiated it may be explained that in suitable subjects if a suggestion is given in hypnosis that a certain action be performed later after waking, the subject will, at the appointed time, carry out the suggested idea; or perhaps more correctly, the suggested idea will complete itself without the subject knowing why he does the action, which sometimes is performed in an absentminded way without his even knowing he has done it. Sometimes the subject enters a semi-hypnotic state at the moment of carrying out the command.

When Miss Beauchamp, as she and B II reported, found herself unable to read and threw down the book, she carried out a command that I had given for therapeutic purposes to Chris, unknown to the other selves. I had told Chris, rather carelessly, that she was to prevent Miss B. from reading, without suggesting how the thing was to be accomplished. Chris, who later explained the phenomenon at length, claimed to have been the author of this automatic action on Miss B.'s part, and to have taken this drastic method of carrying out my suggestion, thereby showing considerable subconscious independence, and, I think, logical reasoning. It is worth noting how sharply differentiated were the volitions of the two personalities at this early date. Later, I personally witnessed similar phenomena on numerous occasions. It may be here stated that though often, for the purposes of a continuous narrative, phenomena are noted as having occurred, on the strength of the statements of the subject, these, when important, were accepted only after searching inquiry; and secondly, examples of every phenomenon described have been *personally witnessed,* at one time or another, over

536

and over again.

To resume: B II [hearing the scratching of my pencil taking notes]. "What are you doing?"

Q. "What do you think?"

A. "You are scratching something, so—" [Illustrating.] "What is it?"

Q. "Don't you know what I am doing?"

A. "No, I·don't know."

Q. "Are you awake or asleep?"

A. [Evidently puzzled.] "I can hear what you say and I can talk, but I can't see you." [Her eyes are closed.]

Q. "What do you infer from this?"

A. [Evidently puzzled—does not know what to answer.] "I never saw such a person as you are for asking questions."

Q. "Are you awake or asleep?"

A. [Still puzzled, but finally apparently catching the suggestion.] "Asleep, I suppose; yes, asleep."

Q. "What is the difference between you now and when you are not here?"

A. "I am asleep now."

Q. "Are you the same person?"

A. [Emphatically.] "Of course I am the same person." [This answer should be compared with the answer of Chris later given.]

Q. "Do you know everything that happens to you when you are awake?"

A. "Yes, everything."

Q. "When awake do you know everything that happens when you are asleep?"

A. "No, nothing, and I do not think it quite fair."

Q. "Why?"

A. "Because I like to know things. It is just that— [with a finger makes a sign imitating my method of hypnotizing] and I go to sleep."

Q. "Do you feel that you are exactly the same person?"

A. "Of course. Why should I feel differently?"

It is interesting to compare the general straightforward, direct tone of these answers with those of Chris, now to be given. The change is easily recognized.

B II is now more deeply hypnotized,—to use a common but incorrect expression,[1]—and Chris appears, as shown by the usual change of manner.

Q. "Why do you let your arms move so?" [Patient is fidgeting and moving her hands and arms. Shakes her head as a negative response, and keeps her lips tightly closed.]

Q. "Why don't you speak?"

A. "I d-d-d-don't want t-t-to."

Question repeated.

A. "I d-d-d-d-don't know."

I ask her another question. She replies by shaking her head in the negative, as if unable to answer.

Q. "Why do you stutter?"

A. [Annoyed.] "I d-d-d-d-don't st-st-st-stutter. If I ch-ch-choose t-t-to st-st-stutter I shall."

Q. "Why have you suddenly changed?"

A. "I have not ch-ch-changed at all."

Q. "You were not stuttering a minute ago."

A. "I was n-n-not t-t-t-talking a m-m-m-minute ago; 'She' was."

Q. "Who is 'she'?"

A. [Showing irritation and annoyance.] "I won't g-g-g-go through that n-n-nonsense again. I t-t-told you t-t-ten d-d-days ago. If you d-d-don't know any better now I sha'n't t-t-tell you."

[These answers were given with a good deal of resentment.]

Q. "What is your name?"

A. "I sha'n't t-t-tell you."

---

[1] The correct way of describing the process would be, B II was by a device changed to Chris.

Q. "Can't you for politeness?"

A. "I d-d-don't ch-ch-choose t-to be p-p-polite. I have t-t-told you many t-t-times."

Q. "Why do you stutter?"

A. "I d-d-don't stutter—only something wrong with my t-t-tongue."

Q. "Did you ever stutter in your life?"

A. "No, and *She* did not either."

[It will be noticed how quick B III was to make the distinction between herself and "she" at this time. I here tried to catch her by the use of the word "you," but failed.]

Q. "Tell me once more your name."

A. [After some hesitation and thought.] "Chris L." [Her real name, we will say, is Christine L. Brown.]

Q. "What more?"

A. "Th-that is all. You had b-b-better make a note of it and remember it."

Q. "What does L. stand for?"

A. "N-n-not at all n-necessary th-th-that you sh-should know."

Q. "Does it stand for Brown?"[1]

A. [Irritated.] "N-n-no, her name is Brown. I t-told you th-that yesterday."

Q. "Well, I shall call you Miss Brown."

A. "If you ch-choose t-t-to c-c-call me Miss Brown you c-can. I shall have n-nothing t-t-to d-do with you."

Q. "How did you get the name of Chris?"

A. [Objects to answering, dodges the question and evades—then says:] "You th-think you c-can make me t-tell everything b-b-because you c-c-can make her."

I change my tone, upbraiding her for not being frank and then explain that my only object is to test her memory; I add that I know how she got it, and she knows that

---

[1] That is, I mentioned the real name of Miss Beauchamp for which "Brown" is here substituted.

I know, and I know that she knows, so she might as well tell, as it is merely a test of continuity of memory. Subject becomes more placid and says: "You suggested it to me one day, and I remember everything." [That is correct.]

The peculiar character traits manifested by Chris, which distinguished her so unmistakably from Miss Beauchamp, both when awake and when hypnotized as B II, naturally gave rise to the suspicion that Chris might be an artificial product, the result of her own self-suggestion, or simply hypnotic acting. It seemed possible that Miss Beauchamp might as a result of reading have acquired some information about the bizarre behavior of certain types of secondary personalities, and that the ideas thus originated might have developed themselves afterwards in the hypnotic state in such a way as to lead Miss Beauchamp in this state to act out a character after some preconceived theory; or, if not deliberate acting, as the psychological development of auto-suggested ideas. On this theory Miss Beauchamp was closely questioned on her past reading and knowledge of psychological phenomena. Nothing was elicited, however, that in any way supported this theory. I never discovered that she had any knowledge of the literature of abnormal psychology, or knew anything about modern researches in this field of inquiry, including hypnotism, multiple personality, etc. Thinking possibly that she had read something which might have been forgotten in the waking state, B II was similarly catechised, and finally Chris was put through the same cross-examination. But in no state was there any memory of Miss Beauchamp's having read any book or acquired any information which could have worked itself out as suspected. The final developments of the case, as will appear, completely negatived such a hypothesis.

540

MORTON PRINCE (b.-Boston, Mass., Dec. 21, 1854; d.-Aug. 31, 1929).

Prince graduated Harvard in 1875, and received his M.D. from the Harvard Medical College in 1879. He studied further at Strassbourg, Paris, Nancy, and Vienna, with such men as Charcot, Janet, Liébeault, and Bernheim. Over the years 1882-1913 he was a practicing physician in Boston. During 1895-1898 he taught neurology at Harvard; he was appointed Professor at Tufts Medical College in 1902, and became Emeritus in 1912. In 1906 he founded the *Journal of Abnormal Psychology* (later *Journal of Abnormal and Social Psychology*). In 1926 he returned to Harvard for two years, as Associate Professor of Abnormal and Dynamic Psychology.

Prince is included here not so much for the greatness of his own contributions to psychopathology, but because that species of human psychological ailment, to which he devoted most of his professional career, has always intrigued mankind more than any of the other bizarre forms of psychic disorganization. This is the multiple personality, the multiple or conscious, as Prince called it. It is now generally classified under the hysterias.*

Perhaps these cases are so intriguing (or threatening) because of their manifest expression of deeply buried wishes in all civilized men. The suppression of libidinal and aggressive drives, inherent in the acculturization process, leaves with it a residual ache, a need to seek expression in other than the socially acceptable forms,—which are never entirely satisfactory. The very existence of sublimation in itself attests to the continued strength of the well-spring of primitive needs. The multiple personality is the very image of all of us, the Faust story in its truest sense.

The present selection consists in two chapters from Prince's most famous case.

PRINCE, M. *The dissociation of a personality. A biographical study in abnormal personality*. N. Y.: Longmans, Green and Co., 1908 (1905). Part I: "The development of the personalities." Chap. II "Miss Beauchamp", Chap. III "The birth of Sally". Reprinted by permission of the publisher.

---

* EDITOR'S NOTE: "schizophrenia", meaning "split brain", describes a much more severe psychotic state, and is not to be confused, as it often is, with the present neurotic condition.

See also:

PRINCE, M.
  a) *The unconscious; the fundamentals of human personality, normal and abnormal.* N. Y.: Macmillan, 1914.
  b) *Clinical and experimental studies in personality.* Cambridge, Mass.: Sci-Art Pub., 1929. Edited A. A. Roback.

MURRAY, H. A. "Morton Prince." J. *Abnorm. & Soc. Psychol.* 1956, 52:291-295.

CAMPBELL, C. M. et al. (ed.) *Problems of personality.* London: Kegan Paul, 1925. Biblio. of Prince—p. 420-427.

THE EFFECT OF MALARIA ON PROGRESSIVE PARALYSIS

Julius Wagner von Jauregg

Although progressive paralysis was considered not so long ago a disease against which physicians were practically powerless (see for instance the discussion by Kraft-Ebbing in Nothnagel's *Handbook,* 1894, and most of the psychiatric textbooks of that day), there has been a reversal of opinion in the last few years, reports having come in from various sources concerning successful attempts at improving this condition.

Two kinds of treatment are used, the specific and the non-specific.

Specific methods of treatment are based on the fact that progressive paralysis is the result of syphilitic infection, and they therefore use the same means as in other manifestations of syphilis, namely, salvarsan, mercury and iodine in different forms.

The non-specific methods are empiric in origin, based on the observation that cases of progressive paralysis have often been improved by acute attacks of infectious disease, and they attempt to reproduce artificially the elements of these diseases, to which the improvement is ascribed, such as fever or leucocytosis, by the use of tuberculin and other bacterial products, sodium nucleinate, milk injections, etc.

The correct procedure is undoubtedly a combination of specific and non-specific treatment, as I first stated in my report on the tuberculin-mercury treatment.

We do not, however, limit ourselves, in our Vienna clinic, to a single course of tuberculin-mercury injections, but repeat it after six months in favorable cases in order to prevent relapses as much as possible, and also fill in the time between the two courses of treatment with other

543

therapeutic measures, such as single or repeated series of neosalvarsan injections, intravenous staphyloccocus vaccine, and iodine cures.

I distinguish between three groups of non-specific methods: those using material that is not the result of bacterial activity (milk, proteins, sodium nucleinate); those that do result from such activity (tuberculin and different kinds of vaccines); and finally the infectious diseases themselves.

I include the last group for the reason that I observed, in the numerous cases of paralysis that I have treated in the past twelve years, that it happened comparatively often that remissions were especially long-continued and complete when some kind of infectious disease happened to attack the patient during the course of his treatment.

I am also inclined to consider these three non-specific treatment groups of unequal value in their effects, the first being the least intensive in its effects, the second more so, and the last-named, the infectious disease itself, the most valuable. This conviction induced me to try an experiment that I had long ago suggested (*Psychiatrische Jahrbucher*, 1888, volume 7), and bring on, in a patient suffering from such a disease as progressive paralysis, some infection that was quite safe, on account of its own slight danger and because it could be successfully treated.

In July, 1917, I inoculated three paralytics with the blood of a patient with tertian malaria who had already had several typical attacks and in whose blood the presence of tertian plasmodia had been microscopically proved. The inoculation was made by taking blood from a vein in the arm during an attack of fever and spreading it on small scarifications in the arm of the paralytic.

In order to prevent any danger to the environment, I had numerous mosquitoes caught in the gardens around the clinic, and convinced myself that there were no

Anopheles, only Culex, in that neighborhood.

Two of the three patients first inoculated showed a reaction, the third did not.

Blood was again drawn twice from the arm of the same malaria patient, during attacks of fever and 1 cc. of it injected subcutaneously into the back of the paralytic patients. The results were the same as before.

Other paralytics were then inoculated at three different times with blood from the paralytics that had acquired malaria, and one of the former supplied blood for still two more, the plasmodia in this last case having thus passed through three persons. All these later inoculations were successful.

In all these patients tertian plasmodia were microscopically demonstrated in the blood during attacks of fever.

One fact of interest was that the period of incubation was gradually decreased by this passage through several human bodies. The period lasted about 17.5 days in the original cases, infected by mosquitoes; 12.3 days in those whose plasmodia has already passed through two persons; and 9. 5 days in those whose plasmodia had passed through three persons.

It was further observed that most of the patients inoculated had repeated rises in temperature, up to 37.5 and 38, during the incubation period, and that these were of the tertian type, before they had any distinctly malaria attacks with chills, fever and perspiration.

Furthermore, only one of the cases of fever in the paralysis patients remained strictly of the tertian type, the others going over very soon into the quotidian type, one of them remaining permanently altered after the fourth attack, while the others only at times changed back into the tertian.

In all but one case, in which the patient died of a paralytic attack during his malaria, bisulphate of quinine was given in 1 gram doses daily, for three days, after from seven to twelve attacks, then in 0.5 doses daily, for fourteen consecutive days. After that the patients were given at intervals of one week three doses of 0.3, 1.45 and 0.6 grams of neosalvarsan intravenously.

The fever ceased in every case after the first dose of quinine; no malaria relapse has occurred in any of them since then, that is to say, during a whole year.

During the attacks of fever the patients were very low, with anemia and edema of the face and legs. The body weight was peculiarly altered, falling at first, then rising on account of the edema, then falling again at the beginning of convalescence, and finally rising as the physical condition improved, which happened rather quickly under the quinine and salvarsan treatment. In almost all cases the final weight was above the original one. Psychic improvement was much slower, so slow, in fact, that in most cases doubts arose, that later proved to be unfounded, as to whether the treatment would really do any good. In five cases another series of seven injections of polyvalent staphylococcus vaccine were therefore given a few weeks after the salvarsan treatment, at two-day intervals and in doses of 10 to 1,000 bacilli.

Full remission occurred so early and definitely in three of the nine cases that there was no further question of treatment. These patients were discharged as able to take up their regular occupations from two to six months after the beginning of the treatment, and are yet, after about a year, still satisfactorily carrying on.

A fourth patient was also discharged after about four months, but relapsed after a few weeks into paralytic melancholia. This case is also otherwise peculiar, as the history will show.

In two other cases improvement was very slow, but did progress to such an extent that the patients could be discharged after about a year. One, a soldier, could be used as a helper, while the other, a railway employee, was at least able to take care of himself, whether at his old occupation remains to be seen.

In only two cases was there no trace whatever of remission; the patient had to be placed in insane asylums.

I am now adding brief reports on the different cases, as follows.

CASE 1.—T. M., Actor. Previously treated for gastric attacks at the clinic in 1916, with 3.0 neosalvarsan and 0.85 Hg. salic. At the time suspected of paralysis on account of poor memory and epileptiform attacks.

Readmitted to the clinic on May 24, 1917; could no longer go on with his work on account of loss of memory and paralytic attacks. Had lost his sense of direction, and was unable to concentrate his attention. Speech hesitating; pupils unlike, the right larger than the left; the left reacting poorly to light. Patellar and Achilles reflexes lacking. Repeated epileptiform attacks at the clinic.

First attack of malaria on July 6, after inoculation (1) on June 14. The malaria was cut after nine attacks. The epileptiform attacks permanently absent after the sixth malaria attack.

Gradual improvement, up to complete disappearance of all symptoms, during the following months. The patient, who was unable to work on entering the clinic, improved to such an extent that he was able during the period of August to November, to appear often as reciter, and vaudeville singer at the entertainments that were given once a week at the clinic for soldiers with head wounds, using a large repertory that he was able to give most successfully from memory and with complete control.

The Wassermann reaction of the serum was positive both before and after treatment; it was weakly positive for the spinal fluid on November 16th, with 1 cell per cubic millimeter; the Nonne-A. reaction was slightly positive.

The patient was discharged on December 4, 1917.

CASE 2.—B. F., 54 years, postal employee. Behavior altered during the past few weeks; irritable, talked foolishly; had been discharged from his post for stealing food supplies.

On admission, had difficulty in thinking, was pretty low; unaware of being sick; stumbled on syllables; pupils equal, the left one reacting poorly to light; patellar reflexes unaffected; movements awkward. Later on, continued depressed, was aways stealing the other patients' food.

June 14. Malaria inoculation (1). July 2, epileptiform attack. July 3, first attack of fever. The first four were of the tertian type, the rest quotidian. July 16, attempted suicide by hanging, motivated by weakmindedness.

July 22. Death in an epileptiform attack.

Wassermann, reaction of the serum, positive on June 14; weakly positive on July 17.

CASE 3.—D. F. 34 years old, street car conductor, soldier since 1915. Spent some time at the Italian front, and said to have lived through a snowslide there. Returned from the front in 1916 on account of sickness, then served in the rear. His wife noticed in 1917 that his handwriting became illegible. Sent to the clinic on June 11 on account of a supposed traumatic neurosis.

On admission disoriented, confused in his statements, made bad mistakes in calculation. Often escaped from the open ward and went home; his wife found him very stupid; he had therefore to be placed in the closed ward.

Distinct syllable stuttering; pupils unequal, the right larger than the left; they reacted insufficiently to light, particularly the right one. Lively patellar and achilles reflexes. Malaria inoculation (1) on June 26, 1917. After having many high temperatures, up to 38.0 beginning with the third day, he had a first attack of malaria on July 16. He then had nine malaria attacks up to July

548

29, after which came a pause, followed on August 8 and 9 by two slighter ones. Malaria treatment was begun on August 17.

The patient became excited and confused in the incubation period, wanted to dress and go out at night, became hypochondriacal and cried like a child.

Soon after the end of the treatment he became clear and reasonable again, understood his condition, told of the foolishness he had done at home, but remained pessimistic and easily excited, and was quite undependable in mental efforts such as writing or counting.

Improvement was slow but continuous. In October, he could already be permitted to go out walking alone.

A course of treatment with polyvalent staphylococcus vaccine was given in December. His condition continued to improve slowly but regularly; he began to take a lively and intelligent part in all the work of the clinic; his mental activities also began to improve.

He was at last discharged at his own request on July 18, 1918, to unarmed service in his regiment.

Wassermann reaction of the serum positive on June 19, and November 1, 1917. Lumbar puncture on October 29, 1917; Wassermann of the fluid positive, with 13 cells per cubic millimeter, and the Nonne-A. positive, even in triple dilution. Lumbar puncture again on July 15, 1918. Wassermann for the spinal fluid slightly positive, 8 cells per cmm., Nonne-A. positive in quadruple dilution. Wassermann reaction of the serum negative on July 16, 1918.

CASE 4.—A. T., 36 years old, soldier, can speak only Italian. Transferred to the clinic from a military neurological center on June 29, 1917, with the diagnosis of progressive paralysis.

He was completely disoriented and demented on admission; for instance, he was practically unable to give any information about the war or his experiences in it.

549

Distinct syllable stammering; unequal pupils, the left larger than the right, did not react to light; the patellar and achilles reflexes slightly clonic, more so on the right side; Babinsky positive on both sides; slight attacks of Jacksonian epilepsy in the left arm from time to time.

Malaria inoculation (1) on July 2, 1917. Rise in temperature on July 15 and 17; first malarial attack July 19; quinine treatment begun July 28, after seven attacks of malaria.

The patient fell into a demented manic condition, with illusions of greatness and a collecting mania. The speech improved, but a staphylococcus treatment was of no use. He was sent on December 12, 1917, to an insane asylum, where the demented condition with illusions still continued, according to reports, in May 1918.

The Wassermann serum reaction was weakly positive both before and after treatment. The Wassermann for the spinal fluid was positive on December 14, 1917, with 4 cells to the cmm., and the Nonne-Appel reaction was weakly positive in a quintuple dilution. Total albumen, 0.5 v.T.

CASE 5.—A. Sch., sergeant, 29 years old, first admitted to the clinic on July 4, 1915, in a manic stage of progressive paralysis. Very talkative, optimistic, with exaggerated self-importance, making big plans for the future, excitable, importunate, no distinct disturbance of the intelligence, none of speech.

The right pupil larger than the left, the left reacting poorly to light; patellar and Achilles reflexes lively, more so on the right than on the left; Wassermann positive for the blood.

The manic excitement slowly decreased as the result of a course of mercury-tuberculin treatments; the Wassermann of the blood became negative. The patient was sent back to his division on September 15, adapted to light service. As he was then discharged from the army

550

due to the military hospital diagnosis of progressive paralysis he obtained a position with a business concern, holding it until June, 1917, more than a year and a half.

He was sent back to the clinic on July 7, 1917, as he had been behaving conspicuously for two weeks, throwing away money, riding around in carriages, talking much and loud, and getting excitable and rough. He arrived at the clinic dressed in a fantastic uniform, with a Boer cap, lively, self-important, full of big plans. No noticeable disturbance of the intelligence, no speech defects. The right pupil smaller than the left; the left pupil unable to react to light, the right one only at times. The tendon reflexes normal. Wassermann positive for the blood.

Malaria inoculation (passage II., taken from Case 2) on July 9, 1917. Rise in temperature up to 38.2, beginning July 17. First attack of malaria on July 20; 18 attacks up to August 12, the first four tertian, the rest mostly quotidian. Quinine and neosalvarsan from August 15 on.

Wassermann for the blood negative on September 17.

The patient's manic excitement continued; he was perfectly able to reason; stole continually from the other patients. Treatment with staphylococcus vaccine in October.

The manic condition had entirely disappeared in November; complete comprehension of illness; no intelligence defect; both pupils rigid. The patient was discharged on November 20, 1917, and went back to his position with the business firm. Lumbar puncture on October 28, with 4 cells per cmm., and the Nonne-Appel reaction positive in quadruple dilution.

However, remission lasted only a short time in this case. He was brought back again to the clinic on May 15, 1918, in a severe stupor, that is at present disappearing.

CASE 6.—F. B., 39 years old, civil employee, admitted on July 13, 1917. The anamnesis stated that he had been excitable for a long time. At the beginning of July he had a beginning manic attack with delusions of grandeur. The patient talked about million dollar deals he had in hand, made wild purchases and debts, began to write to chorus girls and ladies, had impossible marriage plans, indulged in immoral practices.

At the clinic he was in a manic condition that made it impossible to keep him in the quiet section. His delusions of grandeur became wilder all the time. He made mistakes in writing and counting. Intelligence defects clearly evident; defective attention, but no alterations of speech. Pupils equal, the left reacting slightly to light, the right not at all. Patellar reflexes present and equal; practically no Achilles reflexes obtainable; Wassermann reaction in the blood positive.

July 15, 1917, malaria inoculation (II, from Case I). First malaria attack on July 27, with no fever during incubation. Then ten more tertian attacks, several of which lasted for an unusually long time, more than twelve hours. Quinine treatment from August 14, salvarsan later.

The manic condition continued after the end of the treatment, but to a much less degree, so that the patient could be transferred to the quiet ward. Both pupils reacted promptly to light by the middle of August. By the end of September the patient had got over most of his delusions of grandeur. He was perfectly well-behaved and no longer showed any intelligence defects. He was discharged on November 24, fully aware of his condition, and with no traces of mental disturbances.

The spinal fluid gave a positive Wassermann reaction on October 26, 1917, with 6 cells per cmm. Nonne-Appel positive in sextuple dilution.

The patient went back to his former occupation soon after discharge, and is still holding his position successfully. As the Wassermann for the blood was moderately positive on April 15, 1918, he was given a course of neosalvarsan in May, with one dose each, of 0.3 and 0.45, and three doses of 0.6.

CASE 7.—J. Sch., 44 years of age, actor. He was admitted as a vagrant to the Rudolfspital in Vienna, where his condition was diagnosed as progressive paralysis and an attempt made at treatment with four doses of 0.3 neosalvarsan. He was then sent to the psychiatric clinic on July 21, 1917, as he could not longer be kept at the hospital on account of his excited condition.

He was admitted to the clinic in a slightly manic condition, but with no distinct delusions of grandeur. There were clear signs of dementia, mistakes in writing and counting, disturbance of attention, evident difficulty in speech. Pupils unequal, the left larger than the right, but with good reaction in both. Patellar and Achilles reflexes present, and equal on both sides. Movements awkward; Wassermann for the blood positive.

Malaria inoculation (II, from Case 3) on July 27, 1917. Slight rise in temperature on July 29; paralytic attack in the form of a passing aphasic disturbance. Slight rises in temperature up to 37.8 also on August 6 and 8. First malaria attack on August 10, followed at once by others of quotidian type and so severe (temperature of 41.5) that the patient quickly fell very low. Quinine and salvarsan treatment was therefore begun after the sixth attack, on August 15.

After the treatment the patient remained in a condition of euphoria, with no comprehension of his condition and with beginning dementia. A slight difficulty of speech also remained.

Later on his intelligence improved, he became quieter and better behaved, so that an attempt was made to let him go out by himself, to find employment. But it turned out that he merely used his liberty to hold up his friends and acquaintances for money, so that the permission had

553

to be taken away from him. He was finally sent to the Steinhof Insane Asylum on May 3.

The Wassermann reaction of the spinal fluid was positive both on November 24, 1917, and January 14, 1918, the first time with 31 cells per cmm., and the second time with 76. The Nonne-Appel reaction was positive the first time in an octuple dilution, and the second time when ten times diluted. The Wassermann reaction of the blood remained weakly positive after treatment.

CASE 8.—L. S., 45 years, railway employee, admitted August 10, 1917. Said to have been quite confused for six weeks, buying things foolishly, neglecting his person, making mistakes in his work.

He had some consciousness of illness on being admitted, trying to connect his nervous condition with a railway accident. Fairly apathetic; makes bad mistakes in counting; has some indication of syllable stammering. Pupils unequal, left larger than right; reacting neither to light nor to accommodation. Patellar reflexes present, the same on both sides. Wassermann reaction of the blood slightly positive.

Malaria inoculation on August 13, 1917 (III, from Case 6). Fever of 37.8 August 15 and 20. First malaria attack August 21; one attack daily until the 29th, except on the 24th. Finally almost continuous fever. Quinine and salvarsan begun on the 29th.

Euphoria, with no consciousness of illness, at the decline of the fever; manic excitement and delusions of grandeur from September 12. Stammering ceased. The delusions vanished in October, but the patient remained slightly manic, bustling about, and buying things right and left. Staphylococcus treatment in November.

Improvement continued, so that the experiment was made of placing the patient in a private home. But he was brought back the next day, as he drank and stole. A second attempt was equally unsuccessful.

The spinal fluid gave a positive Wassermann reaction on January 3, 1918, with 14 cells to the cmm.; Nonne-Appel positive in a decuple dilution.

The patient did not really realize his condition until April, and was definitely discharged on May 10, 1918.

CASE 9.—F. R., 24 years old. Waitress. Admitted to the clinic on August 9, 1917. Had been absentminded for a month, forgetful, doing everything wrong, had headaches at night. For the past week very lively, gave away her things, borrowed money, bought ridiculous objects, thought she had a fortune, trailed around in the streets, began to drink. At the clinic she was highly excited, with beginning delusions.

Syllable stammering on test words; pupils equal, reacting to light, lively patellar and Achilles reflexes, Wassermann positive for the blood.

Malaria inoculation on August 13 (III. from Case 6). Light fever as early as August 14, up to 37.6. First attack of malaria on August 24; seven attacks from then on until September 2. Quinine and salvarsan from September 1.

Euphoria still present during the middle of September, but the delusions of grandeur disappearing. Complete recognition and good behavior during October, with no more speech defects. Was discharged as fully capable on October 18, 1917.

The patient returned to the clinic from time to time, so that it was possible to make sure of the permanency of the remission and the working capacity.

The spinal fluid was positive to the Wassermann test on March 4, 1918, with 133 cells to the cmm. Nonne-Appel positive in octuple dilution. On account of this the patient was advised to have another salvarsan cure, which she did in April and May, 1918 (one dose of 0.3 and seven of 0.45). The psychic condition remained good during and after the treatment.

Since these cases were reported in the Psychiatrisch-Neurologische Wochenschrift of August 3, 1918, reports have come in on three of the cases described, showing that the improvement was only temporary.

Patient 1 was admitted in August to the University Psychiatric Clinic at Frankfort-a-M. According to reports he had a severe relapse with clonic attacks, complete insanity and extreme excitement. He is at present somewhat more quiet, but appears clearly insane.

It is reported that patient 8 shot himself on August 14, which no doubt indicates a relapse with depression.

Patient 9 was readmitted to the clinic on September 7, 1918. She presented a condition of manic excitement with mental confusion but no delusions.

Thus of the nine cases treated, four showed improvement complete enough to permit return to active life (1, 5, 6, 9), while two more (3 and 8) improved sufficiently to permit their independent existence outside the clinic. Although only two of these (3 and 6) still remain permanent so far, the completeness and length of time of the remissions in cases 1 and 9 was remarkable.

It therefore seems to me that further experiments of this kind are to be recommended, and I hope that the results will be even better when a thorough specific treatment is combined with the malaria, as was not done in the above cases. For it is perfectly evident that the three neosalvarsan injections given to cut the fever in my cases do not amount to specific therapy, when one takes into account the experience otherwise obtained as to the results in the treatment of progressive paralysis with salvarsan.

Such a course of treatments with malaria is perfectly proper in any region free from Anopheles mosquitoes, as this eliminates the possibility of the mosquitoes carrying the artificially produced infection to others.

Finally, a word about the effects of the described treatment on the serum and spinal fluid reactions. This effect seemed to be favorable particularly as regards the pleocytosis, as in cases 1, 3, 4, 6, 8 (with respectively 13, 4, 6, and 14 cells per cmm.); the globulin reaction was also noticeably weak in most of the cases, but the Wassermann reaction of the spinal fluid remained positive in every case, becoming "weakly positive" in only one of them. As for the Wassermann reaction of the serum, it became negative in only two cases. I was, however, unable to find that the degree to which the spinal fluid and the serum were affected corresponded in any way with the degree of improvement of the general condition. For instance, in case 4, that had the poorest results, the Wassermann of the serum was only moderate and the condition of the fluid good, while in case 9, in which there was a fine remission lasting for months, the serum and the fluid both had quite strong reactions. I found the same lack of connection between clinical condition and blood and spinal fluid condition in the remissions of paralysis treated with tuberculin (Therapeutische Monatshefte, volume 28, 1914). This undoubtedly changes if the remission lasts for years, the reactions in such cases becoming almost or entirely negative.

JULIUS RITTER, VON WAGNER-JAUREGG (b.—Wels, Upper Austria, Mar. 7, 1857; d.—Vienna, ca. Sept. 27, 1940).

Wagner-Jauregg received his M.D. from Vienna in 1881. He was Professor of Psychiatry and Neurology at Graz from 1883 to ca. 1886. He was Professor at Vienna ca. 1893-1928 (or 1902 on). He was also Director of the Psychiatric Clinic and Asylum at Troppau. He received the Nobel Prize in physiology and Medicine in 1927.

Wagner-Jauregg's accidental discovery of the positive therapeutic effects of malaria infection with psychotic patients occurred in 1887 and was reported that same year (v.i.). His first deliberate injection of blood from a victim of malaria into a patient suffering from paralytic and epileptic-form attacks due to advanced syphilitic infection occurred on June 14, 1917.

In the area of psychiatric therapy, the one treatment—and it is a biochemical one—upon which full confidence may be placed, and by means of which uniquely reliable results may be obtained, is the malarial therapy developed by Wagner-Jauregg. Though it is perhaps not entirely clear, in nosological terms, that syphilis is a psychiatric disorder from the modern conception of its etiology, nevertheless its symptoms in advanced stages are pre-eminently psychopathological ones.

Actually, it is the hope of the whole field of psychiatry (it was the hope, even, of Freud), that such profound success as Wagner-Jauregg experienced might be duplicated in all areas of psychopathology. The field is split ambivalently today, because of the inherent difficulty in demonstrating etiology exclusively on the psychic level. There are those who advocate talking cures, on the one hand, and those who advocate the organic approach, on the other. The next years of development in psychiatry will see a great shifting of camps, as the balance between these two approaches tilts and sways. From the point of view of philosophical theory, this is again the familiar balance of the mind-body problem, seen in a peculiarly dynamic equilibrium.

The foregoing selection consists in Wagner-Jauregg's first and most important publications on his malarial treatment.

WAGNER-JAUREGG, J. "The effect of malaria on progressive paralysis." *Psychiat. Neuro. Wochenschr.* 1918, 20: 132-134; 251-255. The original typescript of this excellent translation is held by the library of the New York Academy of Medicine. It is dated 11-4-25, with the translator's initials given, possibly as "VS." As the present library staff at the Academy is unable to locate the translator, we can only express our gratitude in his absence. It is reprinted here in its entirety.

See also:

WAGNER-JAUREGG, J. *Fieber- und infektionstherapie. Ausgewählte Beiträge 1887-1935, mit Verknüpfenden und abschliessenden Bemerkungen.* Wien: Verlag für Medizin, Weidmann & Co., 1935 This contains a reprint of Wagner-Jauregg's first paper: "Uber die Einwirkung Fieberhafter Erkrankungen auf Psychosen."

THE PHARMACOLOGICAL SHOCK TREATMENT
OF SCHIZOPHRENIA

Manfred Sakel

THERAPEUTIC MECHANISM OF
PHARMACOLOGICAL SHOCK:
WORKING HYPOTHESIS*

In my study of the theory of drug addiction I assumed that the nerve cell is called into action through the influence of some excitant hormone. The degree of activity of the nerve cell depends on the one hand on its sensitivity to this excitant hormone, and on the other hand on the amount of excitant hormone which is acting on it.

The actual reaction of the nerve cell to stimuli, as I pictured it, followed along certain pathways which are adequate to each stimulus, within the nerve cell itself. When a normal pathway, representing the last and therefore most recent order of development, was destroyed by some toxin, the reaction of the nerve cell to a stimulus had to follow a pathway which had been previously obliterated or else a pathway which was pathologically distorted.

If we could succeed then in blockading the cell against these excitant hormones, and thus prevent all reaction to stimuli, I imagined, then, that the cell would have a chance to rest and recuperate. The therapeutic effect could therefore be pictured somewhat as follows:

1. Neutralization of the excitant hormone and blockade of the nerve cell. In this way stimuli are kept away from the cell which has been reacting abnormally so that it has the time and opportunity to "polarize" the normal pathway. As the number of stimuli reaching the cell diminish, the activity of the pathological pathways cannot be sustained, for the abnormal pathways are not yet deeply

---

* Deleted is a short introductory statement.—*Editor.*

entrenched and are therefore again superseded after a while by the revived normal pathways, which are more deeply entrenched.*

2. Shock. Perhaps the elementary assault, verging almost on the destruction of the cell, serves to shatter or destroy every pathway which is not firmly established so that every possible defensive resource of the cell is provoked and reactivated, in order to save the cell by reestablishing normal conditions in face of this attack. When the cell revives, after termination of the hypoglycemic shock, the original physiological normal functions and pathways again take precedence, and can again be polarized in the right direction as treatment continues.

3. Neutralization of toxins in the total organism may be helped by influencing the entire metabolic sphere, as well as the metabolism within the cell. Glycogen storage in the liver is increased, and the liver is supported in its action against the poisonous disintegration products of metabolism, especially those involved in digestion and resorption, all of which have a toxic effect on the nerve cell.

To elucidate points one and two I should like to describe the hypothetical considerations which have influenced the development of the pharmacological shock treatment.

I have compared† the physiological activity of the nerve cell to the action of a fuel engine, with the excitant hormone representing the catalyst or spark necessary for combustion. Under normal physiological conditions both the supply of excitant hormone (catalyst for the fuel) as well as the reaction it produces (combustion) are sustained at a certain level, and the cell remains at a normal level of function and activity.

---

* See my "Theorie der Sucht" for analogies. (*Zeit. f. d. g. Neur. u. Psych.*, 129: 639, 1930.)

† "Theorie der Sucht."

Under pathological conditions disturbances may occur affecting both the supply of excitant hormone (increased or diminished), as well as the cellular reaction to the same (combustion). Thus the cell develops an exaggerated (or diminished) activity, becomes oversensitive to the normal stimuli of the outside world, and elaborates these stimuli excessively. The result is that something comparable to the racing of a motor develops, and the cellular function is thereby disrupted. To restore normal conditions again one has to either limit the supply of excitant material, or else diminish combustion in the cell by muffling it. This amounts to a blockade of the cell, or a vagotonic condition* in the sense of Hoff. The action of insulin therefore consists in: (1) neutralization of the excitant hormone and (2) vagotonic muffling of the cell.

In order to utilize this theory of nerve cell function for an understanding of mental disease I have had to create still another picture for myself, which again served a useful function as a working theory.

Nerve cells normally react to stimuli in a way which is adequate for a particular stage of development. Every reaction to any given stimulus runs a definite course which is specific to the stimulus and which, when necessary, involves other cells by means of similar juxtaposed pathways in a definite pattern so as to perform a certain function. (Perception, etc.) These pathways are definitely fixed at different levels of development, and they guarantee a normal course of even the most complicated mental processes in response to adequate stimuli. Every nerve pathway pattern is adequate to the corresponding stimulus. However, in the course of long periods of evolution these "stimuli" have changed considerably, so that in the course of time new pathway patterns are developed which become established through epochs of continuous use, and which supersede the previous phylogenetically

* "Theorie der Sucht."

more ancient nerve pathway patterns which have preceded them. These earlier patterns are thus completely overshadowed and finally eliminated. We thus have the so-called "normal attitude" of an individual to the realities of the outside world; whereby we must remember that the attitude is adequate for a certain epoch only and would be abnormal in another epoch, since the reaction involves pathway patterns which would be appropriate to stimuli of a previous epoch but which would be abnormal and inappropriate for the present existing stimuli, and would imply a reactivation and reestablishment of outmoded and obliterated pathways.

When the cell reacts abnormally, obsolete pathways can be reactivated again or else—depending on the severity of the disturbance—the pathways themselves may become distorted and criss-crossed so that there are false transferences to neighboring cells or functional organs. As a result we either see a tolerably well integrated but primitive behavior pattern which is inappropriate to the complicated stimuli of an advanced stage of development; or else we see disorientation and delusions. In other words, when the pathways are shattered a single stimulus releases reactions—because of the dislocation of the pathways—over a number of false, inappropriate and divergent pathways at the same time. Pathways are thereby employed which would ordinarily not be involved by the given stimulus. The patient apprehends these reactions, however false and confused they may be, and experiences an actual sensation which he may at first hesitate to accept (hallucination). Where the cellular dysfunction continues and the same stimuli continue to invoke the same confused reactions involving the same confusion of pathways, the dissociated and false pathways become fixated. When this continues for a long time the result is that the pathological pathways become more deeply intrenched and finally supersede the normal pathway patterns (psychotic deterioration).

This hypothetical pathophysiological picture of the structure of a psychosis was suggested by the phenomena of the pharmacological shock treatment and can be conveniently related to Stransky's theory of intrapsychic ataxia. We must expect that under normal conditions the last nerve pathway patterns are also phylogenetically the most recently developed, and are also the most complicated, because of the increased complexity of the stimuli. It follows therefore that the most complicated and phylogenetically most recent nerve pathway patterns and organs are most sensitive to injurious influences and are most easily affected. Whenever, therefore, some toxin, for example, acts upon the nerve cell, it is clear that the most recent pathways are the first to be injured. The stronger the harmful influence, the more and more deeply seated pathways are successively involved and eliminated, until such phylogenetically ancient pathway patterns are reached, that they prove to be resistant to the toxic influences. In this case, the new stimuli now involve these archaic nerve pathway patterns which had up to now been overshadowed, and these are again activated. The functional injury of the nerve cell thus leads to a tolerably well integrated reaction pattern which is, however, no longer appropriate to the actual stimuli (personality, and character changes as well as defects in psychotics).

If the injury to the nerve cell becomes more severe the nerve pathways between the cells touch and cross each other and are partially distorted. The result is a disturbance in the course of every reaction, regardless of the pathways from which it originates. Because of the confusion of nerve pathways the reaction to any given stimulus is, so to speak, short-circuited onto other pathways which cross the original pathway's course. The result is a reaction which is abnormal for the stimulus involved. This process can repeat itself again and again as more

563

and more different short circuits are involved, so that reactions occur for which there are no corresponding adequate stimuli at all.

By means of this ... representation we can more easily visualize all sorts of abnormal mental states ranging from the abnormal attitude of the psychotic to the outside world, to the phenomenon of complete deterioration, and we may thus find it easier, perhaps, to understand the pathogenesis involved.

For the sake of completeness I should like to add that syntonic manic-depressive pictures do not fit into the scheme. In patients of this type the reactions follow adequate pathways under adequate stimuli. The nerve pathways as such are not disturbed throughout their course, and they are not dislocated or distorted or confused (short-circuited) in relation to each other. The reactions differ from normal reactions only in their speed and intensity. If the changes from the normal described above could be called qualitative, these changes can be described as merely quantitative. The course of the reactions in the cell is either slowed down or speeded up by some sort of central regulation, of the total cell function. This may be due, for example, in the depressed phase—in contrast to the manic phase,—to some vagotonic condition or to exhaustion of the cell in the central nervous system.

In accordance with these assumptions I am inclined to believe that the seat of action in my treatment lies largely in the sphere of the vegetative centers. It is at the same time tempting though premature to also look to the subcortical centers for the primary seat of the disturbance of which the abnormal psychotic symptoms are secondary manifestations. In accordance with the former assumption I believe we can succeed in "blockading" the cells through the vegetative centers so that the injured or confused pathways are not exposed to further stimuli.

By means of this artificial rest the nerve cell pathways are no longer activated and the pathological pathways recede, while the normal pathways recuperate and attain their former prominence.

We ought to try to influence the intensity and speed of the reactions along normal pathways by similar pharmacological means, and to reduce them to normal proportions. It ought to be theoretically possible, with *the right pharmacological preparations,* to reduce the exaggerated vagotonia and eliminate the associated inhibition. But experiments in this direction are still so little advanced that we can say nothing about them as yet. Without discussing further the action or potentialities of the pharmacological preparations that I have tried, I should simply like to repeat what I have already said in my "Neue Behandlung der Morphinsucht" (1930) : "In combination with insulin the drugs I have experimented with are the following: gynergen, cholin, atropine, ephetonin, scopolamine, strychnine and salyrgan. These substances are supposed to diminish sympathetic hyperexcitability either by direct action on the sympathetic, or by stimulation of the parasympathetic system, so as to produce an equilibrium (bipolarity). I cannot now discuss any further the exact mode of action of these drugs. My experiences and experiments have been too incomplete to permit me to say anything definitely about the mode and site of action. In any case there is much to indicate that the equilibrium in ion relationships (potassium and calcium) as well as osmotic conditions and water metabolism are all important factors. I have attempted to explain the appearance of contrary vegetative symptoms [*i.e.,* sympathetic symptoms from parasympathetic drugs] by what I have called the 'reversal of function.' It is erroneous to assume a change in the composition or mode of action of the 'excitant substances.' Withdrawal symptoms usually involve an increased excitability of that portion of the

565

vegetative system which was most active in the ordinary normal life of the individual. But in either case insulin has proved to be of great benefit in restoring the equilibrium of the vegetative system.

"The auxiliary drugs, however, have a different effect. In cases where the sympathetic tone was pronounced I have used gynergen-cholin with good results. In cases where the parasympathetic component was prominent I have had almost equal success with atropin-scopolamine. I cannot give exact doses until I have had further experience."

In concluding these theoretical remarks I should like to say that in my method of treatment the insulin is used not only as a medicine but also to a considerable extent— if I may say so—as an instrument: success with the treatment, like success in an operation, depends not only on the tools employed but also on the skill of the guiding hand.*

CLINICAL OBSERVATIONS AND CONCLUSIONS

In addition to the description of the method and course of treatment which I have given, I should like to add a few observations which are of considerable interest in spite of the fact that they may, so far as we can see at present, have no direct relation to the therapy as such. I should at first like to describe some symptoms which occur as a result of the low blood sugar or low cellular sugar content. Among these are the aphasic phenomena which develop at certain stages of hypoglycemia.

Aphasia

I have already described the stage by stage revival of the different layers of the central nervous system as the patient awakens from a wet shock after having been given

---

* Deleted is a comment on the importance of adrenalin; and an extensive quotation of cases on blood sugar levels.

some sugar solution by tube. We said above that the various functions return in reverse order to the order in which they disappeared as the patient went into coma. I was not thinking at all of anatomical or architectonic relations, but rather of the developmental functional relations. If the patient no longer has any active reflexes in coma he begins after a while—as he begins to absorb the sugar—to show pathological reflexes again (Babinski, Oppenheim). Then his swallowing and corneal reflexes return and his coarser motor functions are revived. He then begins to make coordinated motions and later more delicately organized movements and at about the same time slowly acquires the capacity to perceive his surroundings. He then passes through a stage in which he shows aphasic disturbances; he then acquires the capacity to talk in a coordinated way and finally again establishes good contact. I said above that I regarded this process as a progressive reactivation of the entire series of successive functions of the central nervous system in the order of their development.

As the patients awaken one can see for example that they at first begin to groan and mutter primitive sounds. Then they begin to babble inarticulately and in many cases indeed actually begin to talk like children. During this short period their entire behavior may become childish. When this occurs the impression it conveys is not that of hysterical infantile behavior, but rather of a faithful and in every sense accurate reproduction of some previous stage of development which has long since passed. The infantile features do not merely involve the mental and emotional spheres, or merely the faculty of speech, but involve a completely infantile and typically clumsy coordination of muscular function, such as we can observe only in children who have not yet learned the finer motor activities: this type of clumsiness cannot be successfully imitated in adult life. Within a very short

567

space of time we witness the step by step transition to a later stage of development. At this later stage the patients are able to respond to simple and repeated commands. One gets the impression that the patients at first are unable to understand the meaning of these commands; it is only later that they begin to comprehend them. But they are able to respond promptly and effectively as long as they are not required to express themselves in speech. After another few minutes the patients begin to pronounce recognizable words, but their choice of words is very limited and they keep using the same words in attempting to answer different questions. Here, too, one is again reminded of a certain stage in the child's development when the child knows but a few words which it tries to use for every occasion. These patients do not give one the impression that they are embarrassed at this time by any amnesia for the other words, but they act instead like children who are glad that they can already use these few words. When one attempts somewhat later to establish contact with the patients one gets the definite impression that the patients hear everything and want to react, but that they are unable to grasp the meaning of the questions which are put to them. They do best when they are asked to repeat sentences, but even then they tend to cling to the first few words and keep repeating these same words even when they are asked to repeat other sentences. Finally the patients begin to understand the words they are hearing, but they continue to respond inappropriately or slowly at times in spite of the fact that they seem to understand.

As soon as the patients have emerged far enough out of hypoglycemia to begin to talk, many of them at this time too begin to behave for a short time in a way which is actually infantile or childish. It is only gradually that they make the transition from infantile to appropriate adult behavior. In a few cases one can see the individual's

568

entire ontogenetic development partially and briefly recapitulated. Occasionally, in a few cases, if one succeeds in establishing contact with the patient at this particular point before this transitional period is ended, and the patient is asked at this point how old he is, he will usually mention an age which is much younger than his actual years. His expression and behavior will also correspond to the age he mentions, and the patient will also imagine at the same time that he is in the same surroundings he actually was in at this earlier age.

An adult patient, for example, will say that he is six years old. His entire behavior is childish. His voice and intonation are absolutely infantile. He misidentifies the examiner and mistakes him for the childhood doctor that he actually had when he was young. He asks in a childish, peevish way when he may go to school. He says he has a "tummyache," etc. These transitional stages may take as little time as a few seconds, or at most a few minutes. If one has seen enough such cases and has observed them carefully, some such transitory stage will be found in every case. The transitional stage may manifest itself with a range of symptoms varying from a few scattered phenomena to an entire recapitulation of the personality development. This phenomenon, which lasts but a few minutes, before leading to more normal behavior, seems to me to be due to the same factors which cause the gradual reawakening of the function of speech: namely, the revival, layer by layer, of the successive functional levels of the central nervous system in their developmental order. It was instructive for me to hear an intelligent patient once describe his own sensations during the process of awakening, about two minutes after he was fully aroused. "What could have happened, doctor?" he said. "I saw you perfectly clearly and I heard you talk and I recognized your voice very clearly but it was impossible for me to understand what you wanted of me or what you were asking for, in spite of the fact that I recognized your voice. How was that possible? And then later even though I understood you I could not find enough words to answer your questions sensibly. And then I realized that I was not telling you the things I wanted to say. I felt sort of blocked in my head. Finally I realized that you were asking me something about the time I came to the clinic; but everything seemed so timeless to me. I had no appreciation for any periods of time or any time relationships. I could not even talk about them. Everything seemed really timeless. Even you, doctor, and your questions seemed so far away and unreal . . . sort of unrelated to space.''

I have ventured to give this brief description, but I realize that it has not by any means exhausted the interesting material which the aphasic disturbances in the course of awakening from hypoglycemia present. It seemed important, however, to at least call attention to these phenomena without attempting to exhaust the subject. I repeat again, that the chronological order in which the various functional integrative levels of the central nervous system resume their activity seems to correspond to the actual order of their development. I am inclined to assume that these total functions respond to the same influences which affect the single nerve pathways in the separate cells, and that the more complex functions are more sensitive to sugar deprivation. As a result the functions which are phylogenetically and ontogenetically most recent are most sensitive to hypoglycemia. When hypoglycemia has reached a certain depth or has lasted a certain time, and when the cellular sugar content has reached a certain level which no longer allows normal activity of biological functions, it is these functions which begin to disappear. As soon as sugar is absorbed from the digestive tract again and the hypoglycemia ends, these functions are again resumed. The phylogenetically most recent functions are, in accordance with this assumption, the last to be activated. Before this happens, the less sensitive phylogenetically older functional areas are revived, and predominate until they are displaced by the next higher integrative levels. This happens not only because the most recent functions are most easily harmed by the sugar deprivation (or insulin blockade) but also quite possibly because they need a longer rest period and more favorable conditions than the older functions before they can act normally again. This behavior is very striking in many cases. In one case I was not only able to observe entire functional integrative levels of the central nervous system in isolation, but I have also observed that one hemisphere sometimes needs more time to recuperate than the other. One patient, for example, while awakening from coma began to show his reflex reactions again, but had a right-sided hemiplegia with all the classical accompanying symptoms, which lasted 45 minutes before it disappeared. Whereas the left side of the body was quickly revived the right-sided hemiplegia lasted for 30 minutes longer than all the other disturbances which were observed. Function was then gradually and completely restored in much the same way as in other recoverable hemiplegias, except that it all happened within the space of a few minutes. This phenomenon seems to be best explained on the assumption that the left hemisphere is dominant and is therefore more sensitive to sugar deprivation.

Psychotic Reactions During Hypoglycemia (Activation of Psychosis)

I have already observed several thousand hypoglycemic states but in spite of the variety of the psychotic reactions during hypoglycemia (or sometimes after termination), it is possible to speak of a certain connection between the physiological hypoglycemic state and the reactivation of psychotic symptoms. The physiological changes occurring during hypoglycemia activate a latent psychotic process or render a chronic process more acute in perhaps the same way that irritative agents activate an infectious process that is latent or that has become chronic, in order to again arouse the defensive powers of the organism. I am inclined to assume that the manner in which any individual reacts to hypoglycemia gives us some information about the psychic constitution or mental disposition of the individual.

I have already mentioned the striking fact that early in treatment hypoglycemia often produces lucidity before the onset of somnolence and coma. It is by no means uncommon to observe complete lucidity, even if only for a short time, before coma supervenes. The symptoms which occur during hypoglycemia vary considerably in different phases of treatment. Patients who show a short period of lucidity during hypoglycemia during the early phase of treatment, only to remain psychotic for the entire remainder of the day, later show a complete reversal of reaction and remain symptom-free throughout the day, but may show a certain reactivation of their psychosis during hypoglycemia. Patients in this latter phase are clear and quiet throughout the day but become psychotic during hypoglycemia. It seems justifiable to speak of a reversal of psychotic reaction to hypoglycemia in the course of treatment. But before I elaborate this point I should like to briefly describe a few typical hypoglycemic reactions. . . .

The first of these reactions is an important factor in the actual management of the treatment. This is the so-called hunger excitement . . . ; but it should be emphasized that this reaction does not represent a psychotic reaction in the ordinary sense.

Something which is superficially similar but is fundamentally quite different sometimes occurs when a patient who is calm and clear and perspiring rather freely during hypoglycemia begins to show signs of a definite psychosis more or less colored by manic features. In many cases one is almost tempted to say that the mental picture represents a quick resume of the entire course of the previous psychosis. Patients who are otherwise perfectly quiet, now begin to grow very excited and confused and begin to hallucinate, and when one consults their case records one sees that they have acted more or less similarly at the outset of their psychosis. One gets the impression that the patient is reproducing all the various phases of his previous psychosis in resume, with the psychotic symptoms in usually about the same order as that of their first appearance in the previous psychosis. Many patients at this time again show definitely manic or silly psychotic symptoms, sometimes combined with infantile hysterical features.

These observations of reactivated psychotic symptoms during hypoglycemia apply mostly to patients who have already improved considerably in the course of treatment and are otherwise fairly normal in the non-hypoglycemic periods, or one may see a reactivation of past psychotic material in chronic cases that have already become empty.

It is important never to terminate hypoglycemia during the short period of activated psychosis unless there is some vital indication, or unless one wishes to render the psychosis more acute and productive. I have found that in several cases where I have had to do this for certain reasons that the activated psychotic symptoms were often fixated. Many of these cases had already shown much improvement up to this point, but grew considerably worse after this had happened, again with the exception of previously unproductive psychoses (*i.e.,* inhibited and empty). In most cases, carbohydrate administration ought to be deferred at least until the activated psychotic symptoms have subsided.

It was further observed that the same patients showed different reactivated psychotic pictures during hypoglycemia in various phases of their illness. I observed that as patients improved their psychotic symptoms during hypoglycemia tended to subside and that when they approached full recovery their hypoglycemic symptoms practically disappeared. Patients, for example, who had at first shown florid psychotic symptoms during hypoglycemia later had negligible hypoglycemic psychotic reactions or none at all. I have therefore come to believe that there is a certain relation between a patient's mental condition and his reaction to hypoglycemia. This again is meant to imply that each hypoglycemic state serves to activate the latent psychotic residua and thus to render the clinical picture more acute. As the patient improves and the defensive capacities of the organism are again and again aroused these psychotic residues are finally diminished until finally the latent vestiges are themselves finally eliminated. I have, however, up to now had little experience with the hypoglycemic mental reactions of normal individuals, so that I cannot definitely assume that hypoglycemia specifically activates a latent psychosis, even in predisposed but apparently normal individuals. But if I had sufficient experience with mentally normal persons, I should be tempted to conclude that hypoglycemia constitutes an actual test for the predisposition to psychosis. My experiences with my own case material points in that direction and I have therefore generally preferred to continue treatment even in cases which are perfectly normal otherwise until the patient reaches a point where he no longer shows psychotic symptoms during hypoglycemia before the onset of coma. This procedure is, however, only applicable to cases in which a full recovery may be expected.

574

I should like to call attention to another phenomenon which occurs during hypoglycemia in many patients as they begin to improve and which is even more difficult to explain than the phenomenon just described: this is a reaction which looks more or less like an hysterical picture. In one such case this reaction during hypoglycemia almost reached the point of an actual hysterical psychosis. In this case it was possible to completely relieve the symptoms, which had lasted for a few hours, with a single psychotherapeutic session. In a few cases I was able to completely relieve the condition with a single session of hypnosis.

I cannot explain this type of reaction. It must be remembered that the patients after shock treatment are in a very labile mental condition, for the various functions of the central nervous system are more or less paralyzed during hypoglycemia and are only gradually reactivated when the patient first awakens. It is possible that in this process the various developmentally differentiated functional integrative levels show various degrees of resistance to the process, corresponding to their own developmental age, so that all the functions are not awakened at the same time and do not simultaneously resume their normal activity. It may well be that the developmentally deeper functions sometimes achieve their normal activity while the developmentally more highly developed and more sensitive regions have still not attained equilibrium, so that they cannot yet resume that control of the lower centers which they had once attained at a later stage of development. The result is that their dominance is temporarily displaced. It may very well be that this condition corresponds to an extent to what we would regard as an hysterical personality in another individual, though it was produced in one case by the temporary elimination of a functional integrative level of a more highly devel-

575

oped stage of the personality development. I cannot say whether this condition is produced by the state of psychological sensitivity which occurs in the course of treatment or whether the patient's condition in the course of recovery happens at some point to coincide with what we customarily call the hysterical constitution. I have not been able to make a sufficient number of observations of this sort to decide with certainty, and wish to call the attention of other observers to the occurrence of hysterical phenomena on a pathophysiological basis, for further confirmation and elaboration.

Amnesia

I have already briefly mentioned the posthypoglycemic phenomenon of amnesia, but it seems to me to be a matter of considerable importance for the further development of the pharmacological shock treatment. In a few cases which had a series of particularly severe epileptic seizures which were not readily interrupted the amnesia has been particularly complete and extensive.

The cases I have in mind were treated at a time when the method first began to be applied, and when I was not yet entirely sure of when and how the hypoglycemia ought to be interrupted. *Multiple* epileptic seizures seem to occur only after there has been a protracted sugar deprivation of the tissues, so that the reversibility and capacity for restitution are already considerably endangered. In a few cases where the hypoglycemia was terminated only with intravenous glucose, because of insufficient experience the patient would then be left alone for hours at a time, as soon as he had awakened, without realizing the danger to which he was exposed. In spite of the insufficient amount of sugar administered, the sudden awakening of the patient was misleading, and because the hypoglycemia was thought to be definitely terminated, the patients would then be left alone. As a result of such

576

apparently dangerous and involuntarily protracted hypoglycemic shocks, multiple severe epileptic convulsions occurred (status epilepticus). With appropriate intervention these patients could still be saved.

These cases would then show a complete retrograde amnesia which extended back a long time—in one of my cases as far back as five months. After this patient's *status epilepticus* had been ended, he showed the picture of a postepileptic twilight state which continued for a few days and gradually diminished. Meanwhile his psychotic symptoms had completely disappeared. As this twilight state was relieved, the patient had a complete amnesia for the happenings of the past five months. It was during this forgotten period that the patient's psychosis had first developed. The patient acted as if these five months had not yet passed: when asked for the date he would name a date five months back. When the patient saw the correct date in the newspaper and realized from his surroundings that he was in a clinic, he would attempt to explain the discrepancy between his own recollection and the actual facts by reasoning it out as well as his intelligence allowed. The patient for example remembered that he took a motorcycle trip from Munich to Vienna (in May, 1933). Since he realized he was now in a hospital in spite of the fact that he did not feel sick, he thought he must have had a motorcycle accident and some head injury which kept him from remembering what had happened in the past few months. This patient's amnesia was complete.

After a few days had passed the period for which the patient had an amnesia began to contract, and a week later the patient was able to recall something which had happened only three months ago. He said he remembered that he got a letter from Germany at that time, so that he knew he could not have had an accident on his trip from Germany. This amnesic period continued to grow shorter

577

thereafter but still included the period of the outbreak of his psychosis.

Later as my technique improved and the dangers of protracted shock could be avoided, I continued to observe amnesic phenomena in some of my patients, but these were less marked and less extensive. Even after rather innocuous shocks (coma as well as epileptic seizure) one could sometimes observe that the patient had a hazy recollection for things which had just been bothering him so much. It seemed as if the reality and intensity of the patient's abnormal thought processes began to grow dim. Without developing a complete amnesia, the dominance of the previous psychotic compulsive ideas and thoughts disappeared, so that the normal personality could again become dominant. In these cases I do not so much mean an amnesia in the ordinary psychological sense, as a physiological amnesia in which the more recent pathophysio logical processes (and their psychological manifestations) lose their dominance and retreat in the background. The result is that the more rigid psychotic personality is dislodged and superseded by the older normal personality. These observations suggested the tempting possibility of relieving psychoses by inducing so severe a shock that the patients would develop an amnesia complete enough to shatter both their psychosis and their psychotic behavior pattern. But up to now it seemed inadvisable to protract the shock unduly. Because of the uncertainty concerning the permissible limits of long protracted shock, and the point at which reversible and irreversible pathological anatomical tissue changes begin or end, I would not at present recommend the use of such heroic procedures on any large scale. It will be a task for the future to determine how long hypoglycemia can be protracted without injury so that irreversible changes can these factors, which I regard as very specially significant. be avoided. When this is known we can again reconsider

578

Professor Hitzenberger has reported another case which may be cited in this connection: A diabetic who was given an overdose of insulin, went into hypoglycemic coma which was mistaken by the attending physician for diabetic coma so that the patient was given still more insulin. When the patient was aroused he showed a retrograde amnesia which covered several years. Professor Potzl also believes that some of the amnesic phenomena in general paresis as well as the *ictus amnesique* of cerebral arteriosclerotics may be attributable to hypoglycemia.

At any rate it seems to me that this factor cannot be overemphasized, and as our knowledge of the hypoglycemic mechanisms increases, it may be possible to deliberately produce and extend amnesia at will. It should then be at least theoretically possible to eliminate any psychotic reaction no matter how long it has lasted, provided always of course that it is not based on an irreversible pathological anatomical change, but is due to reversible factors. I have up to now avoided undertaking anything of this sort in the treatment of schizophrenia because I have had sufficient success in recent cases with the relatively harmless system of treatment by phases. Further work in the course of time will allow us to diminish the danger of these severe shocks, and in certain cases to attempt to produce an amnesia which would cover the entire period of the psychosis. (Prolonged shocks, do well as protracted treatments repeated at intervals, have all been in use too short a time to justify their inclusion here.)

Results

I have attempted in this book to describe the exact details and principles of the pharmacological shock treatment and I have also ventured a theoretical explanation. The actual results of the treatment as well as a description of its limitations and potentialities have been included in another study by Dussik and myself based on the cases which have been treated at the clinic during the year 1933-34.

It should be emphasized again that we have had our best statistical results in recent cases of schizophrenia. In our series approximately 50 of our cases were recent: these patients were diagnosed as schizophrenic for the first time on admission. Of these 50 cases over 70% showed a full remission (apparently cured) and another 18% showed social remissions following treatment. Only those cases who returned to their *former work* were counted as social remissions. In other words 88% of our recent cases showed positive results after treatment. The exact statistical material will be found in the paper already mentioned.

MANFRED JOSHUA SAKEL (b.-Nadvorna, Austria, June 6, 1900; d.-New York City, Dec. 2, 1957).

In 1920, Sakel graduated from the college in Brno (Brünn), Czechoslovakia. He received his M.D. from the University of Vienna in 1925. From 1925 to 1927 he was Associate Physician at the Vienna Hospital. (He also received some post-graduate training at the Vienna Hospital.) In 1927 Sakel became Research Fellow at Urban Hospital in Berlin. In this same year, he became Professor in Experimental Psychiatry at the Lichterfelde Hospital in Berlin. He remained here until 1933, when he became Associate in Neuro-psychiatry at the University Clinic in Vienna. In 1936, he came to New York City and entered private practice.

Sakel dates the introduction of insulin shock therapy as June, 1927. In Sept. 1957, a Symposium was held in Vienna in his honor, and to commemorate the 30th anniversary of the first public revelation of his work.

The strength and the omnipresence of the physical universe constantly attracts our search for causes. Even the most abstract patterns of psychic functioning may, we hope, be founded in firm, rigid patterns of biochemical organization. This hope that psychopathology can be attacked on a physical level, perhaps represents more our confidence in the greater efficiency of physical events than our real conviction of the unity of mind and body.

It should be emphasized, however, that there is inherent in the whole concept of 'shock therapy', the icy plunge and the pit of snakes, against which Pinel so gallantly fought. There may be a danger here that we take success for understanding, and as a substitute for the moral treatment of insanity.

Insulin shock therapy, in general, does indeed work. Many thousands of people owe to it the inestimable blessing of mental health and of socially acceptable perceptions of realtity. However, that it does not work in a predictable manner, that its effects are not lasting in all instances, that it is still without a sound theoretical foundation, only serves to make more impressive the genuine isolation of the psychic realm.

This realization in no way lessens our gratitude to Sakel. The biochemical approach to mental disorders dominates the field today, and there is little doubt that Sakel's achievement stands out as the most brilliant. He is mentor, certainly, to the vast majority of the present generation of psychiatrists all over the world.

SAKEL, M. *The pharmacological shock treatment of schizophrenia.* N.Y.: Nervous and Mental Disease Pub. Co., 1938. Trans. J. Wortis. (Enlarged version of a series of articles from *Wien. med. Wochenschr.*, 1934-1935). Chap. VII: "Therapeutic mechanism of pharmacological shock: working hypothesis." Chap. VIII: "Clinical observations and conclusions." Published with the gracious permission of the Trustees of the Smith Ely Jelliffe Trust.

See also:

SAKEL, M.

a) "Neue Behandlung der Morphinsucht." *Z. Neurol. Psychiat.* 1933, 143:50r.
b) "Neue Behandlung der Schizophrenie." *Berlin med. Wochenschr.* 1933, Sept. 5.
c) "The classical Sakel shock treatment: a reappraisal." *J. clin. and exper. Psychopath.*, 1954, 15:255-317.

ON AFFECTIONS OF SPEECH FROM DISEASE
OF THE BRAIN

(John) Hughlings Jackson

It is very difficult for many reasons to write on affections of speech. So much, since the memorable researches of Dax and Broca, has been done in the investigation of these cases of disease of the brain, that there is an *embarras de richesse* in material. To refer only to what has been done in this country, we have the names of Gairdner Moxon, Broadbent, William Ogle, Bastian, John W. Ogle, Thomas Watson, Alexander Robertson, Ireland, Wilks, Bristowe, Ferrier, Bateman, and others. To Wilks, Gairdner, Moxon, Broadbent, and Ferrier, I feel under great obligations. Besides recognizing the value of Broadbent's work on this subject, I have to acknowledge a particular indebtedness to him. Broadbent's hypothesis, a verified hypothesis, is, I think, essential to the methodical investigation of affections of speech. Let me give at once an illustration of its value. It disposes of the difficulty there otherwise would be in holding (1) that loss of speech is, on the physical side, loss of nervous arrangements for highly special and complex articulatory *movements,* and (2) that in cases of loss of speech the articulatory *muscles* are not paralysed, or but slightly paralysed. I shall assume that the reader is well acquainted with Broadbent's researches on the representation of certain movements of the two sides of the body in each side of the brain; the reader must not assume that Broadbent endorses the applications I make of his hypothesis. The recent encyclopaedic article on Affections of Speech, by Kussmaul, in Ziemssen's "Practice of Medicine," is very complete and highly original. It is worthy of most careful study.

The subject has so many sides—psychological,

anatomical, physiological, and pathological—that it is very difficult to fix on an order of exposition. It will not do to consider affections of speech on but one of these sides. To show how they mutually bear, we must see each distinctly. For example, we must not confound the physiology of a case with its pathology, by using for either the vague term "disease." Again, we must not ignore anatomy when speaking of the physical basis of words, being content with morphology, as in saying that words "reside" in this or that part of the brain. Supposing we could be certain that this or that grouping of cells and nerve-fibres was concerned in speech, from its being always destroyed when speech is lost, we should still have to find out the anatomy of the centre. Even supposing we were sure that the psychical states called words, and the nervous states in the "centre for words," were the same things, we should still have the anatomy of that centre to consider. The morphology of a centre deals with its shape, with its "geographical" position, with the sizes and shapes of its constituent elements. A knowledge of the anatomy of a centre is knowledge of the parts of the body represented in it, and of the ways in which these parts are therein represented. Whilst so much has been learned as to the morphology of the cerebrum—cerebral topography—it is chiefly to the recent researches of Hitzig and Ferrier that we are indebted for our knowledge of the anatomy of many of the convolutions, that is, a knowledge of the parts of the body these convolutions represent. It is supposed that the anatomy of the parts of the brain concerned with words is that they are cerebral nervous arrangements representing the articulatory muscles in very special and complex movements. Similarly, a knowledge of the anatomy of the centres concerned during visual ideation is a knowledge of those regions of the brain where certain parts of the organism (retina and ocular muscles) are represented

583

in particular and complex combinations. A merely materialistic or morphological explanation of speech or mind, supposing one could be given, is not an anatomical explanation. Morphologically, the substratum of a word or of a syllable is made up of nerve-cells and fibres; anatomically speaking, we say it is made up of nerve-cells and fibres representing some particular articulatory movement.

Unless we most carefully distinguish betwixt psychology and the anatomy and physiology of the nervous system in this inquiry, we shall not see the fundamental similarity there is betwixt the defect often described in psychological phraseology as "loss of memory for words," and the defect called ataxy of articulation. A method which is founded on classifications which are partly anatomical and physiological, and partly psychological, confuses the real issues. These mixed classifications lead to the use of such expressions as that an *idea* of a word produces an *articulatory movement;* whereas a psychical state, an "idea of a word" (or simply "a word") cannot produce an articulatory movement, a physical state. On any view whatever as to the relation of mental states and nervous states such expressions are not warrantable in a *medical* inquiry. We could only say that discharge of the cells and fibres of the anatomical substratum of a word produces the articulatory movement. In all our studies of diseases of the nervous system we must be on our guard against the fallacy that what are physical states in lower centres fine away *into* psychical states in higher centres; that, for example, vibrations of sensory nerves *become* sensations, or that somehow or another an idea produces a movement.

Keeping them distinct, we must consider now one and now another of the several sides of our subject; sometimes, for example, we consider the psychical side—speech—and at other times the anatomical basis of speech. We cannot go right on with the psychology, nor with the anatomy, nor with the pathology of our subject. We must consider now one and now the other, endeavouring to trace a correspondence betwixt them.

I do not believe it to be possible for anyone to write methodically on these cases of disease of the nervous system; without considering them in relation to other kinds of nervous disease; nor to be desirable in a medical writer if it were possible. Broadbent's hypothesis is exemplified in cases of epilepsy and hemiplegia, as well as in cases of affections of speech, and can only be vividly realized when these several diseases have been carefully studied. Speech and perception ("words" and "images") co-operate so intimately in mentation (to use Metcalfe-Johnson's term) that the latter process must be considered. We must speak briefly of imperception, loss of images, as well as of loss of speech—loss of symbols. The same general principle is, I think, displayed in each. Both in delirium (partial imperception) and in affections of speech the patient is reduced to a more automatic condition; respectively reduced to the more organized relations of images and words. Again, we have temporary loss or defect of speech after certain epileptiform seizures; temporary affections of speech after these seizures are of great value in elucidating some difficult parts of our subject, and cannot be understood without a good knowledge of various other kinds of epileptic and epileptiform paroxysms, and post-paroxysmal states. After a convulsion beginning in the (right) side of the face or tongue, or in both these parts, there often remains temporary speechlessness, although the articulatory muscles move well. Surely we ought to consider cases of discharge of the centres for words as well as cases in which these centres are destroyed, just as we consider not only hemiplegia but hemispasm. Before trying to analyse that very difficult symptom called ataxy of articulation, we should try to understand the more easily studied disorder of co-ordination, locomotorataxy, and before that, the least difficult disorder of co-ordination of movements resulting from ocular paralysis. Unless we do, we shall not successfully combat the notion that there are centres for co-ordination of words which are something over and above centres for special and complex movements of the articulatory muscles, and that a patient can, from lesion of such a centre, have a loss of co-ordination, without veritable loss of some of the movements represented in it.

It might seem that we could consider cases of aphasia, as a set of symptoms at least, without regard to the pathology of different cases of nervous disease. We really could not. It so happens that different morbid processes have what, for brevity, we may metaphorically call different seats of election: thus, that defect of speech with which there are frequent mistakes in words is nearly always produced by local cerebral softening; that defect which is called ataxy of articulation, is, I think, most often produced by hæmorrhage. Hence we must consider hemiplegia in relation to affections of speech; for it so happens that the first kind of defect mostly occurs, as Hammond has pointed out, without hemiplegia, or without persistent hemiplegia, a state of things producible by embolism and thrombosis, and the latter mostly with hemiplegia and persistent hemiplegia, a state of things usually produced by hæmorrhage. From ignoring such considerations, the two kinds of defects are by some considered to be absolutely different, whereas on the anatomico-physiological side they are but very different degrees of one kind of defect.

There are certain general principles which apply not only to affections of speech, but also to the commonest variety of paralysis, to the simplest of convulsive seizures, and to cases of insanity.

The facts that the speechless patient is frequently

reduced to the use of the most general propositions "yes" or "no," or both; that he may be unable to say "no" when told, although he says it readily in reply to questions requiring dissent; that he may be able ordinarily to put out his tongue well, as for example to catch a stray crumb, and yet unable to put it out when he tries, after being asked to do so; that he loses intellectual language and not emotional language; that although he does not speak, he understands what we say to him; and many other facts of the same order illustrate exactly the same principles as do such facts from other cases of disease of the nervous system as that in hemiplegia the arm suffers more than the leg; that most convulsions beginning unilaterally begin in the index-finger and thumb; that in cases of post-epileptic insanity there are degrees of temporary reduction from the least towards the most "organized actions," degrees proportional to the severity of the discharge in the paroxysm, or rather to the amount of exhaustion of the highest centres produced by the discharge causing the paroxysm. In all these cases, except in the instance of convulsion, which, however, illustrates the principle in another way, there are, negatively, degrees of loss of the most voluntary processes with, positively, conservation of the next most voluntary or next more automatic; otherwise put, there are degrees of loss of the latest acquirements with conservation of the earlier, especially of the inherited acquirements. Speaking of the physical side, there are degrees of loss of function of the least organized nervous arrangements with conservation of function of the more organized. There is in each reduction to a more automatic condition; in each there is dissolution, using this term as Spencer does, as the opposite of evolution.[1]

---

[1] Here I must acknowledge my great indebtedness to Spencer. The facts stated in the text seem to me to be illustrations from actual cases of disease, of conclusions he has arrived at deductively in his "Psychology." It is not affirmed that we have

In *defects* of speech we may find that the patient utters instead of the word intended a word of the same class in meaning, as "worm-powder" for "cough-medicine," or in sound, as "parasol" for "castor oil." The presumption is that the patient uses what is to him a more "organized" or "earlier" word, and if so, dissolution is again seen. But often there is no obvious relation of any sort betwixt the word said and the one appropriate, and thus the mistake does not appear to come under dissolution. If, however, we apply the broad principles which we can, I think, establish from other cases of dissolution —viz., from degrees of insanity, especially the slight degrees of the post-epileptic insanity just spoken of—we shall be able to show that many of the apparently random mistakes in words are not real exceptions to the principle of dissolution.

For the above reasons I shall make frequent references to other classes of nervous disease. The subject is already complex without these excursions, but we must face the complexity. Dr. Curnow has well said (*Medical Times and Gazette*, November 29, 1873, p. 616), "The tendency to appear exact by disregarding the complexity of the factors is the old failing in our medical history."

Certain provisional divisions of our subject must be made. The reader is asked to bear in mind that these are admittedly arbitrary; they are not put forward as scientific distinctions. Divisions[1] and arrangements are easy. Distinctions and classifications are difficult. But in

the exact opposite of evolution from the apparently brutal doings of disease; the proper opposite is seen in healthy senescence, as Spencer has shown. But from diseases there is, in general, the corresponding opposite of evolution.

[1] "How often would controversies be sweetened were people to remember that 'distinctions and divisions are very different things,' and that 'one of them is the most necessary and conducive to true knowledge that can be; the other, *when made too much of*, serves only to puzzle and confuse the understanding.' Locke's words are the germ of that wise aphorism of Coleridge: 'It is a dull or obtuse mind that must divide in order to distinguish; but it is a still worse that distinguishes in order to divide.' And if we cast our eyes back over time, it is the same spirit as that which led Anaxagoras to say, 'Things in this one connected world are not cut off from one another as if with a hatchet.'" [*Westminster Review* (art. Locke), January, 1877 (no italics in original).]

the study of a very complex matter we must first divide and then distinguish. This is not contradictory to what was said before on the necessity of encountering the full complexity of our subject. Harm comes, not from dividing and arranging, but from stopping in this stage, from taking provisional divisions to be real distinctions, and putting forward elaborate arrangements, with divisions and subdivisions, as being classifications. In other words we shall, to start with, consider our subject empirically, and afterwards scientifically. We first arbitrarily divide and arrange for convenience of obtaining the main facts which particular cases supply, and then try to classify the facts, in order to show their true relations one to another, and consider them on the physical side as defects of mind, and on the physical side as defects of the nervous system. Empirically we consider the cases of affection of speech we meet with, as they *approach* certain nosological types (most frequently occurring cases); scientifically we classify the facts thus obtained, to show how affections of speech are *departures from* what we know of healthy states of mind and body. The latter study is of the cases as they show different degrees of nervous dissolution.

Let us first of all make a very rough popular division. When a person "talks" there are three things going on, speech, articulation, and voice. Disease can separate them. Thus from disease of the larynx, or from paralysis of its nerves, we have loss of voice, but articulation and speech remain good. Again, in complete paralysis of the tongue, lips, and palate, articulation is lost, but speech is not even impaired; the patient remains able to express himself in writing, which shows that he retains speech— internal speech—that he propositionizes well. Lastly, in extensive disease in a certain region in one half of the brain (left half usually) there is loss of speech, internal and external, but the articulatory muscles move well.

Let us make a wider division. Using the term "language" we make two divisions of it, intellectual and emotional. The patient, whom we call speechless (he is also defective in pantomime), has lost intellectual language and has not lost emotional language.

The kind of case we shall consider first is that of a man who has lost speech and whose pantomime is impaired, but whose articulatory muscles move well, whose vocal organs are sound, and whose emotional manifestations are unaffected. This is the kind of case to be spoken of as No. 2.

The term "aphasia" has been given to affections of speech by Trousseau; it is used for defects as well as for loss of speech. I think the expression affections of speech (including defects and loss) is preferable. Neither term is very good, for there is, at least in many cases, more than loss of *speech;* pantomime is impaired; there is often a loss or defect in symbolizing relations of things in any way. Dr. Hamilton proposes the term "asemasia," which seems a good one. He derives it from "*a,* and *onpaivu,* an inability to indicate by signs or language." It is too late, I fear, to displace the word aphasia. Aphasia will be sometimes used as synonymous with affections of speech in this article.

We must at once say briefly what we mean by speech, in addition to what has been said by implication when excluding articulation, as this is popularly understood, and voice. To speak is not simply to utter words, it is to propositionize. A proposition is such a relation of words that it makes one new meaning; not by a mere addition of what we call the separate meanings of the several words; the terms in a proposition are modified by each other. Single words are meaningless, and so is any unrelated succession of words. The unit of speech is a proposition. A single word is, or is in effect, a proposition, if other words in relation are implied. The English tourist at a French *table d'hote* was understood by the waiter to be asking for water when his neighbours thought he was crying "oh" from distress. It is from the use of a word that we judge of its propositional value. The words "yes" and "no" are propositions, but only when used for assent and dissent; they are used by healthy people interjectionally as well as propositionally. A speechless patient may retain the word "no," and yet have only the interjectional or emotional, not the propositional use of it; he utters it in various tones as signs of feeling only. He may have a propositional use of it, but yet a use of it short of that healthy people have, being able to reply "no" but not to say "no" when told; a speechless patient may have the full use of it. On the other hand, elaborate oaths, in spite of their propositional structure, are not propositions, for they have not, either in the mind of the utterer or in that of the person to whom they are uttered, any meaning at all; they may be called "dead propositions." The speechless patient may occasionally swear. Indeed he may have a recurring utterance, e.g. "Come on to me," which is propositional in structure but not, to him, propositional in use; he utters it on any occasion, or rather on no *occasion,* but every time he tries to speak.

Loss of speech is, therefore, the loss of power to propositionize. It is not only loss of power to propositionize aloud (to talk), but to propositionize either internally or externally, and it may exist when the patient remains able to utter some few words. We do not mean by using the popular term "power" that the speechless man has lost any "faculty" of speech or propositionizing; he has lost those words which serve in speech, the nervous arrangements for them being destroyed. There is no "faculty" or "power" of speech apart from words revived or revivable in propositions, any more than there is a "faculty" of co-ordination of movements apart from movements represented in particular ways. We must here say, too, that besides the use of words in speech there is a service of words which is not speech; hence we do not use the expression that the speechless man has lost words, but that he has lost those words which serve in speech. In brief, speechlessness does not mean entire wordlessness.

It is well to insist again that speech and words are psychical terms; words have, of course, anatomical substrata or bases as other psychical states have. We must as carefully distinguish betwixt words and their physical bases as we do betwixt colour and its physical basis; a psychical state is always accompanied by a physical state, but nevertheless the two things have distinct natures. Hence we must not say that the "memory of words" is a *function* of any part of the nervous system, for function is a physiological term (*vide infra*). Memory or any other psychical state arises *during* not *from* —if "from" implies continuity of a psychical state with a physical state—functioning of nervous arrangements, which functioning is a purely physical thing—a discharge of nervous elements representing some impressions and movements. Hence it is not to be inferred from the rough division we have just made of the elements of "talking," and from what is said of their "separation" by disease, that there is anything in common even for reasonable contrast, much less for comparison, betwixt loss of speech (psychical loss) and immobility of the articulatory muscles from, say disease of the medulla oblongata, as in "bulbar paralysis" (a physical loss). As before said, we must not classify on a mixed method of anatomy, physiology, and psychology, any more than we should classify plants on a mixed natural and empirical method, as exogens, kitchen-herbs, graminaceæ, and shrubs. The things comparable and contrastable in a rough division are (1) the two physical losses: (*a*) loss of function of certain nervous arrangements in the cerebrum, which are not speech (words used in speech), but the anatomical substrata of speech and (*b*) loss of function of nervous arrangements in the medulla oblongata. (2) The comparison, on the psychical side, fails. There is no psychical loss in disease of the medulla oblongata to compare with loss of words, as this part of the nervous system, at least as most suppose,[1] has no psychical side; there is nothing psychical to be lost when nervous arrangements in the medulla oblongata are destroyed.

The affections of speech met with are very different in degree and kind, for the simple reason that the exact position of disease in the brain and its gravity differ in different cases; different amounts of nervous arrangements in different positions are destroyed with different rapidity in different persons. There is, then, no single well-defined "entity"—loss of speech or aphasia—and thus, to state the matter for a particular practical purpose, such a question as, "Can an aphasic make a will?" cannot be answered any more than the question, "Will a piece of string reach across this room?" can be answered. The question should be, "Can this or that aphasic person make a will?" Indeed, we have to consider degrees of affection of language, of which speech is but a part. Admitting the occurrence of numerous degrees of affection of language, we must make arbitrary divisions for the first part of our inquiry, which is an empirical one.

Let us divide roughly into three degrees: (1) *Defect of speech.*—The patient has a full vocabulary, but makes mistakes in words, as saying "orange" for "onion", "chair" for "table"; or he uses approximative or quasi-

---

[1] I, however, believe, as Lewes does, that in so far as we are physically alive we are psychically alive; that some psychical state attends every condition of activity of every part of the organism. This is, at any rate, a convenient hypothesis in the study of diseases of the nervous system.

metaphorical expressions, as "Light the fire up there" for "Light the gas." "When the warm water comes, the weather will go away," for "When the sun comes out, the fog will go away." (2) *Loss of speech.*—The patient is practically speechless, and his pantomime is impaired. (3) *Loss of language.*—Besides being speechless, he has altogether lost pantomime, and emotional language is deeply involved.

To start with, we take the simplest case, one of *loss of speech,* No. 2 ("complete aphasia"). Cases of defect of speech (1) are far too difficult to begin with, and so, too, are those cases (3) in which there is not only loss of speech, but also deep involvement of the least special part of language which we call emotional language. Moreover, we shall deal with a case of permanent speechlessness. I admit that making but three degrees of affection of language, and taking for consideration one kind of frequently occurring case, is an entirely arbitrary proceeding, since there actually occur very numerous degrees of affection of language, many slighter than, and some severer than, that degree (No. 2) we here call one of loss of speech. But as aforesaid, we must study objects so complex as this empirically before we study them scientifically; and for the former kind of study we must have what are called "definitions" by type, and state exceptions. This is the plan adopted in every work on the practice of medicine with regard to all diseases. Let us give an example of the twofold study: Empirically or clinically, that is for the art of medicine, we should consider particular cases of epilepsy, as each *aproaches this or that nosological type* ("le petit mal, le grand mal," &c.). For the science of medicine we should, so far as is possible, consider cases of epilepsy, as each is dependent on a "discharging lesion" of this or that part of the cortex cerebri, and thus as it is a *departure from healthy states* of this or that part of the organism. We cannot do the

latter fully yet, but the anatomico-physiological researches of Hitzig and Ferrier have marvelously helped
us in this way of studying epilepsies, as also have the
clinical researches of Broadbent, Charcot, Duret, Carville, and others.[1]

The following are brief and dogmatic statements about
a condition which is a common one—the kind of one we
call loss of speech, our second degree (No. 2) of affection
of language. The statements are about two equally important things: (1) of what the patient has lost in language—his negative condition—and (2) of what he retains of language—his positive condition. Here, again, is
an illustration of a general principle which is exemplified
in many, if not all, cases of nervous disease, and one of
extreme importance, when they are scientifically considered as instances of nervous dissolution. We have
already stated the duality of many symptomatic conditions. . . . Without recognizing the two elements in all
cases of affections of speech, we shall not be able to
classify affections of speech methodically. If we do not
recognize the duplex (negative and positive) condition,
we cannot possibly trace a relation betwixt Nos. 1, 2,
and 3. . . . There can be no basis for comparison betwixt
the wrong utterances in No. 1 and the non- utterances in

---

[1]See Moxon, "On the Necessity for a Clinical Nomenclature of Disease," *Guy's
Hospital Reports,* 870, vol. xv, p. 479. In this paper Moxon shows conclusively
the necessity of keeping the clinical, or what is above called empirical—not
using that term in its popular bad signification—and scientific studies of
disease distinct. After reading this paper, my eyes were opened to the confusion which results from mixing the two kinds of study. It is particularly
important to have both an empirical arrangement and a scientific classification
of cases of insanity. An example of the former is the much criticized arrangement of Skæ; the scientific classification of cases of insanity, like that of affections of speech, would be regarding them as instances of dissolution; the
dissolution in insanity begins in the highest and most complex of all cerebral
nervous arrangements, the dissolution causing affections of speech in a lower
series. The one kind of classification is for diagnosis (for direct "practical
purposes"), the other is for increase of knowledge, and is worthless for immediate practical purposes. The fault of some classifications of insanity is that
they are mixed, partly empirical and partly scientific.

Nos. 2 and 3—betwixt a positive and a negative condition —betwixt speech, however bad, and no speech. There is a negative and a positive condition in each degree; the comparison is of the three degrees of the negative element and the three degrees of the positive element; the negative and positive elements vary inversely. The condition of the patient No. 1, who made such mistakes as saying "chair" for "table," was duplex; (*a*) negatively in not saying "table," and (*b*) positively, in saying "chair" instead; there is in such a case *loss* of some speech, with *retention* of the rest of speech. Hence the term "defect of speech" applied to such a case is equivocal; it is often used as if the actual utterance was the *direct* result of the disease. The utterance is wrong in that the words of it do not fit the things intended to be indicated; but it is the best speech under the circumstances, and is owing to activity of healthy (except, perhaps, slightly unstable) nervous elements. The real, the primary, fault is in the nervous elements which do not act, which are destroyed, or are for the time *hors de combat*. If, then, we compare No. 1 with No. 2, we compare the two negative conditions, the inability to say "table," &c. (the loss of some speech), in No. 1, with the loss of nearly all speech in No. 2, saying the latter is a greater degree of the former, and we compare the two positive conditions, the retention of inferior speech (the wrong utterances) in No. 1, with in No. 2 the retention of certain recurring utterances, and with the retention of emotional language, saying the latter is a minor or lower degree of language than the former. Unless we take note of the duplex condition in imperception (delirium and ordinary insanity) we shall not be able to trace a correspondence betwixt it and other nervous diseases. There are necessarily the two opposite conditions in all degrees of mental affections, from the slightest "confusion of thought" to dementia, unless the dementia be total.

The Patient's Negative Condition.

(1) *He does not speak.*—He can, the rule is, utter some jargon, or some word, or some phrase. With rare exceptions, the utterance continues the same in the same patient: we call these recurring utterances. The exceptions to the statement that he is speechless are two. (*a*) The recurring utterance may be "yes" or "no," or both. These words are propositions when used for assent or dissent, and they are so used by some patients who are for the rest entirely speechless. (*b*) There are occasional utterances. Under excitement the patient may swear; this is not speech, and is not exceptional; the oath means nothing; the patient cannot repeat it, he cannot *say* what he has just *uttered.* Sometimes, however, a patient, ordinarily speechless, may get out a phrase appropriate to some simple circumstance, such as "good-bye" when a friend is leaving. This is an exception, but yet only a partial exception; the utterance is not of high speech value;[1] he cannot *say* it again, cannot repeat it when entreated; it is inferior speech, little higher in value than swearing. However, sometimes a patient, ordinarily speechless, may get out an utterance of high speech value; this is very rare indeed.

(2) *He cannot write.*—That is to say, he cannot express himself in writing. This is called agraphia (William Ogle). It is, I think, only evidence of the loss of speech, and might have been mentioned in the last paragraph. Written words are symbols of symbols. Since he cannot

---

[1] What is meant by an utterance of high speech value, and by inferior speech, will later on be stated more fully than has been just now stated by implication. When we cease dealing with our subject empirically and treat it scientifically, we hope to show that these so-called exceptions come in place under the principle of dissolution. We may now say that speech of high value, or superior speech, is new speech, not necessarily new words and possibly not new combinations of words; propositions symbolizing relations of images new to the speaker, as in carefully describing something novel. It is the *latest* propositionizing. By inferior speech is meant utterances like, "Very well," "I do not think so," ready fitted to very simple and common circumstances, the nervous arrangements for them being well organized.

write, we see that the patient is speechless, not only in the popular sense of being unable to talk, but altogether so; he cannot speak internally. There is no fundamental difference betwixt external and internal speech; each is propositionizing. If I say "gold is yellow" to myself, or think it, the proposition is the same; the same symbols referring to the same images in the same relation as when I say it aloud. There is a difference, but it is one of degree; psychically "faint" and "vivid," physically "slight" and "strong" nervous discharges. The speechless patient does not write because he has no propositions to write. The speechless man may write in the sense of penmanship; in most cases he can copy writing, and can usually copy print into writing, and very frequently he can sign his name without copy. Moreover, he may write in a fashion without copy, making, or we may say drawing, a meaningless succession of letters, very often significantly the simplest letters, pothooks. His handwriting may be a very bad scrawl, for he may have to write with his left hand. His inability to write, in the sense of expressing himself, is loss of speech; his ability to make ("to draw") letters, as in copying, &c., shows that his "image series" (the materials of his perception) is not damaged.

Theoretically there is no reason why he should not write music without copy, supposing, of course, that he could have done that when well; the marks (artificial images) used in noting music, have no relation to words any way used. On this matter I have no observations. Trousseau writes in his lecture on Aphasia (*New Sydenham Society's Transactions,* vol. i, p. 270), "Dr. Lasegue knew a musician who was completely aphasic, and who could neither read nor write, and yet could note down a musical phrase sung in his presence."

(3) In most cases the speechless patient *cannot read at all,* obviously not aloud, but not to himself either, including what he has himself copied. We suppose our pa-

598

tient cannot read. This is not from lack of sight, nor is it from want of perception; his perception is not itself in fault, as we shall see shortly.

(4) His power of making signs is impaired (panto-mimic propositionizing). We must most carefully distinguish pantomime from gesticulation. Throwing up the arms to signify "higher up," pantomime, differs from throwing the arms when surprised, gesticulation, as a proposition does from an oath.

So far we have, I think, only got two things, loss of speech (by simple direct evidence, and by the indirect evidence of non-writing and non-reading) and defect of pantomime. There are in some cases of loss of speech other inabilities: the most significant are that a patient cannot put out his tongue when he tries, or execute other movements he is told, when he can move the parts concerned in other ways quite well.

The Patient's Positive Condition.

(1) He can understand what we say or read to him; he remembers tales read to him. This is important, for it proves that, although speechless, the patient is not wordless. The hypothesis is that words are in duplicate; and that the nervous arrangements for words used in speech lie chiefly in the left half of the brain; that the nervous arrangements for words used in understanding speech (and in other ways) lie in the right also. Hence our reason for having used such expressions as "words serving in speech"; for there is, we now see, another way in which they serve. When from disease in the left half of the brain speech is lost altogether, the patient understands all we say to him, at least on matters simple to him. Further, it is supposed that another use of the words which remain is the chief part of that service of words which in health precedes speech; there being an unconscious or subconscious revival of words in relation before

599

that second revival which is speech. Coining a word, we may say that the process of verbalizing is dual; the second "half" of it being speech. It is supposed also that there is an unconscious or subconscious revival of relations of images, before that revival of images in relation which is perception.

(2) His articulatory organs move apparently well in eating, drinking, swallowing, and also in such utterances as remain always possible to him (recurring utterances), or in those which come out occasionally. Hence his speechlessness is not owing to disease of those centres in the medulla oblongata for immediately moving the articulatory muscles; for in other cases of nervous disease, when these centres are so damaged that the articulatory muscles are so much paralysed that *talking* is impossible, the patient remains able to *speak* (to propositionize) as well as ever; he has internal speech, and can write what he speaks.

The following dicta may be of use to beginners. Using the popular expression "talk," we may say that if a patient does not talk because his brain is diseased, he cannot write (express himself in writing), and can swallow well; if he cannot talk because his tongue, lips, and palate are immovable, he can write well and cannot swallow well.

(3) His vocal organs act apparently well; he may be able to sing.

(4) His emotional language is apparently unaffected. He smiles, laughs, frowns, and varies his voice properly. His recurring utterance comes out now in one tone and now in another, according as he is vexed, glad, &c.; strictly, we should say he sings his recurring utterance; variations of voice being rudimentary song (Spencer); he may be able to sing in the ordinary meaning of that term. As stated already, he may swear when excited, or get out more innocent interjections, simple or compound

600

(acquired parts of emotional language). Although he may be unable to make any but the simplest signs, he gesticulates apparently as well as ever, and probably he does so more frequently and more copiously than he used to do. His gesticulation draws attention to his needing something, and his friends guess what it is. His friends often erroneously report their guessing what he wants when his emotional manifestations show that he is needing something, as his expressing what thing it is that he wants.

So far for the negative and positive conditions of language in our type case of loss of speech—No. 2 in defect of language.

Words are in themselves meaningless, they are only symbols of things or of "images" of things; they may be said to have meaning "behind them." A proposition symbolizing a particular relation of some images[1]

We must, then, briefly consider the patient's condition in regard to the images symbolized by words. For although we artificially separate speech and perception, words and images co-operate intimately in most mentation. Moreover, there is a morbid condition in the image series (imperception), which corresponds to aphasia in the word series. The two should be studied in relation.

The speechless patient's perception (or "recognition," or "thinking") of things (propositions of images), is unaffected, at any rate as regards simple matters. To give examples: He will point to any object he knew before his illness which we name; he recognizes drawings of all

---

[1] The term "image" is used in a psychical sense, as the term "word" is. It does not mean "visual" images only, but covers all mental states which represent things. Thus we speak of auditory images. I believe this is the way in which Taine uses the term "image." What is here called "an image" is sometimes spoken of as "a perception." In this article the term "perception" is used for a *process*, for a "proposition of images," as speech is used for propositions, i.e., particular inter-relations of words. The expression "organized image" is used briefly for "image," the *nervous arrangements for which* are "organized" correspondingly for "organized word," &c.

objects he knew before his illness. He continues able to play at cards or dominoes; he recognizes handwriting, although he cannot read the words written; he knows poetry from prose, by the different endings of the lines on the right side of the page. One of my patients found out the continuation of a series of papers in a magazine volume, and had the right page ready for her husband when he returned from his work; yet she, since her illness, could not read a word herself, nor point to a letter nor could she point to a figure on the clock. There is better and simpler evidence than that just adduced that the image series is unaffected; the foregoing is intended to show that the inability to read is not due to loss of perception nor to non-recognition of letters, &c., as particular marks or drawings, but to loss of speech. Written or printed words cease to be symbols of words used in speech for the simple reason that those words no longer exist to be symbolized; the written or printed words are left as symbols of nothing, as mere odd drawings. The simplest example showing the image series to be undamaged is that the patient finds his way about; this requires pre-conception, that is, "propositions of images" of streets, &c. Moreover, the patient can, if he retains the propositional use of "yes" and "no," or if he has the equivalent pantomimic symbols, intelligently assent or dissent to simple statements, as that "racehorses are the swiftest horses," showing that he retains organized nervous arrangements for the images of the things "swiftness" and "horse"; this has already been implied when it was asserted that he understands what we say to him, a process requiring not some of his words only, but also some of his "images" of things, of which the words are but symbols.

Such facts as the above are sometimes adduced as showing that the patient's "memory" is unaffected. That expression is misleading, if it implies that there is a general faculty of memory. There is no faculty of memory apart from things being remembered; apart from having, that is, now and again, these or those words, or images, or actions (faintly or vividly). We may say he has not lost the memory of images, or better, that he has the images actually or potentially, the nervous arrangements being intact and capable of excitation did stimuli come to them; we may say that he has lost the memory of those words which serve in speech. It is better, however, to use the simple expression that he has not lost images, and that he has lost the words used in speech.

These facts as to retention of images are important as regards the writing of speechless patients. The printed or written letters and words are images, but they differ from the images of objects, in being artificial and arbitrary, in being acquired later; they are acquired after speech and have their meaning only through speech; written words are symbols of images. The aphasic patient cannot express himself in writing because he cannot speak; but the nervous arrangements for those arbitrary images which are named letters are intact, and thus he can reproduce them as mere drawings, as he can other images, although with more difficulty, they, besides lacking their accustomed stimulus, being less organized. He can copy writing, and he can copy print into writing. When he copies print into writing, obviously he derives the images of letters from his own mind (physically his own organization). He does not write in the sense of expressing himself, because there are no words reproduced in speech to express. That series of artificial images which make up the signature of one's name has become almost as fully organized as many ordinary images; hence in many cases the speechless man who can write nothing else without copy can sign his name.

For the perception (or recognition or thinking) of things, at least in simple relations, speech is not necessary, for such thought remains to the speechless man. Words are required for thinking, for most of our thinking at least, but the speechless man is not wordless; there is an automatic and unconscious[1] or subconscious service of words.

It is not, of course, said that speech is not required for thinking on novel and complex subjects, for ordinary images in new and complex relations (i.e., to the person concerned), and thus the process of perception in the speechless, but not wordless, man may be defective in the sense of being inferior from lack of co-operation of speech; it is not itself in fault, it is left unaided.

To understand anything novel and complex said to him, the healthy man speaks it to himself, e.g., repeats, often aloud, complex directions of route given to him.

The word "thing" has not been used as merely synonymous with "substance"; nor is it meant that anybody has nervous arrangements for the images of "swiftness" and "horse," but only for images of some swiftly moving thing or things, and for images of some particular horse or horses.

It may be well here to give a brief recapitulation of some parts of our subject and, also very briefly, an anticipation of what is to come; the latter is given partly as an excuse for having dwelt in the foregoing on some points not commonly considered in such an inquiry as this, and partly to render clearer some matters which

---

[1] The expression "unconscious reproduction of words," involves the same contradiction as does the expression, "unconscious sensation." Such expressions may be taken to mean that energizing of lower, more organized, nervous arrangements, although unattended by any sort of conscious state, is essential for, and leads to, particular energizings of the highest and least organized—the now organizing nervous arrangements, which last-mentioned energizing is attended by consciousness. I, however, think (as Lewes does) that some consciousness or "sensibility" attends energizing of all nervous arrangements (I use the term "subconscious" for slight consciousness). In cases where from disease the highest nervous arrangements are suddenly placed *hors de combat,* as in sudden delirium, the next lower spring into greater activity, and then, what in health was a subordinate subconsciousness, becomes a vivid consciousness, and is also the highest consciousness there then can be.

were only incidentally referred to.

The division into internal and external speech . . . is not that just made into the dual service of words. Internal and external speech differ in degree only. Such a difference is insignificant in comparison with that betwixt the prior unconscious, or subconscious, and automatic reproduction of words and the sequent conscious and voluntary reproduction of words; the latter alone is speech, either internal or external. Whether I can show that there is this kind of duality or not, it remains certain that our patient retains a service of words, and yet ordinarily uses none in speech. The retention of that service of words which is not a speech use of words, is sometimes spoken of as a retention of "memory of" words, or of "ideas of" words. But as there is no memory or idea of words apart from having words, actually or potentially, it is better to say that the patient retains words serving in other ways than in speech; we should say of his speechlessness, not that he has lost the memory of words, but simply that he has lost those words which serve in speech.

When we consider more fully the duality of the verbalizing process, of which the second "half" is speech, we shall try to show that there is a duality also in the revival of the images symbolized; that perception is the termination of a stage beginning by the unconscious or subconscious revival of images which are in effect "image symbols"; that we think not only by aid of these symbols, ordinarily so-called (words), but by aid of symbol-images. It is, I think, because speech and perception are preceded by an unconscious or subconscious reproduction of words and images, that we seem to have "faculties" of speech and of perception, as it were, above and independent of the rest of ourselves. We seem to have a memory or ideas[1]

---

[1] The so-called *idea* of a word, in contradistinction to *the* word, is itself a word subconsciously revived, or revivable, before the conscious revival or revivability of the same word, which latter, in contradistinction to the so-called *idea* of a word, is the so-called *word itself—the* word.

of words *and* words; having really the two kinds of service of words. The evidence of disease shows, it is supposed, that the highest mentation arises out of our whole organized states, out of ourselves, that will, memory, &c., "come from below," and do not stand autocratically "above," governing the mind; they are simply the now highest, or latest, state of our whole selves. In simple cases of delirium (partial imperception with inferior perception) as when a patient takes his nurse to be his wife, we find, I think, a going down to and a revelation of what would have been when he was sane, the lower and earlier step towards his true recognition or perception of the nurse.

The first step towards his recognition of her when he was sane would be the unconscious or subconscious, and automatic reproduction of his, or of one of his, well-organized symbol-images of woman; the one most or much organized in him would be his wife. To say what a thing is, is to say what it is like; he would not have known the nurse even as a woman, unless he had already an organized image of at least one woman. The popular notion is, that by a sort of faculty of perception, he would recognize her without a prior stage in which, he being passive, an organized image was roused in him by the mere presence of the nurse; the popular notion almost seems to imply the contradiction that he first sees her, in the sense of recognizing her, and then sees her as like his already acquired or organized image of some woman. We seem to ourselves to perceive, as also to will and to remember, without prior stages, because these prior stages are unconscious or subconscious. It seems to me that in delirium the patient is reduced to conditions which are revelations of, or of parts of, the lower earlier and prior stages; the lower or earlier stages are then conscious. They are the *then* highest or *latest* conscious states. When the patient becomes delirious, he takes the nurse to be his wife. More

606

or fewer of the highest nervous arrangements being then exhausted, the final stage is not possible. There is only the first stage; the reproduction of his well-organized symbol-image is all there is, and that is all the nurse can be to him; she is, to him, his wife. The symbol-image is then vividly reproduced because the centres next lower than those exhausted are in abnormally great activity (note that there are two conditions, one negative and the other positive). There is a deepening of consciousness in the sense of going down to lower earlier and more or- ganized states, which in health are mostly unconscious or subconscious, and precede higher or later conscious states; in other words, with loss with or defect of object consciousness, even in sleep dreaming, there is increasing subject consciousness; on the physical side, increasing energizing of those lower centres which are in the daytime more slightly energizing during that unbroken subcon- scious "dreaming," from which the serial states, consti- tuting our latest or highest object consciousness, are the continual "awakenings."

It is supposed that the well-organized images spoken of, in effect arbitrary images, symbol-images, those which *become* vivid and are "uppermost" in delirium, and then cease to be mere symbols, constitute what seems to be a "general notion" or "abstract idea" of such things as "horse," "swiftness," &c.; their particularity (that they are only images of some horse or horses, of some swift moving thing or things) not appearing, because they are unconscious or subconscious; they served once as images of particular things, and at length as symbol-images of a class of images of things, as well as images of the par- ticular things.

[Previously] . . . we spoke of the right half of the brain as being the part during the activity of which the most nearly unconscious and most automatic service of words

607

begins, and of the left as the half during activity of which there is that sequent verbal action which is speech. The division is too abrupt; some speech—voluntary use of words—is, as we have seen when alluding to occasional utterances, possible to the man who is rendered practically speechless by disease in the left half. Again, from disease of the right half, there is not loss of that most automatic service of words which enables us to understand speech. The thing which it is important to show is, that mentation is dual, and that physically the unit of function of the nervous system is double the unit of composition; not that one-half of the brain is "automatic" and the other "voluntary."

Having now spoken of the kind of case we shall consider, and having added remarks, with the endeavour to show how the several symptoms—negative and positive—are related one to another, we shall be able to give reasons for excluding other kinds of cases of speechlessness.

We are not concerned with cases of all persons who do not speak. We shall not, for example, deal with those untrained deaf-mutes who never had speech, but with the cases of those persons only who have had it, and lost it by disease. The condition of an untrained deaf-mute is in very little comparable with that of our arbitrarily taken case of loss of speech. The deaf-mute's brain is not diseased, but, because he is deaf, it is uneducated (or in anatomical and physiological phraseology undeveloped) so as to serve in speech. Our speechless patient is not deaf. Part of our speechless patient's brain is destroyed; he has *lost* nervous arrangements which had been trained in speech. Moreover, our speechless man retains a service of words which is not speech; untrained deaf-mutes have no words at all. Further, the untrained deaf-mute has his natural system of signs, which to him is of speech value as far as it goes. He will think by aid of these symbols as we do by aid of words.[1] Our speechless patient is defective even in such slight pantomime as we may reasonably suppose to have been easy to him before his illness. The deaf-mute may have acquired for talking and thinking the common arbitrary system of deaf-mute signs (finger-talk), or he may have been taught by the new method to speak as we do, and thus have ceased to be mute. But when not taught to speak, he is not in a condition even roughly comparable with that of a man who has *lost* speech. No doubt by disease of some part of his brain the deaf-mute might lose his natural system of signs, which are of some speech value to him, but he could not lose speech, having never had it. Much more like our speechless patient's condition is that of the little child which has been taught to understand speech, and has not yet spoken.

There is another set of cases of so-called loss of speech, which we shall not consider as real loss of speech. I prefer to say that these patients *do* not speak: cases of some persons are meant, who do not talk and yet write perfectly. This may seem to be an arbitrary exclusion. There is in most of these cases an association of symptoms, which never arises from any local disease of any part of the nervous system; the so-called association is a mere jumble of symptoms. Let us state the facts. The patients are nearly always boys or unmarried women. The bearing of this is obvious. The so-called loss of speech is a total non-utterance, whereas it is an excessively rare thing for a patient who does not speak, because his brain is locally diseased, to have no utterance whatever; I do not remember seeing one such case in which there was not some utterance (recurring utterance) a few days or a few weeks after the onset of the illness; the absolute pseudo-speech-

[1] We must not confound the finger-talk with the "natural" system of signs. They are essentially different. No one supposes that words are essential for thought, but only that some symbols are essential for conceptual thought, although it may be that people with "natural" symbols do not reach that higher degree of abstract thinking which people do who have words.

lessness may remain for months. They cannot be mute from paralysis of the articulatory muscle, because they swallow well. Frequently there is loss of voice also—they get out no sounds except, perhaps, grunts, &c.—and yet they cough ringingly and breathe without hoarseness or stridor; there is no evidence of laryngeal disease. Now loss of voice never occurs with loss of speech from local disease of one side of the brain. No disease of the larynx would cause loss of speech or loss of articulation. The patients often "lose" their speech after calamity or worry. In these cases there is no hemiplegia and no other one-sided condition from first to last. They often, after months of not speaking, recover absolutely and immediately after some treatment which can have no therapeutical effect, e.g., a liniment rubbed on the back, a single faradaic stimulation of the vocal cords or of the neck. Dr. Wilks has reported a case of "cure" of a girl who had not spoken for months; she had also "lost" the use of her legs. Knowing well what was the general nature of the case, Dr. Wilks, by speaking kindly to her, and giving her an excuse for recovery in the application of faradization, got her well in a fortnight. Sometimes the so-called speechless patient speaks inadvertently when suddenly asked a question, and then goes on talking; is well again. Sometimes speech is surprised out of her. Thus a woman, whose case is recorded by Durham, when told to cry "Ah!" when the spatula was holding down her tongue, pushed his hand away, saying, "How can I, with that thing in my mouth?" She then said, "Oh! I have spoken." She was "cured." I believe that patients, "speechless" as described, might be "cured" by faradization of the vocal cords, or by a thunderstorm, or by quack medicines or appliances, or by mesmerism, or by wearing a charm, or—not speaking flippantly—by being "prayed over."

610

Sometimes these cases are spoken of as cases of "emotional aphasia"—the speechlessness is said to be "caused by" emotional excitement, because it often comes on *after* emotional disturbance.

I submit that the facts that the patients do not talk and *do* write and *do* swallow are enough to show that there is no disease at all, in any sense except that the patients are hysterical (which is saying nothing explanatory), or that they are pretending. There can be no *local* disease, at any rate.

These cases are spoken of at length, although they are excluded, because they are sometimes adduced as instances of aphasia, or loss of speech proper, with ability to write remaining. I confess that were I brought face to face with a man whom I believed to *have* local disease of his brain, who did not *talk,* and yet wrote well, I should conclude that he did *speak* internally although he could not talk. To say that *he* cannot speak, and yet can express himself in writing is equivalent, I think, to saying *he* cannot speak and yet *he* can speak.

(JOHN) HUGHLINGS JACKSON (b.-Providence Green, Yorkshire, England, April 4, 1835; d.-Manchester Square, London, Oct. 7, 1911.)

Jackson began his medical education at the York Medical and Surgery School, and continued at St. Bartholomew's Hospital. He matriculated at London University and qualified as Member of the Royal College of Surgery in 1856. Until 1859, he was house surgeon to the dispensary at York. In 1859 he was appointed to the staff of the Metropolitan Free Hospital, and he began his great lectures on neural pathology at the London Hospital. In 1860 he earned his M.D. from St. Andrews. In 1863 he was appointed Assistant Physician to the London Hospital, from where he issued his first "London Hospital Report" in 1864. It was in these irregular hospital reports that all of Jackson's work was first published.

The field of neurology and of its associated behavioral and sensory disorders is dominated today by the concepts and ideas of Jackson.

One of the primary clues to neurological injury is through disorders in the use and interpretation of language in all its various aspects. Jackson devoted much of his life to the elucidation of these problems. It is from this work that we reprint here.

JACKSON, H. "On affections of speech from disease of the brain." *Brain,* 1879, 1:304-. This is the first part of Jackson's great essay, which was later completed in three parts (i.e. *Ibid,* 1880, II: 203-, 323-.) The present selection is taken from the readily available collection of Jackson's essays recently republished in *Brain* (1915, 38:1-190; in particular pp. 107-129). It is with particular pleasure that I thank Dr. W. L. H. Jackson, of Auckland, New Zealand, for his gracious permission to reprint.

See also:

JACKSON, H. Selected Writings of John Hughlings Jackson. London: Hodder & Stoughton, Ltd., 1931-32, 2 vol. Edited for the Guarantors of *Brain* by J. Taylor, with assistance from G. Holmes & F.M.R. Walshe.

HEAD, H. "Aphasia: An historical review." *Brain.* 1920, 40: 390-411.

THE INTEGRATIVE ACTION
OF THE
NERVOUS SYSTEM

SIR CHARLES SCOTT SHERRINGTON

Lecture IX

THE PHYSIOLOGICAL POSITION AND
DOMINANCE OF THE BRAIN*

The Primitive Reflex-Arc

If we seek for a reflex-arc of simplest construction it is true we find in some unicellular organisms, e.g. *Vorticella,* a mechanism which resembles a nervous arc and is quite simple. This mechanism, composed from a single cell, shows differentiation into three parts respectively—*receptive, conductive,* and *effective.* In *Vorticella* the receptive element is the ciliated peristome; a stimulus reaching these cilia at the free end of the cell excites contraction of the myoid filament at the fixed end of the cell. . . . In multicellular organisms of low organization like mechanisms occur. In *Actinia* there are ectoderm cells which have externally a receptive hairlet and internally a contractile fibre, and this latter contracts when the receptive hairlet is stimulated.

In view of such cases it might have seemed likely that in more highly developed organisms examples would have been forthcoming in which the differentiation of the parts of a single cell would have advanced further still and produced something yet more akin to a simple reflex-arc such as is considered typical of the true nervous system itself. That expectation is not realized. What we

---

*Deleted is a short introductory statement—Editor.

find as the simplest arc in the organisms which possess a true nervous system, is that the conductor mediating between receptor and effector is itself a separate cell intercalated between a receptive cell and an effector cell. At each end this separate conductive cell breaks up into branches. The branching at the receptive end places it in communication not with one but with several receptor cells. This must allow stimuli at a number of receptive points to combine by summation to a conjoint effect. By this means the threshold of reaction will be lowered and the organism in that respect become more sensitively reactive to the environment. At the deep, i.e. effector, end the branching of the conductive stem places it in touch not with one effective cell but with many. Thus, again, there must result lowering of the threshold—of what we may term the effective threshold. The contraction of a single muscle-fibre in a muscle is practically ineffective where the resistance and mass of the muscle and its load are great as compared with the power of a single muscle-fibre. But by its branching the motor neurone obtains hold of many muscle-fibres. This must tend to lower the effective threshold of reaction, and thus again the organism is rendered more delicately responsive to stimulation by its environment.

But—and it is a striking fact—we do not know of any reflex-arc in which in fact the nervous conductor connecting receptor to effector is formed from end to end of one single neurone. The length of the conductor seems always to include *at least* two neurones in succession. A moment's reflexion reminds us that such arrangements as *Vorticella,* . . . and the neuro-muscular cells of . . . *Actinia* do not exhibit the germ of a feature that we have already considered fundamental in the construction of the reflex-nervous system. The cases do not exhibit even in germ the co-ordinative mechanism which is attained by the principle of the *common path.* Such cases confine each

614

effector to the use of one receptor only and confine each receptor to the use of one effector only. But we saw that a great principle in the plan of the nervous system is that an effector shall be at the behest of many receptors, and that one receptor shall be able to employ many effectors. We saw further in respect to this that there are two conditions which the nervous system satisfies. One is that the effector is at the behest of various receptors which can use it simultaneously and use it harmoniously all in more or less the same way. Thus an advantage accrues in that their reactions sum, even though the receptors may be of different modality; and by summation the threshold is lowered and the organism more sensitized to the environment. This arrangement cannot be obtained by the unicellular mechanisms instanced above. It can only be obtained by the formation of a common path, and the formation of a common path can only be rendered possible by having a conductor of pluricellular length. And there is another condition which the nervous system satisfies. The unicellular reflex-arc— if reflex-arc it can be called—not only admits no opportunity for *pluricellular summation* but also none for the second function of the jointed reflex-arc of pluricellular length, namely *interference*. In animals of complex organization the activity of one effector may interfere with the function of another, e.g. in the case of muscles which when contracting pull in opposite directions at the same lever. We have seen how this wasteful confusion is avoided by one receptor having power not only to throw a particular effector into action but also to throw the opposed effector out of action. We saw that this action it exercises not peripherally but within the nervous system, at the entrance to a common path. The unicellular reflex-arc allows no common path. It lacks, therefore, the mechanism which renders possible the two great co-ordinative processes of *pluriceptive summation* and of *interference.* Without these the nervous system is shorn of its chief powers to integrate a set of organs or an organism.

It is therefore a significant thing that in the nervous system there is not only no instance of the reflex triune —receptor, conductor, and effector—being formed of one cell only, but also no indubitable instance where the middle link, the conductor, is even itself formed of one cell (one neurone) only. In other words, we know of no instance in the nervous system of a reflex-arc so constructed as not to include a junction between one neurone and another neurone. And the rule is apparently always that at such junctions not only does one neurone meet another, but several neurones converge upon another and make of the latter a common path.

The Diffuse Nervous System, The Grey-Centred Nervous System, The Central Nervous System a Part of the Latter

The term 'nerve-centre' is sometimes abused, yet seems in several ways apt. A keynote regarding that part of the nervous system which is termed 'the central' seems that it is wholly pieced together into one system. The nervous system in its simplest forms is diffuse—a number of scattered mechanisms performing merely local operations with much autonomy save that they have communication with their immediate neighbours across near boundaries. The co-ordination effected by the diffuse nervous system is not adapted to compass the quickly combined action of distant parts. It is slow, and it throws *en route* the effectors of intermediate regions into action. It is ill suited, therefore, to produce the integration of a large and complex individual as a whole, or even to integrate large differentiated portions of an individual. Yet the co-ordination it brings about in its own local

616

field may be strikingly effective. A co-adjustment though simple and restricted may be not less perfect than one involving wide and complex neural mechanism. The co-ordination of a peristaltic movement of the bowel is, as shown by Bayliss & Starling, even when managed exclusively by the local diffuse nervous system, capable of the perfect taxis of two muscular coats arranged antagonistically in the viscus. It directs a relaxation of the one co-ordinately with a contraction of the other; it exhibits a primitive but none the less perfect form of 'reciprocal innervation'.

This diffuse system seems the only one in such an organism as Medusa. But in higher animals a system of longer direct connexions is developed. And this latter is 'synaptic', that is, possesses the adjustable junctions which belong characteristically to 'grey matter'. This *synaptic* system co-existing with the *diffuse* in various places dominates the latter. Thus it controls and oversees the actions of the local nervous system of the viscera, and heart, and blood-vessels, which even in the highest animal forms remain diffuse.

The synaptic nervous system has developed as its distinctive feature a central organ, a so-called *central nervous system;* it is through this that it brings into *rapport* one with another widely distant organs of the body, including the various portions of the diffuse nervous system itself.

That portion of the synaptic system which is termed 'central' is the portion where the nervous paths from the various peripheral organs meet and establish paths in common, i.e. *common paths*. It is therefore in accord with expectation that we find the organ in which this meeting occurs situated fairly midway among them all, i.e. centrally. In bilaterally symmetrical animals this organ would be expected to lie where it does, namely, equidistant from the two lateral surfaces of the animal, and to exhibit as it does, laterally symmetrical halves united by a number of nervous cross-ties bridging the median line. This central nervous organ contains almòst all the junctions existent between the multitudinous arcs. In it the afferent paths from receptor-organs become connected with the efferent paths of effector-organs, not. only those adjacent to their own receptors but, through *internuncial* (J. Hunter, 1778) paths, with efferent paths to effector-organs remote. This central 'exchange' organ is therefore well called the *central* nervous system. In the higher Invertebrata it is known as the longitudinal nerve-cord with ganglia, supraoesophageal, suboesophageal, etc.; in Vertebrata it is known as the spinal cord and brain. Under these different anatomical names the same physiological organ is designated. . . . We have seen that it is not merely a meeting place where afferent paths conjoin with efferent, but is, in virtue of its physiological properties, an organ of reflex reinforcements and interferences, and of refractory phases, and shifts of connective pattern; that it is, in short, an *organ of co-ordination* in which from a concourse of multitudinous excitations there result orderly acts, reactions adapted to the needs of the organism, and that these reactions occur in arrangements (*patterns*) marked by absence of confusion, and proceed in *sequences* likewise free from confusion.

By the development of these powers the synaptic system with its central organ is adapted to more speedy, wide, and delicate co-ordinations than the diffuse nervous system allows. Out of this potentiality for organizing complex integration there is evolved in the synaptic nervous system a functional grading of its reflex-arcs and centres. Thus, with allied reflexes, the mechanism of the common path knits together by plurireceptive summation not only the separate individual stimuli of similar kind, e.g. tangoreceptive or photo-receptive received from

618

some agent as this latter becomes prepotent in the environment; but it knits together separate stimuli of even wholly different receptive species. C. J. Herrick has shown that in *Ameiurus nebulosus* (cat-fish) the reaction of the animal to stimulation of the barblets by meat is a reaction to a twofold stimulus, a chemical and a mechanical, and he finds that these two reactions mutually reinforce. . . . v. Uexkull finds that the *Giftzangen* of *Echinus acutus* react only when a chemical and a mechanical stimulus are combined. The several qualitatively different properties of an object which is acting as stimulus are thus combined and reinforce each other in eliciting appropriate reaction. By this summation reflex complication in Herbart's sense is made possible. A touchstone for rank of a centre in this neural hierarchy is the degree to which paths from separate loci and of different receptive modality are confluent thither. Indicative of high rank is such functional position as relieves from 'local work' and involves general responsibility, e.g. for a series of segments or for the whole body. The 'three levels', of Hughlings Jackson is an expressive figure of this grading of rank in nerve-centres.

Integrative Action of the Nervous System in the Segment and in the Segmental Series

In animal organisms of any considerable complexity a division of the body into segments, metameres, is widely found. By the occurrence of separating constrictions or sepiments, or through the regular repetition of appendicular structures, subdivisions of the body are established which severally possess analogues of functions possessed more or less similarly by the other subdivisions but also severally possess functional unity. Such is this functional unity and completeness that in some instances a metamere comes to be independent of the total organism, and able to lead a separate existence. The nervous system it is which largely gives functional solidarity to the composite collection of unit lives and organs composing the individual metamere. Further, the linkage of the several metameres into one functional whole is largely of nervous nature. The integrative function of the nervous system is seen to perfection in the welding together of metameres into the unity of an animal individual. The kind of nervous system employed for this is the *synaptic* system. Although the nerve-net system is retained even in the highest vertebrates, it is then confined to unsegmentally arranged musculature, e.g. visceral and vascular. In the skeletal musculature, where segmental arrangement holds, the nervous system is *synaptic*. It is not surprising therefore that in metameric animals the nervous system, especially its synaptic part, should strikingly exhibit that metamerism.

Various schemes of metamerism have been evolved. Where it is radiate so that each segment bears exactly similar relations to the common axis and to the other segments, the opportunity for dominance of one segment over the rest is slight. The conditions of life for each segment are practically those which are the average for all. The mouth, for instance, lies equidistant from them all. Evolution toward higher differentiation of the whole metameric individual and toward more intricate welding of its parts into one, is at a disadvantage in these radiate forms as compared with its opportunity in the great groups of Arthropoda and Vertebrata where the metameres are ranged serially along a single axis, the longitudinal axis of the organism. With fore and aft arrangement of its segments the animal body has its first opportunity for really high differentiation. Certain of the segments of necessity lie nearer to the mouth than do others; moreover certain segments come to habitually

620

lead, that is to say go foremost, during the animal's active locomotion.

In the integrating function of the nervous system a segmental arrangement of its functions is frequently apparent. It makes itself felt in two ways. Firstly, the various separate and different elements of the segment are knit together by nervous ties. Secondly, where kindred functions are exercised in successive segments, so that throughout a series of segments one set of organs forms a more or less functionally homogeneous system, these organs are combined by interrelated nervous arcs. But particular systems of organs common to all or many metameres of an individual present special differentiation of their function in particular metameres. In this manner the organism is built up of component segments possessing resemblance one to another, but presenting also specializations peculiar to certain segments. Hence the segmental arrangement forms a convenient basis not merely for anatomical but for physiological description. And in dealing with the special problems of integration by the nervous system, especially those of the synaptic nervous system, analysis can employ two co-ordinate sets of descriptive factors—one the segment, the other the line of organs of analogous function scattered along the series of segments. In the two great animal groups just mentioned the latter ordinate is longitudinally extended, while the individual segment is extended transversely. The analysis thus proceeds formally somewhat in the same way as the analysis of a plane figure by rectangular co-ordinates.

The Receptive Fields

The *central* nervous system, though divisible into separate mechanisms, is yet one single harmoniously acting although complex whole. To analyse its action we turn to the receptor-organs, for to them is traceable the initiation of the reactions of the centres. These organs fall naturally into three main groups, distributed in three main fields, each field being differently circumstanced.

Multicellular animals regarded broadly throughout a vast range of animal types are cellular masses presenting to the environment a surface sheet of cells, and under that a cellular bulk more or less screened from the environment by the surface sheet. Many of the agencies by which the environment acts on the organism do not penetrate to the deep cells inside. Bedded in the surface sheet are numbers of *receptor* cells constituted in adaptation to the stimuli delivered by environmental agencies. The *underlying* tissues devoid of these receptors are not devoid of *all* receptor-organs; they have other kinds apparently specific to them. Some agencies act not only at the surface of the organism but penetratively through its mass. Of these there are for some apparently no receptors adapted, for instance, none for the Roentgen rays. For others of more usual occurrence receptors are adapted. The most important of these deep adequate agents seems to be mass acting in the mode of weight and mechanical inertia involving mechanical stresses and mechanical strain. Moreover, the organism, like the world surrounding it, is a field of ceaseless change, where internal energy is continually being liberated, whence chemical, thermal, mechanical, and electrical effects appear. ... In its depths lie receptor-organs adapted consonantly with the changes going on in the microcosm itself, particularly in its muscles and their accessory apparatus (tendons, joints, walls of blood-vessels, and the like).

There exist, therefore, two primary distributions of the receptor-organs, and each constitutes a field in certain respects fundamentally different from the other. The deep field we have called the *proprioceptive* field, because its stimuli are, properly speaking, events in the micro-

622

cosm itself, and because that circumstance has important bearing upon the service of its receptors to the organism.

Richness of the Extero-Ceptive Field in Receptors;
Comparative Poverty of the Intero-Ceptive

The surface receptive field is again subdivisible. It presents two divisions. Of these one lies freely open to the numberless vicissitudes and agencies of the environment. That is to say, it is co-extensive with the so-called *external* surface of the animal. This subdivision may be termed the *extero-ceptive field.*

But the animal has another surface, its so-called *internal,* usually alimentary in function. This, though in contact with the environment, lies however less freely open to it. It is partly screened by the organism itself. For purposes of retaining food, digesting and absorbing it, an arrangement of common occurrence in animal forms is that a part of the free surface is deeply recessed. In this recess a fraction of the environment is more or less surrounded by the organism itself. Into that sequestered nook the organism by appropriate reactions gathers morsels of environmental material whence by chemical action and by absorption it draws nutriment. This surface of the animal may be termed the *intero-ceptive.* At its ingress several species of receptors are met with whose 'adequate' stimuli are chemical (e.g. taste organs). Lining this digestive chamber, this kitchen, the intero-ceptive surface is adapted to *chemical* agencies to a degree such as it exhibits nowhere else. Comparatively little is yet known of the receptor-organs of this surface, though we may suppose that they exhibit refined adaptations. But the body-surface in this recess, though possessed of certain receptors specific to it, is sparsely endowed as contrasted with that remainder of the surface (the *extero-ceptive* surface) lying open fully to the influences of the

623

great outer environment. The afferent nerve-fibres in the sympathetic system as judged by their number in the white rami are comparatively few; Warrington's recent observations show this conclusively. The poverty of afferent paths from the *intero-ceptive* field is broadly indicated by the fact that we know no wholly afferent nerve-trunk in the sympathetic (Langley's 'autonomic') system, though such are common enough in the nervous system subserving the extero-ceptive arcs; and that in the latter system we know no wholly efferent nerve-trunk, whereas in the sympathetic such exist, e.g. the cervical sympathetic trunk.

The extero-ceptive field far exceeds the intero-ceptive in its wealth of receptor-organs. This seems inevitable, for it is the extero-ceptive surface, facing outward on the general environment, that feels and has felt for countless ages the full stream of the varied agencies forever pouring upon it from the outside world. . . . It contains specific receptors adapted to mechanical contact, cold and warmth, light, sound, and agencies inflicting injury (*noxa*). Almost all these species of receptors are distributed to the *extero-ceptive* field exclusively; they are not known to exist in the intero-ceptive or in the proprio-ceptive fields.

It is an instructive exercise to try to classify the stimuli adequate for the receptors of the extero-ceptive field. Each animal has experience only of those qualities of the environment which as stimuli excite its receptors; it analyses its environment in terms of them exclusively. Doubtless certain stimuli causing reactions in other animals are imperceptible to man; and in a large number of cases his reactions are different from theirs. Hence it is impossible for man to conceive the world in terms more than partially equivalent to those of other animals. Humanly, the classification of adequate stimuli can be made with various departments of natural knowledge as its basis. Physics and chemistry can be taken as basis usefully in a number of cases where the sources of stimulation are known to those more exact branches of experimental science. But in several ways a physico-chemical scheme of classification of stimuli lacks significance for physiology. Thus, in the case of noci-ceptive organs of the skin, those receptors —probably naked nerve-endings—are *non-selective* in the meaning that they are excitable by physical and chemical stimuli of diverse kind, radiant, mechanical, acid, alkaline, electrical, and so on, so that a classification according to mode of exciting energy on the one hand fails to differentiate them from each of a number of more specialized other groups (tango-receptors, chemo-receptors, etc.) from which biologically they are quite different, and on the other hand that classification apportions them, though physiologically a single group, to a whole series of different classes. A physiological classification deals with them more satisfactorily. Physiological criteria can be applied which at once separate them from other receptors and yet show their affinity one to another. Thus, physiologically the stimulus which excites these end-organs must, whatever its physical or chemical nature, possess, in order to stimulate them, the quality of tending to do immediate harm to the skin. Further, the reflex they excite (i) is *prepotent;* (ii) tends to *protect* the threatened part by escape or defence; (iii) is *imperative*; and (iv) if we include psychical evidence and judge by analogy from introspection, is accompanied by *pain*.

Here what we may call the physiological scheme of classification proves the more useful at present. ... The key to the physiological classification lies in the reaction which is produced. But the physico-chemical basis of classification also has its uses, and especially with those manifold receptors of the extero-ceptive field which possess highly developed accessory structures that render them selectively receptive—and among these are some

625

of the most highly adapted and important receptors, e.g. photo-receptors, possessed by the organism. It is to the extero-ceptive field that these belong.

Nervous Integration of the Segment

The edifice of the whole central nervous system is reared upon two neurones—the afferent root-cell and the efferent root-cell. These form the pillars of a fundamental reflex arch. And on the junction between these two are superposed and functionally set, mediately or immediately, all the other neural arcs, even those of the cortex of the cerebrum itself. The private receptor paths and the common effector paths are in the Chordata gathered up in a single nerve-trunk for each segment. Close to the central nervous organ, however, there occurs in the segmental nerves of many vertebrates a cleavage of the private receptor paths from the common effector paths. A dorsal spinal nerve of centripetal conduction and a ventral of centrifugal conduction results. Among the afferent root-cells (afferent spinal root of vertebrates) in each segment are quota from the *extero-ceptive* (cutaneous) and from the *proprio-ceptive* (deep) fields. In many segments there is a third quotum, *intero-ceptive*, from the visceral field. This visceral constituent of the spinal ganglion is not present in all segments and is probably, even in those segments in which it is present, numerically the weakest of the three components. Cranial, caudal, and other segments exist, therefore, in which the total afferent nerve of the segment is extero-ceptive and proprio-ceptive but not intero-ceptive. In the remaining segments it is intero-ceptive as well as extero-ceptive and proprio-ceptive, and in these its function is therefore fundamentally threefold.

The efferent segmental nerve conversely radiates outward from the central end of the afferent nerve and the central nervous organ to the various effector organs at

626

the surface and in the depth of the segment. Function does not, however, strictly respect the ancestral boundaries of segments. Among the efferent fibres in the ventral root are a number that extend quite beyond the boundaries of the segment in which the spinal root is placed. These pass to the viscera and muscles of the skin. They embouch not directly into their effector organs, e.g. intestinal muscle-wall, pilomotor muscle, etc., but into ganglia of the sympathetic system. In these ganglia, although not grey matter in the same sense as spinal cord and brain, axone-endings, perikarya, and dendrites are nevertheless found. By its distribution to the cells in such a ganglion and by being distributed in many cases to more than one such ganglion, a single constituent efferent path in the ventral spinal root obtains access to a very large number of effector organs. These ganglia seem, therefore, mechanisms for the *distribution* of nerve-impulses. We have seen . . . how by such widening of distribution the threshold of effective reaction is lowered. But though adapted for distribution of nerve-impulses there is no evidence that these ganglia can serve for the *regulation* of them in the same sense as does the grey matter of the spinal cord with its synapses of *variable* resistance and connexion. Prominent among the integrating connexions intrinsic to each segment itself are conducting paths from the extero-ceptive field to the 'final common paths' for the skeletal musculature. Thus, in the mammal we laid it down (Lect. V) . . . as a general rule that "for each afferent root there exists in immediate proximity to its own place of entrance into the cord, i.e. in its own segment, a reflex motor path from skin to muscle of as low resistance as any open to it anywhere."

The extero-ceptive arcs appear in most segments less closely connected with the visceral musculature than with the skeletal musculature. The intero-ceptive arcs appear in most segments less closely connected with the skeletal

627

musculature than with the visceral. In physiological parlance a resistance to conduction seems intercalated between the two. But both extero-ceptive and intero-ceptive fields easily influence through their nervous arcs the musculature of the blood-vascular organs. So also do the receptors of the proprio-ceptive field itself; and these latter are in particularly close touch with the skeletal musculature, exerting tonic influence on it. In certain segments these general relations are modified in special ways. Thus, in those segments where the intero-ceptive and extero-ceptive fields conjoin, e.g. at the mouth and the cloaca, closer nervous connexions exist between the intero-ceptive arcs and the skeletal musculature, and conversely between the extero-ceptive arcs and the visceral musculature. Thus stimuli acting on the pharyngeal receptors evoke or inhibit activity of skeletal muscles subserving respiration and deglutition; stimuli to the cloacal mucosa evoke movements of the caudal skeletal muscles; and so forth.

It is not merely specific difference between the receptors of the extero-ceptive field and those of the intero-ceptive which brings the former into closer relationship with the skeletal musculature. Receptors of the one and the same species, if they lie in the extero-ceptive field, work skeletal musculature; if they lie in the intero-ceptive, work visceral musculature. Thus the chemo-receptors on the outer surface of the head (gustatory of the barblets of fish) excite reflexes which move the body around, bringing the mouth to the morsel; while the similar chemo-receptors within the mouth excite reflex swallowing without outward movement of the animal (C. J. Herrick).

Receptors of the *same* specific system, where they lie close together, mutually reinforce reaction. On the contrary, where members of two *different* systems lie close together, e.g. tango-receptor and noci-ceptor, in one and the same piece of skin, they, as mentioned above, often have conflicting mutual relation. One relationship between receptor arcs of the same species may be particularly noted. Receptors symmetrically placed on opposite sides of the segment, especially if distant from the median plane, excite reactions which mutually 'conflict'. Thus, when a noci-ceptor is stimulated on the right side of the tail of the spinal dog or cat or lizard, the reaction moves the organ to the left. The symmetrical receptor on the left side does the converse. The two reactions thus conflict. And the like holds true for many right and left symmetrical receptors which initiate exactly converse reactions.

But a group of special cases is formed by reactions initiated from receptors distributed at or near to the median line. Stimulation of such a small group of receptors at the median line in many cases evokes a bilateral movement which is symmetrical, e.g. a touch on the decerebrate frog's lip in the median line causes both fore-limbs to sweep forward synchronously over the spot. The median overlap of the distribution of the afferent fibres of the dorsal spinal roots may be connected with this.

Special Refinements of the Receptors of the "Leading" Segments

As the receptors that are excitable by the various adequate agencies, e.g. mechanical impact, noxa, radiant energy, chemical solutions, etc., are traced along the series of segments, it is found that in one region of the longitudinal segmental series remarkable developments exist.

In motile animals constituted of segments ranged along a single axis, e.g. Vertebrata, when locomotion of the animal goes on, it proceeds for the most part along a line continuous with the long axis of the animal itself, and more frequently in one direction of that line than in the other. The animal's locomotor appendages and their musculature are favourably adapted for locomotion in that habitual direction. In the animal's progression certain of its segments therefore *lead*. The receptors of these leading segments predominate in the motor taxis of the animal. They are specially developed. Thus, in the earthworm, while all parts of the external surface are responsive to light, the directive influence of light is greatest at the anterior end of the animal. The leading segments are exposed to external influences more than are the rest. Not only do they receive *more* stimuli, meet *more* 'objects' demanding pursuit or avoidance, but it is they which usually *first* encounter the agents beneficial or hurtful of the environment as related to the individual. Pre-eminent advantage accrues if the receptors of these leading segments react sensitively and differentially to the agencies of the environment. And it is in these leading segments that remarkable developments of the receptors, especially those of the extero-ceptive field, arise. Some of them are specialized in such degree as almost obscures their fundamental affinity to others distributed in other segments. Thus, among the system of receptors for which radiation is the adequate agent, there are developed in one of the leading segments a certain group, the *retinal,* particularly and solely, and extraordinarily highly, amenable to radiations of a certain limited range of wave-length. These are the *photo-receptors,* for which light and only light, e.g. not heat, is the adequate stimulus. In like manner a certain group belonging to the system receptive of mechanical impacts attains such susceptibility for these as to react to the vibrations of water and air that constitute physical sounds. The retina is thus a group of glorified 'warm-spots', the cochlea a group of glorified 'touch-spots'. Again, a group belonging to the system adapted to chemical stimuli reach in one of the leading segments such a pitch of delicacy that particles in quantity un-

630

weighable by the chemist, emanating from substances called odorous, excite reaction from them.

The Refined Receptors of the Leading Segments are 'Distance-Receptors.' The After-Coming Segments Form a Motor Train Actuated Chiefly by the 'Distance-Receptors'

It is in the leading segments that we find the *distance-receptors*. For so may be called the receptors which react to *objects* at a distance. These are the same receptors which, acting as sense-organs, initiate sensations having the psychical quality termed *projicience*. The receptor-organs adapted to odours, light, and sound, though stimulated by the external matter in direct contact with them—as the vibrating ether, the vibrating water or air, or odorous particles,—yet generate reactions which show 'adaptation', e.g. in direction of movements, etc., to the environmental *objects* at a distance, the *sources* of those changes impinging on and acting as stimuli at the organism's surface. We know that in ourselves sensations initiated through these receptors are forthwith 'projected' into the world outside the 'material me'. The projicience refers them, without elaboration by any reasoned mental process, to directions and distances in the environment fairly accurately corresponding with the 'real' directions and distances of their actual sources. None of the sensations initiated in the proprio-ceptive or intero-ceptive fields possess this property of projicience. And with the distance-receptors considered simply as originators of reflex actions, their reflexes are found to be appropriate to the stimuli as regards the direction and distance of the sources of these latter. Thus, the patch of light constituting a retinal image excites a reflex movement which turns the eyeball toward the source of the image and adjusts ocular accommodation to the distance of that source from the animal itself. Even a negative stimulus suffices. The shadow of the hand put out to seize the tortoise excites, as it blots the retinal illumination, withdrawal of the animal's head to within the shelter of the shell.

How this result of 'distance' has been acquired is hard to say. The net effect is reached in various ways, and with very various gain in the degree of 'distance' acquired. By long vibrissae certain tango-receptors obtain excitation from objects still at a distance from the general surface of the organism. By reduction of their threshold value of stimulus, certain other receptors akin to tactual, inasmuch as their adequate stimuli are mechanical, become responsive to vibratory movements of water and air so as to react to physical sounds whose sources lie remote from the animal. Certain chemo-receptors acquire so low a threshold that they react not merely to food and other substances in contact with them in mass, but react to almost inconceivably diluted traces of such, traces which drift off from the objects and permeate the environment through long distances, as so-called odours, before impinging upon the delicate receptors in question. The leading segments thus come to possess not only taste, but taste at a distance, namely smell. In such cases it seems chiefly by lowering of their threshold that these receptors of the leading segments have been brought to react to objects still remote from the organism.

The 'distance-receptors' seem to have peculiar importance for the construction and evolution of the nervous system. In the higher grades of the animal scale one part of the nervous system has, as Gaskell insists, evolved with singular constancy a dominant importance to the individual. That is the part which is called the brain. *The brain is always the part of the nervous system which is constructed upon and evolved upon the 'distance-recep-*

632

tor' organs. Their effector reactions and sensations are evidently of paramount importance in the functioning of the nervous system and of the individual. This seems explicable, at least partly, in the following manner.

An animal organism is not a machine which merely transforms a quantum of energy given it in potential form at the outset of its career. It has to replenish its potential energy by continued acquisition of suitable energy-containing material from the environment, and this material it has to incorporate in itself. Moreover, since death cuts short the career of the individual organism, the species has to be maintained, and for that in most higher organisms there is required accession of material (gametic) from another organism (of like species) to rejuvenesce a portion of the adult, which portion then cast off leads a new individual existence. To satisfy, therefore, the primary vital requirements of an animal species, actual material contact with certain objects is necessary; thus, for feeding, and in many cases for sexual reproduction.

In these processes of feeding and conjugation the non-distance-receptors play an important and essential part. But ability on the part of an organism to react to an object when still distant from it allows an interval for preparatory reactive steps which can go far to influence the success of attempt either to obtain actual contact or to avoid actual contact with the object. Thus, we may take in illustration the two sets of selective chemo-receptors, the gustatory and the olfactory. Both are responsive to certain chemical stimuli which reach them through solution in the moist mucous membranes of the mouth and nose. No odorous substance appears to be tasteless, and if the threshold value for olfaction and for taste be measured respectively, the threshold for the former as determined in weight of dissolved material is lower than for the latter. The former is the distance-receptor. Animal behaviour shows clearly that in regard to these two groups of receptors the one subserves differentiation of reaction, i.e. swallowing or rejection, of material already found and acquired, e.g. within the mouth. The other, the distance-receptor, smell, initiates and subserves far-reaching complex reactions of the animal anticipatory to swallowing, namely, all that train of reaction which may be comprehensively termed the quest for food. The latter foreruns and leads up to the former. This precurrent relation of the reaction of the distance-receptor to the non-distance-receptor is typical.

The 'distance-receptors' initiate anticipatory, i.e. pre-current, reactions. I ventured above to use the word 'attempt'. Just as a salient character of most of the reactions of the non-projicient receptors taken as sense-organs is *affective tone*, i.e. physical pain or physical pleasure, so *conative feeling* is salient as a psychical character of the reactions which the projicient or distance-receptors, taken as sense-organs, guide. As initiators of reflex movements the action of these latter is character-ized by tendency to work or control the musculature of the animal as a *whole*—as a single machine—to impel locomotion or to cut it short by the assumption of some *total* posture, some attitude which involves steady posture not of one limb or one appendage alone, but of all, so as to maintain an attitude of the body as a whole. Take, for instance, the flight of a moth toward a candle, the dash of a pike toward a minnow, and the tense steadiness of a frog about to seize an insect. These reactions are all of them excited by distance-receptors, though in the one case the musculature is impelled to locomotion toward the stimulus (positive phototropism), in the other re-strained (inhibited) from locomotion. Whether the reac-tion be movement toward or movement away from (positive or negative) or whether it be motion or its restraint (excito-motor or inhibito-motor) does not matter here. The point here is that in both reactions the skeletal musculature is treated practically as a *whole* and in a manner suitably anticipatory of a later event. That is far less the case with the non-projicient receptors. The decerebrate frog changes the whole direction of its path of locomotion when a visual obstacle is set in its way, but a skin impact excites a movement in a small field of musculature only, e.g. the eyelid blinks on corneal contact, the foot flexes at a digital *noxa;* where the part itself cannot well move itself, musculature accessory to it but distant from it is moved. Thus the hind-limb is swept over the flank on irritation there, or the fore-limb over the snout on irritation there. But in these cases the movement induced is merely local and does not affect the body as a whole. Sufficient intensity (we may include summation under intensity) of a stimulus can of course impel the whole creature to movement even through a non-projicient receptor. A decerebrate frog touched lightly between the scapulae will lower its head at first touch, and again more so at a second; at a third will, besides lowering the head, draw the front half of its trunk slightly backward; at a fourth the same movement with stronger retraction; at a fifth give an ineffectual sweep with its hind- or fore-foot; at a sixth a stronger sweep; at a seventh a feeble jump; at an eighth a free jump, and so forth. Considerable intensity or summation is required to evoke a reflex action of the skeletal musculature as a whole from these cutaneous receptors. The projicient receptors and their reflexes once gone, even intense stimuli do not *readily* move or arrest the creature as a whole. It is relatively difficult to get the 'spinal' frog to spring or swim. Co-ordinate movement of the creature as a whole is *then* obtained by general stimulation (i.e. plurireceptive summation), or if by localized stimulation the stimulus must be intense. Thus the spinal frog will swim when placed in water at 36° C. The warm water forms a noci-ceptive

635

stimulus to the receptors of the immersed body-surface generally.

Extensive Internuncial Paths of 'Distance-Receptors'

Conformably with the power of the 'distance-receptors' to induce movements or postures of the individual as a whole we find the neural arcs from these receptors particularly wide and far-reaching. The nerve-fibre that starts from the receptor does not in many of these cases itself extend to, or send processes to, the mouths of the *final common paths*. Instead of doing so it ends often far short of them, and forms connexion with other nerve-fibres (internuncial paths), which in their turn reach distant 'final common paths'. This arrangement involves an intercalation of grey matter between the 'private receptor' path and the 'final common path' not only at the mouth of the latter, but also where the internuncial path itself commences. The *significance of this seems that the internuncial path is itself a 'common path,' and therefore a mechanism of accommodation*. Its community of function is not so extensive as that of a 'final common path', not co-extensive for instance with all the receptors of the body, as would appear the case with a motor-nerve to a skeletal muscle. Yet it furnishes a path for use by certain sets of receptors in common. In *Mustelus* the nerve paths from the retinal and from the olfactory receptors converge toward the roof-nucleus of the mid-brain, whence passes the long mesencephalo-spinal path to the spinal motor nuclei. The inference is that conjoint stimulation of eye and nose exert a combined influence and impinge together on the spinal motor machinery. Similarly the Reissner fibre may serve as an internuncial path between paths coming in from olfactory and visual receptors on the one hand and the spinal motor common paths from the spinal cord to the muscles on the other. Another instance of an internuncial path is the so-called 'pyramidal

636

tract' characteristic of the mammalian nervous system It furnishes a path of internuncial character common to certain arcs that have arisen indirectly from various receptors of various species and are knitted together in the cerebral hemisphere. Another instance is the path from the thalamus to the post-central convolution (Mott, Tschermak, and others).

Precurrent Reactions. Consummatory Reactions

It might seem at first that all motor reflexes may be grouped into those that tend to prolong the stimulus and those that tend to cut it short. Consideration shows that such a grouping expresses the truth but partially. We argued above that the 'distance-receptors' induce anticipatory or precurrent reactions, that is, precurrent to *final* or consummatory reactions. The reflexes of certain non-projicient receptors stand in very close relation to 'consummatory' events. Thus the tango-receptors of the lips and mouth initiate reflex movements that immediately precede the act which for the individual creature viewed as a *conative and a sentient agent* is the final consummatory one in respect to nutriment as a stimulus, namely, swallowing. Similarly with the gustato-receptors and their reactions. The sequence of action initiated by these non-projicient receptors is a short one: their reflex leads immediately to another which is consummatory. Those receptors of the chelae of *Astacus, Homarus*, etc., which initiate the carrying of objects to the mouth, or again the tango-receptors of the hand of the monkey when it plucks fruit and carries it to the lips, give reactions a step further from the consummatory than those just instanced. *These reactions are all steps toward final adjustments, and are not themselves end-points*. The series of actions of which the distance-receptors initiate the earlier steps form series much longer than those initiated by the non-projicient. Their stages, moreover, continue to be guided

637

by the projicient organs for a longer period between initiation and consummation. Thus in a positive phototropic reaction the eye continues to be the starting place of the excitation, and in many cases guides change in the direction not only of the eyeball but of the whole animal in locomotion as the reflex proceeds. The mere length of their series of steps and the vicissitudes of relation between bodies in motion reacting on one another at a distance conspire to give to these precurrent reflexes a multiformity and complexity unparalleled by the reflexes from the non-projicient receptors. The reaction started by 'distance-receptors' where positive not only leads up to the consummatory reactions of the non-projicient, but on the way thither associates with it stimulation of other projicient receptors, as when, for instance, a phototropic reaction on the part of a Selachian brings the olfactory organs into range of an odorous prey, or, conversely, when the beagle sees the hare after running it by scent. In such a case the visual and olfactory receptor arcs would be related as 'allied' arcs . . . , and reinforce each other in regard to the mesencephalo-spinal path, or in higher mammals the 'pyramidal' or other pallio-spinal. path. It is easy to see what copious opportunity for adjustment and of side connexion such a reaction demands, consisting as it does of a number of events in serial chain, each link a modification of its predecessor.

Strong Affective Tone an Accompaniment of Consummatory Reactions

We may venture to turn briefly to the psychical aspect of such sequences. To consummatory reactions affective tone seems adjunct much more than to the anticipatory, especially the remotely anticipatory of the projicient sense-organs. Thus the affective tone of 'tastes' is strong. The reaction initiated by a *noci-ceptor* . . . is to be re-

638

garded as consummatory. The application of an irritant to the flank of a frog evokes a movement of the leg adapted to remove at once that stimulus from the skin of the flank. Or again, an irritant applied to the skin of the foot evokes a movement of the foot away from that stimulus. In both cases the reaction is a consummatory one, because it is calculated of itself to be final. To judge by our own introspection the affective tone adjunct to these reactions is strong. They instance strong affective tone pertaining to consummatory reactions. The affective tone of the reactions of the projicient receptors is less marked: physical pleasure or pain can hardly be said to accompany them. Not of course that they are wholly unrelated to affective tone. The relative haste with which an animal when hungry approaches food offered to the visual field suggests that conation attaches to the visual reaction by association through memory with affective tone. By associative memory a tinge of the affective tone of the consummatory reaction may suffuse the anticipatory. The latter becomes indirectly a pleasure-pain reaction. The neutral tango-receptive reactions of the feet of the tortoise hastening stumblingly towards its food may in this way be imbued with a tinge of affective tone derived from the affective tint of the leading reflex, namely the visual, which itself has thus memorial association with a consummatory reflex of strong affective tone. Examples of this type of reaction furnished by new-born animals are given by Lloyd Morgan. When "after a few days the new-born chick leaves ladybirds unmolested while he seizes wasp-larvae with increased energy" he affords evidence that reactions of his projicient receptors have acquired a new value, and that value is made up *mediately* of affective tone. How they have acquired it or what exact nature their new attribute has is not our question. It is enough here that in regard to certain stimuli the new value—the meaning—which the projicient sensation has obtained has reinforced greatly the conative intensity of the reaction to the stimulus. It has given the stimulus increased force as a spring of precurrent actions aimed at a final consummatory one. It has given this not by altering the external stimulus, nor the receptor-organ, but by, among other alterations, altering internal connexions of the receptor arc. Thus it is that, be it by associative memory or other processes, the reactions of the 'distance-receptors' come in higher animals to reveal a conative driving force which is perhaps the end for which these psychoses exist.

Nor are the series of reactions, short though they be, which the non-projicient receptors initiate wholly *devoid* of conative appearance. They show adaptation as executive of steps toward an end. Food, sexual consummation, suitable posture, preservation from injury, are ends to which their direction leads, as with the longer series of actions due to projicient receptors reacting to objects at a wider horizon. It is rather that the latter afford a freer field for the winning of more subtle adjustments with wider application of associative memory. In the latter there is more scope for the play of mind—mind it may be of such elementary grade as to be difficult for us to picture in its operations.

We may suppose that in the time run through by a course of action focussed upon a final consummatory event, opportunity is given for instinct, with its germ of memory however rudimentary and its germ of anticipation however slight, to evolve under selection that mental extension of the present backward into the past and forward into the future which in the highest animals forms the prerogative of more developed mind. Nothing, it would seem, could better ensure the course of action taken in that interval being the right one than memory and anticipatory forecast: and nothing, it would seem, could tend to select more potently the individuals taking the right course than the success which crowns that course, since the consummatory acts led up to are such— e.g. the seizure of prey, escape from enemies, attainment of sexual conjugation, etc.—as involve the very existence of the individual and the species. The problem before the lowlier organism is in some slight measure shadowed to us by the difficulties of adjustment of reaction shown by the human child. The child, although his reactions are perfect within a certain sphere of his surroundings, shows himself at the confines of that sphere a little blunderer in a world of overwhelming meaning. Hence indeed half the pathos and humour derivable from childhood.

It is the long serial reactions of the 'distance-receptors' that allow most scope for the selection of those brute organisms that are fittest for survival in respect to elements of mind. *The 'distance-receptors' hence contribute most to the uprearing of the cerebrum.* Swallowing was above termed a consummatory reaction. Once through the maw, the morsel is, we know by introspection, under normal circumstances lost for consciousness. But it nevertheless continues to excite receptors and their nervous arcs. The significant point is that the object has passed into such a relation with the surface of the organism that 'conation' is no longer of advantage. The naive notion that when we have eaten and drunken we have *fed* is justified *practically*. No *effort* can help us to incorporate the food further. Conation has then done its all and has no further utility in respect to that food taken. It is significant that all direct psychical accompaniment of the reactions ceases abruptly at this very point. The immediately precedent reactions that were psychically suffused with strong affective colour pass abruptly over into reactions not merely affectively neutral but void—normally —of psychical existence altogether. The concomitance between certain nervous reactions and psychosis seems an alliance that strengthens the restless striving of the

641

individual animal which is the passport of its species to continuance of existence.

Receptive Range

The ascendency of 'distance-receptors' in the organization of neural function may be partly traceable to the relative *frequency* of their use. Although it would be incorrect to assess the value of an organ by the mere frequency with which it is of service, yet *ceteris paribus* that seems a fair criterion. The frequency with which a receptor meets its stimuli is, other things being equal, proportionate to the size of the slice of the external world which lies within its *receptive range*. Although in a fish, for instance, the skin with its tango-receptors is much larger in area than are the retinae with their photo-receptors, the restricted 'receptive-range'—the adequate stimulus requiring actual proximity—of the former gives a far smaller slice of the stimulus-containing world to the skin than pertains to the eyes. In the case of the eye not only is the slice of environment pertaining to it at even a short distance more wide and high than that of the skin, but it is at each moment multiplied by the third dimension. There arise in it, therefore (*ceteris paribus*), in unit of time many more stimulations, with the result that the receptor-organ of 'distant' species receives many more fresh stimuli per unit of time than does the receptor-organ of restricted receptive range. The greater richness of the neural construction of the photo-receptive system than of the tango-receptive accords with this. Thus in the photo-receptive system the so-called 'optic nerve' (which since it is the second neural link and therefore to some extent a 'common path', presents numerical reduction from the first or private path in the retina itself) contains more conductive channels (nerve-fibres) in man (1,000,-000, Krause) than are contained in the whole series of afferent spinal roots of one side of the body put together

(634,000, Ingbert), and of these latter the cutaneous afferent fibres form only a part, and of that part the tango-receptive fibres themselves form only a fraction. The large number of the channels in the retinal path is no doubt primarily indicative of spatial differentiations of the receptive surface, but that spatial differentiation is itself indicative of the numbers of the stimuli frequenting that receptive field.

Locomotion and 'Receptive Range'

Locomotive progression and distance receptivity are two phenomena so fundamentally correlated that the physiology of neither can be comprehended without recognition of the correlation of the two. Evidence is forthcoming from ontogeny and phylogeny. The elaborateness of the photo-receptive organs of the flying Insecta corresponds with the great power of these forms to traverse space. When the Brachiopod passes from a motile wandering life to a fixed sedentary one its 'eyes' degenerate and go. The free-swimming *Ascidia* with fin-like motor organs and semi-rigid axial notochord, affording elasticity and leverage, bears at its anterior end a well-formed photo-receptor organ (eye) and a well-formed otocyst (head proprioceptor). Connected with the nerves of these, the anterior end of its truly vertebrate central nervous system has a relatively large 'brain'. Thence extends backward along the body a spinal cord. Suddenly its free-swimming habit is exchanged for a sedentary; by adhesive projections from its head, it attaches itself permanently to some fixed object. At once there ensues a readaptive metamorphosis. Degeneration sets in concurrently in its locomotive musculature, its eye, its otocyst, its brain, and its cord. These vanish as by magic save that a fraction of the brain remains as a small ganglion near the mouth. The sessile creature re-

643

tains, so far as can be judged from their microscopic structure, only some gustatory (?) receptors round the mouth, and some tango-receptors (? noci-ceptors) in the tegument, connected doubtless with an irregular diffuse subtegumental layer of unstriped muscle tissue. Experimental observations seem wanting on the point, but we may presume that in this metamorphosis the *receptive range of Ascidia* dwindles from dimensions measurable by all the distance through which its free motile individual floats and swims, to a mere film of the external world, say 1 mm. deep, at its own surface, especially round its mouth, and unextended by succession of time, save passively by the mere flowing of the water. Such instances illustrate the fundamental connexion between the function of the skeletal musculature and that of the 'distance-receptors'. Did we know better the sensual aspects of these cases the more significant doubtless would be the comparison.

The 'Head' as Physiologically Conceived

As regards the objects acting on the organism at any moment through its receptors, the extension of environmental space—the animal's *receptive range*—is not equal in all directions as measured from the organism itself. The extension is greater in the direction about the 'leading' pole. Thus, the reactions initiated at the eye precede reactions (cf. Loeb's *Ketten reflexe*) that will in due time come to pass through other receptor-organs. The visual receptors are usually near the leading pole, and so placed that they see into the field whither progression goes. And similarly with the olfatcory receptors. The motor train behind, the elongated motor machinery of the rest of the body, is therefore from this point of view a motor appendage at the behest of the distance-receptor organs in front. The segments lying at the leading pole of the animal, armed as they are with the great 'distance' sense-organs, constitute what is termed the 'head'.

The Proprio-Ceptive System and the Head

We may now attempt to enquire whether this dominance of the leading segments which is traceable in the receptors of the extero-ceptive field applies in the field of reception which we termed the proprio-ceptive. We arrived earlier at the notion that the field of reception which extends through the depth of each segment is differentiated from the surface field by two main characters. One of these was that while many agents which act on the body surface are excluded from the deep field as stimuli, an agency which does act there is mass, with all its mechanical consequences, such as weight, mechanical inertia, etc., giving rise to pressures, strains, etc., and that the receptors of this deep field are adapted for these as stimuli. The other character of the stimulations in this field we held to be that the stimuli are given in much greater measure than in the surface field of reception, by actions of the organism itself, especially by mass movements of its parts. Since these movements are themselves for the most part reactions to stimuli received by the animal's free surface from the environment, the proprioceptive reactions themselves are results in large degree habitually secondary to surface stimuli. The immediate stimulus for the reflex started at the deep receptor is thus supplied by some part of the organism itself as agent.

In many forms of animals, e.g. in vertebrates, there lies in one of the leading segments a receptor-organ (the labyrinth) derived from the extero-ceptive field, but later recessed off from it; and this is combined in action with receptors of the proprio-ceptive field of the remaining segments. This receptive organ, like those of the proprioceptive field, is adapted to mechanical stimuli. It consists of two parts, both endowed with low receptive

645

threshold and with refined selective differentiation. One part, the otolith organ, is adapted to react to changes in the incidence and degree of pressure exerted on its nerve-endings by a little weight of higher specific gravity than the fluid otherwise filling the organ. The other part, the semicircular canals, reacts to minute mass movements of fluid contained within it. These two parts constitute the labyrinth. The incidence and degree of pressure of the otoliths upon their receptive bed change with changes in the *position* of the segments in which the labyrinth lies, relatively to the horizon line. *Movements* of the segment likewise stimulate the labyrinthine receptors through the inertia of the labyrinthine fluid and the otoliths. By the labyrinth are excited reflexes which adjust the segment (and with it the head is usually immovably conjoined) to the horizon line. And other parts are similarly reflexly adjusted by it. Thus, the refined photo-receptive patches in the head—the retinæ—which conduct reflexes delicately differential in regard to space, appropriate for stimuli higher or lower or to right or to left in the photo-receptive patch, depend in their conduct of these upon a more or less constant standardization of their own normals of direction in regard to the horizon line. These photo-receptive patches are set movably in the head; by the action of muscles they can retain their bearings to the horizon, although the head itself shifts its relation to the horizon. The control of these muscles lies largely with the labyrinth. The labyrinth produces a compensatory eyeball reflex. Thus in the head segments the labyrinth effects reflex movements analogous to that which the proprio-receptive nerves from the extensor muscles of the knee excites in the leg segments, reflexes restoring an habitual posture that has been departed from.

And from the above it seems clear that there is another feature of resemblance between the labyrinthine receptor and the proprio-ceptors of the limb. Stimulation of the labyrinth must in preponderant measure be given not by external agents directly but by the reaction of the organism itself. Posture and movement of the head are the immediate causes which stimulate the labyrinth, whether or not they be part of a total movement or posture of the whole individual. Such movement is most frequently an active one on the part of the animal itself. Thus, when *Ascidia* becomes sedentary and its locomotor musculature atrophies its otocyst disappears. But an animal's active movement is in its turn usually traceable as a reaction to an environmental stimulus affecting the receptors at the surface of the animal. Thus the labyrinthine receptors like the proprio-ceptors in other segments, are stimulated by the animal itself as agent, though secondarily to stimulation of the animal itself via some extero-ceptor.

And there is another point of likeness between labyrinth reflexes and those of the proprio-ceptors of the limb and other segments. The proprio-ceptors of the limbs appear productive of certain continuous, that is *tonic,* reflexes. Thus, in the decerebrate dog the tonic extensor rigidity of the leg appears reflexly maintained by afferent neurones reaching the cord from the deep structures of the leg itself. Similarly, if the knee-jerk be accepted as evidence in the spinal animal of a spinal tonus in the extensor muscle, this tonus seems maintained by afferent fibres from the extensor muscle itself, since the knee-jerk is extinguished by severance of those fibres. Again, the rapidity of onset of rigor mortis in a muscle is speedier when its tonus prior to death has been high. Section of the afferent roots of the limb prior to death delays onset of rigor mortis in that limb as judged by stiffness at the knee; but that delay is not observable when skin-nerves only have been severed. The labyrinthine receptors appear likewise to be the source of certain maintained, that is tonic, reflexes. Destruction of the labyrinth also delays

647

the onset of rigor mortis in the muscles to which its field of tonus can be traced. Ewald has shown that each labyrinth maintains tonus especially in the neck and trunk muscles and in the extensor-abductor limb-muscles of the homonymous side.

In regard to these tonic reflexes it is difficult to see how a steady mechanical stimulus can continue to elicit a reflex constantly for long periods. If we take sensation as a guide, a touch excited by constant mechanical pressure of slight intensity fades quickly below the threshold of sensation. It is said that a spinal frog may even be crushed by mechanical pressure without exciting from it a reflex movement provided that the pressure be applied by very slowly progressive increments. The office of a receptor would seem to be, placed across the line of a stream of energy, to react under the transference of energy across it, as for instance from the environment to the organism, or vice versa. We have many instances in which the living material adapts itself to, and maintains its own equilibrium under, different grades of environmental stress, treating each fairly continuous or slowly altering grade as a normal zero. The slow changes of barometric pressure on the body surface originate no skin-sensation, though they are much above the threshold value for touch. There constantly streams from the body through the skin a current of thermal energy above the threshold value of stimuli for warmth sensations; yet this current evokes under ordinary circumstances no sensation. It is the stationary condition, the fact that the transference of energy continues at constant speed, which makes it unperceived. The receptor apparatus is not stimulated unless there is a change of rate in the transference, and that change of rate must occur in most cases with considerable quickness, otherwise there is a mere unperceived shift in the stationary equilibrium which forms the resting zero of the sensual apparatus.

Over and over in the elicitation of reflexes as well as in the artificial excitation of nerve or muscle we meet this same feature. Both for sensation and for reflex action a function in the threshold value of stimulus is time, as well as intensity and quantity. If a weak agent is to stimulate, its application must be abrupt. But in the tonic reflexes whose source lies at the proprio-ceptors and the labyrinth, a weak stimulus, although apparently unchanging, seems to continue to be an effective stimulus.

The proprio-ceptors and the labyrinthine receptors seem to have in common this, that they both originate and maintain tonic reflexes in the skeletal muscles. And they, at least in some instances, reinforce one another in this action. Thus the tonus of the extensor muscle of the knee in the cat and dog appears to have a combined source in the proprio-ceptors of that muscle itself and in the receptors of the homonymous labyrinth. The tonus of skeletal muscles is an obscure problem. Its mode of production, its distribution in the musculature, its purposive significance, are all debatable. The steadiness and slight intensity of the contraction constituting the tonus render its detection difficult. Part of the discrepancy between the experimental findings may be traced to the supposition that a reflex tonus if present is present in all muscles at all times. A single muscle examined for reflex tonus has been taken to represent all muscles under all conditions, although the answer has been sometimes positive and sometimes negative.

It appears to me likely that reflex tonus is the expression of a neural discharge concerned with the maintenance of *attitude*. In many reflex reactions the effect is movement and the muscles are dealt with as organs of motion. In these cases the stimuli and the reactions both of them are short-lived events. But much of the reflex reaction expressed by the skeletal musculature is postural. The bony and other levers of the body are main-

649

tained in certain attitudes both in regard to the horizon, to the vertical, and to one another. The frog as it rests squatting in its tank has an attitude far different from that which gravitation would give it were its musculature not in action. Evidently the greater part of the skeletal musculature is all the time steadily active, antagonizing gravity in maintaining the head raised, the trunk semi-erect, and the hind-legs tautly flexed. Innervation and co-ordination are as fully demanded for the maintenance of a posture as for the execution of a movement. This steady co-ordinate innervation antagonizes gravitation and other forces, e.g. as in currents of water. In these tonic as in other reflexes, antagonistic muscles co-operate co-ordinately. There is nothing to show that reciprocal innervation does not obtain in the one class of reflex as in the other. If so, it becomes easily intelligible that the slight reflex contraction termed *skeletal tonus* should under given conditions be found in some muscles and not in others. The slight reflex contraction will be accompanied by reflex inhibition of the antagonistic muscles. For reflex tonus to be the expression of a neural discharge which maintains attitude accords well with the ascription of its source to the proprio-ceptors, including the labyrinth. Those are exactly the receptors which, functioning as sense-organs, initiate sensations of posture and of attitude (Bonnier). And it accords also with the share in the production and regulation of skeletal tonus which the cerebellum has (Luciani's *atonia*) and the cerebrum.

Naturally, the distinction between reflexes of attitude and reflexes of movement is not in all cases sharp and abrupt. Between a short lasting attitude and a slowly progressing movement the difference is hardly more than one of degree. Moreover, each posture is introduced by a movement of assumption, and after each departure from the posture, if it is resumed, it is reverted to by a

650

movement of compensation. Hence the taxis of attitude must involve not only static reactions of tonic maintenance of contraction, but innervations which execute reinforcing movements and compensatory movements. In all this kind of function the proprio-ceptors of the body generally and the labyrinthine receptors in the head, appear to co-operate together and form functionally one receptive system.

This system as a whole may be embraced within the one term 'proprio-ceptive'. Our inquiry regarding it is now, whether that part of it which is situate in the leading segments, namely its labyrinthine part, exerts preponderance in the system as do the extero-ceptors situate in the leading segments in the extero-ceptive system. It must be remembered of the extero-ceptive system that even in the segments which are not the leading segments its receptors considered as sense organs produce sensations that have *some* projicience; and that in animals provided with outstanding skin appendages, e.g. hair, the tango-reflexes are to a slight extent reactions to objects at a distance. This germ of distance reaction and projicience of sensation in the extero-ceptors of the ordinary body-segments is developed in the extero-ceptors of the leading segments into the vast distance-reactions of the eye and the absolute projicience of vision. But the proprio-ceptors of the limb and body segments exhibit no germ of distance-reaction nor of projicience of sensation. And the specialized proprio-ceptor organ of the leading segment (the labyrinth) is similarly not a distance-receptor; although some of its sensations seem projected into the environment as well as referred to the organism itself, to the 'material me'. Any predominance this proprio-ceptor in the leading segments may exhibit in the proprio-ceptive system is not therefore in virtue of the quality of reaction at a distance. If pre-eminently important to the organism as a whole, its preeminence of importance rests on other grounds than does the importance of the great distance-receptors—the olfactory, the visual, and the auditory.

A posture of the animal as a whole—a total posture—is as much a complex built up of postures of portions of the animal—segmental postures (Bonnier)—as is the total movement of the animal—its locomotion—compounded of segmental movements. With the hinder part of its spinal cord alone intact the frog maintains a posture in its hind-limbs. These limbs are kept flexed at hip, knee, and ankle. When displaced from that posture they return to it. But if the animal be rolled over on its back it makes no attempt to right itself. The decerebrate frog with its labyrinths intact and their arcs still in connection with the skeletal musculature maintains the well-known attitude before mentioned. If inverted it at once reverts to that. The labyrinth keeps the world right-side up for the organism by keeping the organism right-side up to its external world. The cranial receptors control the animal's *total* posture as do receptors of the hinder musculature the *segmental* posture of the hind-limbs when but the hind end of the spinal cord remains.

Thus the labyrinthine proprio-ceptors are largely the equilibrators of the head, and since the retinal patches are movably attached (in mobile eyeballs) to the head, and since each retina has its normals of direction conforming with those of the head, these equilibrators of the head are closely connected by nervous arcs with the musculature maintaining the postures of the eyeballs. The posture of the head in many animals is dependent on the musculature not of the head segments themselves but of a long series of segments behind the head. In many forms the motor organs that steadily maintain or passingly modify the position of the head in regard to the external world—conveniently indexed by the line of direction of gravitation—are contributed to by the skeletal musculature of many post-cranial segments. Hence the labyrinthine receptor is in touch with all the segments of the body, and these in a measure may be regarded as appended to the otic segment. Destruction of the labyrinth in the fish, the frog, the pigeon, and the dog produces not only malposture of the eyeball and the head, but of the limbs and body as a whole. The 'knock-out blow', where the lower jaw conveys concussion to the otocyst, reduces in a moment a vigorous athlete to an unstrung bulk of flesh whose weight alone determines its attitude, if indeed a reactionless mass can be described as possessing attitude at all.

The labyrinthine receptors and their arcs give the animal its definite attitude to the external world. The muscular receptors give to the segment—e.g. hind-limb—a definite attitude less in reference to the external world than in reference to other segments, e.g. the rest of the animal. Our own sensations from the *labyrinth* refer to some extent, as said above, to this environment, that is, have some projected quality; our *muscular* sensations refer to the body itself, e.g. contribute to perceptions of the relative flexions or extensions of our limbs. The arcs of the proprio-receptor of the leading segments control vast fields of the skeletal musculature and deal with it as a whole, while the arcs of the proprio-ceptors of the other segments work with only limited vegians of the musculature. Hence, in conformity with this the proprio-ceptor of the leading segments possesses long internuncial paths, for instance, bulbo-spinal from Deiter's nucleus proceeding to all levels of the spinal cord.

We traced the reactions of proprio-ceptors of the limb to bear habitually a secondary relation to the reactions of the extero-ceptors of the limb. Similar secondary relation is evident also between the reactions of the proprio-ceptor of the leading segments (the labyrinth) and the reactions of the extero-ceptors of those segments. These latter

653

extero-ceptors were seen to be distance-receptors, and the reactions of distance-receptors were seen to be signalized by their anticipatory character. From secondary association with these distance-receptors the reactions of the labyrinth come in their turn to have anticipatory character. They retain, however, their own special features of equilibration and tonus. The locomotion of an animal impelled by its eye toward its prey involves co-operation of the labyrinth with the retina. And the tonic labyrinthine reflex which maintains an attitude may be just as truly an anticipatory reaction as any movement is. The steady flexed posture of the frog directed toward a fly seen on the aquarium wall is a co-ordinate innervation securing preparedness for the seizure of the food. Its character is as truly anticipatory as is that of any movement. We might speak of the animal as 'at rest', but it is the tense quietude of the hunter watching quarry rather than rest, such as supervenes in sleep and other conditions where active innervation is actually relaxed or reflex action is truly in abeyance.

Nervous Integration of a Segmental Series

By longitudinal integration *short* series of adjoining segments become in respect to some one character combined together, so as to form in respect to that character practically a single organ. It is convenient to speak of such reflex reactions, confined from start to finish to a single integrated set of segments, as 'short reflexes' giving '*local* reactions'. Thus the vertebrate appendages called limbs are plurisegmental, but the individual segments constituting the limb form in respect of the limb a functional group of such solidarity that their reactions in the limb are at any one time unitary.

The reflexes that extend beyond the limit of such a group are on the other hand conveniently termed '*long reflexes'*. And it is in the integration of long series, or of the *whole* series, of segments, one with another, that, apart from psychical phenomena, the nervous system seems to reach its acme of achievement. Here it is that we see eminently what Herbert Spencer has insisted on, namely, that integration keeps pace with differentiation.

In the segmental series the nervous concatenation of the segments repeats broadly the kind of association evidenced within each segment taken singly. Broadly taken, each segment has on the one hand a piece of the extero-ceptive field, a piece of the proprio-ceptive field, and a piece of the intero-ceptive field though this last is wanting in not a few segments. On the other, it has fractions of the skeletal, of the vascular, and of the visceral effector organs. Each segment has musculature and glands on its outer and visceral surfaces. Some segments have also secretors discharging into body spaces. Each of these sets of features of the segments has in the series of segments a nervous system of some functional homogeneity. With these plurisegmental systems as with their unisegmental pieces in the single segment the same harmonies of interconnexion are observable. Thus, the nervous arcs embouching into the skeletal musculature start chiefly in the extero-ceptive field in so far as concerns execution of passing movements, in the proprio-ceptive field in so far as concerns tonic postures; and so on, as sketched above. If the receptors of the extero-ceptive field are regarded from the point of view of the nature of the agency adequate for each of their species, representatives of each species are found in almost every segment. In this way the functional properties of the extero-ceptive field form not one but several multisegmental organs or systems of organs. In each segment exist receptors responsive to mechanical, chemical, and radiant agencies respectively. There is thus formed a tango-ceptive system to which practically every segment

655

contributes, a thermo-ceptive system, a noci-ceptive system; so also a musculo-ceptive system, and probably the receptors of the intero-ceptive surface similarly constitute a homogeneous system, prominent among their adequate agencies being those of chemical quality. These systems of receptive arcs present, though more or less compound, a solidarity of action in each system that gives each some rank as a physiological entity.

Restriction of Segmental Distribution a Factor in Integration

The impulse to nervous integration given by regional restriction of a peculiar species of organ to a single segment has especial force where that organ is of especial importance. This is the case with effector organs subserving important actions of consummatory . . . type, e.g. a sexual appendage, or the mouth. Such organs as these are of restricted regional distribution and subserve important reactions of consummatory type. With the mouth is associated differentiation of organs around it. Many postures and movements of the organism are advantageous or disadvantageous to the animal's existence mainly inasmuch as they improve or disimprove the position or attitude of the mouth in regard to objects in the external world. Much of the long series of movements and other reactions initiated and guided by 'distance-receptors' themselves is by-play on the way to a consummatory reaction which requires an appropriate placing and attitude of the mouth. That there is only one mouth and that of limited segmental extent involves coordination of the activities of many other segments with the oral. Integration of plurisegmental activity is effected here, as in the other cases, mainly by the synaptic nervous system. The fact that the mouth is usually placed near the leading segments of the anterior pole is therefore a further factor in differentiating the segments at that end from the after-coming train. Thus it comes about that in many cases the animal consists of two portions broadly different in character but complemental the one to the other, the *head* and the *trunk*.

It is noteworthy that the increase of susceptibility instanced by the distance-receptors is in each case restricted to a special patch, quite limited in area. Given a synaptic nervous system, no single item of functional arrangement more enforces integration of an individual from its segments than the restriction of a special kind of receptor to a single area or segment in the whole series. The motor apparatus of many segments has then to subserve a single segment, since that segment is provided with a receptor of a species not otherwise possessed by the individual at all. For integrative co-ordination of that kind, the synaptic nervous system affords the only instrument in the animal economy. Only by the formation of common paths can due advantage be reaped from a specially refined recipient path (private path) of locally restricted situation.

Further, the condensed setting of a group of specialized receptors favours their simultaneous stimulation in groups together. Stimuli even of small area then cover a number of receptive points in the receptive sheet. Thus, ocular images of various two-dimensional shape tend to be better differentiated by the photo-receptors the more closely the individual photo-receptors lie together. More data are thus gained as a basis for differential reaction.

Further, the juxtaposition of groups of specially refined receptors in one set of segments, the leading or head segments, conduces toward their simultaneous stimulation by several agencies emanating from one and the same environmental object. Thus, the property of brightness and the property of odour belonging to an object of prey may then better excite in unison a reaction in the distant reagent, or excite more potently than would either property alone. And movements of the reagent itself are then more apt to intensify simultaneously the reactions of its two kinds of receptors. The collocation of the disparate receptors in one region will favour that which psychologists in describing sensations term 'complication', a process which in reflex action has a counterpart in the conjunction of reflexes excited by receptors of separate species but of allied reaction. This alliance of reaction we have seen finds expression as mutual reinforcement in action upon a final common path. Thus a reaction is synthesized which deals with the environmental object not merely as a stimulus possessing one property but as a 'thing' built up of properties. A reflex is attained which has its psychological analogue in a sense percept.

The Cerebellum is the Head Ganglion of the Proprio-ceptive System

If the basis taken for classification of receptors be a physiological one with, as its criterion, the type of reaction which the receptors induce, separate receptive systems may be traced running throughout the whole series of segments composing the total organism. We have seen that such separate receptive systems may be treated as functional unities, extending through the segmental series. In any such system there is evident a tendency for its central nervous mechanisms, that is to say, the components of the central nervous organ which specially accrue to the system in question, to be gathered chiefly where the most important contribution to its receptive paths enters the central nervous system. The receptive system in question has as it were its focus at that place. Thus receptive neurones which can influence respiratory movement enter the central nervous organ at various segments, but the chief respiratory centre lies in the bulb where the receptive neurones from the lung itself make entrance and central connexion, the vagal receptors being preponderantly regulative in that function. And we have seen that a proprio-ceptive organ (the labyrinth) in the head segments seems preponderantly regulative in those functions which the proprio-ceptive system sub-serves. The central neural mechanism belonging to the proprio-ceptive system is preponderantly built up over the central connexions of this proprio-ceptive organ (the labyrinth) belonging to the head. Thither converge inter-nuncial paths stretching to this mechanism from the central endings of various proprio-ceptive neurones situ-ate in all the segments of the body. There afferent contributions from the receptors of joints, muscles, liga-ments, tendons, viscera, etc., combine with those from the muscular organs of the head and with those of the laby-rinthine receptors themselves. A central nervous organ of high complexity results. Its size from animal species to animal species strikingly accords with the range and complexity of the habitual movements of the species; in other words, with the range and complexity of the habitual taxis of the skeletal musculature. This central organ is the cerebellum.

The symptoms produced by its destruction or injury in whole or in part in many ways resemble, therefore, the disturbances produced by injury of the labyrinth itself. It also influences tonus very much as do the simple pro-prio-ceptive arcs themselves. It is closely connected struc-turally and functionally with the so-called motor region of the cerebral hemisphere, just as the simpler proprio-ceptive arcs and reflexes are closely associated with the mechanisms of extero-ceptive reactions. Knowledge is not ripe as yet for an adequate definition of the function of the cerebellum. Many authorities have defined it as the centre for the maintenance of the mechanical equilibrium of the body. Others regard it as the organ for co-ordination of volitional movement. Spencer suggested that it was the organ of co-ordination of bodily action in regard to space, the cerebrum he suggested being the organ of co-ordination of bodily action in respect of time. Lewandowski considers it the central organ for the 'muscular sense'. Luciani, the universally acknowledged authority on the physiology of the cerebellum, describes it as the organ which by unconscious processes exerts a continual reinforcing action on the activity of all other nerve-centres.

It is instructive to note how all these separate pronouncements harmonize with the supposition that the organ is the chief co-ordinative centre or rather group of centres of the reflex system of proprio-ception. The cerebellum may indeed be described as the head ganglion of the proprio-ceptive system, and the head ganglion here, as in other systems, is the main ganglion.

The Cerebrum is the Ganglion of the 'Distance-Receptors'

By the 'distance-receptors' are initiated and guided long series of reactions of the animal as a whole. Other receptive reactions integrate individual segments; the reactions of the distance-receptors integrate the whole series of segments. It is in the sphere of reactions of these 'distance-receptors' that the most subtle and complex adjustments of the animal therefore arise. In their neural machinery not only short arcs but long arcs, involving extensive internuncial tracts, figure largely. Chains of reaction conducive to a final reaction relatively remote are more evident with them than with other arcs. If appeal to psychical evidence be ventured on, it is to the field of operation of the arcs of these distance-receptors that higher feats of associative memory accrue, and, though the phrase is hardly permissible here except

660

with curtailed scope, conation becomes more intelligent. Finally, in harmony with the last inference, it is over these 'distance-receptors' and in connexion with their reflexes and arcs that the cerebrum itself is found. The cerebrum constitutes, so to say, the ganglion of the 'distance-receptors'. Langendorff has pointed out that a blinded frog resembles in its reactions a frog with the cerebrum removed: the elasmobranch without its olfactory lobes behaves as if it had lost its fore-brain. Edinger traces the genesis of the cerebral cortex to a distance-receptor, namely the olfactory organ.

The integration of the animal associated with these 'distance-receptors' of the leading segments can be briefly with partial justice expressed by saying that the rest of the animal, so far as its motor machinery goes, is but the servant of them. We might imagine the form of the individual and the disposition of the sense-organs as primitively very simple; for instance, a spheroid with a digestive cavity and sense-organs distributed especially over the external surface. Such an imaginary form we should expect under evolution to become modified. If a motile organism, its contractile mechanisms would obtain mechanical advantage (leverage) by its elongation in certain directions. The lengthwise extension of the vertebrate body and of its lateral motor appendages, e.g. limbs, are in so far such as might be argued *a priori*. Under evolution in motile animals adaptations securing appropriate leverage for the contractile apparatus appear, and length along certain axes is always a consideration in them. In animals with segments ranged along a single axis, the animal for the greater part of its length comes to be one great motor organ, complex and able to execute movements in various ways, but still a unity. The pole at which the great 'distance-receptors' (visual, olfactory, auditory) lie is that which, in the habitual locomotion of the animal under the action of the motor train attached, 'leads'. The animal therefore moves habitually into that part of environmental space which has been already explored by the distance-receptors of its own leading segments.

The head is in many ways the individual's greater part. It is the more so the higher the individual stands in the animal scale. It has the mouth, it takes in the food, including water and air, it has the main receptive organs providing data for the rapid and accurate adjustment of the animal to time and space. To it the trunk, an elongated motor organ with a share of the digestive surface and the skin, is appended as an apparatus for locomotion and nutrition. The trunk must of necessity lie at the command of the great receptor-organs of the head. The co-ordination of the activities of the trunk with the requirements of the head is a cardinal function of the synaptic nervous system. Conducting arcs must pass from the cephalic receptors to the contractile masses of the body as a whole. The spinal cord contains these strands of conductors in vertebrates and is from this point of view a mere appendage of the brain. A salient feature of these conducting arcs is that the nerve-fibres from the cephalic receptors do not run, as might perhaps *a priori* have been thought natural, direct from their cephalic segment backwards to reach the common effector paths upon which they embouch. Instead of having that arrangement, these fibres, starting in the cephalic receptors, end in the gray matter of the central nervous axis not far from their own segment. Thence the conducting arc is continued backward by another strand of fibres, and these reach (perhaps directly) the mouths of the final common paths in the grey matter of segments of the spinal cord. This is the arrangement exemplified by the pulmono-phrenic and other respiratory arcs, the depresso-splanchnic arcs, the olfacto-phrenic respiratory arcs, the arcs between the otic labyrinth and the muscles maintaining posture in the

662

trunk, and practically that of the retino-motor arcs connecting the retina with the muscles of the neck. It gives at least one synapsis more than the first alternative would do. And each *synapse is an apparatus for co-ordination;* it introduces a *'common path'*. And it is in the exercise of the distance-receptors with their extensive range overlapping that of other receptors that the reflexes which relate to 'objects' in the sense that they are reflexes synthesized from receptors of separate species, become chiefly established. The ramifications of the central neurones attached to these receptors are so extensive and the reactions they excite are so far spreading in the organism that their association with the reactions and central mechanisms of other receptors is especially frequent and wide.

The distance-receptors are the great inaugurators of reaction. The reduced initiation of action which ensues on ablation of the cerebrum seems explicable by that reason. The curtailment which ensues is indicative of damage which their removal inflicts on reactions generated by the distance-receptor organs. By a high spinal transection the splendid motor machinery of the vertebrate is practically as a whole and at one stroke severed from all the universe except its own microcosm and an environmental film some millimetres thick immediately next its body. The deeper depression of reaction into which the higher animal as contrasted with the lower sinks when made spinal signifies that in the higher types more than in the lower the great distance-receptors actuate the motor organ and impel the actions of the individual. The deeper depression shows that as the individual ascends the scale of being, the more reactive does it become as an individual to the circumambient universe outside itself. It is significant that spinal shock hardly at all affects the nervous reactions of the intero-ceptors (visceral system); and that it does not affect the intero-ceptive arcs appreciably more in the monkey than in the

663

frog. Its brunt falls, as we have seen before, on the reactions of the skeletal musculature. Not that in the highest
animal forms the 'distance-receptor' merely *per se* has
necessarily reached more perfection or more competence
than in the lower. In the lower types, as in fish, are found
'distance-receptors' of high perfection, but their ablation
does not in lower types cripple in the *same way* as in
higher types. It is that in the higher types there is based
upon the 'distance-receptors' a relatively enormous neural superstructure possessing million-sided connexions
with multitudinous other nervous arcs and representing
untold potentialities for redistribution of so-to-say stored
stimuli by *associative recall*. The development and elaboration of this internal nervous mechanism attached to
the organs of distance-reception has, so far as we can
judge, far outstripped progressive elaboration of the
peripheral receptive organs themselves. Adaptation and
improvement would seem to have been more precious
assets in the former than in the latter. And, as related to
the former rather than to the latter, must be regarded
the parallelism of the ocular axes and the overlapping
of the uniocular fields of photo-reception which in mammals has gradually reached its acme in the monkey and
in man. This overlapping yields, in virtue one would think
of some process akin to Herbart's 'complication', an
important additional datum for visual space. This, together with promotion of the fore-limb from a simple
locomotor prop to a delicate explorer of space in manifold
directions, together also with the organization of mimetic
movement to express thoughts by sounds, have, with the
developments of central nervous function which they connote and promote, been probably the chief factors in
man's outstripping other competitors in progress toward
that aim which seems the universal goal of animal behaviour, namely to dominate more completely the environment. Remembering these conditions, it need not surprise

664

us that the distance-receptors more and more exert preponderant directive influence over the whole nervous system. To say this is to say no more than that the motile and consolidated individual is driven, guided, and controlled by, above all organs, its cerebrum. The integrating power of the nervous system has in fact in the higher animal, more than in the lower, constructed from a mere collection of organs and segments a functional unity, an individual of more perfected solidarity. We see that the distance-receptors integrate the individual not merely because of the wide ramification of their arcs to the effector organs through the lower centres; they integrate especially because of their great connexions in the high cerebral centres. Briefly expressed, their special potency is because they integrate the animal through its brain. The cerebrum itself may be indeed regarded as the ganglion of the distance-receptors.

SIR CHARLES SCOTT SHERRINGTON (b.—London, November 27, 1857; d.—March 4, 1952).

Sherrington matriculated in the Gonville and Caius College, Cambridge in 1880. In 1884 he was a student at St. Thomas' Hospital in London, and in the same year he worked in the Physiological Institute at Strassburg. In 1887 he became Lecturer in Systematic Physiology at St. Thomas' Hospital. In 1891 he was a Professor-Superintendent of the Brown Institute. He received his M.D. in 1892. In 1893 he was elected a Fellow of the Royal Society, of which he was later President from 1920 to 1925. In 1895 he was appointed Holt Professor of Physiology at Liverpool. It was while in this position that he gave the great Silliman Memorial Lectures at Yale, in 1904, which constitute his magnum opus. In 1913 he became Waynflete Professor of Physiology at Oxford, where he remained until his retirement in 1935. In 1932 he shared the Nobel Prize with E. D. Adrian, for "discoveries regarding the neurons."

Sherrington's contributions to psychology lie in the dynamic picture which he created of the nervous system, and of its role in psychophysiological functions. It is his flexible description of the higher nervous system, which gives him so special a place in modern psychological theory. Such conceptual neurology is a major aid in our thinking about sensory phenomena and about the distinctions between voluntary and reflex behavior. An understanding of Sherrington's contributions is essential to progress in this area. The present essay is of particular interest to psychologists because of its discussion of the senses, its distinction between proprioception and distance-receptors, and between physiological and psychological conceptualizations of the brain.

SHERRINGTON, C. S. *The integrative action of the nervous system.* New Haven: Yale University Press, 1952 (1906—Scribner's Sons). The Silliman Lectures. (The new edition contains Sherrington's bibliography.) Lect. IX: "The physiological position and dominance of the brain." Reprinted by permission of the publisher.

See also:

SHERRINGTON, C. S. *The brain and its mechanism.* Cambridge: Cambridge Univ. Press, 1933.

ELVIDGE, A. R. & PENFIELD, W. "Sir Charles Sherrington." *Arch. Neurol. & Psychiat.* 1935, 34: 1299-1309.

STUDIES ON HYSTERIA
ON THE PSYCHICAL MECHANISM OF HYSTERICAL PHENOMENA: PRELIMINARY COMMUNICATION

Josef Breuer and Sigmund Freud

I

A chance observation has led us, over a number of
years, to investigate a great variety of different forms
and symptoms of hysteria, with a view to discovering
their precipitating cause—the event which provoked the
first occurrence, often many years earlier, of the phenomenon in question. In the great majority of cases it is
not possible to establish the point of origin by a simple
interrogation of the patient, however thoroughly it may
be carried out. This is in part because what is in question
is often some experience which the patient dislikes discussing; but principally because he is genuinely unable
to recollect it and often has no suspicion of the causal
connection between the precipitating event and the pathological phenomenon. As a rule it is necessary to hypno-
tize the patient and to arouse his memories under hypnosis of the time at which the symptom made its first
appearance; when this has been done, it becomes possible
to demonstrate the connection in the clearest and most
convincing fashion.

This method of examination has in a large number of
cases produced results which seem to be of value alike
from a theoretical and a practical point of view.

They are valuable theoretically because they have
taught us that external events determine the pathology
of hysteria to an extent far greater than is known and
recognized. It is of course obvious that in cases of 'trau-

matic' hysteria what provokes the symptoms is the accident. The causal connection is equally evident in hysterical attacks when it is possible to gather from the patient's utterances that in each attack he is hallucinating the same event which provoked the first one. The situation is more obscure in the case of other phenomena.

Our experiences have shown us, however, that the most various symptoms, which are ostensibly spontaneous and, as one might say, idiopathic products of hysteria, are just as strictly related to the precipitating trauma as the phenomena to which we have just alluded and which exhibit the connection quite clearly. The symptoms which we have been able to trace back to precipitating factors of this sort include neuralgias and anaesthesias of very various kinds, many of which had persisted for years, contractures and paralyses, hysterical attacks and epileptoid convulsions, which every observer regarded as true epilepsy, *petit mal* and disorders in the nature of *tic,* chronic vomiting and anorexia, carried to the pitch of rejection of all nourishment, various forms of disturbance of vision, constantly recurrent visual hallucinations, etc. The disproportion between the many years' duration of the hysterical symptom and the single occurrence which provoked it is what we are accustomed invariably to find in traumatic neuroses. Quite frequently it is some event in childhood that sets up a more or less severe symptom which persists during the years that follow.

The connection is often so clear that it is quite evident how it was that the precipitating event produced this particular phenomenon rather than any other. In that case the symptom has quite obviously been determined by the precipitating cause. We may take as a very commonplace instance a painful emotion arising during a meal but suppressed at the time, and then producing nausea and vomiting which persists for months in the form of hysterical vomiting. A girl, watching beside a sick-bed in a torment of anxiety, fell into a twilight state and had a terrifying hallucination, while her right arm, which was hanging over the back of her chair, went to sleep; from this there developed a paresis of the same arm accompanied by contracture and anaesthesia. She tried to pray but could find no words; at length she succeeded in repeating a children's prayer in English. When subsequently a severe and highly complicated hysteria developed, she could only speak, write and understand English, while her native language remained unintelligible to her for eighteen months.—The mother of a very sick child, which had at last fallen asleep, concentrated her whole will-power on keeping still so as not to waken it. Precisely on account of her intention she made a 'clacking' noise with her tongue. (An instance of 'hysterical counter-will'.) This noise was repeated on a subsequent occasion on which she wished to keep perfectly still; and from it there developed a *tic* which, in the form of a clacking with the tongue, occurred over a period of many years whenever she felt excited.—A highly intelligent man was present while his brother had an ankylosed hip-joint extended under an anaesthetic. At the instant at which the joint gave way with a crack, he felt a violent pain in his own hip-joint, which persisted for nearly a year.—Further instances could be quoted.

In other cases the connection is not so simple. It consists only in what might be called a 'symbolic' relation between the precipitating cause and the pathological phenomenon—a relation such as healthy people form in dreams. For instance, a neuralgia may follow upon mental pain or vomiting upon a feeling of moral disgust. We have studied patients who used to make the most copious use of this sort of symbolization. In still other cases it is not possible to understand at first sight how they can be determined in the manner we have suggested. It is precisely the typical hysterical symptoms which fall

669

into this class, such as hemi-anaesthesia, contraction of the field of vision, epileptiform convulsions, and so on. An explanation of our views on this group must be reserved for a fuller discussion of the subject.

Observations such as these seem to us to establish an analogy between the pathogenesis of common hysteria and that of traumatic neuroses, and to justify an extension of the concept of traumatic hysteria. In traumatic neuroses the operative cause of the illness is not the trifling physical injury but the affect of fright—the psychical trauma. In an analogous manner, our investigations reveal, for many, if not for most, hysterical symptoms, precipitating causes which can only be described as psychical traumas. Any experience which calls up distressing affects—such as those of fright, anxiety, shame or physical pain—may operate as a trauma of this kind; and whether it in fact does so depends naturally enough on the susceptibility of the person affected (as well as on another condition which will be mentioned later). In the case of common hysteria it not infrequently happens that, instead of a single, major trauma, we find a number of partial traumas forming a *group* of provoking causes. These have only been able to exercise a traumatic effect by summation and they belong together in so far as they are in part components of a single story of suffering. There are other cases in which an apparently trivial circumstance combines with the actually operative event or occurs at a time of peculiar susceptibility to stimulation and in this way attains the dignity of a trauma which it would not otherwise have possessed but which thenceforward persists.

But the causal relation between the determining psychical trauma and the hysterical phenomenon is not of a kind implying that the trauma merely acts like an *agent provocateur* in releasing the symptom, which thereafter leads an independent existence. We must presume rather

670

that the psychical trauma—or more precisely the memory of the trauma—acts like a foreign body which long after its entry must continue to be regarded as an agent that is still at work; and we find the evidence for this in a highly remarkable phenomenon which at the same time lends an important *practical* interest to our findings.

For we found, to our great surprise at first, that *each individual hysterical symptom immediately and permanently disappeared when we had succeeded in bringing clearly to light the memory of the event by which it was provoked and in arousing its accompanying affect, and when the patient had described that event in the greatest possible detail and had put the affect into words*. Recollection without affect almost invariably produces no result. The psychical process which originally took place must be repeated as vividly as possible; it must be brought back to its *status nascendi* and then given verbal utterance. Where what we are dealing with are phenomena involving stimuli (spasms, neuralgias and hallucinations) these re-appear once again with the fullest intensity and then vanish for ever. Failures of function, such as paralyses and anaesthesias, vanish in the same way, though, of course, without the temporary intensification being discernible.[1]

It is plausible to suppose that it is a question here of

---

[1] The possibility of a therapeutic procedure of this kind has been clearly recognized by Delbœuf and Binet, as is shown by the following quotations: 'On s'expliquerait dès lors comment le magnétiseur aide a la guérison. Il remet le sujet dans l'état où le mal s'est manifesté et combat par la parole le même mal, mais renaissant.' ['We can now explain how the hypnotist promotes cure. He puts the subject back into the state in which his trouble first appeared and uses words to combat that trouble, as it now makes a fresh emergence.'] (Delbœuf, 1889.)—'. . . peut-être verra-t-on qu'on reportant le malade par un artifice mental au moment même où le symptome a apparu pour la première fois, on rend ce malade plus docile a une suggestion curative.' ['. . . we shall perhaps find that by taking the patient back by means of a mental artifice to the very moment at which the symptom first appeared, we may make him more susceptible to a therapeutic suggestion.'] (Binet, 1892, 243.)—In Janet's interesting study on mental automatism (1889), there is an account of the cure of a hysterical girl by a method analogous to ours.

unconscious suggestion: the patient expects to be relieved of his sufferings by this procedure, and it is this expectation, and not the verbal utterance, which is the operative factor. This, however, is not so. The first case of this kind that came under observation dates back to the year 1881, that is to say to the 'pre-suggestion' era. A highly complicated case of hysteria was analysed in this way, and the symptoms, which sprang from separate causes, were separately removed. This observation was made possible by spontaneous auto-hypnoses on the part of the patient, and came as a great surprise to the observer.

We may reverse the dictum *'cessante causa cessat effectus'* ['when the cause ceases the effect ceases'] and conclude from these observations that the determining process continues to operate in some way or other for years—not indirectly, through a chain of intermediate causal links, but as a *directly* releasing cause—just as a psychical pain that is remembered in waking consciousness still provokes a lachrymal secretion long after the event. *Hysterics suffer mainly from reminiscences.*[2]

II

At first it seems extraordinary that events experienced so long ago should continue to operate so intensely—that their recollection should not be liable to the wearing away process to which, after all, we see all our memories succumb. The following considerations may perhaps make this a little more intelligible.

The fading of a memory or the losing of its affect

---

[2] In this preliminary communication it is not possible for us to distinguish what is new in it from what has been said by other authors such as Moebius and Strümpell who have held similar views on hysteria to ours. We have found the nearest approach to what we have to say on the theoretical and therapeutic sides of the question in some remarks, published from time to time, by Benedikt. These we shall deal with elsewhere.

depends on various factors. The most important of these is *whether there has been an energetic reaction to the event that provokes an affect*. By 'reaction' we here understand the whole class of voluntary and involuntary reflexes—from tears to acts of revenge—in which, as experience shows us, the affects are discharged. If this reaction takes place to a sufficient amount a large part of the affect disappears as a result. Linguistic usage bears witness to this fact of daily observation by such phrases as 'to cry oneself out' [*'sich ausweinen'*], and to 'blow off steam' [*'sich austoben'*, literally 'to rage oneself out']. If the reaction is suppressed, the affect remains attached to the memory. An injury that has been repaid, even if only in words, is recollected quite differently from one that has had to be accepted. Language recognizes this distinction, too, in its mental and physical consequences; it very characteristically describes an injury that has been suffered in silence as 'a mortification⦁ [*'Krankung'*, lit. 'making ill'].—The injured person's reaction to the trauma only exercises a completely 'cathartic' effect if it is an *adequate reaction*—as, for instance, revenge. But language serves as a substitute for action; by its help, an affect can be 'abreacted' almost as effectively. In other cases speaking is itself the adequate reflex, when, for instance, it is a lamentation or giving utterance to a tormenting secret, e.g. a confession. If there is no such reaction, whether in deeds or words, or in the mildest cases in tears, any recollection of the event retains its affective tone to begin with.

'Abreaction', however, is not the only method of dealing with the situation that is open to a normal person who has experienced a psychical trauma. A memory of such a trauma, even if it has not been abreacted, enters the great complex of associations, it comes alongside other experiences, which may contradict it, and is subjected to rectification by other ideas. After an accident, for instance, the memory of the danger and the (mitigated) repetition of the fright becomes associated with the memory of what happened afterwards—rescue and the consciousness of present safety. Again, a person's memory of a humiliation is corrected by his putting the facts right, by considering his own worth, etc. In this way a normal person is able to bring about the disappearance of the accompanying affect through the process of association.

To this we must add the general effacement of impressions, the fading of memories which we name 'forgetting' and which wears away those ideas in particular that are no longer affectively operative.

Our observations have shown, on the other hand, that the memories which have become the determinants of hysterical phenomena persist for a long time with astonishing freshness and with the whole of their affective colouring. We must, however, mention another remarkable fact, which we shall later be able to turn to account, namely, that these memories, unlike other memories of their past lives, are not at the patients' disposal. On the contrary, *these experiences are completely absent from the patients' memory when they are in a normal psychical state, or are only present in a highly summary form.* Not until they have been questioned under hypnosis do these memories emerge with the undiminished vividness of a recent event.

Thus, for six whole months, one of our patients reproduced under hypnosis with hallucinatory vividness everything that had excited her on the same day of the previous year (during an attack of acute hysteria). A diary kept by her mother without her knowledge proved the completeness of the reproduction . . . Another patient, partly under hypnosis and partly during spontaneous attacks, re-lived with hallucinatory clarity all the events of a hysterical psychosis which she had passed through ten

674

years earlier and which she had for the most part forgotten till the moment at which it re-emerged. Moreover,
certain memories of aetiological importance which dated
back from fifteen to twenty-five years were found to be
astonishingly intact and to possess remarkable sensory
force, and when they returned they acted with all the
affective strength of new experiences.

This can only be explained on the view that these memories constitute an exception in their relation to all the
wearing-away processes which we have discussed above.
*It appears, that is to say, that these memories correspond
to traumas that have not been sufficiently abreacted;* and
if we enter more closely into the reasons which have
prevented this, we find at least two sets of conditions
under which the reaction to the trauma fails to occur.

In the first group are those cases in which the patients
have not reacted to a psychical trauma because the nature
of the trauma excluded a reaction, as in the case of the
apparently irreparable loss of a loved person or because
social circumstances made a reaction impossible or because it was a question of things which the patient wished
to forget, and therefore intentionally repressed from his
conscious thought and inhibited and suppressed. It is
precisely distressing things of this kind that, under hypnosis, we find are the basis of hysterical phenomena (e.g.
hysterical deliria in saints and nuns, continent women
and well-brought-up children).

The second group of conditions are determined, not by
the content of the memories but by the psychical states in
which the patient received the experiences in question.
For we find, under hypnosis, among the causes of hysterical symptoms ideas which are not in themselves significant, but whose persistence is due to the fact that they
originated during the prevalence of severely paralysing
affects, such as fright, or during positively abnormal
psychical states, such as the semi-hypnotic twilight state

675

of day-dreaming, auto-hypnoses, and so on. In such cases it is the nature of the states which makes a reaction to the event impossible.

Both kinds of conditions may, of course, be simultaneously present, and this, in fact, often occurs. It is so when a trauma which is operative in itself takes place while a severely paralysing affect prevails or during a modified state of consciousness. But it also seems to be true that in many people a psychical trauma *produces* one of these abnormal states, which, in turn, makes reaction impossible.

Both of these groups of conditions, however, have in common the fact that the psychical traumas which have not been disposed of by reaction cannot be disposed of either by being worked over by means of association. In the first group the patient is determined to forget the distressing experiences and accordingly excludes them so far as possible from association; while in the second group the associative working-over fails to occur because there is no extensive associative connection between the normal state of consciousness and the pathological ones in which the ideas made their appearance. We shall have occasion immediately to enter further into this matter.

It may therefore be said that the ideas which have become pathological have persisted with such freshness and affective strength because they have been denied the normal wearing-away processes by means of abreaction and reproduction in states of uninhibited association.

III

We have stated the conditions which, as our experience shows, are responsible for the development of hysterical phenomena from psychical traumas. In so doing, we have already been obliged to speak of abnormal states of consciousness in which these pathogenic ideas arise, and to emphasize the fact that the recollection of the operative psychical trauma is not to be found in the patient's normal memory but in his memory when he is hypnotized. The longer we have been occupied with these phenomena the more we have become convinced that *the splitting of consciousnss which is so striking in the well-known classical cases under the form of* 'double conscience' *is present to a rudimentary degree in every hysteria, and that a tendency to such a dissociation, and with it the emergence of abnormal states of consciousness (which we shall bring together under the term 'hypnosis') is the basic phenomenon of this neurosis.* In these views we concur with Binet and the two Janets, though we have had no experience of the remarkable findings they have made on anaesthetic patients.

We should like to balance the familiar thesis that hypnosis is an artificial hysteria by another—the basis and *sine qua non* of hysteria is the existence of hypnoid states. These hypnoid states share with one another and with hypnosis, however much they may differ in other respects, one common feature: the ideas which emerge in them are very intense but are cut off from associative communication with the rest of the content of consciousness. Associations may take place between these hypnoid states, and their ideational content can in this way reach a more or less high degree of psychical organization. Moreover, the nature of these states and the extent to which they are cut off from the remaining conscious processes must be supposed to vary just as happens in hypnosis, which ranges from a light drowsiness to somnambulism, from complete recollection to total amnesia.

If hypnoid states of this kind are already present before the onset of the manifest illness, they provide the soil in which the affect plants the pathogenic memory with its consequent somatic phenomena. This corresponds to *dis-*

677

positional hysteria. We have found, however, that a severe trauma (such as occurs in a traumatic neurosis) or a laborious suppression (as of a sexual affect, for instance) can bring about a splitting-off of groups of ideas even in people who are in other respects unaffected; and this would be the mechanism of *psychically acquired* hysteria. Between the extremes of these two forms we must assume the existence of a series of cases within which the liability to dissociation in the subject and the affective magnitude of the trauma vary inversely.

We have nothing new to say on the question of the origin of these dispositional hypnoid states. They often, it would seem, grow out of the day-dreams which are so common even in healthy people and to which needlework and similar occupations render women especially prone. Why it is that the 'pathological associations' brought about in these states are so stable and why they have so much more influence on somatic processes than ideas are usually found to do—these questions coincide with the general problem of the effectiveness of hypnotic suggestions. Our observations contribute nothing fresh on this subject. But they throw a light on the contradiction between the dictum 'hysteria is a psychosis' and the fact that among hysterics may be found people of the clearest intellect, strongest will, greatest character and highest critical power. This characterization holds good of their waking thoughts; but in their hypnoid states they are insane, as we all are in dreams. Whereas, however, our dream-psychoses have no effect upon our waking state, the products of hypnoid states intrude into waking life in the form of hysterical symptoms.

IV

What we have asserted of chronic hysterical symptoms can be applied almost completely to hysterical *attacks*.

678

Charcot, as is well known, has given us a schematic description of the 'major' hysterical attack, according to which four phases can be distinguished in a complete attack: (1) the epileptoid phase, (2) the phase of large movements, (3) the phase of *'attitudes passionnelles'* (the hallucinatory phase), and (4) the phase of terminal delirium. Charcot derives all those forms of hysterical attack which are in practice met with more often than the complete *'grande attaque'*, from the abbreviation, absence or isolation of these four distinct phases.

Our attempted explånation takes its start from the third of these phases, that of the *'attitudes passionnelles'*. Where this is present in a well-marked form, it exhibits the hallucinatory reproduction of a memory which was of importance in bringing about the onset of the hysteria —the memory either of a single major trauma (which we find *par excellence* in what is called traumatic hysteria) or of a series of interconnected part-traumas (such as underlie common hysteria). Or, lastly, the attack may revive the events which have become emphasized owing to their *coinciding* with a moment of special disposition to trauma.

There are also attacks, however, which appear to consist exclusively of motor phenomena and in which the phase of *attitudes passionnelles is absent*. If one can succeed in getting into *rapport* with the patient during an attack such as this of generalized clonic spasms or cataleptic rigidity, or during an *attaque de sommeil* [attack of sleep]—or if, better still, one can succeed in provoking the attack under hypnosis—one finds that here, too, there is an underlying memory of the psychical trauma or series of traumas, which usually comes to our notice in a hallucinatory phase.

Thus, a little girl suffered for years from attacks of general convulsions which could well be, and indeed were, regarded as epileptic. She was hypnotized with a view

679

to a differential diagnosis, and promptly had one of her attacks. She was asked what she was seeing and replied 'The dog, the dog's coming!'; and in fact it turned out that she had had the first of her attacks after being chased by a savage dog. The success of the treatment confirmed the choice of diagnosis.

Again, an employee who had become a hysteric as a result of being ill-treated by his superior, suffered from attacks in which he collapsed and fell into a frenzy of rage, but without uttering a word or giving any sign of a hallucination. It was possible to provoke an attack under hypnosis, and the patient then revealed that he was living through the scene in which his employer had abused him in the street and hit him with a stick. A few days later the patient came back and complained of having had another attack of the same kind. On this occasion it turned out under hypnosis that he had been re-living the scene to which the actual onset of the illness was related; the scene in the law-court when he failed to obtain satisfaction for his maltreatment.

In all other respects, too, the memories which emerge, or can be aroused, in hysterical attacks correspond to the precipitating causes which we have found at the root of *chronic* hysterical symptoms. Like these latter causes, the memories underlying hysterical attacks relate to psychical traumas which have not been disposed of by abreaction or by associative thought-activity. Like them, they are, whether completely or in essential elements, out of reach of the memory of normal consciousness and are found to belong to the ideational content of hypnoid states of consciousness with restricted association. Finally, too, the therapeutic test can be applied to them. Our observations have often taught us that a memory of this kind which had hitherto provoked attacks, ceases to be able to do so after the process of reaction and associative correction have been applied to it under hypnosis.

The motor phenomena of hysterical attacks can be interpreted partly as universal forms of reaction appropriate to the affect accompanying the memory (such as kicking about and waving the arms and legs, which even young babies do), partly as a direct expression of these memories; but in part, like the hysterical stigmata found among the chronic symptoms, they cannot be explained in this way.

Hysterical attacks, furthermore, appear in a specially interesting light if we bear in mind a theory that we have mentioned above, namely, that in hysteria groups of ideas originating in hypnoid states are present and that these are cut off from associative connection with the other ideas, but can be associated among themselves, and thus form the more or less highly organized rudiment of a second consciousness, a *condition seconde*. If this is so, a chronic hysterical symptom will correspond to the intrusion of this second state into the somatic innervation which is as a rule under the control of normal consciousness. A hysterical attack, on the other hand, is evidence of a higher organization of this second state. When the attack makes its first appearance, it indicates a moment at which this hypnoid consciousness has obtained control of the subject's whole existence—it points, that is, to an acute hysteria; when it occurs on subsequent occasions and contains a memory, it points to a return of that moment. Charcot has already suggested that hysterical attacks are a rudimentary form of a *condition seconde*. During the attack, control over the whole of the somatic innervation passes over to the hypnoid consciousness. Normal consciousness, as well-known observations show, is not always entirely repressed. It may even be aware of the motor phenomena of the attack, while the accompanying psychical events are outside its knowledge.

The typical course of a severe case of hysteria is, as we know, as follows. To begin with, an ideational content

681

is formed during hypnoid states; when this has increased to a sufficient extent, it gains control, during a period of 'acute hysteria', of the somatic innervation and of the patient's whole existence, and creates chronic symptoms and attacks; after this it clears up, apart from certain residues. If the normal personality can regain control, what is left over from the hypnoid ideational content recurs in hysterical attacks and puts the subject back from time to time into similar states, which are themselves once more open to influence and susceptible to traumas. A state of equilibrium, as it were, may then be established between the two psychical groups which are combined in the same person: hysterical attacks and normal life proceed side by side without interfering with each other. An attack will occur spontaneously, just as memories do in normal people; it is, however, possible to provoke one, just as any memory can be aroused in accordance with the laws of association. It can be provoked either by stimulation of a hysterogenic zone or by a new experience which sets it going owing to a similarity with the pathogenic experience. We hope to be able to show that these two kinds of determinant, though they appear to be so unlike, do not differ in essentials, but that in both a hyperaesthetic memory is touched on.

In other cases this equilibrium is very unstable. The attack makes its appearance as a manifestation of the residue of the hypnoid consciousness whenever the normal personality is exhausted and incapacitated. The possibility cannot be dismissed that here the attack may have been divested of its original meaning and may be recurring as a motor reaction without any content.

It must be left to further investigation to discover what it is that determines whether a hysterical personality manifests itself in attacks, in chronic symptoms or in a mixture of the two.

It will now be understood how it is that the psycho-therapeutic procedure which we have described in these pages has a curative effect. *It brings to an end the operative force of the idea which was not abreacted in the first instance, by allowing its strangulated affect to find a way out through speech; and it subjects it to associative correction by introducing it into normal consciousness (under light hypnosis) or by removing it through the physician's suggestion, as is done in somnambulism accompanied by amnesia.*

In our opinion the therapeutic advantages of this procedure are considerable. It is of course true that we do not cure hysteria in so far as it is a matter of disposition. We can do nothing against the recurrence of hypnoid states. Moreover, during the productive stage of an acute hysteria our procedure cannot prevent the phenomena which have been so laboriously removed from being at once replaced by fresh ones. But once this acute stage is past, any residues which may be left in the form of chronic symptoms or attacks are often removed, and permanently so, by our method, because it is a radical one; in this respect it seems to us far superior in its efficacy to removal through direct suggestion, as it is practised to-day by psycho-therapists.

If by uncovering the psychical mechanism of hysterical phenomena we have taken a step forward along the path first traced so successfully by Charcot with his explanation and artificial imitation of hystero-traumatic paralyses, we cannot conceal from ourselves that this has brought us nearer to an understanding only of the *mechanism* of hysterical symptoms and not of the internal causes of hysteria. We have done no more than touch upon the aetiology of hysteria and in fact have been able to throw light only on its acquired forms—on the bearing of accidental factors on the neurosis.

SIGMUND FREUD (b.-Freiberg, Austria, May 6, 1856; d.-England, Sept. 23, 1939).

At the age of 4 years, Freud moved with his family to Vienna, where he lived until 1938 when he was forced to flee, in the Nazi times. To avoid persecution, Freud went to England, and died there a year later.

Freud received his M.D. from Vienna in 1881. From 1885 to 1902 he was Dozent in Neuropathology. The most important event in Freud's education was his attendance at Charcot's famous *Lecons du Mardi* at the Salpetrière, from Oct. 20, 1885 to Feb. 23, 1886. Freud later made the first translation of Charcot's lectures into German (*Poliklinisch Vorträge,* 1887-1888). From 1902 to 1920 Freud was Ausserordentlicher Professor at Vienna. In 1920 he became Ordentlicher Professor.

Freud gave his first public lecture on Charcot's proof of hysteria in the male, upon his return to Vienna from Paris. The day was Oct. 15, 1886. To a man of Freud's temperament, it was no small fact that he was publicly ridiculed and condemned for this idea. He took it as a special challenge, and within a few weeks was able to find, and to present an actual case of conversion hysteria in an Austrian male before the medical society. Freud's later life, in many ways, was a repetition of this rebuff, of his perceiving the challenge, and of his striving for complete and overwhelming victory.

One of the deepest motivations in Freud's life may have come from just such a challenge, tortuously created again and again within himself. Freud is said to have admitted the uncanny into the realm of his personal psychic experience only in one instance. Whenever he was unable to intellectually grasp and rationally describe the feelings and emotions of a fellow man: "whenever he was unable to gauge someone else's emotions through his own" (v. i., Jones, v. 2, p. 226), then and only then did he know the uncanny. Actually, in Freud's own essay on the uncanny, he explicitly denies *ever* having experienced this peak of human terrors. He denied what, in fact, was probably his everyday fate. He certainly experienced it,—man cannot escape it,—but even more than most of us. Freud was known, among his colleagues as a very poor judge of man ("Menschenkenner" —v.i., Jones, v. 2, p. 412). That which he dreaded most, to fail in the deeper knowledge of his fellowmen, this he was known to fail again and again. His life thus resembles that of Sisyphus. This cosmic tragedy may indeed have been the wellspring of his greatness.

Freud had tried to discuss with Charcot, Breuer's later famous case of "Anna O." But the great man's "thoughts seemed to be elsewhere." The realization of the importance of this case, in spite of Charcot's indifference, reflected Freud's first insight into what was soon to be known as psychoanalysis. The study of this case led Freud, and Breuer, to the present formulation of the theory of hysteria, which is generally credited as being the first formal statement of the Psychoanalytical Movement.

BREUER, J. & FREUD, S. Studies on Hysteria. London: Hogarth Press and the Institute of Psychoanalysis, 1956 (1925- German edition). Trans. James & Alex Strachey. Chap. I: "On the psychical mechanism of hysterical phenomena: preliminary communication." This is reprinted here in its entirety with permission of Basic Books, Inc., holders of the copyright in the United States. The present selection was originally published in: *Neurologisches Centralblatt*. 1893, 12: 4-10, 43-47, in Berlin. This essay was subsequently included in the *Studien Uber Hysterie*. Leipzig u. Wien: Deuticke, 1895, as the first chapter. The Standard Edition of the Complete Psychological Works of Sigmund Freud includes this in Vol. II. In the International Psycho-Analytic Library (edited by the late Ernest Jones) this is #50.

See also:

FREUD, S.
   a) *The basic writings of* . . . N.Y.: Modern Library, 1938. Trans. A. A. Brill. The most conveniently available collection.
   b) Project for a scientific psychology. Appended to: Freud, S. *The origins of psychoanalysis*. N. Y.: Basic Books, 1954. Ed. M. Bonaparte, A. Freud, E. Kris. Trans. E. Mosbacher & J. Strachey. This is a very revealing attempt by Freud to examine, for himself, some of the more traditional psychological issues. It reads much like Herbart, and is essential reading for anyone wishing to examine the broader historical picture.

BERNFELD, S. "Freud's earliest theories and the school of Helmholtz" *Psychoanal. Quart.* 1944, 13:341-362.

JONES, E. The life and work of Sigmund Freud. N.Y.: Basic Books, 1953-1957, 3 vol. This is the definitive biography. It contains excellent references to the more technical histories of psychoanalysis. The complete bibliography of Freud is readily available, e.g. Grinstein.

FREUD, M. Sigmund Freud, man and father. N.Y.: Vanguard, 1958. An interesting biography by Freud's son, to be contrasted with the book of E. Jones.

Murchison (b-Vol. III, p. 591-605).

Grinstein (Vol. I, p. 578-646).

JOSEF BREUER (b.-1842; d.-Vienna, June 1925)

Breuer began his studies at Vienna in 1859. In 1867 he became Dozent. In 1868 he began some work in otology and in the vestibular sense, with the psychophysiologist Ewald Hering. In 1881 he received his M.D.

Breuer was a long time personal friend of Ernst Mach, who had a marked influence on him. It was his growing friendship with Freud, however, which induced him to bring to Freud's attention his very intelligent but curious patient known under the pseudonym of Anna O. She was Breuer's patient from Dec. 1880 to June 1882. Thenceforth, together with Freud, Breuer helped to elaborate the theory of hysteria, built largely about this patient.

THE PRACTICE AND THEORY
OF INDIVIDUAL PSYCHOLOGY

Alfred Adler

New Leading Principles for the Practice of Individual-Psychology

I. Every neurosis can be understood as an attempt to free oneself from a feeling of inferiority in order to gain a feeling of superiority.

II. The path of the neurosis does not lead in the direction of social functioning, nor does it aim at solving given life-problems but finds an outlet for itself in the small family circle, thus achieving the isolation of the patient.

III. The larger unit of the social group is either completely or very extensively pushed aside by a mechanism consisting of hyper-sensitiveness and intolerance. Only a small group is left over for the manoeuvres aiming at the various types of superiority to expend themselves upon. At the same time protection and the withdrawal from the demands of the community and the decisions of life are made possible.

IV. Thus estranged from reality, the neurotic man lives a life of imagination and phantasy and employs a number of devices for enabling him to side-step the demands of reality and for reaching out toward an ideal situation which would free him from any service for the community and absolve him from responsibility.

V. These exemptions and the privileges of illness and suffering give him a substitute for his original hazardous goal of superiority.

VI. Thus the neurosis and the psyche represent an attempt to free oneself from all the constraints of the community by establishing a counter compulsion. This latter is so constituted that it effectively faces the peculiar nature of the surroundings and their demands. Both of these convincing inferences can be drawn from the manner in which this counter compulsion manifests itself and from the neuroses selected.

VII. The counter-compulsion takes on the nature of a revolt, gathers its material either from favourable affective experiences or from observations. It permits thoughts and affects to become preoccupied either with the above-mentioned stirrings or with unimportant details, as long as they at least serve the purpose of directing the eye and the attention of the patient away from his life-problems. In this manner, depending upon the needs of the situation, he prepares anxiety-and compulsion-situations, sleeplessness, swooning, perversions, hallucinations, slightly pathological affects, neurasthenic and hypochondriacal complexes and psychotic pictures of his actual condition, all of which are to serve him as excuses.

VIII. Even logic falls under the domination of the counter-compulsion. As in psychosis this process may go as far as the actual nullification of logic.

IX. Logic, the will to live, love, human sympathy, co-operation and language, all arise out of the needs of human communal life. Against the latter are directed automatically all the plans of the neurotic individual striving for isolation and lusting for power.

X. To cure a neurosis and a psychosis it is necessary to change completely the whole up-bringing of the patient and turn him definitely and unconditionally back upon human society.

XI. All the volition and all the strivings of the neurotic are dictated by his prestige-seeking policy, which is continually looking for excuses which will enable him to leave the problems of life unsolved. He consequently automatically turns against allowing any community-feeling to develop.

XII. If therefore we may regard the demand for a complete and unified understanding of man and for a comprehension of his (undivided) individuality as justi-fied—a view to which we are forced both by the nature of reason and the individual-psychological knowledge of the urge toward an integration of the personality—then the method of *comparison,* the main tool of our method, enables us to arrive at some conception of the power-lines along which an individual strives to attain superi-ority. The following will serve as the two contrasting-poles for comparison:

1. Our own attitude in a situation similar to that of a patient hard-pressed by some demand. In such a case it is essential for the practitioner to possess, in a considerable degree, the gift of *putting himself in the other person's place.*

2. The patient's attitudes and anomalies dating from early childhood. These can always be shown as dominated by the relation of the child to his en-vironment, by his erroneous and in the main gener-alized evaluation (of himself), by his obstinate and deep-rooted feeling of inferiority and by his striving after power.

3. Other types of individuals, particularly those spe-cifically neurotic. In these cases we shall come upon the patent discovery that what one type attains by means of neurasthenic troubles, another endeav-ours to obtain by means of fear, hysteria, neurotic-

compulsion or psychosis. Traits of character, affects, principles and nervous symptoms, pointing toward the same goal and, when torn from their context, frequently giving a contrary significance, all these serve as a protection against the shock caused by the demands of the community.

4. Those very demands of the community which the nervous individual, in varying degrees, sidesteps, such as co-operation, fellow-feeling, love, social adaptation and the responsibilities of the community.

By means of this individual-psychological investigation we realize that the neurotic individual, far more than the ordinary normal man, arranges his psychic-life in accordance with the desire for power over his fellow-men. His longing for superiority enables him continually and extensively to reject all outside compulsion, the demands made upon him by others and the responsibilities imposed by Society. The realization of this basic fact in the psychic-life of the neurotic, so lightens the task of obtaining an insight into psychic inter-connections that it is bound to become the most useful working-hypothesis in the investigation and curing of neurotic diseases, until a more profound understanding of the individual enables us to disentangle and grasp in their full significance, the real factors involved in each case.

What irritates the healthy man in this type of argument and the conclusions drawn therefrom, is the suggestion that an imagined goal constructed by an emotionally-conditioned superiority, can possess greater force than rational deliberation. But we can find this inversion of an ideal frequently enough both in the life of healthy individuals as in that of whole nations. War, political abuses, crimes, suicide, ascetic penances, provide us with similar surprises. A good many of our sufferings and tortures we ourselves originate and take upon ourselves under the influence of some idea.

That a cat should catch mice, that without ever having been taught to do so, should be prepared for it even in the first days of its existence, is no more remarkable than that the neurotic individual, according to his nature and destiny, his position and his self-evaluation, should evade and find unbearable every form of compulsion; that he should secretly or openly, consciously or unconsciously look for excuses to free himself, frequently originating them himself.

The reason for the intolerance of the neurotics toward the constraints of society, as the history of their childhood shows, is to be sought in the continuous conflict-attitude that has been practised for many years against the environment. This is forced upon the child, without there being any real justification for its expressing itself in just such a reaction, by the bodily or psychically conditioned position it occupies and from which the child receives either lasting or intensified feelings of inferiority. The object of the conflict-attitude is the conquest of power and importance, an ideal of superiority constructed with an infant's incapacity and over-evaluation and the fulfilment of which presents compensations and super-compensations of a most general kind, in the pursuit of which there always occurs a victory over the constraints of society and over the will of the environment. As soon as this conflict has taken on more acute forms it evolves, from within itself, an antagonism against compulsions of all kinds, whether they be education, reality, common interest, external force, personal weakness, as well as all the compulsions presented by such factors as work, cleanliness, acceptance of nourishment, normal urination and defecation, sleep, treatment of disease, love, tenderness, friendship, loneliness and its opposite, sociability. In toto we get the picture of a

691

man who does not want to play the game, a dog in the manger. Where antagonism is directed against the awakening of feelings of love and comradeship there arises a fear of love and marriage that can assume many and manifold degrees and forms. At this place let me call attention to a number of forms of compulsion hardly perceivable to the normal individual, which are nevertheless almost regularly prevented from developing by the appearance of a nervous or psychotic condition. These compulsions are:—to recognize this compulsion, to be attentive, to subordinate oneself, to tell the truth, to study or to pass examinations, to be punctual, to entrust oneself to a person, a carriage, the railroad; to confide the household, business, children, spouse, or oneself to other people; to become a landlord or adopt a profession; to marry, to acknowledge the correctness of the other man's view, to be grateful, to bring children into the world, to play a proper sexual role or recognize proper love-responsibilities; to rise in the morning, to sleep at night, to recognize the equal rights and equality of others, the rights of women, to keep a measure in everything, to be loyal, etc. All these idiosyncrasies may be conscious or unconscious but they are never grasped by the patient in all their bearings.

This examination teaches us two things:

1. The concept of compulsion in the neurotic has been tremendously enlarged and embraces relationships, even if only from a logical point of view, that a normal individual does not include under the category of compulsion.

2. The antagonism is no final-phenomena but extends further. It has a continuation and is followed by a state of fermentation. It signifies at all times a conflict-attitude and shows us as though at an apparent resting point, the striving of the neurotic to triumph over others, the striving for a directed violent twisting of the logical

inferences drawn from human communal life. "Non me rebus, sed mihi res subigere conor". In this passage taken from a letter of Horace to Maecenas, the former shows in what this infuriated lust for importance ends: in a headache and sleeplessness.

A patient, thirty-five years old, complained to me that he had for a number of years been suffering from sleeplessness, from brooding and masturbation-compulsions. The latter symptom was particularly significant, for the patient was married, the father of two children and on excellent marital relations with his wife. Among other torturing phenomena he spoke of a kind of "rubber-fetichism". From time to time, in any exciting situation, the word "rubber" forced itself to his lips.

The results of an extensive individual-psychological examination led to the following facts: starting from a period in childhood characteristized by marked depression, at a time when the patient used to wet his bed and was regarded as a stupid child because of his clumsiness, he had developed *along the guiding-line of ambition* to such an extent that the latter had grown into a *megalomania*. The pressure of his environment, which actually did exist in a very high degree, brought close to him the picture of a *definitely inimical external world* and invested him with a permanently pessimistic outlook upon life. In such a mood he felt all the demands of the external world as unbearable compulsions and retorted by wetting his bed and by clumsiness, until he met a teacher in whom, for the first time in his life, he came into contact with the counterpart of a good fellowman. He then began to mitigate his defiance and rage at the demands of others and his conflict-attitude toward the community, to the extent of it becoming possible for him to stop wetting his bed, of developing into a "gifted" student and to work for the highest of ideals in life. His hostility against the compulsion of others he solved, in the manner of a

693

poet and a philosopher, by a flight into the transcendental. He developed an emotionally-steeped idea as if *he were the only human being in existence,* and that everything else, particularly human beings, were merely appearances. The relationship with the ideas of Schopenhauer, Fichte, Kant is not to be dismissed. The deeper purpose, however, lay in his robbing existence of value in order to obtain a feeling of security, and escape "the scorn and questionings of our times". All of this was to have been accomplished by *magic,* comparable to that which unreliant children use when they wish to deprive facts of their power. In this way the *rubber-erasure* became the symbol and sign of his power, because to the child, as the destroyer of the visible, the rubber appeared like a possibility fulfilled. The whole situation called for over-evaluation and generalization, and thus the word and concept "rubber" became the conquering watchword, whenever school, the parental household and later on man or woman, wife or child, presented any difficulties or threatened him with coercion.

So, in a well-nigh poetical manner, he arrived at the goal of the isolated hero, fulfilled his striving after power and renounced society. His steadily improving position in the world prevented him, however, from entirely pushing aside the actual and ever-present communal feelings. Little was consequently lost *of the love and the logic that binds us all together,* and so he was spared the fate of developing a *paranoiac disease.* He went only as far as a compulsion-neurosis.

His love was not based upon pure communal feeling. In fact it came under the attraction of the main line of his striving after power. Since the concept and the feeling "power" were united with the magic word "rubber", he sought and found a catchword that would free him from his sexuality in the picture of a *rubber-girdle.* Not a woman but a rubber girdle, in other words, not a

694

personal but an impersonal object influenced him. And thus while making his power-intoxication and his derogatory attitude toward women secure, he became a fetichist, for these traits are found regularly as the starting point of fetichism. Had the belief in his own virility been slighter we would have seen suggestions of homosexuality, gerontophily, necrophily and similar traits appear.

His masturbation-compulsion had the same basic character. It likewise served to enable him to escape from the compulsion of love, from the "magic" of women.

The sleeplessness was directly caused by his brooding-compulsion, the latter struggling against the constraint of sleep. An unquenchable ambition compelled him to spend the night solving the problems of the day. Has he not like another Alexander accomplished so little as yet? This sleeplessness had however another side to it. It weakened his energy and his power of action; became the justification for his disease. What he had so far accomplished had been done so to speak with one hand, had been done despite his sleeplessness. What might he not have done had he been able to sleep! But he was not able to sleep and in this way, by means of this nocturnal brooding-compulsion, he obtained an alibi. Thus he rescued his uniqueness and his god-likeness. All blame for any deficiency could now no more be attributed to his character but to the puzzling and fatal circumstance of his not having been able to sleep. Thus his invalid state had become a disagreeable accident, and for its continuation not he but the insufficient knowledge of the physicians, was responsible. If he is not able to prove his greatness, it will be the concern of the physicians to do so. As can be seen it was of no small importance to him to remain an invalid and he was not going to make the task of the physicians easy.

It is interesting to see how he solves the problem of life and death in order to save his god-likeness. He still has the feeling that his mother, who has been dead for twelve years, is alive. But there is a marked uncertainty about this assumption, manifesting itself more strongly than that tender feeling which so frequently appears shortly after the death of a near relative. This doubt concerning his wild assumption does not at all emanate from cold logic. It is to be explained through the insight given by individual-psychology. If everything is but appearance then his mother has not died. If she is alive, however, then the idea of his being unique falls to the ground. He has no more solved this problem than philosophy has the idea of the universe as an appearance. He answers the compulsion and mischief of death with a doubt.

The interconnection of all the manifestations of his disease he regards as a justification for securing all his privileges as against his wife, his relatives and his inferiors. His high opinion of himself can never come to harm, for taking his sufferings into consideration, he is always greater than he appears to be and he can always evade difficult undertakings by pointing to his disease. But he can also act differently. Toward his superiors he can be the most conscientious, the most industrious and the most obedient official and enjoy their complete approbation although secretly always aspiring to surpass them.

This over-intense striving after the sensation of power had made him ill. His emotional and sensational life, his initiative and his capacity for work, even his power of reasoning, fell under the self-imposed compulsion of his lust for omnipotence, so that his feelings for humanity and with it love, friendship and adjustment to society, all disappeared. A cure could only have been attained by dismantling his whole prestige-mechanism and by inducing the development of a feeling for society.

Individual Psychology, its Assumptions and its Results

A survey of the views and theories of most psychologists indicates a peculiar limitation both in the nature of their field of investigation and in their methods of inquiry. They act as if experience and knowledge of mankind were, with conscious intent, to be excluded from our investigations and all value and importance denied to artistic and creative vision as well as to intuition itself. While the experimental psychologists collect and devise phenomena in order to determine types of reaction—that is, are concerned with the physiology of the psychical life properly speaking——other psychologists arrange all forms of expression and manifestations in old customary, or at best slightly altered, systems. By this procedure they naturally rediscover the interdependence and connection in individual expressions, implied from the very beginning in their schematic attitude toward the psyche.

Either the foregoing method is employed or an attempt is made by means of small, if possible measurable individual phenomena of a physiological nature, to construct psychical states and thought by means of an equation. The fact that all subjective thinking and subjective immersion on the part of the investigator are excluded—although in reality they dominate the very nature of these connections—is from this viewpoint regarded as an advantage.

The method employed, and the very importance it seems to possess as a preparation for the human mind, reminds us of the type of natural science completely antiquated today, with its rigid systems, replaced everywhere now by views that attempt to grasp living phenomena and their variations as connected wholes, biologically, philosophically, and psychologically. This is also the purpose of that movement in psychology that I have

697

called *"comparative individual-psychology"*. By starting with the assumption of the *unity of the individual,* an attempt is made to obtain a picture of this unified personality regarded as a variant of individual life-manifestations and forms of expression. The individual traits are then compared with one another, brought into a common plane, and finally fused together to form a composite portrait that is, in turn, individualized.[1]

It may have been noticed that this method of looking upon man's psychic life is by no means either unusual or even particularly daring. This type of approach is particularly noticeable in the study of child-psychology, in spite of other lines of inquiry also used there. It is the essence and the nature above all of the work of the artist, be he painter, sculptor, musician, or particularly poet, so to present the minute traits of his creations that the observer is able to obtain from them the great principles of personality. He is thus in a position to reconstruct those very things that the artist when thinking of his *finale* had previously hidden therein. Since life in any given society, life without any of the preconceptions of science, has always been under the ban of the question "whither?", we are warranted in definitely stating that, scientific views to the contrary notwithstanding, no man has ever made a judgment about an event without endeavouring to strain toward the point which seems to bind together all the psychic manifestations of an individual; even to an *imagined goal* if necessary.

When I hurry home, I am certain to exhibit to any observer the carriage, expression, the gait, and the gestures that are to be expected of a person returning home. My reflexes indeed might be different from those anticipated, the causes might vary. The essential point to be grasped psychologically and the one which interests us

---

[1] William Stern has come to the same conclusions starting from a different method of approach.

exclusively and practically and psychologically more than all others, *is the path followed.*

Let me observe that if I know the goal of a person I know in a general way what will happen. I am in a position to bring into their proper order each of the successive movements made, to view them in their connections, to correct them and to make, where necessary, the required adaptations for my approximate psychological knowledge of these associations. If I am acquainted only with the causes, know only the reflexes, the reaction-times, the ability to repeat and such facts, I am aware of nothing that actually takes place in the soul of man.

We must remember that the person under observation would not know what to do with himself were he not orientated toward some goal. As long as we are not acquainted with the objective which determines his "lifeline", the whole system of his recognized reflexes, together with all their casual conditions, can give us no certainty as to his next series of movements. They might be brought into harmony with practically any psychic resultant. This deficiency is most clearly felt in association-tests. I would never expect a man suffering from some great disappointment to associate "tree" with "rope". The moment I knew his objective, however, namely suicide, then I might very well expect that particular sequence of thoughts—expect it with such certainty that I would remove knives, poison, and weapons from his immediate vicinity.

If we look at the matter more closely, we shall find the following law holding in the development of all psychic happenings: *we cannot think, feel, will, or act without the perception of some goal.* For all the causalities in the world would not suffice to conquer the chaos of the future nor obviate the planlessness to which we would be bound to fall a victim. All activity would persist in the stage of uncontrolled gropings; the economy visible in our psychic life unattained; we should be unintegrated and in every aspect of our physiognomy, in every personal touch, similar to organisms of the rank of the amœba.

No one will deny that by assuming an objective for our psychic life we accommodate ourselves better to reality. This can be easily demonstrated. For its truth in individual examples, where phenomena are torn from their proper connections, no doubt exists. Only watch from this point of view, the attempts at walking made by a small child or a woman recovering from a confinement. Naturally he who approaches this whole matter without any theory is likely to find its deeper significance escape him. Yet it is a fact that before the first step has been taken the objective of the person's movement has already been determined.

In the same way it can be demonstrated that all psychic activities are given a direction by means of a previously determined goal. All the temporary and partially visible objectives, after the short period of psychic development of childhood, are under the domination of an imagined terminal goal, of a final point felt and conceived of as definitely fixed. In other words the psychic life of man is made to fit into the fifth act like a character drawn by a good dramatist.

The conclusion thus to be drawn from the unbiased study of any personality viewed from the standpoint of individual-psychology leads us to the following important proposition: *every psychic phenomenon, if it is to give us any understanding of a person, can only be grasped and understood if regarded as a preparation for some goal.*

To what an extent this conception promotes our psychological understanding, is clearly apparent as soon as we become aware of the *multiplicity of meaning of those psychical processes that have been torn from their proper context*. Take for example the case of a man with a "bad memory". Assume that he is quite conscious of this fact and that an examination discloses an inferior capacity for the repetition of meaningless syllables. According to present usage in psychology, which we might more properly call an abuse, we would have to make the following inference: the man is suffering, from hereditary or pathological causes, from a deficient capacity for repetition. Incidentally, let me add, that in this type of investigation we generally find the inference already stated in different words in the premises. In this case *e.g.* we have the following proposition: if a man has a bad memory, or if he only remembers a few words—then he has an inferior capacity for repetition.

The procedure in individual-psychology is completely different. After excluding the possibility of all organic causes, we would ask ourselves what is the objective of this weakness of memory? This we could only determine if we were in possession of an intimate knowledge of the whole individual, so that an understanding of one part becomes possible only after we have understood the whole. And we should probably find the following to hold true in a large number of cases: this man is attempting to prove to himself and to others that for certain reasons of a fundamental nature, that are either not to be named or have remained unconscious, *but which can most effectively be represented by poorness of memory,* he must not permit himself to perform some particular act or to come to a given decision (change of profession, studies, examination, marriage). We should then have unmasked this weakness of memory as tendentious and could understand its importance as a weapon against a contemplated undertaking. In every test of ability to repeat we should then expect to find the deficiency due to the secret life-plan of an individual. The question then to be asked is how such deficiencies or evils arise. They may be simply

701

"arranged" by purposely underlining general physiological weaknesses and interpreting them as personal sufferings. Others may succeed either by subjective absorption into an abnormal condition or by pre-occupation with dangerous pessimistic anticipations, in so weakening their faith in their own capacities, that their strength, attention or will-power are only partially at their disposal.

A similar observation may be made in the case of affects. To give one more example, take the case of a woman subject to outbreaks of anxiety recurring at certain intervals. As long as nothing of greater significance than this was discernible, the assumption of some hereditary degeneration, some disease of the vaso-motor system, of the vagus nerve, etc., sufficed. It is also possible that we might have regarded ourselves as having arrived at a fuller understanding of the case, if we had discovered in the previous history of the patient, some frightful experience, or traumatic condition and attributed the disease to it. As soon, however, as we examined the personality of this individual and inquired into her directive-lines we discovered an excess of will-to-power, with which anxiety as a weapon of aggression had associated itself, an anxiety which was to become operative as soon as the force of the will-power had abated and the desired resonance was absent, a situation occurring, for example, when the patient's husband left the house without her consent.

Our science demands a markedly individualizing procedure and is consequently not much given to generalizations. For general guidance I would like to propound the following rule: *as soon as the goal of a psychic movement or its life-plan has been recognized, then we are to assume that all the movements of its constituent parts will coincide with both the goal and the life-plan.*

This formulation, with some minor provisos, is to be

702

maintained in the widest sense. It retains its value even if inverted: *the properly understood part-movements must when combined, give the picture of an integrated life-plan and final goal.* Consequently we insist that, without worrying about the *tendencies, milieu and experiences,* all psychical powers are under the control of a directive idea and all expressions of emotion, feeling, thinking, willing, acting, dreaming as well as psycho-pathological phenomena, are permeated by one unified life-plan. Let me, by a slight suggestion, prove and yet soften down these heretical propositions: more important than tendencies, objective experience and milieu is *the subjective evaluation,* an evaluation which stands furthermore in a certain, often strange, relation to realities. Out of this evaluation however, which generally results in the development of a permanent mood *of the nature of a feeling of inferiority* there arises, depending upon the unconscious technique of our thought-apparatus, an imagined goal, an attempt at a planned final compensation and a life-plan.

I have so far spoken a good deal of men who have "grasped the situation". My discussion has been as irritating as that of the theorists of the "psychology of understanding" or of the psychology of personality, who always break off just when they are about to show us what exactly it is they have understood, as for instance, Jaspers. The danger of discussing briefly this aspect of our investigations namely, *the results of individual-psychology,* is sufficiently great. To do so we should be compelled to force the dynamics of life into static words and pictures, overlook differences in order to obtain unified formulas, and have, in short, in our description to make that very mistake that in practice is strictly prohibited: of approaching the psychic life of the individual with a dry formula, as the Freudian school attempt.

This then being my assumption, I shall in the following

present to you the most important results of our study of psychic life. Let me emphasize the fact that the dynamics of psychic life that I am about to describe hold equally for healthy and diseased. What distinguishes the nervous from the healthy individual is the stronger safeguarding tendency with which the former's life-plan is filled. With regard to the "positing of a goal" and the life-plan adjusted to it there are no fundamental differences.

I shall consequently speak of a general goal of man. A thorough-going study has taught us that we can best understand the manifold and diverse movements of the psyche as soon as our *most general pre-supposition*, that the psyche has as its objective the *goal of superiority*, is recognized. Great thinkers have given expression to much of this; in part everyone knows it, but in the main it is hidden in mysterious darkness and comes definitely to the front only in insanity or in ecstatic conditions. Whether a person desires to be an artist, the first in his profession, or a tyrant in his home, to hold converse with God or humiliate other people; whether he regards his suffering as the most important thing in the world to which everyone must show obeisance, whether he is chasing after unattainable ideals or old deities, over-stepping all limits and norms, at every part of his way he is guided and spurred on by his longing for superiority, the thought of his godlikeness, the belief in his special magical power. In his love he desires to experience his power over his partner. In his purely optional choice of profession the goal floating before his mind manifests itself in all sorts of exaggerated anticipations and fears, and thirsting for revenge, he experiences in suicide a triumph over all obstacles. In order to gain control over an object or over a person, he is capable of proceeding along a straight line, bravely, proudly, overbearing, obstinate, cruel; or he may on the other hand prefer, forced by experience, to resort to by-paths and circuitous routes, to gain his

704

victory by obedience, submission, mildness and modesty. Nor have traits of character an independent existence, for they are also adjusted to the individual life-plan, really representing the most important preparations for conflict possessed by the latter.

This goal of complete superiority, with its strange appearance at times, does not come from the world of reality. Inherently we must place it under "fictions" and "imaginations". Of these Vaihinger (*The Philosophy of 'As If'*) rightly says that their importance lies in the fact that whereas in themselves without meaning, they nevertheless possess in practice the greatest importance. For our case this coincides to such an extent that we may say *that this fiction of a goal of superiority so ridiculous from the view-point of reality, has become the principal conditioning factor of our life as hitherto known.* It is this that teaches us to differentiate, gives us poise and security, moulds and guides our deeds and activities and forces our spirit to look ahead and to perfect itself. There is of course also an obverse side, for *this goal introduces into our life a hostile and fighting tendency,* robs us of the simplicity of our feelings and is always the cause for an estrangement from reality since it puts near to our hearts the idea of attempting to over-power reality. Whoever takes this goal of godlikeness seriously or literally, will soon be compelled to flee from real life and compromise, by seeking a life within life; if fortunate in art, but more generally in pietism, neurosis or crime.

I cannot give you particulars here. A clear indication of this super-mundane goal is to be found in every individual. Sometimes this is to be gathered from a man's carriage, sometimes it is disclosed only in his demands and expectations. Occasionally one comes upon its track in obscure memories, phantasies and dreams. If purposely sought it is rarely obtained. However, every bodily or mental attitude indicates clearly its origin in a striving for power and carries within itself the ideal of a kind of perfection and infallibility. In those cases that lie on the confines of neurosis there is always to be discovered a reinforced pitting of oneself against the environment, against the dead or heroes of the past.

A test of the correctness of our interpretation can be easily made. If everyone possesses within himself an ideal of superiority, such as we find to an exaggerated degree among the nervous, then we ought to encounter phenomena whose purpose is the oppression, the minimizing and undervaluation of others. Traits of character such as intolerance, dogmatism, envy, pleasure at the misfortune of others, conceit, boastfulness, mistrust, avarice,—in short all those attitudes that are the substitutes for a struggle, force their way through to a far greater extent, in fact, than self-preservation demands.

Similarly, either simultaneously or interchangingly, depending upon the zeal and the self-confidence with which the final goal is sought, we see emerging indications of pride, emulation, courage, the attitudes of saving, bestowing and directing. A psychological investigation demands so much objectivity that a moral evaluation will not disturb the survey. In fact *the different levels of character-traits* actually neutralize our good-will and our disapproval. Finally we must remember that these hostile traits, particularly in the case of the nervous, are often so concealed that their possessor is justifiably astonished and irritated when attention is drawn to them. For example, the elder of two children can create quite an uncomfortable situation in trying to arrogate to himself through defiance and obstinacy, all authority in the family. The younger child pursues a wiser course, poses as a model of obedience and succeeds in this manner in becoming the idol of the family and in having all wishes gratified. As ambition spurs him on, all willingness to obey becomes destroyed and pathological-compulsion phenomena de-

706

velop, by means of which every parental order is nullified even when the parents notice that the child is making efforts to remain obedient. Thus we have an act of obedience immediately nullified by means of a compulsion-thought. We get an idea of the circuitous path taken here in order to arrive at the same objective as that of the other child.

The whole weight of the personal striving for power and superiority passes, at a very early age in the case of the child, into the form and the content of its striving, its thought being able to absorb for the time being only so much as the eternal, real and physiologically rooted *community-feeling* permits. Out of the latter are developed tenderness, love of neighbor, friendship and love, the desire for power unfolding itself in a veiled manner and seeking secretly to push its way along the path of group consciousness.

At this place let me go out of my way to endorse an old fundamental conception of all who know human nature. Every marked attitude of a man can be traced back to an origin in childhood. In the nursery are formed and prepared all of man's future attitudes. Fundamental changes are produced only by means of an exceedingly high degree of introspection or among neurotics by means of the physician's individual psychological analysis.

Let me, on the basis of another case, one which must have happened innumerable times, discuss in even greater detail the positing of goals by nervous people. A remarkably gifted man who by his amiability and refined behaviour had gained the love of a girl of high character, became engaged to her. He then forced upon her his ideal of education which made severe demands upon her. For a time she endured these unbearable orders but finally put an end to all further ordeals by breaking off relations. The man then broke down and became a prey to nervous attacks. The individual-psychological examination of the case showed that the superiority-goal in the case of this patient—as his domineering demands upon his bride indicated—had long ago pushed from his mind all thought of marriage, and that his object really was to secretly work toward a break, secretly because he did not feel himself equal to the open struggle in which he imagined marriage to consist. *This disbelief in himself* itself dated from his earliest childhood, to a time during which he, an only son, lived with an early widowed mother somewhat cut off from the world. During this period, spent in continuous family quarrels he had received the ineradicable impression, one he had never openly admitted to himself, that he was not sufficiently virile, and would never be able to cope with a woman. These psychical attitudes are comparable to a permanent inferiority-feeling and it is easily understood how they had decisively interfered in his life and compelled him to obtain prestige along other lines than those obtainable through the fulfilment of the demands of reality.

It is clear that the patient attained just what his concealed preparations for bachelordom aimed at, and what his fear of a life-partner, with the quarrels and restless relationship this implied, had awakened in him. Nor can it be denied that he took the same attitude toward both his bride and his mother, namely the wish to conquer. This attitude induced by a longing for victory has been magnificently misinterpreted by the Freudian school as the permanently incestuous condition of being enamoured of the mother. As a matter of fact this reinforced childhood-feeling of inferiority occasioned by the patient's painful relation to his mother, spurred this man on to prevent any struggle in later life with a wife by providing himself with all kinds of safeguards. Whatever it is we understand by love, in this particular case it is simply *a means to an end* and that end is the final securing of a triumph over some suitable woman. Here we have the reason for the continual tests and orders and for the cancelling of the engagement. This solution had not just "happened", but had on the contrary been artistically prepared and arranged with the old weapons of experience employed previously in the case of his mother. A defeat in marriage was out of the question because marriage was prevented.

Although we consequently realize nothing puzzling in the behaviour of this man and should recognize in his domineering attitude simply aggression *posing as love,* some words of explanation are necessary to clear up the less intelligible nervous break-down. We are here entering upon the real domain of the psychology of neuroses. As in the nursery so here our patient has been worsted by a woman. The neurotic individual is led in such cases to strengthen his protections and to retire to a fairly great distance from danger. Our patient is utilizing his breakdown in order to feed an evil reminiscence, to bring up the question of guilt again, to solve it in an unfavourable sense for the woman, so that in future he may either proceed with even greater caution or take final leave of love and matrimony! This man is thirty years old now. Let us assume that he is going to carry his pain along with him for another ten or twenty years and that he is going to mourn for his lost ideal for the same length of time. He has thereby protected himself against every love-affair and permanently saved himself from new defeat.

He interprets his nervous break-down by means of old, now strengthened, weapons of experience, just as he had as a child refused to eat, sleep or to do anything and played the role of a dying person. His fortunes ebb and *his beloved carries all the stigma,* he himself rises superior to her in both culture and character, and lo and behold: he has attained that for which he longed, for he is the superior person, becomes the better man and his partner like all girls is the guilty one. Girls cannot cope with the man in him. In this manner he has consummated what as a child he had already felt, the duty of demonstrating his superiority over the female sex.

We can now understand that this nervous reaction can never be sufficiently definite or adequate. *He is to wander through the world as a living reproach against women.*

Were he aware of his secret plans he would realize how ill-natured and evil-intentioned all his actions have been. However he would, in that case, not succeed in attaining his object of elevating himself above women. He would see himself just as we see him, falsifying the weights and how everything he has done has only led to a goal previously set. His success could not be described as due to "fate" nor assuredly would it represent any increased prestige. But his goal, his life-plan and his life-falsehood demand this prestige! In consequence it so "happens" that the *life-plan remains in the unconscious,* so that the patient may believe that an *implacable fate* and not a long prepared and long meditated plan for which he alone is responsible, is at work.

I cannot go into a detailed description of what I call the "distance" that the neurotic individual places between himself and the final issue, which in this case is marriage. . . . I should like to point out here however that the "distance" expresses itself clearly in the "hesitating attitudes," the principles, the point of view and the life-falsehood. In its evolution neurosis and psychosis play leading roles. The appropriation for this purpose of perversions and every type of impotence arising from the latter is quite frequent. Such a man concludes his account and reconciles himself with life by constructing one or a number of "if-clauses". "If conditions had been different. . . ."

The importance of the educational questions that arise and upon which our school lays the greatest stress . . . follows from what has been discussed.

From the method of presentation of the present work it is to be inferred that as in the case of a psychotherapeutic cure, our analysis proceeds backwards; examining first the *superiority-goal,* explaining by means of it the type of *conflict-attitude*[1] adopted particularly by nervous patients and only then attempting to investigate the sources of the vital psychic mechanism. One of the bases of the psychical dynamics we have already mentioned, the presumably unavoidable artistic trait of the psychical apparatus which, by means of the *artistic artifice of the creation of a fiction and the setting of a goal,* adjusts itself to and extends itself into the world of possible reality. I shall now proceed to explain briefly how the goal of godlikeness transforms the relation of the individual to his environment into hostility and how the struggle drives an individual towards a goal either along a direct path such as aggressiveness or along byways suggested by precaution. If we trace the history of this aggressive attitude back to childhood we always come upon the outstanding fact that *throughout the whole period of development, the child possesses a feeling of inferiority in its relations both to parents and the world at large.* Because of the immaturity of his organs, his uncertainty and lack of independence, because of his need for dependence upon stronger natures and his frequent and painful feeling of subordination to others, a sensation of inadequacy develops that betrays itself throughout life. This feeling of inferiority is the cause of his continual restlessness as a child, his craving for action, his playing of roles, the pitting of his strength against that of others, his anticipatory pictures of the future and his physical as well as mental preparations. The whole potential educability of the child depends upon this feeling of insufficiency. In this way the future becomes transformed

---

[1]The "struggle for existence", the "struggle of all against all", etc., are merely other perspectives of the same kind.

into the land that will bring him compensations. His conflict-attitude is again reflected in his feeling of inferiority; and only conflict does he regard as a compensation which will do away permanently with his present inadequate condition and will enable him to picture himself as elevated above others. Thus the child arrives at the positing of a goal, an imagined goal of superiority, whereby his poverty is transformed into wealth, his subordination into domination, his suffering into happiness and pleasure, his ignorance into omniscience and his incapacity into artistic creation. The longer and more definitely the child feels his insecurity, the more he suffers either from physical or marked mental weakness, the more he is aware of life's neglect, the higher will this goal be placed and the more faithfully will it be adhered to. He who wishes to recognize the nature of this goal, should watch a child at play, at optionally selected occupations or when phantasying about his future profession. The apparent change in these phenomena is purely external for in every new goal the child imagines a predetermined triumph. A variant of this weaving of plans, one frequently found among weakly aggressive children, among girls and sickly individuals, might be mentioned here. This consists of so misusing their frailties that they compel others to become subordinate to them. They will later on pursue the same method until their life-plan and life-falsehood have been clearly unmasked.

The attentive observer will find the nature of the *compensatory dynamics* presenting a quite extraordinary aspect as soon as he permits the sexual role to be relegated to one of minor importance and realizes that it is the former that is impelling the individual toward superhuman goals. In our present civilization both the girl and the youth will feel themselves forced to extraordinary exertions and manœuvres. A large number of these are admittedly of a distinctively progressive nature. To preserve this progressive nature but to ferret out those by-paths that lead us astray and cause illness, to make these harmless, that is our object and one that takes us far beyond the limits of medical art. It is to this aspect of our subject that society, child-education and folk-education may look for germs of a far-reaching kind. *For the aim of this point-of-view is to gain a reinforced sense of reality, the development of a feeling of responsibility and a substitution for latent hatred of a feeling of mutual goodwill, all of which can be gained only by the conscious evolution of a feeling for the common weal and the conscious destruction of the will-to-power.*

He who is looking for the power-phantasies of the child will find them drawn with a master hand by Dostoevsky in his novel entitled *A Raw Youth.* I found them blatantly apparent in one of my patients. In the dreams and thoughts of this individual the following wish recurred repeatedly: others should die so that he might have enough room in which to live, others should suffer privations so that he might obtain more favourable opportunities. This attitude reminds one of the inconsiderateness and heartlessness of many men who trace all evil back to the fact that there are already too many people in the world; impulses that have unquestionably made the world-war more palatable. The feeling of certainty, in fictions of this kind, has been taken over in the above-mentioned case from the basic facts of capitalistic trade, where admittedly, the better the condition of one individual the worse that of another. "I want to be a grave-digger", said a four-year-old boy to me; "I want to be the person who digs graves for others".

ALFRED ADLER (b.—Vienna, Feb. 7, 1870; d.—Aberdeen, Scotland, May 28, 1937).

Adler received his M.D. from Vienna in 1894, after which he became Dozent at the Vienna State Institute of Pedagogy. Most of his life was devoted to private practice, though he was Visiting Professor at Colum-

713

bia in 1929-30. He began in the specialty of Ophthalmology and changed to Psychiatry only later, largely through the inspiration of Freud.

Adler takes his importance primarily from his contrast with Freud. In 1902, Adler first joined with Freud in the Psychoanalytic Movement. As an active socialist, as well as psychoanalyst, Adler naturally turned towards the social (as opposed to the sexual) bases of human motivation. It was this widening emphasis of Adler's, which finally caused a formal break with Freud in 1911. By this time, Adler described the Oedipus complex as being entirely a power struggle between father and son, and denied the sexual motivation altogether. Adler, and his associates, subsequently founded many child guidance clinics in Munich, Vienna, and Berlin. Adler soon founded his own journal: *Individual Psychologie.* In 1935, he settled permanently in the United States. The American Society of Adlerian Psychology is active today under his continuing influence.

Adler's contributions to the theory and therapy of neurotic behavior are among the most penetrating in modern psychiatry,—precisely because of his ascription of behavior to socially derived motives. The present selection consists in the most important, and earliest, statement of this position.

ADLER, A. *The practice and theory of individual psychology.* London: Routledge & Kegan Paul, Ltd., 1955 (1923). Trans. P. Radin. Chap. III: "New leading principles for the practice of individual psychology." 1913. Chap. I: "Individual psychology, its assumptions and its results." These two essays are reprinted in their entirety by permission of the publisher.

See also:

ADLER, A.
  a) "A study of organ inferiority and its psychical compensation." *Nerv. Ment. Dis. Monogr.* 1917, 24: 1-186 (1907).
  b) *Problems of neurosis.* London, K. Paul, Trench, Truber, 1929. Ed. P. Mairet.
  c) *Social interest.* London: Faber & Faber, 1938 (1935). Trans. J. Linton & R. Vaughn.

ANSBACHER, H. L. & R. R. *The individual psychology of Alfred Adler. A systematic presentation in selections from his writings.* N. Y.: Basic Books, 1956.

BOTTOME, P. *Alfred Adler, a portrait from life.* N. Y.: Putnam, 1939. (Vanguard, 1958.)

WAY, L. *Adler's place in psychology.* N. Y.: Macmillan, 1950.

MURCHISON (b—Vol. II, p. 297; b—Vol. III, p. 584-586).

GRINSTEIN (Vol. I, p. 20-27).

TWO ESSAYS IN ANALYTICAL PSYCHOLOGY
C. G. JUNG

THE PERSONAL UNCONSCIOUS AND THE SUPER-PERSONAL OR COLLECTIVE UNCONSCIOUS

AT this point the fourth stage of our investigation begins. We pursued the analytical elucidation of the infantile transference phantasies until it became quite clear to the patient that he had made his physician stand for father, mother, uncle, guardian, and teacher, in a word for each and all of the parental authorities. But, as experience repeatedly demonstrates, other phantasies begin to appear, which represent the physician as saviour or as a god-like being. Obviously this is in complete contradiction to healthy conscious reasoning. It transpires, further, that these divine attributes go far beyond the bounds set by the Christian conceptions in which we have all grown up, and assume heathen characteristics, very often, indeed, animal forms.

The transference is in itself nothing but a projection of unconscious contents. At first the so-called superficial contents of the unconscious are projected, and under these circumstances the physician is interesting as a possible lover ... Then he appears as the father, either in the good sense, or as the 'thunderer,' according to the qualities with which the patient endowed his actual father. At times the physician has a maternal significance for the patient, a fact of extraordinary implication, but still within the framework of the possible. All these phantasy-projections are dependent upon personal reminiscences.

But now there come up forms of phantasy that have an extravagant and impossible character.[1] The physician

---

[1] I must emphasize the fact that, as a rule, these phantasies do not, in uncomplicated cases, appear in young people, but usually in mature adults, for whom the physician can no longer normally play the role of father.

then suddenly appears endowed with uncanny powers, somewhat like a magician, or a demoniacal criminal, or as the corresponding personification of goodness, a saviour. Again he may appear as an incomprehensible mixture of both aspects. Of course it is to be understood that the physician does not appear in this guise to the consciousness of the patient, only that phantasies ·which picture him thus come up to the surface. If, as not infrequently happens, the patient cannot perceive at once that this way of seeing the doctor is a projection from his (the patient's) unconscious, he behaves somewhat foolishly. At this point one often encounters great difficulties, demanding much good will and great patience on both sides. There are even, in exceptional cases, patients who cannot restrain themselves, and begin to spread all sorts of stupid tales concerning the doctor. Such patients simply will not accept the fact that their phantasies really come from themselves and have little or nothing to do with the character of the doctor. This persistent mistake arises from the fact that there are present no foundations of personal memory for this class of projection. One can sometimes show that similar phantasies had, at a certain time in childhood, involved the father or mother, neither mother nor father, however, having actually given justification for them.

Freud has shown in a brief essay how Leonardo da Vinci was influenced in his later life by the fact that he had two mothers. The fact of the two mothers, or of a double origin, was real in Leonardo's case, but it has also played a role in the lives of other artists, as in that of Benvenuto Cellini who in phantasy devised such an origin for himself. In general it is a mythological theme and many heroes are endowed by legend with two mothers. The phantasy does not come from the actual fact that the heroes have two mothers, but is a generally disseminated 'primordial image' belonging to the secrets of the common mental history of humanity, and not to the field of personal memory.

There are present in every individual besides his personal memories the great 'primordial images' as Jacob Burckhardt once aptly called them, those potentialities of human representations of things as they have always been, inherited through the brain structure from one generation to the next. The fact of this inheritance explains also the really amazing phenomenon, that certain legends and themes repeat themselves the whole world over in identical forms. It explains, further, why it is that our mentally diseased patients can reproduce exactly the same images and associations as those we are familiar with in old texts. . . . I do not by any means assert the inheritance of ideas, but only of the possibilities or germs of ideas, something markedly different.

In this further stage of the transference, then, when these phantasies that no longer depend on personal memories are reproduced, we have to do with the manifestations of the deeper layers of the unconscious, where sleep the primordial images common to humanity.[1]

This discovery leads now to the fourth stage of the new conceptual scheme, that is, to the recognition of two levels in the unconscious. We have to differentiate between a personal unconscious[2] and an impersonal or super-personal unconscious. We speak of the latter also as the collective unconscious, because it is apart from the personal and quite universal. For its contents can be found in all minds, and this is obviously not the case with personal contents.

---

[1] To these images I also apply the term archetypes (*Urbilder*).

[2] The personal unconscious, of which I also speak as the 'subconscious,' in contrast to the absolute or collective unconscious, contains forgotten memories, suppressed (purposely forgotten) painful ideas, apperceptions sometimes described as below the threshold (subliminal), that is, sensory perceptions that were not strong enough to reach consciousness, and, finally, contents that are not yet ripe for consciousness.

The primordial images are the deepest, the most ancient, and the most universal thoughts of humanity. They are as much feelings as thoughts, and have indeed an individual, independent existence, somewhat like that of the 'partial souls' which we can easily discern in all those philosophical or gnostic systems which base themselves upon the apperception of the unconscious as the source of knowledge, as, for example, Steiner's anthroposophical *Geisteswissenschaft*. The conception of angels, archangels, "principalities and powers" in St. Paul, of the *archontes* and kingdoms of light in the gnostics, of the heavenly hierarchies in Dionysius the Areopagite, all come from the perception of the relative independence of the archetypes, or dominants of the collective unconscious.

We have now found the object chosen by the libido when freed from the personal-infantile form of transference. It sinks into the depths of the unconscious, and there activates what has lain sleeping from the beginning. It has discovered the buried treasure from which mankind has ever and always created, out of which have been drawn its gods and its demons, and all those most urgent and mighty thoughts without which man ceases to be man.

Let us take as an example one of the greatest thoughts which the nineteenth century brought to birth, the idea of the conservation of energy. Robert Mayer, the real creator of this idea, was a physician, and not a physicist or 'natural philosopher,' for whom the making of such a concept would have been more appropriate. But it is worth knowing that, strictly speaking, the concept was not made by Mayer. Neither did it come into existence through the coalescence of ideas or scientific hypotheses then extant, but it actually made him its creator. He writes about it in the following way to Griesinger (1844): "I have by no means hatched out the theory at my writing desk." He then reports certain physiological observations which he had made in 1840-41 as ship's doctor. "Now if one wants to be clear on matters of physiology," he continues in his letter, "some knowledge of physical processes is indispensable, unless one prefers to develop the matter from the metaphysical side, a way that disgusts me utterly. I therefore held fast to physics, and stuck to the subject with such interest that I paid but little attention to the remote quarter of the globe in which we were. Many may laugh at me for this, but the fact remains that I was happiest when I could stay on board and work without interruption. For there I had many an hour of inspiration the like of which I cannot remember either before or since. Some flashes of thought that came to me while in the roads of Surabaja were at once carefully followed up, and these in turn led to new subjects. Those times have passed, but the gradual testing of the idea that then came to birth in me has taught me that it is a truth, which was not only subjectively felt but which can be objectively proved. It remains to be seen whether this can be done by a man so little versed in physics as I am."

In his book on energetics, Heim sets forth the view that "Robert Mayer's new idea has not been slowly disentangled from the traditional concepts of force by deeper reflection on them, but belongs to those ideas that are grasped intuitively, ideas that, arising in another mental domain, immediately take possession of thought and force it to reshape the traditional beliefs in accordance with them."

The question is whence comes the new idea that presses itself upon consciousness with such elemental force? And whence did it derive the power that could so seize upon consciousness that attention was completely withdrawn from the manifold impressions of a first voyage to the tropics? These questions are not easy to answer. If we apply our theory to this case, the explanation must be as follows: the idea of energy and of its conservation must be a primordial image that has been latent in the collective unconscious. This conclusion forces us further to demonstrate that there has actually been a primordial image of this kind in existence in the mental history of the human race, and that it has been in operation through the ages. This proof can, as a matter of fact, be produced without much difficulty, for the most primitive religions in the most widely separated regions of the earth are founded upon this image (*Bild*). These are the religions, sometimes called dynamistic or pre-animistic, whose unique and determining idea is to the effect that there exists a generally disseminated magical power[1] to which everything is subordinated. Tylor, the well-known English investigator, as well as Frazer, have misunderstood this idea as animism. Primitives do not in reality mean souls or spirits by their conception of power, but something which the American investigator Lovejoy[2] has appropriately called 'primitive energetics.' This concept corresponds to the idea of soul, spirit, God, health, bodily strength, fertility, magic, influence, power, prestige, and methods of healing, as well as to certain states of feeling which are characterized by the release of affects. Among certain Polynesians, '*mulungu,*' that is, this primitive concept of energy is spirit, soul, a dæmonic being, magic, and prestige; and when anything astonishing happens, the people cry out '*Mulungu!*' This concept of energy is also the first form of the concept of God among primitive races, and is an image which has developed in ever new variations during the course of history. In the Old Testament the magical force shines in the burning bush, and in the countenance of Moses; in the Acts of the Apostles it appears in the pouring forth of the Holy Ghost from

---

[1] The so-called *mana*. Compare Soderblom: *Das Werden des Gottesglaubens*, Leipzig, 1916.
[2] *The Monist*, vol. xvi., p. 363.

heaven in the form of tongues of flame. In Heraclitus it appears as world energy, as ever-living fire; in Persian religion it is the glow of fire, *haoma*, the divine grace; among the Stoics it is *heimarmene*, the power of fate. Again, in mediæval legends it appears as the aura, or the halo that blazes up as a great flame from the roof of the hut in which a saint is lying in a state of ecstasy. In the faces of the saints men see the sun of this power, the fullness of light. According to an ancient point of view, the soul itself is this power; in the idea of its immortality there lies its conservation. The Buddhistic and primitive view of metempsychosis (transmigration of souls) contains the notion of the soul's unlimited power of transformation together with a constant conservation.

This image, then, has been stamped upon the human brain for æons of time, and so lies ready in the unconscious of every man. It needs only certain conditions in order to reappear. These conditions were evidently fulfilled in the case of Robert Mayer. The greatest and best ideas are formed out of these primordial images which are the ancient common property of all humanity.[1]

Having fully discussed this example to show the origin of new ideas out of the treasury of the primordial

---

[1] I have often been asked whence come these archetypes or primordial images (the *eidola* of Plato). It seems me that their origin can be explained in no other way than by regarding them as the deposits of the oft-repeated experiences of humanity. A common, yet, at the same time, most impressive experience is the daily apparent movement of the sun. We certainly cannot discover anything about it in the unconscious, in so far as the physical processes known to us are concerned, but we do find the sun myth there in all its innumerable modifications. It is this myth that forms the sun archetype, and not the physical process. The same can be said of the phases of the moon. The archetype is a disposition to produce over and over again the same, or similar mythical conceptions. According to this it seems as though what was impressed upon the unconscious was exclusively the subjective phantasy-ideas aroused by the physical process. Therefore we may assume that archetypes are the oft-repeated impressions of subjective reactions. Obviously this hypothesis merely pushes the problem further back without solving it. Nothing prevents us, however, from assuming that certain archetypes are already present in animals; that they are involved in the peculiarities of the living organism itself, and are, therefore, immediate expressions of life whose nature cannot be further explained.

images, we will now take up the further presentation of the process of transference. We saw that the libido of the patient had, for its new object, seized upon those apparently absurd and singular phantasies, namely, the contents of the collective unconscious. As I have already said, the unrecognized projection of primordial images upon the physician involves a danger to the further treatment which is not to be underrated. The images contain not only every beautiful and great thought and feeling of mankind, but also every wicked deed of shame or devilry of which men have been capable. If, then, the patient cannot distinguish the personality of the physician from these projections, every possibility of an understanding is lost, and a human relation becomes impossible. But if the patient avoids this Charybdis, he falls into the Scylla of introjecting the images, that is, he ascribes them not to the doctor but to himself. This danger is just as disastrous. If he projects, he vacillates between an exaggerated and pathological deification of the doctor, and a contempt of him that bristles with hate. If he introjects the images, he achieves a laughable self-deification, or a moral self-laceration.

The mistake that he makes comes from taking to himself personally the contents of the collective unconscious. Thus he makes himself either god or devil. Herein lies the psychological reason why men must always have demons and cannot live without gods. No doubt we must make the exception of some peculiarly clever specimens of the *homo occidentalis* of yesterday and the day before—supermen whose god is dead; wherefore they themselves become gods, that is, rationalistic fake-gods with thick skulls and cold hearts. The concept of god is simply a necessary psychological function of an irrational character which has nothing to do with the question of the existence of god. The human intellect can never answer this question, and still less can it give

722

any proof of god. Furthermore, such proof is altogether superfluous, for the idea of an all-powerful divine being is present everywhere, if not consciously recognized, then unconsciously accepted, because it is an archetype. Something or other in our souls is of superior power, and if it is not consciously a god, it is at least the 'belly,' as St. Paul says. Therefore I consider it wiser to recognize the idea of god consciously; otherwise, something else becomes god, as a rule something quite inappropriate and stupid, such as only an 'enlightened' consciousness can devise. Our intellect has long known that one cannot think god, much less conceive in what fashion he really exists, if indeed at all. Just as little can one achieve a process that is not causally conditioned. Theoretically there can be no accidents, yet in practical life one is continually stumbling on accidents. It is the same with the idea of the existence of god; it is once and for all an impossible problem, but the *consensus gentium* has spoken of gods for æons of time, and will still be speaking of them æons hence. No matter how beautiful and perfect man may believe his reason to be, he can always be certain that it is only one of the possible mental functions and covers only that one aspect of the phenomena of life which corresponds to it. There lies on every hand the irrational, that which does not fit in with reason. And this irrational is equally a psychological function, the collective unconscious in a word; while the function of consciousness is essentially rational. Consciousness must have reason, first, in order to discover some system in the chaos of irregular, individual events occurring in the universe; and secondly, at least in the domain of human affairs, in order to act. We have the praiseworthy and useful ambition to root out the chaos of the irrational within and without us as completely as possible, and have apparently advanced some distance in the achievement of this aim. A mental patient once said to me:

"Doctor, I disinfected the whole heavens last night with sublimate, but have not discovered any god." Something of the same kind has happened to us.

Old Heraclitus, who was indeed a very wise man, discovered the most extraordinary of all psychological laws, namely, the regulating function of the opposites. He called it *enantiodromia* (a running contrary ways), by which he meant that everything tends sooner or later to go over into its opposite. . . . Thus the rational attitude of culture necessarily goes over into its opposite, the irrational devastation of culture.[1]

One must not identify oneself with reason, because man is not and cannot be wholly rational, nor will he ever become so. This is a fact which should be noted by all pedants of culture. The irrational cannot and must not be wiped out. The gods cannot and must not die. I said just now that there seems to be something, a superior force, in the soul of man and that if this is not the idea of god, then it is the belly. I was seeking to express what seems to me the fact, that one or other basic instinct, or complex of ideas, consistently attracts the greatest amount of psychical energy, whereby it forces the ego into its service. Generally the ego is sucked into this focus of energy to such a degree, that it becomes identified with it and thinks that it wishes and needs nothing further. But in this way there develops a craze, a monomania or possession, a most exaggerated one-sidedness which endangers the psychical equilibrium most seriously. Without doubt the capacity for such one-sidedness is the secret of success; wherefore our culture has striven assiduously to foster it. The passion, or the heaping up of energy which is invoked in such monomanias is what the ancients called a god, and our common speech of to-day still does

---

[1]This sentence was written during the world war. Although the war is over. I have let it remain in its original form because it contains a truth which is verifiable again and again in the course of history.

the same. Do we not say "he makes a god of this or that"? A man believes that he wills and chooses, and does not notice that he is already possessed, that his greatest interest has become a master who has arrogated to himself the power. These interests are gods of a kind, and, when recognized by many, gradually lead to the formation of a church and draw about them a herd of the faithful. We call this an organization. Thus grew up the state, the army, the financial system and similar bugbears, and consequently the anarchic reactions which seem to try to drive out the devil with Beelzebub. The enantiodromia, which always threatens if a movement attains undisputed power, offers no solution of the problem; for the disorganizing movement is quite as blind as that of organization.

The only person who escapes the gruesome law of enantiodromia is the man who knows how to separate himself from the unconscious, not by repressing it, for then it merely lays hold of him from behind, but by making it clear to himself that it is something different from himself. In doing this, the solution of the Scylla and Charybdis problem, which I pictured above, is achieved. The patient must learn to distinguish in his thoughts between what is the ego and what is the non-ego, or collective unconscious. In this way he obtains the material with which, from this moment on and for a long time afterwards, it will be his task to come to terms. His energy, that before was flowing into inappropriate, pathological channels, has now found its real sphere. Part of the differentiation of the psychological ego from the non-ego consists in the ability of a man to stand with feet firmly planted in his ego-function; that is, he must fulfil his duty towards life completely, so that in every respect he is a vital member of human society. All that he neglects in this respect falls into the unconscious, and reinforces the latter, with the result that he is often in danger of being swallowed up by it, if his ego-function is not firmly established. Heavy punishments threaten one here. As Synesius suggested, it is just the 'inspired' soul (*pneumatike psyche*) that becomes god and demon, and suffers divine punishment, being torn asunder, like Zagreus. Nietzsche experienced this at the beginning of his mental sickness, when, in *Ecce Homo,* the god against whom he had armed himself in front by a desperate scepticism fell upon him from behind. The enantiodromia is the being torn asunder between the pairs of opposites, which, being attributes of deity, also belong to the divine man, who owes his god-likeness to the overcoming of his gods.

As soon as we begin to speak of the collective unconscious we find ourselves in a sphere, and concerned with a problem, which is quite precluded in the practical analysis of young people, or of those who have remained infantile too long. Whenever the father and mother imagos still need to be transferred over to the analyst, whenever there remains a single phase of outer life, naturally experienced by the average man, which must be conquered by the patient, then it were better not to mention the collective unconscious or the problem of the pairs of opposites. But when the parental transferences and the youthful illusions have been mastered, or are, at least, ripe for mastery, then we are forced to speak of the problem of the opposites and of the collective unconscious. Here we find ourselves outside the domain covered by the views of Freud and Adler, for we are no longer concerned with the question of how to deal with the obstacles that hinder a man in the practice of a calling, in marrying, or in anything that means the further expansion of life. Instead, we are confronted with the task of finding a meaning which will make possible the very continuance of life, in so far as it is to be more than mere resignation and mournful retrospection.

Our life is like the course of the sun. In the morning the sun gains continually in strength until it blazes forth in the zenith-heat of high noon; then comes the enantio-dromia: its continued movement forward does not mean an increase but a decrease in strength. Thus our task in handling young people is different from that presented by people who are getting on in years.

In the case of the former, it is enough if we remove all the hindrances that make expansion and the upward way difficult; but for the latter, the older people, we must summon up all that gives support to the downward journey. An inexperienced youth thinks, indeed, that one can let the old people go, because in any case there is nothing much that can be done with them: life is behind them, and they cannot be considered as much more than petrified pillars of the past. But it is a great error to assume that the meaning of life is exhausted in the period of sexual youth and growth; that, for example, a woman who has passed the menopause is 'finished.' The afternoon of life is just as full of meaning as the morning, only its meaning and purpose is a wholly different one. Man has two aims: the first is the aim of nature, the begetting of children and all the business of protecting the brood; to this period belongs the gaining of money and social position. When this aim is satisfied, there begins another phase, namely, that of culture. For the attainment of the former goal we have the help of nature, and moreover of education; but little or nothing helps us towards the latter goal. Indeed, often a false ambition survives, in that an old man wants to be a youth again, or at least feels he must behave like one, although within himself he can no longer make believe. It is this that makes the transition from the natural to the cultural phase terribly difficult and bitter for many people. They cling to the illusions of youth, or at least to their children, in order to preserve in this way a fragment of illusion. One sees this in mothers, who find in their

727

children their only justification, and who imagine they have to sink away into empty nothingness when they give them up. It is no wonder, then, that many bad neuroses develop at the beginning of the afternoon of life. It is a kind of second puberty period, a like repetition of storm and stress, not infrequently accompanied by all the tempests of passion, the 'dangerous age.' But the problems which appear in this age are no longer to be solved by the old rules; the hand of the clock cannot be turned back; what youth found and must find outside, the man of middle life must find within himself. Here we face new problems which often cause the physician no little cudgelling of the brains.

The transition from morning to afternoon is a revaluation of earlier values. There comes the necessity of examining into the values of the opposites of our previous ideals, of becoming aware of the error in our former convictions, of recognizing the falsehood in what had before been truth, and of feeling how much hate lay in that which we had till now accepted as love. Of those who are drawn into the conflict of the problem of the opposites, not a few throw overboard everything that had previously seemed to them valuable and worth striving for, and try to live a life as opposite as possible to that of the former ego. Changes of profession, divorces, religious conversions and apostasies of every sort are the symptoms of this swinging over into one's opposite. The disadvantage of a radical conversion into the opposite is that the previous life now suffers repression. Thus just as unbalanced a condition is brought about as existed before, when the opposites of the conscious virtues and values were still repressed and unconscious. As in earlier years neurotic disturbances came about because of the unconsciousness of opposing phantasies, so there again develop disturbances of even a worse sort perhaps, due to the repression of former idols. Obviously it is a fundamental mistake to think that when we recognize the non-value in a value, or the falsehood in a truth, the value or the truth then ceases to exist. It has only become relative. Everything human is relative, because everything depends on a condition of inner antithesis; for everything subsists as a phenomenon of energy. Energy depends necessarily upon a pre-existing antithesis, without which there could be no energy. There must always be present height and depth, heat and cold, etc., in order that the process of equalization—which is energy—can take place. All life is energy and therefore depends on forces held in opposition. This makes the tendency to deny all previous values in favour of their opposites just as pathological as the original one-sidedness; moreover, in so far as a generally recognized and indubitable value comes into question and is cast aside, a manifestly fatal loss occurs. One who so acts throws himself overboard with his values, as Nietzsche also came to see.

The solution of the problem lies not in a conversion into the opposite, but in the retaining of the former values together with a recognition of their opposites. This naturally means conflict and division within oneself, and it is intelligible that one should shrink from it, philosophically as well as morally. Therefore, more often than a conversion into the opposite, a rigid stiffening in the viewpoint previously held is sought as a solution. One must admit that in this attitude so often displayed by elderly men, and which appears so unsympathetic, there is yet a merit worthy of recognition. At least these men do not become renegades; at least they remain erect and fall neither into indefiniteness, nor into the mire. They are not defaulters, merely slowly dying trees, or to put it more generously, 'witnesses of the past.' But the accompanying symptoms, the rigidity, the petrifaction, the narrow-mindedness, the lagging behind of these *laudatores temporis acti* are undesirable manifestations. Indeed they are definitely harmful, for the way in which such people support a truth, or any worthy aim, is so inflexible and violent that one is more repelled by their unmannerliness than drawn by the merit of the case, so that the result is the opposite of the good intended. The fundamental cause of their stiff and numbed condition is anxiety concerning the problem of the opposites. They feel a presentiment and secret fear of the 'sinister brother of Medardus.' Therefore there can be one truth only, and that must be absolute, or it can afford no protection against the threatened overthrow, which is sensed everywhere save in oneself. But actually we have the most dangerous revolutionary within ourselves, and this must be realized by anyone who would pass over safely into the second half of life. As soon as we take cognizance of this rebel within ourselves, we exchange the apparent safety that we have so far enjoyed for a condition of uncertainty, of internal division and of contradictory convictions. The worst feature of this condition is that it seems to offer no outlet. '*Tertium non datur,*' says Logic, 'There is no middle way.'

The practical necessities arising in the treatment of the sick have therefore forced us to look for ways out of this intolerable situation. If a man is constantly confronted by an apparently insurmountable psychological obstacle, he draws back—*reculer pour mieux sauter*— making what is known technically as a regression. He turns back to times when he found himself in similar situations, and seeks to apply again the methods that helped him then. But what was helpful in youth does not avail in old age.... So the regression continues back to childhood: hence the childishness of many elderly neurotics! Finally it reaches the time before childhood. This may sound strange, but actually we are speaking of something that is not only logical, but altogether possible. We have already said that the unconscious contains, as it were, two layers; first the personal, and secondly the collective.

The personal layer does not go further than the earliest memories of infancy; the collective unconscious, on the other hand, is all time before the actual dawn of infancy, that is, the residue of the life of the ancestors. While the memory-images of the personal unconscious have some detailed form, since they consist of images that have been experienced, such detail is lacking in the memory-traces of the collective unconscious, since they have not been experienced individually. If the regression of the psychical energy, retreating before an insurmountable object, goes back even further than the time of early infancy, it reaches the traces or deposits of ancestral life, and mythological images awaken. An inner mental world, whose existence we never before suspected, unfolds and displays contents which are perhaps in sharpest possible contrast to our previous conceptions. These images are of such intensity as to make it quite intelligible to us that millions of cultured people should have plunged into theosophy and anthroposophy. The reason is that these modern gnostic systems meet the desire for the expression and formulation of these inner worldless experiences more satisfactorily than any of the existing forms of the Christian religion, not excepting Catholicism. Our consciousness is now so thoroughly permeated with Christianity, so completely fashioned by it, that the unconscious counter-position cannot find acceptance therein. Thus an antithesis to Christianity is sought for, and it is found in the eastern religions of Buddhism, Brahmanism, and Taoism. The extraordinary syncretism of theosophy, its astonishing amalgamations and combinations, go a long way towards meeting this need, and the numerical success of theosophy is thus explained. But, in this easy way an individual experience is supplanted by images and words borrowed from a foreign psychology. Conceptions, ideas and forms that are not the growth of our soil cannot be understood by our hearts, only by our heads. Indeed,

731

even our thought cannot clearly grasp them, since they were never discovered by us. It is a case of stolen goods which do not bring prosperity. Just so far, then, as these ideas are foreign to us the satisfaction felt in them is a stupefying self-deception. Such a surrogate makes the people who make use of it shadow-like and unreal; they put empty words in the place of living realities, whereby, rather than endure the tension of the opposites, they coil themselves up in a pale, two-dimensional, phantom world, where every living and creative thing withers and dies.

The wordless experiences, which are evoked by the regression into the pre-infantile period, demand no surrogate, but rather an individual shape and expression within each man's life and work. These images have grown out of the life, the sorrows and joys of our ancestors, and they strive to return to life not as experiences only, but as deeds. On account of their opposition to the conscious they cannot be translated directly into our present world; hence a way must be found that can mediate between the conscious and the unconscious.

THE DOMINANTS OF THE COLLECTIVE UNCONSCIOUS

THERE now lies before us the task of raising to the subjective plane the unconscious relations that have hitherto been taken objectively. To this end we must once more separate them from their objects and take them as referring to images of a subjective nature, to complexes in the unconscious of the patient herself. If we interpret Mrs. X[1] subjectively we find in her the image of what the patient fears yet unconsciously desires. Mrs. X. thus represents what the patient would like to become, and yet resists becoming. In a certain sense Mrs. X. is a picture of the patient's future character. The uncanny artist cannot very well be brought on to the subjective

[1]Mrs. X is a patient previously discussed.—*Editor.*

plane, because the element of unconscious artistic capacity lying dormant in the patient has already been taken up in the figure of Mrs. X. It would be right to say that the artist is the image of the masculine element in the patient which, not being consciously realized, remains in the unconscious. This is true in a certain sense, for the patient does indeed deceive herself in this respect. She seems to herself particularly delicate, sensitive, and feminine, with nothing in the least masculine about her. She was therefore indignantly amazed when I called her attention to her masculine traits. But the element of uncanniness, of fascination, cannot be explained through her masculine characteristics. It is apparently entirely lacking in her; yet it must be in her somewhere, because she herself produced this very feeling.

Whenever such an element as this cannot be discovered, experience teaches us that it has always been projected. But into whom? Is it still projected into the artist? He has long since disappeared out of the circle of the patient's acquaintance, and cannot very well have taken the projection with him, since it lies anchored in the unconscious of the patient. No, such a projection is always actual, that is, there must be some one upon whom this portion of libido is at present projected, else she would be able to perceive it in herself.

Here we again reach the objective plane, for otherwise we cannot work out this projection. The patient knows no man who means anything especial to her, save myself, who as her doctor mean a good deal to her. Probably then she has projected this part of her libido upon me, though I must say I had noticed nothing of the sort. These subtler elements never appear on the surface, but always come to light outside the clinical hour. Therefore I questioned her cautiously thus: "Tell me, how do I seem to you when you are not with me? Am I just the same?" Reply: "When I am with you, you are very pleasant, but when

733

I am by myself, or have not seen you for some time, then you change for me often in a remarkable way. Sometimes you appear quite idealized, and then again different." Here she hesitated, and I helped her out by saying: "Yes, but in what way different?" Reply: "Often you seem quite dangerous, uncanny like an evil magician, or a demon. I don't know how I ever get such ideas—you are not a bit like that."

So this element is in me as part of the transference, and that is why it is missing in her inventory. We thus recognize a further important fact. I was contaminated (identified) with the artist; then she naturally plays the role of Mrs. X. with me in her unconscious phantasy. I could easily prove to her this fact by means of material previously brought to light—sexual phantasies. But I myself then am the obstacle, the crab, that is hindering her from getting across. If in this singular case we were to limit ourselves to the objective plane the position would be serious indeed. Of what use would it be to say: "But I am not in any sense this artist, nor am I in the least uncanny, nor an evil magician." That would leave the patient quite cold, because she knows all that as well as I; the projection would exist as before, and I should be still the obstacle to her further progress.

It is at this point that many a treatment has come to a standstill. There is no way for the doctor to help the patient out of such an entanglement with the unconscious other than by lifting himself to the subjective plane, where he is to be regarded as an image. An image of what? Here arises the greatest difficulty of all. "Yes," the doctor will say, "an image of something in the unconscious of the patient." Whereupon she will say, "What, I am a man, and an uncanny, fascinating one at that, a wicked magician or a demon? No, I cannot accept that; it is nonsense. I would sooner believe that you are all that." She is right: it is preposterous to want to transfer such things over to her, for she can as little submit to be made into a demon as the doctor. Her eyes flash; an evil expression appears on her face, the gleam of an unknown hate never seen before; something snake-like seems to creep up in her. I am suddenly faced by the possibility of a fatal misunderstanding. What is it? Is it disappointed love? Does she feel offended—depreciated? There lurks in her glance something of the beast of prey, something really demoniacal. Is she then really a demon? Or am I myself the beast of prey, the demon, and is there sitting before me a terrified victim, trying to defend herself against my evil spells with the brute strength of despair? All this must surely be nonsense—fantastic delusion. What have I touched upon? What new string is vibrating? Yet it is only a passing moment. The expression on the patient's face becomes quiet again, and, as though relieved, she says: "It is extraordinary; I've just had a feeling that you have touched the point which I could never get over in relation to my friend. It's a horrible feeling, something inhuman, evil, cruel. I cannot describe how queer this feeling is. It makes me hate and despise my friend when it comes, although I struggle against it with all my might."

This utterance threw an explanatory light on what had gone before; I have taken the place of the friend. The friend has been overcome. The ice of the repression has been broken and the patient has unwittingly entered upon a new phase of her existence. Now I know that I shall inherit all that was painful and evil in the relation to her friend. What was good will fall to me also, but it will be in violent conflict with that mysterious unknown x that the patient has never been able to master. A new phase of the transference has begun, which, however, does not as yet show clearly the nature of the x that has been projected upon me.

It is certain that if the patient cannot get beyond this

form of the transference, the most troublesome misunderstandings threaten, for she must treat me as she has
treated her friend; that is, the x will be continually in the
air giving rise to misunderstandings. It will inevitably
fall out that she sees the wicked demon in me, since she
cannot accept it in herself. All insoluble conflicts come
about in this fashion. And an insoluble conflict means
bringing life to a standstill.

But there is still another possibility: the patient could
use her old defence mechanism in the new difficulty, and
could look over and beyond the obscure point. That is,
she could begin to repress the material again, instead of
keeping it conscious, which is the necessary and obvious
demand of the whole method. By such repression nothing
is gained; on the contrary, the x now threatens from the
unconscious, where it is even more unpleasant.

Whenever such an unacceptable content emerges, one
must consider carefully whether or no this element is to
be thought of as human. 'Magician' and 'demon' may
represent qualities that are thus designated in order that
they may be at once recognized as not personal and
human, but mythological qualities. 'Magician' and 'demon' are mythological figures which express the unknown, 'non-human' feeling which swept over the patient.
These attributes are not applicable to a human personality, although they are constantly being projected upon
our fellow-beings, generally as intuitive judgments not
subjected to criticism, and inevitably doing serious injury
to human relations.

Such attributes always show that contents of the supra-
personal or collective unconscious have been projected.
Personal memories cannot account for 'demons,' nor for
'wicked magicians,' although every one has, of course, at
some time or other heard or read of these things. Although one has heard of rattlesnakes one would not
describe a lizard or a slow-worm as a rattlesnake and

show all the corresponding affect, simply because one was startled by the rustling of a lizard. Similarly one would not describe a fellow-man as a demon, even though a sort of demonic effect is actually associated with him. If the demonic effect were really a part of his personal character, it would show itself everywhere and then the person would be indeed a demon, a sort of werewolf. But that is mythology, and arises from the collective, not the individual psyche. Inasmuch as through our unconscious we have a share in the historical collective psyche, we naturally live unconsciously in a world of werewolves, demons and magicians, etc., these being things which the ages before us have invested with a tremendous effect. We have just as much a part in gods and devils, saviours and criminals, but it would be absurd to make oneself personally responsible for these possibilities present in the unconscious. It is therefore essential to differentiate as sharply as possible between the personal and the impersonal attributes of the psyche. This is by no means intended to deny the occasional great effects due to the existence of the contents of the collective unconscious, but as contents of the collective psyche they are contrasted with the individual psyche and differentiated from it. Simple-minded people have of course never separated these things from individual consciousness, because the projection of gods, demons, etc., has not been understood as a psychological function, but the projections have simply been accepted as realities, and their true character never recognized. Not till the age of enlightenment was it discovered that the gods did not really exist, but were only projections. They were thus disposed of, but the psychological function which corresponds to them was by no means disposed of; it merely lapsed into the unconscious and began to poison men with a surplus of libido formerly given to the service of a divine image. Obviously the depreciation and repression of so powerful a function

737

as that represented by religion has serious consequences for the psychology of the individual. The unconscious is prodigiously strengthened by the reflux of this libido, and through the activation of its archaic collective contents, begins to exert a powerful, compulsive influence upon consciousness. The period of enlightenment closed, as we know, with the horrors of the French Revolution, and at the present time we are again experiencing an uprising of the unconscious destructive forces of the collective psyche. The result has been unparalleled mass-murder. It was actually this towards which the unconscious was tending. This tendency had previously been inordinately strengthened by the rationalism of modern life, which, by depreciating everything irrational, caused the function of the irrational to sink into the unconscious, where it works unceasing havoc, like an incurable illness whose invisible focus cannot be eradicated. Then the individual and the nation alike are compelled to live irrationally, devoting even their highest idealism and their best wits to giving form as completely as possible to the madness of the irrational. In a small way we can see this happening in our patient, who fled from a possibility of life that seemed irrational to her (Mrs. X.), only to live it in a pathological form, to her own loss, in relation to an unsuitable object.

There is no possible alternative but to recognize the irrational element as a necessary, because ever present, psychological function. Its contents are not to be taken as concrete realities—that would be a regression—but as psychological realities. They are realities because they are effective things, that is, things that work (*Wirklichkeiten*). The collective unconscious is the deposit of the world experience of all times, and therefore it is an image of the world that has been forming for æons, an image in which certain features, the so-called dominants, have been elaborated through the course of time. These dominants and the ruling powers, the gods, that is, representations of dominating laws and principles, of average regularities in the sequence of secular processes. In so far as the images laid down in the brain are relatively true productions of psychical events, their dominants, that is, their general characteristics emphasized by the accumulation of similar experiences, correspond to certain fundamental physical facts that are also universal. Hence it is possible to take over unconscious images as intuitive conceptions of physical events. We can see an example of this in the æther, the primordial breath, or soul-substance, the notion of which appears in man's conceptions the whole world over; a further example is energy, magic power, an equally widespread intuition.

On account of their connection with physical things the dominants usually appear as projected—appear, indeed, when the process is unconscious, as projected upon the persons of the immediate environment, usually in the form of abnormal, under- or over-valuations which give rise to misunderstandings, quarrels, infatuations and every kind of folly. People say 'He makes a god of So-and-so,' or 'So-and-so is the *bete noire* of X.' Also there grow up in this way modern myth-formations, that is, fantastic rumours, suspicions, and prejudices.

The dominants of the collective unconscious are therefore extremely important things of significant effect, to which we must give our utmost attention; they are not to be simply repressed, but must be most diligently pondered. Since they appear for the most part as projections, and since, on account of the kinship between unconscious images and the object, projections are only attached where some external inducement exists, the evaluation of them is especially difficult. If some one projects the dominant of 'devil' upon a fellow human being, it is because the man has something in him to which this dominant can be attached. But that is by no means to say that the man is therefore, so to speak, a devil; on the contrary, he may be a particularly good fellow, but antipathetic to the person making the projection, so that a 'devilish effect' arises between them. Nor is he who projects necessarily a devil, although he must recognize that he too has in himself a devilish element which he has just stumbled upon, inasmuch as he projected it; but that does not make him a devil; indeed, he may be just as decent a man as the other. The appearance of the devil dominant in such a case means that the two people are incompatible, now and for the near future; wherefore the unconscious forces them apart and holds them away from one another.

One of the dominants that is almost always met with in the analysis of projections from the collective unconscious, is the 'magical demon' with overwhelming and uncanny power. Meyrink's *Golem* is a good example of this; also the Tibetan wizard in Meyrink's *Fledermause*, who kindles the world-war by magic. Obviously Meyrink formed this image freely and independently out of his unconscious, by giving word and picture to a feeling similar to that which my patient projected upon me. The magician dominant appears also in Zarathustra, while in Faust it is, so to speak, the hero himself.

The image of this demon is the lowest and most ancient form of the concept of god. It is the dominant of the primitive tribal magician or medicine man, a peculiarly gifted individual invested with magical power.[1] This figure appears very often in the unconscious products of my patients as dark-skinned, and of Mongolian type. These things were familiar to me long before Meyrink wrote.

With the recognition of the dominants of the collective

---

[1] The idea of the medicine man, who associates with spirits and has control over magical powers, is so deeply rooted in many primitives that they believe 'doctors' are to be found also among animals. Thus the North Californian Achumanis speak of ordinary coyotes, and 'doctor' coyotes.

unconscious an important step forward is made. The magical or demonic effect of the fellow-being disappears when the uncanny feeling is traced to a definite content of the collective unconscious. Now, however, we have an entirely new and unsuspected task before us: that is, the question how the ego is to be reconciled with this psychological non-ego. Can we content ourselves with the statement of the active existence of unconscious dominants, and for the rest let the matter take care of itself? That would be to induce a condition of permanent dissociation in the subject, a split between the individual psyche and the collective psyche. On the one side we should have the differentiated modern ego, while the other side would represent a sort of negro-culture, a thoroughly primitive condition. We should then have set clearly before our eyes, what really does exist, a veneer of civilization over a dark-skinned brute. But such a dissociation requires an immediate synthesis and development of what has remained undeveloped. There must be a unification of the two parts.

Before entering upon this new question, let us return to the dream that was our point of departure. Through our discussion we have attained a widened understanding of the dream, and especially of an essential part of it, that is, the fear. This fear is a demonic dread of the dominants of the collective unconscious. We saw that the patient identified herself with Mrs. X., and thereby showed that she also had some relation to the uncanny artist. It was apparent that she identified the doctor (myself) with the artist, and further we saw that I became, on the subjective plane of interpretation, an image for the magician-dominant of the collective unconscious.

All this is covered in the dream by the symbol of the crab that walks backwards. The crab is the living content of the unconscious that can in no way be exhausted nor rendered inoperative by analysis on the objective plane.

But what we could do was to separate the mythological or collective psychological contents from the objects of consciousness, and to consolidate them as psychological realities outside the individual psyche.

So long as the collective unconscious and the individual psyche are coupled together without differentiation no progress can take place; or, to speak in terms of the dream, the boundary cannot be crossed. If the dreamer does nevertheless prepare to cross the boundary, then what was unconscious becomes activated, seizes her and drags her under. The dream and its material characterize the collective unconscious both as a lower animal living hidden in the depths of the water, and also as a dangerous illness that can be cured only by a timely operation. To what extent this characterization is apt has already been seen. As we said, the animal-symbol points especially to what is extra-human, that is supra-personal; for the contents of the collective unconscious are not merely the archaic residue of specifically human ways of functioning, but also the residue of functions of the animal ancestry of mankind, whose duration in time must have been infinitely greater than the relatively brief epoch of specifically human existence.[1] These residues, or, to speak in Semon's terms, these engrammes, are extremely liable, when active, not only to arrest the progress of development, but to divert the libido into regressive channels until the store of energy that has activated the collective unconscious has been used up. But the energy becomes once more available, in so far as the conscious position that is contraposed to the collective unconscious can take it into account. Religions have produced this energic cycle in a concretistic way[2] through cultural communication

---

[1] In his philosophical dissertation on Leibnitz' theory of the unconscious H. Ganz has used the *engramme* theory of Semon as an explanation of the collective unconscious. The concept of the collective unconscious advanced by me coincides in essentials with Semon's concept of the phylogenetic *mneme*.
[2] Concretistic=thought of as objectively real.

742

with the gods—the dominants of the collective unconscious. This method is too much at variance with our intellectual morality for us to accept it as an adequate, or even possible, solution of the problem. If, however, we apprehend the figures of the unconscious as collective unconscious dominants, hence as collective psychological phenomena or functions, this hypothesis does no violence to our intellectual conscience. This solution is rationally acceptable, and by means of it we secure the possibility of coming to terms with the activated residues of our racial history. This reconciliation makes feasible the crossing of the confining boundary, and is, therefore, appropriately called the transcendent function. It is synonymous with a forward development into a new attitude, which in the dream is indicated by the other side of the stream.

In all this parallels with hero myths are manifest. The typical battle of the hero with the monster (the unconscious content) frequently takes place on the shore of a body of water, or perhaps at a ford, as is the case in the Indian myths, familiar to us in Longfellow's *Hiawatha*. In the decisive battle, the hero (like Jonah) is always swallowed by the monster, as has been shown by Frobenius[1] in a wealth of material. Inside the monster the hero begins in his own way to deal with the beast, while the creature is swimming eastward with him to the rising sun. What he does is to cut out an essential piece of the viscera, the heart for instance, by virtue of which the monster lives, that is, the valuable energy by which the unconscious was activated. He thus kills the monster, which then drifts to land, where the hero, new-born through the transcendent function (the 'night-journey under the sea' of Frobenius), steps forth, often in company with all those whom the monster had previously

---

[1] *Das Zeitalter des Sonnengottes*, Berlin, 1904.

devoured. Thus the normal condition is restored; for the unconscious, having been robbed of its energy, no longer occupies the dominating position. In this way the myth, a people's dream, graphically describes the problem which, in its individual setting, was also the problem of our patient.

I must now emphasize the not unimportant fact, which must also have struck the reader, that in my patient's dream the collective unconscious appears under a very negative aspect, as something dangerous and harmful. This is a consequence of the richly developed, indeed over-luxuriant, phantasy-life of the patient, which is connected with her literary gift. Her heightened power of phantasy is a symptom of illness in that she revelled in it too freely, while letting real life pass her by. Any more mythology would be dangerous for her, because her external life had not been adequately lived. She has still too little hold upon real life to risk all at once a reversal of standpoint. The collective unconscious had overcome her, and threatened to draw her away from a reality still insufficiently fulfilled. The collective unconscious must therefore, as the dream indicates, present itself to her as something dangerous, otherwise she would have made out of it, all too readily, a refuge from the demands of life. I do not wish, however, by this negative example to convey the impression that the unconscious plays this dubious role in all cases. I will therefore add two dreams of a young man, which illuminate another and more favourable side of the function of the unconscious. I do this the more gladly since the solution of the problem of the opposites is only possible through the irrational way indicated by contributions from the unconscious, such as dreams.

First, I must make the reader in some measure acquainted with the personality of the dreamer; for without this acquaintance one can hardly place oneself in the

744

peculiar atmosphere of the dreams. There are dreams which are pure poems, and which therefore can only be understood through the mood they convey as a whole. The dreamer is a youth a little over twenty years old, but still wholly boyish in appearance. There is even a suggestion of girlishness in his looks and in his modes of expression. He is intelligent, with pronounced intellectual and æsthetic interests. His æsthetic interests predominate: one feels at once his good taste and fine appreciation of all forms of art. His feelings are tender and delicate, somewhat fantastic, of the character pertaining to puberty, but of a feminine nature. The feminine element obviously predominates; there is no trace of the boorishness often found at puberty. He is clearly too young for his age, apparently therefore a case of retarded development. Another indication of this is the fact that he came to me on account of homosexuality. The night preceding his first visit he had the following dream:

"I find myself in a great cathedral filled with a mysterious twilight. It is said to be the cathedral of Lourdes. In the middle is a deep, dark well into which I ought to descend."

The dream is plainly a coherent expression of a mood. The dreamer's comments are as follows: "Lourdes is the mystical fountain of healing. Naturally I thought of that yesterday, since I was coming to you for treatment and was in search of a cure. There is said to be such a well at Lourdes. Probably it is very unpleasant to go down into this water. The well in the church was ever so deep."

What does this dream say? Apparently it is quite clear, and one might be content to take it as a kind of poetic formulation of the mood of the preceding day. But we should not stop there because experience shows that these dreams are much deeper and more significant. One might suppose from this dream that the dreamer came to the doctor in a very poetic mood, that he entered upon the treatment as though it were a sacred religious act to be performed in the mystical half light of an awe-inspiring sanctuary. But this in no way corresponds to the fact. The patient merely came to the doctor in order to be treated for an unpleasant matter—his homosexuality, which is far indeed from being poetical. At any rate from the actual mood of the day before it would hardly be intelligible to us why he should dream so poetically, if we were to accept so direct a causality in the origin of the dream. But perhaps we could assume that the stimulus to the dream was just the extremely unpoetical occasion which impelled the patient to seek treatment. We might hazard the supposition that the patient dreamed in such a highly poetic way just by reason of the lack of poetry in his mood the day before, somewhat as a man who has fasted by day may dream at night of an abundant feast. It must be admitted that in the dream the thought recurs of the treatment, of the cure with its unpleasant procedure; but all this reappears with a poetical illumination, that is, in a form that meets most effectively the vivid æsthetic and emotional needs of the dreamer. He is inevitably lured on by this attractive picture, despite the fact that the well is dark, deep, and cold. Something of the mood of this dream would persist after sleep, and continue into the morning of the day on which he must submit himself to an unpleasant and unpoetical duty. Perhaps drab reality would be irradiated with a bright, golden reflection from the dream feeling.

Is this, then, the aim of the dream? That is quite possible, for according to my experience by far the greater number of dreams have a compensatory character. They emphasize another side in each particular case, in order to maintain the psychic equilibrium. But compensation of mood is not the only aim of the dream picture. A correction in the understanding of the situation is also involved. The patient had naturally no adequate notion of the treatment to which he was about to submit himself. But the dream gives him an image that indicates in poetical metaphor the essence of the treatment he is to undergo. This is at once apparent if we follow up his associations and comments on the image of the cathedral.

"The cathedral," he says, "brings to my mind the cathedral of Cologne. I have been greatly interested in it from childhood. I remember that my mother first told me about it. I also remember that, whenever I saw a village church, I used to ask if that were the cathedral of Cologne. I wanted to be a priest in such a cathedral."

The patient is here describing a very important event of his youth. As in most cases of this kind, there was in him an especially close bond with his mother. We must not understand from this an especially satisfactory or intense conscious relation with the mother, but rather a secret subterranean bond that perhaps only expressed itself in consciousness through the retardation of character development—a relative infantilism. In its development the personality struggles away from such an unconscious infantile tie, for nothing is more fatal to development than persistence in an unconscious, or, as one might say, psychically embryonic condition. Therefore the instinct seizes the first opportunity to supplant the mother by another object. In order that this object may be a valid substitute for the mother, it must bear some analogy to her, and in the case of our patient this is true in the fullest sense. The intensity with which his childish phantasy seized upon the symbol of the Cologne cathedral corresponds to the strength of the unconscious need to find a substitute for his mother. The unconscious need is naturally intensified in a case where the infantile bond threatens to become injurious. Therefore it is that his childish imagination took up the idea of the Church with such enthusiasm, the Church being in the fullest sense and in every meaning a mother. We speak not only of

747

Mother Church, but even of the womb of the Church. In the ceremony known in the Catholic Church as *benedictio fontis,* the baptisimal font is actually spoken of as *"immaculatus divini fontis uterus"* (the immaculate womb of the divine fountain-head). We believe, of course, that such meanings must be consciously known before they could be effective in individual phantasy, and that it is impossible that they should affect a child unacquainted with them. These analogies certainly do not work by way of the conscious, but in quite another fashion.

The Church presents a high spiritual surrogate for the merely natural or 'carnal' tie to the parents. The individual is thus freed from an unconscious natural relation that, strictly speaking, is no relation, but a condition of primordial unconscious identity which, on account of its unconsciousness, has an extraordinary inertia and offers the greatest resistance to every higher spiritual development. It is hard to know wherein such a condition can be distinguished from that of an animal. To promote and make possible the liberation of the individual from his original, animal-like condition is by no means the special prerogative of the Christian Church. The role played by the latter is merely the modern, more especially the Western, form of an instinctive striving that is probably as old as mankind itself—a striving that exists in the most varied forms among all primitive peoples who are in any way developed and have not again degenerated. It corresponds to the institution, or rite, of initiation into manhood. At the time of puberty, the youth is brought into the 'men's house' or some similar place of consecration, where he is systematically alienated from his family. At the same time he is initiated into religious secrets, and is thus not only brought into quite new relations, but also introduced to a wholly new world, he himself having become *"quasi modo genitus,"* a renewed and changed personality. The initiation is often attended with all

748

kinds of tortures, circumcision and similar rites being not uncommon. These practices are undoubtedly very ancient and have left their traces in our unconscious just as have many other primitive experiences. They have almost become instinctive mechanisms, so that they continually reproduce themselves, quite apart from any external urge, as in student fraternity baptisms (*Fuxtaufen*), or the more extravagant forms of initiation found among American students. They are engraved in the unconscious as a primordial image, as an archetype, as St. Augustine says.

When the mother spoke to her little son about the cathedral of Cologne, this primordial image was stirred and awakened to life. But no priestly educator was at hand to develop what had thus begun, and so the child remained in the hands of the mother. Yet the longing for a man's leadership kept on growing in the boy, in the form of a homosexual tendency it is true, a faulty development which might never have come about if a man had developed his childish phantasy further. At any rate the deviation into homosexuality has many historical precedents. In ancient Greece, as in many primitive communities, homosexuality and education were, so to speak, identical. Viewed in this light the homosexuality of adolescence, though invariably misunderstood, is none the less a purposeful reaching out toward the man.

According to the sense of the dream, the submission to the treatment signifies for the patient the fulfillment of the meaning of his homosexuality, that is, his entrance into the world of adult men. All that we are forced to explain here by means of tedious and circuitous discussion, has been condensed by the dream into a few expressive metaphors creating a picture that works far more effectively upon the imagination, feeling, and understanding of the dreamer than would a learned discourse. The patient was thus more adequately and ingeniously

749

prepared for the treatment than if he had been over-whelmed with medical and pedagogical maxims. It is for this reason that I regard the dream not only as a valuable source of information, but also as an extraordinarily effective instrument of education and treatment.

We come now to the second dream, and I must explain in advance that, in the first consultation, I did not refer in any way to the dream we have just been discussing. The dream itself was not mentioned, nor in general was there a word said that could have been remotely con-nected with what has been considered above. The second dream was as follows:

"I am in a great Gothic cathedral. At the altar stands a priest. I stand before him with my friend, holding in my hand a small Japanese figure of ivory, and I have the feeling that it should be baptized. Suddenly an elderly lady appears, and taking from my friend his fraternity ring, puts it on her own finger. My friend is afraid that he may be in some way bound by this. But at the same moment wonderful organ music is heard."

I will here only bring out briefly those points that continue and complete the dream of the preceding day. The second dream is clearly connected with the first: the dreamer is again in the church, that is, in a position to undergo initiation into manhood. A new figure has, how-ever, been added, the priest, whose absence in the previous situation we have already noted. The dream affirms, then, that the unconscious meaning of his homosexuality is fulfilled, and thus a further development can ensue. The essential act of initiation can now begin, that is, baptism. The dream symbol confirms what I have already said: it is not the prerogative of the Christian Church alone to bring about such transitions and spiritual transformations. Be-hind the ceremonies of the Church there looms a primor-dial image which under certain conditions can also com-pel such transformations.

750

That which, according to the dream, is to be baptized, is a small Japanese figure of ivory. In regard to it the patient commented: "It was a little, grotesque, dwarf-like man, reminding me of the *membrum virile*. It is most curious that this should be baptized; yet with the Jews, circumcision is a sort of baptism. This must have to do with my homosexuality, because the friend standing with me before the altar is the one with whom I am homosexually connected. He is in the same fraternity with me. The fraternity ring obviously stands for our relation."

It is known that in common usage, a ring is a symbol of a bond or relation, for example, the wedding ring. We can therefore safely take the fraternity ring in this case as a metaphor for the homosexual relation, the dreamer's appearance together with his friend being yet another indication of this relation.

The malady that is to be cured is homosexuality. The dreamer is to be led out of this relatively childish condition, and brought into the adult state by means of a kind of circumcision ceremony under the supervision of the priest. These ideas correspond exactly to my analysis of the previous dream. Thus far the development would proceed logically and intelligibly in conformity with archetypal images. But now a disturbing factor appears to enter. An elderly lady suddenly takes possession of the fraternity ring; in other words, she draws to herself what has hitherto been a homosexual relation, and by her act excites in the dreamer fears of being entangled in a new relation involving responsibility. Since the ring is now on the hand of a woman, a kind of marriage has been contracted, that is, the homosexual relation seems to have passed over into a heterosexual one. It is, however, a heterosexual relation of a peculiar kind since it is an elderly lady who is involved. "She is my mother's friend," the patient comments. "I like her very much, in fact she is to me a kind of motherly friend."

From this declaration we can see what has happened in the dream: by virtue of the initiation the homosexual bond is cut, and a heterosexual relation substituted for it, a platonic friendship with a motherly kind of woman. In spite of resembling her, this woman is not yet the mother, so that the relation means a step forward toward masculinity—toward liberation from the mother and mastery of adolescent homosexuality.

The fear of the new tie is easily understood as fear arising from the resemblance to the mother; it might appear that because of the dissolution of the homosexual relation there had been a complete regression to the mother. Or the fear might be of the new and unknown implicit in the adult heterosexual state, with its possible responsibilities, such as marriage, etc. That we are in fact concerned here not with a regression but with an advance seems to be confirmed by the music that now peals forth. The patient is musical and especially susceptible to solemn organ music. Music therefore signifies for him a very positive feeling, and, in this case, a harmonious conclusion to the dream which is again fitted to spread over the coming morning a beautiful, holy feeling.

If now we recall the fact that up to this moment the patient had seen me in only one consultation, in which little more was discussed than a general clinical anamnesis, it will be evident that both dreams make amazing anticipations. They throw on the patient's situation a singular light, and one strange to the conscious viewpoint, while at the same time an aspect is lent to the banal clinical situation that is uniquely adapted to the dreamer's whole mental peculiarity, and fitted to stimulate in the highest degree his æsthetic, intellectual, and religious interests. No better conditions for treatment could be imagined than those thus created. From the analysis of these dreams one almost receives the impression that the patient came to the treatment with the utmost readiness and hopefulness, quite prepared to cast aside his boyishness and become a man. In reality this was by no means the case. Consciously he was full of hesitations and resistances; moreover, in the further course of the treatment he constantly showed himself antagonistic and difficult, ever ready to slip back into his former infantilism. The dreams stand therefore in definite contrast to his conscious behaviour; they move along progressive lines and take the part of the teacher. To my way of thinking they display most plainly the peculiar function of dreams. I have called this function one of compensation. The unconscious progressive tendency forms with the conscious regressive tendency a pair of opposites, which maintains a balance in the scales: the influence of the educator is the needle-index on the scales.

The positive character of the role played by the images of the collective unconscious throughout the case of this young man results apparently from the fact that the youth has no dangerous inclinations to turn to a phantasy-substitute for reality, and to squander his life therein. The effect of the unconscious images has something of fate in it; one can say of these images: '*Volentem ducunt, nolentem trahunt*' (they lead the willing, they drag the unwilling). Perhaps—who knows?—these eternal images may be the reality of what is called fate.

The archetype is, of course, operative always and everywhere, but practical treatment, especially that of young people, may not allow one to bring the patient into relation with it. In the case of older people, on the contrary, it is necessary to give special attention to the images of the collective unconscious, since they are the only source from which, in these cases, hints may be drawn for the solution of the problem of the pairs of opposites. Through the conscious elaboration of this material, the transcendent function reveals itself as a mode of apprehension made possible by the archetypes, and effecting the reconciliation of the opposites. I should have given examples of this, but since in this field we are advancing upon almost unexplored, new territory, it is better not to subject these delicate phenomena to an overhasty formulation. I must content myself here with the statement that through tension between the opposites, the collective unconscious brings forth images, which as symbols make possible an irrational union of the opposites.

CARL GUSTAV JUNG (b.-Basel, Switzerland, July 26, 1875.)

Jung received his training at the University of Basel, Zürich, and Paris. He earned his M.D. in 1900 from Basel. Jung then became Bleuler's assistant at the University of Zürich, to continue his studies in psychiatry. Under Bleuler's inspiration, some of his first and greatest contributions were made in the field of schizophrenia (v.i.). In his association with Psychoanalysis, he was the first president of the International Psychoanalytic Society. His break with Freud came in 1913. From 1905 to 1909, he was Head Physician at the Psychiatric Clinic in Zürich. Jung was Professor of Psychology at the University of Technology, Zürich, 1933-1940. In 1945 he became Professor of Medical Psychiatry at the University of Basel. Most of his energies, however, were devoted to his private practice. He lives today on Lake Zürich, at Kusnacht.

One of the most penetrating writers of our time, Jung contributes regularly to our knowledge of the Occult, the Mystic, and the Primitive in the religious motives of men. In the present essays, he has stated his most basic tenets in their earliest, and most fundamental form. The influence of these concepts, particularly upon scholars in neighboring fields such as anthropology, and the breadth of the controversies to which they have led, is hardly surpassed by any others in recent years.

JUNG, C. G. *Two essays in analytical psychology*. London: Ballière, Tindall, & Cox, 1928. Authorized trans. H. G. & C. F. Baynes. Chap. V. "The personal unconscious and the super-personal or collective unconscious" (p. 65-82). Chap. VII: "The dominants of the collective unconscious" (p. 83-115). The present essays were revised from an essay which first appeared in 1912. They first appeared in book form in 1916. The present translation is from the 1926 edition, and is printed in its entirety by the permission of the publishers.

See also:

JUNG, C. G.

a) *Zur psychologie und pathologie sogenannter occulter Phän-omene.* Leipzig: Druck v.o. Mutze, 1902.

b) *The psychology of dementia praecox.* Nervous & Mental Disease Pub. Co., 1936 (1907). Trans. A. A. Brill.

c) *The theory of psychoanalysis.* N. Y.: Nerv. & Ment. Dis. Pub. Co., 1915. The 1912 lectures at Fordham Univ., in N.Y.C.

d) "Psychoanalysis" *Trans. Psycho-Medical Soc.* 1913, 3(II): 1-19. This is a clear and simple statement of Jung's growing emphasis on religious motives, while still strongly espousing the Psychoanalytical position.

e) *Studies in word association; experiments in the diagnosis of psychopathological conditions carried out at the Psychiatric Clinic of the University of Zürich.* N.Y.: Moffat, Yard & Co., 1919. Trans. M. D. Eder.

f) *An analysis of the prelude to a case of schizophrenia.* London: Routledge & Kegan Paul, Ltd.; 1956.

g) *Modern man in search of a soul.* N.Y.: Harcourt, Brace & Co., 1933. Trans. W. S. Dell & C. F. Baynes.

JACOBI, J. *The psychology of Jung.* New Haven: Yale Univ. Press, 1943. Trans. K. W. Bash.

The Bollingen Foundation is in the process of publishing a collected edition of all Jung's works, in 17 vol. The last volume (18) will contain a complete bibliography.

MURCHISON (b-Vol. 3, p. 1174-1175).

GRINSTEIN (Vol. II, p. 1033-1047).

CONDITIONED REFLEXES

AN INVESTIGATION OF
THE PHYSIOLOGICAL ACTIVITY
OF THE
CEREBRAL CORTEX

Ivan Petrovich Pavlov

LECTURE I

The development of the objective method in investigating the physiological activities of the cerebral hemispheres.

THE cerebral hemispheres stand out as the crowning achievement in the nervous development of the animal kingdom. These structures in the higher animals are of considerable dimensions and exceedingly complex, being made up in man of millions upon millions of cells—centres or foci of nervous activity—varying in size, shape and arrangement, and connected with each other by countless branchings from their individual processes. Such complexity of structure naturally suggests a like complexity of function, which in fact is obvious in the higher animal and in man. Consider the dog, which has been for so many countless ages the servant of man. Think how he may be trained to perform various duties, watching, hunting, etc. We know that this complex behaviour of the animal, undoubtedly involving the highest nervous activity, is mainly associated with the cerebral hemispheres. If we remove the hemispheres in the dog [Goltz[1] and others[2]], the animal

---

[1] F. Goltz, "Der Hund ohne Grosshirn," Pflüger's *Archiv*, V. li. p. 570, 1892.
[2] M. Rothmann, "Der Hund ohne Grosshirn." *Neurologisches Centralblatt*, V. xxviii. p. 1045, 1909.

becomes not only incapable of performing these duties but also incapable even of looking after itself. It becomes in fact a helpless invalid, and cannot long survive unless it be carefully tended.

In man also the highest nervous activity is dependent upon the structural and functional integrity of the cerebral hemispheres. As soon as these structures become damaged and their functions impaired in any way, so man also becomes an invalid. He can no longer proceed with his normal duties, but has to be kept out of the working world of his fellow men.

In astounding contrast with the unbounded activity of the cerebral hemispheres stands the meagre content of present-day physiological knowledge concerning them. Up to the year 1870, in fact, there was no physiology of the hemispheres; they seemed to be out of reach of the physiologist. In that year the common physiological methods of stimulation and extirpation were first applied to them [Fritsch and Hitzig[1]]. It was found by these workers that stimulation of certain parts of the cortex of the hemispheres (motor cortex) regularly evoked contractions in definite groups of skeletal muscles: extirpation of these parts of the cortex led to disturbances in the normal functioning of the same groups of muscles. Shortly afterwards it was demonstrated [Ferrier,[2] H. Munk[3]] that other areas of the cortex which do not evoke any motor activity in response to stimulation are also functionally differentiated. Extirpation of these areas leads to definite defects in the nervous activity associated with certain receptor organs, such as the retina of the eye, the organ of Corti, and the sensory nerve-endings in the skin. Searching investigations have been made, and still are being

---

[1]Fritsch und E. Hitzig, "Ueber die elektrische Erregbarkeit des Grosshirns." *Archiv für (Anatomie und) Physiologie*, p. 300, 1870.

[2]D. Ferrier, *Functions of the Brain*, London, 1876.

[3]H. Munk, *Ueber die Functionen der Grosshirnrinde*, Berlin, 1890 and 1909.

made, by numerous workers on this question of localization of function in the cortex. Our knowledge has been increased in precision and filled out in detail, especially as regards the motor area, and has even found useful application in medicine. These investigations, however, did not proceed fundamentally beyond the position established by Fritsch and Hitzig. The important question of the physiological mechanism of the whole higher and complex behaviour of the animal which is—as Goltz showed—dependent upon the cerebral hemispheres, was not touched in any of these investigations and formed no part of the current physiological knowledge.

When therefore we ask the questions: What do those facts which have up to the present been at the disposal of the physiologist explain with regard to the behaviour of the higher animals? What general scheme of the highest nervous activity can they give? or what general rules governing this activity can they help us to formulate?— the modern physiologist finds himself at a loss and can give no satisfactory reply. The problem of the mechanism of this complex structure which is so rich in function has got hidden away in a corner, and this unlimited field, so fertile in possibilities for research, has never been adequately explored.

The reason for this is quite simple and clear. These nervous activities have never been regarded from the same point of view as those of other organs, or even other parts of the central nervous system. The activities of the hemispheres have been talked about as some kind of special psychical activity, whose working we feel and apprehend in ourselves, and by analogy suppose to exist in animals. This is an anomaly which has placed the physiologist in an extremely difficult position. On the one hand it would seem that the study of the activities of the cerebral hemispheres, as of the activities of any other part of the organism, should be within the compass of physiology, but on the other hand it happens to have been annexed to the special field of another science—psychology.

What attitude then should the physiologist adopt? Perhaps he should first of all study the methods of this science of psychology, and only afterwards hope to study the physiological mechanism of the hemispheres? This involves a serious difficulty. It is logical that in its analysis of the various activities of living matter physiology should base itself on the more advanced and more exact sciences—physics and chemistry. But if we attempt an approach from this science of psychology to the problem confronting us we shall be building our superstructure on a science which has no claim to exactness as compared even with physiology. In fact it is still open to discussion whether psychology is a natural science, or whether it can be regarded as a science at all.

It is not possible here for me to enter deeply into this question, but I will stay to give one fact which strikes me very forcibly, viz. that even the advocates of psychology do not look upon their science as being in any sense exact. The eminent American psychologist, William James, has in recent years referred to psychology not as a science but as a *hope* of science. Another striking illustration is provided by Wundt, the celebrated philosopher and psychologist, founder of the so-called experimental method in psychology and himself formerly a physiologist. Just before the War (1913), on the occasion of a discussion in Germany as to the advisability of making separate Chairs of Philosophy and Psychology, Wundt opposed the separation, one of his arguments being the impossibility of fixing a common examination schedule in psychology, since every professor had his own special ideas as to what psychology really was. Such testimony seems to show clearly that psychology cannot yet claim the status of an exact science.

If this be the case there is no need for the physiologist

759

to have recourse to psychology. It would be more natural that experimental investigation of the physiological activities of the hemispheres should lay a solid foundation for a future true science of psychology; such a course is more likely to lead to the advancement of this branch of natural science.

The physiologist must thus take his own path, where a trail has already been blazed for him. Three hundred years ago Descartes evolved the idea of the reflex. Starting from the assumption that animals behaved simply as machines, he regarded every activity of the organism as a *necessary* reaction to some external stimulus, the connection between the stimulus and the response being made through a definite nervous path: and this connection, he stated, was the fundamental purpose of the nervous structures in the animal body. This was the basis on which the study of the nervous system was firmly established. In the eighteenth, nineteenth and twentieth centuries the conception of the reflex was used to the full by physiologists. Working at first only on the lower parts of the central nervous system, they came gradually to study more highly developed parts, until quite recently Magnus,[1] continuing the classical investigations of Sherrington[2] upon the spinal reflexes, has succeeded in demonstrating the reflex nature of all the elementary motor activities of the animal organism. Descartes' conception of the reflex was constantly and fruitfully applied in these studies, but its application has stopped short of the cerebral cortex.

It may be hoped that some of the more complex activities of the body, which are made up by a grouping together of the elementary locomotor activities, and which enter into the states referred to in psychological phrase-

---

[1] R. Magnus, *Koerperstellung*, Berlin, 1924.
[2] C. S. Sherrington, *The Integrative Action of the Nervous System*, London, 1906.

ology as "playfulness," "fear," "anger," and so forth, will soon be demonstrated as reflex activities of the subcortical parts of the brain. A bold attempt to apply the idea of the reflex to the activities of the hemispheres was made by the Russian physiologist, I. M. Sechenov, on the basis of the knowledge available in his day of the physiology of the central nervous system. In a pamphlet entitled "Reflexes of the Brain," published in Russian in 1863, he attempted to represent the activities of the cerebral hemispheres as reflex—that is to say, as *determined*. Thoughts he regarded as reflexes in which the effector path was inhibited, while great outbursts of passion he regarded as exaggerated reflexes with a wide irradiation of excitation. A similar attempt was made more recently by Ch. Richet,[1] who introduced the conception of the psychic reflex, in which the response following on a given stimulus is supposed to be determined by the association of this stimulus with the traces left in the hemispheres by past stimuli. And generally speaking, recent physiology shows a tendency to regard the highest activities of the hemispheres as an association of the new excitations at any given time with traces left by old ones (associative memory, training, education by experience).

All this, however, was mere conjecture. The time was ripe for a transition to the experimental analysis of the subject—an analysis which must be as objective as the analysis in any other branch of natural science. An impetus was given to this transition by the rapidly developing science of comparative physiology, which itself sprang up as a direct result of the Theory of Evolution. In dealing with the lower members of the animal kingdom physiologists were, of necessity, compelled to reject anthropomorphic preconceptions, and to direct all their effort towards the elucidation of the connections between

---

[1] Ch. Richet, *Réflexes Psychiques. Réflexes Conditionels. Automatisme Mental.* Pavlov's *Jubilee Volume*, Petrograd, 1925.

the external stimulus and the resulting response, whether locomotor or other reaction. This led to the development of Loeb's doctrine of Animal Tropisms;[1] to the introduction of a new objective terminology to describe animal reactions [Beer, Bethe and Uexkull[2]]; and finally, it led to the investigation by zoologists, using purely objective methods, of the behaviour of the lower members of the animal kingdom in response to external stimuli—as for example in the classical researches of Jennings.[3]

Under the influence of these new tendencies in biology, which appealed to the practical bent of the American mind, the American School of Psychologists—already interested in the comparative study of psychology—evinced a disposition to subject the highest nervous activities of animals to experimental analysis under various specially devised conditions. We may fairly regard the treatise by Thorndyke, *The Animal Intelligence* (1898),[4] as the starting point for systematic investigations of this kind. In these investigations the animal was kept in a box, and food was placed outside the box so that it was visible to the animal. In order to get the food the animal had to open a door, which was fastened by various suitable contrivances in the different experiments. Tables and charts were made showing how quickly and in what manner the animal solved the problems set it. The whole process was understood as being the formation of an association between the visual and tactile stimuli on the one hand and the locomotor apparatus on the other. This method, with its modifications, was subsequently applied by numerous

---

[1] J. Loeb, *Studies in General Physiology,* Chicago, 1905.

[2] Beer, Bethe und Uexküll, "Vorschläge zu einer objectivirenden Nomenklatur in der Physiologie des Nervensystems," *Biologisches Centralblatt,* V. xix, p. 517, 1899.

[3] H. S. Jennings, *The Behavior of Lower Organisms,* New York, 1906.

[4] E. L. Thorndyke, *The Animal Intelligence. An Experimental Study of the Associative Processes in Animals,* New York, 1898.

authors to the study of questions relating to the associative ability of various animals.

At about the same time as Thorndyke was engaged on this work, I myself (being then quite ignorant of his researches) was also led to the objective study of the hemispheres, by the following circumstance: In the course of a detailed investigation into the activities of the digestive glands I had to inquire into the so-called psychic secretion of some of the glands, a task which I attempted in conjunction with a collaborator. As a result of this investigation an unqualified conviction of the futility of subjective methods of inquiry was firmly stamped upon my mind. It became clear that the only satisfactory solution of the problem lay in an experimental investigation by strictly objective methods. For this purpose I started to record all the external stimuli falling on the animal at the time its reflex reaction was manifested (in this particular case the secretion of saliva), at the same time recording all changes in the reaction of the animal.

This was the beginning of these investigations, which have gone on now for twenty-five years—years in which numerous fellow-workers on whom I now look back with tender affection have united with mine in this work their hearts and hands. We have of course passed through many stages, and only gradually has the subject been opened up and the difficulties overcome. At first only a few scattered facts were available, but to-day sufficient material has been gathered together to warrant an attempt to present it in a more or less systematized form. At the present time I am in a position to present you with a physiological interpretation of the activities of the cerebral hemispheres which is, at any rate, more in keeping with the structural and functional complexity of this organ than is the collection of fragmentary, though very important, facts which up to the present have represented all the knowledge of this subject. Work on the

763

lines of purely objective investigation into the highest nervous activities has been conducted in the main in the laboratories under my control, and over a hundred collaborators have taken part. Work on somewhat similar lines to ours has been done by the American psychologists. Up to the present, however, there has been the one essential point of difference between the American School and ourselves. Being psychologists, their mode of experimentation, in spite of the fact that they are studying these activities on their external aspect, is mostly psychological—at any rate so far as the arrangement of problems and their analysis and the formulation of results are concerned. Therefore—with the exception of a small group of "behaviourists"—their work cannot be regarded as purely physiological in character. We, having started from physiology, continue to adhere strictly to the physiological point of view, investigating and systematizing the whole subject by physiological methods alone. As regards other physiological laboratories a few only have directed their attention to this subject, and that recently; nor have their investigations extended beyond the limits of a preliminary inquiry.

I shall now turn to the description of our material, first giving as a preliminary an account of the general conception of the reflex, of specific physiological reflexes, and of the so-called "instincts." Our starting point has been Descartes' idea of the nervous reflex. This is a genuine scientific conception, since it implies necessity. It may be summed up as follows: An external or internal stimulus falls on some one or other nervous receptor and gives rise to a nervous impulse; this nervous impulse is transmitted along nerve fibres to the central nervous system, and here, on account of existing nervous connections, it gives rise to a fresh impulse which passes along outgoing nerve fibres to the active organ, where it excites a special activity of the cellular structures. Thus a stimulus appears to be connected of necessity with a definite response, as cause with effect. It seems obvious that the whole activity of the organism should conform to definite laws. If the animal were not in exact correspondence with its environment it would, sooner or later, cease to exist. To give a biological example: if, instead of being attracted to food, the animal were repelled by it, or if instead of running from fire the animal threw itself into the fire, then it would quickly perish. The animal must respond to changes in the environment in such a manner that its responsive activity is directed towards the preservation of its existence. This conclusion holds also if we consider the living organism in terms of physical and chemical science. Every material system can exist as an entity only so long as its internal forces, attraction, cohesion, etc., balance the external forces acting upon it. This is true for an ordinary stone just as much as for the most complex chemical substances; and its truth should be recognized also for the animal organism. Being a definite circumscribed material system, it can only continue to exist so long as it is in continuous equilibrium with the forces external to it: so soon as this equilibrium is seriously disturbed the organism will cease to exist as the entity it was. Reflexes are the elemental units in the mechanism of perpetual equilibration. Physiologists have studied and are studying at the present time these numerous machine-like, inevitable reactions of the organism—reflexes existing from the very birth of the animal, and due therefore to the inherent organization of the nervous system.

Reflexes, like the driving-belts of machines of human design, may be of two kinds—positive and negative, excitatory and inhibitory. Although the investigation of these reflexes by physiologists has been going on now for a long time, it is as yet not nearly finished. Fresh reflexes are continually being discovered. We are ignorant of the properties of those receptor organs for which the effective stimulus arises inside the organism, and the internal reflexes themselves remain a field unexplored. The paths by which nervous impulses are conducted in the central nervous system are for the most part little known, or not ascertained at all. The mechanism of inhibitions confined within the central nervous system remains quite obscure: we know something only of those inhibitory reflexes which manifest themselves along the inhibitory efferent nerves. Furthermore, the combination and interaction of different reflexes are as yet insufficiently understood. Nevertheless physiologists are succeeding more and more in unravelling the mechanism of these machine-like activities of the organism, and may reasonably be expected to elucidate and control it in the end.

To those reflexes which have long been the subject of physiological investigation, and which concern chiefly the activities of separate organs and tissues, there should be added another group of inborn reflexes. These also take place in the nervous system, and they are the inevitable reactions to perfectly definite stimuli. They have to do with reactions of the organism as a whole, and comprise that general behaviour of the animal which has been termed "instinctive." Since complete agreement as regards the essential affinity of these reactions to the reflex has not yet been attained, we must discuss this question more fully. We owe to the English philosopher, Herbert Spencer, the suggestion that instinctive reactions are reflexes. Ample evidence was later advanced by zoologists, physiologists, and students of comparative psychology in support of this. I propose here to bring together the various arguments in favour of this view. Between the simplest reflex and the instinct we can find numerous stages of transition, and among these we are puzzled to find any line of demarcation. To exemplify this we may take the newly hatched chick. This little creature reacts by pecking to any stimulus that catches the eye, whether it be a real

766

object or only a stain in the surface it is walking upon. In what way shall we say that this differs from the inclining of the head, the closing of the lids, when something flicks past its eyes? We should call this last a defensive reflex, but the first has been termed a feeding instinct: although in pecking nothing but an inclination of the head and a movement of the beak occurs.

It has also been maintained that instincts are more complex than reflexes. There are, however, exceedingly complex reflexes which nobody would term instincts. We may take vomiting as an example. This is very complex and involves the co-ordination of a large number of muscles (both striped and plain) spread over a large area and usually employed in quite different functions of the organism. It involves also a secretory activity on the part of certain glands which is usually evoked for a quite different purpose.

Again, it has been assumed that the long train of actions involved in certain instinctive activities affords a distinctive point of contrast with the reflex, which is regarded as always being built on a simple scale. By way of example we may take the building of a nest, or of dwellings in general, by animals. A chain of incidents is linked together: material is gathered and carried to the site chosen; there it is built up and strengthened. To look upon this as reflex we must assume that one reflex initiates the next following—or, in other words, we must regard it as a chain-reflex. But this linking up of activities is not peculiar to instincts alone. We are familiar with numerous reflexes which most certainly fuse into chains. Thus, for example, if we stimulate an afferent nerve, *e.g.* the sciatic nerve, a reflex rise of blood pressure occurs; the high pressure in the left ventricle of the heart, and first part of the aorta, serves as the effective stimulus to a second reflex, this time a depressor reflex which has a moderating influence on the first. Again, we may take one of the

767

chain reflexes recently established by Magnus. A cat, even when deprived of its cerebral hemispheres, will in most cases land on its feet when thrown from a height. How is this managed? When the position of the otolithic organ in space is altered a definite reflex is evoked which brings about a contraction of the muscles in the neck, restoring the animal's head to the normal position. This is the first reflex. With the righting of the head a fresh reflex is evoked, and certain muscles of the trunk and limbs are brought into play, restoring the animal to the standing posture. This is the second reflex.

Some, again, object to the identification of instincts with reflexes on this ground: instincts, they say, frequently depend upon the internal state of an organism. For instance, a bird only builds its nest in the mating season. Or, to take a simpler case, when an animal is satiated with eating, then food has no longer any attraction and the animal leaves off eating. Again, the same is true of the sexual impulse. This depends on the age of the organism, and on the state of the reproductive glands; and a considerable influence is exerted by hormones (the products of the glands of internal secretion). But this dependence cannot be claimed as a peculiar property of "instincts." The intensity of any reflex, indeed its very presence, is dependent on the irritability of the centres, which in turn depends constantly on the physical and chemical properties of the blood (automatic stimulation of centres) and on the interaction of reflexes.

Last of all, it is sometimes held that whereas reflexes determine only the activities of single organs and tissues, instincts involve the activity of the organism as a whole. We now know, however, from the recent investigations of Magnus and de Kleijn, that standing, walking and the maintenance of postural balance in general, are all nothing but reflexes.

It follows from all this that instincts and reflexes are

768

alike the inevitable responses of the organism to internal
and external stimuli, and therefore we have no need to
call by them by two different terms. Reflex has the better
claim of the two, in that it has been used from the very
beginning with a strictly scientific connotation.

The aggregate of reflexes constitutes the foundation of
the nervous activities both of men and of animals. It is
therefore of great importance to study in detail all the
fundamental reflexes of the organism. Up to the present,
unfortunately, this is far from being accomplished, especially, as I have mentioned before, in the case of those
reflexes which have been known vaguely as "instincts."
Our knowledge of these latter is very limited and fragmentary. Their classification under such headings as
"alimentary," "defensive," "sexual," "parental" and
"social" instincts, is thoroughly inadequate. Under each
of these heads is assembled often a large number of individual reflexes. Some of these are quite unidentified;
some are confused with others; and many are still only
partially appreciated. I can demonstrate from my own
experience to what extent the subject remains inchoate
and full of gaps. In the course of the researches which
I shall presently explain, we were completely at a loss on
one occasion to find any cause for the peculiar behaviour
of an animal. It was evidently a very tractable dog, which
soon became very friendly with us. We started off with
a very simple experiment. The dog was placed in a stand
with loose loops round its legs, but so as to be quite comfortable and free to move a pace or two. Nothing more
was done except to present the animal repeatedly with
food at intervals of some minutes. It stood quietly enough
at first, and ate quite readily, but as time went on it
became excited and struggled to get out of the stand,
scratching at the floor, gnawing the supports, and so on.
This ceaseless muscular exertion was accompanied by
breathlessness and continuous salivation, which persisted

at every experiment during several weeks, the animal getting worse and worse until it was no longer fitted for our researches. For a long time we remained puzzled over the unusual behaviour of this animal. We tried out experimentally numerous possible interpretations, but though we had had long experience with a great number of dogs in our laboratories we could not work out a satisfactory solution of this strange behaviour, until it occurred to us at last that it might be the expression of a special *freedom reflex,* and that the dog simply could not remain quiet when it was constrained in the stand. This reflex was overcome by setting off another against it—the reflex for food. We began to give the dog the whole of its food in the stand. At first the animal ate but little, and lost considerably in weight, but gradually it got to eat more, until at last the whole ration was consumed. At the same time the animal grew quieter during the course of the experiments: the freedom reflex was being inhibited. It is clear that the freedom reflex is one of the most important reflexes, or, if we use a more general term, reactions, of living beings. This reflex has even yet to find its final recognition. In James's writings it is not even enumerated among the special human "instincts." But it is clear that if the animal were not provided with a reflex of protest against boundaries set to its freedom, the smallest obstacle in its path would interfere with the proper fulfilment of its natural functions. Some animals as we all know have this freedom reflex to such a degree that when placed in captivity they refuse all food, sicken and die.

As another example of a reflex which is very much neglected we may refer to what may be called the *investigatory reflex.* I call it the "What-is-it?" reflex. It is this reflex which brings about the immediate response in man and animals to the slightest changes in the world around them, so that they immediately orientate their appropriate receptor organ in accordance with the perceptible quality in the agent bringing about the change, making full investigation of it. The biological significance of this reflex is obvious. If the animal were not provided with such a reflex its life would hang at every moment by a thread. In man this reflex has been greatly developed with far-reaching results, being represented in its highest form by inquisitiveness—the parent of that scientific method through which we may hope one day to come to a true orientation in knowledge of the world around us.

Still less has been done towards the elucidation of the class of negative or inhibitory reflexes (instincts) which are often evoked by any strong stimulus, or even by weak stimuli, if unusual. Animal hypnotism, so-called, belongs to this category.

As the fundamental nervous reactions both of men and of animals are inborn in the form of definite reflexes, I must again emphasize how important it is to compile a complete list comprising all these reflexes with their adequate classification. For, as will be shown later on, all the remaining nervous functions of the animal organism are based upon these reflexes. Now, although the possession of such reflexes as those just described constitutes the fundamental condition for the natural survival of the animal, they are not in themselves sufficient to ensure a prolonged, stable and normal existence. This can be shown in dogs in which the cerebral hemispheres have been removed. Leaving out of account the internal reflexes, such a dog still retains the fundamental external reflexes. It is attracted by food; it is repelled by nocuous stimuli; it exhibits the investigatory reflex, raising its head and pricking up its ears to sound. In addition it exhibits the freedom reflex, offering a powerful resistance to any restraint. Nevertheless it is wholly incapable of looking after itself, and if left to itself will very soon die. Evidently something important is missing in its present nervous make-up. What nervous activities can it have lost?

771

It is easily seen that, in this dog, the number of stimuli evoking reflex reaction is considerably diminished; those remaining are of an elemental, generalized nature, and act at a very short range. Consequently the dynamic equilibrium between the inner forces of the animal system and the external forces in its environment has become elemental as compared with the exquisite adaptability of the normal animal, and the simpler balance is obviously inadequate to life.

Let us return now to the simplest reflex from which our investigations started. If food or some rejectable substance finds its way into the mouth, a secretion of saliva is produced. The purpose of this secretion is in the case of food to alter it chemically, in the case of a rejectable substance to dilute and wash it out of the mouth. This is an example of a reflex due to the physical and chemical properties of a substance when it comes into contact with the mucous membrane of the mouth and tongue. But, in addition to this, a similar reflex secretion is evoked when these substances are placed at a distance from the dog and the receptor organs affected are only those of smell and sight. Even the vessel from which the food has been given is sufficient to evoke an alimentary reflex complete in all its details; and, further, the secretion may be provoked even by the sight of the person who brought the vessel, or by the sound of his footsteps. All these innumerable stimuli falling upon the several finely discriminating distance receptors lose their power for ever as soon as the hemispheres are taken from the animal, and those only which have a direct effect on mouth and tongue still retain their power. The great advantage to the organism of a capacity to react to the former stimuli is evident, for it is in virtue of their action that food finding its way into the mouth immediately encounters plenty of moistening saliva, and rejectable substances, often nocuous to the mucous membrane, find a layer of pro-

772

tective saliva already in the mouth which rapidly dilutes and washes them out. Even greater is their importance when they evoke the motor component of the complex reflex of nutrition, *i.e.* when they act as stimuli to the reflex of seeking food.

Here is another example—the reflex of self-defence. The strong carnivorous animal preys on weaker animals, and these if they waited to defend themselves until the teeth of the foe were in their flesh would speedily be exterminated. The case takes on a different aspect when the defence reflex is called into play by the sights and sounds of the enemy's approach. Then the prey has a chance to save itself by hiding or by flight.

How can we describe, in general, this difference in the dynamic balance of life between the normal and the de-corticated animal? What is the general mechanism and law of this distinction? It is pretty evident that under natural conditions the normal animal must respond not only to stimuli which themselves bring immediate benefit or harm, but also to other physical or chemical agencies—waves of sound, light, and the like—which in themselves only *signal* the approach of these stimuli; though it is not the sight and sound of the beast of prey which is in itself harmful to the smaller animal, but its teeth and claws.

Now although the *signalling stimuli* do play a part in those comparatively simple reflexes we have given as examples, yet this is not the most important point. The essential feature of the highest activity of the central nervous system, with which we are concerned and which in the higher animals most probably belongs entirely to the hemispheres, consists not in the fact that innumerable signalling stimuli do initiate reflex reactions in the animal, but in the fact that under different conditions these same stimuli may initiate quite different reflex reactions; and conversely the same reaction may be initiated by different stimuli.

In the above-mentioned example of the salivary reflex, the signal at one time is one particular vessel, at another time another; under certain conditions one man, under different conditions another—strictly depending upon which vessel had been used in feeding and which man had brought the vessel and given food to the dog. This evidently makes the machine-like responsive activities of the organism still more precise, and adds to it qualities of yet higher perfection. So infinitely complex, so continuously in flux, are the conditions in the world around, that that complex animal system which is itself in living flux, and that system only, has a chance to establish dynamic equilibrium with the environment. Thus we see that the fundamental and the most general function of the hemispheres is that of reacting to signals presented by innumerable stimuli of interchangeable signification.

LECTURE II

Technical methods employed in the objective investigation of the functions of the cerebral hemispheres.

In the previous lecture I gave an account of the reasons which led us to adopt, for the investigation of the functions of the cerebral hemispheres, the purely objective method used for investigating the physiological activity of the lower parts of the nervous system. In this manner the investigation of the cerebral hemispheres is brought into line with the investigations conducted in other branches of natural science, and their activities are studied as purely physiological facts, without any need to resort to fantastic speculations as to the existence of any possible subjective state in the animal which may be conjectured on analogy with ourselves. From this point of view the whole nervous activity of the animal must be regarded as based firstly on inborn reflexes. These are regular causal connections between certain definite external stimuli acting on the organism and its necessary reflex actions. Such inborn reflexes are comparatively few in number, and the stimuli setting them in action act close up, being as a rule the general physical and chemical properties of the common agencies which affect the organism. The inborn reflexes by themselves are inadequate to ensure the continued existence of the organism, especially of the more highly organized animals, which, when deprived of their highest nervous activity, are permanently disabled, and if left to themselves, although retaining all their inborn reflexes, soon cease to exist. The complex conditions of everyday existence require a much more detailed and specialized correlation between the animal and its environment than is afforded by the inborn reflexes alone. This more precise correlation can be established only through the medium of the cerebral hemispheres; and we have found that a great number of all sorts of stimuli always act through the medium of the hemispheres as temporary and interchangeable signals for the comparatively small number of agencies of a general character which determine the inborn reflexes, and that this is the only means by which a most delicate adjustment of the organism to the environment can be established. To this function of the hemispheres we gave the name of "signalization."

Before passing on to describe the results of our investigation it is necessary to give some account of the purely technical side of the methods employed, and to describe the general way in which the signalizing activity of the hemispheres can be studied. It is obvious that the reflex activity of any effector organ can be chosen for the purpose of this investigation, since signalling stimuli can get linked up with any of the inborn reflexes. But, as was mentioned in the first lecture, the starting point for the present investigation was determined in particular by the study of two reflexes—the food or "alimentary" reflex, and the "defence" reflex in its mildest form, as observed when a rejectable substance finds its way into the mouth of the animal. As it turned out, these two reflexes proved a fortunate choice in many ways. Indeed, while any strong defence reflex, *e.g.* against such a stimulus as a powerful electric current, makes the animal extremely restless and excited; and while the sexual reflexes require a special environment—to say nothing of their periodic character and their dependence upon age—the alimentary reflex and the mild defence reflex to rejectable substances are normal everyday occurrences.

It is essential to realize that each of these two reflexes—the alimentary reflex and the mild defence reflex to rejectable substances—consists of two distinct components, a motor and a secretory. Firstly, the animal exhibits a reflex activity directed towards getting hold of the food and eating it or, in the case of rejectable substances, towards getting rid of them out of the mouth; and secondly, in both cases an immediate secretion of saliva occurs, in the case of food, to start the physical and chemical processes of digestion and, in the case of rejectable substances, to wash them out of the mouth. We confined our experiments almost entirely to the secretory component of the reflex: the allied motor reactions were taken into account only where there were special reasons. The secretory reflex presents many important advantages for our purpose. It allows of an extremely accurate measurement of the intensity of reflex activity, since either the number of drops in a given time may be counted or else the saliva may be caused to displace a coloured fluid in a horizontally placed graduated glass tube. It would be much more difficult to obtain the same accuracy of measurement for any motor reflex, especially for such complex motor reactions as accompany reflexes to food or to rejectable substances. Even by using most delicate instru-

776

ments we should never be able to reach such precision in measuring the intensity of the motor component of the reflexes as can easily be attained with the secretory component. Again, a very important point in favour of the secretory reflexes is the much smaller tendency to interpret them in an anthropomorphic fashion—*i.e.* in terms of subjective analogy. Although this seems a trivial consideration from our present standpoint, it was of importance in the earlier stages of our investigation and did undoubtedly influence our choice.

For the purpose of registering the intensity of the salivary reflex all the dogs employed in the experiments are subjected to a preliminary minor operation, which consists in the transplantation of the opening of the salivary duct from its natural place on the mucous membrane of the mouth to the outside skin. For this purpose the terminal portion of the salivary duct is dissected and freed from the surrounding tissue, and the duct, together with a small portion of the mucous membrane surrounding its natural opening, is carried through a suitable incision, to the outside of the cheek in the case of the parotid gland, or under the chin in the case of the submaxillary gland. In this new position the duct is fixed by a few stitches which are removed when the wound has healed. As a result of the operation the saliva now flows to the outside, on to the cheek or chin of the animal, instead of into the mouth, so that the measurement of the secretory activity of the gland is greatly facilitated. It is only necessary for this purpose to adjust a small glass funnel over the opening of the duct on to the skin, and for this we find a special cement prepared according to a formula of Mendeleeff[1] most useful. As an alternative, very suitable and accurate as a recording apparatus is a hemispherical bulb which also can be hermetically sealed

---

[1] *Mendeléeff's cement*: Colophonium, 50 grammes; ferric oxide, 40 grammes; yellow beeswax, 25 grammes.

on to the skin. From the bulb project two tubes, one pointing up and the other pointing down. The latter tube is used for drawing off the saliva which collects during each observation, while the former tube connects by air transmission with a horizontal graduated glass tube filled with coloured fluid. As the saliva flows into the hemispherical bulb the coloured fluid is displaced along the graduated tube, where the amount of secretion can be read off accurately. Further, it is not difficult to fix up an automatic electrically-recording device which will split up the dis-

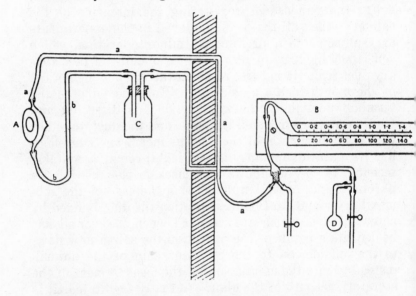

Fig. 1.—The apparatus used for recording the salivary secretion in experiments on conditioned reflexes. *A*, hemispherical bulb which is fixed over the fistula. *aaa*, connecting tube leading through the partition separating the animal's room from the experimenter and connecting the bulb *A* to the registering apparatus, *B. bb*, tube connecting the bulb with bottle, *C*.

After each observation a vacuum is created in the bottle *C* by depression of the rubber balloon *D*; the saliva accumulating in *A* is thus sucked away. During the observation *A* is automatically disconnected from *C* and connected with the registering apparatus. During the aspirations of the saliva from bulb *A* the latter is automatically disconnected from the registering apparatus.

placed fluid into drops of exactly equal volume and reduce any lag in the movement of the fluid to a minimum.[1]

To come to the general technique of the experiments, it is important to remember that our research deals with the highly specialized activity of the cerebral cortex, a signalizing apparatus of tremendous complexity and of most exquisite sensitivity, through which the animal is influenced by countless stimuli from the outside world. Every one of these stimuli produces a certain effect upon the animal, and all of them taken together may clash and interfere with, or else reinforce, one another. Unless we are careful to take special precautions the success of the whole investigation may be jeopardized, and we should get hopelessly lost as soon as we begin to seek for cause and effect among so many and various influences, so intertwined and entangled as to form a veritable chaos. It was evident that the experimental conditions had to be simplified, and that this simplification must consist in eliminating as far as possible any stimuli outside our control which might fall upon the animal, admitting only such stimuli as could be entirely controlled by the experimenter. It was thought at the beginning of our research that it would be sufficient simply to isolate the experimenter in the research chamber with the dog on its stand, and to refuse admission to anyone else during the course of an experiment. But this precaution was found to be wholly inadequate, since the experimenter, however still he might try to be, was himself a constant source of a

[1]In almost all the experiments quoted in these lectures the amount of salivary secretion is, for the sake of uniformity, given in drops. It was, however, only in the very earliest period of the research—before the separation of the experimenter from the animal was made—that the actual number of drops falling from a small funnel fixed over the fistula was counted, and only a few of these experiments are given. In the great majority of the experiments the salivary secretion was measured by the displacement of water in a graduated tube or by the electric recorder, allowing a much greater accuracy of measurement. The readings so obtained have been converted, in the tables, into drops. Thus, in some experiments it will be noticed that the number of drops is given to an accuracy of one-tenth.

large number of stimuli. His slightest movements—blinking of the eyelids or movement of the eyes, posture, respiration and so on—all acted as stimuli which, falling upon the dog, were sufficient to vitiate the experiments by making exact interpretation of the results extremely difficult. In order to exclude this undue influence on the part of the experimenter as far as possible, he had to be stationed outside the room in which the dog was placed, and even this precaution proved unsuccessful in laboratories not specially designed for the study of these particular reflexes. The environment of the animal, even when shut up by itself in a room, is perpetually changing. Footfalls of a passer-by, chance conversations in neighbouring rooms, slamming of a door or vibration from a passing van, street-cries, even shadows cast through the windows into the room, any of these casual uncontrolled stimuli falling upon the receptors of the dog set up a disturbance in the cerebral hemispheres and vitiate the experiments. To get over all these disturbing factors a special laboratory was built at the Institute of Experimental Medicine in Petrograd, the funds being provided by a keen and public-spirited Moscow business man. The primary task was the protection of the dogs from uncontrolled extraneous stimuli, and this was effected by surrounding the building with an isolating trench and employing other special structural devices. Inside the building all the research rooms (four to each floor) were isolated from one another by a cross-shaped corridor; the top and ground floors, where these rooms were situated, were separated by an intermediate floor. Each research room was carefully partitioned by the use of sound-proof materials into two compartments—one for the animal, the other for the experimenter. For stimulating the animal, and for registering the corresponding reflex response, electrical methods or pneumatic transmission were used. By means of these arrangements it was possible to get something of that stability of environmental conditions so essential to the carrying out of a successful experiment.

Another point should be mentioned—although in this respect the means at our disposal still leave something to be desired. In analysing the exceedingly complex influence of the external environment upon the animal, the experimenter must be able to exercise full control over all the conditions obtaining during the course of any experiment. He should therefore have at his disposal various instruments for affecting the animal by different kinds of stimuli, singly or combined, so as to imitate simple natural conditions. But we were often handicapped by the conditions in which we had to work and by the shortcomings of the instruments at our disposal, for we always found that the cerebral hemispheres were sensitive to far finer gradations of stimulus than we could furnish.

It is possible that the experimental conditions I have described may raise somewhere the objection of being abnormal and artificial. However it is hardly likely, in view of the infinite variety of stimuli met with under natural conditions, that we shall hit on one that is quite unprecedented in the life of the animal. Moreover, in dealing with any phenomenon of vast complexity it is absolutely necessary to isolate the different single factors involved, so as to study them independently, or in arbitrary groups in which we can keep the individual units under control. But as a matter of fact the same objection and the same answer apply equally to the whole of animal physiology. For instance, the methods of vivisection and of the study of isolated organs and tissues, which aim at the same isolation of different individual functions, have been constantly employed, and we may safely say that the greater part of the achievements of physiology are due to the successful application of such methods of control. In our experiments it is the whole animal which is placed under a limited number of rigidly defined conditions, and only by this method is it possible to study the reflexes independently of one another.

The foregoing remarks give an idea of our general aim and of the technical side of our methods. I propose to introduce you to the first and most elementary principles of the subject matter of our research by means of a few demonstrations:

Demonstration.—The dog used in the following experiment has been operated upon as described previously. It can be seen that so long as no special stimulus is applied the salivary glands remain quite inactive. But when the sounds from a beating metronome are allowed to fall upon the ear, a salivary secretion begins after 9 seconds, and in the course of 45 seconds eleven drops have been secreted. The activity of the salivary gland has thus been called into play by impulses of sound—a stimulus quite alien to food. This activity of the salivary gland cannot be regarded as anything else than a component of the alimentary reflex. Besides the secretory, the motor component of the food reflex is also very apparent in experiments of this kind. In this very experiment the dog turns in the direction from which it has been customary to present the food and begins to lick its lips vigorously.

This experiment is an example of a central nervous activity depending on the integrity of the hemispheres. A decerebrate dog would never have responded by salivary secretion to any stimulus of the kind. It is obvious also that the underlying principle of this activity is signalization. The sound of the metronome is the signal for food, and the animal reacts to the signal in the same way as if it were food; no distinction can be observed between the effects produced on the animal by the sounds of the beating metronome and showing it real food.

Demonstration.—Food is shown to the animal. The salivary secretion begins after 5 seconds, and six drops are collected in the course of 15 seconds. The effect is the same as that observed with the sounds of the metronome. It is again a case of signalization, and is due to the activity of the hemispheres.

That the effect of sight and smell of food is not due to an inborn reflex, but to a reflex which has been acquired in the course of the animal's own individual existence, was shown by experiments carried out by Dr. Zitovich in the laboratory of the late Prof. Vartanov. Dr. Zitovich took several young puppies away from their mother and fed them for a considerable time only on milk. When the puppies were a few months old he established fistulae of their salivary ducts, and was thus able to measure accurately the secretory activity of the glands. He now showed these puppies some solid food—bread or meat—but no secretion of saliva was evoked. It is evident, therefore, that the sight of food does not in itself act as a direct stimulus to salivary secretion. Only after the puppies have been allowed to eat bread and meat on several occasions does the sight or smell of these foodstuffs evoke the secretion.

The following experiment serves to illustrate the activity of the salivary gland as an inborn reflex in contrast to signalization:

Demonstration.—Food is suddenly introduced into the dog's mouth; secretion begins in 1 to 2 seconds. The secretion is brought about by the physical and chemical properties of the food itself acting upon receptors in the mucous membrane of the mouth and tongue. It is purely reflex.

This comparatively simple experiment explains how a decerebrate dog can die of starvation in the midst of plenty, for it will only start eating if food chances to come into contact with its mouth or tongue. Moreover, the elementary nature of the inborn reflexes, with their limitations and inadequacy, are clearly brought out in these experiments, and we are now able to appreciate the fundamental importance of those stimuli which have the character of *signals*.

Our next step will be to consider the question of the nature of signalization and of its mechanism from a purely physiological point of view. It has been mentioned already that a reflex is an inevitable reaction of the organism to an external stimulus, brought about along a definite path in the nervous system. Now it is quite evident that in signalization all the properties of a reflex are present. In the first place an external stimulus is required. This was given in our first experiment by the sounds of a metronome. These sounds falling on the auditory receptor of the dog caused the propagation of an impulse along the auditory nerve. In the brain the impulse was transmitted to the secretory nerves of the salivary glands, and passed thence to the glands, exciting them to active secretion. It is true that in the experiment with the metronome an interval of several seconds elapsed between the beginning of the stimulus and the beginning of the salivary secretion, whereas the time interval for the inborn reflex secretion was only 1 to 2 seconds. The longer latent period was, however, due to some special conditions of the experiment, as will come out more clearly as we proceed. But generally speaking the reaction to signals under natural conditions is as speedy as are the inborn reflexes. We shall be considering the latent period of signalization in fuller detail in a further lecture.

In our general survey we characterized a reflex as a necessary reaction following upon a strictly definite stimulus under strictly defined conditions. Such a definition holds perfectly true also for signalization; the only difference is that the type of the effective reaction to signals depends upon a greater number of conditions. But this does not make signalization differ fundamentally from the better known reflexes in any respect, since in the latter, variations in character or force, inhibition and absence of reflexes, can also be traced to some definite change in the conditions of the experiment.

Thorough investigation of the subject shows that accident plays no part whatever in the signalizing activity of the hemispheres, and all experiments proceed strictly according to plan. In the special laboratory I have described, the animal can frequently be kept under rigid experimental observation for 1 to 2 hours without a single drop of saliva being secreted independently of stimuli applied by the observer, although in the ordinary type of physiological laboratory experiments are very often distorted by the interference of extraneous and uncontrolled stimuli.

All these conditions leave no grounds for regarding the phenomena which we have termed "signalization" as being anything else than reflex. There is, however, another aspect of the question which at a first glance seems to point to an essential difference between the better known reflexes and signalization. Food, through its chemical and physical properties, evokes the salivary reflex in every dog right from birth, whereas this new type claimed as reflex—"the signal reflex"—is built up gradually in the course of the animal's own individual existence. But can this be considered as a fundamental point of difference, and can it hold as a valid argument against employing the term "reflex" for this new group of phenomena? It is certainly a sufficient argument for making a definite distinction between the two types of reflex and for considering the signal reflex in a group distinct from the inborn reflex. But this does not invalidate in any way our right logically to term both "reflex," since the point of distinction does not concern the character of the response on the part of the organism, but only the mode of formation of the reflex mechanism. We may take the telephonic installation as an illustration. Communication can be effected in two ways. My residence may be connected directly with the laboratory by a private line, and I may call up the laboratory whenever it pleases me to do so; or on the other hand, a connection may have to be made through the central exchange. But the result in both cases is the same. The only point of distinction between the methods is that the private line provides a permanent and readily available cable, while the other line necessitates a preliminary central connection being established. In the one case the communicating wire is always complete, in the other case a small addition must be made to the wire at the central exchange. We have a similar state of affairs in reflex action. The path of the inborn reflex is already completed at birth; but the path of the signalizing reflex has still to be completed in the higher nervous centres. We are thus brought to consider the mode of formation of new reflex mechanisms. A new reflex is formed inevitably under a given set of physiological conditions, and with the greatest ease, so that there is no need to take the subjective states of the dog into consideration. With a complete understanding of all the factors involved, the new signalizing reflexes are under the absolute control of the experimenter; they proceed according to as rigid laws as do any other physiological processes, and must be regarded as being in every sense a part of the physiological activity of living beings. I have termed this new group of reflexes *conditioned reflexes* to distinguish them from the inborn or *unconditioned reflexes*. The term "conditioned" is becoming more and more generally employed, and I think its use is fully justified in that, compared with the inborn reflexes, these new reflexes actually do depend on very many conditions, both in their formation and in the maintenance of their physiological activity. Of course the terms "conditioned" and "unconditioned" could be replaced by others of arguably equal merit. Thus, for example, we

786

might retain the term "inborn reflexes," and call the new type "acquired reflexes"; or call the former "species reflexes" since they are characteristic of the species, and the latter "individual reflexes" since they vary from animal to animal in a species, and even in the same animal at different times and under different conditions. Or again we might call the former "conduction reflexes" and the latter "connection reflexes."

There should be no theoretical objection to the hypothesis of the formation of new physiological paths and new connections within the cerebral hemispheres. Since the especial function of the central nervous system is to establish most complicated and delicate correspondences between the organism and its environment we may not unnaturally expect to find there, on the analogy of the methods used by the technician in everyday experience, a highly developed connector system superimposed on a conductor system. The physiologist certainly should not object to this conception seeing that he has been used to employing the German conception of "Bahnung," which means a laying down of fresh physiological paths in the centres. Conditioned reflexes are phenomena of common and widespread occurrence: their establishment is an integral function in everyday life. We recognize them in ourselves and in other people or animals under such names as "education," "habits," and "training"; and all of these are really nothing more than the results of an establishment of new nervous connections during the post-natal existence of the organism. They are, in actual fact, links connecting definite extraneous stimuli with their definite responsive reactions. I believe that the recognition and the study of the conditioned reflex will throw open the door to a true physiological investigation probably of all the highest nervous activities of the cerebral hemispheres, and the purpose of the present lectures is to give some account of what we have already accomplished in this direction.

We come now to consider the precise conditions under which new conditioned reflexes or new connections of nervous paths are established. The fundamental requisite is that any external stimulus which is to become the signal in a conditioned reflex must overlap in point of time with the action of an unconditioned stimulus. In the experiment which I chose as my example the unconditioned stimulus was food. Now if the intake of food by the animal takes place simultaneously with the action of a neutral stimulus which has been hitherto in no way related to food, the neutral stimulus readily acquires the property of eliciting the same reaction in the animal as would food itself. This was the case with the dog employed in our experiment with the metronome. On several occasions this animal had been stimulated by the sound of the metronome and immediately presented with food—*i.e.* a stimulus which was neutral of itself had been superimposed upon the action of the inborn alimentary reflex. We observed that, after several repetitions of the combined stimulation, the sounds from the metronome had acquired the property of stimulating salivary secretion and of evoking the motor reactions characteristic of the alimentary reflex. The first demonstration was nothing but an example of such a conditioned stimulus in action. Precisely the same occurs with the mild defence reflex to rejectable substances. Introduction into the dog's mouth of a little of an acid solution brings about a quite definite responsive reaction. The animal sets about getting rid of the acid, shaking its head violently, opening its mouth and making movements with its tongue. At the same time it produces a copious salivary secretion. The same reaction will infallibly be obtained from any stimulus which has previously been applied a sufficient number of times while acid was being introduced into the dog's mouth. Hence a first and most essential requisite for the formation of a new conditioned reflex lies in a coincidence in time of the action of any previously neutral stimulus with some definite unconditioned stimulus. Further, it is not enough that there should be overlapping between the two stimuli; it is also and equally necessary that the conditioned stimulus should begin to operate before the unconditioned stimulus comes into action.

If this order is reversed, the unconditioned stimulus being applied first and the neutral stimulus second, the conditioned reflex cannot be established at all. Dr. Krestovnikov performed these experiments with many different modifications and controls, but the effect was always the same. The following are some of his results:

In one case 427 applications were made in succession of the odour of vanillin together with the introduction of acid into the dog's mouth, but the acid was always made to precede the vanillin by some 5 to 10 seconds. Vanillin failed to acquire the properties of a conditioned stimulus. However, in the succeeding experiment, in which the order of stimuli was reversed, the odour, this time of amyl acetate, became an effective conditioned stimulus after only 20 combinations. With another dog the loud buzzing of an electric bell set going 5 to 10 seconds after administration of food failed to establish a conditioned alimentary reflex even after 374 combinations, whereas the regular rotation of an object in front of the eyes of the animal, the rotation beginning before the administration of food, acquired the properties of a conditioned stimulus after only 5 combinations. The electric buzzer set going before the administration of food established a conditioned alimentary reflex after only a single combination.

Dr. Krestovnikov's experiments were carried out on five dogs, and the result was always negative when the neutral stimulus was applied, whether 10 seconds, 5 seconds or only a single second after the beginning of the unconditioned stimulus. During all these experiments not only the secretory reflex but also the motor reaction of

789

the animal was carefully observed, and these observations always corroborated one another. We thus see that the first set of conditions required for the formation of a new conditioned reflex encompasses the time relation between the presentation of the unconditioned stimulus and the presentation of that agent which has to acquire the properties of a conditioned stimulus.

As regards the condition of the hemispheres themselves, an alert state of the nervous system is absolutely essential for the formation of a new conditioned reflex. If the dog is mostly drowsy during the experiments, the establishment of a conditioned reflex becomes a long and tedious process, and in extreme cases is impossible to accomplish. The hemispheres must, however, be free from any other nervous activity, and therefore in building up a new conditioned reflex it is important to avoid foreign stimuli which, falling upon the animal, would cause other reactions of their own. If this is not attended to, the establishment of a conditioned reflex is very difficult, if not impossible. Thus, for example, if the dog has been so fastened up that anything causes severe irritation, it does not matter how many times the combination of stimuli is repeated, we shall not be able to obtain a conditioned reflex. A somewhat similar case was described in the first lecture—that of the dog which exhibited the *freedom reflex* in an exaggerated degree. It can also be stated as a rule that the establishment of the first conditioned reflex in an animal is usually more difficult than the establishment of succeeding ones. It is obvious that this must be so, when we consider that even in the most favourable circumstances the experimental conditions themselves will be sure to provoke numerous different reflexes—*i.e.* will give rise to one or other disturbing activity of the hemispheres. But this statement must be qualified by remarking that in cases where the cause of these uncontrolled reflexes is not found out, so that we are not able

790

to get rid of them, the hemispheres themselves will help us. For if the environment of the animal during the experiment does not contain any powerful disturbing elements, then practically always the extraneous reflexes will with time gradually and spontaneously weaken in strength.

The third factor determining the facility with which new conditioned reflexes can be established is the health of the animal. A good state of health will ensure the normal functioning of the cerebral hemispheres, and we shall not have to bother with the effects of any internal pathological stimuli.

The fourth, and last, group of conditions has to do with the properties of the stimulus which is to become conditioned, and also with the properties of the unconditioned stimulus which is selected. Conditioned reflexes are quite readily formed to stimuli to which the animal is more or less indifferent at the outset, though strictly speaking no stimulus within the animal's range of perception exists to which it would be absolutely indifferent. In a normal animal the slightest alteration in the environment—even the very slightest sound or faintest odour, or the smallest change in intensity of illumination—immediately evokes the reflex which I referred to in the first lecture as the investigatory reflex—"What is it?"—manifested by a very definite motor reaction. However, if these neutral stimuli keep recurring, they spontaneously and rapidly weaken in their effect upon the hemispheres, thus bringing about bit by bit the removal of this obstacle to the establishment of a conditioned reflex. But if the extraneous stimuli are strong or unusual, the formation of a conditioned reflex will be difficult, and in extreme cases impossible.

It must also be remembered that in most cases we are not acquainted with the history of the dog before it came into the laboratory, and that we do not know what sort

791

of conditioned reflexes have been established to stimuli which appear to be of the simplest character. But in spite of this we have, in a large number of cases, found it possible to take a strong stimulus which evoked some strong unconditioned response of its own, and still succeed in converting it into a conditioned stimulus for another reflex. Let us take for example a nocuous stimulus, such as a strong electric current or wounding or cauterization of the skin. These are obviously stimuli to vigorous unconditioned defence reflexes. The organism responds by a violent motor reaction directed towards removal of the nocuous stimulus or to its own removal from it. But we may, nevertheless, make use even of these stimuli for the establishment of a new conditioned reflex. Thus in one particular experiment a strong nocuous stimulus—an electric current of great strength—was converted into an alimentary conditioned stimulus, so that its application to the skin did not evoke the slightest defence reaction. Instead, the animal exhibited a well-marked alimentary conditioned reflex, turning its head to where it usually received the food and smacking its lips, at the same time producing a profuse secretion of saliva. The following is a record taken from a research by Dr. Erofeeva:

Time	Distance of secondary coil in cms.	Part of Skin Stimulated	Secretion of Saliva in drops during 30 secs.	Motor Reaction
4.23 p.m.	4	usual place	6	In all cases the motor reaction displayed was that characteristic of an alimentary reflex; there was no slightest trace of any motor defence reflex.
4.45 ,,	4	,, ,,	5	
5.7 ,,	2	new place	7	
5.17 ,,	0	,, ,,	9	
5.45 ,,	0	,, ,,	6	

After each stimulation the dog was allowed to eat food
for a few seconds.

Similar results were obtained from dogs in which cauterization or pricking of the skin deep enough to draw blood was made to acquire the properties of an alimentary conditioned stimulus. These experiments have been apt to upset very sensitive people; but we have been able to demonstrate, though without any pretension of penetrating into the subjective world of the dog, that they were labouring under a false impression. Subjected to the very closest scrutiny, not even the tiniest and most subtle objective phenomenon usually exhibited by animals under the influence of strong injurious stimuli can be observed in these dogs. No appreciable changes in the pulse or in the respiration occur in these animals, whereas such changes are always most prominent when the nocuous stimulus has not been converted into an alimentary conditioned stimulus. Such a remarkable phenomenon is the result of diverting the nervous impulse from one physiological path to another. This transference is dependent, however, upon a very definite condition—namely, upon the relative strengths of the two unconditioned reflexes.

Successful transformation of the unconditioned stimulus for one reflex into the conditioned stimulus for another reflex can be brought about only when the former reflex is physiologically weaker and biologically of less importance than the latter. We are led to this conclusion from a consideration of Dr. Erofeeva's experiments. A nocuous stimulus applied to the dog's skin was transformed into a conditioned stimulus for the alimentary reflex. This, we consider, was due to the fact that the alimentary reflex is in such cases stronger than the defence reflex. In the same way we all know that when dogs join in a scuffle for food they frequently sustain skin wounds, which however play no dominant part as stimuli to any defence reflex, being entirely subordinated to the reflex for food. Nevertheless there is a certain limit—there are stronger reflexes than the alimentary reflex. One is the reflex of self-preservation, of existence or non-existence, life or death. To give only one example, it was found impossible to transform a defence reaction into an alimentary conditioned reflex when the stimulus to the unconditioned defence reaction was a strong electric current applied to skin overlying bone with no muscular layer intervening. This signifies that the afferent nervous impulses set up by injury to the bone, and signalizing far greater danger than those set up by injury to the skin, cannot acquire even a temporary connection with the part of the brain from which the alimentary reflex is controlled. Nevertheless, on the whole, the foregoing considerations emphasize the advantage of using the alimentary reflex for most of our experiments, since in the hierarchy of reflexes this holds a very high place.

While, as we have seen, very strong and even specialized stimuli can under certain conditions acquire the properties of conditioned stimuli, there is, on the other hand, a minimum strength below which stimuli cannot be given conditioned properties. Thus a thermal stimulus of 45° C. applied to the skin can be made into an alimentary conditioned reflex, whereas at 38° to 39° C. (approximately 2° C. above the skin temperature in the dog) a thermal stimulus is ineffective [experiments of Dr. Solomonov]. Similarly, while with the help of a very strong unconditioned stimulus it is possible to convert a very unsuitable stimulus—for example, one which naturally evokes a different unconditioned reflex—into a conditioned stimulus, it is exceedingly difficult or even impossible with the help of only a weak unconditioned stimulus to transform even a very favourable neutral stimulus into a conditioned stimulus. Even where such a conditioned reflex is successfully established, its occurrence results only in a very small reflex response. Some unconditioned stimuli may be permanently weak, others may display a weakness which is only temporary—varying with the condition of the animal. As an example of the last we may take food. In the hungry animal food naturally brings about a powerful unconditioned reflex, and the conditioned reflex develops quickly. But in a dog which has not long been before fed the unconditioned stimulus has only a small effect, and alimentary conditioned reflexes are not formed at all or are established very slowly.

By complying with all the conditions which · I have enumerated—which is not a very difficult task—a new conditioned reflex is infallibly obtained. We apply to the receptors of the animal rigidly defined stimuli; these stimuli necessarily result in the formation of a new connection in the hemisphere with a consequent development of a typical reflex reaction.

To sum up, we may legitimately claim the study of the formation and properties of conditioned reflexes as a special department of physiology. There is no reason for thinking about all these events in any other way, and it is my belief that in these questions prejudices blunt the intellect and that generally speaking the preconceptions of the human mind stand in the way of any admission that the highest physiological activity of the hemispheres is rigidly determined. The difficulty is mainly due to the tremendous complexity of our subjective states; and, of course, these cannot yet be traced to their primary causations.

IVAN PETROVICH PAVLOV (b.—Ryazan, Russia, Sept. 26, 1849; d.—Feb. 27, 1936).

Pavlov received his M.D. in 1883 from the Military Medical Academy of the University of St. Petersburg (Leningrad). In 1884-1886 he studied physiology at Leipzig and Breslau. In 1890 he was elected Professor of Pharmacology at the St. Petersburg Medical Academy. In 1891 he established a division of experimental surgery at the newly founded Institute of Experimental Medicine. In 1897 he became Professor of Physiology at the Military Medical Academy. He received the Nobel Prize in Physiology in 1904 for his work on the digestive glands (v.i.). He became director of the Physiological Laboratories of the Russian Academy of Sciences in 1907.

The first paper on Conditioned Reflexes was delivered by Pavlov before the International Medical Congress in Madrid, 1903. It was entitled: "Experimental psychology and psychopathology of animals." Pavlov was certainly one of the foremost experimental physiologists of all time. Both in surgical technique and in brilliant experimental design, he was unsurpassed. Sticking hard to the positivist position, Pavlov believed only in what he could demonstrate in objective physiology. Throughout his life, politically as well as scientifically, he was a terror to meet in open debate. His unbending adherence to high scientific principles has made him both the idealized mentor of Soviet Psychology today, as well as the primary target for world wide attacks upon the strict physiological approach to psychological issues.

The present essays describe his basic concepts. They were first given as lectures in 1924 at the Military Medical Academy of Petrograd, and are rendered here in the definitive English translation by G. V. Anrep of Cambridge. Though Pavlov's ideas have contributed substantially to our understanding of practically all the psycho-physiological functions of man, his blunt rejection of introspection and phenomenology has prevented them from being accepted by the majority of psychologists concerned more directly with the intangibles of the human psyche. To evaluate his final place in the history of ideas is to fiid the solution to the mind-body problem, and so perhaps will ever escape us.

PAVLOV, I. P. *Conditioned reflexes: an investigation of the physiological activity of the cerebral cortex.* Oxford: Oxford University Press, Humphrey Milford, 1927 (1926). Trans. and edited: G. V. Anrep. Lect. I: "The development of the objective method in investigating the physiological activities of the cerebral hemispheres" (p. 1-15). Lect. II: "Technical methods employed in the objective investigation of the functions of the cerebral hemispheres" (p. 16-32). Reprinted by permission of the publisher.

See also:

PAVLOV, I. P.:

a) *The work of the digestive glands.* London: Griffin, 1902 (1897).

b) *Lectures on conditioned reflexes. Twenty-five years of objective study of the higher nervous activity (behaviour) of animals.* N. Y.: Liveright Pub. Co., 1928. Trans. W. H. Gantt, with the collaboration of G. Volboth. This contains his first paper delivered at Madrid, his Nobel Prize address, as well as an

796

excellent collection of his important scientific papers, illustrating the wide field of their application. Also a bibliography of the field.

c) *Experimental psychology and other essays.* N. Y.: Philosophical Library, 1957. Edited: Kh. S. Koshtoyants. This also contains the critical early essays, though in a new translation. Of especial interest are the additional essays reporting Pavlov's comments on the other major trends in his science, e.g. Behaviorism, Gestalt Psychology, and so forth.

BABKIN, B. P. *Pavlov, a biography.* Chicago: Chicago University Press, 1947.

MURCHISON (b—Vol. 2, p. 1222-1228).

PSYCHOLOGY AS THE BEHAVIORIST VIEWS IT

John B. Watson

Psychology as the behaviorist views it is a purely objective experimental branch of natural science. Its theoretical goal is the prediction and control of behavior. Introspection forms no essential part of its methods, nor is the scientific value of its data dependent upon the readiness with which they lend themselves to interpretation in terms of consciousness. The behaviorist, in his efforts to get a unitary scheme of animal response, recognizes no dividing line between man and brute. The behavior of man, with all of its refinement and complexity, forms only a part of the behaviorist's total scheme of investigation.

It has been maintained by its followers generally that psychology is a study of the science of the phenomena of consciousness. It has taken as its problem, on the one hand, the analysis of complex mental states (or processes) into simple elementary constituents, and on the other the construction of complex states when the elementary constituents are given. The world of physical objects (stimuli, including here anything which may excite activity in a receptor), which forms the total phenomena of the natural scientist, is looked upon merely as means to an end. That end is the production of mental states that may be 'inspected' or 'observed.' The psychological object of observation in the case of an emotion, for example, is the mental state itself. The problem in emotion is the determination of the number and kind of elementary constituents present, their loci, intensity, order of appearance, etc. It is agreed that introspection is the method *par excellence* by means of which mental states may be manipulated for purposes of psychology. On this assumption, behavior data (including under this term everything which goes under the name of **comparative** psychology) have no value *per se*. They possess significance only in so far as they may throw light upon conscious states.[1] Such data must have at least an analogical or indirect reference to belong to the realm of psychology.

Indeed, at times, one finds psychologists who **are** sceptical of even this analogical reference. Such scepticism is often shown by the question which is put to the student of behavior, "what is the bearing of animal work upon human psychology?" I used to have to study over this question. Indeed it always embarrassed me somewhat. I was interested in my own work and felt that it was important, and yet I could not trace any close connection between it and psychology as my questioner understood psychology. I hope that such a confession will clear the atmosphere to such an extent that we will no longer have to work under false pretenses. We must frankly admit that the facts so important to us which we have been able to glean from extended work upon the senses of animals by the behavior method have contributed only in a fragmentary way to the general theory of human sense organ processes, nor have they suggested new points of experimental attack. The enormous number of experiments which we have carried out upon learning have likewise contributed little to human psychology. It seems reasonably clear that some kind of compromise must be effected: either psychology must change its viewpoint so as to take in facts of behavior, whether or not they have bearings upon the problems of 'consciousness'; or else behavior must stand alone as a wholly separate and independent science. Should human psychologists fail to look with favor upon our overtures and refuse to modify their position, the behaviorists will be driven to using human beings as subjects and to employ methods of investigation which

---

[1] That is, either directly upon the conscious state of the observer or indirectly upon the conscious state of the experimenter.

are exactly comparable to those now employed in the animal work.

Any other hypothesis than that which admits the independent value of behavior material, regardless of any bearing such material may have upon consciousness, will inevitably force us to the absurd position of attempting to *construct* the conscious content of the animal whose behavior we have been studying. On this view, after having determined our animal's ability to learn, the simplicity or complexity of its methods of learning, the effect of past habit upon present response, the range of stimuli to which it ordinarily responds, the widened range to which it can respond under experimental conditions,—in more general terms, its various problems and its various ways of solving them,—we should still feel that the task is unfinished and that the results are worthless, until we can interpret them by analogy in the light of consciousness. Although we have solved our problem we feel uneasy and unrestful because of our definition of psychology: we feel forced to say something about the possible mental processes of our animal. We say that, having no eyes, its stream of consciousness cannot contain brightness and color sensations as we know them,—having no taste buds this stream can contain no sensations of sweet, sour, salt and bitter. But on the other hand, since it does respond to thermal, tactual and organic stimuli, its conscious content must be made up largely of these sensations; and we usually add, to protect ourselves against the reproach of being anthropomorphic, "if it has any consciousness." Surely this doctrine which calls for an analogical interpretation of all behavior data may be shown to be false: the position that the standing of an observation upon behavior is determined by its fruitfulness in yielding results which are interpretable only in the narrow realm of (really human) consciousness.

This emphasis upon analogy in psychology has led the

800

behaviorist somewhat afield. Not being willing to throw off the yoke of consciousness he feels impelled to make a place in the scheme of behavior where the rise of consciousness can be determined. This point has been a shifting one. A few years ago certain animals were supposed to possess 'associative memory,' while certain others were supposed to lack it. One meets this search for the origin of consciousness under a good many disguises. Some of our texts state that consciousness arises at the moment when reflex and instinctive activities fail properly to conserve the organism. A perfectly adjusted organism would be lacking in consciousness. On the other hand whenever we find the presence of diffuse activity which results in habit formation, we are justified in assuming consciousness. I must confess that these arguments had weight with me when I began the study of behavior. I fear that a good many of us are still viewing behavior problems with something like this in mind. More than one student in behavior has attempted to frame criteria of the psychic—to devise a set of objective, structural and functional criteria which, when applied in the particular instance, will enable us to decide whether such and such responses are positively conscious, merely indicative of consciousness, or whether they are purely 'psychological.' Such problems as these can no longer satisfy behavior men. It would be better to give up the province altogether and admit frankly that the study of the behavior of animals has no justification, than to admit that our search is of such a 'will o' the wisp' character. One can assume either the presence or the absence of consciousness anywhere in the phylogenetic scale without affecting the problems of behavior by one jot or one tittle; and without influencing in any way the mode of experimental attack upon them. On the other hand, I cannot for one moment assume that the paramecium responds to light; that the rat learns a problem more quickly by working at the task five times a day than once a day, or that the human child exhibits plateaux in his learning curves. These are questions which vitally concern behavior and which must be decided by direct observation under experimental conditions.

This attempt to reason by analogy from human conscious processes to the conscious processes in animals, and *vice versa*: to make consciousness, as the human being knows it, the center of reference of all behavior, forces us into a situation similar to that which existed in biology in Darwin's time. The whole Darwinian movement was judged by the bearing it had upon the origin and development of the human race. Expeditions were undertaken to collect material which would establish the position that the rise of the human race was a perfectly natural phenomenon and not an act of special creation. Variations were carefully sought along with the evidence for the heaping up effect and the weeding out effect of selection; for in these and the other Darwinian mechanisms were to be found factors sufficiently complex to account for the origin and race differentiation of man. The wealth of material collected at this time was considered valuable largely in so far as it tended to develop the concept of evolution in man. It is strange that this situation should have remained the dominant one in biology for so many years. The moment zoology undertook the experimental study of evolution and descent, the situation immediately changed. Man ceased to be the center of reference. I doubt if any experimental biologist today, unless actually engaged in the problem of race differentiation in man, tries to interpret his findings in terms of human evolution, or ever refers to it in his thinking. He gathers his data from the study of many species of plants and animals and tries to work out the laws of inheritance in the particular type upon which he is conducting experiments. Naturally, he follows the progress of the work upon race differentiation in man and in the descent of man, but he looks upon these as special topics, equal in importance with his own yet ones in which his interests will never be vitally engaged. It is not fair to say that all of his work is directed toward human evolution or that it must be interpreted in terms of human evolution. He does not have to dismiss certain of his facts on the inheritance of coat color in mice because, forsooth, they have little bearing upon the differentiation of the *genus homo* into separate races, or upon the descent of the *genus homo* from some more primitive stock.

In psychology we are still in that stage of development where we feel that we must select our material. We have a general place of discard for processes, which we anathematize so far as their value for psychology is concerned by saying, "this is a reflex"; "that is a purely physiological fact which has nothing to do with psychology." We are not interested (as psychologists) in getting all of the processes of adjustment which the animal as a whole employs, and in finding how these various responses are associated, and how they fall apart, thus working out a systematic scheme for the prediction and control of response in general. Unless our observed facts are indicative of consciousness, we have no use for them, and unless our apparatus and method are designed to throw such facts into relief, they are thought of in just as disparaging a way. I shall always remember the remark one distinguished psychologist made as he looked over the color apparatus designed for testing the responses of animals to monochromatic light in the attic at Johns Hopkins. It was this: "And they call this psychology!"

I do not wish unduly to criticize psychology. It has failed signally, I believe, during the fifty-odd years of its existence as an experimental discipline to make its place in the world as an undisputed natural science. Psychology, as it is generally thought of, has something esoteric in its methods. If you fail to reproduce my findings, it is not due to some fault in your apparatus or in the control of your stimulus, but it is due to the fact that your introspection is untrained.[1] The attack is made upon the observer and not upon the experimental setting. In physics and in chemistry the attack is made upon the experimental conditions. The apparatus was not sensitive enough, impure chemicals were used, etc. In these sciences a better technique will give reproducible results. Psychology is otherwise. If you can't observe 3-9 states of clearness in attention, your introspection is poor. If, on the other hand, a feeling seems reasonably clear to you, your introspection is again faulty. You are seeing too much. Feelings are never clear.

The time seems to have come when psychology must discard all reference to consciousness; when it need no longer delude itself into thinking that it is making mental states the object of observation. We have become so enmeshed in speculative questions concerning the elements of mind, the nature of conscious content (for example, imageless thought, attitudes and Bewusstseinslage, etc.) that I, as an experimental student, feel that something is wrong with our premises and the types of problems which develop from them. There is no longer any guarantee that we all mean the same thing when we use the terms now current in psychology. Take the case of sensation. A sensation is defined in terms of its attributes. One psychologist will state with readiness that the attributes of a visual sensation are *quality, extension, duration,* and *intensity.* Another will add *clearness.* Still another that of *order.* I doubt if any one psychologist can draw up a set

---

[1]In this connection I call attention to the controversy now on between the adherents and the opposers of imageless thought. The 'types of reactors' (sensory and motor) were also matters of bitter dispute. The complication experiment was the source of another war of words concerning the accuracy of the opponents' introspection.

of statements describing what he means by sensation which will be agreed to by three other psychologists of different training. Turn for a moment to the question of the number of isolable sensations. Is there an extremely large number of color sensations—or only four, red, green, yellow and blue? Again, yellow, while psychologically simple, can be obtained by superimposing red and green spectral rays upon the same diffusing surface! If, on the other hand, we say that every just noticeable difference in the spectrum is a simple sensation, and that every just noticeable increase in the white value of a given color gives simple sensations, we are forced to admit that the number is so large and the conditions for obtaining them so complex that the concept of sensation is unusable, either for the purpose of analysis or that of synthesis. Titchener, who has fought the most valiant fight in this country for a psychology based upon introspection, feels that these differences of opinion as to the number of sensations and their attributes; as to whether there are relations (in the sense of elements) and on the many others which seem to be fundamental in every attempt at analysis, are perfectly natural in the present undeveloped state of psychology. While it is admitted that every growing science is full of unanswered questions, surely only those who are wedded to the system as we now have it, who have fought and suffered for it, can confidently believe that there will ever be any greater uniformity than there is now in the answers we have to such questions. I firmly believe that two hundred years from now, unless the introspective method is discarded, psyhcology will still be divided on the question as to whether auditory sensations have the quality of 'extension,' whether intensity is an attribute which can be applied to color, whether there is a difference in 'texture' between image and sensation and upon many hundreds of others of like character.

The condition in regard to other mental processes is just as chaotic. Can image type be experimentally tested and verified? Are recondite thought processes dependent mechanically upon imagery at all? Are psychologists agreed upon what feeling is? One states that feelings are attitudes. Another finds them to be groups of organic sensations possessing a certain solidarity. Still another and larger group finds them to be new elements correlative with and ranking equally with sensations.

My psychological quarrel is not with the systematic and structural psychologist alone. The last fifteen years have seen the growth of what is called functional psychology. This type of psychology decries the use of elements in the static sense of the structuralists. It throws emphasis upon the biological significance of conscious processes instead of upon the analysis of conscious states into introspectively isolable elements. I have done my best to understand the difference between functional psychology and structural psychology. Instead of clarity, confusion grows upon me. The terms sensation, perception, affection, emotion, volition are used as much by the functionalist as by the structuralist. The addition of the word 'process' ('mental act as a whole,' and like terms are frequently met) after each serves in some way to remove the corpse of 'content' and to leave 'function' in its stead. Surely if these concepts are elusive when looked at from a content standpoint, they are still more deceptive when viewed from the angle of function, and especially so when function is obtained by the introspection method. It is rather interesting that no functional psychologist has carefully distinguished between 'perception' (and this is true of the other psychological terms as well) as employed by the systematist, and 'perceptual process' as used in functional psychology. It seems illogical and hardly fair to criticize the psychology which the systematist gives us, and then to utilize his terms

806

without carefully showing the changes in meaning which are to be attached to them. I was greatly surprised some time ago when I opened Pillsbury's book and saw psychology defined as the 'science of behavior.' A still more recent text states that psychology is the 'science of mental behavior.' When I saw these promising statements I thought, now surely we will have texts based upon different lines. After a few pages the science of behavior is dropped and one finds the conventional treatment of sensation, perception, imagery, etc., along with certain shifts in emphasis and additional facts which serve to give the author's personal imprint.

One of the difficulties in the way of a consistent functional psychology is the parallelistic hypothesis. If the functionalist attempts to express his formulations in terms which make mental states really appear to function, to play some active role in the world of adjustment, he almost inevitably lapses into terms which are connotative of interaction. When taxed with this he replies that it is more convenient to do so and that he does it to avoid the circumlocution and clumsiness which are inherent in any thoroughgoing parallelism.[1] As a matter of fact I believe the functionalist actually thinks in terms of interaction and resorts to parallelism only when forced to give expression to his views. I feel that *behaviorism* is the only consistent and logical functionalism. In it one avoids both the Scylla of parallelism and the Charybdis of interaction. Those time-honored relics of philosophical speculation need trouble the student of behavior as little as they trouble the student of physics. The consideration of the mind-body problem affects neither the type of problem selected nor the formulation of the solution of that problem. I can state my position here no better than by saying

---

[1] My colleague, Professor H. C. Warren, by whose advice this article was offered to the REVIEW, believes that the parallelist can avoid the interaction terminology completely by exercising a little care.

that I should like to bring my students up in the same ignorance of such hypotheses as one finds among the students of other branches of science.

This leads me to the point where I should like to make the argument constructive. I believe we can write a psychology, define it as Pillsbury, and never go back upon our definition: never use the terms consciousness, mental states, mind, content, introspectively verifiable, imagery, and the life. I believe that we can do it in a few years without running into the absurd terminology of Beer, Bethe, Von Uexkull, Nuel, and that of the so-called objective schools generally. It can be done in terms of stimulus and response, in terms of habit formation, habit integrations and the like. Furthermore, I believe that it is really worth while to make this attempt now.

The psychology which I should attempt to build up would take as a starting point, first, the observable fact that organisms, man and animal alike, do adjust themselves to their environment by means of hereditary and habit equipments. These adjustments may be very adequate or they may be so inadequate that the organism barely maintains its existence; secondly, that certain stimuli lead the organisms to make the responses. In a system of psychology completely worked out, given the response the stimuli can be predicted; given the stimuli the response can be predicted. Such a set of statements is crass and raw in the extreme, as all such generalizations must be. Yet they are hardly more raw and less realizable than the ones which appear in the psychology texts of the day. I possibly might illustrate my point better by choosing an everyday problem which anyone is likely to meet in the course of his work. Some time ago I was called upon to make a study of certain species of birds. Until I went to Tortugas I had never seen these birds alive. When I reached there I found the animals doing certain things: some of the acts seemed to work

808

peculiarly well in such an environment, while others seemed to be unsuited to their type of life. I first studied the responses of the group as a whole and later those of individuals. In order to understand more thoroughly the relation between what was habit and what was hereditary in these responses, I took the young birds and reared them. In this way I was able to study the order of appearance of hereditary adjustments and their complexity, and later the beginnings of habit formation. My efforts in determining the stimuli which called forth such adjustments were crude indeed. Consequently my attempts to control behavior and to produce responses at will did not meet with much success. Their food and water, sex and other social relations, light and temperature conditions were all beyond control in a field study. I did find it possible to control their reactions in a measure by using the nest and egg (or young) as stimuli. It is not necessary in this paper to develop further how such a study should be carried out and how work of this kind must be supplemented by carefully controlled laboratory experiments. Had I been called upon to examine the natives of some of the Australian tribes, I should have gone about my task in the same way. I should have found the problem more difficult: the types of responses called forth by physical stimuli would have been more varied, and the number of effective stimuli larger. I should have had to determine the social setting of their lives in a far more careful way. These savages would be more influenced by the responses of each other than was the case with the birds. Furthermore, habits would have been more complex and the influences of past habits upon the present responses would have appeared more clearly. Finally, if I had been called upon to work out the psychology of the educated Europeans, my problem would have required several lifetimes. But in the one I have at my disposal I should have followed the same general line of attack. In the main, my desire in all such work is to gain an accurate knowledge of adjustments and the stimuli calling them forth. My final reason for this is to learn general and particular methods by which I may control behavior. My goal is not "the description and explanation of states of consciousness as such," nor that of obtaining such proficiency in mental gymnastics that I can immediately lay hold of a state of consciousness and say, "this, as a whole, consists of gray sensation number 350, of such and such extent, occurring in conjunction with the sensation of cold of a certain intensity; one of pressure of a certain intensity and extent," and so on *ad infinitum*. If psychology would follow the plan I suggest, the educator, the physician, the jurist and the business man could utilize our data in a practical way, as soon as we are able experimentally, to obtain them. Those who have occasion to apply psychological principles practically would find no need to complain as they do at the present time. Ask any physician or jurist today whether scientific psychology plays a practical part in his daily routine and you will hear him deny that the psychology of the laboratories finds a place in his scheme of work. I think the criticism is extremely just. One of the earliest conditions which made me dissatisfied with psychology was the feeling that there was no realm of application for the principles which were being worked out in content terms.

What gives me hope that the behaviorist's position is a defensible one is the fact that those branches of psychology which have already partially withdrawn from the parent, experimental psychology, and which are consequently less dependent upon introspection are today in a most flourishing condition. Experimental pedagogy, the psychology of drugs, the psychology of advertising, legal psychology, the psychology of tests, and psychopathology are all vigorous growths. These are sometimes wrongly called "practical" or "applied" psychology. Surely there was never a worse misnomer. In the future there may grow up vocational bureaus which really apply psychology. At present these fields are truly scientific and are in search of broad generalizations which will lead to the control of human behavior. For example, we find out by experimentation whether a series of stanzas may be acquired more readily if the whole is learned at once, or whether it is more advantageous to learn each stanza separately and then pass to the succeeding. We do not attempt to apply our findings. The application of this principle is purely voluntary on the part of the teacher. In the psychology of drugs we may show the effect upon behavior of certain doses of caffeine. We may reach the conclusion that caffeine has a good effect upon the speed and accuracy of work. But these are general principles. We leave it to the individual as to whether the results of our tests shall be applied or not. Again, in legal testimony, we test the effects of recency upon the reliability of a witness's report. We test the accuracy of the report with respect to moving objects, stationary objects, color, etc. It depends upon the judicial machinery of the country to decide whether these facts are ever to be applied. For a 'pure' psychologist to say that he is not interested in the questions raised in these divisions of the science because they relate indirectly to the application of psychology shows, in the first place, that he fails to understand the scientific aim in such problems, and secondly, that he is not interested in a psychology which concerns itself with human life. The only fault I have to find with these disciplines is that much of their material is stated in terms of introspection, whereas a statement in terms of objective results would be far more valuable. There is no reason why appeal should ever be made to consciousness in any of them. Or why introspective data should ever be sought during the experimentation, or published

811

in the results. In experimental pedagogy especially one can see the desirability of keeping all of the results on a purely objective plane. If this is done, work there on the human being will be comparable directly with the work upon animals. For example, at Hopkins, Mr. Ulrich has obtained certain results upon the distribution of effort in learning—using rats as subjects. He is prepared to give comparative results upon the effect of having an animal work at the problem once per day, three times per day, and five times per day. Whether it is advisable to have the animal learn only one problem at a time or to learn three abreast. We need to have similar experiments made upon man, but we care as little about his 'conscious processes' during the conduct of the experiment as we care about such processes in the rats.

I am more interested at the present moment in trying to show the necessity for maintaining uniformity in experimental procedure and in the method of stating results in both human and animal work, than in developing any ideas I may have upon the changes which are certain to come in the scope of human psychology. Let us consider for a moment the subject of the range of stimuli to which animals respond. I shall speak first of the work upon vision in animals. We put our animal in a situation where he will respond (or learn to respond) to one of two monochromatic lights. We feed him at the one (positive) and punish him at the other (negative). In a short time the animal learns to go to the light at which he is fed. At this point questions arise which I may phrase in two ways: I may choose the psychological way and say "does the animal see these two lights as I do, *i.e.*, as two distinct colors, or does he see them as two grays differing in brightness, as does the totally color blind?" Phrased by the behaviorist, it would read as follows: "Is my animal responding upon the basis of the difference in intensity between the two stimuli, or upon the difference in wave-lengths?'' He nowhere thinks of the animal's response in terms of his own experiences of colors and grays. He wishes to establish the fact whether wave-length is a factor in that animal's adjustment.[1] If so, what wave-lengths are effective and what differences in wave-length must be maintained in the different regions to afford bases for differential responses? If wave-length is not a factor in adjustment he wishes to know what difference in intensity will serve as a basis for response, and whether that same difference will suffice throughout the spectrum. Furthermore, he wishes to test whether the animal can respond to wave-lengths which do not affect the human eye. He is as much interested in comparing the rat's spectrum with that of the chick as in comparing it with man's. The point of view when the various sets of comparisons are made does not change in the slightest.

However we phrase the question to ourselves, we take our animal after the association has been formed and then introduce certain control experiments which enable us to return answers to the questions just raised. But there is just as keen a desire on our part to test man under the same conditions, and to state the results in both cases in common terms.

The man and the animal should be placed as nearly as possible under the same experimental conditions. Instead of feeding or punishing the human subject, we should ask him to respond by setting a second apparatus until standard and control offered no basis for a differential response. Do I lay myself open to the charge here that I am using introspection? My reply is not at all; that while I might very well feed my human subject for a right choice and punish him for a wrong one and thus produce the response if the subject could give it, there

---

[1] He would have exactly the same attitude as if he were conducting an experiment to show whether an ant would crawl over a pencil laid across the trail or go round it.

is no need of going to extremes even on the platform I suggest. But be it understood that I am merely using this second method as an abridged behavior method.[1] We can go just as far and reach just as dependable results by the longer method as by the abridged. In many cases the direct and typically human method cannot be safely used. Suppose, for example, that I doubt the accuracy of the setting of the control instrument, in the above experiment, as I am very likely to do if I suspect a defect in vision? It is hopeless for me to get his introspective report. He will say: ''There is no difference in sensation, both are reds, identical in quality.'' But suppose I confront him with the standard and the control and so arrange conditions that he is punished if he responds to the 'control' but not with the standard. I interchange the positions of the standard and the control at will and force him to attempt to differentiate the one from the other. If he can learn to make the adjustment even after a large number of trials it is evident that the two stimuli do afford the basis for a differential response. Such a method may sound nonsensical, but I firmly believe we will have to resort increasingly to just such a method where we have reason to distrust the language method.

There is hardly a problem in human vision which is not also a problem in animal vision: I mention the limits of the spectrum, threshold values, absolute and relative, flicker, Talbot's law, Weber's law, field of vision, the

---

[1] I should prefer to look upon this abbreviated method, where the human subject is told in words, for example, to equate two stimuli; or to state in words whether a given stimulus is present or absent, etc., as the *language method* in behavior. It in no way changes the status of experimentation. The method becomes possible merely by virtue of the fact that in the particular case the experimenter and his animal have systems of abbreviations or shorthand behavior signs (language), any one of which may stand for a habit belonging to the repertoire both of the experimenter and his subject. To make the data obtained by the language method virtually the whole of behavior—or to attempt to mould all of the data obtained by other methods in terms of the one which has by all odds the most limited range—is putting the cart before the horse with a vengeance.

Purkinje phenomenon, etc. Every one is capable of being worked out by behavior methods. Many of them are being worked out at the present time.

I feel that all the work upon the senses can be consistently carried forward along the lines I have suggested here for vision. Our results will, in the end, give an excellent picture of what each organ stands for in the way of function. The anatomist and the physiologist may take our data and show, on the one hand, the structures which are responsible for these responses, and, on the other, the physico-chemical relations which are necessarily involved (physiological chemistry of nerve and muscle) in these and other reactions.

The situation in regard to the study of memory is hardly different. Nearly all of the memory methods in actual use in the laboratory today yield the type of results I am arguing for. A certain series of nonsense syllables or other material is presented to the human subject. What should receive the emphasis are the rapidity of the habit formation, the errors, peculiarities in the form of the curve, the persistence of the habit so formed, the relation of such habits to those formed when more complex material is used, etc. Now such results are taken down with the subject's introspection. The experiments are made for the purpose of discussing the mental machinery[1] involved in learning, in recall, recollection and forgetting, and not for the purpose of seeking the human being's way of shaping his responses to meet the problems in the terribly complex environment into which he is thrown, nor for that of showing the similarities and differences between man's methods and those of other animals.

The situation is somewhat different when we come to a study of the more complex forms of behavior, such as imagination, judgment, reasoning, and conception. At present the only statements we have of them are in con-

---

[1] They are often undertaken apparently for the purpose of making crude pictures of what must or must not go on in the nervous system.

815

tent terms.[1] Our minds have been so warped by the fifty-
odd years which have been devoted to the study of states
of consciousness that we can envisage these problems only

---

[1]There is need of questioning more and more the existence of what psychology
calls imagery. Until a few years ago I thought that centrally aroused visual
sensations were as clear as those peripherally aroused. I had never accredited
myself with any other kind. However, closer examination leads me to deny
in my own case the presence of imagery in the Galtonian sense. The whole
doctrine of the centrally aroused image is, I believe, at present, on a very
insecure foundation. Angell as well as Fernald reach the conclusion that an
objective determination of image type is impossible. It would be an interesting
confirmation of their experimental work if we should find by degrees that we
have been mistaken in building up this enormous structure of the centrally
aroused sensation (or image).

The hypothesis that all of the so-called 'higher thought' processes go on in
terms of faint reinstatements of the original muscular act (including speech
here) and that these are integrated into systems which respond in serial order
(associative mechanisms) is, I believe, a tenable one. It makes reflective processes as mechanical as habit. The scheme of habit which James long ago
described—where each return or afferent current releases the next appropriate
thought processes there are faint contractions of the systems of musculature
involved in the overt exercise of the customary act, and especially in the still
finer systems of musculature involved in speech. If this is true, and I do not
see how it can be gainsaid, imagery becomes a mental luxury (even if it really
exists) without any functional significance whatever. If experimental procedure
justifies this hypothesis, we shall have at hand tangible phenomena which may
be studied as behavior material. I should say that the day when we can study
reflective processes by such methods is about as far off as the day when we can
tell by physico-chemical methods the difference in the structure and arrangement of molecules between living protoplasm and inorganic substances. The
solutions of both problems await the advent of methods and apparatus.

After writing this paper I heard the addresses of Professors Thorndike and
Angell, at the Cleveland meeting of the American Psychological Association. I
hope to have the opportunity to discuss them at another time. I must even here
attempt to answer one question raised by Thorndike.

Thorndike (see this issue) casts suspicions upon ideo-motor action. If by
ideo-motor action he means just that and would not include sensori-motor action
in his general denunciation, I heartily agree with him. I should throw out
imagery altogether and attempt to show that practically all natural thought
goes on in terms of sensori-motor processes in the larynx (but not in terms of
'imageless thought') which rarely come to consciousness in any person who has
not groped for imagery in the psychological laboratory. This easily explains
why so many of the well-educated laity know nothing of imagery. I doubt if
Thorndike conceives of the matter in this way. He and Woodworth seem to
have neglected the speech mechanisms.

It has been shown that improvement in habit comes unconsciously. The first
we know of it is when it is achieved—when it becomes an object. I believe that
'consciousness' has just as little to do with *improvement* in thought processes.
Since, according to my view, thought processes are really motor habits in the
larynx, improvements, short cuts, changes, etc., in these habits are brought

816

in one way. We should meet the situation squarely and say that we are not able to carry forward investigations along all of these lines by the behavior methods which are in use at the present time. In extenuation I should like to call attention to the paragraph above where I made the point that the introspective method itself has reached a *cul-de-sac* with respect to them. The topics have become so threadbare from much handling that they may well be put away for a time. As our methods become better developed it will be possible to undertake investigations of more and more complex forms of behavior. Problems which are now laid aside will again become imperative, but they can be viewed as they arise from a new angle and in more concrete settings.

Will there be left over in psychology a world of pure psychics, to use Yerkes' term? I confess I do not know. The plans which I most favor for psychology lead practically to the ignoring of consciousness in the sense that that term is used by psychologists today. I have virtually denied that this realm of psychics is open to experimental investigation. I don't wish to go further into the problem at present because it leads inevitably over into metaphysics. If you will grant the behaviorist the right to use consciousness in the same way that other natural scientists employ it—that is, without making consciousness a special object of observation—you have granted all that my thesis requires.

In concluding, I suppose I must confess to a deep bias on these questions. I have devoted nearly twelve years to experimentation on animals. It is natural that such a one

---

about in the same way that such changes are produced in other motor habits. This view carries with it the implication that there are no reflective processes (centrally initiated processes): The individual is always *examining objects,* in the one case objects in the now accepted sense, in the other their substitutes, viz., the movements in the speech musculature. From this it follows that there is no theoretical limitation of the behavior method. There remains, to be sure, the practical difficulty, which may never be overcome, of examining speech movements in the way that general bodily behavior may be examined.]

should drift into a theoretical position which is in harmony with his experimental work. Possibly I have put up a straw man and have been fighting that. There may be no absolute lack of harmony between the position outlined here and that of functional psychology. I am inclined to think, however, that the two positions cannot be easily harmonized. Certainly the position I advocate is weak enough at present and can be attacked from many standpoints. Yet when all this is admitted I still feel that the considerations which I have urged should have a wide influence upon the type of psychology which is to be developed in the future. What we need to do is to start work upon psychology, making *behavior,* not *consciousness,* the objective point of our attack. Certainly there are enough problems in the control of behavior to keep us all working many lifetimes without ever allowing us time to think of consciousness *an sich.* Once launched in the undertaking, we will find ourselves in a short time as far divorced from an introspective psychology as the psychology of the present time is divorced from faculty psychology.

Summary

1. Human psychology has failed to make good its claim as a natural science. Due to a mistaken notion that its fields of facts are conscious phenomena and that introspection is the only direct method of ascertaining these facts, it has enmeshed itself in a series of speculative questions which, while fundamental to its present tenets, are not open to experimental treatment. In the pursuit of answers to these questions, it has become further and further divorced from contact with problems which vitally concern human interest.

2. Psychology, as the behaviorist views it, is a purely objective, experimental branch of natural science which needs introspection as little as do the sciences of chem-

istry and physics. It is granted that the behavior of animals can be investigated without appeal to consciousness. Heretofore the viewpoint has been that such data have value only in so far as they can be interpreted by analogy in terms of consciousness. The position is taken here that the behavior of man and the behavior of animals must be considered on the same plane; as being equally essential to a general understanding of behavior. It can dispense with consciousness in a psychological sense. The separate observation of 'states of consciousness' is, on this assumption, no more a part of the task of the psychologist than of the physicist. We might call this the return to a non-reflective and naive use of consciousness. In this sense consciousness may be said to be the instrument or tool with which all scientists work. Whether or not the tool is properly used at present by scientists is a problem for philosophy and not for psychology.

3. From the viewpoint here suggested the facts on the behavior of amœbæ have value in and for themselves without reference to the behavior of man. In biology studies on race differentiation and inheritance in amœbæ form a separate division of study which must be evaluated in terms of the laws found there. The conclusions so reached may not hold in any other form. Regardless of the possible lack of generality, such studies must be made if evolution as a whole is ever to be regulated and controlled. Similarly the laws of behavior in amœbæ, the range of responses, and the determination of effective stimuli, of habit formation, persistency of habits, interference and reinforcement of habits, must be determined and evaluated in and for themselves, regardless of their generality, or of their bearing upon such laws in other forms, if the phenomena of behavior are ever to be brought within the sphere of scientific control.

4. This suggested elimination of states of consciousness

819

as proper objects of investigation in themselves will remove the barrier from psychology which exists between it and the other sciences. The findings of psychology become the functional correlates of structure and lend themselves to explanation in physico-chemical terms.

5. Psychology as behavior will, after all, have to neglect but few of the really essential problems with which psychology as an introspective science now concerns itself. In all probability even this residue of problems may be phrased in such a way that refined methods in behavior (which certainly must come) will lead to their solution.

JOHN BROADUS WATSON (b.—Greenville, South Carolina, Jan. 9, 1878; d.—Woodbury, N.Y., Sept. 25, 1958).

Watson graduated from Furman College in 1900, with an M.A. He then went to the University of Chicago, studying with John Dewey, and received his Ph.D. in 1903. Immediately thereafter (1904) he became Assistant in Experimental Psychology at Chicago. Later in 1904 he came to the Johns Hopkins University as Instructor. In 1908 he became Professor of Experimental and Comparative Psychology at Johns Hopkins, and Director of the Laboratory. Watson was editor of the *Psychological Review* 1908-1915, and the *Journal of Experimental Psychology* 1915-1926. He was elected President of the American Psychological Association in 1915. He left Johns Hopkins at the end of 1919, and lectured subsequently at the New School for Social Research. After this time, except for sporadic scientific activity, his time was devoted to industry. (J. Walter Thompson Co., Baltimore. In 1936 he became a vice president of William Esty & Co.)

It is hard to over-estimate the influence which Watson has had on the subsequent development of psychology in America. Though his influence elsewhere was less, literally generations of American students were nurtured on his ideas. His popular appeal was even greater.*

---

*Woodworth (*Contemporary schools of psychology.* London: Methuen & Co. Ltd., 1931 (1956), p. 93) quotes the *N. Y. Times* on Watson's *Behaviorism,* "It marks an epoch in the intellectual history of mankind"; the *N. Y. Tribune,* "Perhaps this is the most important book ever written. One stands for an instant blinded with a great hope."

Though most behaviorists today do not take all his words at face value (*e.g.* Bergmann), they nevertheless vigorously defend his basic ideas. An objective science of human behavior is, in fact, a very great ideal. Watson took major steps in this direction.

The present essay, the first formal statement of behaviorism, grew out of invited lectures at Columbia University, undertaken during the previous year.

WATSON, J. B. "Psychology as a behaviorist views it." *Psychol. Rev.* 1913, 20: 158-177. This is reproduced in its entirety with the kind permission of the American Psychological Association.

See also:

WATSON, J. B.:

a) *Behavior: an introduction to comparative psychology.* N. Y.: Holt, 1914.

b) *Psychology from the standpoint of a behaviorist.* Philadelphia: Lippincott, 1919.

c) *Behaviorism.* N. Y.: People's Inst. Pub. Co., 1924-25.

d) "Behaviorism." In: *Encyclo. Brit.* 1926, 12 (supp. I of Vol. 13): 345-347.

BERGMANN, G. "The contribution of John Watson." *Psychol. Rev.* 1956, 63: 265-276.

MURCHISON (a—Vol. 3, p. 271-281; b—Vol. 2, p. 268-270; b—Vol. 3, p. 528-530).

MIND, MECHANISM AND ADAPTIVE BEHAVIOR[1]

Clark L. Hull

Introduction

Since the time of Charles Darwin it has become clear not only that living organisms have gradually evolved through immense periods of time, but that man is evolution's crowning achievement. It is equally clear that man's preeminence lies in his capacity for adaptive behavior. Because of the seemingly unique and remarkable nature of adaptive behavior, it has long been customary to attribute it to the action of a special agent or substance called 'mind.' Thus 'mind' as a hypothetical entity directing and controlling adaptive behavior attains biological status possessing survival value and, consequently, a 'place in nature.' But what is this mysterious thing called mind? By what principle does it operate? Are these principles many or are they few? Are they those of the ordinary physical world or are they of the nature of spiritual essences—of an entirely different order, the non-physical?

It will, perhaps, be most economical to begin our examination of this important problem by passing briefly in review some typical phenomena of adaptive behavior which have led to the assumption of a special psychic entity. Among these may be mentioned the following: When obstacles are encountered, organisms often persist in making the same incorrect attempt over and over again; they vary their reactions spontaneously; they display anticipatory reactions antedating the biological emergencies to which the reactions are adaptive; they present the phenomena of disappointment and discouragement;

---

[1]Presidential Address delivered before the American Psychological Association, Hanover, New Hampshire, September 4, 1936.
The author is indebted to Professor Max Wertheimer for a critical reading of this paper.

they strive to attain states of affairs which are biologically advantageous; they transfer to new problem situations adaptive behavior acquired in situations which, objectively considered, are totally different. The behavior of organisms is purposive in that they strive for goals or values, and in so doing manifest intelligence or insight and a high degree of individual freedom from current coercion of the environment. Whatever may be the final conclusion as to the ultimate nature of these phenomena, their biological significance in terms of survival must be immense. The task of understanding and controlling them is surely worthy of the best cooperative efforts of the biological and social sciences.

THE CONTROVERSY REGARDING ADAPTIVE BEHAVIOR IS THEORETICAL, NOT FACTUAL

Historically, two main views have been held as to the ultimate nature of adaptive behavior. The most widely accepted of these, at the present time, is also the most ancient; its roots lie far back in primitive animism. According to this view, the principles governing adaptive behavior are essentially, non-physical, mental, or psychic. The second view, despite its austerity, has received a certain amount of favor among men of science. It assumes that adaptive behavior operates ultimately according to the principles of the physical world. In our consideration of these contrasting views, it will be convenient to begin with the latter.

The physical or mechanistic view of the nature of adaptive behavior can best be stated by quoting the beautiful presentation of the raindrop analogy written by the late Albert P. Weiss:

We may best visualize the relationship between the responses that make up the so-called purposive behavior category by the raindrop analogy. We may start with the assumption that every drop of rain in some way or other gets to the ocean. . . . Anthropomorphizing this condition we may say that it is the *purpose* of every drop of rain to get to the ocean. Of course, this only means that virtually every drop *does* get there eventually. . . . Falling from the cloud it may strike the leaf of a tree, and drop from one leaf to another until it reaches the ground. From here it may pass under or on the surface of the soil to a rill, then to a brook, river, and finally to the sea. Each stage, each fall from one leaf to the next, may be designated as a *means* toward the final end, the sea, . . . Human behavior is merely a complication of the same factors.[2]

The nub of Weiss's statement lies in his concluding remark that adaptive behavior is merely a 'complication' of the same factors as those which are involved in the behavior of a drop of water finding its way from an inland cloud to the sea. Obviously, Weiss did not mean to say that the several forms of seeking and striving behavior characteristic of the higher organisms are brought about by the various compoundings of such processes as evaporation, condensation, splashing, and flowing. The context of the quotation shows that he meant that ultimately the complex forms of purposive behavior would be found to derive from the same *source* as those from which the raindrop phenomena are derived; *i.e.*, from the basic entities of theoretical physics, such as electrons and protons. He discusses these latter concepts explicitly and at length.

Passing to the more orthodox view, that adaptive behavior is essentially non-physical, or psychic, the words of A. S. Eddington may be taken as a point of departure. In his book, 'The nature of the physical world,'[3] Eddington remarks:

Conceivably we might reach a human machine interacting by reflexes with its environment; but we cannot reach rational man morally responsible. [P. 343.] . . . In a world of æther and electrons we might perhaps encounter *nonsense*; we could not encounter *damned nonsense*.

---

[2]Albert P. Weiss, A theoretical basis of human behavior, Columbus, Ohio; R. G. Adams and Company, 1925, pp. 346-347.

[3]New York: The Macmillan Company, 1929, p. 345.

The significance of Eddington's statement centers around the word *reach*. From the present point of view, he seems to be saying that we cannot reach the highest forms of adaptive behavior, such as complex problem solution (rational behavior) and certain complex forms of social behavior involving the implicit verbal coercion of the behavior of the individual (moral behavior) if we start out merely with æther and electrons; we must begin with something non-physical, or psychic — presumably consciousness.

Thus the issue is joined. We are presented with the paradox of Eddington, the physicist, apparently insisting that the higher forms of behavior are at bottom non-physical, whereas Weiss, the psychologist, insists that they are fundamentally non-psychological!

But what, exactly, is the issue? Is it, for example, a difference as to an ordinary matter of observed fact? Do Eddington and those who share his view claim to have made certain observations which are in conflict with a corresponding set of observations supposed to have been made by Weiss and those with a mechanistic leaning? The dispute involves nothing of this nature. It is clear that the controversy is definitely a theoretical one. Eddington seems to be implying that we *can not* reach a sound theory of rational, purposive and moral behavior if we set out with nothing but æther and electrons. Weiss is saying, by implication, that a sound theory of such behavior *can* be reached by setting out with nothing but electrons and protons.

THE METHODOLOGY OF SCIENTIFIC THEORY DIFFERENTIATED FROM THAT OF PHILOSOPHICAL SPECULATION

Having located definitely in the field of theory the contrasted views represented in a general way by Weiss and Eddington, we face at once the critical question of whether the problem lies within the range of the operation of scientific methodology. If it does, what is that methodology? How is it to be applied to the question before us in a way which will avoid the interminable wrangles and philosophical futilities so long associated with the mind-body problem? It will be necessary to go into the matter of methodology rather thoroughly, in part because of its central importance for our present problem, but in part also because of the widespread misconceptions regarding it due to our early associations with philosophy. With the question of methodology clarified we shall return to Weiss and Eddington in the hope of demonstrating its concrete application.

The essential characteristics of a sound scientific theoretical system, as contrasted with ordinary philosophical speculation, may be briefly summarized under three heads:

1. A satisfactory scientific theory should begin wtih a set of explicitly stated postulates accompanied by specific or 'operational' definitions of the critical terms employed.

2. From these postulates there should be deduced by the most rigorous logic possible under the circumstances, a series of interlocking theorems covering the major concrete phenomena of the field in question.

3. The statements in the theorems should agree in detail with the observationally known facts of the discipline under consideration. If the theorems agree with the observed facts, the system is probably true; if they disagree, the system is false. If it is impossible to tell whether the theorems of a system agree with the facts or not, the system is neither true nor false; scientifically considered, it is meaningless.

Since concrete example is more illuminating and more convincing than abstract statement, there is reproduced below a small scientific theoretical system in which an attempt has been made to conform to the above principles. There may be found . . . a number of definitions, which are followed . . . by six postulates. The system concludes with a series of thirteen theorems . . . each derived from the postulates by a process of reasoning analogous to that ordinarily employed in geometry.

At first sight the formal characteristics of scientific theory look very much like those of philosophical speculation and even of ordinary argumentation, from which philosophical speculation can scarcely be distinguished. At their best, both scientific theory and philosophical speculation set out from explicit postulates; both have definitions of critical terms; both have interlocking theorems derived by meticulous logic. Consider, for example, Spinoza's 'Ethic,' a philosophical work of the better sort. This has all of the above characteristics in almost exactly the same form as the miniature scientific system which is presented below. Where, then, lie the great difference and superiority of the scientific procedure?

The answer, while extending into many complex details, rests upon a single fundamental principle. The difference is that *in philosophical speculation there is no possibility of comparing a theorem with the results of direct observation.* An obvious example of this impossibility is seen in Spinoza's famous pantheistic theorem, Proposition XIV, from Part One of his 'Ethic':

Besides God no substance can be, nor can be conceived.

It is difficult to imagine subjecting such a theorem as that to an observational test.

Consider, by way of contrast, a really scientific procedure, one carried out by Galileo at about the same time that Spinoza was writing. The Copernican hypothesis concerning the nature of the solar system was then in violent dispute. From this hypothesis, together with a few familiar principles concerning the behavior of light, it follows logically as a theorem that the planet Venus, like the moon, should show the crescent and all the other stages between the full and dark phases. Presumably led by this deduction, Galileo, with a telescope of his own construction, made the necessary observations on Venus and found the phases exactly as demanded by the theorem. Here we have the indispensable observational check demanded by science but lacking in philosophy.

But why, it will be asked, is it so imperative to have an observational check on the theorems of a system if the system is to merit serious consideration by scientists? To answer this question adequately it will be necessary to consider in a little detail the characteristics of postulates, the procedure in selecting them, and the methodology of their substantiation.

It is important to note at the outset that in scientific theory postulates tend to be of two kinds. First, there are postulates which are mere matters of fact; *i.e.*, they are matters of relatively simple and direct observation. Second, there are postulates which by their nature cannot conceivably be matters of direct observation. The classical investigation of Galileo just considered contains examples of both types. The principles of light and shadow upon which lunar and planetary phases depend are obviously matters of ordinary, everyday, direct terrestrial observation, and so represent postulates of the first type. On the other hand, the Copernican hypothesis as to the relative movements of the several components of the solar system is not susceptible to direct observation, and so represents postulates of the second type.

In scientific theory, owing to the continuous checking of theorems arived at deductively against the results of direct observation, both types of postulates are constantly receiving *indirect* verification or refutation. Thus postulates capable of the direct approach are susceptible of two independent kinds of test, the direct and the indirect. But the continuous indirect test is of special importance for the postulates incapable of the direct approach. Were it not for this they would be subject to no observational verification at all, and scientific theory would in this respect have no more safeguard against erroneous basic assumptions than has philosophical speculation. Thus Galileo's brilliant observations of the phases of Venus not only gave the scientific world some new facts but, of far greater importance, they substantiated in a convincing, though indirect, manner the fundamental Copernican hypothesis.[4]

Whenever a theorem fails to check with the relevant facts, the postulates which gave rise to it must be ruthlessly revised until agreement is reached. If agreement cannot be attained, the system must be abandoned. In this constant revision there is a definite tendency to choose and formulate the postulates in a way which will make them yield the deductions desired. Such a procedure involves an obvious element of circularity. This is particularly the case where the system is small and where the postulates are purely symbolic constructs or inventions and therefore not subject to direct investigation. Even so, the choice of postulates to fit the facts is methodologically legitimate and, upon the whole, desirable. One important reason for this is that a postulate or hypothesis so arrived at may lead to a *direct,* experimental confirmation in case it is capable of the direct

---

[4]Many persons have been puzzled by the paradox that in science a deduction frequently sets out with postulates which are by no means securely established, whereas in ordinary argumentation there is the greatest insistence upon the certainty of the premises upon which the argument is based. The explanation of this paradox lies largely in the difference of objective in the two cases. Argument ordinarily seeks to convince by a deductive procedure of something which under the circumstances is not directly observable; otherwise there would be no point in performing the deduction. It is clear that if the person to whom the argument is directed does not agree with the premises he will not agree with the conclusion and the whole procedure will be futile. In science, on the other hand, the situation may be almost completely reversed; the conclusion (or theorem) may be known observationally at the outset, but the premises (or postulates) may at first be little more than conjectures and the logical process quite circular. For the methodology of resolving this circularity, see below.

approach.[5] In such an event, of course, all circularity disappears.

But if the system is truly scientific in nature, the circularity just considered is only a temporary phase even when one or more of the postulates are insusceptible to direct investigation. It is precisely in this connection that scientific method shows its incomparable superiority over philosophical speculation. A sound set of postulates should lead to the deduction of theorems representing phenomena never previously investigated quite as logically as of theorems representing phenomena already known when the postulates were formulated. When a theorem representing novel phenomena receives direct observational confirmation there is no possibility of circularity; as a consequence the probability that the postulates directly involved are sound is very definitely increased.[6] Thus the fact that Venus shows lunar phases could not have been known to Copernicus when he formulated his epoch-making hypothesis, because the telescope had not yet been invented. Accordingly their discovery by

---

[5]From the experimental point of view the process of developing systematic theory thus leads in two directions. On one hand it leads to the investigation of theorems derived from postulates of the system, and on the other to the direct investigation of postulates which appear to be required as assumptions for the deductive explanation of facts already known. Since phenomena of the latter type are fundamental in a strict sense, their investigation is of the highest significance. A background of systematic theory thus often directly suggests fundamental investigations which might be indefinitely delayed under the usual procedure of random, and even of systematic, exploration.

[6]A single unequivocal disagreement between a theorem and observed fact is sufficient to assure the incorrectness of at least one of the postulates involved. But even if the postulates of a system generate a very long series of theorems which are subsequently confirmed without exception, each new confirmation merely adds to the *probability* of the truth of such postulates as are incapable of direct observational test. Apparently this indirect evidence never reaches the crisp certainty of a deductive conclusion in which the postulates are directly established, except in the highly improbable situation where all the possible deductions involving a given postulate have been tested with positive results. According to the theory of chance, the larger the sample from this possible total which has been tried and found without exception to be positive, the greater the probability that a new deduction based on the same set of postulates will be confirmed when tested.

830

Galileo constituted strong positive evidence of the essential soundness of the Copernican hypothesis regarded as a postulate. This classical example of the observational but indirect confirmation of the soundness of postulates will serve as a fitting conclusion for our general consideration of theoretical methodology.

The Recognized Scientific Methodology Has Not Been Applied To The Behavior Controversy

We turn now to the question of whether the recognized scientific methodology is really applicable to a resolution of the controversy concerning the basic nature of adaptive behavior. At first glance the prospect is reassuring. It becomes quite clear, for example, what Weiss and Eddington should have done to substantiate their claims. They should have exhibited, as strict logical deductions from explicitly stated postulates, a series of theorems corresponding in detail to the concrete manifestations of the higher forms of human behavior. Then, and only then, they might proceed to the examination of the postulates of such system. To substantiate his position Weiss would have to show that these postulates concern essentially the behavior of electrons, protons, etc.; and Eddington to support his assertions would need to show that the postulates of a successful system are primarily phenomena of consciousness.[7] The formal application of the methodology is thus quite clear and specific.

But here we meet an amazing paradox. In spite of the calm assurance of Weiss as to the truth of his statement that purposive behavior is at bottom physical, we find that he neither presents nor cites such a system. Indeed, he

---

[7]It is here assumed as highly probable that if the two approaches are strictly in conflict, only one would be successful. In the course of the development of scientific theoretical systems, however, it is to be expected that during the early stages several different systems may present appreciable evidences of success. See The conflicting psychologies of learning—A way out, PSYCHOL. REV., 42, 1936; especially pp. 514-515.

seems to be quite oblivious of such a necessity. Turning to Eddington, we find exactly the same paradoxical situation. Notwithstanding his positive, even emphatic, implications that moral behavior must be conscious or psychic in its ultimate nature, we find him neither presenting nor citing a theoretical system of any kind, much less one derived from psychic or conscious postulates. This paradox is particularly astonishing in the case of Eddington because he has been active in the field of physical theory and should, therefore, be sophisticated regarding the essential methodology involved in scientific theory in general. Surely the same logic which demands strict deduction from explicitly stated postulates in physical theory demands it for the theory of adaptive and moral behavior. And surely if we demand it of a mechanistic theory of the more recondite forms of human behavior, as Eddington seems emphatically to do, there is no hocus-pocus whereby a psychic view of such behavior may be maintained without the same substantial foundation.

A Demonstration of the Application of Theoretical Methodology to Adaptive Behavior

But if neither Weiss nor Eddington, nor any other writer in this field, has been able to bring forward the indispensable systematic theory as a prerequisite of the logical right to express a valid conclusion concerning the ultimate nature of higher adaptive behavior, may this not mean that the attainment of such a system is impossible, and that, consequently, the problem still remains in the realm of philosophical speculation? There is reason to believe that this is not the case. The ground for optimism lies in part in the small theoretical system which is presented below. . . .

By way of introduction to the system we may begin with the consideration of Theorem I. . . . In brief, this theorem purports to show that Pavlov's conditioned reaction and the stimuli-response 'bonds' resulting from Thorndike's so-called 'law of effect' are in reality special cases of the operation of a single set of principles. The major principle involved is given in Postulate 2. Briefly, this postulate states the assumption of the present system concerning the conditions under which stimuli and reactions become associated. The difference in the two types of reaction thus turns out to depend merely upon the accidental factor of the temporal relationships of the stimuli to the reactions in the learning situation, coupled with the implication that R_G, which in part serves to mark a reinforcing state of affairs, is also susceptible of being associated with a new stimulus.[8] The automatic, stimulus-response approach thus exemplified is characteristic of the remainder of the system.

A consideration of Theorem II will serve still further as an orientation to the system before us. We find this theorem stating that both *correct* and *incorrect* reaction may be set up by the conditioning or associative process just referred to. Our chief interest in this theorem, as an introduction to the system, concerns the question of whether the terms 'correct' and 'incorrect' can have any meaning when they refer to reaction tendencies which are the result of a purely automatic process of association such as that presented by Postulate 2. It is believed that they have a very definite meaning. Definitions 7 and 8 state in effect that correctness or incorrectness is determined by whether the reaction tendency under given conditions is, or is not, subject to experimental extinction. Such purely objective or behavioral definitions of numerous terms commonly thought of as applying exclusively to experience, as distinguished from action, are characteristic of the entire system.

---

[8] In effect this deduction purports to show that the Pavlovian conditioned reflex is a special case under Thorndike's 'law of effect,' though Thorndike might not recognize his favorite principle as formulated in Postulate 2. For a fuller but less formal discussion of this point see *Psychol. Bull.*, 1935, 32, 817-822.

With this general orientation we may proceed to the theorems more specifically concerned with adaptive behavior. The proof of the first of these, Theorem III, shows that under certain circumstances organisms will repeatedly and successively make the same incorrect reaction. At first sight this may seem like a most commonplace outcome. However, when considered in the light of the definition of correctness given above it is evident that this theorem differs radically from what might be deduced concerning the behavior of a raindrop or a pebble moving in a gravitational field.[9]

Theorem IV states that after making one or more incorrect reactions an organism will spontaneously vary the response even though the environmental situation remains unchanged. This theorem is noteworthy because it represents the classical case of a form of spontaneity widely assumed, as far back as the Middle Ages, to be inconceivable without presupposing consciousness.

Theorem V states that when an organism originally has both correct and incorrect excitatory tendencies evoked by a single stimulus situation, the correct tendency will at length be automatically selected in preference to stronger incorrect ones.[10] This theorem, also, has been widely regarded as impossible of derivation without the presupposition of consciousness. Otherwise (so it has been

---

[9]It may be suggested that if water should fall into a hollow cavity on its way to the sea, it might at first oscillate back and forth vigorously and then gradually subside, each oscillation corresponding to an unsuccessful attempt and the gradual cessation, to experimental extinction. In all such cases the discussion as to whether the observed parallelism in behavior represents an essential similarity or a mere superficial analogy requires that both phenomena possess a thorough theoretical basis. *If the two phenomena are deducible from the same postulates and by identical processes of reasoning, they may be regarded as essentially the same, otherwise not.* But if one or both lacks a theoretical basis such a comparison cannot be made and decision can ordinarily not be reached. Much futile argument could be avoided if this principle were generally recognized.

[10]See Simple trial-and-error learning: A study in psychological theory, PSYCHOL. REV., 1930, 37, 241-256; especially pp. 243-250.

argued) how can the organism know which reaction to choose?

Theorem VI represents the deduction that in certain situations the organism will give up seeking, *i.e.*, cease making attempts, and thus fail to perform the correct reaction even when it possesses in its repertoire a perfectly correct excitatory tendency. The substance of this proof lies in the expectation that the extinction resulting from repeated false reactions will cause indirectly a critical weakening of a non-dominant but correct reaction tendency. This theorem is of unusual importance because it represents the deduction of a phenomenon not as yet subjected to experiment. As such it should have special significance as a test of the soundness of the postulates.

With Theorems VII and VIII we turn to the problem of anticipatory or preparatory reactions. The proof of Theorem VII derives, from the principles of the stimulus trace and conditioning (Postulates 1 and 2), the phenomenon of the antedating reaction. The substance of this theorem is that after acquisition, learned reactions tend to appear in advance of the point in the original sequence at which they occurred during the conditioning process.[11] Pursuing this line of reasoning, Theorem VIII shows that in the case of situations demanding flight, such antedating reactions become truly anticipatory or preparatory in the sense of being biologically adaptive to situations which are impending but not yet actual. Thus we arrive at behavioral foresight, a phenomenon evidently of very considerable survival significance in animal life and one frequently regarded as eminently psychic, and inconceivable without consciousness.[12]

Passing over Theorem IX, which lays some necessary

---

[11]See A functional interpretation of the conditioned reflex, Psychol. Rev., 1929, 36, 498-511; especially pp. 507-508.

[12]See Knowledge and purpose as habit mechanisms, Psychol. Rev., 1930, 37, 511-525; especially pp. 514-516.

groundwork, we come to Theorem X. Here we find a deduction of the existence of the fractional anticipatory goal reaction. Of far greater significance from our present point of view, the deduction purports to show that through the action of mere association the fractional anticipatory reaction tends automatically to bring about on later occasions the state of affairs which acted as its reinforcing agent when it was originally set up. For this and other reasons it is believed that the anticipatory goal reaction is the physical basis of expectation, of intent, of purpose, and of guiding ideas.[13]

Theorem XI represents a deduction of the phenomenon of behavioral disappointment[14] as manifested, for example, by Tinklepaugh's monkeys. When these animals had solved a problem with the expectation of one kind of food they would tend to refuse a different kind of food, otherwise acceptable, which had been surreptitiously substituted.[15]

Theorem XII purports to be the deduction of the principle that organisms will strive actively to attain situations or states of affairs which previously have proved to be reinforcing. The automaticity deduced in the proof of Theorem X has here reached a still higher level. This is the capacity to surmount obstacles. But with the ability to attain ends in spite of obstacles comes automatically a genuine freedom (Definition 18), of great biological value but in no way incompatible with determinism.[16]

---

[13]See Goal attraction and directing ideas conceived as habit phenomena, PSYCHOL. REV., 1931, 38, 487-506.

[14]It is to be observed from a comparison of Definitions 9 and 16 that *Disappointment* necessarily presupposes a specific expectation or intent (r_G), whereas *Discouragement* does not.

[15]O. L. Tinklepaugh, An experimental study of representative factors in monkeys, *J. Comp. Psychol.*, 1928, 8, 197-236. See especially p. 224 ff.

[16]An additional element of interest in this theorem is the fact that the fundamental phenomenon of motivation seems to have been derived from the ordinary principle of association (Postulate 2). If this deduction should prove to be sound, it will have reduced the two basic categories of motivation and learning to one, the latter being primary.

Theorem XIII is also derived with the aid of the fractional anticipatory goal reaction. This theorem represents the phenomenon of the adaptive but automatic transfer of learned reactions to situations having, as regards *external* characteristics, nothing whatever in common with the situations in which the habits were originally acquired. This, once more, is a form of adaptive behavior of the greatest survival significance to the organism, and one supposed in certain quarters to be impossible of derivation from associative principles. This is believed to be a low but genuine form of insight and a fairly high order of the 'psychic.'

This concludes the list of formally derived theorems. They have been selected from a series of fifty or so which are concerned with the same subject. None of these theorems 'reaches' Eddington's 'rational man morally responsible.' They accordingly are not offered as a basis for deciding the ultimate nature of such behavior. They *are* offered as a concrete and relevant illustration of the first and most essential step in the methodology which must be followed by Eddington, or anyone else who would determine the basic nature of the higher forms of behavior. Incidentally they are offered as specific evidence that such problems, long regarded as the peculiar domain of philosophy, are now susceptible of attack by a strictly orthodox scientific methodology.

ADAPTIVE BEHAVIOR—A SCIENTIFIC THEORETICAL SYSTEM IN MINIATURE [17]

Definitions

1. A *reinforcing state of affairs* (Postulate 3) is one which acts to give to the stimulus-trace component (Postulate 1) of preceding or following temporal coincidences consisting of a stimulus trace and a reaction, the capacity to evoke the reaction in question (Postulate 2).

---

[17]The author is greatly indebted to Dr. E. H. Rodnick and Mr. D. G. Ellson for detailed criticisms and suggestions during the original preparation of the system which follows. Thanks are also due Professor K. F. Muenzinger, Dr. R. T. Ross, and Dr. R. K. White for criticisms given since the presentation at Hanover.

2. *Experimental extinction* is the weakening of a conditioned excitatory tendancy resulting from frustration or the failure of reinforcement (Postulate 4).

3. *Frustration* is said to occur when the situation is such that the reaction customarily evoked by a stimulus complex cannot take place (Postulate 4).

4. *Seeking* is that behavior of organisms in trial-and-error situations which, upon frustration, is characterized by varied alternative acts all operative under the influence of a common drive (S_D).

5. An *attempt* is a segment of behavior the termination of which is marked by either reinforcement or extinction.

6. A *simple trial-and-error situation* is one which presents to an organism a stimulus complex which tends to give rise to multiple reaction tendencies which are mutually incompatible, one or more of them being susceptible to reinforcement and one or more of them not being so susceptible.

7. A *correct* or 'right' reaction is a behavior sequence which results in reinforcement.

8. An *incorrect* or 'wrong' reaction is a behavior sequence which results in experimental extinction.

9. *Discouragement* is the diminution in the power of one excitatory tendency to evoke its normal reaction, this diminution resulting from one or more unsuccessful attempts involving a second reaction.

10. A behavior sequence is said to be *directed* to the attainment of a particular state of affairs when there appears throughout the sequence a characteristic component (r_G) of the action (R_G) closely associated with the state of affairs in question and this component action (r_G) as a stimulus tends to evoke an action sequence leading to the total reaction (R_G) of which the component constitutes a part.

11. Striving is that behavior of organisms which, upon frustration, displays varied alternative action sequences, all *directed* by an intent (r_G) to the attainment of the same reinforcing state of affairs.

12. A *goal* is the reinforcing state of affairs towards the attainment of which a behavior sequence of an organism may be directed by its intent (r_G).

13. An organism is said to *anticipate* a state of affairs when there is active throughout the behavior sequence leading to the state of affairs a fractional component (r_G) of the action associated with the state of affairs in question.

14. *Success* is the culmination of striving which is characterized by the occurrence of the full reaction (R_G) of which the fractional anticipatory component (r_G) is a part.

15. *Failure* is the culmination of striving which is characterized by the lack of the enactment of the full reaction (R_G) of which the fractional component (r_G) is a part.

16. *Disappointment* is the diminution in the power of one reinforcing situation to evoke appropriate consummatory reaction, this diminution (Postulate 4) resulting from the failure of a second reaction sequence directed (by an intent, or r_G) to a different reinforcing situation from that to which the first was directed, both being based on the same drive (S_D).

17. A *habit-family hierarchy* consists of a number of habitual behavior sequences having in common the initial stimulus situation and the final reinforcing state of affairs.

18. *Individual freedom* of behavior, so far as it exists, consists in the absence of external restraint.

Postulates

1. The adequate stimulation of a sense organ initiates within the organism a neural reverberation which persists for some time after the stimulus has ceased to act, the absolute amount of the reverberation diminishing progressively to zero but at a progressively slower rate. (Stimulus trace.)

2. When a reaction and a given segment of a stimulus-trace (Postulate 1) repeatedly occur simultaneously and this coincidence occurs during the action of a drive (S_D) and temporally close to a reinforcing state of affairs (Definition 1), this and stronger segments of the stimulus trace tend progressively to acquire capacity to evoke the reaction, the strength of the association thus acquired manifesting a negatively accelerated diminution with distance of the associates from the reinforcing state of affairs. (Positive association.)

3. A characteristic stimulus-reaction combination ($S_G \text{ ---} \rightarrow R_G$) always marks reinforcing states of affairs (Definition 1). The particular stimulus-response combination marking the reinforcing state of affairs in the case of specific drives is determined empirically, *i.e.*, by observation and experiment. (Mark of reinforcing state of affairs.)

4. When a stimulus evokes a conditioned (associative) reaction (Postulate 2) and this event does not occur within the range of the reinforcing state of affairs (Definition 1 and Postulate 3), or when an excitatory tendency in a behavior sequence encounters a situation which makes the execution of the act impossible (Definition 3), the excitatory tendency in question undergoes a diminution in strength with a limit below the reaction threshold (Definition 2), this diminution extending in considerable part to other excitatory tendencies which may be operative at the same time or for some time thereafter. (Negative association or experimental extinction.)

839

5. The strength of any given increment of either positive or negative association (Postulates 2 and 3) diminishes with the passage of time, and the portion remaining shows a progressively greater resistance to disintegration with the increase in time since its acquisition, a certain proportion of each increment being permanent. (Negative retention or forgetting.)

6. Each reaction of an organism gives rise to a more or less characteristic internal stimulus. (Internal stimulation.)

S = an adequate stimulus together with the resulting trace (Postulate 1).

S_D = the stimulus associated with a drive, such as hunger.

S_G = the stimulus associated with the goal or reinforcing state of affairs.

s = an internal stimulus resulting from a reaction.

R = a reaction.

R_G = the reaction associated with the goal or reinforcing state of affairs.

r_G = a fractional component of the goal reaction.

— — → = excitatory tendency from stimulus to reaction.

→ = causal connection of a non-stimulus-reaction nature.

... = a continuation or persistence of a process, as of a drive

Distance from left to right represents the passage of time.

Theorems

I

The Pavlovian conditioned reaction and the Thorndikian associative reaction are special cases of the operation of the same principles of learning.

1. Suppose that in the neighborhood of a sensitive organism stimuli S_G and S_G occur in close succession, that these stimuli in conjunction with the drive (S_D) evoke reactions R_G and R_G respectively, that S_m coincides in time with S_G while S_n coincides in time with S_G, and that (Postulate 1) the stimulus trace of S_m extends to R_G, and the stimulus trace of S_n extends to R_G.

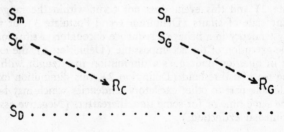

2. From (1) and Postulate 1, it follows that one phase of the stimulus trace of S_m will coincide with R_o and one phase of the stimulus trace of S_n will coincide with R_o.

3. Now, by Postulate 3, the combination $S_o - - - \rightarrow R_o$ marks a reinforcing state of affairs.

4. From (1), (2), (3), and Postulate 2 it follows, among other things, that the trace of S_n will become conditioned to R_o, and the trace of S_m will be conditioned to R_o, yielding the following excitatory tendencies:

$$S_m - - - \rightarrow R_o$$
$$S_n - - - \rightarrow R_o$$

5. But by (3) and (4) the reaction of the newly acquired excitatory tendency $S_n - - - \rightarrow R_o$ is that intimately associated with the reinforcing state of affairs, which identifies it as a conditioned reaction of the Pavlovian type.

6. On the other hand, by (3) and (4) the reaction of the excitatory tendency $S_m - - - \rightarrow R_o$ is a reaction distinct from that of the reinforcing state of affairs, which identifies it as an associative reaction of the Thorndikian type.

7. By (5) and (6) both the Pavlovian and the Thorndikian types of reaction have been derived from (1), (2), (3), and (4) jointly, and these in turn from the same principles of learning (Postulates 1, 2, 3).

8. From (7) the theorem follows.

Q.E.D.

II

Both correct (right) and incorrect (wrong) reactions may be set up by the conditioning (associative) process.

1. Let it be supposed that an organism capable of acquiring associative reactions (Postulate 2) is, a number of times, stimulated simultaneously by S_A, S_B, S_C, and S_D; that S_C evokes reaction R_C; that the stimulus trace (Postulate 1) of S_A and S_B extend as far as R_C; that the object represented by S_B, in conjunction with act R_C, produces (causes) in the external world the event yielding the stimulus S_G; and finally that S_G evokes R_G.

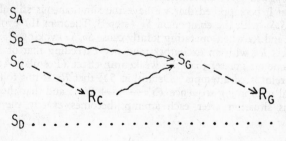

841

2. By Postulate 3, S_G — — → R_G marks a reinforcing state of affairs.

3. From (1), (2), and Postulates 1 and 2, it follows that among other associative tendencies the following must be kept up:

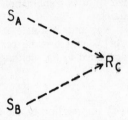

4. Now suppose that at a later time, S_B *alone* should evoke R_C. It follows from (1) that S_B, in conjunction with R_C, will cause to occur the event in the external world which will yield the stimulus S_G which, in turn, will evoke R_G.

5. But, once more, by Postulate 3, S_G — — → R_G marks a reinforcing state of affairs from which it follows that under the special new conditions of (4) the reaction tendency S_B — — → R_C will still be reinforced.

6. From (5) and Definition 7 it follows that S_B — — → R_C must be a correct or 'right' reaction.

7. Let us suppose, on the other hand, that S_A *alone* should evoke R_C. It follows from (1) that the external event giving rise to S_G will not occur (S_B being absent), and the excitatory tendency S_A — — → R_C will not be reinforced and, by Postulate 4, will suffer experimental extinction.

8. From (7) and Definition 8 it follows that S_A — — → R_C will be an incorrect or 'wrong' reaction.

9. From (6) and (8) the theorem follows.

Q.E.D.

III

Simple trial-and-error situations may arise in which the organism will make repeated incorrect reactions.

1. Let it be supposed that we have the simultaneous stimulus situation $S_T S_B S_D$ with the component S_B (step 3, Theorem II) evoking R_C; that S_B and R_C when operating jointly cause S_G, S_G evoking R_G, whereas S_T evokes R_V with an excitatory tendency exceeding that of S_B to R_C by an amount greater than the weakening effect (Postulate 4) of several unreinforced attempts (Definition 5); that R_V is not followed by its usual reinforcing sequence (S'_G — — → R'_G); and that the external stimulus situation after each attempt becomes exactly the same as before.

842

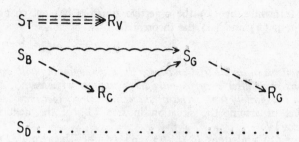

2. From (1) it follows that reaction R_V will take place at once after the organism encounters the compound stimulus $S_T S_B S_D$.

3. Now, by (1) the situation is such that R_V cannot be followed by its accustomed reinforcing sequence, so that this behavior sequence must be interrupted.

4. From (3) and Postulate 4, the excitatory tendency from S_T to R_V will be weakened by experimental extinction.

5. By (4) and Definition 8, R_V is an incorrect reaction.

6. By (1) and (2) the stimulus situation after the first R_V reaction must be the same as the beginning, and the excitatory tendency to R_V must still be considerably in excess of that to R_C, from which it follows that R_V will occur a second time, and so on.

7. But, by (2), we have a first reaction (R_V), which, by (5) is incorrect and by (6) we have a repetition of this incorrect reaction, from which the theorem follows.

Q.E.D.

IV

Organisms in simple trial-and-error situations may manifest spontaneous variability of reaction, the objective situation remaining constant.

1. Suppose the situation in (1) of Theorem III with the additional assumption that excitatory tendency $S_B \text{------} \rightarrow R_C$ shall be strong enough to resist all generalized inhibitory effects (Postulate 4) sufficiently to escape becoming subliminal.

2. By (1) and Theorem III, it follows that reaction R_V will take place repeatedly.

3. By (1) and (2), reaction $S_T \text{------} \rightarrow R_V$ will not be followed by reinforcement (neither $S'_G \text{------} \rightarrow R'_G$ nor $S_G \frown \frown \rightarrow R_C$), which failure (Postulate 4) will progressively weaken the tendency to R_V.

4. From (1) and (3) it follows that the reaction tendency to R_V must finally become weaker than that to R_C, at which point the stimulus complex $S_T S_B S_D$ will evoke reaction R_C.

5. But the shift from reaction R_V (2) to R_C (4) constitutes a variability of reaction.

843

6. Meanwhile, by (1) the objective situation has not changed.

7. From (5) and (6) the theorem follows.

Q.E.D.

V

Organisms in simple trial-and-error situation beginning with erroneous reactions may, after a sufficiently large number of attempts, come to give an indefinitely long series of successive correct reactions.

1. Let us assume the situation in step (1) of the deduction of Theorem IV.

2. By (1) and steps (2), (3), and (4) of Theorem IV, reaction tendency R_V will be progressively weakened by extinction until it is below the level of R_0, when the latter will take place.

3. Moreover, by (1), R_0 in conjunction with S_B causes S_G; and S_G evokes R_0 which, by Postulate 3, marks a reinforcing state of affairs.

4. It follows from (2), (3), and Postulate 2 that the excitatory tendency $S_B \text{---} \to R_0$ will be reinforced, and therefore strengthened.

5. But a certain amount of time must elapse while reaction R_0 is taking place; by Postulate 5, this time must permit a certain amount of spontaneous recovery from experimental extinction on the part of R_V.

6. Now, the rate of the spontaneous recovery of R_V (5) may be either (*A*) more rapid than the gain in strength of R_0 through the latter's reinforcement, or (*B*) it may be less rapid, or (*C*) the two processes may take place at the same rate. If it is less rapid, or if the two processes take place at the same rate, R_0 will maintain its dominance, thus giving an indefinitely long series of correct reactions (Definition 7); from which the theorem follows.

7. But suppose, on the other hand, that the rate of the spontaneous recovery of R_V *from its* experimental extinction is faster than the gain in strength of R_0 through its reinforcement (6). It follows that on this alternative R_V must again become dominant.

8. From (7) it follows by reasoning analogous to that in (2) that R_V will occur repeatedly until depressed by further experimental extinction below the strength of R_0 when the latter will again occur, to be further reinforced, and so on.

9. Now it follows from (4) and (8) together with Postulate 5, that after each complete cycle of reversal of R_V and R_0, the former will retain a certain amount of its weakening which will not yield to spontaneous recovery and the latter will retain a certain amount of the strengthening which will not yield to forgetting.

10. It follows from (9) that if the cyclical alternation were to go on indefinitely, the tendency to R_V must be weakened to zero and that to R_0 must be strengthened to its maximum.

11. It is evident from (10) that at some point in the progressive

shift in the basic strengths of R_V and R_O the two movements must cross, at which point R_O will be permanently dominant over R_V irrespective of spontaneous recovery or forgetting, and there will then follow an indefinitely long series of successive correct reactions.

12. From (6) and (11) the theorem follows.

Q.E.D.

VI

In simple trial-and-error learning situations, failure of final correct reaction will, under certain conditions, result from discontinued effort.

1. Suppose the situation in (1) of Theorem III except that the excitatory tendency $S_B \text{---} \to R_O$ is at the outset only a little above the reaction threshold.

2. From (1) and Theorem III, false reaction R_V will be made repeatedly.

3. By (1) and (2), reaction tendency $S_T \text{---} \to R_V$ will not be followed by reinforcement, which failure (by Postulate 4) will, if not interrupted, gradually weaken $S_T \text{---} \to R_V$ to zero.

4. By (3) and Postulate 4, the weakening of $S_T \text{---} \to R_V$ will extend in considerable part to $S_B \text{---} \to R_O$.

5. Now, by (1) the super-threshold margin of strength of $S_B \text{---} \to R_O$ may be smaller than any assigned finite value, from which it follows that it may be smaller than the depressing effects (4) arising from the extinction of $S_T \text{---} \to R_V$.

6. It follows from (5) that before $S_T \text{---} \to R_V$ may be extinguished beneath the level of $S_B \text{---} \to R_O$ the latter will also have been depressed below the reaction threshold so that when $S_T \text{---} \to R_V$ reaches zero and causes action, the potentially correct reaction tendency, $S_B \text{---} \to R_O$, will also be unable to function even though without any competition whatever.

7. But the depression of both the tendency to R_V and R_O as shown in (6) will bring about a cessation of attempts (Definition 5), the latter of which (1) would have been a correct reaction (Definition 7).

8. From (3), (4), and (7) the theorem follows.

Q.E.D.

Corollary I.

Organisms capable of acquiring competing excitatory tendencies will manifest discouragement.

This follows directly from Theorem VI and Definition 9.

VII

Reactions conditioned to a late segment of a stimulus trace will subsequently occur as antedating reactions.

1. Suppose that stimulus S_B precedes stimulus S_O by several times the latency of conditioned reactions; that S_C evokes reaction R_C; that the

845

stimulus trace of S_B extends as far as R_G; that the physical event responsible for S_G, jointly with reaction R_C, causes S_G; that S_G evokes R_G; and that S_D begins at S_C and persists throughout the remainder of the process.

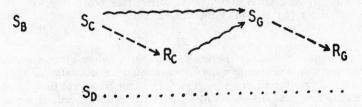

2. From (1) and Postulate 1, a segment of the stimulus trace initiated by S_B will coincide with R_C.

3. By (1) and Postulate 3, $S_G \text{---} \rightarrow R_G$ marks a reinforcing state of affairs and follows the coincidence of R_C with the trace of S_B.

4. By (2), (3), and Postulate 2, reaction R_C will become conditioned to a late coinciding segment of the trace of stimulus S_B, i.e., that portion which coincides temporally with R_C.

5. Now, by Postulate 1, stimulus trace S_B at the point of the onset of the stimulus is substantially the same as the segment conditioned to R_C, except that it is stronger.

6. From (5) and Postulate 2 it follows that once R_C has been conditioned to a late segment of the trace of stimulus S_B with a supraliminal strength, the reaction will be evoked by any portion of the same trace which is as strong as, or stronger than, the segment conditioned.

7. But since, by (1), the initial portion of the stimulus trace of S_B will occur several times the latency of such a reaction in advance of the original point of the occurrence of R_C, it follows from (5) and (6) that after conditioning, R_C will be evoked in advance of the point of its original occurrence.

8. From (7) the theorem follows.

Q.E.D.

VIII

Organisms capable of acquiring trace conditioned reactions will be able to execute successful defense reactions.

1. Let it be supposed that an organism capable of acquiring trace conditioned reaction is stimulated by S_B, that the external world event responsible for S_B initiates a causal sequence several times the length of a conditioned reaction latency, which sequence terminates in S_G and S_D, the two latter jointly constituting an injury and evoking R_G, a flight reaction, which terminates their impact on the organism; and that the stimulus trace of S_B reaches well beyond the point at which R_G occurs.

846

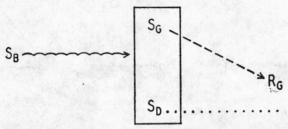

2. From (1) and Postulates 1 and 2 it follows that R_G will be conditioned to the trace of S_B.

3. From (1), (2), and Theorem VII it follows that if S_B occurs on a later occasion, reaction R_G will occur in advance of situation S_GS_D, which if it impinges on the organism, will be injurious.

4. But, by (1), R_G is a flight reaction. It follows from (3) that the organism will not be present when the situation otherwise giving rise to S_GS_D occurs and so will escape the injury, thus:

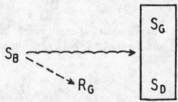

5. From (1) and (4) the theorem follows.

Q.E.D.

IX

In stable behavior sequences terminating in reinforcement, each reaction, in general, becomes conditioned (A) to the proprioceptive stimulus arising from the action immediately preceding it, and (B) to the drive stimulus (S_D), each with an intensity diminishing according to a negatively accelerated rate with distance from the reinforcing state of affairs.

1. Let it be supposed that there impinges on an organism a uniform sequence of external stimuli S_1, S_2, S_3, etc.; that these stimuli evoke in the organism reactions R_1, R_2, R_3, etc.; that these reactions produce (Postulate 6) proprioceptive stimuli s_1, s_2, s_3, etc.; that R_3 by an external causal sequence produces a state of affairs which includes S_G; that S_G evokes R_G; that the combination $S_G \text{---} \rightarrow R_G$ marks (Postulate 3) a reinforcing state of affairs; and that throughout the sequence there occurs the persisting drive stimulus S_D.

847

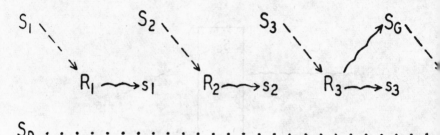

S_D · · · · · · · · · · · · · · · · · ·

2. By Postulates 1 and 2 the situation supposed in (1) will give rise to an association between each proprioceptive stimulus and the reaction immediately following thus:

$$s_1 \dashrightarrow R_2$$
$$s_2 \dashrightarrow R_3$$
$$s_3 \dashrightarrow R_G$$

3. Also, since by (1) S_D occurs at every point throughout the series, it follows from (1) and Postulate 2 that S_D will be conditioned to every reaction in the series, thus:

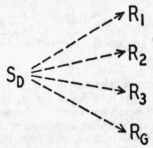

4. By (2) and Postulate 2, $s_3 \dashrightarrow R_G > s_2 \dashrightarrow R_3 > s_1 \dashrightarrow R_2$

and $(s_3 \dashrightarrow R_G) - (s_2 \dashrightarrow R_3) > (s_2 \dashrightarrow R_3) - (s_1 \dashrightarrow R_2)$

5. Also by (3) and Postulate 2, $S_D \dashrightarrow R_G > S_D \dashrightarrow R_3 > S_D \dashrightarrow R_2 > S_D -$

and $(S_D \dashrightarrow R_G) - (S_D \dashrightarrow R_3) > (S_D \dashrightarrow R_3) - (S_D \dashrightarrow R_2) > (S_D \dashrightarrow R_2) - (S_D \dashrightarrow R$

848

6. But the expressions in (4) and (5) represent negatively accelerated excitatory gradients diminishing with distance from the reinforcing state of affairs.

7. From (2), (3), and (6) the theorem follows.

X   Q.E.D.

A fractional anticipatory goal reaction as a stimulus will tend to bring about the reinforcing state of affairs with which the total goal reaction, of which it is a constitutent part, is associated.

1. Suppose the situation in (1) of Theorem IX with the additional assumption that the goal reaction (R_G) is composed of two components, a major one which cannot take place without the aid of the object represented by S_G and which is incompatible with the several acts of the sequence preceding it, and a minor one (r_G) which is not mechanically dependent on S_G and which may take place simultaneously with the antecedent reactions of the series.

2. Now, by Theorem IX, S_D is conditioned to R_G and, since by (1) r_G is a constituent part of R_G, S_D is also conditioned to r_G.

3. Since, by (1), S_D occurs throughout the series, it follows that it will evoke r_G at all points in the behavior sequence R_1, R_2, R_3, etc.

4. From (3) and Postulates 1 and 6 it follows that the trace of the internal stimulus produced by r_G, *i.e.*, s_G, will tend to occur in conjunction with all the reactions of the sequence R_1, R_2, R_3, etc.

5. Now, each time the situation represented in (4) occurs it is followed (1) by the reinforcing state of affairs marked by $S_G \relbar\relbar\longrightarrow R_G$, from which it follows by Postulate 2 that s_G will ultimately become associated with all of the reactions of the sequence, thus: very much as in the case of S_D (Theorem IX).

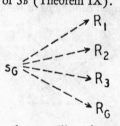

6. From (5) it follows that s_G will tend, on subsequent occasions, to bring about reactions R_1, R_2, R_3. By (1), R_3 causes S_G, and S_G evokes R_G.

7. But by (1), r_G is a constituent part of R_G which, with its S_G, marks (*i.e.*, is associated with) the reinforcing state of affairs.

8. But if (6 and 7) r_G, through the action of s_G, brings about the inevitable mark of its reinforcing state of affairs ($S_G \relbar\relbar\longrightarrow R_G$), it must at the same time bring about the reinforcing state of affairs itself.

9. From (7) and (8) the theorem follows.

Q.E.D.

849

XI

Organisms capable of acquiring functionally potent anticipatory reactions intimately associated with the reinforcing state of affairs, will manifest a weakened tendency to the consummatory reaction if at the completion of the action sequence, the state of affairs then presented does not permit the occurrence of the complete reaction of which the anticipatory reaction is a constituent part.

1. Suppose that an organism which has been in a situation such as (1) in Theorem IX later finds itself in the same situation with the exception that the terminal conditions, instead of permitting reaction $S_G ———→ R_G$, permit a different reaction, $S'_G \frown \frown → R'_G$, which is appropriate to the same drive (S_D) and is in the repertoire of the organism in question but has a strength only slightly above the reaction threshold.

2. By step (1) of the proof of Theorem IX, together with Theorem IX itself, the customary stimulus complex giving rise to the terminal reaction must be:

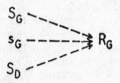

3. Now, by (1) and Theorem IX, the s_G of (2) represents r_G, and r_G (Definition 13) is both a reaction anticipatory of, and a fractional component of, R_G.

4. On the other hand, by (1), (2), and Theorem IX, the excitatory tendencies under the changed conditions of the present theorem will be:

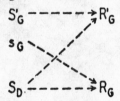

5. From (1) and (4) it follows that the excitatory tendencies leading to R_G must be frustrated (Definition 3) which (by Postulate 4) will set up experimental extinction at the point in question.

6. From (5) and Postulate 4 it follows that as a result of the extinction of the tendencies to R_G there will occur simultaneously a weakening of the tendency to reaction R'_G.

7. But by (1) the tendencies to R'_g may be as small as desired and therefore smaller than the generalized extinction of (6), from which it follows that under these circumstances the excitatory tendencies to R'_g will pass below the reaction threshold.

8. From (3) and (7) the theorem follows.

Q.E.D.

Corollary 1.

Organisms will display disappointment.

This follows directly from Theorem XI and Definition 16.

XII

Organisms capable of acquiring anticipatory goal reactions will strive to bring about situations which are reinforcing.

1. Let it be assumed that an organism has acquired a habit-family hierarchy (Definition 17) of two distinct action sequences of the type described in (1) of Theorem X, both originating in the external stimulus situation S_1, terminating in the reinforcing situation S_g — — $\rightarrow R_g$ and associated with the drive S_D; that the initial acts of one of the sequences are R_1, R_{11}, etc., and those of the other are R_1, R_2, etc.; that the excitatory tendency initiating the sequence beginning with R_1 is dominant over that beginning with R_1, but that the tendency to R_1 is far enough above the reaction threshold to survive the weakening effect which would result (Postulate 4) from the frustration of the tendency to R_1.

2. Now suppose that an obstacle is interposed which effectually prevents the completion of R_1 and the remainder of that sequence (1). It follows from Postulate 4 that this excitatory tendency will suffer extinction, with no limit above zero.

3. From (1) and (2) it follows that the sequence beginning with R_1 and terminating with R_g will be executed after the frustration of the excitatory tendency leading to R_1.

4. Now, from (1) it follows by reasoning strictly analogous to steps (2), (3), (4), (5), and (6) of the deduction of Theorem X, that s_g will acquire during the acquisition of the habit-family the tendency to evoke (A) reaction sequence R_1 and all those acts following it in the sequence leading to R_g, and (B) reaction sequence R_1 together with all those leading from it to R_g.

5. From (2), (3), (4), and Definition 10 it follows that under these circumstances the introduction of a barrier will cause the organism to shift from one behavior sequence *directed* to a reinforcing state of affairs to another *directed to the same* reinforcing state of affairs.

6. But by (5) and Definition II, when the interposition of an obstacle leads an organism to choose an alternative action sequence *directed* to the same reinforcing state of affairs as that interrupted by the obstacle,

851

the behavior in question is striving.

7. From (6) the theorem follows.

Corollary 1

Organisms will strive for goals.

This follows directly from Theorem XII and Definitions 11 and 12.

XIII

When an organism has attained a reinforcing state of affairs in a situation which, objectively considered, is totally novel, but by means of a member of a previously established habit-family hierarchy, there may follow without specific practice a tendency to a transfer to the new situation of the behavior tendencies represented by one or another of the remaining members of the habit-family hierarchy in question.

1. Let it be assumed that an organism has acquired a habit-family hierarchy (Definition 17) of two distinct action sequences of the type described in (1) of Theorem X, both originating in the external stimulus situation S_1, terminating in the reinforcing situation $S_G - - \to R_G$ and associated with the drive stimulus S_D; that the initial act of one of the sequences is R_1 and that of the other is R_1.

2. From (1) it follows by reasoning strictly analogous to steps (2), (3), (4), (5), and (6) of the deduction of Theorem X, that s_G will acquire during the acquisition of the habit family the tendency to evoke (*A*) reaction sequence R_1 and all those acts following it in the sequence leading to R_G, and (*B*) reaction sequence R_1 together with all those leading from it to R_G.

3. Now, suppose that this same organism in a novel external situation S'_1 and acting under the same drive stimulus S_D reaches, a few times, by the process of trial and error the reinforcing state of affairs marked by $S_G - - \to R_G$, by an action sequence the same as that beginning with R_1 of one of the members of the habit-family hierarchy of (1).

4. From (3) it follows by reasoning similar to steps (2) and (3) of the deduction leading to Theorem X, that r_G will be present throughout the behavior sequence beginning with S'_1.

5. It follows from (4) that there will be a coincidence of r_G and the stimulus trace of S'_1.

6. Since by (3) the coincidence of the stimulus trace of S'_1 and r_G (5) is followed by $S_G - - \to R_G$, it follows by Postulates 1 and 2 that there will be set up the excitatory tendency $S'_1 - - \to r_G$.

7. From (6), (2), and Postulate 6 it follows that S'_1 will tend to initiate the behavior sequence (omitting internal stimuli after R_1):

$$S'_1 - - \to r_G \rightsquigarrow s_G - - \to R_1 - - \to R_2 - - \to R_3 \rightsquigarrow s_G - - \to R_G$$

and also

$$S'_1 \dashrightarrow r_G \rightsquigarrow s_G \dashrightarrow R_I \dashrightarrow R_{II} \dashrightarrow R_{III} \rightsquigarrow s_G \dashrightarrow R_G$$

or, combining the two sequences,

$$S'_1 \dashrightarrow r_G \rightsquigarrow s_G \Big\langle \begin{array}{l} R_I \dashrightarrow R_2 \dashrightarrow R_3 \\ R_I \dashrightarrow R_{II} \dashrightarrow R_{III} \end{array} \Big\rangle s_G \dashrightarrow R_G$$

8. Now, suppose that at this point an obstacle is interposed such that R_1 cannot take place, and that $s_G \dashrightarrow R_1$ is far enough above the reaction threshold to resist the weakening effect of the frustration of the excitatory tendency to R_1. With the competition of R_1 thus removed from the excitatory tendency to R_1, s_G will initiate R_1 (7); this will lead to R_{II}, this to R_{III}, etc., and finally to $S_G \dashrightarrow R_G$.

9. But the shift from the sequence beginning with R_1 to that beginning with R_1 as in (8) is a transfer without specific practice from an old to a new situation because R_1, R_{II}, etc., have never taken place in the external stimulus situation beginning with S'_1.

10. From (9) the theorem follows.

Q.E.D.

The Nature of Adaptive Behavior as Indicated by the Postulates of the Present System

We come now to the second step in our exposition of the procedure which should have been carried out by Eddington and Weiss before they presumed to state the ultimate nature of the more complex forms of adaptive and moral behavior. In this step we turn, mainly for purposes of illustration, to the direct examination of the postulates which gave rise to the system, to see whether they are, in fact, physical or psychic. Let us pass them in review. Postulate I states that the physiological effects of a stimulus persists for a certain time even after the stimulus has ceased. Postulate 2 indicates the conditions under which stimuli and reactions become associated or conditioned. Postulate 3 gives the marks of reinforcing situations. Postulate 4 states the conditions under which associations are unlearned. Postulate 5 gives the conditions under which positive and negative learning are lost. Postulate 6 states the well-known fact of internal stimulation.

At first glance most persons would probably say that these postulates represent the behavior of what has always been regarded as physical. Moreover, the postulates appear to be phenomena of physical structures which most theoretical physicists believe will ultimately be derived, i.e., deduced, by them from electrons, protons, neutrons, etc. According to this view the theoretical physicists will ultimately deduce as theorems from electrons, protons, etc., the six postulates which we have employed as the basis for the deduction of adaptive behavior. If this deduction were accomplished we should have an unbroken logical chain extending from the primitive electron all the way up to complex purposive behavior. Further developments may conceivably extend the system to include the highest rational and moral behavior. Such is the natural goal of science. This is the picture which a complete scientific monism would present. Unfortunately, theoretical physics is very far from this achievement, and judgement regarding its ultimate accomplishment must be indefinitely suspended. At most such a view, attractive as it is, can be regarded only as a working hypothesis.[18]

---

[18]There is conceivable, however, a kind of experimental shortcut to the determination of the ultimate nature of adaptive behavior. Suppose it were possible to construct from inorganic materials, such as the theoretical physicists have already succeeded in deriving from electrons and protons, a mechanism which would display exactly the principles of behavior presented in the six postulates just examined. On the assumption that the logic of the above deductions is sound, it follows inevitably that such a 'psychic' machine, if subjected to appropriate environmental influences, must manifest the complex adaptive phenomena presented by the theorems. And if, upon trial, this *a priori* expectation should be verified by the machine's behavior, it would be possible to say with assurance and a clear conscience that such adaptive behavior may be 'reached' by purely physical means. A beginning in the direction of such constructions has already been made. See R. G. Krueger and C. L. Hull, An electro-chemical parallel to the conditioned reflex, *J. Gen. Psychol.*, 1931, 5, 262-269; G. K. Bennett and L. B. Ward, Synthesis of conditioned reflex, *Amer. J. Psychol.*, 1933, 45, 339; D. G. Ellson, A mechanical synthesis of trial-and-error learning, *J. Gen. Psychol.*, 1935, 13, 212-218.

But What of Consciousness?

But what of consciousness, of awareness, of experience —those phenomena of which the philosophers and the-ologians have made so much and upon the priority of which they are so insistent? An inspection of the postu-lates of the miniature system of adaptive behavior pre-sented above certainly shows no trace of any such phenomena. It is clear, therefore, that so far as that considerable array of complex behavior is concerned, consciousness or experience has no logical priority. In the field of scientific theory no other form of priority is of primary significance.

What, then, shall we say about consciousness? Is its existence denied? By no means. But to recognize the existence of a phenomenon is not the same thing as in-sisting upon its basic, *i.e.*, logical, priority. Instead of furnishing a means for the solution of problems, con-sciousness appears to be itself a problem needing solution. In the miniature theoretical system, no mention of con-sciousness or experience was made for the simple reason that no theorem has been found as yet whose deduction would be facilitated in any way by including such a pos-tulate. Moreover, we have been quite unable to find any other scientific system of behavior which either has found consciousness a necessary pre-supposition or, having assumed it, has been able to deduce from it a system of adaptive behavior or moral action.[19] There is, however, no reason at all for not using consciousness or experience

---

[19]It is rather hoped and expected that this statement wil be challenged. In the interest of the clarification of an important problem, it is desirable that the challenge be accompanied by a formal exhibition of the structure of the system supposed to manifest the critical characteristics. As illustrated above, a theo-retical system is a considerable sequence of interlocking theorems, all derived from the same set of postulates. Too often what pass as systems in psychology are merely informal points of view containing occasional propositions which, even if logically derived, would be nothing more than isolated theorems. Some authors are prone to the illusion that such propositions could be deduced with rigor in a few moments if they cared to take the trouble. Others assert that

as a postulate in a scientific theoretical system if it clearly satisfies the deductive criteria already laid down. If such a system should be worked out in a clear and unambiguous manner the incorporation of consciousness into the body of behavior theory should be automatic and immediate. The task of those who would have consciousness a central factor in adaptive behavior and in moral action is accordingly quite clear. They should apply themselves to the long and grinding labor of the logical derivation of a truly scientific system. Until such a system has been attained on a considerable scale, the advancement of science will be favored by their limiting their claims to statements of their hopes and wishes as such. Meanwhile, one cannot help recalling that for several centuries practically all psychological and philosophical theorists have set out precisely with the assumption of the priority of consciousness or experience. Considering the practically complete failure of all this effort to yield even a small scientific system of adaptive or moral behavior in which consciousness finds a position of logical priority as a postulate, one may, perhaps, be pardoned for entertaining a certain amount of pessimism regarding such an eventuality.

In view of the general lack of the kind of evidence which would be necessary to show the logical priority of consciousness, it may naturally be asked why there is such insistence upon its central significance. While there are many contributing factors, it can scarcely be doubted that an important element in the situation is found in the perseverative influences of medieval theology. During the Middle Ages, and for centuries thereafter, social or moral control was supposed to be effected largely through promises of rewards or punishments after death. Therefore something had to survive death to reap these re-

---

the logic has all been worked by them 'in their heads,' but that they did not bother to write it out; the reader is expected to accept this on faith. Fortunately, in science it is not customary to base conclusions on faith.

wards. Consciousness as a non-physical entity was considered incorruptible and thus immune to the disintegration of the flesh. Consequently it offered a logical possibility of something surviving physical death upon which scores might be evened among the shadows beyond the river Styx. But to be convincing, it was necessary for the thing rewarded or punished to be an essentially causal element in the determination of moral conduct or behavior. Thus it was imperative not only that consciousness be non-physical, but also that it be the basic factor in determining action. Such a view is incompatible with the belief that the more complex forms of human behavior could be derived without any reference whatever to consciousness. Tradition is strong, especially when fostered by powerful institutions. Accordingly, the frequent insistence on the logical priority of consciousness is not surprising, even when coming from persons who have no clear notion as to the origin of their feelings in the matter.

Thus it can hardly be doubted that psychology in its basic principles is to a considerable degree in the thrall of the Middle Ages, and that, in particular, our prevailing systematic outlook in the matter of consciousness is largely medieval. The situation depicted in a remarkable panel of the fresco by Orozco in the Dartmouth Library gives a powerful artistic representation of this. There, lifeless skeletons in academic garb assist solemnly at the gruesome travail of a reclining skeleton in the act of reproducing itself. What a picture of academic sterility! Fortunately the means of our salvation is clear and obvious. As ever, it lies in the application of scientific procedures. The methodology is old and tried; it goes back even to the time of Galileo. The present paper is, in reality, an expression of the specific application of this technique in a systematic manner to the problems of complex adaptive behavior. Galileo practiced this methodology at the imminent risk of imprisonment, torture, and death. For us to apply the methodology, it is necessary only to throw off the shackles of a lifeless tradition.

CLARK LEONARD HULL (b.-Akron, N.Y. May 24, 1884; d.-May 10, 1952.)

Hull graduated from the University of Michigan in 1913. He received his PhD. from the University of Wisconsin, in 1918, after having been turned down for graduate study at both Yale and Cornell. He was a teaching assistant at Wisconsin in Experimental Psychology from 1916 to 1920; 1920-1922, Assistant Professor; 1922-25, Associate Professor; 1925-29, Professor of Psychology and Director of the Laboratory. During this time he had made application for a grant to study in Europe, but was turned down (Murchison-a, Vol. 4, p. 143-162). So instead, Hull arranged to bring Kurt Koffka to Wisconsin for one year of lectures on Gestalt Psychology (1926-1927). In 1929 Hull was invited to the Institute of Human Relations at Yale University as Research Professor in Psychology. At the time of his death he was Sterling Professor of Psychology.

One of the uniquely American contributions to psychology has been the area now known as "learning theory". The single leading statement in this field is the present paper by Hull (Address as retiring President, delivered before the American Psychological Association in Hanover, N. H., Sept. 1936). All Hull's later writings, and influence,—now so widespread as to have fostered dedicated departments all over the world,—stem directly from this work.

Learning theory is still in its immaturity as an approach to the basic problems of psychology. However, as it reaches beyond the limited problems of rote-learning, which it first described, and tackles the richer, more subtle, and more relevant problems of human experience, it reveals itself more and more to possess the stature of a genuinely important contribution to human thought. As it stands even today, it is certainly the closest that psychology has yet come to a perfectly logical system of postulates, theorems, and experimental verifications. At the very least it sets an ideal for rigor of thought, and beauty, which all of future psychology should strive to emulate.

HULL, C. L. "Mind, mechanism, and adaptive behavior." *Psychol. Rev.* 1937, 44:1-32. This essay is reproduced in its entirety, with the kind permission of the American Psychological Association.

See also:

HULL, C. L. a) "Quantitative aspects of the evolution of concepts." *Psychol. Monogr.* 1920, 28 (1): Thesis, PhD., Univ. Wisconsin, 1918.

b) "Modern behaviorism and psychoanalysis." *Trans. N. Y. Acad. Sci.* 1937, I (II): 78-82.

c) *Principles of behavior; an introduction to behavior theory.* N.Y.: D. Appleton-Century Co., 1943.

d) *Essentials of behavior.* New Haven: Yale Univ. Press, 1951.

e) *A behavior system, an introduction to behavior theory concerning the individual organism.* New Haven: Yale Univ. Press, 1952.

HULL, C. L. et al. *The mathematico- deductive theory of rote-learning: a study in scientific methodology.* New Haven: Yale Univ. Press, 1940.

HILGARD, E. R. *Theories of learning.* New York: Appleton-Century-Crofts, 1956 (2nd ed.).

HOVLAND, C. I. "Clark Leonard Hull (1884-1952)". *Psychol. Rev.* 1952, 59:347-350.

MURCHISON (b-Vol. 3, p. 245).

MENTAL TESTS AND MEASUREMENTS

James McK. Cattell

Psychology cannot attain the certainty and exactness of the physical sciences, unless it rests on a foundation of experiment and measurement. A step in this direction could be made by applying a series of mental tests and measurements to a large number of individuals. The results would be of considerable scientific value in discovering the constancy of mental processes, their interdependence, and their variation under different circumstances. Individuals, besides, would find their tests interesting, and, perhaps, useful in regard to training, mode of life or indication of disease. The scientific and practical value of such tests would be much increased should a uniform system be adopted, so that determinations made at different times and places could be compared and combined. With a view to obtaining agreement among those interested, I venture to suggest the following series of tests and measurements, together with methods of making them.[1]

The first series of ten tests is made in the Psychological Laboratory of the University of Pennsylvania on all who present themselves, and the complete series on students of Experimental Psychology. The results will be published when sufficient data have been collected. Meanwhile, I should be glad to have the tests, and the methods of making them, thoroughly discussed.

---

[1] Mr. Francis Galton, in his Anthropometric Laboratory at South Kensington Museum, already uses some of these tests, and I hope the series here suggested will meet with his approval. It is convenient to follow Mr. Galton in combining tests of body, such as weight, size, colour of eyes, &c., with psychophysical and mental determinations, but these latter alone are the subject of the present discussion. The name (or initials) of the experimentee should be recorded, the nationality (including that of the parents), and the age, sex, occupation and state of health.

The following ten tests are proposed:

    I. Dynamometer Pressure.

    II. Rate of Movement.

    III. Sensation-areas.

    IV. Pressure causing Pain.

    V. Least noticeable difference in Weight.

    VI. Reaction-time for Sound.

    VII. Time for naming Colours.

    VIII. Bi-section of a 50 cm. line.

    IX. Judgment of 10 seconds time.

    X. Number of Letters remembered on once Hearing.

It will be noticed that the series begins with determinations rather bodily than mental, and proceeds through psychophysical to more purely mental measurements.[1]

The tests may be readily made on inexperienced persons, the time required for the series being about an hour. The laboratory should be conveniently arranged and quiet, and no spectators should be present while the experiments are being made. The amount of instruction the experimentee should receive, and the number of trials he

---

[1]Sharpness of sight (including colour-vision) and hearing might, perhaps, be included in the list. I have omitted them because it requires considerable time to discover the amount and nature of the defect (which is usually bodily, not mental), and because abundant statistics have been published, and are being collected by oculists and aurists.

should be given, are matters which ought to be settled in order to secure uniformity of result. The amount of instruction depends on the experimenter and experimentee, and cannot, unfortunately, be exactly defined. It can only be said that the experimentee must understand clearly what he has to do. A large and uniform number of trials would, of course, be the most satisfactory, the average, average variation, maximum and minimum being recorded. Time is, however, a matter of great importance if many persons are to be tested. The arrangement most economical of time would be to test thoroughly a small number of persons, and a large number in a more rough-and-ready fashion. The number of trials I allow in each test is given below, as also whether I consider the average or 'best' trial the most satisfactory for comparison.

Let us now consider the tests in order.

1. *Dynamometer Pressure.* The greatest possible squeeze of the hand may be thought by many to be a purely physiological quantity. It is, however, impossible to separate bodily from mental energy. The 'sense of effort' and the effects of volition on the body are among the questions most discussed in psychology and even in metaphysics. Interesting experiments may be made on the relation between volitional control or emotional excitement and dynamometer pressure. Other determinations of bodily power could be made (in the second series I have included the 'archer's pull' and pressure of the thumb and forefinger), but the squeeze of the hand seems the most convenient. It may be readily made, cannot prove injurious, is dependent on mental conditions, and allows comparison of right- and left-handed power. The experimentee should be shown how to hold the dynamometer in order to obtain the maximum pressure. I allow two trials with each hand (the order being right, left, right,

862

left), and record the maximum pressure of each hand.

II. *Rate of Movement.* Such a determination seems to be of considerable interest, especially in connexion with the preceding. Indeed, its physiological importance is such as to make it surprising that careful measurements have not hitherto been made. The rate of movement has the same psychological bearings as the force of movement. Notice, in addition to the subjects already mentioned, the connexion between force and rate of movement on the one hand and the 'four temperaments' on the other. I am now making experiments to determine the rate of different movements. As a general test, I suggest the quickest possible movement of the right hand and arm from rest through 50 cm. A piece of apparatus for this purpose can be obtained from Clay & Torbensen, Philadelphia. An electric current is closed by the first movement of the hand, and broken when the movement through 50 cm. has been completed. I measure the time the current has been closed with the Hipp chronoscope, but it may be done by any chronographic method. The Hipp chronoscope is to be obtained from Peyer & Favarger, Neuchatel. It is a very convenient apparatus, but care must be taken in regulating and controlling it. . . .

III. *Sensation-areas.* The distance on the skin by which two points must be separated in order that they may be felt as two is a constant, interesting both to the physiologist and psychologist. Its variation in different parts of the body (from 1 to 68 mm.) was a most important discovery. What the individual variation may be, and what inferences may be drawn from it, cannot be foreseen; but anything which may throw light on the development of the idea of space deserves careful study. Only one part of the body can be tested in a series such as the present. I suggest the back of the closed right hand, between the tendons of the first and second fingers, and in a longitudinal direction. Compasses with rounded wooden or rubber tips should be used, and I suggest that the curvature have a radius of .5 mm. This experiment requires some care and skill on the part of the experimenter. The points must be touched simultaneously, and not too hard. The experimentee must turn away his head. In order to obtain exact results, a large number of experiments would be necessary, and all the tact of the experimenter will be required to determine, without undue expenditure of time, the distance at which the touches may just be distinguished.

IV. *Pressure causing Pain.* This, like the rate of movement, is a determination not hitherto much considered, and if other more important tests can be devised they might be substituted for these. But the point at which pressure causes pain may be an important constant, and in any case it would be valuable in the diagnosis of nervous diseases and in studying abnormal states of consciousness. The determination of any fixed point or quantity in pleasure or pain is a matter of great interest in theoretical and practical ethics, and I should be glad to include some such test in the present series. To determine the pressure causing pain, I use an instrument (to be obtained from Clay & Torbensen) which measures the pressure applied by a tip of hard rubber 5 mm. in radius. I am now determining the pressure causing pain in different parts of the body; for the present series I recommend the centre of the forehead. The pressure should be gradually increased, and the maximum read from the indicator after the experiment is complete. As a rule, the point at which the experimentee says the pressure is painful should be recorded, but in some cases it may be necessary to record the point at which signs of pain are shown. I make two trials, and record both.

V. *Least noticeable difference in Weight.* The just noticeable sensation and the least noticeable difference in sensation are psychological constants of great interest. Indeed, the measurement of mental intensity is probably the most important question with which experimental psychology has at present to deal. The just noticeable sensation can only be determined with great pains, if at all: the point usually found being in reality the least noticeable difference for faint stimuli. This latter point is itself so difficult to determine that I have postponed it to the second series. The least noticeable difference in sensation for stimuli of a given intensity can be more readily determined, but it requires some time, and consequently not more than one sense and intensity can be tested in a preliminary series. I follow Mr. Galton in selecting 'sense of effort' or weight. I use small wooden boxes, the standard one weighing 100 gms. and the others 101, 102, up to 110 gms. The standard weight and another (beginning with 105 gms.) being given to the experimentee, he is asked which is the heavier. I allow him about 10 secs. for decision. I record the point at which he is usually right, being careful to note that he is always right with the next heavier weight.

VI. *Reaction-time for Sound.* The time elapsing before a stimulus calls forth a movement should certainly be included in a series of psychophysical tests: the question to be decided is what stimulus should be chosen. I prefer sound; on it the reaction-time seems to be the shortest and most regular, and the apparatus is most easily arranged. I measure the time with a Hipp chronoscope, but various chronographic methods have been used. There is need of a simpler, cheaper and more portable apparatus for measuring short times. Mr. Galton uses an ingenious instrument, in which the time is measured by the motion of a falling rod, and electricity is dispensed with, but this method will not measure times longer than about ⅓ sec.

In measuring the reaction-time, I suggest that three valid reactions be taken, and the minimum recorded. Later, the average and mean variation may be calculated.

VII. *Time for naming Colours.* A reaction is essentially reflex, and, I think, in addition to it, the time of some process more purely mental should be measured. Several such processes are included in the second series; for the present series I suggest the time needed to see and name a colour. This time may be readily measured for a single colour by means of suitable apparatus . . . , but for general use sufficient accuracy may be attained by allowing the experimentee to name ten colours and taking the average. I paste coloured papers (red, yellow, green and blue) 2 cm. square, 1 cm. apart, vertically on a strip of black pasteboard. This I suddenly uncover and start a chronoscope, which I stop when the ten colours have been named. I allow two trials (the order of colours being different in each) and record the average time per colour in the quickest trial.

VIII. *Bisection of a 50 cm. Line.* The accuracy with which space and time are judged may be readily tested, and with interesting results. I follow Mr. Galton in letting the experimentee divide an ebony rule (3 cm. wide) into two equal parts by means of a movable line, but I recommend 50 cm. in place of 1 ft., as with the latter the error is so small that it is difficult to measure, and the metric system seems preferable. The amount of error in mm. (the distance from the true middle) should be recorded, and whether it is to the right or left. One trial would seem to be sufficient.

IX. *Judgment of 10 sec. Time.* This determination is easily made. I strike on the table with the end of a pencil, and again after 10 seconds, and let the experimentee in turn strike when he judges an equal interval to have

866

elapsed. I allow only one trial and record the time, from which the amount and direction of error can be seen.

X. *Number of Letters repeated on once Hearing.* Memory and attention may be tested by determining how many letters can be repeated on hearing once. I name distinctly and at the rate of two per second six letters, and if the experimentee can repeat these after me I go on to seven, then eight, &c.; if the six are not correctly repeated after three trials (with different letters), I give five, four, &c. The maximum number of letters which can be grasped and remembered is thus determined. Consonants only should be used in order to avoid syllables.

Experimental psychology is likely to take a place in the educational plan of our schools and universities. It teaches accurate observation and correct reasoning in the same way as the other natural sciences, and offers a supply of knowledge interesting and useful to everyone. I am at present preparing a laboratory manual which will include tests of the senses and measurements of mental time, intensity and extensity, but it seems worth while to give here a list of the tests which I look on as the more important in order that attention may be drawn to them, and co-operation secured in choosing the best series of tests and the most accurate and convenient methods. In the following series, fifty tests are given, but some of them include more than one determination.

Sight.

1. Accommodation (short sight, over-sight, and astigmatism).
2. Drawing Purkinje's figures and the blind-spot.
3. Acuteness of colour vision, including lowest red and highest violet visible.
4. Determination of the field of vision for form and colour.

5. Determination of what the experimentee considers a normal red, yellow, green and blue.

6. Least perceptible light, and least amount of colour distinguished from grey.

7. Least noticeable difference in intensity, determined for stimuli of three degrees of brightness.

8. The time a colour must work on the retina in order to produce a sensation, the maximum sensation and a given degree of fatigue.

9. Nature and duration of after-images.

10. Measurement of amount of contrast.

11. Accuracy with which distance can be judged with one and with two eyes.

12. Test with stereoscope and for struggle of the two fields of vision.

13. Errors of perception, including bisection of line, drawing of square, &c.

14. Colour and arrangement of colours preferred. Shape of figure and of rectangle preferred.

Hearing.

15. Least perceptible sound and least noticeable difference in intensity for sounds of three degrees of loudness.

16. Lowest and highest tone audible, least perceptible difference in pitch for C, C′, C″, and point where intervals and chords (in melody and harmony) are just noticed to be out of tune.

17. Judgment of absolute pitch and of the nature of intervals, chords and dischords.

18. Number and nature of the overtones which can be heard with and without resonators.

19. Accuracy with which direction and distance of sounds can be judged.

20. Accuracy with which a rhythm can be followed and complexity of rhythm can be grasped.

21. Point at which loudness and shrillness of sound become painful. Point at which beats are the most disagreeable.

22. Sound of nature most agreeable. Musical tone, chord, instrument and composition preferred.

Taste and Smell.

23. Least perceptible amount of cane-sugar, quinine, cooking salt and sulphuric acid, and determination of the parts of the mouth with which they are tasted.

24. Least perceptible amount of camphor and bromine.

25. Tastes and smells found to be peculiarly agreeable and disagreeable.

Touch and Temperature.

26. Least noticeable pressure for different parts of the body.

27. Least noticeable difference in pressure, with weights of 10, 100 and 1000 gms.

28. Measurement of sensation-areas in different parts of the body.

29. Accuracy with which the amount and direction of the motion of a point over the skin can be judged.

30. Least noticeable difference in temperature.

31. Mapping out of heat, cold and pressure spots on the skin.

32. The point at which pressure and heat and cold cause pain.

Sense of Effort and Movement.[1]

33. Least noticeable difference in weight, in lifting weights of 10, 100 and 1000 gms.

---

[1]Organic sensations and sensations of motion, equilibrium and dizziness, should perhaps be included in this series.

34. Force of squeeze of hands, pressure with thumb and forefinger and pull as archer.

35. Maximum and normal rate of movement.

36. Accuracy with which the force, extent and rate of active and passive movements can be judged.

Mental Time.

37. The time stimuli must work on the ear and eye in order to call forth sensations.

38. The reaction-time for sound, light, pressure and electrical stimulation.

39. The perception-time for colours, objects, letters and words.

40. The time of naming colours, objects, letters and words.

41. The time it takes to remember and to come to a decision.

42. The time of mental association.

43. The effects of attention, practice and fatigue on mental time.

Mental Intensity.

44. Results of different methods used for determining the least noticeable difference in sensation.

45. Mental intensity as a function of mental time.

Mental Extensity.

46. Number of impressions which can be simultaneously received.

47. Number of successive impressions which can be correctly repeated, and number of times a larger number of successive impressions must be heard or seen in order that they may be correctly repeated.

48. The rate at which a simple sensation fades from memory.

49. Accuracy with which intervals of time can be remembered.

50. The correlation of mental time, intensity and extensity.

JAMES McKEEN CATTELL (b.—Easton, Pennsylvania, May 25, 1860; d.—Lancaster, Pennsylvania, January 20, 1944.)

Cattell was one of the most widely educated of American psychologists. He received his Ph.D. from the University of Leipzig in 1886, where he had gone specifically to study under Wundt. He also studied at the Universities of Gottingen, Paris, Geneva, Cambridge, and the Johns Hopkins University in Baltimore. In 1891 he founded the psychology laboratory at Columbia University. In 1894 he founded the *Psychological Review,* together with J. M. Baldwin. His collection, *American Men of Science* (1906), has gone through many editions, and is today the standard reference in the field.

His work was encouraged and greatly influenced by the English scientist Francis Galton, to whom Cattell often pays deference. Cattell was the pioneer of the field of individual differences. Many of the methods which he introduced were new with him, though having inspiration in Wundt and Galton. The very term "mental measurements" is his own, being introduced in the present selection. This essay is Cattell's first formal statement, and constitutes the important description of the major concepts of intelligence prevalent before the work of Binet.

CATTELL, J. M. "Mental tests and measurements." *Mind.* 1890, XV: 373-381. This selection is reprinted, deleting only the appended comments of Galton, with the permission of the editor of *Mind.*

See also:

CATTELL, J. McK. "Statistics of American psychologists." *Amer. J. Psychol.* 1903, 14: 310-328.

FULLERTON, G. S. & CATTELL, J. McK. "On the perception of small differences." *Pub. Univ. Penn., Phil. Series.* 1892, 2: 1-159. This is probably Cattell's most important experimental paper.
"On errors of observation." *Amer. J. Psychol.* 1893, 5: 285-293.

WOODWORTH, R. S. "James McKeen Cattell." *Psychol. Rev.* 1944, 51: 1-10.

MURPHY, G. *Historical introduction to modern psychology.* Harcourt Brace & Co., 1949, p. 160-165.

The most complete collection of Cattell's writings, some 15,000 pages, has recently been deposited in the Library of Congress.

THE
DEVELOPMENT OF INTELLIGENCE
IN CHILDREN

Alfred Binet and Theodore Simon

UPON THE NECESSITY OF ESTABLISHING A SCIENTIFIC DIAGNOSIS OF INFERIOR STATES OF INTELLIGENCE[1]

We here present the first rough sketch of a work which was directly inspired by the desire to serve the interesting cause of the education of subnormals.

In October 1904, the Minister of Public Instruction named a commission which was charged with the study of measures to be taken for insuring the benefits of instruction to defective children. After a number of sittings, this commission regulated all that pertained to the type of establishment to be created, the conditions of admission into the school, the teaching force, and the pedagogical methods to be employed. They decided that no child suspected of retardation should be eliminated from the ordinary school and admitted into a special class, without first being subjected to a pedagogical and medical examination from which it could be certified that because of the state of his intelligence, he was unable to profit, in an average measure, from the instruction given in the ordinary schools.

But how the examination of each child should be made, what methods should be followed, what observations taken, what questions asked, what tests devised, how the child should be compared with normal children, the com-

---

[1] *L'Année Psychologique*, 1905, pp. 163-191.

mission felt under no obligation to decide. It was formed to do a work of administration, not a work of science.

It has seemed to us extremely useful to furnish a guide for future Commissions' examination. Such Commissions should understand from the beginning how to get their bearings. It must be made impossible for those who belong to the Commission to fall into the habit of making haphazard decisions according to impressions which are subjective, and consequently uncontrolled. Such impressions are sometimes good, sometimes bad, and have at all times too much the nature of the arbitrary, of caprice, of indifference. Such a condition is quite unfortunate because the interests of the child demand a more careful method. To be a member of a special class can never be a mark of distinction, and such as do not merit it, must be spared the record. Some errors are excusable in the beginning, but if they become too frequent, they may ruin the reputation of these new institutions. Furthermore, in principle, we are convinced, and we shall not cease to repeat, that the precision and exactness of science should be introduced into our practice whenever possible, and in the great majority of cases it is possible.

The problem which we have to solve presents many difficulties both theoretical and practical. It is a hackneyed remark that the definitions, thus far proposed, for the different states of subnormal intelligence, lack precision. These inferior states are indefinite in number, being composed of a series of degrees which mount from the lowest depths of idiocy, to a condition easily confounded with normal intelligence. Alienists have frequently come to an agreement concerning the terminology to be employed for designating the difference of these degrees; at least, in spite of certain individual divergence of ideas to be found in all questions, there has been an agreement to accept *idiot* as applied to the lowest state, *imbecile* to the

873

intermediate, and *moron* (debile)* to the state nearest normality. Still among the numerous alienists, under this common and apparently precise terminology, different ideas are concealed, variable and at the same time confused. The distinction between idiot, imbecile, and moron is not understood in the same way by all practitioners. We have abundant proof of this in the strikingly divergent medical diagnoses made only a few days apart by different alienists upon the same patient.

Dr. Blin, physician of the Vaucluse Asylum, recently drew the attention of his fellow physicians to these regrettable contradictions. He states that the children who are sent to the colony come provided with several dissimilar certificates. "One child, called imbecile in the first certificate, is marked idiot in the second, feeble-minded (debile) in the third, and degenerate in the fourth."[1] M. Damaye, former house surgeon of Dr. Blin, adds this observation: "One would have only to look through several folders of records belonging to children of the colony, in order to collect almost the same number of different diagnoses."[2] Perhaps this last affirmation is a little exaggerated, but a statistical study would show the exact truth on this point.

We cannot sufficiently deplore the consequence of this state of uncertainty recognized today by all alienists. The simple fact, that specialists do not agree in the use of the technical terms of their science, throws suspicion upon

---

*The French word *débile* (weak) is used by Binet to designate the highest grade of mental defectives, called in England feeble-minded. In America the term feeble-minded has been used in the same sense, but unfortunately it is also applied generically to the entire group of mental defectives. To obviate this ambiguity, we coined the word MORON (Greek Moros, foolish) to designate the highest grade of mental defect. We have accordingly translated *débile* by moron, except in a few instances where the context requires a different term.—EDITOR.

[1]Blin, Les débilités mentales, *Revue de psychiatrie.* Aout, 1902.
[2]Damaye, *Essai de diagnostic entre les états de débilité mentale.* Thèse de Paris, Steinheil, 1903.

their diagnoses, and prevents all work of comparison. We ourselves have made similar observations. In synthesizing the diagnoses made by M. Bourneville upon patients leaving the Bicetre, we found that in the space of four years only two feeble-minded individuals have left his institution although during that time the Bureau of Admission has sent him more than thirty. Nothing could show more clearly than this change of label, the confusion of our nomenclature.

What importance can be attached to public statistics of different countries concerning the percentage of backward children if the definition for backward children is not the same in all countries? How will it be possible to keep a record of the intelligence of pupils who are treated and instructed in a school, if the terms applied to them, feeble-minded, retarded, imbecile, idiot, vary in meaning according to the doctor who examines them? The absence of a common measure prevents comparison of statistics, and makes one lose all interest in investigations which may have been very laborious. But a still more serious fact is that, because of lack of methods, it is impossible to solve those essential questions concerning the afflicted, whose solution presents the greatest interest; for example, the real results gained by the treatment of inferior states of intelligence by doctor and educator; the educative value of one pedagogical method compared with another; the degree of curability of incomplete idiocy, etc. It is not by means of *a priori* reasonings, of vague considerations, of oratorical displays, that these questions can be solved; but by minute investigation, entering into the details of fact, and considering the effects of the treatment for each particular child. There is but one means of knowing if a child, who has passed six years in a hospital or in a special class, has profited from that stay, and to what degree he has profited; and that is to compare his certificate of entrance with his certificate of dismissal, and by that means ascertain if he shows a special amelioration of his condition beyond that which might be credited simply to the considerations of growth. But experience has shown how imprudent it would be to place confidence in this comparison, when the two certificates come from different doctors, who do not judge in exactly the same way, or who use different words to characterize the mental status of patients.

It might happen that a child, who had really improved in school, had received in the beginning the diagnosis of moron (debile), and on leaving, the prejudicial diagnosis of imbecile, simply because the second doctor spoke a different language from the first. If one took these certificates literally, this case would be considered a failure. On the contrary, the appearance of amelioration would be produced if the physician who delivered the certificate of dismissal had the habit of using higher terms than the one who furnished the certificate of entrance. One can even go further. The errors which we note, do not necessarily emanate from the disagreement of different physicians. It would suffice for the same physician to deliver the two certificates, if he did not employ for each one the same criterion; and it would certainly be possible for him to vary unconsciously after an interval of several years if he had nothing to guide him but his own subjective impressions. Might not the same thing also happen if his good faith as a physician happened to be in conflict with the interests of the institution which he directed? Might he not unconsciously as it were, have a tendency to lower the mental status of patients on entering and to raise it on dismissal, in order to emphasize the advantages of the methods which he had applied? We are not incriminating anyone, but simply calling attention to methods actually in use which, by their lack of precision, favor the involuntary illusions of physicians and relatives, in a word, of all those who, having an interest in the amelioration of the condition of the defective child, would have a tendency to confound their desires with the reality.

Perhaps someone will raise an objection and say this uncertainty has no special application to diagnosis of the degrees of mental debility; it is also to be found in mental pathology and, in a general way, in the diagnosis of all maladies; it is the result of the empirical nature which is characteristic of clinical studies. It might be added, that, if anyone took the trouble to make a statistical study of the divergence in the diagnosis of different physicians upon the same patient, it would probably be found that the percentage of disagreement is very great in all branches of medicine.

We believe it worth while to examine their objection because it permits us to enter more deeply into the analysis of the question. The disagreements of practitioners might come from three very different classes of causes:

1. Ignorance, that is, the lack of aptitude of certain physicians. This is an individual failure, for which abstract science is not responsible. It is certain that, even when the symptoms of a disease are absolutely clear, such a physician might fail to recognize them through incapacity. There are many accountants who make mistakes in calculation, but these errors do not discredit mathematics. A physician might not be able to recognize a "p. g." if he is himself a "p. g."

2. The variable meaning of terms. Since the same expression has a different sense according to the person who uses it, it is possible that the disagreement of diagnosis may be simply a disagreement of words, due to the use of different nomenclature.

3. Lack of precision in the description of the symptoms which reveal or which constitute a certain particular malady; different physicians do not examine the same patient in the same manner and do not give the symptoms

the same importance; or, it may be they make no effort to find out the precise symptoms, and no effort to analyze carefully in order to distinguish and interpret them.

Of these three kinds of error, which is the one that actually appears in the diagnosis of inferior states of intelligence? Let us set aside the first. There remain the faults of nomenclature, and the insufficiency of methods of examination.

The general belief seems to be that the confusion arises wholly from an absence of a uniform nomenclature. There is some truth in this opinion. It can be proved by a comparison of terms used by authors belonging to the different countries. Even in France the terms differ somewhat according to the physician, the order of the admitted subdivisions not being rigorously followed. The classification of Magnan is not that of Voisin, and his, in turn, differs from that of Bourneville. Undoubtedly it would be a good work to bring about a unification of this nomenclature as has been done for the standard of measurements and for electric units. But this reform in itself is not sufficient and we are very sure that they deceive themselves who think that at bottom this is only a question of terminology. It is very much more serious. We find physicians who, though using the same terminology, constantly disagree in their diagnosis of the same child. The examples cited from M. Blin prove this. There the doctors had recourse to the terminology of Morel, who classifies those of inferior intelligence as idiots, imbeciles and *"debiles."* Notwithstanding this use of the same terms, they do not agree in the manner of applying them. Each one according to his own fancy, fixes the boundary line separating these states. It is in regard to the facts that the doctors disagree.

In looking closely one can see that the confusion comes principally from a fault in the method of examination. When an alienist finds himself in the presence of a child

878

of inferior intelligence, he does not examine him by bringing out each one of the symptoms which the child manifests and by interpreting all symptoms and classifying them; he contents himself with taking a subjective impression, an impression as a whole, of his subject, and of making his diagnosis by instinct. We do not think that we are going too far in saying that at the present time very few physicians would be able to cite with absolute precision the objective and invariable sign, or signs, by which they distinguish the degrees of inferior mentality.

A study of the historical side of the question shows us very clearly that what is lacking is a *precise basis for differential diagnosis.*

NEW METHODS FOR THE DIAGNOSIS OF THE INTELLECTUAL LEVEL OF SUBNORMALS[1]

Before explaining these methods let us recall exactly the conditions of the problem which we are attempting to solve. Our purpose is to be able to measure the intellectual capacity of a child who is brought to us in order to know whether he is normal or retarded. We should therefore, study his condition at the time and that only. We have nothing to do either with his past history or with his future; consequently we shall neglect his etiology, and we shall make no attempt to distinguish between acquired and congenital idiocy; for a stronger reason we shall set aside all consideration of pathological anatomy which might explain his intellectual deficiency. So much for his past. As to that which concerns his future, we shall exercise the same abstinence; we do not attempt to establish or prepare a prognosis and we leave unanswered the question of whether this retardation is curable, or even improvable. We shall limit ourselves to ascertaining the truth in regard to his present mental state.

---

[1] *L'Année Psychologique*, 1905, Vol. XII, pp. 191-244.

Furthermore, in the definition of this state, we should make some restrictions. Most subnormal children, especially those in the schools, are habitually grouped in two categories, those of backward intelligence, and those who are unstable. This latter class, which certain alienists call moral imbeciles, do not necessarily manifest inferiority of intelligence; they are turbulent, vicious, rebellious to all discipline; they lack sequence of ideas, and probably power of attention. It is a matter of great delicacy to make the distinction between children who are unstable, and those who have rebellious dispositions. Elsewhere we have insisted upon the necessity of instructors not treating as unstable, that is as pathological cases, those children whose character is not sympathetic with their own. It would necessitate a long study, and probably a very difficult one, to establish the distinctive signs which separate the unstable from the undisciplined. For the present we shall not take up this study. We shall set the unstable aside, and shall consider only that which bears upon those who are backward in intelligence.

This is not, however, to be the only limitation of our subject because backward states of intelligence present several different types. There is the insane type—or the type of intellectual decay—which consists in a progressive loss of former acquired intelligence. Many epileptics, who suffer from frequent attacks, progress toward insanity. It would be possible and probably very important, to be able to make the distinction between those with decaying intelligence on the one hand, and those of inferior intelligence on the other. But as we have determined to limit on this side also, the domain of our study, we shall rigorously exclude all forms of insanity and decay. Moreover we believe that these are rarely present in the schools, and need not be taken into consideration in the operation of new classes for subnormals.

Another distinction is made between those of inferior

intelligence and degenerates. The latter are subjects in whom occur clearly defined, episodical phenomena, such as impulsions, obsessions, deliriums. We shall eliminate the degenerates as well as the insane.

Lastly, we should say a word upon our manner of studying those whom most alienists call idiots but whom we here call of inferior intelligence. The exact nature of this inferiority is not known; and today without other proof, one very prudently refuses to liken this state to that of an arrest of normal development. It certainly seems that the intelligence of these beings has undergone a certain arrest; but it does not follow that the disproportion between the degree of intelligence and the age is the only characteristic of their condition. There is also in many cases, most probably a deviation in the development, a perversion. The idiot of fifteen years, who, like a baby of three, is making his first verbal attempts, can not be completely likened to a three-year old child, because the latter is normal, but the idiot is not. There exists therefore between them, necessarily, differences either apparent or hidden. The careful study of idiots shows, among some of them at least, that whereas certain faculties are almost wanting, others are better developed. They have therefore certain aptitudes. Some have a good auditory or musical memory, and a whole repertoire of songs; others have mechanical ability. If all were carefully examined, many examples of these partial aptitudes would probably be found.

Our purpose is in no wise to study, analyze, or set forth the aptitudes of those of inferior intelligence. That will be the object of a later work. Here we shall limit ourselves to the measuring of their general intelligence. We shall determine their intellectual level, and in order the better to appreciate this level, we shall compare it with that of normal children of the same age or of an analogous level. The reservations previously made as to the true conception of arrested development, will not prevent our finding great advantage in a methodical comparison between those of inferior and those of normal intelligence.

To what method should we have recourse in making our diagnosis of the intellectual level? No one method exists, but there are a number of different ones which should be used cumulatively, because the question is a very difficult one to solve, and demands rather a collaboration of methods. It is important that the practitioner be equipped in such a manner that he shall use, only as accessory, the information given by the parents of the child, so that he may always be able to verify this information, or, when necessary, dispense with it. In actual practice quite the opposite occurs. When the child is taken to the clinic the physician listens a great deal to the parents and questions the child very little, in fact scarcely looks at him, allowing himself to be influenced by a very strong presumption that the child is intellectually inferior. If, by a chance not likely to occur, but which would be most interesting some time to bring about, the physician were submitted to the test of selecting the subnormals from a mixed group of children, he would certainly find himself in the midst of grave difficulties and would commit many errors especially in cases of slight defect.

The organization of methods is especially important because, as soon as the schools for subnormals are in operation, one must be on his guard against the attitude of the parents. Their sincerity will be worth very little when it is in conflict with their interests. If the parents wish the child to remain in the regular school, they will not be silent concerning his intelligence. "My child understands everything," they will say, and they will be very careful not to give any significant information in regard to him. If on the contrary, they wish him to be admitted into an institution where gratuitous board and lodging are furnished, they will change completely. They will be

882

capable even of teaching him how to simulate mental debility. One should, therefore, be on his guard against all possible frauds.

In order to recognize the inferior states of intelligence we believe that three different methods should be employed. We have arrived at this synthetic view only after many years of research, but we are now certain that each of these methods renders some service. These methods are:

1. *The medical method,* which aims to appreciate the anatomical, physiological, and pathological signs of inferior intelligence.

2. *The pedagogical method,* which aims to judge of the intelligence according to the sum of acquired knowledge.

3. *The psychological method,* which makes direct observations and measurements of the degree of intelligence.

From what has gone before it is easy to see the value of each of these methods. The medical method is indirect because it conjectures the mental from the physical. The pedagogical method is more direct; but the psychological is the most direct of all because it aims to measure the state of the intelligence as it is at the present moment. It does this by experiments which oblige the subject to make an effort which shows his capability in the way of comprehension, judgment, reasoning, and invention.

I. THE PSYCHOLOGICAL METHOD

The fundamental idea of this method is the establishment of what we shall call a measuring scale of intelligence. This scale is composed of a series of tests of increasing difficulty, starting from the lowest intellectual level that can be observed, and ending with that of average normal intelligence. Each group in the series corresponds to a different mental level.

This scale properly speaking does not permit the measure of the intelligence, because intellectual qualities are not superposable, and therefore cannot be measured as linear surfaces are measured, but are on the contrary, a classification, a hierarchy among diverse intelligences; and for the necessities of practice this classification is equivalent to a measure. We shall therefore be able to know, after studying two individuals, if one rises above the other and to how many degrees, if one rises above the average level of other individuals considered as normal, or if he remains below. Understanding the normal progress of intellectual development among normals, we shall be able to determine how many years such an individual is advanced or retarded. In a word we shall be able to determine to what degrees of the scale idiocy, imbecility, and moronity correspond.

The scale that we shall describe is not a theoretical work; it is the result of long investigations, first at the Salpetriere, and afterwards in the primary schools of Paris, with both normal and subnormal children. These short psychological questions have been given the name of tests. The use of tests is today very common, and there are even contemporary authors who have made a specialty of organizing new tests according to theoretical views, but who have made no effort to patiently try them out in the schools. Theirs is an amusing occupation, comparable to a person's making a colonizing expedition into Algeria, advancing always only upon the map, without taking off his dressing gown. We place but slight confidence in the tests invented by these authors and we have borrowed nothing from them. All the tests which we propose have been repeatedly tried, and have been retained from among many, which after trial have been discarded. We can certify that those which are here presented have proved themselves valuable.

We have aimed to make all our tests simple, rapid,

convenient, precise, heterogeneous, holding the subject in continued contact with the experimenter, and bearing principally upon the faculty of judgment. Rapidity is necessary for this sort of examination. It is impossible to prolong it beyond twenty minutes without fatiguing the subject. During this maximum of twenty minutes, it must be turned and turned about in every sense, and at least ten tests must be executed, so that not more than about two minutes can be given to each. In spite of their interest, we were obliged to proscribe long exercises. For example, it would be very instructive to know how a subject learns by heart a series of sentences. We have often tested the advantage of leaving a person by himself with a lesson of prose or verse after having said to him, "Try to learn as much as you can of this in five minutes." Five minutes is too long for our test, because during that time the subject escapes us; it may be that he becomes distracted or thinks of other things; the test loses its clinical character and becomes too scholastic. We have therefore reluctantly been obliged to renounce testing the rapidity and extent of the memory by this method. Several other equivalent examples of elimination could be cited. In order to cover rapidly a wide field of observation, it goes without saying that the tests should be heterogeneous.

Another consideration. Our purpose is to evaluate a level of intelligence. It is understood that we here separate natural intelligence and instruction. It is the intelligence alone that we seek to measure, by disregarding in so far as possible, the degree of instruction which the subject possesses. He should, indeed, be considered by the examiner as a complete ignoramus knowing neither how to read nor write. This necessity forces us to forego a great many exercises having a verbal, literary or scholastic character. These belong to a pedagogical examination. We believe that we have succeeded in completely disregarding the acquired information of the subject. We give him nothing to read, nothing to write, and submit him to no test in which he might succeed by means of rote learning. In fact we do not even notice his inability to read if a case occurs. It is simply the level of his natural intelligence that is taken into account.

But here we must come to an understanding of what meaning to give to that word so vague and so comprehensive, "the intelligence." Nearly all the phenomena with which psychology concerns itself are phenomena of intelligence; sensation, perception, are intellectual manifestations as much as reasoning. Should we therefore bring into our examination the measure of sensation after the manner of the psycho-physicists? Should we put to the test all of his psychological processes? A slight reflection has shown us that this would indeed be wasted time.

It seems to us that in intelligence there is a fundamental faculty, the alteration or the lack of which, is of the utmost importance for practical life. This faculty is judgment, otherwise called good sense, practical sense, initiative, the faculty of adapting one's self to circumstances. To judge well, to comprehend well, to reason well, these are the essential activities of intelligence. A person may be a moron or an imbecile if he is lacking in judgment; but with good judgment he can never be either. Indeed the rest of the intellectual faculties seem of little importance in comparison with judgment. What does it matter, for example, whether the organs of sense function normally? Of what import that certain ones are hyperesthetic, or that others are anesthetic or are weakened? Laura Bridgman, Helen Keller and their fellow-unfortunates were blind as well as deaf, but this did not prevent them from being very intelligent. Certainly this is demonstrative proof that the total or even partial integrity of the senses does not form a mental factor equal to judgment. We may measure the acuteness of the sensibility of subjects; nothing could be easier. But we should do this, not so much to find out the state of their sensibility as to learn the exactitude of their judgment.

The same remark holds good for the study of the memory. At first glance, memory being a psychological phenomenon of capital importance, one would be tempted to give it a very conspicuous part in an examination of intelligence. But memory is distinct from and independent of judgment. One may have good sense and lack memory. The reverse is also common. Just at the present time we are observing a backward girl who is developing before our astonished eyes a memory very much greater than our own. We have measured that memory and we are not deceived regarding it. Nevertheless that girl presents a most beautifully classic type of imbecility.

As a result of all this investigation, in the scale which we present we accord the first place to judgment; that which is of importance to us is not certain errors which the subject commits, but absurd errors, which prove that he lacks judgment. We have even made special provision to encourage people to make absurd replies. In spite of the accuracy of this directing idea, it will be easily understood that it has been impossible to permit of its regulating exclusively our examinations. For example, one can not make tests of judgment on children of less than two years when one begins to watch their first gleams of intelligence. Much is gained when one can discern in them traces of coordination, the first delineation of attention and memory. We shall therefore bring out in our lists some tests of memory; but so far as we are able, we shall give these tests such a turn as to invite the subject to make absurd replies, and thus under cover of a test of memory, we shall have an appreciation of their judgment.

MEASURING SCALE OF INTELLIGENCE

General recommendations. The examination should

take place in a quiet room, quite isolated, and the child should be called in alone without other children. It is important that when a child sees the experimenter for the first time, he should be reassured by the presence of someone he knows, a relative, an attendant, or a school superintendent. The witness should be instructed to remain passive and mute, and not to intervene in the examination either by word or gesture.

The experimenter should receive each child with a friendly familiarity to dispel the timidity of early years. Greet him the moment he enters, shake hands with him and seat him comfortably. If he is intelligent enough to understand certain words, awaken his curiosity, his pride. If he refuses to reply to a test, pass to the next one, or perhaps offer him a piece of candy; if his silence continues, send him away until another time. These are little incidents that frequently occur in an examination of the mental state, because in its last analysis, an examination of this kind is based upon the good will of the subject.

We here give the technique of each question. It will not suffice simply to read what we have written in order to be able to conduct examinations. A good experimenter can be produced only by example and imitation, and nothing equals the lesson gained from the thing itself. Every person who wishes to familiarize himself with our method of examination should come to our school. Theoretical instruction is valuable only when it merges into practical experience. Having made these reservations, let us point out the principal errors likely to be committed by inexperienced persons. There are two: the first consists in recording the gross results without making psychological observations, without noticing such little facts as permit one to give to the gross results their true value. The second error, equally frequent, is that of making suggestions. An inexperienced examiner has no idea of the influence of words; he talks too much, he aids his subject, he

888

puts him on the track, unconscious of the help he is thus giving. He plays the part of pedagogue, when he should remain psychologist. Thus his examination is vitiated. It is a difficult art to be able to encourage a subject, to hold his attention, to make him do his best without giving aid in any form of an unskillful suggestion.

THE SERIES OF TESTS

1. *"Le Regard"*[1]

In this test the examiner seeks to discover if there exists that coordination in the movement of the head and the eyes which is associated with the act of vision. If such coordination does exist it proves that the subject not only sees but more than that he "regards" (that is he is able to follow with his eyes a moving object).

Procedure. A lighted match is slowly moved before the eyes of the subject in such a way as to provoke a movement of the head or of the eyes to follow the flame. If a first attempt does not succeed the experiment should be tried again after a little while. It is preferable to operate in a quiet place where no kind of distraction is likely to occur. It is not important that the subject follow the movements of the match constantly for any length of time or persistently. The least sign of coordination of the movements of vision is sufficient, if it leaves no doubt in the mind of the examiner.

Additional remarks. The observation of a few spontaneous phenomena may well be noted. Thus it is possible sometimes for the examiner, by fixing his gaze steadily upon the child, to satisfy himself that the child really coordinates for a moment. If the subject is afflicted with or suspected of blindness, the visual stimulus may be replaced by an auditory stimulus. For example, call him

---

[1]*Goddard's note:* We have here retained the word used by Binet, because in the English there is no one word exactly synonymous with it. The word literally translated means "the ability to follow with the eyes a moving object."

889

loudly, or better, ring a little bell behind his head and notice if he turns his head toward the sound, or if he has any peculiar facial expression which would indicate that he hears. The reaction of attention to sound seems to develop later than the reaction to light. We have observed children who, when a bell was rung behind the head, would not make a single movement in order to hear better, and yet would follow with their eyes the lighted match. It is scarcely necessary to add that the child who hides his face behind his hand when questioned, or who replies to your smile by a smile, or who walks about the room without knocking against obstacles, stove, chairs, wall, table, proves by his behaviour that he coordinates the movements of vision, and thus he has passed the first test.

2. *Prehension Provoked by a Tactile Stimulus*

Here the purpose is to discover whether the coordination exists between a tactile stimulus of the hand, and the movement of seizing and carrying to the mouth.

Procedure. A small object, easily handled, for example a piece of wood, is placed in contact with the hand of the child in order to determine if he succeeds in seizing the object, holding it in his hand without letting it fall, and carrying it to his mouth. It is well to stimulate the contact either on the back of the hand or on the palm, and note the results. It is possible that the subject, after having taken the little object, loosens his fingers and lets it fall. It is necessary in that case to try again with a little patience, in order to learn if the letting go came of a chance distraction, or if the subject is not capable of performing the muscular act which would consist in carrying it to his mouth.

3. *Prehension Provoked by a Visual Perception*

Here the purpose is to find whether coordination exists between the sight of an object and its prehension, when the object is not placed in contact with the hand of the subject.

890

Procedure. The object is presented to his view and within reach of his hand, in a manner to provoke an intentional movement of his hand to take it. This third test is passed when the subject, following a visual perception of the object, makes a movement of the hand towards the object, reaches, seizes and carries it to his mouth. A small cube of white wood, easy to handle is used. In these presentations it is not forbidden to speak and hence the object is offered to the child as follows: "Here is a little object, take it, it is for you—Come now, pay attention, etc." If the subject understands, so much the better for him; if he does not understand the sound of these words has the advantage of attracting his attention. Moreover the examiner makes gestures and makes them more naturally if he talks at the same time.

4. *Recognition of Food*

Here the purpose is to discover whether the subject can make the distinction by sight between familiar food and what can not be eaten.

Procedure. A piece of chocolate (half a bar) and a little cube of white wood of similar dimensions are successively presented. The test is to see if the subject, by sight alone, makes the distinction between the two objects before carrying them to his mouth. Does he carry only the chocolate to his mouth and begin to eat it? Does he refuse to take the piece of wood, or having taken it does he push it away, or again does he hold it in his hand without putting it to his mouth?

Tests 3 and 4 can be made rapidly as a single experiment. A piece of chocolate is first shown to the child and his attention is drawn to it. Note whether he tries to take it or not. If he makes no effort to attain it, and is not distracted by anything, place the chocolate in the palm of his hand, and note what happens. If on the contrary he takes the chocolate which is shown him and carries it to his mouth, the chocolate is taken from him, and the piece of wood put in its place, to see if he carries this new object also to his mouth.

Although these tests succeed with very many children by appealing to their greediness, it often happens that a willful child, or one frightened by the sight of the examiner whom he does not know, turns away from him and refuses to look at what is shown him. These movements of defense indicate already a mentality that corresponds most likely to the fourth degree. The experimenter must be armed with patience and gentleness. He may have a relative, an attendant, or any other person who knows the child, present the chocolate, but he must carefully note the behavior of the child throughout the operation. If the attack of anger, or tears, or fear lasts too long, the examination is necessarily suspended to be taken up at a more favorable time. These are the disappointments to which alienists are accustomed.

5. *Quest of Food Complicated by a Slight Mechanical Difficulty*

This test is designed to bring into play a rudiment of memory, an effort of will, and a coordination of movements.

Procedure. First be sure that the child recognizes the candy or bonbon to be used in this experiment. Then while he is watching you, wrap the bonbon in a piece of paper. Present it to him and carefully note his movements. Does he remember that the paper contains a bonbon? Does he reject it as a useless object, or does he try to pull it apart? Does he carry the covered morsel to his mouth? Does he eat the paper or does he make some effort to unfold it? Does he completely succeed in unfolding it, or does he seem satisfied with one attempt? Does he present the covered morsel to some one else as if to ask his aid?

892

6. *Execution of Simple Commands and Imitation of Simple Gestures*

This test involves various motor coordinations, and associations between certain movements, and the understanding of the significance of certain gestures. In these tests the subject enters for the first time into social relations with the experimenter and it is therefore necessary that he understand the will and desires of the latter. It is the beginning of inter-psychology.

Procedure. As soon as the subject enters the room say good morning to him with expression, give him your hand with accentuated gesture to see if he understands the salutation and if he knows how to shake hands. In cases where the subject walks in, ask him to be seated; this permits one to see whether he understands the meaning of the invitation and if he knows the use of a chair. Throw some object on the floor and request him by gestures as well as by speech to pick it up and give it back. Make him get up, shut the door, send him away, call him back. So much for commands. Imitation of simple gestures is accomplished by fixing his attention by repeating several times, "Look at me carefully," and when his attention is gained, by saying "Do as I do." The examiner then claps his hands together, puts them in the air, on the shoulders, behind the back; he turns the thumbs one about the other, raises the foot, etc. All this mimicry must be conducted gaily with the air of play. It is sufficient if a single well marked imitation is provoked; the rest is unnecessary. Do not confound the inaptitude for imitation, with bad humor, ill-will, or timidity.

7. *Verbal Knowledge of Objects*

The object of this test is to discover if associations exist between things and their names. Comprehension and the first possibilities of language are here studied. This test is a continuation of the previous one and represents the second degree of communication between individuals; the first degree is made through imitation, the second through words.

Procedure. This test is composed of two parts. In the first place the examiner names a part of the body and asks the child to point to it. The questions may relate to the head, the hair, the eyes, the feet, the hands, the nose, the ears, the mouth. Ask the child with a smile "Where is your head?" If he seems embarrassed or timid, encourage him by aiding him a little. "There is your head," pointing it out and touching it if the child does not seem to understand what is wanted of him. On the other hand if he replies by a correct designation to the first question go no further, because if he knows where his head is he should know equally well where are his ears and his mouth. Give him therefore some more difficult questions, for example, his cheek, his eyebrow, his heart.

The second part of the experiment consists in making him designate familiar objects, a string, a cup, a key. Bring the child to the table and by means of gestures indicate the objects and turn his attention to them. When his attention is fixed upon the objects tell him to give you the one you name. "Give me the cup. Give me the key, etc." The cup, the key, the string are the three objects asked for. It is of little importance that he shows awkwardness in taking and presenting them. The essential is that by the play of the countenance and gestures, he indicates clearly that he distinguishes these objects by their names. It is preferable to keep these three objects, others less familiar should be rejected, as for instance a box of matches, a cork, etc. The test is made with three objects in order to avoid the right designation by simple chance. With backward children the following facts may present themselves. They do not know the name of the object presented to them, but having understood that they are

894

to designate an object, they point to anything that is on the table. This is a manner of reacting very common among idiots and imbeciles. They make mistakes but they do not realize it, being in fact very well satisfied with their achievements. Here is another source of error to be avoided. In consequence of their extreme docility, many backward children may be bewildered by the least contradiction. When they have handed you a cup, if you ask them "Isn't this a key?" some might make a sign of acquiescence. This is a test of suggestibility of which more will be said further on. To a blind child, give objects to be recognized by the sense of touch.

8. *Verbal Knowledge of Pictures*

This exercise is the same as the preceding one with this difference only, that the objects are replaced by pictures which, in consequence of the diminished size and the reduction to a plane surface, are a little more difficult to recognize than in nature, and more than this in a picture the objects must be sought for.

Procedure. We make use of a print borrowed from the picture-book of Inspector Lacabe and Mlle. Goergin. This print in colors represents a complex family scene. We show the print to the child and ask him to designate successively the following objects: the window, mamma, big sister, little sister, little girl, cat, broom, basket, bouquet, duster, coffee-mill. The questions are asked in this way: "Where is the window?" or "Tell me where the window is," or "Show me the window," or "Put your finger on the window."

The last suggestion is generally unnecessary because the child has a tendency to place his forefinger, generally a dirty one, upon the detail which is named for him. If he makes an error in designation be careful not to correct it, but make a note of it. In a psychological examination of this kind, one must never point out to a child the errors which he makes. The examiner is not a pedagogue. It is rare that those who take an interest in the picture can not designate the principal details named to them. The incapable ones give no attention to the picture and do not seem to comprehend what is wanted of them. It is interesting to study the attitude of a child during this test. There are two acts to be accomplished, one a search for the object, the other the recognition of the object. At once in the search the aptitudes or inaptitudes betray themselves. Many defective persons show an excess of eagerness to designate the object, which in itself is a sign of faulty attention. They point out at once without waiting to comprehend. They sometimes point out before one has finished the sentence. "Where is the —," said with a suspension in the voice, and already their finger is placed haphazard upon the picture. Such as these do not hunt with care and are incapable of suspending their judgment. This is, it seems to us, a striking characteristic of a weak mind. The child must be closely studied in order to find if, in spite of this special manner, he really knows the names of the objects. A reprimand gently given will sometimes put him on his guard, "No, no, pay attention, you go too fast," and if the question is repeated he will often give a correct answer.

In other cases, errors are sometimes made through suggestibility. The subject seems to imagine that he will commit a fault if he does not designate some object when the question is asked, and out of compliance or of timidity, he makes an erroneous designation for an object whose name he does not know, or which he does not succeed in finding. Notice again, the more reasonable attitude of those who, not knowing the name of the object, refrain from pointing it out but continue the search or reply distinctly, "I do not know." It is rare that an imbecile uses that little phrase. The avowal of ignorance is a proof of judgment and is always a good indication.

9. *Naming of Designated Objects*

This test is the opposite of the preceding one. It shows the passing from the thing to the word. It also is executed by the use of pictures.

Procedure. Here we make use of another colored print borrowed from the same collection as the preceding. We place it before the eyes of the child and designate with a pencil different objects while asking each time, "What is this?" The objects upon which we place the pencil are the little girl, the dog, the boy, the father, the lamp-lighter, the sky, the advertisement. For the lamp-lighter we ask what he does. Here as elsewhere it is unnecessary to exhaust the complete series of questions unless the subject fails. One or two positive replies are sufficient to satisfy the requirements of the test. This test permits us to know the vocabulary and the pronunciation of the child. Defects of pronunciation, so frequent in the young, are a serious source of embarrassment. It often requires a very indulgent ear to recognize the right word in an indistinct and very brief murmur, and in a case of this sort the examiner will do well to use an interrogation point. Added to the difficulties which proceed from faulty pronunciation, are those brought about by a special vocabulary. Many little children though normal use a vocabulary invented or deformed by them, which is understood only by themselves and their parents.

Additional remarks. Tests 7, 8, and 9 do not constitute differing degrees in the rigorous sense of the word, that is to say they are not tests corresponding to different levels of intelligence. We have ascertained that generally with subnormals those who can pass test 7, pass 8 and also 9. These would therefore be tests of equal rank. We have kept them, however, because these tests occupy an important place in our measuring scale of intelligence, as they constitute a borderline test between imbecility and idiocy. It is useful to have this borderline solidly placed and all these tests will serve as buttresses.

Observations, such as one may make every day on those afflicted with general paralysis, aphasia, or simply people very much fatigued, show that it is much more difficult to pass from the object to the word than it is to pass from the word to the object, or we may say, that one recognizes a word more easily than one finds it. It does not seem clear up to the present that this observation is also applicable to inferior states of intelligence.

10. *Immediate Comparison of Two Lines of Unequal Lengths*

As we enter the field of what may properly be called psychological experimentation, we shall find it difficult to define which mental functions are being exercised because they are very numerous. Here the child must understand that it is a question of comparison, that the comparison is between two lines that are shown to him; he must understand the meaning of the words, ''Show me the longer.'' He must be capable of comparing, that is of bringing together a conception and an image, and of turning his mind in the direction of searching for a difference. We often have illusions as to the simplicity of psychical processes, because we judge them in relation to others, still more complex. In fact here is a test which will seem to show but little mentality in those who are able to execute it; nevertheless when analyzed it reveals a great complexity.

Procedure. The subject is presented successively with three pieces of paper upon each of which two lines, drawn in ink, are to be compared. Each piece of paper measures 15 by 20 cm.; the lines are drawn lengthwise of the paper, on the same level, and separated by a space of 5 mm. The lines are respectively 4 and 3 cm. in length and one-half of a millimeter in width. On the first sheet the longer line is at the right and on the other two at the left. Each sheet is shown to the subject while saying to him, "Which is the longer line?" Note if his reply is correct but do not tell him. In order to eliminate haphazard replies, it is well to repeat the whole series at least twice. The end is not to discover just how far the accuracy of the child's glance may go, but simply to find if he is capable of making a correct comparison between two lines. Many subnormals are incapable of this; but they act as though they were capable; they seem to understand what is said to them and each time put the finger upon one of the lines saying, "This one." It is necessary to recognize those subjects whose errors are not, strictly speaking, faults of comparison but absence of comparison. It often happens that the subject constantly chooses the line on the same side for the longer, for example always the one on the right side. This manner of reacting would be a sign of defect were it not that one encounters the same thing with some normals.

11. *Repetition of Three Figures*

This is a test of immediate memory and voluntary attention.

Procedure. Looking the subject squarely in the eye to be sure his attention is fixed, one pronounces three figures, after having told him to repeat them. Choose figures that do not follow each other, as for instance, 3, 0, 8, or 5, 9, 7. Pronounce the three figures in the same voice without accentuating one more than the others and without rhythm, but with a certain energy. The rapidity to be observed is two figures per second. Listen carefully and record the repetition which is made. Often the first attempt is unsuccessful because the subject has not clearly understood and commences to repeat the first figure the moment he hears it; he must be made to be quiet, renew the explanation and commence the pronunciation of another series of figures. There are certain subjects who can not repeat a single figure; in general these are the ones whose mental condition is such that they have not understood anything at all of what is asked of them. Others repeat only a single figure, the first or the last; others pronounce more than three. Special attention must be given to those whose error consists in pronouncing a greater number of figures than that which is said, or in pronouncing a series of figures in their natural order. An individual who, when asked to repeat 3, 0, 8, replies 2, 3, 4, 5, commits a serious error, which would cause one to suspect mental debility. But on the other hand it is true that all feeble-minded and all imbeciles do not commit this error, and that many young normals may commit it. Be careful to notice also if the subject seems satisfied with his reply when this is obviously and grossly false; this indicates an absence of judgment which constitutes an aggravated condition.

Let us say, apropos of this test, that it is important to make a distinction between errors of attention and of adaptation on the one hand, and errors of judgment on the other. When a failure is produced by distraction it is not very important. Thus it may happen that a subject does not repeat the three figures the first time. Begin again and if he succeeds the second time in retaining them he should be considered as having passed the test. A little farther on we shall have to deal with tests of judgment properly so-called, and three or four difficulties will be presented for solution. In this last case, failure will be much more serious, because it can not be due to inattention and the test cannot be considered as passed unless the solutions are given complete.

12. *Comparison of Two Weights*

This is a test of attention, of comparison and of the muscular sense.

Procedure. Place side by side on the table before the subject two small cubical boxes having the same dimensions, (23 mm. on a side) and the same color, but of different weights. The boxes, weighted by grains of lead rolled in cotton and not perceptible by shaking, weigh 3 grams and 12 grams respectively. The subject is asked to find out which is the heavier. The operation terminated, two other cubes of 6 and 15 grams respectively are given him to compare, and again 3 grams and 15 grams. If the subject hesitates or seems to be going haphazard, start over again mixing the cubes in order to be sure that he really compares the weights.

At the injunction, "See the two boxes, now tell me which is the heavier," many young subjects designate haphazard one of the two boxes without testing the weights. This error, all the more naive since the two are exactly alike in appearance, does not prove that the subject is incapable of weighing them in his hand and of judging of the weights while exercising muscular sense. One must then order him to take the boxes in his hand and weigh them. Some are very awkward, and put the two boxes into one hand at the same time to weigh them. One must again interfere and teach him how to put a box in each hand and weigh the two simultaneously.

Additional remarks. Following this weighing of two boxes of different weight and equal volume, one can propose to weigh two boxes of equal weight but different volume. The illusion which is produced under these circumstances is well known. With the weights equal, the larger box will appear lighter; and the apparent difference of weight increases with the difference of volume. Investigations have been made to determine whether this illusion takes place with backward children, and it has been observed by Demoor that there are certain ones who are not affected by it, something which we ourselves have recently verified. We put before the defective children long boxes of white wood, of the same weight, the largest one 24 x 4 x 4 cm., the smallest 12 x 2 x 2 cm., the medium one 18 x 3 x 3 cm. Like many normal children our subnormals, when given two for comparison and asked "Which is the heavier," pointed out the larger. The first naive response has but little significance. If one insists, if one tells the subject to weigh them in his hand, it sometimes happens that subnormals either cling to their first designation, or abandon it altogether and find the smaller one the heavier; in the latter case they are sensitive to the illusion. It seems to us that before declaring that a subnormal is not sensitive, one must first find if he can compare two weights, and whether he is able to judge which is the heavier of two weights, and whether he is able to judge which is the heavier of two weights having the same volume. Having made this preliminary test, one will perceive that very many subnormals are insensible to the illusion because they are incapable of comparing weights. What they lack therefore is a more elementary aptitude.

13. *Suggestibility*

Suggestibility is by no means a test of intelligence, because very many persons of superior intelligence are susceptible to suggestion, through distraction, timidity, fear of doing wrong, or some preconceived idea. Suggestion produces effects which from certain points of view closely resemble the natural manifestations of feeble-mindedness; in fact suggestion disturbs the judgment, paralyzes the critical sense, and forces us to attempt unreasonable or unfitting acts worthy of a defective. It is therefore necessary, when examining a child suspected of retardation, not to give a suggestion unconsciously, for thus artificial debility is produced which might make the diagnosis deceptive. If a person is forced to give an absurd reply by making use of an alternative pronounced in an authoritative voice, it does not in the least prove

902

that he is lacking in judgment. But this source of error being once recognized and set aside, it is none the less interesting to bring into the examination a precise attempt at suggestion, and note what happens. It is a means of testing the force of judgment of a subject and his power of resistance.

Procedure. The proof of suggestibility which we have devised does not give rise to a special experiment: it complicates by a slight addition other exercises which we have already described.

(*a*) *Designation of objects named by the experimenter.* When we ask the child (test 7) to show us the thread, the cup, the thimble, we add, "Show me the button." On the empty table there is no button, there are only the three preceding objects and yet by gesture and look we invite the subject to search for the button on the table. It is a suggestion by personal action, developing obedience. Certain ones obey quickly and easily, presenting to us again the cup or no matter what other objects. Their suggestibility is complete. Others resist a little, pout, while feigning to hunt for it on the table, or in the cup; they do not reply, but cover their embarrassment by a search which they continue indefinitely if not interrupted. One should consider this attitude as a sufficient expression of resistance, and go no further. It would be unnecessary as we are not seeking a victory over them. Lastly, those least affected by suggestion, reply clearly, "I do not know," or "There is no button." Some laugh.

(*b*) *Designation of parts of a picture named by the experimenter.* When the child has looked at the picture and we have asked him to point out the window, etc., at the very last say, "Where is the patapoum?" and then "Where is the nitchevo?" words that have no sense for him. These demands are made in the same manner as the preceding ones. Here again we find the three types, children who docilely designate any object whatever, others

903

who search indefinitely without finding anything, and again others who declare, "There is none."

(c) *Snare of lines.* Following the three pairs of unequal lines, which serve to show the correctness of comparison, we place before the subject three other similar sheets each containing two equal lines. We present them saying, "And here?" Led on by the former replies he has a tendency, an acquired force, for again finding one line longer than the other. Some succumb to the snare completely. Others stop at the first pair and declare, "They are equal," but at the second and third they say one of the lines is longer than the other. Others find them all equal but hesitate. Others again fall into the snare without a shadow of hesitation.

14. *Verbal Definition of Known Objects*

Vocabulary, some general notions, ability to put a simple idea into words, are all brought to light by means of this test.

Procedure. Ask the child what is a house, a horse, a fork, a mamma. This is the conversation that takes place: "Do you know what a —— is?" If the child answers yes then ask him: "Very well, then tell me what it is." Try to overcome his silence a little and his timidity. Aid him, only when necessary, by giving him an example: "A dog, it barks," and then see if the child understands and approves that definition.

Very young normal children of two or three years, reply to questions of this kind with enthusiasm. They ordinarily reply in terms of use, "A fork is to eat with." This is typical. Record the answer verbatim. Some will keep silent, some give absurd, incomprehensible replies, or again will repeat the word, "A house, it is a house."

15. *Repetition of Sentences of Fifteen Words*

This is a test of immediate memory, so far as it concerns the recollection of words; a proof of voluntary attention, naturally because voluntary attention must accompany all psychological experiments; lastly it is a test of language.

Procedure. First be sure that the child is listening carefully, then, after having warned him that he will have to repeat what is said to him, pronounce slowly, intelligibly, the following sentence: *I get up in the morning, I dine at noon, I go to bed at night.* Then make a sign for him to repeat. Often the child, still not very well adapted, has not fully understood. Never repeat a sentence but go on to another. When the subject repeats it write down verbatim what he says. Many even among normals make absurd repetitions, for example: "I go to bed at noon." Often the child replaces the cultured expression "I dine" with a more familiar form, "I eat." The fact of being able to repeat the sentence correctly after the first hearing is a good sign. The second sentence is easier than the first, *In the summer the weather is beautiful; in winter snow falls.* Here is the third, *Germaine has been bad, she has not worked, she will be scolded.* Now we give five sentences quite difficult to understand:

The horse-chestnut tree in the garden throws upon the ground the faint shade of its new young leaves.

The horse draws the carriage, the road is steep and the carriage is heavy.

It is one o'clock in the afternoon, the house is silent, the cat sleeps in the shade.

One should not say all that he thinks, but he must think all that he says.

The spirit of criticism must not be confounded with the spirit of contradiction.

16. *Comparison of Known Objects from Memory*

This is an exercise in ideation, in the notion of differences, and somewhat in powers of observation.

Procedure. One asks what difference there is between paper and cardboard, between a fly and a butterfly, between a piece of wood and a piece of glass. First be sure that the subject knows these objects. Ask him, "Have you seen paper?" "Do you know what cardboard is?" Thus ask him about all the objects before drawing his attention to the difference between them. It may happen that little Parisians, even though normal, and eight or nine years old, have never seen a butterfly. These are examples of astounding ignorance, but we have found, what is still more extraordinary, Parisians of ten years who have never seen the Seine.

After being assured that the two objects to be compared are known, demand their difference. If the word is not understood, take notice and afterward choose more familiar language. "In what are they not alike? How are they not alike?" Three classes of replies may be expected. First, that of the children who have no comprehension of what is desired of them. When asked the difference between cardboard and paper, they reply, "The cardboard." When one has provoked replies of this kind, the explanation must be renewed with patience to see if there is not some means of making oneself understood. Second, the absurd replies, such as, "The fly is larger than the butterfly." "The wood is thicker than the glass," or "The butterfly flies and so does the fly." Third, the correct reply.

17. *Exercise of Memory on Pictures*

This is a test of attention and visual memory.

Procedure. The subject is told that several pictures will be shown to him, which he will be allowed to look at for thirty seconds, and that he must then repeat the names of the objects seen, from memory. There are thirteen pictures, each 6 by 6 centimeters, representing the following objects: clock, key, nail, omnibus, barrel, bed, cherry, rose, mouth of a beast, nose, head of a child, eggs, landscape. These pictures are pasted on two cardboards and are shown simultaneously. Measure the time of exposure with the second hand of the watch. In order that the subject shall not become absorbed in one picture, say to him, "Make haste. Look at all." The thirty seconds passed, the examiner writes from dictation the names of the pictures the subject recalls.

This test does indeed give an idea of the memory of a person, but two subjects may have very unequal memories of the same picture; one of them may recall only one detail while another recalls the whole. Moreover there is a weak point in this test in that it may be affected by failure of attention. It is sufficient that a fly should alight, a door should open, a cock should crow, or for the subject to have a desire to use his handkerchief during the thirty seconds to disturb the work of memorizing. If the result is altogether lacking, the test should be repeated with another collection of pictures to find whether the first error was the result of distraction.

18. *Drawing a Design from Memory*

This is a test of attention, visual memory, and a little analysis.

Procedure. The subject is told that two designs will be shown to him, which he will be allowed to look at for ten seconds, and which he must then draw from memory.

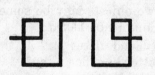 

DESIGN TO BE DRAWN FROM MEMORY AFTER BEING STUDIED 10 SECONDS

Excite his emulation. The two designs which we reproduce here, are shown to him and left exposed for ten seconds. (Regulate the time by the second hand of a watch; the time must be exact within one or two seconds.) Then see that the subject commences the reproduction of the design without loss of time.

Marking the results of this test, that is the errors committed, is a delicate operation. Simply note if the reproduction is absolutely correct; or if without being correct it resembles the model; or if, on the contrary, it bears no resemblance whatever to it.

19. *Immediate Repetition of Figures*

This is a test of immediate memory and immediate attention.

Procedure. This is the same as for the three figures, see above. Here the errors noted for the three figures take on greater proportions. One must be on the watch for errors of judgment. A normal may fail but the manner is different.

20. *Resemblances of Several Known Objects*
Given from Memory

This is a test of memory, conscious recognition of resemblances, power of observation.

Procedure. This test closely resembles test 16, except that here resemblances are to be indicated instead of differences. It may be surprising to learn that children have a good deal of trouble noting resemblances; they much more willingly find differences in the objects given them to compare. One must insist a good deal and show them that although unlike two objects may be somewhat similar. Here are the questions to be asked:

In what are a poppy and blood alike?
How are a fly, an ant, a butterfly, a flea alike?
In what way are a newspaper, a label, a picture alike?
Under test 16 we have indicated the precautions that

908

must be taken, notably that of assuring oneself that the child knows the objects to be compared. There are little Parisians who have never seen poppies or ants.

21. *Comparison of Lengths*

This is a test in exactness of glance in rapid comparison.

Procedure. In this test one presents a series of pairs of lines. One line of each pair is 30 mm. long and the other varies from 31 to 35 mm. These lines are drawn on the pages of a blank book, 15 by 30 cm.; there are only two lines on a page. They extend in the same direction, end to end, separated by 5 mm. The longer occupies first the right then the left of the page. There are fifteen pairs. After placing them in order one begins by showing the pair where the difference is greatest. The subject is asked to point out the longer of the two lines.

We then present, in another blank book, a series of pairs of lines very much more difficult to estimate. The pages of this book are 20 by 30 cm.; the constant line is 100 mm. long, the variable ranging from 101 to 103 mm. The exact comparison of such long lines is beyond the ability of many adults. The number of pairs is twelve.

22. *Five Weights to be Placed in Order*

This test requires a direct concentration of attention, an appreciation of weight, and the memory of judgment.

Procedure. Five little boxes of the same color and volume are placed in a group on the table. They weigh respectively 3, 6, 9, 12, and 15 grams. They are shown to the subject while saying to him: "Look at these little boxes, they have not the same weight; you are going to arrange them here in their right order. Here to the left first the heaviest weight; next, the one a little less heavy; here one a little less heavy; here one a little less heavy; and here the lightest one." This explanation is difficult to give in childish terms. It must be attempted, however, and repeated if one perceives that it is not understood.

The explanation terminated, one must observe with

909

attention the attitude of the child. One child does not understand, puts nothing in order; another arranges the weights very well but does not compare them; he takes one at random and puts it at the left as the heaviest, without comparing it with the others, and places those remaining without weighing them. A third tries them a little, but noticeably goes at it blindly. The reading of the weights which is inscribed on each, shows us the errors.

There are three classes to distinguish. First, the subject who goes at random without comparing, often committing a serious error, four degrees for example. Second, the subject who compares, but makes a slight error of one or two degrees. Third, the one who has the order exact. We propose to estimate the errors in this test by taking account of the displacement that must be made to reestablish the correct order. Thus in the following example: 12, 9, 6, 3, 15,—15 is not in its place, and the error is of four degrees because it must make four moves to find the place where it belongs. All the others must be changed one degree. The sum of the changes indicates the total error which is of eight degrees. It is necessary to make a distinction between those who commit slight errors of inattention, and those who by the enormity of an error of 6 or 8 prove that they act at random.

23. *Gap in Weights*

As soon as the subject has correctly arranged the weights and only then, tell him that one of the weights is to be taken away while he closes his eyes, and that he is to discover which has been taken away by weighing them in his hand. The operation demanded of him is delicate. One must note that he does not cheat by reading the marking on the box. If there is any fear of this, wrap the boxes in paper.

24. *Exercises upon Rhymes*

This exercise requires an ample vocabulary, suppleness

910

of mind, spontaneity, intellectual activity.

Procedure. Begin by asking the subject if he knows what a rhyme is. Then explain by means of examples: "Rhymes are words that end in the same way. Thus 'grenouille' rhymes with 'citrouille,' because it is the same sound 'ouille.' 'Compote' rhymes with 'carotte,' they both end with 'ote.' 'Baton' rhymes with 'macaron,' and with 'citron.' Here the rhyme is on 'on.' Do you now understand what a rhyme is? Very well, you must find all the rhymes you can. The word with which you must find rhymes is 'obeissance.' Come, begin, find some." In order to accomplish this test, the subject must not only find rhymes, which is partly a matter of imagination, but he must understand the preceding explanation, which is a matter of judgment. There are subjects who remain silent who either have not understood or are unable to find rhymes. Others are more loquacious but the false rhymes they cite prove that they have not comprehended. The minute having elapsed, renew the explanation and try the test again.

25. *Verbal Gaps to be Filled*

This test thought out and proposed by Professor Ebbinghaus of Berlin, varies in significance according to its mode of use. It consists essentially in this: a word of a text is omitted and the subject is asked to replace it. The nature of the intellectual work by which the gap is filled, varies according to the case. This may be a test of memory, a test of style, or a test of judgment. In the sentence: "Louis IX was born in ——" the gap is filled by memory. "The crow —— his feathers with his beak;" in this the idea of the suppressed word is not at all obscure, and the task consists in finding the proper word. We may say in passing, that according to the opinion of several teachers before whom we have tried it, this kind of exercise furnishes excellent scholastic training. Lastly, in sentences of the nature of those we have chosen, the filling of the gaps requires an attentive examination and an appreciation of the facts set forth by the sentence. It is therefore an exercise of judgment.

Procedure. We have simplified it by suppressing all explanations. The words forming the gap are intentionally placed at the end of the sentence. It is sufficient to read the text with expression, then suspend the voice with the tone of interrogation when one arrives at the gap. The subject naturally fills in the gap. If he does not do so spontaneously, urge him a little by saying, "Finish. What must one say?" Once the operation is set going it continues easily.

The operator knows the true words of the text which have been suppressed. He should not yield to the temptation of considering those the only correct ones. He must examine and weigh with care all the words that are given him. Some are good, others altogether bad, nonsensical or absurd. There will be all degrees.

Here is the text with the gaps. The words to be suppressed are in italics.

The weather is clear, the sky is (1) *blue.* The sun has quickly dried the linen which the women have spread on the line. The cloth, white as snow, dazzles the (2) *eyes.* The women gather up the large sheets which are as stiff as though they had been (3) *starched.* They shake them and hold them by the four (4) *corners.* Then they snap the sheets with a (5) *noise.* Meanwhile the housewife irons the fine linen. She takes the irons one after the other and places them on the (6) *stove.* Little Mary who is dressing her doll would like to do some (7) *ironing,* but she has not had permission to touch the (8) *irons.*

26. *Synthesis of Three Words in One Sentence*

This exercise is a test in spontaneity, facility of invention and combination, aptitude to construct sentences.

Procedure. Three words are proposed: Paris, river, fortune. Ask that a sentence be made using those three words. It is necessary to be very clear, and to explain to those who may not chance to know what a sentence is. Many subjects remain powerless before this difficulty, which is beyond their capacity. Others can make a sentence with a given word but they can not attain to the putting of three words in a single sentence.

27. *Reply to an Abstract Question*

This test is one of the most important of all, for the diagnosis of mental debility. It is rapid, easily given, sufficiently precise. It consists in placing the subject in a situation presenting a difficulty of an abstract nature. Any mind which is not apt in abstraction succumbs here.

Procedure. This consists in reading the beginning of a sentence and suspending the voice when one arrives at the point, and repeating, "What ought one to do?" The sentences are constructed in such a manner that the slight difficulty of comprehension which they present, comes from the ideas rather than from the words. The child who does not understand, is hindered less by his ignorance of the language than by his lack of ability to seize an abstract idea. There are twenty-five questions. The first are very easy and tend to put the subject at his ease. We do not reproduce them here as they will be found farther on with the results. Here are only four of the sentences. They are among those of medium difficulty.

1. When one has need of good advice—what must one do?

2. Before making a decision about a very important affair—what must one do?

3. When anyone has offended you and asks you to excuse him—what ought you to do?

4. When one asks your opinion of someone whom you know only a little—what ought you to say?

It is often a delicate matter to estimate the value of a reply. Sometimes the subject does not gather all the shades of the question and the reply is too simple, not absolutely adequate to the demand. Nevertheless one must be satisfied if it expresses sense, if it proves that the general bearing of the question has been grasped.

In other cases the reply is equivocal; it would be excellent if it came from a dilettante, or a decadent, because of the double meaning which is ironically evoked. It is of no value in the mouth of a school child. Thus to the first question, "When one has need of good advice—" a child replied, "one says nothing." We suppose he has not understood but if this had been an ironical reply, one might have found in it a curious meaning. As a matter of fact, these uncertainties, which are truly matters of conscience with the examiner, present themselves but rarely. Ordinarily the interpretation is easy because one knows already about what to expect from his subject.

28. *Reversal of the Hands of a Clock*

This is a test of reasoning, attention, visual imagery.

Procedure. First ask the subject if he knows how to tell time. In case his answer is in the affirmative, put him to the test because it is not best to trust his word. There are imbeciles who say they know how to tell time and give extravagant answers when a watch is given them to read. It is important to note this error in judgment. Having found that the subject knows how to tell time, remind him that the long hand indicates the minutes and the short hand the hours. Then say to him, "Suppose that it is a quarter of three, do you clearly see where the long hand is, and the short hand? Very well, now suppose the long hand is changed to the place where the short hand is, and the short hand to the place of the long, what time is it?" Reverse the hands for the following hours: twenty minutes past six; four minutes of three. The correct solutions are, half past four, and a quarter past eleven.

The subject must not see the face of a watch, nor make the design upon paper, or his cuff or his nail to aid his imagination. As the experiment is made individually, supervision is easy.

When the subject gives the two solutions correctly, one can push him a little further, imposing a question much more difficult. Say to him, "For each of the hours the you have indicated, the reversal of the hands brings about the result that you have found; nevertheless this result is not altogether correct. The transposition indicated is not altogether possible. By analyzing the case with care, tell me why."

This test permits of varying degrees of accuracy in the replies. First, certain ones are not able to make any transposition; they give no solution, or else it is absolutely incorrect. Others who come nearer the truth give a solution which is partially correct; for example, only one of the hands is rightly placed, or perhaps an error of symmetry has been committed, one has put to the right what ought to have been at the left or inversely. The third category is that of subjects who give correct solutions. Finally the fourth is composed of those who give a correct solution and are capable of criticizing the slight inaccuracies.

29. *Paper Cutting*

This exercise calls for voluntary attention, reasoning, visual imagery, but not for vocabulary.

Procedure. Take two sheets of white paper of the same dimensions. Call the attention of the subject to their equality. "You see they are alike." Lay the first one on the table, fold the other into two equal parts slowly before the subject, then fold again into two equal parts at right angles to the first fold. The sheet is now folded in four equal divisions. On the edge that presents a single fold, cut out with the scissors, a triangle. Take away the triangular piece of paper without allowing the subject to study it, but show him the folded paper, and say to him: "The sheet of paper is now cut. If I were to open it, it would no longer resemble the first sheet of paper here on the table; there will be a hole in it. Draw on this first sheet of paper what I shall see when I unfold this one." It is important that the experimenter say neither more nor less than our text, and that he compel himself to employ the words chosen by us although scarcely exact and accurate. The subject now draws upon the first sheet the result of the cutting which he has just witnessed. He should not be allowed to handle the perforated sheet. Some subjects look a little at the perforation, others rely upon their imagination and begin at once to draw. The less intelligent simply draw an angle placed no matter where on the white page, or perhaps a triangle whose form and dimensions are not those of the cut. A little closer observation causes some to consider the form and dimensions. Somewhat better is the triangle replaced by a diamond drawn in the center of the page. Although better, it is still not the correct result, for to be correct two diamonds must be drawn, one in the center of each half of the paper. This test interests everybody. It requires no development of style. It has nothing literary, and rests upon entirely different faculties than those required by preceding tests. Moreover the correctness of the result is easy to grade.

30. *Definitions of Abstract Terms*

This test resembles closely those which consist in replying to an abstract question. It differs especially in that it requires a knowledge of vocabulary.

Procedure. Without preliminaries, one asks of the subject, ''What difference is there between esteem and affection? What difference is there between weariness and sadness?'' Often the subject does not reply. He sometimes gives an absurd or nonsensical answer.

We conclude here the list of tests we have used. It would have been easy to continue them by rendering them more complicated, if one had wished to form a hierarchy among normal children. One could even extend the scale up to the adult normal, the average intelligent, the very intelligent, the hyper-intelligent and measure, or

916

try to measure, talent and genius. We shall postpone for another time this difficult study.

When a subnormal, or a child suspected of being such, is questioned, it is not necessary to follow the exact order of tests. A little practice enables one to cut short, and put the finger upon the decisive test.

The solutions given by the subjects can be put into four categories:

1. *Absence of solution.* This is either a case of mutism, or refraining from making an attempt, or an error so great that there is nothing satisfactory in the result. We indicate the absence of result by the algebraic sign minus (—).

2. *Partial solutions.* A part of the truth has been discovered. The reply is passable. This is indicated by a fraction; the fraction in use is ½. When the test permits several degrees one can have ¼ or ¾, etc.

3. *Complete solution.* This does not admit of definition. It is indicated by the algebraic sign plus (+).

4. *Absurdities.* We have cited a great number of examples and insist upon their importance; they are indicated by the exclamation sign (!).

The cause for certain defective replies can sometimes be grasped with sufficient clearness to admit of classification.

Besides the failure to comprehend the tests as a whole, we encounter:

1. Ignorance; the subject does not know the sense of a word or has never seen the object of which one speaks. Thus a child does not know a poppy. We write an I.

2. Resistance to the examination because of bad humor, unwillingness, state of nerves, etc. We write an R.

3. Accentuated timidity. We write a T.

4. The failure of attention, distraction. We write a D. The distraction may be of different kinds. There is an

accidental distraction, produced by an exterior excitant or an occasional cause. For example, the case of a normal who spoils a memory test because he must use his handkerchief. There is constitutional distraction frequent among subnormals. We have ascertained among them the following types: Distraction from scattered perceptions. Distraction from preoccupation. Distraction from inability to fix the attention.

ALFRED BINET (b.-Nice, France, ca. July 8, 1857; d.-Paris, Oct. 18, 1911).

Binet was originally trained for the law. His life-long hobby was the writing of plays for the Paris theater, for which he wrote several. Binet began his studies of children with his own two daughters, while working in association with Charcot at the Salpetrière. In 1894, Binet received his DSc. from the Sorbonne, and became Director of the first psychology laboratory there. In 1895, together with Beaunis, he founded the journal *L'année psychologique*. It is in this journal that all of Binet's early studies on intelligence were published. The immediate stimulus to the development of the test was Binet's appointment to a special commission, established by the Minister of Public Education of Paris, in 1904, to find a way to distinguish between normal and subnormal children.

The present selection consists in the first tentative form of the famous intelligence test. Though substantially modified in later edition, this early form is by far the most revealing in terms of the problems which had to be defined and overcome. It is brilliant in conception, and never loses sight of the delicate problems of human evaluation with which it is dealing.

BINET, A. & SIMON, TH. *The development of intelligence in children.* Pub. #11, Training School, Vineland, N. J. May 1916,—Williams & Wilkins Co., Baltimore. Trans. E. S. Kite, from various essays in *L'année psychol.*

    (a) "Upon the necessity of establishing a scientific diagnosis of inferior states of intelligence." (p. 9-14).

    (b) "New methods for the diagnosis of the intellectual level of subnormals" (p. 37-69).

I am particularly grateful to Miss Alice M. Whiting (niece of the late Dr. Henry Goddard who held the copyright to this translation), for permission to reprint it here.

918

See also:

BINET, A. *L'étude expérimentale de l'intelligence.* Paris: Schleicher Frères & Cie., 1903.
La fatigue intellectuelle, with V. Henri. Paris: Schleicher Frères & Cie., 1898.
Les idées modernes sur les enfants. Paris: E. Flammarien, 1910.
The intelligence of the feebleminded, with Th. Simon. Baltimore: Williams & Wilkins Co., 1916. Trans. E. S. Kite.
Introduction a la psychologie expérimentale, with P. Courtier & V. Henri. Paris: F. Alcan, 1894.
The psychology of reasoning. Chicago: Open Court Pub. Co., 1899 (1886). Trans. A. G. Whyte.

BERTRAND, F.-L. *Alfred Binet et son Oeuvre.* Paris. F. Alcan, 1930. This contains a complete bibliography of Binet's writings, pp. 317-330.

VARON, E. J. "The development of Alfred Binet's psychology." *Psychol. Monogr.* 1935, XLVI: 1-129.
Also contains an excellent bibliography.

VARON, E. J. "Alfred Binet's concept of intelligence." *Psychol. Rev.* 1936, XLIII: 37-58.

THEODORE SIMON (b.-Dijon, France, July 10, 1873; d.- ?)
Simon received his M.D. from the University of Paris. All his subsequent life he was in active private practice. From 1908 on, he was physician at the Hospital for the Insane at Saint Yon. Upon Binet's death, Simon took over the presidency of the Society for the Experimental Study of Intelligence. Simon's reputation for kindness, skill and vision was widespread. He numbers Jean Piaget, among others, among his pupils.

PSYCHODIAGNOSTICS

A DIAGNOSTIC TEST BASED ON PERCEPTION

Hermann Rorschach

I. THE METHOD.

1. *Apparatus.*

The experiment consists in the *interpretation of accidental forms,* that is, of non-specific forms. . . .

The production of such accidental forms is very simple: a few large ink blots are thrown on a piece of paper, the paper folded, and the ink spread between the two halves of the sheet. Not all figures so obtained can be used, for those used must fulfill certain conditions. In the first place, the forms must be relatively simple; complicated pictures make the computations of the factors of the experiment too difficult. Furthermore, the distribution of the blots on the plate must fulfill certain requirements of composition or they will not be suggestive, with the result that many subjects will reject them as "simply an ink-blot" without consideration of other possible interpretations.

Every figure in the series has to fulfill certain special requirements as well as these general ones, and each, as well as any whole series, must be thoroughly tried out before it can be used as apparatus for the test. . . . The construction of a suitable series of ten figures is not so simple as might appear at first glance.

From the method of preparation it will be apparent that the figures will be symmetrical, with very little difference between the two halves. Asymmetrical figures are rejected by many subjects; symmetry supplies part of the necessary artistic composition. It has a disadvantage in that it tends to make the answers somewhat stereotyped. On the other hand, symmetry makes conditions the same for right- and left-handed subjects; furthermore, it facilitates interpretation in certain inhibited and blocked subjects. Finally, symmetry makes possible the interpretation of whole scenes.

Figures which are asymmetrical and show poor composition could add new factors to the results of the experiment but would require testing on normal control groups. But the problem cannot be further discussed here. The examination of individual sensibility to composition is a problem in itself.

The order of the plates within the series is determined by empirical results. . . .

2. *Procedure.*

The subject is given one plate after the other and asked, "What might this be?" He holds the plate in his hand and may turn it about as much as he likes. The subject is free to hold the plate near his eyes or far away as he chooses; however, it should not be viewed from a distance. The length of the extended arm is the maximum permissible distance. Care must be taken that the subject does not catch a glimpse of the plate from a distance, since this would alter the conditions of the experiment. For instance, Plate I is frequently interpreted "the head of a fox" when seen at a distance of several meters; at a closer range this answer is almost never given. Once the subject has interpreted the plate as the head of a fox it becomes very difficult for him to see anything else when it is brought nearer.

An attempt is made to get at least one answer to every plate, though suggestion in any form is, of course, avoided. Answers are taken down as long as they are produced by the subject. It has proved unwise to set a fixed time for exposure of the card. Coercion should be avoided as much as possible.

Occasionally it becomes necessary to show a suspicious subject how the figures are prepared, ad oculos. In general, however, rejection of the test is relatively rare, even among suspicious and inhibited patients.

3. Interpretation of the Figures as Perception.

Almost all subjects regard the experiment as a test of imagination. This conception is so general that it becomes, practically, a condition of the experiment. Nevertheless, the interpretation of the figures actually has little to do with imagination, and it is unnecessary to consider imagination a prerequisite. It is true, however, that those gifted with imagination react differently from those not so gifted. On the other hand, it makes little difference whether one encourages the subject to give free rein to his imagination or not; the results will be little changed. Those who have imagination show it, those who do not have it may apologize for the lack, but the results may be compared without taking richness or poverty of imagination into account.

The interpretation of the chance forms falls in the field of perception and apperception rather than imagination. . . . *

If perception can also be called an associative integration of available engrams (memory-pictures) with recent complexes of sensations, then the interpretation of chance forms can be called a perception in which the effort of integration is so great that it is realized consciously as an effort. This intrapsychic realization that the complex of sensations and the engrams are not perfectly identical gives the perception the character of an interpretation.

All answers given by the subjects are not interpretations in this sense, however. Most organic cases (senile dements, paretics), epileptics, many schizophrenics, most manics, almost all the feebleminded subjects, and even many normals are not aware of the assimilative effort. These subjects do not interpret the pictures, they name them. They may even be astonished that someone else is able to see something different in them. We deal in these

---

*Deleted is a quotation from Bleuler defining perception—*Editor.*

cases not with an interpretation but with a perception in the strict sense of the word. They are as unconscious of the associative-assimilative performance as a normal person is of the process of seeing a familiar face or in perceiving a tree. From the above discussions, we conclude that there must be a kind of threshold beyond which perception (assimilation without consciousness of assimilative effort) becomes interpretation (perception with consciousness of assimilative effort). This threshold must be very high in cases of senile dementia, in manic states, in feeblemindedness, etc.

Where this threshold is low, it is to be expected that even the simplest, most commonplace perception brings with it the consciousness of assimilative effort. This is the case in certain pedants who demand an absolutely exact correspondence between sensation complex and engrams for their perceptions. It is even more apparent in some depressed subjects. Here the assimilative effort may have become so great that it can no longer be overcome and everything they perceive seems "changed" and "strange". Pedantic and depressed subjects show just this in the test; they search for those details in the figures that happen to have distinct counterparts in nature, frequently going on to say: "I know that I am interpreting and that actually it must be something else."

Normal subjects frequently speak of the "interpretation" of the figures spontaneously.

Cases showing congenital or acquired defects of intelligence want to "recognize" the pictures.

These different ways of handling the figures indicate that the difference between interpretation and perception lies in associative factors. Furthermore, reactions of subjects in elated moods show more of a perceptive character, while in depressed moods the reaction is more interpretative. Finally, it is apparent that the difference cannot be said to be due only to associative processes; emotional factors may also shift the boundary between perception and interpretation.

In summary, we may conclude that *the differences between perception and interpretation are dependent on individual factors, not on general ones; that there is no sharp delineation, but a gradual shifting of emphasis; and that interpretation may be called a special kind of perception.* There is, therefore, no doubt that this experiment can be called a test of the perceptive power of the subject. . . .

II. THE FACTORS OF THE EXPERIMENT.

1. *Statement of Problems.*

In scoring the answers given by subject, the content is considered last. It is more important to study the *function* of perception and apperception. The experiment depends primarily on the pattern.

Protocols of the experiment are examined according to the following scheme:

1. How many responses are there? What is the reaction time? How frequently is refusal to answer encountered for the several plates?

2. Is the answer determined only by the form of the blot, or is there also appreciation of movement or color?

3. Is the figure conceived and interpreted as a whole or in parts? Which are the parts interpreted?

4. What does the subject see?

The conclusions in this work are based on experimental observations which have been obtained with the series of plates accompanying this book. The following table gives a summary of the material collected:

	Male	Female	Total
Normal, educated	35	20	55
Normal, uneducated	20	42	62
Psychopathic personality . .	12	8	20
Alcoholic cases	8	—	8
Morons, Imbeciles	10	2	12
Schizophrenics	105	83	188
Manic-depressives	4	10	14
Epileptics	17	3	20
Paretics	7	1	8
Senile dements	7	3	10
Arteriosclerotic dements . .	3	2	5
Korsakoff and similar states	3	—	3
Total	231	174	405

In addition to this, many experiments have been conducted using earlier, but now discarded, figures. These cannot be considered here because comparative scoring is possible only when observations are obtained with the same series of plates, or with a parallel series.

The totals indicated above are far too small, especially in the groups of uneducated normals and the common psychoses. The small number of the common psychoses studied is partly due to the fact that an institution serving a country canton offers little variety of material. Before the printing of the plates the number of experiments was limited because the figures were damaged by passing through hundreds of hands. . . .*

5. Form, Movement and Color Responses: Their Relation to the Perceptive Process.

Most interpretations are determined by the form of the blot alone, both in normal and abnormal subjects. The subject searches among his visual memories for that one which in form, especially in outline, most closely resem-

---

*Deleted are sections 2—number of responses; 3—reaction time; 4—Failure to answer.

925

bles the entire figure or one of its details. In accomplishing this, he does not visualize the object "seen" as moving, but as a fixed form. Such *Form-answers* will be designated hereafter as F.

In contrast to these, we have "Movement" and "Color" responses. The *Movement responses,* designated M, are those interpretations in which it can be established that *kinaesthetic* engrams (visual memories of movements observed, imagined or executed previously) have had a determining influence in addition to the consciousness of the form of the blot. The subject imagines the object "seen" as moving. *Color responses,* designated C, are those interpretations in which it can be established that the color as well as the form, or the color alone, of the figure has determined the answer. The frequency with which these three types of answers occur, and especially their relative proportions to each other are very important. They show characteristic, typical variations which are significant in normals as well as in the various illnesses.

a) Form Responses (F).

Most interpretations are determined by the form of the blots. This is the case generally as well as in each individual test. The evaluation of these form responses thus becomes a significant problem; in order to avoid subjective evaluation statistical methods were used. Form answers given by a large number of normal subjects (100) were used as the norm and basis. From this a definite range of normal form visualization could be defined, and a large number of frequently recurring answers were collected. These were called "good forms" (F+). In this process, many forms which would not, on subjective estimation, have been called good, were so designated. Those answers which are better than these, are called F+ also; those which are less clear are F—. Even though the normal range is statistically fixed, judgment

926

of what is better or worse than the good normal response remains a matter for subjective evaluation to a certain extent. However, this evaluation can be made with relative certainty. The form answers having been evaluated, 5% more or less F+ should not be considered significant in calculating the F+ percentage, since the evaluation is purely empirical and not absolutely objective. Nevertheless, the F+ percentage provides useful leads in the study.

Table I is a summary of the empirical relationships found in the cases. Only rough averages are given. Naturally, the perception of form by a schizophrenic depends on what it was before he became ill. Furthermore, the adjective "intelligent" is used loosely; as is demonstrated below, however, the test is capable of evaluating the individual components of what is called "intelligence." One of these components is sharpness of form visualization. The Table requires no special comment except to call attention to a few points. It is noteworthy that depression improves the sharpness of form visualization, while elation dulls it. Certain groupings already seen earlier in the study are repeated in the table. Those subjects who were most conscious of the assimilative effort in interpreting, namely the pedants and mild and severe depressions, are all to be found in the group which saw forms most clearly. . . . On the other hand, those whose interpretations were simply perceptions occupy the lower half of the table; these are the manics, the epileptics, the feebleminded, and the organic cases. Thus, acuteness in the perception of objects and a marked consciousness of assimilative effort in the experiment are seen to go hand in hand; the converse of this statement is also true, that lack of acuity in the perception of objects goes with freedom from a sense of effort in the test. Probably only in schizophrenics can this relationship be disturbed.

Table I.

Form Responses

	Normal	Feebleminded	Schizophrenic	Manic-Depressive	Epileptic	Organic
100—80% F+	Intelligent Pedantic Depressive	—	Apparently well preserved paranoid cases, latent and recovered	—	—	—
80—70% F+	Intelligent but careless Mod. intelligent	—	Relatively well preserved	—	—	—
70—60% F+	Unintelligent «normal» elated mood	—	Scattered	—	Epileptoid	Korsakoffs, arteriosclerotic dements
60—50% F+	—	Morons	Very scattered, originally morons	Manic	Epileptic	—
50—30% F+	—	Morons Imbeciles	Originally morons, abulic	—	Demented epileptic	Paretic
30—0% F+	—	Low grade imbecile	—	—	—	Senile dements

928

b) Movement Responses (M).

Movement Responses are those interpretations which are determined by *form perceptions plus kinaesthetic factors*. The subject imagines the object interpreted to be in motion. For instance, in Plate I he sees two angels with fluttering wings; in Plate II, two carnival clowns dancing with each other, their knees bent; in Plate III, two waiters bowing to each other, etc. Frequently the gestures of the subject during the test will indicate whether or not kinaesthetic influences are in play. He makes the movements which he is interpreting or indicates them by involuntary innervations.

One should not be misled, however, into considering each movement described or even demonstrated by the subject as indicating that the answer is kinaesthetically determined. These are subjects who indicate not a few animated objects but whose answers, nevertheless, may not be considered as determined by movement. Responses such as "a duck going into the water," "a dog snapping at a butterfly," "a bird in flight," "an airplane in flight," a "volcano in eruption," etc., are not M answers in many cases. These are form answers, determined by the form alone, and the indication of motion is often only a rhetorical embellishment of the answer, a *secondary* association. This may be the case even if the movement is demonstrated in some way. We deal here not with movement sensed in the figure, but with an association of the movement designated. . . .*

The following may be taken as a rule: answers may be considered as kinaesthetically determined practically only when human beings or animals capable of motion similar to that of human beings (monkeys, bears) are seen in the figures.

Interpretations involving human beings are not always

---

*Deleted is a comment concerning the origin of motility.

M answers. The question always is, does the movement indicated play a primary role in the determination of the answer? Do we deal with an actual *sensation of motion,* or simply the conception of a form that is secondarily interpreted as moving? Plate III is important for this consideration. It is usually interpreted as "Two waiters carrying a champagne bucket," or something similar. In this interpretation the black fish-shaped forms below and laterally are thought of as the legs of the waiters, and the legs are, as may be seen, separated from the body. Primary kinaesthetic factors are very probably necessary to make it possible for the subject to overlook this separation. Such answers are, then, to be considered as kinaesthetically determined. To be sure, very many subjects will give the answer "two men," but they do not indicate the fish-like figures as the legs, but tend rather to point out the "arms" of the waiters carrying the champagne bucket. These subjects are interpreting primarily by form alone; they perceive the heads and necks of the men, and fabricate the rest without the participation of kinaesthesias.

Other subjects frequently answer, "a sketch of men," or "caricatures." Such answers are almost never M's. "Skeletons" is the answer given by others; this also is not an M answer according to my experience.

Sometimes it is difficult to determine whether an answer is F or M. Intelligent subjects can generally say with reasonable certainty whether or not kinaesthetic factors have contributed to the response; one should wait until after the completion of the test before asking the question, however; otherwise attention is drawn to kinaesthetic factors too strongly. Occasionally unintelligent subjects and patients will give clues on careful questioning. In other cases, comparison of the interpretation under question with answers clearly F or M will make differentiation possible. (An M answer, the designation of which is definitely established, is compared with the interpretation in question, and the same procedure is carried through with an F answer.) There are some subjects who can perceive movement not only in human figures and animals with certain human characteristics but in all kinds of animals, plants, geometric figures, and even in single lines. In such cases the differentiation is usually not difficult, however, for the subjects are nearly always good at self-observation and can give the necessary information.

The experience and practice of the examiner using the same series of test blots counts heavily in scoring the M answers. Apparently the speed and certainty with which experience is acquired varies widely from individual to individual. If the observer himself has a personality too inclined to make kinaesthetic interpretations or lies at the opposite extreme, it will be difficult for him to judge properly. At any rate, the scoring of the M answers is the thorniest problem in the entire experiment. The personal equation of the observer, dependent upon his "imagery-type," can warp the results most easily here. Some statistical method might be introduced to avoid false subjective conclusions based on analogies. If there be too much schematization, however, many correct subjective conclusions will be stifled at the start.

There are considerable differences in the number of M answers given, in normals as well as in patients. The number ranges between 0 and 15, is rarely higher. See Table II.

Table II is a rough compilation which nevertheless allows certain conclusions to be drawn. In normals, the number of M responses rises in proportion to the "productivity of the intelligence," the wealth of associations, the capacity to form new associative patterns. Stereotyped and feebleminded subjects have no M's. The rule is the same for schizophrenics; the more productive the

Table II.

Movement Responses

	Normal	Feebleminded	Schizophrenic	Manic-Depressive	Epileptic	Organic
More than 5 M	Good, productive intelligence. Imaginative. Intelligent + «normal» elated mood.	—	Most inhibited catatonics. Most productive paranoids.	Manic	Epileptics with early dementia.	Korsakoff
3—5 M	Average intelligence. Unintelligent + «normal» elated mood.	—	Inhibited catatonics. Productive paranoids.	Manic	Epileptics with slow dementia.	—
1—2 M	Intelligence predominantly reproductive.	Morons + «normal» elated mood.	Unproductive catatonics + hebephrenics. Depressive.	—	Epileptics with later dementia. Epileptoid.	Paretics
0 M	Unintelligent. Pedantic. «Normal» depressive mood.	Morons, Imbeciles	With simple dementia. Stereotyped. Some querulous cases.	Depressed	Epileptoid	Arteriosclerotic and Senile Dementa.

associative life of the patient, the more M's; the more stereotyped the thinking, the fewer M answers. Elated mood increases, depressed mood decreases the number of M's so that in psychotic depressions, there are no M answers. In depressions in a schizophrenic setting, a few M's appear; in psychogenic depressions, the number may remain rather large. More M's occur in hypomanics than in manics, but in the hypomanic states of organic cases, there is little or no increase. Depressed and pedantic subjects are again found together, showing few or no M's.

The results with epileptics are extraordinary. The most demented of them show the highest number of M answers, while cases in which the dementia has developed slowly, over the course of many years, produce the least.

Comparison of tables I and II shows a few clear relationships. In normals, the number of M's is, in general, clearly proportional to the acuity of form visualization. Pedants and depressed subjects do not conform to this proportion; they can combine the most acute clarity of form visualization with no M's at all. No definite conclusions can be drawn from the rough compilation in the case of schizophrenics, and this would be possible only if individual symptoms were the basis of comparison. Such a study would go beyond the plan of this treatise. In organic cases, the results are identical with the normals; the poorer the forms, the fewer the M's. The fact that arteriosclerotic patients do not react as do the normals in this respect is due to emotional factors.

The normal relation, i.e., the better the forms, the more M's, is entirely inverted in all cases in which there is mood disturbance. In elated or depressed moods of normals, in manic-depressive insanity and in arteriosclerotic depressions, the proportion reads, the better the form, the fewer the M's. The reverse of this is also true in these cases; the poorer the forms, the more M's. Epileptics show this inverse proportion also.

933

The answers determined by kinaesthetic factors can, as was the case in the form answers, be divided into good and poor M's (M+ and M—). Those answers which correspond poorly to the form of the figure are to be considered M—. Many of these M— answers occur in the protocols of manics and epileptics but are rare in schizophrenics. A few M— answers may occur in elated normals and in subjects with Korsakoff's psychosis. M— answers are practically impossible in normal tests; however, M— responses may occur in a normal subject who knows the test and is ambitious to produce as many M's as possible; this ambition is betrayed by a few M— responses.

The movement answers are further divided into primary and secondary. In most M answers it appears that the form and kinaesthetic engrams have mixed very rapidly in the assimilative process, so that the form and motion of the objects seem to reach perception simultaneously (primary M). In other cases, it appears that first the form and later the motion of the figure reaches perception (secondary M). For example, an epileptic may see a human form in Plate III and begin to maneuver his body, bending and stretching until his position conforms to the lines of the figure. Then he gives his answer; it may be well or poorly visualized.

Is this reaction in epileptics different from that of normals because of an inherent slowness of associative processes in epilepsy? Manics show the same sort of reaction, but with much greater rapidity. They, too, may give well or poorly visualized M answers. In the manic there is no slowing of the associative process to account for this so that it must be concluded that there are other factors at work. Suffice it to say that there are differences which must be examined more fully, and will be expressed in terms of "primary" and "secondary" M answers for the present.

Frequently the responses of morons and delirious patients are similar to these secondary M's. They often describe movements that they simply imagine, and the forms they use do not correspond to any part of the figure. Subjects of these groups may see a human head and then imagine a body, or even a whole story full of movements. Such answers are not to be considered as M's, but as F's, or entirely separately, as "confabulatory F—M's."

In conclusion, it is instructive to examine the movement answers, especially in normals, to see whether they indicate flexion or extension. Subjects who usually see extension movements are fundamentally different from those who see only bent, burdened or twisted figures. In Plate V, held vertically, one of the first type saw a danseuse stretching herself upwards and backwards, making passionate movements, while one of the second type saw a bent old woman carrying two umbrellas under her arm. Subjects who see extension movements are active individuals with strong drive toward self-assertion, though they often show neurotic inhibitions. Those who see flexion movements are passive, resigned, neurasthenic individuals. Control experiments made with plates selected so that extension and flexion movements could be perceived with equal ease would be helpful in this case. . . .*

6. Mode of Apperception of the Figures.

a) Statement of Problems.

The normal subject goes at the experiment in somewhat the following manner. He first tries to interpret a given plate as a whole, searching his store of visual memories for something which coincides as far as possible with the entire figure on the plate. If his search is successful, we have a "Whole Answer," hereafter designated as W. This done, he goes on to the separate parts of the figure. He keeps to those parts which are most

*Deleted are sections c—color responses; d—incidence of M and C in the same interpretation.

935

prominent because of their arrangement. We then have one or more "Detail Answers" (D). When the most striking details are exhausted, he goes on to the smallest details of the figure and gives, perhaps, one or more interpretations of these "Small Detail Answers" (Dd). The next figure is treated in the same way and the sequence W-D-Dd is repeated, and so on through the entire series as regularly as possible. A normal subject interpreting the plates in this schematic manner would give, perhaps, ten whole answers, twenty detail answers, and thirty small detail answers; a total of about sixty interpretations. Every plate would be conceived in the sequence W-D-Dd.

If there were a subject who would react exactly in this way, he would be so "normal" that he could no longer be considered normal at all in any practical sense. Among my many subjects not one has reacted in this "normal" manner. It is possible that some day such a subject will turn up. Basing my conclusions on observations of subjects most closely approaching the fictitious "normal," this man would have a psychological make-up something like this:—He would be a know all, have a large store of available associations, and would show a logic far beyond the range of anything that might be called healthy common sense. He would constantly impress one as tyrannical, grumbling, impatient and pedantic. He would also be very proud of his power and stamina of thinking, especially of his logical reasoning ability, but he would show no originality of reasoning nor sense for practical things. He would be original only in his desire to know and do everything. He would have almost no capacity to form rapport, would be empty of any temperament, but full of self-righteousness and pride. In fine, he would be a proud but sterile technician of logic and memory. Such would be this "normal" individual.

Actually the problem is more complicated. There are

many associative and emotional factors which tend to modify this fictitious normal type. . . .

b) Scoring the Mode of Apperception

The scoring of Whole answers (W) is self-evident. Examples of this type of answers are: Plate I interpreted as a butterfly or as two angels giving aid to a woman; Plate V as a bat; and Plate VI as the skin of an animal or a leaf; Plate IX (inverted) as a volcano. Further differentiation among the W answers is necessary, however, for there are *primary* and *secondary* answers of this type. The examples given above are of the primary type. The differentiation can best be explained by comparison of the two types. There are, moreover, further differentiations within the secondary whole answers.

The "confabulated" whole answer is the most common type of secondary W. In this type of answer a single detail, more or less clearly perceived, is used as the basis for the interpretation of the whole picture, giving very little consideration to the other parts of the figure. For instance, in Plate I, the small claw-like figures (medial top) lead many subjects to call the whole figure a "cray-fish." The primary whole answer interprets the figure primarily as a whole, using as many and disregarding as few details as possible. Between this type and the confabulated secondary W there are many intermediate types. When the phenomenon of confabulation is as clear as in the example above, it is advisable to score the answer, not W, but DW, DW indicating that the Whole is arrived at from a detail. Naturally the result of DW visualization is unclear conception of form. These answers occur in many unintelligent normals, in morons, in epileptics, in organic cases, and in schizophrenics.

There are, in addition, *successive-combinatory answers*, also secondary Wholes. In these the subject first interprets a few details and then combines them into a whole answer. In Plate I, for example, the subject may say,

937

"Two men (sides) and a woman (middle)," adding, "The men are quarreling about the woman."

In contrast to these successive-combinatory answers, there are *simultaneous-combinatory* Wholes. The latter differ from the former only in the greater rapidity of the associative process, and should be added to the primary W's in scoring. Plate I interpreted as "Two men taking an oath on an altar" furnishes an example. Both types of answers are characteristic of imaginative subjects and are very frequently F+ or M+. Successive-combinatory answers of varying degree appear also, of course, in protocols of Korsakoffs, manics, etc.

In the psychoses, *confabulatory-combined* whole answers are more common. These are amalgamations of confabulation and combination in which the forms are vaguely seen and the individual objects interpreted are combined without any real consideration for their relative positions in the picture. An example is Plate VIII interpreted as "Two bears climbing from a rock, over an iceberg, onto a tree trunk." Here the forms are F+, but the position of the objects in the picture is neglected. Such answers are frequently given by unintelligent normal subjects. Confabulating morons, Korsakoff cases, and delirious patients are able to invent whole stories in this way. Less frequently such responses are seen in manics and schizophrenics.

Contaminated whole answers are found only in schizophrenics. A catatonic subject sees in Plate IV, "The liver of a respectable statesman." This response would be incomprehensible had not many other experiments furnished the key to it. The plate is not infrequently conceived as a degenerated organ, perhaps a liver or a heart, but it is also frequently seen as a broad man sitting on a column-like stool. The schizophrenic interprets the figure twice, once as a liver and once as a man, and then contaminates the two with each other, at the same time

938

tossing in the associated ideas, "respectable" and "statesman." Schizophrenics give many interpretations in which confabulation, combination and contamination are mixed in together. Thus, an old paranoid catatonic tells the following story in interpreting Plate IX: "This is Weinfelden (lower red = spilled wine = C answer). It was there I was married. At that time the Bodensee reached to Weinfelden. There is the Bodensee (greenish-blue = C), and here is the door of the hotel where we stayed (indicating a tiny section of the middle line). There were two men sitting and drinking wine from a bottle (the brown figures at the top = M), and here is the cup from which we drank, too (the intermediate figure, center, between the brown and green) and here is the wine that they spilled (back to the lower red again)."

Detail answers (D) must be separated from the small detail answers (Dd). The differentiation carries with it certain difficulties, but it is important since D is the normal detail. Dd, however, whenever occurring in large numbers, is more or less abnormal. The normal is generally finished with the plate when he has given a few D's; he rarely goes on to give Dd answers.

D's are those details which, because of their position in the figure, are the most striking. One can define them statistically, as was the case with the forms, but the procedure is unnecessary because after the test has been given to 50 normals one knows most of the normal details. The final theoretical differentiation between D and Dd answers rests on factors not yet fully studied. The principal research indicated is examination of the individual sensitivity to spatial rhythms. It is certain that factors of this sort are effective in the experiment. Certain small details have to be considered normal because of the frequency with which they are interpreted; this is the case with the black points above the middle white part in Plate II and the intermediate figure between the blue squares in Plate VIII. Both these lie in the midline about the same height on the card.

The D's are by far the most frequent answers. Primary and secondary answers—and various classes of the latter—may be distinguished among the D's as was the case with the W answers, but in practice the differentiation has proved superfluous.

The small-detail answers are those which remain after the statistically common D's are subtracted from the total. Occasionally large parts of the figures have to be designated Dd; this is the case where very unusual sections of a figure are picked out, or where an ordinary detail is interpreted peculiarly and with unusual associations. However, Dd's are usually the smallest details of the picture almost always overlooked by normal subjects. Classification of these would add nothing. It is only necessary to do a test with a scattered schizophrenic or a notorious grumbler to understand very quickly what is meant by a Dd answer.

There are only two special forms of Dd diagnostically important enough to be distinguished and scored separately. These are the *intermediate form* (S) and the *oligophrenic detail* (Do).

Intermediate forms (S) are those answers in which the white spaces are interpreted rather than the black or colored parts of the figure which surround them. If there occurs more than one S in a protocol [it] gives reason for suspicion. S are most common in stubborn, eccentric normals and in negativistic, scattered schizophrenics. They are seen less frequently in epileptics, and tend, in this group, to be changed to color-form or form-color answers. S answers always indicate some sort of *tendency to opposition*.

Oligophrenic (oligophrenic = feebleminded) *small detail answers* (Do) are those interpretations in which only a part of the body is seen by a subject, though others see

940

the whole body clearly in the same part of the figure in question. In Plate I, for instance, the central figure is frequently called a female body; if a subject interprets only hands or legs we deal with Do answers. In Plate III the same applies if only heads or legs of the figures are pointed out. Do answers are found primarily in morons and imbeciles, less frequently in anxious or depressed subjects. They are almost invariably present in protocols of compulsion neurotics. . . .*

HERMANN RORSCHACH (b.—Zurich, Switzerland, Nov. 8, 1884; d.—April 2, 1922).

Rorschach received his M.D. from Berlin, after having studied also in Neuenburg, Zurich, and Berne. He went immediately into clinical practice at the asylum in Muensterlingen. He spent about a year (1913) as physician at a private sanatorium in Moscow. In 1914 he returned to Switzerland to the psychiatric clinic at Berne-Waldau. In 1915 he became an assistant physician in Herisau, and remained here until his death.

Eugen Bleuler was the mentor of Rorschach, and said of him after his death at so young an age, in a famous encomium that "Rorschach was the hope of an entire generation of Swiss Psychiatry."

Rorschach dates his work from early experiments in 1911. The concept of projection, emphasized so strongly by Jung's work on word-association, is the basic theme of Rorschach's great idea. To have established, over so short a span of years, the essential concept of the controlled and formalized psychiatric interview, is an achievement of the highest magnitude. The regulated and consistent examination of patients is at the heart of the whole medical profession. Rorschach may be said to have established this as a component of the psychiatric armamentarium. His test has, subsequently, served as a model for quite literally hundreds of similar diagnostic instruments, but is to this day still the foremost single guide upon which the psychiatrist may rely.

The present selection constitutes only a short introduction to his thought and to his method of approach. A full understanding of the strength of this test, and of its wide ramifications, can only come through careful study, and a mastering of the literature, which now probably numbers in the thousands.

*Deleted are sections c—Number of W, D, Dd, etc.; d—Apperceptive Types e—Sequence in the Modes of Apperception.

RORSCHACH, H. *Psychodiagnostics: a diagnostic test based on perception.* Berne, Switzerland: Hans Huber, 1951 (1942). Trans. P. Lemkau and B. Kronenberg (1921 edition). This contains a complete bibliography of Rorschach, and a bibliography on the test to date. Reprinted with the gracious permission of the publisher.

See also:

KLOPFER, B. & KELLEY, D. M. *The Rorschach technique.* N. Y.: World Book Co., 1946 (1942).

WAYWARD
YOUTH

AUGUST AICHHORN

THE MEANING OF THE REALITY PRINCIPLE
IN SOCIAL BEHAVIOUR

... Experience teaches us how to take care of ourselves; education has the further task of expanding this primitive adjustment to reality to such a point that we are capable of adaptation to the demands of society. Although we know that experience and education are inextricably interwoven in their effect on the child, let us assume a division in their work for the sake of our discussion. This enables us to make certain assumptions about education which will clarify one of the important aspects of remedial training. We must remember, however, that this division is only schematic.

Let us expand the conception ... and assign to education the further work of preventing the development of anti-social potentialities. We can now turn our attention to those psychic processes which enable the small child to develop gradually from a being concerned almost exclusively with gratification of instinctual drives to one capable of taking his place in society.

Freud in his investigation of instincts raised the question whether we can recognize the existence of a purpose in the functioning of our mental apparatus. He has found that this purpose is the attainment of pleasure. It appears to him that all mental activity aims at the securing of pleasure and the avoidance of pain. He explains how mental acts are regulated automatically by a tendency which he names the "pleasure principle."

When we hear about the pleasure principle for the first

time, we are inclined to repudiate it, for we have learned from our own experience that the end result of a mental operation is often connected with pain. However, let us not be too hasty in our criticism but seek first to understand what Freud means. For this purpose we need only to follow his arguments. We have learned from him that the unconscious is the original source of all mental life and that instincts as well as wishes arise from the unconscious. Here the pleasure principle rules exclusively. What does this mean? Freud has observed that everything arising in the unconscious is directed toward the attainment of pleasure. The outer world, however, takes no cognizance of our need for pleasure, sometimes granting it, sometimes refusing it, according to the existing circumstances. In this way situations often arise which do not correspond to the striving for pleasure but run directly counter to it. Let us take for example the infant who is still wholly dominated by unconscious functions. Its repose is disturbed by the imperious demands of physical needs arising from its instincts, which it strives to satisfy in order to avoid discomfort. It lives according to its instinctual demands, which are directed exclusively toward the attainment of pleasure and which ignore reality. Consequently the small child is subjected repeatedly to disappointments. The expected satisfaction is not achieved and pain instead of pleasure is experienced. At the same time, the child's psychic apparatus is undergoing changes that come with growth. The psychic apparatus is thereby forced to adapt itself to reality and, making the best of a poor bargain, it strives toward those adaptations which are the least dangerous to the personality. Naturally this adjustment is not achieved all at once. It is rather the result of a long process of development. From the unconscious, the ego receives information about physical functions, and through the sense organs about events in the outer world. Thus gradually it becomes capable of conforming to the demands of life. An important aspect of this development consists in a modification of the striving for pleasure. Pleasure may have to be postponed or renounced because of difficulties that stand in the way of instinctual gratification or because of the pain that may result from the gratification of instincts in a manner prohibited by society. This leads to the suppression of instinctual desires. The task of avoiding pain soon becomes as important as that of attaining pleasure. This renunciation of pleasure establishes a second principle which forces the conscious ego to regulate the unbridled pleasure impulses of the unconscious and to modify them in such a way that their satisfaction is harmless. This second tendency, which takes account of outer circumstances, Freud has named the "reality principle." The establishment of this principle means important progress in mental development. From this time on, the pleasure principle and the reality principle rule all mental processes: the reality principle in consciousness, the pleasure principle in the unconscious. While the pleasure ego seeks only pleasure and avoids pain, the reality ego strives for practical advantages and protects itself from harm. With an increase in the strength of the reality principle, the ego can defend itself better against instinctual demands. The earlier the individual recognizes the dangers which threaten him because of the contradiction between his instinctual desires and the demands of reality, the more capable he is of meeting reality.

When we understand these postulates of Freud, we see that the reality principle leads the growing child from his unreal world of pleasure into reality and enables him to make adjustments between his desire for pleasure and the demands of life. When the child is small and his capacity for adjustment to reality is still weak, the ego demands immediate instinctual satisfaction and is less able to forego pleasure and to endure pain. We can define the different stages of the child's development according to the degree in which the pleasure principle predominates over the reality principle. Although the reality principle acts as a safeguard to the ego, it does not require the ego to renounce all pleasure. The reality principle, too, has pleasure as its goal, but it takes reality into consideration and contents itself with postponed pleasure or with a smaller degree of pleasure.

This explains the apparent contradiction that one can suffer pain while under the domination of the pleasure principle. Pain is endured under the reality principle in order to achieve more assured pleasure later. Pain may also arise from the encounter of an immature ego with reality; that is to say, the instinctual desires, regulated by the pleasure principle, break through prematurely in an individual not yet capable of dealing with them in relation to reality. Another possibility is that what is experienced in consciousness as pain may be experienced simultaneously as pleasure in the unconscious.

The educator must recognize clearly that the establishment and development of the reality principle result from the factors in the outer world which force the child to restrict his instinctual demands. However, we must not assume that the reality principle increases in strength in direct proportion to the amount of renunciation forced on the child. To assume this would be to disregard elements present in the child and to take only the outer factors into account. We must consider not only what the outer difficulties are but also how far these have been recognized and experienced by the child as such. Deprivations which are significant for one child may have no effect on another. Each child reacts according to his own inherent tendencies.

What I have just said does not imply that we have such control over an individual child that we can arbitrarily regulate the deprivations he must endure in order to influence his adaptation to reality. Although we can influence these deprivations appreciably, it is dangerous to increase or decrease them beyond certain limits. In our discussion of the disturbances which lead to delinquency, we shall learn what happens when a child is subjected prematurely to extreme harshness or to extreme solicitude. How does a normally developed individual try to compensate himself for the pleasure denied him by reality? The ego does not submit without protest to the demands of reality when these demands are too great. Instead it takes refuge in a part of consciousness which is cut off from reality and which remains under the domination of the pleasure principle. I am sure you know to what mental process I refer. I mean fantasy, with which you are already acquainted. It begins in the child's play and continues later in daydreams. If an individual is not contented with the meagre satisfactions which he can wrest from life, he enjoys in fantasy the freedom which he has long ago relinquished in reality.

We have intimated that experience and education have certain functions to perform in the development of the child's inherent potentialities. We have learned that the first adaptations to reality are biologically determined and that their expression is influenced by the circumstances in the outer world. This is the primitive adjustment to reality. Further development toward social adaptability is achieved through education. Thus the individual becomes capable of recognizing and submitting to the demands of society, and of co-operating in the maintenance and the advance of civilization. However, the ability to cope with reality and to further the work of civilization depends not only upon experience and education but also upon the individual himself. The capacity of the individual for adjustment to reality is determined less by the nature of the renunciations required of him than by the strength of the ego to meet them. In the same way, the capacity of an individual for education is determined chiefly by his constitutional endowment. In favourable cases the educator can so modify the environmental circumstances that they present the most advantageous conditions for development. The final result, however, depends on the child's ability to avail himself of the opportunities offered.

By social adaptation we mean the expansion of our first primitive adjustments to the stage of our present civilization. The educator of the child can only assist this developmental process, which the ego is forced to make in order to conform to reality. This aid consists in providing incentives for the conquest of the pleasure principle in favour of the reality principle. The long road mankind has travelled in attaining the present cultural level could not be traversed by the child in the short span of his growing up, without the help of education.

We now see what the incentives provided by education must do. Adaptation to reality involves renunciation. In order to bring about this adaptation the educator must proceed in conformity with life itself and erect dams that curb immediate instinctual gratification or make the gratification impossible. In this way he influences the child to suppress his instinctual demands, to postpone or renounce pleasure, and to endure pain. This method seems to contradict the present popular belief that the best education means letting the child do as he likes. Such a conception results either from confusing the means of education with its goal or from an attitude toward the problem which is coloured by our emotional experiences. It is incorrect to think that education means letting the child do as he pleases. Everyone who has had anything to do with little children knows that restraint and prohibition of momentary impulses belong to the order of the day and that the child must continually submit to limitations of his freedom. We ask ourselves: Is it true that the child has so many wishes that must be denied him? Could we not avoid prohibitions altogether? Let us imagine what a two-year-old child would do, if he met no hindrances. For example, he might pull the table cover off, break the dishes, climb up on the chairs and table without realizing he could fall and hurt himself. Is there anything a child would not try to put in his mouth, pry into, or break up if all his impulses were given free rein? How could we ever train him to be clean if we did not overcome his resistance to bodily care? We consider that these continual limitations of his freedom are in the child's interest, even though they seem to him violent attempts to hinder him in the satisfaction of his impulses. Naturally the child cannot renounce pleasure for reality without a struggle, but he must do this if he is to become socially acceptable. The educator will make this training as easy as possible and will at times offer no opposition because he understands that the little child is still dominated by the pleasure principle and that immediate pleasure is his most natural aim. However, he does this with the realization that such procedure is not education because it does not teach the child to renounce pleasure. . . .

A demand which leads to renunciation is effective only when it is recognized as such by the child, that is, when it corresponds to a similar wish in the child. The educator must choose between two possibilities in order to bring this about: either he allows the child to experience increased pain following forbidden instinctual satisfaction or he permits a substitute gratification. In both cases, he forces the child to renounce the desired pleasure. He accomplishes this either through punishment when the child will not give in or through recognition and love when he does give in. Thus the same end is attained by two diametrically opposed means, the fear of punishment and the reward of love. This fact has confused many people. To bring the child to renunciation through the reward of approval instead of through threats of punishment does not mean that we are indulging his desire for pleasure.

Generally speaking we have two methods of education. The one works with rewards, the other with punishment. As a matter of fact, both methods obtain results. Some people become social because they fear punishment; others because they seek approval. Both methods, however, can result in failure as well as success.

If we were now concerned with the rearing of children and not with the *re-education of delinquents,* our present task would not be to decide which of these two methods we prefer, but rather to investigate in concrete cases which is the more advantageous.

Mistakes made in bringing up children interest us because of the part they may play in causing delinquency. We learned in the first chapter that all dissocial behaviour cannot be traced to poor upbringing. We shall consider later the fact that some unavoidable circumstances in life can produce situations the results of which may indicate that the child's training has been at fault.

It might be assumed that education will succeed in direct proportion to the love the child receives from his parents and educators. Within certain limits this is true. When these limits are exceeded, however, rewards as well as punishment not only lose their effectiveness, but even bring about results contrary to those desired. Let us not overlook the fact that rewards are useful only as stimuli or as means to achieve renunciation of pleasurable desires. If the parents bestow affection without asking any return by way of renunciation, the child does not need to exert himself. Assured of love, he lacks the incentive to give up pleasure in favour of reality. He thus retains the pleasure of direct instinctual gratification as well as the gratuitous love of his parents. A well-known example of this kind of training is the spoiled only child. He develops physically, but remains under the domination of the pleasure principle just as in his early childhood. This domination breaks down only when outer circumstances bring him unavoidable pain, or when the parents make an occasional demand on him in return for their love.

Let us now examine the second method of training in which indulgence in undesirable instinctual satisfactions is met with threat of punishment. If the child suffers too much from punishment or severity and is not compensated for this by the parents' love, he is forced into opposition and has no further incentive to submit to their demands and thus to subject himself to the reality principle. His main object is to resist authority. Rebellion against his parents, teachers, and society—the assertion of his ego against them—becomes just as great a source of pleasure to him as the gratification of his instincts. In this case, a counter-impulse may lead to persistence in childishness or, what is more likely, it may lead to a later rebellion which will destroy the effect of what had at first seemed successful training.

When either of these two methods of education goes astray, failure is inevitable. The over-powerful pleasure principle calls forth psychic reactions in undisciplined children that are different from those of normally developed children of the same age. Their behaviour makes them so conspicuous that we can easily see which of them need remedial training. We must help them when their undisciplined search for pleasure brings them into conflict with society. This thirst for pleasure we have long recognized as characteristic of the delinquent, and we have now found an explanation of this in the residue of childishness not yet given up.

The delinquent is like the child also in that he is not able to give up immediate pleasure in favour of later pleasure. He does and says things which are normal for an earlier stage of childhood development, but which make him appear abnormal and dissocial because they bring him into conflict with society. When we consider the various symptoms of delinquency in this light, they become understandable. In the training school as well as in the nursery there are incessant outbreaks of jealousy and constant quarreling, not only among the younger children but also among the older ones. Most of them are like little children in regard to their physical care; uncombed hair and soiled clothes do not disturb them. A great many traits which the delinquents show can be interpreted as childish behaviour, even if greatly distorted. Like children, their interest span is short and their judgment is poor. They react immediately to any stimulus and give way to their feelings without restraint.

It seems as though only a part of the ego of the delinquent had succeeded in making the transition from the unconscious pleasure world of the small child to that of reality. Why have they remained immature in one part of their ego? Because another part of their ego has developed to a maturity corresponding to or exceeding their chronological age. Every delinquent shows this cleavage in the ego. A part of the personality of the delinquent is dominated by the over-powerful pleasure principle; the remaining part of the personality may react in a reasonable and mature way. The delinquent often shows himself especially adept in conforming to reality in situations where the bare struggle for existence is involved. One type of delinquent shows under-developed sexuality. The others are normally developed, or precocious. They are seldom perverse or inverted.

We now understand the delinquent as one disturbed in his ego development. We recognize the origin of this disturbance, but as yet we do not understand how it arose. If we draw an analogy to a neurosis, we arrive at a general explanation. Two possibilities must be considered. In one instance the phases of development have not run a normal course because of faulty training; for instance, mental functions or parts of them remain at an earlier developmental stage. This we designate as an "inhibition of development." In the second instance, parts of mental functions which had already reached a higher level of development are for some reason pushed back to a lower level. This we call "regression." In brief, we may say: Delinquency is the consequence of an inhibition of development or of a regression, which takes place somewhere along the path from primitive reality adaptation to social adaptation. What is meant will be clearer when we compare the delinquency which develops gradually with the delinquency which breaks out suddenly in a previously normal individual. We must remember that the delinquent is capable of primitive reality adaptation and that his difficulties arise in his progress from this point toward social conformity. His inability to assert himself in an acceptable manner brings him into conflict with society.

We shall examine more closely the two most striking types of delinquency, "delinquency caused by excess of love" and "delinquency caused by excess of severity," and I shall try to show you what remedial training must do in these cases.

The type "delinquent due to excess of love" is not often seen in the training school. However, he is found disproportionately often in middle-class homes and is the source of great sorrow and despair, though this is rarely admitted by the parents. These cases are frequently brought to the child-guidance clinic. I have seen many cases of "only children" in which the delinquency was caused by an excess of affection. We might assume that this indulgence results from a natural solicitude for an only child, or it may have other causes. For example, a woman who has lost her husband gives her whole love to the child, or divorced parents compete with each other in demonstrations of their love in order to win the child. More frequently, we find that the mother feels that she receives too little love from her husband. In some instances this feeling may be justified; in others it may arise from an excessive need for love which cannot be satisfied in a normal way. Occasionally we find a woman with an illegitimate daughter married to a man who is not the child's father. In these cases the stepfather often shows great devotion to his stepdaughter. When these marriages remain childless, the woman is usually inconsolable because she has borne her husband no children, and she cites as proof of her husband's desire for children his tender interest in the stepdaughter. She maintains that she spoils the daughter to please her husband.

This type of delinquency develops because the mother, or in some instances, the father, is not equal to the task of rearing the child. Mothers of this kind are well known to you and are not difficult to characterize. Since such a mother is ready to do anything to keep her darling from suffering the slightest discomfort, she is unable to subject him to any denials. Punishment upsets her more than it does the child. Weighed down by cares for him, she worries continually about his welfare and cannot demand from him any postponement or renunciation of pleasure. She clears out of his way all disappointments and obstacles which the child must learn to face and overcome in later life and thus she robs the child of initiative. His moods are endured with inexhaustible patience, and his naughtiness is admired as an indication of unusual individuality. Any criticism of him is as painful as a personal insult. The child's playmates are very severely criticized, especially if they offer resistance to his having his own way.

This child is the centre of interest and lives without

restraint according to the wishes of his pleasure ego. Reality does not exist for him because his mother shuts it out. Since he is unable to modify the pleasure principle, reality is pushed further and further away. There are renunciations even for him, but they are always in the wrong place. His mother hinders him in his activity when there is any danger of bodily harm. He might fall down and hurt himself, he might take cold, he might upset his stomach, or get a headache! The child cannot understand these restrictions which stand in such contrast to his freedom in other respects, and he consequently rebels. But the mother lacks insight into this behaviour also. She tries to win his compliance with bribes of affection or with greater concessions in another direction. These methods soon lose their effectiveness, and the rebelliousness increases. Finally the child makes demands which the mother cannot meet. He can no longer be kept away from reality and when he has to meet it suddenly, he is unprepared for the force of its demands. This encounter either leads to neurosis or it kindles a rebellion which is beyond the control of the parents and which finds expression in all kinds of dissocial acts.

Delinquency of this type cannot be completely explained by the unconquered pleasure principle. We must also take into consideration libidinal relationships, which may not have been dealt with normally in earlier childhood. In our present discussion I shall disregard the latter factor as I wish to consider delinquency only from the point of view of the pleasure principle.

In the training school we find much more frequently the second type of delinquency: that which results from an excess of severity. We can recognize a third type also, in which the delinquency is the result of the practice of the two extremes of training at the same time, excess of severity and excess of affection. At first glance this may seem impossible, but it is easy to understand when we realize that two persons, mother and father, share in the child's training. Usually the father is too severe and the mother too indulgent.

Since childhood experiences are so significant for later life, we can understand the significance to the child of the normally strict father and the normally kind mother. The father usually represents the stern demands of reality and the mother softens these demands. This enables the child who develops normally to meet the later demands of reality with less pain.

When the father is too severe and the mother too indulgent, the mother will alter the father's demands not only in their form but also in their content, and thus the child escapes the father's demands through flight to the mother. When the mother makes certain demands in the interest of his physical protection which run counter to the pleasure principle, then the child can escape them through flight to the father. In this instance, the child conforms with the wishes of his father; but he suffers thereby no instinctual deprivation because he is acting in accordance with the pleasure principle. Whether he turns to his father or to his mother, the child avoids reality, attains his pleasurable desires, and remains under the control of the pleasure principle. Thus he comes to rebel against both parents and finally becomes delinquent. The attitude of this type of delinquent can be epitomized thus: "Whatever I do, nothing can happen to me." This is clearly the result of the upbringing.

Such delinquency does not necessarily arise from actual experience of severity. Some children are as much affected by a quiet, cold attitude lacking in tenderness as others are by corporal punishment. We know that subjective reactions are decisive for the origin of delinquency. This must be kept in mind; otherwise we shall go astray in cases where the objective severity is lacking.

When a child is too strictly treated, or when through

fate he experiences a crass encounter with reality too early, he is not able at this stage of his development to make the necessary adjustment to reality. A premature adaptation to reality is not accomplished, but as often happens, regression which takes the form of delinquency sets in after a period of apparently successful training. Thus the pleasure principle again achieves the mastery, as on the earlier level of development. We know from experience that when a child is thus forced back to an earlier developmental level to achieve satisfaction, he finds it more difficult to advance from this point than in the normal course of development. This child is progressively less amenable to force. The harshness of the child's training and life, which may have been borne patiently at one time, now leads to conscious opposition which often manifests itself in insubordination. This progresses to open rebellion, and in adolescents can lead to acts of violence. . . .

Remedial training has the same task in all three types. It must help the child to overcome the failures in his development so that he can exchange a childish level, where the pleasure principle predominates, for a level corresponding to his age, where the reality principle is effective. The educator must so guide the delinquent that he learns to exercise judgment; that is, the delinquent must develop the reality principle so that he is able before acting to decide between *immediate pleasure with later pain, and postponement or renunciation with later assured pleasure*. During the course of his training, the delinquent must learn that the amount of pleasure obtained from social conformity is greater than the sum of small pleasures derived from dissocial acts even when the accompanying discomfort of conformity is taken into account.

There is another important consideration which will enable us to avoid mistakes in judgment of dissocial behaviour. We do not have to find a neurotic factor in every case of delinquency. Sometimes the child's training is incomplete. The child's training may have failed to give him sufficiently strong incentives for the recognition of reality, or have made it possible for him to avoid unpleasantness, and thus the necessary development may have been interrupted or not made at all. We do not always have to assume that the unpleasant consequences of stealing give the delinquent unconscious pleasure, nor that every theft is due to unconscious guilt feelings. In many cases it seems probable that the delinquent is basically under the domination of a powerful pleasure principle and that, driven by his instincts, he automatically seeks satisfaction for his desires. *He is controlled by his pleasure ego; reality with its later unpleasant consequences does not exist for him at the moment.* Possibly this conception will arouse opposition. It is, however, the inevitable conclusion derived from observed facts, as well as from our theoretical considerations. We have by no means exhausted the question of the retraining of delinquents when we say that the problem consists in retrieving a neglected part of normal education. It is a far more complicated problem. To regard delinquency as the result of a failure in the child's upbringing is only one aspect of the problem.

A certain amount of instinctual deprivation is necessary for social adaptation. If this deprivation is too great or too little, the normal course of development does not follow. Thus it becomes the task of remedial training to make good this mistake.

Since we have decided that remedial training must help the child to a renunciation of his instinctual demands it is not difficult to outline the procedure we must follow with the various types of delinquency in order to arouse the necessary incentives for renunciation.

The first and second types did not learn how to control

their instincts because there was no need for them to do so; the third type failed because of their rebellion against restriction. These facts give us a point of attack.

The individual who was always certain of love at home, or who could turn from one parent to the other, must be held in the institution through a certain inner compulsion dependent on the sympathy and goodwill of the counsellor, which will spur him on to achievements and to the overcoming of his difficulties. This inner compulsion is not immediately established. It will be developed through the transference situation. Normally, however, it arises from the fact that the educator offers the reward of recognition only for some achievement on the part of the pupil.

The spoiled child who was allowed everything and who had all difficulties cleared out of his way defends himself against every outer force which demands the slightest deprivation, and refuses the simplest requests of the educator if they run counter to the wishes of his pleasure ego. This is not surprising or serious; it is the natural reaction to a new situation. If we did not endanger the results of our treatment we could wait until the transference is so positively established that the child is willing to forfeit direct pleasure because of his love for the counsellor. In this way, the domination of the pleasure principle is broken down rather than repressed. However, we cannot always wait for this process to take place. In the training school many insuperable difficulties arise which proceed from the pupil himself and from his parents. The pupil brought to the institution against his will has so many unpleasant experiences in the beginning that he can see no advantage in staying there. In this situation, he reacts just as he has at home; either he runs away from the institution or, more frequently, he writes to his parents urging them to take him away. In this letter he usually tells them about the abuse and discomforts which he must endure. He complains of the bad food, his failing health, and the cruelty of the teachers, and is full of promises of good behaviour if he is allowed to come home. As a last resort, he uses the most effective means to get what he wants; he threatens to kill himself if his parents do not come. The parents are alarmed and horrified over what they have done and they come in the greatest excitement to see whether their darling is alive or dead. When they find him living and far from emaciated, they overwhelm him with affection. They pour out their indignation on our heads, instead of on his. We cannot convince them off the unreasonableness of the boy's complaints because they themselves are not rational. It is especially difficult to make the mother see that her indulgence at home has caused the delinquency and that his gross exaggerations were meant to arouse their solicitude and force them to take him home. The parents remain incredulous and are convinced that their boy is not understood and that he is in an unsuitable environment. "There must be some truth in his statements," one hears continually. The parents cannot see that this is a natural reaction to the inevitable discomfort which must arise when a child is no longer allowed to realize his instinctual demands. The child triumphs, and he is taken home. Neither the child nor the parents realize that in a short time he will be as impossible at home as he was before.

The child whose delinquency is the result of too great severity at home comes from a *milieu* which, both subjectively and objectively, has offered him nothing but opposition to his desires. We must take an attitude toward him entirely different from that toward the delinquents described above. Here we must strive for a reconciliation with him; we must make good the love of which he has been deprived. Everything which we have said about the happy atmosphere of the institution is especially applicable to this boy. He needs the friendly, cheerful counsellor. He belongs in an environment where the adolescent's need for pleasure is satisfied. This environment must be so constituted that it gradually leads the child to an adjustment to the real world in which pain as well as pleasure exists.

Roughly expressed, each of these types of delinquent should find in the training school conditions exactly opposite to those of the former environment. The old style reformatory attempted through force, through fear of punishment, and without rewards of love to make the delinquent socially acceptable. Since most of their charges belong to the type just described, they only exaggerated what the parents had already begun and consequently they were doomed to failure.

That the modern training school uses another method is not especially praiseworthy. To the educator, this method is obvious because of the changed conception of the child's place in the family. It is correct as far as the type last described is concerned. However, this method is just as false for the first type as the old training-school methods were for the last.

I must emphasize that I am not presenting a theory of delinquency. I have done no more than to describe several striking features of delinquency and have discussed these from one point of view, which seems important for a first approach to the whole problem of delinquency.

The study of delinquency only from the pleasure principle is one-sided and not exhaustive. I have done this intentionally in order to offer you quite specific new insights.

AUGUST AICHHORN (b.-Vienna, July 27, 1878).

Aichhorn was not trained as a physician, as many have thought; he was, above all else, a gifted and beloved teacher. Because of his great love of children, he sought naturally to work with the most difficult, the delinquent child,—"Verwahrloste , as he called them with greater justice. Aichhorn studied psychoanalysis, as a layman, with Paul Federn. He founded child guidance clinics throughout Vienna, and, in particular, the institute for delinquent boys, at Oberhollabrunn.

Aichhorn pioneered in applying the methods and findings of psychoanalysis to areas outside the clinic. The fields of special education, social work and delinquency, were developing, about the turn of the twentieth century, as legitimate areas of professional concentration, under the aegis of the same intellectual insights which were causing the great social and political upheavals of this period. And Aichhorn's major literary effort, from which the present selection is taken, embodies these insights in their highest form. This book, first delivered as a series of lectures before the Vienna Psychoanalytical Society, is one of the earliest contributions to our understanding of the wayward child,—and one of the most important.

AICHHORN, A. *Wayward youth.* N. Y.: Viking Press, Inc., 1951 (1935, 1925). Chap. 9: "The meaning of the reality principle in social behavior." This selection is reprinted, substantially complete, with the permission of the publishers.

See also:

EISSLER, K. R. (ed.) *Searchlights on delinquency.* N. Y.: International Universities Press, 1949. A bibliography of Aichhorn's writings is given on pp. 455-456.

GRINSTEIN (Vol. 1, p. 29-31).

ADOLESCENCE: ITS PSYCHOLOGY AND ITS RELATIONS TO PHYSIOLOGY, ANTHROPOLOGY, SOCIOLOGY, SEX, CRIME, RELIGION, AND EDUCATION

G. Stanley Hall

We here face problems both more complex and more inaccessible than those connected with the somatic changes. The most important and basal of these are connected with the fact that powers and faculties, essentially non-existent before, are now born, and of all the older impulses and instincts some are reenforced and greatly developed, while others are subordinated, so that new relations are established and the ego finds a new center. In connection with the reproduction function, love is born with all its attendant passions—jealousy, rivalry, and all the manifold phenomena of human courtship. All the previous religious sentiments are regenerated and some now arise for the first time, motivating a wide plexus of new psychic relations between the individual and the race, and irradiating to the cosmos. Nature is felt and plays upon the soul with all its rich orchestra of influences. Art at this time may become an enthusiasm and is now first deeply and truly felt, even though it had been known and practiced before. The ethical life is immensely broadened and deepened, because now a far deeper possibility and sense of sin and impurity arises. The floodgates of heredity are thrown open again somewhat as in infancy. As in the prenatal and infant stage man hears from his remoter forebears back perhaps to primitive organisms, now the later and higher ancestry takes up the burden of the song of life, and the voices of our extinct and perhaps forgotten, and our later and more human ancestry, are heard in the soul. Just as in the first birth the gifts of nature are of fundamental psycho-physic qualities, which are later elaborated and

963

differentiated by development, so now her rich dotations are generic, and the accessory qualities that are unfolded out of them arise slowly from the feelings, instincts, impulses, dispositions, *Anlangen* and *Triebe,* which are the products of this later heritage.

In some respects, early adolescence is thus the infancy of man's higher nature, when he receives from the great all-mother his last capital of energy and evolutionary momentum. Thus the child is father of the man, far older and conditioning his nature. He is at the same time reduced back to a state of nature, so far as some of the highest faculties are concerned, again helpless, in need not only of guidance but of shelter and protection. His knowledge of self is less adequate and he must slowly work out his salvation. Character, temperament, emotions, and appetites are changed; the youth moves about in both an inner and an outer world unrealized. The parent and teacher must understand that mother nature has again taken her child upon her knee and must stand off a little to see and make room for her more perfect education. These years again, like infancy, should be sacred to heredity, and we should have a good warrant indeed before we venture to interfere with its processes.

Psychic adolescence is heralded by all-sided mobilization. The child from nine to twelve is well adjusted to his environment and proportionately developed; he represents probably an old and relatively perfected stage of race-maturity, still in some sense and degree feasible in warm climates, which, as we have previously urged, stands for a long-continued one, a terminal stage of human development at some post-simian point. At dawning adolescence this old unity and harmony with nature is broken up; the child is driven from his paradise and must enter upon a long viaticum of ascent, must conquer a higher kingdom of man for himself, break out a new sphere, and evolve a more modern story to his psychophysical nature. Because his environment is to be far more complex, the combinations are less stable, the ascent less easy and secure; there is more danger that the youth in his upward progress, under the influence of this "excelsior" motive, will backslide in one or several of the many ways possible. New dangers threaten on all sides. It is the most critical stage of life, because failure to mount always means retrogression, degeneracy, or fall. One may be in all respects better or worse, but can never be the same. The old level is left forever. Perhaps the myth of Adam and Eden describe this epoch. The consciousness of childhood is molted, and a new, larger, better consciousness must be developed, or increased exposure and vulnerability will bring deterioration. Before this, boys and girls have been interested largely in those of their own age and have had little interest in their future or in the life of adults. Their own life is too varied, intense and absorbing. But the soul now realizes in a deeper sense the meaning of maturity and is protensive toward its higher plateau. Slowly the color and life fade from juvenile interests, which are deciduous like foliage or like milk teeth. Vocations beckon first faintly, and then more and more imperatively. Hero worship arises; youth aspires to excel, first perhaps by the order of nature in athletic contests, then in those of the mind. The young savage can not attain his new name or be initiated into adolescence until he has shown prowess or won some fame as a doer of deeds, as e.g., by killing some large animal or in successful head-hunting. It is perhaps on the athletic field that youth has his first taste of gratified ambition and is fired thereby to constant discontent and *Sehnsucht* thereafter. He longs to struggle, make an effort, combat, loves a hard and strenuous and scorns an easy life. The great deeds and lives and prizes in the human world never shine so bright, seem so near, or beckon so alluringly. The youth wills all that he must or

965

can; would be wise, strong, famous, talented, learned, rich, loved, and withal good and perfect. When the thought of death forces its presence upon his soul, though at first cast down, he reacts by immortal longings. The transcendental world opens before him; he dreams of an ideal future of the race or of a heaven where all his wishes shall be realized in the glory of the world to be; and in these "vague snatches of Uranian antiphony," instead of its finding reminiscences of the preexistent state of the soul, the more progressive Occidental world sees anticipations of a future immortality, as it has taken its conceptions of paradise from the past where antiquity placed them, and reconstructed them and set them up in the future.

This long pilgrimage of the soul from its old level to a higher maturity which adolescence recapitulates must have taken place in the race in certain of its important lines long before the historic period, because its very nature seems to involve the destruction of all its products and extinction of all records. Just as the well-matured adult, as is elsewhere shown has utterly lost all traces and recollection of the perturbations of the storm and stress period, because they are so contradictory and mutually destructive and because feelings themselves can not be well remembered, so the race must have gone through a long heat and ferment, of which consciousness, which best develops in stationary periods, was lost, partly because growth was so rapid. Incidents are never better remembered by the individual, but they are never more transformed and changed, and just so the precious but often grotesque myths and legends of races, sacred to them but often meaningless to others, afford the only traces of ethnic adolescence which races retain. They are told about camp fires, perhaps laboriously and allegorically interpreted or developed into literary form with the same gusto with which the man recounts in ever more mythic form the most vivid incidents his memory has rescued from the turmoil of these years of transformation and reconstruction, when nature's first call is heard to go out from the home to some promised land or career, to establish a new domicile for body and soul, and to be the progenitor of offspring of both, that to the inflamed youthful heart seem like the stars of heaven in number.

Youth loves intense states of mind and is passionately fond of excitement. Tranquil, mild enjoyments are not its forte. The heart and arteries are, as we have seen, rapidly increasing in size, and perhaps heightened blood pressure is necessary to cause the expansion normal at this stage. Nutritive activities are greatly increased; the temperature of the body is probably a trifle higher. After its period of most rapid growth, the heart walls are a little weak, and peripheral circulation is liable to slight stagnation, so that in the interests of proper irrigation of the tissues after the vascular growth has begun, tension seems necessary. Although we do not know precisely the relation between blood pressure and the strong instinct to tingle and glow, some correlation may safely be postulated. It is the age of erectile diathesis, and the erethism that is now so increased in the sexual parts is probably more or less so in nearly every organ and tissue. The whole psycho-physic organism is expanding, stretching out, and proper elasticity that relaxes and contracts and gives vaso-motor range is coordinated with the instinct for calenture or warming up, which is shown in phenomena of second breath in both physical and mental activity. In savage life this period is marked by epochs of orgasm and carousal, which is perhaps one expression of nature's effort to secure a proper and ready reflex range of elasticity in the circulatory apparatus. The "teens" are emotionally unstable and pathic. It is the age of natural inebriation without the need of intoxicants, which made Plato define youth as spiritual drunkenness. It is a natural impulse to experience hot and perfervid psychic states, and is characterized by emotionalism. This gives a sense of vitality and the hunger for more and fuller life. This desire to feel and to be very much alive, and the horror of inertness and apathy, is . . . one of the chief features which incline youth to intoxicants. Indeed, everything men strive for—fame, wealth, knowledge, power, love—are only specialized forms of the will to attain and to feel the maximum of vitality. Hence comes the proclivity to superlativeness, to high, lurid color and fast life, because youth must have excitement, and if this be not at hand in the form of moral and intellectual enthusiasms, it is more prone, on the principle of kinetic equivalents, to be sought for in sex or in drink. Athletic enthusiasm, the disposition of high school and college youth to yell and paint the town, to laugh, become boisterous and convivial, are better than sensuality and reduce temptation to it. Better that a few of the most promising youth should be maimed or even killed on the gridiron or in college rushes, or lose standing in their devotion to teams and to emotional culture, than that they should find excesses, some forms of which seem necessary now, in the lower life of sinful indulgence, which is so prone to stunt and arrest the precious last stages of growth in mind and body. More or less of this erethic diathesis is necessary and inevitable, and one of the chief problems of education is to prevent its lower forms and give it ever higher vents and fields. Interest in and devotion to all that is good, beautiful, and true is its loftiest expression, but it is often best cultivated on a lower plane, to be applied later on the higher.

We here see the instability and fluctuation now so characteristic. The emotions develop by contrast and reaction into the opposite. We will specify a few of its antithetic impulses now so marked.

968

1. There are hours, days, weeks, and perhaps months of over-energetic action. The young man trains with ardor; perhaps breaks a record; sleep may be reduced; he studies all night in a persistent cram; is swept away by some new fad; is exalted and hilarious and then reacts; is limp, languid, inert, indifferent, fatigued, apathetic, sleepy, lazy; feels the lack of motive power, and from overwork and excessive effort, when he goaded himself to do or die, he relapses to a dull state of relaxation and doubts whether anything is really worth while in the world. Thus youth now is really and easily overworked; is never so fresh or more rested as when at the top of its condition, but very easily wearied and exhausted with the languor due to overtraining. We have seen that early adolescent years are prone to be sickly, although the death rate is now lowest, and this is closely connected with the changes from overefficiency to low tension so frequent. Sometimes the stage of torpor comes first or predominates and causes friends to be anxious. Many great men ... loitered in their development, dawdled in their work and seemed to all about them entirely unpromising; but later woke up, went to work, made up for lost time, and outstripped their fellows. These changes are perhaps in slight degree modified by weather, like moods, and have no doubt a physiological basis. Sometimes it is as if anemia and hyperemia followed each other with extreme sloth and then almost convulsive activity of motor centers. There are periods when one can do easily twice the ordinary task without fatigue. Girls of fifteen or sixteen would often like to sleep or rest a week, and seem incapable of putting forth real effort, and then there are fevers of craving hard and disagreeable work. Many returns show that in the spring there is very often great loathing to exert one's self, but this is occasionally broken by hours, days, or even weeks of supernormal activity, when stints are not only com-

pleted, but extra and self-imposed tasks are done with alacrity and satisfaction. Often there is a periodicity of activity in young men that suggests a monthly and sometimes a seasonal rhythm. The regular changes of day and night do not suffice, but this is complicated by some larger cycle of alternating recuperative and energetic periods of latent and patent, or inner and outer work. This, like so much else, suggests an atavistic trace of savage life, more controlled by moon and tides and warm and cold seasons. Indeed, diurnal regularity of work, play, food, and sleep is a recent thing in the development-history of man, is hard to establish, and in the vagrant, criminal, vicious, and pauper class is often never reached. But spells of overactivity, alternating with those of sluggishness and inertness, still seem in these years like neural echoes of ancient hunts and feasts, fasts and famines, migration and stagnation. Now at least nature pushes on her work of growth by alternation, now centering her energies upon function, now upon increase in size of organs, and perhaps by this method of economy attains a higher level than would be reached by too much poise, balance, and steadiness. It is as if the momentum of growth energies had to overcome obstacles at every point, by removing now this, now that hindrance, where if its energies had been applied to all simultaneously they would have been less effective.

2. Closely connected with this are the oscillations between pleasure and pain—the two poles of life, its sovereign masters. The fluctuations of mood in children are rapid and incessant. Tears and laughter are in close juxtaposition. Their emotional responses to impressions are immediate. They live in the present and reflect all its changes, and their feelings are little affected by the past or the future. With the dawn of adolescence, the fluctuations are slower and often for a time more extreme, and recovery from elation and especially from depression is

970

retarded. The past, and still more the future, is involved, and as the mental life widens, either tendency acquires more momentum. Youth can not be temperate, in the philosophical sense. Now it is prone to laughter, hearty and perhaps almost convulsive, and is abandoned to pleasure, the field of which ought gradually to widen with perhaps the pain field, although more. There is gaiety, irrepressible levity, an euphoria that overflows in every absurd manifestation of excess of animal spirits, that can not be repressed, that danger and affliction, appeals to responsibility and to the future, can not daunt nor temper. To have a good time is felt to be an inalienable right. The joys of life are never felt with so keen a relish; youth lives for pleasure, whether of an epicurean or an esthetic type. It must and ought to enjoy life without alloy. Every day seems to bring passionate love of just being alive, and the genius for extracting pleasure and gratification from everything is never so great.

But this, too, reacts into pain and disphoria, as surely as the thesis of the Hegelian logic passes over to its antithesis. Young people weep and sigh, they know not why; depressive are almost as characteristic as expansive states of consciousness. The sad Thanatopsis mood of gloom paints the world in black. Far-off anticipations of death come in a foreboding way, as it is dimly felt, though not realized, that life is not all joy and that the individual must be subordinated and eventually die. Hence statistics show, as we have seen, a strange rise in the percentage of suicides. Now there is gloom and anon spontaneous exuberance. In 766 of Lancaster's returns, thirteen had thought seriously of suicide, although only three had successfully attempted it. Perhaps elation precedes and depression comes as a reaction in the majority of cases, although this is not yet clear. Some feel despondent on awakening, at school time, or at noon, suggesting nutritive changes. "The curve of despondency starts at eleven, rises steadily and rapidly till fifteen, culminates at seventeen, then falls steadily till twenty-three.'' Young people are often unaccountably pleased with every trifle. They can shout for joy from the very fact of being alive. The far-off destiny of senescence looms up, and in fatigue the atrabiliar psychic basis of pessimism clouds life for a time and brings into dominance a new set of associations like another personality. Youth fears inadequacy of its powers to cope with the world. How this is connected with the alternating extremes of sexual tension, we have seen, although this by no means explains all. Sometimes the tears are from no assignable cause, and often from factitious motives. Suspicion of being disliked by friends, of having faults of person or character that can not be overcome; the fancy of being a supposititious child of their parents, of having unwittingly caused calamity to others, of hopeless love; failure in some special effort; a sense of the necessity of a life of work and hardship—these bring moods that may be more or less extreme according to environment, heredity, temperament, and other causes, may succeed each other with greater or less frequency, and may threaten to issue in brooding, depression, and melancholy, or in a careless and blind instinct to live for the day; but these, too, are due to the fact that the range of pleasure and pain is increased, so that there are new motives to each, and perhaps a long period with occasional special dangers must elapse before a final adjustment.

This is the age of giggling, especially with girls, who are at this stage of life farthest from Vassey's[1] view that man is not originally a laughing animal and that the gentleman and lady should never laugh, but only smile. If convulsive laughter is an epilepsy, it is one that begins in the highest regions and passes down the meristic

---

[1] The Philosophy of Laughing and Smiling. London, 1877, p. 194.

levels.[1] Goethe well says, that nothing is more significant of men's character than what they find laughable. The adolescent perhaps is most hilarious over caricature of nationalities, teachers, freshmen, the other sex, etc., who are mimicked, burlesqued, and satirized. Ridicule is now a powerful weapon of propriety. Again, the wit of the ephebos sometimes provokes a mental ticklishness about certain sacred and sometimes sexual topics, which may make jocularity and waggishness almost a plague. Another of the chief butts of adolescent fun is what is naive and unconscious; the blunders of the greeny, the unsophisticated way not only of the freshman, but of the countryman, the emigrant, and the *Bachfisch* girl now abound, while the simple idea of disaster or misfortune, which constitutes the humor of nine-tenths of the professional joke-makers, is rare. The horror of old or even once-told jests is never so intense, nor the appreciation for novelty so keen.

3. Self-feeling is increased, and we have all degrees of egoism and all forms of self-affirmation. The chief outcrop may be vanity and a sense of personal beauty and attractiveness, that is felt to be stunning to the other sex. It may be expressed in swagger ways; thrusting one's self into conspicuous places; talking, acting, dressing, to attract notice; or in complacency and even conceit for supposed superiority over others. Impudence, affront, insult, and sometimes even physical aggressiveness are forms of it. Growth of mind and body is so rapid that it is felt to the point of overestimation. Self-feeling is fed by all the compliment and sweet flattery of affection, which is the food often really tasted for the first time with true gusto, on which it shoots up with mushroom growth. The wisdom and advice of parents and teachers is overtopped, and in ruder natures may be met by blank

[1]The Psychology of Tickling, Laughing, and the Comic, by G. Hall and the late Arthur Allin. Am. Jour. of Psy., October, 1897, vol. ix, pp. 1-41.

contradiction. It is all a new consciousness of altitude and the desire to be, and to be taken for, men and women; to be respected, consulted, and taken into confidence. The new sense of self may be so exquisitely delicate that a hundred things in the environment, that would never rankle before, now sting and irritate. This is sometimes expressed in more or less conscious and formulated codes of honor, which among youth is often a strange and wondrous thing which must be defended by the wager of battle, with fists, or among German students with the sword, with all the punctilio of chivalry. Sometimes the formulæ by which honor and self-respect may be gained, maintained, impaired, and restored are detailed. Courage, honesty, parents, especially the mother, and perhaps a sweetheart, are involved, and the youth must perhaps represent honor for two. Ideals are so high and the tedious labor by which they are attained so constitutionally ignored that the goal seems very near and attainable if the purpose is high, so that the spirited, mettlesome ephebos or cadet summarily demands the world to take him on credit, as if the promise of his ambition were already fulfilled. The youth who has been amenable to advice and even suggestion, now becomes obstreperous, recalcitrant, filled with a spirit of opposition, and can not repress a sense of top-lofty superiority to the ways and persons of his environment. Age is often made to suffer discourtesy, and it sometimes seems as though the faculties of reverence and respect, to say nothing of admiration, were suddenly gone.

But the ebb of this tide is no less pronounced, and may precede in time its flood. The same youth with all his brazen effrontery may feel a distrust of self and a sinking of heart, which all his bravado is needed to hide. He doubts his own powers, is perilously anxious about his future, his self-love is wounded and humiliated in innumerable ways keenly felt, perhaps at heart resented, but with a feeling of impotence to resist. The collapsing moods bring a sense of abasement and humiliation, which sometimes seems like a degree of complacency to all that comes, suggesting spiritlessness. Youth often fears itself lacking in some essential trait of manhood or womanhood, or wanting the qualities of success. He is often vanquished in innumerable rivalries and competitions that now make so much of life, and loses heart and face. The world seems all the more hopeless because of the great demands which the opposite mood has imposed. Sometimes a sense of shame from purely imaginary causes is so poignant as to plunge the soul for a time into the deepest and most doleful dumps; fancied slights suggest despair, and in place of wonted self-confidence there is a retiring bashfulness, which no coaxing or encouragement of friends can overcome or fathom, and which may express itself only in some secret diary or perhaps in prayer. This, too, of course, often shades into elation and depression from moral causes.

Youth, too, may become overfastidious and effeminate, and this may pervade toilet, manners, care for health, or even take the form of moral nicety, overscrupulousness, and casuistry. Time was when the freshman was really green, awkward, inept in speech, without repose, but now too often the sub-freshman is a polished gentleman, confident and at home everywhere, though happily often betraying in some respects the earmarks of the native roughness which goes along with strength, in the midst of the overrefinement, suggestive of weakness.

4. Another clearly related alternation is that between selfishness and altruism. Before puberty, children are fed, clothed, sheltered, instructed, and done for, so that all the currents in their environment, especially with parents who follow Froebel's injunction to live for their children, have flowed toward and converge in them. Now currents in the opposite direction arise and should nor-

mally gather strength until they predominate. Life is sacrifice, and in trite parlance, we really live for what we die for. Before, youth must be served; now, it must serve. Its wants, perhaps even its whims, have been supreme, but in the matin song of love the precepts of renunciation are heard. Just as the embryonic cell grows large till it can no longer be nourished from without and must then divide or die, so the individual must be subordinated to society and posterity. Life is no longer egocentric, but altro-centric. Politeness and courtesy, and respect for the feelings of others, are often hard at first, but are a school of minor morals graduating into that of the higher virtues. Sympathy, and especially love, wither the individual, until self-subordination may become a passion. Youth devotes himself, perhaps by a vow, to a lifetime of self-denial or painful servitude to some great cause, or a career in which some of the deepest of human instincts must be mortified and eradicated. He or she would go on missions; labor for the sick, ignorant, depraved, and defective classes; espouse great philanthropic causes, and very often practice in secret asceticisms in the common and harmless pleasures and comforts of life, in food, drink, sleep, it may be, to the point of impairment of health, as if now glimpsing from afar the universal law which makes all individual good merely ancillary to the welfare of the species. Self-sacrifice may be exorbitant and vows gifts; humiliations are enthusiastic; selfishness seems mean; the ideal becomes a "pure life ruled by love alone"; the unselfishness may sometimes come in streaks and is often secreted, young people giving food or sweetmeats, staying at home to give others pleasure, without telling. There is, on the one hand, increase of self-confidence, a sense that the individual "is important enough to be noticed anywhere"; but this is not incompatible with helping others as never before, and even performing disagreeable tasks for them, associating with the bad in order to make them better, and greater readiness to give up any individual good. Our returns here show outcrops of the grossest selfishness and greediness side by side with a generosity and magnanimity rarely found in adult life save in poetry and romance. Others' rights of possession, food, and clothing sometimes are rudely trampled under foot, while the most delicate attentions and services, involving both forethought and hardship, are carried out to others or perhaps to the same persons. It seems as if expressions of extremely puerile selfishness were now particularly prone to be compensated for by extremes of the opposite nature, and *vice versa;* that often those most tender and considerate, most prone to take pains, to prefer others' enjoyment to their own, and to renounce ease, abandon cherished plans, and conquer the strongest natural desires in doing this, were those most liable occasionally to fall lowest in gloating self-gratification at the expense of others.[1]

Here, too, parents and teachers sometimes alternate between hope and despair for the young, before they slowly settle to fixed characteristics and conduct. Moreover, there is often arrest before the process of self-effacement is duly complete, so that we see in adults noble lives and acts veined with petty meannesses, which are the residual and unreduced organs of childhood.

5. Closely connected with the above are the alternations

---

[1]The ego, Fichte argued, created not only its own consciousness but the objective world, and is therefore sovereign lord of all. The self only exists, and all else, even other persons, are phantasmic projections of it. On this basis Max Stirner (Das Ich und sein Eigenthum) bases his monstrous ethics of absolute selfishness. Each must get every possible pleasure and seek his own aggrandizement in every way. Fame, property, sense, and enjoyment must be striven for by every means that can be successful, and all ideas of morality, truthfulness, duty, are utter nullities evolved from the brain of superior individuals in furtherance of this aim. Nietzsche's "will to power" is a no less crass reversion to the egoism of savagery. Lust of power is glorified to the point of tyranny and to the actual disparagement of tenderness and humanity. Whatever truth there is in this view, it has its best outcrop in this age.

between good and bad conduct generally. Perhaps at no time of life can goodness be so exotically pure and true, virtue so spotless, and good works spring from such a depth of good-will, which, since Kant, is often made the source of all real morality. Conscience, though not new-born, now can first begin to play a leading role. It awakens with a longing hunger and thirst for righteousness, prompts to highest aspiration and resolve. Benevolence and love to all persons and all being is fresh from its original source, and there are hearty good wishes for the general and special weal of others and ingenuity in anticipating and gratifying their desires, so that for brief periods youths and maidens sometimes seem too good for this earth.

But we need have no fear. From the same soil in which these budding virtues spring and bloom so delicately arise rank weeds; physical appetites are grossly indulged naively, even though they may sometimes seem almost bestial; propensities to lie break out, perhaps irresistibly, for a time. Anger slips its leash and wreaks havoc. Some petty and perhaps undreamed meanness surprises the onlooker. The common constraints of society are ruptured, or there are spasms of profanity; perhaps a sudden night of debauch, before knowledge had put up proper defenses; perhaps some lapse from virtue, which seems almost irretrievable, but which in fact should never be so readily pardoned and forgotten. The forces of sin and those of virtue never struggle so hotly for possession of the youthful soul. As statistics show, the age of most frequent conversions to true religion is precisely the years of the largest percentage of first commitments to houses of detention for crime. Now some new manifestations of vice surprise the soul in the midst of its ideal longings for absolute perfection, and wring it with grief and remorse. It seems a law of psychic development, that more or less evil must be done to unloose the higher powers of constraint and to practise them until they can keep down the baser instincts. The religious struggles of this stage bear abundant evidence to the violence of these storms and counter currents of which the human soul is now the arena. Temptations hitherto unknown to sins hitherto impossible bring redeeming agencies also new into action, and while the juvenile offender and the debauchee is arrested in his development and remains through life under the power of evil, growth is benign, and those who achieve normal maturity domesticate their baser instincts into the service of goodness.

6. The same is true of the great group of social instincts, some of which rest upon the preceding. Youth is often bashful, retiring, in love with solitude; perhaps wanders alone and communes with stars, sea, forest, animals; prefers nature to man; loves midnight walks; shuns the face of man, and especially the other sex; becomes interested in its own inner states and careless of the objective while sunken in the subjective life. Some youth take to drink chiefly or solely to gain through it the courage to go into society. They know not how, or if they do so, find it hard to assert themselves sufficiently to do justice to their ideas of their own merits. This is most common among country youth, but it is also frequent enough in the city. Others spring into a new love of companionship; friendships are cemented; "mashes" and "crushes" occur; the gregarious passion vents itself in all kinds of convivial associations, in organizations of many kinds, sometimes in riotous bouts and carousals; some can never be alone and seem to have for a time no resources in themselves, but to be abjectly dependent for their happiness upon their mates. They lose independence, and not only run, but think and feel, with the gang and the class. Alone, they are uninteresting and uninterested, but with others, vivacious, lively, and entertaining. To the inner circle of their chosen associates they bare

their inmost soul. There are no reserves or secrets, but a love of confessional outpourings in intimate hours together or sometimes in letters. The desire to please dominates some, and that to rule and lead, others; while the more passive and inert gradually lose the power of independent action, thought, or impulse, and come into the settled habits of dependent henchmen and followers. The psychology of crowds shows us how all human qualities are kept in countenance and developed, when like is paired with like; how joys are doubled and pains divided; how responsibility is attenuated until the greatest outrages are perpetrated by masses, from which every individual would revolt. Alternations between these two extremes of excessive or defective sociability are less frequent in the same individual, and if they occur, are at longer intervals.

At times, young people feel that those who are liked fail to appreciate or even dislike them. They are repelled by society, feel sinful and lonely, and perhaps need a good cry, which quite relieves them. We find, too, admiration and contempt strangely mingled; now appreciation, which almost becomes abject hero worship or fanaticism for great and new ideas, gushing devotion to literary and art products, etc., but all alternating with satire, burlesque, and parody, which seem to indicate that the power of reverence is lost and all the charm and modesty, which Plato found so becoming in youth, for a season quite extinct.

There is always a wide range of change between more and less before a center of gravity is found and a definite social character established. Both, of course, are necessary, and there is much that is true in the Baconian adage, that character is perfected in solitude and talent in society. City life, the innumerable clubs, business aggregations, sodalities, political and religious fraternization, seem a characteristic of this growingly urban age, and have no doubt perturbed the oscillations of the compass, so that it settles more slowly toward the pole of man's destiny than in other historic periods. We have seen these phenomena unusually accented in the early lives of Savonarola, Newton, Shelley, Patrick Henry, Keats, Hawthorne, Gifford, Jeffries, Boyeson, Nansen, and in the scores of our returns from men and women unknown to fame.

7. Closely akin to this are the changes from exquisite sensitiveness to imperturbability and even apathy, hardheartedness, and perhaps cruelty. Many youthful murderers, callous to the sufferings of their victims, have had the keenest sympathy with pets and even with children. Most criminals are unfeeling and unhumane. They can not pity, and the susceptibility to pathos is alien to them. The juvenile torturers often seem to have specialized psychic zones, where tenderness is excessive, as if to compensate for their defect. They weep over the pain, actual or imaginary, of their pets, while utterly hardened to the normal sentiments of kindness and help for suffering. The development of sympathy, as Sutherland has shown, has been slow and hard in the world, but it is basal for most of the factors of morality.

8. Curiosity and interest are generally the first outcrop of intellectual ability. Youth is normally greedy for knowledge, and that, not in one but in many directions. There is eagerness, zest, enthusiasm, which inspires corresponding activity to know that and only that which is of the highest worth. Wherever a new mine of great and fruitful discovery of truth is opened, a new field of activity appears, or new motives of self-sacrifice are made operative, there youth is in its element. It is the age of questioning, exploration, investigation, testing ideas, men, and the world. Expectation is at its best and the impulse to be ready for any new occasion is at its strongest. Now first it is really felt that knowledge is power,

and the noetic fever sometimes becomes too hot for the convenience of others, for conventionality, the routine of life, or even for health.

But the opposite is no less germane to these years. Here we find the inert moods and types, which are apathetic, which can not be profoundly stirred, that regard passionate mental interest as bad form, and cultivate indifference, that can not and will not admire. No devoted teacher need attempt to arouse and fire the mind in this condition. Sometimes this is all an affectation, mental posing, provoked by fashion or environment, and unconsciously imitative. Sometimes, alas! it is the direct result of excess, which saps the springs of life and brings senescent inertia before its time. It may be a product of fatigue and reaction from excessive effort, as in the case of Stuart Mill. It is not pain or pessimism, although, if real, it is the raw material out of which the latter is made. To the wise adult this is always pathetic, for what is youth without enthusiasm? These states always need wise diagnosis, because if they are recuperative, they should be let alone, and if results of dissipation, they should be drastically treated. Institutions, especially the tone and traditions of colleges and high schools, differ widely in their prevailing atmosphere in this regard. Here, too, a considerable range is no doubt normal.

9. Another vacillation is between knowing and doing. Now the life of the study charms, and the ambition is to be learned, bookish, or there is a passion to read. Perhaps there is a love of poetic intoxication or of contemplation, such as Scott, Bryant, Fulton, Franklin, Newton, etc., experienced. This afferent, more passive, receptive mood is necessary, because in the civilized state youth always lives in the midst of a far higher culture than it could produce. But a reaction is almost always inevitable where this receptive passion is extreme, and soon either unconscious instinct or else purpose takes the youth out of

doors, because he has fallen in love with nature, or, it may be, to cultivate muscle. His tastes and plans turn to active occupation. He would achieve rather than learn. He feels sometimes, more or less unconsciously, the vanity of mere erudition, and wishes to storm the world of reality and win his spurs, make his mark, and become an active and perhaps creative cause.

10. Less often we see one or more alternations between dominance by conservative and by radical instincts. The young man finds the world out of joint and would reform the church, school, perhaps social and family life; is sick at heart at the hollowness of established conventionality; is fired at the tyranny of wealth or trusts, and would himself reconstruct by doubting, casting out everything which does not seem to his own fledgling intelligence good, true, and beautiful. Some do and all ought to react from the party of progress to that of order, from burning the products of the past to worshipping them, to caring and working that no good already attained be lost; they should at some period feel the force of conventionalities, the truth of highly saturated creeds, the value of established institutions, despite their possible betterment. There is especial danger that temperament or environment will destroy this balance and precipitate the mind for life into one or another of these camps where extreme views are so easy and simple, and moderate ones so hard and complex. This is especially seen in the religious sphere, to which we shall turn later. The equipoise between atheism and bigotry is almost always disturbed; there is excess of skepticism or of credulity, affirmation or denial, doubt or faith, and youth is especially prone to be distracted between the instincts that make the devotee and those that make the heretic.

11. We find many cases of signal interest in which there is a distinct reciprocity between sense and intellect, as if each had its nascent period. We have already seen

how the senses are acuminated and sense interests modified and generally enhanced, so that occasionally youth is passionately devoted to seeing and hearing new things, is all eye, ear, taste, and would widen the surface of contact with the external world to the maximum, as if laying in stock for future mental elaboration; but there are also periods of inner absorption and meditation, when reality fades and its very existence is questioned, when the elements that make the content of the sensory shoot together into new unities. The inner eye that sees larger correspondences in time and space is opened; the bearings of familiar facts appear; wisdom is sought from books or friends, and is assimilated with amazing facility, so that a new consciousness is born within or above the old, and the attention is attracted to inner states which demand explanation. It is as if the projective system, which acts and reacts upon the external world, had now its innings, to be later followed by a period when the energy of psychic growth is largely turned to the associative fibers, both ends of which are in the brain.

12. Closely connected with this is the juxtaposition of wisdom and folly. Now there are high intuitions that anticipate maturity and even the best mental products of old age, an attitude of mind that seems to have anticipated the experiences of a lifetime, and to have found rest in the true goal of wisdom. Yet, interspersed with all this precocious philosophy, we find pitfalls of collapsing and childish folly. This may be ethical, in the form of irritability, greed, causeless and irrational freakishness and abandon to the lower impulses, or downright silliness. Those precocious in some are often arrested in other respects.

We have already seen that body growth is not symmetrical, but to some extent the parts, functions, and organs grow in succession, so that the exact normal proportions of the body are temporarily lost, to be regained later on a new plan. The mind now grows in like manner. It is as if the various qualities of soul were developed successively; as if the energy of growth now stretched out to new boundaries, now in this and now in that direction. This is biological economy, as well as recapitulatory, because in some way that we do not understand nature follows in the psychic field the familiar mechanical principle we must so often appeal to by which power is best developed over a large surface, to be later best applied at a point. The human plant circumnutates in a wider and wider circle, and the endeavor should be to prevent it from prematurely finding a support, to prolong the period of variation to which this stage of life is sacred, and to prevent natural selection from confirming too soon, the slight advantage which any quality may temporarily have in this struggle for existence among many faculties and tendencies within us. The educational ideal is now to develop capacities in as many directions as possible, to indulge caprice and velleity a little, to delay consistency for a time, and let the diverse prepotencies struggle with each other. Now everything psychic tends in its turn to be intense to the point of illusion or positive obsession, but nature's rhythm, if allowed to have its due course, prevents stagnation and hebetude, and the passion to change keeps all powers fluent and plastic, gives elasticity and develops power of sanification. Sometimes there seem almost to be dual or multiplex personalities. The venerable four temperaments of the phrenologists seem contending with each other for dominance, but the soul should make some place for all of them in its many mansions. It is veritably like a batrachian, or insect struggling to get out of its last year's skin or chitin, or like sloughing off the old consciousness of childhood for the new one of maturity. It is thus that the soul explores the maximum area possible of human experience. This is now the meaning of the freedom of the will, and captious though it often seems, it is thus that the foundations of wise choices that first hear from all parts and parties are preformed. The mind is now in what the biologists call its generalized form. It is as if man were polyphyletic in his origin and now the different ethnic stocks were successively harked back to. The possibility of variation in the soul is now at its height. Especially in races of mixed blood, our returns convince me, that more prepotencies clash or coincide, as the case may be, and we can often detect the voices of our forebears of very different races in the soul. Psychic life is thus for a term greatly perturbed. When the youth takes the helm of his own being, he navigates a choppy sea. Thus it would appear in nature's economy he must strive, fight, and storm his way up, if he would break into the kingdom of man. Here, too, many an impulse seeks expression, which seems strong for a time, but which will never be heard of later. Its function is to stimulate the next higher power that can only thus be provoked to development, in order to direct, repress, or supersede it. Never is it so true that nothing human is alien from each individual, as in this fever of ephebeitis, which has so many peculiar features in the American temperament.

The popular idea, that youth must have its fling, implies the need of greatly and sometimes suddenly widened liberty, which nevertheless needs careful supervision and wise direction, from afar and by indirect methods. The forces of growth now strain to their uttermost against old restrictions. It is the age of bathmism, or most rapid variation, which is sometimes almost saltatory. Nearly every latency must be developed, or else some higher power, that later tempers and coordinates it, lacks normal stimulus to develop. Instead of the phenomena of alternate generation, where certain potentialities lie dormant in one generation to appear in the next, we have corresponding psychic phenomena in one and the same individual by which faculties and impulses, which are denied legitimate expression during their nascent periods, break out well on in adult life—falsetto notes mingling with manly bass as strange puerilities. The chief end in view must now be to bring out all the polyphonous harmonies of human nature. The individual can never again expand his nature to so nearly compass the life of the species. The voices of extinct generations, sometimes still and small, sometimes strident and shrill, now reverberate, and psychic development is by leaps and bounds, of which psychological science has so far been able to know but very little.

Mental unity comes later. Consistency then has its place. The supreme Aristotelian virtue of temperance and the golden mean—which is courage well poised between timidity and foolhardiness, liberality midway between the extremes of avarice and prodigality, modesty which combines the good and rejects the evil by excess of bashfulness and impudence, self-respect which is neither vainglory nor self-abasement—slowly knits up the soul, coordinates its many elements, represses illusions, and issues in settled character. The logical as contrasted with the genetic ideal now arises and prompts to reason, consistency, and coordinations in ever higher associations as cosmos rises from chaos. We see over and over again that the metamorphic stages of early adolescence are forgotten, and how impossible it is for the mature mind to remember or even credit, when they are noted or told by others, the preceding phases of instinctive transformations. In one sense, youth loses very much in becoming adult. The ordered, regular life of maturity involves necessarily more or less degeneration for simple tendencies. Indeed, the best definition of genius is intensified and prolonged adolescence, to which excessive or premature systematization is fatal. Even in commonplace lives, higher qualities, and often the very highest, appear in the teens for a brief flitting moment, or at least they barely hint their existence and then fade, sometimes because the demands of adulthood are too early or too insistently enforced.

This law of a period of freedom that leans a little toward license before the human colt is haltered and broken to any of the harnesses of severe discipline, is favored by every aspect of the bionomic law. It is a fact of great significance not only unexplored but hitherto unnoted, that even as the psychic perturbations of this stage of multifarious impulsions are lost to recollection, because they are so inconsistent and blind, since they lack the intellectual factor of experience, just so the phyletic stages in the development of the race that correspond to puberty fall largely in the unhistoric period—the darkest of all dark ages, during which brute became man. Science explores the simian forms of life, but here our sense of ignorance is increasingly painful. The distribution of the gorilla is rapidly narrowing toward early extinction, and we know far less of its characteristics, or those of the gibbon, ourang, and chimpanzee, than we do of the lowest races of men. The interval between the highest anthropoid brain of 550 cubic centimeters, and that of the lowest man, 1,150 cubic centimeters, is almost as lost as a sunken Atlantis. If we take Canstadt man, perhaps the lowest in Europe, as the point of reemergence of man's phyletic history, we find the most radical transformations.

In the interval that separates the pithecoid from the troglodyte, many changes, perhaps more momentous than any in the historic period, took place. Arboreal life and a diet of fruits, nuts, and buds was exchanged for a life well adjusted to fluvial and littoral conditions. The shore —the most changing of all the life areas, the great feeding-ground of aquatic and terrestrial forms, where all land animals originally came from their primordial home in the sea, after long amphibian apprenticeship, and where the whale, seal, and other backsliders to aquatic life reverted after long experience on the land—had already been the highway of extended migration; and man, especially if monophyletic and if the qualities that gave him supremacy over the brutes were developed in a single narrow area, had multiplied rapidly; had learned the use of fire and cooking, thus freeing energy, hitherto needed for digestion, to higher uses; had entered the paleolithic stage of chipped stone for spear and arrow heads; had asserted his dominion over the mammoth, cave-bear, hyena, woolly rhinoceros, Irish elk; had invested himself with the freedom of the world; had become the most migratory of all species, thus favoring amphimixis and variation by exogamy, and knew no barrier because only man stops man. He had been forced from some primitive home or cunabula, perhaps by the slow submergence of Sclater's Lemuria, or driven from his pristine habitat on the high table-lands north of the Himalayas, and had already begun his career over the globe. During this period many of the scores of domestic animals had been tamed—perhaps mostly, as O. T. Mason thinks—by women who began pastoral life. Many of the two hundred and forty-nine species of plants of which de Candolle traces the history—all phanerogamous —were brought under culture also perhaps first by women, and thus settled agricultural life had been introduced. The hand had been developed much in structure, and far more in function, from a simple prehensile organ to a tool and weapon user and even maker. Dress had evolved, a momentous change had come about by focusing development upon intelligence as soon as its high survival and selective value made itself felt, leaving the body relatively unchanged while mind evolved enormously, if not disproportionately, like the giraffe's neck. Infancy had been prolonged, and, with it, parental care, love and home, and the possibilities of education unfolded Speech and tradition had been acquired. From this point all is relatively easy of explanation, for as Lyell said, if all but one race of men in a single spot of the globe were exterminated, they would soon people the earth again though they were as low as the Eskimo or South Sea Islander. Perhaps primitive man had already grown to gigantic stature, as Principal Dawson conjectures, and did and dared at sea, in hunting, and in crossing barriers, that which modern man would not. Perhaps he was a pigmoid, as the horse has grown from the orohippus of fox size; perhaps he was Broca's estromelian, half monster and half man; or more akin to Lombroso's degenerate mattoid, or to Sergi's hominidæ. Perhaps McRitchie's conjecture that fairies were primitive dwarfs or mid-men is valuable; it is in line with the wide-spread superstition that arrow-heads are fairy darts. He may have been pliocene, diluvial, or even tertiary.

My own belief, as I have set forth elsewhere,[1] is that man early became the wanderer and the exterminator *par excellence*. Less than any other animal, can man tolerate rivals in the struggle for existence. The instinct which impelled him to exterminate the North sea-cow in 1767, and, in the nineteenth century, the great awk in 1840, the African quagga in 1870, and scores of other animals and birds that in recent times have gone forever even beyond the reach of the collector, that is now rapidly reducing to the vanishing point the American bison, the Indian lion and rhinoceros, the walrus, the zebra-giraffe, halibut, oyster, lobster, etc., and that prepares and sells the skins of two million birds a year, which are dying out that man may have food, safety, or sport, is the same instinct which in prehistoric times destroyed chiefly or with aid of other causes the gigantic extinct mammals, and has

---

[1] The Relation of Civilization and Savagery. Proc. Mass. Hist. Soc., January, 1903.

forever scarred man's soul with fear, anger, and wanton cruelty. The same enmity against the lower races, which in our day has exterminated forever the Boethuks, the Tasmanians, and is reducing so many lower human ethnic stocks to make way for favored races, is but a relic of the rage which exterminated the missing links and made man for ages the passionate destroyer of his own pedigree, so to that no trace of it is left.

A great number of the phyletic corollates of some of the most marked stages by which prepubescent boyhood passes to maturity exist only in the later phases of this transition from anthropoid to savage life, although many are found earlier and others later yet. To much in this dark interval early adolescence is the only key, but even here the record is so distorted, falsified, so often inverted, so mingled with what belongs to later phases, that we know as yet but little how to use this key. To-day youth is passed in an environment of culture, nearly every element of which is far superior to anything that it could produce. The powers of imitation and appropriation are so developed and perhaps hypertrophied that it is impossible to distinguish what comes from indigenous and what from acquired sources. The past and future contend with each other for mastery. In his elegiac moods, youth seems to long for a lost idea in a way that suggests transmigration of a Platonic Wordsworthian type, as plants dream of the sun, and on the other hand, his esthetic sensibilities are presentiments of a superior stage of the race that will develop out of the present human type which it is the function of art to prophesy and anticipate. The processes last to be attained are least assured by heredity and most dependent upon individual effort, in aid of which nature gives only propulsion, often less defined the later it can be acquired, like the Kantian pure autonomous "oughtness," which the individual must laboriously shape by a wise use of heteronymous and consciously regulated motives. While adolescence is the great revealer of the past of the race, its earlier stages must be ever surer and safer and the later possibilities ever greater and more prolonged, for it, and not maturity as now defined, is the only point of departure for the superanthropoid that man is to become. This can be only by an ever higher adolescence lifting him to a plane related to his present maturity as that is to the well-adjusted stage of boyhood where our puberty now begins its regenerating metamorphoses.

(GRANVILLE) STANLEY HALL (b.-Ashfield, Massachusetts, Feb. 1, 1848; d.-April 24, 1924).

Hall received his Ph.D. from Havard in 1878, having studied under James. He then went to Leipzig for two years where he worked with Wundt in particular, and also with Helmholtz. From 1881 to 1888 he was Professor at the Johns Hopkins University, where he founded the first laboratory in psychology in the United States, in 1882, modeled after Wundt's. In 1887 Hall founded the *American Journal of Psychology*. In 1889 he was appointed first President of the newly founded Clark University in Worcester, Massachusetts. Here, he was also Professor of Psychology and Pedagogy.

Through the establishment of a renowned invited lecture series, Hall can be credited with introducing psychoanalysis to the United States, by extending the first invitation to Sigmund Freud, in December 1908, to celebrate the twentieth anniversary of the founding of Clark. More directly, Hall is widely noted for his theoretical contributions to the understanding of the psychology of youth and adolescence. His writings in this field bear the stamp of the highest genius. The present selection is taken from his most important book in this field.

HALL, G. S. *Adolescence: its psychology and its relations to physiology, anthropology, sociology, sex, crime, religion, and education.* New York: D. Appleton & Co., 1925 (1904), 2 vol. Chap. 10: "Evolution and the feelings and instincts characteristic of normal adolescence." Reprinted, with deletions, by permission of the publisher.

See also:

HALL, G. S.

a) *Senescence, the last half of life.* N. Y.: D. Appleton & Co., 1922 (1884).

b) *Aspects of German culture.* Boston: J. R. Osgood & Co., 1887.

c) *The contents of children's minds on entering school.* N. Y.: E. L. Kellogg & Co., 1893.

d) *Aspects of child life and education.* Boston: Ginn & Co., 1907. Ed. T. L. Smith.

e) *Educational problems.* N. Y.: D. Appleton & Co., 1911.

993

THE LANGUAGE AND THOUGHT
OF THE CHILD
JEAN PIAGET

The problem which we propose to solve can be stated as follows: What are the intellectual interests or, if one prefers, the *logical functions* to which the questions of a given child testify, and how are those interests to be classified? In order to solve this problem it is sufficient to make a list extending over a certain stretch of time, if not of all the questions asked by a child, at least of those asked of the same person, and to classify these questions according to the sort of answer which the child expects to receive. But this classification is a nicer matter than one would think, and we shall therefore be more concerned with the creation of an instrument of research than with its practical application.

The material on which we shall work consists of 1125 spontaneous questions asked of Mlle. Veihl over a period of ten months by Del, a boy between 6 and 7 (6; 3 to 7; 1). These questions were taken down in the course of daily talks lasting two hours; each talk was a sort of lesson by conversation, but of a very free character during which the child was allowed to say anything he liked. These talks had begun long before lists were made of the questions, so that the child found himself in a perfectly natural atmosphere from the start. Also, what is more important, he never suspected that his questions were being noted in any way. Mlle. Veihl possessed the child's full confidence, and was among those with whom he best liked to satisfy his curiosity. No doubt the subject-matter of the lessons (reading, spelling, general knowledge) had a certain influence on the questions that were asked, but that was inevitable. The chance occurrences of walks or games— which, incidentally, played their own small part in these interviews—had just as much influence in directing the subject's interests. The only way to draw a line between what is occasional and what is permanent in the curiosity of a child is to multiply the records in conditions as similar as possible. And this is what we did. Finally, it need hardly be said that we abstained as carefully from provoking questions as from picking and choosing among those that were asked.

Neverthelesss, as this investigation was originally destined to help only in the study of 'whys,' these alone have been taken down in their entirety during the first interviews in which the experimenter was at work. For a few weeks, all other questions were only taken down intermittently. On some days, it goes without saying, all questions were taken down without any exception, but on others, only the 'whys' were taken into account. Questions 201 to 450, 481 to 730, and 744 to 993, however, represent a complete account of all the questions asked during the corresponding periods of time. The statistical part will therefore deal with these three groups of 250 questions each, or else with the 'whys.'

I. 'Whys'

Before broaching the difficult problem presented by the types of questions asked by Del, let us try, by way of introduction, to solve a special and more limited problem—that of the different types of 'whys.'

The question of children's 'whys' is more complex than it at first appears to be. It is well known that the whys which appear somewhere about the age of 3 (Stern mentions them at 2; 10, 3; 1 etc., Scupin at 2; 9, Rasmussen between 2 and 3 etc.), are extremely numerous between this age and that of 7, and characterize what has been called the second age of questions in the child. The first age is characterized by questions of place and name, the second by those of cause and time. But its very abundance leads us to look upon the 'why' as the maid-of-all work among questions, as an undifferentiated question, which in reality has several heterogeneous meanings. Stern was right in pointing out that the earliest 'whys' seem more affective than intellectual in character, *i.e.,* that instead of being the sign of verbal curiosity, they rather bear witness to a disappointment produced by the absence of a desired object or the non-arrival of an expected event. But we have yet to ascertain how the child passes from this affective curiosity, so to speak, to curiosity in general, and finally to the most subtle forms of intellectual interest such as the search for causes. Between these two extremes there must be every shade of intervening variety, which it should be our business to classify.

There is a certain category of childish 'whys' which do seem from a superficial point of view, to demand a causal explanation for their answer. Such an one is this, one of the earliest questions of a boy of 3: *"Why do the trees have leaves?"* Now, if such a question were asked by an adult, educated or otherwise, it would imply at least two groups of answers. One group of answers, the finalistic, would begin with the word 'to' ("to keep them warm," "to breathe with," etc.), the other, the causal or logical, would begin with the word 'because' ("because they are descended from vegetables which have leaves" or "because all vegetables have leaves"). It is, therefore, not possible to see at first which of these two shades of meaning is uppermost in the child's question. There may even be a quantity of other meanings which elude our understanding. The question may be merely verbal, and indicate pure astonishment without calling for any answer. This is often the case with the questions of children; they are asked of no one, and supply in effect a roundabout way of stating something without incurring contradiction. Very often, if one does not answer a child immediately, he will not wait, but answer himself. We

996

have already come across several of these ego-centric questions, which are strictly speaking pseudo-questions. But this will not be taken into account in the classification which follows. However egocentric a question may be, it is always interesting that it should have been expressed in the form of a question, and the type of logical relation (causality, finalism, etc.), which it presupposes is always the same as that which would characterize the question if it were asked of anyone. In this connexion, the question which we quoted admits of many more meanings for the child than for the adult. The child may have wanted to know, from anthropomorphism and apart from any interest in the tree itself, "who put the leaves on the trees." (Why have the trees got leaves? Because God put them there.) He may have purposive or utilitarian ideas in relation to humanity. (Why . . . etc.—So that it should look pretty. So that people might sit in its shade, etc.), or in relation to the tree itself, which the child would endow with more or less explicit aims (because it likes to, etc.). In a word, a large number of interpretations are always possible when a child's 'why' is isolated from its context.

The lists of 'whys' belonging to the same child, such as we are going to discuss, will therefore by the mere fact that they make comparisons possible, help to solve the two following problems, which without this method are insoluble: 1. What are the possible types of 'whys,' classified according to the logical type of answer which the child expects or which he supplies himself? 2. What is the genealogy of these types?

§ 1. PRINCIPAL TYPES OF 'WHYS.'—There are three big groups of children's 'whys'—the 'whys' of *causal explanation* (including *finalistic* explanation), those of *motivation,* and those of *justification.* Inside each group further shades of difference may be distinguished. After a certain age (from 7 to 8 onwards) there are also the whys of *logical justification,* but they hardly concern us at the age of Del, and they can be included in the "whys of justification" in general.

The term *explanation* is to be taken in the restricted sense of causal or finalistic explanation. For the word 'explain' carries with it two different meanings. Sometimes it signifies giving a 'logical' explanation, *i.e.,* connecting the unknown with the known, or giving a systematic exposition (explaining a lesson or a theorem). 'Whys' referring to logical explanation ("Why is half 9, 4.5?") are to be classified as "logical justification." Sometimes, on the contrary, the word 'explain' means carrying back our thought to the causes of a phenomenon, these causes being efficient or final according as we are dealing with natural phenomena or with machines. It is in the second sense only that we shall use the word explanation. 'Whys' of causal explanation will therefore be recognizable by the fact that the expected answer implies the idea of cause or of final cause. Here are some examples taken from Del: *"Why do they* [bodies] *always fall?"*—*"Lightning . . . Daddy says that it makes itself all by itself in the sky. Why?* [does it make itself in this way]"—*"Why haven't they* [little goats] *got any milk?"* —*"Why is it so heavy* [a two-franc piece]*?"*

Let us designate as *motivation* that sort of explanation which accounts, not for a material phenomenon, as in the last category, but for an action or a psychological state. What the child looks for here is not, strictly speaking, a material cause, but the purpose or the motive which guided the action, sometimes also the psychological cause. 'Whys' of motivation are innumerable, and easy to classify: *"Are you going away? Why?"*—*"Why do we always begin with reading?"*—*"Why doesn't daddy know the date? He is quite grown up."*

Finally, let us designate as "whys" of *justification* those which refer to some particular order, to the aim,

not of some action, but of a rule. "Why do we have to
. . . etc." These 'whys' are sufficiently frequent in the
case of Del to justify the formation of a separate category. The child's curiosity does not only attach itself to
physical objects and the actions of human beings, it goes
out systematically to all the rules that have to be
respected—rules of language, of spelling, sometimes of
politeness, which puzzle the child and of which he would
like to know the why and the wherefore. Sometimes he
seeks for their origin, i.e., his idea of it, the object of the
'grown-ups' who have decided that it should be so, sometimes he looks for their aim. These two meanings are
confused in the same question—"why . . . etc.?" We
have here a collection of interests which can be united
under the word 'justification' and which differ from
the simple interest in psychological motivation. Here are
examples of it, some less obvious than others: *"Why not
'an' [in the spelling of a word]? You can't tell when it is
'an' or 'en.'"—"Why not 'in' [in 'Alain']? Who said it
shouldn't be, the grownups in Paris?"—"Why do people
'strayed,' does it mean lost?"—"Black coffee, why black?
All coffee is black. . . ."*

These, then, are the three great classes of 'whys' which
it is possible to establish straight away. But it need hardly
be said that these are 'statistical' types, i.e., that between
them there exists every kind of intermediate variety. If
all the existing transitional types could be arranged in
order, and their shades of difference expressed in numbers, then the three main types would simply represent
the three crests of a graph of frequency. Between these
summits there would be the intermediate zones. . . .

It is obvious, for instance, that between the "causal
explanation" of physical objects .called forth by the
questions of the first group, and psychological 'motivation', there are two intermediate types. Alongside of the
explanations which the child himself considers as physical

(the cloud moves because the wind drives it along) there are those which he looks upon as mixed up with motivation (the river is swift because man or God wanted it to be), and there are those which we ourselves consider mixed (the two-franc piece is heavy because it is in silver, or because it was made to weigh more than a one-franc piece, etc.). Causal explanation therefore often inclines to motivation. But the converse also happens. In addition to the "whys of motivations" which refer to a momentary intention (Why are you going away?) there are those which involve explanations of a more psychological nature, and appeal no longer to an intention, but to cause properly so-called (Why does Daddy not know the date?), which brings us back to the first type of question. The result is that we can give no fixed form to the criterion used to distinguish causal explanation from motivation. The decision in each case as to whether the child wanted to be answered with a causal explanation or with a motivation would be too arbitrary. The criterion can only be practical, and will have to adapt itself to the contents of the question. When the question refers to physical objects (natural phenomena, machines, manufactured objects, etc.), we shall class it among the 'whys' of causal explanation; when the question refers to human activities, we shall class it among the 'whys' of motivation. This classification is a little arbitrary, but the convention is easy to follow. In our opinion the attempt to define the child's motive too closely would be still more arbitrary, for that would be to put the purely subjective judgment of each psychologist in the place of conventions, which may be rigid, but which are known to be only conventions.

The distinction between motivation and justification, on the other hand, is even more difficult to establish with any precision. In the main, 'whys' of justification imply the idea of rules. But this idea is far less definite in the

1000

child than in us, so that here again we are obliged to use a criterion bearing on the matter rather than on the form of the question. The justification of a rule is very closely allied to motivation, to the search for the intention of him who knows or who established the rule. We shall therefore say that 'whys' of justification are those which do not bear directly on a human activity, but on language, spelling and, in certain cases to be more closely defined, on social conventions (bad manners, prohibitions, etc.).

If we insist upon this third class of 'whys,' it is because of the following circumstance. We have shown throughout the last three chapters that before 7 or 8 the child is not interested in logical justification. He asserts without proving. Children's arguments in particular consist of a simple clash of statements, without any justification of the respective points of view. The result is that the word 'because,' corresponding to a logical demonstration ('because' connecting two ideas of which one is the reason for the other) is rarely used by the child, and . . . is even imperfectly understood by him; in a word, it is alien to the habits of thought of the child under 7 or 8. Now, corresponding to this group of logical relations, to the 'because' which unites two ideas, there is obviously a group of 'whys of justification' whose function is to find the logical reason for a statement; in other words, to give a proof or to justify a definition. For example, "why is 4.5 half of 9?" This is not a case of causal or psychological motivation, but quite definitely one of logical reasoning. Now, if the observations made in the course of the last chapters are correct, we shall expect—and our expectation will prove to be justified—this type of 'why' to be very rare under the age of 7 or 8, and not to constitute a separate class. But—and this is why we wish to keep the 'whys of justification' in a separate category—there is for the child only a step from a rule of spelling or grammar to the definition of a word, etc., and from the definition of a word to a genuine "logical reason." Everyone knows that childish grammar is more logical than ours, and that the etymologies spontaneously evolved by children are perfect masterpieces of logic. Justification in our sense is therefore an intermediate stage between simple motivation and logical justification. Thus, in the examples quoted, " *Why do people say 'strayed'?*" (instead of saying lost) inclines to the 'whys' of motivation; "*Why black coffee, all coffee is black*" seems to appeal to a logical reason (which would be a link between a reason and conclusion); and the other two seem to be intermediate 'whys' which appeal to a certain form of spelling, etc.

To sum up. "Whys of justification" are an undifferentiated class before the age of 7 or 8. After the age of 7 or 8 this class is replaced—such at least is our hypothesis—by two other classes. One of these, "logical justification or reason," is to be contrasted with causal explanation and motivation. The other, "justification of rules, customs, etc.," can be considered as intermediate between logical justification and motivation. Before the age of 7 to 8, these two classes can therefore be united into one. This gives us the following table:

	Form of the question	Matter of the question
Explanation (causal)	Cause . . . . . . End	Physical objects
Motivation	Motive	Psychological actions
Justification	Justification proper . . .	Customs and rules
	Logical reason . Classification and connexion of ideas	

In addition to this, it should be pointed out that there are certain classes of questions beginning with such words as 'how,' 'what is,' 'where . . . from,' etc., which correspond word for word with the classes of 'whys' of which we have just spoken. This will supply us with a very useful counter-proof.

§ 2. "Whys of Causal Explanation." Introduction and Classification by Material. . . .*

"Whys of causal explanation" raise a number of problems which are of paramount importance in the study of the child intelligence. It is indeed a matter for conjecture whether a child feels in the same degree as we do the need for a causal explanation properly so-called (efficient cause as opposed to finalism). We ought therefore to examine the possible types of causality which could take the place of causality properly so-called. Stanley Hall has shown that out of some hundreds of questions about the origin of life (birth) 75% are causal. But he never stated his criteria. He simply pointed out that among these causal questions a large number are artificialistic, animistic, etc. The difficulty therefore still remains of classifying these types of explanation and of finding their mutual relations to each other.

Now we had occasion . . . to show that the child between 6 and 8 takes very little interest in the "how" of phenomena. His curiosity reaches only the general cause, so to speak, in contrast to the detail of contacts and of causal sequences. This is a serious factor in favour of the *sui generis* character of "whys of explanation" in the child. Let us try to classify those of Del, starting from the point of view of their contents, and not bothering about their form.

Classifying these 'whys' by their contents consists in grouping them according to the objects referred to in the question.

In this connexion, out of the 103 "whys of causal explanation" 81 refer to nature and 22 to machines or manufactured articles. The 81 'whys' concerning nature can be subdivided into 26 questions about inanimate

*Deleted is a short comment on the vastness of the subject of causality.—*Editor.*

objects (inanimate for the adult), 10 about plants, 29 about animals and 16 about the human body.

What is most remarkable about this result is the feeble interest shown in inanimate physical objects. This circumstance should put us on our guard from the first against the hypothesis according to which Del's 'whys' would refer to causality in the same sense as ours. A certain number of the peculiarities exhibited by the 'whys' concerning the physical world will enable us to state the problem more precisely.

In the first place, some of Del's questions bear witness to the well-known anthropomorphism of children. It may be better described as *artificialism,* but nothing is known as yet about its origin or its duration. For example: *"Why* [does the lightning make itself by itself in the sky]? *Is it true? But isn't there everything that is needed to light a fire with up in the sky?"* These artificialistic questions, which are rarely quite clear, obviously do not presuppose an efficient mechanistic causation analogous to ours.

Other and more interesting 'whys' raise the problem of *chance* in the thought of the child. These for example: Del had thought that Bern was on the lake. "The lake does not reach as far as Bern."—*"Why?"* or *"Why does it not make a spring in our garden?"* etc. Mlle. V. finds a stick and picks it up. *"Why is that stick bigger than you?"* —*"Is there a Little Cervin and a Great Cervin?"*—No.— *"Why is there a Little Saleve and a Great Saleve?"* Questions of this kind abound with this child; we shall come across many more, and they will always surprise us. We are in the habit of allotting a large part to chance and contingency in our explanations of phenomena. All "statistical causality," which for us is simply a variety of mechanical causality, rests on this idea of chance, *i.e.,* of the intersection of two independent causal sequences. If there are no springs in the garden, it is because the series of motives which lead to the choice of the garden's locality is independent of the series of causes which produced a spring a little distance away. If the two lines of sequences had crossed, it would only be by chance, as there is very little likelihood of their crossing. But it is clear that this idea of chance is derivative: it is a conclusion forced upon us by our powerlessness to explain. The result is that the child is slow in reaching the sort of agnosticism of ordinary adult life. For lack of a definite idea of chance, he will always look for the why and wherefore of all the fortuitous juxtapositions which he meets with in experience. Hence this group of questions. Do these questions then point to a desire for causal explanation? In a sense they do, since they demand an explanation where none is forthcoming. In another sense they do not, since obviously a world in which chance does not exist is a far less mechanical and far more anthropomorphic world than ours. Besides, we shall meet this problem of causality again, in connexion with other varieties of 'why.'

The following questions, however, seem to really belong to the order of physical causality:

(1) *"Why do they* [bodies] *always fall?"* (2) *"It* [water] *can run away, then why* [is there still some water in the rivers]?" (3) "[The water goes to the sea]— *Why?"* (4) *"There are waves only at the edge* [of the lake]. *Why?"* (5) *"Why does it always do that* [stains of moisture] *when there is something there* [fallen leaves]?" (6) *"Will it always stay there* [water in a hole worn away in the sandstone]?—No, the stone absorbs a lot.—*Why? Will it make a hole?*—No.—*Does it melt?"* (7) *"Why does it get colder and colder as you go up* [as you go north]?" and (8) *"Why can you see lightning better at night?"*

It is worth noting how difficult it is to determine what part is played by finalism in these questions and what by mechanical causality. Thus 'whys' 3, 7, and 8 could easily be interpreted as finalistic questions: you see the lightning better in order to...etc. It is only in questions 1, 4, 5, and 6 that we can be at all sure of any desire for a causal explanation, because the objects are uncircumscribed, and clearly independent of human or divine intervention. Lightning, on the other hand, is, as we have just seen, spontaneously conceived of as 'manufactured' in the sky; rivers, as we shall show later on, are thought of as put into action by man, etc.

In a word, these questions asked about the physical world are far from being unambiguously causal. Questions about plants do not throw much light on the matter. Some point to a certain interest in the circumstances of the flower's habitat: *"Why are there not any* [bluebells] *in our garden?"* Others, more interesting, refer to the life and death of plants: *"Has it rained in the night?—* No.*—Then why have they* [weeds] *grown?" "Why do we not see those flowers about now* [the end of summer]*?"—"They* [roses on a rose-tree] *are all withered, why? They shouldn't die, because they are still on the tree."—"Why does it* [a rotten mushroom] *drop off so easily?"* We shall come across this preoccupation with 'death' in connexion with other questions, which will show that this interest is of great importance from the point of view of the idea of chance. The first group of questions raises the same problems as before: the child is still very far from allowing its share to chance in the nexus of events, and tries to find a reason for everything. But is the reason sought for causal, or does it point to a latent finalism?

Questions on animals are naturally very definite in this connexion. About half of them refer to the intentions which the child attributes to animals. *"Does the butterfly make honey?—No.—But why does it go on the flowers?"* —*"Why do they* [flies] *not go into our ears?"* etc. These

1006

'whys' ought to be classified as "whys of motivation," but we are confining this group to the actions of human beings. If it were extended to include animals, there would be no reason for not extending it to include the objects which at 6 or 7 the child still openly regards as animated, such as ... stars, fire, rivers, wind, etc. Among the other questions, only four are causal, and curiously enough, are again concerned with death:

"They [butterflies] *die very soon, why?"*—*"Will there still be any bees when I grow up?*—Yes, those that you see will be dead, but there will be others.—*Why?"*—*"Why do they* [animals] *not mind* [drinking dirty water]?"*—*"It* [a fly] *is dead, why?"*

The rest of the questions about animals are either finalistic, or else those 'whys' about special fortuitous circumstances or about anomalies for which the child wishes to find a reason.

"Why is it [a pigeon] *like an eagle, why?"*—*"If they* [snakes] *are not dangerous, why have they got those things* [fangs]?"*—*"Why has a cockchafer always got these things* [antennæ]?"*—*"It* [an insect] *sticks to you, why?"*—[Looking at an ant]: *"I can see green and red, why?"*—*"It* [a cockchafer] *can't go as far as the sun, why?"*—[Del draws a whale with the bones sticking out of its skin]. "You shouldn't see the bones, they don't stick out."—*"Why, would it die?"*

Some of these questions mean something, others (those about the pigeon, the ant, etc.) do not. That is because in the second case we bring in chance by way of explanation. If our idea of chance is really due to the impotence of our explanation, then this distinction is naturally not one that can be made *a priori*. The child, therefore, can have no knowledge of these shades of difference; hence his habit of asking questions in season and out of season. Shall we adopt Groos' view that curiosity is the play of attention, and interpret all these questions as the outcome of

1007

invention? But this would not explain their contents. If childish questions strike us as uncouth, it is because for the child, everything can *a priori* be connected with everything else. Once the notion of chance, which is a derivative notion, is discarded, there is no reason for choosing one question rather than another. On the contrary, if everything is connected with everything else it is probable that everything has an end, and an anthropomorphic end at that. Consequently no question is absurd in itself.

Questions referring to the human body will help us to understand more clearly this relation between finalism and those 'whys' which are the negation of chance. Here is an example of a definitely finalistic 'why' where we would have expected a purely causal one: Del asks in connexion with Negroes: *"If I stayed out there for only one day, would I get black all over?"* (This question without being a 'why' appears to be definitely causal. The sequel shows that it is nothing of the kind).—"No."— *Why are they made to be* [exist] *like that?* Although too much stress must not be laid on the expression "are they made to," it obviously points to a latent finalism. There is therefore every likelihood that the following questions will be of the same order:

"Why have you got little ones [ears] *and I have big ones although I am small?"* and *"Why is my daddy bigger than you although he is young"*—*"Why do ladies not have beards?"*—*"Why have I got a bump* [on the wrist]?"*—*"Why was I not born like that* [dumb]?"*— *"Caterpillars turn into butterflies, then shall I turn into a little girl?—No.—Why?"*—*"Why has it* [a dead caterpillar] *grown quite small? When I die shall I also grow quite small?"*

Now here again, most of the questions are put as though the child were incapable of giving himself the answer: "By chance." At this stage, therefore, the idea of the fortuitous does not exist; causality presupposes a

1008

'maker,' God, the parents, etc., and the questions refer
to the intentions which he may have had. Even those of
the preceding questions which come nearest to causality
presuppose a more or less definite finalism. Organic life
is, for the child, a sort of story, well regulated according
to the wishes and intentions of its inventor.

We can now see what is the part played by questions
about death and accidents. If the child is at this stage
puzzled by the problem of death, it is precisely because
in his conception of things death is inexplicable. Apart
from theological ideas, which the child of 6 or 7 has not
yet incorporated into his mentality, death is the fortuitous
and mysterious phenomenon *par excellence*. And in the
questions about plants, animals, and the human body, it
is those which refer to death which will cause the child
to leave behind him the stage of pure finalism, and to
acquire the notion of statistical causality or chance.

This distinction between the causal order and the order
of ends is undoubtedly a subtle one if each case be examined in detail, but we believe that the general conclusions
which can be drawn from it hold good. Del has a tendency
to ask questions about everything indiscriminately, because he inclines to believe that everything has an aim.
The result is that the idea of the fortuitous eludes him.
But the very fact that it eludes him leads him to a preference for questions about anything accidental or inexplicable, because accident is more of a problem for him than
for us. Sometimes, therefore, he tries to do away with
the accidental element as such, and to account for it by
an end; sometimes he fails in this attempt, and then,
recognizing the fortuitous element for what it is, he tries
to explain it causally. When, therefore, we are faced with
a child's question that appears to be causal, we must be
on our guard against any hasty conclusion, and see by
careful examination whether the finalistic interpretation
is excluded. It is not always possible to come to a conclu-

sion, and out of the 81 'whys' referring to nature, only one-tenth can be said to be definitely causal. This is very little. Classification of the questions by their contents cannot therefore correspond term for term with a formal classification: the interest shown in natural objects does not constitute a direct proof of interest in mechanical or physical causality.

Before enquiring any further into the nature of childish causality, let us examine the 'whys' that relate to the *technical appliances* of human beings; we mean machines or manufactured articles. Out of 22 such questions, two-thirds are simply about the intention of the maker: *"Why are the funnels* [of a boat] *slanting?"—"Why have two holes been made in this whistle?"* These are the questions which are continuous with the "whys of motivation," but easily distinguishable from them, since the question refers to the manufactured object. Only in a few cases can there be any doubt as to the particular shade of meaning. For example, before a picture of a woman handing a cabbage to a little girl: *"Why does it always stay like that?"* Does Del wish to know the psychological intention of the artist or of the woman, or is he asking why the drawing represents movement by fixing a single position into immobility?

The other 'whys' are more interesting: they refer to the actual working of the machines, or to the properties of the raw materials that are used:

"Why has it [a crane] *got wheels?"—"There are lamps in our attic at home. When there's a thunderstorm the electricity can't be mended. Why?"* After leaning too heavily with his pencil on a sheet of paper: *"Why can you see through?"* He traces a penny: *"Why is this one all right and not the other one?"* His name had been written in pencil on his wooden gun. The next day it did not show any more: *"Why do wood and iron rub out pencil marks?"* While he is painting: *"When I mix red*

and orange it makes brown, why?"

Several of these questions do seem to call for a causal explanation. But here, as in the questions about nature, the definitely causal questions are concerned almost exclusively with the element of accident, whereas those which refer to a customary event (the question about the crane or about the colours) seem as much concerned with utility or motive as with cause. At any rate, we have not found one indisputably causal question, even among those concerning the working of machines. In this respect, therefore, the questions of this group confirm our previous findings.

§ 3. STRUCTURE OF THE "WHYS OF EXPLANATION."— The reader can now see for himself how complex is the problem of causality in the child, and how much a classification based on the contents of the questions differs from a formal classification, *i.e.*, one relating to the structure of 'whys' and to the different types of causality. We should like to be able to give such a formal classification which would be homogeneous with the rest of our work. Unfortunately, the present conditions of knowledge render this impossible. To carry out such a scheme, it would have been necessary to examine Del in detail on all the natural phenomena about which he had asked questions, and thus establish a parallel between his questions and the types of explanation which he gave. An enquiry which has since been set on foot, and is now being carried out with the collaboration of Mlle. Guex, will perhaps yield the desired result. In the meantime, and pending the establishment of formal types of "whys of explanation," let us content ourselves with bringing some system into the preceding considerations, and let us try to indicate what is the general structure of Del's "whys of explanation."

There are five principal types of adult explanation. First of all there is *causal explanation* properly so-called, or *mechanical explanation*: "the chain of a bicycle revolves because the pedals set the gear-wheel in motion." This is causation by spatial contact. Then there is *statistical explanation,* in a sense a special case of the former, but relating to the sum of these phenomena which are directly or indirectly subject to the laws of chance. *Finalistic explanation* is used by common sense in connexion with the phenomena of life: "Animals have legs to walk with." *Psychological explanation,* or explanation by *motive,* accounts for purposive actions: "I read this book because I wished to know its author." Finally, *logical explanation,* or *justification,* accounts for the reason of an assertion: "$X1$ is larger than $Y1$, because all x's are larger than y's." These various types naturally encroach upon each other's territory, but in the main they are distinct in adult thought and even in ordinary common sense.

Now what we purpose to show is that in the child before the age of 7 or 8, these types of explanation are, if not completely undifferentiated, at any rate far more similar to one another than they are with us. Causal explanation and logical justification in particular are still entirely identified with motivation, because causation in the child's mind takes on the character of finalism and psychological motivation far rather than that of spatial contact, and because, moreover, logical justification hardly ever exists in an unadulterated form, but always tends to reduce itself to psychological motivation. We shall designate by the name of *precausality* this primitive relation in which causation still bears the marks of a quasi-psychological motivation. One of the forms taken by this precausality is the anthropomorphic explanation of nature. In this case, the causes of phenomena are always confused with the intentions of the Creator or with those of men, who are the makers of mountains and rivers. But even if no 'intention' can be detected in this

1012

anthropormorphic form, the 'reason' which the child tries to give for phenomena is far more in the nature of a utilitarian reason or of a motive than of spatial contact.

It will be easier to understand the nature of this precausality if we explain it at once by means of one of the most important phenomena of the mental life of the child between the years of 3 and 7; we mean that which was discovered by specialists in the drawings of children, and which has been most successfully characterized by M. Luquet as "logical realism," or, as he now calls it, "intellectual realism." The child, as we all know, begins by drawing only what he sees around him—men, houses, etc. In this sense, he is a realist. But instead of drawing them as he sees them, he reduces them to a fixed schematic type; in a word, he draws them as he knows them to be. In this sense, his realism is not visual, but intellectual. The logic of this primitive draughtsmanship is childish but entirely rational, since it consists, for instance, in adding a second eye to a face seen in profile, or rooms to a house seen from the outside. Now this intellectual realism has a significance which . . . extends beyond the sphere of drawing. The child thinks and observes as he draws. His mind attaches itself to things, to the contents of a chain of thought rather than to its form. In deductive reasoning he examines only the practical bearing of the premises, and is incapable of arguing as we do, *vi formae,* on any given 'data.' He does not share the point of view of his interlocutor . . . . He contradicts himself rather than lose his hold on reality. In this sense, he is a realist. But, on the other hand, this reality to which he clings so continuously is the outcome of his own mental construction rather than the fruit of pure observation. The child sees only what he knows and what he anticipates. If his powers of observation seem good, it is because his trains of thought, which are very different from ours, cause him to see things which do not interest us, and which it therefore

1013

astonishes us that he should have noticed. But on closer observation one is struck by the extent to which his vision is distorted by his ideas. If a child believes that rivers flow backwards, he will see the Seine or the Rhone flowing upwards towards their sources; if he believes the sun to be alive, he will see it walking about in the sky; if he believes it to be inanimate, he will see it always motionless, etc. In a word, the child observes and thinks as he draws: his thought is realistic, but intellectually so.

The structure of childish precausality will now be clear. Children's 'whys' are realistic in the sense that in Del's language ... there are no genuine "whys of logical justification." Curiosity is concentrated always on the causes of phenomena (or actions), and not logical deductions. But this causation is not visual or mechanical, since spatial contact plays in it only a very restricted part. Everything happens as though nature were the outcome, or rather the reflexion of a mental activity whose reasons or intentions the child is always trying to find out.

This does not mean that the whole of nature is, for the child, the work of a God or of men. These reasons and intentions are no more referred to one single mental activity than they are in the prelogical mentality of primitive races. What is meant is that instead of looking for an explanation in spatial contact (visual realism) or in logical deduction of laws and concepts (intellectualism), the child reasons, as he draws, according to a sort of "internal model," similar to nature, but reconstructed by his intelligence, and henceforth pictured in such a fashion that everything in it can be explained psychologically, and that everything in it can be justified or accounted for (intellectual realism). Thus the child invokes as the causes of phenomena, sometimes motives or intentions (finalism), sometimes pseudo-logical reasons which are of the nature of a sort of ethical necessity hanging over everything ("it always must be so"). It is in this sense that the explanations of children point to intellectual realism and are as yet neither causal (spatial contact) nor logical (deduction), but precausal. For the child, an event leading to an event, a motive leading to an action, and an idea leading to an idea are all one and the same thing; or rather, the physical world is still confused with the intellectual or psychical world. This is a result which we shall frequently meet with in our subsequent investigations.

Three independent groups of facts seem to confirm our analysis of precausality in the child. The first is the rareness of 'whys' of pure causation and of 'whys' of justification or logical reason properly so-called. We showed in the last paragraph that out of 103 "whys of causal explanation" only about 13, *i.e.*, an eighth or a seventh, could be interpreted as 'whys' of causation properly so-called, or of mechanical causation. We shall show . . . that "whys of logical reason" are even rarer. Thus childish thought is ignorant both of mechanical causality and of logical justification. It must therefore hover between the two in the realm of simple motivation, whence arises the notion of precausality.

In addition to this, what was said about the notion of chance and the element of fortuitousness also favours the hypothesis of precausality. The child asks questions as if the answer were always possible, and as if chance never intervened in the course of events. The child cannot grasp the idea of the 'given,' and he refuses to admit that experience contains fortuitous concurrences which simply happen without being accounted for. Thus there is in the child a tendency towards justification at all costs, a spontaneous belief that everything is connected with everything else, and that everything can be explained by everything else. Such a mentality necessarily involves a use of causality which is other than mechanical, which tends to justification as much as to explanation, and thus once more gives rise to the notion of precausality.

It should be remembered, however, that this tendency to justify, though it is an essential factor in the precausal explanation, is dependent in its turn upon a wider phenomenon which we studied . . . under the name of 'syncretism.' The incapacity for conceiving of the fortuitous as such, or of the 'given' in experience, is reflected in the verbal intelligence of the child. We have shown elsewhere that up till the age of about 11, the child cannot keep to a formal chain of argument, *i.e.*, to a deduction based on given premises, precisely because he does not admit the premises as given. He wants to justify them at all costs, and if he does not succeed, he refuses to pursue the argument or to take up the interlocutor's point of view. Then, whenever he does argue, instead of confining himself to the data, he connects the most heterogeneous statements, and always contrives to justify any sort of connexion. In a word, he has a tendency, both in verbal intelligence and in perceptive intelligence (and the tendency lasts longer in the former than in the latter type of mental activity), to look for a justification at any cost of what is either simply a fortuitous concurrence or a mere 'datum.' Now in verbal intelligence this tendency to justify at any cost is connected with the fact that the child thinks in personal, vague and unanalysed schemas (syncretism). He does not adapt himself to the details of the sentence, but retains only a general image of it which is more or less adequate. These schemas connect with one another all the more easily owing to their vague and therefore more plastic character. In this way, the syncretism of verbal thought implies a tendency to connect everything with everything else, and to justify everything. Exactly the same thing happens in perceptive intelligence. If the precausal questions of the child have a tendency to justify everything and connect everything with everything else, it is because perceptive intelligence is syncretistic, at any rate before the age of 7 or 8. In view of this, intellectual realism can be thought of as necessarily connected with syncretism by a relation of mutual dependence. Syncretism, as we have already shown, is the characteristic of confused perception which takes in objects as a whole, and jumbles them together without order. The result of this is that since objects are perceived in a lump and constitute general schemas, instead of being diffused and discontinuous, childish realism can only be intellectual and not visual. For lack of an adequate vision of detail, and in particular of spatial and mechanical contacts, syncretistic perception is bound to make the child connect things together by thought alone. Or, conversely, it can be maintained that it is because the child's realism is intellectual and not visual, that his perception is syncretistic. Be that as it may, there is a relation of solidarity between syncretism and intellectual realism, and enough has been said to show how deeply rooted is the childish tendency to precausal explanation, and to the negation of anything fortuitous or 'given.'

Finally, a third group of facts compels us to adopt the hypothesis of precausality. A great number of 'whys' of causal explanation seem to demand nothing but an interpretation of the statements made. When Del, for example, asks: *"Daddy says that it* [lightning] *makes itself by itself in the sky. Why?"* it looks as though he were asking: "Why does Daddy say that?" Or, when he asks why the lake does not reach as far as Bern, it may seem that Del is simply looking for the reasons which may exist for making this assertion. As a matter of fact, this is far from being the case. Del cares very little whether statements put forward are proved or not. What he wants to know is something quite different. When he asks: *"Why is it* [a pigeon] *like an eagle?"* or *"Why do I see* [on an insect] *red and green colours?"* the question, though it has the same form, can obviously not receive the same

1017

interpretation. Sully and his commentators will help us to understand cases of this kind. This author has rightly pointed out that if the questions of children frequently relate to new and unexpected subjects, it is very often because the child wants to know whether things are really as he sees them, whether the new elements can be made to fit into the old framework, whether there is a 'rule.' But what should be especially noticed is that this rule is not merely factual: it is accompanied by a sort of ethical necessity. The child feels about each assertion that "it must be so," even though he is unable precisely to find any definite justification for it. Thus at a certain stage of development (from 5 to 6), a boy who is beginning to understand the mechanism of a bicycle, does not concern himself with the contact of the different pieces of the machine, but declares them all to be necessary, and all equally necessary. It is as though he said to himself: "it is necessary since it is there." The feeling of necessity precedes the explanation. Its meaning is just and as finalistic as it is causal, just as ethical as it is logical. As a general rule, moreover, the child confuses human necessity (moral and social, the 'decus') with physical necessity. (The idea of law has long retained the traces of this complex origin.) A great many of the 'whys' of children, therefore, do no more than appeal to this feeling of necessity. It is probable that the answer to the last few 'whys' we have quoted is not only "because it always is so" but also "because it should be, because it must be so." The connexion will now be seen between this type of explanation and precausality, which is precisely the result of a confusion between the psychical or intellectual world, or the world of ethical or logical necessity and the world of mechanical necessity.

§ 4. "WHYS OF MOTIVATION."—We have shown that among the 'whys' relating to nature and manufactured articles there are several which are not really 'whys' of causal explanation properly so-called, but questions connected more or less with motives, and therefore leading back to the present category. This category therefore predominates in Del's questions, numbering altogether 183/360 of the total.

Many of these questions are concerned only with the motive of a chance action or of an indifferent phrase, and are not, therefore, particularly interesting. Here are some examples:

"Are you having lunch here?—No, I can't to-day.— Why?"—"Does this caterpillar bite?—No.—Then why did Anita tell me it did? Horrid of her!"—"What is your drawing supposed to be?—*You want to know everything. That's greedy of you. Why do you want to know everything, teacher? Do you think I am doing silly things?"—"Why is she frightened?"* etc.

It is in this category that we find the earliest 'whys' of indirect interrogation: *"Do you know why I would rather you didn't come this afternoon?"*

Other "whys of motivation" relate less to purely momentary intentions than to psychological explanation properly so-called. It is in such cases as these that the term 'motive' takes on its full meaning, both causal and finalistic, for to explain an action psychologically is really to consider its motive both as its cause and as its aim. We can extend this meaning of "why of motivation" to cover all questions concerning the cause of an unintentional act or psychological event. For example: *"Why do you never make a mistake?"* Between a motive and the cause of a psychological action there are numerous transitional stages. We can talk of the motive of a fear as well as of its cause, and though we may not be able to speak of the motive of an involuntary error, we can do so in the case of one that is semi-intentional. In a word, short of making them definitely separate, we shall agree to place among the "whys of motivation" all questions

1019

relating to psychological explanation, even when it is causal. Here are some examples:

"Why do you teach me to count?"—"Why does Daddy not know [what day of the month it is], *he is a grownup?"—"And does my Mummy* [love the Lord Jesus]*?—Yes, I think so.—Why are you not sure?" "Why shall I be able to defend you even if I don't take it* [an iron bar]? *Because I am a boy?"—"Why are angels always kind to people? Is it because angels don't have to learn to read and do very nasty things? Are there people who are wicked because they are hungry?"—"Why can I do it quickly and well now, and before I did it quickly and badly?"*

In all these cases we can see that the cause of the actions referred to in the 'why' is inextricably bound up with their aim and with the intention which has directed them. The phenomenon is the same as in the 'whys' relating to nature, but in this case it is justified, since these 'whys' relate to human actions. We may therefore assert that among all the questions of the child, "whys of motivation" are those which are the most correctly expressed and the least removed from our own manner of thinking.

Between these 'whys' and those relating to momentary intentions there is naturally every intermediate shade of meaning. For instance: "I like men who swim that way.—*Why?"—"Why are you not pleased that I should have killed him?"* Thus it would appear possible to establish two sub-categories among the "whys of motivation," one relating to momentary intentions, the other to psychological states of a more lasting character. The distinction, however, is unimportant. What would be more interesting would be to bring greater precision into the relation between "whys of motivation" and "whys of justification." At times, it seems as though the explanation required by the child as an answer to his 'why' were something between logical explanation (one idea bringing another idea in its wake) and psychological explanation (a motive bringing about an action). For example: *"Do you like mice best, or rats?—Why?—Because they are not so fierce and because you are weak."* Cases like these help us to understand how "whys of logical justification," which we shall study presently, have gradually separated themselves from "whys of motivation."

To the "whys of motivation" must also be added a fairly abundant group of 'whys' (34 out of 183): we mean those which the child expresses simply in order to contradict a statement or a command which annoys him. If these questions are taken literally and seriously, they would seem to constitute "whys of motivation" properly so-called, and at times even "whys of logical justification" in the sense we have just instanced. But, as a matter of fact, we are dealing here, not with genuine questions as before, but with affirmations, or rather disguised negations, which assume the form of questions only as a matter of politeness. The proof of this is, that the child does not wait for an answer. Here are some examples: *"Anita wouldn't, so I hit her.—*You should never hit a lady.—*Why? She isn't a lady . . ."* etc.—"Up to here.—*Why?"*—"Draw me a watch.—*Why not cannons?"* etc. The child is apparently asking: "Why do you say this?" or "Why do you want this?" etc. As a matter of fact the question simply amounts to saying: "That's not true" or "I don't want to." But it goes without saying that between 'whys' of contradiction and those relating to intentions there is a whole series of transitional types.

Finally, mention must be made of a class of 'whys' which hover between "whys of motivation" and "whys of causal explanation," and which may be called *whys of invention*. In these the child tells stories, or personifies in play the objects which surround him, and it is in connexion with this romancing that he asks questions which, incidentally, do not admit of any possible answer: *"Why do you do that* [rub with an india-rubber] *to the poor little table? Is it still old?" "Do you know why I don't kill you? It's because I don't want to hurt you."*

§ 5. "WHYS OF JUSTIFICATION."—"Whys of justification" are interesting in many connexions. They are a sign of the child's curiosity about a whole set of customs and rules which are imposed from outside, without motive, and for which he would like to find a justification. This justification is not a causal, nor even a strictly finalistic explanation. It is more like the motivation of the last group which we described, but is to be distinguished from it by the following characteristic: what the child looks for under the rules is not so much a psychological motive as a reason which will satisfy his intelligence. If, therefore, we place the 'whys' of this category in a special group, it is because they form the germ which after the age of 7 or 8 will develop into "whys of logical reason." In the case of Del we can even see this gradual formation taking place.

Del's "whys of justification" can be divided into three sub-groups easily distinguishable from one another. They are 'whys' relating 1 to social rules and customs, 2 to rules appertaining to lessons learnt in school (language, spelling), and 3 to definitions. Of these, three, the third alone contains "whys of logical reason." The first is still closely connected to psychological motivation, the second constitutes an intermediate group.

Out of the 74 "whys of justification," 14 relate to social customs. Among these, some point simply to psychological curiosity and might just as well be classed under "whys of motivation." For example: *"Why in some churches are the gowns black, and* [in] *others they are coloured?"* Others come nearer to the idea of a rule: *"Why is it forbidden* [to open letters]? *Would he* [the postman] *be sent to prison?"* etc.

1022

This first group, as may be seen, is hardly in the right place among "whys of justification." If we have classified it in this way, it is simply because it is connected through a chain of intermediate links with the 'whys' relating to scholastic rules. Here is a transitional case: *"Why not 'in'* [in Alain]," or in connexion with the spelling of 'quatre': *"k?*—No.—*Who said not, was it the grown-ups in Paris?"*—The 'grown-ups' who settle the spelling of words are thus more or less on the same level as those who make police regulations and send postmen to prison.

The 'whys' genuinely relating to scholastic rules (55 out of 74) are much further removed from the 'whys' of psychological motivation. Here are some examples: *"Why* [are proper names spelt with capitals]? *I want to know."*—"You must always put a 'd' at the end of grand.'—*Why, what would happen if you didn't put any?"*—"*Why is it* ['*bon soir*'] *not spelt with a 'c,' that makes coi?"*—"You don't have to put a dot on a capital I.—*Why?"*—"*Why do you put full-stops here* [at the end of sentences], *and not here* [at the end of words]? *Funny!"*

It is well known that in spelling and in grammar children are more logical than we are. The large number of "whys of justification" furnishes additional proof of this. They are the exact parallel of the "whys of causal explanation" with which we have already dealt. Language, like nature, is full of freaks and accidents, and the explanation of these must be *sui generis* and must take into account the fortuitous character of all historical development. The child, devoid alike of the notion of chance and of the notion of historical development, wants to justify everything immediately, or is surprised at his inability to do so.

If we lay stress once more upon this rather trivial fact, it is because these "whys of justification," added to the already abundant "whys of causal explanation," and showing the same tendency to justify at any cost, make it all the more extraordinary that Del's questions should be so poor in "whys of logical reason." One would have thought that since Del and the children of his age are inclined to justify everything, their language would be full of deductive arguments, of the frequent use of 'because' and 'why' connecting one idea to another, and not a fact to an idea or a fact to a fact. But this is not in the least what happens. Out of the 74 "whys of justification," only 5 are "whys of logical justification or reason." It is needless to repeat the reason for this paradox: the child is not an intellectualist, he is an intellectual realist.

Let us rather try to analyse the nature of this logical justification, and find out how it differs from other 'whys.' 'Whys' relating to language furnish us with several transitional cases along the path leading to the true logical 'why.' These are the etymological 'whys': *"Why do you say 'strayed' when it means lost?"*—*"Why are there lots of words with several names, the lake of Geneva, Lake Leman?"*—*"Why is it* [a park in Geneva] *called Mon Repos?"*—*"Why 'black coffee,' all coffee is black?"* Just at first, it looks as though these were genuine "whys of logical justification," connecting a definition to an idea which serves as a reason for it. This is true of the last of these 'whys,' which we shall therefore class along with four subsequent examples under logical justification. But the others aim chiefly at the psychological intention. They are, moreover, still tainted with intellectual realism. It is well known that, for the child, the name is still closely bound with the thing; to explain an etymology is to explain the thing itself. Del's slip, "words with several names" is significant in this connexion. Therefore we cannot talk here about one idea being connected to another: the ideas are connected to the objects themselves.

The only cases, then, in which one can say that there is

logical justification are cases of pure definition, and cases of demonstration, in which the mind tries to establish a proof in such a way as to render strict deductions possible.

In definition, the question falls under the following schema: "If you call all objects having such-and-such characteristics x, why do you call this object x?" Here the connexion is really between one idea and another, or, to speak more accurately, between one judgment recognized as such (an x is . . . etc.) and another (I call such-and-such an object x), and not between one thing and another. This distinction, however subtle it may appear, is of the greatest importance from the point of view of genetic psychology. Up till now, the mind has dealt solely with things and their relations, without being conscious of itself, and above all without being conscious of deducing. In logical justification, thought becomes conscious of its own independence, of its possible mistakes, and of its conventions, it no longer seeks to justify the things in themselves, but its own personal judgments about them. Such a process as this appears late in the psychological evolution of the child. The earlier chapters have led us not to expect it before the age of 7 or 8. The small number of "whys of logical justification" asked by Del confirms our previous treatment of the subject.

Similarly, in all demonstration the connexion holding between 'because' and 'why' relates to judgments and not to things. In the following example:—"Why does the water of the Rhone not flow upwards?" if an explanation is expected the answer must be: "Because the weight of the water drags it along in the direction of the slope." But if a demonstration is expected, the answer must be: "Because experience shows that it does" or "Because all rivers flow downwards." In the first case the connexion connects the direction of the water to the downward slope; it relates to the actual things themselves and

1025

is causal. In the second case the connexion relates to the judgments as such, and is logical. Therefore all 'whys' of demonstrations are "logical whys." But demonstration rarely operates before the age of 7 or 8. The first two chapters showed us that in their arguments, children abstained from any attempt to check or demonstrate their statements.

In short, "logical whys" can by rights relate to anything, since they include all 'whys' which refer to definitions or demonstrations. Here are the only questions of Del's which can be said to belong to this group (in addition to the example about the black coffee which we have just recalled):

"*Why* [do you say 'tom cat']? *A she-cat is a mummy cat. A cat is a baby cat. . . . I want to write 'a daddy cat.'*"—"They are torrents.—*Why not rivers?*"—"That isn't a bone, it's a bump.—*Why? If I was killed, would it burst?*"—"*Is that snow?* [question of classification]—No, it is rocks.—*Then why is it white?*"

The last of these 'whys' is ambiguous; it is probably an elliptical form, meaning: "Why do you say it is rocks, since it is white?" At the same time, it may very well be a simple "why of causal explanation." There are therefore only four authentic "whys of logical reason." They can be recognized by the fact that under the interrogative word itself the phrase "why do you assert that . . ." can be understood; and this is never so in the other categories. In a word, *"whys of logical justification" look for the reason of a judgment which is recognized as such, and not of the thing to which the judgment relates.* 'Whys' of this kind are therefore very rare before the age of 7 or 8. The child, while he tries to justify everything, yet neglects to use the one legitimate justification, that of opinions and judgments as such. After the age of 7 or 8, however, these questions will probably be more frequent. We have fixed at 11-12 the age where formal thought first makes

1026

its appearance, *i.e.*, thought relating to hypotheses which are held as such, and only seeking to ascertain whether the conclusions drawn from these hypotheses are justified or not, simply from the point of view of deduction and without any reference to reality. Between the period of pure intellectual realism (up till 7 or 8) and the beginnings of formal thought there must therefore be an intermediate stage, in which children try to justify judgments as such, yet without for that matter being able to share the interlocutor's point of view nor, consequently, to handle formal deduction. The presence of "whys of logical justification" must correspond to this intermediary stage.

In conclusion, the results of this section confirm those reached in our study of the "why of causal explanation." In the case of Del, there are no more "whys of logical reason" than there are "whys" of pure causality. Consequently, Del's mind must have interests which are intermediate between mechanical explanation and logical deduction. It is in this failure to distinguish between the causal and the logical point of view, both of which are also confused with the point of view of intention or of psychological motive, that we see the chief characteristic of childish precausality.

Finally, it may be of interest to point out a curious phenomenon which supports the hypothesis that the child often confuses notions which in our minds are perfectly distinct. The peculiarity we are speaking of is that Del occasionally takes the word 'why' in the sense of 'because,' and thus uses the same word to express the relation of reason to consequence and that of consequence to reason. Here is an example which happens precisely to be concerned with a logical 'why' or 'because': "Rain water is good—*Is it why* [=because] *it is a spring?*" Now, this is a phenomenon which we have already noticed in connexion with explanations between one child and an-

1027

other ... and which we shall meet with again in our study of the conjunctions of causality ....It occurs frequently in ordinary life in children from 3 to 6. We remember in particular a little Greek boy of 5 years who learnt French very well, but systematically used the word 'why' instead of the word 'because' which is absent from his vocabulary: "Why does the boat stay on top of the water"— "*Why* [=because] *it is light*," etc. As a matter of fact this phenomenon indicates only a confusion of words. But this confusion shows how hard it is for a child to distinguish between relations which language has differentiated.

§ 6. CONCLUSIONS.—The complexity of Del's 'whys' will now be apparent, as will also the necessity for classifying them partly according to material, since it is impossible to say straight away to which type of relation (strictly causal, finalistic or logical explanation, etc.) they refer. The frequencies obtained out of our 360 'whys' are summed up in the following table:

		Numbers (roughly)	%
Whys of causal explanation (in the wide sense)	Physical objects	26	
	Plants	10	
	Animals	29	
	Human body	16	
	Natural objects	— 81	22%
	Manufactured objects	22	6%
	Total	103	29%
Whys of psychological motivation	Properly so-called	143	
	Contradiction	34	
	Invention	6	
	Total	— 183	50%
Whys of justification	Social Rules	14	
	Scholastic Rules	55	
	Rules	— 69	19%
	Logical reason or justification	5	1%
	Total	74	21%

Thus the "whys of motivation" outnumber all the others. Does this preponderance indicate that the other types of 'why' radiate from this group as from a common centre? This would seem to be the case, for the "whys of causal explanation" are connected with motivation through a whole series of anthopomorphic 'whys,' finalistic 'whys,' and 'whys' which reveal precausality itself. The "whys of justification," on their side, are connected with those of motivation by the series of 'whys' relating to social usage and to rules conceived of as obeying psychological motives. The relations between the two groups of causal explanation and justification are not so close. The idea of precausality certainly presupposes a confusion between causal explanation and logical justification, but this confusion is only possible owing to the fact that both are, as yet, insufficiently differentiated from psychological motivation. In a word, the source of Del's 'whys' does seem to be motivation, the search for an intention underlying every action and every event. From this source there would seem to arise two divergent currents, one formed of 'whys' which try to interpret nature as a thing of intentions, the other formed of those which relate to customs and to the rules associated with them. Between those finalistic 'whys' and the 'whys' of justification interaction would naturally be possible. Finally, causality proper would emerge from the 'whys' of precausality, and true logical justification from the 'whys' of justification. Such, approximately, would be the genealogy of the whys asked by Del. We shall try to sum it up in a table.

GENETIC TABLE—DEL'S WHYS

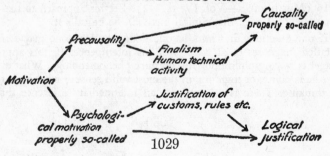

1029

Is such a systematization as this the result of an individual mentality of a particular type, or does it mark the general character of child thought before 7 or 8 years of age? The answer to this question will have to be supplied by other monographs. What we know of other lines of research leads us to believe that the schema is a very general one, but this supposition must serve for the present only as a working hypothesis.

JEAN PIAGET (b.—Neuchatel, Switzerland, Aug. 9, 1896).

Piaget received his Ph.D. at Neuchatel in 1918 for a thesis on the 'Distribution of the Different Varieties of Mollusks in the Valaisian Alps,' having actually published in the scientific literature on mollusks since the age of 15. (Piaget's early interest in mollusks has stayed with him throughout his life.) He then went to Zurich, and attended the lectures of Lipps, Bleuler, and Jung. In 1919 Piaget went to the Sorbonne for two years, and worked with Piéron. He received a Dr.Sci.Nat. in 1921. He soon became associated with Simon, on problems of the intelligence and psychopathology of children, at Binet's experimental Grade School (Rue de la Grangeaux-Belles, Paris). He also worked at the Salpetrière. In 1921, at the invitation of Claparède, Piaget returned to Geneva as Director of Studies at the Maison des Petits of the Institute of Jean Jacques Rousseau. At the same time, he became Privatdozent at the Faculté des Sciences, Geneva. In 1925 he became Professor of Philosophy at Neuchatel. In 1929 he returned to Geneva as Professor in the History of Scientific Thought, and Assistant Director of the J. J. Rousseau Institute. In 1932 he became Co-director. In 1939 he moved back to Geneva as Professor of Sociology. In 1940 he was appointed to the Chair of Experimental Psychology, and made Director of the laboratories. He continues, today, his role as a Swiss delegate to Unesco.

Piaget's approach to psychology is closely parallel to that of the Gestalt school. He himself has said that he would have been a Gestaltist had he but known of the work of Wertheimer and Köhler in 1912-1915 (Murchison, a—Vol. IV, p. 242). Yet his approach to the child is uniquely his own, the 'clinical method,' he he calls it.

If one questions the child, as one does a patient, one may arrive at detailed diagnoses of all aspects of his intelligence. In this approach, Piaget is relying philosophically on pure phenomenology. What a child says he is doing, or thinking, in the most valid sense *is* what he is doing or thinking. There is no need for an intermediary inference through physiology into behavior, or vice versa. The great body of Piaget's work is thus in sharp contrast to the positivist philosophy.

Let the child speak for himself, he will tell his own story. Piaget's genius lies in seeing so clearly the problems left unsolved by previous students in the field, in being able to let them emerge in the beautifully simple tasks which he poses to the child, in asking the child the very special question at the right moment. And, above all, in watching and listening. "This clinical method . . . does not confine itself to superficial observations, but aims at capturing what is hidden behind the immediate appearance of things. It analyses down to its ultimate constituents the least little remark made by the young subjects. It does not give up the struggle when the child gives incomprehensible or contradictory answers, but only follows closer in chase of the ever-receding thought, drives it from cover, pursues and tracks it down till it can seize it, dissect it and lay bare the secret of its composition." So speaks Claparède in his introduction to Piaget's first book, from which we take our selection.

The present selection is perhaps the most inherently interesting of all of Piaget's work. It is taken from his first book in child psychology, published just two years after he began his work at the Institute.

PIAGET, J. *The language and thought of the child.* N. Y.: Humanities Press, Inc., 1926 (1923). Trans. M. Gabain. Chap. 5, no. 1: "The questions of a child of six. Whys." This section of the chapter is reproduced substantially complete by permission of the publisher.

See also:

PIAGET, J.

    a) *The child's conception of the world.* London: Routledge & Kegan Paul, 1929.

    b) *The child's conception of physical causality.* London: Routledge & Kegan Paul, 1930.

    c) *The moral judgment of the child.* London: Routledge & Kegan Paul, 1932.

    d) *Logic and psychology.* Manchester, Eng.: Manchester Univ. Press, 1953, Trans. W. Mays & F. Whitehead.

    e) *The child's conception of space.* London: Routledge & Kegan Paul, 1956. Trans. F. J. Langdon & J. L. Lunzer.

HUANG, I. "Children's explanations of strange phenomena." *Psychol. Forsch.* 1930-31, 14: 63-182.

INHELDER, B. & PIAGET, J. *The growth of logical thinking from childhood to adolescence.* N. Y.: Basic Books, 1958.

BERLYNE, D. E. Recent developments in Piaget's work. *Brit. J. educ. Psychol.* 1957, 27: 1—12.

MURCHISON (a—Vol. IV, p. 237-256; b—Vol. 2, p. 548; b—Vol. 3, p. 1182-1183).

EXPERIMENTAL STUDIES ON THE SEEING
OF MOTION[1]

MAX WERTHEIMER

Introduction

One sees motion: an object has moved from one position to another. One describes the physical circumstances: up to the time t_1 the object was in the position p_1 (in the location l_1; from the time t_n onwards, it has been in position p_n (in the location l_n). In the interval between t_1 and t_n, the object was situated successively in the intermediate positions between p_1 and p_n, and, with spatial and temporal continuity, has reached p_n through them.

One sees this motion. One does not merely see that the object is now some place else than before, and so knows that it has moved (as one knows that a slowly moving clock hand is in motion), rather one [actually] sees the motion.[2] What is psychically given?

One is tempted to say, in a simple analogy to the physi-

---

[1] Editor's note. This paper is particularly difficult to translate because of Wertheimer's deliberate use of words and phrases in a novel manner, i.e. as symbols of the event (e.g. "stationary-position-character") rather than as simple names or descriptions. In those cases, and they are many, where the shade of meaning seems to be particularly delicate, I give the original German word in brackets. Because of the length of this paper, extensive deletions have been necessary. These are as follows: #2—deletion of the description of the slide apparatus, #4—deletion of subsections 1—(tachistoscopic elimination of eye-movements), 2—(fixation of eyes), 3—(after-image to fix retinal image), 4—(short exposure time); #6—On the [self-] identity of that which moves; #7—On dual part motion; #8—On inner motion; #9—On singular motion; #10—On singular motion with three objects; #11—On the postures of attention [*Aufmerksamkeitsstellungen*]; #12—On the actual nature [givenness: *Gegebenheit*] of the two stimuli; #13—On special motions; #19—A discussion of Marbe-Linke; #22—Appendix on spatial orientation. It is my hope that these deletions do not mar the essay to any great extent. The basic experiment is, I believe, still largely intact.

[2] Exner asserted in principle the direct impression of motion with regard to peripheral perception, quantitative relations, etc. in Uber das Sehen von Bewegung. *Wiener Sitz.—Ber.* 72, Abt. 3, 1875.

cal circumstances, that the seeing of motion occurs when the seen-thing, the psychic visual object, also arrives at p_n from the seen-position p_1, through continuous intermediate spatial positions: hence, as such a sequence of intermediate positions is psychically given, so the seeing of motion is given.

If this seeing of motion were achieved as an "illusion," i.e. if physically, first really only one stationary [*ruhende*] position was given, and afterwards, another stationary position was presented at a definite distance from the first, then some subjective supplementation [*Erganzung*] would have taken place on the basis of the sensations of the two stationary objects, and in conjunction with them: namely, the passage, the perception of the intermediate positions, was somehow supplied subjectively.

The following investigation deals with impressions of motion which can be achieved even when two such successive positions are presented at a considerable spatial distance from one another.

* * *

It is known that when the conditions of exposure are adequate, the successive presentation of stationary individual positions produces "illusions of motion." The motion picture projector achieves motion in this manner (similar to the older stroboscope, in which the conditions are complicated by the rotation of the object strips).[3] Exner achieved motion . . . by the successive lighting of two sparks[4]; Marbe [achieved motion] in experiments with small stationary lamps lit in succession[5]; Schumann has observed a sudden turning, a rotation, with the suc-

---

[3] I refer to the considerable literature on the "stroboscopic illusion." It is largely summarized in Ebbinghaus (*Psychologie*, 3rd ed., p. 531f.) and in individual papers, e.g. Fischer (*Philos. Studien*, vol. 3) and Linke (*Ibid*); cf. Marbe (*Theorie der kinematogr. Projektionen*. Leipzig, 1910.).

[4] Exner: cf. footnote 2.
[5] Marbe: cf. footnote 3, pp. 61 and 66.

cessive tachistoscopic presentation first of a vertical line and then of a horizontal line.[6]

There are a great number of scattered papers on other, different illusions of motion.[7] Elementary quantitative investigations have been made on the conditions for seeing motion.[8]

There are a number of theoretical views on the seeing of motion; in particular, an extensive discussion exists on the question of whether the seeing of motion "can be determined and deducted without a remnant from a kind of combined space-time perception",[9] based on a special kind of sensation[10] or on a higher psychic process[11]; whenever one attempts to analyze the seeing of motion theoretically the problem of explaining the illusions of motion naturally plays a role.[12] A survey of the theories reveals the following existing ones: the trace [*Nachbild*] theory, which attempts to explain the essence of seen motion by the proportional rise and fall of the stimulation of adjacent points on the retina;[13] the eye-movement theory, which stresses the role of the sensations of eye movements in the creation of the impression of motion;[14] the theory of the sensation of change, which deduces the impression of motion from something elementary, a

---

[6]Schumann: *II Kongress für exp. Psychologie. Bericht.* Leipzig, 1907, p. 218.

[7]Literature, e.g., in Ebbinghaus, *op. cit.,* p. 534; v. Kries, *Hndb. d. physiol. Optik,* pp. 226ff. Cf. the recent summary: H. Hanselmann, *Uber optisches Bewegungswahrnehmung.* Zürich, Disc., 1911.

[8]Aubert: Die Bewegungsempfindung. *Pflüger's Archiv.* 39, 40. . . .

[9]Ebbinghaus: *Gründzüge der Psychologie.* Leipzig, 1902, pp. 466. Cf. Dürr, in the new, 3rd ed. of Ebbinghaus' *Psychologie,* pp. 531ff.

[10]Exner: *Entwurf zu einer physiologischen Erklärung der psychischen Erscheinungen.* Leipzig-Vienna; Stern: *Psychologie der Veränderungsauffassung,* Breslau, 1906; Cornelius; *Psychologie,* p. 132.

[11]See footnotes 16 and 17 below.

[12]Cf. the numerous papers by Exner. Mach: *Analyse der Empfindungen,* Leipzig. Haman: Die psychologischen Grundlagen des Bewegungsbegriffs. *Z. f. Psychol.* 45: p. 231 and p. 341. . . .

[13]Marbe: *Z. f. Psychol.* 46: p. 345; 47: p. 321, etc.

[14]Wundt: *Physiol. Psychol.* II, p. 577.

specific feeling of the changes of sense impressions;[15] the fusion theory, which presupposes here a kind of apperceptive fusion[16]; and, finally, the *Gestalt—* or *Komplexqualitat* theory.[17]. Explanations are offered, based principally on peripheral processes on the one hand, and, on the other hand, based on higher processes lying beyond the periphery. The view that central processes must be used to explain definite impressions of motion is represented by Exner[18]; also Marbe[19]; and Linke. Schumann represents the view that we are operating here with a centrally produced content of consciousness, whether we call it sensation of motion with Exner, or *Gestaltqualitat* with Ehrenfels.

1. The three primary stages

One draws simply, two objects on the object strip of a stroboscope. For example, a 3 cm. horizontal line at the beginning of the strip and a second line in the middle of the strip about 2 cm. lower. With a relatively very slow rotation of the stroboscope, first one horizontal line appears and then the other; they both appear clear, successive and as two. With much faster rotation, one sees them simultaneously one above the other; they are there together, at the same time. With a medium speed one sees a definite motion: a line moves clearly and distinctly from an upper position into a lower one, and back.

Alternately, one places an inclined line in the beginning of the object strip and again a horizontal line in the middle. In the extreme successive stage, the inclined line

---

[15]Stern, *op. cit.*, Exner: *Zentralb. f. Physiol.* 24: p. 1169.

[16]Wundt, *op. cit.*, p. 578 and 580f.; Linke, *op. cit.*, p. 544, etc.

[17]Ehrenfels: Uber Gestaltqualitäten. *Vierteljahrsschr. f. wiss. Philos.* 15: p. 263f. Cornelius: Uber Verschmelzung und Analyse. *Ibid.* 17: pp. 45ff. There is also, as I discovered after completion of the present paper, a special concept-production theory, as given in Witasek: *Psychologie der Raumwahrnehmung des Auges.* Heidelberg, 1910.

[18]See footnote 10.

[19]Marbe: *Philos. Studien.* 14: 1898, p. 400.

appears first, and then the horizontal. In the extreme simultaneous stage, they are given together, and one sees an angle. In the motion stage, between the two extreme stages, a line rotates out of the inclined position (about its end point as vertex) into the horizontal position, and reverses. And analogously with other objects, forms and positions... .

The question of seeing the passage [*Vorubeziehens*] of objects can be dealt with easily: it is a question of seeing up and down motion, rotation or rest, with regard to the direction which is given by the relative positions of the two objects. ... Further complications arise with the use of the stroboscope; the three "distinguished stages"—succession, optimal motion and simultaneity—could as easily be observed with other experimental arrangements in which there [also] is no [actual] passage of the objects. This was the case with the chief experiments here: the tachistoscopic exposure of two successive static stimuli by means of Schumann's tachistoscope. ...

This sensibly clear and distinctly given impression of the motion of a [self] identical [object] [*eine Identischen*], is psychologically mysterious. What is psychically given when one sees motion?

Is it possible (by successive experimental approaches) to advance towards the solution of the problem: what is the psychic reality, what is the essence of this impression?

Observations with the stroboscope suggested to me the first technical experimental question: how is the stage of optimum motion produced? How does it develop from the simultaneous and from the successive stages? How does it divide into them? What occurs on the way between these three stages? Are there, perhaps, qualitatively individual and specifically characteristic impressions of the intermediate stages which could throw some light on the qualitative development and the psychological nature of the optimal impression of motion?

Next, what happens in the "field of motion"[20]? Is it possible to determine what is "given" in the space between the first and the second position (in the angle experiment, for example, in the angular space between the two angle legs)?

Also, are peripheral conditions or eye movements basically [*Konstitutiv*] decisive?

Are conditions of attention and of comprehension basically of importance? Do the different postures of attention [*Aufmerksameitsstellungen*] play a role? What[21]?

What are the manners of appearance and effects of the process? And so on.

From the vantage point of such questions, we arrived at the following special variations in the experimental conditions:

1. Observations during the transition from one of the three main stages to another, with variations of the time interval, t, between the exposures of the two objects; variations in the exposure time.

2. Appropriate variations in the arrangement of the objects, their position, their relative spacing (distance), their form, color, and so on, and in the use of different kinds of objects in special ways.

3. Variations with respect to subjective behavior: [eye] fixation, posture of attention, set [*Einstellung*].

4. Introduction of a third object, and more, into the exposure field, with complicating factors to be eliminated by suitable control experiments.

5. Investigation of after effects.

---

[20]This question was already put by Schumann, *op. cit.*, p. 218.

[21]Cf. the role played by variations of attention: Schumann: *Beiträge zur Analyse der Gesichtswahrnehmungen*, Heft 1; Von Aster: Z. *f. Psychol.*, 53: p. 161; Karpinska: Z. *f. Psychol.*, 57: p. 1; Jaensch: Z. *f. Psychol. Supple.* vol. IV.

2. Experimental comparison of actual motion and successive exposure

I have selected this slide arrangement here since the experiment can thus be carried out simply and the facts can be clearly demonstrated. (It does make certain demands on the experimenter's manual dexterity to ensure correct sliding; for further experiments and for the possibility of exact time setting, purely mechanical operation could easily be provided in various ways.)

First one selects a suitable rhythmic speed, which can be found quickly as an optimum between "imperfect" impressions of too slow or too fast slide motion, and then one permits the subject to observe, while maintaining this rhythm. . . .

The experiment can also be performed so that there is only a single succession. However, this makes it more difficult to find both the suitable exposure time for each slit and the interval between the exposures. Furthermore, the observation requires a concentration of attention onto the moment of exposure as well as some training in tachistoscopic observations, for it soon becomes obvious that even with lengthy, careful and repeated observations, it is a rather difficult problem to distinguish between the impressions produced by actual slit motions, on the one hand, and by successive exposures on the other. It is also better for internal reasons . . . that the observer perform his observations quietly, i.e. with a prolonged alternating exposure which exhibits the back and forth movement of the stripes.

The result was:

In most cases, actual and "apparent" motion could not be distinguished at all; not even by observers who had been trained for months by numerous tachistoscopic experiments in the most accurate observation of stimuli in instantaneous exposure. In most cases after many exposures of the same target and after long observations of the motion they were at last correctly recognized. However, one was not denoted as motion and the other as non-motion; rather, there [only] existed a qualitative difference between the seen motions. There was a different "impression of motion"... or there was a difference, relatively, in the visibility of the objects. ... Often statements were made, like "one motion differed from the other by being so strong, so energetic; it was the best motion of all"; and these statements actually were not made about the exposure of real motion but about the exposure of two stationary stimuli. . . .

In all these procedures, different methods of observation are possible. The observer can try to follow the motion with his eyes, or his glance can be fixed on a certain definite point. During prolonged exposure, the place of observation may be changed back and forth—a good optimal impression of motion was achieved in all cases. . . .

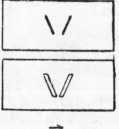

Analogously, impressions of motion of a different kind occurred, resulting from different arrangements of the objects: with arrangements of the slits diagonally to each other (Fig. 1),[22] [we have] rotations of angles and curves (Fig. 2 and Fig. 3), and so on.

[22]Editor's note. In the original manuscript, most of the figures were presented at the end of the text. In the present translation, all of the figures which have been retained, are included directly in the text.

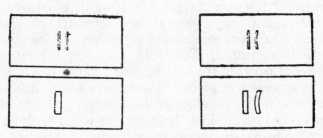

Let it be noted, concerning the speed of the apparent motion, that the actual objective speeds of the successions of positions are not so extraordinarily fast as one

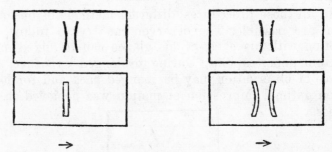

might suspect at first sight from the rate of the succession, e.g. $t=50\sigma$[23]. Analogous speeds occur every day in seeing the actual motions of real life: they correspond to the rapid walking (not running) of a man, or to the trotting of a horse. It was also shown . . . that under certain circumstances a much slower motion ("colossally slow but optimal"), can be obtained. . . .[24]

3. Concerning the main experiments

I at first made numerous observations on the transition between the three main stages on a simple stroboscope: with increasing and decreasing speeds, and in the selec-

---

[23]Editor's note. $\sigma = 0.001$ seconds.

[24]The *apparent speed* of such an "illusory" motion should be distinguished from the physical-objective [speed] in other things also. Factors of apparent speed which play a part here (as also of apparent magnitude and apparent distance), are a special problem in themselves.

tion of a particular speed; with variations such as the introduction of a diaphragm, fixation of the glance, setting the attention on special places; with different simple objects and suitable variations thereof, introduction of a definite third object, use of definite differences in the form, color, size and position of the objects. These observations produced special results, which were confirmed by the observations of Dr. W. Köhler.

Prof. Schumann was kind enough to place his well-known tachistoscope at my disposal (with the special device which he had installed to study the effects of two successive exposures), so as to enable me to carry out my experiments under technically precise and exactly measurable conditions. The experiments described in this paper were conducted in the fall and winter of 1910 in the Institute of Psychology at Frankfurt am Main. What follows, in the first place, is a report on the results of the main experiments achieved with the aid of Schumann's tachistoscope. These [results] could also be observed, in essence, with different experimental arrangements.

The Schumann apparatus, which permits the selection of a single successive exposure under exactly measurable conditions, may be described as follows. Close to the disc of the tachistoscope wheel, behind the objective of the telescope, through which one looks, a prism is erected which covers the lower half of the objective in such a way that the rays fall normal on to the upper half of the objective and fall at some angle on to the lower half of the objective. One exposure slit on the wheel frees the upper half [of the objective], and a second [slit] frees the lower half; if the distances between the prism and the objective are slight, the entire circular area of each exposure field is seen in each of the two exposures. If the wheel of the tachistoscope is rotated, first one and then the other of the exposure fields is presented.

It proved to be advisable to use black exposure fields

1041

to which white or colored objects (stripes, etc.) were attached, in order to counteract the change in the brightness of the visual field and the eventual contribution of its border.

The length of the exposure times, α and β, could be varied on the one hand by the slit length and on the other by the rate of rotation of the wheel. The length of the interval between the two successive exposures was varied, analogously, by the rate of rotation and the distance between the two slits. In essence, I used an exposure slit equal in length to 6°—12° of the circumference of the wheel, where the distance between them was, respectively, 3°, 6°, 12°, and 16° of the circumference. . . .

In tachistoscopic investigations it is generally advisable to use high speeds of wheel rotation and relatively long slits in order to achieve an instantaneous appearance and disappearance of the exposure. In the present instance, there is an additional reason: the slow passage of the slit edges produces special apparent motions of a different kind.

The following assistants at the Institute kindly served as regular experimental subjects: Dr. Wolfgang Köhler, Dr. Koffka, and afterwards, the latter's wife, Dr. Klein-Koffka.

On a number of occasions, especially with the slide experiments made under especially convenient observation conditions, I also used other subjects, quite untrained in psychological observation.

The essential observations were all made naively; the results of the experiments were revealed to the subjects only after they themselves had spontaneously expressed them.

It proved to be unnecessary to obtain a large number of subjects, since the characteristic phenomena appeared in every case unequivocally, spontaneously and compellingly. . . .

The objective distance of the exposure fields from the prism was about 80 cm.; both exposure fields were black or dark; each was illuminated by a lamp from the side. The [stimulus] objects (stripes etc. . . . . of 1 x 6 cm., or larger or smaller; white, or of other colors), were placed in the exposure fields, and their position was set for objective simultaneous exposure (simultaneous and common opening of the slits). The luminosity was equated by [adjusting] the positions of the two lamps. The luminosity, form, and size, and the [spatial] separation of the stimulus objects from each other (in contrast to their position), are also of some relevance.[25] Thus, the range of the time intervals, t, within which the optimal [motion] impression appeared, proved to be more extensive (both longer and shorter) with smaller separations than with greater separations. In this case, for example, if one wishes to obtain the extreme stage of stationary simultaneity (by shortening t) or that of stationary succession (by lengthening t), while starting from the stage of optimal motion, one must use definitely larger positive and negative increments of t, than one need use with greater separations. Correspondingly, in the case of the specially prepared slide (Fig. 4), a different stage ap-

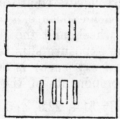

peared (for the same speed and the same t) with the objects at greater separations (by increasing from the optimal conditions); while with the objects of smaller

[25]Cf. Marbe, *op. cit.*, p. 65; Linke, *op. cit.*, p. 494.

separation, the optimal [stage] was still present. The influence of separation also appears in another way: the smaller of the two existing separations of the lines generally ... favors the impression of motion.

I used separations of 1, 3, 5 cm. and more, between the parallel (Fig. 5) and inclined objects (e.g. Fig. 10, *v.i.*).

Under the present circumstances, the exposures led, as a rule, to optimal impressions of motion with the magnitude of the interval (between the two exposures) of $t=60\sigma$; stationary simultaneity appeared with $t=30\sigma$; stationary succession appeared in the region of $t=200\sigma$.

To illustrate the time values, I present some tables, showing the results obtained for the three principal observers, about equally trained in tachistoscopic observation and instructed in an unequivocal manner. ... In some experiments, especially at the beginning, individual differences played some part ...; but, generally speaking, all the tachistoscopic experiments yielded analogous time values. ... In the following tables, the results are arranged according to time.

The time values are calculated as follows. For example: if the slit length of each exposure, $a = b$, is 7° on the circumference of the wheel, and the length of the space interval between the exposure slits is 16°, then the total length (time of total exposure) is 30° [i.e. 7° + 7° + 16° = 30°]. The components of the complete rotation, $\dfrac{360°}{x}$, are respectively 51.4, 22.5, and 12. If the measurement of the time for 20 rotations is, e.g., 20.4 seconds in a given case, then the time of a single rotation is 1020σ [i.e. ($\dfrac{20.4}{20}$) x 1000]; the total exposure time $\gamma = 85c$

[i.e. 1020/12]; the exposure time of any single stimulus $\alpha = \beta = 20\sigma$ [i.e. 1020/51.4]; and the interval between the exposures of a and b, $t = 45\sigma$ [i.e. 1020/22.5].

First Example. Objects: two white stripes (1.5 by 8.7 cm.) on a black ground, inclined diagonally towards one another at an angle of 45° and touching at the vertex; . . . the horizontal stripe (a) on the exposure field (A), the inclined stripe (b) on the exposure field (B). The stage of optimal motion consisted in a rotation of the a—stripe from the horizontal position into the inclined position.

Single exposures of ab were presented, with pauses of about two minutes. . . . Uniform conditions of observa-tion: [eye] fixation, and posture of attention [*Auf-merksamkeitspostierung*] . . . on the common vertex—as established by previous exposures of a alone.

The period of rotation changed step by step and was measured during the two minute pauses. [The results are given in Table I.]

TABLE 1†

		t	σ	β	γ
Subject 1	Stationary simultaneity	32	5	5	42
	Dual total motion††	53	7	7	67
	Identity, rotation, optimal motion	59	7	7	73
	. . . slow motion††	116	14	14	144
	Stationary succession	178	22	22	222
Subject 2	Stationary simultaneity	36	5	5	46
	Identity, rotation, optimal motion	74	9	9	92
Subject 3	Stationary simultaneity	31	8	8	47
	Part simultaneity††	40	10	10	60
	Part motion††	50	13	13	75
	Dual total rotation††	58	15	15	87
	Identity rotation††	62	16	16	93
	" "	64	16	16	97

†[Time is given in d.]
††[See text below.]

Second Example. Analogous to Example I, with longer and with unequal σ, β . . . [The results are given in Table 2.]

1045

		t	σ	β	γ
Subject 1	Identity, optimal rotation	45	33	33	111
Subject 2	Stationary simultaneity	33	17	8	58
	Identity rotation	54	28	14	96
	Slower rotation	61	31	16	108
	. . . Slower rotation	131	67	33	231
	Simultaneity††	45	6	8	59
	Identity rotation	70	9	13	94
	Identity rotation, slower	90	11	17	118
	Stationary succession	153	19	28	200
Subject 3	Stationary simultaneity	32	15	15	62
	Part motion††	45	20	20	85
	Identity rotation	49	22	22	93
	Part motion††	105	57	57	200
	Stationary simultaneity	322	17	9	58
	Identity rotation	50	25	12	87
	" "	53	28	14	95

†[Time is given in d.]
††[See text below.]

One sees here, that the stages depend in the first place on t (values of t for the optimal rotations are: 59, 45; 74, 54, 70; 62, 49, 50σ)[26]. The exposure times α, β can be varied greatly under these conditions, without the impression of motion being materially reduced. (It is noteworthy that certain [other] motion phenomena also occur when the exposure times [actually] overlap—v.i. . . . .)

All the subsequently presented experiments (with a few exceptions . . .) utilize a γ varying from a maximum of $\gamma = 0.1$ sec. $= 100σ$ ($= \alpha + \beta + t$), to a minimum of $\gamma = 4^0 s$ (simultaneity stage), and are thus analogous to the time values given here[27].

---

[26]These are specifically valid for the experimental conditions used here.

[27]It was technically important in the basic experiments to operate under conditions such that the total time of exposure should not exceed 100 σ, so that, on the one hand, the stimuli were easily perceived, and, on the other, for external reasons, so that the rotation speed of the tachistoscope did not become so great that the selection of a definite exposure [time] for each successive stimuli became uncertain or impossible. All this was achieved by the conditions outlined above.

In addition to the main experiments with the tachisto-scope, I employed a series of other experimental arrange-ments: the slide experiments described . . . [above] in their several variations . . ., with and without projection; an arrangement of the focal-tachistoscope type; a shadow experiment suitable for demonstration purposes.[28] [I also used,] for serial exposures, (in addition to the ordi-nary stroboscope and the symmetrical slit arrangement of the Schumann tachistoscope), a combination of a tachistoscope with a rotating kymograph drum, . . ., or a spoked wheel . . ., or the well-known [expanding] spiral . . .; [also] a motion picture projector; for haploscopic purposes, [I used] a double tube arrangement with the tachistoscope . . .; and, [finally, I used] a mirror ar-rangement which was convenient for demonstration pur-poses. . . .

An examination of the question of eye motions was finally achieved by the use of *several simultaneous* suc-cessive exposures. Given Fig. 6a, *a* and *a* belonging to the

first exposure, *b* and *b* to the second; the exposure re-sulted in two opposite yet simultaneous motions [as in Fig. 6b] (and analogously, with variations of forms and positions). It was also possible to achieve two *opposite*

---

[28]In its most primitive form, which is not very exact because of the change in luminosity, the shadow experiment is arranged as follows: shadows of one or two standing rods are thrown, at a distance from one another, by two electric lamps. They are projected either from the front onto a white wall, or from the rear onto a milk glass plate or a taut piece of paper. Then one or the other lamp is [successively] lit and darkened in a rhythmic manner, by an alternating contact. In the optimal stage one sees a shadow passing back and forth. Different arrangements of the lengths and strengths of the shadows give many possibilities for variation. It is also possible to achieve a single succession of *ab*.

simultaneous motions in the same field of motion (Fig. 7), with tachistoscopic single (or multiple) exposures

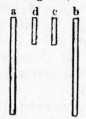

(analogously, also with the slide Fig. 8). It soon became

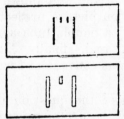

obvious that one could achieve *several*—three, four—disparate and differently directed impressions of motion simultaneously, and a limit seems to be given only by the narrowness of consciousness or of the range of attention. Thus there appeared (Fig. 9) three or even four definite

motions simultaneously, and similarly with other experiments under different conditions. (This occurred not only after training with the particular objects, but also on the first exposure and in totally naive procedures.) Some subjects did require previous training, in the sense of extending their range of comprehension to [include] many disparate, clear motions in such a brief exposure time; but this was not done with the same experimental arrangements. Thus, all the subjects achieved the three

1048

simultaneous motions clearly in the first (and surprising) use of three real and complex objects—e.g. the exposure of a small cage, a plant and a bunch of grapes together in different successive positions.

Should one wish to explain these impressions of motion by eye movements, it would be necessary to assume several disparate, even opposite eye movements.

(Even with the lesser assumption of so-called "eye movement innervations" or "eye movement memories", it would still be necessary to assume that several, even contradictory ones, were effective simultaneously.)

Finally, let us recall motion pictures and the seeing of real motions, how complex and simultaneously differently directed motions can be *seen* and [recall] what requirements this necessitates for eye movements or for "innervations".

The fact that the phenomenon of motion is present between the two stimuli, [even] with the eye steadily fixed, essentially excludes—given some spatial separation between the two objects—explanations of this phenomenon (of motion within the span of that separation) based upon the mere process of rising and falling of the excitation in the two stimulated places of the retina. (Such processes, of rise and fall, may have to be taken into account with adjacent positions of the two retinal points, namely when the successive phase-images are superimposed; but, the phenomenon here is seen in the span of separation between the two object positions[29].)

5. Deduction of two theses

The facts are these:

Two objects were successively given as stimuli. These were perceived. First *a* was seen, then *b;* between them, a "motion from *a* to *b* was seen", without the corresponding motion or the spatially and temporally continu-

---

[29]Cf. Marbe: *Theorie der kinematographischen Projektionen,* 1910, p. 64.

ous positions between a and b actually being exposed as stimuli.

The psychic state of affairs can be called—without prejudice—$a\phi b$. ϕ designates something that exists outside the perceptions of a and b; what happens between a and b, in the space interval between a and b; what is added to a and b.

The considerations outlined [previously] would thus give rise to two basic theses; and as long as one conceived the seeing of motions in the sense common to all the foregoing theories . . ., at least *one* of these two [basic] theories is objectively required, even if in varied form and direction.

I. ϕ is something which uniformly concerns a and b, something which is built on them, which both embraces and unites them.

II. The prenomenal content of ϕ is given by subjective supplementation (or on the basis of a subjective supplementation) of the between positions which are not objectively manifest as spatially and temporally continuous.

One would, therefore, have to say: ϕ is plainly a matter which concerns a and b, and, moreover, concerns them *uniformly* and *binds* them uniformly; and a and b must be thought of as necessary, as the essential content that is the foundation and the framework for ϕ; and finally, ϕ exists in the sense that the space interval between the positions a and b is supplied subjectively.

The [actual] observation of these phenomena, however, pointed in a different direction. Our progress [in the experiments] showed ever more clearly that something compelling and specific must be present here; it led step by step to an investigation which challenged, as necessary, the apparent absolute concurrence of $a\phi b$.

14. On leaving out one stimulus object

In accordance with Thesis I, one would say: ϕ is built on a and b, the objectively primary, the data on which the ϕ-impression is founded. In whatever way these two may be given—separately or fused into the whole $a\phi b$—must not the impressions a and b actually be present (the perceptions of the two objects), if the impression of motion is to result?

1. I refer to the cases of the angle arrangement . . .: e.g. a vertical and b horizontal was given in the temporal conditions of optimal (or dual) full motion. But the result was that the experimental subject did not see one of the objects at all. In the most extreme sense: the experimental subject had no idea in such cases that a vertical [line] was actually exposed. After all, we often operated during the experiments with interposed single exposures of only one object. . . . And so the experimental subjects could have repeatedly expressed the opinion in these cases that only one object was exposed and that the other object, which was not seen, was in fact not exposed (it had been removed in the interval)—as did actually happen on a number of occasions.

And what of the other, the seen object? From the thesis that ϕ is founded on the perception of [both] a and b, it must follow that a ϕ-impression cannot be obtained here, that this other object will appear stationary.

During the experiments several such instances occurred in which one of the two exposed objects was simply not seen, it was not even present as a concept; and the subject concluded that only one object was exposed. As regards the other, perceived object, a motion, ϕ, was sensibly clear, from out of its position (a) or towards its final position (b). For example: given a the vertical, b the horizontal (in the motion stage) and a psychically not there. Then b carries out a part motion, e.g. there exists, with respect to b, a ϕ-rotation in the region of 45° to the horizontal; as a larger or a smaller arc, b exhibits a small motion. . . .

(Such a result was also obtained several times with a

subliminal unilateral shortening of the exposure time of one of the objects, and also with a unilateral lowering of the luminosity of one of the exposure fields.)

This is essential: in the production of this (part-) ϕ, the other object was not seen, was not given in the observation, not even as a concept. ϕ had not emerged, however, from the position of the not seen a, but only from the region of 45° or further (analogously with b).

Such a case occurred, for example, in the angle experiment of Fig. 10 (90°). The observer said that: "there is

a small but distinct movement towards the vertical line from the right, a rotation of about 40°, there is nothing else present. The horizontal? They must have taken it away." I immediately changed the arrangement, without the knowledge of the subject, and actually took the horizontal line away so that only the vertical was left. The exposure still produced the same result: only the vertical was present, with motion.

It was possible, through various arrangements, to regularly obtain such ϕ-phenomena in which only one object was given objectively. For example: the angle arrangement, a the vertical, b the horizontal, was given in the good motion stage several times in succession, with short pauses of 1 to 5 seconds. During one of the intervals, the vertical was taken away without the subject knowing it (or else the exposure field A was covered up). The next two or three exposures, presenting only one of the objects, produced a smaller motion, a rotation into the horizontal. In the first of such exposures this rotation was of about 45°, in the second it was a smaller arc, until, only the third or fourth exposure brought complete rest.

This phenomenon can hardly represent a mere error of

judgment: it appeared in both the naive and the sophisticated procedures, regularly and clearly observable.

This unique, lawful and quantitatively measurable effect, was also produced in experiments of a different kind: if *ab* was given in the motion stage several times in a succession of short intervals, and then, if either *a* or *b* was exposed alone (in either the sophisticated or the naive procedure), an impression of motion still occurred, with regard to the single object, though admittedly smaller in extent [than with *ab*]. It became still smaller in successive exposures, yet complete rest appeared only with the third, fourth and sometimes even the fifth exposure.

An effective arrangement for obtaining the ϕ-phenomena in a definite field, also appeared in a simple way in the following experiments: I presented a rather long horizontal line as one object and a line standing on its middle as the other (Fig. 11a). When the middle line

stood inclined towards the right—by about 20° to 80°—under the given conditions of exposure ($t = 70\sigma$), a rightward rotation (Fig. 11b) occurred under normal

circumstances (that is, upon the first exposure of this arrangement), i.e. in the sense of the acute angle. When the line was inclined towards the left—by about 100° to 170°—then, correspondingly, a leftward rotation occurred (Fig. 11c). . . .

If the exposures were now given one after the other, so that *a* was successively exposed first inclined to the right at about 30°, then inclined at 40° then at 50°, and so on, one could go *far beyond* 90° without a reversal occurring in the direction [of apparent motion]. For example, the setting at 120° still produced a rightward rotation, over the longer stretch, through the obtuse angle (Fig. 11d).

When one is set on a definite direction (or a definite rotation to one side) one often tries vainly to rid oneself of the rotation towards this side, appearing in so very unlikely a position. It is no use: the phenomenon may sometimes appear, for example, in the extremely unlikely position of 160°! The strength of this arrangement appears to be dependent upon individual differences, and upon the number of [previous] experiments with the same arrangement. It proved to be lawful, and easily measurable: I arranged *a* to be rotatable, and experimented step by step, proceeding from left to right and from right to left. The reversal occurred in several experimental sessions at about 160° for subject number 1; with subject number 2 it occurred at about 130°; but up to 175° could also be obtained [with] stronger more effective arrangements!

In other words: a ϕ, which has occurred several times in a specific exposure field, consequently predisposes the production of ϕ in successive exposures of this field, so that a ϕ occurs even under unlikely conditions, which would not have been produced without the previous settings.

In addition to the motions of a single exposed object . . ., one should take account of occasional phenomena, where, *without* previous settings, the objects would not be perceived at all, and where the subject would say: "There was nothing but a strong rotation (showing the correct direction); but I don't know what was there, I have seen nothing of the objects...."[30]

15. Insertion

In view of certain theoretical possibilities, the following results are significant:

1. Even with *longer* exposure time, e.g. $\sigma = \beta = 2$ seconds, impressions of motion can occur with [particular] arrangements ... and with favorable conditions of attention. ...

2. Even with a form of tachistoscope exposure slit (as in Fig. 12, #2, 3 or even 4), in which there is a super-

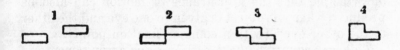

imposition in time of the two exposures, or in which *ab* are exposed at the same time, clear impressions of motion do occur. ...

3. The appearance of motion, even optimal whole motion, often occurs after prolonged observation when the two fixed slit lines are themselves visible at the slide[32] (i.e. when the fixed disc of the slide facing the observer, is not so much in darkness that the two slit lines cannot be seen without exposure); a bright line moves from one slit to the other.

---

[30]Similar results were obtained with experiments of a special design in which, without previous settings, only one object (*b*) was used and, in place of the other [object], a change [was made] below the threshold, in the peripheral parts of the other visual field; also in investigations with the lowering of the two stimuli below the threshold. Both these kinds of experiment extend the range to further complicating problems. ...

Analogous results occurred with exposures of *a* and *b* in different colors (Fig. 13). Instead of *a,* one saw the

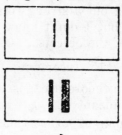

line, now red, now blue, moving between positions *a* and *b,* with the red now above, now below. (Similarly, though more complex effects occurred when both slides were presented simultaneously in several different colors.)

4. In a different direction, it is important as a matter of principle that the appearance of motion can also be produced when one object is given to one eye and the other to the other eye[31] (with a common fixation point).

This was confirmed here with various arrangements.

1. By observing tachistoscopic exposures through two tubes, arranged in such a way that one exposure was presented only to one eye, and the other [exposure] to the other.

2. By placing a screen between the slide slits so that only the left [slit] was visible to the left eye, and the right to the right eye.

3. This fact can also be demonstrated in a way that is very simple, though less exact. For example, if one leans one's head against a standing book cover, so that the visual fields of the two eyes are separated, and if one places a small rod to the right and one to the left (in not quite symmetrical positions), and binocularly fixates some common

---

[31]This fact, of the haploscopic impression of motion, was already shown in an experiment by Exner, (Binokularstroboskop, *Biol. Zentralbl.* 8).

point; then, with a rhythmical and alternating occlusion of each eye, motion of the rod soon appears. (Since, when viewing nearby solid objects, the visual fields of the two eyes are considerably different, one can also achieve motion, a shaking, etc., with all kinds of objects, through alternating monocular observation. This can also be achieved with two fingers; the double images show motion.)[32] It is even more convenient to assume a position in front of a mirror which produces a separation of the visual fields. Finally, the phenomenon also appears with a simple mirror haploscope: one arranges two mirrors at an angle to one another, with the vertex line at the tip of the nose, in such a way that one eye can look into one mirror and the other eye into the other; opposite each mirror stands a screen to which one attaches an object, etc.

16. On the phenomenon of pure motion

What is psychically given in the field of motion? The thesis previously quoted . . . said that the intermediate positions of the object are subjectively supplied. (One could also quote the *à priori* argument, that motion is unthinkable unless an object, a thing, a seen-thing moves.)

If only fully optimal motion occurred, in the sense that the object moved or rotated clearly and distinctly (from the initial position, through the field, to the final position), then this assertion could be demonstrated easily.

But it appears that the essence of the passage across or of the rotation, has nothing to do with subjective intermediate positions. There are cases where ϕ, the motion across, the rotation, is clearly given, without a line being present in the field of motion in any way. The initial and final positions were present, and between them the mo-

[32]See Ebbinghaus, *Gr. d. Psych.*, p. 469, etc.

tion[33], but in the field of motion, no optical supplementation, no seeing or imagining of the intermediate positions of the rod. This occurred spontaneously with all the observers; in the experimental arrangement . . . (below) this "pure" ϕ (without any supplementation of intermediate positions) could be demonstrated in a simple way.

During the impression of unitary whole motion, the following appeared many times, with more acute observation of what was actually present in the field of motion: if, for example, in the angle- or in the parallel-experiments, a and b were white stripes and the ground was black, and if there existed unitary motion from a to b, it [the motion] was present, although clearly, in no sense was there a stripe in passage through the intermediate positions in the field of motion, not even the color of the stripe, except in the positions, a,b themselves and perhaps on the borders of the field of motion.

For example: angle arrangement, a horizontal, b vertical, red stripe on black ground: "very clear unitary rotation, sensibly clear to describe the horizontal stripe visibly rotates part of the way, the vertical [rotates] somewhat into its final position; but the whole is a unity, not a disjointed motion, but a whole rotation clearly seen from a to b; concerning the center, it can be said that, optically, there was nothing of a stripe, nothing of red." And, similarly, for example, with white stripes: "it is curious that I don't see the white bar anywhere during the motion; true, in the last part of the motion, about 15°, where the white is already present, it makes the final part of the motion; but before that it is not there, I could never see the white bar anywhere in the region of 45°." Or, further: a vertical: "a kind of clear, compelling motion occurs, a rotation of about 90°, it is impossible to

---

[33]Cf. Schumann, *op. cit.*, p. 218: ". . . the image of the vertical bar maintains its vertical position and there is, nonetheless, an impression of rotation".

think of it as a succession; it is not the white vertical that moves, but there simply is a process, a transition; one sees the horizontal 'lie down'; earlier positions of the stripe, or of white, e.g. in the region of 45°, were certainly not apparent, not as such; nevertheless, though nothing white rotates, and though no object rotates, motion is still clearly given and, separately, even the final part of the motion [is given] in the 'lying down' of the horizontal".

And, in many cases, spontaneously: "the stripes *a* and *b* are seen, clear motion between them, between *a* and *b* nothing of intermediate positions; the stripe (its color, or the object itself) has not passed through the field, the ground remained quite blank—but the motion goes across". And, finally, similarly in some cases where the two stripes, *a* and *b*, were completely at rest—and between them nothing other than motion. (Particularly convincing were all those cases, with greater distances between *a* and *b,* in which the observation gave unitary clear motion through the field while optically there was nothing of *ab* present at all.)

Thus, these cases showed that not even the thought that "an object has moved across" was present. What was apparent, of the objects, was given in the two positions. Neither one or the other of them, or anything similar, embodied the motion; but motion was given between them; not an object-motion. Nor was it: "that the object moves across, only I don't see it." But there was, simply, motion; without reference to an object.

In this field, where there was nothing to be seen of other optical qualities (except for the blank ground); where no conception was supplied of a stripe passing through the places; and where there was no thought that the stripe was passing across—what, then, was it that was psychically given?

Wherever the attention was concentrated, the impression [of motion] occurred there even more strongly. . . .

1059

Nothing else optical was present; in no sense was there anything of a passage of the stripe through the intermediate positions; nevertheless there was "a strong unitary motion here in this field; a specific, compelling 'passage across' or 'rotation' ".

I presented the 90° angle arrangement, in an optimal-identity rotation; and added on the exposure field, *B*, in the region of 45°, a shorter stripe, *c*, of the same color, which did not reach the vertex (Fig. 14), that is, in a

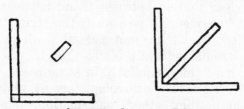

place where any stripe supplemented in the intermediate positions would have to pass over. For example, if *a* and *b* were white stripes of 1/2 or 1 cm. by 6 or 8 cm., then *c* was just as wide but shorter, 1 or 2 cm., etc., (something like a piece of a central stripe). Attention would be focused on *c* or on its inner end, or on the distance between it and the vertex. The motion *ab*, whole rotation by 90°, remained optimal. Was the white stripe *c* supplemented in any way? Does *c* appear somewhat lengthened for a moment, by the passage of a supplemented moving stripe or does a shimmer glide by in the place between *c* and the vertex? Numerous observations always yielded this characteristic result: there was a clear, compelling motion of about 90°, the specific "across" could be observed clearly; nothing of white glides through the place between *c* and the vertex, the ground remains quite black in this place, no supplementation occurred there, even for a moment; but there was an "across" in that place—not the "across" of the stripe, but simply an "across", a "rotation".

I have also arranged this experiment with a slide (Fig. 15). Analogous results occurred with an arrangement in

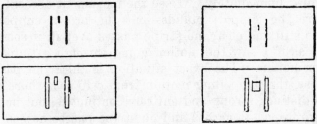

the tachistoscopic experiments, in which *c* was affixed identically to both exposure fields of the tachistoscope; and also in the slide of Fig. 8, in which *c* remained continuously illuminated.

But it is even simpler to demonstrate. One places a slide before oneself (in a manner described above . . .), for example Fig. 16. Then one places an object between

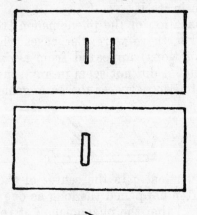

the two slits, e.g. a visible little rod or something similar, and fixates it. Or, analogously, on a larger scale: the slide slits may be projected in optimal motion in a not quite darkened room, onto a white wall. Between the two projected images (the distance from each other being,

1061

say, 60 cm. or 30 cm.), stands a light brown wooden support about 10 cm. wide. Several times the subjects exclaimed immediately: "I see the movement across! Also where the support stands—but the brown support is quite still and clear, no stripe passes over it, it seems at first as if I saw the motion going through a tunnel!"[34] Then again: "The exact situation is this: the passage across, the compelling motion from a to b, is there clear and distinct, strong and entirely continuous, but nothing of white passes across and no stripe passes across."

And also: "the ground remains entirely clear on the right and on the left of the support, nothing slips across it"; "I see whiteness only in the stripes in the initial and in the final positions of the back and forth motion, in between there is only this curious passage across given in the space between a and b." "But there is no passage across of the stripe itself! Only the passage across, a strong motion in itself —— !"

In this separation of the phenomenon from the visual objects a and b, there were also cases where two pure ϕ-motions (rotations) appeared from a *single a*, and in such a way that it did not seem in any sense as if a was being split into two parts. In the arrangement of Fig. 17,

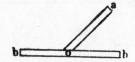

(the shorter vertical a in the center of the longer horizontal b) it often happened (as long as one direction was not favored ...) that the phenomenon of rotation clearly

[34]Von Kries occasionally notes a "tunnel observation" in connection with ghost-experiments, Z. f. Psychol., 29, p. 81; see also Linke, II. *Konger*, p. 217: "The observer now believed (with stroboscopic wheel rotation) that the wheel was suddenly covered during its rotation by a screen or a shadow, and then uncovered again immediately afterwards. The rotatory motion was not inferred, but—and this is most important—it was seen directly". See also Wundt, *Physiol. Psych.*, II, p. 582, etc.

appeared, both to the left and to the right at the same time (rotation by 90° towards the right and towards the left). But it did not at all appear as if the vertical itself turned, let alone as if two lines were turning in opposite directions. Rather, both the vertical and horizontal lines were seen, and the two φ-rotations. Eventually, the horizontal (b) participated in the very last part of the rotations; but, as with the clear immobility of the lines, the φ-phenomenon was between them. Occasionally [these rotations appeared] in different strength; thus, when the right side was favored . . .: "two rotations, a strong one to the right and at the same time a weaker and a less compelling one to the left." This occurred not only with the right-angle arrangement, but also with the a line in the diagonal position (e.g. on the right, motion in an arc of 135°; on the left, motion in one of 45°), and so forth.

This φ-phenomenon, this "across" or "rotation", was present several times so strongly in the tachistoscopic experiments, especially with novel arrangements or reversals from ab into ba, that the observer could report nothing about the objects themselves . . .: "I can say nothing about what kind of objects there were; I have seen a strong motion (showing the correct direction) but I know nothing of the objects, and to my knowledge I have seen nothing of the objects." Similarly, with the arrangement in Fig. 14b where, in the naive procedure, a right-angle was exposed as b and a stripe (in the 45° position of this b-angle) was exposed as a: "a motion was there, at its conclusion there stood a right-angle; there was a rotating motion about the vertex downwards to the horizontal in the lower part of the right angle; I don't know what has turned—the horizontal was lying still, so was the vertical, and it was not as if the horizontal had rotated in its position."

By virtue of these experiments, we must contend not only with a theoretical argument, namely that φ may also

1063

occur without any supplementation of the intermediate positions of the objects and that the characteristics of the ϕ-process do not appear at all to be influenced by the absence of a supplementation of the intermediate positions, but [we must also contend] with a crucial experiment in the literal sense [*Demonstrations experiment in pragnantem Sinn*][35], in which the pure ϕ-process appears.

Apart from the color of the ground, nothing of the ordinary optical qualities appears in the field of motion; there is nothing in the process of color or of contour; in the ordinary optical sense, nothing has changed in the region of the intermediate field, the ground. The observer, here, does not say that the line moves across, nor does he believe that the line moves across (from a to b), or even that it seems to move across. But, rather: "I see a, I see b, I see motion between the two, I see the 'across', the 'rotation'—not that of the line or lines, which are in their locations a and b—but a relatively stronger or a weaker 'across' in itself." "I see motion; thus (illustrating) not an across of something." And this occurs with the fullest concentration of attention on the field and with the most critical observation; the stronger the attention, the more centrally it is concentrated in the field, the better.

One might think, that, where nothing of a supplementation appeared, nothing of a thought-motion [*gedachter Bewegung*] (that an object itself moved across), nothing of intermediate positions of the object, the "illusion" of motion would disappear. But, on the contrary, the motion is present compellingly and characteristically in its specific nature; it is given clearly and distinctly and is always observable.

These motion phenomena may appear in stronger or weaker intensity. They are given in the extremes as two

---

[35]Editor's note. This is not yet the well-known concept of *Prägnance*.

simultaneous appearances; for example, as in Fig. 17, where the arrangement is adjusted for the right to be the greater angle: to the right, a colossally strong [motion occurs], while to the left, a weak ϕ-phenomenon occurs at the same time.

They also vary characteristcally with the nature of the experiment: a "rapid across", a "lazy, slow rotation", a "quiet rotation", a "rotation with a jerky beginning and end", etc.

They also show specific motion-curves . . ., and appear with definite spatial localization.[36]

These are psychic phenomena,[37] which are directed in the same way as the actual sensed form and color contents (appearing objectively, not subjectively). Contrary to other psychic data they are dynamic, not static in nature; they have their psychological flesh and blood in the specific characteristic "across", etc., and this cannot be composed from the usual optical content.

17. Analogy to the seeing of actual motion

If one turns from such experiments to the seeing of actual motion in real life, then one sees that the things to which we have been led by the apparently unrealistic experimental arrangements are by no means so strange, exceptional, or untrue to life. They can be observed everywhere when looking at motion. The eye is so sharp-

---

[36]In the experiments considered here, this localization was in one spatial section of the field plane. In order to see whether a ϕ-phenomenon is present under complicated circumstances in a definite plane, I projected two slide slits, each one on a wall at different distances in space (Fig. 18a—view of the arrangement from above). The observer stood on the side, and a distinct motion phenomenon occurred (Fig. 18b).

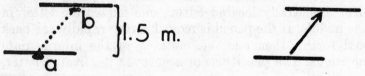

[37]The expression "psychic phenomena" is used here in the simple sense of what is specifically and observably given.

ened that it can see the characteristic ϕ-phenomena in motions, even in opposition to the perception of actual positions or successions of positions. In actual motion, too, it is very often not the spatial and temporal continuity of the intermediate visual positions which is given, but rather a pure ϕ-phenomenon. One sees, for example, how construction workers throw bricks to one another; one sees (when one fixates upon a definite point) the characteristic motions of the arm against the background of a white wall; one continually sees the upward swing, from the given position of the arm (while grasping the brick) to the final position above; one sees both final positions; one sees the motion. Nothing appears of the spatial and temporal continuity of the positions between the initial and the final position, except perhaps in the first jerk of the motion and in the very last—and yet one sees the entire compelling motion. Here, too, one might at first think in terms of illusion; but when one has made such observations often and has trained one's eye to perceive in small time intervals (as in the above experiments), it becomes clear that there is no illusion of judgment here, no conclusion, but a living seeing of motion. Similarly with the shadow of a man striding over asphalt, or when seeing a metronome beating time at a certain speed. One can observe a similar thing in a very simple experiment: a pencil[38] is held vertically above a piece of paper (at a convenient viewing distance) on which one or more letters are printed, and is moved (about 10 cm.) horizontally (once or several times, or even back and forth) from a place at the left to another one at the right over a centrally located letter; one fixates the letter in the middle. If the pencil is moved across rapidly (or back and forth), then one sees nothing of the intermediate positions. The pencil is not seen over the fixated letter,

---

[38]More exactly, any very thin object.

it does not, as such, pass over it; and, generally, neither the pencil nor its color have been perceived between the initial and the final positions, that is to say, they have not been seen at all. None the less, not only is the succession of the seen initial position and of the seen final position present, but the motion is also present. The physical "being in the place" (for example, over the fixated letter), was not seen here. If one oscillates (using the same speed) over a *small* span between initial and final positions, then fully optimal motion appears. One sees the pencil and its color passing back and forth through the field of motion. If one retains a larger span and moves the pencil *more slowly,* one eventually sees it passing across continuously. . . . But with still slower motion, it characteristically often occurs, that one believes that he really saw the pencil in all positions in a continuous sequence, in which case the characteristic impression of *motion itself* is often absent. The paradox occurs that, in so far as the space-time series of the intermediate positions is really present psychically, the motion itself very often appears only as something concluded, as mere inference; and a careful self-observation reveals that one has seen the occupation of positions— here, here, and here—without interruption; but the specific really *seen motion* was not present.

Concomitant Successive Exposures

Enduring continuous and concomitant successive exposures may be obtained, for example, in the following manner:

A simple slit or several symmetrically placed slits were affixed to the tachistoscope wheel (without the prism device...). A Zimmerman kymograph drum was set up in the exposure field and a number of lines were drawn on the drum, parallel to its axis of rotation. The tachistoscope wheel and the kymograph drum were rotated; the tachistoscope wheel was rotated at such a speed so that the visible parallel lines remained completely stationary during a single exposure. Then, according to the phase relation of the two rotations (the sequence of the exposures, on the one hand, and the rotation speed of the kymograph, on the other), three things could be obtained with prolonged observation under optimal conditions: (1) the seeing of the continuous motion of the parallel lines in *the sense of the actual motions of the kymograph drum;* (2) standing, enduring, immobility of the lines in the field of vision, or a state of liability; and (3) the seeing of continuous *motion in the opposite direction.*

If the exposures proceed in such a way, for example, that the positions *abcd* are exposed in the first exposure and the positions *a'b'c'd'* in the second exposure (i.e. during the interval the kymograph lines have moved up one quarter of the distance between the lines), as in Fig. 19a, then motion is seen in the sense of the actual motion

of the kymograph lines (Fig. 19b). If the lines have

moved up in the time between the exposures by *three quarters* of the distance (Fig. 19c), then a *motion in the opposite direction* is seen. According to the law of the smaller distance, an *a:b* motion occurs as in Fig. 19d,

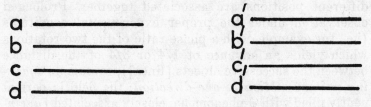

i.e. a descending motion is seen. If the kymograph lines have moved up in the time between the exposures by the entire distance between the lines, then no motion of the lines is seen (*b′* has taken the place of a, etc., as in Fig. 19e); because of the inexactness of the rotation relations,

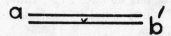

a small upward or downward motion may appear according to whether *b′* has reached a position slightly above or below that of *a*. If the lines have moved up in the interval between the exposure by *one half* of the distance (Fig. 19f), then, with any slight inexactness of the rotation

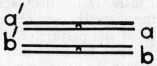

relations, the resulting distance [i.e. not exactly half] could be decisive. Otherwise, both directions of motion are objectively equally favored, and what decides [between them] are the conditions of *set* and the *posture of the attention*. An upward or a downward motion may

1069

occur, or one [line] may slide over into the other.[39]

In all these experiments, successive exposures of different positions are associated together. Prolonged observation under the proper experimental conditions (i.e., for example, with a phase ratio of the two rotations which yields an advance of 1/4 or 3/4 of the distance between the successive objects [lines]), reveals an *enduring unitary motion in one direction*: the field is permanently filled with ϕ-phenomena, closely associated [*aneinanderschliessenden*] and moving in the same direction, which flow into one another, completely, homogeneously; a continuous "sinking", "rising", "rotation", etc., appears in the field.

Moreover, in the optimal impression, the individual positions . . . are no longer imposing as such. There is an enduring unitary motion, without any definite "positions" standing out as such; . . . thus, the transition to the seeing of slow, quietly continuous real motion is achieved here.

Analogous results occurred with the use of a spinning-spoked-wheel instead of a kymograph drum. In a simple tachistoscopic successive exposure of two intersecting lines, the smaller separations are at first decisive. With a single successive exposure, motion appears over the smaller angle; with serial exposure, a back and forth motion is seen there. If the lines stand normal to one another, and the distances are objectively equally favored, then it is set and posture of attention (e.g. to the top of the angle, or to the side) that proved decisive in determining whether the rotation was seen towards the *right* or towards the *left*. If we operate in this arrangement with a spoked-wheel with two or more spokes, the results are analogous to those obtained with the kymograph lines. Given a phase-ratio of the two rotations,

---

[39]An extended observation often exhibits a strange state of liability, a vacillating, an uncertainty. . . .

for example, that entailed the advance of the wheel by that number of degrees which corresponded to three fourths of the angle between the two spokes, then continuous rotary motion occurred in a direction opposite to the actual [direction].[40]

The well-known spiral disk (Fig. 21) was also used

instead of the spoked-wheel. The (slowly) rotating spiral gives the compelling impression of an enduring "expansion" from the center or a "contraction" to the center. This is explained in a simple way by the above mentioned laws for the production of the ϕ-phenomena: there is little or no reason for the production of ϕ *in the direction of the spiral line* (or in the circular direction); but there is good reason for the production of ϕ-phenomena from places on the line to radially neighboring places[41]; and closely associated, radial, centripetally or centrifugally

---

[40]With simple accurate observation of the actual motion of rotating spoked wheels, it is possible to observe the ϕ-phenomena occurring in an opposite direction (with suitable speeds and different postures of attention); e.g. let a motion to the right be the actual direction, then an apparent sudden turning back in the opposite direction occurs (Fig. 20). An essential cause of the well-known, mysterious "wheel-spoke phenomenon" (a rotating wheel suddenly appears to rotate in the opposite direction, and in broad daylight) may be given here in a very simple way. If a spoked-wheel is rotated at various speeds, then there first appears certain stationary phenomena . . ., e.g. at the hub, and then, with rather different speeds, the retrograde ϕ-phenomena.

[41]Cf. recently Stumpf, "Uber die Abhängigkeit der vis. Bewegungsempf." Z. f. Psychol. 59: p. 324.

directed ϕ-phenomena, are regularly produced. There is an "expansion" or a "shrinking". Schematically: it is as if the rotating spiral first gave the position of the solid line of Fig. 21; then, after a rotation of say 90°, it

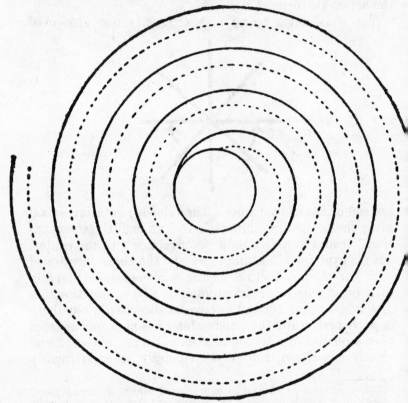

reached the position indicated by the dotted line. (By mistake [*sic*], the dotted line in the figure represents a different spiral!)

After-image

In the prolonged observations mentioned above, the field is permanently filled by the unitary appearance of closely associated ϕ-phenomena moving in the same direction (even with relatively large separations between the successively exposed positions).

If one looks for some time at an enduring ϕ-motion in one direction, and then looks at appropriate immobile objects, or an immobile field, then the opposite motion appears spontaneously. This demonstrated the theoretically important fact, that the ϕ-phenomena (with sufficient duration and consistency of direction) yields a *negative after-image,* in analogy to the well-known after-image in the seeing of real motion.

Exner[42] has already achieved negative after-images with "apparent motion". Analogous results were obtained here (even where the motion first seen was opposite to the real motion ...), but in a much stronger manner (completely analogous to the after-images of "actual" motion), by using the spiral experiment (as above) and, finally, by the *motion picture* presentation of the rotating spiral.

Enduring closely associated ϕ-phenomena moving in the same direction in the same field, yield an intense negative after-image (motion in the opposite direction).

18. Summary

Reviewing the results as a whole, we obtain:

1. With appropriate successive exposure of two stationary stimuli at a distance from one another, motion was seen[43] which cannot be accounted for by the eye motions or by the relative rise and fall of excitation in the two stimulated points of the retina.

With fixated eyes, two separate points on the retina would be stimulated successively. Under the given conditions ..., with a time *interval of succession* equal to about 30σ, the two stimulus objects would be seen in

---

[42]Z. *f. Psychol.* 21: p. 388, 1899. Exner: "Nachbild einer vorgetäuschten Bewegung".

[43]Cf. Pleikart Stumpf, *op. cit.,* p. 321, Gesetze I.

stationary simultaneity; with an interval of 200σ, they would appear in stationary succession; with an interval of 60σ as a rule, motion would appear from one position into another. The production of this effect appears to be a function, in the first place, apart from the time relations, of the size of the *separation* of the two objects: a smaller distance, for example, allows a wider range of time-interval magnitudes over which optimal motion can be obtained. Prolonged observation and set have a specific regulatory influence.

2. The impression of motion need not essentially be connected with the identity of a and b. In the stages, running from the simultaneous downwards, as a rule, first motion and then identity appeared; running from the optimal upwards, as a rule, the identity $a = b$ first disappeared, even before immobility was obtained.

3. Between the appearance of whole motion (from position a to position b) and the extreme stages (e.g. stationary simultaneity) there were dual part motions, i.e. motions of the two objects, each in itself.

Between the appearance of [self-] identical whole motion and the extreme stationary stages, *special characteristic qualitative* impressions occur: the [self-] identity of the two stimulus objects was present only in the stage of optimal motion; beyond this (e.g. in the process of shortening the time interval), motion appeared *without [self-] identity of the objects,* in addition to the special phenomenon of *part motion,* i.e. two smaller motions referring to each of the two objects in itself. Such dual part motions were of greater or smaller extent: with the further shortening of the time intervals towards the stage of stationary simultaneity, there was a diminution of both ranges of motion. Close to the simultaneity stage yet another phenomenon appeared (no longer dependent on the span of separation), i.e. internal motion (motion phenomena within the objects) and, in some cases, displacement.

4. Impressions of motion occurred in which one of the two objects remained unmoved and at rest, while the other exhibited a (part-) motion (*singular motion*).

5. The *posture of attention* and the *set* have a regulatory influence on the production and kind of effects produced.

Special factors proved to be of influence in the observations: duration, set and posture of attention had special effects; thus, the direction of attention towards the span of separation, for example, was favorable to impressions of motion. Experimentally varied set produced quantitative measurable influences on the place and the kind of motion.

6. There were impressions of motion (as part motion) in which one of the two objects was not psychically perceived or was no longer objectively present as a stimulus.

7. The impression of motion is materially not constructed from the subjective supplementation of the intermediate positions of the object. In certain experiments, though there was nothing seen or even thought of the objects or of the optical qualities of the objects in the span of separation, nevertheless the impression of motion over the field was itself compellingly present (even with pure duality and immobility of the two objects). The ϕ-phenomenon exists separately from the appearances of the two stimulus objects.

(8. A third smaller object placed in the field of motion of two such objects (at the optimal stage), remained stationary, under certain circumstances, without disturbing the motion as regards the other two objects; or, in other circumstances, exhibited a small singular motion. Two neighboring successive exposures exhibited a definite influence on one another.)

9. Under the given circumstances, the duration of *exposure* of the individual stimuli themselves could be

varied considerably. The question of whether a time interval, between the *end* of the first stimulus and the beginning of the second, was absolutely necessary for the production of impressions of motion, was decided in the sense that impressions of motion (part motions) can appear even with a partial temporal overlapping of the stimulus times, though with greater difficulty; also, [this was decided] by stimulating one of the two stimulated places in a different manner, *at the same time* that the other was being stimulated. Special experiments confirmed that if one stimulus was presented *to one eye and the other stimulus to the other eye,* impressions of motion would result.

10. The optimal motion resulting from successive stimulation appears *qua motion,* equal in value to the seeing of motion which occurs with the exposure of a corresponding actually moved object. It appeared equally as strong, and, under certain circumstances, more compelling.

11. In various experimental arrangements, the *transition to the impression of continuously enduring motion* appeared with the concomitance of successive exposures of stationary positions, which were exposed in spatial separation from each other. It was also confirmed in special experiments that the impression of motion resulting from such successive exposures has a *negative after-image* (analogous to the after-image phenomena of actual motion seen for a longer time).

20. Application of existing theories of attention to the findings

If one considers the various theories . . . in the light of the results of these investigations, one obtains the following:

1. The *trace* [after-image] theory or *trace-stripe theory,* which deduces the phenomena of motion from the event of the fading of the excitation in the stimulated

points of the retina, cannot be taken into account here as a constituent factor, where there is no successive stimulation of several neighboring retinal points. Here we have impressions which are produced at a *considerable distance* from the two stimulated places (with the eyes fixated . . .) and which are essentially phenomena occurring in the span of separation itself, *between the stimulated places*. (There is no juxtaposition of fading phases in neighboring retinal points).[44]

2. Regarding the constitutive foundation on *eye motions* [see above]. . . .[45] Even if one retreats to "innervations", the special consequences given there still apply.

3. As to the question of whether we are dealing with *illusions of judgment,* the following essential points should be raised. Here it cannot be a question of illusion over something physically real, but rather an illusion over something given psychically. It is not a matter of: "I am deceived over something physically present", but: "I am deceived in the judgment of something seen. I have actually seen only the stationary *a* and *b*, the deception lies in my believing that I have also seen the motion". One might observe here that the chief reason, *ad hominem,* for such a deception is absent: appearances of motion occur *without* apparent [self-] identity. . . .

Moreover: the distinct, detailed, compelling appearance of the seen motion between *a* and *b*, is revealed by the testimony of self-observation. Time and again [motion appears], although the observer *knows* that he is dealing with two stationary stimuli in separation and succession. *With repeated, careful* observation, with *prolonged* observation, with *attention concentrated* on what

---

[44]Inasmuch as such processes have to be taken into account when using the stroboscope, it is necessary to deal with them in any exhaustive treatment of the facts, and Marbe's theory of elementary stimuli can be usefully applied here.

[45]Quite apart from the fact that a number of other illusions of motion argue against explanations by eye motions; e.g. the Plateau-Dvorak experiment with several spirals.

is actually given, with *careful training* in the observation of tachistoscopic phenomena, with thorough *experience* (after all, one has learned the various phenomena, even the stationary succession, etc., in all their numerous variations)—illusions of judgment should grow weaker and finally disappear, but this is not the case; rather the contrary occurs. . . .

In addition to these general arguments, there are the special ones: with attention concentrated on the most critical place of the illusion (the place where the purest "illusion product" should play its part, in setting one's attention on the span of separation, the angle space) the illusion nevertheless is not decreased, but rather strengthened and improved. Moreover, after special attention to one of the two objects, during a single exposure, not only was this object not free from illusion, but all the more, it exhibited part motions.

And then there is the pure ϕ-*experiment* . . .: where it is really *clear* that *nothing* is to be seen of an intermediate position, a color, an object in motion through the span of separation, and where one does not even think that the object itself moves—must not the illusion finally disappear. . .?! Remarkable, also, is the curious 2ϕ-phenomenon . . . where two [simultaneous] motions were seen: for example, in the angle space, a rightward rotation was seen to the right, and a leftward rotation was seen to the left; but the line, a was not in the least split, and did not appear to move in one of the two (or both!) directions.

Furthermore: the sequence of qualitatively different phenomena would naturally have to be explained by the theory; e.g. how after the change of t [exposure time] to whole motion, the way led through the phenomena of the intermediate stages to simultaneity. In each *individual* case a *special, plausible explanation* could finally be thought out—since by its nature an illusion of judgment can be freely postulated—*but what of the correlation* with the changes in *t*? One would have to draw upon a great abundance of hypotheses to explain the phenomena of a part motion, for example, or of a singular motion;[47] but how then [would we explain] the continuous step by step transition from optimal motion through the phenomena to the extreme stage of stationary simultaneity?

Finally, there would still remain the lawful *negative after-image* of the concomitant ϕ-phenomena.

4. As regards the conception of these motion phenomena as a *fusion* of the stimulus contents, we have:

I. *a* and *b* do not necessarily fuse into a [self-]iden-tity, there are phenomena in which the motion is indeed present, but without the identity of the two contents (e.g. the dual whole motions . . ., and the part motions).

II. ϕ is not necessarily something that embraces the *two contents a* and *b*, but in the case of part motion it concerns each of them by itself, without the two fusing in any sense. Consider also, part motions with two contents being of different colors or of different shapes without any impression of change [in them], e.g. where the red moves above, and the blue moves below. . . .

III. In singular motion ϕ concerns *only the one object* in itself, the other object remains quite untouched. . . .

IV. Consider those cases . . . where there is *no* stimulus material for fusion; or the cases . . . where *both objects* remain untouched by the ϕ-phenomenon, i.e. dual, stationary. . . .

5. Regarding the conception of these phenomena in the sense of the usual definitions of a *Gestaltqualität* or of a *Komplexqualität* . . ., there are several analogous considerations. They require the facts of the aforementioned Thesis I. (1) ϕ would have to concern *a* and *b* in a

---

[47]Specially complicated bases would have to be found for the special "motion-curves". . . .

way that is phenomenally unitary; however, it was shown above . . . that φ appeared as a part motion, as an event which phenomenally concerned each of the two "basic stimuli" purely for itself. (2) φ would have to concern both *a* and *b*; but this contrasts with singular motion. . .; (3) and *a* and *b* would have to be present, i.e. the basic contents—"*at least two*"—would have to be somehow present in the experience; but this was contraindicated [above]. . . .

Apart from all this, the theory would have to explain the other lawful phenomena that occurred; e.g. the dual part motion *as an intermediate* stage on the way between whole motion and the simultaneous stage, etc. . . .

6. Is φ based upon a process (passage across, motion) of attention? First *a* would present itself to the attention, then *b*; the viewpoint of the attention which first grasps *a* is torn from *a* and drawn over to *b*. One might suggest that this passing across of attention is the phenomenon of motion.

Attention can be understood in several ways. *Attention is understood here in the special sense of* that experimentally used datum . . . *in which the observer concentrates in such a way on some definite place, so that he observes the phenomena* and the events in such a place most sharply, and these appear to him most clearly and distinctly "in the center of consciousness". Apart from the fact that the observer in the pure φ-experiment sees the φ-process differently from the well-known, well-learned phenomenon of a mere passing across the center of the attention from one place to another, we then obtain the following:

I. The situation is similar to that with fixation of the eye. . . . The question is: is it possible to hold the posture of the attention rigidly during the experiment? If so, what is the effect? The experimental testing required a good deal of training of the observers. In exercises of shifting the posture of the attention, it soon occurred that the subjects could state with certainty whether their posture of attention had suffered a change or not. In the beginning—as with the fixation experiment—it often happened that after the seen-motion, the place on which the attention was concentrated was *different* from that at the beginning of the experiment; the attention had been "drawn across", and was finally at *b* or even beyond *b*. But it soon came about that the posture of attention *stayed quietly* in one place (we operated with different positions . . .), and the motion phenomena performed in the same way (across the place, from it, towards it, peripherally to it, etc.). . . .[48]

III. Finally, in order to account for the phenomenal appearances of the ϕphenomena, one would have to ascribe to the phenomenal passage across of attention, very far-reaching, numerous and unusual achievements when . . ., for example, two motions in opposite directions were simultaneously obtained in the same field of motion (without any phenomenal presence of a figural unification *Aa:bB*); or, similarly, when . . ., *several opposite motions* appeared; or, finally, when three and four disparate motions were obtained, ununified, in the

---

[48]Additional recognition experiments suggested themselves: thus, an instantaneous exposure of *XAM* (Fig. 22) did not produce a tendency to read *"XAM"* but *"MAX"* etc.

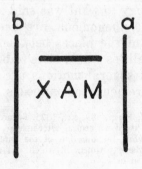

same field. One would have to reckon here with several isolated simultaneous passages across of the attention [*Aufmerksamkeithinubergangen*].

One soon sees that the ϕ-phenomena themselves have nothing to do *directly* with "clarity and distinctness" in a particular place. *They themselves* may be more or less clear and distinct, and play either on peripheral or more central places of the attention. *Passage-across-of-attention, in the sense this phrase is used here,* appears rather *as a plus,* which may be present in addition to the seen-motion. It appears explicitly under simple conditions, as a constituent not as a requisite.

(If "attention" is not understood in the sense defined above, but in another manner: *as any central factor on which the production of the ϕ-phenomena is based,* then ... *the central processes themselves must in some way be explained*).[49]

If one wishes to prescind from attention, in the usual sense of that word (in its relation to clarity and distinctness), and to believe, *on purely logical grounds,* in a "process" as necessarily meaning *"a process of something",* then there is this to be said against it: this is *not* founded on psychological data, and why should not pure dynamic phenomena exist? There is no internal reason why something that is psychologically "dynamic" should have to be deduced *à priori* from something "static".

(Note: In analogy to what was said above, ... it could be said that the ϕ-phenomena are based upon *"a successive grasping* of the places between *a* and *b*". However, ... what qualities would have to be required of such a *grasping,* when several motions are seen at the same time? This requirement, too, appears as a plus—which

---

[49]Exner, *Arch. f. Physiol.* 11: p. 589, etc., 1875. Regarding the possible recourse to the constituent effects of a "central after-image", I refer to . . . the impressions of motion when the duration of the stimulus *a* extends over the appearance of *b,* and the experiment in which *a* is seen in a different color, also during the duration of *b.*

need not necessarily be deduced from these experiments—especially when one considers that all the (positions) places between the several different a and b objects that come into account, would have to be grasped in succession. A phenomenal "across" (actually a "passage over or across", through the distance ab) does, indeed, exist; but each additional requirement represents a plus which leads to too great demands on what can be psychically achieved. Consider, finally, the experiment [above] . . . of two simultaneous and opposite motions in the same field and the one [footnote 48] in which "successive grasping" in the direction towards the left should lead to the approximation of "MAX".)

21. Sketch of a physiological hypothesis

In essence, in the foregoing experiments, two points on the retina which were separated from one another were successively stimulated. Eye motions, and the conditions of the rise and fall of the excitation in the specifically stimulated retinal points themselves, . . . cannot be considered as the fundamental constituents.

Exner has already explained (in 1875) that central factors have to be drawn upon as the basis of these phenomena, as a conclusion from the results which he obtained with his "double stroboscope"[50]; from another viewpoint, Marbe[51] came to the same conclusion on the basis of Durr's experiments with the falling out of the phases[52]; also Wundt[53]; then Linke, as a conclusion from

---

[50]Exner, Exper. Untersuchungen der einfachsten psychischen Prozesse, *Arch. f. Physiol.* 11: 1875, p. 589: "This impression of motion either always occurs, or does so at least in certain cases, in the zone that is common to both eyes," etc.

[51]*Phil. Stud.*, vol. 14, 1898, p. 400: "the most important part of these processes, the stroboscopic motion phenomena, are also founded on the fact that we cannot notice the dyssynchronism of the motion-phases because of purely central conditions".

[52]Dürr, *Phil. Stud.*, vol. 15.

[53]Wundt, *Phys. Psychol.*, II.

the phenomena treated [above] . . .; and Schumann on the basis of "motion without change of place of the stimulating objects"[54]. The experiment . . . in which the phenomenon of motion occurred in *haploscopic* observation at the tachistoscope, in analogy to Exner's experiments, and *without* moving glance, clearly shows that it is not sufficient to draw upon pure peripheral processes in relation to a single eye: we must have recourse to processes "which lie behind the retina"[55,56].

A physiological theory has two functions in connection with the experimental investigation: on the one hand it must encompass the diverse individual results and their regularity in a unified manner and make them deducible; on the other hand, and this seems the essential—this unified summation must serve the further *advance of investigation* by leading to the posing of concrete *experimental questions,* which at first test the theory itself and which are then appropriate to the further penetration into the regularities of the phenomena.

In this sense, it is possible to sketch here a brief outline of the physiological basis. This outline was used by me for a comprehensive deduction of the results obtained and on the posing of special further questions in the course of the investigation; it has proved itself heuris-

[54]Schumann, II. *Kongr,* p. 218.

[55]In a different way, the regularities . . . of the determining influences of attention and set also point to a central basis.

[56]NB: I note a recent pathological case (an affection of both occipital lobes) which seems to argue for a central basis for the seeing of motion: In the *Wien. klin. Wochenschr.,* 24: 1911, p. 518, Dr. Potzl reports, of a female patient: "if one lets a strong source of light act upon her in slower or faster motion, then she appears not to apperceive the motion of the object and she describes what she sees as several lights". In May 1911 I contacted Dr. Potzl and had an opportunity in the summer of that year to test his patient both with various actual motions, and with slide experiments. The conditions of stringency suffered somewhat from the lowered intelligence of the subject; nonetheless, time and again, the seeing of motion did not occur, in spite of the recognition of the color, etc. The subject, when helped by acoustic impressions (rustling, etc.), spoke of "fluttering back and forth". The color of the moving object was recognized.

tically correct in later work. If this hypothesis treads upon difficult or unknown ground, this seems to be required by the facts of the case; this seems necessary, and permissible, since the hypothesis itself leads to concrete problems that can be solved experimentally. I limit myself to the sketching of the essential features: . . . It is a question of certain central processes, physiological "transverse functions" of a special kind, which serve as the physiological correlate of the ϕ-phenomena.

According to recent neurophysiological investigations it must be assumed as probable that the excitation of a central point a sets up a physiological disturbance in a definite circle around it. If two points a and b, are thus excited, there would result a similar circular disturbance in both cases; this circle is then predisposed for excitation processes.

If the point a is stimulated, and within some specific short time, the neighboring point b,[57] then there would occur a kind of *psychological short-circuit* from a to b. A specific passage of excitation occurs in the span between the two points. If, for example, the amount of circular disturbance from a, has reached the peak of its time process curve and the circular disturbance from b now occurs, then excitation flows over (a physiologically specific event), the direction of which is given by the fact that a and its circular disturbance occurred first.

The closer the two points ab are[57] to one another, the more favorable are the conditions for the creation of the ϕ-phenomenon (cf. . . . the various cases of the law of the smaller distance).

If t, the time interval between the entry of the excita-

_____
[57] It is immaterial here whether this "neighborhood" is thought of simply geometrically (as in the sense of the theories of "retinal projection"), or whether it is only a question of functional linkage. Even if one does not admit any [central] image of the retina, the neighboring points of the retina must be thought of as being in a special, specially strong, and specially "near", reciprocal functional connection with corresponding afferent central points.

tion into the two successively stimulated points a and $b,$ is *too great,* then the circular disturbance around a has already subsided when that from b enters (stage cf *succession*) ; if the time interval is shorter, so that the circular disturbance of a is still present, and is actually at the peak of its process curve when that of b enters, then the crossing of excitation occurs; if t is very short, then the circular disturbances from a and b occur simultaneously (or else that around a has not reached sufficient height at the critical moment), which makes the *directed* short-circuit impossible (stage of stationary simultaneity)....

In whatever way the basic central role of attention may be conceived, the formulation must always be thus: *that one place toward which* the fundamental attention is directed has a *heightened disposition for* excitation (be it only a higher excitability or higher conductivity, or a higher state of excitation). This is only in simple accord with the•results ... : the setting of attention onto the span of separation (between a and b) favored the phenomenon; setting it onto the place of one of the two objects favored (part) motions of it, etc. ...

The circular disturbances are naturally strongest in the neighborhood of the stimulated points. If optimal conditions are not present, e.g. a t between the optimal and the simultaneous stages, then the phenomenon acts most strongly on the borders of the two objects, and is subliminal in the center (dual part motion). Moreover, for fully optimal motion (and part motion, in the sense of a motion of the object), the qualitative influence of a or of b comes into consideration. But there need be no such influence: to the pure ϕ-phenomenon ... there would correspond a passage across of excitation without a qualitative influence of a and b. ...

With regard to the more special phenomena . . ., the following need be said: it is always a question here of the

1086

later appearance of the exposure of *b* or of the earlier disappearance of that of *a*. The circular disturbance (part motion) can also become effective through repetition of the stimulation, through dispositional factors, through longer exposure time, and through temporal overlap. The fact that the effect may still occur with a different stimulus *a* (in the presence of *b*), can also be explained by the foregoing conception.

The ... effects achieved by the ϕ-process under certain circumstances on an object in the field of motion and on a neighboring successive stimulation, are also in accord with the nature of this physiological process.

It is to be expected that several disturbances that are too weak in themselves become stronger in their summation, and, likewise, that many repeated actual presentations of the specific psychological process should favor its entrance. ...

On the other hand: if a strong across appears for a long time in a definite direction, it is to be expected that afterwards, when the stimulation to the across is absent, a flooding back, a compensation in the opposite direction will occur; there is a *negative after-image*. ...

With concomitant successive exposures ... under optimal conditions, ... the resulting ϕ-phenomena continuously join one another, and produce a *unitary continuous whole-process*; the "position-character" ... disappears. This would seem to be the clue to the seeing of actual enduring motion: a progressive diminution of "separations" leads directly to the physical conditions of actual motion. In this case, *the uniformly passing across ϕ process* comes into account, *in addition to the reception of the stimulus* itself (and the process directly conditioned by it). The fact that with actual motion there is a *far greater range of optimal times* (and thus also of speeds of motion) can be explained simply. The smaller the "separation" becomes, the greater the resulting range of optimal t times. If the distance is small or if we operate with continuous stimulus successions (and if, in the case of concomitant exposures, the stationary-position-character of the exposed positions is not favored by too great a duration, etc. of the δ, β ... times), then we must draw *upon quite excessive accelerations or decelerations* of the succession (decreases and increases of t) in order to reach one of the extreme stages—successive or simultaneous stationary positions—from optimal motion.[58]

MAX WERTHEIMER (b.—Prague, April 15, 1880: d.—New Rochelle, New York, Oct. 12, 1943.)

After studying at the Universities of Prague and Berlin, Wertheimer received his Ph.D. from the University of Wurzburg in 1904. Having studied earlier with Stumpf at Berlin, Wertheimer returned there until 1910, at which time he went to Psychologische Institut of the Akademie für Socialwissenschaften at Frankfurt. There, also, were Wolfgang Köhler and Kurt Koffka, who participated as principle subjects in Wertheimer's epochal experiment. From 1912-1914 Wertheimer was Privatdozent at the Akademie. In 1914 he became Privatdozent at the University of Frankfurt till 1916. From there he went to the University of Berlin, where, by 1922, he had become Ausserordentlicher Professor in Philosophy and Psychology. He returned to the University at Frankfurt as Ordentlicher Professor in 1929 and remained there until 1933. He was forced to leave Germany in 1933 by the political situation. He joined the staff of the University in Exile at the New School for Social Research as Professor of Psychology and Philosophy, where he was at his death.

The present selection is a condensation of the paper which is usually considered to have launched the *Gestalt movement*. It was the first formal experimental report, and the inaugural effort of the three men who later made the most important contributions to Gestalt theory. It was, approximately, Wertheimer's ninth published paper (cf. Murchison). Probably, it is the most widely quoted single experimental study

---

[58]From this, one may also specify a condition for the operation of the motion picture projector: a mere increase of the "phase images" in number is not in itself a favorable factor for the impression of motion. On the one hand, it acts favorably only when the exposure times of the single phases are short enough so as not to favor the "position" impressions themselves; on the other hand, there is no need for the motion itself to be compelling . . ., the favorable effect may be conditioned, in the first instance, by the fact that small distances are used which allow a large range of possibilities for different speeds.

in the field, and is rendered here for the first time in the English language. It is to such work as this that Wertheimer always referred when he insisted that the Gestalt-theory was solidly grounded in experimental facts; for him, it was never an abstract, idealized formulation.

WERTHEIMER, M. "Experimentelle Studien über das Sehen von Bewegung." Z. Psychol. 1912, 61:161-265.

See also:

WERTHEIMER, M.
   a) *Drei Abhandlungen zur Gestalttheorie*. Neuhrsg.: Erlangen, Philosophische Akad., 1925.
   b) "On truth." *Social Research*. 1934, 1:135-146.
   c) *Productive thinking*. N. Y., Harper & Bros., 1945.

ELLIS, W. D. *A source book in Gestalt psychology*. N. Y.: Harcourt, Brace & Co., 1939. Translations of many papers.

KOHLER, W. "Max Wertheimer." *Psychol. Rev.* 1944, 51:143-146.

FOCHT, M. *What is Gestalt-theory?* N. Y.: Columbia University Ph.D. thesis, 1935. Abstracts of three early papers, in translation.

PETERMANN, B. *The Gestalt theory and the problem of configuration*. Trans. M. Fortes. London: Kegan Paul, Trench & Trubner, 1932.

MURCHISON (b—Vol. 2, p. 479; b—Vol. 3, p. 888).

THE MENTALITY OF APES

Wolfgang Köhler

THE MAKING OF IMPLEMENTS

Building

WHEN a chimpanzee cannot reach an objective hung high up with *one* box, there is a possibility that he will pile two or more boxes on top of one another and reach it in that way. Whether he *actually* does this seems a simple question that can soon be decided. But if experiments are made, it is quickly seen that the problem for the chimpanzee falls into two very distinct parts: one of which he can settle with ease, whilst the other presents considerable difficulties. We think the first is the *whole* problem; where the animal's difficulties begin, we do not, at first, see any problem at all. If in the description this curious fact is to be emphasized as much as it impressed itself on the observer, the report of the experiment should be divided into two parts in accordance with this fact. I shall begin with the answer to the question that seems to be the only one.

In one of the experiments described previously . . . Sultan came very near putting one box on the top of another, when he found one insufficient; but instead of placing the second box, which he had already lifted, upon the first, he made uncertain movements with it in the air around and above the other; then other methods replaced these confused movements. The test is repeated (8.2)*; the objective is placed very high up, the two boxes are not very far away from each other and about four metres away from the objective; all other means of reaching it have been taken away. Sultan drags the bigger of the two

---

*Feb. 2—editor.

boxes towards the objective, puts it just underneath, gets up on it, and looking upwards, makes ready to jump, but does not jump; gets down, seizes the other box, and, pulling it behind him, gallops about the room, making his usual noise, kicking against the walls and showing his uneasiness in every other possible way. He certainly did not seize the second box to put it on the first; it merely helps him to give vent to his temper. But all of a sudden his behaviour changes completely; he stops making a noise, pulls his box from quite a distance right up to the other one, and stands it upright on it. He mounts the somewhat shaky construction, several times gets ready to jump but again does not jump; the objective is still too high for this bad jumper. But he has achieved the essential part of his task.

. . . Some days previously Chica and Grande learnt from Sultan and myself how to use *one* box; they do not yet know how to work with *two*. The situation is the same as in Sultan's experiment. Each of the animals forthwith seizes a box; first Chica, then Grande, will stand under the objective with her box, but there is no sign of an attempt to put one on top of the other. On the other hand, they hardly get up on their own boxes; though their feet are lifted, they put them down again as soon as they glance upwards. It is certainly not a matter of accident, but the result of that upward glance at the objective, when both Chica and Grande proceed to stand the box upright . . .; a measurement of the distance with the eye leads to this change of plan; it is a sudden and obvious attempt to meet the needs of the situation. Finally, Grande seizes her box and tears about the room with it, in a rage, as Sultan did before. Just as he did, she calms down un-expectedly, pulls her box close to the other one, after a glance at the objective, lifts it with an effort, puts it clumsily on the lower one, and quickly tries to get up on it; but when the upper box slips to one side during this operation, she makes no move, and lets it fall altogether, quite discouraged. In principle Grande solved the problem too, so the box is lifted by the observer, placed firmly on the lower one, and held there, while Grande climbs up and reaches the objective. But she does all this with the greatest mistrust.

(22.2) Grande, Chica, and Rana are present. Grande carries first one, then the other box underneath the objective, but handles them in such a way as to create the impression that she is perplexed; she does not put one box on the other. This looks very like the condition of "lack of direction" which sometimes influenced Sultan and Chica when dealing with the two bamboo sticks. Suddenly Chica springs up beside Grande, puts one box on the other without further delay, and gets up on top. It is hard to say whether this was an after-effect of the previous attempt and Grande's example, or an independent solution, helped perhaps by Grande's "messing around".

A new objective is hung up; Rana now puts one of the boxes flat underneath the objective and the second one immediately on top of it (also flat); but the arrangement is too low, and the animals prevent each other from improving it, as they now all want to build on their own, and at the same time. Knowing Rana, I am inclined to assume that this is a case of imitation of what she has just seen, or, at any rate, what she saw was of great help to her; but this question is not important here.

A number of further experiments, which, however, did not quickly lead to greater assurance, as in other cases, will be described later. After the animals had become accustomed to putting one box on another as soon as the situation called for it, the question arose as to whether they would make further progress in the same direction.

The tests (higher objective, three boxes at some distance) first resulted in Sultan carrying out more difficult constructions, with two boxes on top of each other, perpendicularly so that they looked like columns, and, of course, enabled him to reach very high (8.4); he took the third box, to begin with, to the place of construction, but left it standing beside him without using it, as he could then reach the objective by means of his column without it.

(9.4) The objective hangs still higher up; Sultan has fasted all the forenoon and, therefore, goes at his task with great zeal. He lays the heavy box flat underneath the objective, puts the second one upright upon it, and, standing on the top, tries to seize the objective. As he does not reach it, he looks down and round about, and his glance is caught by the third box, which may have seemed useless to him at first, because of its smallness. He climbs down very carefully, seizes the box, climbs up with it, and completes the construction.

Grande in particular progressed with time. Of the smaller animals she was the strongest and by far the most patient. She would not allow herself to be diverted by any number of mishaps, the collapse of the structure, or any other difficulties (partly created involuntarily by herself), and soon was able to put three boxes on top of each other, like Sultan. She even managed once (30.7. 1914) a beautiful construction of four boxes when she found a fairly big cage near by, whose flat surface allowed of the addition of the three remaining parts with safety. When, in the spring of 1916, an opportunity was again given for making higher constructions, Grande was sill, even after this long interval, relatively the best of them all and quite as good an architect as before. High constructions composed of four objects gave her some difficulty, but with obstinate effort she managed them with considerable success.

Chica also builds towers composed of three boxes without too many mishaps, but has not become so expert as Grande, because, impatient and quick by nature, she prefers dangerous jumps (with or without a stick) from the floor or from some low structure to the slow process of building. And in these she is often successful, while Grande in her own way has still a good deal of hard work to get done. Rana scarcely gets beyond two boxes. Whenever she has got so far, she stops, and either goes on endlessly trying out miniature vaulting-poles, or else (a frequent occurrence) she places the upper box open side up, and then carries out an irresistible impulse to sit down beside it; once she is there, she feels too comfortable to get up again and to continue building. Konsul never built, Tercera and Tschego got not further than some feeble attempts, Nueva and Koko died before they could be experimented with.

Without doubt, constructions such as those achieved by Grande are considerable feats, especially when one considers that the constructions of insects (ants, bees, spiders) and other vertebrates (birds, beavers), though they may, when finished, be more perfect, yet are built by a very different and much more primitive process, from an evolutionary point of view. The following accounts will show that the difference between the clever but clumsy constructions of a gifted chimpanzee, and the firm and objectively elegantly-spun web of a spider, for instance, is one of *genus,* which, of course, should be obvious from what has been already said. But, unfortunately, I have been asked by otherwise intelligent spectators of these constructions, "whether this is not instinct"? Therefore I feel obliged to emphasize the following particularly: the spider and similar artists achieve true wonders, but the main *special* conditions *for this particular work alone* are within them, long before the incentive to use them occurs. The chimpanzee is not simply provided for life with any special disposition which will help him to attain objects placed high up, by heaping up any building material, and yet he can accomplish this much by his own efforts, when circumstances require it, and when the material is available.

Adult human beings are inclined to overlook the chimpanzee's real difficulty in such construction, because they assume that adding a second piece of building material to the first is only a repetition of the placing of the first one on the ground (underneath the objective); that when the first box is standing on the ground, its surface is the same thing as a piece of level ground, and that, therefore, in the building-up process the only new factor is the actual lifting up. So the only questions seem to be, whether the animals proceed at all "tidily" in their work, whether they handle the boxes very clumsily, and so forth. I myself never expected to be faced, through my observations, by a wider, and very much more important, question. That another special difficulty exists, however, should become obvious from the further details of Sultan's first attempt at building. May I repeat: When Sultan for the first time fetches a second box and lifts it (28.1), he waves it about enigmatically above the first, and does not put it on the other. The second time (8.2) . . . he places it upright on the bottom one, seemingly without any hesitation, but the construction is still too low, as the objective has accidentally been hung too high up. The experiment is continued at once, the objective hung about two metres to one side at a lower spot in the roof, and Sultan's construction is left in its old place. But Sultan's failure seems to have a disturbing after-effect; for a long time he pays no attention at all to the boxes, quite contrary to other cases, where a new solution was found and usually repeated readily (though Koko once forgot a solution). It may well be that for the chimpanzee (as for man) the practical "success" of a method is more important as an estimate of its value, than is really justifiable. (This is judging *ex eventu* in the bad sense.)

[It occasionally happens that one will start working

1095

at a mathematical or physical problem with perfectly correct premises, and calculate or think up to a point where one gets lost. The whole proceeding is then rejected, and only later will one discover that the method was quite right, and that the difficulty was only a superficial one and could easily have been overcome. If, when the difficulty occurred, the logical relations had been the sole determinant, and if these had been carefully examined, the obstacle would at once be found unimportant. The less one takes into consideration all the relevant conditions, the more one will be embarrassed by an apparent failure. And so, it is not surprising that the chimpanzee, who does not grasp certain parts of the situation at all clearly, is influenced just as much by a mistake methodologically unimportant, as by an error in principle, and will then, because subsidiary circumstances spoiled the first attempt, give up the whole thing in despair. Grande furnishes a good example, when she suddenly puts a second box on the first one; the solution is not only objectively good in principle, it also appears with the character of genuineness; but as luck would have it, a corner of the top box is upon a board nailed across the surface of the lower one, so that when the animal begins to climb up, the box slips sideways, and then Grande lets it fall altogether, and shows distinctly by her behaviour that, for her, the *whole method* is now completely spoiled. But such incidents can only happen under one condition, i.e. that one side of the situation is not clearly grasped, and so we arrive at our chief point: the experiment with two boxes involves conditions which the chimpanzee does not quite understand.]

Further on in the experiment a curious incident occurs: the animal reverts to older methods, wants to lead the keeper by his hand to the objective, is shaken off, attempts the same thing with me, and is again turned away. The keeper is then told that if Sultan tries to fetch him again, he is apparently to give in, but, as soon as the animal climbs on his shoulders, he is to kneel down very low. Soon this actually happens: Sultan climbs on to the man's shoulders, after he has dragged him underneath the objective, and the keeper quickly bends down. The animal gets off, complaining, takes hold of the keeper by his seat with both hands, and tries with all his might to push him up. A surprising way to try to improve the human implement!

When Sultan now takes no further notice of the box, since he once discovered the solution by himself, it seems justifiable to remove the cause of his failure. I put the boxes on top of each other for Sultan, underneath the objective, exactly as he had himself done the first time, and let him pull down the objective.

[As to Sultan's effort to push the keeper into an erect position, I should like at the very beginning to rebut the reproach of "misunderstanding", of "reading into the animal"; the procedure has merely *been described,* and there is no possibility at all of its being misunderstood. But lest suspicions should arise, this case being an isolated one (an unjustifiable suspicion in any case, considering that Sultan tries to utilize both the keeper and me, not once, but over and over again, as a footstool), I shall briefly add a description of similar cases: (19.2) Sultan cannot solve a problem, in which the objective is outside the bars beyond reach; I am near him inside. After vain attempts of all sorts, the animal comes up to me, seizes me by the arm, pulls me towards the bars, at the same time pulling my arm with all his might down to himself, and then pushes it through the bars towards the objective. As I do not seize it, he goes to the keeper, and tries the same thing with him. Later (26.3) he repeats this proceeding, with the only difference that he first has to call me with plaintive pleading to the bars, as this time I am standing outside. In this case, as in the first, I offered so much resistance that the animal could barely overcome it, and he did not release me until my hand was actually on the objective; but I did not do him the favour (in the interests of future experiments) of bringing it in.—I must mention further, that one hot day the animals had had to wait longer than usual for their water "course", so that finally they simply grabbed hold of the keeper's hand, foot, or knee, and pushed him with all their strength towards the door, behind which the water-jug usually stood. This became their custom for some time; if the man tried to continue feeding them on bananas, Chica would calmly snatch them out of his hand, put them aside, and pull him towards the door (Chica is always thirsty).—It would be erroneous to consider the chimpanzee unenlightened and stupid in these matters. I must add that the animals understand the human body particularly easily in its local costume of shirt and trousers without any coat. If anything puzzles them, they will investigate it on occasion, and any large change in the manner of dressing or appearance (e.g. a beard) will make Grande and Chica undertake an immediate and very interested examination.]

After the encouraging assistance to Sultan, the boxes are again put aside. A new objective is hung in the same place on the roof. Sultan immediately builds up both boxes, *but at the place where the objective had been hung at the very beginning of the experiment and where his own first construction had stood.* In about a hundred cases of using boxes for building, this is the only one in which a stupidity *of this kind* was committed. Sultan is quite confused while doing this, and is probably quite exhausted, as the experiment has lasted over an hour in this hot place.[1] As Sultan keeps on pushing the boxes to and fro quite aimlessly, they are once more put on top

---

[1] I only noticed later that I used to strain the animals a little too much during the first months; only with time did I develop the slowness of procedure adequate to the apes and to the climate.

of each other underneath the objective; Sultan reaches it, and is allowed to go. Only on *one* occasion did I see him similarly confused and disturbed.

The next day (9.2) it is clear that a particular difficulty must lie in the problem itself. Sultan carries one box underneath the objective, but does not bring the second one; finally it is built up for him and he attains the goal. The new one immediately replacing it (the construction was again destroyed) does not induce him to work at all; he keeps on trying to use the observer as a footstool; so once more the construction is made for him. Underneath the third objective Sultan places a box, pulls the other one up beside it, but stops at the critical moment, his behaviour betraying complete perplexity; he keeps on looking up at the objective, and meanwhile fumbling about with the second box. Then, quite suddenly, he seizes it firmly, and with a decided movement places it on the first. His long uncertainty is in the sharpest contrast to this sudden solution.

Two days later the experiment is repeated; the objective is again hung at a new spot. Sultan places a box a little aslant underneath the objective, brings the second one up, and has begun to lift it, when, all the while looking at the objective, he lets it drop again. After several other actions (climbing along the roof, pulling the observer up) he again starts to build; he carefully stands the first box upright underneath the objective, and now takes great pains to get the second one on top of it; in the turning and twisting, it gets stuck on the lower one, with its open side caught on one of the corners. Sultan gets up on it, and straightaway tumbles with the whole thing to the floor. Quite exhausted, he remains lying in one corner of the room, and from here gazes at both box and objective. Only after a considerable time does he resume work; he stands one box upright and tries to reach his goal thus; jumps down, seizes the second, and finally, with tenacious zeal, succeeds in making it stand upright also, on the first one; but it is pushed so far to one side that, at every attempt to climb up, it begins to topple. Only after a long attempt, during which the animal obviously acts quite blindly, letting everything depend on the success or failure of planless movements, the upper box attains a more secure position, and the objective is attained.

After this attempt Sultan always used the second box at once and, above all, was never uncertain as to where he had to put it.

The report shows that after the first independent solution, the boxes were arranged on top of each other for Sultan *four* times; in the experiments on Grande, Chica, and Rana, I gave the same amount of assistance three times after the first solution, which proved a good incentive to the animals to go on with that method. If I had let them get very hungry and then put them time and again into the same situation, they would probably have developed their building process without this interference. But what seemed to me more important, after my first experiences (instead of trying to see whether the chimpanzees would keep on building without encouragement, proceeding to constructions of three and four parts), was to examine minutely their *method* of building; that was why, after they had once solved the first essentials of the problem, I encouraged them as much as possible to continue.

If putting the second box on the first were nothing more than a repetition of the simple use of boxes (on the ground) on a higher level, one would expect—after the other experiences—that the solution once found would simply be repeated. To Sultan and Grande it is quite a matter of custom—in the days of these experiments—to attain objectives by means of *one* box, as the tests show; but neither succeeded easily in reproducing his *building* methods, and one glance at the description of the experi-

1100

ments will show that the first failure (merely practical) is not alone to be blamed for it. Neither is a quite external factor the chief cause: it is true that the boxes are heavy for the little animals, and there are moments in the course of the experiments when they simply cannot manage the weight. But one has only to see with what energy and success they generally carry and lift their burden, when they build at all, and how completely perplexed they become, too, even when they have the second box high enough (from a human point of view) merely to let it sink on to the lower one, to realize that the animals do *not* omit further building merely on account of the physical effort. Rather, they will be a little clumsy to begin with. But too much stress must not be laid on this; for probably the abandoning of the method after the first trial, is connected, internally, with their other strange behaviour, their sudden fits of perplexity before the two boxes; and this behaviour has nothing to do with clumsiness. The animal does not behave then like somebody accomplishing a task clumsily, but like someone to whom the situation does not offer any definite lead toward a particular action.

This inhibition, perplexity, or whatever one likes to call it, which may befall the animals in their first attempts, when obviously the solution "put second box up" has already appeared and they are proceeding to carry it out, was observed three times in Sultan, twice in Grande, and clearest of all, later (in the spring of 1916) in the adult Tschego, on the occasion when she was to place one box on the other for the first time. I want to emphasize again that at first everything goes well; as soon as the animals are quite familiar with the situation, and are convinced that they cannot attain the objective with *one* box, a moment arrives when the second box is suddenly "drawn into the task". They then drag it up (Tschego) or carry it just to the first box and all of a sudden stop and hesitate. With uncertain movements they wave the second one to and fro over the first (unless they let it drop to the ground immediately, not knowing what to do with it, as Sultan once did) and if you did not know that the animals see perfectly well in the ordinary sense of the word, you might believe that you were watching extremely weak-sighted creatures, that cannot clearly see where the first box is standing. Especially does Tschego keep lifting the second box over the first and waving it about for some time, without either box touching the other for more than a few seconds. One cannot see this without saying to oneself: "Here are two problems; the one ('put the second box up') is not really a difficult task for the animals, provided they know the use to which a box can be put; the other (*add one box to the other, so that it stays there firmly, making the whole thing higher*) *is extremely difficult.*" For therein lies the one essential difference between using one box on the ground and adding a second to the first: In the *former* case, on the homogeneous and shapeless ground, which does not claim any special requirements, a compact form is simply put down or else it is just dragged along (till underneath the objective) without being taken off the ground at all. In the *latter* case a limited body of special shape is to be brought into contact with a similar one, in such a way that a particular result is obtained; and this is where the chimpanzee seems to reach the limit of his capacity.

A glance in retrospect will show immediately that the experiments before described with *one* box only on level ground, get over this difficulty; but they are misleading, and, therefore, cannot give an adequate idea of the chimpanzee. Either the little animal *pulls* his box almost underneath the objective, or he *rolls* it there. In neither case does it matter whether the box is some centimetres or even decimetres to the right, left, in front, or behind. The ground is the same level everywhere, and the objective, in spite of these small differences in position, is easily attainable[1] and, therefore, in the hands of the chimpanzee (who does not see any problem at all) the box automatically, with a few quick movements, reaches a position of equilibrium, in which it can be used. Quite different is the experiment with *two* boxes. Here the chimpanzee already meets a *static problem* which he must solve[2], since the first and second box do not solve it by themselves, as the first box and the level ground did.

[These observations and discussions lead to the conclusion that the chimpanzee will, without effort, place a small box on a very big box under the objective (the surface of the big box being both optically and physically more like the ground); and, as a matter of fact, once, where a big cage formed the lower part of the structure, the second small box was immediately put firmly on top of it.]

There are two kinds of statics involving insight, just as there are ... two ways of mastering lever action. The one kind, the physicist's (centre of gravity, movement of a force, etc.), does not come into question here any more than in those countless cases in which man "correctly" lays or stands some things on others. Unfortunately, psychology has not yet even begun to investigate the physics of ordinary men, which from a *purely biological standpoint,* is much more important than the science itself, as not only statics and the function of the lever, but also a great deal more of physics exist in two forms, and the non-scientific form constantly determines our whole behaviour.

---

[1]Considerable mistakes of this nature, with reference to the objective, are easily and "genuinely" corrected (compare Koko); no factor of shape of any higher degree enters into consideration here, but simply "distance."

[2]Probably he seldom solves it "genuinely"; but it seems remarkable to me that cases occur (as those described) where at least the problem as a problem has an effect upon the chimpanzee and keeps him perplexed, since the solution does not appear. He could, after all, just let the second box drop somehow on to the first, and need not hesitate; uncertainty may also be a good sign, on occasion.

However the naive statics of man may have arisen, even the most superficial observation will show that "gravity" on the one hand and visual forms in space on the other, play just as important a part in it as forces and distances, considered abstractly, in strictly physical statics. At least *one* of those "components" must be in a very undeveloped state in the chimpanzee; for the total impression of all observations made repeatedly on the animals leads to the conclusion that *there is practically no statics to be noted in the chimpanzee.* Almost everything arising as "questions of statics" during building operations, he solves not with insight, but by trying around blindly. And there can be no more striking contrast than that between genuine solutions arrived at suddenly and in one sequence, and the blind groping about with one box on the other, which is the procedure of construction when no lucky chance (like those described above) brings box on box, surface to surface. "Bringing a second box above the first one" (or a third or fourth—not realized as numbers, but as "more" or "others") no doubt still comes into the category of "genuine solutions", but the expression "to set one on top of the other" should be used with great caution, when meant to denote what the chimpanzee really does. These words suggest our (not necessarily scientific) human statics, and the animal possesses extremely little of this.

One may observe very similar facts in the first years of childhood. Very young children also, in attempting to pile one thing on another, try, by holding, and sometimes pressing, one against the other, to fix them in different and often curious positions. It is quite obvious that they too lack that kind of statics. But while human children, when about three years old, begin to develop the elements of this naive physics of equilibrium, the chimpanzee does not seem to make any essential progress in this direction,

1104

even when he has plenty of opportunity to practise. For, although his uncertainty in the sphere of spatial forms and gravity soon discourages him less than at first (when he gives up all effort, in face of the conglomeration of boxes), yet even after success has strengthened his confidence, his gaily-undertaken work remains as much "mere trying" as at the beginning: a turning, pulling, twisting, tipping of the upper box on the lower, so that the animals, especially Grande, arouse admiration by their patience. One must not think that such a construction, even of three boxes only, can be accomplished in a few seconds; the more scope the boxes give for various accidents, the smaller they are, the more boards they are made of, the longer the animals will have to work, and it has happened that Grande kept on building up her structure for ten minutes at a time, then tumbling down with it, beginning again, and so on, until she was quite exhausted, and altogether unable to continue at all.

In the confusion of this method of construction some features are particularly characteristic. If the upper box is brought into a position in which it stands quite satisfactorily from a static point of view, but in which it may still wobble a little (this motion having no significance), it is often taken, or turned, out of this good position, if either hand or foot discover the oscillation; for the optics of the position has here no further noticeable significance for the chimpanzee's control over the situation. If by chance, or in any other way, the upper box comes into any position where it does not for the moment wobble, the chimpanzee will certainly climb up, even though a mere touch or friction at some point has for the moment steadied the box; really it may be quite unsteady and may fall over at once if weight is put on it. Thus Sultan, quite as a matter of course, once tried to climb up on the second box when it was precariously balanced on one corner only of the under one. Whether one box, for example, projects quite far out sideways from the rest of the structure or not, seems to be a matter of indifference to the chimpanzee—and sometimes the third box does not fall, only as long as the fourth and the animal remain on top of it and steady it by their weight. So one sees what happens when the chimpanzee deviates for the first time quite definitely from his optically-led treatment of the situation; probably because it no longer serves to meet his needs. Structures grow under his hand, and often enough he can climb them, but they are structures which, according to the rules of statics, seem to us almost impossible. For all structures that *we* know (and are familiar with optically) are achieved by the apes by chance at best, and, as it were, by the "struggle for not wobbling."

From this description it will be seen that the animals partly replace the missing (everyday) statics of human beings by a third kind—that of their own bodies, which is taken care of automatically by a special neuro-muscular machinery. In this respect, the chimpanzee, it seems to me, is even superior to man, and he obviously draws an advantage from this gift. When he is standing on a structure, the balance of which would fill an onlooker with fear, the first suspicious wobbling of the structure is counteracted in the most masterly fashion by an instantaneous altering of the balance of the body, by lifting his arms, bending his trunk, etc., so that the boxes, under the animal, to a certain extent, share the statics of his labyrinth and cerebellum. It can be said that in a great number of these constructions the animal itself, with the delicately-balanced distribution of its weight, contributes a certain element, without which the structure would collapse. But this is chiefly a *physiological* movement, in the narrower sense of the word; there is no question of a real "solution". I must express a warning against an explanation which is too easy and quite inadequate in face of the actual facts, which would consider the animals

1106

merely too untidy and careless to build anything more stable. The animals' work may make this impression on a novice, but longer observation of the tireless energy which Grande displays—as much in pulling down well-built structures because one part wobbles, as in building up structures which do not statically balance—will convince anyone that the real explanation lies deeper, and that, at least, those animals up till now observed, are chiefly hindered by the limits of their "visual insight"[1].

If the animals cannot even intelligently combine the building materials into one whole, it is not astonishing if they often are unable to understand or deal with an existing structure; for the corresponding (naive) human faculties are missing, and can only be acquired with difficulty; nor is there any question of mere haste or untidiness here. So it will sometimes happen that Grande (and others too), while standing on one box, will try to lift another up in spite of its being open on one side, and a corner of the first box projecting into it. So, at least in part, Grande by her own weight, which rests on both boxes, hinders the lifting of the second box, but in spite of that she takes the greatest pains to drag it up, tearing and shaking it until, in a rage, she finally gives up trying to accomplish what she herself, without realizing it, is preventing. In the same way it may happen that Grande will be standing on a box supported at each end by two others, like pillars,[2] and that then one of the lower boxes

[1]Nueva dealt with shapes in space so much more sensibly than any of the others, that one was led to think that she might have built differently, had she ever got as far as building experiments. That there is an *"optical* weakness" must be taken for granted in any case, because even in the simple "gravitational physics", *"gravity"* is for the most part determined optically.

[2]Such a thing can *only* come about by chance. Not once did the animals purposely pile up their boxes on the *bridge principle*, although in several experiments I tried to suggest such a proceeding to them, by hanging the objective high up, by placing heavy, solid pedestals at its right and left, and laying a stout board handy, so that they had only to place it across in order to reach the objective by standing on its centre. The board was always used (by Sultan and Chica) as a jumping-stick. Similarly all other experiments failed, in which the principle of using *two* factors at the same time plays any role.

will strike her as suitable for building purposes; if she can, she calmly pulls this out at the side, and is very much startled when, together with the box on which she is standing, she tumbles to the ground (as must happen). I saw this even in 1916; there is simply no perceptible improvement.

[On the other hand the animals seem to learn that it is well not to turn the open side of a box upward in building, although this is not a matter of great importance; many constructions were built in which the second box lay firmly across the open end of the first. Nevertheless, this method of construction gradually occurs less and less.

Piling higher boxes on lower ones may be done from the ground or from the protruding edges of the *lower* boxes, but also in such a way that the animal, standing on the *topmost* one, pulls the next box up to it. The former proceeding is generally more practical, since the architect does not stand in his own way, as he easily may in the latter case. The animals all adopted it at the beginning. But in the building activities to be described later, in which the whole company joined, too much depended on keeping possession of the top, and so the second proceeding became customary.]

Sometimes it seems advisable to take one of the facts developed by observation, and demonstrate it in sharp outline by an extreme test. For this purpose the animals were confronted with the following situation: the objective is placed very high, a box lies near by, but the ground underneath the objective is covered with a heap of average-sized stones on which a box can hardly be placed firmly. (11.4 1914) Chica gets up on the stone-heap and endeavours in vain to reach the objective with her hand, and later with the stick; she does not pay any attention to the box, and, after a short time, not even to the objective. A second experiment, several hours later on the same day, proceeds in exactly the same way. This tells us nothing. It seems to me completely impossible that Chica should immediately see the stone-heap as an obstacle, as she never reached such clearness of conception in much ruder obstacle-experiments; in any case she would at least make a try with the box. The test with the most intelligent of the animals, Sultan, had an entirely clear result, in the same situation and on the same day. He immediately pulls the box on to the stone-heap, but does not succeed in making it stand up; he drags a big cage from a distance, tips it onto the stones, sets the first one on top of it, and reaches the objective after fifteen minutes of very hard labour, though on a construction that stands crookedly up in the air. The stones are now heaped up into a pointed pyramid. But this time Sultan, by a series of lucky accidents, fixes his box onto the heap in a certain way in a few minutes, and again reaches the objective. At the third repetition—the pyramid having been built up again—he is not successful, and soon gives up his efforts. He did not make the least attempt, during the experiments, to move the stones and clear a level foundation.

On the following day the stones are replaced by a number of preserve-tins which are laid underneath the objective in rolling position. Sultan immediately seizes the box and attempts to put it on the tins, whereat the box rolls off to the side over and over again. After fussing about with the box for some time, he pushes the tins (accidentally) a little sideways from the objective, so that a free place is made between them, big enough to place the box perpendicularly. But he makes further hard efforts to stand the box on the tins without paying the least attention to this free place. Nothing in his behaviour indicates any endeavour to remove the rolling tins, although he could do it in a few seconds without the least trouble. Finally the box is put accidentally on the ground and partly on the tins, aslant it is true, yet fairly firm, and Sultan reaches the objective. [The experiment with Sultan becomes all the more important as this animal takes out of the box the stones which weigh it down the moment he realizes that it cannot be moved; he thus removes obstacles which he understands to be such. The same earlier experiment also showed that the chimpanzee did not have so much respect for obstacles set up "by the master" that he would not remove them. *This* is an anthropomorphism. Sultan does not consider at all how it comes about that strange objects lie under the objective, and as far as respect goes, he generally reserves that for the moment when, after an offence, the sad consequences actually occur; unless it is a matter which has been frequently forbidden, such as climbing along the wire-netting of the roof; which eventually did not happen often in my presence.]

In March, 1916, the same test was accidentally successful, Grande being the animal experimented with. Chica had in vain jumped for the objective with a short stout tree-trunk, and had then left it lying under the goal. Grande began to build, and at first on free ground; but when, on fussing about with the boxes, one of them tumbled under the objective and thus fell on the trunk, the animal changed its plan, and chose this box as a base. She took all sorts of pains to erect a structure on it, but, all the while, the foundation kept tipping and toppling on the trunk. Grande threw not one glance at the obstacle, any more than Sultan had at the tins.

According to these results, one can construct *a priori* a type of further observations. When the chimpanzee solves problems genuinely, which are only problems of "rough distance" from the goal, and at the same time hardly possesses or learns anything of our naive statics, "good errors" are bound to occur, in which the animal makes real attempts to conquer the distance better—that is the good in it—but unconsciously aims at a static impossibility—that is the error.

The first of these good mistakes was observed in only two cases; it has a startling effect. (12.2) Chica tries in vain, in the first experiments, to attain the objective with one box; she soon realizes that even her best jumps are of no avail, and gives up that method. But suddenly she seizes the box with both hands, holds it by a great effort as high as her head, and now presses it to the wall of the room, close to which the objective hangs. If the box would "stick" to the wall, the problem would be solved; for Chica could easily climb up and reach the goal by standing on it. In the same experiment, later on, Grande puts a box under the objective, lifts her foot to climb, but lets it drop again, discouraged, when she looks up. Suddenly she seizes the box and presses it, still looking up towards the objective, to the wall at a certain height, just as Chica had done. The attempt at solution is genuine: the sequence of movements, from "lifting up the foot" to "pressing the box to the wall" contains an abrupt break between "dropping of the foot" and "seizing the box"; and the proceeding "seizing—resolutely lifting it to about 1 m. high—pressing it to the wall," forms one single whole. Exactly the same applies to Chica's behaviour. It would be a wrong interpretation to say that the animals wanted to knock down the objective with the box. If that were their intention, they would deal with it quite differently, make different movements with it, and would lift the box straight up in the direction of the objective, not press it sideways to the wall, as both did from the very beginning. I will refer again later to this proceeding, for once really containing naive statics, even though chimpanzee-like and extremely primitive. [One might think that Grande was imitating what she had seen Chica do, but this seems very improbable to anyone more familiar with the chimpanzees' power of imitation. Furthermore, Grande's procedure is that of a genuine attempt at solution, and nothing

1111

would be changed if she had copied it; *it is most difficult for chimpanzees to imitate anything, unless they themselves understand it.*]

If the chimpanzee cannot reach his objective from a box placed flat, he often turns it upright, after measuring the distance with a glance. There is a further development of this, which only has the defect that it is not compatible with the laws of statics. The animal stands on one box and places another in front of him and on top of the first, but a glance at the goal shows that the distance is too great. Then the upper of the two boxes is turned and turned again out of its position of equilibrium and "diag-

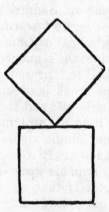

Fig. 1

onally" (cf. Fig. 1); the animal tries meanwhile with grave concentration to ascend the heightened pinnacle. This attempt at solution can be repeated *ad infinitum* as the box certainly moves under the ape's hands, but remains in balance itself, to a certain extent, without much effort on his part. With an amazing stubbornness and minute care, Grande repeated this "good error" for years.

To the preceding two a third example may be added, which, though not concerned with building, contains nevertheless a problem of statics. Chica tries to combine her jumping-stick procedure with building; she either begins her lightning-like climb from the top of the structure while the pole stands beside it, or she tries to prop up the pole *on the boxes,* if the building is firm enough, though, of course, she does not control it visually. If the boxes are so arranged that the top one lies with the opening uppermost, then the highest portions are the narrow edges of the boards composing its sides. *So Chica does not put her pole inside the open box,* but with all care *on its highest portion,* that is, on a point at the edge of the box, a surface about 15 mm. wide. Fortunately the pole always slips down before she has begun to climb properly, or she might easily have a bad fall. She does everything to invite this catastrophe, and always props her pole on the edge. This is a "good" error, arising from understanding of some factors (height and approach to the objective) and complete blank innocence of others (statics).

The setting up of a ladder is, as a task, so like the piling up of boxes that I will pass on to it here. In both cases, when once decided these tools shall be used, there arises the special problem of making them ready for use: a quite independent task of arrangement and statics. However, the ape's treatment of ladders brings out two points not conspicuous in the problem of the boxes.

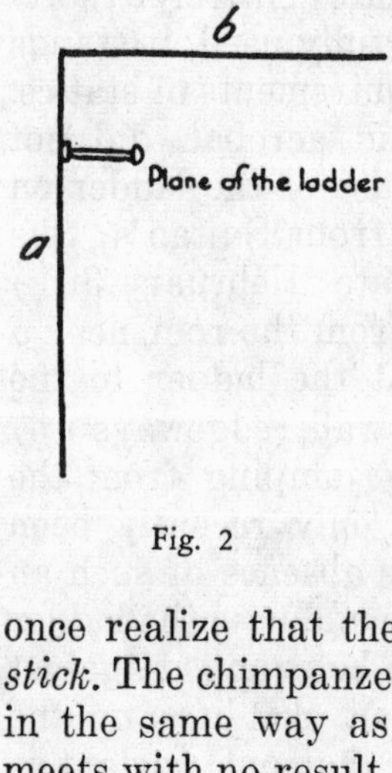

b

Plane of the ladder

a

Fig. 2

When Sultan first made use of the ladder (instead of a box or a table . . .) his handling of it looked very strange. Instead of leaning it against the wall near which the fruit was hanging from the roof, he set it up in the open space directly under the objective in a vertical position, and tried to climb up it. If the observer is already acquainted with the animal's habits, he will at once realize that the ladder is here used as a *jumping-stick.* The chimpanzee tries to use this long wooden frame in the same way as sticks and planks. As this method meets with no result, it is altered. Sultan leans the ladder against the neighboring wall *a* (cf. Fig. 2), but quite differently from the way we do, so that one of the uprights rests against the wall, the plane of the ladder extending into the room. He then ascends the ladder. As

1113

the objective is hung from the roof close to one of the corners of the room, and the animal in mounting the ladder has the other wall *b* close before him, he succeeds on the lower rungs in preserving both the ladder's equilibrium and his own, by resting one arm against the wall *b*. But before he reaches the prize, the ladder falls, and after Sultan has had several such tumbles, he lies still for a while in annoyance. Then he returns to the task, and after long trying, finds a position more similar to that in human use in which he succeeds in climbing the ladder and securing the prize. But in this case, as in the previous efforts, he gives the impression of not aiming at placing the ladder against the wall in a human fashion, but, as far as possible, *fitting it to the wall,* while remaining more or less under the objective. The first tendency is the more pronounced and sometimes predominates entirely: therefore, even when the ladder is successfully used, it stands much *too vertically* for our human requirements of statics.

Grande, the exceedingly indifferent acrobat, did not care to do pole-jumping, and so her use of the ladder on the first occasion differed entirely from Sultan's. She had not been present at his test. (Date: February 3rd.) The objective was again suspended from the roof near a corner of the room. Grande brought the ladder to the spot, laid it horizontally against the wall (edgeways up) and tried to reach the objective by jumping from the upright that lay topmost. She had only recently been initiated into the use of boxes; in the absence of such an article, it is easy to see that she places and uses the ladder as a sort of *defective box,* that has to be propped against the wall. But in the next experiment she lifts up the ladder as Sultan did, in such a way that one upright is propped against the wall and the rungs protrude vertically from it into space. The end of the upright got just enough support against the rough wall to keep it in position, but as Grande began her ascent, it slipped of

1114

course and so did she. Nevertheless she often repeated the effort, keeping to the same position of the ladder until at last and purely by chance, the upright was caught and supported by a little roughness in the wall, long enough for her to climb up (the ladder almost in the air, to our notions) and reach the goal. I repeated this test with, Grande three months later (May 14th). She set up the ladder in almost exactly the same position as before, only at a slightly less vertical angle. The caution and dexterity with which she balanced the swaying of the ladder by movements of her own body, were wonderful and admirable, for as before, the ladder was precariously supported by the end of one upright only, and the whole proceeding looked almost super-static.

Sultan kept to this procedure till 1916. As Chica also prefers this position (and but rarely presses the flat side of the ladder against the wall) this manner of placing it can hardly be mere coincidence. Equally it will be no coincidence that the normal human method of placing a ladder in position was never perfectly carried out— i.e. unmistakably and at once, as a real solution.

1. If we exclude Sultan's attempt to use the ladder as a jumping-stick, we must admit, from the other efforts, that chimpanzees do possess a very modest understanding of statics, and that we can only speak of an *almost* absolute lack of insight in this respect. Both Grande and Chica press a box that is too low, sideways against the wall; they do not try to suspend it *in vacuo*. Sultan, Grande, and Chica try to put the ladder into contact with the wall, as soon as they perceive the need for firmness, but at first contact is purely *visual;* and, therefore, not much depends on whether, in their subsequent attempts, an *actual* and practically useful contact is established as well, as long as the ladder will somehow stick to the wall. Even in their procedure with the jumping-stick the same point could be noticed: none of

1115

the animals tried to hold too short a stick or a second one, added for length . . . simply higher up *in the air;* the end must be in touch with something or, at least appear to be in optical contact. Thus the dangerous venture of Chica in putting the end of her pole on the narrow edge of the open box showed not only lack of clearness in statics, but also, by the very minute attention and precision with which she placed the pole just there, and not blindly *in the air,* a plain static need.

But the pressing of the boxes against the vertical wall proved again that this need has not evolved much beyond visual and physical contact. The placing of the ladder has certainly been decided by the urge to bring about visual contiguity between ladder and wall, and therefore is not the outcome of mere trying around; but since only this visual factor comes into consideration, the procedure remains odd to our eyes. The ladder which is in contact with the wall by the length of one upright, or by the whole face of the rungs, is *optically in closer contact* than if it were supported at four points—the two extremities of each upright—as in our human fashion. It is then statically rightly placed, but probably appears to the chimpanzee to be "not firm", just as *his* favourite position does to *us.* Unfortunately this visual factor, too, is never fully evolved: in box-piling there is no attempt at a real fitting of forms, and even "rough contact" is ignored to some extent when, for example, boxes project considerably beyond their pedestals. There is probably, in problems in which full insight will not in any case be attained, a tendency to neglect even the possible degree, and so the ape merely "tries around." In the case of the ladder the task is a little easier: the relation "homogeneous wall—simple total shape of the ladder" is more easily comprehensible to an ape than the relation of two boxes. Here, a certain statics of contact is quite indisputable, though it varies from human ideas and is

1116

very "unpractical." The particular position of the ladder with one upright against the wall and the rungs projecting vertically into space is probably determined by the *position of the fruit*. Had the first tests in this series been arranged with the objective attached to the wall, pressing the rungs of the ladder to the wall would perhaps have been the only procedure adopted.[1]

[As this essay treats as little as possible of theory, I will give only a brief suggestion of the manner in which the habits of the chimpanzee positively hinder the evolution of statics. We know[2] that in human beings the absolute visual orientation in space which makes complete reversal of forms appear as a strong alteration, develops gradually in children. The hypothesis that this (normal) *absolute spatial orientation,*[3] this fixed "above" and "below," is a product of the *habitual* upright posture of our heads, appears plausible, whether we wish to attribute the formation of these facts to "experience", or (like the author) are inclined to admit a direct physiological influence of gravity upon the optical processes in certain parts of the working nervous system (as in this upright posture). In any case, we should not have developed *this absolute orientation in space* to such an extent, if we, like the chimpanzees held our heads just as often in other positions as vertically erect. If we consider the fundamental dependence of our statics on the generally firm orientation of "above" and "below", the "vertical" and "horizontal" (a child too has no statics as long as it lacks this absolute orientation), it will be evident that the chimpanzee lives under very unfavourable circumstances to the development of statics.

On the other hand, his natural life is eminently calculated to exercise the functions of the labyrinth and

---

[1]Subsequent tests about this point gave no definite results.
[2]W. Stern, *Zeitschrift fur angewandte Psychologie,* 1909; F. Oetjen, *Zeitschr. f. Psychol.,* vol. 71, 1915.
[3]M. Wertheimer, *Zeitschr. f. Psychol.,* vol. 61, p. 93 seq.

cerebellum, and to make him so muscularly dexterous and agile that the least expert acrobat among chimpanzees need not fear human rivalry. Thus in the manipulations with ladders and boxes, he lacks a powerful incentive to the development of statics, for he is physically able to cope with structures to which no human adult would trust himself.]

2. When an inexperienced observer comes into contact with the chimpanzees and wishes to test them in any way, his method is, very often, to give them carefully designed and specialized human implements, e.g. ladders, hammers, tongs, etc., and to inquire whether they utilize these. And then, if such an inexperienced observer sees a chimpanzee using a ladder, he is amazed at the high degree of intelligence and development displayed. But we must quite distinctly understand that the chimpanzee is *not using a "ladder" in the human sense* of the term (which connotes both a special *form* and a special *function*), and that, for the ape, a ladder has no particular advantages over a strong plank, a pole, or a tree-trunk, all of which he utilizes in much the same way,[1] for he only apprehends the rough qualities of the whole object and its most primitive functions.

But the observer is far less impressed by the utilization of tree-trunk, pole or plank, just because he was dazzled and misled by the *external* "humanness" of the chimpanzee's employment, of a "real ladder", though the trunk, pole, and plank are, for the chimpanzee, absolutely equivalent to the ladder. We must be very careful in this case, as always in investigating the ape's nature, *to distinguish between the external impression of humanness—possibly only due to the instrument used—and the*

---

[1]This, although he certainly *sees them as "different things"* and, as this whole book proves, does not simply pass through diffuse streams of phenomena. (Volkelt, *Vorstellungen der Tiere* (1914)—where lower forms of animal life are considered). I admit that the objects perceived by the chimpanzee have not all the qualities of *our* objects.

degree of insight and the level of achievement displayed.
The two are not, by any means, necessarily parallel. I
must explicitly state, in order to dispel any misconceptions, that I do not recognize any difference in value
between the employment of a ladder and of a jumping-
stick by the chimpanzees; and I consider that there is
only a minute difference in that respect between the
placing of a ladder *under the objective,* and the same
procedure with a strong plank. Ladder and board are both
utilized in the same manner and are *practically the same*
to the chimpanzee, as he grips with his feet. For us
humans, they are quite different, and while the chimpanzee's jumping-stick would be a wretched implement for
most human beings, it is even more convenient for the
chimpanzee than the ladder. External resemblance to
human procedure is no criterion here.

We must always first consider the *function* of the tool,
the purpose and manner in which it is used *by the chimpanzee;* we must analyse and determine what qualities
and properties he *realizes.* And, having learnt the *range
of functions,* within whose limits the chimpanzee is able
to understand the utility of any object, we shall prefer
to investigate his achievements and methods of arriving
at his solutions in this clear and simple domain, instead
of bringing him into contact with the complex products
of human craftsmanship. For in such products—e.g. even
in ladders, hammers, tongs—there are combined a great
number of delicate functional points of view. The ape will
always leave uncomprehended and unrecognized full half
of what to us, are the essential requisites in such a tool.
He will make, on the one hand, an impression of dullness
or confusion, because he uses the tool wrongly, and, on
the other, he will look imposingly "human", just because
he "handles ladders, hammers, and tongs." The experimental tests furnish clearer and more valuable results,
both for the estimate of the chimpanzee's stage of

1119

development and for the psychological theories one wishes to base on such research, if we do not employ as "material" the complicated tools of human invention, but confine ourselves to the most primitive objects— primitive both as regards form and function. Otherwise we only confuse both the animals and ourselves as observers. Only as long as the region of simple intelligent treatment of the surroundings is not even superficially investigated, can one fail to see that we must study the simplest functions which can be grasped with insight, before the animals are overwhelmed with whole conglomerations of problems at once.

The position is somewhat different in respect of another class of problems: when there is no longer a question of discovering what the chimpanzee is able to achieve by his unaided efforts. When once we are to some extent in a position to judge this, we can pass on to further tests with more intricate conditions and material, in which we offer him all possible teaching and assistance, in order to see how far he learns to understand. We human beings, too, did not discover all the methods of acting intelligently in a day, but learnt much by the aid of instruction. And so it would be a significant problem to solve, whether the chimpanzee could learn to comprehend the human use of the ladder, or whether eventually he could—with human help—realize the essential function of a pair of tongs.

Supplement: Building in Common.

After the chimpanzees available in our researches were already familiar with the process of piling one box on another, the whole group was often afforded opportunity to build up boxes towards an objective suspended at a considerable height in the playground. In time this became a favourite amusement. But we must not suppose that this "co-operative building" represents any systematic collaboration, with any strict division of labour

1120

among individuals. This is, rather, the procedure: The objective is hung in position, and the assembled chimpanzees gaze around for material to use as tools. In a minute they have all rushed under it, one with a pole, another armed with a box; sometimes they drag their tools along the ground, but Chica prefers to lift her box up in her arms or to balance her plank on her shoulder like a workman. Then several of the animals want to ascend at the same time, each behaves as if he alone were about to "build", or had himself erected any "pediment" that may exist, and wished to complete the structure quite unaided. If one ape has already begun this constructional exercise, with others building close beside him, as frequently happens, a box is unhesitatingly pilfered from the neighbour's store and the rival architects come to blows; this is apt to interrupt the progress of the work, as the higher the structure, the keener the competition to mount it. The result is generally that the object of the struggle is itself destroyed in the struggle—knocked over in the melee. So the melee. So the apes have to start again from the beginning, and thus, Chica, Rana, and Sultan often give up the labour and struggle, while Grande, the oldest, strongest, and most patient of the four, is left to complete it. In this way she has gradually acquired the most skill in building, although the more impatient animals, Chica and Sultan, are distinctly superior to her in intelligence.

It is only rarely that one animal *helps* another, and when this happens, we must carefully consider the meaning of such action. As Sultan was much more expert than the others, in the beginning, he was often obliged to be present without helping, as I wished to ascertain the capabilities of the others. If the observer's vigilance is at all relaxed, and the veto on building not continuously renewed, Sultan does not venture to enter fully into the work, but he cannot keep from "lending a hand" here and there, supporting a box that threatens to fall under some adventurous and decisive sort of another animal, or otherwise taking a less important part in the work. On one occasion when we had forbidden him to participate in the building, he could not keep to the role of passive spectator, when Grande had piled one box on the other, and was still unable to reach the prize. He quickly fetched a third box from a distance of about twelve metres and put it close to the pile; *then he squatted down again and watched,* although he had not been reminded of my prohibition by either word or gesture[1]. But we must guard against misconceptions: Sultan's motive is not the wish to help his fellow, at least not predominantly. When we watch him, squatting beside the other animal, following all Grande's movements with his eyes and often with slight sketchy movements of arm and hand, there can be no doubt that these proceedings *in themselves interest him,* and to a very high degree; that he follows and "feels" the movements himself, and all the more keenly as they grow more difficult and crucial. The "help" he offers at the critical moment is simply *a heightening of his already indicated participation in the process;* and interest in the other animal can play only a very secondary part, for Sultan is a pronounced egoist. We are all acquainted with similar states of mind. It is difficult for anyone who, as a result of long practice understands any form of work, to stand aside while another bungles it: his fingers itch to intervene and "do the job". And we human beings, too, are far from wishing to help such a bungler from motives of pure altruism (our feelings towards him at the moment are not particularly cordial). Neither do we see some external advantage for ourselves: *the work* attracts and dominates us. Sometimes I think that in these traits of character

---

[1] I have already said what is necessary on the subject of "reading into" and "anthropomorphism". There was no ambiguity whatever in Sultan's behaviour on this occasion.

the chimpanzee resembles us even more closely than in the realm of intelligence in the narrower sense;—but we should be on our guard against a mere *intellectualist* interpretation of them. (A fine example of this resemblance in minor traits is the habit of "passing on" a punishment that has been suffered to an habitually unpopular or uncongenial animal: Sultan often does this to Chica.)

Sometimes the behaviour of the animals strongly resembles collaboration in the strictly human sense, without, however, entirely carrying conviction. (Date: 15th February.) The little ones had made repeated efforts to reach an elevated objective, without success. At some distance stood a heavy cage, which had never before been used in the tests. Suddenly Grande's attention was caught by this cage; she shook it to and fro, to turn it over and roll it towards the objective. but could not move it. Rana forthwith came up, and laid hold of the cage in the most adequate way, and the two were in the act of lifting and rolling it, when Sultan joined them and, seizing one side of the cage, "helped" with great energy. Alone, none of the three could have stirred the cage from its place, but under their united efforts—which were "timed" together perfectly—it rapidly approached the goal. It was still at a little distance when Sultan bounded upon it and then, with a second spring, secured and tore down the fruit. The others received no reward, but then, they had worked for themselves and not for Sultan, who had good reason to take a sudden dash forward, for otherwise he might have been "done out of it." Rana certainly understood Grande's intentions when she first began to move the distant cage, and took a hand in her own interests just as Sultan did. As all three had the same aim, and as the moving cage prescribed to all of them the form of procedure, the box was rapidly rolled on its way.

1123

The following examples are pendants to Sultan's behaviour when he saw others building and was excluded from the competition. As he is, generally speaking, much in advance of the other animals, he is sometimes permitted to be present when they are undergoing tests with which he is already familiar. He pays close attention—as in the building experiments—but is not allowed to take part. If the test is one in which the animal under observation is on the opposite side of a grating—for Sultan watches from *outside* the bars—and the objective is outside on the ground, no stick being available, Sultan watches the other animal's ill-adapted efforts quietly for a time. Then he disappears, to return with a stick in his hand. With this stick he scrapes sand together, at a distance from the objective, but near the bars, or pokes through the bars. If the other ape tries to grasp it, he pulls it away seemingly to tease, and thus there develops a to and fro game, *which tends to leave the stick in the neophyte's hand, if no prohibition on my part intervenes.*

In one of these tests the neophyte could have supplied himself with a stick by breaking up the lid of a box which stood near the bars. Sultan was sitting outside, but the other chimpanzee failed to solve the problem. Suddenly Sultan began to shuffle towards the bars, until he was quite close to them. He cast a few cautious glances at the observer, stretched his hand between the bars, and tore a loose board from the lid. The further course of this test was an exact repetition of the one just described.

In both cases, as in the building examples, Sultan's behaviour shows no trace of "altruism", but, though he takes no part in the procedure, we feel his complete comprehension of it, and his imperative impulse to *do something* towards the solution which remains so long undiscovered.

It is clearly proved by the following instance that he really sees the task to be carried out, *from the standpoint*

1124

of the other animal. I was endeavouring to teach Chica the use of the double stick. I stood outside the bars, Sultan squatted at my side, and gazed seriously, slowly scratching his head meanwhile. As Chica absolutely failed to realize what was required, I finally gave the two sticks to Sultan, in the hope that he would make things clear. He took the sticks, fitted one into the other, and did not himself appropriate the fruit, but pushed it, in a leisurely manner, towards Chica at the bars. (Had he been very hungry, his behaviour would probably have been quite different.)

Mutual obstruction is more frequent than co-operation. Tercera and Konsul do not take part in the building operations; they sit on some point of vantage, and watch the others at work. But when the building is in full swing, they give striking proof of their comprehension. They love to creep up behind the back of the busy architect, especially when he is perched precariously high, and, with one vigorous push knock both building and constructor to the ground. They then flee at top speed. Konsul was a master of this game as well as of every grotesque contortion. With an expression of comic rage, stamping, rolling his eyes and gesticulating, he prepared his fell design behind the innocent constructor. It is impossible to describe happenings of this sort; I have seen observers shed tears of helpless mirth as they watched them.

The emotional foundation of this behaviour is a little difficult to understand; in that described below it seems clearer and also has been frequently observed. One of the animals has just completed his building; then suddenly another, the redoubtable Grande for instance, approaches, with unmistakable intent to use the first animal's efforts for her own advantage. A pitched battle seems inadvisable, but the smaller animal does not at once take to flight, leaving the field clear. Instead, he sits on the edge of the topmost box and slides off it in such

1125

a way that the whole structure overbalances and collapses. This proceeding differs totally from that usually adopted in descending and must be intentional; flight follows and rage on the part of the outwitted aggressor.

WOLFGANG KÖHLER (b.-Reval, Estonia, Jan. 21, 1887.)

Köhler studied at the University of Tübingen (1905-1906); at Bonn (1906-1907). He received his Ph.D. from the University of Berlin in 1909. In 1910 he was appointed Assistant to Schumann at the University of Frankfurt. In 1912 he became Privatdozent. In 1913, the Prussian Academy of Sciences appointed him director of the Anthropoid Research Station on the Spanish island of Tenerife, which position he held from late 1913 to the early summer of 1920.* The Academy had set up the Research Station at Tenerife because the climate was supposed to be comfortable for both the apes and the scientific investigator. Köhler returned to the University of Berlin in 1920 as Substitute Director of the Psychology Institute. In 1922, he was appointed Professor of Psychology and Director of the Institute at Berlin. During this period he was Visiting Professor of Clark University, 1925-1926. In the fall of 1934, he left Berlin and delivered the William James lectures at Harvard. At this time, he came permanently to the United States, to Swarthmore College, as Professor of Psychology. In 1945 he was appointed Research Professor in Psychology and Philosophy at Swarthmore, where he is today.

Köhler is perhaps one of the greatest scientists of the century. Few men of this century have held the basic philosophical issues in such a clear grasp while at the same time conducting the most complex and adroit experiments in physiological psychology. Köhler's ability to disentangle the great continuing nexus of psychological and physiological facts, and to spread before us the hidden assumptions, the historical prejudices, and the philosophical nuances, is unique. He is unsurpassed as experimenter, teacher, and philosopher. His work at Tenerife set entirely new standards in the fields of comparative psychology and animal behavior. It is, to this day, the most important single body of experiments within the Gestalt School, and has major ramifications for perception and learning theory. The full implications

---

*To clear up a misunderstanding of many people (e.g. Sargent, S. S. *Basic teachings of the great psychologists*. N.Y.: Barnes and Noble, Inc., 1944, p. 322; Murphy, G. *Historical introduction to modern psychology*. N. Y.: Harcourt and Brace, 1949, p. 291 says Kohler was "marooned"; as do others): during World War I Kohler was "never interned by the Spanish or anybody else". (private communication to the Editor).

of this work for educational theory are yet to be drawn. In addition, Köhler's philosophical writings (v.i.) constitute the fundamental arguments on which the Gestalt School is based.

The present selection is one of the most fascinating chapters from Köhler's work with the apes at Tenerife.

KÖHLER, W. *The mentality of apes.* London: Routledge and Kegan Paul, Ltd., 1948 (1925, 1921, 1917). Trans. E. Winter, from the 2nd German edition (1927, 1925). Chap. V, 2: "The making of implements-building" (pp. 135-172). This selection is reprinted substantially complete by permission of the publisher.

See also:

KÖHLER, W.

a) *Die physischen Gestalten in Ruhe und im stationären Zustand. Eine naturphilosophische Untersuchung.* Braunschweig: Vieweg, 1920. In part translated in Ellis, W. D. *A sourcebook in Gestalt Psychology.* N. Y.: Harcourt, Brace and Co., 1939, p. 17-54.

b) *The place of value in a world of facts.* N. Y.: Liveright Pub. Co., 1938. The William James lectures.

c) *Dynamics in psychology.* N. Y.: Liveright Pub. Co., 1940.

d) *Gestalt psychology: an introduction to new concepts in modern psychology.* N. Y.: Liveright Pub. Co., 1947 (1929).

e) The American Psychological Association Distinguished Scientific Contribution Awards for 1956. *Amer. J. Psychol.* 1957, 12 (a): 125-133. This contains a bibliography of Köhler's writing to date, on pp. 132-133.

MURCHISON (b—Vol. 2, p. 441-442; b—Vol. 3, p. 827-837).

PERCEPTION: AN INTRODUCTION TO THE *GESTALT-THEORIE*.

KURT KOFFKA

When it was suggested to me that I should write a general critical review of the work recently carried on in the field of perception, I saw an opportunity of introducing to American readers a movement in psychological thought which has developed in Germany during the last ten years. In 1912 Wertheimer stated for the first time the principles of a *Gestalt-Theorie* which has served as the starting point of a small number of German psychologists. Wherever this new method of thinking and working has come in touch with concrete problems, it has not only showed its efficiency, but has also brought to light startling and important facts, which, without the guidance of this theory, could not so easily have been discovered.

The *Gestalt-Theorie* is more than a theory of perception: it is even more than a mere psychological theory. Yet it originated in a study of perception, and the investigation of this topic has furnished the better part of the experimental work which has been done. Consequently, an introduction to this new theory can best be gained, perhaps, by a consideration of the facts of perception.

Since the new point of view has not yet won its way in Germany, it is but fair to state at the outset that the majority of German psychologists still stands aloof. However, much of the work done by other investigators contains results that find a place within the scope of our theory. Accordingly I shall refer to these results as well as to those secured by the *Gestalt*-psychologists proper; for I wish to demonstrate the comprehensiveness of our theory by showing how readily it embraces a number of facts hitherto but imperfectly explained. For the same

1128

reason I shall occasionally go farther back and refer to older investigations. On the other hand, I cannot hope to give a complete survey of the work on perception, and I shall therefore select my facts with reference to my primary purpose.

Since my chief aim is to invite a consideration of the new theory, I shall try first of all to make my American readers understand what the theory purports to be. So far there exists no general presentation of the theory which marshals all the facts upon which it rests; indeed, the general field of psychology has not, as yet, been treated from this point of view. For this reason the understanding of the theory has met with serious difficulties, and numerous misunderstandings have occasioned a great deal of the disapprobation which the theory has met. And yet, a theory which has admittedly inspired so many successful investigations may surely claim the right to be at least correctly understood.

My plan in detail is the following: After giving a short sketch of the chief concepts of current psychology as they present themselves to the mind of a *Gestalt*-psychologist, I shall introduce the newer concepts by demonstrating how appropriate they are in the solution of a very old psychological problem. I shall then proceed by developing a fundamental distinction made by the new theory which is quite contrary to the traditional view, and I shall also show the wide application of this distinction. . . .

When I speak of perception in the following essay, I do not mean a specific psychical function; all I wish to denote by this term is the realm of experiences which are not merely "imagined," "represented," or "thought of." Thus, I would call the desk at which I am now writing a perception, likewise the flavor of the tobacco I am now inhaling from my pipe, or the noise of the traffic in the street below my window. That is to say, I

wish to use the term perception in a way that will exclude
all theoretical prejudice; for it is my aim to propose a
theory of these everyday perceptions which has been
developed in Germany during the last ten years, and to
contrast this theory with the traditional views of psychology. With this purpose in mind, I need a term that
is quite neutral. In the current textbooks of psychology
the term perception is used in a more specific sense, being
opposed to sensation, as a more complex process. Here,
indeed, is the clue to all the existing theories of perception which I shall consider in this introductory section,
together with a glance at the fundamental principles of
traditional psychology. Thus I find three concepts, involving three principles of psychological theory, in every
current psychological system. In some systems these are
the only fundamental concepts, while in others they are
supplemented by additional conceptions; but for a long
time the adequacy of these three has been beyond dispute.
The three concepts to which I refer are those of *sensation, association,* and *attention.* I shall formulate the
theoretical principles based upon these concepts and indicate their import in a radical manner so as to lay bare
the methods of thinking which have been employed in
their use. I am fully aware, of course, that most, if not all,
the writers on this subject have tried to modify the assertions which I am about to make; but I maintain, nevertheless, that in working out concrete problems these
principles have been employed in the manner in which I
shall state them.

I

Sensation: All present or existential consciousness
consists of a finite number of real, separable (though not
necessarily separate) elements, each element corresponding to a definite stimulus or to a special memory-residuum
(see below). Since a conscious unit is thus taken to be a
bundle of such elements, Wertheimer, in a recent paper

1130

on the foundations of our new theory, has introduced the name "bundle-hypothesis" for this conception (65). These elements, or rather, some of them, are the sensations, and it is the first task of psychology to find out their number and their properties.

The elements, once aroused in the form of sensations, may also be experienced in the form of images. The images are also accepted as elements or atoms of psychological textures and are distinguishable from sensations by certain characteristic properties. They are, however, very largely a dependent class, since every image presupposes a corresponding sensation. Thus the concept of image, though not identical with that of sensation, rests upon the same principle, namely, the bundle-hypothesis.

In accordance with the method by which sensations have been investigated, it has been necessary to refer to the stimulus-side in defining the principle which underlies this concept. More explicitly, this relation of the sensation to its stimulus is expressed by a generally accepted rule, termed by Köhler the "constancy-hypothesis" (34); that the sensation is a direct and definite function of the stimulus. Given a certain stimulus and a normal sense-organ, we know what sensation the subject must have, or rather, we know its intensity and quality, while its "clearness" or its "degree of consciousness" is dependent upon still another factor, namely, *attention.*

What the stimulus is to the sensation, the residuum is to the image. Since each separate sensation-element leaves behind it a separate residuum, we have a vast number of these residua in our memory, each of which may be separately aroused, thus providing a certain independence of the original arrangement in which the sensations were experienced. This leads to the theory of the "association mixtures" (*associative Mischwirkungen*) propounded by G. E. Müller (44) and carried to the extreme in a paper by Henning (14).

2. Association: Even under our first heading we have met with the concept of memory. According to current teaching, the chief working principle of memory is association, although the purest of associationists recognize that it is not the only principle. It may suffice to point out in this connection that Rosa Heine (12) concludes from experiments performed in G. E. Müller's laboratory, that recognition is not based upon association; for she failed to detect in recognition any trace of that retroactive inhibition which is so powerful a factor in all associative learning. Likewise, Muller himself, relying upon experiments by L. Schluter (54) acknowledges the possibility of reproduction by similarity. Yet, despite all this, association holds its position as the primary factor governing the coming and the going of our ideas, and the law of association is based upon the sensation-image concept. Our train of thought having been broken up into separate elements, the question is asked by what law does one element cause the appearance of another, and the answer is, association, the tie that forms between each element and all those other elements with which it has ever been in contiguity. As Wertheimer (65) again has pointed out, the core of this theory is this, that the necessary and sufficient cause for the formation and operation of an association is an original existential connection—the mere coexistence of a and b gives to each a tendency to reproduce the other. Meaning, far from being regarded as one of the conditions of association, is explained by the working of associations, which in themselves are meaningless.

Another feature of this theory is its statistical nature. At every moment, endless associations are working, reinforcing and inhibiting each other.[3] Since we can never

---

[3]That the facts of reinforcement and inhibition are far from fitting into the theory can be mentioned only incidentally. The reader is referred to the work of Shepard and Fogelsonger (58), and to that of Fringa (8).

have a complete survey of all the effective forces, it is impossible in any single case to make accurate prediction. As the special laws of association can be discovered by statistical methods only, so our predictions can be only statistical.

3. Attention: It is a recognized fact, that, clear and simple as association and sensation appear to be, there is a good deal of obscurity about the concept of attention.[4] And yet, wherever there is an effect that cannot be explained by sensation or association, there attention appears upon the stage. In more complex systems attention is the makeshift, or the scapegoat, if you will, which always interferes with the working out of these other principles. If the expected sensation does not follow when its appropriate stimulus is applied, attention to other contents must have caused it to pass unnoticed, or if a sensation does not properly correspond to the stimulus applied, the attention must have been inadequate, thus leading us to make a false judgment. We meet with like instances over and over again which justify the following general statement, that attention must be added as a separate factor which not only influences the texture and the course of our conscious processes, but is also likely to be influenced by them.

Modern psychology has endeavored to give a physiological foundation to its psychological conceptions. Let us therefore glance at the physiological side of these three principles. The substratum of sensation (and image) is supposed to be the arousal of a separate and circumscribed area of the cortex, while the substratum for association is the neural connection established between such areas. Again attention holds an ambiguous position, for some see its essence as a facilitation and some as an inhibition of the nervous processes. Without going more into detail, let us examine the nature of this psycho-

---

[4]Compare Titchener's recent discussion (62).

physical correspondence. Methodologically the physiological and the psychological aspects of these three principles are in perfect harmony; the cortex has been divided into areas, the immediate experience has been analyzed into elements, and connections are assumed to exist between brain areas as between the elements of consciousness. Furthermore, the nervous processes may be altered functionally and their corresponding psychological elements are subject to the functional factor of attention. Evidently the psychological and the physiological are interdependent, and are not sensation, association, and attention, factual? Do not cortical areas exist, and likewise nervous tracts, and the facilitation and inhibition of excitations? Certainly facts exist which have been interpreted in these ways, but we believe it can be proved that this interpretation is insufficient in the face of other and more comprehensive facts. Furthermore, we maintain that the insufficiency of the older theory cannot be remedied by supplementing the three principles, but that these must be sacrificed and replaced by other principles. It is not a discovery of the *Gestalt-psychologie* that these three concepts are inadequate to cover the abundance of mental phenomena, for many others have held the same opinion, and some have even begun experimental work with this in mind. I need but mention v. Ehrenfels and the Meinong school as one instance, Kulpe and Wurzburg school as another. But they all left the traditional concepts intact, and while trying to overcome the difficulties by the expedient of adding new concepts, they could not check the tendency involved in these new concepts to modify the old ones. I must, however, warn the reader not to confound the old term of *Gestalt-Qualitat* with the term *Gestalt* as it is employed in the new theory. It was to avoid this very confusion that Wertheimer in his first paper avoided the term (64) and introduced a totally neutral expression for the perception of movement—the *phi-phenomenon.*

1134

Just a line at this point upon certain recent tendencies in American psychology. Behaviorism, excluding as it does all forms of consciousness from its realm, strictly speaking denies the use of these three principles altogether. Therefore we do not find the terms attention and sensation in the behaviorist's writings, and even association has disappeared from the explanation in the sense of a tie that can be formed as an original act. And yet, as I have shown in a paper which discusses the fundamental differences between Wertheimer's theory and that of Meinong and Benussi (26), despite the restriction in his use of terms, the outfit of the Behaviorist is essentially the same as that of the traditional psychologist. He says "reaction" where the latter said "sensation," and in so doing includes the effector side of the process, but apart from this he builds his system in exactly the same manner, joining reflex arcs to reflex arcs entirely in accordance with the method of the "bundle-hypothesis."

However, I find a radical abandonment of this hypothesis in Rahn's monograph (52) and also in a recent paper by Ogden (48). With both of these I can in large measure agree, and both of these writers, it seems to me, could readily assimilate the fundamental working principle of the *Gestalt-Psychologie*.

II

In order to demonstrate the clash of the old and new methods of thinking, I have chosen a very elementary example, which I have discussed in a recent paper (30). No field of psychological research, perhaps, has been better clarified than that pertaining to the differential threshold and Weber's Law. Yet when we come to the theory, we are far from finding unanimity among psychologists. I need but recall to the reader's mind Stumpf's famous old argument (60) which, abbreviated, may be stated in the following form: It is always possible to produce three sensations, a, b, and c, so that a and b are judged equal, likewise b and c, whereas a and c are judged to be different (either a $>$ b or b $>$ a). Stumpf concludes that in reality a $\neq$ b and b $\neq$ c, that is to say, our judgments of equality were based upon our incapacity to *notice* very small yet actual differences, the consequence of this conclusion being that the differential threshold as measured by our methods appears to be a fact, not of sensation, but of our capacity of perceiving. Others, such as Cornelius, Ebbinghaus, Titchener, have not been so ready to abandon the sensationalistic interpretation. The explanations of Ebbinghaus and Titchener may be summarized in the word "friction." The nervous excitation corresponding to sensation *a* has a certain amount of inertia, so that a second but slightly different stimulus is incapable of arousing a slightly different sensation, but only the first sensation *a*. If, however, we apply a stimulus that is considerably different, the inertia will be overcome, and a different sensation result. This, at the first flush, would appear to be a sufficient explanation, but for the following result: When we apply two slightly different stimuli a $>$ b a great number of times, we get four different kinds of judgment: (1) a equals b; (2) a $>$ b; (3) a $<$ b; (4) uncertain. Now the "friction" theory, although it covers 2 and 4, does not explain case 3.

Two attempts have been made to overcome this difficulty. The first is G. E. Müller's theory of the "chance-error" (43) which maintains that the final result of a stimulus is never the effect of this stimulus alone, for there are external or internal processes always at work to modify either the sensation itself or our apprehension of it (In so far, Müller's theory is in harmony with Stumpf's unnoticed sensations). Therefore it may well happen that though a $>$ b, a$-d <$ b$+d$. According to Müller, one of the causes of these chance processes is attention.

To understand the second attempt, made by Cornelius (4), we must analyze the "friction" and the "chance-error" hypotheses in their interpretation of Stumpf's paradox. Stumpf introduced his "function of perceiving" in order to avoid a contradiction. If a=b and b=c, it is contradictory that a $\neq$ c. However, the whole argument rests upon a tacit assumption. We have three different stimuli in a > b > c. According to the classic theories a sensation corresponds to each of these; let us call them *a, b, c*. Now in reality we have also three different sets of experiments (or groups of experiments): *a* compared with *b, b* compared with *c*, and *a* with *c*. Stumpf's contradiction arises only if a sensation is regarded as being a function of its stimulus alone, that is, if the constancy hypothesis holds in its strictest form. If, however, a sensation is also a function of the general experimental setting, then the contradiction disappears. Should stimulus a correspond in accordance with the special experiment to one of the sensations a_1, a_3, stimulus b to b_1, b_2, and stimulus c to c_2, c_3, then as a result of our experiments we might have the following non-contradictory facts: $a_1=b_2$, $b_3=c_3$, $a_3 \vartriangle c_3$. Long ago this was pointed out by Cornelius and has been admitted, since, by Stumpf, who nevertheless maintains his position, *viz*: $a_1=a_3$, $b_1=b_2$, and $c_2=c_3$, because it seemed to him ever so much simpler than any other assumption.[5] Yet the "friction" and the "chance-error" theories both abandon Stumpf's position. Friction requires that c^2 at least must be different from c^3, and the chance-error theory, insofar as it touches sensation and not apprehension merely, allows variability to all sensations. But both these theories strive to remain as close as possible to the constancy-hypothesis, the latter even more so than the former; for according to it, the true stimulus always evokes the same sensation although additional processes may increase or decrease its effect.

---

[5] Full quotations in (30).

Now Cornelius excludes the constancy-hypothesis from his theory. He assumes that to a single definite stimulus there corresponds, not a single definite sensation, but one of a number of several different ones (he denies also the continuity of the sensation-series). His theory therefore implies the general rule that sensation is not a function of the stimulus alone, and again it is attention that determines which of the many possible sensations will be aroused.

We have therefore a number of different explanations, which, however, apart from the role ascribed to attention, all possess one common element: namely, they all start from the relation between a single stimulus and a single sensation, though this relation is modified by the friction-theory and still more by Cornelius. This modification, however, involves an addition of new factors, and accordingly we get a sum of different effects instead of a single effect.

Shall we then say that all in all the problem has been solved; that the minor differences of opinion are negligible? My answer is no, for with no one of the existing theories can we predict a single case. Therefore, if we accept them, we must either exclude single predictions altogether from our programme—as chance can be only statistically predicted—or we must await a discovery of the laws of attention, the outlook for which is not very hopeful when we consider how ill-defined the concept of attention now is.

Let us, therefore, try another method, and, returning to the simplest facts, without prepossession, look the data underlying all these theories in the face. What is my experience when I say this gray is lighter than that, this line longer, or this sound louder, than that? The old theories assume without question that we are dealing with gray a and gray b, line a and line b, sound a and sound b. Whenever the bare existence of two sensations have seemed insufficient to explain a judgment of comparison, psychologists have searched, and not in vain, for other elements. Schumann (56) long ago attacked this problem, and was able to supplement the descriptive side of comparison, but he could only find what he was seeking, and it was in this way that he discovered the accessory impressions (*Nebeneindrucke*)—those transitional sensations (*Ubergangsempfindungen*) which have not yet ceased to play an important part in psychological theory. Other authors have turned to the *relations* as separate autonomous or dependent (*unselbstandig*) elements,[6] and these again have been either rejected or reduced by the analysis of other psychologists. Thus, current teaching has reached no agreement concerning the descriptive side of this problem.

Let us, therefore, turn to the experience itself. Upon a black cloth two squares of gray cardboard lie side by side. I am to judge whether or not they are of equal grayness. What is my experience? I can think of four different possibilities (1) I see on a black surface one homogeneous gray oblong with a thin division line which organizes this oblong into two squares. For simplicity's sake we shall neglect this line, although it has varying aspects. (2) I see a pair of "brightness steps" ascending from left to right. This is a very definite experience with well-definable properties. Just as in a real staircase the steps may have different heights, so my experience may be that of a steep or a moderate ascent. It may be well-balanced or ill-balanced, the latter *e.g.* when there is a middle gray on the left and a radiant white on the right. And it has two *steps*. This must be rightly understood. If I say a real stair has two steps, I do not say there is one plank below and another plank above. I may find out later that the steps are planks, but originally I saw no

---

[6] A full discussion of this problem of relation may be found in the papers by Gelb (10) and Hofler (16).

planks, but only steps. Just so in my brightness steps: I see the darker left and the brighter right not as separate and independent pieces of color, but as steps, and as steps ascending from left to right. What does this mean? A plank is a plank anywhere and in any position; a step is a step only in its proper position in a scale. Again, a sensation of gray, for traditional psychology, may be a sensation of gray anywhere, but a gray step is a gray step only in a series of brightnesses. Scientific thought, concerned as it is with real things, has centered around concepts like "plank" and has neglected concepts like "step."[7] Consequently the assertion has become true without qualification that a "step" is a "plank". Psychology, although it is concerned with experiences, has invariably taken over this mode of procedure. But since the inadequacy occasioned by the neglect of the step-concept is much more conspicuous in psychology than it is in physics, it is our science that first supplied the impulse to reconsider the case. And when we do reconsider, we see at once that the assertion "a sensation of gray is a sensation of gray anywhere" loses all meaning, and that the assertion that a real step is a plank is true only with certain qualifications.

But our previous description must be still further supplemented, or, rather, amplified; for, speaking of "steps" I mean not only two different levels, but the rise itself, the upward trend and direction, which is not a separate, flighty, transitional sensation, but a central property of this whole undivided experience. Undivided does not mean uniform, for an undivided experience may be articulated and it may involve an immense richness of detail, yet this detail does not make of it a sum of many experiences. The direction upward or downward under certain conditions, *e.g.*, under brief exposure, may be the chief

---

[7]The reason for this trend in the formation of our concepts is discussed by Köhler (38, p. 48f).

1140

moment of the total experience; in extreme cases, this direction may be present and nothing else, the plank-character of the steps having entirely vanished. In this connection I may refer to a result of Seifert's. He worked with tachistoscopically exposed figures that were composed either of full lines or of isolated dots. But this made no difference in the appearance of the total figure, and although Seifert accepts the distinction of a fundamental and a superstructure, he is constrained to acknowledge an "ungratefulness" toward the elements (57, p. 74). To return to our own case, we may say that the experience described as *direction* may be entirely dynamic, and that it is always partially so.[9]

Let us now return to the remaining possible experiences which can arise in the comparison of two gray squares. (3) I see a pair of brightness-steps with the reverse direction. (4) I see neither the uniform oblong nor the steps, but something indefinite, vague, not tending towards uniformity, nor towards an ascending or descending step, since it never quite consolidates itself.

It is evident what judgments will follow from each of these experiences: (1) Judgment of equality; (2) left darker (or right brighter)[10]; (3) left brighter (right darker), and (4) uncertain. Thus the four types of judgment which we met previously are reduced to four different experiences.

..While in the former passage we made the four types correspond to the same pair of (subliminally different) stimuli, we shall now consider cases in which typically different pairs of stimuli provoke these different judg-

---

[9]Wertheimer has introduced the distinction of static and dynamic phenomena (64, p. 227), recognizing that the latter are no less real than the former.

[10]These two judgments are psychologically different, and to each there corresponds a different stepwise phenomenon, as a rise to the right, or a fall to the left. We have, for simplicity's sake, neglected this difference, and shall continue to do so in what follows. The reader can easily supplement the discussion in order to make it cover this distinction also.

ments. What, then, follows theoretically from our pure description? We find that our description *explains* the comparison. Comparison is no longer a new act supervening upon the given sensations. The question how the two sensations can be compared no longer exists, because the two sensations themselves do not exist. What we find is an undivided, articulated whole. Let us call these wholes "structures," and we can then assert that an unprejudiced description finds such structures in the cases underlying all psycho-physical experiments, but never any separate sensations.

Our theory finds confirmation in a crucial experiment, which shows, moreover, that these simple structures, far from being a peculiarity of the human species, are a very primitive form of reaction. As the question is put by Köhler (36), if an animal is confronted with two stimuli and is trained to react positively to the one and negatively to the other, what has it learned? The traditional theory would reply: the animal has formed a connection between the one sensation corresponding to the first stimulus and the positive reaction and likewise between the other sensation and the negative reaction; our theory, however, would say that the animal has learned to react to a certain structure. Köhler then introduced an experimental variation to solve the dilemma as to which explanation is the more apt. His method was as follows: b and c, one lighter, the other darker, were placed before the animal, their spatial arrangement being varied. From the one, say b, food could be taken, but not from the other. The training was continued until the animal, in a fixed number of trials, invariably chose the positive b. Then this pair of stimuli was replaced by another pair a and b, a being lighter than b. According to the old theory the behavior of the animal should be as follows: Since it has to choose between the well-known and positive b, connected by pre-

1142

vious training with a positive movement, and a new and neutral a with which it has formed no connection at all, we should expect that in the majority of cases b would be chosen. From our theory, however, we should make a contrary prediction. Having learned to react positively to the higher step of a brightness-scale, the animal will do the same thing when confronted with a new pair, and choose a. The experiments were performed with fowls, chimpanzees and a three-year-old child. In the vast majority of cases gray a was chosen, while further variations in the experiment indicated the reason for every b reaction. In exceptional cases the absolute factor, b, was dominant, though even then it could not be regarded a sensation in the traditional meaning of the term, but only as a structure of a kind to be discussed in the next section. As compared with the structural component the absolute factor as a cue to reaction has a very weak hold upon the memory, and with an increase of the time-interval between the training and the critical experiments, the number of a-choices was found to increase. The same problem was attacked with different sizes of objects and yielded the same results. The experiments were very carefully executed, all possible errors being excluded, while certain objections, which were nevertheless raised, have been set aside by subsequent tests (35, 37).

Though the results of these experiments are unimpeachable, psychologists have not all been ready to accept Köhler's theory. Jaensch, for instance, who reported upon similar experiments with fowls two years after Köhler's publication (21), turns to Schumann's transitional sensations for an explanation of his results, as do Buhler (2) and Lindworsky (41) in their criticism of Köhler's experiments. I have shown at some length in my book on mental development (33) that this attempt at an explanation is quite unsatisfactory, but here I must pass the matter over. Structures, then, are very elementary reactions, which phenomenally are not composed of constituent elements, their members being what they are by virtue of their "member-character," their place in the whole; their essential nature being derived from the whole whose members they are.

Here the argument may be anticipated that, in the analysis, parts must determine the whole; you lay the lighter gray at the left and you have a different brightness gradation than when you lay it at the right! But what does this argument really prove? Remember, you must not substitute your sensations for your stimuli. If you are careful not to do this, your argument must be that the arrangement of the single stimuli determines the whole structure. But you have not proved that the part phenomena have determined the whole phenomenon; for if you react at all by way of a stepwise phenomenon its nature must depend, of course, upon the stimuli which provoked the reaction. Very good, you may say, but what is the advantage of this new way of describing simple experiences? It seems on the face of it so much more complicated, so much less systematic, than the old way. This, indeed, is a fundamental question. But it cannot be answered by argument,—only by facts. It must be shown that in all fields as well as in the field of choice-training (*Wahldressuren*) this new description explains the facts of experience more easily and better than they can be explained by the traditional view.

Let us, therefore, turn back to our threshold-problem, and to Stumpf's paradox which is now easily solved, while the solution leads us to two important laws of structure. With the two subliminally different stimuli, a and b, what will be the O.'s reaction? Most probably experience 1 or 4; which of these two will depend upon circumstances.

1144

If the observer is not acting as the subject of a psychological experiment and is neither suspicious of deception nor otherwise prepared to look for the finest shades of difference, he will react with experience 1; which means that the structure corresponding to two very slightly different stimuli will be one of uniformity. Next you present the supraliminally different stimuli a and c and he will react with experience 2 or 3, as the case may be, that is, he will experience a true stepwise phenomenon. Mathematically, a plane surface can be defined as an aggregate of steps of infinitely small gradation; in mathematics, therefore, we can have a continual transition from steps to plane-surface. But not so in our experience, for here a plane is never a step nor is there any mediation between the two—our experience being neither a step nor a plane but a very labile and indefinite experience. This means that if we neglect for the moment experience 4, we shall have either one of two totally distinct experiences, each of which is a "good" structure. A real ladder with steps one mm. high would not be a good ladder, and, excepting under artificial conditions, such scales do not as a rule exist in our experience nor in the real world either. If, on the other hand, the difference between two stimuli is too great to permit a plane-experience, then we shall have a good stepwise-phenomenon; loosely expressed the experienced difference is exaggerated as compared with the stimulus-difference, and this can be proved wherever we have organs that are adapted to reproduce the stimuli.

We can sum up these facts in two special laws of structure: the law of leveling or assimilation, and the law of emphasis. Later on we shall see that these are both special cases of a more general law.

From these two laws we can infer that the "goodness" of the scale has also a maximum or upper limit. Therefore,

1145

with an increasing stimulus-difference the step-height-experience will become less and less emphasized until an indifference point is reached, where the objective and the phenomenal difference coincide. At this point the emphasis will be replaced by an assimilative leveling, since the phenomenal difference has become less than the real one. If in a real scale we raise the height of the steps more and more we come at length to a point where we no longer have a scale. Two planks at levels ten meters apart are no longer two steps, and the same thing may happen on the phenomenal side. From the chirping of a cricket to the thundering of a sixteen-inch gun there is no scale, for they cannot be compared in the same sense in which we compare two strokes of a hammer.

To complete our survey by answering some other questions, let us turn to *attention*. Attention influences the differential limen which is lowered by a high and raised by a low degree of attention. What does this mean? (1) We see that assimilation is a less developed reaction than emphasis which demands special conditions and a special readiness on the part of the reacting organism. Accordingly, fatigue raises the threshold and reduces the efficiency of the organism. (2) What is it that a high degree of attention really does in such cases? I mentioned above that, under normal conditions, where we are not called upon to make comparisons, our reaction to subliminally different stimuli will be that of equality, whereas in psychophysical experiments equality-judgments are very rare, being replaced by judgments of uncertainty, or even those of "greater," "smaller." So Fernberger (7) reports of a subject, who, in a series of twelve hundred judgments, did not judge a single pair to be equal. How is this difference of behavior explained? We may describe the facts by stating that judgments of equality or "level-experiences" which are descriptively clear are interfered with by experimental conditions, since these conditions always favor some sort of emphasis. We must therefore endeavor to find out the specific character of the experimental conditions. The O. has the task of comparing and judging, *i.e.*, of asserting a relation. So far we have not distinguished between the relational and the structural consciousness. This was in the interest of a simplification which must now be corrected to some extent. A pure stepwise phenomenon would lead us to a judgment of "crescendo" or "diminuendo," which, in accordance with the experience will refer to an undivided whole. The judgment "A is greater than B" presupposes a somewhat different experience, for the two steps of the scale are more prominent, more independent; they are not only steps in the scale but also its limiting platforms. Somehow, they stand apart and a greater "tension" between these two members of the whole is a consequence; a tension which does not exist at all in an assimilative phenomenon of the level-type. This, as Kohler (36) has pointed out, is, grossly speaking, our comparing experience. A comparing attitude in itself will therefore tend to separate the two members by producing a tension, which decreases the chance that a phenomenon of the level-type will occur. This explains the preponderance of judgments of uncertainty over those of equality in psychological experiments.

But the experimental attitude is often still more specialized. Even if we include judgments of equality and uncertainty under the same head, they may be remarkably rare. Fernberger (7) has clearly pointed out the reason for this in the subject's attitude which makes him tend toward a specific judgment of "greater or smaller." In the terms of our theory, the instruction facilitates the stepwise and impedes the assimilative phenomena. This can be experimentally proved, and Fernberger has demonstrated how one of Brown's experiments furnishes

1147

this proof. Brown impressed upon his subject that he ought to be able to find a difference, *i.e.*, he emphasized the stepwise attitude, and the result was that practically no equality-judgments were made in a long series of experiments. Fernberger himself arranged the following experiment with lifted weights: One group of seven subjects was given the customary instruction which presumably facilitates the stepwise phenomenon, while another group of seven received different instructions in which the three categories "greater", "smaller," and "equal" received the same value. Fernberger gives no tables to show the frequency of these judgments, nor does he differentiate between equality- and uncertainty-judgments, which for our present purpose would have been very advantageous, but he calculates the intervals of uncertainty and finds that "the interval of uncertainty for group two is considerably more than half as large again as the first group" (page 541).

I may in this connection refer also to Washburn's experiments upon the effect of verbal suggestion in tactual space perception (63). She stimulated twice successively the same region of the volar side of the O.'s wrist with rubber-tipped compass points which were always 15 mm. apart, the O. being instructed to compare the distance between the two points in two successive contacts. In one group of experiments the O. was told the distance would always be smaller or greater, while in a second group the possibility of equality was also included. The results show a marked rise in the number of equality judgments in the second group over the first. Out of eighty judgments only five were of equality in the first group, while there were twenty such in the second.

What can we make of these facts? They show that the organism's structural reaction to a pair of stimuli depends upon its attitude. If we generalize from all the data the attitude may be such as to favor either a stepwise or an assimilative structure (each to the detriment of the other), or it may be indifferently advantageous to either one. From a consideration of the stepwise attitude we can now draw the following conclusions: before the subject is confronted with the stimulus, the structure that eventually will ensue must be prepared for by a mental attitude, and this attitude consists mainly in a readiness to carry out a certain structural process. "Attitude" has now become a well-defined term as distinguished from "attention." It means that in entering a given situation the organism has in readiness certain modes of response, these modes being themselves what we have called "structures." Having such a process in readiness may be a mere nuisance, and it may not help the final response to the stimulus at all—as when I am prepared for an ascending scale and receive stimuli that determine a descending one— but the attitude may also be very effective. If a structural process is thus adequately prepared for, it may come to its full effect under conditions which of themselves would have provoked a different structural process. This is a very important law, embracing as it does many of the facts imperfectly formulated by the ancient law of association. Take again the ascending scale attitude, with reference to a pair of subliminally different stimuli a and b. By themselves, these would provoke a structure of the level-type; now, however, they give rise to the ascending-scale phenomena, a   b. In this way the typically false judgments are explained, or, at least, all those that cannot be explained by the absolute impression (*absoluter Eindruck*).

Thus we see that all chance means is that our customary experimental conditions leave room for an uncontrollable change of attitude inasmuch as they do not determine the status of the reacting organism. It is therefore an experimental task of the highest importance to fix the conditions so that they will also govern these attitudes.

I owe the reader a proof of this general law, and I shall give it by a reference to two experiments of Wertheimer (64) which I have elsewhere considered from this point of view (31). In the tachistoscope Wertheimer exposes in succession, with a short interval between them, the two lines, a and b, of Figure 1.

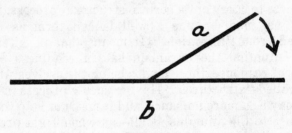

a

b

Fig. 1

The O. sees one line turning in the direction of the arrow. This experiment is repeated several times and then the position of line a is gradually changed, the angle between a and the right half of b becoming less and less acute until it is a right angle, and finally a more and more obtuse angle; let the direction of the turning movement remain constant, as indicated in the second figure.

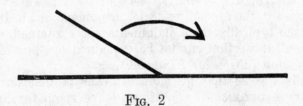

Fig. 2

Had the experiment been begun with the last pattern first, then, of course, the O. would have seen the opposite movement. The effect is always produced by the O.'s

1150

attitude, and depends upon the strength of the original movement-structure. Again, expose a,b in the pattern Figure 3, and repeat it a great number of times. Then suddenly remove a so that b alone is exposed. What will the O. see? b resting in its true position? Not at all! The O. sees a line moving in the same direction as before only over a smaller angle, say like Figure 4, and if you repeat the exposure of b alone, at short intervals, this movement may persist several times, though each time the angle grows smaller. Now a single line like b exposed under no specific movement attitude will, of course, give rise to no experience of movement at all, yet in our last experiment the readiness of the movement-structure process is such that it can be touched off by a totally inadequate

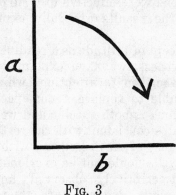

Fig. 3

stimulus. This demonstrates the reality of structural preparations or anticipations. We find the same in cases of perseveration[11] and of suggestion. A striking example of the latter is found in the experiments of Edwards (5). Working in different sense-realms he employed the following method of experimentation: a stimulus was

---

[11] This has been proved by Lewin who speaks of a "readiness to act" *(Tatigkeits-bereitschaft)* (40).

given and then gradually changed in some definite
direction; the O. had to announce when he noticed the
change, but in the suggestion-experiments he was always
given a false direction. So when a gray disc was darkened,

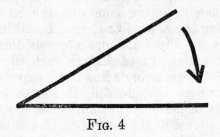

FIG. 4

he was instructed to give notice of the first brightening.
These suggestions were effective in a surprising number
of cases, and the results are fully explained by our
hypothesis.

With this concept of attitude as a readiness to carry out
a structural process, we have explained a number of
facts hitherto ascribed to attention; which means that
we have been able to replace a non-specific, ill-defined
cause by one which is both specific and well-defined. The
explanation is also consistent with the rest of our theory,
and this consistency of the descriptive with the functional
concepts employed should not be overlooked. A stepwise
phenomenon, descriptively observed, and a stepwise
process, functionally deduced, are thus brought into
intimate connection. The structural process prepared by
the attitude functions during the presence of a phenomenon as its physiological correlate, and this physiological hypothesis is determined by psychological observation; for we maintain that the physiological processes
which underlie the structural phenomena must themselves
possess the character of structures. This may seem to
be a problem rather than a solution, but we shall presently

see that even this problem has been successfully attacked.

No discussion of the differential threshold can pass by Weber's law; we shall therefore next consider the bearing of our theory upon this classic generalization. Although the theory of the Weber-Fechner law has long been controversial, we can now say that the physiological interpretation has won the field.[12] This supposes that the function connecting the stimulus with the nervous excitation which underlies the sensation is the logarithmic factor. Since our theory abandons sensation, the usual interpretation of Weber's law must be remodeled; which again shows that we are not dealing with a mere change of names, but with a very active agent. In order to elucidate this part of our theory we must enter into certain details of physiological chemistry. Let us suppose, following Köhler's inferences (38, page 6 ff and 211 ff), that our entire field of vision is filled with a uniform gray, our whole optical sense-organ being homogeneously stimulated; we should then see a gray wall or nebula, but what may the process in our brain be like? Without entering the region of mere speculation, the following assertion can be made: the chemical reaction that will take place after we have become adapted to the stimulus will be a stationary one, that is, the concentration of all the substances concerned will be held constant during the whole time. It can further be shown that, owing to the chemical composition of our nervous system, ions will take part in this process, so that a given degree of concentration would imply a definite amount of free ions. Let us now change our stimulus to one composed of two differently colored parts, say dark and light, meeting in an entirely arbitrary curve. Can the new process be fully described as two stationary processes corresponding to these two areas? An affirmative answer to this question would imply that no connection whatever exists between

---

[12] A full discussion is given in Pauli's monograph (49).

the two parts of the brain which are being differently excited, and since their border line was quite arbitrary it would also mean that each brain element is a miniature system insulated from each and every other element. This assumption is obviously untenable. Upon purely physicochemical grounds we must therefore conclude that between the two regions with their different concentrations, there must take place an adjustment (*Ausgleich*) of osmotic pressure, since with a certain concentration of substance there also belongs a certain concentration of ions. As ions must take part in this process of diffusion and since different ions move with different velocities, there must arise, instantaneously, along the whole border line, a leap in the electrostatic potential. The absolute potential of each of the two areas is thus determined by the amount of this potential difference. It is not at all as though we had two areas independent on one another, each having its fixed potential, from which the potential difference arises. The opposite is true, since the fact of these two differently reacting areas coming together and forming one system is the cause for the arousal of the leap of potential and thereby determines the single potentials themselves. The term "potential difference" instead of misleading us, ought to furnish a striking analogy to our physiological stepwise phenomenon; for just as the step is a step only in a scale, so here each area has its potential only by virtue of the system in which it occurs, and just as the "upward (downward) direction" of the scale is a central property of the experience, so here the leap of potential is a central factor of the optical function.

Let us go a bit further, and put this question: how does the potential difference $o^1 - o^2$ depend upon the two concentrations C^1 and C^2? From Nernst's theory of galvanic chains the following formula can be deduced: $o^1 - o^2 =$

$$\text{const. log. } \frac{C^2}{C^1},$$

and this is precisely Fechner's formula for Weber's law.

We can now state the structural theory of the Weber-Fechner law. The logarithmic law does not refer at all to single sensations, but to the whole structure; and from our deduction we must even infer that the concentration of ions in one area is a linear function of the intensity of the stimulus. Furthermore, what psychologists have called the process or function of comparing is not a third or "higher" factor accruing to the two sensations compared, but a moment inseparable from the whole structural system, which has been falsely singled out, just as the sensations have been falsely separated. In truth, comparison is always determined by a system in which one step necessitates another.

The closest analogy in its essentials, even an identity, exists between our psychological description and our physico-chemical deduction, although the latter in no wise presupposes the former. We have, therefore, full justification for our previous assertion that the physiological process must also be structural, for the system of the two reacting areas with their potential difference is a true structure in the strictest sense. Von Ehrenfels, in his famous article (6) gave two criteria for his *Gestaltqualitaten,* which, though imperfect, may be applied to our structures, both the psychological and the physiological. These criteria were (1) that structures cannot be composed out of elements, but (2) they can be transposed like melodies.

Our conception has now been further enlarged; for while our deductions are in no wise dependent upon physiological assumptions, they are found applicable to purely physico-chemical facts. We may therefore accept the fact that structures exist also in the realm of inorganic nature.

Before leaving the topic of the differential limen, I wish to mention a very interesting result from some experiments with lifted weights which Borak has recently published (1). Though his paper gives a mere statement of fact, and makes no reference to structural principles, it may be referred to here for two reasons. (1) The new fact puts a new problem before structural psychology, which, as I have reason to know, has been vigorously and successfully attacked. (2) It is very surprising that this fact has not been discovered before, since it ought to have appeared in almost any of the innumerable investigations made with the method of constant stimuli. The fact is the following: the sensibility to an increase in weight is greater than that of a decrease in weight, and, within certain limits, this difference increases with the time-interval within the two lifts. I quote the results from one of Borak's tables:

Weights in Ascending Sequence	Number of Right Judgments	Weights in Descending Sequence	Number of Right Judgments
400:420	16	420:400	2
400:430	27	430:400	10
400:440	30	440:400	16
400:450	33	450:400	20
400:460	45	460:400	35

n=50

Both thresholds, the ascending and the descending, obey Weber's law.

III

In the last section I have tried to give an impression of what "structure" means, descriptively and functionally. In this part of my essay I shall report a number of experiments performed in various fields, which show the fruitfulness of our conception. First of all, let us turn to a special structure of great significance. Keeping close to the discussion of the last section, I put this question: What are the phenomena which appear when

1156

we investigate an absolute threshold, say in the auditory field? Is it not correct to say in this connection that we try to find the smallest stimulus-energy that can give rise to a single sensation? Let us seek our answer in a pure description of the phenomenal data observable during the course of the experiment. The O. sits in a noiseless room and awaits a faint sound. Is there anything auditory in his consciousness? The question would have appeared very different if we had chosen the visual field, for then the O. would be sitting in a dark room waiting for a faint light, and darkness is admittedly a visual phenomenon. But is "stillness" auditory? Let the following rhythm be beaten:—..—..—..—.., do we hear anything between the dactyllic groups? Our question now appears to be more difficult, but my answer is that the intermetric intervals belong quite as much to the whole experience as do the intrametric intervals, only they belong to it in a different manner. Or take a visual analogy: In Figure 5 the intervals ab, bc, are different from the intervals aa, bb, cc, though both belong to the "fence-phenomenon." In trying to describe this difference we find one very striking feature which we shall here single out. The white spaces in the intervals ab, bc, cd, form part of the total white space, whereas the white spaces in the other intervals are limited to the regions between their respective black lines; they do not extend beyond these regions, nor do they form a part of the white space round about. Practised observers can even describe the curves that mark off these white stripes, which are slightly convex toward the interior. We see, then, that the white surface of our pattern, though objectively the same throughout, gives rise to two different phenomena, one being limited to the "stripes," while the other comprises all the rest of the experience. We have two expressive terms to indicate this difference: we call the one phenomenon a

1157

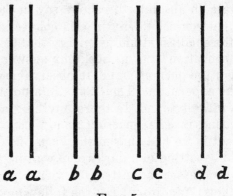

$a\ a\quad b\ b\quad c\ c\quad d\ d$

F<small>IG</small>. 5

"figure" and the other its "ground"; on recognizing at once that no visual figure can occur without a ground upon which it appears.

Let us return now, to our auditory example. The situation is very similar, for we have two kinds of intervals, the inter- and the intra-metric. Does our distinction apply here? Clearly the intrametric intervals belong to the rhythmic group itself, i.e., to the "figure," but can we say that the intermetric ones belong to the "ground" in the same sense in which the intervals between the stripes constitute a visual ground? My observation tells me that we can, and that there exists a ground in the auditory field as well as in the visual field, or in any other sensory field. This ground may be "stillness" or it may be the mixture of street-noises which, in a city, never cease during the day-time. And now mark this: When you leave the city for the country, and sit down to work at your desk, you may be startled by a strange phenomenon, for you may "hear" the stillness. The auditory ground of your work has altered and this alteration strikes you forcibly.

To show that this is not a description made up in accordance with a predetermined theory, I may quote an unprejudiced witness. At the beginning of Ibsen's last play, "When We Dead Awaken," Mrs. Maja says, "Do listen how still it is here," and Professor Rubeck replies a little later, "One can, indeed, hear the stillness."

Returning to our threshold problem, we may therefore conclude that when the O. awaits the appearance of a faint sound, he is conscious not of auditory nothingness, but of an auditory ground; and what he is looking for is the appearance of an auditory figure, though in this case, because of its faintness, the figure may be ill-defined.

If we consult experimental procedure, this is strongly confirmed. In measuring auditory thresholds the chief consideration is not always to have the room as quiet as possible, but to have it as uniformly noisy as possible. If both postulates can be combined, well and good, but as a rule we are not able to exclude irregular outbursts of faint noises. Therefore, instead of keeping the room still, the experimenter fills it with a constant noise which is intensive enough to drown all irregular incoming sounds; as, for instance, Peters has done (50). The O.'s task is then well defined. Upon this auditory ground he is instructed to await the appearance of a circumscribed noise-quality which does not belong to the ground.

An artificial ground has been created because a constant and uniform ground is a most important condition in testing absolute thresholds. But does not this mean a reduction of absolute to differential limens? Are not the objective conditions quite similar in the two cases—a constant stimulus, and a slightly greater test-stimulus? For just as I compare the weight N with the weight N plus Δ, so here I compare the constant sound-intensity A with the slightly increased one (fall of a shot) A plus Δ. This interpretation, however, misses the psychological point; for it overlooks the characteristic phenomenal difference between the two experiences. In absolute-threshold experiments we do not work with stepwise phe-

1159

nomena, as we do in differential limens, for our experience oscillates between one of a uniform ground alone, and one of a quality that stands out from the ground. Our assimilative phenomenon of the "level" which lies at the basis of all quality-judgments in the differential tests, is different from what we now call a pure *ground* experience. The "level" phenomenon is always experienced with a figure lying on a ground, and although the figure itself may be inarticulated, it is nevertheless distinct from its ground.

The difference between absolute and differential thresholds is therefore well-founded, and our principles of structure enable us to comprehend it fully. The distinction is also corroborated by experiments which indicate that the two function quite differently. Specht (59) has shown that alcohol lowers the absolute and raises the differential threshold, and we can infer from this a functional difference between the two structures—the one, a figure against a ground, and the other, a part against another part of a figure.

Having discovered this figure-ground-structure in the absolute threshold, we must now consider it more closely. Let us revert to our fence-phenomenon. We found that the white intervals belonging to the figure were bounded, while those belonging to the ground were not, though objectively there was no border line in either case. Here

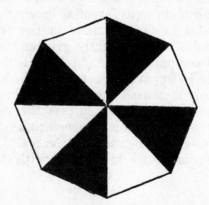

1160   FIG. 6

we have a very general characteristic, namely, that the ground is always less "formed," less outlined, than the figure. Rubin (53) was the first to investigate these facts systematically, and the following statements are largely taken from his work. His method was peculiarly well-adapted to bring out the differences of figure and ground, in employing geometrical patterns which are phenomenally equivocal as to their figure-ground structure. A simple example of such a pattern has already been discussed by Schumann (55). If we make the distances in our fence, aa, bb, .. equal to ab, bc, .. we have a striking instance. For now bb may be a stripe, bc a piece of the ground, or inversely, bc may be a stripe, and bb a piece of the ground. In either case we find our old difference, that the stripes are always bounded, whether they are formed by bb or bc, while the intervals are not. Another example is offered by the so-called subjective rhythm, whether auditory or visual, which corresponds to an objectively equal series of beats or flashes. In such a phenomenal series we again meet with the difference of inter- and intra-metric intervals, and again their co-ordination with the objective intervals is ambiguous. The cross in Figure 6, reproduced from Rubin, may be experienced either as a white cross on a black ground, or as a black cross on a white ground (neglecting other less important effects). Compare either cross with its ground and you can clearly recognize that the latter is always less definitely structured than the former; either the ground has no distinct shape at all, or else it approaches the comparatively simple form of a square.

Hand in hand with higher degrees of structure there goes a greater "liveliness" or vividness of the figure. As Schumann observed, the white space inside a figure is "whiter" than that outside, which can also be easily seen in the equidistant fence-design. A striking example of this is afforded by a certain kind of drawings, used

1161

frequently for advertising posters, where the contour is not fully drawn, but where, nevertheless, no gap appears in the figure. I may refer the reader to Jastrow's *Editor,* reproduced in Pillsbury's textbook (51, p. 158).

These last examples show what has already been pointed out, namely, that phenomenal figures have boundary lines even when the corresponding objective figures have none. A good figure is always a "closed" figure, which the boundary line has the function of closing. So this line, separating the fields of figure and ground, has a very different relation to each of these, for though it bounds the figure, it does not bound the ground. The ground is unaffected by the contour and is partly hidden by the figure, yet it lies without interruption behind the figure. The cross of the accompanying figure (Figure 7) will make this description clear. Look at the fields with the arcs for filling. When forming a cross, these become true arcs, *i.e.,* cut-off pieces of circles, but when forming the ground they look quite differently, for they are no longer cut off, becoming now the visible parts of a phenomenal series of complete circles.

This property of the ground, that the figure's contour does not affect it, is closely related to the first characteristic we mentioned, namely, its lesser degree of structure. In our last instance this fact is revealed by the observation that the whole circles when they constitute a ground are simpler structures than the arcs which are necessary to the formation of the cross; for in place of each single circle there appear four arcs. The lesser degree of structure leads also to another indication noted by Rubin of the difference between ground and figure: the ground has more of a substance- and the figure more of a thing-character.

Let us return to the boundary line. From its variable relation to figure and ground there follows the inference that it must have two different sides, an inside and an outside; the one includes, the other excludes, or to use terms in this more general sense which have been suggested by v. Hornbostel (19), the one is concave, and the other is convex. Though these words are not psychological terms they are meant to indicate true psychological descriptions. Look at the left line-b in our fence-figure and you will understand what is meant by this description,

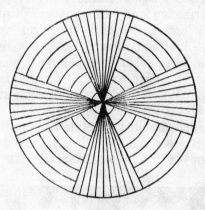

Fig. 7

for its left side is hard and repelling, whereas its right side is soft and yielding. Very full descriptions of these properties are given by v. Hornbostel who reduces the illusions of reversible perspective to a change in these properties: to reverse a figure is to make concave what was convex, and convex what was concave.

One remark here to the reader who may raise the objection that our terms do not designate the existential properties of visual phenomena, but only their intentional meanings. I have said that I wished to point out true properties. Now consider that these properties need not be like those of traditional psychology, "dead" attributes, possessing a "so-being" only, but that many of them are alive and active, possessing a "so-functioning."

A beam of wood, lying unused on the floor, may look like a beam carrying weight, yet an accurate description would have to note this fact by giving heed to the state of tension which must then exist. More generally speaking, a state of rest with an absence of force is different from a state of rest with an equilibrium of force, and the same thing holds true, in the writer's opinion, for phenomena. The border line of a figure performs a function, and this performance is one of its visual properties. Traditional psychology has *defined* the term "visual property" so as to include "dead" properties only. Consequently in looking for visual properties it has found only these. But this definition was arbitrary, and it proves to be inadequate, since it makes the investigator blind to facts of the highest significance.

Lest the reader should be inclined to consider the distinction hitherto offered as trivial, artificial, and secondary, we may turn to experiments with ambiguous

Fig. 8

patterns, where the different structures correspond to two totally different forms, whereas in the previous examples the same form, a fence or a cross, appeared in both cases. Well-known puzzle pictures fall under this head, one of which is produced by Titchener (61, p. 278)—a brain with fissures which assimilate as babies, while another example is given in Pillsbury's book (51, p. 162) as a duck's or a rabbit's head. The best example of this which I know was used by Rubin. It is a goblet, whose contours also form the profiles of two faces. Many similar patterns were employed by Martin (42). We need not, however, search for examples, since everyday life supplies us with any number of them. The simplest, perhaps, is an ordinary chessboard pattern, where at least six different phenomena may be aroused, and many others are frequently found in lace or wallpaper designs. Figure 8 is reproduced from the edging of a table cloth. You can see either the black T-shaped forms or the white leaves. On the actual frieze it is hardly possible to see both at the same time, though in our sample this is easier. Whenever you see one of the figures only, the remainder becomes a ground of the simplest possible description.

This difference has not escaped the psychologist, but has been discussed at length. The clearest statement is given by Titchener (61), whose report I shall closely follow in my interpretation. He would say that in the beginning the black T's are at the upper level of consciousness, while the rest is at a lower level. Suddenly a change takes place, the T's drop clear away from the upper level, and the white leaves stand out with all imaginable clearness, while the form of the T's is no clearer than the feel of the book in your hand. Had he written the last sentence only there would be no disagreement between us, for the "feel of the book" belongs truly to the "ground" of the whole situation. But what he does say leaves the existence of the T-phenomenon untouched by the change in its phenomenal aspect. It has merely shifted its level, having dropped from the crest of attention to its base, from whence the leaves have now risen.

In objecting to this interpretation (which has also been vigorously attacked by Rahn), and at the same time arguing against Wundt, Rubin states most emphatically that when the T's have disappeared and we see in their place a mere ground, the T's have indeed no clearness at all, for they have become nonexistent.

1165

In Titchener's report we recognize the typical attempt of traditional psychology to elucidate phenomena by means of the cardinal concepts stated at the beginning of this paper. Something which ought to be there phenomenally, since a corresponding stimulus does exist, is not observable, and this contradiction is overcome with the aid of attention. Yet this is no longer a description of fact, but a hypothetical interpretation.[14] For I can describe only what I can observe, what is there before me, and to say that a figure is at so low a level of consciousness that it is not observable is not a description of what is present, even though in the next moment I can reexperience what at the time was nonexistent. If I wish to describe truly I must report positively what that part of the total phenomenon looks like which lies at the so-called basis of attention; for it is not a description of it to tell how it does not look.

To infer how something looks when it is not observable from the data of its appearance when at the crest of the attention-wave, means the acceptance of the constancy-hypothesis and a final abandonment of every effort to obtain a factual verification. As Kohler has pointed out (34), if we stand by description proper, i.e., by verifiable description, we must recognize that the T's have ceased to exist the moment we see the leaves, and that the T-phenomenon has been replaced by a totally different ground-phenomenon, which corresponds to the same part of the stimulus-complex. We see now what an enormous change has been effected when a figure "emerges" from its ground. Rubin gives a striking description of the shock of surprise felt again and again in such a transition, even when he tried to imagine in advance what the new phenomenon would be like.

We have seen how the concept of attention has pre-

---

[14]Titchener, though he recognizes that he is interpreting, seems not to be fully aware of the totally hypothetical character of his interpretation.

vented the recognition and vitiated the pure description of a very marked phenomenal difference. Yet a connection exists between the figure-ground consciousness and the attention, so-called. But, by observing the facts, what we find is a functional dependency, instead of a descriptive identity. As a rule the figure is the outstanding kernel of the whole experience. Whenever I give attention to a particular part of a field, this part appears in the figure-character. I have frequently performed the following classroom experiment: using a photographic shutter I project Figure 8 for a short time upon the wall, and instruct beforehand one-half the audience to watch the white, and one-half the black parts of the picture. I then ask the whole audience to make sketches of what they have seen. Invariably the "black" half of the audience draws the T's, and the "white" half the leaves.

Is it possible to describe the attitude of the observer which is produced by the instruction to "watch"? Again we may refer to v. Hornbostel's inversion experiments. He finds that it is more difficult to invert the convex into the concave than the concave into the convex, because whatever I am looking at, watching, acting upon, stands forth, grows fixed, becomes an object, while the rest recedes, grows empty, and becomes the ground. He also adds that since the objects obtrude themselves upon me, and come toward me, it is *they* I notice and watch rather than the holes between them. (19, p. 154.) We need only to apply this general description to our special case, and we shall see that attention has now a very definite meaning; for, in attending to the black parts, we adopt a "figure attitude" toward them by making them the center of our interest. At the same time, the part that has become the figure itself strives to become the center of our experience. This notion of the "center" will play an important part in the later expositions of our theory; here we have simply replaced the vague concept of attention with one which is well-defined.

The functional connection of figure- and center-consciousness is not absolute. Though it is natural to "attend" to the figure we can, for a time, at least, attend to the ground, and let the figure recede. If we continue this attitude too long, however, we run the risk of a change in the phenomenon; but that such an attitude is possible— and many observations reported in the foregoing prove that it is—again demonstrates that the figure-ground distinction cannot be identified with a mere difference of the attention-level.

All good psychological descriptions must find their justification in functional facts. Phenomena that are different in description must also prove to be different in function, if the description is tenable. So we turn to

Fig. 9

the functional facts which underlie the figure-ground distinction.

Two sets of experiments have been performed by Rubin, both employing patterns of the type of Figure 9. These patterns are ambiguous, either the enclosed white space or the enclosing black space may appear as the figure. Let us call the first the positive, the second the negative reaction. According to the instructions given, it is possible for the O.'s to assume either a positive or a negative attitude before the exposure of the pattern. After some practice the attitude assumed will in most cases be effective, *i.e.*, a positive reaction will ensue from a positive attitude, and *vice versa*. In his first series of experiments, Rubin presented a number of such patterns with either positive or negative instructions. After a certain interval the experiment was repeated with instructions prescribing an indifferent attitude, neither positive nor negative. The result was that in the majority of cases a pattern once reacted to in a certain manner was reacted to the next time in the same manner. Rubin calls this a "figural after-effect" (*figurale Nachwirkung*). It proves that the structure by which we react to a given stimulus-complex remains in the memory of the individual, a fact of paramount importance for the theory of learning, as I have elsewhere (33) shown. The problem of the second series was to find out if a pattern seen the first time under one attitude, positive or negative, will be recognized when it is seen the second time under the reversed attitude. The procedure was similar to that of the previous experiment, except that the instruction of the test-series was either positive or negative. The result was in full accordance with the descriptive distinction, for when the reverse instruction was effective no recognition took place. By overlooking this fact many troublesome mistakes are committed even in everyday life.

We have assigned to the figure a "thing"-character, and to its ground a "substance"-character. This description has also been justified by experiments, for we learn from Gelb's investigation (11) that the color-constancy commonly called memory-color is dependent upon the color's "thing"-character and not upon its "surface"-character. This was clearly proved by two patients with brain lesions who saw no surface-colors (*Oberflachenfarben*) and yet they made the same brightness-equations between a lighted and an unlighted color as did normal O.'s. They reacted differently only in case of a shadow, and this was because their visual apprehension was not sufficiently restored to enable them to recognize a dark spot as a shadow cast upon an object.

Before Gelb's paper had been published the connection between color-constancy and "thing"-character was suggested to Rubin by the researches of Katz (24), and Rubin concluded that because of this connection the figure-ground difference ought also to appear when the color-constancy is altered. To test this conclusion he planned two ingenious experiments. In the shadow-experiment he used a cross of the type of Figure 6, and cast a light shadow upon one of the white sectors. His O.'s reported this shading to be stronger when the white sector was part of the ground than when it was part of the cross. In the color experiment the cross was colored and observed through differently colored glasses. The result was again that the figure offered a stronger resistance to change of color than did the ground.

Starting from the greater vividness of the figure as described, I devised the following experiment (32). I tested the power of figure and ground to resist so-called retinal rivalry. On the left side of a stereoscope I put a Rubin cross like that of Figure 6, composed of alternate blue and yellow sectors, while on the right side there was a regular blue octagon of homogeneous surface (comp. Figure 10). The left cross can appear either as a blue cross on a yellow ground, or as a yellow cross on a blue ground, and in looking through the stereoscope it is easy to see either, since the left image, with its richer detail is superior in rivalry to the right image. Beginning with the yellow cross which is a very stable phenomenon, you can accentuate the right image by moving it, or by pointing at it with a pencil, without disturbing the yellow cross. But let the blue cross on the yellow field involuntarily

1170

appear, and then accentuate the right image but slightly and the cross will disappear as the blue octagon emerges.

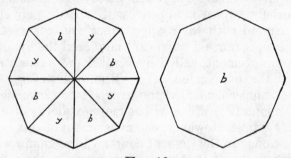

Fig. 10

The explanation is simple enough. There is a constant rivalry between the yellow sectors on the left and the corresponding blue space on the right, yet so long as the yellow forms the figure in the left image the structure is so strong and so fixed that it resists attack. When yellow is the ground, however, it is but loosely formed and can therefore be easily defeated by the right image. So the better formed the field is, the more vivid and more impressive (*eindringlich*) it will be, a fact which has been theoretically explained by Kohler (38, p. 206f). Discussing the electrical processes occurring in the optical system during stimulation, and making the well-founded assumption that the entire optical sector, periphery, optical tract, and cortical area together form one system, Kohler comes to the conclusion that the density of energy is always much greater in the figure-field than it is in the ground-field, and that the current (*Stromung*) is much more concentrated in the former than in the latter. It is this condition of energy which helps figures to attain their phenomenal vividness, and also, as we can say after our last experiment, their superiority in rivalry.

Phenomenally, the figure is always a stronger and more resistant structure than the ground, and in extreme cases the ground may be almost formless, a mere background. For this distinction we have also found a functional counterpart. Kenkel (25) has discovered that figures, when briefly exposed, appear with specific movements which expand with their appearance and contract with their disappearance. I have (27) advanced the hypothesis that this movement, called by Kenkel the *gamma move-ment,* is the expression of a structural process. This hypothesis has been tested and proved by an investigation of Lindemann (28) which will be more explicitly discussed in a later article. However, one experiment of this investigation belongs in the present context. Lindemann worked also with patterns that were ambiguous in their figure-ground structure. His figures were of the type of Figure 9 and of the goblet pattern described above. If Figure 9 is positively apprehended the O. sees violent outward movements of the white teeth, whereas, if observed negatively, the black indentures, particularly the lower claw-like one, move vigorously inwards. The goblet pattern behaves similarly. If the goblet is seen, it performs extensive expansions and contractions, whereas, if the profiles appear they tend toward one another, the direction of the movement being reversed, but, on account of the close proximity of these two structures movement is in this case notably checked. These experiments show that the gamma movement takes place in the figure and not in the ground, and since they reveal a constructing process, they prove that functionally the figure is better formed than the ground.

I shall repeat here another experiment performed in the Giessen Psychological Laboratory, which has not yet been published. Hartmann (29) has investigated the laws governing the fusion of two stimuli separated by a dark interval. The O. looked through a telescope, or in most of the experiments through a blackened tube, behind which the Schumann tachistoscope was rotating. In the

1172

rim of the wheel there were two slits, separated by a variable interval. Behind the wheel was the object which in this procedure was twice exposed during one revolution. The objects were transparent figures getting their light from the rear. In accordance with the facts known about the Talbot fusion (for instance, rotating discs), Hartmann found that the critical speed of the wheel was a direct function of the intensity of the stimulus which could easily be regulated by varying the amount of light passing through the exposed objects. By "critical" speed is meant that speed which is just capable of bringing about a complete fusion, after the last bit of flicker has disappeared. Hartmann then worked with Figure 6 as one of his objects, and he found a marked difference in the critical speed for the two phenomena, black cross on white ground and white cross on black ground. For instance, the time of revolution in the first case was 1.65 seconds while in the second case it was 1.3 seconds. Now the black sectors are no blacker than the dark interval, hence the flicker is produced by the white sectors alone; consequently the same field fuses under Hartmann's conditions more easily when it is a ground than when it is a figure. This proves again the close connection between construction or "formedness" and vividness or intensity. And this proof seems all the more convincing because it is based upon an effect which has hitherto been considered a purely physiological process of the retina. Besides, this experiment is not only qualitative, it is also quantitative, since the difference of critical speed for the two different phenomena corresponding to the same stimulus-intensity can be matched with another difference in critical speed between two corresponding phenomena (black vs. white cross) with different stimulus-intensities.

I believe that the functional facts I have adduced are sufficient to prove the essential difference between the figure and ground phenomena. This difference is fundamental and the figure-ground structure must therefore be considered one of the most primitive of all structures. I have (33) defended the view that this structure is also the first phenomenon experienced by the human infant; for instance a light patch on a dark ground instead of the various sensations with which, according to the traditional view, the baby's consciousness is supposed to be filled. This genetic consideration raises still another question. We have said that a figure cannot exist without a ground. Can a ground exist without a figure? In another connection (33, p. 97) I have tried to prove that it cannot, and that mere ground would be equivalent to no consciousness at all.

So far our observations have shown a superiority of the figure-phenomenon over the ground-phenomenon. This, however, must not lead us to disregard the latter, for the ground has a very important function of its own; it serves as a general level (*niveau*) upon which the figure appears. Now figure and ground together form a structure, consequently the former cannot be independent of the latter. On the contrary the quality of the figure must be very largely determined by the general level upon which it appears. This is a universal fact, observed in such products of culture as fashion and style. The same dress which is not only smart, but nice to look at, almost a thing of beauty, may become intolerable after the mode has passed. Again, put a heavy modern leather club-chair into a rococo salon and the effect will be hideous. Music offers any number of examples as to the influence exerted by the general level. Each tone, each harmony, has a specific meaning, inherent in its "sound" for a given key only; but this meaning changes with the key, so that G is the tonic of G major, but the dominant of C major.

The influence of the ground appears in many psychological experiments. As Hering (15) has shown, the question of the functional dependence of the brightness of a gray upon the amount of light reflected into our eyes is unanswerable because it is incompletely stated. To solve this problem we must determine the general level. If we allow the level to vary the same amount of light in the figure may arouse a black, a gray or a white, as can easily be proved by Hering's "hole method," and the same is true if we take color into consideration. Witness the following experiment with Hering's hole method which I have often used as demonstration in a classroom. Put a white screen (of about 50 x 50 cm.) with a hole in it of about 5 cm. diameter before a white wall. Put one or two ordinary electric lamps between screen and wall so that they throw their reddish-yellowish light on the wall, and close the shutters of the room. The wall will look fairly white, so will the hole in the screen so long as you perceive it as part of the wall, seen through the hole in the screen. But you can also see the hole as part of the screen, which then becomes its ground; in which case the hole will seem to protrude somewhat from the screen and will have a distinct yellow tinge. Now throw on the screen white light from the arc-lamp of a projection lantern and arrange the intensities so that the amount of light upon the wall and upon the screen is approximately equal. The filling of the hole is then forced into the plane of the screen and has a fairly saturated color of a warm reddish-yellow. It is much more colored than it was before, while the screen now looks to be a light gray with a slight blue-greenish tint. Cover and uncover alternately the objective lens of the lantern and you can easily observe a great change in the hole's color. Now fixate the wall, looking right under the lower edge of the screen. Again open and close your lantern. In this case you will see the fairly white wall suffering but very little change, whereas when the screen is lit up with a clear blue-green color, the hole becomes invisible.

You may object that this experiment involves a combination of memory-color and contrast. But in the first place, Jaensch has proved that these are not two different effects, but special cases of one and the same law; in the second place these terms are not an explanation of the phenomena and the facts mentioned do not readily submit to the current theories of contrast.[15]

Let us describe the facts by means of our level-concept. Consider that objectively the filling of the hole is but slightly altered by the turning on of the lantern light, which only causes it to grow a little whiter. Since this effect is opposed to the phenomenon we have described, we may for simplicity neglect it altogether. But why does the "white" wall, when illumined by the yellowish lamp, still look fairly white? There is but one sort of light in the room, excepting the traces of daylight that are not excluded by the shutters.

The light-level of the room is therefore solely determined by the lamps, and the lighted part of the room is homogeneously colored. Let us now make the assumption that every general color-level tends to look white, that, in other words, white (including gray and black) is the characteristic level-color. This will explain our fact. Now, as to the hole in the dark screen: it remains white when it appears as part of the wall, for it then belongs to this general level. But, if it appears on the screen it lies at the screen's level, and since the screen reflects no lamplight but only certain traces of daylight, the screen will therefore look almost black (white-level). As a consequence, the hole as a figure upon this ground, reflecting a light which is different from its ground, can no longer retain the same color; accordingly it appears yellowish. The color-effect is not very marked because of the great difference in brightness between the ground and the figure. The explanation for this, which also involves a law of structure, will be given in the following article.

---

[15]Compare Jaensch (22, 23) and Kroh (39).

When the screen is illuminated by the white lantern light, it forms a pronounced level, and since by the conditions of the experiment the brightness-difference between ground and figure has been decreased, the figure now appears to have the color of the lamps behind the screen. The screen, reflecting white light only, does not look like a pure gray, but being much smaller than the wall, it is therefore influenced by the wall's general level, as the wall is also influenced by the "level" of the screen. Therefore the screen looks slightly blue-greenish, while the wall, in turn, is tinged with yellow. If the screen were larger, so as to cover the entire wall, it would look pure gray and the hole still more yellowish. The difference in illumination between screen and wall determines, primarily, a color-distance or a system of color-steps, the actual position of the steps being dependent upon other factors.

Turn to the second experiment. Here one remains at the unchanged level of the wall. The screen becomes now the figure upon this constant level, and since the objectively yellowish level of the wall looks almost white, the screen must appear of a pronounced bluish color, though it, too, is objectively white.

In other words, objective white looks white when it is the "ground" of the observation, and objective yellow looks yellow when it is a "figure" upon this "ground." Similarly, objective white looks bluish when it appears upon an objectively yellow ground, and objective yellow looks white when it forms a ground—all of which may take place under the same objective conditions. From this we can draw the conclusion that a field, reflecting a certain amount and quality of light, depends for its phenomenal color-quality upon the ground on which it appears.

Thus our experiments are arguments in favor of our initial assumption, and this assumption furnishes a true psychological interpretation of the observation of Helmholtz, who maintained that we are unable to recognize a true white without comparison. Since, according to his theory, a sensation of white is composed of the sensations of the three cardinal colors mixed in certain proportions of intensity, and since the comparison of the intensities of colors is difficult and uncertain, therefore, in the absence of a true standard, we are very often mistaken and judge a sensation to be white, when in reality it is not white, but colored.

Our conception (*Begriff*) of white, is thus subject to change, while the sensation remains constant (13, II, p. 223f, 1st ed., p. 396f). This theory involves the constancy-hypothesis, deducing the actual though misjudged sensation from the nature of its stimulus. Furthermore, it draws a distinction between the true sensation and our judgment of it. Having abandoned this position, we can resolve the statement of Helmholtz into our own terms by saying that if the general level is produced by a colored light, then we *see* it as white. Helmholtz characteristically bases his theory upon a number of experiments similar to those from which we started. Let us return to our experiments and leave everything unaltered except that instead of a white light, we throw saturated yellow light upon the screen. If the intensities upon the screen and the wall are fairly equal the objectively yellow hole will appear to be distinctly bluish. The explanation follows from what has already been said. In a third experiment we use the same arrangement as in the first—white light on the screen, both wall and screen receiving approximately the same intensity—and we see a hole slightly lighter or darker than the screen and of a different color. Now slowly change the illumination of the screen, for instance by moving the objective lens of the projection lantern, and a distinct change will take place in the objectively unaltered hole, whereas a change upon the screen is hardly noticeable.

This experiment shows that the general level offers a greater resistance to changes in the objective conditions than does a single figure. The physiological explanation follows from the general physiological theory of the figure-ground structure. Since the density of energy is greater in the figure-field than in the ground-field, any change of the whole system will appear with greater strength in the figure than in the ground. This relative stability of a general level is probably the fundamental fact in all our so-called "color-transformations." Nor does this fact contradict the results of the experiments previously described, in which the figure, by virtue of its "thing-character" proved to be the more constant; for in these other experiments the general level of the whole experience was never involved.

In the realm of space the general level plays a role no less important. Witasek (66) has described the following method of testing the single "space-values" of the retina. One single point of light in a totally dark room is presented in different positions with head and eyes fixated. Under these so far unrealized conditions Witasek expected to secure an exact determination of pure space (local) sensations. Try this experiment yourself and you will find it altogether impossible; for after you have stayed some time in total darkness, a single point of light has no definite position at all; if continually exposed, it wanders about, even when fixated, making so-called autokinetic movements.[16]

If the exposure is only momentary the point of light is neither clearly nor fixedly localized, and the crudest mistakes in localization occur. After watching these autokinetic movements for some time, the floor under your feet, the very chair you sit on, begin to lose their hold.

All this means that a definite single phenomenal posi-

---

[16]Compare, for instance, Wertheimer (64).

tion exists only within a fixed spatial level. If the conditions for the formation and conservation of such a level are absent, localization is no longer possible; for just as the level grows unstable so does the single point within it.

The spatial level has, however, a marked tendency to remain constant, together with the common directions of "above" and "below," "right" and "left." We shall see in the next article what a strong influence these common directions exercise upon the formation of structure. For our present purpose we need only point out that "above" is not necessarily something depicted upon the vertical meridian of the eye below the fovea, since this is true only when the eyes are in a special position with head erect and eyes looking straight forward. When writing at my desk, for instance, this same part of my retina gives the impression of that which is farther away. It comes, to be sure, from the upper part of my manuscript but this is not "above" me. As a rule, the general level remains unaltered, despite changes in phenomena produced by movements of the eye, the head, the whole body, or indeed movements of the surrounding objects. But let yourself be rapidly turned around several times, or let the surroundings be revolved about you, and everything is changed; all orientation is lost and giddiness results. The effect when your surroundings revolve is produced by visual influences alone, but when you are yourself moved, the vestibular organs play a part. This, however, does not impair our theoretical position for it only goes to show that spatial level is dependent upon these sense-organs.

A third system upon which our spatial level depends is formed by the sense-organs of skin and muscles. In a very ingenious investigation, Garten (9) has tested our capacity to recognize the position of the body relative to the vertical. He constructed a special tilt-table which could be immersed in water so that the effect of gravity could be almost totally neutralized. Under these conditions, orientation was considerably disturbed, which again indicates the importance of the sensory systems named.

The term "spatial level" (*Raumlage*) in the specific meaning here employed was used for the first time by Wertheimer (64) who also maintained that the Aubert phenomenon (A-P) depends largely upon a shifting of this level. This phenomenon and a number of related facts have been extensively investigated of late by G. E. Muller (46), but before we turn to these facts we must introduce some of the concepts used by Muller to explain the A-P, which are also applicable in our determination of the spatial level. Muller, investigating the localization of visual images (45), found that an ego-centric localization can be referred to three different systems of coordinates: the visual (*Blick*) system (*V.* system), the head system (*H. system*), and the "standpoint" system (*S. system*). The V system may be defined by the three main axes of Hering's imaginary "Cyclopean" eye; the H. system is represented by the head, one axis being the basal line, the other two lying in the median plane of the head at right angles to the first; while the S. system is determined by the normal position of the trunk. In normal positions of trunk, head and eye the three systems fall together, while in other positions they may differ so that each in turn may determine the localization. Muller inferred these systems primarily from results obtained with images, but he could show also that they play a part in perception and recognition, for instance in reading.[17]

In the following consideration of the A-P we shall refer merely to the V. and S. systems. An O., inclining his head, say 90° sidewards, in a totally dark room, is shown a single vertical line of light (*Leuchtlinie*). He sees this line not as vertical, but inclined in a manner contrary to the incination of his head. The inclination, considerable

[17]See Muller (46, p. 238f). Oetjen (47).

though it may be, never, or at least very rarely, reaches the full degree of the head's inclination, even when we deduct the effect produced by the compensatory swivel-rotation of the eye. This is the gross phenomenon of the A-P; it can be described, using Muller's terminology, in the following manner: The apparent position of the vertical line lies between the two positions which it would have if either the V. or the S. system were alone operative. The V. system would make the line vertical, since it is parallel to the basal line which now is vertical, while the S. system would make the line horizontal, since normally a line cast upon the horizontal meridian of the eyes, as this vertical line now is, would be a horizontal line. For simplicity's sake we shall neglect the swivel rotation. Muller explains the actual apparent position of the line as a compound effect resulting from the competition of the two systems, and speaks, therefore, of the V. and S. components. This explanation is corroborated by another form of the phenomenon appearing mainly with slighter inclinations of the head, which we shall here omit.

For Muller these systems are a product of experience and they work according to the general law of association. They can also be expressed by ascribing to each retinal point, not one, but two, values, a V. and an S. value. We see that Muller does not use our concept of a spatial level but operates with single elementary effects, the V. and S. components (resulting from corresponding space-values) which enter into an additive combination. But, like all theories of this sort, it must be supplemented, as we shall presently see, by the employment of such concepts as "apprehension" and "judgment." We may proceed by reporting from Muller's monograph (46) which contains an excellent summary of the existing literature, as well as a number of further facts.

1. We saw above that 'in eye- or head-movements our general level is not changed. Consequently objects do

1182

not seem to move when we move our head or eyes. But this holds only at a fixed level where the visual field contains points of "anchorage" (*Verankerungspunkte*). In the dark, where such points are missing, a single vertical line of light may appear to be moving about a vertical axis in a direction contrary to that of the head's movement. This shows that the effect of head-movements on visual objects is a function of the fixity of the spatial level, since, as we have already seen, in total darkness this level loses its stability.

2. If we observe the line of light with head inclined in a lighted room it appears to be vertical when the light is turned out, and with many O.'s it maintains at first its initial vertical position, and then passes gradually into its final oblique position. Muller considers this to be the effect of a general spatial perseverative tendency (*Beharrungstendenz*). But what is it that perseveres; is it the line itself, or is it primarily the initial space-level of the lighted room? All the facts here adduced speak for the latter interpretation and against the former which Muller accepts. (See particularly No. 5, below.)

3. Some authors maintain that the A-P also appears, though in a lesser degree, when the head remains erect, if the rest of the body is turned about its sagittal axis. This result, which has not been confirmed by all investigators, seems largely dependent upon individual differences and upon the method by which the position of the body is maintained. Yet like Muller, we have no reason to doubt that it may occur. Muller explains it by the associative law of substitution. I cannot here set forth the reasons why I am unable to accept this explanation, but the reader will understand that the *Gestalt* theory is fundamentally incompatible with the associationist's principles. According to our conception the fact under discussion signifies that the spatial level may be altered by unnatural positions of the body, even if the head

1183

remains in a normal position, and that this change of level is similar to that of the A-P proper. The individual differences, and the differences between the results of different authors, can then be also understood for the stability of the spatial level is very different with different individuals, as has been clearly shown by Wertheimer (64), and different experimental conditions will therefore not be of equal effectiveness in producing a uniform change of level.

4. Many O.'s report that they feel very uncertain in judging the position of the line, since they have lost their standard of the vertical, and the same O.'s show great variability in their final judgments. Apparently Muller considers this only as a matter of judgment, but again we cannot accept the distinction he draws between the phenomenon itself and the judgment of it, in which marked properties of the judgment are not considered to be founded in the phenomenon. We must ask, instead, what are the properties of the phenomenon, and what are the causes of these properties which lead to an uncertain and variable judgment? Our answer is that such judgments are based upon uncertain and variable phenomena. "Uncertainty" or "undeterminateness" may quite well be a property of visual phenomena, as Katz (24) maintained for the "distance" of his so-called "film-" colors (*Flachenfarben*), and both the undeterminatedness and the variability of this phenomenon are readily explained from our point of view. We have recognized the paramount importance of visual points of anchorage for the spatial level. When these are lacking, the level loses its hold, since the position of any single object depends upon the general level, and if the O. no longer has this, the position itself is no longer fixed or unanimously determined. Instead of employing this descriptively and functionally well-defined concept of the spatial level Muller and his followers distinguish between the phen-

omenon and the means whereby we orientate ourselves to it, the absence of points of anchorage being for P. Busse (3, p. 19), the absence of objects that can give us information about the inclination of the observed line.

5. During a longer observation, the line of light does not, as a rule, maintain its position. In the majority of cases its angle of inclination is increased toward the vertical. Muller suggests several explanations for this, maintaining that the V. component loses in weight, since with the passing of time the impression of the head's inclination loses in intensity; since, however, this explanation is insufficient, he also suggests a tendency to decrease the influence of the V. component which is purely visual in origin. Yet the observed fact fits very readily into our explanations; for the longer the points of anchorage are lacking, the more the spatial level will change, and in consequence of its great instability the more it will deviate from its normal standard. The rarer cases in which a change takes place in the opposite direction simply prove again the general condition of instability; for they can be fully explained only when we know in detail all the factors upon which the level depends. In this connection we are reminded of the vestibular and the skin-muscle systems, to both of which we would ascribe a direct influence upon the level, and not merely an indirect influence upon our judgment concerning the head's inclination, as Muller states the case with reference to the vestibular organ.

6. Some O.'s, particularly those who report uncertainty of judgment, show a tendency to persist in judging the line vertical. Again Muller explains this as a tendency to judge "without sufficient foundation," but he also admits the possibility of an illusory perception, caused by the O.'s imagination, which, in some persons, exercises a strong influence over the apparent position of the line. He calls this the "vertical tendency." From this vertical

tendency he distinguishes such cases as those in which the O., with head but slightly inclined, judges the line of light, when momentarily exposed as either uncertain or vertical. In cases of this sort he says that the line was not apprehended long enough. Apart from this method of interpretation the facts are as follows: When the level is unstable —and the influence of the imagination is nothing but an expression of its instability—the O. can see the line at will in different positions; the more prominent character of the vertical direction can then be influential. A momentary exposure is a favorable condition for instability because the peripheral (stimulus-determined) conditions of the whole (physiological) process, comprising the entire optical system, are weakened. Such a weakening always increases the effectiveness of purely structural factors. This has appeared clearly in Lindemann's investigations (28).

The conclusion we draw from these facts is not that Muller's theory is altogether wrong; for when we discard from it the concepts of apprehension, judgment, imagination and association[18], the competition among the two or three components remains. Only we would refer their effect to the general spatial level and not directly to the line. The components, therefore, find a place in our system as functional but not as descriptive facts.

Experimentally, we can destroy a fixed spatial level; we can also make one level give place to another, as has been shown by an experiment of Wertheimer's (64). Put a mirror in an inclined position upon a table. That part of the room seen in the mirror will then look abnormal. Objectively vertical lines will be inclined, and if a person visible in the mirror drops an object, it does not appear to

---

[18]That association is quite out of place here will appear when in our next article we are able to prove that the principal directions of space do not owe their prominence to experience and habit, but to an imminent law of structure, in consequence of which Muller's three systems cannot be accepted as habitual tendencies.

fall vertically. Now hold a tube to your eyes excluding the whole "real" room from your vision and continue looking into the mirror. Let other persons walk about and do things in the visible section of the room. Very soon everything will be all right again; the floor will assume its horizontal position, the chairs will stand vertically upon it and objects will no longer be seen in an angle smaller than 90°. You can measure the change by executing an apparently vertical line at the beginning and at the end of the experiment, and then determine the angle between these two.

In the three systems, the V., the H., and the S. system, we have found factors which enter into the constitution of our spatial level, and this last experiment has shown that the visible world itself is a concurrent factor. This is a fact of very general significance. Standing in a room of average size the direction "straight ahead" is not under all conditions the sagittal axis of my Cyclopean eye; for the most part it is the direction toward the wall, with which the plane of my face forms the smallest angle. It is I who am turned out of the main direction when I gaze obliquely towards the wall. This influence of the objective room-structure upon the space level is very different with different individuals. Yet the normal effect for the majority of persons can be shown by the following experiment. Since the discovery of v. Hornbostel and Wertheimer (20), we know that the apparent direction of a noise depends upon the time-difference with which the sound-waves strike the two ears. By inserting pipes of variable length, like trombone pipes, between the source of the sound and each ear one can, by drawing out or pushing in these pipes, readily make the noise wander from one side of the head to the other. One can also try to bring it to the middle or straight ahead. After some practice, this can be done with great precision and subjective certainty if one sits in a "good" position, i.e., if one

1187

of the walls of the room serves as a frontal-parallel orientation. But if a wall is lacking, or if one sits somewhat obliquely, the same task becomes very trying. When I had acquired an enormous practice after several thousand experiments, working with closed eyes, I was still unable to find a good middle position for the sound under these conditions. The auditory middle, the phenomenon provoked by the time-difference zero, coincides with the sagittal axis of the Cyclopean eye, but in an oblique position this was not "straight ahead" for me, since the walls of the room influenced my spatial level, and consequently the auditory cue failed. Referring back to the beginning of this paragraph, I may add that these experiments also indicate descriptively the existence of an auditory space-level; for when the noise of a metronome stroke occurs, it enters into a thus far empty, yet phenomenally existing auditory space. We find, too, that the stability of objects within a given level depends upon the quality of the object. Thus Busse (3) found that fine black vertical threads were much less stable than thicker brown ones which carried red and black wooden beads at fixed distances.

The conclusion is that normally we possess a general spatial level within which we are anchored. When we lose this anchorage, we are practically lost. Yet even this effect of optical vertigo has been explained by experience! When a room is rotated around us, "experience" should tell us that the room is fixed and that consequently we are ourselves rotative. Think of the man who daily operates such a machine of deception and who knows by experience of long standing that the room does move; will this man entering the rotating chamber with his knowledge grow giddy, or will he not? Practice in the room may no doubt modify the effect, just as does practice on the merry-go-round. But it is only by practice and not by knowledge or experience that the individual can succeed in maintaining a fixed level of any sort under these trying circumstances. With the aid of our level-concept we can also understand the so-called (physiological) relativity of movement. A person looking from a bridge into a rapid stream soon has the impression of being himself moved. Seated in a train which is standing in a station, we are often unable to decide whether it is our train or the one on a neighboring track which is beginning to move. One explanation of the former effect actually maintains that the movement of a small piece of the bridge which belongs to one's field of vision is *more probable* than the movement of so large a surface as that of the stream! But we should say that normally there is no choice as to where we shall place our anchorage; for, in most cases, even with the strongest impulse of our will, we cannot alter this anchorage (see Wertheimer [64]). Normally it is something quite independent of our will—a compulsory perception founded in properties of the objective field which determine for us what parts are to appear as figures and what parts as ground; as v. Hornbostel (19) puts it: *things* are not holes in the world of experience. On the other hand ambiguous situations occur in which two or more anchorages are equally possible, though here, too, law reigns and not chance. The chief rule for these ambiguous cases is this: that the objects which form the (dynamic) center of our visual world are at the same time our points of anchorage. When I am playing cards in my compartment I see the train move on the next track even if it is in reality my own train which is moving, but when I am looking at the other train, searching perhaps for an acquaintance in the coach, then it is my own train which seems to be moving. Psychologically, *i.e., phenomenally,* there is no relativity of movement.[19]

---

[19]Nor of size either, as Wertheimer (64) has shown.

But our level-concept has still a wider application. We have already referred to certain instances, such as fashion and style. Experimental psychology has also studied certain facts about the phenomenon of the level without recognizing them to be such. What I mean is best explained by referring to some of Hollingworth's experiments upon the indifference-point (I.P.) (17, 18). Many investigators, testing a scale of magnitudes, have found the existence of an I.P.; that is, while most members of the scale were estimated with a constant error, positive or negative, small magnitudes being overestimated and large ones underestimated, there comes a point where no constant error occurs. Though the fact has been confirmed over and over again, and in very different fields, yet, strangely enough, there has been a wide divergence of opinion as to the absolute position of the I.P. This startling fact suggested to Hollingworth the idea that there must be a mistake somewhere in the way the question is put. Is there, he asks, an absolute I.P. independent of the position and extent of the test-series, or is this I.P. a function of the total scale? He was able to demonstrate by a number of ingenious experiments that the latter is the correct assumption. Working with the reproduction of hand-and-arm movements, he arranged three series of experiments; A, including magnitudes of 10 to 70 mm. (with increments of 10 mm.); B, magnitudes of 30 to 150 mm. (with increments of 20 mm.); and C, magnitudes of 70 to 250 mm. (with increments of 30 mm.); each scale consisting of seven different magnitudes. Upon a given day only one of these series was used. The I.P. of series A fell at about 40 mm., of B, at about 75 mm., and of C at about 1^{2}5 mm., that is, it was always found to be approximately at the center of the scale. Smaller magnitudes were overestimated and larger ones underestimated. There was no absolute I.P. The magnitude of 70 mm., being the upper limit of A, and the lower limit of C, and near the middle of B, was underestimated in A (minus 10.2), overestimated in C (plus 16.5), and reproduced fairly accurately in B (plus 1.7; p.e. 10.3). To check this result, four months later, the three magnitudes of 10 mm. (always overestimated), 250 mm. (always underestimated) and 70 mm. (variable with the series) were tested singly on occasions several days apart, but for none of these three did a constant error occur.

In still another very clear experiment, the shifting of the I.P. itself was demonstrated. A set of standard magnitudes was prepared ranging from 10mm. to 60mm. (by increments of 10), from 60 mm. to 150 mm. (by increments of 15) and on to 250 mm. (by increments of 20). The standards of the 10 mm.—60 mm. were now given and reproduced in chance order, five trials being given for each magnitude. Then, without the knowledge of the O., the next magnitude was added and again five trials made of each standard. This was continued until the whole series of seventeen standards had been offered. The success of this experiment was remarkable. The I.P. rose with the introduction of each new standard magnitude; constant errors which were positive from the beginning, increased throughout the series, while constant errors which were negative in the beginning likewise underwent a continual change, decreasing to the zero point and emerging again as positive increments.

Hollingworth concludes, "that the phenomenon of the indifference point . . . is of purely central origin" (17 p. 21), and this theory is as close to the one we propose as the general theoretical position of psychology at the time of his investigation would admit. According to his results, the I.P.-phenomenon belongs not to memory but to perception, and as an analogy he refers to type-concepts, such as race and class (18, p. 468). He also speaks of a "mental set", meaning by this "that we are adjusted for or tend to expect the average magnitude, and to assimilate all other magnitudes toward it, to accept them in place of it" (17, p. 39). But he insists on employing the term "judgment"; the error to which this tendency leads, he says, "is distinctly an error of judgment, and is quite independent of sensory or physiological conditions" (18, p. 469).

Again the distinction drawn between sensory components and judgments of peripheral and central factors vitiates his theory. Leaving these out of account . . . we may here draw the following conclusions. In reacting to a definite scale of stimuli we establish a general level which, in the case described, as in many others, is both motor and sensory. The effect of each single stimulus is dependent upon this level, much as the figure is dependent upon its ground. And secondly, the general level holds together the whole group of phenomena corresponding to the scale of stimuli. Although they may rise or fall from this level, the phenomena never lose their existential connection with it, and being attracted by the level, the result is often a wrong judgment or a false reproduction. This attracting or assimilating effect of the level is a special case of our general law of levelling (discussed above). We see further that this level adapts itself automatically to the scale and this process of adaptation must therefore be explicable in terms of our general physiological theory.

Hollingworth rightly gives a wide application to his results, comparing the I.P.'s of different investigators with the range of their scales, and he has himself confirmed his "law of central tendency" in a purely sensory field by experiments upon the size of gray squares. I may also add in this connection that what G. E. Muller calls the "absolute impression" (*Absoluter Eindruck*) is just such a rise or fall from a general level. Whenever an O. makes a judgment that is not based upon a comparison between two stimuli, he is reacting not to a stepwise phenomenon, but to an emergence from the general level. With this I must bring my first article to a close.

REFERENCES

1. BORAK, J. Uber die Empfindlichkeit für Gewichtsunterschiede bei abnehmender Reizstärke. *Psychol. Forsch.*, 1922, 1, 374-389. 2. BÜHLER, K. *Die geistige. Entwicklung des Kindes.* Jena: Fischer. 2 Aufl., 1921, pp. xvi+463. 3. BUSSE, P. Uber die Gedächtnisstufen und ihre Beziehung zum Aufbau der Wahrnehmungswelt. Uber die Vorstellungswelt der Jugendlichen und den Aufbau des intellektuellen Lebens. Eine Untersuchung über Grundfragen der Psychologie des Vorstellens und Denkens. *Zeits. f. Psychol.*, 1920, 84, 1-66. 4. CORNELIUS, H. *Psychologie als Erfahrungswissenschaft.* Leipzig, Teubner, 1897, pp. xv+445. 5. EDWARDS, A. S. An Experimental Study of Sensory Suggestion. *Amer. J. of Psychol.*, 1915, 26, 99-129. 6. v. EHRENFELS, CH. Uber Gestaltqualitaten. *Vierteljahrschr. f. wissensch. Philos.* 1890. 14. 7. FERNBERGER, S W. The Effect of the Attitude of the Subject Upon the Measure of Sensibility. *Amer. J. of Psychol.*, 1914, 25, 538-543. 8. FRINGS, G. Uber den Einfluss der Komplexbildung auf die effektuelle und generative Hemmung. *Arch. f. d. ges. Psychol.*, 1913, 30, 415-479. 9. GARTEN, S. Uber die Grundlagen unserer Orientierung im Raume. *Abh. d. math.-phys. Kl. d. süchs. Akad. d. Wissensch.*, 1920, 36, 433-510. 10. GELB, A. Theoretisches über "Gestaltqualitäten." *Zeits. f. Psychol.*, 1911, 58, 1-58. 11. GELB, A. Uber den Wegfall der Wahrnehmung von "Oberflächen farben." Beiträge zur Farbenpsychologie auf Grund von Untersuchungen am Fällen mit erworbenen, durch zerebrale Läsionen bedingten Farbensinnstorungen. Psychologische Analysen hirnpathologischer Fälle auf Grund von Untersuchungen Hirnverletzter. *Zeits. f. Psychol.*, 1920, 84, 193-257. Also contained in *Psychologische Analysen* u.s.w. Bd. I. Leipzig: Barth. 1920, pp. 561. 12. HEINE, R. Uber Wiederkennen und rückwirkende Hemmung. *Zeits. f. Psychol.*, 1914, 68, 161-236. 13. v. HELMHOLTZ, H. *Handbuch der physiologischen Optik.* 3 Aufl. Erg. u. her. in Gemeinschaft mit *A. Gullstrand* und *J. v. Kries* von *W. Nagel.*† 3 Bde. Hamburg & Leipzig, 1909-1911 (l. Aufl. 1856-1866). 14. HENNING, H. Experimentelle Untersuchungen zur Denkpsychologie. I. Die assoziative Mischwirkung, das Vorstellen von noch nie Wahrgenommenem und deren Grenzen. *Zeits. f. Psychol.*, 1919, 81, 1-96. 15. HERING, E. *Grundzüge der Lehre vom Lichtsinn.* Berlin: Springer, 1905-1920, pp. v+294. Sonderabdruck a. d. Handbuch d. Augenheilkunde (*Graefe-Sämisch*) I. Teil, XII Kop. 16. HOFLER, A. Gestalt und Beziehung—Gestalt und Auschanung. *Zeits. f. Psychol.*, 1912, 60, 161-228. 17. HOLLINGSWORTH, H. L. The Inaccuracy of Movement With Special Reference to Constant Errors. *Arch. of Psychol.*, 1909, No. 13, Columbia Contrib. to Philos. & Psychol., 17, pp. 87. 18. HOLLINGSWORTH, H. L. The Central Tendency of Judgment. *J. of Philos., Psychol. and Sci. Meth.*, 1910, 7, 461-469. 19. v. HORNBOSTEL, E. M. Uber optische Inversion. *Psychol. Forsch.*, 1922, 1, 130-156. 20. v. HORNBOSTEL, E M. UND WERTHEIMER, M. Uber die Wahrnehmung der Schallrichtung. *Sitzungsber. d. Preuss. Akad. d. Wissensch.*, 1920, 20, 388-396. 21. JAENSCH, E. R. Einige allgemeinere Fragen der Psychologie und Biologie des Denkens, erläutert an der Lehre vom Vergleich. (Mit Bemerkungen über die Krisis in der Philosophie der Gegenwart.) *Arb. z. Psychol. und Philos.* Leipzig: Barth, 1920, 1, pp. 31. 22. JAENSCH, E. R. UND MÜLLER, E. A. Uber die Wahrnehmung farbloser Helligkeiten und den Helligkeitskontrast. Uber Grundfragen der Farbenpsychologie. Zugleich ein Beitrag zur Theorie der Erfahrung. Hn. v. *E. R. Jaensch* I. *Zeits. f. Psychol.*, 1920, 83, 266-341. (Auch separat bei Barth.) 23. JAENSCH, E. R. Uber den Farbenkontrast und

1193

die so genannte Berücksichtigung der farbigen Beleuchtung. Uber Grundfragen u.s.w. III. *Zeits. f. Sinnesphysiol.*, 1921, 52, 165-180. 24. KATZ, D. Die Erscheinungsweisen der Farben und ihre Beimflussung durch die individuelle Erfahrung. *Erg. Bd. d. Zeits. f. Psychol.* Leipzig: Barth, 1911, pp. xviii+425. 25. KOFFKA, K. *Beiträge zur Psychologie der Gestalt.* I. Untersuchungen über den Zusammenhang zwischen Erscheinungsgrosse und Erscheinungsbewegung bei einigen sagenannten optischen Täuschungen, von *F. Kenkel. Zeits. f. Psychol.*, 1913, 67, 358-449. 26. KOFFKA, K. The same. III. Zur Grundlegung der Wahrnehmungspsychologie. Eine Auseinandersetzung mit V. Benussi, von *K. Koffka. Zeits. f. Psychol.*, 1915, 73, 11-90. 27. KOFFKA, K. The same. IV. Zur Theorie einfachster gesehener Bewegungen. Ein physiologisch-mathematischer Versuch von *K. Koffka. Zeits. f. Psychol.*, 1919, 82, 257-292. Beiträge I-IV also separate, as Beiträge, etc. Vol. I, Leipzig: Barth, 1919, pp. v.+323. 28. KOFFKA, K. The same. VII. Experimentelle Untersuchunger über das Entsteher & Vergehen von Gestalten, von *E. Lindemann. Psychol. Forsch.*, 1922, 2, 5-60. 29. KOFFKA, K. The same. VIII. Uber die Verschmelzung von zwei Reizen (title not definitely settled), von *L. Hartmann*, to appear in *Psychol. Forsch.* 30. KOFFKA, K. Probleme der experimentellen Psychologie. I. Die Unterscheidsschwelle. *Die Naturwissensch.*, 1917, 5, 1-5, 23-28. 31. KOFFKA, K. The same. II. Uber den Einfluss der Erfahrung auf die Wahrnehmung (Behandelt am Problem des Sehens von Bewegungen). *Die Naturwissensch.*, 1919, 7, 597-604. 32. KOFFKA, K. Die Prävalenz der Figur. Kleine Mitteilungen a. d. psychol. Inst. d. Univ. Giessen, 3. *Psychol. Forsch.*, 1922, 2, 147-148. 33. KOFFKA, K. *Die Grundlagen der psychischen Entwicklung. Eine Einführung in die Kinderpsychologie.* Osterwieck a/H: Zickfeldt, 1921, pp. vii+278. 34. KOHLER, W. Uber unbemerkte Empfindungen und Urteilstäuschungen. *Zeits. f. Psychol.*, 1913, 66, 51-80. 35. KOHLER, W. Die Farbe der Sehdinge beim Schimpansen und beim Haushuhn. *Zeits. f. Psychol.*, 1917, 77, 248-255. 36. KOHLER, W. Nachweis einfacher Strukturfunktionen beim Schimpansen und beim Haushuhn. Uber eine neue Methode zur Untersuchung des bunten Farbensystems. Aus der Anthropoidenstation auf Teneriffe IV. *Abh. d. Preuss. Akad. d. Wissenschaft*, 1918, phys.-math. Klasse. No. 2, pp. 101 (Einzelausgabe). 37. KOHLER, W. Zur Psychologie der Schimpansen. Psychol. Forsch., 1922, 1, 2-46. 38. KOHLER, W. *Die physischen Gestalten in Rube und im stationären Zustand. Eine naturphilosophische Untersuchung.* Braunschweig: Vieweg, 1920, pp. xx+263. 39. KROH, O. Uber Farbenkonstang und Farbenstraus formation. Uber Grundfragen u.s.w. (s. No. 22), her. v. *E. R. Jaensch.* IV. *Zeits. f. Sinnesphysiol.*, 1921, 52, 181-186. 40. LEWIN, K. Das Problem der Willensmessung und das Grundgesetz der Assoziation. *Psychol. Forsch.*, 1922, 1, 191-302, 2, 65-140. 41. LINDWORSKY, J. Referat über *Kohler* (36), *Stimmen der Zeit*, 1919, 97, 62-68. 42. MARTIN, L. J. Uber die Abhängigkeit visueller Vorstellungsbilder vom Denken. Eine experimentelle Untersuchung. *Zeits. f. Psychol.*, 1914-15, 70, 212-275. 43. MÜLLER, G. E. *Zur Grundlegung der Psychophysik.* Berlin: Grieben, 1878, pp. xvi+424. 44. MÜLLER, G. E. UND PILZECKER, A. Experimentelle Beiträge zur Lehre vom Gedächtnis. *Erg. Bd. I, d. Zeits. f. Psychol.* Leipzig: Barth, 1900, pp. xiv+300. 45. MÜLLER, G. E. *Zur Analyse der Gedächtnistätigkeit und des Vorstellungsverlaufes.* II. *Teil. Erg. Bd. 9 d. Zeits. f. Psychol.* Leipzig: Barth, 1917, pp. xii+682. 46. MÜLLER, G. E. Uber das Aubertsche Phänomen. *Zeits. f. Sinnesphysiol.*, 1916, 49, 109-244. 47. OETJEN, F. Die Bedeutung der Orientierung des Lesestoffes für das Lesen und der Orientierung von sinnlosen Formen für das Wiedererkennen der Letzteren. *Zeits. f. Psychol.*, 1915, 71, 321-355. 48. OGDEN, R. M. Are there any Sensations? *Amer. J. of Psychol.*, 1922, 33, 247-254. 49. PAULI, R. *Uber Psychische Gesetzmässigkeit, insbesondere über das Weber'sche Gesetz.* Jena: Fischer, 1920, pp. 88. 50. PETERS, W. Aufmerksam-

1194

keit und Reizschwelle. Versuche zur Messung der Aufmerksamkeitskonzentration. *Arch. f. d. ges. Psychol.*, 1906, 8, 385-432. 51. PILLSBURY, W. B. *The Essentials of Psychology.* New York: Macmillan Co., 1911, pp. ix+362. 52. RAHN, C. The Relation of Sensation to other Categories in Contemporary Psychology. A Study in the Psychology of Thinking. *Psychol. Monog.*, 1913, 16(1), pp. 131. 53. RUBIN, E. *Synsoplovede Figurer. Studier i psykologisk Analyse.* 1 del. Kobenhavn og Kristiania: Gyldendal, 1915, pp. xii+228. German edition: *Visuell wahrgenommen Figuren. Studien in psychologischer Analyse.* 1 Teil. Kobenhavn, Christiania, Berlin, London: Gyldendal, 1921, p. xii+244. 54. SCHLÜTER, L. Experimentelle Beiträge zur Prüfung der Auschauungs-und der Ubersetzungsmethode bei der Einführung in einen fremdsprachlichen Wortschatz. *Zeits. f. Psychol.*, 1914, 68, 1-114. 55. SCHUMANN, F. Beiträge zur Analyse der Gesichtswahrnehmungen. I. Einige Beobachtungen über die Zusammenfassung von Gesichtseindrücken zu Einheiten. *Zeits. f. Psychol.*, 1900, 23, 1-32. 56. SCHUMANN, F. Beiträge etc. III. Der Successivvergleich. *Zeits. f. Psychol.*, 1902, 30, 241-291 and 321-339. 57. SEIFERT, F. Zur Psychologie der Abstraktion und Gestaltauffassung. *Zeits. f. Psychol.*, 1917, 78, 55-144. 58. SHEPARD, G. F., and FOGELSONGER, H. M. Studies in Association and Inhibition. *Psychol. Rev.*, 1913, 20, 290-311. 59. SPECHT, W. Die Beeinflussung der Sinnesfunktionen durch geringe Alkoholmengen. I. Das Verhalten von Unterschiedschwelle und Reizschwelle im Gebiet des Gehorsinnes. *Arch. f. d. ges. Psychol.*, 1907, 9, 180-295. 60. STUMPF, C. Tonpsychologie. I. Leipzig: Hirzel, 1883, pp. xiv+ 427. 61. TITCHENER, E. B. A Text-Book of Psychology. New York: Macmillan Co., 1910, pp. xx+565. 62. TITCHENER, E. B. Functional Psychology and the Psychology of Act II. *Amer. Jour. of Psychol.*, 1922, 33, 43-83. 63. WASHBURN. M. F. An Instance of the Effect of Verbal Suggestion on Tactual Space Perception. Notes from the Psychological Laboratory of Vassar College. II. *Amer. J. of Psychol.*, 1909, 20, 447-448. 64. WERTHEIMER, M. Experimentelle Studien über des Sehen von Bewegung. *Zeits. f. Psychol.*, 1912, 61, 161-265. 65. WERTHEIMER, M. Untersuchungen zur Lehre von der Gestalt. I. Prinzipielle Bemerkungen. *Psychol. Forsch.*, 1922, 1, 47-58. 66. WITASEK, St. Psychologie der Raumwahrnehmung des Auges.—Die Psychologie in Einzeldarstellungen, her. v. *H. Ebbinghaus* † und *E. Meumann*, II. Heidelberg: Winter, 1910, pp. viii+454.

KURT KOFFKA (b.—Berlin, March 18, 1886; d.—November 22, 1941).

Koffka entered the University of Berlin in 1903. He spent one year at Edinburgh, 1904-1905. Then returning to Berlin, he received his Ph.D. in 1908. He subsequently worked with v. Kries in physiology for one semester. Then he went to the University of Wurzburg, as assistant to Kulpe and Marbe. In 1910 he joined Köhler at Frankfurt, also as Assistant to Schumann. In 1911 he became Privatdozent at the University of Giessen. In 1918 he was appointed Ausserordentlicher Professor. In 1924-25 he was Visiting Professor of Education at Cornell. In 1925 he was at Chicago. In 1926-27 he was invited to Wisconsin by Clark Hull. He was William Allen Neilson Professor of Psychology at Smith College, Northampton, Massachusetts, from 1927 until his death.

Koffka worked closely with Wertheimer and Köhler in the development of Gestalt Psychology. Together with Köhler, he was an observer in Wertheimer's study on the perception of movement (q.v.).

The present essay constitutes the first complete statement of the Gestalt psychology in English. As such, it was probably more influential in the history of psychology in America than any other single work in this field.

KOFFKA, K. "Perception: an introduction to the *Gestalt-Theorie.*" *Psychol. Bull.* 1922, 19:531-585. This essay is reproduced substantially in its entirety with the kind permission of the American Psychological Association.

See also:

KOFFKA, K.

a) *The growth of the mind: an introduction to child psychology.* London: Routledge, Kegan Paul, Ltd., 1925 (1921). Trans. R. M. Ogden.

b) *Principles of gestalt psychology.* London: Routledge, Kegan Paul, Ltd., 1935. This book constitutes the definitive classical statement.

HARROWER-ERICKSON, M. R. "Kurt Koffka (1886-1941)." *Amer. J. Psychol.* 1942, 55: 278-281. This contains a recent bibliography, thus completing the one in Murchison.

MURCHISON (b—Vol. 2, p. 131-132, b—Vol. 3 p. 285-287).

A
TREATISE
ON THE
MEDICAL JURISPRUDENCE
OF
INSANITY.

Issac Ray

CHAPTER VIII.

LEGAL CONSEQUENCES OF MANIA.

§ 166. MAN, being destined for the social condition, has received from the author of his being the faculties necessary for discovering and understanding his relations to his fellow-men, and possesses the liberty, to a certain extent, of regulating his conduct agreeably or directly opposed to their suggestions. For the manner in which this power is used he is *morally* responsible, the elements of responsibility always being the original capacity, the healthy action, and the cultivation of the moral and intellectual faculties,—the measure of the former being in proportion to the degree in which the latter are possessed. In *legal* responsibility, the last element above mentioned is not admitted, and the first to a very limited extent only, the second alone being absolutely essential....

§ 167. The influence of this condition on responsibility will obviously be proportioned to its severity and the extent of its action, and though we cannot hope to become acquainted with all its grades, there is no reason why we may not be able to recognise and identify some of the more common and prominent. If men had agreed to receive some particular analysis and arrangement of the

affective and intellectual faculties, and to assign to each
a particular portion of the brain as its material organ,
we might then discuss the question how far disease of
one cerebral organ affects the actions of the rest, with
the prospect of arriving at something like definite results.
But as no such unanimity exists, we can only consider the
observations that have been made on the derangement of
particular faculties, and thus form our opinions relative
to their influence, by the general tenor of experience.
Analogy would lead us to expect that this inquiry would
result in establishing the principle; first, that each and
every kind and degree of mania does not equally diminish
legal responsibility; and secondly, that the effect of mania
in this respect must be estimated not merely by the severity of its outward symptoms, but also in reference to the
particular faculty affected. If now, these results are confirmed by the evidence of facts, we have only to keep
them steadily in view, in order to avoid much of the
difficulty usually complained of, in arriving at satisfactory conclusions on this much vexed and agitated subject.

SECTION I.

Legal Consequences of Intellectual Mania.

§ 168. The common law relating to insanity, as before
intimated, is open to censure, not so much on account of
the manner in which it modifies the civil and criminal
responsibilities of the lunatic, as of the looseness, incon-
sistency, and incorrectness of the principles on which the
fact of the existence of the disease is judicially established. The disabilities it imposes on this unfortunate
class of our fellow-men are founded in the most humane
and enlightened views, and have for their object the promotion of their highest welfare. To incapacitate a person
from making contracts, bequeathing property, and performing other civil acts, who has lost his natural power
of discerning and judging, who mistakes one thing for

another, and misapprehends his relations to those around him, is the greatest mercy he could receive, instead of being an arbitrary restriction of his rights.

§ 169. In opposition to that principle of the common law, which makes the lunatic who commits a trespass on the persons or property of others, amenable in damages to be recovered by a civil action,[1] Hoffbauer declares, that if the patient is "so deranged that he is no longer master of his actions, he is under no responsibility, nor obliged to make reparation for injuries."[2] He gives no reason for this opinion, and we are unable to see how it can be even plausibly supported. To the maniac, who, when restored to his senses, discovers that during his derangement he has committed an injury to his neighbor's property, indemnity for which will strip him of his own possessions and reduce him to absolute beggary, his recovery must seem indeed like escaping from one evil only to encounter a greater. Such a possible consequence of madness, it is certainly painful to think of; but as the damage is produced and must be borne by one party or the other, we cannot hesitate which it should be; for though it may be hard for a person thus to suffer for actions committed while utterly unconscious of their nature, it would manifestly be the height of injustice to make another suffer, who was equally innocent and perhaps equally unconscious of the act.

§ 170. There is one operation of the common law, however, which is justly a cause of complaint, namely, that by which lunatics, even when under guardianship, are subject to be imprisoned like others, in default of satisfying a civil execution obtained against them;[3] because, whether such imprisonment be considered as a penal or

---

[1]Weaver v. Ward, Hobart's Reports, 134.
[2]Op. cit. § 131, p. 139.
[3]Shelford on Lunacy, 407; Ex parte Leighton, 14 Mass. Rep. 207.

a merely coercive measure, it is altogether inapplicable to the insane. It cannot coerce one who has no control over his own property, and whose mental condition is supposed to be such that he is unable to see any relation between the means and the end; and to punish a person, for what he himself had no agency whatever in doing, is a violation of the first principles of justice. To incarcerate some madmen in a common jail would, in all probability, aggravate their disorder, and if the confinement were protracted to the extent which the law would allow, render it utterly incurable.

§ 171. The civil disabilities above-mentioned are not incurred by every one laboring under mental derangement; the measure of insanity necessary to produce this effect, or in legal phrase, the fact of the party's being *compos,* or *non compos mentis,* is a question to be submitted to judicial investigation, the result of which will depend on the views of individuals relative to the effect of insanity on the mental operations, and to the respect due to opinions and decisions already promulgated. General intellectual mania, as we have represented it, should be followed, to the fullest extent, by the legal consequences of insanity; but partial intellectual mania does not necessarily render a person *non compos,* or so impaired in mind as to be no longer legally responsible for his acts, any more than every disease of the lungs or stomach prevents a patient from attending to his ordinary affairs, and enjoying a certain measure of health. The question when mania invalidates a person's civil acts and annuls criminal responsibility, and when it does not affect his liability in these respects, has occasioned considerable discussion, and is certainly the most delicate and important that the whole range of this subject embraces. No general principles concerning it are to be found in the common law, and cases seem to have been decided with but little reference to one another, according to the medi-

cal or legal views which happened at the time to possess
the minds of the court and jury. As insanity has become
better known, decisions have occasionally been more correct, but as the prevalence of these improvements has
not been universal, this branch of jurisprudence has often
retrograded, and thus the mind of the inquirer is confused by an array of opinions diametrically opposed.
General principles on this subject, therefore, are yet to
be established; and in furtherance of this object, we shall
endeavor to lay down such legal consequences of partial
intellectual mania, as seem to be warranted by correct
medical knowledge of madness and by enlightened principles of justice.

§ 172. We see some persons managing their affairs
with their ordinary shrewdness and discretion, evincing
no extraordinary exaltation of feeling or fancy, and on
all but one or a few points, in the perfect enjoyment of
their reason. It has been elsewhere remarked, that strange
as it may appear, it is no less true, that notwithstanding
the serious derangement of the reasoning power which a
person must have experienced, who entertains the strange
fancies that sometimes find their way into the mind, it
may be exercised on all other subjects, so far as we can
see, with no diminution of its natural soundness. To deprive such a one of the management of his affairs, or to
invalidate his contracts, under the show of affording him
protection, would be to inflict a certain and a serious
injury for the purpose of preventing a much smaller one
that might never occur. The principle that we would in-
culcate is, that monomania invalidates a civil act only
when such act comes within the circle of the diseased
operations of the mind. The celebrated Pascal believed
at times that he was sitting on the brink of a precipice
over which he was momentarily in danger of falling, and
a German professor of law, mentioned by Hoffbauer,
thought the freemasons were leagued against him, while

1201

he discharged the duties of his chair with his usual ability, and numberless are the instances of worthy people who have imagined their heads turned round, or their limbs made of butter or glass, but who nevertheless manage their concerns with their ordinary shrewdness. No one, however, following the dictates of his own judgment, would seriously propose to invalidate such of these men's acts as manifestly have no reference to the crotchets they have imbibed.

§ 173. It is not to be understood however that in every case of partial mania we have only to ascertain the insane delusion and then decide whether or not the act in question could have come within the range of its influence. In many instances the delusion is frequently changing, in which case, it is not only difficult to determine how far it may have been connected with any particular act, but the mind, in respect to other operations, has lost its original soundness, to such a degree that it cannot be trusted in the transaction of important affairs. Still this is not a sufficient reason against applying the general principle, where it can be done without fear of mistake. In doubtful instances we must be governed by the circumstances of the case, and this course, with all its objections, seems far more rational than the practice of universal disqualification.

§ 174. The validity of a marriage contracted in a state of partial mania, is not to be determined exactly upon the above principles. Here it is not sufficient to consider merely the connexion of the hallucination with the idea of being married, nor should we form any conclusion in favor of the capacity of the deranged party, from the propriety with which he conducts himself during the ceremony. The mere joining of hands and uttering the usual responses are things not worth considering; it is the new relations which the married state creates, the new responsibilities which it imposes, that should fix our

1202

attention, as the only points in regard to which the question of capacity can be properly agitated. In other contracts, all the conditions and circumstances may be definite and brought into view at once, and the capacity of the mind to comprehend them determined with comparative facility. In the contract of marriage, on the contrary, there is nothing definite or certain; the obligations which it imposes do not admit of being measured and discussed; they are of an abstract kind, and constantly varying with every new scene and condition of life. With these views we are obliged to dissent from the principle, laid down by the Supreme Judicial Court of Massachusetts, in a case of libel for divorce for insanity of the wife at the time of the marriage, that "the fact of the party's being able to go through the marriage ceremony with propriety, was *prima facie* evidence of sufficient understanding to make the contract."[1] If by making the contract is meant merely the giving of consent and the execution of certain forms, then indeed the fact of the party's going through the ceremony with propriety may be some evidence of sufficient understanding to make it; but if the expression includes the slightest idea of the nature of the relations and duties that follow, or even of the bonds and settlements that sometimes accompany it, then the fact here mentioned is no evidence at all of sufficient capacity. Sir John Nicholl, looking at the subject in a different light, has very properly said, that "going through the ceremony was not sufficient to establish the capacity of the party; and that foolish, crazy persons might be instructed to go through the formality of the ceremony, though wholly incapable of understanding the marriage contract."[2] In a similar case, Lord Stowell, then Sir William Scott, had previously observed, on the fact given in evidence, that the party "had manifested

---

[1]4 Pickering's Reports, 32.
[2]Browning *v.* Reade, 2 Phillimore's Eccl. Rep. 69.

perfect propriety of behavior" during the ceremony, "that much stress was not to be laid on the circumstance; as persons, in that state, will nevertheless often pursue a favorite purpose, with the composure and regularity of apparently sound minds.'"[1]

§ 175. The principles that should regulate the legal relations of the partially insane are few and simple. While they should be left in possession of every civil right that they are not clearly incapable of exercising, they should be subjected to the performance of no duties involving the interests or comfort of individuals, which may be equally well discharged by others. In the former instance we continue the enjoyment of a right that has never been abused; in the latter, we refrain from imposing duties on people who are not qualified to perform them. We cannot therefore agree with Hoffbauer, that a monomaniac should be allowed to manage the affairs of another, or be appointed to the office of guardian, however much we might be inclined to respect the validity of his civil acts. In some instances it is impossible to know or to conjecture, beforehand, how the predominant idea in his mind may be affected by his connexion with persons and things that have hitherto been foreign to his thought; while in others, it is far within the range of probability that the consequences will be ruinous to himself and others. Here for example, is a man who has long believed that he has an eel in his stomach, but on no other point has he manifested the slightest mental impairment. If a monomaniac is ever a suitable person to manage the affairs of another, it would seem, at first thought, that this one certainly is; yet nothing would be more injudicious than to entrust him with any such duty, for in all probability, though perfectly upright in his dealings, he would be irresistibly impelled to dissipate the property of others, as he always has his own earnings, in constant

---

[1]Turner *v.* Meyers, 1 Hagg. Con. Rep. 414.

journeyings from one empiric to another, in purchasing medicines, and consulting physicians, for the purpose of getting relieved from his fancied tormenter. This exclusion, as Chambeyron the French translator of Hoffbauer, justly remarks, does the monomaniac no wrong, it frees him from a great responsibility, it prevents dangers, possible at least, either to the ward or to him.

§ 176. The above views, though not yet distinctly received in courts, are countenanced by many distinguished physicians and jurists. Hoffbauer supports them to the fullest extent, Esquirol sanctions them, by interposing no word of disapprobation, and Georget admits them in application to civil cases. Paris and Fonblanque have explicitly recognised their correctness in the following passage. "When a man suffers under a partial derangement of intellect, and on one point only, it would be unjust to invalidate acts which were totally distinct from, and uninfluenced by this so-limited insanity; but if the act done bear a strict and evident reference to the existing mental delusion, we cannot see why the law should not also interpose a limited protection, and still less why courts of equity, which in their ordinary jurisdiction relieve against mistake, should deny their aid in such cases."[1]

§ 177. Mr. Evans, the translator of Pothier's Treatise on Obligations, expresses an opinion on this subject, no less positive and precise. "I cannot but think," he says, "that a mental disorder operating on partial subjects, should, with regard to those subjects, be attended with the same effects as a total deprivation of reason; and that on the other hand, such a partial disorder operating only upon particular subjects, should not in its legal effects, have an influence more extensive than the subjects to which it applies; and that every question should be reduced to the point, whether the act under consideration

---

[1] Medical Jurisprudence, 302.

proceeded from a mind fully capable, in respect of that act, of exercising free, sound and discriminating judgment; but in case the infirmity is established to exist, the tendency of it to direct or fetter the operations of the mind should be in general regarded as sufficient presumptive evidence, without requiring a direct and positive proof of its actual operation."[1]

§ 178. It has been already remarked that the practice of the English courts in regard to partial insanity has been regulated by no settled principles. Of the truth of this remark we have a striking illustration in Greenwood's case, which has been so often cited. Mr. Greenwood was bred to the bar and acted as chairman at the quarter sessions, but becoming diseased, and receiving in a fever a draught from the hand of his brother, the delirium, taking its ground then, connected itself with that idea; and he considered his brother as having given him a potion, with a view to destroy him. He recovered in all other respects, but that morbid image never departed; and that idea appeared connected with the will by which he disinherited his brother. Nevertheless, it was considered so necessary to have some precise rule, that, though a verdict had been obtained in the common pleas against the will, the judge strongly advised the jury to find the other way, and they did accordingly find in favor of the will.

Farther proceedings took place afterwards and concluded in a compromise.[1] No one would be hardly enough to affirm that Greenwood's mind was perfectly rational and sound, and as his insanity displayed itself on all topics relating to his brother, every act involving this brother's interests, to go no farther, ought consequently to have been invalidated. A plainer case cannot well be imagined.

§ 179. More enlarged and correct views prevailed in

---

[1]2 Pothier on Obligations, Appendix, 24.
[2]Lord Eldon, in White *v.* Wilson, 3 Vesey's Reports, 88.

the able and elaborate judgment delivered by Sir John Nicholl, in the case of Dew v. Clark,[1] where the existence of partial mania is recognised, and the necessity of bearing in mind the fact of its partial operation on the understanding, while determining its influence on the civil acts of the individual, is strongly inculcated. The point at issue was the validity of the will of one Stott (who left personal property nearly amounting to £40,000), bequeathing the complainant, who was his daughter and only child, a life-interest in a small portion of his estate, the most of which was devised to his nephews. The object of inquiry was whether the extraordinary conduct and feelings of the deceased towards his daughter had any real cause, or was solely the offspring of delusion in a disordered mind, and to this end an unparalleled mass of evidence was offered by each party. It was proved by the nephews that the testator had considerable practice as a surgeon and medical electrician from 1785 to 1820, and that at all times down to the latter period when he had a paralytic stroke, he managed the whole of his pecuniary and professional affairs in a rational manner, and rationally conducted all manner of business. They admitted that he was a man of an irritable and violent temper; of great pride and conceit; very precise in all his domestic and other arrangements; very impatient of contradiction, and imbued with high notions of parental authority. They represented him to have entertained rigid notions of the total and absolute depravity of human nature and of the necessity of sensible conversion, and contended that all the singularities of his conduct could be attributed to his peculiar disposition and belief, without resorting to insanity for an explanation. By the daughter, it was shown by a body of evidence that placed the fact beyond the shadow of a reasonable doubt, that from an early period of her life, he manifested an insane

---

[1] 3 Addams's Reports, 79.

aversion towards her. It appears that he was in the habit of describing her, even to persons with whom he was not intimately acquainted, as sullen, perverse, obstinate, and given to lying; as a fiend, a monster, a very devil, the special property of Satan; and charging her with vices, of which it was impossible that a girl of her age could be guilty. The peculiar and unequalled depravity of his child, her vices, obstinacy, and profligacy were topics on which he was constantly dwelling, and his general deportment towards her not only negatived all idea of natural affection, but betrayed a most fiend-like temper. His manner towards her was fiery and terrific; the instant she appeared, his eye flashed with rage and scorn, and he spurned her from him as he would a reptile. He compelled her to do the most menial offices, such as sweeping the rooms, scouring the grates, washing the linen and the dishes; to live in the kitchen and be sparingly fed. He once stripped her naked, when ten or eleven years old, tied her to a bed-post, and after flogging her severely with a large rod intertwisted with brass wire, rubbed her back with brine. Repeatedly, and on the most trivial occasions, he struck her with his clenched fists, cut her flesh with a horsewhip, tore out her hair, and once aimed at her a blow with some weapon which made a dent in a mahogany table, and which must have killed her, had she not avoided it. Now it was abundantly proved that there existed no real cause whatever for this strange antipathy, but that the daughter was of an amiable, obliging, and docile disposition—that she had always shown a great filial affection for her father—that she conducted at home and abroad with the utmost propriety and decorum—that she was a person of strictly moral and religious habits, and was so considered and known to be by the friends of the deceased and others of high reputation and character. The court, in making up its decision, declared that the question at issue was, ''not whether the deceased's in-

1208

sanity in certain *other* particulars, as proved by the daughter, should have the effect of defeating *a* will, *generally,* of the deceased, or even *this* identical will—but whether his insanity, on the subject of his daughter, should have the effect of defeating, not so much *any* will (*a* will *generally*) of the deceased, as this identical will.'' Accordingly, considering it proved that the will was the direct, unqualified offspring of that morbid delusion concerning the daughter, thus put into act and energy, it was pronounced to be *null* and *void* in law. In this decision we see the prevalence of those more correct and profound views of insanity, which have resulted from the inquiries of the last few years.

The same principle had been previously laid down in the following case which was adjudicated in Kentucky, in 1822. George Moore made his will in April 1822, and shortly after died. It was the validity of this will which was the point at issue. About twenty-four years previous to his death, he had a dangerous fever, during which he imbibed a strong antipathy towards his brothers, imagining that they intended to destroy or injure him, though they attended him throughout his illness, and never gave the slightest foundation for his belief. This antipathy continued to the day of his death, with a single exception, when he made a will in their favor, but afterwards cancelled it. When asked by one of the witnesses why he disinherited his brothers, he became violently excited, and declared that they had endeavored to get his estate before his death. The court, in its decision, observed, that, ''he cannot be accounted a free agent in making his will, so far as his relatives are concerned, although free as to the rest of the world. But however free he may have been as to other objects, the conclusion is irresistible, that this peculiar defect of intellect did influence his acts in making his will, and for this cause it ought not to be sustained. It is not only this groundless hatred or malice to his

1209

brethren that ought to affect his will, but also his fears of them, which he expressed during his last illness, conceiving that they were attempting to get away his estate before his death, or that they were lying in wait to shoot him, while on other subjects he spoke rationally; all which are strong evidences of a derangement in one department of his mind, unaccountable indeed, but directly influencing and operating upon the act which is now claimed as the final disposition of the estate.'"[1]

Esquirol has related a case of a very similar kind, where a person conceived an antipathy against his brothers, sisters, and other relatives, who, he believed were seeking to destroy him. Under the influence of this delusion he made testamentary dispositions, and Esquirol being consulted respecting their validity, gave it as his opinion that the testator was laboring under insanity.[2]

§ 180. In criminal as well as civil cases, it is important to consider the operation of the predominant idea, and its influence on the act in question. There certainly is no reason why a person should be held responsible for a criminal act that springs from a delusion which would be sufficient to invalidate any civil act to which it might give rise. A monomaniac's sense of the *fitness of things* is not different when he signs a ruinous contract, from what it is when he commits a criminal deed; and if the inability to discern the true relations of things is the ground on which the former is invalidated, it ought equally to annul criminal responsibility; unless it can be shown that the abstract conceptions of the nature and consequences of crime are never affected in insanity, or are compatible with a degree of mental soundness that would incapacitate a person from buying a house or selling a piece of land. It is yet a disputed point however, whether partial mania should have the full legal effect

---

[1] Johnson *v.* Moore's heirs, 1 Littel's Reports, 371.
[2] Annales d'Hygiène Publique, vol. 3, p. 370.

of insanity, in criminal cases. By Hoffbauer, Fodere and some other writers, it is contended that the same principle which determines the effect of mania in civil, should also determine its effect in criminal cases; that is, that criminal responsibility should be annulled only when the act comes within the range of the diseased operations of the mind. In favor of this view, it may be urged, that the connexion of the morbid delusion with the criminal act is generally very direct, and not easily mistaken. A remote and circuitous association of the predominant idea with the deed in question, presents fair ground for suspicion, because the farther the thoughts of the monomaniac wander from the object of his delusion, the less are they affected by its influence. If a man who imagines his legs are made of glass, should see another approaching him with a stick for the purpose of breaking them, he could not help resisting even to bloodshed, in what would be to him an act of self-defense, but it would require a very peculiar concatenation of circumstances to warrant us in considering a rape or theft as the offspring of this hallucination, because the idea of these acts would carry the thoughts far beyond the reach of its influence.

§181. Against these views it may be objected, that it is not always easy to trace the connexion between the predominant idea and the criminal act. The links that connect the thoughts which rise in succession in the sound mind defy all our penetration, and the few laws we have established are totally inapplicable to the associations of the insane mind. No one will be bold enough to affirm that a certain idea cannot possibly be connected with a certain other idea in a healthy state of the mind, least of all when it is disordered by disease, so that the existence of partial insanity once established, it is for no human tribunal to arbitrarily circumscribe the circle of its diseased operations. We must remember also that sometimes the predominant idea is frequently changing, and

1211

at others, is obstinately concealed by the patient, and is not ascertained till after his restoration to health. The views here objected to have also found a strong opponent in Georget whose practical knowledge of the subject and acknowledged acuteness in observing the manners of the insane, entitle his opinions to great consideration, if not to entire belief. The following observations of his should never be forgotten in forming conclusions on this disputed point. "In conversing," says he, "with patients on topics foreign to their morbid delusions, you will generally find no difference between them and other people. They not only deal in common-place notions, but are capable of appreciating new facts and trains of reasoning. Still more, they retain their sense of good and evil, right and wrong, and of social usages, to such a degree, that whenever they forget their moral sufferings and their delusions, they conduct, in their meetings, as they otherwise would have done, inquiring with interest for one another's health, and maintaining the ordinary observances of society. They have special reasons even for regarding themselves with a degree of complacency; for the most part they believe that they are victims of arbitrary measures, fraudulent contrivances, and projects of vengeance or cupidity, and thus they sympathize with one another in their common misfortunes. Accordingly the inmates of lunatic asylums are rarely known to commit those reprehensible acts which are regarded as crimes when dictated by sound reason, though the most of them enjoy considerable freedom. They often talk very sensibly of their interests, and some even manage their property perfectly well."

"Those patients who are insane on one point only more or less limited, may have experienced some severe moral disorders which influence the conduct and actions of the individual, without materially injuring his judgment. Those who conduct themselves so well in the

1212

asylum, in the midst of strangers with whom they have no relations, and against whom they have conceived no prejudice nor cause of complaint, and in quiet submission to the rule of the house, are no sooner at liberty, in the bosom of their families, than their conduct becomes insupportable; they are irritated by the slightest contradiction, abusing and threatening those who address to them the slightest observation, and working themselves up to the most intolerable excesses. And whether the reprehensible acts they then commit are really foreign to the predominant idea or not, ought we to make a being responsible for them whose *moral* nature is so deeply affected?"[1] These facts, it cannot be denied, furnish strong ground for the remark with which Georget closes his observations on this point, namely, that if, in following the rule that partial mania excludes the idea of culpability, "the moralist and the criminal judge run the risk of committing injustice by sparing a really guilty person, certainly, the opposite course would lead them into still greater errors."

§ 182. Hoffbauer has not only limited the exculpatory effects of partial mania to the acts which clearly come within its influence, but has laid down the principle that in the criminal jurisprudence of this condition, the predominant idea shoud be considered as true; that is, that the acts of the patient should be judged as if he had really been in the circumstances he imagined himself to be when they were committed. It is based on the common, but erroneous notion, that insane people always reason correctly from wrong premises, and therefore it is inapplicable to the numerous instances where the premises and inferences are all equally wrong. If a person imagines he heard the voice of God commanding him to immolate his only child and he accordingly obeys, it may be said indeed that he is not responsible for the bloody deed.

---

[1]Discussion medico-légale sur la Folie, pp. 10, 14

because it would have been perfectly proper, had he really heard the command; but are we to be told, that if he had killed his neighbor for a fancied petty injury, he is not to be absolved from punishment, because, the act would have been highly criminal, even though he might have really received the injury? It must not be overlooked that in cases like the latter, the insanity manifests itself, not only in the fancied injury, but in the disproportionate punishment which he inflicts upon the offender, and it is absurd to consider one manifestation as a delusion, and the other a crime.

§ 183. In the English courts there has been a great diversity of practice on this subject, according as it has been affected by the speculative opinions of the judge, the eloquence of counsel, the magnitude of the criminal act, and the ignorance or humanity of juries. If we carefully examine the cases tried within the last hundred years, as they are brought together in the various treatises on lunacy and on criminal law, the utmost respect for authority will not prevent us from observing the want of any definite principle as the ground of the difference of their results. Amid the mass of theoretical and discordant speculations on the psychological effects of insanity, and of crude and fanciful tests for detecting its presence, which these trials have elicited, the student who turns to them for the purpose of informing his mind on this branch of his profession, finds himself completely disheartened and bewildered. Instead of inquiring into the effect produced by the peculiar delusions of the accused on his ordinary conduct and conversations, and especially of their connexion with the criminal act in question, the courts in these cases, have been contented with laying down metaphysical dogmas on the consciousness of right and wrong, of good and evil, and the measure of understanding still possessed by the accused. Under the influence of the doctrines of Lord Hale, partial insanity has seldom been considered as sufficient, *per se,* to annul responsibility for crime. When received as an exculpatory plea, it has generally been in those cases where the principal delusions were of a religious nature, though the reason of this preference it might be difficult to assign.

§ 184. The practice of the American courts, judging from the few cases that have come to our knowledge, has been guided by more liberal doctrines. In the trial of Lawrence, at Washington, in 1835, for shooting at president Jackson, the jury were advised by the court to regulate their verdict by the principles laid down in the case of Hadfield, which had been stated to them by the district-attorney.[1] In the case of Theodore Wilson, tried in York county, Maine, in 1836, for the murder of his wife in a paroxysm of insanity, the court charged the jury that if they were satisfied the prisoner was not of *sound memory* and *discretion* at the time of committing the act, they were bound to return a verdict of acquittal. This is all that could be wished; and considering that two highly respectable physicians had given their opinion in evidence that the prisoner had some consciousness of right and wrong, and that the attorney-general, though he admitted the existence of insanity in some degree, denied that it was of sufficient extent to exempt him from punishment, supporting his assertion on the authority of the leading English cases relating to insanity, this decision indicates an advance in the criminal jurisprudence of insanity that does credit to the humanity and intelligence of that court.

Section II.

Legal Consequences of Moral Mania.

§ 185. General moral mania furnishes good ground

---

[1] Nile's Register, vol. 48, p. 119. The principle adopted in Hadfield's case was, that a person is not responsible for whatever criminal act is committed under the influences of delusion.

for invalidating civil acts, for notwithstanding the apparent integrity of the intellectual powers, it is probable that their operation is influenced to a greater or less extent, by a derangement of the moral powers. The mutual independence of these two portions of our spiritual nature is not absolute and unconditional, but is always liable to be affected by the operation of the organic laws. The animal economy is a whole; no part of it can exist without the rest, nor be injured or abstracted without marring the energy or harmony of the whole system; and though each part is so far independent of the others as to contribute its distinct share in the production of the general result, even sometimes when surrounded by the ravages of disease, yet the general law is, that disease in one part modifies more or less the action of all the rest, and especially of those connected with it by contiguity or by resemblance of function. Nature has established a certain adaptation of the moral and intellectual faculties to one another, leading to that harmony of action which puts them in proper relation to external things, and we can scarcely conceive of any disturbance of their equilibrium, that will not more or less impair the general result. Amid the chaos of the sentiments and passions produced by moral mania, the power of the intellect must necessarily suffer, and instead of accurately examining and weighing the suggestions of the moral powers, it is influenced by motives which may be rational enough, but which would never have been adopted in a perfectly healthy state. It is hard to conceive, indeed, that with an understanding technically sound, the relations of a person should be viewed in an entirely different light, the circle of his rights and duties broken and distorted, and his conduct turned into a course altogether foreign to his ordinary habits and pursuits. Notwithstanding the correctness of his conversation, and his plausible reasons for his singular

1216

conduct, a strict scrutiny of his actions, if not his words, obscured and perverted, and that his own social position will convince us that his notions of right and wrong are is viewed through a medium which gives a false coloring to its whole aspect. Now, though such a person may not be governed by any blind, irresistible impulse, yet to judge his acts by the standard of sanity and attribute to them the same legal consequences as to those of sane men, would be clearly unjust, because their real tendency is not and cannot be perceived by him. Not that his abstract notions of the nature of crime are at all altered, for they are not, but the real character of his acts being misconceived, he does not associate them with their ordinary moral relations. No fear of punishment restrains him from committing criminal acts, for he is totally unconscious of violating any penal laws, and therefore, the great end of punishment, the prevention of crime, is wholly lost in his case. If there were no other reason for withholding punishment in cases of moral mania, this alone would be sufficient, that the fear of it, which with others is a powerful preventive of crime, or at least is supposed to be, in the most popular theories of criminal law, does not and cannot exert its restraining influence on the mind. No one would think of attributing moral guilt to Earl Ferrers for entertaining the insane idea that his steward was a villain conspiring with the earl's relatives against his comfort and interests . . . ; why then should it be charged to him as a crime, that, amid the tumult of his passions disturbing the healthy exercise of his understanding, he considered himself as the proper avenger of his own wrongs? Each delusion was alike the offspring of the same derangement, and it is unjust and unphilosophical to regard one with indifference as the hallucination of a madman, and be moved with horror at the other and visit it with the utmost terrors of the law, as the act of a brutal murderer.

§ 186. Liberty of will and of action is absolutely essential to criminal responsibility, unless the constraint upon either is the natural and well-known result of immoral or illegal conduct. Cupability supposes not only a clear perception of the consequences of criminal acts, but the liberty, unembarrassed by disease of the active powers which nature has given us, of pursuing that course which is the result of the free choice of the intellectual faculties. It is one of those wise provisions in the arrangement of things, that the power of perceiving the good and the evil, is never unassociated with that of obtaining the one and avoiding the other. When, therefore, disease has brought upon an individual the very opposite condition, enlightened jurisprudence will hold out to him its protection, instead of crushing him as a sacrifice to violated justice. That the subject of homicidal insanity is not a free agent, in the proper sense of the term, is a truth that must not be obscured by theoretical notions of the nature of insanity, nor by apprehensions of injurious consequences from its admission. Amid the rapid and tumultuous succession of feelings that rush into his mind, the reflective powers are paralyzed, and his movements are solely the result of a blind, automatic impulse with which the reason has as little to do, as the movements of a new-born infant. That the notions of right and wrong continue unimpaired under these circumstances, proves only the partial operation of the disease; but in the internal struggle that takes place between the affective and intellectual powers, the former have the advantage of being raised to their maximum of energy by the excitement of disease, which, on the other hand, rather tends to diminish the activity of the latter. We have seen that generally after the fatal act has been accomplished, and the violence of the paroxysm subsided, the monomaniac has gone and delivered himself into the hands of justice, as if, overwhelmed with horror at the

1218

enormity of his action, he either considered his own life the only compensation he could offer in return; or it may be, felt that the presence of his fellow men, though it would seal his own fate, would be a welcome relief from the crushing agony of his own spirit. It is not to be wondered at, however, if occasionally, the tide of feeling takes a different course, and the murderer is prompted to avoid what he cannot help thinking to be the just consequence of his act, by flying from the bloody scene, and even denying his agency in it altogether. Considering the diversity of habits, sentiments and education, uniformity in an unessential phenomenon like this is not to be expected. That flying from pursuit indicates a consciousness of having committed a reprehensible act, and also a fear of punishment, is not denied, but it has never been contended that the opposite course implies the absence of all ideas of this kind from the mind of the homicidal monomaniac. The real point at issue is, whether the fear of punishment or even the consciousness of wrong doing destroys the supposition of insanity, and this is settled by the well-known fact that the inmates of lunatic asylums, after having committed some reprehensible acts, will often persist in denying their agency in them, in order to avoid the reprimand or punishment which they know would follow their conviction. If insane persons have any rational ideas at all, and it is not denied that they have, it is not strange that they sometimes are conscious of the penal consequences of their acts and use the intelligence of a brute in order to avoid them. Besides, in moral insanity the intellectual faculties are supposed not to be impaired, and when the fury of the paroxysm which has borne him on in spite of every attempt at resistance has subsided, the homicidal monomaniac returns, in some degree at least, to his ordinary habit of thinking and feeling. He regrets the havoc he has made, foresees its disgraceful consequences to himself, shudders at the sight and flies, like the most hardened criminal, to avoid them.

§ 187. In medical science, it is dangerous to reason against facts. Now we have an immense mass of cases related by men of unquestionable competence and veracity, where people are *irresistibly* impelled to the commission of criminal acts while fully conscious of their nature and consequences; and the force of these facts must be overcome by something more than angry declamation against visionary theories and ill-judged humanity. They are not fictions invented by medical men (as was rather broadly charged upon them in some of the late trials in France), for the purpose of puzzling juries and defeating the ends of justice, but plain, unvarnished facts as they occurred in nature; and to set them aside without a thorough investigation, as unworthy of influencing our decisions, indicates any thing rather than that spirit of sober and indefatigable inquiry which should characterize the science of jurisprudence. We need have no fear that the truth on this subject will not finally prevail, but the interests of humanity require that this event should take place speedily.

§ 188. The distinction between crimes and the effects of homicidal monomania is too well-founded to be set aside by mere declamation, or appeals to popular prejudices, as has been repeatedly done in courts of justice. On the trial of Papavoine for the murder of two young children near Paris, in 1823, the advocate-general, in reply to the counsel of the prisoner who had pleaded homicidal insanity in his defence, declared that Papavoine committed the crime, in order "to gratify an inveterate hatred against his fellow-men, transformed at first, into a weariness of his own life, and subsequently into an instinct of ferocity and a thirst of blood. Embittered by his unhappy condition, excited by a sense of his sufferings and misfortunes, irritated by the happiness of others

1220

which awakened in him only ideas of fury, and drove him into seclusion which increased the perversity of his depraved propensities, he arrived at that pitch of brutal depravity where destruction became a necessity and the sight of blood a horrible delight. His hateful affections, after being long restrained, finally burst forth and raised in his bosom a necessity of killing, which, like a young tiger, he sought to gratify."[1] That beings in human shape have lived who delighted in the shedding of blood, and found a pastime in beholding the dying agonies of their victims, is a melancholy fact too well established by the Neros and Caligulas of history. For such we have no disposition to urge the plea of insanity, for though we are willing to believe them to have been unhappily constituted, we have no evidence that they labored under cerebral disease, and they certainly exhibited none of its phenomena. Motives, the very slightest no doubt, generally existed for even their most horrid atrocities, and even when they were entirely wanting, there was still a conformity of their bloody deeds with the whole tenor of their natural character. They followed the bent of their dispositions as manifested from childhood, glorying in their preeminent wickedness and rendered familiar by habit with crime; and though conscience might have slumbered, or opposed but a feeble resistance to the force of their passions, yet it was not perverted by diseased action so as to be blind to the existence of moral distinctions. In homicidal insanity, on the contrary, every thing is different. The criminal act for which its subject is called to account, is the result of a strong and sudden impulse, opposed to his natural habits and generally preceded or followed by some derangement of the healthy actions of the brain or other organ. The advocate-general himself represented Papavoine, "as having been

---

[1] Georget: Examen des proces criminelles.

noted for his unsocial disposition, for avoiding his fellow-laborers, for walking in retired, solitary places, appearing to be much absorbed in the vapors of a black melancholy.'' This is not a picture of those human fiends to whom he would assimilate Papavoine, but it is a faithful one of a mind over which the clouds of insanity are beginning to gather. Where is the similarity between this man, who, with a character for probity and in a fit of melancholy, is irresistibly hurried to the commission of a horrible deed, and those wretches who, hardened by a life of crime, commit their enormities with perfect deliberation and consciousness of their nature.

§189. It has been also urged that the subjects of homicidal insanity are, no less than criminals, injurious to society, the safety of which implicitly requires their extermination, upon the same principle that we do not hesitate to destroy a dog that has been so unfortunate as to go mad. Sane, or insane, criminal or not, such monsters should be cut off from the face of the earth, and it is a misplaced humanity to reserve them for a different fate. Such language might have been expected from people who are moved only by the feelings, that are immediately raised by the sight of appalling crimes, but it is an humiliating truth that the opinions of those who are in the habit of discriminating between various shades of guilt and of canvassing motives, are too often but an echo to the popular voice. If the old custom of smothering under a feather bed the miserable victims of hydrophobia be now considered as a specimen of the most revolting barbarity, we cannot see why the punishment of insane offenders should be regarded under a more favorable aspect. Society has a right to protect itself against the aggressions of the dangerously insane, but unnecessary severity in its protective measures defeats the very purpose in view, and indicates a want of humanity and intellectual enlightenment. While confinement in prisons and mad-houses furnishes all the restraint which the necessity of their case requires, it is idle to urge the infliction of death as the only means by which society can be effectually shielded from a repetition of their terrible enormities.

§ 190. One of the principal objects of punishments should be to deter from the commission of crime, by impressing the mind with ideas of physical and moral suffering as its certain consequence; and whenever it is found to produce a very different effect, it is the part of enlightened legislation to devise some other means of prevention. Nothing can be more absurd than to inflict the very punishment which the delusion of the monomaniac often impels him to seek,—to put *him* to death who voluntarily surrenders himself and imploringly beseeches it as the only object he had at heart in perpetrating a horrid crime. What is it but converting a dreadful punishment into the dearest boon that earth can offer? In religious monomania, it is not uncommon for the patient to believe that the joys of heaven are in store for him, and under the excitement of this insane idea, to murder a fellow-creature, in order that he may the sooner enter on their fruition. To execute one of this class, is to perpetuate an evil which needs only a change of penal consequences to be effectually remedied. A kind of delusion has sometimes prevailed in certain parts of Europe which persuades its unfortunate subjects that eternal happiness can be gained by being executed for the murder of some innocent person. The idea is that suicide being itself a sin will not be followed by the happiness they seek, but that murder, though a greater crime, can be repented of before the time of execution. This delusion prevailed epidemically in Denmark, during the middle of the last century, and to avoid sending an unprepared person out of the world, the victim generally selected was a child. Death, of course, was no punishment in this case, and

1223

at last, the king issued an ordinance directing that the guilty should be branded on the forehead with a hot iron and whipped, and be imprisoned for life with hard labor. Every year, on the anniversary of their crime, they were to be whipped.[1] Lord Dover, in his Life of Frederic, relates that such was the severity of discipline among the Prussian troops at Potsdam, that many wished for death to finish their intolerable sufferings, and murdered children, which they had enticed within their power, in order to obtain from justice the stroke they dared not inflict upon themselves.[2] Abolish capital punishment in such cases, and the delusion will disappear with it; continue it, and no one can tell when the latter will end

§ 191. Not only is the moral effect of punishment totally lost when inflicted on the subjects of homicidal insanity, since it does not deter other madmen from committing similar acts, but by a curious law of morbid action, every publicity obtained for them by the trial and execution of the actors, leads to their repetition to an almost incredible extent. At a sitting of the Royal Academy of Medicine in Paris, August 8th, 1826, Esquirol stated that since the trial of Henriette Cornier, which occurred not two months before, he had become acquainted with six instances of a parallel nature. Among these was a Protestant minister who became affected with the desire of destroying a favorite child. He struggled against this terrible inclination for fifteen days, but was at last driven to the attempt on his child's life, in which he fortunately failed. Several other physicians, on the same occasion, bore similar testimony relative to the effect of that trial, and the newspapers about that period teemed with cases of child-murder which had originated in the same way.

---

[1]London Quarterly Review, vol. 12, p. 219.
[2]Discussion medico-légale esur la Folie, 126.

§ 192. It should not be forgotten, that well-grounded suspicion that the homicidal act was the result of physical disease, instead of moral depravity, is so horrid as to excite, in whatever mind it arises, feelings of distrust and jealousy towards the law and its ministers, infinitely more to be dreaded than the occasional acquittal of a supposititious maniac. When, on the contrary, the distinction is carefully made between the acts of a sound and those of an unsound mind, and a decision in doubtful cases is dispassionately and deliberately formed upon every species of evidence calculated to throw light upon it, the mind is impressed with a new sense of the wisdom and majesty of the laws and with a feeling of security under their discriminating operation. The numerous trials for witchcraft in a former age, and the occasional condemnation of a maniac in the present, have done more to lessen men's respect for the laws, than all its overruled decisions have to weaken their confidence in its certainty. Insanity is a disease, before the prospect of which the stoutest heart may quail, but how much more appalling is it made by the reflection, that in some wild paroxysm it may be followed by legal consequences, that will consign its unhappy subjects to an ignominious death. In cases of simulated madness, the purposes of justice are more fully answered by receiving and examining all the evidence and patiently showing its value and bearings, and thus laying open the imposition to the conviction of all, than by repelling the plea with idle declamation on its injurious tendency. Not only does the criminal obtain his deserts, by such a course, but the most cunning device of his ingenuity is seen to be baffled, and the plea that should ever shield innocence from destruction is ineffectually urged to protect the guilty. Every murmur at the injustice of the sentence is hushed, all scruples are removed and all fears are dissipated, that a fellow-being has been sacrificed, whose only crime was the misfortune of laboring under disease of the brain. Besides, what, if amid the obscurity in which a case may sometimes be involved, a guilty person do escape—though this event must be of very rare occurrence,— is it not a maxim in legal practice that it is better for ten guilty persons to escape punishment than one innocent person to suffer? But though he escape the sentence of the law, yet society is perfectly secure from the effects of mistake, because the very plea by which he obtains his acquittal, consigns him to confinement and surveillance.

§ 193. In those cases where there are some but not perfectly satisfactory indications of insanity, the trial or sentence should be postponed, in order that opportunity may be afforded to those who are properly qualified, for observing the state of the prisoner's mind. Where the moral powers have become so deranged as to lead to criminal acts, without, however, any perceptible impairment of the intellect, time only is necessary in the greater proportion of cases to furnish indubitable evidence of mental derangement. And whatever may be the result, the ends of justice are not defeated by waiting a few months, while the scruples of the over humane are removed, and the acquiescence of the ministers of the law in measures calculated to establish innocence rather than guilt, gains for them a confidence and respect that the conviction of guilt never can. Many instances might be mentioned where the accused, whose insanity was doubtful on trial, has, during the confinement subsequent to his acquittal on a criminal prosecution, become most manifestly insane. Hadfield, who was tried for shooting at the king and acquitted on the ground of insanity, though during the trial he displayed no indications of disordered mind, spent the remainder of his life in Bedlam hospital, and for thirty years showed scarcely any signs of mental alienation, except once, when suddenly and without any known cause, he became so furious that they were obliged to chain him in his cell. This paroxysm lasted but a short time, when he recovered his ordinary state of health.

§ 194. Another reason for delay is, that insanity is sometimes so completely veiled from observation, as never to be suspected even by the most intimate associates of the patient. An instructive case is related by Georget, in which the existence of insanity, though of several years duration, was not recognised till after the death of the subject. The circumstances were briefly these. Bertet, a revenue-officer, exercised the duties of his office for three years, in the manufactory of M. M. Ador and Bonnaire, at Vaugirard, where he was only noticed for his unaccommodating disposition, melancholic temperament and fondness for seclusion. One day while M. Ador was conversing with some of the workmen, he was requested by Bertet to affix his signature to certain papers. He proceeded to his room for this purpose, and while in the act of writing, was shot dead by Bertet, who immediately afterwards blew out his own brains. Among his papers were found several addressed to the advocate-general, bearing the most singular titles, such as *my last reflections, my last sighs,* in which he declared that he had been poisoned several years before, and gave a minute account of the numerous remedies he had ineffectually used, insisting at the same time that his head was not turned, that he acted deliberately, and giving very coherent reasons to prove it. He announced that four victims were required, namely, the two heads of the establishment, a woman who was living in it, and his old housekeeper, and that in case he should be contented with one, he would leave to justice the charge of obtaining the others. Some of these papers he finishes with saying, "To day my pains are less acute,—I feel better,—my vengeance is retarded," or "my pains are renewed—with them my thoughts of vengeance." Among other wild fancies, he made a description of the funeral monument to be raised to one of his victims, which was to be a gibbet covered with figures of instruments of punishment. He also described his own funeral procession. He wished the four corners of the pall to be carried by the four persons above-mentioned, in case he should not have sacrificed them; that the advocate-general should follow the cortege; and that when it reached the cemetery, the latter should prepare a large ditch in which they should first cast him, Bertet, and then the four pall-bearers. In another paper, he said he designed for each of his victims two gilt balls, as an emblem of their ambition and thirst of gold, and some pulverized cantharides, as an image of the torments which he suffered. Bertet had never shown any signs of mental alienation in his official letters and reports. He was sometimes abstracted and loved to be alone, but his disposition, in this respect, had been of long standing and seemed to be owing to the state of his health, of which he was constantly complaining, though judging from his exterior he seemed to be well enough. He had always discharged the duties of his office satisfactorily, and, by his own solicitation, had just before obtained a more profitable place. Had not Bertet recorded his insane fancies, but failing in his suicidal attempt, had been brought to trial for the murder of M. Ador, the plea of insanity would have fallen on the most incredulous ears, and he would have paid the last penalty of the law. In a state of confinement and seclusion, however, nothing but time would have been necessary to reveal the true nature of his case.

§ 195. Homicidal monomania presents us with one of those remarkable phenomena, the existence of which men are slow to believe, long after the evidence in its favor has accumulated to such an extent as to render incredulity any thing but a virtue. The facts themselves cannot be denied, and the various methods of explaining them on the hypothesis of a sound understanding, though every

1228

phase of human character and every spring of human action has been resorted to for the purpose, are little calculated to diminish the confidence of impartial minds in the correctness of the above views. Strongly impressed as we are with their importance, we may have devoted more attention to the objections that have been urged against them, than they really deserve; we shall therefore say but little more on this part of the subject. Against Georget's proposition relative to the homicide committed by Henriette Cornier, that "an act so atrocious, so contrary to human nature, committed without interest, without passion, opposed to the natural character of the individual, is evidently an act of madness";[1] it has been seriously objected that though we may be unable to discover motives, yet this is not a positive proof that there actually are no motives. This objection depends upon a question of fact, and we shall content ourselves with putting it to every criminal lawyer to answer for himself, whether a criminal act, committed by a person whose motives defy all penetration or rational suspicion while his mind evinces no signs of impairment, is not one of the most uncommon occurrences in the world—so uncommon perhaps, as to have never fallen within their experience?

§ 196. By those who delight not in metaphysical subtleties, a more summary, if not more philosophical, explanation of homicidal monomania has been furnished in the idea that it is to be attributed to an instinct of ferocity; to unnatural depravity of character; to a radical perversity. That such qualities do exist as the too common result of a defective constitution, or a vicious education, is proved by the testimony of every day's experience, even if we had not the best authority for believing that the heart may be "desperately wicked." But even where they exist to the fullest extent, the actions to which they

---

[1] Discussion medico-légale sur la Folie, 126.

prompt have always some immediate motive, slight as it may be, of pleasure sought, or pain avoided; or if they can claim no higher title than that of *instinct*, it is one of no sudden, transitory character, but a constant and consistent portion of the constitution. It is an anomalous instinct that manifests itself but once or twice in a person's life; and therefore, we cannot, without indulging in the most unwarrantable use of language, apply this term to those uncontrollable, abnormal influences that lead to acts of fury and destruction. What resemblance can we detect between the Domitians and Neros of history, and the Papavoines and Corniers, whose terrible acts have been commemorated in the records of criminal jurisprudence? In the former, this instinct of ferocity appeared in their earliest youth; it imparted a zest to every amusement, and excited ingenuity to contrive new means for heightening the agonies of the wretched victims of their displeasure. In the latter, the character was mild and peaceable, and their days were spent in the quiet and creditable discharge of the duties belonging to their station, till a cloud of melancholy enveloped their minds and under its shadow they perpetrated a single deed, at the very thought of which they would have previously shuddered with horror. In short, all our knowledge of human nature, all our experience of the past, forces us to the conclusion, that "the presence of mental alienation should be admitted in him who commits a homicide without positive interest, without criminal motives, and without a reasonable passion."

§ 197. After what has been said on the subject of homicidal monomania, it will be scarcely necessary to enter into particulars relative to the legal consequences of the other forms of partial moral mania. Completely annulling, as we believe they do, all moral responsibility for acts committed under their influence, the law can rightfully inflict no punishment on their unfortunate subjects, though it should adopt every measure of precaution that the interests of society require. To punish the thief and the incendiary for acts which are the result of disease is not only unjust, but it serves to aggravate their disorder, and to prepare them, when their term of punishment has closed, for renewing their depradations on society with increased perseverance. The only proper course to pursue with this class of offenders when brought into courts of justice, is to place them, or obtain a guaranty from their friends that they shall be placed, where judicious medical treatment will be used for the purpose of restoring their moral powers to a sounder condition, and where they will be secluded from society until this end shall be accomplished.

If the doctrines here laid down relative to moral insanity and its legal consequences are correct, it would seem to follow as a matter of course, that they should exert their legitimate influence on judicial decisions. Nevertheless, it is contended—and that too by some who do not question the truth of these doctrines—that they ought not to have this practical effect, for the reason that insanity would thereby be made the ground of defence in criminal actions, to a most pernicious extent. This objection, stated in the plainest and strongest terms we presume to be this. If these doctrines should be recognised in our courts of justice, and suffered to influence their decisions, almost every criminal would resort to a defence, the tendency of which is invariably to puzzle and distract the minds of the jury, and to produce the acquittal of many a wretch, who would first hear the mention of his own derangement from the lips of ingenious counsel. Now, even if we were disposed to accord to this objection all the weight that is claimed for it, it would not seem to warrant the inference that is drawn from it. Are we to take from the maniac the defence which the law of nature secures to him, because it may be sometimes offered by those who use it as a means of deception? Are the innocent to be made to suffer for the devices of the guilty? To avoid this cruel injustice, therefore, without at the same time inflicting a positive evil on society, we would deduce from this objection an inference of a totally different kind. It is, to let the right of the accused party to make his defence be cumbered with no restrictions, expressed or implied; let the plea of insanity, if he choose to make it, be attentively listened to, the facts urged in its support closely scrutinized, the accused carefully and dispassionately examined, and his character and history investigated. If this duty be performed as it should be, and always may be, the case will seldom happen, when the truth will not be established to the satisfaction of every unprejudiced mind. If the accused be really insane, we have the satisfaction of reflecting, that an enlightened investigation of his case has saved an innocent person from an ignominious fate, while on the other hand, if he be simulating insanity, every doubt will be dissipated as to the justice of his sentence, and the conviction will be strengthened in the popular mind, that the law will prevail over every false pretence, and expose the guilty even in their most secret refuge.

ISSAC RAY (b.—Beverly, Mass., January 16, 1807; d.—Philadelphia, March 31, 1881.)

Ray studied at Phillips Andover Academy, and the Bowdoin College, in Maine. In 1827 he received his M.D. from Harvard, and returned to Portland, Me. to practice. The years 1828-1829 he spent in England and France. In 1841 Ray became medical superintendent of the State Hospital for the Insane in Augusta, Me. In 1844, he was one of the thirteen original founders of the Association of Medical Superintendents of American Institutions for the Insane (later the American Psychiatric Association). From Augusta, Ray went to the Butler Hospital in Providence, R. I., where he held a similar position. He remained there some 20 years, and then retired to Philadelphia.

Ray formulated, and grappled with some of the major, still unsolved, problems in social psychology: the nature of moral responsibility (culpability), of guilt, of punishment, of the legal aspects of human motiva tions. Within these areas, the problems of the insane are among the most poignant and the most difficult. Ray's book is certainly one of the important historical documents in this field. Though not the very first one to discuss these issues, he was the first to do so in such a complete manner. He can probably be credited with having founded this specialized branch of forensic medicine. His book went through a great many editions, and was quoted in the technical literature up into the twentieth century. His influence, not only through his book, but through his many strong critiques and legal opinions, and his many formal testaments, extended widely over the world. Psychiatrists today still struggle with his ideas.

RAY, I. *A treatise on the medical jurisprudence of insanity.* Boston: C. C. Little and J. Brown, 1838. Chap. 8: "Legal consequences of mania."

See also:

RAY, I.

   a) "Shakespeare's delineations of insanity." *Amer. J. Insanity.* 1846-47, 3:289—.
   b) *Education in its relation to the physical health of the brain. A lecture.* Boston: Tickner, Reed & Fields, 1851.
   c) "Insanity of King George III." *Amer. J. Insanity.* 1855, 12: 1—. (July).
   d) *Mental hygiene.* Boston: Tickner & Fields, 1863.
   e) "The Angell will case, rceently adjudicated in Providence, R. I." *Amer. J. Insanity.* 186³, 20:145. (Oct.).
   f) *Contributions to mental pathology.* Boston: Little, Brown & Co., 1873.

Maudsley, H. *Responsibility in mental disease.* N. Y.: D. Appleton and Co., 1874.

ZILBOORG, G. "Legal aspects of psychiatry." In Hall.

INTENTION, WILL AND NEED[1]

Kurt Lewin

I. A FEW FACTS[2]

1. *The Influence of Time on the Effect of the Intention; the Immediate Cessation of the Effect after Consummatory Action*

INTENTIONAL ACTIONS are usually considered the prototype of all acts of will. Theoretically a complete intentional action is conceived of as follows: its first phase is a *motivation process,* either a brief or a protracted vigorous struggle of motives; the second phase is an act of choice, decision, or intention, terminating this struggle; the third phase is the consummatory intentional action itself, following either immediately or after an interval, short or long. The second phase, the act of intending, is considered the central phenomenon of the psychology of will. The problem is: how does the act of intending bring about the subsequent action, particularly in those cases in which the consummatory action does not follow immediately the act of intending? It has been demonstrated that in such cases the act of intending need not be repeated before the action.

Indeed, Ach's[3] experiments have shown that an instruction given in hypnosis is carried out upon a posthypnotic signal without the subject's knowledge of the instruction. When the occasion (Ach's "referent-presen-

---

1. Editor's note. Deleted is the introduction, which sets the stage for the work which is to follow. It is entitled: "The changed significance of intention in the modern training of the will." It discusses the education of children in relation to problems of discipline, motivation, and the "pedagogy of the will."
2. For a detailed survey and discussion of the available experimental investigations into the psychology of will, see: Lindworsky, *Der Wille.* 3. Aufl., Leipzig, 1923.
3. Ach: *Über die Willenstätigkeit und das Denken.* Gottingen. 1905.

tation") implied in the act of intending occurs, it suffices to initiate the intended consummatory action (Ach's "goal-presentation"). For instance, an optic signal will initiate the pressing of a lever. The question is: what are the further characteristics of this after-effect of the act of intending?

According to prevailing theory, the act of intending creates such a relationship between the "referent-presentation" and "goal-presentation" that the appearance of the former results in an action consistent with the latter. According to the association theory,[4] an association of the referent- and goal-presentations is the cause of this process. Even the theory of the determining tendency, which denies the associative character of this relationship, assumes that a coupling created by the act of intending between the referent- and goal-presentations is the cause of the intentional action.

The origin of such theories becomes clear if it is remembered that the experimental analysis started with so-called reaction experiments, in which the intention was to carry out certain actions upon arbitrarily chosen signals, which had nothing or very little to do with the actions themselves.

Let us open up the problem by raising an apparently extraneous question: what role is played by the length of time elapsing between the act of intending and the consummatory action? Does the after-effect of the intention decrease progressively as associations do, according to the so-called curve of forgetting? It must be said right away that this after-effect persists over astonishingly long time-spans, even for relatively unimportant and outright nonsensical intentions.

Students were instructed: "Coming to the next laboratory hour (8 days hence), you will twice go up and down

---

4. Müller, G. E. Zur Analyse der Gedächtnistätigkeit und des Vorstellungsverlaufs. Part III, *Z.f. Psychol.* 1913, 8:.

the stairs leading to the Psychological Institute." An astonishingly high percentage of the students carried out the instruction, even though they did not renew the intention in the intervening period.

Following certain processes, however, this after-effect ceases in a typical and abrupt fashion. For instance, someone intends to drop a letter into a mailbox. The first mailbox he passes serves as a signal and reminds him of the action. He drops the letter. The mailboxes he passes thereafter leave him altogether cold. In general, the *occurrence of the occasion* (referent-presentation) as a rule *has no effect once the intentional action has been* "*consummated.*"

The apparent obviousness of this statement makes it especially necessary that its theoretical implications be made explicit. According to the laws of association, dropping the letter into the first mailbox should create an association between the mailbox and the dropping of the letter; the forces, whether associative or any other kind, which lead to dropping the letter, should also be reinforced by it. This is a stumbling block for association psychology; moreover it casts doubt on whether the coupling between occasion and consummation (referent- and goal-presentations) plays really the essential role here. If the effect of the act of intending is that a tendency toward consummation arises when the occasion implied in the act of intending occurs, then it is hard to see why on a second occasion this tendency should not appear to the same and even to a greater degree. (The actual absence of the letter, after it was mailed, would prevent full consummation; yet the inhibitory effect of this failure would be expected only at the third mailbox, unless very complex auxiliary hypotheses were employed.) To explain the phenomenon we cannot fall back on a time-decrement of the intention-effect, since when repetitive action *is* intended (for example, to paste an announcement on each mailbox) the intention becomes effective on each occasion. In the case of the intention to mail a letter, however, the forces directed toward action seem suddenly exhausted once the letter is mailed. Thus, the cause of the process does not seem to be simply that the coupling between the referent and goal-presentations drives toward action when the occasion arises.

A mailbox may elicit the tendency to drop the letter—or at least to check whether or not it has been dropped—even after it has been mailed. This happens mainly with important letters. Such cases are amenable to experimental study.

In studies using reaction experiments for this purpose, the following considerations must be kept in mind. If the subject is instructed, "You will press the lever when you see this signal," the signal will not play the role which a meaningful occasion, objectively connected with the action, would. It will play the role of a "signal" which may acquire the meaning of "command," and may therefore have repeated effects. The repetition of the signal then amounts to the verbal instruction: "Repeat the task again." (For instance, the policeman's raised hand amounts to a direct command.) We shall discuss such cases again. If the subject is given the task to nail together a frame, and the occasion for this is so chosen that it fits meaningfully into the process-whole—that is, it becomes an occasion and not a command—typically no tendency to repeat the completed task appears. For instance, if the occasion for this frame to be nailed together is when Mr. X. brings in a nail box, there will be no tendency to repeat nailing the frame if Mr. X. brings in the nail box again.

2. *The Effect of Intentions when Occasion and Consummatory Action Are Not Predetermined, or when the Occasion Fails to Appear*

It is usually assumed that, in the prototype of intentional action, the act of intending defines a *quite specific* occasion and a *specific* consummatory action. The reaction experiments, which were the point of departure for the experimental investigation of will, may serve as a useful paradigm. The referent-presentation may, for instance, be an optical signal and the goal-presentation the pressing of a lever.

Not in every act of intending are occasion and consummatory action so specifically defined.

First of all, *the consummatory action may remain quite indeterminate.* For instance, a person may intend to talk someone into doing a certain thing; the act of intending may leave it entirely open what words and arguments he will use, whether he will first go for a walk with him to make friends without even mentioning the matter, and so forth. The intention to avoid a ball *may* contain the provision that one will veer left; but it may leave it entirely open whether one will veer right or left, jump, or duck.

Such general intentions are more the rule than the exception, and they are not less effective than specific intentions. On the contrary, it is usually more purposeful to let the mode of consummation grow from the total *concrete consummatory situation* than to define it beforehand unequivocally. . . .

The same holds for the precise definition of the occasion in the act of intending. Actually, vitally important and far-reaching intentions, like the decision to pursue an occupational goal or to be a well-behaved child, are extraordinarily indefinite on this point. The actions to be executed and the occasions therefore are left wide open. Indeed, *the very same intention* may give rise, according to the conditions, *to quite contrary actions.* "Good behavior" requires now action, now foregoing of action.

But even where the act of intending predetermines definite occasion and consummatory action, we often encounter the astounding phenomenon that the intention takes effect all of a sudden *in response to quite other occasions and by different consummatory actions.*[5] This, however, is rare where there is no meaningful objective relationship between occasion and consummatory action, as in the so-called reaction-experiments. But it is frequent where, as in everyday life, there is an *objective* connection between the occasion and the consummatory action implied.

Somebody resolves to write a postal card to an acquaintance soon after returning home in the evening. In the afternoon he gets to a telephone, it reminds him to communicate with the acquaintance, and he does. Or: I resolve to drop a letter in the mailbox when I leave. A friend comes to see me, and I ask him to take care of the letter.

Two points in these examples seem important. In the first case an experience (seeing the telephone) very different from the occasion implied by the act of intending (the return home) actualizes the forces emanating from or connected with the intention. This experience assumes the role of the intended occasion: it initiates a consummatory action, though another than that implied in the act of intending. It is an action which from the vantage point of the act of intending is a *substitute action,* or more correctly, an equivalent action "appropriate to the situation."

In order to maintain the view that the forces striving toward the intentional action derive from a coupling between the occasion and the consummation created by the act of intending, and that these forces are released by the occurrence of the occasion, one might attempt to explain the effectiveness of the "substitute occasion" and the

5. Concerning the range and the displacement of such actualizing-stimuli, see Lewin: Das Problem der Willensmessung und das Grundgesetz der Assoziation. *Psychol. Forsch.* 2: 90.

occurrence of the substitute action by assuming that they are special cases of the same "general idea" to which both the intended occasion and consummatory action belong. It has been demonstrated, however, by the psychology of thinking that such a theory of general ideas is in contradiction to concrete psychological facts.[6]

The main objection to the concept of coupling is that it leaves unexplained why, after such *substitute actions*, the later actual occurrence of the intended occasion generally *no longer arouses a tendency* to consummate the intended action. Why is it that once the letter is entrusted to a friend the mailbox no longer challenges one, though a hundred different interpolated actions will not destroy the effects of the intention? There is no doubt that it is a salient characteristic of intention-effects that they usually cease, once the intended action or its equivalent is consummated. This, however, is not understandable once the forces driving toward the intentional action are conceived of as arising from couplings either of an associative or a non-associative sort.

The following example demonstrates the difficulties of this conception even more clearly. Somebody resolves to tell something to an acquaintance who is about to visit; but the visit is canceled. When *the occasion* fails to occur, the intention-effect is not simply canceled, instead new occasions are sought. This shows directly that *here a state of tension is pressing toward discharge by means of a specifically directed action.*

The objection does not hold that in such cases the original intention is general (to communicate something to the acquaintance) and not specific (to communicate on a certain occasion). There are such general intentions, but certainly there are specific ones also. Occasionally, the intentional action will not take place after the intended occasion has failed to occur: in such cases the intended

---

6. Selz: *Gesetze des geordneten Denkverlaufs.* Stuttgart, 1913.

action is "forgotten." Such exceptions will be discussed later on.

The internal tensions may initiate the consummatory action when the expected occasion is delayed too long. For instance, in a race there is a strong tendency to *start prematurely*. Reaction experiments show similar phenomena. In political life also we observe *premature* acting before the intended occasion had occurred.

The effect of intentions in which both occasion and consummatory action are left indeterminate; the effect of occasions different from those implied by the act of intending (substitute occasions appropriate to the situation); the occurrence of objectively equivalent actions; the search for new occasions and the premature actions when the expected occasion fails to occur; the cessation of the intention-effect once the intended action or its substitute has been consummated—all indicate that it is unsatisfactory to describe the causes of intentional actions as forces which on definite occasions drive to definite actions connected with them by a *coupling*.

3. *The Resumption of Interrupted Activities*

Another group of related phenomena should be discussed in greater detail.[7]

The consummation of an intended action is [initiated but] interrupted. Were the coupling between occasion and consummation decisive, nothing would happen without a repeated occurrence of the occasion, provided that the initiation of the consummatory action creates no new forces. The experimental setting used makes it possible to compare the results with those cases in which the effect of the intention is exhausted by the response to the first occasion. I shall mention only a few of Ovsiankina's results which are relevant to our present subject.

The activities used in the experiment were in general

---

7. These phenomena have been studied by Miss Ovsiankina at the Berlin Psychological Institute.

not particularly *interesting*: for example, reproduction of a figure by colored building-stones, copying a rank-order correlation table, threading beads, making an animal from plasticine.

In the moment the activity is interrupted, a strong, *acute* effect is observed. Subjects *resist* interruption even of not particularly agreeable activities. This assumes occasionally quite stubborn forms. The forces opposing interruption appear to be closely connected with, among other things, the course, structure, and whole-quality of the activity.

In our present context it is of particular interest what happens when the subject, following instructions, interrupts one activity to start and *complete another*. In brief *a strong tendency to resume the first activity is observed*

The experiments used two kinds of interruption. First *incidental interruptions*: the lights go out, presumably due to power failure; the experimenter drops a box of small objects and the polite subject helps to pick them up, and so on. Second, interruptions by direct instruction to start *another activity*.

Though often the incidental interruptions took as much as twenty minutes, the original activity was resumed without exception. After the interruptions by other tasks, resumption was frequent, at times even after a full hour. The subjects knew that the experimenter did not expect resumption; indeed, in some cases the experimenter actually *prohibited it*.

The *act of resumption* is of particular interest to us. The resumption tendency is reinforced when the subject catches sight of the material of the interrupted first activity, for instance, of the piece of paper on which he began to draw. *But even when there is no such external stimulus, the tendency to resumption is present*. The behavior observations and the subjects' self-observations indicate that a few seconds after the interrupting activity is fin-

1242

ished, there appears an urge to resume the first activity, even if the subject did not think of it while engaged in the other. This urge appears first in an indefinite form, "There is still something to be done," without the subject's knowing what it actually is.

This is usually not a *persistence* of activity, such as occurs in continuous rhyming of nonsense syllables, but rather a typical tendency toward the consummation of an action, that is, toward the equilibration of an inner tension. Accordingly, the resumption tendency is more often absent if the interrupted activity is a continuous, rather than an end-activity.

. . . The intensity of the resumption tendency does not depend directly upon the intensity of the intention which preceded the activity[8] but rather upon *the subject's internal attitude toward that activity*. "Pure experimental subjects"—that is, subjects who "do everything the experimenter wants," subordinating their will to his— show little or no resumption tendency. The subject must actually have the will to carry out the specific activity.

The *central goals of will* which prompt the subject to accept the instructions of the experimenter are also important here. If the subject is asked to do some work because the experimenter needs it in other experiments, then the subject accepts this work not as a "subject" but as a person who wants to do a favor for the experimenter —that is, as a professional colleague or a social being. This is then a "serious activity," and the resumption tendency is much stronger in it than a mere "experimental activity."

---

8. This finding agrees with the results of many other investigations. *Cf.* Lindworsky, *op. cit.*—Lewin: Die psychische Tätigkeit bei der Hemmung von Willensvorgängen und das Grundgesetz der Assoziation. *z.f. Psychol.* 1917, 77: 236-. —Boumann, L.: Experimentelle Untersuchungen über den Willen bei Normalen u. Psychopathen. *Psychiat. en Neurol. Bladen.* 1919, 5 & 6:. —Sigmar: Uber die Hemmung bei der Realisation eines Willensaktes. *Arch. f. d. ges. Psychol.* 1925, 52:.

We are faced with the following facts: a force is demonstrated which drives, even after relatively long intervals, toward the completion of interrupted activity. The manifestation of the force does not require an external stimulus to prompt resumption of the task; frequently the resumption occurs spontaneously.

Further examples: Questions discussed but not settled in a meeting, usually continue to preoccupy us and may lead to long soliloquies, particularly if the questions are personally important. If we are interrupted in helping a school-child with a mathematical problem, it may recur to us for a long while even if quite uninteresting. If we slip into reading some stupid fiction but do not finish it, it may pursue us for years. The important experimental findings is that "interest" is not the decisive factor in such cases.

Finally, a few words about those theoretically important cases in which, because of a specific objective relationship between the original activity and the interrupting activity, no resumption tendency appears. A child telling a story is interrupted and told to draw the content of the story. No resumption tendency appears, obviously because the drawing somehow completed the interrupted storytelling. This is a substitute consummation. Such cases seem to be particularly revealing of the forces active in the execution of intentions. Even in real resumption the completing activity need not be the missing part of the original activity. It may be a quite differently structured activity directed "toward" the goal, or only playful handling of the material of the original activity.

4. *The Forgetting of Intentions*

An obvious, and in one sense, direct approach to the study of intention-effects is the investigation of the forgetting of intentions.

Two concepts of forgetting must be carefully distinguished. The first pertains to the usual conception of *memory*: the ability to reproduce knowledge once possessed. The ability to repeat an action once performed we will also consider reproduction, though in some respects it is an essentially different process.[9]

The second concept of forgetting pertains to *intentions which are not carried out.* In everyday life we call it "forgetfulness." It is obvious that we usually remember the content of the intention, even though we have forgotten to carry it out. In such cases the memory-knowledge of the act of intending is extant. A good memory, ability to reproduce knowledge and actions, need not be accompanied by the virtue of not being "forgetful" in carrying out intentions—though some connections between the two may exist. . . .[10]

Our concern here is the second concept of forgetting, the *failing to carry out an intention.*

We will disregard those cases where forgetting of intentions is due to momentary strong preoccupation with other matters. The remaining cases promise immediate insight into the conditions under which intentions fail.

As mentioned, intention effects do not seem to show a time-decrement. *The passage of time can no more be considered the cause of real happening in psychology than in physics.* Progressive time-decrements are usually referable to normal life processes. But even then the question remains: what in the whole life process is the *concrete cause,* for instance, of the forgetting of a given intention.

In an experimental investigation of the forgetting of intentions[11] the subject was to do a number of tasks and,

---

9. Lewin: *op. cit.,* footnote 5, p. 125ff.
10. Translator's note. In the omitted section Lewin discusses "forgiving" (the opposite of "holding things against people" tenaciously) as a kind of "forgetting." Clinically, both the relation of such tenacity to suspicion and other paranoid traits, and the relation to denial of an extreme tendency to forgive, are familiar. Lewin's reminder holds out the hope that these clinically familiar relationships may be approached some day from a new angle permitting systematic treatment of their "formal characteristics."
11. These experiments were conducted by Mrs. Birenbaum at the Berlin Psychological Institute.

at the end (or at another definite point) of each, sign and date the paper used. After the completion of each task the sheet was handed over to the experimenter.

The following results were obtained:

a. Generally, an intention is not an isolated fact in the psyche, but *belongs*, rather, *to a definite action-whole*, to a definite *region of the personality*. Thus, for instance, the signature is usually not embedded in the "objective work" of the task, but rather in that "personal" region which is involved in "handing the work over" to the experimenter.

Thus the transition from the action-region in which the intention is *embedded* to another may bring about the forgetting of the intention. An example from these experiments: the signature is often forgotten when six *similar* activities are followed by a seventh which is different.

A region of intention-effects may be sealed off simply by a pause of a few minutes. After the pause the signature is often forgotten. It is clear that we are not dealing here with a time-decrement of the intention since, even without renewal of the intention, the signing is usually not forgotten when the subject works on ever-new tasks without pauses, and, since the signature is usually still affixed, even when the "pause" lasts not five minutes but a whole day.

The apparent reason for this paradox is that, in a continuous series of experiments, a pause of five minutes is a very considerable interruption; after it, the subject enters a new region, as it were, in which the previous intentions hold little or not at all. If, however, a second group of the experiments takes place the next day, then for the subject it is a "resumption of yesterday's experiments," and not, as in the first case, a "proceeding to new experiments." Therefore, the subject reenters the situation of the preceding day without difficulty. In fact, it is not necessary to repeat the experimental instructions on the second day in other experiments either: in preparing himself subjectively for the experiment, the subject again accepts the previous instructions.

Such embedded intentions are not forgotten if—but only if—the action-region to which they belong is alive. This is true for everyday life also. Forgetting of an intention, or rather unresponsiveness of an intention to the intended occasion or another proper one, is observed when the occasion presents itself at a time or in a situation where those psychic complexes in which the intention is embedded are not alive. The most frequent cases of forgetting, which we usually attribute to being preoccupied with something else, are probably not solely due to the *intensity of the other experience*. If these intensive experiences belong to the *same* psychic complex, they may even reinforce the intention. Furthermore, forgetting may occur without intensive preoccupation if the momentarily prevailing psychological region is sufficiently distant from the intention. Yet pure intensity-relationships do seem to play some role.

b. The *occasion*, also, is of significance for the problem of forgetting. For instance, the subject will forget to sign his name, quite regularly, if he must change to signing on a larger paper or on one of a different color. Obviously, the paper reminds the subject of the intention, as does the mailbox of the letter to be mailed, or the knot in the handkerchief of something not to be forgotten; they have what I would like to call a *valence*. We have discussed cases in which, though the intentions were quite specific, a whole varied series of events and objects had valences (mailbox-friend). The valence may be fixated, however, as in the example of the paper, to a very specific object....

c. One of the tasks in the experiments mentioned was the drawing of the subject's own monogram. In this task the subjects regularly forget to sign their names. Asso-

1247

ciation theory would have us expect the opposite: due to the strong coupling between the monogram and the signature, forgetting of the intention to sign should be particularly rare on this task.

Detailed analysis indicates, however, that this is a kind of *substitute consummation*. In view of the whole situation, the subject could hardly have assumed that the monogram would sufficiently identify his work for the experimenter. Actually the signature is "forgotten" without further consideration. The need to sign, established by the act of intending, is apparently somehow satisfied by this monogram signature (though other factors are also at play here). It is significant that monogram writing done as "craft work," and not as "writing one's own monogram," does not have the effect of substitute consummation.

Such substitute- or even part-consummations are frequent causes of forgetting in everyday life also. I shall mention two examples that actually occurred. A man wishes to buy collar buttons. He forgets it repeatedly. Now he makes a detour, to go by a street in which there certainly are men's stores. He is satisfied and happy that he did "not forget his shopping." He arrives at the library and notices that he did not buy the buttons.

A teacher resolves to ask her pupil about a certain matter. About the middle of the study hour she remembers it, and is glad that "she remembered it just in time." She ends up without having carried out the intention. (In these cases, as in those of everyday life in general, there is naturally no unequivocal proof that going through the street or the mere remembering of the intention, as substitute consummations, were really the causes of forgetting.)

It is often observed that even making a written note of an intention is conducive to forgetting it, though according to the association theory it should reinforce the coupling between the referent- and the goal-presentation. Making a note is somehow a consummation, a discharge. We rely on the note to remind us in due time and weaken thereby the inner need not to forget. This case is similar to the one where remembering the intention to ask something acts as a fulfillment, so that the question is never actually asked.

There are, however, cases where taking notes, even if they are never seen again, facilitates remembering. In these cases the note-taking may, for instance, connect the intended action with a certain personality region (such as the region of occupation) or a certain style of living (such as orderliness), so that the total energy of this region partakes in carrying out the intention.

d. When not a result of substitute consummation, forgetting can often be traced to natural *counter-needs*. The intention to write an unpleasant letter often remains ineffective even if repeated: we forget it whenever we have leisure for it. Freud has called attention to these hidden resistances. Even though not all forgetting can be traced to such natural—and certainly not always to sexual —needs, nevertheless it is of central significance for our problem that *the after effect of an intention proves to be a force, which may clash with and be made ineffective by needs.*

We have already discussed the positive relation of intention effects to the needs from which the intention itself arose. (See, for instance, the resumption of "serious" activities.) The ease of forgetting depends upon the intensity of the genuine-need underlying the intention. Signatures were much less frequently forgotten in mass experiments than in experiments with individual subjects. The need to distinguish one's work (other factors being equal) is much greater in a mass experiment.

Whether or not an intention is carried out in the face

of obstacles *depends not on the intensity of the act of intending, but rather on the broader goals of will, or natural needs, on which the intention rests.* The study of forgetting has also shown that calm, affect-free acts of intending are usually more effective than those of particularly great or vehement intensity. This may be related to the fact that affective and vehement actions—in general, but with certain exceptions—have less achievement-effect than calm actions.

Under what conditions does an act of intending, and particularly an intensive act of intending, occur? An instructive though exaggerated adage says: "What one intends, one forgets." This means that only *when there is no natural need for an action,* or when there is a natural counter-need, *is it necessary to form an intention.* If the act of intending is not based on a genuine-need, it promises little success. It is precisely when there is no genuine-need that we attempt to substitute for it an "intensive act of intending." (To put it paradoxically: either there is no need to make a certain intention, or it promises little success.)

Wilde (*Dorian Gray*) is acute when he says, "Good intentions are useless attempts to meddle with the laws of nature. Their origin is mere vanity and their results are absolute zero."

II.. THE THEORY OF INTENTIONAL ACTION

1. *The Effect of the Act of Intending Is a Quasi-Need*
The experiments on forgetting of intentions, and even more those on resumption of interrupted activities, prove that the [after-effect of] intention is a force. To take effect, this force does not require the actual occurrence of the occasion anticipated in the act of intending in order to elicit the intentional action as its consequence.

There exists rather an internal pressure of a definite direction, an internal tension-state which presses to carry out the intention even if no predetermined occasion invites the action.

The clearest subjective experience of this state of affairs occurs in the resumption of interrupted tasks, when after completion of the interrupting activity a general pressure—that "there is still something I want to do"—appears. In this case, which is frequent in everyday life also, the content of the intention is not yet clear and only the internal tension as such is perceived. Only later does the goal, that is, what one wants to do, become conscious. Indeed, it happens in everyday life that, in spite of searching for it, one cannot remember what he really wanted. (Such indeterminate tensions occur sometimes even where a predetermined occasion by itself reminds one of the intentional activity.)[12] But in such cases consummatory activities often occur under internal pressure without the stimulation of specific occasions.

It could be argued that in the experiments mentioned the fact that there is nothing definite to do at the completion of the interrupting activity serves as the "proper occasion." . . . Indeed the "completion of a certain activity" *may* actually acquire the genuine valence of an occasion, for instance, if the intention is to do a certain thing at the completion of an activity.

As a rule, however, "not having anything to do" cannot be considered as an occasion with a definite valence, as is the mailbox for mailing a letter. The effect of momentarily "not being particularly occupied" is only that certain inner tensions pressing toward the motor region penetrate more easily when the motor region is not otherwise heavily taxed. (The conditions are naturally quite different in the case of real boredom.)

The state of tension arising from the act of intending need not be continuously expressed in conscious tension-experiences. As a rule, it exists over long periods of time,

---

12. *Cf.* Ach: *Uber den Willensakt und das Temperament.* Leipzig, 1910.

only in latent form, as during the interrupting activity, but that does not make it less real. These facts are related to the psychic function of the motor-region and of consciousness, as well as to the structuring of the psyche into relatively segregated complexes. These latent tension-states may break through momentarily into consciousness even during the interrupting activity, as an experience of pressure toward the original activity.

(A) MISSING AND UNFORESEEN OCCASIONS. The recognition that the driving-force of intentional activity is not an associative coupling but an internal tension-state—that is, a directed internal pressure—makes it possible to explain the various phenomena we described.

Now it becomes understandable why, when the occasion fails to occur, another is sought out, and why, when one keeps waiting too long for the occasion and the internal pressure is too great, premature action results.

We also understand now why the intention is responsive not only to the intended occasions, but also to entirely different objects and events (mailbox and friend). The internal state of tension breaks through as soon as there is a possibility to eliminate or at least decrease the tension, that is to say, as soon as a situation appears to permit activity in the direction of the goal.

(B) THE CESSATION OF PSYCHOLOGICAL FORCES FOLLOWING CONSUMMATION. As soon as the presence of internal tension, and not an associative coupling, is considered the decisive cause of the consummatory action, the disappearance of the valence of the intended occasion after consummation can also be deduced. In the extreme case, the effect of the intended occasion fails to occur altogether, because the internal tension is discharged in a "substitute consummation."

Clearly, the forces arising from acts of intending are closely related in type to those psychological forces which we usually called *needs,* and these in turn derive either

1252

from drives or from central goals of will, such as the will to pursue a vocation.

(C) PARALLEL PHENOMENA IN GENUINE- AND IN QUASI-NEEDS. (v) *Genuine-Needs and Natural Valences. Drive-needs*, such as hunger, are internal tensions, directed pressures, driving toward so-called "satisfying actions." For drive-needs, also, certain "occasions" play an essential role; they too respond to certain alluring objects and events which have a *valence* for them.

Our psychologically given environment does not consist of a sum of optical, acoustic, and tactile sensations, but of objects and events.[13] The recognition of this has slowly established itself in psychology. It is traditional to attribute certain feeling-tones to these objects and events; they are pleasant or unpleasant, pleasurable or painful.

Furthermore, it is common knowledge that the objects and events of the environment are not neutral toward us in our role of *acting* beings. Not only does their very nature facilitate or obstruct our actions to varying degrees, but we also encounter many objects and events which face us with a will of their own: *they challenge us to certain activities.* Good weather and certain landscapes entice one to a walk. A stairway stimulates the two-year-old child to climb it and jump down; doors, to open and to close them; small crumbs, to pick them up; dogs, to pet them; building stones, to play with them; the chocolate and a piece of cake want to be eaten. This is not the place to discuss in detail the nature, kinds, and functions of these "objects and events" which have valences. We will refer here only to a few of their basic characteristics, and will avoid discussing the role which experience and habit play in establishing them.

13. For a detailed discussion of this issue see Katz: Die Erscheinungsweisen der Farben. *Z.f. Psychol.* 1911,7:,*Z.f. angew. Psychol.* 1917, 12: 440 *Cf.* also Giese: *Hndb. d. psychotechn. Eignungsprüfungen.* Halle, 1925.

The intensity with which objects and events challenge us varies greatly. The shadings of such challenge range from "irresistible temptations," to which child as well as adult yields unthinkingly and against which self-control helps little if at all, to those which have the character of "command," to the weaker "urgings" and "attractions," which can be easily resisted and become noticeable only when the person tries to find something to do. The term "valence" comprises all these shadings.

We distinguish positive and negative valences, according to whether we are attracted by something (a good concert, an interesting man, a beautiful woman) or repelled by it (a discomfort, a danger). This dichotomy is correct in that the valences of the first group all press us to *approach* the objects and events in question, while those of the second press us to *retreat* from them. It would be, however, a mistake to assume that this is the crucial feature of valences. It is much more characteristic for valences that they press toward definite *actions*, the range of which may be narrow or broad, and that these actions may be of a great variety even within the group of positive valences. The book entices to reading, the cake to eating, the ocean to swimming, the mirror to looking, a confused situation to decisive action.

The valence of a structure is usually not constant, but depends greatly—in its kind and degree—on the internal and external situation of the person. The study of the vicissitudes of valences reveals their nature.

The meaning of a structure having a valence is transparent enough in certain basic cases: in these the objects which have the valence are *direct means of need satisfaction* (the cake, the concert if one goes to listen and not to be seen, etc.). In such cases we speak of *independent valences*.

There are, besides, objects and events which have valences due to their relation to the direct means of need

1254

satisfaction in the given situation; for instance, they can facilitate satisfaction. They are means to an end and have only a momentary significance. Other such *derivative valences* arise from a space or time extension of structures which have original valences. The house, the street, and even the city in which the beloved lives, may each acquire a valence. The transition between these two kinds of valences is naturally fluid, and the concept of independent valence is also relative.

A valence may undergo great changes, depending on the action-whole in which the object or event in question appears: the mirror which has just enticed the subject to take a look at her hair-do and dress becomes a neutral "instrument" as soon as she is given a task involving the use of the mirror. Similar changes of a most extreme sort occur with the objects of a landscape in war at the time of battle.[14] Besides their dependence upon the momentarily prevailing action, valences have other vicissitudes: greatly tempting delicacies become uninteresting as soon as one is *satiated*. In fact, *oversatiation* typically changes the sign of the valence: what was attractive prior to it, repels after it. Oversatiation may even lead to a lasting fixation of a negative valence. (Now and then it happens that for years one will avoid a favorite dish after once getting sick on it.) In general, however, a rhythmic rise and fall, following the periodicity of the corresponding needs, is typical for valences.

The vicissitudes of certain valences may be followed over long periods of time, for instance, those which accompany the development of the individual from infancy, through childhood and adolescence into adulthood, and old age. Their course corresponds to the changes in needs and interests, and plays a fundamental

---

14. See Lewin, Kriegslandschaft, *Z. F. angen. Psychol.* 1917, 12:440. Cf. also Aiese, *Hdbd. psychotech. Eignungsprüfungen.*

role in development. The development of the achievement-abilities of an individual does not depend only on the potentialities of "endowment." For instance, the development of speech or of intellectual achievements is basically influenced by the degree and direction of such "inclinations," which are the motors of psychic processes.

These vicissitudes, the exploration[15] of which has only begun, seem to be similar to the vicissitudes of valences which accompany changes in the general goals of will that govern the individual. The will to follow an occupation is an example of such general goals of will. Once a choice of an occupation is made, certain things which have until then been neutral obtain a positive or a negative valence..[16] Much that at first would seem "natural" inborn inclination or disinclination—preference for a certain kind of work, tendency to cleanliness and meticulousness—can be derived from the occupational goal of the individual.

A man's world changes fundamentally when his fundamental goals of will change. This holds not only for the great upheavals which follow a decision to take one's life or change one's occupation, but even for those temporary suspensions of the usual goals of will which occur when one is on vacation. Familiar things may then suddenly acquire a new look; those which went unnoticed a hundred times become interesting, and important occupational matters turn indifferent.

This change of strong positive or negative valences to complete indifference is often astonishing even to the person concerned, and has frequently been described in poetry, particularly in relation to the erotic sphere. Such change of valence is often the first indication of a

---

15. Spranger: *Psychologie des Jugendalters*. Leipzig, 1924.—Charlotte Bühler: *Das Seelenleben des Jugendlichen*. Jena, 1922. —Lau: *Beiträge zur Psychologie der Jugend in der Pubertätszeit*. Langensalza, 1924.
16. *Cf.* Lau, *op. cit.*

change in one's internal situation, and may even precede awareness of change in inclinations. The occurrence or absence of a change of valence is frequently the actual criterion of whether a decision—for instance, "to begin a new life in some way"—is apparent or *real;* that is, whether the decision occurred only in subjective experience or is a psychologically effective dynamic change. Conversions are particularly far-reaching and abrupt changes of this sort: "persecute what you have worshipped and worship what you have persecuted."

The structure of the relation between valences and these general goals of will is thus basically the same as that between valences and the goals of single activities.

These brief considerations show that the natural valences are most closely related to certain inclinations and needs, some of which derive from the so-called "drives," and others from central goals of will of varying degrees of generality. Indeed, since a change of valence corresponds to every change of need, *the proposition that "such-and-such a need exists" is to a certain extent equivalent to the proposition that "such-and-such a region of structures has a valence for such-and-such actions."*

2) *The Effects of Quasi-Needs and Genuine-Needs.* The relation of genuine needs and natural valences, however, is not such that to each need there always belongs a definite structure with a corresponding valence. It is typical for new needs which have not yet been frequently satisfied, and thus particularly for needs previous to their first real gratification, that they have a broad range of possible valences. For instance, for the purpose of systematic study the prototype of sexual and erotic inclinations is not that stage at which a firm fixation on one or more definite people and a specialization of satisfying action has already taken place, but one at which the inclination is diffuse and the region of valences is broad

1257

and indefinite.[17] Yet development does not always proceed from a diffuse to a differentiated and specialized stage. There are processes in which an inclination, at first specific, diversifies. For instance, a child of a year and a half likes at first to "open and close" only a certain clock-case, and only gradually takes to opening and closing of doors, closets and chests of drawers. A diffuse phase followed by gradual specialization and consolidation may also be the course of needs related to general goals of will—for instance, occupational will. (Yet a highly specialized goal may be present from the beginning.)

In the case of such diffuse drive-or central-needs, the *situation* to a great extent determines the valence which will have an effect and the actions which will be carried out. The need to "get ahead in an occupation" implies little or nothing for or against any specific kind of consummatory action. It remains quite indefinite whether one should write or telephone, do activity A or a quite different activity B. Even jobs considered typically "beneath the dignity of one's occupation" and therefore usually avoided (for instance, letter-filing by a bookkeeper), may be considered an honor and done with delight in certain situations (for instance, when a bookkeeper is entrusted to file particularly confident documents). Thus activities of identical achievement may appear now highly desirable and now taboo, depending on their occupational significance. Even for quite specialized and fixated needs there usually exists a certain, and mostly not even a narrow, range of valences, the actual evocation of which depends only on the concrete situation.

The situation is quite similar to that which obtains for intentions, where occasion and consummatory action

---

17. v. Allesch: Bericht über die drei ersten Lebensmonate eines Schimpansen. *Sitz. d. preuss. Akad. d. Wiss.* 1921, 672f.

are often quite indeterminate. There, too, exists a certain latitude of valences eliciting the intention effects, even when the act of intending has established definite occasions.

This parallel between the effect of a genuine-need and the effect of an intention extends also to many other essential points which will be discussed below. Because of this parallel, whenever an intention is extant we will assume that a quasi-need is present.

Both for genuine-needs and intention-effects there exist certain objects or events of valence, which when encountered arouse a tendency to definite actions. In neither case is valence and action so related that an associative coupling between the two is the cause of the action. The action-energy of drive-needs also originates essentially in certain *internal tensions,* the significance of external drive-stimuli notwithstanding. Where occasions and means of drive satisfaction do not appear from the outside they are *actively sought out,* just as in the case of intention effects.

As an argument against this conception, the so-called *habits* could be marshaled. In fact, popular psychology, and until recently scientific psychology also, considered habits as couplings between certain occasions and actions, and these couplings as the energy source of habit actions. The examples marshaled to support the theory were of this sort: we are not always hungry when we take our meal at set hours. According to recent experimental results,[18] such cases can be understood if we assume that the action in question is embedded, as a dependent part, in a broader action-complex—for instance, in the "daily routine" or "style of life"—so that its energy, the motor of the action, derives from other need sources. It seems to me that even in such habit actions and special fixations,

18. Lewin. *op. cit.,* 1922.—Sigmar, *op. cit.*

the structure of the driving forces is still rather clearly discernible: *the significance of external drive-stimuli notwithstanding, needs imply states of tension which press toward satisfaction.* Satisfaction eliminates the tension-state and may, therefore, be described as psychological "satiation."

The valences which a region of structures and events has before satisfaction (in the "hunger state") are eliminated by satiation. The region becomes neutral. Needs and intentions are analogous in this respect also; we have described the sudden neutralization of the valence of a structure by the "consummation" of the intentional action. This basic phenomenon of the intention-effect, which a theory of associative couplings can hardly explain without complex auxiliary hypotheses, becomes understandable if the intention-effect is considered to be the arising of a quasi-need and *the consummation of the intention to be its "satisfaction," that is, satiation.*

In fact, *satisfaction experiences* occur very frequently at the end of consummatory actions, even in experimental investigations.

Over and above the phenomenal relationship of consummation and satisfaction experience, the thesis concerning quasi-needs gains support by affording a dynamic explanation and derivation of the characteristics of intention-effects.

If a latent tension-state pressing toward equilibration (satisfaction) plays the primary role here, then the intention effect should be elicited *by every objectively relevant occasion* and not only by that implied in the act of intending—provided that these occasions exist psychologically and are not paralyzed by counter-forces. If the occasion fails to occur, it is—as a result of the latent state of tension—*actively sought out,* just as in the case of drive-needs and other genuine-needs. If the tension-state is too intensive, then here also inexpedient actions

1260

akin to "premature start" come about.

Genuine-needs and quasi-needs show a great deal of agreement also in their special relations to valences. (Since the following data derive only from observations of everyday life, they are in urgent need of experimental exploration, for which they should be considered only as points of departure.)

Increase in the intensity of the genuine-need usually broadens the region of valences also. In states of extraordinary hunger, objects which are otherwise unpalatable and disgust-arousing may attain positive valence. In extremes, earth is eaten and anthropophagy becomes frequent. (In such cases people partly obey the need with inner disgust, but partly the phenomenal valences are changed.) Even in less extreme instances, increasing need-intensity results in a noticeable spread of valences. The same holds for the so-called intellectual needs. . . . There are similar observations concerning quasi-needs also. The region of occasions other than the intended one to which the intention also responds, usually spreads as the tension resulting from the intention increases. For dispatching an important letter urgently, the visit of a friend or any other occasion is more likely to be utilized than when the letter is an indifferent one. (Later on I shall discuss exceptions related to the nature of vehement activity.)

3) *Fixation in Genuine-Needs and Quasi-Needs. Fixation* is one of the crucial phenomena pertaining to the relation between valences and genuine-needs. It denotes the occasional narrowness of the region of valences in comparison to the region of objects or events which "per se" would seem relevant.

For instance, a child who has several dolls will play always with one and the same doll, or give it disproportionate preference. The child will maintain that the doll "is always well behaved," or "she never lies." Even when the child is out of sorts and pays little attention to the other dolls, she will still love this one.

The fixation on *certain* valences and on *certain* modes of satisfaction plays a great and significant role in psychic life. It is known how extraordinarily intense the fixation of any genuine-need can be, to a human being, or an occupation, or a certain work, and how exclusive a role that fixation may play, and how difficult it often is to resolve.

Such fixations result apparently in an unusually strong valence of the structure in question and have a certain *exclusive function*: other structures lose their valence, entirely or partly. Similarly with the fixation to certain modifications of the satisfying *activity*.

Something quite analogous may be observed in quasi-needs also. An occasion implied by the act of intending may have a fixating effect, narrowing the range of the objectively relevant occasions to which less specific intentions might have been responsive. This holds for consummatory actions too: for instance, without the specific intention to bring up certain arguments, one would argue in a discussion appropriately to the situation and therefore purposively; but specific fixation of the arguments by a preceding act of intending often results in statements inappropriate to the situation. But, as a rule, fixation does not have an entirely exclusive effect, either for genuine- or for quasi-needs. In spite of the fixation a certain range of other valences usually persists, particularly if the pressure of the genuine- or quasi-need is strong.

With genuine-needs, the occasion and kind of the *first satisfaction* has a particularly fixating effect (first love). This is also true for those intentions which press toward repetitive action. If several occasions are possible before the first consummation, then later this first occasion will stand out from the others. This holds for the first satisfy-

1262

ing consummatory action too,[19] and plays therefore a considerable role in the so-called training process. In this, which is by no means a uniform process psychologically, valences and their vicissitudes are of great significance.[20] In learning any activity (for example, turning a lathe) many things lose their natural valences: large wheels or sudden events which are at first frightening become neutral. In turn, other structures and events, at first unnoticed, obtain definite and clear valences when embedded in the new total context.

In repeating intentional actions, usually certain modes of consummation crystallize. In this crystallization process, frequently called "automatization," the course of activity becomes rigid and lifeless. The quasi-need in early repetitions compares to that in later ones, as a young organism does to an old one. All the potentialities which together provide the conditional-genetic definition of the quasi-need actually exist in the beginning: the need is responsive to a variety of occasions and its form of consummation readily *adapts to the situations*. In later repetitions, however, the *form of consummation* becomes *relatively rigid*: historical factors limit the range of possible modes of behavior. (In some cases, as mentioned, fixation seems to exist from the beginning on.)

As a rule, a *growing independence* of the need- or quasi-need action accompanies, and may even be the prerequisite of, this ossification. A relatively independent specific organism comes about, which acts without requiring the control of the total personality and whose communication with other needs and quasi-needs is limited.

The experiments on the measurement of will may serve

---

19. This may be the origin of "latent attitudes" and "activity readinesses". See Koffka: *Zur Analyse der Vorstellungen und ihrer Gesetze.* Leipzig, 1912.
20. Lewin, *op. cit., Psychol. Forsch.* 1924, 2:.—Blumenfeld: Das Suchen von Zahlen im begrenzten ebenen Felde und das Problem der Abstraktion. *Z.f. angew. Psychol.* 1925, 26.

as an example.[21] In these experiments the process—for instance, the occurrence of intended errors (habit-errors)—depends only indirectly on the underlying needs, but directly on the specific form of consummation: a definite "activity-readiness"—implying a definite form of consummation—and not the presence of a definite quasi-need, decides whether or not a habit-error will occur.

But even in such ossified quasi-needs the energy-source remains the quasi-need itself, that is, in final analysis, the genuine-need underlying it.

Whether it is the act of intending or the course of the first consummations which *establishes* the valences and consummatory actions, the process establishing them is closely related to that of fixation of genuine-needs. It differs in essential points from *associations* as encountered in learning syllables by rote or in any other "change of the stock of knowledge."[22]

It makes no difference whether the association is conceived as one between occasion and consummation, or one between the occasion and its valence accrued from the intention. The valence of an object, just like its figural Gestalt (though the former varies more than the latter), is not independent of it as a second psychic structure. The valence of an object is as much a part of its essence as its figural Gestalt. In order to avoid misunderstandings, it would be better to speak not of changes in the valence of the object, but of *different* structures which are only figurally and externally identical. A structure whose valence has changed with the change in situation—for example, the mailbox before and after mailing the

21. Ach, *op. cit.;* Lewin, *op. cit.*
22. Selz, cited in footnote 6; also *Zur Psychologie des produktiven Denkens und des Irrtums,* 1922.—Lewin: *Psychol. Forsch.* 2: 135.

letter—*is* psychologically a different structure. . . .[23]

The following consideration appears at first contrary to our conception. We saw that consummation of the intended action—satiation of the quasi-need—as a rule eliminates the valence, since it leaves no real tension driving toward consummation. Everyday observations, however, seem to indicate that such valences can persist for a while even after consummation. It does happen that, though the letter has been mailed, a mailbox subsequently passed again reminds us to mail it.

It is conceivable that this is the inverse of those cases discussed below, in which a *substitute satisfaction* causes the forgetting of the intended action. Here mailing the letter, while objectively achieving the desired result, did not have the *psychic* effect of satisfaction; at any rate, it did not completely eliminate the tension of the quasi-need. Our concern is not with the external activity as such, but with the elimination of tensions.

The same question arises for valences related to genuine-needs:

When a small child refuses some food, bringing the spoon to his mouth is often enough to make him start eating. The older child displays greater control over the direct valence to which the younger yields as to a drive: he shuts his mouth tight, turns his head, and so on. Yet the same result can be attained by distracting the older child's attention. (Above a certain age, not even distraction avails.)

Two factors are essential to this phenomenon. First, the valence has a *stronger effect* if it is not "attended to." Increased "attention" prevents the direct effect of this "stimulus" (valence). We explain this seemingly paradoxical state of affairs by assuming that the field-forces

---

23. Translator's note. In the omitted section Lewin again stresses that an association theory based on repetition frequencies cannot explain the disappearance, after consummation, of valences once created.

exert their effect more directly when distraction weakens the controls.

The case of distraction is complicated by the negative valence of the food.

Secondly, the full spoon near the mouth has a valence for the child even if he dislikes the food. Popular psychology would explain this as a "habit," a frequent label, anyway, for fixation effects. Since there is no need present for the food in question, the valence must be that of the spoon or that of the spoon's being brought near the mouth in this situation. It appears that the valence has an effect here, even in the absence of a momentary need. Similarly, in everyday life we often do with reluctance things which on other occasions we have done with pleasure.

It is justifiable to ask: is there some genuine- or quasi-need for the activity in these cases even if the major need is absent? It is possible that here we have tensions which are intermediary forms between genuine- and quasi-needs and are related to those general goals of will which shape our everyday life: arising, dressing, taking meals, going to sleep. This assumption is supported by the observation that such valences will persist as a rule only for a short while in the face of contrary needs, which in the long run will change the "style of life."

Only experimental analysis can answer the question whether these explanations hold for all cases, or whether under certain conditions—as in fixations—valences persist in spite of the satiation of the quasi-need.

Fixations play an important role in psychic life and our discussion of them in genuine- and quasi-needs is not meant to be a systematic theory. Nor do we assert here that genuine associative couplings have no role in fixation.

We advance only a few fundamental propositions: the restriction of a valence to a definite occasion and the fixation of a specific mode of consummation are extremes in a continuum in which broad regions of events and structures have valences. The theory of quasi-needs, in contrast to the customary conception, considers that the pure and fundamental form of intention processes is found in those cases which are free of specializing fixations limiting the effect of other objectively feasible occasions. The energy sources of these processes are the genuine- or quasi-needs underlying them, and the fixated valences are also mainly related to these. The fixation is not itself the source of the action, but only the determiner of its form or occasion. Even if the relation of occasion and consummatory action were actually an associative coupling, this relation would not be analogous to the association of syllables or other kinds of knowledge, but rather to the fixation of a valence to a definite occasion. . . .[24]

4) *Substitute Consummation.* If a quasi-need and not an associative coupling between occasion and consummation is the source of intentional action, then some basic problems of *substitute consummation* are also easily clarified.

Genuine-needs too have substitute satisfactions. Genuine-needs and quasi-needs both have a whole variety of substitute consummations. The differences between these varieties are in part fundamental, but it is not easy to define them conceptually because of the transitions between them, and the mixed types among them. We will use the term *substitute consummation* for all of them, and will refer only to a few main variants, without discussing the important questions they raise.

(a) *Consummation appropriate to the situation* is objectively equivalent to the intended consummation and

---

24. Translator's note. In the omitted section Lewin demonstrates, by means of data taken from his association studies . . . that fixated valences also weaken by repeated consummation. His point is that habit-strength need not correlate positively with repetition-frequency, and under certain conditions correlates with it negatively.

is adapted to the situation. Example: instead of mailing the letter as originally intended, we ask a friend to take care of it. This is not really a substitute consummation; the course of the consummatory action alone is different from that which was anticipated. We know that this is actually the common form of intentional acts, since genuine as well as quasi-needs usually leave the mode of consummation wide open. The theory of quasi-needs (in contrast to that of associative couplings) has no difficulties with this kind of substitute consummation, in which the goal of the original need is actually reached. The consummatory action eliminates the tension (satiates the quasi-need) and causes the valences to disappear. This holds, we repeat, for genuine needs also.

(b) "Pars pro toto" *consummation*. Example: instead of buying an object, we go through the street where we can buy it; instead of actually carrying out an intention, we record it in a notebook. The consummatory action goes "in the direction of" the original goal, but apparently halts somewhere along the line. Yet the typical dynamic effects of incomplete consummation do not appear and the need-tensions are rather well equilibrated, though the consummation proper did not take place and may, for instance, have been forgotten. Specific satisfaction experiences following partial consummation seem to contribute to the failure of the consummation proper to occur. . . .

(c) *Unreal consummation, apparent consummation,* and the closely related *surrogate consummation*. Example (from Miss Dembo's experiments): failing to throw a ring over a certain bottle, one throws it over another more easily reached, or over any near-by hook. There is no action toward the real goal here. The goal itself is not brought nearer, but the consummatory action resembles somehow that of the genuine consummation. Usually a certain momentary satisfaction results, which

1268

however soon yields to the original need. It is relatively easy to produce such cases experimentally—for instance, as "avoidance actions" in difficult tasks.

How can need-tensions press to actions which are not even in the direction of eliminating the need? This important question will not be discussed here in detail. The assumption that we have here a tendency "just to do something" (as in affective restless-activity) would be an insufficient explanation. Various assumptions are possible, such as "spread" of the original need to actions of identical type, or actual satisfaction of the original need by the substitute action (based on the identity of the consummatory action). In the latter case, the occasional perseverance of the need would be explained as its revival due to recurring stimulation (valence). (This does not exhaust the possible theories: for example, there is a clear relation here to the easily misunderstood Freudian "symbol" concept).

Surrogate satisfactions occur even with drive-needs or central goals of will, when the satisfying-action proper encounters obstacles: we are "satisfied with less," and reduce our aspirations. There exist all degrees of such surrogates, from satisfactions which are not quite complete to those which are mere sham or shadow. Someone who likes to give commands but has no authority will often want to "have his say" at least or even just "be in on it." The youngster who cannot signal the train will shout "Ready, Go" after the station-master. A child who would like to escape from an orphanage has instead a burning desire for a traveling bag. A student who cannot afford to buy a piano collects piano catalogs instead.

In cases like the last, the action may attain independence, giving rise to "substitute needs." (The concept of sublimation is relevant to this point.)

(d) *Hidden apparent consummations.* The second bottle mentioned in (c) may be replaced by a Teddy-bear

1269

or something similar, and the type of action itself may "change" until it is hardly recognizable. This may occur when the situation demands that the substitute consummation be concealed, for instance when it is embarrassing.

Besides the intensity of the tension underlying the need in question, *the general level of satisfaction or frustration of the subject* is also crucial in evoking substitute consummations. The experiments on forgetting already mentioned have demonstrated this. The signature is more readily forgotten when the subject is particularly satisfied with his other achievements. . . .

(4) THE REAL RELATIONS BETWEEN QUASI-NEEDS AND GENUINE NEEDS.

1) *Quasi-Needs and Counter-Needs.* To consider the intention-effect a quasi-need amounts to more than creating a formal analogue to genuine-needs: *it makes a real relationship between intention-effect and genuine-need demonstrable.*

The various natural needs may conflict with each other: their tension-systems are not completely isolated. In part they are subordinate factors of a general tension-state, and in part there is some real communication between them, corresponding to the connections of the spheres and complexes in question with the psyche as a whole. (This has often been disregarded in the treatment of drives.)

Similar considerations hold for the real relations of quasi-needs to each other and to genuine-needs. This explains the ready "forgetting of intentions" when pitted against a strong genuine *counter-need.*

The relation and the clashing of quasi-needs and genuine needs lead us to the problem of *"freedom"* of *intentions.* The extraordinary liberty which man has to intend any, even nonsensical actions—that is, his freedom to create in himself quasi-needs—is amazing. This is characteristic of civilized man. Children, and probably

1270

also preliterates, have it to an incomparably lesser degree. It is likely that this freedom distinguishes man from kindred animals more than does his higher intelligence. (This distinction is obviously related to the problem of "control.")

Yet, one cannot arbitrarily intend "just anything" if the criterion of intending is the formation of an actual quasi-need. Without a real need one cannot resolve to kill oneself or an acquaintance, or even to do something serious against one's true interests. Not even under the pressure of hypnosis are such intentions carried out. These examples make the real relations between quasi-needs and genuine-needs particularly clear.

In children the range of the apparent arbitrariness of intentions is even narrower. Often they cannot endow even relatively neutral objects or events with positive valence by means of a quasi-need. The actions they want to intend must arise in part at least from natural valences. (These issues play a great role in the education of the small child.)

2) *Quasi-Needs and Genuine-Needs of Identical Direction.* The real relation between quasi-needs and genuine-needs explains the unanimous result, at first paradoxical, of various experimental investigations, *that the intensity of the act of intending does not decide the effectiveness of the intention.*

The fact that particularly intensive acts of intending are often less effective than weaker ones is, as said before, in part due to the general ineffectiveness of *vehement* as compared to controlled activity. Here the act of intending itself is considered as an action.

More important is the following consideration. The tensions and valences to which the act of intending gives rise are not primary. They derive from some genuine-needs, which in turn arise from drives or general goals of will. After a *quasi-need* arises from a genuine-need, it

1271

still remains *in communication with the complex of tensions implicit in the genuine-need*. Even if the intentions to drop a letter in the mailbox, to visit an acquaintance, yes, even to learn a series of nonsense syllables as an experimental subject, are relatively closed and segregated activities, the forces underlying them are not isolated, but arise from general needs, such as the will to do one's occupational work, to get ahead in one's studies, or to help a friend. The effectiveness of the intention does not depend on the intensity of the act of intending but, other factors being equal, rather on the *intensity* (vital nature) and *depth* of the genuine-need, in which the quasi-need is embedded.

The *genuine-needs* in question are those which give rise to the intention, that is, those which lead one to decide for the action. In the intention to mail a letter, the decisive need is to inform somebody, and this in turn arises from a more general goal of will.

In the course of the consummatory action, however, tensions and forces become frequently manifest which had little or no role in forming the intention. Once an intention is set up or an action is initiated, often the "whole person" becomes immediately engaged in it; thus communication is established with tensions related to "self-esteem" and "fear of insufficiency." There are great individual differences in the ease with which such auxiliary forces connect with intentional actions, and become at times their sole driving force: for instance, to persist as far as possible with a decision once made, is the corollary of a certain life-ideal. The *situation* too has a significant influence in determining the role of these auxiliary forces. For instance, Mrs. Birenbaum's finding, that the signature is less easily forgotten in *mass experiments* than in individual ones, is probably to be explained as the effect of such forces.

The communication with various genuine-needs may be

1272

extant from the beginning on, as in the case of the mass experiments. Frequently, however, it is not yet present at the act of intending, and arises only subsequently. This relation of needs is not merely theoretical, like that which obtains between different yet conceptually comparable types of needs. It is a *real communication* between concrete tension-systems. One can establish only from case to case, but not in general, when communication between systems is extant or absent. Such communication of systems comes about at a definite time, by a real process, which may progress slowly or break through suddenly.

Whether or not, besides these genuine-needs, there is an individually variable *reservoir of active energy,* used by intentional action not based on genuine-needs, is an open question awaiting experimental exploration. Some observations on encephalitics (their quick transition to micrography, their "getting stuck" after a brief spurt) are conducive to such explanation.

The idea that the effectiveness of intentions depends not on their intensity, but rather on the depths of the underlying genuine-need, is in agreement with Lindworsky's repeatedly quoted studies. He too rejects the idea that the repetition of an act necessarily strengthens its driving force. To him, the decisive factor is the relation of the intention to certain values of the individual.[25]

An individual's valuation of an object or event undoubtedly exerts crucial influence on his motivation processes and total behavior. But we will have to keep in mind that it is not an objective scale of values which is relevant to our problem, but rather the subjective momentary valuations like those which a child has for a pet dog or a piece of chocolate. These valuations always vary with the changing situation and with the person's "degree of satiation" at the moment. Two facts, how-

---

25. Translator's note. In the omitted section Lewin discusses the dangers inherent in the historical load of the concept "value."

ever, must be stressed: a) The value of an object is not simply identical with its valence. (A sum of gold somewhere may represent a great value for one person without tempting him to steal it, while for another person it may have a strong valence prompting to steal.) Naturally, valuations and valences can be related; at times, however, they are independent. b) Not values, but *definite, real psychic tensions, psychic systems, are the energy-sources of processes.* These energy systems are the *dynamic* facts which determine the course of processes. . . .[26]

The experimental subject's "acceptance of an instruction" implies dynamically an intention which is hardly distinguishable phenomenally from mere understanding. Often the mere "thought," that "this could be done in such a way" or "it would be nice if this would happen," fulfills the function of an intention.

Dostoevski[27] describes an extreme case of this kind in which, though there is no act of intending and a decision is impossible, suddenly the *dynamically real* psychic factors lie exactly as they would subsequent to a decision: "He felt it distinctly and suddenly, he knew it with a full clarity, that he would flee, yes, that he really would flee, but he knew also that he was now completely unable to answer the question whether he should flee *before* or *after* [murdering] Shatoff. And he felt that he would surely not flee '*before* Shatoff,' but rather absolutely only '*after* Shatoff,' and that it was so decided, signed and sealed." . . .

In other cases, which are—at least phenotypically— very similar, no such effect occurs. It seems to make a great deal of difference whether a need remains at the

---

26. Translator's note. The omitted section restates the dependence of quasi-need affects on genuine-needs, and ther relative independence from the intensity of the act of intending.
27. Dostoevski: *Die Dämonen.* München, 1919, Bd. II, 343.

stage of mere *wish* or crystallizes into a definite quasi-need. The crucial difference seems to be that crystallization of a quasi-need creates, in principle, an avenue to the motor-region which did not exist before. But not even here is the clear experience of "I really want it" crucial, but rather whether or not a real avenue to the motor-region is created.

3) *The Dynamic Independence (Segregation) of Quasi-Needs.* The degree to which other needs influence a quasi-need in the course of the consummatory action varies greatly.

A subject is instructed to touch two copper cords with two fingers of one hand and to press with the other a lever which closes the circuit. The subject suffers a strong electric shock. There are subjects who, having once decided to do this task, give one a particularly "factual" impression. The course of action becomes very direct (some observers say it becomes "soldierly"). The subjects' introspections corroborate these observations. For example, one subject's experience was that she acted "as in a dream," and had strikingly little more to report.

Other subjects' behavior follows a much less direct course. The internal vacillation and contradictory tensions preceding the decision continue even *after* the decision to accept the instructions. Here the decision does not set a sharp dividing line after the preceding processes, as in the subjects of the "factual" type. Paradoxically, however, it is not the subjects of the "factual" type who have little anxiety about the electrical shock; their fear of pain is considerably greater than that of the more "subjective" type.

The difference illustrated by this example always plays an important role in the consummation of intentions, and is related to general and fundamental problems of psychic structure which can be merely touched upon here. The psyche of an individual is not a homogeneous unity in which every structure and event is equally related to every other; nor does the mutual influence of these psychic structures and processes depend solely on their intensity, power, or significance. There are psychic regions and complexes which are most closely related to each other, while they are engaged in various degrees from other psychic complexes. The extent to which a psychic event or force influences other psychic structures depends on whether they are embedded in the same or in different complexes.

The independence and segregation of a complex varies from case to case. An example from the motor sphere: a beginner in moving-picture photography stops involuntarily on any sudden and unexpected happening in the field of the picture, and is influenced even by events outside of it, such as every movement of his own head and other hand, all of which prevent his turning the handle of his machine evenly. The experienced operator is undisturbed by all these influences. He has segregated the movement of his arm, the procedure of turning the handle, from his other hand movements and impressions, and has developed it into *a relatively independent action organism*. . . .

Such cases are usually described as "mechanical" action. In the present context, however, it is not the *reflex character or stereotype* of the action which is essential. Even in activities of irregular course, for instance, in catching irregularly thrown balls, or in turning a handle the friction of which is changing, a correction may "quite mechanically" take place by changes in the catching movement or in muscle tension. The mechanism often works like a real organism in which "perceptual basis" and "motor sphere" are tuned together. (Naturally, as with many other organisms under given conditions a mechanism too may change from a natural flexibility to rigid automatism.)

1276

The crucial fact here is that an *independent "action-organism"* came about, not that it is mechanical. With a beginner, the turning of the handle is a subordinate part of the motor-region as a whole (which is tuned to the perception-basis as a whole); with the experienced moving-picture photographer, the turning of the handle is an independent partial motor-region, which is segregated from the rest of the motor region and tuned together with a previously subordinate part of the perception-basis into an independent action-organism. The kind and intensity of Gestalt-ties, of system-relations, undergoes a dynamic change: old bonds are dissolved and a new, relatively closed structure is formed.

The previous example of the decision-effect implies an analogous process. In the subject to whom the task was especially painful, and whose consummatory activity was nevertheless particularly factual and direct, the tensions of the quasi-need arising from the act of decision are far more strongly *segregated from the rest of the ego* than in the other subjects. The boundary created between this quasi-need and the other psychic complexes has a double effect. It renders the consummatory action more independent from the other psychic tensions (therefore its directness), and it also affords the individual greater protection against the painfulness of the process (therefore, its dream-character). Thus it becomes understandable that the objectification and isolation of this specific psychic complex occurred precisely in those subjects who were particularly afraid of the pain.

In war, in the course of battle, there often is opportunity to make such observations on the so-called "plucky" soldier.

The degree of independence of the quasi-need from other need tensions thus shows great situational and individual variability.

(E) REMEMBERING FINISHED AND UNFINISHED ACTIVITIES.

1277

The effects of tension-states may be observed not only in the intentional actions to which they give rise, but also indirectly in facts of memory-psychology. We may ask, for instance, which is remembered better—an intentional action that is completed, or one that is not completed. At first one would assume that the completed ones will be remembered, because the subject was longer at them.

The experiment[28] shows something quite different. The subject is given twenty tasks to do in an experimental hour. The experimenter interrupts part of these before their completion. Shortly after the subject has done the last of the tasks, he is tested to see which of them he remembers.

The results show that *the interrupted tasks are remembered, on an average, 50 percent better than the completed ones.* There are characteristic differences for various kinds of activities (end-activity versus continuous activity, interesting activity versus indifferent activity), and for various types of subjects. In the present context we must remain quite general, and state only that the *tension-state* which persists after the interruption of the intentional action expresses itself not only in a tendency to resume the action, but also in memory.

These tensions do not always, or for all subjects, cause a better remembering; they may also result in *repression phenomena.* However, particularly in subjects of a certain childish type, these tensions favor remembering.

2. *The Conditions of Intention-Formation; Intentional Action, "Will Action" (Controlled Action), and "Drive-" (Field-) Action*

If we make a gross estimate of the frequency of intentions in everyday life, considering at first only those intentions which are attended by an experience of a specific act of intending, we find to our surprise that *acts*

---

28. These experiments were carried out by Mrs. Zeigarnik at the Berlin Psychological Institute.

of intending are not very frequent. True, the day often begins with an act of intending. Usually about 50 percent of students state that their rising that morning was preceded by the specific intention to get up. But throughout the rest of the day, while dressing, breakfasting, going to work, acts of intending are rare.

This scarcity of intending is not explained alone by the assumption that habits or generalized intentions determine the daily routine. Children at play in new situations do not give the impression of frequent acts of intending, not even when they play roughly or fight. Not even the changes which occur when something new attracts them, or when they want something the other child has, are mediated by acts of intending; instead we observe immediate responses, usually described as "drive-like" or "involuntary." *In cases where genuine-needs are directly in play, it is typical that no acts of intending preceded the action.* (Under such conditions, in terms of the theory of quasi-needs, an act of intending would make no sense.)

But not all actions which are not preceded by an act of intending are drive-like. In a conversation, for instance, the answers and the exchanges in general are rarely preceded by specific acts of intending, which occur mainly when one is about to lie or to conceal something. Yet we must realize that such talk—questions and answers without preceding acts of intending—is not all drive-like, but mostly of a volitional character. There are many other everyday actions, for instance occupational, which, though not preceded by specific acts of intending, are neither automatized nor uncontrolled and drive-like. These and other facts, a discussion of which would lead us too far afield, contradict the view that intentional action is the prototype of will action. To establish the action-type to which a psychological event belongs, we will have to regard the character of its course, rather

1279

than whether it has been preceded by another act.

Accordingly, the following cases are typically not "drive-actions" but "will-actions": when one does not shun menacing danger or pain, but faces or even goes forth to meet it; when one takes an insult calmly; when one is cool and unfriendly toward a friendly person. This type of action, on which our attention now centers, is *controlled action.*[29]

If we disregard the *automatized* and—in the strict sense of the term—*reflex-like* actions, the use of the term "drive" proves equivocal. By *drive-action* we mean first of all an "involuntary action, directed by forces *not under the control* of the individual."

Such action is not always an instant effect of a stimulus-constellation and may be preceded by delay, yet sudden response to a stimulus-constellation is indeed often the sign of an uncontrolled reaction. Thus the second meaning of the concepts "drive-like, involuntary, impulsive" is, that the action they qualify is the *opposite* of those *preceded by a specific act of intending.*

It must be stressed that genuine intentional action, preceded by a specific act of intending, is not always of that controlled character which would be the opposite of drive-action in the first sense. Naturally an intentional action may take the form of controlled action. When a child decides to go past a dog of which he is afraid, the walking past is occasionally a controlled action; then the child passes the dog with a controlled and calm, though cautious, bearing. *The intentional action is, however, often not a controlled action,* or may show only little control. For instance, in the example given, the intention is often carried out in the form of entirely uncontrolled running past the dog.

In this case, the course of events is as though the intention were a force simply added to the others of

---

29. *Cf.* also Klages, A: *Prinzipien der Characterologie.* Leipzig, 1921.

the situation (the psychological field), and as though the action ensued in accordance with the force-distribution so created in an altogether drive-like, uncontrolled fashion.

Such uncontrolled or little controlled consummatory action is frequent in intentional actions, and is—in some respects—more characteristic of them than is controlled consummation. The common, simple reaction experiment —certainly a genuine intentional action, based solely on the preceding intention of the subject—is usually, to judge by the consummation and the events following the signal, the pure type of an uncontrolled activity. (Only failures tend to change it into controlled action.) We find it particularly in successful intentions that the action following the appearance of the occasion (dropping the letter in to the mailbox) is involuntary, that is, closer to uncontrolled than to controlled actions. Like the term "drive action," its opposite term "voluntary action" has two meanings. It may refer to intentional as well as to controlled action. Thus it will be desirable, for the sake of conceptual clarity, to avoid using the terms "will" and "drive" wherever there is the slightest chance for misunderstanding. Instead of these terms one might use: (a) *controlled action,* and its counterpart "uncontrolled" or "field action," as I prefer to call it (action directly determined by the field forces)[30]; (b) *intentional action,* which does not imply any definite type of consummatory action, but only a preceding act of intending, that is, its origin in a quasi-need.

We can be certain of the following. The character of the consummatory action is not determined by the fact that it originated in an intention. The consummation *may* take the form of controlled action, but it is the rela-

---

30. Naturally, controlled activity, too, is subject to the forces of the total field. However, it is characteristic of controlled activity that the whole person does not enter the field; he maintains a certain degree of reserve and perspective and therefore has the activity in hand. In other words, the demarcation of the psychic systems differ here from that in uncontrolled activity: the "ego systems" have a greater independence, or their dominance is firmer.

tively uncontrolled forms which are characteristic and theoretically essential, since in many respects the intention-effects become particularly clear in these. Objects and events, to which otherwise the person would have remained indifferent, attain a valence due to the intention, and directly initiate uncontrolled pure field-actions. (The theory of determining tendencies, also, emphasizes particularly these cases.)

Now it is clear the essential achievement of the intention is one of preparation.[31] Due to the act of intending, at some subsequent time a psychological field appears which otherwise would not have existed, or at least not in the same form. *Forming an intention creates conditions which allow us later simply to abandon ourselves to the effects of the field* (letter and mailbox), or permit a [psychological] field to be so transformed, or so supplied with additional forces, that a controlled action becomes feasible or easier.

Now we can state the conditions under which intentions arise. The intention is not characteristic of will-action in its sense of controlled action. An intention, in the narrower sense, arises only where there is a certain *foresight* (which need not imply a precise picture of the future), and the situation as aforeseen does not include those valences which by themselves would bring about the desired actions in the form of pure field-actions. An intention also arises when the foreseen situation by itself would lead to field-actions contrary to the desired action.

A typical example, from experiments Miss Dembo undertook for another purpose, follows. The subject was forbidden to leave a certain place, yet would like to; she does not dare to, that is, cannot carry out her leaving in the form of a controlled action. Her way out is to form the intention: "I will go as soon as the clock gets into

---

31. This is also G. E. Müller's view (*op. cit.*) of intentions, though his theory is fundamentally different from that presented here.

this or that position." (Similar occurrences are frequent in everyday life.) Thus she creates valences for the future, which will then directly press her to leave, and bring about or facilitate the intended action. (It is an interesting question why, when it is impossible to leave immediately, it is possible to form such an intention. We cannot enter this problem here.)

The following cases are also related to the fact that intentions aim at influencing future situations. It does happen that, in fear of certain anticipated events and situations, we "armor ourselves with firm intentions." If the actual situation proves harmless, we then get the feeling of having hammered at an open door. The relation between intention and foresight becomes particularly clear in such cases, where the *knowledge* of the future was erroneous, and the actual situation does not have the counterforces expected. . . .

Concomitant to the intention is usually another process, which is called *decision*. The main functional effect of this process is that it opens or facilitates for the internal tension an access to activity, to motility, either momentarily or in principle (that is, for a future situation). Thus, decision does not create new psychic tensions (if they accompany it, they are not its essence); rather, it creates for an already existing tension a new *access*, in a form previously not extant, *to the* motor-region. The pure phenomenological expression of this dynamic fact of decision is the experience, "I really want it,"[32] "fiat!"[33] meaning "this is how I will do it." When in a person there are several simultaneous tension-systems of opposing directions, a decision often amounts to the effecting of some kind of equilibrium among them, or to

---

32. Ach, *op. cit.*
33. James, W. *Psychologie.* 1909, 415.

isolating some of them.[34] At any rate, the internal situation created is one in which a more or less unitary tension-system controls the atcion. Occasionally in such cases, an internal vacillation is observed before the decision (the so-called struggle of motives).

In this connection it is customary to speak of choice, the implication of which is that in the interest of clear-cut action it is often necessary to suppress some of the tension-systems competing for the access to the motor region. This is not always completely successful, however; then, in spite of the choice, the tensions originating from the suppresed systems will make themselves mildly noticeable in the action. Thus unpurposeful mixed actions may come about, resulting in an inhibition or weakening of the activity.

Decisions as here functionally defined, like intentions, have no unequivocal indicators in [subjective] experience. The firmness of a decision and the intensity of the act of decision are not directly related, and even functionally essential decisions may occur without clear-cut decision-experiences.

Intentions in the functional sense (formation of quasi-needs), and decisions in the functional sense (the suppression or equilibration of simultaneous internal tensions in their claims for control of action), appear at times as closely related, and only conceptually separable, functional components of a [psychic] process; at other times they appear separately in relatively pure forms. The internal decision, the choice of a certain direction, may result in a specific intention for a certain form of consummation. But the intention, the arising quasi-need, usually implies in principle an access of its own to the

_____

34. *Cf.* Koffka: "Psychologie" In *Die Philosophie in ihren Einzelgebieten.* Berlin, 1925.—Claparède: "Does the will express the entire personality?" In *Problems of Personality, Studies in Honour of Dr. Morton Prince.* London, 1925, pp. 39-43.

motor-region, and unless there are internal counter-tensions, requires no specific act of decision for this purpose.[35]

Intentional action is not the prototype of will-action. It occurs in all forms of transition from controlled action to uncontrolled, drive-like, field-action. . . . **All in all,** intentional actions belong more to the field-actions than to the controlled actions.

Accordingly, the majority of controlled (will) actions are not preceded by an act of intending. Intentional actions are relatively rare. They are prepared actions, where the act of intending, which is as a rule controlled, prepares an *uncontrolled field-action.*

The effects of intentions are twofold. One of these effects is the *creation* or transformation of certain *future psychic fields;* the other, the creation of immediate or future access to the motor-region for certain psychic tensions. These effects appear frequently together, but at times also separately.

The first of these effects, as a functional factor, may be designated as "intention" in the strict sense, the second as "decision" in the strict sense.

The *decision* equalizes tensions of differing directions which already exist in the total person, or at least changes the internal situation so that the action will be controlled by relatively homogeneous tensions.

Another effect of the intention is that occasions which

---

35. Translator's note. The omitted part applies to quasi-needs the considerations pertaining to conditional-genetic concepts . . . Its salient statement is: "In contrast to the usual procedure, we want to stress that similar concepts will have to be applied to drives and other genuine-needs, also. The pressure of needs always leaves open a certain region of concrete consummatory activities and possible occasions (excepting the cases of pronounced fixation), and *only need and situation* (where the latter is not considered as momentary in time) *together determine unequivocally the phenotypical aspect of the concrete process."*

would have remained neutral without the act of intending acquire valence and issue in certain consummatory actions. In individual cases, the *occasions* as well as the *consummatory actions* may be unequivocally established and limited by the act of intending. But these cases are not the prototype of intention; and even in them, the forces underlying the intentional action cannot be considered associative couplings, established by the act of intending between the idea of the occasion and the idea of consummation.

The act of intending often leaves the consummation action, as well as the occasions to which it is to respond, indeterminate. In these cases, and as a rule even where the act of intending implies a definite occasion, the intention may respond to various occasions not foreseen, which have certain objective relations to the intention, or rather to the need underlying it. The same holds for consummatory actions.

Dynamically the intention is defined as the formation of a quasi-need, of a tension-state, which is very similar to and has real relationships with genuine-needs.

(a) To each quasi-need (just as to each genuine-need) there corresponds a certain region of objects and events which have a valence that entices to actions (satisfying actions of the need, which satiate the quasi-need, that is, discharge the tension).

The consummatory actions of a quasi-need vary with the concrete consummatory situation. The quasi-need may press to a single or to repetitive action.

(b) The extent of the region of structures which have a valence depends, among other things, on the strength of the quasi-need. Where this region is unnaturally narrow, the situation is similar to that where genuine-needs are fixated on certain occasions and satisfactions. Fixation may come about by the act of intending or by the (first) consummation, but is not always reinforced by repetition.

1286

(c) The *need-tension* is the primary fact: if sufficiently intensive, and the occasion is delayed, it leads to premature beginning of the consummatory action; when the occasion fails to appear, to actively seeking it out; and when the action is interrupted, to resume it or better retain it in memory.

(d) When the quasi-need is satiated, the valences in general disappear, even in cases of fixation. The valences of the occasion implied by the act of intending usually disappear, even if the consummation occurs in a form or on an occasion not foreseen in the act.

(e) Genuine consummation may be replaced by various forms of substitute consummation. To some extent these have the same effects as consummation proper, and thus may lead to forgetting an intention and failure to resume an interrupted activity.

(f) The quasi-need, created by the act of intending, is not an isolated structure in the whole psyche, but is usually embedded in a *certain* psychic complex or region of the personality. It is in communication with other quasi-needs and genuine-needs derived from certain general goals of will, or drives. The intensity of the intention-effect depends on the intensity and centrality of these needs. The needs to which the quasi-need has real relationships are not necessarily those which have led to the act of intending. The effect of a quasi-need may be inhibited by contrary genuine-needs.

(g) The phenomenal intensity of the act of intending and its other phenomenal characteristics have no decisive significance [for the occurrence and manner of consummation].

KURT LEWIN (b.-Mogilno, Germany, Sept. 9, 1890; d.-Newtonville, Mass., U.S.A., Feb. 12, 1947).

Lewin studied at a variety of schools: University of Freiburg-1908, University of Munich-1909. He received his Ph.D. in 1914 from the University of Berlin. Here he gradually came under the influence of the

Gestalt School. In 1919 Lewin became Instructor in Philosophy at Berlin; in 1926 he was appointed Professor of Philosophy and Psychology. He came to the United States in 1932 as Visiting Professor of Psychology at Stanford University. For two years (1933-1935) he was Acting Professor at Cornell. In 1935 he became Professor of Child Psychology at the University of Iowa, where he developed the famous Child Welfare Research Center. In 1945 he founded the Research Center for Group Dynamics at the Massachusetts Institute of Technology (now at the University of Michigan). He remained director until his death.

Lewin's thought ranged widely. Embodying the insights of Gestalt Psychology, Lewin gave it a sharp twist of his own. His penetrating insight into personal and social dynamics has fostered a great body of experimental and theoretical work. The large number of his students have expanded the complex components of his ideas into pedagogy, learning theory, memory, intelligence, personality dynamics, and, above all, social psychology. The later field of study has taken on an entirely new and richer aspect since the Lewinian concepts of field, boundary, drive, force, personality structuring, goal, level of aspiration, dedifferentiation, and situational tensions have been brought to bear on the issues of racial prejudice, small group structure (so-called group dynamics), communication patterns, and social mobility. The very basis of the democratic way of life has come to be understood for the first time in psychological rather than political terms. The practical applications have already extended from Labor-Management relations through summer camps to individual psychopathology. It can be said without exaggeration that much of the power and strength of social psychology, as an approach to the encouragement of peaceful solutions to aggressive intergroup tensions, stems from the inspiration of Kurt Lewin. His gift to the world is very great.

The present essay is Lewin's earliest, most complete, and most concise statement of basic principles.

LEWIN, K. "Intention, will and need." In Rappaport, D. *Organization and pathology of thought.* N.Y.: Columbia University Press; Austin Riggs Foundation Monogr. No. 1, 1951, Chap. 5 (pp. 95-153). Trans. D. Rappaport from: "Vorsatz, Wille und Bedurfnis". *Psychol. Forsch.* 1926, 7:330-385. It is with special pleasure that I thank Mrs. Kurt Lewin, David Rappaport, and the Columbia University Press for permission to reprint. This essay is substantially complete; however, the illuminating footnotes of Rappaport have necessarily been deleted for reasons of space.

See also:

LEWIN, K.

    a. *A dynamic theory of personality.* N.Y.: McGraw-Hill, 1935.

    b. *Principles of topological psychology,* N.Y.: McGraw-Hill, 1936. Trans. F. & G. M. Heider.

    c. "The conceptual representation and measurement of psychological forces." *Contri. Psychol. Theory.* 1938, I (4).

    d. *Resolving social conflicts.* N. Y.: Harper and Bros., 1948. Edited: G. W. Lewin.

    e. *Field Theory in social science.* N.Y.: Harper and Bros. 1951. Edited: D. Cartwright. An important collection of Lewin's essays.

LIPPITT, R. "An experimental study of the effect of democratic and authoritarian group atmospheres." *Univ. Iowa Stud. Child Welf.* 1940, 16 (3): 45-195.

TOLMAN, E. C. "Kurt Lewin (1890-1947)." *Psychol. Rev.* 1948, 55:1-4.

MURCHISON (b-Vol. 2, p. 447; b-Vol. 3, p. 836-837).

AN INTRODUCTION TO

SOCIAL PSYCHOLOGY

WILLIAM McDOUGALL, F.R.S.

THE MENTAL CHARACTERS OF MAN OF PRIMARY IMPORTANCE
FOR HIS LIFE IN SOCIETY

*The Nature of Instincts and Their Place in
the Constitution of the Human Mind*

The human mind has certain innate or inherited tendencies which are the essential springs or motive powers
of all thought and action, whether individual or collective,
and are the bases from which the character and will of
individuals and of nations are gradually developed under
the guidance of the intellectual faculties. These primary
innate tendencies have different relative strengths in the
native constitutions of the individuals of different races,
and they are favoured or checked in very different degrees
by the very different social circumstances of men in
different stages of culture; but they are probably common
to the men of every race and of every age. If this view,
that human nature has everywhere and at all times this
common native foundation, can be established, it will
afford a much-needed basis for speculation on the history
of the development of human societies and human institutions. For so long as it is possible to assume, as has often
been done, that these innate tendencies of the human mind
have varied greatly from age to age and from race to race,
all such speculation is founded on quicksand and we
cannot hope to reach views of a reasonable degree of
certainty.

The evidence that the native basis of the human mind,
constituted by the sum of these innate tendencies, has

this stable unchanging character is afforded by comparative psychology. For we find, not only that these tendencies, in stronger or weaker degree, are present in men of all races now living on the earth, but that we may find all of them, or at least the germs of them, in most of the higher animals. Hence there can be little doubt that they played the same essential part in the minds of the primitive human stock, or stocks, and in the pre-human ancestors that bridged the great gap in the evolutionary series between man and the animal world.

These all-important and relatively unchanging tendencies, which form the basis of human character and will, are of two main classes—

(1) The specific tendencies or instincts;

(2) The general or non-specific tendencies arising out of the constitution of mind and the nature of mental process in general, when mind and mental process attain a certain degree of complexity in the course of evolution.

Contemporary writers of all classes make frequent use of the words "instinct" and "instinctive," but with very few exceptions, they use them so loosely that they have almost spoilt them for scientific purposes. On the one hand, the adjective "instinctive" is commonly applied to every human action that is performed without deliberate reflexion; on the other hand, the actions of animals are popularly attributed to instinct, and in this connexion instinct is vaguely conceived as a mysterious faculty, utterly different in nature from any human faculty, which Providence has given to the brutes because the higher faculty of reason, has been denied them. Hundreds of passages might be quoted from contemporary authors, even some of considerable philosophical culture, to illustrate how these two words are used with a minimum of meaning, generally with the effect of disguising from the writer the obscurity and incoherence of his thought. The following examples will serve to illustrate at once this abuse and the hopeless laxity with which even cultured authors make use of psychological terms. One philosophical writer on social topics tells us that the power of the State "is dependent on the instinct of subordination, which is the outcome of the desire of the people, more or less distinctly conceived, for certain social ends": another asserts that ancestor-worship has survived amongst the Western peoples as a "mere tradition and instinct": a medical writer has recently asserted that if a drunkard is fed on fruit he will "become instinctively a teetotaler": a political writer tells us that "the Russian people is rapidly acquiring a political instinct": from a recent treatise on morals by a distinguished philosopher two passages, fair samples of a large number, may be taken; one describes the "notion that blood demands blood" as an "inveterate instinct of primitive humanity"; the other affirms that "punishment originates in the instinct of vengeance": another of our most distinguished philosophers asserts that "popular instinct maintains" that "there is a theory and a justification of social coercion latent in the term 'self-government.' " As our last illustration we may take the following passage from an avowedly psychological article in a recent number of the *Spectator*: "The instinct of contradiction, like the instinct of acquiescence, is inborn. . . . These instincts are very deep-rooted and absolutely incorrigible, either from within or from without. Both springing as they do from a radical defect, from a want of original independence, they affect the whole mind and character." These are favourable examples of current usage, and they justify the statement that these words "instinct" and "instinctive" are commonly used as a cloak for ignorance when a writer attempts to explain any individual or collective action that he fails, or has not tried, to understand. Yet there can be no understanding of the development of individual character or of individual and collec-

1292

tive conduct unless the nature of instinct and its scope and function in the human mind are clearly and firmly grasped.

It would be difficult to find any adequate mention of instincts in treatises on human psychology written before the middle of last century. But the work of Darwin and of Herbert Spencer has lifted to some extent the veil of mystery from the instincts of animals, and has made the problem of the relation of instinct to human intelligence and conduct one of the most widely discussed in recent years.

Among professed psychologists there is now fair agreement as to the usage of the terms "instinct" and "instinctive." By the great majority they are used only to denote certain innate specific tendencies of the mind that are common to all members of any one species, racial characters that have been slowly evolved in the process of adaptation of species to their environment and that can be neither eradicated from the mental constitution of which they are innate elements nor acquired by individuals in the course of their lifetime. A few writers, of whom Professor Wundt is the most prominent, apply the terms to the very strongly fixed, acquired habits of action that are more commonly and properly described as secondarily automatic actions, as well as to the innate specific tendencies. The former usage seems in every way preferable and is adopted in these pages.

But, even among those psychologists who use the terms in this stricter sense, there are still great differences of opinion as to the place of instinct in the human mind. All agree that man has been evolved from pre-human ancestors whose lives were dominated by instincts; but some hold that, as man's intelligence and reasoning powers developed, his instincts atrophied, until now in civilised man instincts persist only as troublesome vestiges of his pre-human state, vestiges that are comparable

1293

to the vermiform appendix and which, like the latter, might with advantage be removed by the surgeon's knife, if that were at all possible. Others assign them a more prominent place in the constitution of the human mind; for they see that intelligence, as it increased with the evolution of the higher animals and of man, did not supplant and so lead to the atrophy of the instincts, but rather controlled and modified their operation; and some, like G. H. Schneider[1] and William James,[2] maintain that man has at least as many instincts as any of the animals, and assign them a leading part in the determination of human conduct and mental processes. This last view is now rapidly gaining ground; and this volume, I hope, may contribute in some slight degree to promote the recognition of the full scope and function of the human instincts; for this recognition will, I feel sure, appear to those who come after us as the most important advance made by psychology in our time.

Instinctive actions are displayed in their purest form by animals not very high in the scale of intelligence. In the higher vertebrate animals few instinctive modes of behaviour remain purely instinctive—*i.e.*, unmodified by intelligence and by habits acquired under the guidance of intelligence or by imitation. And even the human infant, whose intelligence remains but little developed for so many months after birth, performs few purely instinctive actions; because in the human being the instincts, although innate, are, with few exceptions, undeveloped in the first months of life, and only ripen, or become capable of functioning, at various periods throughout the years from infancy to puberty.

Insect life affords perhaps the most striking examples of purely instinctive action. There are many instances of insects that invariably lay their eggs in the only places

---

[1]"Der thierische Wille." Leipzig, 1880.
[2]"Principles of Psychology," London, 1891.

where the grubs, when hatched, will find the food they need and can eat, or where the larvæ will be able to attach themselves as parasites to some host in a way that is necessary to their survival. In such cases it is clear that the behaviour of the parent is determined by the impressions made on its senses by the appropriate objects or places: *e.g.*, the smell of decaying flesh leads the carrion-fly to deposit its eggs upon it; the sight or odour of some particular flower leads another to lay its eggs among the ovules of the flower, which serves as food to the grubs. Others go through more elaborate trains of action, as when the mason-wasp lays its eggs in a mud-nest, fills up the space with caterpillars, which it paralyses by means of well-directed stings, and seals it up; so that the caterpillar remains as a supply of fresh animal food for the young which the parent will never see and of whose needs it can have no knowledge or idea.

Among the lower vertebrate animals also instinctive actions, hardly at all modified by intelligent control, are common. The young chick runs to his mother in response to a call of peculiar quality and nestles beneath her; the young squirrel brought up in lonely captivity, when nuts are given him for the first time, opens and eats some and buries others with all the movements characteristic of his species; the kitten in the presence of a dog or a mouse assumes the characteristic feline attitudes and behaves as all his fellows of countless generations have behaved. Even so intelligent an animal as the domesticated dog behaves on some occasions in a purely instinctual fashion; when for example, a terrier comes across the trail of a rabbit, his hunting instinct is immediately aroused by the scent; he becomes blind and deaf to all other impressions as he follows the trail, and then, when he sights his quarry, breaks out into the yapping which is peculiar to occasions of this kind. His wild ancestors hunted in packs, and, under those conditions, the characteristic bark emitted on sighting the quarry served to bring his fellows to his aid; but when the domesticated terrier hunts alone, his excited yapping can but felicitate the escape of his quarry; yet the old social instinct operates too powerfully to be controlled by his moderate intelligence.

These few instances of purely instinctive behaviour illustrate clearly its nature. In the typical case some sense-impression, or combination of sense-impressions, excites some perfectly definite behaviour, some movements or train of movements which is the same in all individuals of the species and on all similar occasions; and in general the behaviour so occasioned is of a kind either to promote the welfare of the individual animal or of the community to which he belongs, or to secure the perpetuation of the species.[1]

In treating of the instincts of animals, writers have usually described them as innate tendencies to certain kinds of action, and Herbert Spencer's widely accepted definition of instinctive action as compound reflex action takes account only of the behaviour or movements to which instincts give rise. But instincts are more than innate tendencies or dispositions to certain kinds of movement. There is every reason to believe that even the most purely instinctive action is the outcome of a distinctly mental process, one which is incapable of being described in purely mechanical terms, because it is a psycho-physical process, involving psychical as well as physical changes, and one which like every other mental process, has, and can only be fully described in terms of, the three aspects of all mental processes—the cognitive, the affective, and the conative aspects; that is to say, every instance of instinctive behaviour involves a

---

[1]In many cases an instinct is excitable only during the prevalence of some special organic condition (*e.g.*, the nest-building and mating instinct of birds, the sitting instinct of the broody hen; and some writers have given such organic conditions an undue prominence, while neglecting the essential part played by sense-impressions.

knowing of some thing or object, a feeling in regard to it, and a striving towards or away from that object.

We cannot, of course, directly observe the threefold psychical aspect of the psycho-physical process that issues in instinctive behaviour; but we are amply justified in assuming that it invariably accompanies the process in the nervous system of which the instinctive movements are the immediate result, a process which, being initiated on stimulation of some sense organ by the physical impressions received from the object, travels up the sensory nerves, traverses the brain, and descends as an orderly or co-ordinated stream of nervous impulses along efferent nerves to the appropriate groups of muscles and other executive organs. We are justified in assuming the cognitive aspect of the psychical process, because the nervous excitation seems to traverse those parts of the brain whose excitement involves the production of sensations or changes in the sensory content of consciousness; we are justified in assuming the affective aspect of the psychical process, because the creature exhibits unmistakable symptoms of feeling and emotional excitement; and, especially, we are justified in assuming the conative aspect of the psychical process, because all instinctive behaviour exhibits that unique mark of mental process, a persistent striving towards the natural end of the process. That is to say, the process, unlike any mere mechanical process, is not to be arrested by any sufficient mechanical obstacle, but is rather intensified by any such obstacle and only comes to an end either when its appropriate goal is achieved, or when some stronger incompatible tendency is excited, or when the creature is exhausted by its persistent efforts.

Now, the psycho-physical process that issues in an instinctive action is initiated by a sense-impression which, usually, is but one of many sense-impressions received at the same time; and the fact that this one

1297

impression plays an altogether dominant part in determining the animal's behaviour shows that its effects are
peculiarly favoured, that the nervous system is peculiarly
fitted to receive and to respond to just that kind of
impression. The impression must be supposed to excite,
not merely detailed changes in the animal's field of sensation, but a sensation or complex of sensations that has
significance or meaning for the animal; hence we must
regard the instinctive process in its cognitive aspect as
distinctly of the nature of perception, however rudimentary. In the animals most nearly allied to ourselves
we can, in many instances of instinctive behaviour,
clearly recognise the symptoms of some particular kind
of emotion such as fear, anger, or tender feeling; and
the same symptoms always accompany any one kind of
instinctive behaviour, as when the cat assumes the
defensive attitude, the dog resents the intrusion of a
strange dog, or the hen tenderly gathers her brood
beneath her wings. We seem justified in believing that
each kind of instinctive behaviour is always attended
by some such emotional excitement, however faint, which
in each case is specific or peculiar to that kind of
behaviour. Analogy with our own experience justifies
us, also, in assuming that the persistent striving towards
its end, which characterises mental process and distinguishes instinctive behaviour most clearly from mere
reflex action, implies some such mode of experience as
we call conative, the kind of experience which in its
more developed forms is properly called desire or
aversion, but which, in the blind form in which we
sometimes have it and which is its usual form among the
animals, is a mere impulse, or craving, or uneasy sense
of want. Further, we seem justified in believing that
the continued obstruction of instinctive striving is always
accompanied by painful feeling, ·its successful progress
towards its end by pleasurable feeling, and the achieve-

ment of its end by a pleasurable sense of satisfaction.

An instinctive action, then, must not be regarded as simple or compound reflex action if by reflex action we mean, as is usually meant, a movement caused by a sense-stimulus and resulting from a sequence of merely physical process in some nervous arc. Nevertheless, just as a reflex action implies the presence in the nervous system of the reflex nervous arc, so the instinctive action also implies some enduring nervous basis whose organisation is inherited, an innate or inherited psycho-physical disposition, which, anatomically regarded, probably has the form of a compound system of sensori-motor arcs.

We may, then, define an instinct as an inherited or innate psycho-physical disposition which determines its possessor to perceive, and to pay attention to, objects of a certain class, to experience an emotional excitement of a particular quality upon perceiving such an object, and to act in regard to it in a particular manner, or, at least, to experience an impulse to such action.

It must further be noted that some instincts remain inexcitable except during the prevalence of some temporary bodily state, such as hunger. In these cases we must suppose that the bodily process or state determines the stimulation of sense-organs within the body, and that nervous currents ascending from these to the psycho-physical disposition maintain it in an excitable condition.[1]

---

[1] Most definitions of instincts and instinctive actions take account only of their conative aspect, of the motor tendencies by which the instincts of animals are most clearly manifested to us; and it is a common mistake to ignore the cognitive and the affective aspects of the instinctive mental process. Some authors make the worst mistake of assuming that instinctive actions are performed unconsciously. Herbert Spencer's definition of instinctive action as compound reflex action was mentioned above. Addison wrote of instinct that it is "an immediate impression from the first Mover and the Divine Energy acting in the creatures." Fifty years ago the entomologists, Kirby and Spence, wrote: "We may call the instincts of animals those faculties implanted in them by the Creator, by which, independent of instruction, observation, or experience, they are all alike impelled to the performance of certain actions tending to the wellbeing of the individual and the preservation of the species." More recently Dr. and Mrs. Peckham, who

The behaviour of some of the lower animals seems to be almost completely determined throughout their lives by instincts modified but very little by experience; they perceive, feel, and act in a perfectly definite and invariable manner whenever a given instinct is excited—*i.e.*, whenever the presence of the appropriate object coincides with the appropriate organic state of the creature. The highest degree of complexity of mental process attained by such creatures is a struggle between two opposed instinctive tendencies simultaneously excited. Such behaviour is relatively easy to understand in the light of the conception of instincts as innate psycho-physical dispositions.

While it is doubtful whether the behaviour of any

have observed the behaviour of wasps so carefully, have written: "Under the term 'instinct' we place all complex acts which are performed previous to experience, and in a similar manner by all members of the same sex and race." One modern authority, Professor Karl Groos, goes so far as to say that "the idea of consciousness must be rigidly excluded from any definition of instinct which is to be of practical utility." In view of this persistent tendency to ignore the inner or psychical side of instinctive processes, it seems to me important to insist upon it, and especially to recognise in our definition its cognitive and affective aspects as well as its conative aspect. I would reverse Professor Groos's dictum and would say that any definition of instinctive action that does not insist upon its psychical aspect is useless for practical purposes, and worse than useless because misleading. For, if we neglect the psychical aspect of instinctive processes, it is impossible to understand the part played by instincts in the development of the human mind and in the determination of the conduct of individuals and societies; and it is the fundamental and all-pervading character of their influence upon the social life of mankind which alone gives the consideration of instincts its great practical importance.

The definition of instinct proposed above does not insist, as do many definitions, that the instinctive action is one performed without previous experience of the object; for it is only when an instinct is exercised for the first time by any creature that the action is prior to experience, and instinctive actions may continue to be instinctive even after much experience of their objects. The nest-building or the migratory flight of birds does not cease to be instinctive when these actions are repeated year after year, even though the later performances show improvement through experience, as the instinctive actions of the higher animals commonly do. Nor does our definition insist, as some do, that the instinctive action is performed without awareness of the end towards which it tends, for this too is not essential; it may be, and in the case of the lower animals, no doubt, often is, so performed, as also by the very young child; but in the case of the higher animals some prevision of the immediate end, however vague, probably accompanies an instinctive action that has often been repeated; *e.g.*, in the case of the dog that has followed the trail of game many times, we may properly regard the action as instinctive, although we can hardly doubt that, after many kills, the creature has some anticipation of the end of his activity.

animal is wholly determined by instincts quite unmodified by experience, it is clear that all the higher animals learn in various and often considerable degrees to adapt their instinctive actions to peculiar circumstances; and in the long course of the development of each human mind, immensely greater complications of the instinctive processes are brought about, complications so great that they have obscured until recent years the essential likeness of the instinctive processes in men and animals. These complications of instinctive processes are of four principal kinds, which we may distinguish as follows:—

(1) The instinctive reactions become capable of being initiated, not only by the perception of objects of the kind which directly excite the innate disposition, the natural or native excitants of the instinct, but also by ideas of such objects, and by perceptions and by ideas of objects of other kinds:

(2) the bodily movements in which the instinct finds expression may be modified and complicated to an indefinitely great degree:

(3) owing to the complexity of the ideas which can bring the human instincts into play, it frequently happens that several instincts are simultaneously excited; when the several processes blend with various degrees of intimacy:

(4) the instinctive tendencies become more or less systematically organised about certain objects or ideas. . . .

In order to understand these complications of instinctive behaviour we must submit the conception of an instinct to a more minute analysis. It was said above that every instinctive process has the three aspects of all mental process, the cognitive, the affective, and the conative. Now, the innate psycho-physical disposition, which is an instinct, may be regarded as consisting of three corresponding parts, an afferent, a central, and a motor or efferent part, whose activities are the cognitive, the affective, and the conative features respectively of the total instinctive process. The afferent or receptive part of the total disposition is some organised group of nervous elements or neurones that is specially adapted to receive and to elaborate the impulses initiated in the sense-organ by the native object of the instinct; its constitution and activities determine the sensory content of the psycho-physical process. From the afferent part the excitement spreads over to the central part of the disposition; the constitution of this part determines in the main the distribution of the nervous impulses, especially of the impulses that descend to modify the working of the visceral organs, the heart, lungs, blood-vessels, glands, and so forth, in the manner required for the most effective execution of the instinctive action; the nervous activities of this central part are the correlates of the affective or emotional aspect or feature of the total psychical process. The excitement of the efferent or motor part reaches it by way of the central part; its constitution determines the distribution of impulses to the muscles of the skeletal system by which the instinctive action is effected, and its nervous activities are the correlates of the conative element of the psychical process, of the felt impulse to action.

Now, the afferent or receptive part and the efferent or motor part are capable of being greatly modified, independently of one another and of the central part, in the course of the life history of the individual; while the central part persists throughout life as the essential unchanging nucleus of the disposition. Hence in man, whose intelligence and adaptability, are so great, the afferent and efferent parts of each instinctive disposition are liable to many modifications, while the central part alone remains unmodified: that is to say, the cognitive processes through which any instinctive process may be initiated exhibit a great complication and variety; and the actual bodily movements by which the instinctive process achieves its end may be complicated to an indefinitely great extent; while the emotional excitement, with the accompanying nervous activities of the central part of the disposition, is the only part of the total instinctive process that retains its specific character and remains common to all individuals and all situations in which the instinct is excited. It is for this reason that authors have commonly treated of the instinctive actions of animals on the one hand, and of the emotions of men on the other hand, as distinct types of mental process, failing to see that each kind of emotional excitement is always an indication of, and the most constant feature of, some instinctive process.

Let us now consider very briefly the principal ways in which the instinctive disposition may be modified on its afferent or receptive side; and let us take, for the sake of clearness of exposition, the case of a particular instinct, namely the instinct of fear or flight, which is one of the strongest and most widely distributed instincts throughout the animal kingdom. In man and in most animals this instinct is capable of being excited by any sudden loud noise, independently of all experience of danger or harm associated with such noises. We must suppose, then, that the afferent inlet, or one of the afferent inlets of this innate disposition consists in a system of auditory neurones connected by sensory nerves with the ear. This afferent inlet to this innate disposition is but little specialised, since it may be excited by any loud noise. One change it may undergo through experience is specialisation; on repeated experience of noises of certain kinds that are never accompanied or followed by hurtful effects, most creatures will learn to neglect them; their instinct of flight is no longer excited by them; they learn, that is to say, to discriminate between these and other noises; this implies that the perceptual disposition, the afferent inlet of the instinct, has become further specialised.

1303

More important is the other principal mode in which the instinct may be modified on its afferent or cognitive side. Consider the case of the birds on an uninhabited island, which show no fear of men on their first appearance on the island. The absence of fear at the sight of man implies, not that the birds have no instinct of fear, but that the instinct has no afferent inlet specialised for the reception of the retinal impression made by the human form. But the men employ themselves in shooting, and very soon the sight of a man excites the instinct of fear in the birds, and they take to flight at his approach. How are we to interpret this change of instinctive behaviour brought about by experience? Shall we say that the birds observe on one occasion, or on several or many occasions, that on the approach of a man one of their number falls to the ground, uttering cries of pain; that they infer that the man has wounded it, and that he may wound and hurt them, and that he is therefore to be avoided in the future? No psychologist would now accept this anthropomorphic interpretation of the facts. If the behaviour we are considering were that of savage men, or even of a community of philosophers and logicians, such an account would err in ascribing the change of behaviour to a purely intellectual process. Shall we, then, say that the sudden loud sound of the gun excites the instinct of fear, and that, because the perception of this sound is constantly accompanied by the visual perception of the human form, the idea of the latter becomes associated with the idea of the sound, so that thereafter the sight of a man reproduces the idea of the sound of the gun, and hence leads to the excitement of the instinct by way of its innately organised afferent inlet, the system of auditory neurones? This would be much nearer the truth than the former account; some such interpretation of facts of this order has been offered by many psychologists and very generally accepted. Its acceptance

1304

involves the attribution of free ideas, of the power of representation of objects independently of sense-presentation, to whatever animals display this kind of modification of instinctive behaviour by experience—that is to say, to all the animals save the lowest; and there are good reasons for believing that only man and the higher animals have this power. We are therefore driven to look for a still simpler interpretation of the facts, and such a one is not far to seek. We may suppose that, since the visual presentation of the human form repeatedly accompanies the excitement of the instinct of fear by the sound of the gun, it acquires the power of exciting directly the reactions characteristic of this instinct, rather than indirectly by way of the reproduction of the idea of the sound; *i.e.*, we may suppose that, after repetition of the experience, the sight of a man directly excites the instinctive process in its affective and conative aspects only; or we may say, in physiological terms, that the visual disposition concerned in the elaboration of the retinal impression of the human form becomes directly connected or associated with the central and efferent parts of the instinctive disposition, which thus acquires, through the repetition of this experience, a new afferent inlet through which it may henceforth be excited independently of its innate afferent inlet.

There is, I think, good reason to believe that this third interpretation is much nearer the truth than the other two considered above. In the first place, the assumption of such relative independence of the afferent part of an instinctive disposition as is implied by this interpretation is justified by the fact that many instincts may be excited by very different objects affecting different senses, prior to all experience of such objects. The instinct of fear is the most notable in this respect, for in many animals it may be excited by certain special impressions of sight, of smell, and of hearing, as well as by all loud noises (perhaps also by any painful sense-impression), all of which impressions evoke the emotional expressions and the bodily movements characteristic of the instinct. Hence, we may infer that such an instinct has several innately organised afferent inlets, through each of which its central and efferent parts may be excited without its other afferent inlets being involved in the excitement.

But the best evidence in favour of the third interpretation is that which we may obtain by introspective observation of our own emotional states. Through injuries received we may learn to fear, or to be angered by, the presence of a person or an animal or thing towards which we were at first indifferent; and we may then experience the emotional excitement and the impulse to the appropriate movements of flight or aggression, without recalling the nature and occasion of the injuries we have formerly suffered; *i.e.*, although the idea of the former injury may be reproduced by the perception, or by the idea, of the person, animal, or thing from which it was received, yet the reproduction of this idea is not an essential step in the process of re-excitement of the instinctive reaction in its affective and conative aspects; for the visual impression made by the person or thing leads directly to the excitement of the central and efferent parts of the innate disposition. In this way our emotional and conative tendencies become directly associated by experience with many objects to which we are natively indifferent; and not only do we not necessarily recall the experience through which the association was set up, but in many such cases we cannot do so by any effort of recollection.[1]

Such acquisition of new perceptual inlets by instinctive

---

[1] In this way some particular odour, some melody or sound, some phrase or trick of speech or manner, some peculiar combination of colour or effect of light upon the landscape, may become capable of directly exciting some affective disposition, and we find ourselves suddenly swept by a wave of strong emotion for which we can assign no adequate cause.

dispositions, in accordance with the principle of association in virtue of temporal contiguity, seems to occur abundantly among all the higher animals and to be the principal mode in which they profit by experience and learn to adapt their behaviour to a greater variety of the objects of their environment than is provided for by their purely innate dispositions. In man it occurs still more abundantly, and in his case the further complication ensues that each sense-presentation that thus becomes capable of arousing some emotional and conative disposition may be represented, or reproduced in idea; and, since the representation, having in the main the same neural basis as the sense-presentation, induces equally well the same emotional and conative excitement, and since it may be brought to mind by any one of the intellectual processes, ranging from simple associative reproduction to the most subtle processes of judgment and inference, the ways in which any one instinctive disposition of a developed human mind may be excited are indefinitely various.

There is a second principal mode in which objects other than the native objects of an instinct may lead to the excitement of its central and efferent parts. This is similar to the mode of reproduction of ideas known as the reproduction by similars; a thing, or sense-impression, more or less like the specific excitant of an instinct, but really of a different class, excites the instinct in virtue of those features in which it resembles the specific object. As a very simple instance of this, we may take the case of a horse shying at an old coat left lying by the roadside. The shying is, no doubt due to the excitement of an instinct whose function is to secure a quick retreat from any crouching beast of prey, and the coat sufficiently resembles such a crouching form to excite the instinct. This example illustrates the operation of this principle in the crudest fashion. In the human mind it works in a

1307

much more subtle and wide-reaching fashion. Very delicate resemblances of form and relation between two objects may suffice to render one of them capable of exciting the emotion and the impulse which are the appropriate instinctive response to the presentation of the other object; and in order that this shall occur, it is not necessary that the individual shall become explicitly aware of the resemblance between the two objects, nor even that the idea of the second object shall be brought to his consciousness; though this, no doubt occurs in many cases. The wide scope of this principle in the human mind is due, not merely to the subtler operation of resemblances, but also to the fact that through the working of the principle of temporal contiguity, discussed on the foregoing page, the number of objects capable of directly exciting any instinct becomes very considerable, and each object then serves as a basis for the operation of the principle of resemblance; that is to say, each object that in virtue of temporal contiguity acquires the power of exciting the central and efferent parts of an instinct renders possible the production of the same effect by a number of objects more or less resembling it. The conjoint operation of the two principles may be illustrated by a simple example: a child is terrified upon one occasion by the violent behaviour of a man of a peculiar cast of countenance or of some special fashion of dress; thereafter not only does the perception or idea of this man excite fear, but any man resembling him in face or costume may do so without the idea of the original occasion of fear, or of the terrifying individual, recurring to consciousness.

As regards the modification of the bodily movements by means of which an instinctive mental process achieves,[1]

---

[1] It would, of course, be more correct to say that the creature strives to achieve its end under the driving power of the instinctive impulse awakened within it, but, if this is recognised, it is permissible to avoid the repeated use of this cumbrous phraseology.

or strives to achieve, its end, man excels the animals even to a greater degree than as regards the modification of the cognitive part of the process. For the animals acquire and use hardly any movement-complexes that are not natively given in their instinctive dispositions and in the reflex co-ordinations of their spinal cords. This is true of even so intelligent an animal as the domestic dog. Many of the higher animals may by long training be taught to acquire a few movement-complexes—a dog to walk on its hind legs, or a cat to sit up; but the wonder with which we gaze at a circus-horse standing on a tub, or at a dog dancing on hind legs, shows how strictly limited to the natively given combinations of movements all the animals normally are.

In the human being, on the other hand, a few only of the simpler instincts that ripen soon after birth are displayed in movements determined purely by the innate dispositions; such are the instincts of sucking, of wailing, of crawling, of winking and shrinking before a coming blow. Most of the human instincts ripen at relatively late periods in the course of individual development, when considerable power of intelligent control and imitation of movement has been acquired; hence the motor tendencies of these instincts are seldom manifested in their purely native forms, but are from the first modified, controlled, and suppressed in various degrees. This is the case more especially with the large movements of trunk and limbs; while the subsidiary movements, those which Darwin called serviceable associated movements, such as those due to contractions of the facial muscles, are less habitually controlled, save by men of certain races and countries among whom control of facial movement is prescribed by custom. An illustration may indicate the main principle involved: One may have learnt to suppress more or less completely the bodily movements in which the excitement of the instinct of pugnacity naturally finds

1309

vent; or by a study of pugilism one may have learnt to render these movements more finely adapted to secure the end of the instinct; or one may have learnt to replace them by the habitual use of weapons, so that the hand flies to the sword hilt or to the hip-pocket, instead of being raised to strike, whenever this instinct is excited. But one exercises but little, if any, control over the violent beating of the heart, the flushing of the face, the deepened respiration, and the general redistribution of blood-supply and nervous tension which constitutes the visceral expression of the excitement of this instinct and which are determined by the constitution of its central affective part. Hence in the human adult, while this instinct may be excited by objects and situations that are not provided for in the innate disposition, and may express itself in bodily movements which also are not natively determined, or may fail to find expression in any such movements owing to strong volitional control, its unmodified central part will produce visceral changes, with the accompanying emotional state of consciousness, in accordance with its unmodified native constitution; and these visceral changes will usually be accompanied by the innately determined facial expression in however slight a degree; hence result the characteristic expressions or symptoms of the emotion of anger which, as regards their main features, are common to all men of all times and all races.

All the principal instincts of man are liable to similar modifications of their afferent and motor parts, while their central parts remain unchanged and determine the emotional tone of consciousness and the visceral changes characteristic of the excitement of the instinct.

It must be added that the conative aspect of the psychical process always retains the unique quality of an impulse to activity, even though the instinctive activity has been modified by habitual control; and, this felt impulse, when it becomes conscious of its end, assumes the character of an explicit desire or aversion.

Are, then, these instinctive impulses the only motive powers of the human mind to thought and action? What of pleasure and pain, which by so many of the older psychologists were held to be the only motives of human activity, the only objects or sources of desire and aversion?

In answer to the former question, it must be said that in the developed human mind there are springs of action of another class, namely, acquired habits of thought and action. An acquired mode of activity becomes by repetition habitual, and the more frequently it is repeated the more powerful becomes the habit as a source of impulse or motive power. Few habits can equal in this respect the principal instincts; and habits are in a sense derived from, and secondary to, instincts; for, in the absence of instincts, no thought and no action could ever be achieved or repeated, and so no habits of thought or action could be formed. Habits are formed only in the service of the instincts.

The answer to the second question is that pleasure and pain are not in themselves springs of action, but at the most of undirected movements; they serve rather to modify instinctive processes, pleasure tending to sustain and prolong any mode of action, pain to cut it short; under their prompting and guidance are effected those modifications and adaptations of the instinctive bodily movements which we have briefly considered above.[1]

---

[1]None of the doctrines of the associationist psychology was more profoundly misleading and led to greater absurdities than the attempt to exhibit pleasure and pain as the source of all activities. What could be more absurd than Professor Bain's doctrine that the joy of a mother in her child, her tender care and self-sacrificing efforts in its behalf, are due to the pleasure she derives from bodily contact with it in the maternal embrace? Or what could be more strained and opposed to hundreds of familiar facts than Herbert Spencer's doctrine that the emotion of fear provoked by any object consists in faint revivals, in some strange cluster, of ideas of all the pains suffered in the past upon contact with, or in the presence of, that object? (cf. Bain's "Emotions and the Will," chap. vi.; and H. Spencer's "Principles of Psychology," vol. i. part iv. chap. viii. 3rd Ed.)

We may say, then, that directly or indirectly the instincts are the prime movers of all human activity; by the conative or impulsive force of some instinct (or of some habit derived from an instinct), every train of thought, however cold and passionless it may seem, is borne along toward its end, and every bodily activity is initiated and sustained. The instinctive impulses determine the ends of all activities and supply the driving power by which all mental activities are sustained; and all the complex intellectual apparatus of the most highly developed mind is but a means towards these ends, is but the instrument by which these impulses seek their satisfactions, while pleasure and pain do but serve to guide them in their choice of the means.

Take away these instinctive dispositions with their powerful impulses, and the organism would become incapable of activity of any kind; it would lie inert and motionless like a wonderful clockwork whose mainspring had been removed or a steam-engine whose fires had been drawn. These impulses are the mental forces that maintain and shape all the life of individuals and societies, and in them we are confronted with the central mystery of life and mind and will. . . .

The Principal Instincts and the Primary Emotions of Man

Before we can make any solid progress in the understanding of the complex emotions and impulses that are the forces underlying the thoughts and actions of men and of societies, we must be able to distinguish and describe each of the principal human instincts and the emotional and conative tendencies characteristic of each one of them. This task will be attempted in the present chapter. . . .

In the foregoing chapter it was said that the instinctive mental process that results from the excitement of any

1312

instinct has always an affective aspect, the nature of which depends upon the constitution of that most stable and unchanging of the three parts of the instinctive disposition, namely the central part. In the case of the simpler instincts, this affective aspect of the instinctive process is not prominent; and though, no doubt, the quality of it is peculiar in each case, yet we cannot readily distinguish these qualities and we have no special names for them. But, in the case of the principal powerful instincts, the affective quality of each instinctive process and the sum of visceral and bodily changes in which it expresses itself are peculiar and distinct; hence language provides special names for such modes of affective experience, names such as anger, fear, curiosity; and the generic name for them is "emotion."

Each of the principal instincts conditions, then, some one kind of emotional excitement whose quality is specific or peculiar to it; and the emotional excitement of specific quality that is the affective aspect of the operation of any one of the principal instincts may be called a primary emotion. This principle . . . proves to be of very great value when we seek to analyse the complex emotions into their primary constituents.

In adapting to scientific use a word from popular speech, it is inevitable that some violence should be done to common usage; and in adopting this rigid definition of emotion, we shall have to do such violence in refusing to admit joy, sorrow, and surprise (which are often regarded, even by writers on psychology, as the very types of emotions) to our list whether of simple and primary or of complex emotions. At this stage I will only point out that joy and sorrow are not emotional states that can be experienced independently of the true emotions, that in every case they are qualifications of the emotions they accompany, and that in strictness we ought rather to speak always of a joyful or sorrowful emotion—*e.g.*,

1313

a joyful wonder or gratitude, a sorrowful anger or pity.

In considering the claim of any human emotion or impulse to rank as a primary emotion or simple instinctive impulse, we shall find two principles of great assistance. First, if a similar emotion and impulse are clearly displayed in the instinctive activities of the higher animals, that fact will afford a strong presumption that the emotion and impulse in question are primary and simple; on the other hand, if no such instinctive activity occurs among the higher animals, we must suspect the affective state in question of being either a complex composite emotion or no true emotion. Secondly, we must inquire in each case whether the emotion and impulse in question occasionally appear in human beings with morbidly exaggerated intensity, apart from such general hyper-excitability as is displayed in mania. For it would seem that each instinctive disposition, being a relatively independent functional unit in the constitution of the mind, is capable of morbid hypertrophy or of becoming abnormally excitable, independently of the rest of the mental dispositions and functions. That is to say, we must look to comparative psychology and to mental pathology for confirmation of the primary character of those of our emotions that appear to be simple and unanalysable.[1]

The Instinct of Flight and the Emotion of Fear

The instinct to flee from danger is necessary for the survival of almost all species of animals, and in most of the higher animals the instinct is one of the most

[1]That the emotion as a fact of consciousness may properly be distinguished from the cognitive process which it accompanies and qualifies is, I think, obvious and indisputable. The propriety of distinguishing between the conative element in consciousness, the impulse, appetite, desire, or aversion, and the accompanying emotion is not so obvious. For these features are most intimately and constantly associated, and introspective discrimination of them is usually difficult. Nevertheless they show a certain degree of independence of one another; e.g., with frequent repetition of a particular emotional situation and reaction, the affective aspect of the process tends to become less prominent, while the impulse grows stronger.

powerful. Upon its excitement the locomotory apparatus is impelled to its utmost exertions, and sometimes the intensity and long duration of these exertions is more than the visceral organs can support, so that they are terminated by utter exhaustion or death. Men also have been known to achieve extraordinary feats of running and leaping under this impulse; there is a well-known story of a great athlete who, when pursued as a boy by a savage animal, leaped over a wall which he could not again "clear" until he attained his full stature and strength. These locomotory activities are accompanied by a characteristic complex of symptoms, which in its main features is common to man and to many of the higher animals, and which, in conjunction with the violent efforts to escape, constitutes so unmistakable an expression of the emotion of fear that no one hesitates to interpret it as such; hence popular speech recognises the connection of the emotion with the instinct that determines the movements of flight in giving them the one name *fear*. Terror, the most intense degree of this emotion, may involve so great a nervous disturbance, both in men and animals, as to defeat the ends of the instinct by inducing general convulsions or even death. In certain cases of mental disease the patient's disorder seems to consist essentially in an abnormal excitability of this instinct and a consequent undue frequency and intensity of its operation; the patient lives perpetually in fear, shrinking in terror from the most harmless animal or at the least unusual sound, and surrounds himself with safeguards against impossible dangers.

In most animals this instinct may be excited by a variety of objects and sense-impressions prior to all experience of hurt or danger; that is to say, the innate disposition has several afferent inlets. In some of the more timid creatures it would seem that every unfamiliar sound or sight is capable of exciting it. In civilised man,

1315

whose life for so many generations has been more or less sheltered from the dangers peculiar to the natural state, the instinct exhibits (like all complex organs and functions that are not kept true to the specific type by rigid selection) considerable individual differences, especially on its receptive side. Hence it is difficult to discover what objects and impressions were its natural excitants in primitive man. . . .

In most animals instinctive flight is followed by equally instinctive concealment as soon as cover is reached, and there can be little doubt that in primitive man the instinct had this double tendency. As soon as the little child can run, his fear expresses itself in concealment following on flight; and the many adult persons who seek refuge from the strange noises of dark nights, or from a thunderstorm by covering their heads with the bed-clothes, and who find a quite irrational comfort in so doing, illustrate the persistence of this tendency. It is, perhaps, in the opposed characters of these two tendencies, both of which are bound up with the emotion of fear, that we may find an explanation of the great variety of, and variability of, the symptoms of fear. The sudden stopping of heart-beat and respiration, and the paralysis of movement in which it sometimes finds expression, are due to the impulse to concealment; the hurried respiration and pulse, and the frantic bodily efforts, by which it is more commonly expressed, are due to the impulse to flight.

That the excitement of fear is not necessarily, or indeed usually, the effect of an intelligent appreciation or anticipation of danger, is especially well shown by children of four or five years of age, in whom it may be induced by the facial contortions or playful roarings of a familiar friend. Under these circumstances, a child may exhibit every symptom of fear even when he sits upon his tormentor's lap and, with arms about his neck, beseeches him to cease or to promise not to do it again.

And many a child has been thrown into a paroxysm of terror by the approach of some hideous figure that he knew to be but one of his playfellows in disguise.

Of all the excitants of this instinct the most interesting, and the most difficult to understand as regards its mode of operation, is the unfamiliar or strange as such. Whatever is totally strange, whatever is violently opposed to the accustomed and familiar, is apt to excite fear both in men and animals, if only it is capable of attracting their attention. It is, I think, doubtful whether an eclipse of the moon has ever excited the fear of animals, for the moon is not an object of their attention; but for savage men it has always been an occasion of fear. The well-known case of the dog described by Romanes, that was terrified by the movements of an object jerked forward by an invisible thread, illustrates the fear-exciting powers of the unfamiliar in the animal world. The following incident is instructive in this respect: A courageous child of five years, sitting alone in a sunlit room, suddenly screams in terror, and, on her father hastening to her, can only explain that she saw something move. The discovery of a mouse in the corner of the room at once explains and banishes her fear, for she is on friendly terms with mice. The mouse must have darted across the peripheral part of her field of vision, and this unexpected and unfamiliar appearance of movement sufficed to excite the instinct. This avenue to the instinct, the unfamiliar, becomes in man highly diversified and intellectualised, and it is owing to this that he feels fear before the mysterious, the uncanny, and the supernatural, and that fear, entering as an element into the complex emotions of awe and reverence, plays its part in all religions.

Fear, whether its impulse be to flight or to concealment, is characterised by the fact that its excitement, more than that of any other instinct, tends to bring to an end at once all other mental activity, riveting the attention

1317

upon its object to the exclusion of all others; owing, probably, to this extreme concentration of attention, as well as to the violence of the emotion, the excitement of this instinct makes a deep and lasting impression on the mind. A gust of anger, a wave of pity or of tender emotion, an impulse of curiosity, may co-operate in supporting and re-enforcing mental activities of the most varied kinds, or may dominate the mind for a time and then pass away, leaving but little trace. But fear, once roused, haunts the mind; it comes back alike in dreams and in waking life, bringing with it vivid memories of the terrifying impression. It is thus the great inhibitor of action, both present action and future action, and becomes in primitive human societies the great agent of social discipline through which men are led to the habit of control of the egoistic impulses.

The Instinct of Repulsion and the Emotion of Disgust

The impulse of this instinct is, like that of fear, one of aversion, and these two instincts together account probably for all aversions, except those acquired under the influence of pain. The impulse differs from that of fear in that, while the latter prompts to bodily retreat from its object, the former prompts to actions that remove or reject the offending object. This instinct resembles fear in that under the one name we, perhaps, commonly confuse two very closely allied instincts whose affective aspects are so similar that they are not easily distinguishable, though their impulses are of different tendencies. The one impulse of repulsion is to reject from the mouth substances that excite the instinct in virtue of their odour or taste, substances which in the main are noxious and evil-tasting; its biological utility is obvious. The other impulse of repulsion seems to be excited by the contact of slimy and slippery substances with the skin, and to express itself as a shrinking of the

1318

whole body, accompanied by a throwing forward of the hands. The common shrinking from slimy creatures with a "creepy" shudder seems to be the expression of this impulse. It is difficult to assign any high biological value to it (unless we connect it with the necessity of avoiding noxious reptiles), but it is clearly displayed by some children before the end of the first year; thus in some infants furry things excite shrinking and tears at their first contact. In others the instinct seems to ripen later, and the child that has handled worms, frogs, and slugs with delight suddenly evinces an unconquerable aversion to contact with them.

These two forms of disgust illustrate in the clearest and most interesting manner the intellectualisation of the instincts and primary emotions through extension of the range of their objects by association, resemblance, and analogy. The manners or speech of an otherwise presentable person may excite the impulse of shrinking in virtue of some subtle suggestions of sliminess. Or what we know of a man's character—that it is noxious, or, as we significantly say, is of evil odour—may render the mere thought of him an occasion of disgust; we say, "It makes me sick to think of him"; and at the same time the face exhibits in some degree, however slight, the expression produced by the act of rejection of some evil-tasting substance from the mouth. In these cases we may see very clearly that this extension by resemblance or analogy does not take place in any roundabout fashion; it is not that the thought of the noxious or "slippery" character necessarily reproduces the idea of some evil-tasting substance or of some slimy creature. Rather, the apprehension of these peculiarities of character excites disgust directly, and then, when we seek to account for, and to justify, our disgust, we cast about for some simile and say, "He is like a snake," or "He is rotten to the core!" The common form of emotion serves as the link between the two ideas.

The Instinct of Curiosity and the Emotion of Wonder
 The instinct of curiosity is displayed by many of the
higher animals, although its impulse remains relatively
feeble in most of them. And, in fact, it is obvious that it
could not easily attain any considerable strength in any
animal species, because the individuals that displayed
a too strong curiosity would be peculiarly liable to meet
an untimely end. For its impulse is to approach and
to examine more closely the object that excites it—a
fact well known to hunters in the wilds, who sometimes
by exciting this instinct bring the curious animal within
the reach of their weapons. The native excitant of the
instinct would seem to be any object similar to, yet
perceptibly different from, familiar objects habitually
noticed. It is therefore not easy to distinguish in
general terms between the excitants of curiosity and
those of fear; for we have seen that one of the most
general excitants of fear is whatever is strange or
unfamiliar. The difference seems to be mainly one
of degree, a smaller element of the strange or unusual
exciting curiosity, while a larger and more pronounced
degree of it excites fear. Hence the two instincts, with
their opposed impulses of approach and retreat, are apt
to be excited in animals and very young children in
rapid alternation, and simultaneously in ourselves. Who
has not seen a horse, or other animal, alternately
approach in curiosity, and flee in fear from, some such
object as an old coat upon the ground? And who has
not experienced a fearful curiosity in penetrating some
dark cave or some secret chamber of an ancient castle?
The behaviour of animals under the impulse of curiosity
maybe well observed by any one who will lie down in
a field where sheep or cattle are grazing and repeat at
short intervals some peculiar cry. In this way one may

1320

draw every member of a large flock nearer and nearer, until one finds oneself the centre of a circle of them, drawn up at a respectful distance, of which every pair of eyes and ears is intently fixed upon the strange object of their curiosity.

In the animals nearest to ourselves, namely, the monkeys, curiosity is notoriously strong, and them it impels not merely to approach its object and to direct the senses attentively upon it but also to active manipulation of it. That a similar impulse is strong in children, no one will deny.

This instinct, being one whose exercise is not of prime importance to the individual, exhibits great individual differences as regards to its innate strength; and these differences are apt to be increased during the course of life, the impulse growing weaker for lack of use in those in whom it is innately weak, stronger through exercise in those in whom it is innately strong. In men of the latter type it may become the main source of intellectual energy and effort; to its impulse we certainly owe most of the purely disinterested labours of the highest types of intellect. It must be regarded as one of the principal roots of both science and religion.

The Instinct of Pugnacity and the Emotion of Anger

This instinct, though not so nearly universal as fear, being apparently lacking in the constitution of the females of some species, ranks with fear as regards the great strength of its impulse and the high intensity of the emotion it generates. It occupies a peculiar position in relation to the other instincts, and cannot strictly be brought under the definition of instinct proposed in the first chapter. For it has no specific object or objects the perception of which constitutes the initial stage of the instinctive process. The condition of its excitement is rather any opposition to the free exercise of any

1321

impulse, any obstruction to the activity to which the creature is impelled by any one of the other instincts. And its impulse is to break down any such obstruction and to destroy whatever offers this opposition. This instinct thus presupposes the others; its excitement is dependent upon, or secondary to, the excitement of the others, and is apt to be intense in proportion to the strength of the obstructed impulse. The most mean-spirited cur will angrily resent any attempt to take away its bone, if it is hungry; a healthy infant very early displays anger, if his meal is interrupted; and all through life most men find it difficult to suppress irritation on similar occasions. In the animal world the most furious excitement of this instinct is provoked in the male of many species by any interference with the satisfaction of the sexual impulse; since such interference is the most frequent occasion of its excitement, and since it commonly comes from other male members of his own species, the actions innately organised for securing the ends of this instinct are such actions as are most effective in combat with his fellows. Hence, also, the defensive apparatus of the male is usually, like the lion's or the stallion's mane, especially adapted for defence against the attacks of his fellows. But the obstruction of every other instinctive impulse may in its turn become the occasion of anger. We see how among the animals even the fear-impulse, the most opposed in tendency to the pugnacious, may on obstruction give place to it; for the hunted creature when brought to bay—*i.e.,* when its impulse to flight is obstructed—is apt to turn upon its pursuers and to fight furiously, until an opportunity for escape presents itself.

Darwin has shown the significance of the facial expression of anger, of the contracted brow and raised upper lip; and man shares with many of the animals the tendency to frighten his opponent by loud roars or bellowings. As with most of the other human instincts, the excitement of this one is expressed in its purest form by children. Many a little boy has, without any example or suggestion, suddenly taken to running with open mouth to bite the person who has angered him, much to the distress of his parents. As the child grows up, as self-control becomes stronger, the life of ideas richer, and the means we take to overcome obstructions to our efforts more refined and complex, this instinct ceases to express itself in its crude natural manner, save when most intensely excited and becomes rather a source of increased energy of action towards the end set by any other instinct; the energy of its impulse adds itself to and reinforces that of other impulses and so helps us to overcome our difficulties. In this lies its great value for civilised man. A man devoid of the pugnacious instinct would not only be incapable of anger, but would lack this great source of reserve energy which is called into play in most of us by any difficulty in our path. In this respect also it is the opposite of fear, which tends to inhibit all other impulses than its own.

The Instincts of Self-abasement (or Subjection) and of Self-assertion (or Self-display), and the Emotions of Subjection and Elation (or Negative and Positive Self-feeling)

The instinct of self-display is manifested by many of the higher social or gregarious animals, especially, perhaps, though not only, at the time of mating. Perhaps among mammals the horse displays it most clearly. The muscles of all parts are strongly innervated, the creature holds himself erect, his neck arched, his tail lifted, his motions become superfluously vigorous and extensive, he lifts his hoofs high in air, as he parades before the eyes of his fellows. Many animals, especially the birds, but also some of the monkeys, are provided with organs of display that are specially disposed on these occasions. Such are the tail of the peacock and the beautiful breast of the pigeon. The instinct is essentially a social one, and is brought into play by the presence of spectators. Such self-display is popularly recognised as implying pride; we say "How proud he looks!" and the peacock has become the symbol of pride. By psychologists pride is usually denied the animals, because it is held to imply self-consciousness, and that, save of the most rudimentary kind, they probably have not. But this denial arises from the current confusion of the emotions and the sentiments. The word "pride" is no doubt most properly to be used as the name of one form of the self-regarding sentiment, and such sentiment does imply a developed self-consciousness such as no animal can be credited with. Nevertheless, popular opinion is, I think, in the right in attributing to the animals in their moments of self-display the germ of the emotion that is the most essential constituent of pride. It is this primary emotion which may be called positive self-feeling or elation, and which might well be called pride, if that word were not required to denote the sentiment of pride. In the simple form, in which it is expressed by the self-display of animals, it does not necessarily imply self-consciousness.

Many children clearly exhibit this instinct of self-display; before they can walk or talk the impulse finds its satisfaction in the admiring gaze and plaudits of the family circle as each new acquirement is practised; a little later it is still more clearly expressed by the frequently repeated command, "See me do this," or "See how well I can do so-and-so"; and for many a child more than half the delight of riding on a pony, or of wearing a new coat, consists in the satisfaction of this instinct, and vanishes if there be no spectators. A little later, with the growth of self-consciousness the instinct may find expression in the boasting and swaggering of boys, the vanity of girls; while, with almost all of us, it becomes the most important constituent of the self-regarding sentiment and plays an all-important part in the volitional control of conduct. . . .

The situation that more particularly excites this instinct is the presence of spectators to whom one feels oneself for any reason, or in any way, superior, and this is perhaps true in a modified sense of the animals; the "dignified" behaviour of a big dog in the presence of small ones, the stately strutting of a hen among her chicks, seem to be instances in point. We have, then, good reason to believe that the germ of this emotion is present in the animal world, and if we make use of our second criterion of the primary character of an emotion, it answers well to the test. For in certain mental diseases, especially in the early stages of that most terrible disorder, general paralysis of the insane, exaggeration of this emotion and of its impulse of display is the leading symptom. The unfortunate patient is perpetually in a state of elated self-feeling, and his behaviour corresponds to his emotional state; he struts before the world, boasts of his strength, his immense wealth, his good looks, his luck, his family, when, perhaps, there is not the least foundation for his boastings.

As regards the emotion of subjection or negative self-feeling, we have the same grounds for regarding it as a primary emotion that accompanies the excitement of an instinctive disposition. The impulse of this instinct expresses itself in a slinking, crestfallen behaviour, a general diminution of muscular tone, slow restricted movements, a hanging down of the head, and sidelong glances. In the dog the picture is completed by the sinking of the tail between the legs. All these features express submissiveness, and are calculated to avoid attracting attention or to mollify the spectator. The nature of the instinct is sometimes very completely expressed in the behaviour of a young dog on the approach of a larger, older dog; he crouches or crawls with legs so bent that his belly scrapes the ground, his back hollowed, his tail tucked away, his head sunk and turned a little on one side, and so approaches the imposing stranger with every mark of submission.

The recognition of this behaviour as the expression of a special instinct of self-abasement and of a corresponding primary emotion enables us to escape from a much-discussed difficulty. It has been asked, "Can animals and young children that have not attained to self-consciousness feel shame?" And the answer usually given is, "No; shame implies self-consciousness." Yet some animals, notably the dog, sometimes behave in a way which the popular mind interprets as expressing shame. The truth seems to be that, while fully-developed shame, shame in the full sense of the word, does imply self-consciousness and a self-regarding sentiment, yet in the emotion that accompanies this impulse to slink submissively we may see the rudiment of shame; and, if we do not recognise this instinct, it is impossible to account for the genesis of shame or of bashfulness.

In children the expression of this emotion is often mistaken for that of fear; but the young child sitting on his mother's lap in perfect silence and with face averted, casting sidelong glances at a stranger, presents a picture very different from that of fear.

Applying, again, our pathological test, we find that it is satisfied by this instinct of self-abasement. In many cases of mental disorder the exaggerated influence of this instinct seems to determine the leading symptoms. The patient shrinks from the observation of his fellows, thinks himself a most wretched, useless, sinful creature, and, in many cases, he develops delusions of having performed various unworthy or even criminal actions;

1326

many such patients declare they are guilty of the unpardonable sin, although they attach no definite meaning to the phrase—that is to say, the patient's intellect endeavours to justify the persistent emotional state, which has no adequate cause in his relations to his fellow-men.

The Parental Instinct and the Tender Emotion
... The maternal instinct, which impels the mother to protect and cherish her young, is common to almost all the higher species of animals. Among the lower animals the perpetuation of the species is generally provided for by the production of an immense number of eggs or young (in some species of fish a single adult produces more than a million eggs), which are left entirely unprotected, and are so preyed upon by other creatures that on the average but one or two attain maturity. As we pass higher up the animal scale, we find the number of eggs or young more and more reduced, and the diminution of their number compensated for by parental protection. At the lowest stage this protection may consist in the provision of some merely physical shelter, as in the case of those animals that carry their eggs attached in some way to their bodies. But, except at this lowest stage, the protection afforded to the young always involves some instinctive adaptation of the parent's behaviour. We may see this even among the fishes, some of which deposit their eggs in rude nests and watch over them, driving away creatures that might prey upon them. From this stage onwards protection of offspring becomes increasingly psychical in character, involves more profound modification of the parent's behaviour and a more prolonged period of more effective guardianship. The highest stage is reached by those species in which each female produces at a birth but one or two young and protects

them so efficiently that most of the young born reach maturity; the maintenance of the species thus becomes in the main the work of the parental instinct. In such species the protection and cherishing of the young is the constant and all-absorbing occupation of the mother, to which she devotes all her energies, and in the course of which she will at any time undergo privation, pain, and death. The instinct becomes more powerful than any other, and can override any other, even fear itself; for it works directly in the service of the species, while the other instincts work primarily in the service of the individual life, for which Nature cares little.

When we follow up the evolution of this instinct to the highest animal level, we find among the apes the most remarkable examples of its operation. Thus in one species the mother is said to carry her young one clasped in one arm uninterruptedly for several months, never letting go of it in all her wanderings. This instinct is no less strong in many human mothers, in whom, of course, it becomes more or less intellectualised and organised as the most essential constituent of the sentiment of parental love. Like other species, the human species is dependent upon this instinct for its continued existence and welfare. It is true that reason, working in the service of the egoistic impulses and sentiments, often circumvents the ends of this instinct and sets up habits which are incompatible with it. When that occurs on a large scale in any society, that society is doomed to rapid decay. But the instinct itself can never die out save with the disappearance of the human species itself; it is kept strong and effective just because those families and races and nations in which it weakens become rapidly supplanted by those in which it is strong.

It is impossible to believe that the operation of this, the most powerful of the instincts, is not accompanied by a strong and definite emotion; one may see the emotion expressed unmistakably by almost any mother among the higher animals, especially the birds and the mammals—by the cat, for example, and by most of the domestic animals; and it is impossible to doubt that this emotion has in all cases the peculiar quality of the tender emotion provoked in the human parent by the spectacle of her helpless offspring. This primary emotion has been very generally ignored by the philosophers and psychologists; that is, perhaps, to be explained by the fact that this instinct and its emotion are in the main decidedly weaker in men than in women, and in some men, perhaps, altogether lacking. We may even surmise that the philosophers as a class are men among whom this defect of native endowment is relatively common.

It may be asked, How can we account for the fact that men are at all capable of this emotion and of this disinterested protective impulse? For in its racial origin the instinct was undoubtedly primarily maternal. The answer is that it is very common to see a character, acquired by one sex to meet its special needs, transmitted, generally imperfectly and with large individual variations, to the members of the other sex. Familiar examples of such transmission of sexual characters are afforded by the horns and antlers of some species of sheep and deer. That the parental instinct is by no means altogether lacking in men is probably due in the main to such transference of a primarily maternal instinct, though it is probable that in the human species natural selection has confirmed and increased its inheritance by the male sex.

To this view, that the parental tenderness of human beings depends upon an instinct phylogenetically continuous with the parental instinct of the higher animals, it might be objected that the very widespread prevalence of infanticide among existing savages implies that primitive man lacked this instinct and its tender emotion. But that would be a most mistaken objection. There is no feature of savage life more nearly universal than the kindness and tenderness of savages, even of savage fathers, for their little children. All observers are agreed upon this point. I have many a time watched with interest a bloodthirsty head-hunter of Borneo spending a day at home tenderly nursing his infant in his arms. And it is a rule, to which there are few exceptions among savage peoples, that an infant is only killed during the first hours of its life. If the child is allowed to survive but a few days, then its life is safe; the tender emotion has been called out in fuller strength and has begun to be organised into a sentiment of parental love that is too strong to be overcome by prudential or purely selfish consideration.

The view of the origin of parental tenderness here adopted compares, I think, very favourably with other accounts of its genesis. Bain taught that it is generated in the individual by the frequent repetition of the intense pleasure of contact with the young; though why this contact should be highly pleasurable he did not explain.[1] Others have attributed it to the expectation by the parent of filial care in his or her old age. This is one form of the absurd and constantly renewed attempt to reveal all altruism as arising essentially out of a more or less subtle regard for one's own welfare or pleasure. If tender emotion and the sentiment of love really arose from a disguised selfishness of this sort, how much stronger should be the love of the child for the parent than that of the parent for the child! For the child is for many years utterly dependent on the parent for his every pleasure and the satisfaction of his every need; whereas the mother's part—if she were not endowed with this powerful instinct—would be one long

---

[1] "Emotions and the Will," p. 82.

succession of sacrifices and painful efforts on behalf of her child. Parental love must always appear an insoluble riddle and paradox if we do not recognise this primary emotion, deeply rooted in an ancient instinct of vital importance to the race. Long ago the Roman moralists were perplexed by it. They noticed that in the Sullan prosecutions, while many sons denounced their fathers, no father was ever known to denounce his son; and they recognised that this fact was inexplicable by their theories of conduct. For their doctrine was like that of Bain, who said explicitly: . . . "The superficial observer has to be told that the feeling [maternal tenderness] in itself as purely self-regarding as the pleasure of wine or of music. Under it we are induced to seek the presence of the beloved objects and to make the requisite sacrifices to gain the end, looking all the while at our own pleasure and to nothing beyond."[1] This doctrine is a gross libel on human nature, which is not so far inferior to animal nature in this respect as Bain's words imply. If Bain, and those who agree with his doctrine, were in the right, everything the cynics have said of human nature would be justified; for from this emotion and its impulse to cherish and protect spring generosity, gratitude, love, pity, true benevolence, and altruistic conduct of every kind; in it they have their main and absolutely essential root, without which they would not be.

Like the other primary emotions, the tender emotion cannot be described; a person who had not experienced it could no more be made to understand its quality than a totally colour-blind person can be made to understand the experience of colour-sensation. Its impulse is primarily to afford physical protection to the child, especially by throwing the arms about it; and that fundamental impulse persists in spite of the immense extension of

---

[1] *Op. cit., p.* 80.

the range of application of the impulse and its incorporation in many ideal sentiments.[1]

Like all the other instinctive impulses, this one, when its operation meets with obstruction or opposition, gives place to, or is complicated by, the pugnacious or combative impulse directed against the source of the obstruction; and, the impulse being essentially protective, its obstruction provokes anger perhaps more readily than the obstruction of any other. In almost all animals that display it, even in those which in all other situations are very timid, any attempt to remove the young from the protecting parent, or in any way to hurt them, provokes a fierce and desperate display of all their combative resources. By the human mother the same prompt yielding of the one impulse to the other is displayed on the same plane of physical protection, but also on the higher plane of ideal protection; the least threat, the smallest slight or aspersion (*e.g.*, the mere speaking of the baby as "it," instead of as "he" or "she"), the mere suggestion that it is not the most beautiful object in the world will suffice to provoke a quick resentment.

This intimate alliance between tender emotion and anger is of great importance for the social life of man, and the right understanding of it is fundamental for a true theory of the moral sentiments; for the anger evoked in this way is the germ of all moral indignation, and on moral indignation justice and the greater part of public law are in the main founded. Thus, paradoxical as it may seem, beneficence and punishment alike have their firmest and most essential root in the parental instinct. For the understanding of the relation of this instinct to moral indignation, it is important to note that the object which is the primary provocative of

[1] It is, I think, not improbable that the impulse to kiss the child, which is certainly strong and seems to be innate, is a modification of the maternal impulse to lick the young which is a feature of the maternal instinct of so many animal species.

1332

tender emotion is, not the child itself, but the child's expression of pain, fear, or distress of any kind, especially the child's cry of distress; further, that this instinctive response is provoked by the cry, not only of one's own offspring, but of any child. Tender emotion and the protective impulse are, no doubt, evoked more readily and intensely by one's own offspring, because about them a strongly organised and complex sentiment grows up. But the distress of any child will evoke this response in a very intense degree in those in whom the instinct is strong. There are women—and men also, though fewer—who cannot sit still, or pursue any occupation, within sound of the distressed cry of a child; if circumstances compel them to restrain their impulse to run to its relief, they cannot withdraw their attention from the sound, but continue to listen in painful agitation.

In the human being, just as is the case in some degree with all the instinctive responses, and as we noticed especially in the case of disgust, there takes place a vast extension of the field of application of the maternal instinct. The similarity of various objects to the primary or natively given object, similarities which in many cases can only be operative for a highly developed mind, enables them to evoke tender emotion and its protective impulse directly *i.e.*, not merely by way of associative reproduction of the natively given object. In this way the emotion is liable to be evoked, not only by the distress of a child, but by the mere sight or thought of a perfectly happy child; for its feebleness, its delicacy, its obvious incapacity to supply its own needs, its liability to a thousand different ills, suggest to the mind its need of protection. By a further extension of the same kind the emotion may be evoked by the sight of any very young animal, especially if in distress; Wordsworth's poem on the pet lamb is the celebration of this emotion in its purest form; and indeed it would be easy to wax enthusiastic in the cause of an instinct that is the source of the only entirely admirable, satisfying, and perfect human relationship, as well as of every kind of purely disinterested conduct.

In a similar direct fashion the distress of any adult (towards whom we harbour no hostile sentiment) evokes the emotion; but in this case it is more apt to be complicated by sympathetic pain, when it becomes the painful, tender emotion we call pity; whereas the child, or any other helpless and delicate thing, may call it out in the pure form without alloy of sympathetic pain. It is amusing to observe how, in those women in whom the instinct is strong, it is apt to be excited, owing to the subtle working of similarity, by any and every object that is small and delicate of its kind—a very small cup, or chair, or book, or what not.

Extension takes place also through association in virtue of contiguity; the objects intimately connected with the prime object of the emotion—such objects as the clothes, the toys, the bed, of the beloved child—become capable of exciting the emotion directly.

But the former mode of direct extension of the field of application is in this case the more important. It is in virtue of such extension to similars that, when we see, or hear of, the ill-treatment of any weak, defenceless creature (especially, of course, if the creature be a child) tender emotion and the protective impulse are aroused on its behalf, but are apt to give place at once to the anger we call moral indignation against the perpetrator of the cruelty; and in bad cases we are quite prepared to tear the offender limb from limb, the tardy process of the law with its mild punishments seeming utterly inadequate to afford vicarious satisfaction to our anger.

How is this great fact of wholly disinterested anger or indignation to be accounted for, if not in the way here suggested? The question is an important one; it supplies

1334

a touchstone for all theories of the moral emotions and sentiments. For, as was said above, this disinterested indignation is the ultimate root of justice and of public law; without its support law and its machinery would be most inadequate safeguards of personal rights and liberties; and, in opposition to the moral indignation of a majority of members of any society, laws can only be very imperfectly enforced by the strongest despotism, as we see in Russia at the present time. Those who deny any truly altruistic motive to man and seek to reduce apparent altruism to subtle and far-sighted egoism, must simply deny the obvious facts, and must seek some far-fetched unreal explanations of such phenomena as the anti-slavery and Congo-reform movements, the anti-vivisection crusade, and the Society for the Prevention of Cruelty to Children.*

WILLIAM McDOUGALL (b.-Chadderton, Lancashire, England, June 22, 1871; d.-Durham, North Carolina, U.S.A., November 28, 1938).

McDougall graduated Queens College, Manchester in 1890. He then spent several years at St. Johns College, Cambridge. In 1894 he became an assistant to Sherrington, at St. Thomas' hospital, until 1898. In this same year he received an M.B. from Cambridge. He then went to Gottingen to work with G. E. Müller, in 1900. He was one of the founders of the British Psychological Association in 1901. From 1902 to 1904 he taught psychology at University College, London. In 1903 he was elected Reader in Mental Philosophy at Oxford, and founded the experimental laboratories. In 1908 he received an M.A. from Oxford. In 1912 he was elected Fellow of the Royal Society. He came to the United States in 1920 as Professor of Psychology at Harvard, till 1927. He was appointed Professor at Duke University, in 1927, where he remained until his death.

Though McDougall began in physiological psychology (with Sherrington) and experimental psychology (with Müller, and then at Oxford), his historical significance consists in his role as the father of Social Psychology. His several books and his lectures established this

---

*Deleted is a criticism of Alexander Bain, and of Shand. Also a discussion of secondary instincts: reproduction, gregariousness, acquisition and construction.

field as a discrete area for the concentration of research and professional careers.

His most famous explanatory principle was the human instinct. And though this concept has fallen into disrepute, an understanding of it is essential to an understanding of modern formulations in the field. The vast majority of later thinkers have used McDougall as a target against which to test the strength and relevance of their own ideas.

MCDOUGALL, W. *An introduction to social psychology.* Methuen and Co., Ltd., 1913 (1908). Section I, Chap. II: "The mental characters of man of primary importance for his life in society. The nature of instincts and their place in the constitution of the human mind." (p. 19-44). Section I, Chap. III: "The principal instincts and the primary emotions of man" (p. 45-76). These essays are reproduced, with some deletions, by the permission of the publisher.

See also:

MCDOUGALL, W.
    a. *Body and mind.* London: Methuen, Ltd., 1911.
    b. *The group mind.* Cambridge: Cambridge University Press, 1920.
    c. *Character and conduct of life.* London: Methuen, Ltd., 1927.

MURCHISON (b-Vol. 2, p. 151-153; b-vol. 3, p. 326-328).

INDEX

A

Ach, 1234, 1235
Adams, John, 512
Adler, Alfred, 687-714, 726
Agassiz, Louis, 223
Aichhorn, August, 943-62
Aldini, 365
Alpin, Prosper, 358
Angell, F., 77
Anrep, G. V., 796
Anvers, Leroi d', 361
Aquinas, Thomas, 1
Aristotle, 51, 53, 54, 62, 63, 68, 242
Arnold, 511
Aubert, 135, 1181
Avenbrugger, 361

B

Babinsky, 415
Bacon, Francis, 51, 73
Bailie, 508
Bain, 77, 1330, 1331
Baldwin, J. M., 871
Ballet, 403
Bastian, 582
Batault, 373
Bateman, 582
Bayliss, 617
Beaunis, 918
Beard, 389
Beer, 762, 808
Beethoven, Ludwig von, 495
Bell, Charles, 7
Bennett, 409
Benussi, 1135

Bergmann, 821
Berkeley, 184, 201
Bernheim, 541
Bethe, 762, 808
Binet, Alfred, 11, 19, 20, 415, 871, 872-919, 1030
Bleuler, Eugen, 415, 417-63, 754, 941, 1030
Blin, 784, 878
Bonnier, 650, 652
Boring, E. B., 21, 77
Bourgoin, 355
Bourneville, 371, 875, 878
Boyeson, 981
Brentano, 231, 232, 240, 242
Breuer, Josef, 667-86
Brewster, 134
Bridgman, Laura, 886
Briquet, 404
Bristowe, 582
Broadbent, 582, 585, 595
Broca, 582, 990
Brown, 1148
Brown, Thomas, 208
Bryant, 982
Buhler, 1144
Burckhardt, Jacob, 717
Busse, 1188

C

Cabanis, 298
Campbell, 191, 409
Condolle, de, 989
Carpenter, 187
Carville, 595
Cattell, James, 11, 77, 860-71

Cellini, Benvenuto, 716
Chambeyron, 1205
Charcot, Jean Martin, 2, 3, 19, 370-416, 462, 541, 595, 681, 684, 918
Chiarugi, Vincenzo, 369
Chrestien, 362
Clapàrede, 1030
Coelius, 334
Cope, 225
Copernicus, 830
Cornelius, 1136, 1137, 1138
Cox, Mason, 362, 366
Crichton, 509
Croce, Benedetto, 1
Cullen, 292
Curnow, 588
Currie, 358

D

Damaye, 874
Darwin, Charles, 5, 140, 144, 147, 148, 366, 802, 1309, 1322
Dax, 582
Debove, 371
Deiter, 650
Democritus, 501
Demoor, 901
Descartes, René, 3, 760, 764
Desportes, 366
Dewey, John, 4, 8, 820
Dostoevski, 1274
Dreisch, 147
Dreyfus, 371
Duret, 595
Durham, 610
Durr, 1083
Dussik, 580

E

Ebbinghaus, 231, 232, 233, 234, 235, 431, 911, 1136
Eddington, A. S., 824, 825, 826, 831, 832, 837, 853
Edinger, 661
Edwards, 1151
Egger, M. V., 212, 214
Ehrenfels, von, 150, 1134, 1155
Erastratus, 334

Erofeeva, 793
Esquirol, Etienne Dominique, 2, 19, 313-69, 1205, 1210
Evans, 1205
Ewald, 648
Exner, 1034, 1035, 1073, 1083, 1084

F

Faria, 366
Fechner, 49, 131
Fernberger, 1146, 1147, 1148
Ferrers, Earl, 1217
Ferrier, 582, 583, 595, 757
Fichte, 49, 694
Fizeau, 119
Fodere, 1211
Forel, 450, 455
Foucalt, 119
Franklin, 982
Frazer, 720
Freud, Sigmund, 2, 11, 415, 558, 667-86, 714, 716, 726, 754, 943, 944, 945, 992, 1249
Fritsch, 757, 758
Frobenius, 743
Froebel, 975
Fulton, 982

G

Gale, H., 77
Galen, 10, 511
Galileo, 51, 827, 828, 829, 831, 857
Gallienus, 334
Galton, Francis, 11, 184, 196, 866, 871
Garten, 1180
Gaskell, 632
Gaubius, 349
Gaynor, Frank, 19
Gelb, 1169, 1170
Georget, 1205, 1212, 1227, 1229
Georgin, 895
Gifford, 981
Gmelin, 365
Goethe, 161, 495, 973
Gogh, Vincent van, 455
Goldstein, 271
Goltz, 142, 756, 758

Gosselin, 386
Gretry, 350
Griesinger, 718
Groos, 1007
Groth, 136
Gutkind, Eric, 21

H

Haen, De, 503
Hale, Lord, 1214
Hall, G. Stanley, 77, 963-93, 1003
Hamilton, 590
Hammond, 586
Heberden, 511
Hegel, 62, 194, 195
Hartmann, Edward von, 248, 1172, 1173
Hawthorne, 981
Heilbronner, 431
Heim, 719
Heine, Rosa, 1132
Helmholtz, Hermann von, 79-127, 133, 159, 217, 223, 992, 1177
Helmont, Van, 309, 359
Henle, Mary, 21
Henning, 1131
Henry, Patrick, 981
Heraclitus, 161, 721, 724
Herbart, Johann Friedrich, 11, 19, 22-50, 62, 63, 77, 619, 664
Hering, Ewald, 102, 137, 138, 140, 141, 686, 1174, 1175
Herrick, C. J., 619, 628
Herzen, 204
Hippocrates, 501
Hitzenberger, 579
Hitzig, 583, 595, 757, 758
Hodgson, Shadworth, 157
Hoff, 561
Hoffbauer, 1199, 1201, 1204, 1205, 1211, 1213
Hoffding, 49
Holderlin, 454
Hollingsworth, 1190, 1191, 1192
Horn, 366
Hornbostel, 1163, 1167, 1187, 1189
Hufeland, 361, 366
Hull, Clark L., 822-59, 1195
Hume, 174, 184

Hunter, John, 508, 618
Huxley, 184

I

Ibsen, Henrik, 1159
Ingbert, 643
Ireland, 582
Irons, 241

J

Jackson, Hughlings, 582-613, 619
Jaensch, 1143, 1176
James, William, 151-223, 228, 231, 241, 242, 759, 770, 992, 1126, 1294
Janet, 154, 155, 156, 415, 541
Jaspers, Karl, 703
Jastrow, 1162
Jeffries, 981
Jennings, H. S., 762
Jones, E., 684
Joubert, 212
Joyce, James, 11
Judd, C. H., 77
Jung, C. G., 13, 446, 715-55, 941, 1030

K

Kant, 6, 13, 49, 51, 102, 209, 242, 694, 978
Katz, 1170, 1184
Keats, John, 981
Keller, Helen, 886
Kenkel, 1172
Kiesow, F., 77
Kinnebrook, 9, 10
Kirschmann, A., 77
Kleijn, de, 768
Klein, 371, 372
Klein-Koffka, 1042
Koffka, Kurt, 858, 1042, 1088, 1128-96
Köhler, Wolfgang, 1030, 1041, 1042, 1088, 1090-1127, 1131, 1142, 1143, 1144, 1147, 1153, 1166, 1171, 1195
Kraepelin, Emil, 77, 457, 458, 464-498
Krause, 642

Krestovnikov, 789
Kries, 1195
Kruegar, F., 77
Külpe, O., 77, 231, 233, 234, 235, 239, 1134, 1195
Kussmaul, 582

L

Lacabe, 895
Lancaster, 971
Lange, 217
Langendorff, 661
Langley, 624
Lapique, 4
Laromiguiere, 330
Lashley, 271
Lefort, 409
Lehmann, H., 77, 234
Leibnitz, 13, 76, 248
Lemoin, 302
Lenz, 455
Lewandowski, 660
Lewes, 201
Lewin, Kurt, 49, 290, 1234-89
Liébeault, 541
Lieutaud, 508
Lindemann, 1172, 1186
Lindworsky, 1144, 1273
Linke, 1035, 1083
Lipps, A. F., 77, 1030
Locke, John, 5, 76, 158, 322
Loeb, 644, 761
Lombroso, 990
Londe, 395
Longfellow, Henry Wadsworth, 743
Lotze, 4, 222, 233
Lovejoy, 720
Luciani, 650, 660
Ludwig, Heinrich, 135
Luys, 392
Lyell, 990

M

McDougall, William, 1290-1336
McRitchie, 990
Mach, Ernst, 128-50, 138, 686
Magnan, 878

Magnus, R., 760, 768
Marbe, 1033, 1035, 1083, 1195
Marble, K., 77
Marie, 415
Martin, 366, 1165
Maskelyne, 9, 10
Mason, O. T., 989
Mayer, Alfred, 135
Mayer, Robert, 718, 719, 721
Meinong, 1134, 1135
Mendeleeff, 777
Metcalfe-Johnson, 585
Meuman, E., 77
Meyrink, 740
Mickell, 508
Mill, J. S., 112, 124, 161, 239, 982
Morel, 878
Morgagni, 364, 508
Morgan, C. Lloyd, 145, 639
Moses, 720
Mott, 637
Moxon, Gairdner, 582
Müller, G. E., 1131, 1132, 1136, 1181, 1182, 1183, 1184, 1185, 1186, 1192, 1335
Müller, Johannes, 7, 77, 130
Munk, H., 757
Münsterberg, H., 77, 234, 235
Murchison, 859, 1030, 1088

N

Nansen, 981
Nernst, 1154
Newton, 119, 134, 981, 982
Nicholl, John, 1203, 1207
Nietzsche, 726, 729
Nuel, 808

O

Odier, 366
Ogden, 1135
Ogle, John W., 582
Ogle, William, 582
Olivier, 371
Oppenheim, 375, 384
Orozco, 857
Ovsiankina, 1241

P

Pace, E. A., 77
Page, 371, 384, 389
Panas, 391
Parinaud, 387
Pascal, Blaise, 1201
Patrick, G. T. W., 77
Paul, St., 723
Pauli, W., 137, 138
Pausanias, 350
Pavlov, Ivan Petrovich, 4, 756-97, 832
Pearson, Karl, 150
Perfect, 365
Pestalozzi, 49
Peters, 1159
Piaget, Jean, 290, 994-1031
Piéron, 1030
Pillsbury, 807, 808, 1162, 1164
Pinel, Philippe, 1, 2, 8, 14, 19, 291-312, 322, 331, 332, 334, 348, 353, 354, 359, 363, 498, 504, 512
Plato, 968
Pothier, 1205
Potzl, 579
Poussin, 301, 306
Prince, Morton, 514-42
Prost, 502
Putnam, 371, 375, 384

R

Rahn, 1135, 1165
Rasmussen, 995
Ray, Issac, 19, 512, 1197-1233
Raymond, 371
Redman, John, 512
Reich, 119
Reil, 342
Reis, 452
Ribot, 228
Richet, Ch., 761
Robertson, Alexander, 582
Rollett, 142
Romanes, 1317
Rorschach, Hermann, 11, 920-42
Rousseau, Jean-Jacques, 321, 329
Royer-Collard, 351
Rubin, 1161, 1162, 1164, 1165, 1166, 1168, 1169, 1170

Runes, Dagobert, 19, 21
Rush, Benjamin, 19, 362, 369, 499-513

S

Sakel, Manfred, 559-581
Sauvages, 292
Savonarola, 981
Scheffel, 455
Schelling, 248
Schluter, L., 1132
Schneider, G. H., 145, 1994
Schopenhauer, 221, 694
Schuele, 437
Schumann, 1033, 1035, 1036, 1041, 1047, 1084, 1126, 1139, 1143, 1161, 1172, 1195
Schumann, Robert, 455
Schuster, P. R., 140
Schweitzer, Albert, 11
Sclater, 989
Scott, Walter, 982
Scott, William, 1203
Scripture, E. W., 77
Scupin, 995
Sechenoy, L. M., 761
Seifert, 1141
Semon, 742
Seneca, 352
Sergi, 990
Shelley, Percy Bysshe, 981
Sherrington, Charles Scott, 4, 613-666, 760, 1335
Shoemaker, 204
Simon, Théodore, 20, 872-919, 1030
Smith, Adam, 59
Socrates, 352
Solomonov, 794
Specht, 452, 1160
Spencer, Herbert, 140, 205, 560, 655, 766, 1296
Spinoza, Baruch, 6, 245, 827
Stark, 503
Starling, 617
Steiner, 718
Stern, William, 243-290, 995, 996
Stevens, 508
Storring, G. W., 77
Stout, 231, 240, 241, 242
Stowell, 1203

1341

Strachey, Lytton, 5, 6
Stransky, 444, 563
Stratton, G. M., 77
Strauss, David, 143
Stumpf, 237, 1088, 1136, 1137, 1144
Sully, 1018
Sutherland, 981
Swieten, Van, 359
Synesius, 726

T

Taine, 220
Talbot, 1173
Tawney, G. A., 77
Theden, 361
Thomsen, 375, 384
Thorndyke, E. L., 762, 763, 833
Tinklepaugh, O. L., 836
Titchener, Edward B., 77, 224-242,
    1136, 1164, 1165, 1166
Trousseau, 590, 598
Tschermak, 637
Tuke, William, 369
Tylor, 720

U

Uexkull, von, 762, 808

V

Vaihinger, 705
Valentin, L., 365
Valsalva, 364
Valtat, 409
Vartanov, 783
Vassey, 972
Vinci, Leonardo da, 135, 136, 716
Voisin, 878

W

Wagner-Jauregg, Julius, 19, 543-558
Walton, 371, 375, 384
Warren, H. Z., 77
Warrington, 624
Washburn, 1148
Watson, John B., 8, 798-821
Watson, Thomas, 582
Weiss, Albert, P., 823, 824, 825, 826,
    831, 832, 853
Weissmann, 141, 145, 146
Wennolt, 365
Wernicke, 433
Wertheimer, Max, 13, 19, 1030, 1032-
    89, 1128, 1130, 1132, 1134, 1135,
    1150, 1181, 1186, 1189, 1195, 1196
Wilde, Oscar, 1250
Wilks, 582, 610
Willis, 336
Wirth, W., 77
Witasek, 1179
Witmer, L., 77
Wolfe, H. M., 77
Wolff, Christian, 62
Wordsworth, William, 1333
Wundt, Wilhelm, 19, 51-78, 233, 234,
    235, 236, 237, 238, 243, 497, 759,
    871, 992, 1083, 1165, 1293
Wurzburg 1134

Y

Yerkes, 817
Young, Thomas, 134

Z

Zagreus, 726
Zeno, 173
Ziehen, 233, 234, 235
Ziemssen, 582
Zitovich, 783